Child Development

THIRD EDITION

LAURA E. BERK

Illinois State University

ALLYN AND BACON

Boston London Toronto Sydney Tokyo Singapore

In loving memory of my parents
Sofie and Philip Eisenberg

VICE-PRESIDENT AND PUBLISHER: Susan Badger
SENIOR EDITOR: Laura Pearson
EDITORIAL ASSISTANT: Marnie Greenhut
COVER ADMINISTRATOR: Linda Knowles
COMPOSITION BUYER: Linda Cox
MANUFACTURING BUYER: Megan Cochran
EDITORIAL-PRODUCTION SERVICE: Sally Stickney
TEXT DESIGNER: Karen Mason
COVER DESIGNER: Susan Paradise

Copyright © 1994, 1991, 1989 by Allyn and Bacon
A Division of Paramount Publishing
160 Gould Street
Needham Heights, Massachusetts 02194

Library of Congress Cataloging-in-Publication Data

Berk, Laura E.
    Child development / Laura E. Berk. — 3rd ed.
        p.   cm.
    Includes bibliographical references and index.
    ISBN 0-205-15027-6
    1. Child development. I. Title.
HQ767.9.B464 1994
305.23'1—dc20   93-39062
                                                 CIP

Printed in the United States of America
10 9 8 7 6 5 4 3 2 1   98 97 96 95 94 93

Brief Contents

Detailed Contents

PART TWO

Foundations of Development

PART THREE

Cognitive and Language Development

Contexts for Development

xiii

ABOUT THE AUTHOR

Laura E. Berk is professor of psychology at Illinois State University, where she has taught child development to undergraduate and graduate students for over twenty years. She received her bachelor's degree in psychology from the University of California, Berkeley, and her master's and doctoral degrees in early childhood development and education from the University of Chicago. She was visiting scholar at Cornell University in 1975–1976, at the University of California, Los Angeles, in 1982–1983, and at Stanford University in 1990–1991. She has published extensively on the effects of school environments on children's development and, more recently, on the development of children's private speech. Her research has been funded by the U.S. Office of Education and the National Institute of Child Health and Human Development. It has appeared in many prominent journals, including *Child Development, Developmental Psychology, Merrill-Palmer Quarterly, Child and Youth Care Quarterly,* and *American Journal of Education.* Currently she serves as research editor of *Young Children* and consulting editor of *Early Childhood Research Quarterly,* journals of the National Association for the Education of Young Children. She is coeditor of *Private Speech: From Social Interaction to Self-Regulation* and author of the chronologically organized textbook, *Infants, Children, and Adolescents,* published by Allyn and Bacon.

Preface

My more than twenty years of teaching child development have brought me in contact with thousands of students having diverse college majors, future goals, interests, and needs. Some are affiliated with my own department, psychology, but many come from other child-related fields—education, home economics, sociology, anthropology, and biology, to name just a few. Each semester, my students' aspirations have proved to be as varied as their fields of study. Many look toward careers in applied work with children—teaching, caregiving, nursing, counseling, social work, school psychology, and program administration. Some plan to teach child development, and a few want to do research. Most hope someday to have children, whereas others are already parents who come with a desire to better understand and rear their own youngsters. And almost all my students arrive with a deep curiosity about how they themselves developed from tiny infants into the complex human beings they are today.

My goal in preparing this third edition of *Child Development* is to provide a textbook that meets the instructional goals of the course as well as the varied needs of students. I aimed for a book that is intellectually stimulating, that provides depth as well as breadth of coverage, and that portrays the complexities of child development in a way that captures student interest while helping them learn. To achieve these objectives, I have grounded this text in a carefully selected body of classic and current theory and research, emphasized how the research process helps solve real-world problems, and paid special attention to policy issues that are critical to the overall condition of children in today's world. I have also used a clear, engaging writing style and provided a unique pedagogical program that assists students in mastering information, integrating the various aspects of development, and applying what they have learned.

TEXT PHILOSOPHY

The basic approach of this book has been shaped by my own professional and personal history as a teacher, researcher, and parent. It consists of six philosophical ingredients that I regard as essential for students to emerge from a course with a thorough understanding of child development. Each theme is woven into every chapter.

1. **An understanding of the diverse array of theories in the field and the strengths and shortcomings of each.** The first chapter begins by emphasizing that only knowledge of multiple theories can do justice to the richness of child development. In each topical domain, I present a variety of theoretical perspectives, indicate how each approach highlights previously overlooked aspects of development, and discuss research that has been used to evaluate them. If one or two theories have emerged as prominent in a particular area, I indicate why, in terms of the theory's broad explanatory power. Discussion of contrasting theories also

serves as the context for an evenhanded analysis of many controversial issues throughout the text.

2. **An appreciation of basic research strategies to investigate child development.** To evaluate theories, students need a firm grounding in basic research design and methodology. I devote an entire chapter to describing and critiquing research strategies. Throughout the book, numerous studies are discussed in sufficient detail for students to use what they have learned to critically assess the findings, conclusions, and implications of research.

3. **Knowledge of both the sequence of child development and the processes that underlie it.** Students are provided a description of the organized sequence of development along with a discussion of processes of change. An understanding of process—how complex combinations of biological and environmental events produce development—has been the focus of most recent research. Accordingly, the text reflects this emphasis. But new information about the timetable of change has also emerged in recent years. In many ways, children have proved to be far more competent beings than they were believed to be in decades past. Recent evidence on the timing and sequence of development, along with its implications for process, is presented in detail throughout the book.

4. **An appreciation of the impact of context and culture on child development.** A wealth of new research indicates more powerfully than ever before that children live in rich physical and social contexts that affect all aspects of their development. In each chapter, students travel to distant parts of the world through a growing body of cross-cultural evidence. The text narrative also discusses many findings on socioeconomically and ethnically diverse children within the United States. Besides highlighting the role of immediate settings, such as family, neighborhood, and school, I make a concerted effort to underscore the impact of larger social structures—societal values, laws, and government programs—on children's well-being.

5. **A sense of the interdependency of all domains of development—physical, cognitive, emotional, and social.** In every chapter, an integrated approach to child development is emphasized. I show how physical, cognitive, emotional, and social development are interwoven. Within the text narrative and in Connections tables at the end of each chapter, students are referred to other sections of the book in order to deepen their understanding of relationships among various aspects of change.

6. **An appreciation of the interrelatedness of theory, research, and applications.** Throughout this book, I stress that theories of child development and the research stimulated by them provide the foundation for sound, effective practices with children. The link between theory, research, and applications is reinforced by an organizational format in which theory and research are presented first, followed by implications for practice. In addition, a new focus in the field—harnessing child development knowledge to shape social policies that support children's needs—is reflected in every chapter. The text addresses the current condition of children in the United States and around the world and shows how theory and research have sparked successful interventions. Many important applied topics are considered—prenatal transmission of AIDS, infant mortality, maternal employment and day care, early intervention for at-risk children, teenage pregnancy and childbearing, information processing and academic learning, bilingual education, effective parenting techniques, children's gender stereotyping, child maltreatment, vocational education in adolescence, and more.

TEXT ORGANIZATION

This text is organized topically, a manner best suited to a comprehensive discussion of theory, research, and applications and an uninterrupted view of development within each domain. The book retains the same basic structure that was praised by users of its previous two editions. It is divided into 5 parts and 15 chapters, each of which develops the six philosophical themes just described.

PART I. THEORY AND RESEARCH IN CHILD DEVELOPMENT. This section provides an overview of the history of the field, twentieth-century theories, and research strategies. **Chapter 1** stresses the importance of theories as organizing frameworks for understanding child development and traces changes in views of childhood from medieval to modern times. The study of child development is depicted as an interdisciplinary endeavor that aims to both understand children and improve their life condition. **Chapter 2** covers strategies for conducting scientifically sound research. Commonly used research methods and both general and developmental research designs are explained and critiqued. The chapter concludes with a consideration of ethics in research on children.

PART II. FOUNDATIONS OF DEVELOPMENT. A trio of chapters introduces students to the foundations of development. **Chapter 3** combines a discussion of genetic mechanisms and prenatal and perinatal environmental influences into a single, integrated discussion of these earliest determinants of development. A concluding section takes up the various ways in which investigators conceive of the relationship between heredity and environment as a prelude to revisiting the nature–nurture controversy in later chapters. **Chapter 4** is devoted to an overview of the rapidly expanding literature on infant capacities. Research on newborn reflexes, states, and learning capacities is reviewed, and early motor and perceptual development is considered. The chapter closes with the question of whether infancy is a sensitive period in which certain experiences must occur to ensure healthy development. **Chapter 5** addresses physical growth, including development of the brain. The close connection between physical and psychological development is emphasized. A variety of hereditary and environmental influences on physical growth are also considered.

PART III. COGNITIVE AND LANGUAGE DEVELOPMENT. Four chapters treat the diverse array of theories and wealth of research on cognitive and language development. **Chapter 6** discusses Piaget's cognitive-developmental theory and Vygotsky's sociocultural theory. Even though questions have been raised about Piaget's stages in recent years, no other individual has contributed more to our understanding of child development. Students are given a thorough grounding in Piagetian theory as a prerequisite for studying language, emotional, and social-cognitive development in later chapters. With its strong emphasis on the social context of cognition, Vygotsky's theory has recently risen to the forefront of the field, stands as a major competing approach to Piaget's, and therefore shares the title of Chapter 6 in this edition. **Chapter 7** introduces information processing, another leading alternative to the Piagetian perspective. General and developmental models of information processing are reviewed along with research on each major facet of the information-processing system. The chapter also discusses recent applications of information processing to children's academic learning and concludes with an analysis of the strengths and weaknesses of the information-processing perspective. **Chapter 8** presents the psychometric approach to children's intelligence. It provides an overview of the intelligence testing movement and addresses a variety of controversial issues and research findings, including racial, ethnic, and social-class differences in IQ, heritability of intelligence, and cultural bias in tests. The concluding section moves beyond IQ to a discussion of creativity and talent. **Chapter 9** provides a comprehensive introduction to language development, including behaviorist, nativist, and interactionist theories. The body of the chapter is organized around the four components of language: phonology, semantics, grammar, and pragmatics. The chapter also addresses such questions as: Can nonhuman primates acquire language? Is there a sensitive period for language learning? How does bilingualism affect children's development?

PART IV. PERSONALITY AND SOCIAL DEVELOPMENT. Coverage of personality and social development is divided into four chapters. **Chapter 10** contains an overview of theory and research on children's expression and understanding of emotion, the origins of temperament and its implications for cognitive and social development, and infant–caregiver attachment. The impact of caregiving and temperament on the attachment bond, fathers as attachment figures, and effects of maternal employment and day care on attachment security are among the issues discussed. **Chapter 11** considers the development of social cognition. The discussion is divided into three sections: children's understanding of self, other people, and relations between people. Among the topics included are self-concept and self-esteem, achievement-related attributions, identity, perspective taking, friendship, and social problem solving. **Chapter 12,** which addresses moral development, includes a review of psychoanalytic, social learning, and cognitive-developmental theories and related research. Child-rearing practices that foster moral internalization, cross-cultural research on moral reasoning, the controversial issue of whether males and females differ in moral understanding, and the development of self-control and aggression are among the topics featured in this chapter. **Chapter 13** focuses on sex-related differences and gender roles. Biological and environmental influences on gender stereotyping and gender-role adoption, diverse theories and research on the development of gender-role identity, and sex-related differences in mental abilities and personality traits are discussed. The chapter also includes an applied section on raising non-gender-stereotyped children.

PART V. CONTEXTS FOR DEVELOPMENT. The final two chapters examine four highly influential contexts for development—family, peers, media, and schooling. **Chapter 14** considers the family from a social systems perspective. The bidirectional nature of parent–child interaction, the importance of links between the family and community for children's optimal development, and styles of child rearing are highlighted. The central portion of this chapter discusses the impact of family transitions in Western industrialized nations on children's development—the trend toward a smaller family size and the high rates of divorce, remarriage, maternal employment, day care, and self-care by school-age children. The chapter concludes with a discussion of child maltreatment. In **Chapter 15,** the social systems perspective is extended to extrafamilial contexts for development. In the section on peer relations, research on the development of peer sociability, peer acceptance, peer groups, and peers as socialization agents is discussed. The middle portion of the chapter addresses the impact of television and computers on social and cognitive development. A concluding section on schooling considers such topics as educational philosophies, school transitions, teacher–pupil interaction, ability grouping, and cross-national research on academic achievement.

NEW COVERAGE IN THE THIRD EDITION

In this edition, I continue to represent a burgeoning contemporary literature, with theory and research drawn from over 900 new citations. To make room for new coverage, I have condensed and reorganized some topics and eliminated others that are no longer as crucial in view of new evidence. The text content includes many major changes:

- Social policy brought to the forefront of the text through a special section in Chapter 1 that provides an overview of the current condition of children in the United States and the social-policy process. A wide variety of social-policy topics are integrated into succeeding chapters.
- A reorganized discussion of history and theory in Chapter 1, in which basic themes and issues are introduced early and used as the basis for comparing and contrasting major perspectives. New coverage of James Baldwin as a historical force in the field, the impact of theories on child-rearing advice to parents, and the role of culture in development.

- Expanded treatment of research strategies in Chapter 2, including new sections on ethnography and the microgenetic design. Many new illustrations of research.
- Updated coverage of prenatal teratogens, preterm and low-birth-weight infants, and cross-national findings on infant mortality in Chapter 3.
- New evidence on cultural variations in infant sleeping arrangements, changes in crying over the first year, sudden infant death syndrome, newborn imitation, development of hearing and vision, linkages between motor skills and perceptual capacities, and long-term consequences of early deprived rearing experiences in Chapter 4.
- Expanded treatment of the psychological impact of pubertal events, teenage sexual activity and childbearing, development of the brain, nutrition and physical growth, and sex-related differences in motor skills; and a new section on sexual orientation in Chapter 5.
- More evaluative commentary on Piaget's stages, new findings on the development of representation and categorization and cultural influences on operational thought; and an expanded section on Vygotsky's sociocultural theory and its educational applications in Chapter 6.
- New work on the development of processing capacity, the controversy over whether the mind is a general or modular device, infantile amnesia, children's eyewitness memory, Siegler's model of strategy choice, cultural differences in mathematical understanding, and development of scientific reasoning in Chapter 7.
- A new section on Gardner's theory of multiple intelligences along with added coverage of componential analyses of intelligence test performance, effects of cultural background and schooling on IQ, the impact of early intervention on intellectual development, and creativity and talent in Chapter 8.
- Expanded discussion of research relevant to nativist theory of language development and new evidence on babbling, children's strategies for acquiring word meaning and grammatical forms, adult support for early language learning, and language development of later-born children in Chapter 9.
- Recent findings on young infants' expression of emotion, development of emotional understanding in childhood, assessment of temperament through physiological reactions, the relative contributions of quality of caregiving and infant temperament to attachment security, and the internal working model concept in Chapter 10.
- A new section on young children's theory of mind and updated evidence on the origins and consequences of achievement-related attributions; cultural influences on self-concept, self-esteem, and adolescent identity; and the development of perspective taking and friendship in Chapter 11.
- A new section on recent psychoanalytic ideas about conscience development and current research on children's reasoning about authority, the relationship of child-rearing practices to moral understanding, the importance of higher education for advanced moral reasoning, cultural influences on moral development, and individual differences in self-control in Chapter 12. Evidence on the development of aggression, including new information on juvenile delinquency, has been moved to this chapter.
- Updated research on the development of gender stereotyping, biological and cultural influences on gender-role adoption, parents' and teachers' encouragement of gender typing, and the development of gender-role identity in Chapter 13. New material on cognitive interventions to reduce gender stereotyping and sex-related differences in vocational development.
- Expanded discussion of the family as a social system, social-class and ethnic variations in child rearing, sibling influences, and development of only children in Chapter 14. Also, new evidence on how parents adapt child rearing to children's growing competence and updated information on divorce,

remarriage, maternal employment, and day-care policies in the United States and other Western nations.

- Greater emphasis on the importance of peer relations, including new primate research on peer-only rearing, new evidence on parental influences on peer sociability, family origins of peer acceptance, subtypes of rejected children, and adolescent peer groups; expanded discussion of policy issues related to improving children's television; and updated research on school transitions, cross-cultural comparisons of academic achievement, and vocational preparation of non-college-bound adolescents in Chapter 15.

PEDAGOGICAL FEATURES

The pedagogical features of the text have been revised and greatly expanded. A highly accessible writing style—one that is lucid and engaging without being simplistic—continues to be one of the text's strong points. In this edition, I frequently converse with students, ask questions, and encourage them to relate what they read to their own lives. In doing so, I hope to make the study of child development even more involving and pleasurable.

CHAPTER INTRODUCTIONS AND END-OF-CHAPTER SUMMARIES. To provide students with a helpful preview of what they are about to read, I begin each chapter with an outline and overview of its content. Chapter introductions have been rewritten to present lively, involving examples of children's development and introduce controversial issues as a means of stimulating student interest. Comprehensive end-of-chapter summaries, organized according to the major divisions of each chapter and highlighting key terms, remind students of important points in the text discussion.

BRIEF REVIEWS. Interim summaries of text content appear at the end of most major sections in each chapter. They enhance retention by encouraging students to reflect on information they have just read before moving on to a new section.

BOXES. Three types of boxes accentuate the philosophical themes of this book. Cultural Influences boxes highlight the impact of context and culture on all aspects of development. Social Issues boxes discuss the condition of children in the United States and around the world and emphasize the need for sensitive social policies to ensure their well-being. From Research to Practice boxes integrate theory, research, and applications. Twenty-five new boxes appear in this edition.

MARGINAL GLOSSARY, END-OF-CHAPTER TERM LIST, AND END-OF-BOOK GLOSSARY. Mastery of terms that make up the central vocabulary of the field is promoted through a new marginal glossary, an end-of-chapter term list, and an end-of-book glossary. Important terms and concepts also appear in boldface type in the text narrative.

MILESTONES TABLES. Milestones tables that provide an overview of the sequence and timing of achievements in each domain of development appear throughout the text. These tables are designed to help students keep track of major developments as they consider a wealth of theory and research. At the same time, each Milestones table reminds students that individual differences exist in the precise age at which milestones are attained, a point made repeatedly throughout the text discussion.

CONNECTIONS TABLES. Each chapter concludes with a Connections table, which encourages students to explore high-interest topics and integrate domains of development by turning to relevant information in other sections of the book. The Connections tables are designed to foster a coherent, unified picture of child development.

ADDITIONAL TABLES, ILLUSTRATIONS, AND PHOTOGRAPHS. New tables are liberally included to help students grasp essential points in the text discussion, extend information on a topic, and consider applications. The many color illustrations depict important theories, methods, and research findings. Photos have been carefully selected to portray text content and represent the diversity of children around the world.

ACKNOWLEDGMENTS

The dedicated contributions of many individuals helped make this book a reality and contributed to refinements and improvements in each of its editions. An impressive cast of reviewers provided many helpful suggestions, constructive criticisms, and encouragement and enthusiasm for the organization and content of the book. I am grateful to each one of them.

Reviewers of the First Edition

Dana W. Birnbaum
University of Maine, Orono
Kathryn N. Black
Purdue University
Cathryn L. Booth
University of Washington
Sam Boyd
University of Central Arkansas
Celia A. Brownell
University of Pittsburgh
Toni A. Campbell
San Jose State University
Beth Casey
Boston College
John Condry
Cornell University
James L. Dannemiller
University of Wisconsin, Madison
Darlene DeSantis
West Chester University of Pennsylvania
Kenneth Hill
Saint Mary's University, Halifax
Alice S. Honig
Syracuse University
Elizabeth J. Hrncir
University of Virginia
Mareile Koenig
George Washington University Hospital
Gary W. Ladd
Purdue University
Frank Laycock
Oberlin College
Robert S. Marvin
University of Virginia

Carolyn J. Mebert
University of New Hampshire
Gary B. Melton
University of Nebraska, Lincoln
Mary Evelyn Moore
Indiana University, Bloomington
Larry Nucci
University of Illinois, Chicago
Carol Pandey
Pierce College, Los Angeles
Thomas S. Parish
Kansas State University
B. Kay Pasley
Colorado State University
Ellen F. Potter
University of South Carolina, Columbia
Kathleen Preston
Humboldt State University
Maria E. Sera
University of Iowa
Beth Shapiro
Emory University
Gregory J. Smith
Dickinson College
Harold Stevenson
University of Michigan, Ann Arbor
Ross A. Thompson
University of Nebraska, Lincoln
Barbara A. Tinsley
University of Illinois, Urbana–Champaign
Kim F. Townley
University of Kentucky

Reviewers of the Second Edition

James Dannemiller
University of Wisconsin, Madison
Darlene DeSantis
West Chester University of Pennsylvania
Claire Etaugh
Bradley University

Katherine Green
Millersville University of Pennsylvania
Daniel Lapsley
University of Notre Dame
Mary D. Leinbach
University of Oregon

Gary Melton
   University of Nebraska, Lincoln
Daniel Reschly
   Iowa State University
Rosemary Rosser
   University of Arizona
Phil Schoggen
   Cornell University

Harold Stevenson
   University of Michigan, Ann Arbor
Ross A. Thompson
   University of Nebraska, Lincoln
Janet Valadez
   Pan American University

Reviewers of the Third Edition

Stephanie Broderick
   University of California, Irvine
James Dannemiller
   University of Wisconsin, Madison
Rebecca Eder
   Bryn Mawr College
Bill Fabricius
   Arizona State University
John Gibbs
   Ohio State University
Janet F. Gillespie
   SUNY College at Brockport
Peter Gordon
   University of Pittsburgh
Claire Kopp
   University of California, Los Angeles

Beth Kurtz-Costes
   University of North Carolina, Chapel Hill
Mary Evelyn Moore
   Illinois State University
Lois Muir
   University of Wisconsin, La Crosse
Rosemary Rosser
   University of Arizona
Jane Rysberg
   California State University, Chico
Robert Siegler
   Carnegie-Mellon University
Ross A. Thompson
   University of Nebraska, Lincoln

In addition, I thank the following individuals for responding to a survey that provided vital feedback for the new edition.

Anne Copeland
   Boston University
Darlene DeSantis
   West Chester University of Pennsylvania
Paul Echandia
   Pace University
Claire Etaugh
   Bradley University
Kathleen Green
   Millersville University of Pennsylvania
Donald Hayes
   University of Maine, Orono
Jim Hittner
   Hofstra University
Elana Joram
   University of California, Los Angeles
Jan Kennedy
   Georgia Southern University

Beth Kurtz-Costes
   University of North Carolina, Chapel Hill
Mary D. Leinbach
   University of Oregon
Suzanne Lovitt
   Bowdoin College
Daniel Reschly
   Iowa State University
Rosemary Rosser
   University of Arizona
John Stabler
   Georgia State University
Ross A. Thompson
   University of Nebraska, Lincoln
Belinda Traughber
   Middle Tennessee State University
Janet Valadez
   Tarleton State University

I am also indebted to colleagues at Illinois State University and Illinois Wesleyan University—Raymond Bergner, Gary Creasey, Elmer Lemke, Carolyn Jarvis, Patricia Jarvis, Benjamin Moore, Leonard Schmaltz, and Mark Swerdlik— for providing consultation in areas of their expertise. Dawn Ramsburg helped with literature reviews and securing permissions for use of copyrighted material. Jennifer Burke, Joan Croce, Eugie Foster, and Jane Wirtz spent many hours indexing the text.

I have been fortunate to work with an outstanding publishing staff at Allyn and Bacon. John-Paul Lenney, my signing editor, guided this project through its first edition with unusual involvement and dedication. Diane McOscar's extensive knowledge and organizational skill contributed to a highly successful second edition. During the past two years, it has been my privilege and pleasure to work with Laura Pearson, Executive Editor, on both the third edition of *Child Development* and the first edition of my chronologically organized text, *Infants, Children, and Adolescents.* Laura's sound judgment, insight into the needs of instructors and students, and keen aesthetic sense are reflected on every page. I especially appreciate her generous moral support, diplomatic problem solving, responsiveness to my many questions, and warm sense of humor. I look forward to working with her for many years to come.

On the production team, Sally Stickney and Karen Mason assumed day-to-day responsibility for the complex, time-consuming tasks that transformed my manuscript into an elegant, finished textbook. I thank Elsa Peterson for obtaining the outstanding photos of culturally diverse children that appear in this edition. Marnie Greenhut, Editorial Assistant, graciously arranged for manuscript reviews, managed the preparation of text supplements, and attended to a wide variety of pressing, last-minute details.

A final word of gratitude goes to my family, whose love, patience, and understanding have enabled me to be wife, mother, teacher, researcher, and text writer since I began this book in 1986. My sons, David and Peter, have provided me with many valuable lessons in child development over the years. I thank them for their good-humored interest in my work ("Unreal! She's *still* working on the same textbook!") and expressions of pride in having a mom who currently writes for their own generation of college students. My husband, Ken, willingly made room for this project in our family life and communicated his belief in its importance in a great many unspoken, caring ways.

Laura E. Berk

Child Development

CHAPTER
1

◆ **Amy B. Atkinson,** *Bubbles*
By courtesy of the City of Manchester Art Galleries

History, Theory, and Applied Directions

Not long ago, I left my midwestern home to live for a year near the small city in northern California where I spent my childhood. One morning, I visited the neighborhood where I grew up—a place I had not been since I was 12 years old. I stood at the entrance to my old schoolyard. Buildings and grounds that had looked large to me as a child now seemed strangely small from my grown-up vantage point. I peered through the window of my first-grade classroom. The desks were no longer arranged in rows but grouped in clusters around the room. A computer rested against the far wall, near the spot where I had once sat. I walked my old route home from school, the distance shrunken by my larger stride. I stopped in front of my best friend Kathryn's house, where we had once drawn sidewalk pictures, crossed the street to play kick ball, produced plays for neighborhood audiences in the garage, and traded marbles and stamps in the backyard. In place of the small shop where I had purchased penny candy stood a neighborhood day-care center, filled with the voices and vigorous activity of toddlers and preschoolers.

As I walked, I reflected on early experiences that contributed to who I am and what I am like today—weekends helping my father in his downtown clothing shop; the year during which my mother studied to become a high school teacher; moments of companionship and rivalry with my sister and brother; Sunday trips to museums and the seashore; and overnight visits to my grandmother's house, where I became someone extra special. As I passed the homes of my childhood friends, I thought of what I knew about their present lives: my close friend

Kathryn, star pupil and president of our sixth-grade class—today a successful corporate lawyer and mother of two children; shy, withdrawn Phil, cruelly teased because of his cleft lip—now owner of a thriving chain of hardware stores and member of the city council; Hulio, immigrant from Mexico who joined our class in third grade—today director of an elementary school bilingual education program and single parent of an adopted Mexican boy; and finally, my next-door neighbor Rick, who picked fights at recess, struggled with reading, repeated fourth grade, dropped out of high school, and (so I heard) moved from one job to another over the following ten years.

As you begin this course in child development, perhaps you, too, have wondered about some of the same questions that crossed my mind during that nostalgic neighborhood walk:

- What determines the features human beings have in common and those that make each of us unique—in physical characteristics, capabilities, interests, and behaviors?
- Are infants' and young children's perceptions of the world much the same as adults', or are they different in basic respects?
- Why do some of us, like Kathryn and Rick, retain the same styles of responding that characterized us as children, whereas others, like Phil, change in essential ways?
- How did Hulio, transplanted to a foreign culture at 8 years of age, master its language and customs and succeed in its society, yet remain strongly identified with his ethnic community?
- In what ways are children's home, school, and neighborhood experiences the same today as they were in generations past, and in what ways are they different? How does generational change—employed mothers, day care, divorce, smaller families, and new technologies—affect children's characteristics and skills?

These are central questions addressed by **child development,** a field devoted to understanding all aspects of human growth and change from conception through adolescence. Child development is part of a larger discipline known as **developmental psychology,** or (as it is referred to in its interdisciplinary sense) **human development,** which includes all changes we experience throughout the life span. Great diversity characterizes the interests and concerns of the thousands of investigators who study child development. But all share a single goal: the desire to describe and identify those factors that influence the dramatic changes in young people during the first two decades of life.

CHILD DEVELOPMENT AS AN INTERDISCIPLINARY, SCIENTIFIC, AND APPLIED FIELD

Child development
A field of study devoted to understanding all aspects of human growth from conception through adolescence.

Developmental psychology
A branch of psychology devoted to understanding all changes that human beings experience throughout the life span.

Human development
An interdisciplinary field of study devoted to understanding all changes that human beings experience throughout the life span.

Look again at the questions just listed, and you will see that they are not just of scientific interest. Each is of *applied,* or practical importance, as well. In fact, scientific curiosity about the vast changes that take place between infancy and adulthood is just one factor that has led child development to become the exciting field of study it is today. Research about development has also been stimulated by social pressures to better the lives of children. For example, the beginning of public education in the early part of this century led to a demand for knowledge about what and how to teach children of different ages. The interest of pediatricians in improving children's health required an understanding of physical growth and nutrition. The social service profession's desire to treat children's anxieties and behavior problems required information about personality and social development. And parents have continually asked for advice from child development specialists about child-rearing practices and experiences that would promote the growth of their child.

Our large storehouse of information about child development is *interdisciplinary*. It has grown through the combined efforts of people from many fields of study. Because of the need for solutions to everyday problems concerning children, academic scientists from psychology, sociology, anthropology, and biology have joined forces in research with professionals from a variety of applied fields, including education, home economics, medicine, and social service, to name just a few. Today, the field of child development is a melting pot of contributions. Its body of knowledge is not just scientifically important, but relevant and useful.

BASIC THEMES AND ISSUES

Before scientific study of the child, questions about children were answered by turning to common sense, opinion, and belief. Systematic research on children did not begin until the late nineteenth and early twentieth centuries. Gradually it led to the construction of theories of child development, to which professionals and parents could turn for understanding and guidance. Although the word *theory* has many definitions, for our purposes we can think of a **theory** as an orderly, integrated set of statements that describes, explains, and predicts behavior. For example, a good theory of infant–caregiver attachment would *describe* the behaviors that lead up to babies' strong desire to seek the affection and comfort of a familiar adult around 6 to 8 months of age. It would also *explain* why infants have such a strong desire. And it might also try to *predict* what might happen if babies do not develop this close emotional bond.

As we will see later on, theories are influenced by the cultural values and belief systems of their times. But theories differ in one important way from mere opinion and belief: a theory's continued existence depends on *scientific verification* (Scarr, 1985). This means that the theory must be tested using a fair set of research procedures agreed on by the scientific community. (We will consider research strategies in Chapter 2.)

Theories are vital tools in child development (and any other scientific endeavor) for several reasons. First, they provide organizing frameworks for our observations of children. In other words, they *guide and give meaning* to what we see. To appreciate this idea, imagine a researcher who observes and measures, with no clear idea of what information is important to collect, at least for the moment, and what is unimportant. Such a person is likely to be overwhelmed by a multitude of trivial and disconnected facts because no "lens" is available to focus, integrate, and help make sense of the data (Thomas, 1992). Theories, then, are essential for imposing orderly, meaningful direction on our research efforts.

Second, theories that are verified by research often serve as a sound basis for practical action. Once a theory helps us *understand* development, we are in a much better position to know *what to do* in our efforts to improve the welfare and treatment of children. When knowledge precedes action, coherent plans replace floundering and groping attempts at solutions.

In the field of child development, there are many theories with very different ideas about what children are like and how they develop. The study of child development provides no ultimate truth, since investigators do not always agree on the meaning of what they see. In addition, children are complex beings; they grow physically, mentally, emotionally, and socially. As yet, no single theory has been able to explain all these aspects. Finally, the existence of multiple theories helps advance knowledge, since researchers are continually trying to support, contradict, and integrate these different points of view.

This chapter traces the emergence of the field of child development and provides an overview of major twentieth-century theories. (We will return to each modern theory in greater detail in later chapters of this book.) Although there are many theories, we can easily organize them, since almost all take a stand on three basic issues about childhood and child development. To help you remember these

Theory
An orderly, integrated set of statements that describes, explains, and predicts behavior.

TABLE 1.1 *Basic Issues in Child Development*	
ISSUE	*QUESTION RAISED ABOUT DEVELOPMENT*
Organismic versus mechanistic child	Are children active beings with psychological structures that underlie and control development, or are they passive recipients of environmental inputs?
Continuous versus discontinuous development	Is child development a matter of cumulative adding on of skills and behaviors, or does it involve qualitative, stagewise changes?
Nature versus nurture	Are genetic or environmental factors the most important determinants of child development and behavior?

controversial issues, they are briefly summarized in Table 1.1. Let's take a close look at each in the following sections.

Organismic versus Mechanistic Child

Recently, the mother of a 16-month-old boy named Angelo reported to me with amazement that her young son pushed a toy car across the living room floor while making a motorlike sound, "Brmmmm, brmmmm," for the first time. "We've never shown him how to do that!" exclaimed Angelo's mother. "Did he make that sound up himself," she inquired, "or did he copy it from some other child at day care?"

Angelo's mother has asked a puzzling question about the nature of children. It contrasts two basic perspectives: the organismic, or *active* position, with the mechanistic, or *passive* point of view.

Organismic theories assume that change is stimulated from *within the organism*—more specifically, that psychological structures exist inside the child that underlie and control development. Children are viewed as active, purposeful beings who make sense of their world and determine their own learning. For an organismic theorist, the surrounding environment supports development, as Angelo's mother did when she provided him with stimulating toys. But since children invent their own ways of understanding and responding to events around them, the environment does not bring about the child's growth.

In contrast, **mechanistic theories** focus on relationships between environmental inputs and behavioral outputs. The approach is called mechanistic because children's development is compared to the workings of a machine. Change is stimulated by the environment, which shapes the behavior of the child, who is a passive reactor. For example, when Angelo's playmate says "Brmmmm," Angelo responds in a likewise way. According to this view, new capacities result from external forces acting on the child. Development is treated as a straightforward, predictable consequence of events in the surrounding world (Miller, 1989; Smith, 1992).

Continuity versus Discontinuity in Development

How can we best describe the differences in capacities and behavior that exist between small infants, young children, adolescents, and adults? As Figure 1.1 illustrates, major theories recognize two possibilities.

On the one hand, babies and preschoolers may respond to the world in much the same way as adults. The difference between the immature and mature being may simply be one of *amount* or *complexity* of behavior. For example, little Angelo's thinking might be just as logical and well organized as our own. Perhaps (as his mother reports) he can sort objects into simple categories, recognize whether there are more of one kind than another, and remember where he left his favorite toy at day care the week before. Angelo's only limitation may be that he cannot perform these skills with as many pieces of information as we can. If this is

Organismic theories
Theories that assume the existence of psychological structures inside the child that underlie and control development.

Mechanistic theories
Theories that regard the child as a passive reactor to environmental inputs.

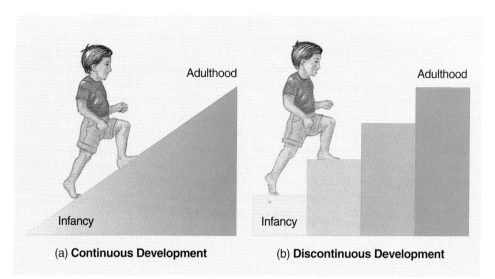

FIGURE 1.1 Is development continuous or discontinuous? (a) Some theorists believe development is a smooth, continuous process. Children gradually add more of the same types of skills. (b) Other theorists think development takes place in abrupt, discontinuous stages. Children change rapidly as they step up to a new level of development and then change very little for a while. With each new step, the child interprets and responds to the world in a qualitatively different way.

true, then Angelo's development must be **continuous**—a process that consists of gradually adding on more of the same types of skills that were there to begin with.

On the other hand, Angelo may have unique ways of thinking, feeling, and behaving that must be understood on their own terms—ones quite different from our own. If so, then development is a **discontinuous** process in which new ways of understanding and responding to the world emerge at particular time periods. From this perspective, Angelo is not yet able to organize objects or remember experiences in the same way as adults. Instead, he will move through a series of developmental steps, each of which has unique features, until he reaches a final transformation that marks the beginning of adulthood.

Theories that accept the discontinuous perspective include a vital developmental concept: the concept of stage. **Stages** are qualitative changes in thinking, feeling, and behaving that characterize particular time periods of development. In stage theories, development is much like climbing a staircase, with each step corresponding to a more mature, reorganized way of functioning than the one that came before. The stage concept also assumes that children undergo periods of rapid transformation as they step up from one stage to the next, followed by plateaus during which they stand solidly within a stage. In other words, change is fairly sudden rather than gradual and ongoing. Finally, stages are always assumed to be universal across children and cultures; that is, stage theories assume that children everywhere follow the same sequence of development.

Does development actually take place in a neat, orderly stepwise sequence that is identical for all human beings? For now, let's note that this is a very ambitious assumption that has not gone unchallenged. We will review some very influential stage theories later in this chapter.

Nature versus Nurture

In addition to describing the course of child development, each theory takes a stand on a major question about its underlying causes: Are genetic or environmental factors most important in explaining developmental change? This is the age-old **nature–nurture controversy.** By *nature*, we mean inborn biological givens—the hereditary information we receive from our parents at the moment of conception that signals the body to grow and affects all our characteristics and skills. By *nurture*, we mean the complex forces of the physical and social world that children encounter in their homes, neighborhoods, schools, and communities.

Although all theories grant at least some role to both nature and nurture, they vary in the emphasis placed on each. For example, consider the following questions: Is the older child's ability to think in more complex ways largely the result of an inborn timetable of growth? Or is it primarily influenced by the way parents

Continuous development
A view that regards development as a cumulative process of adding on more of the same types of skills that were there to begin with.

Discontinuous development
A view in which new and different ways of interpreting and responding to the world emerge at particular time periods.

Stage
A qualitative change in thinking, feeling, and behaving that characterizes a particular time period of development.

Nature–nurture controversy
Disagreement among theorists about whether genetic or environmental factors are the most important determinants of development and behavior.

and teachers stimulate and encourage the child? Do children acquire language because they are genetically predisposed to do so or because parents intensively tutor them from an early age? And what accounts for the vast individual differences among children—in height, weight, physical coordination, intelligence, personality, and social skills? Is nature or nurture more responsible?

In later sections of this chapter and throughout this book, we will see that theories offer strikingly different answers to these questions. To illustrate, take a moment to look back at our discussion of organismic versus mechanistic child. An organismic theorist would never assume that nurture plays a more powerful role in development than nature. And a mechanistic theorist would always stress the importance of nurture. Notice, also, that the stance a theorist takes on nature versus nurture is of great applied significance. If you believe that development is largely due to nature, then providing children with experiences aimed at inducing change would seem to be of little value. If, on the other hand, you are convinced that the environment has a profound impact on development, then you would want to offer a rich variety of learning experiences designed to ensure that children realize their potential.

A Balanced Point of View

Up to now, we have discussed the three basic issues of child development mostly in terms of extremes—solutions on one side or the other. As we trace the unfolding of the field of child development in the rest of this chapter, you will see that the positions of many theories have softened. Modern ones, especially, recognize the merits of both sides. Some theorists take an intermediate stand between an organismic versus mechanistic perspective. They regard both the child and the surrounding environment as active and as collaborating to produce development. Similarly, some contemporary researchers believe that both continuous and discontinuous changes characterize development and alternate with one another. Finally, recent investigators have moved away from asking which is more important—heredity or environment. Instead, they want to know precisely *how nature and nurture work together* to influence the child's traits and capacities.

Brief Review

Child development is a field of study devoted to understanding all aspects of human growth from conception through adolescence. Investigators from many disciplines have contributed to its vast knowledge base, which has been stimulated both by scientific curiosity and by efforts to better the lives of children. Theories lend structure and meaning to observations of children and provide a sound basis for practical action. Almost all theories take a stand on three basic issues about what children are like and how they develop: (1) Is the child an organismic or mechanistic being? (2) Is development a continuous or discontinuous process? (3) Is nature or nurture more important in development?

HISTORICAL FOUNDATIONS

Modern theories of child development are the result of centuries of change in Western cultural values, philosophical thinking about children, and scientific progress. To understand the field as it exists today, we must return to its beginnings—to influences that long preceded scientific child study. We will see that many early ideas about children linger on as important forces in current theory and research.

Medieval Times

In medieval times (the sixth through the fifteenth centuries), little importance was placed on childhood as a separate phase of the life cycle. The idea accepted by many theorists today, that children are unique and different from youths and adults, was much less common then. Instead, once children emerged from infancy, they were regarded as miniature, already formed adults, a view called **preformationism.** This attitude is reflected in the art, everyday entertainment, and language of the times. If you look carefully at medieval paintings, you will see that children are depicted in dress and expression as immature adults. Before the sixteenth century, toys and games were not designed to occupy and amuse children but were for all people. And consider age, so important an aspect of modern personal identity that children can recite how old they are almost as soon as they can talk. Age was unimportant in medieval custom and usage. People did not refer to it in everyday conversation, and it was not even recorded in family and civil records until the fifteenth and sixteenth centuries (Aries, 1962).

Nevertheless, faint glimmerings of the idea that children are unique emerged during medieval times. The Church defended the innocence of children, spoke out against the common practice of infanticide, and encouraged parents to provide spiritual training. Medical works had sections acknowledging the fragility of infants and children and providing special instructions for their care. And some laws recognized that children needed protection from adults who might mistreat or take advantage of them. But even though in a practical sense there was some awareness of the smallness and vulnerability of children, as yet there were no theories about the uniqueness of childhood or separate developmental periods (Borstelmann, 1983; Sommerville, 1982).

The Reformation

In the sixteenth century, a revised image of childhood sprang from the religious movement that gave birth to Protestantism—in particular, from the Puritan belief in original sin. According to Puritan doctrine, the child was a fragile creature of God who needed to be safeguarded but who also needed to be reformed. Born evil and stubborn, children had to be led away from their devilish ways. Therefore, it was necessary to take them firmly in hand and civilize them toward a destiny of

*I*n this medieval painting, the young child is depicted as a miniature adult. His dress, expression, and activities resemble those of his elders. Through the fifteenth century, little emphasis was placed on childhood as a unique phase of the life cycle. (GIRAUDON/ART RESOURCE)

Preformationism
Medieval view of the child as a miniature adult.

virtue and salvation. Schools separated boys of the middle classes from the corrupt world of older youths and adults, extending the period of childhood beyond infancy. Girls and lower-class boys were excluded, their limited childhood much the same as it was in medieval times (Aries, 1962; Shahar, 1990).

Harsh, restrictive child-rearing practices were recommended as the most efficient means for taming the depraved child. Infants were tightly swaddled, and children were dressed in stiff, uncomfortable clothing that held them in adultlike postures. In schools, disobedient pupils were routinely beaten by their schoolmasters (Stone, 1977). Although these attitudes represented the prevailing child-rearing philosophy of the time, it is important to note that they were probably not typical of everyday practices in Puritan families. Recent historical evidence suggests that love and affection for their children made many Puritan parents reluctant to use extremely repressive discipline (Moran & Vinovskis, 1986).

As the Puritans emigrated from England to the United States, they brought with them the belief that child rearing was one of their most important obligations. Although they continued to regard the child's soul as tainted by original sin, they tried to promote reason in their sons and daughters so they would be able to separate right from wrong and resist temptation. The Puritans were the first to develop special reading materials for children that instructed them in religious and moral ideals. As they trained their children in self-reliance and self-control, Puritan parents gradually adopted a moderate balance between discipline and indulgence, severity and permissiveness (Pollock, 1987).

Philosophies of the Enlightenment

The seventeenth-century Enlightenment brought new philosophies of reason and fostered ideals of human dignity and respect. Conceptions of childhood appeared that were more humane than those of centuries past.

JOHN LOCKE. The writings of John Locke (1632–1704), a leading British philosopher, served as the forerunner of an important twentieth-century perspective that we will discuss shortly: behaviorism. Locke viewed the child as **tabula rasa.** Translated from Latin, this means "blank slate" or "white piece of paper." According to this idea, children were not basically evil. They were, to begin with, nothing at all, and their characters could be shaped by all kinds of experiences while growing up. Locke (1690/1892) described parents as rational tutors who could mold the child in any way they wished, through careful instruction, effective example, and rewards for good behavior. In addition, Locke was ahead of his time in recommending to parents child-rearing practices that were eventually supported by twentieth-century research. For example, he suggested that parents not reward children with money or sweets, but rather with praise and approval. Locke also opposed physical punishment: "The child repeatedly beaten in school cannot look upon books and teachers without experiencing fear and anger." Locke's philosophy led to a change from harshness toward children to kindness and compassion.

Look carefully at Locke's ideas, and you will see that he took a firm stand on each of the basic issues we discussed earlier in this chapter. As blank slates, children are viewed in passive, *mechanistic* terms; the course of growth is written upon them by the environment. Locke also regarded development as a *continuous* process. Adultlike behaviors are gradually built up through the warm, consistent teachings of parents. Finally, Locke was a champion of *nurture*—of the power of the environment to determine whether children become good or bad, bright or dull, kind or selfish.

Tabula rasa

Locke's view of the child as a blank slate whose character is shaped by experience.

JEAN-JACQUES ROUSSEAU. In the eighteenth century, babies were no longer swaddled, children were dressed more comfortably, and corporal punishment declined. A new theory of childhood was introduced by the French philosopher of the Enlightenment, Jean-Jacques Rousseau (1712–1778). Children, Rousseau (1792/1955) thought, were not blank slates and empty containers to be filled by adult instruction. Instead, they were **noble savages,** naturally endowed with a sense of right and wrong and with an innate plan for orderly, healthy growth. Unlike Locke, Rousseau thought children's built-in moral sense and unique ways of thinking and feeling would only be harmed by adult training. His was a permissive philosophy in which the adult should be receptive to the child's needs at each of four stages of development: infancy, childhood, late childhood, and adolescence.

Rousseau's philosophy includes two vitally important concepts that are found in modern theories. The first is the concept of *stage,* which we discussed earlier in this chapter. The second is the concept of **maturation,** which refers to a genetically determined, naturally unfolding course of growth. If you accept the notion that children mature through a sequence of stages, then they cannot be preformed, miniature adults. Instead, they are unique and different from adults, and their development is determined by their own inner nature. Compared to Locke, Rousseau took a very different stand on basic developmental issues. He saw children as *organismic* (active shapers of their own destiny), development as a *discontinuous* stagewise process, and *nature* as having mapped out the path and timetable of growth.

Darwin's Theory of Evolution

A century after Rousseau, another ancestor of modern child study—this time of its scientific foundations—emerged. In the mid–nineteenth century, Charles Darwin (1809–1882), a British naturalist, joined an expedition to distant parts of the world, where he made careful observations of fossils and animal and plant life. Darwin (1859/1936) noticed the infinite variation among species. He also saw that within a species, no two individuals are exactly alike. From these observations, he constructed his famous theory of evolution.

The theory emphasized two related principles: *natural selection* and *survival of the fittest.* Darwin explained that certain species were selected by nature to survive in particular parts of the world because they had characteristics that fit with, or were adapted to, their surroundings. Other species died off because they were not well suited to their environments. Individuals within a species that best met the survival requirements of the environment lived long enough to reproduce and pass their more favorable characteristics to future generations. Darwin's emphasis on the adaptive value of physical characteristics and behavior eventually found its way into important twentieth-century theories. For example, later in this chapter we will see that Darwin's ideas are central to ethology, an approach to development that emphasizes the evolutionary origins and adaptive value of human behavior. Jean Piaget, master theorist of children's thinking, was also influenced by Darwin. As will become clear shortly, Piaget believed that as children reason about the world in more mature, effective ways, they achieve a better adaptive fit with their surroundings (Dixon & Lerner, 1992).

During his explorations, Darwin discovered that the early prenatal growth of many species was strikingly similar. This suggested that all species, including human beings, were descended from a few common ancestors. Other scientists concluded from Darwin's observation that the development of the human child, from conception to maturity, followed the same general plan as the evolution of the human species. Although this belief eventually proved to be inaccurate, efforts to chart parallels between child growth and human evolution prompted researchers to make careful observations of all aspects of children's behavior. Out of these first attempts to document an idea about development, the science of child study was born.

Early Scientific Beginnings

Scientific child study evolved quickly during the early part of the twentieth century. As we will see in the following sections, rudimentary observations of single

Noble savage
Rousseau's view of the child as naturally endowed with an innate plan for orderly, healthy growth.

Maturation
A genetically determined, naturally unfolding course of growth.

children were soon followed by improved methods and theoretical ideas. Each advance contributed to the firm foundation on which the field rests today.

FIRST CHILD SUBJECTS: THE BABY BIOGRAPHIES. Imagine yourself as a forerunner in the field of child development, confronted with studying children for the first time. How might you go about this challenging task? Scientists of the late nineteenth and early twentieth century did what most of us would probably do in their place. They selected a convenient subject—a child of their own or of a close relative. Then, beginning in early infancy, they jotted down day-by-day descriptions and impressions of the youngster's behavior. Dozens of these baby biographies were published by the early twentieth century. In the following excerpt from one of them, the author reflects on the birth of her young niece, whose growth she followed during the first year of life:

> Its first act is a cry, not of wrath, . . . nor a shout of joy, . . . but a snuffling, and then a long, thin tearless á——á, with the timbre of a Scotch bagpipe, purely automatic, but of discomfort. With this monotonous and dismal cry, with its red, shriveled, parboiled skin . . . , it is not strange that, if the mother . . . has not come to love her child before birth, there is a brief interval occasionally dangerous to the child before the maternal instinct is fully aroused.
>
> It cannot be denied that this unflattering description is fair enough, and our baby was no handsomer than the rest of her kind. . . . Yet she did not lack admirers. I have never noticed that women (even those who are not mothers) mind a few little aesthetic defects, . . . with so many counterbalancing charms in the little warm, soft, living thing. (Shinn, 1900, pp. 20–21)

Can you tell from this passage why baby biographies have sometimes been upheld as examples of how *not* to study children? These first investigators tended to be emotionally invested in their young subjects, and they seldom began their observations with a clear idea of what they wanted to find out about the child. Not surprisingly, many of the records were eventually discarded as biased. But we must keep in mind that the baby biographers were like explorers first setting foot on alien soil. When a field is new, we cannot expect its theories and methods to be well formulated.

The baby biographies were clearly a step in the right direction. In fact, two theorists of the nineteenth century, Darwin (1877) and the German biologist William Preyer (1882/1888), contributed to these early records of children's behavior. Each charted the development of his son during the first 3 years of life. Preyer, especially, set high standards for making observations. He recorded what he saw immediately, as completely as possible, and at regular intervals. He also tried not to influence the child's behavior or to let his own interests and interpretations distort what he saw. And he checked the accuracy of his own notes against those of a second observer (Cairns, 1983). These are the same high standards that modern researchers use when making observations of children. As a result of the biographers' pioneering efforts, in succeeding decades the child became a common subject of scientific research.

THE NORMATIVE PERIOD OF CHILD STUDY. G. Stanley Hall (1844–1924), one of the most influential American psychologists of the early twentieth century, is generally regarded as the founder of the child study movement (Dixon & Lerner, 1992). Inspired by Darwin's work, Hall and his well-known student Arnold Gesell (1880–1961) developed theories based on evolutionary ideas. These early leaders regarded child development as a genetically determined series of events that unfolds automatically, much like a blooming flower (Gesell, 1933; Hall, 1904).

Hall and Gesell are remembered less for their one-sided theories than for their intensive efforts to describe all aspects of child development. Aware of the limitations of baby biographies, Hall set out to collect a sound body of objective facts about children. This goal launched the **normative approach** to child study. In a normative investigation, measurements of behavior are taken on large numbers of

Normative approach
An approach in which age-related averages are computed to represent the typical child's development.

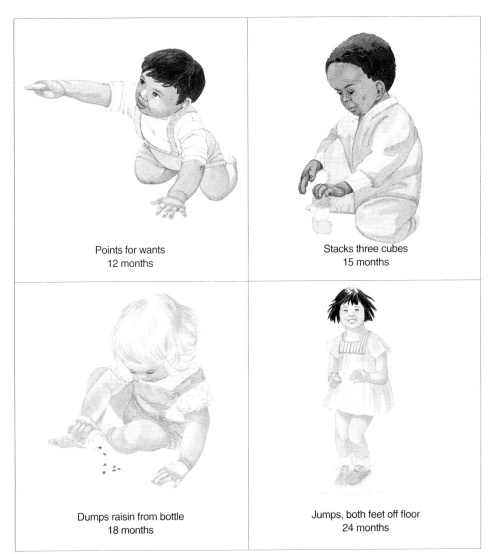

Points for wants
12 months

Stacks three cubes
15 months

Dumps raisin from bottle
18 months

Jumps, both feet off floor
24 months

FIGURE 1.2 Sample milestones from the most recent revision of Gesell's schedules of infant development, which include norms on hundreds of motor, mental, language, and social skills. Gesell's efforts to describe the course of development continue to be useful today. (Adapted from Knobloch, Stevens, & Malone, 1980.)

children. Then age-related averages are computed to represent the typical child's development. Using this approach, Hall constructed elaborate questionnaires asking children of different ages almost everything they could tell about themselves—interests, fears, imaginary playmates, dreams, friendships, favorite toys, and more (White, 1992).

In the same tradition, Gesell devoted a major part of his career to collecting detailed normative information on the behavior of infants and children. His schedules of infant development were particularly complete, and revised versions continue to be used today (see Figure 1.2). Gesell was also among the first to make knowledge about child development meaningful to parents. He provided them with descriptions of motor achievements, social behaviors, and personality characteristics (Gesell & Ilg, 1949). Gesell hoped to relieve parents' anxieties by informing them of what to expect at each age. If, as he believed, the timetable of development is the product of millions of years of evolution, then children are naturally knowledgeable about their needs. His child-rearing advice, in the tradition of Rousseau, was a permissive approach that recommended sensitivity and responsiveness to children's cues (Thelen & Adolph, 1992). Gesell's books were widely read. Along with Benjamin Spock's famous *Baby and Child Care,* they became a central part of a rapidly expanding literature for parents published over this century. (See the From Research to Practice box on page 12.)

Almost all parents—especially new ones—feel a need for sound advice on how to raise their children. To meet this need, the field of child development has long been communicating what it knows to the general public through a wide variety of popular books and magazines. A recent survey looked at the types of advice that experts gave to parents of infants from 1955 to 1984 (Young, 1990). Two widely read sources were carefully examined: *Parents* magazine (to which scholars often contribute articles) and *Infant Care* (a pamphlet written by pediatricians and other child development specialists and published at regular intervals by the United States Children's Bureau).

From the 1950s to the 1980s, advice to parents changed in ways that reflected new social realities, cultural beliefs about children, and scientific discoveries. Prior to the 1970s, the publications emphasized the central role of the mother in healthy infant development. Although mothers were encouraged to include fathers in the care of the baby, they were cautioned not to expect fathers to participate equally. The succeeding decade brought considerably fewer references to the primacy of the mother until, in the mid-1980s, an about-face was evident. Experts suggested that fathers might share in the full range of caregiving responsibilities,

since new evidence revealed that the father's role is unique and important to all aspects of development.

Around this time, information about maternal employment and child care also appeared in the publications. In contrast to the earlier view of the maternal role as a full-time commitment, experts reassured the modern mother that her baby did not require her continuous presence and offered advice about how to select good day care. Recommendations on this score, however, displayed some ambivalence. Mothers were also told that staying with the infant "can be a great human experience," and they were discouraged from entrusting the care of their babies to others. As we will see in Chapter 10, controversy exists in both American culture and in the scientific community about the advisability of placing infants in day care, and it is reflected in contemporary advice to parents.

During the three decades studied, some child-rearing themes did not change. Parents were told repeatedly that they play a large role in guiding their baby's development, that infants are active learners who benefit from a rich variety of physical and social stimulation, and that early experiences have a lasting impact. As you read the rest of this chapter, try to identify major theories of the mid– and late twentieth century that may have prompted these statements.

Although Hall and Gesell's work offered a large body of descriptive facts about children of different ages, it provided little information on *process*—the how and why of development. Yet the child's development had to be described before it could be understood, and the normative approach provided the foundation for more effective explanations of development that came later.

THE MENTAL TESTING MOVEMENT. While Hall and Gesell were developing their theories and methods in the United States, French psychologist Alfred Binet (1857–1911) was also taking a normative approach to child development, but for a different reason. In the early 1900s, Binet and his colleague Theodore Simon were asked to find a way to identify retarded children in the Paris school system who needed to be placed in special classes. The first successful intelligence test, which they constructed for this purpose, grew out of practical educational concerns.

Previous attempts to create a useful intelligence test had met with little success. But Binet's effort was unique in that he began with a well-developed theory. In contrast to earlier views, which reduced intelligence to simple elements of reaction time and sensitivity to physical stimuli, Binet captured the complexity of children's thinking (Siegler, 1992). He defined intelligence as good judgment, planning, and critical reflection. Then he selected test questions that directly measured these abilities, creating a series of age-graded items that permitted him to compare the intellectual progress of different children.

In 1916, at Stanford University, Binet's test was translated into English and adapted for use with American children. It became known as the Stanford-Binet Intelligence Scale. Besides providing a score that could successfully predict school achievement, the Binet test sparked tremendous interest in individual differences in development. The mental testing movement was in motion. Comparisons of the intelligence test scores of children who vary in sex, ethnicity, birth order, family background, and other characteristics became a major focus of research.

Intelligence tests also rose quickly to the forefront of the controversy over nature versus nurture that has continued throughout this century.

JAMES MARK BALDWIN: EARLY DEVELOPMENTAL THEORIST. A final important figure, overlooked in the history of child development for decades but now recognized as having had a major influence, is American psychologist James Mark Baldwin (1861–1934). A theorist rather than an observer of children, Baldwin's (1897) rich interpretations of development are experiencing a revival today. He believed that children's understanding of their physical and social worlds develops through a sequence of stages, beginning with the simplest behavior patterns of the newborn infant and concluding with the adult's capacity to think abstractly and reflectively (Cairns, 1992). Yet in describing the process of change, Baldwin differed from other leaders of his time in adopting a balanced view of child development.

Baldwin regarded neither the child nor the environment as in control of development. Instead, both nature and nurture were granted equal importance. Children, he argued, actively revise their ways of thinking about the world, but they also learn through habit, or simple copying of others' behaviors. As development proceeds, the child and his social surroundings influence each other, forming an inseparable, interwoven network. In other words, children are affected by those around them, but they too affect others' reactions toward them, in a reciprocal fashion.

Consider these ideas, and you will see why Baldwin (1895) argued that heredity and environment should not be viewed as distinct, opposing forces. Instead, he claimed, most human characteristics are "due to both causes working together" (p. 77). As we turn now to an overview of modern theories of child development, you will find Baldwin's ideas represented in several of them, especially the more recent ones.

Brief Review

The modern field of child development has roots dating far back into the past. In medieval times, children were regarded as preformed, miniature adults. By the sixteenth century, childhood became a distinct phase of the life cycle. The Puritan belief in original sin fostered a harsh, authoritarian approach to child rearing. During the seventeenth century Enlightenment, Locke's "blank slate" and Rousseau's "inherently good" child promoted more humane treatment of children. Darwin's evolutionary ideas inspired maturational theories and the first attempts to study the child directly, in the form of baby biographies and Hall and Gesell's normative investigations. Out of the normative approach arose Binet's first successful intelligence test and a concern with individual differences among children. Baldwin's balanced view of the process of development survives in modern theories.

MID–TWENTIETH-CENTURY THEORIES

In the mid–twentieth century, the field of child development expanded into a legitimate discipline. Specialized societies were founded, and research journals were launched. Perhaps the most important group is the Society for Research in Child Development, an interdisciplinary organization of researchers established in 1933 and devoted to advancing our knowledge of children. The society's journal, *Child Development,* is currently in its seventh decade of publication.

As child development attracted increasing interest, a variety of mid–twentieth-century theories emerged, each of which continues to have followers today. In these theories, the European concern with the inner thoughts and feelings of the child contrasts sharply with the focus of American academic psychology on scientific precision and concrete, observable behavior.

Sigmund Freud founded the psychoanalytic movement. His psychosexual theory was the first approach to stress the importance of early experience for later development. (LYRL AHERN)

Psychoanalytic perspective
An approach to personality development introduced by Freud that assumes children move through a series of stages in which they confront conflicts between biological drives and social expectations. The way these conflicts are resolved determines psychological adjustment.

Psychosexual theory
Freud's theory, which emphasizes that how parents manage children's sexual and aggressive drives during the first few years is crucial for healthy personality development.

Id
In Freud's theory, the part of personality that is the source of basic biological needs and desires.

Ego
In Freud's theory, the rational part of personality that reconciles the demands of the id, the external world, and the conscience.

Superego
In Freud's theory, the part of personality that is the seat of conscience and is often in conflict with the id's desires.

The Psychoanalytic Perspective

By the 1930s and 1940s, many parents whose children suffered from serious emotional stress and behavior problems sought help from psychiatrists and social workers. The earlier normative movement had answered the question, What are children like? But child guidance professionals had to address the question, How and why did children become the way they are? to treat their difficulties. They turned for help to the **psychoanalytic perspective** on personality development because of its emphasis on the unique developmental history of each child. According to the psychoanalytic approach, children move through a series of stages in which they confront conflicts between biological drives and social expectations. The way these conflicts are resolved determines the individual's ability to learn, to get along with others, and to cope with anxiety. Although many individuals contributed to the psychoanalytic perspective, two have been especially influential: Sigmund Freud, founder of the psychoanalytic movement, and Erik Erikson.

FREUD'S PSYCHOSEXUAL THEORY. Freud (1856–1939), a Viennese physician, saw patients in his practice with a variety of nervous symptoms, such as hallucinations, fears, and paralyses, that appeared to have no physical basis. Seeking a cure for these troubled adults, Freud found that their symptoms could be relieved by having patients talk freely about painful events of their childhood. Using this "talking cure," he carefully examined the unconscious motivations of his patients. Startling the straitlaced Victorian society in which he lived, Freud concluded that infants and young children were sexual beings and that the way they were permitted to express their impulses lay at the heart of their adult behavior. Freud constructed his **psychosexual theory** of development on the basis of adult remembrances. He emphasized that how parents manage their child's sexual and aggressive drives in the first few years of life is crucial for healthy personality development.

Three Portions of the Personality. In Freud's theory, three parts of the personality—id, ego, and superego—become integrated during a sequence of five stages of development. The **id,** the largest portion of the mind, is inherited and present at birth. It is the source of basic biological needs and desires. The id seeks to satisfy its impulses head-on, without delay. As a result, young babies cry vigorously when they are hungry, wet, or need to be held and cuddled.

The **ego,** the conscious, rational part of personality, emerges in early infancy to ensure that the id's desires are satisfied in accordance with reality. Recalling times when parents helped the baby gratify the id, the ego redirects the impulses so they are discharged on appropriate objects at acceptable times and places. Aided by the ego, the hungry baby of a few months of age stops crying when he sees his mother unfasten her clothing for breast-feeding or warm a bottle. And the more competent preschooler goes into the kitchen and gets a snack on her own.

Between 3 and 6 years of age, the **superego,** or seat of conscience, appears. It contains the values of society and is often in conflict with the id's desires. The superego develops from interactions with parents, who eventually insist that children control their biological impulses. Once the superego is formed, the ego is faced with the increasingly complex task of reconciling the demands of the id, the external world, and the conscience (Freud, 1923/1974). For example, when the ego is tempted to gratify an id impulse by hitting a playmate to get an attractive toy, the superego may warn that such behavior is wrong. The ego must decide which of the two forces (id or superego) will win this inner struggle or work out a reasonable compromise, such as asking for a turn with the toy. According to Freud, the relations established among the id, ego, and superego during the preschool years determine the individual's basic personality.

Psychosexual Development. Freud (1938/1973) believed that over the course of childhood, sexual impulses shift their focus from the oral to the anal to the genital regions of the body. In each stage of development, parents walk a fine line between

TABLE 1.2 Freud's Psychosexual Stages

PSYCHOSEXUAL STAGE	PERIOD OF DEVELOPMENT	DESCRIPTION
Oral	Birth–1 year	The new ego directs the baby's sucking activities toward breast or bottle. If oral needs are not met appropriately, the individual may develop such habits as thumb sucking, fingernail biting, and pencil chewing in childhood and overeating and smoking in later life.
Anal	1–3 years	Young toddlers and preschoolers enjoy holding and releasing urine and feces. Toilet training becomes a major issue between parent and child. If parents insist that children be trained before they are ready or make too few demands, conflicts about anal control may appear in the form of extreme orderliness and cleanliness or disorder and messiness.
Phallic	3–6 years	Id impulses transfer to the genitals, and the child finds pleasure in genital stimulation. Freud's *Oedipus conflict* for boys and *Electra conflict* for girls take place. Young children feel a sexual desire for the opposite-sex parent. To avoid punishment, they give up this desire and, instead, adopt the same-sex parent's characteristics and values. As a result, the superego is formed. The relations between the id, ego, and superego established at this time determine the individual's basic personality orientation.
Latency	6–11 years	Sexual instincts die down, and the superego develops further. The child acquires new social values from adults outside the family and from play with same-sex peers.
Genital	Adolescence	Puberty causes the sexual impulses of the phallic stage to reappear. If development has been successful during earlier stages, it leads to marriage, mature sexuality, and the birth and rearing of children.

permitting too much or too little gratification of their child's basic needs. Either extreme can cause the child's psychic energies to be *fixated*, or arrested, at a particular stage. Too much satisfaction makes the child unwilling to move on to a more mature level of behavior. Too little leads the child to continue seeking gratification of the frustrated drive. If parents strike an appropriate balance, then children grow into well-adjusted adults with the capacity for mature sexual behavior, investment in family life, and rearing of the next generation. Table 1.2 summarizes each of Freud's stages.

Freud's psychosexual theory highlighted the importance of family relationships for children's development and provided a framework for understanding children's emotional problems. It was the first theory to stress the importance of early experience for later development. But Freud's perspective was eventually criticized for several reasons. First, the theory overemphasized the influence of sexual feelings in development. Second, because it was based on the problems of sexually repressed, well-to-do adults, some aspects of Freud's theory did not apply in cultures differing from nineteenth-century Victorian society. Finally, Freud's ideas were called into question because he did not study children directly.

ERIKSON'S PSYCHOSOCIAL THEORY. Several of Freud's followers took what was useful from his theory and stretched and rearranged it in ways that improved upon his vision. The most important of these neo-Freudians for the field of child development is Erik Erikson (b. 1902).

Although Erikson (1950) accepted Freud's basic psychosexual framework, he expanded the picture of development at each stage. In his **psychosocial theory,** Erikson emphasized that social experiences at each Freudian stage do not just lead to an embattled ego that mediates between id impulses and superego demands. The ego is also a positive force in development. At each stage, it acquires attitudes

Psychosocial theory
Erikson's theory, which emphasizes that the demands of society at each Freudian stage not only promote the development of a unique personality, but also ensure that individuals acquire attitudes and skills that help them become active, contributing members of their society.

*E*rik Erikson expanded Freud's theory, emphasizing the psychosocial outcomes of development. At each psychosexual stage, a major psychological conflict is resolved. If the outcome is positive, individuals acquire attitudes and skills that permit them to contribute constructively to society.
(LYRL AHERN)

and skills that make the individual an active, contributing member of society. A basic psychosocial conflict, which is resolved along a continuum from positive to negative, determines healthy or maladaptive outcomes at each stage. As you can see in Table 1.3, Erikson's first five stages parallel Freud's stages. However, Erikson did not regard important developmental tasks as limited to early childhood. He believed that they occur throughout life. Note that Erikson added three adult stages to Freud's model and was one of the first to recognize the life-span nature of development.

Finally, unlike Freud, Erikson pointed out that normal development must be understood in relation to each culture's unique life situation. Societies have evolved ways of imposing new demands at each stage that help children acquire competencies valued and needed by their culture. For example, among the Yurok Indians (a tribe of fishermen and acorn gatherers on the northwest coast of the United States), babies are deprived of breast-feeding for the first 10 days after birth and are instead fed a thin soup from a small shell. At 6 months of age, infants are abruptly weaned, an event enforced, if necessary, by having the mother leave for a few days. These experiences, from our cultural vantage point, seem like cruel attempts to frustrate the child's oral needs. But Erikson pointed out that the Yurok live in a world in which salmon fill the river just once a year, a circumstance that requires the development of considerable self-restraint for survival. In this way, he showed that child-rearing practices can be understood only in the context of the values and requirements of the child's society as a whole.

CONTRIBUTIONS AND LIMITATIONS OF THE PSYCHOANALYTIC PERSPECTIVE. A special strength of the psychoanalytic perspective is its emphasis on the individual's unique life history as worthy of study and understanding (Emde, 1992). Consistent with this view, psychoanalytic theorists accept the *clinical method* (sometimes called the case-study approach) as the most effective way to gather information about development. The clinical method combines data from a variety of sources—interviews with the child, family members, and others who know the child well; responses to psychological tests; and observations in a clinic setting and sometimes in everyday environments as well. The information is synthesized into a detailed picture of the personality functioning of a single child. As we will see in Chapter 2, because information obtained in this way is often selective and subjective, it is risky to rely on it for conclusions about children in general. Nevertheless, clinical records have served as rich sources of ideas that have been tested more precisely with other procedures. Psychoanalytic theories and findings have stimulated a wealth of research on many aspects of emotional and social development, including infant–mother attachment, aggression, sibling relationships, child-rearing practices, morality, gender roles, and adolescent identity.

Despite its extensive contributions, the psychoanalytic perspective is no longer in the mainstream of child development research. There are various speculations as to why this is the case. Psychoanalytic theorists may have become isolated from the rest of the field because they were so strongly committed to the clinical approach that they failed to consider other methods (Sears, 1975). In addition, child development researchers found many psychoanalytic ideas, such as Freud's Oedipal conflict and Erikson's account of basic trust, to be so vague and laden with interpretation that they were difficult or impossible to test empirically (Miller, 1989).

Behaviorism and Social Learning Theory

At the same time that psychoanalytic theory gained in prominence, child study was also influenced by a very different perspective: **behaviorism,** a tradition consistent with Locke's tabula rasa. American behaviorism began with the work of psychologist John Watson (1878–1958) in the early part of the twentieth century. Watson wanted to create an objective science of psychology. Unlike psychoana-

Behaviorism
An approach that views directly observable events—stimuli and responses—as the appropriate focus of study and the development of behavior as taking place through classical and operant conditioning.

16

TABLE 1.3 Erikson's Psychosocial Stages

PSYCHOSOCIAL STAGE	PERIOD OF DEVELOPMENT	DESCRIPTION	CORRESPONDING PSYCHOSEXUAL STAGE
Basic trust versus mistrust	Birth–1 year	From warm, responsive care, infants gain a sense of trust, or confidence, that the world is good. Mistrust occurs when infants have to wait too long for comfort and are handled harshly.	Oral
Autonomy versus shame and doubt	1–3 years	Using new mental and motor skills, children want to choose and decide for themselves. Autonomy is fostered when parents permit reasonable free choice and do not force or shame the child.	Anal
Initiative versus guilt	3–6 years	Through make-believe play, children experiment with the kind of person they can become. Initiative—a sense of ambition and responsibility—develops when parents support their child's new sense of purpose and direction. The danger is that parents will demand too much self-control, which leads to overcontrol, or too much guilt.	Phallic
Industry versus inferiority	6–11 years	At school, children develop the capacity to work and cooperate with others. Inferiority develops when negative experiences at home, at school, or with peers lead to feelings of incompetence and inferiority.	Latency
Identity versus identity diffusion	Adolescence	The adolescent tries to answer the question, Who am I, and what is my place in society? Self-chosen values and vocational goals lead to a secure personal identity. The negative outcome is confusion about future adult roles.	Genital
Intimacy versus isolation	Young adulthood	Young people work on establishing intimate ties to other people. Because of earlier disappointments, some individuals cannot form close relationships and remain isolated from others.	
Generativity versus stagnation	Middle adulthood	Generativity means giving to the next generation through child rearing, caring for other people, or productive work. The person who fails in these ways feels an absence of meaningful accomplishment.	
Ego integrity versus despair	Old age	In this final stage, individuals reflect on the kind of person they have been. Integrity results from feeling that life was worth living as it happened. Old people who are dissatisfied with their lives fear death.	

lytic theorists, he believed in studying directly observable events—stimuli and responses—rather than the unseen workings of the mind (Horowitz, 1992).

TRADITIONAL BEHAVIORISM. Watson was inspired by some studies of animal learning carried out by the famous Russian physiologist Ivan Pavlov. Pavlov knew that dogs release saliva as an innate reflex when they are given food. But he noticed that his dogs were salivating before they tasted any food—when they saw the trainer who usually fed them. The dogs, Pavlov reasoned, must have learned to associate a neutral stimulus (the trainer) with another stimulus (food) that produces a reflexive response (salivation). As a result of this association, the neutral stimulus could bring about the response by itself. Anxious to test this idea, Pavlov successfully taught dogs to salivate at the sound of a bell by pairing it with the presentation of food. He had discovered *classical conditioning.*

Watson wanted to find out if classical conditioning could be applied to children's behavior. In a historic experiment, he taught Albert, a 9-month-old infant, to fear a neutral stimulus—a soft white rat—by presenting it several times with a sharp, loud sound, which naturally scared the baby. Little Albert, who at first had reached out eagerly to touch the furry rat, cried and turned his head away when he caught sight of it (Watson & Raynor, 1920). In fact, Albert's fear was so intense that researchers eventually questioned the ethics of studies like this one (an issue we will take up in Chapter 2). On the basis of findings like these, Watson concluded that environment is the supreme force in child development. Adults could mold children's behavior in any way they wished, he thought, by carefully controlling stimulus–response associations.

After Watson, American behaviorism developed along several lines. The first was Clark Hull's *drive reduction theory.* According to this view, people continually act to satisfy physiological needs and reduce states of tension. As *primary drives* of hunger, thirst, and sex are met, a wide variety of stimuli associated with them become *secondary,* or *learned drives.* For example, a Hullian theorist believes that infants prefer the closeness and attention of adults who have given them food and relieved their discomfort. To ensure adults' affection, children will acquire all sorts of responses that adults desire of them—politeness, honesty, patience, persistence, obedience, and more. In the 1940s and 1950s, an entire theory of social development was based on these principles (Sears, Maccoby, & Levin, 1957).

Another form of behaviorism was B.F. Skinner's (1904–1990) *operant conditioning theory.* Skinner rejected Hull's idea that primary drive reduction is the only way to get children to learn. According to Skinner, a child's behavior can be increased by following it with a wide variety of *reinforcers* besides food and drink, such as praise, a friendly smile, or a new toy. It can also be decreased through *punishment,* such as withdrawal of privileges, parental disapproval, or being sent to be alone in one's room. As a result of Skinner's work, operant conditioning became a broadly applied learning principle in child psychology. We will consider these conditioning principles more fully when we explore the infant's learning capacities in Chapter 4.

B. *F. Skinner rejected Hull's idea that primary drive reduction is the basis of all learning. He emphasized an alternative learning principle, operant conditioning, that has been widely applied in the field of child development.* (LYRL AHERN)

SOCIAL LEARNING THEORY. Psychologists quickly became interested in whether behaviorism might offer a more direct and effective explanation of the development of children's social behavior than the less precise concepts of psychoanalytic theory. This concern sparked the emergence of **social learning theory.** Social learning theorists accepted the principles of conditioning and reinforcement that came before them. They also built on these principles, offering expanded views of how children and adults acquire new responses. By the 1950s, social learning theory had become a major force in child development research.

Several kinds of social learning theory emerged. The most influential was devised by Albert Bandura and his colleagues. Bandura (1967, 1977) demonstrated that modeling, otherwise known as imitation or observational learning, is the basis for a wide variety of children's behaviors. He recognized that children acquire many favorable and unfavorable responses in the absence of direct rewards and punishments, simply by watching and listening to others around them. Why do children mimic the actions of some models more readily than others? Research by Bandura and his followers shows that children are drawn to models who are warm and powerful and who possess desirable objects and characteristics. By behaving like these models, children hope to obtain their valued resources for themselves sometime in the future.

Bandura's work continues to influence much research on children's social development. However, like changes in the field of child development as a whole, today his theory stresses the importance of *cognition,* or thinking. Bandura has

Social learning theory
An approach that emphasizes the role of modeling, or observational learning, in the development of behavior.

shown that children's ability to listen, remember, and abstract general rules from complex sets of observed behavior affects their imitation and learning. In fact, the most recent revision of Bandura's (1986, 1989) theory places such strong emphasis on how children think about themselves and other people that he calls it a *social cognitive* rather than a social learning approach. According to this view, children gradually become more selective in what they imitate. From watching others engage in self-praise and self-blame and through feedback about the worth of their own actions, children develop *personal standards* for behavior and a sense of *self-efficacy*—beliefs about their own abilities and characteristics—that guide responses in particular situations (Grusec, 1992). In Chapters 11 and 12, we will examine the development of children's reasoning about themselves and others, along with its impact on behavior, in greater detail.

CONTRIBUTIONS AND LIMITATIONS OF BEHAVIORISM AND SOCIAL LEARNING THEORY. Like psychoanalytic theory, behaviorism and social learning theory have had a major impact on applied work with children. Yet the techniques used are decidedly different. **Applied behavior analysis** refers to procedures that combine conditioning and modeling to eliminate children's undesirable behaviors and increase their socially acceptable responses. It has been used largely with children who have serious problems, such as persistent aggression and delayed language development (Patterson, 1982; Whitehurst et al., 1989). But it is also effective in dealing with more common difficulties of childhood. For example, in one study, preschoolers' anxious reactions during dental treatment were reduced by reinforcing them with small toys for answering questions about a story read to them while the dentist worked. Because the children could not listen to the story and kick and cry at the same time, their disruptive behaviors subsided (Stark et al., 1989).

Although applied behavior analysis is helpful in treating many problems, we must keep in mind that making something happen through modeling and reinforcement does not mean that these principles offer a complete account of development (Horowitz, 1987). We will see in later sections that many theorists believe that behaviorism and social learning theory offer too narrow a view of important environmental influences. These extend beyond immediate reinforcements and modeled behaviors to the richness of children's physical and social worlds. Finally, we have seen that in emphasizing cognition, Bandura is unique among theorists whose work grew out of the behaviorist tradition in granting children an active role in their own learning. As we will see when we discuss Piaget's theory in the next section, behaviorism and social learning theory have been criticized for underestimating children's contributions to their own development.

Piaget's Cognitive-Developmental Theory

If there is one individual who has influenced the modern field of child development more than any other, it is the Swiss cognitive theorist Jean Piaget (1896–1980). Although American investigators had been aware of Piaget's work since 1930, they did not pay much attention to it until 1960. A major reason is that Piaget's ideas and methods of studying children were very much at odds with behaviorism, which dominated American psychology during the middle of the twentieth century (Beilin, 1992).

Recall that behaviorists did not study the child's mental life. In their view, thinking could be reduced to connections between stimuli and responses, and development was a continuous process, consisting of a gradual increase in the number and strength of these connections with age. In contrast, Piaget did not believe knowledge was imposed on a passive, reinforced child. According to his **cognitive-developmental theory,** children actively construct knowledge as they manipulate and explore their world, and their cognitive development takes place in stages.

Applied behavior analysis
A set of practical procedures that combines reinforcement, modeling, and the manipulation of situational cues to change behavior.

Cognitive-developmental theory
An approach introduced by Piaget that views the child as actively building mental structures and cognitive development as taking place in stages.

PIAGET'S STAGES. Piaget's view of development was greatly influenced by his early training in biology. Central to his theory is the biological concept of *adaptation* (Piaget, 1971). Just as the structures of the body are adapted to fit with the environment, so the structures of the mind develop over the course of childhood to better fit with, or represent, the external world. In infancy and early childhood, children's understanding is very different from that of adults. For example, Piaget believed that young babies do not realize that something hidden from view—a favorite toy or even the mother—continues to exist. He also concluded that preschoolers' thinking is full of faulty logic and fantasy. For example, children younger than age 7 commonly say that the amount of milk or lemonade changes when it is poured into a differently shaped container. And some of them insist that the images in their dreams are real objects that miraculously appear beside their beds at night! According to Piaget, children eventually revise these incorrect ideas in their ongoing efforts to achieve an *equilibrium*, or balance, between internal structures and information they encounter in their everyday worlds (Beilin, 1992; Kuhn, 1992).

In Piaget's theory, children move through four broad stages of development, each of which is characterized by qualitatively distinct ways of thinking. Table 1.4 provides a brief description of Piaget's stages. In the *sensorimotor stage,* cognitive development begins with the baby's use of the senses and movements to explore the world. These action patterns evolve into the symbolic but illogical thinking of the preschooler in the *preoperational stage.* Then cognition is transformed into the more organized reasoning of the school-age child in the *concrete operational stage.* Finally, in the *formal operational stage,* thought becomes the complex, abstract reasoning system of the adolescent and adult.

PIAGET'S METHODS OF STUDY. Piaget devised special methods for investigating how children think. In the early part of his career, he carefully observed his three infant children and also presented them with little problems, such as an attractive object that could be grasped, mouthed, kicked, or searched for when hidden from view. From their reactions, Piaget derived his ideas about cognitive changes that take place during the first 2 years of life.

In studying childhood and adolescent thought, Piaget took advantage of children's ability to describe their thinking. He adapted the clinical method of psychoanalysis, conducting open-ended clinical interviews in which a child's initial response to a task served as the basis for the next question Piaget would ask. We

Through careful observations of and clinical interviews with children, Jean Piaget developed his comprehensive theory of cognitive development. His work has inspired more research on children than any other single theory. (YVES DE BRAINE/BLACK STAR)

TABLE 1.4 Piaget's Stages of Cognitive Development

STAGE	PERIOD OF DEVELOPMENT	DESCRIPTION
Sensorimotor	Birth–2 years	Infants "think" by acting on the world with their eyes, ears, and hands. As a result, they invent ways of solving sensorimotor problems, such as pulling a lever to hear the sound of a music box, finding hidden toys, and putting objects in and taking them out of containers.
Preoperational	2–7 years	Preschool children use symbols to represent their earlier sensorimotor discoveries. Development of language and make-believe play takes place. However, thinking lacks the logical qualities of the two remaining stages.
Concrete operational	7–11 years	Children's reasoning becomes logical. School-age children understand that a certain amount of lemonade or play dough remains the same even after its appearance changes. They also organize objects into hierarchies of classes and subclasses. However, thinking falls short of adult intelligence. It is not yet abstract.
Formal operational	11 years on	The capacity for abstraction permits adolescents to reason with symbols that do not refer to objects in the real world, as in advanced mathematics. They can also think of all possible outcomes in a scientific problem, not just the most obvious ones.

will look at an example of a Piagetian clinical interview, as well as the strengths and limitations of this technique, in Chapter 2.

CONTRIBUTIONS AND LIMITATIONS OF PIAGET'S THEORY. Piaget's cognitive-developmental perspective has stimulated more research on children than any other single theory. It also convinced many child development specialists that children are active learners whose minds are inhabited by rich structures of knowledge. Piaget's emphasis on an active, adaptive child has been especially influential in the recent expansion of research on infant development, which we will address in Chapter 4. And besides investigating children's understanding of the physical world, Piaget began some explorations into how children reason about the social world. As we will see in Chapters 11 and 12, Piaget's stages of cognitive development have sparked a wealth of research on children's conceptions of themselves, other people, and human relationships.

Practically speaking, Piaget's theory encouraged the development of educational philosophies and programs that emphasize discovery learning and direct contact with the environment. A Piagetian classroom contains richly equipped activity areas designed to stimulate children to revise their immature cognitive structures.

Despite Piaget's overwhelming contribution to child development and education, in recent years his theory has been challenged. New evidence indicates that Piaget underestimated the competencies of infants and preschoolers. We will see in Chapter 6 that when young children are given tasks scaled down in difficulty, their understanding appears closer to that of the older child and adult than Piaget believed. This discovery has led many researchers to conclude that the maturity of children's thinking may depend on their familiarity with the investigator's task and the kind of knowledge sampled. For example, in one study a 4-year-old who had learned the names and characteristics of over 40 species of dinosaurs thought about them in a logical, hierarchical fashion, in much the same way as an adult (Chi & Koeske, 1983). Preschoolers with less opportunity or desire to find out about dinosaurs are unlikely to display such advanced classification skills. Finally, many studies show that children's performance on Piagetian problems can be improved with training. This finding raises questions about his assumption that discovery learning rather than adult teaching is the best way to foster development.

Today, the field of child development is divided over its loyalty to Piaget's ideas. Those who continue to find merit in Piaget's approach accept a modified view of his cognitive stages—one in which changes in children's thinking are not sudden and abrupt but take place much more gradually than Piaget believed (Case, 1985, 1992; Fischer & Pipp, 1984). Others have given up the idea of cognitive stages in favor of a continuous approach to development—information processing—that we will take up in the next section.

Brief Review

Three perspectives dominated child development research in the middle of the twentieth century. Child guidance professionals turned to Freud's psychoanalytic approach, and Erikson's expansion of it, for help in understanding personality development and children's emotional difficulties. Behaviorism and social learning theory rely on conditioning and modeling to explain the appearance of new responses and to treat behavior problems. Piaget's stage theory of cognitive development revolutionized the field with its view of children as active beings who take responsibility for their own learning.

RECENT PERSPECTIVES

New ways of understanding children are constantly emerging—questioning, building on, and enhancing the discoveries of earlier theories. Today, a burst of fresh approaches and research emphases, including information processing, ethology, ecological systems theory, and Vygotsky's dialectical perspective, is broadening our understanding of child development.

Information Processing

During the 1970s, child development researchers became disenchanted with behaviorism as a complete account of children's learning and disappointed in their efforts to completely verify Piaget's ideas. They turned to the field of cognitive psychology for new ways to understand the development of children's thinking. Today, a leading perspective is **information processing.** It is a general approach in which the human mind is viewed as a complex, symbol-manipulating system through which information flows (Klahr, 1992). From presentation to the senses at *input* and behavioral responses at *output,* information is actively coded, transformed, and organized.

Information processing is often thought of as a field of scripts, frames, and flowcharts. Diagrams are used to map the precise series of steps individuals use to solve problems and complete tasks, much like the plans devised by programmers to get computers to perform a series of "mental operations." Let's look at an example to clarify the usefulness of this approach. The left-hand side of Figure 1.3 shows the steps that Andrea, an academically successful 8-year-old, used to complete a two-digit subtraction problem. The right-hand side displays the faulty procedures of Jody, who arrived at the wrong answer. The flowchart approach ensures that models of child and adult thinking will be very clear. For example, by comparing the two procedures shown in Figure 1.3, we know exactly what is necessary for effective problem solving and where Jody went wrong in searching for a solution. As a result, we can pinpoint Jody's difficulties and design an intervention to improve her reasoning.

A wide variety of information processing models exist. Some, like the one in Figure 1.3, are fairly narrow in that they track children's mastery of a single task. Others describe the human information-processing system as a whole (Atkinson & Shiffrin, 1968; Craik & Lockhart, 1972). These general models are used as guides for asking questions about broad age-related changes in children's thinking. For example, Does a child's ability to search the environment for information needed to solve a problem become more organized and planful with age? How much new

Information processing

An approach that views the human mind as a symbol-manipulating system through which information flows and that regards cognitive development as a continuous process.

information can preschoolers hold in memory compared to older children and adults? To what extent does children's current knowledge influence their ability to learn more?

Like Piaget's theory, information processing regards children as active, sense-making beings who modify their own thinking in response to environmental demands (Klahr, 1992). But unlike Piaget, there are no stages of development. Rather, the thought processes studied—perception, attention, memory, planning strategies, categorization of information, and comprehension of written and spoken prose—are assumed to be similar at all ages but present to a lesser extent in children. Consequently, the view of development is one of continuous increase rather than abrupt, stagewise change.

Perhaps you can tell from what we have said so far that information-processing research has important implications for education. Investigators have successfully designed instructional procedures that help children overcome cognitive limitations and approach tasks in more advanced ways (Hall, 1989; Resnick, 1989;

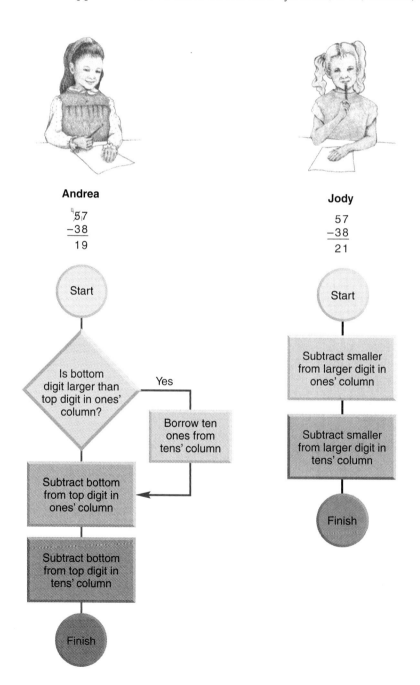

FIGURE 1.3 Information-processing flowcharts showing the steps that two 8-year-olds used to solve a math problem. In this two-digit subtraction problem with a borrowing operation, you can see that Andrea's procedure is correct, whereas Jody's results in a wrong answer.

Konrad Lorenz was one of the founders of ethology and a keen observer of animal behavior. He developed the concept of imprinting. Here, young geese who were separated from their mother and placed in the company of Lorenz during an early, critical period show that they have imprinted on him. They follow him about as he swims through the water, a response that promotes survival. (NINA LEEN/*LIFE* MAGAZINE © TIME WARNER)

Siegler, 1983). But information processing has fallen short in some respects. Aspects of children's cognition that are not linear and logical, such as imagination and creativity, are all but ignored by this approach (Greeno, 1989). In addition, critics complain that information processing isolates children's thinking from important features of real-life learning situations. So far, it has told us little about the links between cognition and other areas of development, such as motivation, emotion, and social experience.

Fortunately, a major advantage of having many child development theories is that they can compensate for one another's weaknesses. A unique feature of the final three perspectives we will discuss is the emphasis they place on *contexts for development.* The impact of context, or environment, can be examined at many levels. We will see that family, school, community, larger society, and culture all affect children's growth. In addition, human capacities have been shaped by a long evolutionary history in which our brains and bodies have adapted to their surroundings. The next theory, ethology, emphasizes this biological side of development.

Ethology

Ethology is concerned with the adaptive, or survival, value of behavior and its evolutionary history (Hinde, 1989). It began to be applied to research on children in the 1960s but has become even more influential today. The origins of ethology can be traced to the work of Darwin. Its modern foundations were laid by two European zoologists, Konrad Lorenz and Niko Tinbergen (Dewsbury, 1992).

Watching the behaviors of diverse animal species in their natural habitats, Lorenz and Tinbergen observed behavior patterns that promote survival. The most well known of these is *imprinting,* the early following behavior of certain baby birds that ensures that the young will stay close to the mother and be fed and protected from danger. Imprinting takes place during an early, restricted time period of development. If the mother is not present during this time, but an object resembling her in important features is, young goslings may imprint on it instead (Lorenz, 1952).

Observations of imprinting led to a major concept that has been widely applied in child development: the *critical period.* It refers to a limited time span during which the child is biologically prepared to acquire certain adaptive behaviors but needs the support of an appropriately stimulating environment. Many researchers have conducted studies to find out whether complex cognitive and social behaviors must be acquired during restricted time periods. For example, if children are deprived of adequate food or physical and social stimulation during

Ethology
An approach concerned with the adaptive, or survival, value of behavior and its evolutionary history.

their early years, will their intelligence be permanently impaired? If language is not mastered during early childhood, is the child's capacity to acquire it reduced? As we address these and other similar questions in later chapters, we will discover that the term *sensitive period* offers a better account of human development than does the strict notion of a critical period (Bornstein, 1989). A **sensitive period** is a time that is optimal for certain capacities to emerge and in which the individual is especially responsive to environmental influences. However, its boundaries are less well defined than those of a critical period. It is possible for development to occur later, but it is harder to induce it at that time.

Inspired by observations of imprinting, the British psychoanalyst John Bowlby (1969) applied ethological theory to the understanding of the human infant–caregiver relationship. He argued that attachment behaviors of babies, such as smiling, babbling, grasping, and crying, are built-in social signals that encourage the parent to approach, care for, and interact with the baby. By keeping the mother near, these behaviors help ensure that the infant will be fed, protected from danger, and provided with stimulation and affection necessary for healthy growth. The development of attachment in human infants is a lengthy process involving changes in psychological structures that lead the baby to form a deep affectional tie with the caregiver (Bretherton, 1992). As we will see in Chapter 10, it is far more complex than imprinting in baby birds. But for now, note how the ethological view of attachment, which emphasizes the role of innate infant signals, differs sharply from the behaviorist drive-reduction explanation we mentioned earlier—that the baby's desire for closeness to the mother is a learned response based on feeding.

Observations by ethologists have shown that many aspects of children's social behavior, including emotional expressions, aggression, cooperation, and social play, resemble those of our primate ancestors. For example, in Chapter 15, we will see that groups of children at play quickly form dominance hierarchies. A 6-year-old can tell you who among classmates playing together at recess is the toughest and who is the weakest. Dominance hierarchies promote survival because they reduce aggression among group members (Pettit et al., 1990; Savin-Williams, 1979). Children lower in the hierarchy seldom attack more highly ranked peers because they are unlikely to win. And as long as they are not threatened, dominant children have no special reason to harm their less powerful agemates.

Ethological research emphasizes the genetic and biological roots of behavior. However, learning is also considered important because it lends flexibility and greater adaptiveness to behavior. Since ethologists believe that children's behavior can best be understood in terms of its adaptive value, they seek a full understanding of the environment, including physical, social, and cultural aspects. The interests of ethologists are broad. They want to understand the entire organism–environment system (Hinde, 1989; Miller, 1989). The next contextual perspective we will discuss, ecological systems theory, serves as an excellent complement to ethology, since it shows how various aspects of the environment, from immediate human relationships to larger societal forces, work together to affect children's development.

Ecological Systems Theory

Urie Bronfenbrenner, an American psychologist, is responsible for a new approach to child development that has risen to the forefront of the field over the past decade. **Ecological systems theory** views the child as developing within a complex system of relationships affected by multiple levels of the surrounding environment. Before Bronfenbrenner's (1979, 1989) theory, most researchers viewed the environment fairly narrowly—as limited to events and conditions immediately surrounding the child. As Figure 1.4 shows, Bronfenbrenner expanded this view by envisioning the environment as a series of nested structures that includes but extends beyond home, school, and neighborhood settings

*U*rie Bronfenbrenner is the originator of ecological systems theory. He views the child as developing within a complex system of relationships affected by multiple levels of the surrounding environment, from immediate settings to broad cultural values, laws, and customs. (COURTESY OF URIE BRONFENBRENNER, CORNELL UNIVERSITY)

Sensitive period
A time span that is optimal for certain capacities to emerge and in which the individual is especially responsive to environmental influences.

Ecological systems theory
Bronfenbrenner's approach, which views the child as developing within a complex system of relationships affected by multiple levels of the environment, from immediate settings of family and school to broad cultural values and programs.

26

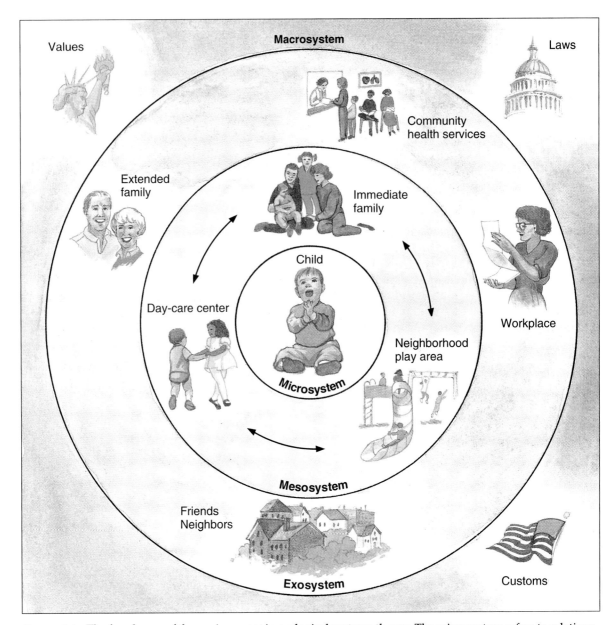

FIGURE 1.4 The four layers of the environment in ecological systems theory. The microsystem refers to relations between the child and the immediate environment, the mesosystem to connections among the child's immediate settings, the exosystem to social settings that affect but do not contain the child, and the macrosystem to values, laws, and customs of the child's culture. (Adapted from Kopp & Krakow, 1982.)

in which children spend their everyday lives. Each layer of the environment is viewed as having a powerful impact on children's development.

THE MICROSYSTEM. The innermost level of the environment is the **microsystem**, which refers to activities and interaction patterns in the child's immediate surroundings. Until recently, researchers emphasized adults' effects on children when studying relationships in the microsystem. Bronfenbrenner emphasizes that to understand child development at this level, we must keep in mind that all relationships are *bidirectional and reciprocal*. In other words, adults affect children's responses, but children's characteristics—their personality styles and ways of thinking—also influence the behavior of adults. For example, a friendly, attentive child is likely to evoke positive and patient reactions from parents, whereas an active, distractible youngster is more likely to be responded to with restriction and punitiveness (Henker & Whalen, 1989). But whether either of these children experi-

Microsystem
In ecological systems theory, the activities and interaction patterns in the child's immediate surroundings.

ence child-rearing practices that enhance or undermine development depends on environmental systems that surround and influence parent–child relationships.

Within the microsystem, interaction between any two individuals is influenced by the presence of third parties. If other individuals in the setting are supportive, the quality of relationships is enhanced. For example, when parents encourage one another in their child-rearing roles, each engages in more effective parenting (Gottfried, Gottfried, & Bathurst, 1988; Simons et al., 1992). In contrast, marital conflict is associated with inconsistent discipline and hostile reactions toward children (Hetherington & Clingempeel, 1992). Child development within the microsystem must be understood in terms of these complex, interacting relationships.

THE MESOSYSTEM. For children to develop at their best, child-rearing supports must also exist in the larger environment. The second level of Bronfenbrenner's model is the **mesosystem.** It refers to connections among microsystems, such as home, school, neighborhood, and day-care center, that foster children's development. For example, a child's academic progress depends not just on activities that take place in classrooms. It is also promoted by parental involvement in school life and the extent to which academic learning is carried over into the home (Stevenson & Baker, 1987). Similarly, parent–child interaction is likely to be affected by the child's relationships with caregivers at day care, and vice versa. Parent–child and caregiver–child relationships are each likely to support development when there are links, in the form of visits and exchange of information, between home and day-care setting.

THE EXOSYSTEM. The **exosystem** refers to social settings that do not contain children but that affect their experiences in immediate settings. These can be formal organizations, such as the parents' workplace or health and welfare services in the community. For example, flexible work schedules, paid maternity and paternity leave, and sick leave for parents whose children are ill are ways that work settings can help parents in their child-rearing roles and, indirectly, foster development. Exosystem supports can also be informal, such as parents' social networks— friends and extended family members who provide advice, companionship, and even financial assistance. Research demonstrates the negative impact of a breakdown in exosystem activities. Families who are socially isolated because they have few personal or community-based ties or who are affected by unemployment show increased rates of conflict and child abuse (Emery, 1989; McLoyd, 1989).

THE MACROSYSTEM. The outermost level of Bronfenbrenner's model is the **macrosystem.** It is not a specific context but instead refers to the values, laws, and customs of a particular culture. The priority that the macrosystem gives to children's needs affects the support they receive at lower levels of the environment. For example, in countries that require high-quality standards for child care and workplace benefits for employed parents, children are more likely to have favorable experiences in their immediate settings. As we will see in greater detail later in this chapter and in other parts of this book, although most European nations have such programs in place, they are not yet widely available in the United States (Kamerman, 1993).

A DYNAMIC, EVER-CHANGING SYSTEM. According to Bronfenbrenner (1989), we must keep in mind that the environment is not a static force that affects children in a uniform way. Instead, it is dynamic and ever-changing. Important events, such as the birth of a sibling, entering school, or moving to a new neighborhood, modify existing relationships between children and their environments, creating new conditions that affect development. In addition, the timing of environmental change affects its impact. The arrival of a new sibling has very different consequences for a homebound toddler than for a school-age child with many satisfying relationships and activities beyond the family.

Mesosystem
In ecological systems theory, connections among children's immediate settings.

Exosystem
In ecological systems theory, settings that do not contain children but that affect their experiences in immediate settings. Examples are parents' workplaces and health and welfare services in the community.

Macrosystem
In ecological systems theory, the values, laws, and customs of a culture that influence experiences and interactions at lower levels of the environment.

Finally, an additional point must be kept in mind to appreciate the complex interplay between person and environment. Children select, modify, and create some of their own settings and experiences. How they do so depends on their age, their physical, intellectual, and personality characteristics, and the environmental opportunities available to them. Therefore, in ecological systems theory, development is neither driven by inner forces nor controlled by environmental circumstances. Instead, children are both products and producers of their environments, both of which form a network of interdependent effects. We will see many more examples of these important principles in later chapters of this book.

INTERVENING IN THE ENVIRONMENT. Perhaps you can already tell that ecological systems theory is of tremendous applied significance, since it suggests that interventions at any level of the environment can enhance development. For example, at the level of the exosystem, providing socially isolated parents of abused children with access to parenting groups where they can discuss their problems and experience gratifying social relationships helps relieve distress and improve conditions for children. Bronfenbrenner (1989) emphasizes that change at the level of the macrosystem is particularly important. Because the macrosystem affects all other environmental levels, revising established values and government programs in ways more favorable to child development has the most far-reaching impact on children's well-being.

Cross-Cultural Research and Vygotsky's Sociocultural Theory

Ecological systems theory, as well as Erikson's psychoanalytic theory, underscores the connection between culture and development. In line with this emphasis, child development research has recently seen a dramatic increase in cross-cultural studies. Investigations that make comparisons across cultures, and between ethnic and social class groups within cultures, provide insight into whether developmental theories apply to all children or are limited to particular environmental conditions. As a result, cross-cultural research helps untangle the contributions of biological and environmental factors to the timing and order of appearance of children's behaviors (Rogoff & Morelli, 1989).

In the past, cross-cultural studies focused on broad cultural differences in development—for example, whether children in one culture are more advanced in motor development or do better on intellectual tasks than children in another. However, this approach can lead us to conclude incorrectly that one culture is superior in enhancing development, whereas another is deficient. In addition, it does not help us understand the precise experiences that contribute to cultural differences in children's behavior.

Today, more research is examining the relationship of *culturally specific practices* to child development. The contributions of the Russian psychologist Lev

*A*ccording to Lev Semanovich Vygotsky, many cognitive processes and skills are socially transferred from more knowledgeable members of society to children. Vygotsky's sociocultural theory helps us understand the wide variation in cognitive competencies from culture to culture. Vygotsky is pictured here with his daughter. (COURTESY OF JAMES V. WERTSCH, CLARK UNIVERSITY)

Semanovich Vygotsky (1896–1934) have played a major role in this trend. Vygotsky's (1934/1986) perspective is called **sociocultural theory.** It focuses on how *culture*—the values, beliefs, customs, and skills of a social group—is transmitted to the next generation. According to Vygotsky, *social interaction*—in particular, cooperative dialogues between children and more knowledgeable members of society—is necessary for children to acquire the ways of thinking and behaving that make up a community's culture (van der Veer & Valsiner, 1991). Vygotsky believed that as adults and more expert peers help children master culturally meaningful activities, the communication between them becomes part of children's thinking. Once children internalize the essential features of these dialogues, they can use the language within them to guide their own actions and accomplish skills on their own (Wertsch & Tulviste, 1992). The young child instructing herself while working a puzzle or tying her shoes has started to produce the same kind of guiding comments that an adult previously used to help her master important tasks (Diaz & Berk, 1992).

Perhaps you can tell from this brief description that Vygotsky's theory has been especially influential in the study of children's cognition. But Vygotsky's approach to cognitive development is quite different from Piaget's. Recall that Piaget did not regard direct teaching by adults as important for cognitive development. Instead, he emphasized children's active, independent efforts to make sense of their world. Vygotsky agreed with Piaget that children are active, constructive beings. But unlike Piaget, he viewed cognitive development as a *socially mediated process*—as dependent on the support that adults and more mature peers provide as children try new tasks. Finally, Vygotsky did not regard all children as moving through the same sequence of stages. Instead, he believed that social interaction leads to continuous, step-by-step changes in children's thought and behavior that can vary greatly from culture to culture.

A major finding of cross-cultural research is that cultures select different tasks for children's learning. In line with Vygotsky's theory, social interaction surrounding these tasks leads to knowledge and skills essential for success in a particular culture. For example, among the Zinacanteco Indians of southern Mexico, girls become expert weavers of complex garments at an early age through the informal guidance of adult experts (Childs & Greenfield, 1982). In Brazil, child candy sellers with little or no schooling develop sophisticated mathematical abilities as the result of buying candy from wholesalers, pricing it in collaboration with adults and experienced peers, and bargaining with customers on city streets (Saxe, 1988). And, as the research reported in the Cultural Influences box on page 30 indicates, adults begin to encourage culturally valued skills in children at a very early age.

Findings like these reveal that children in every culture develop unique strengths that are not present in others. The field of child development has again borrowed from another discipline—anthropology—to achieve this understanding. A cross-cultural perspective reminds us that the majority of child development specialists reside in the United States, and their subjects of study are only a small minority of humankind. We cannot assume that the developmental sequences observed in our own children are "natural" or that the experiences fostering them are "ideal" without looking around the world.

New child development theories are constantly emerging, questioning and building on earlier discoveries. Using computerlike models of mental activity, information processing has brought exactness and precision to the study of children's thinking. Ethology highlights the adaptive, or survival, value of children's behavior and its evolutionary history. Ecological systems theory stresses that adult–child interaction is a two-way street affected by a range of environmental influences, from immediate settings of home and school to broad cultural values and programs. Vygotsky's sociocultural theory takes a closer look at social relationships that foster development. Through cooperative dialogues with mature members of society, children acquire unique, culturally adaptive competencies.

Sociocultural theory
Vygotsky's theory, in which children acquire the ways of thinking and behaving that make up a community's culture through cooperative dialogues with more knowledgeable members of that society.

Brief Review

Interaction between caregivers and infants takes different paths in different cultures. Through it, adults begin to transmit their society's values and skills to the next generation, channeling the course of future development.

Focusing on a culture very different from our own, researchers have studied how caregivers respond to infants' play with objects among the !Kung, a hunting and gathering society living in the desert regions of Botswana, Africa (Bakeman et al., 1990). Daily foraging missions take small numbers of adults several miles from the campground, but most obtain enough food to contribute to group survival by working only 3 out of every 7 days. A mobile way of life also prevents the !Kung from collecting many possessions that require extensive care and maintenance. Adults have many free hours to relax around the campfire, and they spend it in intense social contact with one another and with children (Draper & Cashdan, 1988).

In this culture of intimate social bonds and minimal property, objects are valued as things to be shared, not as personal possessions. This message is conveyed to !Kung children at a very early age. Between 6 and 12 months, grandmothers start to train babies in the importance of exchanging objects by guiding them in handing beads to relatives. The child's first words generally include *i* (here, take this) and *na* (give it to me).

In !Kung society, no toys are made for infants. Instead, natural objects, such as twigs, grass, stones, and nutshells, are always available, along with cooking implements. However, adults do not encourage babies to play with these objects. In fact, adults are unlikely to interact with infants while they are exploring objects independently. But when a baby offers an object to another person, adults become highly responsive, encouraging and vocalizing much more than at other times. Thus, the !Kung cultural emphasis on the interpersonal rather than physical aspects of existence is reflected in how adults interact with the very youngest members of their community.

When you next have a chance, observe the conditions under which parents respond to infants' involvement with

!Kung children grow up in a hunting-and-gathering society in which possessions are a burden rather than an asset. From an early age, children experience rich, warm social contact with adults and are taught the importance of sharing. (IRVEN DEVORE/ANTHRO-PHOTO)

objects in your own society. How is parental responsiveness linked to cultural values? How does it compare with findings on the !Kung?

COMPARING CHILD DEVELOPMENT THEORIES

In the preceding sections, we reviewed theoretical perspectives that are major forces in modern child development research. They differ in many respects.

First, they focus on different aspects of development. Some, such as psychoanalytic theory and ethology, emphasize children's social and emotional development. Others, such as Piaget's cognitive-developmental theory, information processing, and Vygotsky's sociocultural theory, stress important changes in children's thinking. The remaining approaches—behaviorism, social learning theory, and ecological systems theory—discuss factors assumed to affect all aspects of children's functioning.

Second, every theory contains a point of view about what the process of development is like. As we conclude our review of theoretical perspectives, take a moment to identify the stand each theory takes on the three controversial issues presented at the beginning of this chapter. Then check your analysis of theories against the information given in Table 1.5. If you had difficulty classifying any of them, return to the relevant section of this chapter and reread the description of that theory.

Finally, we have seen that theories have strengths and weaknesses. This may remind you of an important point we made earlier in this chapter—that no single

TABLE 1.5 *Stance of Major Developmental Theories on Three Basic Issues in Child Development*

THEORY	ORGANISMIC VERSUS MECHANISTIC CHILD	CONTINUOUS VERSUS DISCONTINUOUS DEVELOPMENT	NATURE VERSUS NURTURE
Psychoanalytic theory	*Organismic:* Relations among structures of the mind (id, ego, and superego) determine personality.	*Discontinuous:* Stages of psychosexual and psychosocial development are emphasized.	*Both:* Innate impulses are channeled and controlled through child-rearing experiences.
Behaviorism and social learning theory	*Mechanistic:* Development is the result of connections established between stimulus inputs and behavioral responses.	*Continuous:* Quantitative increases in learned behaviors occur with age.	*Emphasis on nurture:* Learning principles of conditioning and modeling determine development.
Piaget's cognitive-developmental theory	*Organismic:* Psychological structures determine the child's understanding of the world. The child actively constructs knowledge.	*Discontinuous:* Stages of cognitive development are emphasized.	*Both:* Children's innate drive to discover reality is emphasized. However, it must be supported by a rich, stimulating environment.
Information processing	*Both:* Active processing structures combine with a mechanistic, computerlike model of stimulus input and behavioral output to produce development.	*Continuous:* A quantitative increase in perception, attention, memory, and problem-solving skills takes place with age.	*Both:* Maturation and learning opportunities affect information-processing skills.
Ethology	*Organismic:* The infant is biologically prepared with social signals that actively promote survival. Over time, psychological structures develop that underlie infant–caregiver attachment and other adaptive behavior patterns.	*Both:* Adaptive behavior patterns increase in quantity over time. But sensitive periods—restricted time periods in which qualitatively distinct capacities and responses emerge fairly suddenly—are also emphasized.	*Both:* Biologically based, evolved behavior patterns are stressed, but an appropriately stimulating environment is necessary to elicit them. Also, learning can improve the adaptiveness of behavior.
Ecological systems theory	*Organismic:* Children's personality characteristics and ways of thinking actively contribute to their development.	*Not specified*	*Both:* Children's characteristics and the reactions of others affect each other in a bidirectional fashion. Layers of the environment influence child-rearing experiences.
Vygotsky's sociocultural theory	*Organismic:* Children internalize essential features of social dialogues, forming psychological structures that they use to guide their own behavior.	*Continuous:* Interaction of the child with mature members of society leads to step-by-step changes in thought and behavior.	*Both:* Maturation and opportunities to interact with knowledgeable members of society affect the development of psychological structures and culturally adaptive skills.

theory provides a complete account of development. Perhaps you found that you were attracted to some theories, but you had doubts about others. As you read more about child development research in later chapters of this book, you may find it useful to keep a notebook in which you test your own theoretical likes and dislikes against the evidence. Do not be surprised if you revise your ideas many times, just as theorists have done throughout this century. By the end of the course, you will have built your own personal perspective on child development. It might turn out to be a blend of several theories, since each viewpoint we have discussed has contributed in important ways to what we know about children. And, like researchers in the field of child development, you will be left with some unanswered questions. I hope those questions will motivate you to continue your quest to understand children in the years to come.

NEW APPLIED DIRECTIONS: CHILD DEVELOPMENT AND SOCIAL POLICY

In recent years, the field of child development has become increasingly concerned with applying its vast knowledge base to the solution of pressing social problems faced by children and families. In this final decade of the twentieth century, we know much more than ever before about family, school, and community contexts that foster the development of physically healthy, cognitively competent, and socially mature children. Nevertheless, the condition of millions of children in the United States is much less than satisfactory. Consider the following indicators of the current status of American children.

- *Poverty.* Nearly 22 percent of children in the United States—14.3 million in all—live in poverty, a circumstance that threatens all aspects of development. Nearly half of these children—1 out of 10 American youngsters—is in desperate straits, with a family income of less than half the *poverty line* (earnings judged by the federal government to be necessary for bare subsistence). Today, children are the poorest of any age sector of the American population. Poverty is especially high among ethnic minority children; 38 percent of Hispanic and 44 percent of African-American youngsters are affected (Children's Defense Fund, 1992b).

In the United States, nearly 22 percent of children live in poverty, a circumstance that threatens all aspects of development. Poverty is especially high among ethnic minority children. (BARBARA PFEFFER, PETER ARNOLD INC.)

- *Homelessness.* Compounding the devastating effects of poverty, homelessness has risen dramatically in the United States over the past decade. By the early 1990s, approximately 3 million people had no place to live. Over one-third of America's homeless population is made up of families, and 1 in every 4 homeless individuals is believed to be a child (Milburn & D'Ercole, 1991).

- *Health insurance.* Twenty percent of American children have no health insurance, making them the largest segment of the uninsured population. Among industrialized nations, only the United States and South Africa fail to guarantee every citizen basic health care services (Children's Defense Fund, 1991b; Oberg, 1988).

- *Childhood immunization.* Approximately 40 percent of American preschoolers are not fully immunized against childhood disease. Although immunization rates have risen around the world in recent years, they have declined in the United States. As a result, the rate of preventable infectious illnesses has increased. For example, in 1990 there were over 25,000 cases of measles, 16 times the number in 1983 (American Academy of Pediatrics, 1992; Children's Defense Fund, 1991b).

- *Low birth weight and infant death.* Each year, approximately 7 percent of American infants—about 250,000 babies—are born underweight. Low birth weight is a powerful predictor of serious health difficulties and early death. Nine out of every 1,000 American babies do not survive their first year, a figure that compares dismally to that of other industrialized nations (Wegman, 1992).

- *Teenage parenthood.* Each year, over 300,000 babies are born to American teenagers, who are neither psychologically nor economically prepared to raise a child (Children's Defense Fund, 1992b). The rates of adolescent pregnancy and childbearing in the United States are the highest in the industrialized world. Teenage parenthood is strongly linked to poverty and poses serious risks to the development of both adolescent and child.

- *Divorce.* Family breakdown is common in the lives of American children. One out of every 65 youngsters experiences parental divorce annually, a rate that exceeds that of any other nation in the world (U.S. Bureau of the Census, 1992). In Chapter 14, we will see that marital dissolution is linked to temporary—and occasionally long-term—declines in family income and highly stressful living conditions.

- *Mental illness.* When environments undermine development during the early years, many children reach middle childhood and adolescence with serious mental health problems. Approximately 6 million to 9 million American youngsters suffer from emotional and behavioral difficulties severe enough to warrant treatment (Saxe, Cross, & Silverman, 1988). Chronic anxiety, antisocial behavior, eating disorders, depression, and suicide are among the problems we will discuss in later chapters. Yet only 20 to 30 percent of mentally ill children and adolescents have access to the treatment services they need (Children's Defense Fund, 1992b).

- *Child abuse and neglect.* In 1991, 2.5 million reports of child abuse and neglect were made to juvenile authorities in the United States. The figure greatly underestimates the true number, since many cases go unreported (Children's Defense Fund, 1992b).

- *Day care.* Sixty-five percent of American children under age 6 have mothers who are employed. Yet unlike most European nations, the United States has been slow to move toward a national system of day care. According to recent surveys, much day care in the United States is substandard in quality. Low-income parents, who cannot afford the high cost of day care, often have no choice but to place their children in poor-quality settings (Children's Defense Fund, 1992b).

TABLE 1.6 How Does the United States Compare to Other Nations on Indicators of Child Health and Well-Being?

INDICATOR	U.S. RANK*	SOME COUNTRIES THE UNITED STATES TRAILS
Childhood poverty	8th (among 8 industrialized nations studied)	Australia, Canada, Great Britain, Norway, Sweden, Switzerland, West Germany (before reunification with East Germany in October 1990)
Infant death in the first year of life	21st (worldwide)	Hong Kong, Ireland, Singapore, Spain
Low-birth-weight newborns	28th (worldwide)	Bulgaria, Egypt, Greece, Iran, Jordan, Kuwait, Paraguay, Romania, Saudi Arabia
One-year-old children fully immunized against polio	17th (worldwide)	Chile, Czechoslovakia, Jordan, Poland
Number of school-age children per teacher	19th (worldwide)	Cuba, Lebanon, Libya
Mathematics achievement of college-bound high school students	12th (among 15 nations studied)	Belgium, Canada (Ontario), Finland, Israel, Scotland
Expenditures on education as percentage of gross national product	14th (among 16 industrialized nations studied)	Canada, France, Great Britain, the Netherlands, Sweden
Teenage pregnancy rate	6th (among 6 industrialized nations studied)	Canada, England, France, the Netherlands, Sweden

*Based on the most recent available data.

SOURCE: From *S.O.S. America! A Children's Defense Budget*, 1990b, Washington, DC: Children's Defense Fund. Adapted by permission. *Additional sources:* Children's Defense Fund, 1992b; Jones et al., 1985; McKnight et al., 1987; Wegman, 1992.

- *School achievement.* Many students are graduating from American high schools without the educational preparation they need to contribute fully to society. Although the majority master basic facts and skills, over 90 percent of 17-year-olds have difficulty with complex reasoning and problem solving in reading, writing, mathematics, and science (Mullis et al., 1991).
- *School dropout.* By age 18 or 19, 15 percent of American young people leave high school without a diploma. Those who do not return to finish their education are at risk for lifelong poverty. The dropout rate is especially high among low-income ethnic minority youths. In some inner-city areas, it approaches 50 percent (Children's Defense Fund, 1992b).

Because of global economic conditions, the overall status of children worldwide has also declined, particularly in developing countries (Grant, 1992). But the dire condition of so many American youngsters is particularly disturbing. The United States has the largest gross national product* and the broadest knowledge base for intervening effectively in children's lives of any nation in the world. Yet, as Table 1.6 reveals, it does not rank among the top countries on any key measure of children's health and well-being. Let's consider why this is the case.

The Policy-Making Process

Social policy
Any planned set of actions directed at solving a social problem or attaining a social goal.

Social policy is any planned set of actions directed at solving a social problem or attaining a social goal. The breadth of this definition indicates that social policies

*Gross national product is the value of all goods and services produced by a nation during a specified time period. It serves as an overall measure of a nation's wealth.

can take place at many levels. Policies can be proposed and implemented by small groups or large formal organizations; by private or public institutions, such as schools, businesses, and social-service agencies; and by governing bodies, such as the U.S. Congress, state legislatures, the courts, and city councils.

When widespread social problems arise, nations attempt to solve them by developing a special type of social policy called **public policy**—laws and government programs designed to improve current conditions. Return for a moment to Bronfenbrenner's ecological systems theory on page 25, and notice how the concept of the macrosystem suggests that sound public policies are essential for protecting children's well-being. When governing bodies authorize programs to meet children's health, safety, and educational needs, they serve as broad societal plans for action. Events of the early 1980s provided a dramatic illustration of how critical government support of children and families truly is. When Aid to Families with Dependent Children (the nation's key welfare program) and food, housing, and medical benefits for the poor were cut in the face of rising inflation and unemployment, poverty, hunger, homelessness, and childhood disease climbed substantially (Children's Defense Fund, 1990a; Hayes, 1989).

Why have attempts to help children been more difficult to realize in the United States than in other industrialized nations? To answer this question, we must have some understanding of the complex forces that combine to foster effective public policies. Among the most important are societal values, special interests, economic conditions, and child development research.

SOCIETAL VALUES. The *political culture* of a nation—dominant beliefs about the relationship that should exist between citizen and government—has a major impact on the policy-making process. When you next have a chance, ask several residents of your community the following question: "Who should be responsible for raising young children?" Many Americans respond in ways like these: "If parents decide to have a baby, then they should be ready to care for it." "Most people are not happy about others intruding into family matters."

These statements reflect a widespread opinion in the United States—that the care and rearing of children during the early years is the duty of the parents, and only the parents (Goffin, 1988). This view has a long history, one in which independence, self-reliance, and the privacy of family life emerged as central American values. It is a major reason that the American public has been slow to accept the idea of government-supported health insurance and day care. These programs are broadly available in Europe, largely because European citizens are much more approving of government intervention and control of family services (Wilensky, 1983).

SPECIAL INTERESTS. Of course, not all people hold the same political beliefs. In complex societies, distinct subcultures exist, based on such factors as geographic region, ethnicity, income, and age, that stand alongside a nation's dominant values. The diversity of American society has led *special-interest groups* to play an especially strong role in policy-making. In fact, policies generally arise out of conflicts and compromises among groups of people who have distinct beliefs and desires. In this clash of special interests from which new programs emerge, groups that are well organized, have skilled leadership, contribute to the economic welfare of a nation, and have a large membership are likely to fare much better than those that are poorly organized, a drain on economic reserves, and small in size.

In this effort to jockey for public influence, the needs of children can easily remain unrecognized. Instead of making immediate contributions to the welfare of a nation, children are a costly drain on economic resources that people with quite different interests want for their own pressing needs. In addition, children are not capable of organizing and speaking out to protect their own unique concerns, as adult citizens do. Because they must rely on the goodwill of others for

Public policy
Laws and government programs designed to improve current conditions.

becoming an important government priority, children are constantly in danger of becoming a "forgotten constituency" in the United States (Takanishi, DeLeon, & Pallak, 1983).

ECONOMIC CONDITIONS. Besides dominant values and the demands of special interests, the current state of a nation's economy affects what it does to improve the welfare of children and families. Scarce public resources are commonplace in less developed countries of the world, which depend on economic aid from richer nations like the United States to feed, educate, and provide health care for many citizens. But even in large industrialized nations, the government does not always have enough resources to solve pressing social problems. In times of economic crisis, governments are less likely to initiate new social programs, and they may cut back or even eliminate those that exist. Over the past decade, the U.S. federal deficit tripled, reaching an astronomical $3.1 trillion by the early 1990s (U.S. Office of Management and Budget, 1992). During this period, it is not surprising that federal support for the needs of children and families became very difficult to secure, and funding of many child-related services declined considerably (Garwood et al., 1989).

CHILD DEVELOPMENT RESEARCH. For a policy to be most effective in meeting children's needs, research should guide it at every step along the way—during design, implementation, and evaluation of the program. The recent trend toward greater involvement of child development researchers in the policy process was stimulated by events of the 1960s and 1970s, a time of greater economic prosperity and receptiveness to government-sponsored social services. Investigators quickly realized that they could have a substantial impact on policy formation (Zigler & Finn-Stevenson, 1992).

For example, in 1965, research on the importance of early experience for children's intellectual development played a major role in the founding of Project Head Start, the nation's largest preschool intervention program for low-income families (Hunt, 1961). As we will see in Chapter 8, two decades of research on the long-term benefits of Head Start helped it survive when its funding was threatened and contributed to the increase in support it has received in recent years. In another instance, findings on the severe impact of malnutrition on early brain development stimulated passage by Congress of the Special Supplemental Food Program for Women, Infants, and Children. Since the early 1970s, it has supplied food packages to many poverty-stricken pregnant women and young children (see Chapter 3).

Policy-relevant research, investigators soon realized, has the added benefit of expanding our knowledge base of child development. As researchers started to examine the impact of children's services, they became more aware of the power of settings remote from children's daily lives to affect their well-being. As a result, researchers broadened their focus of study to include development within a wider social context (Bronfenbrenner, 1979, 1989). Throughout this book, we will encounter a wealth of findings on the impact of larger social systems, such as school, workplace, community, mass media, and government. Researchers also began to address the impact of rapid societal change on children—poverty, homelessness, divorce, day care, family violence, and teenage parenthood. All of these efforts have, in turn, helped to forge new policy directions.

Still, as we mentioned earlier, a large gap exists between what we know about children and the application of that knowledge. For several reasons, scientific research does not invariably affect policy-making. First, the impact of research depends on its interactions with other components of the policy process. In the case of both Head Start and the Special Supplemental Food Program, if public sentiments had not been so receptive to helping poor children at the time these policies were proposed, compelling findings on the importance of early education and nutrition might have been less influential (Hayes, 1982). Second, research that sheds light on policy often takes many years to conduct. Large numbers of studies that yield consensus on an issue are generally needed to arrive at an appropriate solution. Third, child development researchers have had to learn how to communicate effectively with policymakers and the general public. Today, they are doing a better job than ever before of disseminating their findings in easily understandable ways, through television documentaries, newspaper stories, and magazine articles as well as direct reports to government officials (McCall, 1987). As a result, they are helping create a sense of immediacy about children's conditions that is necessary to spur a society into action.

Contemporary Progress in Meeting the Needs of American Children

Until very recently, the American child and youth population was relatively plentiful, allowing society to survive despite the sacrifice of many young lives to tragic social conditions (Edelman, 1989). But the number of children in the United States has begun to shrink rapidly. A declining birth rate led the population under age 18 to decrease by more than 5 million over the past two decades, a trend anticipated to continue into the twenty-first century (U.S. Bureau of the Census, 1992). Consequently, the problems affecting children take on even greater significance as they threaten to affect larger proportions of future generations (Wetzel, 1987).

As we will see in later chapters, a wide variety of government-sponsored programs aimed at helping children and families does exist in the United States. But analyses of these programs reveal that the majority have been enacted piecemeal, over a long period of time, with little attention given to their interrelatedness. In addition, they are largely crisis oriented, aimed at handling the most severe family difficulties rather than preventing problems before they happen. Furthermore, funding for these efforts has waxed and waned and been seriously threatened at various times. In most cases, only a minority of needy individuals are being helped (Takanishi, DeLeon, & Pallak, 1983; Zigler & Finn-Stevenson, 1992).

Nevertheless, there are hopeful signs on the horizon. New policy initiatives are under way that promise to improve the status of American children. For example, a 1990 bill granted low-income parents increased tax relief to offset the cost of day care and offered modest funding to the states to enhance the quality and availability of day-care services. A bill signed into law in 1992 provided funds to upgrade treatment programs for children with serious mental health problems. And a 1993 bill granted workers 12 weeks of unpaid employment leave to deal with family emergencies, such as the birth or illness of a child. Furthermore, steps are being taken to upgrade the availability of health care services, including universal immunization against childhood disease.

Additional policies are being initiated by a few businesses, such as on-site or nearby day-care services, and by some state legislatures, such as enforcement of child support payments in divorce cases. Child-related professional organizations are also taking a strong leadership role. In the absence of federal guidelines for high-quality day care, The National Association for the Education of Young Children (NAEYC, an 80,000-member organization of early childhood educators) recently established a voluntary accreditation system for preschool and day-care centers. It grants special professional recognition to programs that meet its rigorous standards of quality. Efforts like these are serving as inspiring models for the nation as a whole.

Finally, child development specialists are joining with concerned citizens to become advocates for children's causes. Over the past two decades, several influential interest groups with children's well-being as their central purpose have emerged in the United States. One of the most vigorous is the Children's Defense

Moments in America

Every 35 seconds a baby is born into poverty.
Every night 100,000 children go to sleep without homes.
Every 14 minutes an infant dies in the first year of life.
Every 64 seconds an infant is born to a teenage mother.
Every month at least 56,000 children are abused.
Every year at least 446,000 youths drop out of school.

(CHILDREN'S DEFENSE FUND, 1991b)

FIGURE 1.5   A public-service poster distributed to American communities by the Children's Defense Fund. (Reprinted by permission of the Children's Defense Fund.)

Many people are not aware of the problems experienced by large numbers of children in the United States. To sensitize the public, the Children's Defense Fund presents dramatic images like these in media ads and nationwide mailings. Besides promoting public awareness, the Children's Defense Fund provides government officials with a steady stream of facts about the status of children and encourages them to support legislation responsive to children's needs.

The Children's Defense Fund is the most avid interest group for children in the United States. To accomplish its goals, it engages in research, public education, legal action, drafting of legislation, congressional testimony, and community organizing. Each year, it publishes *The State of America's Children,* which provides a comprehensive analysis of the current condition of children, government-sponsored programs serving them, and proposals for improving child and family programs. The Children's Defense Fund also supports an extensive network of state and local organizations that have children's needs as their central purpose. Two of its most significant projects are an adolescent pregnancy prevention program and a prenatal care campaign designed to reduce the high rate of death, illness, and developmental disability among poverty-stricken infants in the United States. Dissemination of information on how communities can develop more effective child and family services, publication of a monthly newsletter on what people across the nation are doing to solve children's problems, and public-service announcements (see Figure 1.5) are among its many activities.

The Children's Defense Fund is supported by private foundations, corporate grants, and individual dona-

tions. To inquire about its publications and efforts on children's behalf, contact

The Children's Defense Fund
122 C Street
N.W., Washington, D.C. 20001
Telephone (800) 424-9602.

Fund, a private nonprofit organization founded by Marion Wright Edelman in 1973. To learn more about its activities, refer to the Social Issues box above.

By forging more effective partnerships with government and the general public, the field of child development is playing a significant role in spurring the policy process forward. As these efforts continue, there is every reason to expect increased attention to the needs of children and families in the years to come.

In 1973, Marion Wright Edelman founded the Children's Defense Fund, a private, nonprofit organization that provides a strong, effective voice for American children, who cannot vote, lobby, or speak for themselves. Edelman continues to serve as president of the Children's Defense Fund today. (PHOTO © 1993 TIMOTHY GREENFIELD-SANDERS/CHILDREN'S DEFENSE FUND)

CHAPTER SUMMARY

Child Development as an Interdisciplinary, Scientific, and Applied Field

- **Child development** is the study of human growth and change from conception through adolescence. It is part of a larger discipline known as **developmental psychology** or **human development,** which includes all changes that take place throughout the life span. Research on child development has been stimulated by both scientific curiosity and social pressures to better the lives of children.

Basic Themes and Issues

- **Theories** provide organizing frameworks for our observations of the child and a sound basis for practical action. Major theories can be organized according to the stand they take on three controversial issues: (1) Is the child an **organismic** or **mechanistic** being? (2) Is development a **continuous** process, or does it follow a series of **discontinuous** stages? (3) Is development primarily determined by **nature** or **nurture**? Some theories, especially the more recent ones, take an intermediate stand on these issues.

Historical Foundations

- Modern theories of child development have roots extending far back into the past. In medieval times, children were regarded as miniature adults, a view called **preformationism.** By the sixteenth century, childhood became a distinct phase of the life cycle. However, the Puritan conception of original sin led to a harsh philosophy of child rearing.
- The Enlightenment brought new ideas favoring more humane treatment of children. Locke's **tabula rasa** provided the basis for twentieth-century behaviorism, and Rousseau's **noble savage** foreshadowed the concepts of **stage** and **maturation.** A century later, Darwin's theory of evolution stimulated scientific child study.
- Efforts to observe children directly began in the late nineteenth and early twentieth centuries with baby biographies. Soon after, Hall and Gesell introduced the **norma-**tive approach, which produced a large body of descriptive facts about children. Binet initiated the mental testing movement, an outgrowth of normative child study, which led to the first successful intelligence test. Baldwin's theory was ahead of its time in taking a balanced view on issues of organismic versus mechanistic child and nature versus nurture.

Mid–Twentieth-Century Theories

- In the 1930s and 1940s, child guidance professionals turned to the **psychoanalytic perspective** for help in understanding children with emotional problems. In Freud's **psychosexual theory,** children move through five stages, during which three portions of the personality—**id, ego,** and **superego**—become integrated. Erikson's **psychosocial theory** builds on Freud's theory by emphasizing the development of culturally relevant attitudes and skills and the life-span nature of development.
- Academic psychology also influenced child study. From **behaviorism** and **social learning theory** came the principles of conditioning and modeling and practical procedures of **applied behavior analysis** with children.
- In contrast to behaviorism, Piaget's **cognitive-developmental theory** emphasizes an active child with a mind inhabited by rich structures of knowledge. According to Piaget, children move through four broad stages, beginning with baby's sensorimotor action patterns and ending with the elaborate, abstract reasoning system of the adolescent and adult. Piaget's theory has stimulated a wealth of research on children's thinking and encouraged educational programs that emphasize discovery learning.

Recent Perspectives

- The field of child development continues to seek new directions. **Information processing** views the mind as a complex, symbol-manipulating system, operating much like a computer. This approach helps researchers achieve a clear understanding of what children of different ages do when faced with tasks or problems. Information processing has led to the design of instructional procedures that help children overcome cognitive limitations and approach tasks in more advanced ways.

- Three modern theories place special emphasis on contexts for development. **Ethology** stresses the adaptive or survival value of behavior and its origins in evolutionary history. In **ecological systems theory,** nested layers of the environment, which range from the child's immediate setting to broad cultural values and programs, are seen as major influences on children's well-being. Vygotsky's **sociocultural theory** focuses on how culture is transmitted to the next generation. Through cooperative dialogues with mature members of society, children acquire culturally relevant knowledge and skills.

New Applied Directions:
Child Development and Social Policy

- In recent years, the field of child development has become increasingly concerned with applying its vast knowledge base to the solution of pressing social problems. Millions of children in the United States are growing up under conditions that threaten their well-being.

- A special type of **social policy** called **public policy**—laws and government programs designed to improve current conditions—is essential for protecting children's development. Dominant political values, competing claims of special-interest groups, the state of a nation's economy, and child development research combine to influence the policy-making process. Policy-relevant research not only helps forge new policy directions, but also expands our understanding of child development.

- Although many government-sponsored child and family policies are in effect in the United States, they are largely crisis oriented and do not reach all individuals in need. A variety of new policies are under way, initiated by the federal government, state legislatures, businesses, and professional organizations. In addition, child development researchers are joining with concerned citizens to become advocates for children's causes. These efforts offer hope of improving the well-being of children and families in the years to come.

IMPORTANT TERMS AND CONCEPTS

child development (p. 2)
developmental psychology (p. 2)
human development (p. 2)
theory (p. 3)
organismic theories (p. 4)
mechanistic theories (p. 4)
continuous development (p. 5)
discontinuous development (p. 5)
stage (p. 5)
nature–nurture controversy (p. 5)
preformationism (p. 7)
tabula rasa (p. 8)

noble savage (p. 9)
maturation (p. 9)
normative approach (p. 10)
psychoanalytic perspective (p. 14)
psychosexual theory (p. 14)
id (p. 14)
ego (p. 14)
superego (p. 14)
psychosocial theory (p. 15)
behaviorism (p. 16)
social learning theory (p. 18)
applied behavior analysis (p. 19)

cognitive-developmental theory (p. 19)
information processing (p. 22)
ethology (p. 24)
sensitive period (p. 25)
ecological systems theory (p. 25)
microsystem (p. 26)
mesosystem (p. 27)
exosystem (p. 27)
macrosystem (p. 27)
sociocultural theory (p. 29)
social policy (p. 34)
public policy (p. 35)

CONNECTIONS

CHAPTER
2

♦ **Karel Appel,** *Questioning Children*
1949, Tate Gallery, London/Art Resource

Research
Strategies

One afternoon, Ron, a colleague of mine, crossed the street between his academic department and our laboratory school, the expression on his face reflecting a deep sense of apprehension. After weeks of planning, Ron had looked forward to launching his study on the development of children's peer relations. Thinking back to his own elementary school years, he recalled the anguish experienced by several of his classmates, who were repeatedly ridiculed, taunted, and shunned by their peers. Ron wanted to find ways to help rejected children, many of whom go on to lead unhappy and troubled lives. In view of the importance of his research, Ron was puzzled by the request he had received to appear before the school's research committee.

Ron was joined at the committee meeting by teachers and administrators charged with evaluating research proposals on the basis of their ethical integrity. A third-grade teacher spoke up.

"Ron, I see the value of your work, but frankly, I'm very concerned about your asking my pupils whom they like most and whom they like least. I've got a couple of kids who are soundly disliked and real troublemakers, and I'm doing my best to keep the lid on the situation. If you come in and start sensitizing my class to whom they like and dislike, the children are going to share these opinions. Unfortunately, I think your study is likely to promote conflict and negative interaction in my classroom!"

Imagine the jolt Ron must have felt to hear someone suggest that the research he had been so carefully planning might have to be scrapped. Anyone who has undertaken the time-consuming process of preparing for such a study could commiserate with Ron's dismay. This chapter takes a close look at the research process—the many challenges investigators face as they plan and implement studies of children. Ron had already traveled a long and arduous path before he arrived at the door of the laboratory school, prepared to collect his data. First, he spent many weeks developing a researchable idea, based on theory and prior knowledge about children's peer relations. Next, he had to decide on an appropriate research strategy, which involves two main tasks. First, he had to choose from a wide variety of *research methods,* the specific activities in which subjects will participate, such as taking tests, answering questionnaires, responding to interviews, or being observed. Second, he had to select a *research design,* an overall plan for his study that would permit the best possible test of his research idea. Finally, Ron scrutinized his procedures for any possible harm they might cause to the subjects involved.

Still, as Ron approached a committee charged with protecting the welfare of young research participants, he faced an ethical dilemma. Research on any subjects, whether human or animal, must meet certain standards that protect participants from stressful treatment. Because of children's immaturity and vulnerability, extra precautions must be taken to ensure that their rights are not violated in the course of a research study. In the final section of this chapter, we will see how Ron resolved the committee's earnest challenge to the ethical integrity of his research.

FROM THEORY TO HYPOTHESIS

In Chapter 1, we saw how theories structure the research process by identifying important research concerns and, occasionally, preferred methods for collecting data. We also discussed how theories guide the application of findings to real-life circumstances and practices with children. In fact, research usually begins with a prediction about behavior drawn directly from a theory, or what we call a **hypothesis.** Think back to the various child development theories presented in Chapter 1. Many hypotheses can be drawn from any one of them that, once tested, would reflect the accuracy of the theory.

Sometimes research pits a hypothesis taken from one theory against a hypothesis taken from another. For example, a theorist emphasizing the role of maturation in development would predict that parental encouragement will have little effect on the age at which children utter their first words, learn to count, or tie their shoes. A behaviorist, in contrast, would speculate that these skills can be accelerated through systematic reinforcement.

At other times, research tests predictions drawn from a single theory. For example, ecological systems theory suggests that providing isolated, divorced mothers with social supports will lead them to be more patient with their children. An ethologist might hypothesize that an infant's cry will stimulate strong physiological arousal in adults who hear it, motivating them to soothe and protect a suffering baby.

Occasionally, little or no theory exists on a topic of interest. In these instances, rather than making a specific prediction, the investigator may start with a *research question,* such as: Are children reaching puberty earlier and growing taller than they did a generation ago? Do first-grade girls learn to read more easily and quickly than first-grade boys? Once formulated, hypotheses and research questions offer investigators vital guidance as they settle on research methods and a research design.

At this point, you may be wondering, Why learn about research strategies? Why not leave these matters to research specialists and concentrate on what is already known about the child and how this knowledge can be applied? There are two reasons. First, each of us must be wise and critical consumers of knowledge, not naive sponges who soak up facts about children. Knowing the strengths and weaknesses of various research strategies becomes important in separating dependable information from misleading results. Second, individuals who work directly with children are sometimes in a position to test hypotheses or research

Hypothesis
A prediction about behavior drawn from a theory.

Ideally, researchers and practitioners should collaborate in the quest for knowledge about children. The researcher needs to find out about behavior in the everyday environments in which teachers, caregivers, social workers, and others deal with children. And research questions and plans often benefit from the insights, suggestions, and concerns of practitioners.

In a study carried out by one of my students, this unique partnership happened. Cheryl Kinsman was interested in factors that cause children's behavior to conform to gender roles at an early age. At the same time, Mary Natale, a preschool teacher in our university laboratory school, wondered how to arrange activity centers in her classroom to enhance the social and play experiences of her 4- and 5-year-old pupils. Together, Cheryl and Mary selected two activity centers—the housekeeping and block areas—for special study, since these united their respective interests.

Cheryl devised a plan in which children were observed for a 3-week period under Mary's original arrangement, in which the two centers, located next to each other, were separated by a high wall of shelves. Then the shelves were removed, and changes in boys' and girls' use of each area and the quality of their play were noted.

The findings revealed that boys and girls did not differ in time spent in the two settings, either before or after the shelves were removed. In fact, under each condition, children of both sexes preferred the block area. But changes in aspects of their play were substantial. Before the shelves were removed, play was highly gender-typed. Children largely interacted with same-sex peers, a pattern that was particularly pronounced for boys in blocks and for girls in housekeeping. In addition, when boys entered the housekeeping area, they generally did not use its play materials. Instead, they tended to play in ways that were irrelevant to the basic purpose of the setting, such as acting out themes of King Kong or Batman.

Behavior after the divider was removed was strikingly different. Instead of sex segregation, boys and girls frequently played together. And girls, especially, engaged in more complex play, integrating materials from both settings into their fantasy themes. Finally, negative interactions between children declined after the divider was

In a collaborative study, a researcher and a teacher found that removing a high wall of shelves between the block and housekeeping areas in a preschool classroom enriched children's social and play experiences. Girls, especially, engaged in more complex play. (ROBERT BRENNER/PHOTOEDIT)

removed, perhaps because the more open play space reduced crowding and competition for materials.

Could these changes in children's play partners and styles have been due to sheer passage of time rather than removal of the divider? Possibly; but the chances are unlikely, since alterations in behavior were so abrupt and dramatic. As a result of this study, Cheryl learned that the design of play environments can have major impact on children's gender-role behavior. And Mary rearranged her classroom in ways that extended and enriched her pupils' social and play experiences (Kinsman & Berk, 1979).

questions, either on their own or with an experienced investigator. (See the From Research to Practice box above.) At other times, they may have to provide information on how well their goals for children are being realized to justify continued financial support for their programs and activities. Under these circumstances, an understanding of the research process becomes essential practical knowledge.

COMMON METHODS USED TO STUDY CHILDREN

How does a researcher choose a basic approach to gathering information about children? Common methods in the field of child development include systematic

TABLE 2.1 Strengths and Limitations of Common Research Methods

METHOD	DESCRIPTION	STRENGTHS	LIMITATIONS
Systematic observation			
Naturalistic observation	Observation of behavior in natural contexts	Observations reflect children's everyday lives	Conditions under which children are observed cannot be controlled; presence of observer may influence behavior in unnatural ways
Structured observation	Observation of behavior in a laboratory	Conditions of observation are the same for all children	Observations may not be typical of the way subjects behave in everyday life
Self-reports			
Clinical interview	Flexible interviewing procedure in which the investigator obtains a complete account of the subject's thoughts	Comes as close as possible to the way subjects think in everyday life; great breadth and depth of information can be obtained in a short time	Subjects may not report information accurately; flexible procedure makes comparing subjects' responses difficult
Structured interview, tests, and questionnaires	Self-report instruments in which each subject is asked the same questions in the same way	Standardized method of asking questions permits comparisons of subjects' responses and efficient data collection and scoring	Does not yield the same depth of information as a clinical interview; responses still subject to inaccurate reporting
Clinical method (case study)	A full picture of a single child's psychological functioning, obtained by combining interviews, observations, and test scores	Provides rich, descriptive insights into processes of development	May be biased by researcher's theoretical preferences; findings cannot be applied to individuals other than the subject
Ethnography	Understanding a culture or distinct social group through participant observation; by making extensive field notes, the researcher tries to capture the culture's unique values and social processes	Provides a more complete and accurate description than can be derived from a single observational visit, interview, or questionnaire	Presence of observer may influence behavior in unnatural ways; may be biased by researcher's values and theoretical preferences; findings cannot be applied to individuals and settings other than the ones studied

observation, self-reports, clinical or case studies of a single child, and ethnographies of the life circumstances of a particular group of children. As you read about these methods, you may find it helpful to refer to Table 2.1, which summarizes the strengths and limitations of each.

Systematic Observation

To find out how children actually behave, a researcher may choose *systematic observation*. Observations of the behavior of children, and of the adults who are important in their lives, can be made in different ways. One approach is to go into the field, or the natural environment, and record the behavior of interest, a method called **naturalistic observation.**

A study of children's social development provides a good example of this technique (Barrett & Yarrow, 1977). Observing 5- to 8-year-old children at a summer camp, the researchers recorded the number of times each child provided another person with physical or emotional support in the form of comforting,

Naturalistic observation
A method in which the researcher goes into the natural environment to observe the behavior of interest.

By making structured observations in a laboratory, researchers can ensure that all subjects have the same opportunity to display the behavior of interest. But subjects may not respond in the laboratory as they do in everyday life. (DICK LURIA/FPG)

sharing, helping, or expressing sympathy. They also noted the occurrence of cues from other people nearby, such as a tearful playmate or a harried adult, that indicated a need for comfort or assistance. The great strength of naturalistic observation in studies like this one is that investigators can see directly the everyday behaviors they hope to explain (Miller, 1987).

Naturalistic observation also has a major limitation: Not all children have the same opportunity to display a particular behavior in everyday life. In the study just mentioned, some children happened to be exposed to more cues for positive social responses than others, and for this reason they showed more helpful and comforting behavior. Researchers commonly deal with this difficulty by making **structured observations** in a laboratory. In this approach, the investigator sets up a cue for the behavior of interest. Since every subject is exposed to the cue in the same way, each has an equal opportunity to display the response. In one study, structured observations of children's helping behavior were made by having an adult "accidentally" spill a box of gold stars and recording how each child reacted (Stanhope, Bell, & Parker-Cohen, 1987).

Structured observation permits greater control over the research situation than does naturalistic observation. In addition, the method is especially useful for studying behaviors that investigators rarely have an opportunity to see in everyday life. For example, in a recent study, researchers wanted to find out how the presence of distracting toys influenced children's attention to and learning from educational television. They were particularly interested in hyperactive boys, who have great difficulty sitting still and paying attention. Television viewing, under these conditions, is hard to measure in children's homes. So the researchers furnished a laboratory to look much like a living room, where they could control both TV programming and the presence of distractors. As expected, when toys were available, hyperactive 6- to 12-year-olds found them irresistible; they spent only half as much time watching the TV as did their nonhyperactive counterparts (see Figure 2.1). Yet surprisingly, recall of televised information in the presence of toys was similar for hyperactive and nonhyperactive subjects. The inattentive, overactive boys appeared to learn effectively from TV, even when their attention was frequently diverted. These findings suggest that television may be an especially effective medium of instruction for hyperactive children, who typically do poorly in school (Landau, Lorch, & Milich, 1992). Of course, the great disadvantage of structured observations in studies like this one is that children may not behave in the laboratory as they do in their natural environments.

Structured observation
A method in which the researcher sets up a cue for the behavior of interest and observes that behavior in a laboratory.

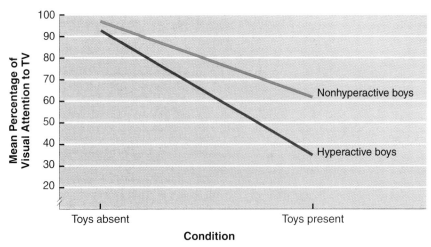

FIGURE 2.1 Results of a study that used structured observations. The researchers wanted to know how the presence of distracting toys influenced hyperactive and nonhyperactive boys' attention to and learning from educational television. When toys were absent, attention to TV in the laboratory by both groups of boys was high. When toys were present, hyperactive boys spent only half as much time attending to TV as did their nonhyperactive counterparts. However, other findings revealed that both hyperactive and nonhyperactive boys remembered just as much information from the programs, suggesting that TV may be an especially effective medium for helping inattentive, overactive children learn. (From "Visual Attention to and Comprehension of Television in Attention-Deficit Hyperactivity Disordered and Normal Boys" by S. Landau, E. P. Lorch, & R. Milich, 1992," *Child Development, 63*, p. 933. © The Society for Research in Child Development, Inc. Reprinted by permission.)

PROCEDURES FOR COLLECTING SYSTEMATIC OBSERVATIONS. The procedures used to collect systematic observations vary, depending on the research problem posed. Some investigators choose the **specimen record,** a description of the subject's entire stream of behavior—everything said and done for a particular time period. In one of my own studies, I wanted to find out how sensitive, responsive, and verbally stimulating caregivers were when they interacted with children in day-care centers (Berk, 1985). In this case, everything each caregiver said and did—even the amount of time she spent away from the children, taking coffee breaks and talking on the phone—was important.

In other studies, information on only one or a few kinds of behavior is needed, and preserving the entire behavior stream is unnecessary. In these instances, researchers may select more efficient observation procedures. One common approach is **event sampling,** in which the observer records all instances of a particular behavior of interest during a specified time period, ignoring other behaviors. In the study of hyperactive children's television viewing just reported, the researchers used event sampling by counting each instance in which the child looked toward the TV set. And, as you saw in Figure 2.1, they also measured the percentage of time that children attended to TV while in the setting.

A second efficient means of observing is **time sampling**. In this procedure, the researcher records whether or not certain behaviors occur during a sample of short time intervals. First, a checklist of the behaviors of interest is prepared. Then the observation period is divided into a series of brief time segments. For example, a half-hour observation period might be divided into 120 15-second intervals. The observer collects data by alternately watching the child for an interval and then checking off behaviors during the next interval, repeating this process until the entire observation period is complete.

Several decades ago, most naturalistic observations were obtained by jotting down notes on a pad of paper. But this technique is cumbersome, and information was missed in instances in which researchers tried to capture a complete account of each subject's behavior. Today, sophisticated equipment and recording devices are available to increase the convenience and accuracy of observational research. Tape recorders with mouthpieces that muffle the sound of an observer's voice

Specimen record

An observational procedure in which the researcher records a description of the subject's entire stream of behavior for a specified time period.

Event sampling

An observational procedure in which the researcher records all instances of a particular event or behavior during a specified time period.

Time sampling

An observational procedure in which the researcher records whether or not certain behaviors occur during a sample of short time intervals.

enable investigators to dictate on-the-spot descriptions of subjects' behavior. Cordless microphones attached to children's collars permit researchers to pick up verbal data that are not easily heard, such as soft-spoken conversations with peers and adults. Videotaping is often used to obtain a complete record of subjects' behavior in the laboratory. It can be used effectively in natural environments as well, if equipment is placed so that subjects are not distracted or made to feel self-conscious by its presence.

LIMITATIONS OF SYSTEMATIC OBSERVATION. A major problem in collecting systematic observations is the influence of the observer on the subject's behavior. The presence of a watchful, unfamiliar individual may cause children and adults to react in unnatural ways. For children below the age of 7 or 8, **observer influence** is generally limited to the first session or two that the unknown adult is present in the setting. Young children cannot stop "being themselves" for very long, and they quickly get used to the observer's presence. Older children and adults often engage in more positive, socially desirable behavior. In these instances, researchers can take subjects' responses as an indication of the best behavior they can display under the circumstances. However, not all subjects will conceal undesirable reactions. In several studies, parents who had developed hostile patterns of family interaction continued to engage in harsh discipline, including physical punishment, even though they were aware that an observer was recording their behavior (Reid, Taplin, & Lorber, 1981).

There are ways that researchers can minimize observer influence. Adaptation periods, in which observers visit the research setting so subjects have a chance to get used to their presence, are helpful. Another approach is to ask individuals who are part of the child's natural environment to do the observing. For example, in several studies, parents have been trained to record their children's behavior. Besides reducing the observer's impact on research participants, this method permits information to be gathered on behaviors that would require observers to remain in the natural setting for a very long time to see them. In one such study, researchers wanted to know what kinds of TV programs children watch with their parents and which ones they watch alone. To find out, they asked parents to keep detailed diaries of the viewing behaviors of all family members for several 1-week periods (St. Peters et al., 1991).

In addition to observer influence, **observer bias** is a serious danger in observational research. When observers are aware of the purposes of a study, they may see and record what is expected rather than subjects' actual behaviors. To guard against this problem, in most research it is wise to have people who have no knowledge of the investigator's hypotheses, or who at least have little personal investment in them, collect the observations.

Finally, although systematic observation provides invaluable information on how children and adults actually behave, it generally tells us little about the thinking and reasoning that underlie their behavior. For this kind of information, researchers must turn to another type of method—self-report techniques.

Self-Reports: Interviews and Questionnaires

Self-reports are instruments that ask subjects to provide information on their perceptions, thoughts, abilities, feelings, attitudes, beliefs, and past behaviors. They range from relatively unstructured clinical interviews, the method used by Piaget to study children's thinking, to highly structured interviews, questionnaires, and tests.

CLINICAL INTERVIEWS. Let's look at an example of a **clinical interview** in which Piaget questioned a 5-year-old child about his understanding of dreams:

> Where does the dream come from?—*I think you sleep so well that you dream.*—Does it come from us or from outside?—*From outside.*—What do we dream with?—*I don't know.*—With the hands? . . . With nothing?—*Yes, with nothing.*—When you are in bed and you dream, where is the dream?—*In my bed, under the blanket. I don't really know. If*

Observer influence
The tendency of subjects to react to the presence of an observer and behave in unnatural ways.

Observer bias
The tendency of observers who are aware of the purposes of a study to see and record what is expected rather than subjects' actual behaviors.

Clinical interview
A method in which the researcher uses flexible, open-ended questions to probe for the subject's point of view.

*U*sing the clinical interview, this
researcher asks a mother to describe her
child's development. The method permits
large amounts of information to be gathered in a relatively short period of time.
However, a major drawback of this method
is that subjects do not always report information accurately. (TONY FREEMAN/PHOTOEDIT)

it was in my stomach, the bones would be in the way and I shouldn't see it.—Is the dream
there when you sleep?—*Yes it is in the bed beside me . . .* —You see the dream when you
are in the room, but if I were in the room, too, should I see it?—*No, grownups don't ever
dream.*—Can two people ever have the same dream?—*No, never.*—When the dream is
in the room, is it near you?—*Yes, there!* (pointing to 30 cm in front of his eyes). (Piaget,
1926/1930, pp. 97–98)

Notice how Piaget used a flexible, conversational style to encourage the child
to expand his ideas. Prompts are given to obtain a fuller picture of the child's reasoning. Piaget's use of the clinical interview to study children's cognition is the
method's most well-known application. But it has also been applied to other areas
of child development. For example, researchers have obtained information on
child-rearing practices by questioning parents in an open-ended format about a
wide range of topics, including their handling of weaning, feeding, aggression,
dependency, exploration, and more (Sears, Maccoby, & Levin, 1957).

The clinical interview has two major strengths. First, it permits subjects to display their thoughts in terms that are as close as possible to the way they think in
everyday life. Second, it can provide a large amount of information in a fairly
brief period of time. For example, in an hour-long session, a wide range of child-
rearing information can be obtained from a parent—much more than could be
captured by observing parent-child interaction for the same amount of time.

LIMITATIONS OF CLINICAL INTERVIEWS. A major limitation of the clinical interview
has to do with the accuracy with which subjects report their own thoughts, feelings, and behaviors. Some subjects, wanting to please the interviewer, may make
up answers that do not represent their actual thinking. And because the clinical
interview depends on verbal ability and expressiveness, it may not accurately
assess individuals who have difficulty putting their thoughts into words. Skillful
interviewers minimize these problems by wording questions carefully and by
watching for cues indicating that a subject may not have clearly understood a
question or may need extra time to feel comfortable in the situation.

Interviews on certain topics are particularly vulnerable to distortion. When parents are asked to recall events during an earlier period of their child's life, they are
likely to speak in glowing terms. In a few instances, researchers have been able to
compare recall of early events with information obtained at the same time the events
occurred. Mothers reported faster development, fewer childhood problems, and
child-rearing practices more in line with current expert advice than with records of
their past behavior (Robbins, 1963; Yarrow, Campbell, & Burton, 1970). Also, most
parents find it difficult to recall specific instances of early events, although they can
report general tendencies—for example, their disciplinary style as "strict" or "permissive." But strictness to one parent may register as permissiveness to another.

Parents often have different definitions of these global terms, making their recollections of child rearing virtually useless as predictors of children's development (Maccoby & Martin, 1983). Parental interviews that focus on current rather than past information and specific characteristics rather than global judgments show a better match with actual behavior. Even so, parents are far from perfect in describing their own practices and their youngsters' personalities, preferences, and cognitive abilities (Kochanska, Kuczynski, & Radke-Yarrow, 1989; Miller & Davis, 1992).

Finally, we mentioned in Chapter 1 that the clinical interview has been criticized because of its flexibility. When questions are phrased differently for each subject, responses may be due to the manner of interviewing rather than real differences in the way subjects think about a certain topic. A second self-report method, the structured interview, reduces this problem.

STRUCTURED INTERVIEWS, TESTS, AND QUESTIONNAIRES. In a **structured interview**, each individual is asked the same set of questions in the same way. As a result, this approach eliminates the possibility that an interviewer might press and prompt some subjects more than others, thereby distorting the results. In addition, compared to clinical interviews, structured interviews are much more efficient. Answers are briefer, and researchers can obtain written responses from an entire class of children or group of children at the same time. Also, when structured interviews use multiple-choice, yes-no, and true-false formats, as is done on many tests and questionnaires, the answers can be tabulated by machine. However, keep in mind that these procedures do not yield the same depth of information as a clinical interview. And they can still be affected by the problem of inaccurate reporting.

The Clinical Method

In Chapter 1, we discussed the clinical method (sometimes called the case-study approach) as an outgrowth of the psychoanalytic perspective, which stresses the importance of understanding the individual child. Recall that the **clinical method** combines a wide range of information on one subject, including interviews, test scores, and observations. The aim is to obtain as complete a picture as possible of that child's psychological functioning and the experiences that led up to it.

Although clinical studies are usually carried out on youngsters who have serious emotional problems, they are sometimes done on well-adjusted children. A recent clinical investigation serves as an example. The researchers wanted to find out what contributes to the accomplishments of children who perform extraordinary intellectual feats—ones that are rare even among adults. Among the six prodigies studied over several years was Adam, a boy who read, wrote, and composed musical pieces before he was out of diapers. Adam's parents were dedicated to engaging his interests. They provided a home exceedingly rich in stimulation, raised him with affection, firmness, and humor, and searched for schools in which he could develop his talents while forming rewarding social relationships. By age 4, Adam was intensely involved in mastering human symbol systems—BASIC for the computer, French, German, Russian, Sanskrit, Greek, ancient hieroglyphs, music, and mathematics. Would Adam have realized his abilities without the chance combination of his special gift with nurturing, committed parents? Probably not, the investigators concluded (Feldman & Goldsmith, 1991). Adam's case illustrates the unique strengths of the clinical method. It yields case narratives that are rich in descriptive detail and that offer valuable insights into factors that affect development.

The clinical method, like all others, has drawbacks. Information is often collected unsystematically and subjectively, permitting too much leeway for researchers' theoretical preferences to bias their observations and interpretations. In addition, investigators cannot assume that the findings of clinical research apply to anyone other than the single child studied. For these reasons, the insights

Structured interview
A method in which the researcher asks each subject the same questions in the same way.

Clinical method
A method in which the researcher attempts to understand the unique individual child by combining interview data, observations, and sometimes test scores.

For many years, the poor school achievement of low-income minority children was attributed to "cultural deficits"—home environments that place little value on education. A recent ethnographic study of Mexican-American families challenges this assumption. Concha Delgado-Gaitan (1992) spent many months getting to know the residents of a Mexican-American community located in a small California city. There she collected extensive field notes on six families, each with a second-grade child. While in their homes, she carefully examined children's experiences related to education.

Although the Mexican-American parents had little schooling themselves, they regarded education as a great privilege and supported their children's learning in many ways. Their homes were cramped, one-bedroom apartments, occasionally shared with relatives. Still, parents did their best to create a stable environment that encouraged children to think positively about school. They offered material rewards for good grades (such as a new book or dinner at a favorite restaurant), set regular bedtime hours, and where possible provided a special place for doing schoolwork. And they frequently spoke to their children about their own educational limitations and the importance of taking advantage of the opportunity to study.

During the week, most parent–child conversations revolved around homework. All parents tried to help with assignments and foster behaviors valued in school. But how well they succeeded depended on social networks through which they could obtain information about educational matters. Some parents relied on relatives who had more experience in dealing with the school system. Others sought out individuals at church or work as advisers.

When social support was available, perplexing school problems were quickly resolved. For example, one parent, Mrs. Matias, received repeated reports from her son Jorge's teacher about his unruly behavior. Finally, a note arrived threatening suspension if Jorge did not improve. Mrs. Matias consulted one of her co-workers, who suggested that she ask for permission to leave during the lunch hour to talk with Jorge's teacher. After a conference revealed that Jorge needed to stay away from certain boys who were provoking him, his fighting subsided.

Despite sincere efforts, lack of familiarity with school tasks often hampered Mexican-American parents' ability to help their children. Mrs. Serna insisted that her poorly achieving daughter Norma do her homework at regularly scheduled times, and she checked to make sure that Norma completed her assignments. But when she tried to assist Norma, Mrs. Serna frequently misinterpreted the instructions. And she did not understand the school environment well enough to contact teachers for information about how to support her child. As a result, Norma's progress remained below average.

Although the Mexican-American families had limited income and material resources, this did not detract from their desire to create a home environment conducive to learning. The major barrier parents faced was how to assist children with actual tasks. Delgado-Gaitan recommends that schools establish open lines of communication with minority parents to make sure they have access to the resources they need to strengthen their children's learning.

---

drawn from clinical investigations need to be tested further using other research strategies before they can be accepted as accurate and generalizable.

Ethnography

Because of a growing interest in the impact of culture, child development researchers have begun to rely increasingly on a method borrowed from the field of anthropology—**ethnography.** Like the clinical method, ethnographic research is largely a descriptive, qualitative technique. But instead of aiming to understand a single individual, it is directed toward understanding a culture or a distinct social group (Winthrop, 1991).

The ethnographic method achieves its goals through *participant observation.* Typically, the researcher lives with the cultural community for a period of months or years, participating in all aspects of its daily life. Extensive field notes, which consist of a mix of observations, self-reports from members of the culture, and interpretations by the investigator, are gathered. Later, these notes are put together into a description of the community that tries to capture its unique values and social processes.

The ethnographic approach assumes that by entering into close and long-term contact with a social group, researchers can understand the beliefs and behavior of its members more accurately, in a way not possible with a single observational

Ethnography
A method in which the researcher attempts to understand the unique values and social processes of a culture or a distinct social group by living with its members and taking field notes for an extended period of time.

visit, interview, or questionnaire. Ethnographies of children from diverse cultures currently exist, and many more are being compiled. In some, investigators focus on all aspects of children's experience, as one researcher did in describing what it is like to grow up in an American small town (Peshkin, 1978). In other instances, the research is limited to one or a few settings, such as home or school life (Chang, 1992; Miller & Sperry, 1987). Because the ethnographic method is committed to trying to understand others' perspectives, it often overturns widely held stereotypes, as the Cultural Influences box on page 52 reveals.

Ethnographers strive to minimize their influence on the culture being studied by becoming part of it. Nevertheless, at times their presence does alter the situation. In addition, as with clinical research, investigators' cultural values and theoretical commitments sometimes lead them to observe selectively or misinterpret what they see. Finally, the findings of ethnographic studies cannot be assumed to generalize beyond the people and settings in which the research was originally conducted (Hammersley, 1992).

Brief Review

Systematic observation, self-reports, clinical studies, and ethnographies are commonly used research methods in the field of child development. Naturalistic observation provides information on children's everyday behaviors. When it is necessary to control the conditions of observation, researchers often make structured observations in a laboratory. The clinical interview provides a wealth of information on the reasoning behind subjects' behavior. However, subjects may not report their thoughts accurately, and comparing subjects' responses is difficult because each is asked questions in different ways. The structured interview is a more efficient method that questions each subject in the same way, but it does not yield the same depth of information as a clinical interview. Clinical studies of individual children provide rich insights into processes of development. However, information obtained is often unsystematic and subjective. In ethnographic research, an investigator tries to understand a culture or distinct social group through participant observation. Like clinical studies, ethnographies can be affected by researchers' theoretical biases, and the findings may not generalize beyond the subjects studied.

RELIABILITY AND VALIDITY:
KEYS TO SCIENTIFICALLY SOUND RESEARCH

Once investigators choose their research methods, they must take special steps to make sure their procedures provide trustworthy information about the topic of interest. To be acceptable to the scientific community, observations and self-reports must be both *reliable* and *valid*—two keys to scientifically sound research.

Reliability

Suppose you go into a classroom and record the number of times a child behaves in a helpful and cooperative fashion toward others, but your research partner, in simultaneously observing the same child, comes up with a very different set of measurements. Or you ask a group of children some questions about their interests, but a week later when you question them again, their answers are much different. **Reliability** refers to the consistency, or repeatability, of measures of subjects' behavior. To be reliable, observations of subjects' actions cannot be unique to a single observer. Instead, observers must agree on what they see. And an interview, test, or questionnaire, when given again within a short period of time (before subjects can reasonably be expected to change their opinions or develop more sophisticated responses) must yield similar results on both occasions.

Reliability
The consistency, or repeatability, of measures of subjects' behavior.

Researchers determine the reliability of data in different ways. In observational research, pairs of observers are often asked to record the same behavior sequences, and agreement between them is assessed. Reliability of self-report instruments can be demonstrated by finding out how similar children's responses are when the same questions are asked on another occasion. Or children's scores can be compared on different forms of the same test. If necessary, reliability can also be estimated from a single testing session by comparing children's scores on different halves of the test.

Validity

For research methods to have high **validity,** they must accurately measure characteristics that the researcher set out to measure. Think, for a moment, about this idea, and you will quickly see that reliability is absolutely essential for valid research. Methods that are implemented carelessly, unevenly, and inconsistently cannot possibly represent what an investigator originally intended to study.

But reliability by itself is not sufficient to ensure that a method will reflect the investigator's goals. Researchers must go further to guarantee validity, and they generally do so in several ways. They may carefully examine the content of observations and self-reports to make sure the behaviors of interest are included. For example, a test intended to measure fifth-grade children's knowledge of mathematics would not be valid if it contained addition problems but no subtraction, multiplication, or division problems (Miller, 1987). Another approach to validity is to see how effective a method is in predicting behavior in other situations that we would reasonably expect it to predict. If scores on a math test are valid, they should be related to how well children do on their math assignments in school or even to how quickly and accurately they can make change in a game of Monopoly.

As we turn now to research designs, you will discover that the concept of validity can also be applied more broadly, to the overall accuracy of research findings and conclusions. If, during any phase of carrying out a study—selecting subjects, choosing research settings and tasks, and implementing procedures—the researcher permits factors unrelated to the hypothesis to influence subjects' behavior, then the validity of the results are in doubt, and they cannot be considered a fair test of the investigator's theory. As you read the following sections, keep a list of the many possible threats to the validity of research that can occur in the course of designing and conducting an investigation.

GENERAL RESEARCH DESIGNS

In deciding which research design to use, investigators choose a way of setting up a study that permits them to test their hypotheses with the greatest certainty possible. Two main types of designs are used in all research on human behavior: correlational and experimental.

Correlational Design

In a **correlational design,** researchers gather information on already existing groups of individuals, generally in natural life circumstances, and no effort is made to alter their experiences in any way. Suppose we want to answer such questions as: Do structure and organization in the home make a difference in children's school performance? Does attending a day-care center promote children's friendliness with peers? Do mothers' styles of interacting with their children have any bearing on the children's intelligence? In these and many other instances, the conditions of interest are very difficult to arrange and control.

The correlational design offers a way of looking at relationships between subjects' experiences or characteristics and their behavior or development. But corre-

Validity
The extent to which measures in a research study accurately reflect what the investigator intended to measure.

Correlational design
A research design in which the investigator gathers information without altering subjects' experiences and examines relationships between variables. Does not permit inferences about cause and effect.

lational studies have one major limitation: We cannot infer cause and effect. For example, if we find in a correlational study that maternal interaction does relate to children's intelligence, we would not know whether mothers' behavior actually causes intellectual differences among children. In fact, the opposite is certainly possible. The behaviors of highly intelligent children may be so attractive that they cause mothers to interact more favorably. Or a third variable that we did not even think about studying, such as the amount of noise and distraction in the home, may be causing both maternal interaction and children's intelligence to change together in the same direction.

In correlational studies, and in other types of research designs, investigators often examine relationships among variables by using a **correlation coefficient,** which is a number that describes how two measures, or variables, are associated with one another. Although other statistical approaches to examining relationships are also available, we will encounter the correlation coefficient in discussing research findings throughout this book. So let's look at what it is and how it is interpreted. A correlation coefficient can range in value from +1.00 to −1.00. The *magnitude, or size, of the number* shows the *strength of the relationship.* A zero correlation indicates no relationship; but the closer the value is to +1.00 or −1.00, the stronger the relationship that exists. For instance, a correlation of −.52 is a stronger relationship than −.25, but correlations of +.50 and −.50 are equally strong. The *sign of the number* (+ or −) refers to the *direction of the relationship.* A positive sign (+) means that as one variable increases, the other also increases. A negative sign (−) indicates that as one variable increases, the other decreases.

Let's take a couple of examples to illustrate how a correlation coefficient works. In one study, a researcher found that a measure of maternal attention at 11 months of age was positively correlated with infant intelligence during the second year of life, at +.60. This is a moderately high positive correlation, which indicates that the more attentive the mothers were to their babies in infancy, the better their children did on an intelligence test several months later (Clarke-Stewart, 1973). In another study, a researcher reported that the extent to which mothers ignored

*I*s warm, attentive parenting related to children's development? A correlational design can be used to answer this question, but it does not permit researchers to determine the precise cause of their findings. (STEPHEN MARKS)

Correlation coefficient
A number, ranging from +1.00 to −1.00, that describes the strength and direction of the relationship between two variables.

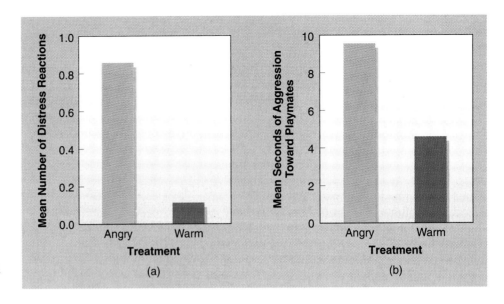

FIGURE 2.2 How does the quality of adult interaction affect 2-year-olds' emotional reactions? A laboratory experiment showed that exposure to angry adult interaction increased children's emotional distress (a) and aggressive behavior (b) toward playmates. (Adapted from Cummings, Iannotti, & Zahn-Waxler, 1985.)

their 10-month-olds' bids for attention was negatively correlated with children's willingness to comply with parental demands 1 year later—at −.46 for boys and −.36 for girls (Martin, 1981). These moderate correlations reveal that the more mothers ignored their babies, the less cooperative their children were during the second year of life.

Both of these investigations found a relationship between maternal behavior in the first year and children's behavior in the second year. Although the researchers suspected that maternal behavior affected children's responses, in neither study could they really be sure about cause and effect. However, if we find a relationship in a correlational study, this suggests that it would be worthwhile to track down its cause with a more powerful experimental strategy, if possible.

Experimental Design

Unlike correlational studies, an **experimental design** permits us to make inferences about cause and effect. In an experiment, the events and behaviors of interest are divided into two types: independent and dependent variables. The **independent variable** is the one anticipated by the investigator, on the basis of a hypothesis or research question, to cause changes in another variable. The **dependent variable** is the one the investigator expects to be influenced by the independent variable. Inferences about cause-and-effect relationships are possible because the researcher directly controls or manipulates changes in the independent variable. This is done by exposing subjects to two or more treatment conditions and comparing their performance on measures of the dependent variable.

In one **laboratory experiment,** researchers wanted to know if the quality of interaction between adults (independent variable) affects young children's emotional reactions while playing with a familiar peer (dependent variable). Pairs of 2-year-olds were brought into a laboratory set up to look much like a family home. One group was exposed to a warm treatment in which two adults in the kitchen spoke in a friendly way while the children played in the living room. A second group received an angry treatment in which positive communication between the adults was interrupted by an argument in which they shouted, complained, and slammed the door. As Figure 2.2(a) reveals, children in the angry condition displayed much more distress (such as freezing in place, anxious facial expressions, and crying). And as Figure 2.2(b) shows, they also exhibited more aggression toward their playmates than did children in the warm treatment

Experimental design

A research design in which the investigator randomly assigns subjects to treatment conditions. Permits inferences about cause and effect.

Independent variable

The variable manipulated by the researcher in an experiment by randomly assigning subjects to treatment conditions.

Dependent variable

The variable the researcher expects to be influenced by the independent variable in an experiment.

Laboratory experiment

An experiment conducted in the laboratory, which permits the maximum possible control over treatment conditions.

(Cummings, Iannotti, & Zahn-Waxler, 1985). The experiment revealed that exposure to even short episodes of intense adult anger can trigger negative emotions and antisocial behavior in very young children.

In experimental studies, investigators must take special precautions to control for characteristics of subjects that could reduce the accuracy of their findings. For example, in the study just described, if a greater number of children who had already learned to behave hostilely and aggressively happened to end up in the angry treatment, we could not tell whether the independent variable or the children's background characteristics produced the results. **Random assignment** of subjects to treatment conditions offers protection against this problem. By using an evenhanded procedure, such as drawing numbers out of a hat or flipping a coin, the experimenter increases the chances that subjects' characteristics will be equally distributed across treatment groups.

Sometimes researchers combine random assignment with another technique called **matching.** In this procedure, subjects are measured ahead of time on the factor in question—in our example, aggression. Then equal numbers of high- and low-aggressive subjects are randomly assigned to each treatment condition. In this way, the experimental groups are deliberately matched, or made equivalent, on characteristics that are likely to distort the results.

Modified Experimental Designs

Most experiments are conducted in laboratories where researchers can achieve the maximum possible control over treatment conditions. But, as we have already indicated, findings obtained in laboratories may not always apply to everyday situations. The ideal solution to this problem is to do experiments in the field as a complement to laboratory investigations. In **field experiments,** researchers capitalize on rare opportunities to randomly assign subjects to treatment conditions in natural settings. In the experiment we just considered, we can conclude that the emotional climate established by adults affects children's behavior in the laboratory. But does it also do so in daily life?

Another study helps answer this question. This time, the research was carried out in a day-care center. A caregiver deliberately interacted differently with two groups of preschoolers. In one condition (the *nurturant treatment*), she modeled many instances of warmth, helpfulness, and concern for others. In a second condition (the *control,* since it involved no treatment), she behaved as usual, with no special concern for others. Two weeks later, the researchers created several situations that called for helpfulness in a room adjoining the day-care center. For example, a visiting mother asked each child to watch her baby for a few moments, but the baby's toys had fallen out of the playpen. The investigators recorded whether or not each child returned the toys to the baby. As Figure 2.3 shows, children exposed to the nurturant treatment behaved in a much more helpful way than those in the control condition (Yarrow, Scott, & Waxler, 1973).

In testing many hypotheses, researchers cannot randomly assign subjects and manipulate conditions in the real world, as these investigators were able to do. Sometimes researchers can compromise by conducting **natural experiments.** Treatments that already exist, such as different school environments, day-care centers, and preschool programs, are compared. These studies differ from correlational research only in that groups of subjects are carefully chosen to ensure that their characteristics are as much alike as possible. In this way, investigators rule out as best they can alternative explanations for the treatment effects. But despite these efforts, natural experiments are unable to achieve the precision and rigor of true experimental research (Achenbach, 1978).

To help you compare the correlational and experimental designs we have discussed, Table 2.2 summarizes their strengths and limitations. Now let's take a close look at designs for studying development.

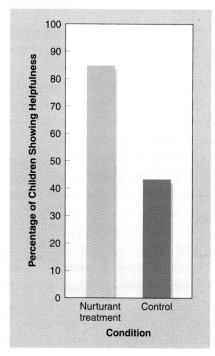

FIGURE 2.3 Does the emotional climate established by adults affect children's behavior in everyday life? In a field experiment conducted in a day-care center, children exposed to a nurturant treatment in which a caregiver modeled helpfulness and concern for others were far more likely than children in the control condition to show helpfulness themselves. (Adapted from Yarrow, Scott, & Waxler, 1973.)

Random assignment

An evenhanded procedure for assigning subjects to treatment groups, such as drawing numbers out of a hat or flipping a coin. Increases the chances that subjects' characteristics will be equally distributed across treatment conditions in an experiment.

Matching

A procedure for assigning subjects with similar characteristics in equal numbers to treatment conditions in an experiment. Ensures that groups will be equivalent on factors likely to distort the results.

Field experiment

A research design in which subjects are randomly assigned to treatment conditions in natural settings.

Natural experiment

A research design in which the investigator studies already existing treatments in natural settings by carefully selecting groups of subjects with similar characteristics.

TABLE 2.2 *Strengths and Limitations of General Research Designs*

DESIGN	DESCRIPTION	STRENGTHS	LIMITATIONS
Correlational design	The investigator obtains information on already existing groups, without altering subjects' experiences	Permits study of relationships between variables	Does not permit inferences about cause-and-effect relationships
Laboratory experiment	Under controlled laboratory conditions, the investigator manipulates an independent variable and looks at its effect on a dependent variable; requires random assignment of subjects to treatment conditions	Permits inferences about cause-and-effect relationships	Findings may not generalize to the real world
Field experiment	The investigator randomly assigns subjects to treatment conditions in natural settings	Permits generalization of experimental findings to the real world	Control over treatment is generally weaker than in a laboratory experiment
Natural experiment	The investigator compares already existing treatments in the real world, carefully selecting them to ensure that groups of subjects are as much alike in characteristics as possible	Permits study of naturally occurring variables not subject to experimenter manipulation	Obtained differences may be due to variables other than the treatment

DESIGNS FOR STUDYING DEVELOPMENT

Scientists interested in child development require information about the way their subjects change over time. To answer questions about development, they must extend correlational and experimental approaches to include measurements of subjects at different ages. Longitudinal and cross-sectional designs are special *developmental* research strategies. In each, age comparisons form the basis of the research plan.

The Longitudinal Design

In a **longitudinal design,** a group of subjects is studied repeatedly at different ages, and changes are noted as they mature. The time span may be relatively short—a few months to several years—or it may be very long—a decade or even a lifetime.

In the early part of this century, several longitudinal studies were begun in which individuals were followed from infancy into the adult years. One well-known example is the Guidance Study, initiated in 1928 at the University of California, Berkeley. The researchers collected a wide range of information on several hundred subjects—physical growth, intelligence, personality, child-rearing practices, and more. Today, this massive data base is still being tapped to answer questions about development. We will use examples from it to highlight three major strengths of longitudinal research.

Longitudinal design
A research design in which one group of subjects is studied repeatedly at different ages.

ADVANTAGES OF THE LONGITUDINAL DESIGN. First, the longitudinal approach is unique in tracking the performance of each subject over time. As a result, researchers can identify common patterns as well as individual differences in the paths children follow to maturity. Data from the Guidance Study on children's mental test performance illustrate the value of this kind of information. In the early part of this cen-

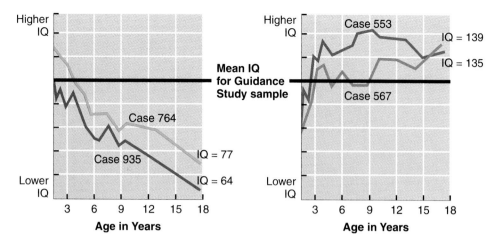

FIGURE 2.4 Individual patterns of change in intelligence test scores for four children in the Guidance Study sample. Cases 935 and 764 showed age-related declines, whereas Cases 567 and 553 showed gradual gains. The amount of change for each of these subjects was dramatic—from 70 to 79 points. Steady decreases in performance were linked to emotional stress and illness, increases to improved adjustment and health. (From "The Stability of Mental Test Performance Between Two and Eighteen Years" by M. P. Honzik, J. W. Macfarlane, & L. Allen, 1948, *Journal of Experimental Education, 17,* p. 319. Adapted by permission.)

tury, intelligence was assumed to be a largely inherited characteristic that remained stable over an individual's lifetime. The Guidance Study offered one of the first challenges to this assumption. Repeated testing revealed that 85 percent of the sample showed changes of 10 or more IQ points and 32 percent showed changes of more than 20 IQ points between 6 and 18 years of age. As the individual developmental trends in Figure 2.4 illustrate, children who changed most usually showed steady gains or declines, not random, haphazard fluctuations (Honzik, Macfarlane, & Allen, 1948). The existence of these stable patterns of change raises intriguing questions about the factors responsible for them.

A second strength of the longitudinal design is that researchers can compare different aspects of development to see whether the timing of change in one resembles the timing of change in another (Wohlwill, 1973). When similarities appear, they often lead to valuable insights into why certain changes occur. For example, the Guidance Study investigators compared information on children's emotional and physical health to their IQ scores. They found that emotional stress and illness were consistently related to declines in IQ, whereas improved adjustment and health often accompanied gains. Although we cannot conclude from this evidence that variations in emotional and physical health cause changes in children's intelligence, the associations present a serious challenge to the view that IQ is largely a reflection of heredity and only minimally affected by the environment.

A third and final advantage of the longitudinal design is that it permits researchers to examine relationships between early and later events and behaviors (Wohlwill, 1973). A group of investigators delved into the archives of the Guidance Study in search of just this kind of information. They wondered whether children who show extreme personality styles in childhood—either angry and explosive or shy and withdrawn—retain the same dispositions when they become adults. In addition, they wanted to know what kinds of experiences promote stability or change in personality and what consequences explosiveness and shyness have for long-term adjustment (Caspi, Elder, & Bem, 1987, 1988).

Results revealed that the two styles were only moderately stable between ages 8 and 30. When stability did occur, it appeared to be due to a "snowballing effect," in which children evoked responses from adults and peers that acted to maintain their dispositions. In other words, explosive youngsters were likely to be treated with anger and hostility (to which they reacted with even greater unruliness), whereas shy children were apt to be ignored.

Persistence of extreme personality styles affected many areas of adult adjustment, but these outcomes were different for males and females. For men, the results of early explosiveness were most apparent in their work lives, in the form of conflicts with supervisors, frequent job changes, and unemployment. Since few women in this sample of an earlier generation worked after marriage, their family lives were most affected. Explosive girls grew up to be hotheaded wives and mothers

59

Cohort effects are a serious threat to the accuracy of longitudinal findings. Suppose a researcher had charted the intellectual development of the children on the left, attending elementary school during the 1950s in a stark, regimented classroom offering few opportunities for active learning. Findings would be unlikely to apply to the school-age children of the 1990s shown on the right, whose development is supported by advances in instructional technology, greater individualization of academic tasks, and hands-on exploration of the environment. Notice, on page 62, how cohort effects can also threaten the validity of cross-sectional research. (LEFT: CAMERIQUE/STOCK PHOTOGRAPHY; RIGHT: ALEX WEBB/MAGNUM PHOTOS, INC.)

who were especially prone to divorce. Sex-related differences in the long-term consequences of shyness were even greater. Men who had been withdrawn in childhood were delayed in marrying, becoming fathers, and developing careers. Because a withdrawn, unassertive style was socially acceptable for females, women who had shy personalities showed no special adjustment problems.

PROBLEMS IN CONDUCTING LONGITUDINAL RESEARCH. Despite their strengths, longitudinal investigations confront researchers with a number of problems. There are practical difficulties, such as obtaining enough financial support and waiting the many years it takes for meaningful results in a long-term study. In addition, many factors can create serious difficulties for the validity of the findings.

Biased sampling is a common problem in longitudinal research. People who willingly participate in research that requires them to be continually observed and tested over many years are likely to have unique characteristics—at the very least, a special appreciation for the scientific value of research. As a result, we cannot easily generalize from them to the rest of the population. Furthermore, longitudinal samples generally become more biased as the investigation proceeds. Subjects may move away or drop out for other reasons, and the ones who remain are likely to be different in important ways from the ones who do not continue.

The very experience of being repeatedly interviewed, observed, and tested can also threaten the validity of a longitudinal study. If the measures concern attitudes or opinions, participants may gradually be alerted to their own thoughts and feelings, think about them, and revise them in ways that have little to do with age-related change (Nunnally, 1982). In addition, with repeated testing, subjects may become "test-wise." Their performance may improve as a result of **practice effects**—better test-taking skills and increased familiarity with the test, not because of factors commonly associated with development.

But the most widely discussed threat to the accuracy of longitudinal findings is cultural-historical change, or what are commonly called **cohort effects.** Longitudinal studies examine the development of cohorts—children born in the same time period who are influenced by a particular set of cultural and historical conditions. Results based on one cohort may not apply to children growing up at other times. For example, children's intelligence test performance may be affected

Biased sampling
Failure to select subjects who are representative of the population of interest in a study.

Practice effects
Changes in subjects' natural responses as a result of repeated testing.

Cohort effects
The effects of cultural-historical change on the accuracy of findings: Children born in one period of time are influenced by particular cultural and historical conditions.

Economic disaster, wars, and periods of rapid social change can profoundly affect people's lives. Glen Elder (1974) capitalized on the extent to which families experienced economic hardship during the Great Depression of the 1930s to study its impact on development. Elder delved into the vast archives of the Oakland Growth Study, a longitudinal investigation begun in the early 1930s that followed 167 adolescents into mature adulthood. He divided the sample into two groups: those whose adolescent years were marked by severe economic deprivation and those whose youth was relatively free of economic strain.

The findings showed that unusual burdens were placed on adolescents from deprived families as their parents' lives changed. Mothers entered the labor force, fathers sought work outside the immediate community, and the stress of economic hardship led to a rising rate of parental divorce and illness. In response, adolescents had to take on family responsibilities. Girls cared for younger siblings and assumed household chores, while boys tried to find part-time jobs. These changes had major consequences for adolescents' future aspirations. Girls' interests focused on home and family even more than was typical for that time period, and they were less likely to think about college and careers. Boys learned that economic resources could not be taken for granted, and they tended to make a very early commitment to an occupational choice.

Relationships also changed in economically deprived homes. As unemployed fathers lost status, mothers were granted greater control over family affairs. This reversal of traditional gender roles often sparked conflict. Fathers sometimes became explosive and punitive toward their children (Elder, Liker, & Cross, 1984). In response, boys turned toward peers and adults outside the family for emotional support. Because girls were more involved in family affairs, they bore the brunt of their fathers' anger. And some fathers may have been especially resentful of their daughters as family power was transferred to women (Elder, Van Nguyen, & Caspi, 1985).

The impact of the Great Depression continued to be apparent as these young people entered adulthood. Girls who grew up in economically deprived homes remained committed to domestic life, and many married at an early age. Men had a strong desire for economic security, and they changed jobs less often than those from nondeprived backgrounds. The chance to become a parent was especially important to men whose lives had been disrupted by the Depression. Perhaps because they felt a rewarding career could not be guaranteed, these men viewed children as the most enduring benefit of their adult lives.

The fact that the Oakland Growth Study subjects were adolescents and, therefore, beyond the early years of intense family dependency may explain why most weathered economic hardship successfully. More recently, Elder and his colleagues conducted a similar investigation of the Guidance Study sample, people who were born later and therefore were much younger when the Great Depression struck. For boys (who, as we will see in later chapters, are especially prone to adjustment problems in the face of family stress), the impact of economic strain was particularly severe. They showed long-term emotional difficulties and poor attitudes toward school and work (Elder & Caspi, 1988; Elder, Caspi, & Van Nguyen, 1986).

Clearly, cultural-historical change does not affect all children in the same way. With respect to the Great Depression, the outcomes varied considerably, depending on the young person's sex and the period of development in which social change took place (Stewart & Healy, 1989).

by differences in the quality of public schooling from one decade to another or by generational changes in parental values regarding the importance of stimulating children's mental development. And a longitudinal study of adolescent social development would probably result in quite different findings if it were carried out in the 1990s, around the time of World War II, or during the Great Depression of the 1930s. (See the Social Issues box above.)

Finally, changes occurring within the field of child development may create problems for longitudinal research covering an extended time period. Theories and methods are constantly changing, and those that first inspired a longitudinal study may become outdated (Nunnally, 1982). For this reason, as well as the others just mentioned, many recent longitudinal studies are short term, spanning only a few months or years in a child's life. In this way, researchers are spared some of the formidable obstacles that threaten longitudinal investigations lasting from childhood to maturity.

The Cross-Sectional Design

The length of time it takes for many behaviors to change, even in limited longitudinal studies, has led researchers to turn toward a more convenient strategy for studying development. In the **cross-sectional design,** groups of subjects differing in age are studied at the same point in time.

A recent investigation provides a good illustration. Children in grades 3, 6, 9, and 12 filled out a questionnaire asking about their sibling relationships. Findings revealed that sibling interaction was characterized by greater equality and less power assertion with age. Also, feelings of sibling companionship declined during adolescence. The researchers thought these age changes were due to several factors. As later-born children become more competent and independent, they no longer need and are probably less willing to accept direction from older siblings. In addition, as adolescents move from psychological dependence on the family to greater involvement with peers, they may have less time and emotional need to invest in their siblings (Buhrmester & Furman, 1990). These intriguing ideas about the impact of development on sibling relationships deserve to be followed up in future research.

Notice how in cross-sectional studies, researchers do not have to worry about many difficulties that plague the longitudinal design. When participants are measured only once, investigators do not need to be concerned about subjects dropping out of the study, "test-wiseness," or changes in the field of child development that might make the findings obsolete by the time the study is complete.

PROBLEMS IN CONDUCTING CROSS-SECTIONAL RESEARCH. Although the cross-sectional design is a very efficient strategy for describing age-related trends, when researchers choose it they are shortchanged in the kind of information they can obtain about development. Evidence about change at the level at which it actually occurs—the individual—is not available. For example, in the study of sibling relationships we just discussed, comparisons are limited to age-group averages. We cannot tell if important individual differences exist in the development of sibling relationships, some becoming more supportive and intimate and others becoming increasingly distant with age.

Furthermore, to conclude from a cross-sectional study that a true age-related change has occurred, researchers must make a special, sometimes unwarranted assumption: that the behavior of the younger subjects reflects what the older subjects were like at an earlier age. In cross-sectional research that covers a large age range, this assumption is especially risky because the separate age groups contain individuals born in widely separated years. Differences found between 10-year-old children born in 1984 and 20-year-old adults born in 1974 may not really represent age-related changes. Instead, they may reflect unique experiences associated with the different time periods in which the age groups were growing up. Thus, the validity of cross-sectional studies can also be threatened by cohort effects, and cross-sectional research is likely to suffer from fewest problems if the age range sampled is fairly narrow.

Improving Developmental Designs

In recent years, researchers have tackled the problems inherent in longitudinal and cross-sectional designs and devised ways of minimizing the weaknesses of each approach while continuing to take advantage of and even building on its strengths. Several modified developmental designs have resulted.

COMBINING LONGITUDINAL AND CROSS-SECTIONAL APPROACHES. To overcome some of the limitations of longitudinal and cross-sectional research, investigators sometimes combine the two approaches. One way of doing so is the **longitudinal-sequential design,** shown in Figure 2.5. It is called a sequential design because it is composed of a sequence of samples, each of which is followed longitudinally for a number of years (Schaie & Hertzog, 1982). In Figure 2.5, two groups are followed: one born in 1982, the other in 1985. Both are tracked longitudinally from 1988 to 1994. The first sample is followed from ages 3 to 9, the second from ages 6 to 12.

The design has three advantages. First, it permits researchers to find out whether cohort effects are operating by comparing children of the same age who

Cross-sectional design
A research design in which groups of subjects of different ages are studied at the same point in time.

Longitudinal-sequential design
A research design with both longitudinal and cross-sectional components in which groups of subjects born in different years are followed over time.

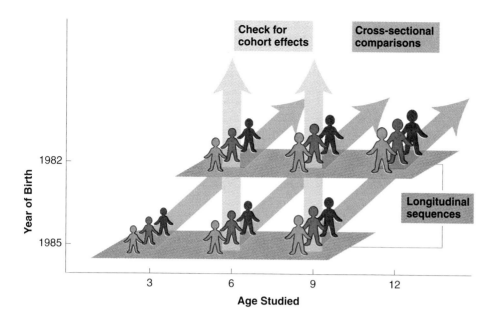

FIGURE 2.5 Example of a longitudinal-sequential design. Two samples of children, one born in 1982 and the other in 1985, are observed longitudinally from 3 to 12 years of age. The design permits the researcher to check for cohort effects by comparing children of the same age who were born in different years. Also, both longitudinal and cross-sectional comparisons can be made.

were born in different years. In Figure 2.5, we can compare the behaviors of the two samples at ages 6 and 9. If they do not differ, we can rule out cohort effects. Second, it is possible to make both longitudinal and cross-sectional comparisons. If outcomes are similar in both, then we can be especially confident about our findings. Third, the design is efficient. In the example shown in Figure 2.5, the researcher can find out about change over a 9-year period by following each cohort for just 6 years. Although the longitudinal-sequential design is used only occasionally, it provides researchers with a convenient way to profit from the strengths of both longitudinal and cross-sectional approaches.

EXAMINING MICROCOSMS OF DEVELOPMENT. Look back at the examples of developmental research we have discussed, and notice how in all instances observations of children are fairly widely spaced. When we observe at ages 4, 6, and 8, we can describe development, but we have little opportunity to capture the processes that produced the changes. A recent modification of the longitudinal approach, called the **microgenetic design,** is becoming more popular because it offers unique insights into how development takes place (Siegler & Crowley, 1991, 1992).

*T*he microgenetic design permits researchers to witness development as it takes place. In this study, a child's mastery of a counting task is tracked over a series of sessions, from the time the task is new until it is fully mastered. (JIM PICKERELL)

Microgenetic design
A research design in which change is tracked from the time it begins until it stabilizes, as subjects master an everyday or novel task.

In microgenetic studies, researchers track change while it is occurring, observing frequently from the time it begins until it stabilizes. Since it is not practical to use this approach over a long developmental period, investigators usually present children with a novel task or a task from their everyday environment and follow their mastery of it over a series of sessions. Within this "microcosm" of development, they see how change occurs. In one microgenetic study, researchers watched how mothers supported their young child's learning of a challenging puzzle problem. Children who progressed the fastest had mothers who sensitively adjusted the help they offered to the child's changing performance on the task. If the child failed in an attempt to place a puzzle piece, the mother provided more direct guidance on the next try. If the child succeeded, she pulled back and gave less direct support, permitting the child to assume greater responsibility for the task (Pratt et al., 1988).

As this example illustrates, microgenetic studies are especially useful for studying cognitive development. At the same time, they are very difficult to carry out. Researchers must pour over hours of videotaped records, analyzing each subject's moment-by-moment behaviors. In addition, the time required for children to change is hard to anticipate. It depends on a careful match between the child's capabilities and the demands of the task (Siegler & Crowley, 1991). Finally, microgenetic studies are subject to practice effects. Repeated exposure to the task may distort developmental trends (Pressley, 1992). But when researchers find ways to surmount these challenges, they reap the benefits of witnessing development as it takes place.

COMBINING EXPERIMENTAL AND DEVELOPMENTAL DESIGNS. Perhaps you noticed that all of the examples of longitudinal and cross-sectional research we have considered provide only correlational, and not causal, inferences about development. Yet ideally, causal information is desirable, both for testing theories and for coming up with ways to improve children's lives. If we find that some aspect of children's experiences and behavior are related in a developmental design, in some instances we can explore the causal relationship between them by experimentally manipulating the experience in a later study. If, as a result, development is enhanced, we would have strong evidence for a causal association between early experience and later behavior. Today, research that combines an experimental strategy with either a longitudinal or cross-sectional approach appears with increasing frequency in the research literature. Such designs are a vital force in helping investigators move beyond correlated variables to a causal account of developmental change. For a summary of the strengths and limitations of developmental research designs, turn to Table 2.3.

Brief Review

A variety of research designs are commonly used to study children. In correlational research, information is gathered on existing groups of individuals. Investigators can examine relationships between variables, but they cannot infer cause and effect. Because the experimental design involves random assignment of subjects to treatment groups, researchers can find out if an independent variable causes change in a dependent variable. Field and natural experiments permit generalization to everyday life, but they sacrifice rigorous experimental control.

Longitudinal and cross-sectional designs are uniquely suited for studying development. Longitudinal research provides information on common patterns as well as individual differences in development and the relationship between early and later events and behaviors. The cross-sectional approach is more efficient, but comparisons are limited to age-group averages. The longitudinal-sequential design permits researchers to reap the benefits of both longitudinal and cross-sectional strategies. A special form of longitudinal research, the microgenetic design, offers unique insights into the processes of development. Experimental approaches can be combined with longitudinal or cross-sectional designs to examine causal influences on development.

TABLE 2.3 Strengths and Limitations of Developmental Research Designs

DESIGN	DESCRIPTION	STRENGTHS	LIMITATIONS
Longitudinal	A group of subjects is studied repeatedly at different ages	Permits study of common patterns and individual differences in development and relationships between early and later events and behaviors	Age-related changes may be distorted because of biased sampling, subject dropout, practice effects, and cohort effects
Cross-sectional	Groups of subjects of different ages are studied at one point in time	More efficient than the longitudinal design	Does not permit study of individual developmental trends; age differences may be distorted because of cohort effects
Longitudinal-sequential	Two or more groups of subjects born in different years are followed over time	Permits both longitudinal and cross-sectional comparisons; reveals existence of cohort effects	May have the same problems as longitudinal and cross-sectional strategies, but the design itself helps identify difficulties
Microgenetic	Change is tracked from the time it begins until it stabilizes, as subjects master a novel or an everyday task	Offers unique insights into the processes of development	Requires intensive study of subjects' moment-by-moment behaviors; the time required for children to change is difficult to anticipate; practice effects may distort developmental trends

ETHICS IN RESEARCH ON CHILDREN

Research into human behavior creates ethical issues because, unfortunately, the quest for scientific knowledge can sometimes exploit people. When children take part in research, the ethical concerns are especially complex. Children are more vulnerable than adults to physical and psychological harm. In addition, immaturity makes it difficult or impossible for children to evaluate for themselves what participation in research will mean. For these reasons, special ethical guidelines for research on children have been developed by the federal government, by funding agencies, and by research-oriented associations such as the American Psychological Association (1982) and the Society for Research in Child Development (1990).

Table 2.4 presents a summary of children's basic research rights drawn from these guidelines. Once you have examined them, think back to the ethical controversy faced by my colleague Ron, described at the beginning of this chapter. Then take a close look at the following research situations, each of which poses an additional ethical dilemma. What precautions do you think should be taken to protect the rights of children in each instance? Is any one of these studies so threatening to children's well-being that it should not be carried out?

- To study children's willingness to separate from their caregivers, an investigator decides to ask mothers of 1- and 2-year-olds to leave their youngsters alone for a brief time period in an unfamiliar playroom. The researcher knows that under these circumstances, some children become very upset.
- In a study of moral development, a researcher wants to assess children's ability to resist temptation by videotaping their behavior without their knowledge. Seven-year-olds are promised an attractive prize for solving some very difficult puzzles. They are also told not to look at a classmate's correct solutions, which are deliberately placed at the back of the room. If the researcher

TABLE 2.4 Children's Research Rights

RESEARCH RIGHT	DESCRIPTION
Protection from harm	Children have the right to be protected from physical or psychological harm in research. If in doubt about the harmful effects of research, investigators should seek the opinion of others. When harm seems possible, investigators should find other means of obtaining the desired information or abandon the research.
Informed consent	All research participants, including children, have the right to have explained to them, in language appropriate to their level of understanding, all aspects of the research that may affect their willingness to participate. When children are subjects, informed consent of parents as well as others who act on the child's behalf (such as school officials) should be obtained, preferably in writing. Children, and the adults responsible for them, have the right to discontinue participation in the research at any time.
Privacy	Children have the right to concealment of their identity on all information collected in the course of research. They also have this right with respect to written reports and in any informal discussions about the research.
Knowledge of results	Children have the right to be informed of research results in language that is appropriate to their level of understanding.
Beneficial treatments	If experimental treatments believed to be beneficial are under investigation, children in control groups have the right to alternative beneficial treatments if they are available.

SOURCES: American Psychological Association, 1982; Society for Research in Child Development, 1990.

has to tell children ahead of time that cheating is being studied or that their behavior is being closely monitored, she will destroy the purpose of her study.

Did you find it difficult to decide on the best course of action in these examples? Virtually every organization that has worked on developing ethical principles for research has concluded that the conflicts raised by studies like these cannot be resolved with simple answers. The ultimate responsibility for the ethical integrity of research lies with the investigator. However, researchers are advised or, in the case of federally funded research, required to seek advice from others. Special committees, like the one that evaluated Ron's research, exist in colleges, universities, and other institutions for this purpose. These committees weigh the costs of the research to the participants in terms of time, stress, and inconvenience against the study's value for advancing knowledge and improving children's conditions of life (Cooke, 1982).

Ron's procedures, the school's research committee claimed, might not offer his subjects sufficient **protection from harm.** If there are any risks to the safety and welfare of participants that the research does not justify, then priority should always be given to the research participants. But occasionally, further inquiry can help resolve perplexing ethical dilemmas. In Ron's case, he provided the research committee with recently published findings showing that asking elementary school pupils to identify disliked peers does not lead them to interact less frequently or more negatively with those children (Bell-Dolan, Foster, & Sikora, 1989). At the same time, Ron agreed to take special precautions when requesting such information. He promised to ask all the children to keep their comments con-

Protection from harm
The right of research participants to be protected from physical or psychological harm.

fidential. Also, he arranged to conduct the study at a time when classmates have limited opportunity to interact with one another—just before a school vacation. With these safeguards in place, the committee felt comfortable with Ron's research, and eventually they approved it.

The ethical principle of **informed consent** requires special interpretation when research subjects are children. The competence of youngsters of different ages to make choices about their own participation must be taken into account. Parental consent is meant to protect the safety of children whose ability to make these decisions is not yet fully mature. Besides parental consent, agreement of other individuals who act on children's behalf, such as institutional officials when research is conducted in schools, day-care centers, or hospitals, should be obtained. This is especially important when studies include special groups, such as abused children, whose parents may not represent their best interests (Thompson, 1990b).

For children 7 years and older, their own informed consent should be obtained in addition to parental consent (National Commission for the Protection of Human Subjects, 1977). Around age 7, changes in children's thinking permit them to better understand simple scientific principles and the needs of others. Researchers should respect and enhance these new capacities by providing school-age children with a full explanation of research activities in language they can understand (Ferguson, 1978; Thompson, 1990b). Extra care needs to be taken when informing children that the information they provide will be kept confidential and that they can end their participation anytime. Children may not understand, and sometimes do not believe, these promises from researchers (Abramovitch et al., 1991).

Finally, young children rely on a basic faith in adults to feel secure in unfamiliar situations. For this reason, some types of research may be particularly disturbing to them. All ethical guidelines advise that special precautions be taken in the use of deception and concealment, as occurs when researchers observe children from behind one-way mirrors, give them false feedback about their performance, or do not tell them the truth regarding what the research is about. When these kinds of procedures are used with adults, **debriefing,** in which the experimenter provides a full account and justification of the activities, occurs after the research session is over. Debriefing should also take place with children, but it often does not work as well. Despite explanations, children may come away from the research situation with their belief in the honesty of adults undermined. Ethical standards permit deception in research with children if investigators satisfy institutional committees that such practices are necessary. Nevertheless, since deception may have serious emotional consequences for some youngsters, many child development specialists believe that its use is always unethical and that investigators should come up with other research strategies when children are involved (Cooke, 1982; Ferguson, 1978).

Informed consent
The right of individuals, including children, to have explained to them, in language they can understand, all aspects of a research study that may affect their willingness to participate.

Debriefing
Providing a full account and justification of research activities to subjects who participated in a study in which deception was used.

CHAPTER SUMMARY

From Theory to Hypothesis
- Research usually begins with a **hypothesis,** or prediction about behavior drawn from a theory. In areas in which there is little or no existing theory, it starts with a research question. On the basis of the hypothesis or question, the investigator selects research methods (specific activities in which each subject will participate) and a research design (overall plan for the study).

Common Methods Used to Study Children
- Common research methods in child development include systematic observation; self-reports; the clinical, or case-study, method; and ethnography. **Naturalistic observations** are gathered in children's everyday environments, whereas **structured observations** take place in laboratories, where investigators deliberately set up cues to elicit the behaviors of interest.
- Depending on the researcher's purpose, observations can preserve the entire behavior stream of the subject, as in the **specimen record.** Or they can be limited to one or a few behaviors of interest, as in **event sampling** and **time sampling.**
- Self-report methods can be flexible and open-ended, like the **clinical interview,** which yields a full picture of each subject's thoughts and feelings. Alternatively, **structured interviews,** questionnaires, and tests, which permit efficient administration and scoring, can be given.
- Investigators use the **clinical method** when they desire an in-depth understanding of a single child. In this approach, interview, test, and observational information is synthe-

sized into a complete description of the subject's development and unique psychological functioning.

- A growing interest in the impact of culture has prompted child development researchers to borrow a method from the field of anthropology—**ethnography.** Like the clinical method, ethnographic research is descriptive and qualitative. But instead of aiming to understand a single individual, it uses participant observation to understand the unique values and social processes of a culture or distinct social group.

Reliability and Validity: Keys to Scientifically Sound Research

- To be acceptable to the scientific community, observations and self-reports must be both reliable and valid. **Reliability** refers to the consistency, or repeatability, of measures of subjects' behavior. A method has high **validity** if, after examining its content and relationships with other measures of behavior, the researcher finds that it reflects what it was intended to measure.
- The concept of validity can also be applied more broadly, to the overall accuracy of research findings and conclusions. In designing a study, investigators must take special precautions to make sure that factors unrelated to the hypothesis do not influence subjects' behavior.

General Research Designs

- Two main types of designs are used in all research on human behavior. The **correlational design** examines relationships between variables as they happen to occur, without any intervention. The **correlation coefficient** is often used to measure the association between variables. Correlational studies do not permit inferences about cause and effect. However, their use is justified when it is difficult or impossible to control the variables of interest.
- An **experimental design** can determine cause and effect. Researchers manipulate an **independent variable** by exposing groups of subjects to two or more treatment conditions. Then they determine what effect this has on a **dependent variable. Random assignment** and **matching** are techniques used to ensure that characteristics of subjects do not reduce the accuracy of experimental findings.
- **Laboratory experiments** usually achieve high degrees of control, but their findings may not apply to everyday life. To overcome this problem, researchers sometimes conduct **field experiments,** in which they manipulate treatment conditions in the real world. When this is impossible, investigators may compromise and conduct **natural experi-**

ments, in which already existing treatments containing subjects who are as much alike as possible are compared. This approach, however, is far less rigorous than a true experimental design.

Designs for Studying Development

- Longitudinal and cross-sectional designs are uniquely suited for studying development. In the **longitudinal design,** a group of subjects is observed repeatedly at different ages. It permits study of individual developmental trends, relationships among different aspects of development, and associations between early and later events and behaviors.
- Researchers face a variety of problems in conducting longitudinal research, including **biased sampling** and **practice effects.** But the most widely discussed threat to the accuracy of longitudinal findings is **cohort effects**—difficulties in generalizing to children growing up during different time periods.
- The **cross-sectional design,** in which groups of subjects differing in age are studied at the same time, offers an efficient approach to studying development. However, it is limited to comparisons of age-group averages. Like longitudinal research, cross-sectional studies can be threatened by cohort effects, especially when they cover a wide age span.
- New designs have been devised to overcome some of the limitations of longitudinal and cross-sectional research. By combining the two approaches, the **longitudinal-sequential design** benefits from the strengths of each and permits researchers to test for cohort effects. In the **microgenetic design,** researchers track change as it occurs. In doing so, they obtain unique insights into the processes of development. When experimental procedures are combined with developmental designs, researchers can examine causal influences on development.

Ethics in Research with Children

- Research involving children raises special ethical concerns. Because of their immaturity, children are especially vulnerable. Ethical guidelines for research and special committees that weigh the costs and benefits of research projects help ensure that children's rights are protected and that they are afforded **protection from harm.** In addition to parental consent, researchers should seek the **informed consent** of children age 7 and older for research participation. The use of deception in research with children is especially risky, since **debriefing** can undermine their basic faith in the trustworthiness of adults.

IMPORTANT TERMS AND CONCEPTS

hypothesis (p. 44)
naturalistic observation (p. 46)
structured observation (p. 47)
specimen record (p. 48)
event sampling (p. 48)
time sampling (p. 48)
observer influence (p. 49)
observer bias (p. 49)
clinical interview (p. 49)
structured interview (p. 51)
clinical method (p. 51)
ethnography (p. 52)

reliability (p. 53)
validity (p. 54)
correlational design (p. 54)
correlation coefficient (p. 55)
experimental design (p. 56)
independent variable (p. 56)
dependent variable (p. 56)
laboratory experiment (p. 56)
random assignment (p. 57)
matching (p. 57)
field experiment (p. 57)

natural experiment (p. 57)
longitudinal design (p. 58)
biased sampling (p. 60)
practice effects (p. 60)
cohort effects (p. 60)
cross-sectional design (p. 62)
longitudinal-sequential design (p. 62)
microgenetic design (p. 63)
protection from harm (p. 66)
informed consent (p. 67)
debriefing (p. 67)

C O N N E C T I O N S

If you are interested in . . .	Turn to . . .	To learn about . . .
Common research methods used to study children 	Chapter 4, pp. 141–147, 154	Research methods for studying infant learning and perception
	Chapter 8, pp. 317–319	Intelligence testing of infants and children
	Chapter 9, p. 355	A clinical study of Genie, a child deprived of early language learning
	Chapter 10, pp. 408–410	Observational, self-report, and physiological assessments of temperament
	Chapter 10, pp. 418–419	The Strange Situation: a laboratory observational procedure for studying the security of infant–caregiver attachment
	Chapter 12, pp. 481–482, pp. 485–487	Clinical interviewing and questionnaire methods for studying moral reasoning
General and developmental research designs 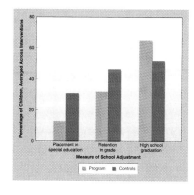	Chapter 4, pp. 170–171	Longitudinal research on the importance of early experience for later development
	Chapter 8, pp. 339–340	Natural experiments on early intervention and intellectual development of at-risk children
	Chapter 14, pp. 563–566	Correlational research on child-rearing styles and children's cognitive and social competence
Ethics in research on children 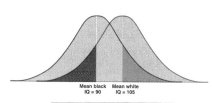	Chapter 3, pp. 87–88	Ethical implications of advances in fetal medicine
	Chapter 8, p. 326	Ethical implications of research on the origins of racial differences in intelligence
	Chapter 14, p. 590	Ethical implications of definitions of child maltreatment

shows combined features of both parents, another resembles just one parent, whereas still a third is not like either parent? These directly observable characteristics are called **phenotypes.** They depend in part on the individual's **genotype**— the complex blend of genetic information that determines our species and influences all our unique characteristics. But phenotypes, as our discussion will show, are also affected by a long history of environmental influences—ones that begin even before the moment of conception.

Next, we trace development during the most rapid phase of growth, the prenatal period, in which complex transactions between heredity and environment begin to shape the course of development. We consider environmental supports that are necessary for normal prenatal growth as well as damaging influences that threaten the child's health and survival. Then we turn to the drama of birth and to developmental risks for infants born underweight or prematurely, before the prenatal phase is complete.

Finally, we take a look ahead. This earliest period introduces us to the operation of the two basic determinants of development: heredity and environment. We will consider how researchers think about and study the relationship between nature and nurture as they continue to influence the individual's emerging characteristics from infancy through adolescence.

GENETIC FOUNDATIONS

Basic principles of genetics were unknown until the mid–nineteenth century, when the Austrian monk and botanist Gregor Mendel began a series of experiments with pea plants in his monastery garden. Recording the number of times white- and pink-flowered plants had offspring with white or pink flowers, Mendel found that he could predict the characteristics of each new generation. Mendel inferred the presence of genes, factors controlling the physical traits he studied. Although peas and humans may seem completely unrelated, today we know that heredity operates in similar ways among all forms of life. Since Mendel's ground-breaking observations, our understanding of how genetic messages are coded and inherited has vastly expanded.

The Genetic Code

Each of us is made up of trillions of independent units called cells. Inside every cell is a control center, or nucleus. When cells are chemically stained and viewed through a powerful microscope, rodlike structures called **chromosomes** are visible in the nucleus. Chromosomes store and transmit genetic information. Their number varies from species to species—48 for chimpanzees, 64 for horses, 40 for mice, and 46 for human beings. Chromosomes come in matching pairs (an exception is the XY pair in males, which we will discuss shortly). Each member of a pair corresponds to the other in size, shape, and genetic functions. One is inherited from the mother and one from the father. Therefore, in humans, we speak of 23 pairs of chromosomes residing in each human cell (see Figure 3.1).

Chromosomes are made up of a chemical substance called **deoxyribonucleic acid, or DNA.** In the early 1950s, James Watson and Francis Crick's (1953) discovery of the structure of the DNA molecule unlocked the genetic code. As Figure 3.2 shows, DNA is a long, double-stranded molecule that looks like a twisted ladder. Notice that each rung of the ladder consists of a specific pair of chemical substances called bases, joined together between the two sides. Although the bases always pair up in the same way across the ladder rungs—A with T, and C with G—they can occur in any order along its sides. It is this sequence of bases that provides genetic instructions. A **gene** is a segment of DNA along the length of the chromosome. Genes can be of different lengths—perhaps one hundred to several thousand ladder rungs long—and each differs from the next because of its special sequence of base pairs. Altogether, about 100,000 genes lie along the human chromosomes.

Phenotype
The individual's physical and behavioral characteristics, which are determined by both genetic and environmental factors.

Genotype
The genetic makeup of the individual.

Chromosomes
Rodlike structures in the cell nucleus that store and transmit genetic information.

Deoxyribonucleic acid (DNA)
Long, double-stranded molecules that make up chromosomes.

Gene
A segment of a DNA molecule that contains genetic instructions.

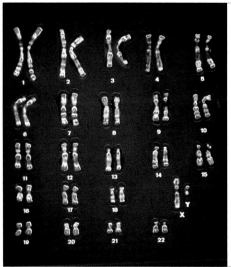

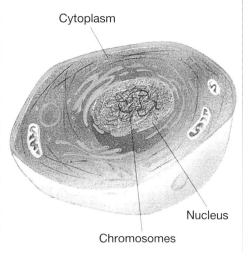

Cytoplasm

Nucleus

Chromosomes

FIGURE 3.1 A *karyotype,* or photograph, of human chromosomes. The 46 chromosomes shown here were isolated from a body cell, greatly magnified, and arranged in pairs according to decreasing size of the upper arm of each chromosome. Notice the 23rd pair, XY. The cell donor is a male. In females, the 23rd pair would be XX. (*Left:* CNRI/Science Photo Library/ Photo Researchers)

FIGURE 3.2 DNA's ladderlike structure. The pairings of bases across the rungs of the ladder are very specific: adenine (A) always appears with thymine (T), and cytosine (C) with guanine (G). Here, the DNA ladder is shown duplicating by splitting down the middle of its ladder rungs. Each free base picks up a new complementary partner from the area surrounding the cell nucleus.

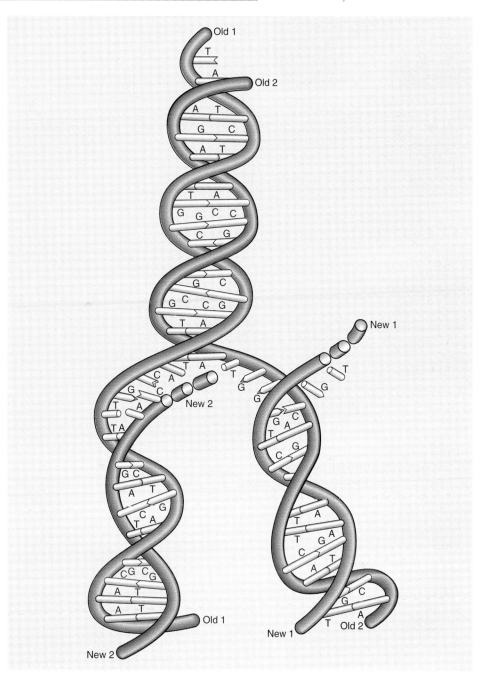

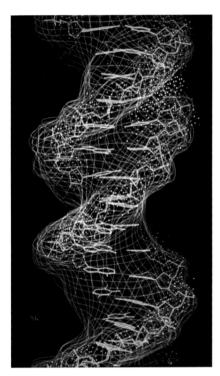

*T*he ladderlike appearance of DNA is evident in this computer-generated model. By simulating and color-coding the structure of DNA on a computer, scientists can rotate the image and study it from different vantage points. (JEAN-CLAUDE REVY/PHOTOTAKE)

Mitosis

The process of cell duplication, in which each new cell receives an exact copy of the original chromosomes.

Gametes

Human sperm and ova, which contain half as many chromosomes as a regular body cell.

Meiosis

The process of cell division through which gametes are formed and in which the number of chromosomes in each cell is halved.

Crossing over

Exchange of genes between chromosomes next to each other during meiosis.

Zygote

The union of sperm and ovum at conception.

Genes accomplish their task by sending instructions for making a rich assortment of proteins to the cytoplasm, the area surrounding the nucleus of the cell. Proteins, which trigger chemical reactions throughout the body, are the biological foundation from which our characteristics and capacities are built.

A unique feature of DNA is that it can duplicate itself. This special ability makes it possible for the one-celled fertilized ovum to develop into a complex human being composed of a great many cells. The process of cell duplication is called **mitosis.** In mitosis, the DNA ladder splits down the middle, opening somewhat like a zipper (refer again to Figure 3.2). Then, each base is free to pair up with a new mate from cytoplasm of the cell. Notice how this process creates two identical DNA ladders, each containing one new side and one old side of the previous ladder. At the level of chromosomes, during mitosis each chromosome copies itself. As a result, each new body cell contains the same number of chromosomes and the identical genetic information.

The Sex Cells

New individuals are created when two special cells called **gametes,** or sex cells—the sperm and ovum—combine. Gametes are unique in that they contain only 23 chromosomes, half as many as a regular body cell. They are formed through a special process of cell division called **meiosis,** which halves the number of chromosomes normally present in body cells.

Meiosis takes place according to the steps in Figure 3.3. First, chromosomes pair up within the original cell, and each one copies itself. Then, a special event called **crossing over** takes place. Chromosomes next to each other break at one or more points along their length and exchange segments, so that genes from one are replaced by genes from another. This shuffling of genes in crossing over creates new hereditary combinations. Next, the paired chromosomes separate into different cells, but chance determines which member of each pair will gather with others and end up in the same gamete. Finally, in the last phase of meiosis, each chromosome leaves its duplicate and becomes part of a sex cell containing 23 chromosomes instead of the usual 46.

In the male, four sperm are produced each time meiosis occurs. Also, the cells from which sperm arise are produced continuously throughout life. For this reason, a healthy man can father a child at any age after sexual maturity. In the female, gamete production is much more limited. Each cell division produces just one ovum. In addition, the female is born with all her ova already present in her ovaries, and she can bear children for only three to four decades. Still, there are plenty of female sex cells. About 1 million to 2 million are present at birth, 40,000 remain at adolescence, and approximately 350 to 450 will mature during a woman's childbearing years (Sadler, 1990).

Look again at the steps of meiosis in Figure 3.3, and notice how they ensure that a constant quantity of genetic material is transmitted from one generation to the next. When sperm and ovum unite at fertilization, the cell that results, called a **zygote,** will again have 46 chromosomes. Can you also see how meiosis leads to variability among offspring? Crossing over and random sorting of each member of a chromosome pair into separate sex cells means that no two gametes will ever be the same. Meiosis explains why siblings differ from each other even though they also share features in common, since their genotypes come from a common pool of parental genes.

The genetic variability produced by meiosis is important in an evolutionary sense. Certain combinations of genes enable individuals to adapt better to the environment. When these individuals reproduce, their favorable genetic makeup has the opportunity to become even better suited to their surroundings. In addition, environments are constantly changing. Genetic variability increases the chances that at least some members of a species will be able to cope with new environmental conditions and survive.

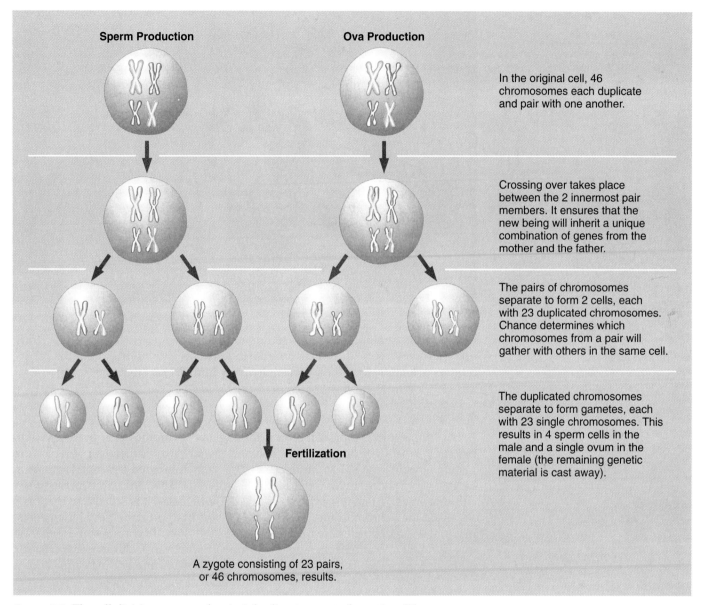

FIGURE 3.3 The cell-division process of meiosis leading to gamete formation. (Here, original cells are depicted with 2 rather than the full complement of 23 chromosome pairs.) Meiosis creates gametes with only half the usual number of chromosomes. When sperm and ovum unite at fertilization, the first cell of the new individual (the zygote) has the correct, full number of chromosomes.

Multiple Offspring

Only under one circumstance do offspring *not* display the genetic variability we have just discussed. Sometimes a zygote that has started to duplicate separates into two clusters of cells that develop into two individuals. These are called **identical,** or **monozygotic, twins** because they have the same genetic makeup. The frequency of identical twins is about the same around the world—4 out of every 1,000 births. Scientists do not know what causes this type of twinning in humans. In animals, it can be produced by temperature changes, variation in oxygen levels, and late fertilization of the ovum (Cohen, 1984).

There is another way that twins can be created. **Fraternal,** or **dizygotic, twins,** the most common type of multiple birth, result when two ova are released at the same time. If both are fertilized, two offspring who are genetically no more alike than ordinary siblings develop. As Table 3.1 shows, a variety of factors are linked

Identical, or monozygotic, twins
Twins that result when a zygote, during the early stages of cell duplication, divides in two. They have the same genetic makeup.

Fraternal, or dizygotic, twins
Twins resulting from the release and fertilization of two ova. They are genetically no more alike than ordinary siblings.

*T*hese identical, or monozygotic, twins were created when a duplicating zygote separated into two clusters of cells, and two individuals with the same genetic makeup developed. Identical twins look alike, and, as we will see later in this chapter, tend to resemble each other in a variety of psychological characteristics. (PORTER/THE IMAGEWORKS)

to fraternal twinning. In the final section of this chapter, we will see that the study of twin resemblance plays a central role in scientists' efforts to sort out the contributions of heredity and environment to many human characteristics.

Boy or Girl?

Using special microscopic techniques, the 23 pairs of chromosomes in each human cell can be distinguished from one another. Twenty-two of them, all of which are matching pairs, are called **autosomes.** They are numbered by geneticists from longest (1) to shortest (22) (refer back to Figure 3.1). The 23rd pair consists of **sex chromosomes.** In females, this pair is called XX; in males, it is called XY. The X is a relatively long chromosome, whereas the Y is short and carries very little genetic material. When gametes are formed in males, the X and Y chromosomes separate into different sperm cells. In females, all gametes carry an X chromosome. The sex of the new organism is determined by whether an X-bearing or a Y-bearing sperm

Autosomes

The 22 matching chromosome pairs in each human cell.

Sex chromosomes

The 23rd pair of chromosomes, which determines the sex of the child. In females, called XX; in males, called XY.

TABLE 3.1 Maternal Factors Linked to Fraternal Twinning

FACTOR	DESCRIPTION
Ethnicity	About 8 per 1,000 births among whites, 12 to 16 per 1,000 among blacks, and 4 per 1,000 among Asians
Age	Rises with maternal age, peaking at 35 years, and then rapidly falls
Nutrition	Occurs less often among women with poor diets; occurs more often among women who are tall and overweight or of normal weight as opposed to slight body build
Number of births	Chances increase with each additional birth
Exposure to fertility drugs	Treatment of infertility with hormones increases the likelihood of multiple fraternal births, from twins to quintuplets

SOURCE: Cohen, 1984.

fertilizes the ovum. In fact, scientists have isolated a single gene on the Y chromosome that triggers male sexual development by switching on the production of male sex hormones. When that gene is absent, the fetus that develops is female (Page et al., 1987).

Patterns of Genetic Inheritance

Two forms of each gene occur at the same place on the autosomes: one inherited from the mother and one from the father. Each different form of a gene is called an **allele.** If the alleles from both parents are alike, the child is said to be **homozygous** and will display the inherited trait. If the alleles are different, then the child is **heterozygous,** and relationships between the alleles determine the trait that will appear.

DOMINANT–RECESSIVE RELATIONSHIPS. In many heterozygous pairings, only one allele affects the child's characteristics. It is called *dominant;* the second allele, which has no effect, is called *recessive.* Hair color is an example of **dominant–recessive inheritance.** The allele for dark hair is dominant (we can represent it with a capital D), whereas the one for blond hair is recessive (symbolized by a lowercase b). Children who inherit either a homozygous pair of dominant alleles (DD) or a heterozygous pair (Db) will be dark haired, even though their genetic makeup is different. Blond hair can result only from having two recessive alleles (bb). Still, heterozygous individuals with just one recessive allele (Db) can pass on that trait to their children. As a result, they are called **carriers** of the trait.

Some human characteristics and diseases that follow the rules of dominant–recessive inheritance are given in Tables 3.2 and 3.3. As you can see, many defects and disorders are the product of recessive alleles. One of the most frequently occurring disorders is *phenylketonuria,* or *PKU.* PKU is an especially good example, since it shows that inheriting unfavorable genes does not always mean that the child's condition cannot be treated.

PKU affects the way the body breaks down proteins contained in many foods, such as cow's milk and meat. Infants born with two recessive alleles lack an enzyme that converts a harmful amino acid (phenylalanine) contained in proteins into a harmless by-product. Without this enzyme, phenylalanine quickly builds up and damages the central nervous system. Around 3 to 5 months, infants with untreated PKU start to lose interest in their surroundings. By 1 year, they are permanently retarded. Most states require that every newborn be given a blood test that, by measuring the level of phenylalanine, detects PKU. If the disease is found, treatment involves placing the baby on a diet low in phenylalanine. Children who receive this dietary treatment achieve an average level of intelligence and have a normal life span. Nevertheless, they display subtle difficulties with planning and problem solving, since the presence of even small amounts of phenylalanine interferes with normal brain functioning (Welsh et al., 1990).

In dominant–recessive inheritance, if we know the genetic makeup of the parents, we can predict the percentage of children in a family who are likely to display a trait or be carriers of it. Figure 3.4 shows one example for PKU. Notice that for a child to inherit the condition, a recessive allele (p) must be transmitted by each parent. One good reason for cultural taboos and laws against marriages between close blood relatives is that related parents have an increased risk of inheriting the same harmful allele from a common ancestor and passing it along to their offspring. Recessive diseases like PKU are more common among children of parents who are first and second cousins (Reed, 1975).

As Table 3.3 suggests, only rarely are serious diseases due to dominant alleles. Think about why this is the case. Children who inherit the dominant allele would always develop the disorder. They would seldom live long enough to reproduce, and the harmful allele would be eliminated from the family's heredity in a single generation. Some dominant disorders, however, do persist. One of them is *Huntington's chorea,* a condition in which the central nervous system degenerates.

Allele

Each of two forms of a gene located at the same place on the autosomes.

Homozygous

Having two identical alleles at the same place on a pair of chromosomes.

Heterozygous

Having two different alleles at the same place on a pair of chromosomes.

Dominant–recessive inheritance

A pattern of inheritance in which, under heterozygous conditions, the influence of only one allele is apparent.

Carrier

A heterozygous individual who can pass a recessive gene to his or her offspring.

TABLE 3.2 *Examples of Dominant and Recessive Characteristics*

DOMINANT	RECESSIVE
Dark hair	Blond hair
Nonred hair	Red hair
Curly hair	Straight hair
Normal hair	Pattern baldness
Facial dimples	No dimples
Normal hearing	Some forms of deafness
Normal vision	Nearsightedness
Farsightedness	Normal vision
Normal vision	Congenital eye cataracts
Normal color vision	Red-green color blindness
Normally pigmented skin	Albinism
Double-jointedness	Normal joints
Thick lips	Thin lips
Extra or fused digits	Five digits
Type A blood	Type O blood
Type B blood	Type O blood
Rh positive blood	Rh negative blood

NOTE: Many normal characteristics that were previously thought to be due to dominant–recessive inheritance, such as eye color, are now regarded as due to multiple genes. For the characteristics listed here, there still seems to be fairly common agreement that the simple dominant–recessive relationship holds.

SOURCE: McKusick, 1990.

TABLE 3.3 *Examples of Dominant and Recessive Diseases*

DISEASE	DESCRIPTION	MODE OF INHERITANCE	INCIDENCE	TREATMENT	PRENATAL DIAGNOSIS	CARRIER IDENTIFICATION[*]
Autosomal Diseases						
Cooley's anemia	Pale appearance, retarded physical growth, and lethargic behavior begin in infancy.	Recessive	1 in 500 births to parents of Mediterranean descent	Frequent blood transfusions; death from complications usually occurs by adolescence.	Yes	Yes
Cystic fibrosis	Lungs, liver, and pancreas secrete large amounts of thick mucus, leading to breathing and digestive difficulties.	Recessive	1 in 2,000 to 2,500 Caucasian births; 1 in 16,000 African-American births	Bronchial drainage; prompt treatment of respiratory infections; dietary management. Advances in medical care allow survival with good life quality into adulthood.	Yes	Yes

*Carrier status detectable in prospective parents through blood test or genetic analyses.

SOURCES: Behrman & Vaughan, 1987; Cohen, 1984; Fackelmann, 1992; Gilfillan et al., 1992; Martin, 1987; McKusick, 1990; Stanbury, Wyngaarden, & Frederickson, 1983.

TABLE 3.3 *Examples of Dominant and Recessive Diseases (continued)*

DISEASE	DESCRIPTION	MODE OF INHERITANCE	INCIDENCE	TREATMENT	PRENATAL DIAGNOSIS	CARRIER IDENTIFICATION[1]
Phenylke-tonuria (PKU)	Inability to neutralize the harmful amino acid phenylalanine, which is contained in many food proteins, causes severe central nervous system damage in the first year of life.	Recessive	1 in 8,000 births	Placing the child on a special diet results in average intelligence and a normal life span. However, subtle difficulties with planning and problem solving are often present.	Yes	Yes
Sickle cell anemia	Abnormal sickling of red blood cells causes oxygen deprivation, pain, swelling, and tissue damage. Anemia and susceptibility to infections, especially pneumonia.	Recessive	1 in 500 African-American births	Blood transfusions, painkillers, prompt treatment of infections. No known cure; 50 percent die by age 20.	Yes	Yes
Tay-Sachs disease	Central nervous system degeneration with onset at about 6 months, leading to poor muscle tone, blindness, deafness, and convulsions.	Recessive	1 in 3,600 births to Jews of European descent	None. Death by 3 to 4 years of age.	Yes	Yes
Huntington's chorea	Central nervous system degeneration leading to muscular coordination difficulties, mental deterioration, and personality changes. Symptoms usually do not appear until age 35 or later.	Dominant	1 in 18,000 to 25,000 North American births	None. Death occurs 10 to 20 years after symptom onset.	Yes	Not applicable
Marfan syndrome	Tall, slender build; thin, elongated arms and legs. Heart defects and eye abnormalities, especially of the lens. Excessive lengthening of the body results in a variety of skeletal defects.	Dominant	1 in 20,000 births	Correction of heart and eye defects sometimes possible. Death from heart failure in young adulthood common.	Yes	Not applicable
Maturity-onset diabetes	A mild form of diabetes first appearing in adulthood that involves glucose intolerance.	Dominant	1 in 60 North Americans	Dietary management.	No	Not applicable
X-Linked Diseases						
Duchenne muscular dystrophy	Degenerative muscle disease. Abnormal gait, loss of ability to walk between 7 and 13 years of age.	Recessive	1 in 3,000 to 5,000 male births	None. Death from respiratory infection or weakening of the heart muscle usually occurs in adolescence.	Yes	Yes
Hemophilia	Blood fails to clot normally. Can lead to severe internal bleeding and tissue damage.	Recessive	1 in 4,000 to 7,000 male births	Blood transfusions. Safety precautions to prevent injury.	Yes	Yes
Diabetes insipidus	A form of diabetes present at birth that is caused by insufficient production of the hormone vasopressin. Results in excessive thirst and urination. Dehydration can cause central nervous system damage.	Recessive	1 in 2,500 male births	Hormone replacement.	No	No

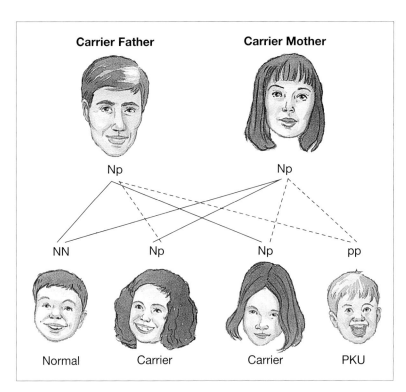

Carrier Father   **Carrier Mother**

Np   Np

NN   Np   Np   pp

Normal   Carrier   Carrier   PKU

FIGURE 3.4 Dominant–recessive mode of inheritance as illustrated by PKU. When both parents are heterozygous carriers of the recessive allele, we can predict that 25 percent of their offspring will be normal, 50 percent will be carriers, and 25 percent will inherit the disorder. Notice that the PKU-affected child, in contrast to his siblings, has light hair. Later in this chapter, we will see that the recessive gene for PKU is *pleiotropic* (affects more than one trait). It also leads to fair coloring.

Why has this disease endured in some families? The reason is that its symptoms usually do not appear until age 35 or later, after the person has passed the dominant gene on to his or her children.

CODOMINANCE. In some heterozygous circumstances, the dominant–recessive relationship does not hold completely. Instead, we see **codominance,** a pattern of inheritance in which both alleles influence the person's characteristics.

The *sickle cell trait*, a heterozygous condition present in many black Africans, provides an example. *Sickle cell anemia* (see Table 3.3) occurs in full form when a child inherits two recessive alleles. They cause the usually round red blood cells to become sickle shaped, a response that is especially great under low oxygen conditions. The sickled cells clog the blood vessels and block the flow of blood. Individuals who have the disorder suffer severe attacks involving intense pain, swelling, and tissue damage. They generally die in the first 20 years of life; few live past age 40. Heterozygous individuals are protected from the disease under most circumstances. However, when they experience oxygen deprivation—for example, at high altitudes or after intense physical exercise—the single recessive allele asserts itself, and a temporary, mild form of the illness occurs (Sullivan, 1987).

The sickle cell allele is common among black Africans for a particular reason. Carriers of it are more resistant to malaria than are individuals with two alleles for normal red blood cells. In Africa, where malaria occurs often, these carriers survived and reproduced more frequently than others, leading the gene to be maintained in the black population. In regions of the world where the risk of malaria is low and the sickle cell trait is harmful rather than adaptive, affected individuals are less likely to reproduce. Among African-Americans, for example, the gene is expected to become less common in future generations, until it is finally eliminated from the gene pool.

Codominance

A pattern of inheritance in which both alleles, in a heterozygous combination, are expressed.

Mutation

A sudden but permanent change in a segment of DNA.

MUTATION. At this point, you may be wondering, How are harmful genes created in the first place? The answer is **mutation,** a sudden but permanent change in a segment of DNA. A mutation may affect only one or two genes, or it may involve many genes, as is the case for the chromosomal disorders we will discuss shortly.

Some mutations occur spontaneously, simply by chance. Others are caused by a wide variety of hazardous environmental agents that enter our food supply or are present in the air we breathe.

For many years, ionizing radiation has been known to cause mutations. Women who receive repeated doses of radiation before conception are more likely to miscarry or give birth to children with hereditary defects (Zhang, Cai, & Lee, 1992). Genetic abnormalities are also higher when fathers are exposed to radiation in their occupations (Schrag & Dixon, 1985). In one instance, men who worked at a reprocessing plant for nuclear fuel in England were fathers of an unusually high number of children who developed cancer. Exposure to radiation at the plant is believed to have damaged chromosomes in the male sex cells, causing cancer in the children years later (Gardner et al., 1990). Does this mean that routine chest and dental X-rays are dangerous to future generations? Research indicates that infrequent and mild exposure to radiation does not cause genetic damage. Instead, high doses over a long period of time appear to be required.

Although virtually all mutations that have been studied are harmful, we should keep in mind that some spontaneous ones (such as the sickle cell allele in malaria-ridden regions of the world) are necessary and desirable. By increasing genetic variability, they help individuals adapt to unexpected environmental challenges. However, scientists seldom go looking for mutations that underlie favorable traits, such as an exceptional talent or an especially sturdy immune system. Instead, they are far more concerned with identifying and eliminating unfavorable genes that threaten the health and survival of new generations.

X-Linked Inheritance. Males and females have an equal chance of inheriting recessive disorders carried on the autosomes, such as PKU and sickle cell anemia. But when a harmful allele is carried on the X chromosome, **X-linked inheritance** applies. Males are more likely to be affected because their sex chromosomes do not match. In females, any recessive allele on one X chromosome has a good chance of being suppressed by a dominant allele on the other X. But males have only one X chromosome, and there are no corresponding alleles on the Y to override those on the X.

Red-green color blindness (a condition in which individuals cannot tell the difference between shades of red and green) is one example of an X-linked recessive trait. It affects males twice as often as females (Cohen, 1984). Return to Table 3.3 and review the diseases that are X-linked. A well-known example is *hemophilia,* a disorder in which the blood fails to clot normally. Figure 3.5 shows its greater likelihood of inheritance by male children whose mothers carry the abnormal allele.

Besides X-linked disorders, many sex-related differences reveal the male to be at a disadvantage. Rates of miscarriage and infant and childhood deaths are greater for males. Learning disabilities, behavior disorders, and mental retardation are also more common among boys (Richardson, Koller, & Katz, 1986). It is possible that these sex differences can be traced to the genetic code. The female, with two X chromosomes, benefits from a greater variety of genes. Nature, however, seems to have adjusted for the male's greater vulnerability. Because the Y-bearing sperm are lighter and swifter, they tend to reach the ovum more quickly. Consequently, about 106 boys are born for every 100 girls, and judging from miscarriage and abortion statistics, an even greater number of males are conceived (Shettles & Rorvik, 1984).

Pleiotropism and Modifier Genes. So far, we have considered only one-to-one relationships between genes and phenotypic characteristics. It is possible for a single gene to affect more than one trait. This is known as **pleiotropism,** and the recessive gene for PKU provides an example. In addition to their potential for central nervous system damage, PKU children usually have light hair and blue eyes. Their fair coloring is due to an inability to convert phenylalanine into tyrosine, an amino acid responsible for pigmentation.

X-linked inheritance
A pattern of inheritance in which a recessive gene is carried on the X chromosome. Males are more likely to be affected.

Pleiotropism
The influence of a single gene on more than one characteristic.

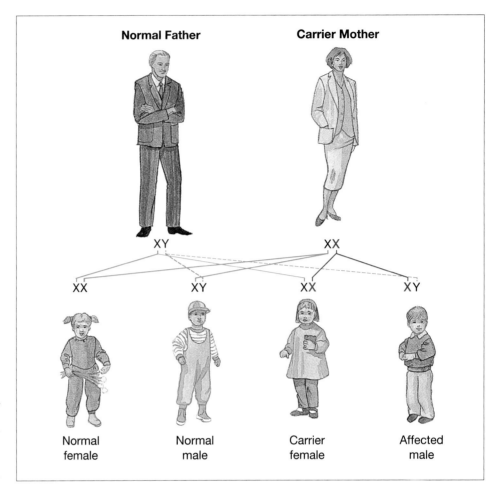

FIGURE 3.5 X-linked inheritance. In the example shown here, the allele on the father's X chromosome is normal. The mother has one normal and one abnormal allele on her X chromosomes. By looking at the possible combinations of the parents' alleles, we can predict that 50 percent of male offspring will have the disorder and 50 percent of female offspring will be carriers of it.

It is also possible for some genes to modify the expression of other genes by either enhancing or diluting their effects. Because of the influence of **modifier genes** on the two recessive alleles for PKU, children differ in the degree to which phenylalanine accumulates in their tissues and in the extent to which they respond to dietary treatment. Other inherited traits and diseases listed in Tables 3.2 and 3.3 also vary in severity, and modifier genes are thought to be responsible.

POLYGENIC INHERITANCE. Nearly 2,000 human characteristics are believed to follow the rules of dominant–recessive inheritance (McKusick, 1990). In most of these cases, people either display a particular trait or do not. These cut-and-dried individual differences are much easier to trace to their genetic origins than characteristics that vary continuously among people. Many traits of interest to child development specialists, such as height, weight, intelligence, and personality, are of this type. People are not just tall or short, bright or dull, outgoing or shy. Instead, they show gradations between these extremes. Continuous traits like these are due to **polygenic inheritance,** in which many genes determine the characteristic in question (Plomin, 1989). Polygenic inheritance is complex, and much about it is still unknown. In the final section of this chapter, we will discuss ways that have been used to infer the influence of heredity on human attributes when knowledge of precise patterns of inheritance is unavailable.

Modifier genes

Genes that modify the effect of another gene on a characteristic by either enhancing or diluting its effects.

Polygenic inheritance

A pattern of inheritance involving many genes that applies to characteristics that vary continuously among people.

CHROMOSOMAL ABNORMALITIES

Besides inheriting harmful recessive alleles, abnormalities of the chromosomes are a major cause of serious developmental problems. Most chromosomal defects are the result of mistakes during meiosis when the ovum and sperm are formed. A chromosome pair may not separate properly, or part of a chromosome may break off. Since these errors involve far more DNA than problems due to single genes, they usually produce disorders with many physical and mental symptoms.

Down Syndrome

The most common chromosomal abnormality, occurring in 1 out of every 800 live births, is *Down syndrome*. In 95 percent of cases, it results from a failure of the 21st pair of chromosomes to separate during meiosis, so the new individual inherits three of these chromosomes rather than the normal two. In other less frequent forms, an extra broken piece of a 21st chromosome is present. Or an error occurs during the early stages of mitosis, causing some but not all body cells to have the defective chromosomal makeup (called a *mosaic* pattern). In these instances, the child's characteristics can vary from practically normal to the typical characteristics of Down syndrome, depending on how much extra genetic material is present (Rosenberg & Pettegrew, 1983).

Children with Down syndrome have distinct physical features—a short, stocky build, a flattened face, a protruding tongue, almond-shaped eyes, and an unusual crease running across the palm of the hand. In addition, infants with Down syndrome are often born with eye cataracts and heart and intestinal defects. Because of medical advances, fewer Down syndrome children die early than was the case in the past, but early death is still common. About 14 percent die by age 1, and 21 percent by age 10. The rest live until middle adulthood (Baird & Sadovnick, 1987).

The behavioral consequences of Down syndrome include mental retardation, speech problems, limited vocabulary, and slow motor development. These problems become more evident with age, since Down syndrome children show a gradual slowing in development from infancy onward when compared to normal children. Most fall within an IQ range of 20 to 50, and only about 5 percent learn to read (Kopp, 1983).

Down syndrome babies are more difficult to care for than are normal infants. Their facial deformities often lead to breathing and feeding difficulties. In addition, they tend to be less emotionally expressive than their normal counterparts. They smile less readily, show poor eye-to-eye contact, and explore objects less persistently. Therefore, caregivers need to be more assertive in getting these

*T*he flattened face and almond-shaped eyes of the younger child in this photo are typical physical features of Down syndrome. Although his intellectual development is impaired, this boy is doing well because he is growing up in a family in which his special needs are met and he is loved and accepted.
(FRANK SITEMAN/STOCK BOSTON)

infants to become engaged in their surroundings (Loveland, 1987; MacTurk et al., 1985). When parents make this effort, their children show better developmental progress. In one study, mothers who actively stimulated and played with their Down syndrome 2-year-olds had children who scored higher in social responsiveness and play maturity (Crawley & Spiker, 1983). Early intervention programs for Down syndrome youngsters also lead to better development, although social, emotional, and motor skills improve more readily than intellectual performance (Gibson & Harris, 1988; Van Dyke et al., 1990). These findings indicate that even though Down syndrome is a genetic disorder, environmental factors play an important role in how well these children fare in the long run.

As Table 3.4 shows, the incidence of Down syndrome rises dramatically with maternal age. The woman's gamete, however, is not always the cause of a Down syndrome child. In about 20 percent of cases, the extra genetic material originates with the father. Like older mothers, older fathers are more likely to have children with the disorder (Hook, 1980; Stene, Stene, & Stengel-Rutkowski, 1981). The occurrence of other chromosomal abnormalities is also age related. Why is this so? Geneticists believe that the sex cells may weaken over time, either because of the aging process or increased exposure to harmful environmental agents. As a result, chromosomes do not separate properly during meiosis. A second possibility is that with age, mothers are less likely to miscarry defective conceptions. At present, the evidence is consistent with both of these hypotheses (Antonarakis, 1992; Warburton, 1989).

Abnormalities of the Sex Chromosomes

Other disorders of the autosomes besides Down syndrome exist, but they usually disrupt development so severely that they account for about 50 percent of miscarriages. When such babies are born, they rarely survive beyond early childhood. In contrast, abnormalities of the sex chromosomes usually lead to fewer problems. The shortness of the Y chromosome leads little genetic material to be involved, and additional X chromosomes may be inactivated early in development. In fact, sex chromosome disorders are often not recognized until adolescence, when, in some of the deviations, puberty is delayed. The most common problems involve the presence of an extra chromosome (either X or Y) or the absence of one X chromosome in females (see Table 3.5). Sometimes, individuals inherit more than one extra chromosome, as in XXXX, XXXY, or XYYY. Defects tend to become more severe as genetic material is added (Plomin, DeFries, & McClearn, 1990).

A variety of myths about individuals with sex chromosome disorders exist. For example, many people think that males with *XYY syndrome* are more aggressive and antisocial than XY males. Yet by examining Table 3.5, you will see that this is not true. Also, it is widely believed that children with sex chromosome disorders are retarded. Yet most are not. The intelligence of boys with XYY syndrome is similar to that of normal children (Netley, 1986; Stewart, 1982). And the intellectual problems of children with *triple X, Klinefelter,* and *Turner syndromes* are very specific. Verbal difficulties (for example, with reading and vocabulary) are common among girls with triple X syndrome and boys with Klinefelter syndrome, each of whom inherits an extra X chromosome. In contrast, Turner syndrome girls, who are missing an X, have trouble with spatial relationships. Their handwriting is poor, and they have difficulty telling right from left and finding their way around the neighborhood during the early school years. When they get to high school, they avoid courses like geometry and those that demand drawing skills (Hall et al., 1982; Netley, 1986; Pennington et al., 1982). These findings tell us that adding to or subtracting from the usual number of X chromosomes results in particular intellectual deficits. At present, geneticists do not know why this is the case.

One exception to the fairly mild consequences of sex chromosome abnormalities is *fragile X syndrome.* In this disorder, the X chromosome is damaged. An abnormal break appears in a special spot. Fragile X syndrome ranks second only to Down syndrome as a major genetic cause of mental retardation. It has also been linked to

TABLE 3.4 *Risk of Giving Birth to a Down Syndrome Child by Maternal Age*

MATERNAL AGE	RISK (PER NUMBER OF BIRTHS)
20	1 in 1900
25	1 in 1200
30	1 in 900
33	1 in 600
36	1 in 300
39	1 in 140
42	1 in 70
45	1 in 30
48	1 in 15

SOURCE: Adapted from Hook, 1982.

TABLE 3.5 Sex Chromosomal Disorders

DISORDER	DESCRIPTION	INCIDENCE	TREATMENT
XYY syndrome	Inheritance of an extra Y chromosome. Typical characteristics are above-average height, large teeth, and sometimes severe acne. Intelligence, development of male sexual characteristics, and fertility are normal.	1 in 1,000 male births	No special treatment necessary.
Triple X syndrome (XXX)	Inheritance of an extra X chromosome. Impaired verbal intelligence. Affected girls are no different in appearance or sexual development from normal age-mates, except for a greater tendency toward tallness.	1 in 500 to 1,250 female births	Special education to treat verbal-ability problems.
Klinefelter syndrome (XXY)	Inheritance of an extra X chromosome. Impaired verbal intelligence. Affected boys are unusually tall, have a body-fat distribution resembling females, and show incomplete development of sexual characteristics at puberty. They are usually sterile.	1 in 500 to 1,000 male births	Hormone therapy at puberty to stimulate development of sexual characteristics. Special education to treat verbal-ability problems.
Turner syndrome (XO)	All or part of the second X chromosome is missing. Impaired spatial intelligence. Ovaries usually do not develop prenatally. Incomplete development of sexual characteristics at puberty. Other features include short stature and webbed neck.	1 in 2,500 to 8,000 female births	Hormone therapy in childhood to stimulate physical growth and at puberty to promote development of sexual characteristics. Special education to treat spatial-ability problems.
Fragile X syndrome	An abnormal break appears at a special place on one or both X chromosomes. Associated with mental retardation and mild facial deformities, including enlarged ears, jaw, and forehead. About 12 percent have infantile autism.	1 in 1,500 male births and 1 in 2,000 female births	Special therapeutic programs for retarded and behavior disordered children.

SOURCES: Bancroft, Axworthy, & Ratcliffe, 1982; Borghraef et al., 1987; Cohen, 1984; Hall et al., 1982; Ho, Glahn, & Ho, 1988; Netley, 1986; Pennington et al., 1982; Schaivi et al., 1984.

infantile autism, a serious emotional disorder of early childhood involving bizarre, self-stimulating behavior and delayed or absent language and communication.

At first, fragile X syndrome was believed to follow X-linked principles of genetic inheritance, since it occurs more often in boys than girls. But recent studies show that it does not always conform to the X-linked pattern. Twenty percent of males who inherit the fragile site display no symptoms at all, whereas 30 percent of females with only one damaged X are affected. Also, recent evidence suggests that the damaged X chromosome must be passed from mother to child to be expressed (Barnes, 1989; Bodurtha, Tams, & Jackson-Cook, 1992). As fragile X syndrome reveals, scientists still have much to learn about even the most basic principles of genetic transmission.

Each individual is made up of trillions of cells. Inside each cell nucleus are chromosomes composed of a molecule called DNA. Genes are segments of DNA that determine our species and unique characteristics. Gametes, or sex cells, are formed through a process of cell division called meiosis, which halves the usual number of chromosomes in human cells. Then, when sperm and ovum unite to form the zygote, each new being has the correct number of chromosomes. Two types of twins—identical and fraternal—are possible. Identical twins have the same genetic makeup, whereas fraternal twins are genetically no more alike than ordinary siblings. A different combination of sex chromosomes establishes whether a child will be male or female. Three patterns of inheritance—dominant–recessive, codominant, and X-linked—underlie many traits as well as disorders. Continuous characteristics, such as height and intelligence, result from the enormous complexities of polygenic inheritance, which involves many genes. Chromosomal abnormalities occur when meiosis is disrupted during gamete formation. Disorders of the autosomes are usually more serious than those of the sex chromosomes.

REPRODUCTIVE CHOICES

In the past, many couples with genetic disorders in their families chose not to bear a child at all rather than risk having an abnormal baby. Today, genetic counseling and prenatal diagnosis permit people to make informed decisions about conceiving or carrying a pregnancy to term.

Genetic Counseling

Genetic counseling helps couples assess their chances of giving birth to a baby with a hereditary disorder. Individuals likely to seek it are those who have had difficulties bearing children, such as repeated miscarriages, or who know that genetic problems exist in their families. When mental retardation, physical defects, or inherited diseases are present in the relatives of prospective parents, then genetic counseling is warranted (Fine, 1990).

The genetic counselor interviews the couple and prepares a *pedigree,* a picture of the family tree in which affected relatives are identified. The pedigree is used to estimate the likelihood that parents will have an abnormal child, using the same genetic principles we discussed earlier in this chapter. In the case of many disorders, blood tests or genetic analyses can reveal whether the parent is a carrier of the harmful gene. Turn back to pages 78–79, and you will see that carrier detection is possible for many of the diseases listed in Table 3.3. A carrier test has recently been developed for fragile X syndrome as well (Bodurtha, Tams, & Jackson-Cook, 1992).

When all of the relevant information is in, the genetic counselor helps people consider appropriate options. These include "taking a chance" and conceiving, adopting a child, or choosing from among a variety of reproductive technologies. The Social Issues box on the following page describes these medical interventions into conception along with the host of legal and ethical dilemmas that have arisen in their application.

Prenatal Diagnosis and Fetal Medicine

If couples who might bear an abnormal child decide to conceive, several **prenatal diagnostic methods**—medical procedures that permit detection of problems before birth—are available (see Table 3.6). Women of advanced maternal age are prime candidates for *amniocentesis* or *chorionic villus sampling* (see Figure 3.6), since the overall rate of chromosomal problems rises sharply after age 35, from 1 in every 100 to as many as 1 in every 3 pregnancies at age 48 (Hook, 1988). Except for

Genetic counseling
Counseling that helps couples assess the likelihood of giving birth to a baby with a hereditary disorder.

Prenatal diagnostic methods
Medical procedures that permit detection of developmental problems before birth.

Some couples decide not to risk pregnancy because of a history of genetic disease. And many others—in fact, one-sixth of all couples who try to conceive—discover that they are sterile. Today, increasing numbers of individuals are turning to alternative methods of conception—technologies that, although fulfilling the wish of parenthood, have become the subject of heated debate.

For several decades, *donor insemination*—injection of sperm from an anonymous man into a woman—has been used to overcome male reproductive difficulties. In the United States alone, it is estimated that over 370,000 individuals have been conceived this way. In addition, two new practices—in vitro fertilization and surrogate motherhood—have become increasingly common.

Since the first "test tube" baby was born in England in 1978, more than 7,000 infants have been created through *in vitro fertilization*. In this method, hormones are used to stimulate the ripening of several ova. These are removed surgically and placed in a dish of nutrients, to which sperm are added. Once an ovum is fertilized and begins to duplicate into several cells, it is injected into the mother's uterus, where, hopefully, it will implant and develop. In vitro fertilization is generally used to treat women whose fallopian tubes (see page 90) are damaged, and it is successful for 20 percent of those who try it. These results are encouraging enough that the method has been expanded. By mixing and matching gametes of donors and recipients, pregnancies can be brought about when either or both partners have a fertility problem. In cases where couples might transmit harmful genes, single cells can be plucked from the duplicating zygote and screened for hereditary defects (Verlinsky et al., 1992). Fertilized ova can even be frozen and stored in embryo banks for use at some future time, thereby guaranteeing healthy zygotes to older women, who run an increased risk of bearing children with chromosomal abnormalities (Edwards, 1991).

Clearly, donor insemination and in vitro fertilization have many benefits. Nevertheless, serious questions have been raised about their use. Many states have no legal guidelines for these procedures. As a result, donors are not always screened for genetic or sexually transmitted diseases. In addition, only a minority of doctors keep records of donor characteristics. Yet the resulting children may someday want information about their genetic background or need it for medical reasons. In some places, doctors report using the same donor for many pregnancies. In these instances, many genetically related children grow up in the same community, creating opportunities for marriage among half-siblings and repetition of hereditary defects (Andrews, 1987; Sokoloff, 1987). Critics also worry that these methods might someday be used for genetic selection as couples strive not just for a healthy baby, but for the "perfect child" (Edwards, 1991).

The most controversial form of medically assisted conception is *surrogate motherhood.* In this procedure, sperm from a man whose wife is infertile are used to inseminate a woman, who is paid a fee for her childbearing services. In return, the surrogate agrees to turn the baby over to the man (who is the natural father). The child is then adopted by his wife. Although most of these arrangements proceed smoothly, those that end up in court highlight the serious risks for all concerned. In one case, both parties rejected the handicapped infant that resulted from the pregnancy. In several others, the surrogate mother changed her mind and wanted to keep the baby. These children came into the world in the midst of family conflict, which threatened to last for years to come. Most surrogates already have children of their own, who may be deeply affected by the experience. Knowledge that their mother would sell a half-sibling for profit may cause these youngsters to question the security of their own family circumstances (McGinty & Zafran, 1988; Ryan, 1989).

Although new reproductive technologies permit many barren couples to rear healthy newborn babies, laws are needed to regulate them (Capron, 1991). In the case of surrogate motherhood, the legal and ethical problems are so complex that 18 U.S. states have sharply restricted the practice, and many European governments have banned it (Belkin, 1992). Finally, at present, practically nothing is known about the psychological consequences of being a product of these procedures. Research on how such children grow up, including what they know and how they feel about their origins, is crucial for weighing the pros and cons of these techniques.

ultrasound and *maternal blood analysis,* prenatal diagnosis should not be used routinely, since each of the other methods described in Table 3.6 has some chance of injuring the developing organism.

Improvements in prenatal diagnosis have led to new advances in fetal medicine. Today, some medical problems are being treated before birth. For example, by inserting a needle into the uterus, drugs can be delivered to the fetus. Surgery has been performed to repair such problems as urinary tract obstructions and neural defects. Nevertheless, these practices remain controversial. Although some babies are saved, the techniques frequently result in complications or miscarriage. Yet when parents are told that their unborn child has a serious defect, they may be willing to try almost any option, even if there is only a slim chance of success. Currently, the medical profession is struggling with how to help parents make

TABLE 3.6 Prenatal Diagnostic Methods

METHOD	DESCRIPTION
Amniocentesis	The most widely used technique. A hollow needle is inserted through the abdominal wall to obtain a sample of amniotic fluid in the uterus. Cells are examined for genetic defects. Can be performed by 11 to 14 weeks after conception; 3 more weeks are required for test results. Small risk of miscarriage.
Chorionic villus sampling	A procedure that can be used if results are desired or needed very early in pregnancy. A thin tube is inserted into the uterus through the vagina or a hollow needle is inserted through the abdominal wall. A small plug of tissue is removed from the end of one or more chorionic villi, the hairlike projections on the membrane surrounding the developing organism. Cells are examined for genetic defects. Can be performed at 6 to 8 weeks after conception, and results are available within 24 hours. Entails a slightly greater risk of miscarriage than does amniocentesis. Also associated with a small risk of limb deformities, which increases the earlier the procedure is performed.
Ultrasound	High-frequency sound waves are beamed at the uterus; their reflection is translated into a picture on a videoscreen that reveals the size, shape, and placement of the fetus. By itself, permits assessment of fetal age, detection of multiple pregnancies, and identification of gross physical defects. Also used to guide amniocentesis, chorionic villus sampling, and fetoscopy.
Fetoscopy	A small tube with a light source at one end is inserted into the uterus to inspect the fetus for defects of the limbs and face. Also allows a sample of fetal blood to be obtained, permitting diagnosis of such disorders as hemophilia and sickle cell anemia as well as neural defects. Usually performed between 15 to 18 weeks after conception. Entails some risk of miscarriage.
Maternal blood analysis	By the second month of pregnancy, some of the baby's cells enter the maternal bloodstream. An elevated level of alpha-fetoprotein may indicate kidney disease, abnormal closure of the esophagus, or neural defects such as anencephaly (absence of most of the brain) and spina bifida (bulging of the spinal cord from the spinal column).

SOURCES: Benacerraf et al., 1988; Burton, 1992; Cohen, 1984; Mastroiacovo & Cavalcanti, 1991; Rhoads et al., 1989.

informed decisions about fetal surgery. One suggestion is that the advice of an independent counselor be provided—a doctor or nurse who understands the risks but is not involved in doing research on or performing the procedure (Kolata, 1989).

Advances in *genetic engineering* also offer new hope for correcting hereditary defects. Genetic repair of the prenatal organism, once inconceivable, is one goal of today's genetic engineers. Researchers are mapping human chromosomes, finding the precise location of genes for specific traits and cloning (duplicating) these genes using chemical techniques in the laboratory. Of the approximately 3,000 known inherited diseases, genes have been found for about 100, including cystic fibrosis, Huntington's chorea, Marfan syndrome, Duchenne muscular dystrophy, and the two forms of diabetes listed in Table 3.3 (NIH/CEPH Collaborative Mapping Group, 1992). Scientists are using this information to identify abnormal conditions with greater accuracy before birth. Eventually, *gene splicing* (replacing a harmful gene with a good one in the early zygote or in cells in the affected part of the body) may permit many defects to be corrected.

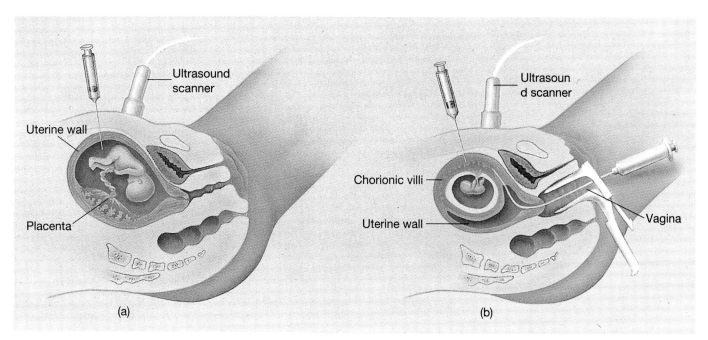

FIGURE 3.6 Amniocentesis and chorionic villus sampling. Today, more than 250 diseases can be detected before birth using these procedures. (a) In amniocentesis, which can be performed by 11 to 14 weeks after conception, a hollow needle is inserted through the abdominal wall into the uterus. Fluid is withdrawn and fetal cells are cultured, a process that takes about 3 weeks. (b) Chorionic villus sampling can be performed much earlier in pregnancy (at 6 to 8 weeks after conception), and results are available within 24 hours. Two approaches to obtaining a sample of chorionic villi are shown: inserting a thin tube through the vagina into the uterus or a needle through the abdominal wall. In both amniocentesis and chorionic villus sampling, an ultrasound scanner is used for guidance. (From K. L. Moore and T. V. N. Persaud, *Before We Are Born* (4th ed.), Philadelphia: W. B. Saunders Company, 1993, p. 89. Adapted by permission of the publisher and the author.)

If prenatal diagnosis shows that the fetus has an abnormal condition that cannot be corrected, parents are faced with the difficult choice of whether or not to have an abortion. The decision to terminate a desired pregnancy is painful for all who have to make it. Parents must deal with the emotional shock of the news and decide what to do within a very short period of time. If they choose abortion, they face the grief that comes with having lost a wanted child, worries about future pregnancies, and possible guilt about the abortion itself. Fortunately, 95 percent of fetuses examined through prenatal diagnosis are normal (Benacerraf et al., 1988). Because modern medicine makes such tests possible, many individuals whose age or family history would have caused them to avoid pregnancy entirely can now have healthy children.

Brief Review

Genetic counseling helps couples who have a family history of reproductive problems or hereditary defects make informed decisions about bearing a child. For those who decide to conceive, prenatal diagnostic methods permit early detection of fetal problems. Advances in fetal medicine enable some disorders to be treated before birth. Progress in genetic engineering means that genetic repair of the prenatal organism may be possible in the near future. Although reproductive technologies have helped many childless couples become parents, they raise serious legal and ethical concerns.

PRENATAL DEVELOPMENT

The sperm and ovum that will unite to form the new individual are uniquely suited for the task of reproduction. The ovum is a tiny sphere, measuring $\frac{1}{175}$ of an inch in diameter, that is barely visible to the naked eye, appearing as a dot the size of a period at the end of this sentence. But in its microscopic world, it is a giant—the largest cell in the human body. The ovum's size makes it a perfect target for the much smaller sperm, which measure only $\frac{1}{500}$ of an inch.

About once every 28 days, in the middle of a woman's menstrual cycle, an ovum bursts from one of her ovaries, two walnut-sized organs located deep inside her abdomen (see Figure 3.7). Surrounded by thousands of nurse cells that will feed and protect it along its path, the ovum is drawn into one of two *fallopian tubes*—long, thin structures that lead to the hollow, soft-lined uterus. While the ovum is traveling, the spot on the ovary from which it was released, now called the *corpus luteum,* begins to secrete hormones that prepare the lining of the uterus to receive a fertilized ovum. If pregnancy does not occur, the corpus luteum shrinks, and the lining of the uterus is discarded in 2 weeks with menstruation.

The male produces sperm in vast numbers—an average of 300 million a day. In the final process of maturation, each sperm develops a tail that permits it to swim long distances, upstream in the female reproductive tract and into the fallopian tube, where fertilization usually takes place. The journey is difficult, and many sperm die. Of the approximately 360 million sperm released during sexual intercourse, only 300 to 500 reach the ovum, if one happens to be present. Sperm have an average life of 48 hours and can lie in wait for the ovum for up to 2 days;

In this photograph of fertilization taken with the aid of a powerful microscope, a tiny sperm completes its journey and starts to penetrate the surface of an enormous-looking ovum, the largest cell in the human body. (Francis Leroy, Biocosmos/Science Photo Library/Photo Researchers)

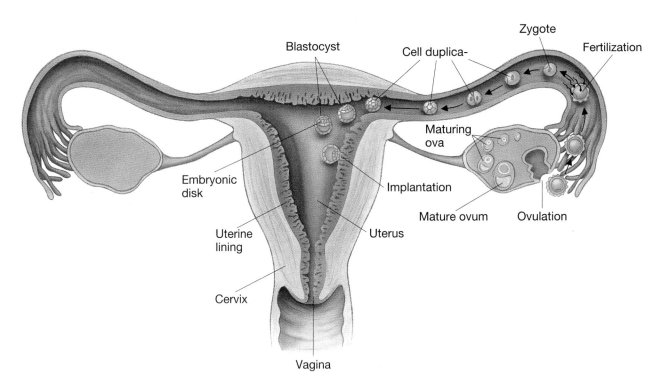

Figure 3.7 Journey of the ovum toward the uterus. Once every 28 days, an ovum matures, is released from one of the woman's ovaries, and is drawn into the fallopian tube. After fertilization, it begins to duplicate, at first slowly and then more rapidly. By the 4th day, it forms a hollow, fluid-filled ball called a blastocyst. The inner cells will become the new organism; the outer cells will provide protective covering. At the end of the 1st week, the blastocyst begins to implant in the uterine lining. (From K. L. Moore and T. V. N. Persaud, *Before We Are Born* (4th ed.), Philadelphia: W. B. Saunders Company, 1993, p. 33. Adapted by permission of the publisher and the author.)

MILESTONES
PRENATAL DEVELOPMENT

Trimester	Period	Weeks	Length and Weight	Major Events
First	Zygote	1		• The one-celled zygote multiplies and forms a blastocyst.
		2		• The blastocyst burrows into the uterine lining. Structures that feed and protect the developing organism begin to form—amnion, chorion, yolk sac, placenta, and umbilical cord.
	Embryo	3–4	$\frac{1}{4}$ inch	• A primitive brain and spinal cord appear. Heart, muscles, backbone, ribs, and digestive tract begin to develop.
		5–8	1 inch	• Many external body structures (e.g., face, arms, legs, toes, fingers) and internal organs form. The sense of touch begins to develop, and the embryo can move.
	Fetus	9–12	3 inches; less than 1 ounce	• Rapid increase in size begins. Nervous system, organs, and muscles become organized and connected, and new behavioral capacities (kicking, thumb sucking, mouth opening, and rehearsal of breathing) appear. External genitals are well formed, and the fetus's sex is evident.
Second		13–24	12 inches; 1.8 pounds	• The fetus continues to enlarge rapidly. In the middle of this period, fetal movements can be felt by the mother. Vernix and lanugo keep the skin from chapping in the amniotic fluid. All of the neurons that will ever be produced in the brain are present by 24 weeks. Eyes are sensitive to light, and the fetus reacts to sound.
Third		25–38	20 inches; 7.5 pounds	• The fetus has a chance of survival if born around this time. Size continues to increase. Lungs gradually mature. Rapid brain development causes sensory and behavioral capacities to expand. In the middle of this period, a layer of fat is added under the skin. Antibodies are transmitted from mother to fetus to protect against disease. Most fetuses rotate into an upside-down position in preparation for birth.

SOURCES: Moore & Persaud, 1993; Nilsson & Hamberger, 1990.

an ovum survives for up to 24 hours. Therefore, the maximum fertile period during each monthly cycle lasts about 72 hours (Nilsson & Hamberger, 1990).

With fertilization, the story of prenatal development beings to unfold. The vast changes that take place during the 38 weeks of pregnancy are usually divided into three phases: (1) the period of the zygote; (2) the period of the embryo; and (3) the period of the fetus. As we look at what happens in each phase, you may find it useful to refer to the Milestones table above.

The Period of the Zygote

The period of the zygote lasts about 2 weeks, from fertilization until the tiny mass of cells drifts down and out of the fallopian tube and attaches itself to the wall of the uterus. The zygote's first cell duplication is long and drawn out; it is not complete until about 30 hours after conception. Gradually, new cells are added at a

*D*uring the period of the zygote, the fertilized ovum begins to duplicate at an increasingly rapid rate, forming a hollow ball of cells, or blastocyst, by the fourth day after fertilization. Here the blastocyst, magnified thousands of times, burrows into the uterine lining between the seventh and ninth day. (© LENNART NILSSON, *A CHILD IS BORN*/BONNIERS)

Amnion

The inner membrane that forms a protective covering around the prenatal organism and encloses it in amniotic fluid, which helps keep temperature constant and provides a cushion against jolts caused by the mother's movement.

Chorion

The outer membrane that forms a protective covering around the prenatal organism. It sends out tiny fingerlike villi, from which the placenta begins to emerge.

Placenta

The organ that separates the mother's bloodstream from the embryo or fetal bloodstream but permits exchange of nutrients and waste products.

Umbilical cord

The long cord connecting the prenatal organism to the placenta that delivers nutrients and removes waste products.

faster rate. By the 4th day, 60 to 70 cells exist that form a hollow, fluid-filled ball called a *blastocyst* (refer again to Figure 3.7). The cells on the inside, called the *embryonic disk,* will become the new organism; the outer ring will provide protective covering.

IMPLANTATION. Sometime between the 7th and 9th day, implantation occurs: the blastocyst burrows deep into the uterine lining. Surrounded by the woman's nourishing blood, it now starts to grow in earnest. At first, the protective outer layer multiplies fastest. A membrane, called the **amnion,** forms that encloses the developing organism in *amniotic fluid.* It helps keep the temperature of the prenatal world constant and provides a cushion against any jolts caused by the mother's movement. A *yolk sac* also appears. It produces blood cells until the developing liver, spleen, and bone marrow are mature enough to take over this function (Moore & Persaud, 1993).

The events of these first 2 weeks are delicate and uncertain. As many as 30 percent of zygotes do not make it through this phase. In some, the sperm and ovum do not join properly. In others, for some unknown reason, cell duplication never begins. By preventing implantation in these cases, nature eliminates most prenatal abnormalities in the very earliest stages of development (Sadler, 1990).

THE PLACENTA AND UMBILICAL CORD. By the end of the 2nd week, another protective membrane, called the **chorion,** surrounds the amnion. From the chorion, tiny fingerlike villi, or blood vessels, begin to emerge.* As these villi burrow into the uterine wall, a special organ called the **placenta** starts to develop. By bringing the mother's and embryo's blood close together, the placenta will permit food and oxygen to reach the developing organism and waste products to be carried away. A membrane forms that allows these substances to be exchanged but prevents the mother's and embryo's blood from mixing directly.

The placenta is connected to the developing organism by the **umbilical cord.** In the period of the zygote, it first appears as a primitive body stalk; but during

*Recall from Table 3.6 on page 88 that chorionic villus sampling is the prenatal diagnostic method that can be performed earliest, 6 to 8 weeks after conception. In this procedure, tissue from the ends of the villi is removed and examined for genetic abnormalities.

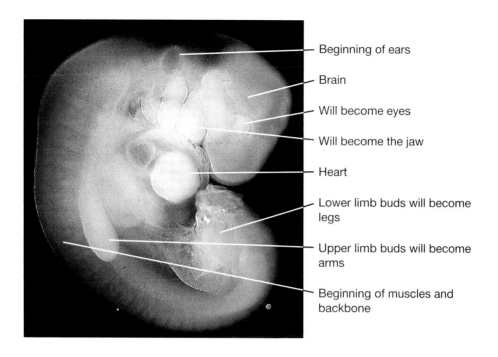

- Beginning of ears
- Brain
- Will become eyes
- Will become the jaw
- Heart
- Lower limb buds will become legs
- Upper limb buds will become arms
- Beginning of muscles and backbone

This curled embryo is about 4 weeks old. In actual size, it is only $\frac{1}{4}$-inch long, but many body structures have begun to form. The primitive tail will disappear by the end of the embryonic period. (© LENNART NILSSON, *A CHILD IS BORN* / BONNIERS)

the course of pregnancy, it grows to a length of 1 to 3 feet. The umbilical cord contains one large artery that delivers blood loaded with nutrients and two veins that remove waste products. The force of blood flowing through the cord keeps it firm, much like a garden hose, so it seldom tangles while the embryo, like a space-walking astronaut, floats freely in its fluid-filled chamber (Rugh & Shettles, 1971).

By the end of the period of the zygote, the developing organism has found food and shelter in the uterus. Already, it is a very complex being. These dramatic beginnings take place before all but the most sensitive woman knows she is pregnant.

The Period of the Embryo

The period of the **embryo** lasts from implantation through the 8th week of pregnancy. During these brief 6 weeks, the most rapid prenatal changes take place, as the groundwork for all body structures and internal organs is laid down. Because all parts of the body are forming, the embryo is especially vulnerable to interference in healthy development. But the fact that embryonic growth takes place over a fairly short time span helps limit opportunities for serious harm to occur.

LAST HALF OF THE FIRST MONTH. In the 1st week of this period, the embryonic disk forms three layers of cells: (1) the *ectoderm*, which will become the nervous system and skin; (2) the *mesoderm*, from which will develop the muscles, skeleton, circulatory system, and other internal organs; and (3) the *endoderm*, which will become the digestive system, lungs, urinary tract, and glands. These three layers give rise to all parts of the body.

At first, the nervous system develops fastest. The ectoderm folds over to form a *neural tube,* or primitive spinal cord. At $3\frac{1}{2}$ weeks, the top swells to form a brain. Production of *neurons* (brain cells that store and transmit information) begins deep inside the neural tube. Once formed, neurons travel along tiny threads to their permanent locations, where they will form the major parts of the brain (Nowakowski, 1987).

While the nervous system is developing, the heart begins to pump blood around the embryo's circulatory system, and muscles, the backbone, ribs, and the digestive tract start to appear. At the end of the 1st month, the curled embryo consists of millions of organized groups of cells with specific functions, although its length is only $\frac{1}{4}$ inch.

Embryo
The prenatal organism from 2 to 8 weeks after conception, during which time the foundations of all body structures and internal organs are laid down.

*B*y *7 weeks, the embryo's posture is more upright. Body
structures—eyes, nose, arms, legs, and internal organs—are
more distinct. An embryo of this age responds to touch. It
can also move, although at less than an inch long and an
ounce in weight, it is still too tiny to be felt by the mother.*
(© LENNART NILSSON, *A CHILD IS BORN* / BONNIERS)

THE SECOND MONTH. In the 2nd month, growth continues rapidly. The eyes, ears,
nose, jaw, and neck form. Tiny buds become arms, legs, fingers, and toes. Internal
organs are more distinct: the intestines grow, the heart develops separate chambers, and the liver and spleen take over production of blood cells so that the yolk
sac is no longer needed. Changing body proportions cause the embryo's posture
to become more upright. Now 1 inch long and weighing $\frac{1}{7}$ of an ounce, the embryo
can already sense its world. It responds to touch, particularly in the mouth area
and on the soles of the feet. And it can move, although its tiny flutters are still too
light to be felt by the mother (Nilsson & Hamberger, 1990).

The Period of the Fetus

Lasting until the end of pregnancy, the period of the **fetus** is the "growth and finishing" phase. During this longest prenatal period, the organism begins to
increase rapidly in size. The rate of body growth is extraordinary, especially from
the 9th to the 20th week (Moore & Persaud, 1993).

THE THIRD MONTH. In the 3rd month, the organs, muscles, and nervous system
start to become organized and connected. The brain signals, and in response, the
fetus kicks, bends its arms, forms a fist, curls its toes, opens its mouth, and even
sucks its thumb. The tiny lungs begin to expand and contract in an early rehearsal
of breathing movements. By the 12th week, the external genitals are well formed,
and the sex of the fetus can be detected with ultrasound. Other finishing touches
appear, such as fingernails, toenails, tooth buds, and eyelids that open and close.
The heartbeat is now stronger and can be heard through a stethoscope.

Prenatal development is often divided into *trimesters,* or three equal periods of
time. At the end of the 3rd month, the first trimester is complete. Two more must
pass before the fetus is fully prepared to survive outside the womb.

THE SECOND TRIMESTER. By the middle of the second trimester, between 17 and 20
weeks, the new being has grown large enough that its movements can be felt by
the mother. If we could look inside the uterus at this time, we would find the fetus
to be completely covered with a white cheeselike substance called **vernix.** It protects the skin from chapping during the long months spent in the amniotic fluid. A

Fetus
The prenatal organism from the
beginning of the 3rd month to the
end of pregnancy, during which
time completion of body
structures and dramatic growth in
size take place.

Vernix
A white, cheeselike substance
covering the fetus and preventing
the skin from chapping due to
constant exposure to the amniotic
fluid.

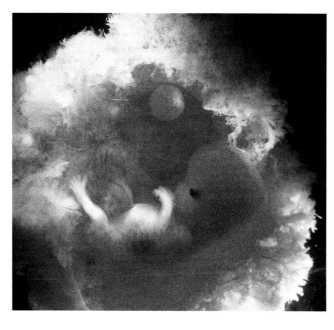

During the period of the fetus, the organism increases rapidly in size, and body structures are completed. At 11 weeks, the brain and muscles are better connected. The fetus can kick, bend its arms, open and close its hands and mouth, and suck its thumb. Notice the yolk sac, which shrinks as pregnancy advances. The internal organs have taken over its function of producing blood cells. (© LENNART NILSSON, *A CHILD IS BORN*/BONNIERS)

white, downy hair covering called **lanugo** also appears over the entire body, help- ing the vernix stick to the skin.

At the end of the second trimester, many organs are quite well developed. And a major milestone is reached in brain development, in that all the neurons are now in place. No more will be produced in the individual's lifetime. However, *glial cells,* which support and feed the neurons, continue to increase at a rapid rate throughout the remaining months of pregnancy, as well as after birth (Nowakowski, 1987).

Brain growth means new behavioral capacities. The 20-week-old fetus can be stimulated as well as irritated by sounds. And if a doctor has reason to look inside the uterus with fetoscopy (see Table 3.6), fetuses try to shield their eyes from the light with their hands, indicating that the sense of sight has begun to emerge (Nilsson & Hamberger, 1990). Still, a fetus born at this time cannot survive. Its

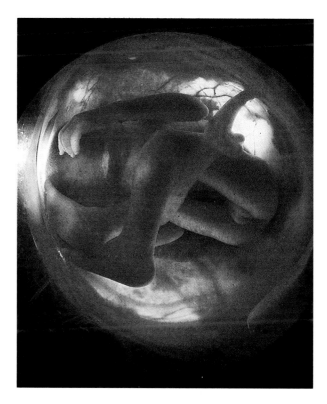

At 22 weeks, this fetus is almost a foot long and slightly over a pound in weight. Its movements can be clearly felt by the mother and by other family members who place a hand on her abdomen. If born at this time, a baby has a slim chance of surviving. (© LENNART NILSSON, *A CHILD IS BORN*/BONNIERS)

Lanugo
A white, downy hair that covers the entire body of the fetus, helping the vernix stick to the skin.

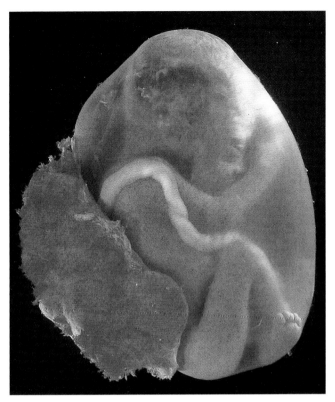

This 36-week-old fetus fills the uterus. To support its need for nourishment, the umbilical cord and placenta have grown very large. Notice the vernix (cheeselike substance), which protects the skin from chapping. The fetus has accumulated a layer of fat to assist with temperature regulation after birth. In another 2 weeks, it will be full term. (© LENNART NILSSON, *A CHILD IS BORN*/BONNIERS)

lungs are too immature, and the brain has not yet developed to the point at which it can control breathing movements and body temperature.

THE THIRD TRIMESTER. During the final trimester, a fetus born early has a chance for survival. The point at which the baby can first survive is called the **age of viability.** It occurs sometime between 22 and 26 weeks (Moore & Persaud, 1993). If born between the 7th and 8th month, breathing would still be a problem, and oxygen assistance would be necessary. Although the respiratory center of the brain is now mature, tiny air sacs in the lungs are not yet ready to inflate and exchange oxygen for carbon monoxide.

The brain continues to make great strides during the last 3 months. The *cerebral cortex*, the seat of human intelligence, enlarges. At the same time, the fetus responds more clearly to sounds in the external world. By 28 weeks, fetuses blink their eyes in reaction to nearby sounds (Birnholz & Benacerraf, 1983). And in the last weeks of pregnancy, they learn to prefer the tone and rhythm of their mother's voice. In one clever study, mothers were asked to read aloud Dr. Seuss's lively book *The Cat in the Hat* to their unborn babies for the last 6 weeks of pregnancy. After birth, their infants were given a chance to suck on nipples that turned on recordings of the mother reading this book or different rhyming stories. The infants sucked hardest to hear *The Cat in the Hat,* the sounds they had come to know while still in the womb (DeCasper & Spence, 1986).

During the final 3 months, the fetus gains more than 5 pounds and grows 7 inches. In the 8th month, a layer of fat is added under the skin to assist with temperature regulation. The fetus also receives antibodies from the mother's blood that protect against illnesses, since the newborn's own immune system will not work well until several months after birth. In the last weeks, most fetuses assume an upside-down position, partly because of the shape of the uterus and because the head is heavier than the feet. Growth starts to slow, and birth is about to take place.

Age of viability

The age at which the fetus can first survive if born early. Occurs sometime between 22 and 26 weeks.

The vast changes that take place during pregnancy are usually divided into three periods. In the period of the zygote, the tiny one-celled fertilized ovum begins to duplicate and implants itself in the uterine lining. Structures that will feed and protect the developing organism begin to form. During the period of the embryo, the foundations for all body tissues and organs are rapidly laid down. The longest prenatal phase, the period of the fetus, is devoted to growth in size and completion of body systems.

PRENATAL ENVIRONMENTAL INFLUENCES

Although the prenatal environment is far more constant than the world outside the womb, many factors can affect the embryo and fetus. In the following sections, we will see that there is much that parents—and society as a whole—can do to create a safe environment for development before birth.

Teratogens

The term **teratogen** refers to any environmental agent that causes damage during the prenatal period. It comes from the Greek word *teras,* meaning "malformation" or "monstrosity." This label was selected because scientists first learned about harmful prenatal influences from cases in which babies had been profoundly damaged.

Yet the harm done by teratogens is not always simple and straightforward. It depends on a number of factors. First, we will see as we discuss particular teratogens that amount and length of exposure make a difference. Larger doses over longer time periods usually have more negative effects. Second, the genetic makeup of the mother and baby plays an important role. Some individuals are better able to withstand harmful environments. Third, the presence of several negative factors at once, such as poor nutrition, lack of medical care, and additional teratogens, can worsen the impact of a single harmful agent. Fourth, the effects of teratogens vary with the age of the developing organism at time of exposure. We can best understand this idea if we think of prenatal development in terms of an important concept introduced in Chapter 1: the *sensitive period.* Recall that a sensitive period is a limited time span in which a part of the body or a behavior is biologically prepared to undergo rapid development. During that time, it is especially vulnerable to its surroundings. If the environment is harmful, then damage occurs that would not have otherwise happened, and recovery is difficult and sometimes impossible.

Figure 3.8 provides a summary of sensitive periods during prenatal development. Look carefully at it, and you will see that some parts of the body, such as the brain and eye, have long sensitive periods that extend throughout the prenatal phase. Other sensitive periods, such as those for the limbs and palate, are much shorter. Figure 3.8 also indicates that we can make some general statements about the timing of harmful influences. During the period of the zygote, before implantation, teratogens rarely have any impact. If they do, the tiny mass of cells is usually so completely damaged that it dies. The embryonic period is the time when serious defects are most likely to occur, since the foundations for all body parts are being laid down. During the fetal period, damage caused by teratogens is usually minor. However, some organs, such as the brain, eye, and genitals, can still be strongly affected.

The effects of teratogens are not limited to immediate physical damage. Although deformities of the body are easy to notice, important psychological consequences are harder to identify. Some may not show up until later in development. Others may occur as an indirect effect of physical damage. For example, a defect resulting from drugs the mother took during pregnancy can change reactions of

Teratogen
Any environmental agent that causes damage during the prenatal period.

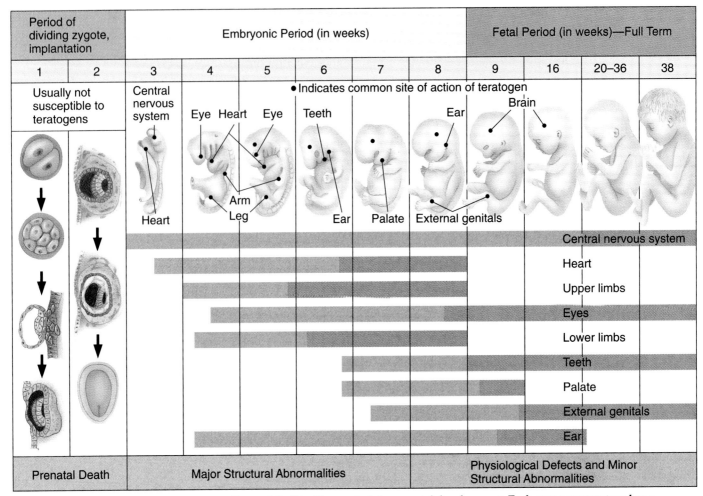

Period of dividing zygote, implantation		Embryonic Period (in weeks)						Fetal Period (in weeks)—Full Term			
1	2	3	4	5	6	7	8	9	16	20–36	38

Figure 3.8 Sensitive periods in prenatal development. Each organ or structure has a sensitive period during which its development may be disturbed. Gray indicates highly sensitive periods. Pink indicates periods that are somewhat less sensitive to teratogens, although damage can still occur. (From K. L. Moore and T. V. N. Persaud, *Before We Are Born* (4th ed.), Philadelphia: W. B. Saunders Company, 1993, p. 130. Reprinted by permission of the publisher and the author.)

others to the child as well as the child's ability to move about the environment. Over time, parent–child interaction, peer relations, and opportunities to explore may suffer. These experiences, in turn, can have far-reaching consequences for cognitive, emotional, and social development (Kopp & Kaler, 1989; Vorhees & Mollnow, 1987). Notice how an important idea about development discussed in Chapter 1 is at work here—that of *bidirectional* influences between child and environment. Now let's take a look at what scientists have discovered about a variety of teratogens.

PRESCRIPTION AND NONPRESCRIPTION DRUGS. Just about any drug a woman takes can enter the embryonic or fetal bloodstream. In the early 1960s, the world learned a tragic lesson about drugs and prenatal development. At that time, a sedative called thalidomide was widely available in Europe, Canada, and South America. Although the embryos of test animals were not harmed by it, in humans it had drastic effects. When taken by mothers between the 4th and 6th week after conception, thalidomide produced gross deformities of the embryo's developing arms and legs. About 7,000 infants around the world were affected (Moore & Persaud, 1993). As children exposed to thalidomide grew older, a large number of them scored below average in intelligence. Perhaps the drug damaged the central nervous system directly. Or the child-rearing conditions of these severely deformed youngsters may have impaired their intellectual development (Vorhees & Mollnow, 1987).

Despite the bitter lesson of thalidomide, many pregnant women continue to take over-the-counter drugs without consulting their doctors. Aspirin is one of the most common. Several studies suggest that regular use of aspirin is linked to low birth weight, infant death around the time of birth, poorer motor development, and lower intelligence test scores in early childhood (Barr et al., 1990; Streissguth et al., 1987). The most frequently consumed drug during pregnancy is caffeine, contained in coffee, tea, and chocolate. Some studies have linked heavy caffeine use to prematurity, miscarriage, and newborn irritability (Aaronson & MacNee, 1989; Fenster et al., 1991). Other research, however, reveals no negative effects (Barr & Streissguth, 1991).

Because children's lives are involved, we must take even tentative findings on the harmful impact of medications seriously. At the same time, it is important to note that we cannot yet be sure that these drugs actually cause the problems mentioned. Often mothers take more than one kind of drug. If the prenatal organism is injured, it is hard to tell which drug might be responsible or if other factors correlated with drug taking are really at fault. Until we have more information, the safest course of action for pregnant women is to cut down on or avoid these drugs entirely.

ILLEGAL DRUGS. The use of highly addictive mood-altering drugs, such as cocaine and heroin, is becoming more widespread, especially in poverty-stricken inner-city areas, where these drugs provide a temporary escape from a daily life of hopelessness. The number of "cocaine babies" born in the United States has reached crisis levels in recent years. In large cities, as many as 25 percent of women giving birth test positive for cocaine in their bloodstreams (Allen et al., 1991).

Babies born to users of heroin, methadone (a less addictive drug used to wean people away from heroin), and cocaine are at risk for a wide variety of problems, including prematurity, low birth weight, physical defects, breathing difficulties, and death around the time of birth. In addition, these infants arrive drug addicted. They are feverish and irritable and have trouble sleeping. Their cries are abnormally shrill and piercing—a common symptom among stressed newborns that we will discuss in Chapter 4 (Allen et al., 1991; Little et al., 1989). When mothers with many problems of their own must take care of these babies, who are difficult to calm down, cuddle, and feed, behavior problems are likely to persist.

Throughout the first year, heroin- and methadone-exposed infants are less attentive to the environment, and their motor development is slow. After infancy, some children get better, whereas others remain jittery and inattentive. The kind of parenting these youngsters receive may explain why there are long-term problems for some but not for others (Vorhees & Mollnow, 1987).

Unlike findings on heroin- and methadone, growing evidence on cocaine suggests that many prenatally exposed babies have lasting difficulties. Cocaine is linked to a specific set of physical defects. These include genital, urinary tract, kidney, and heart deformities as well as brain seizures (Chasnoff et al., 1989). Infants born to mothers who smoke crack (a cheap form of cocaine that delivers high doses quickly through the lungs) appear to be worst off in terms of low birth weight and damage to the central nervous system (Kaye et al., 1989). Fathers also seem to contribute to these effects. Recent research suggests that cocaine can attach itself to sperm, "hitchhike" its way into the zygote, and cause birth defects (Yazigi, Odem, & Polakoski, 1991). Still, it is difficult to isolate the precise damage caused by cocaine, since users often take several drugs and engage in other high-risk behaviors (Coles et al., 1992).

Marijuana is another illegal drug that is used more widely than cocaine and heroin, but less is known about its prenatal effects. Studies examining its relationship to low birth weight and prematurity reveal mixed findings (Fried & O'Connell, 1987; Zuckerman, Frank, & Hingson, 1989). After controlling for other factors, several researchers have linked prenatal marijuana exposure to newborn tremors, startles, an abnormally high-pitched cry, and reduced attention to the environment (Fried & Makin, 1987; Fried, Watkinson, & Dillon, 1987; Lester &

Dreher, 1989). These outcomes certainly put newborn babies at risk for future problems, even though long-term effects have not been established.

CIGARETTE SMOKING. Although smoking has recently declined in the United States, an estimated 28 percent of men and 23 percent of women continue to use cigarettes (U.S. Bureau of the Census, 1992). The most well-known effect of smoking during pregnancy is low birth weight. But the likelihood of other serious consequences, such as prematurity, miscarriage, infant death, and cancer later in childhood, is also increased. The more cigarettes a mother smokes, the greater the chances that her baby will be affected. If a pregnant woman decides to stop smoking at any time, even during the last trimester, she can help her baby. She immediately reduces the likelihood that her infant will be born underweight and suffer from future problems (Aaronson & MacNee, 1989; Stjernfeldt et al., 1992).

Even when a baby of a smoking mother appears to be born in good physical condition, slight behavioral abnormalities may threaten the child's development. Newborns of smoking mothers are less attentive to sounds and display more muscle tension (Fried & Makin, 1987). An unresponsive, restless baby may not evoke the kind of interaction from adults that promotes healthy psychological development. Some long-term studies report that prenatally exposed children have shorter attention spans and poorer mental test scores in early childhood, even after many other factors have been controlled (Fried & Watkinson, 1990; Kristjansson & Fried, 1989). But other researchers have not been able to confirm these findings, so long-term effects remain uncertain (Barr et al., 1990; Streissguth et al., 1989).

Exactly how can smoking harm the fetus? Nicotine, the addictive substance in tobacco, causes the placenta to grow abnormally. As a result, transfer of nutrients is reduced, and the fetus gains weight poorly. Also, smoking raises the concentration of carbon monoxide in the bloodstreams of both mother and fetus. Carbon monoxide displaces oxygen from red blood cells. It damages the central nervous system and reduces birth weight in the fetuses of laboratory animals; similar effects may occur in humans (Aaronson & MacNee, 1989; Nash & Persaud, 1988).

Finally, from one-third to one-half of nonsmoking pregnant women are "passive smokers" because their husbands, relatives, and co-workers use cigarettes. Recent findings suggest that passive smoking is also related to low birth weight, infant death, and possible long-term impairments in attention and learning (Makin, Fried, & Watkinson, 1991; Schwartz-Bickenbach et al., 1987). Clearly, expectant mothers should do what they can to avoid smoke-filled environments, and family members, friends, and employers need to assist them in this effort.

ALCOHOL. Over the past 20 years, thousands of studies have confirmed that heavy prenatal alcohol use produces a set of handicaps so consistent and severe that it has been called **fetal alcohol syndrome (FAS)**. Mental retardation, poor attention, and overactivity are typical of children with the disorder. Distinct physical symptoms also accompany it. These include slow physical growth and a particular pattern of facial abnormalities: widely spaced eyes, short eyelid openings, a small upturned nose, and a thin upper lip. The small heads of these children indicate that the brain has been prevented from reaching full development. Other defects—of the eyes, ears, nose, throat, heart, genitals, urinary tract, and immune system—may also be present. In all babies born with FAS, the mother drank heavily through most or all of her pregnancy.

Sometimes, children do not display all of these abnormalities—only a few of them. In these cases, the child is said to suffer from **fetal alcohol effects (FAE)**. Usually, mothers of these children drank alcohol in smaller quantities. The defects of FAE children vary with the timing and length of prenatal alcohol exposure (Hoyseth & Jones, 1989).

How does alcohol produce its devastating consequences? Researchers believe it does so in two ways. First, alcohol interferes with cell duplication and migration in the primitive neural tube (see page 93). When the brains of FAS babies who did not survive are examined, they show a reduced number of cells and major structural

Fetal alcohol syndrome (FAS)
A set of defects that results when pregnant women consume large amounts of alcohol during most or all of pregnancy. Includes mental retardation, slow physical growth, and facial abnormalities.

Fetal alcohol effects (FAE)
The condition of children who display some but not all of the defects of fetal alcohol syndrome. Usually their mothers drank alcohol in smaller quantities during pregnancy.

abnormalities (Nowakowski, 1987). Second, large quantities of oxygen are needed to metabolize alcohol. When pregnant women drink heavily, they draw oxygen away from the embryo or fetus that is vital for cell growth in the brain and other parts of the body (Vorhees & Mollnow, 1987).

At this point, you may be wondering, How much alcohol is safe during pregnancy? Is it all right to have a drink or two, either daily or occasionally? A recent study found that as little as 2 ounces of alcohol a day, taken very early in pregnancy, was associated with FAS-like facial features (Astley et al., 1992). But recall that other factors—both genetic and environmental—can make some fetuses more vulnerable to teratogens. Therefore, a precise dividing line between safe and dangerous drinking levels cannot be established. Recent research shows that the more alcohol consumed during pregnancy, the poorer a child's motor coordination, intelligence, and achievement during the preschool and school years (Barr et al., 1990; Coles et al., 1992; Streissguth et al., 1989). These dose-related effects indicate that it is best for pregnant women to avoid alcohol entirely.

*T*he mother of this severely retarded boy drank heavily during pregnancy. His widely spaced eyes, thin upper lip, and short eyelid openings are typical of fetal alcohol syndrome. (FETAL ALCOHOL SYNDROME RESEARCH FUND, UNIVERSITY OF WASHINGTON)

HORMONES. Earlier in this chapter, we saw that the Y chromosome causes male sex hormones (called androgens) to be secreted prenatally, leading to formation of male reproductive organs. In the absence of male hormones, female structures develop. Hormones are released as part of a delicately balanced system. If their quantity or timing is off, then defects of the genitals and other organs can occur.

Between 1945 and 1970, a synthetic hormone called *diethylstilbestrol (DES)* was widely used in the United States to prevent miscarriages in women with a history of pregnancy problems. As the daughters of these mothers reached adolescence and young adulthood, they showed an unusually high rate of cancer of the vagina and malformations of the uterus. When they tried to have children, their pregnancies more often resulted in prematurity, low birth weight, and miscarriage than those of non-DES-exposed women. Young men whose mothers took DES prenatally were also affected. They showed an increased risk of genital abnormalities and cancer of the testes (Linn et al., 1988; Stillman, 1982). Because of these findings, pregnant women are no longer treated with DES. But many children whose mothers took it are now of childbearing age, and they need to be carefully monitored by their doctors.

Sometimes mothers take other hormones that could damage the embryo or fetus. For example, occasionally a woman continues to use birth control pills during the early weeks after conception, before she knows she is pregnant. Research has linked oral contraceptives to heart and limb deformities, although additional studies are needed to confirm this relationship (Grimes & Mishell, 1988; Kricker et al., 1986).

RADIATION. Earlier in this chapter, we saw that ionizing radiation can cause mutation, damaging the DNA in ova and sperm. When mothers are exposed to radiation during pregnancy, additional harm can come to the embryo or fetus. Defects due to radiation were tragically apparent in the children born to pregnant Japanese women who survived the atomic bombing of Hiroshima and Nagasaki near the end of World War II. Miscarriage, slow physical growth, an underdeveloped brain, and malformations of the skeleton and eyes were common (Michel, 1989). Even when an exposed child appears normal at birth, the possibility of later problems cannot be ruled out. For example, research suggests that even low-level radiation, as the result of industrial leakage or medical X-rays, can increase the risk of childhood cancer (Smith, 1992).

ENVIRONMENTAL POLLUTION. An astounding number of potentially dangerous chemicals are released into the environment in industrialized nations. In the United States, over 100,000 are in common use, and 1,000 new ones are introduced each year. Although many chemicals cause serious birth defects in laboratory animals, the impact on the human embryo and fetus is known for only a small number of them.

Among heavy metals, mercury and lead are established teratogens. In the 1950s, an industrial plant released waste containing high levels of mercury into a bay providing food and water for the town of Minimata, Japan. Many children born at the time were mentally retarded and showed other serious symptoms, including abnormal speech, difficulty in chewing and swallowing, and uncoordinated movements. Autopsies of those who died revealed widespread brain damage (Vorhees & Mollnow, 1987).

Pregnant women can absorb lead from car exhaust, paint flaking off the walls in old houses and apartment buildings, and other materials used in industrial occupations. High levels of lead exposure are consistently linked to prematurity, low birth weight, brain damage, and a wide variety of physical defects (Dye-White, 1986). Even a very low level of prenatal lead exposure seems to be dangerous. Affected babies show slightly poorer mental development during the first 2 years (Bellinger et al., 1987).

For many years, polychlorinated-biphenyls (PCBs) were used to insulate electrical equipment. In 1977, they were banned by the federal government after research showed that, like mercury, they found their way into waterways and entered the food supply. In one study, newborn babies of women who frequently ate PCB-contaminated fish were compared to newborns whose mothers ate little or no fish. The PCB-exposed babies had a variety of problems, including slightly reduced birth weight, smaller heads (suggesting brain damage), and less interest in their surroundings (Jacobson et al., 1984). When studied again at 7 months of

TABLE 3.7 *Effects of Some Infectious Diseases During Pregnancy*

DISEASE	MISCARRIAGE	PHYSICAL MALFORMATIONS	MENTAL RETARDATION	PREMATURITY AND LOW BIRTH WEIGHT
Viral				
Acquired immune deficiency syndrome (AIDS)	0	?	+	?
Chicken pox	0	+	+	+
Cytomegalovirus	+	+	+	+
Herpes simplex 2 (genital herpes)	+	+	+	–
Mumps	+	?	0	0
Rubella	+	+	+	+
Bacterial				
Syphilis	+	+	+	?
Tuberculosis	+	?	+	+
Parasitic				
Malaria	+	0	0	+
Toxoplasmosis	+	+	+	+

NOTE: + = established finding; 0 = no present evidence; ? = possible effect that is not clearly established.

SOURCE: Adapted from *Clinical Genetics in Nursing Practice* (p. 232) by F. L. Cohen, 1984, Philadelphia: Lippincott. Reprinted by permission. *Additional sources:* Chatkupt et al., 1989; Qazi et al., 1988; Samson, 1988; Sever, 1983; Vorhees, 1986.

AIDS is a relatively new viral disease that destroys the immune system. Infected individuals eventually die of a wide variety of illnesses that their bodies can no longer fight. Adults at greatest risk include male homosexuals and bisexuals, users of illegal drugs who share needles, and their heterosexual partners. Transfer of body fluids from one person to another is necessary for AIDS to spread.

The percentage of AIDS victims who are female has risen dramatically over the past decade, from 3 to 10 percent. When women carrying the virus become pregnant, about 30 percent of the time they pass the disease to the embryo or fetus (Valleroy, Harris, & Way, 1990). The likelihood of transmission is greatest when a woman already has AIDS symptoms, but it can also occur before there are obvious signs of infection. According to the U.S. Centers for Disease Control (1992), over 3,000 childhood cases of AIDS have been diagnosed in the United States since 1981. The large majority (84 percent) are infants who received the virus before birth, often from a drug-abusing mother.

AIDS symptoms generally take a long time to emerge in older children and adults—up to 5 years after infection with the virus. In contrast, the disease proceeds rapidly in prenatally infected babies. Most are born with abnormalities of the immune system (Mayers et al., 1991). By 6 months of age, weight loss, fever, diarrhea, and respiratory illnesses are common. The virus also causes serious brain damage. Infants with AIDS show a loss in brain weight over time, accompanied by seizures, delayed mental and motor development, and abnormal muscle tone and movements. Most survive for only 5 to 8 months after the appearance of these symptoms (Chamberlain, Nichols, & Chase, 1991; Chatkupt et al., 1989).

Prenatal AIDS babies are generally born to urban, poverty-stricken parents. Lack of money to pay for medical treatment, rejection by relatives and friends who do not understand the disease, and anxiety about the child's future cause tremendous stress in these families. Currently, medical services for young children with AIDS and counseling for their parents are badly needed. Also, with no cure at hand, education of adolescents and adults about the disease and outreach programs that get women at high risk for infection into drug-treatment programs are the only ways to stop continued spread of the virus to children (Task Force on Pediatric AIDS, 1989; Weissman, 1991).

age, infants whose mothers ate fish during pregnancy did more poorly on memory tests (Jacobson et al., 1985). A follow-up at 4 years of age showed persisting memory difficulties and lower verbal intelligence test scores (Jacobson, Jacobson, & Humphrey, 1990; Jacobson et al., 1992).

MATERNAL DISEASE. Five percent of women catch an infectious disease of some sort while pregnant. Most of these illnesses, such as the common cold and various strains of the flu, seem to have no impact on the embryo or fetus. However, as Table 3.7 indicates, a few diseases can cause extensive damage.

Rubella (3-day German measles) is a well-known teratogen. In the mid-1960s, a worldwide epidemic of rubella led to the birth of over 20,000 American babies with serious birth defects. Consistent with the sensitive period concept, the greatest damage occurs when rubella strikes during the embryonic period. Over 50 percent of infants whose mothers become ill during that time show heart defects; eye cataracts; deafness; genital, urinary, and intestinal abnormalities; and mental retardation. Infection during the fetal period is less harmful, but low birth weight, hearing loss, and bone abnormalities may still occur (Samson, 1988). Since 1966, infants and young children have been routinely vaccinated against rubella, so the number of prenatal cases today is much less than it was a generation ago. Still, 10 to 20 percent of American women lack the rubella antibody, so new outbreaks of the disease are still possible (Cochi et al., 1989).

The harmful effects of other common viruses are summarized in Table 3.7. The developing organism is particularly sensitive to the family of herpes viruses, for which there is no vaccine or treatment. Among these, cytomegalovirus (the most frequent prenatal infection, transmitted through respiratory or sexual contact) and herpes simplex 2 (which is sexually transmitted) are especially dangerous. In both, the virus invades the mother's genital tract. Babies can be infected either during pregnancy or at birth (Samson, 1988). Acquired immune deficiency syndrome (AIDS) is a relatively new, deadly viral disease that is infecting increasing numbers of newborn babies. To find out about its prenatal transmission, refer to the Social Issues box above.

Also included in Table 3.7 are several bacterial and parasitic diseases. Among the most common is toxoplasmosis, caused by a parasite found in many animals. Pregnant women may become infected from eating raw or undercooked meat or from contact with the feces of infected cats. Only 3 percent of women with the disease transmit it to the developing organism, but when they do, its effects can be devastating. If the disease strikes during the first trimester, it is likely to cause eye and brain damage (Bobak, Jensen, & Zalar, 1989; Marcus, 1983). Expectant mothers can avoid toxoplasmosis by making sure that the meat they eat is well cooked, having pet cats checked for the disease, and turning the care of litter boxes over to other family members.

Other Maternal Factors

Besides teratogens, maternal nutrition and emotional well-being affect the development of the embryo and fetus. In addition, many prospective parents wonder about the impact of a woman's age on the course of pregnancy. We examine each of these influences in the following sections.

NUTRITION. Children grow more rapidly during the prenatal period than at any other phase of development. During this time, they depend totally on the mother for nutrients to support their growth.

During World War II, a severe famine occurred in the Netherlands, giving scientists a rare opportunity to study the impact of nutrition on prenatal development. Findings revealed that the sensitive-period concept operates with nutrition, just as it does with the teratogens discussed earlier in this chapter. Women affected by the famine during the first trimester were more likely to have miscarriages or to give birth to babies with physical defects. When women were past the first trimester, fetuses usually survived, but many were born underweight and had small heads (Stein et al., 1975).

We now know that prenatal malnutrition can cause serious damage to the central nervous system. Autopsies of malnourished babies who died at or shortly after birth reveal fewer brain cells and a brain weight that is as much as 36 percent below average. The poorer the mother's diet, the greater the loss in brain weight, especially if malnutrition occurred during the last trimester. During that time, the brain is growing rapidly in size, and a maternal diet high in all the basic nutrients is necessary for it to reach its full potential (Naeye, Blanc, & Paul, 1973; Parekh et al., 1970; Winick, Rosso, & Waterlow, 1970).

Prenatally malnourished babies enter the world with serious problems. They frequently catch respiratory illnesses, since poor nutrition suppresses development of the immune system (Chandra, 1991). In addition, these infants are irritable and unresponsive to stimulation around them. Like drug-addicted newborns, they have a high-pitched cry that is particularly distressing to their caregivers. The effects of poor nutrition quickly combine with an impoverished, stressful home life. With age, low intelligence test scores and serious learning problems become more apparent (Lozoff, 1989).

Prevention or recovery from prenatal malnutrition is possible only if an adequate diet is provided early in development, while cell duplication is still taking place in the brain. Many studies show that giving pregnant mothers food supplements has a substantial impact on the health of their babies, reducing miscarriage, low birth weight, and respiratory infections. When poor nutrition is allowed to continue throughout pregnancy, infants often require more than dietary enrichment. Their tired, restless behavior leads mothers to be less sensitive and stimulating, and in response, babies become even more passive and withdrawn. Successful interventions must break this cycle of apathetic mother–baby interaction. Some do so by teaching parents how to interact effectively with their infants, whereas others focus on stimulating infants to promote active engagement with their physical and social surroundings (Grantham-McGregor, Schofield, & Powell, 1987; Zeskind & Ramey, 1978, 1981).

Although prenatal malnutrition is highest in poverty-stricken regions of the world, it is not limited to developing countries. Each year, 80,000 to 120,000 American infants are born seriously undernourished. The federal government does provide food packages to impoverished pregnant women through its Special Supplemental Food Program for Women, Infants, and Children. Unfortunately, because of funding shortages, the program serves only 60 percent of those who are eligible (Children's Defense Fund, 1992a).

Finally, the fetuses of some middle-class expectant mothers are also deprived of adequate nourishment. A weight gain during pregnancy of 25 to 30 pounds is normal and helps ensure the health of mother and baby. Yet in the United States, where thinness is the feminine ideal, women often feel uneasy about gaining this much weight, and they may try to limit their food intake. When they do so, they risk the infant's development in all of the ways just described.

EMOTIONAL STRESS. When women experience severe emotional stress during pregnancy, their babies are at risk for a wide variety of difficulties. Intense anxiety is associated with a higher rate of miscarriage, prematurity, low birth weight, and newborn respiratory illness. It is also related to certain physical defects, such as cleft palate and pyloric stenosis (tightening of the infant's stomach outlet, which must be treated surgically) (Norbeck & Tilden, 1983; Omer & Everly, 1988). Extreme prenatal stress may also have lasting consequences for the developing person's ability to cope with anxiety. In one long-term study, offspring born to mothers who experienced the trauma of their husband's death during pregnancy were compared to a control group whose mothers experienced the same loss during the first year of life. By adulthood, the group exposed to prenatal stress showed a much higher rate of emotional disorders (Huttunen & Niskanen, 1978).

How can maternal stress affect the developing organism? To understand this process, think back to how your own body felt the last time you were under considerable stress. When we experience fear and anxiety, stimulant hormones are released into our bloodstream. These cause us to be "poised for action." Large amounts of blood are sent to parts of the body involved in the defensive response—the brain, the heart, and muscles in the arms, legs, and trunk. Blood flow to other organs, including the uterus, is reduced. As a result, the fetus is deprived of a full supply of oxygen and nutrients. Stress hormones also cross the placenta, leading the fetus's heart rate and activity level to rise dramatically. Finally, women who experience long-term anxiety are more likely to smoke, drink, eat poorly, and engage in other behaviors that harm the embryo or fetus. These factors probably contribute to the negative outcomes observed in their babies (Istvan, 1986).

But women under severe emotional stress do not always give birth to infants with problems. The risks are greatly reduced when mothers have husbands, other family members, and friends who offer emotional support. In one study of expectant women experiencing high life stress, those who reported having people on whom they could count for help had a pregnancy complication rate of only 33 percent, compared to 91 percent for those who had few or no social supports (Nuckolls, Cassel, & Kaplan, 1972). These results suggest that finding ways to provide isolated women with supportive social ties during pregnancy can help prevent prenatal complications.

MATERNAL AGE. First births to women in their 30s have increased greatly over the past two decades in the United States (see Figure 3.9). Many more couples are putting off childbearing until their careers are well established and they know they can support a child. Earlier in this chapter, we indicated that women who

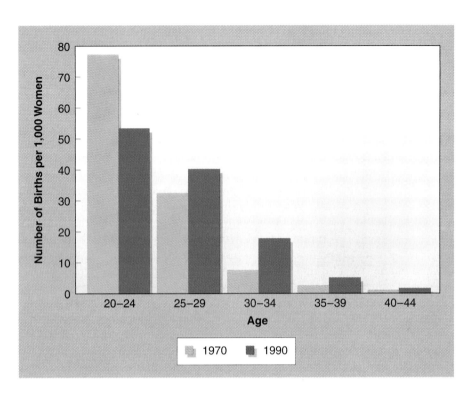

FIGURE 3.9 First births to American women of different ages in 1970 and 1990. The birth rate decreased over this time period for women 20–24 years of age, whereas it increased for women 25 years and older. For women in their 30s, the birth rate more than doubled. (Adapted from Ventura, 1989; U.S. Department of Health and Human Services, 1992a.)

delay having children face a greater risk of giving birth to babies with chromosomal defects. Are other pregnancy problems more common among older mothers?

For many years, scientists thought that aging and repeated use of the mother's reproductive organs increased the likelihood of a wide variety of pregnancy complications. Recently, these ideas have been questioned. When women without serious health difficulties are considered, even those in their 40s do not experience more prenatal problems than those in their 20s (Ales, Druzin, & Santini, 1990; Spellacy, Miller, & Winegar, 1986). And a large study of over 50,000 pregnancies showed no relationship between number of previous births and pregnancy complications (Heinonen, Slone, & Shapiro, 1977). As long as an older woman is in good health, she can carry a baby successfully.

In the case of teenage mothers, does physical immaturity cause prenatal problems? Again, research shows that it does not. A teenager's body is large enough and strong enough to support pregnancy. In fact, as we will see in Chapter 5, young adolescent girls grow taller and heavier and their hips broaden (in preparation for childbearing) before their menstrual periods begin. Nature tries to ensure that once a girl can conceive, she is physically ready to carry and give birth to a baby. Infants of teenagers are born with a higher rate of problems for quite different reasons. Many teenagers do not have access to medical care or are afraid to seek it. In addition, most pregnant teenagers come from low-income backgrounds where stress, poor nutrition, and health problems are common (Ketterlinus, Henderson, & Lamb, 1990; Roosa, 1984).

Brief Review

Teratogens—cigarettes, alcohol, certain drugs, radiation, environmental pollutants, and diseases—can seriously harm the embryo and fetus. The effects of teratogens are complex. They depend on amount and length of exposure, the genetic makeup of mother and baby, and the presence of other harmful environmental agents. Teratogens operate according to the sensitive-period concept. In general, greatest damage occurs during the embryonic phase, when all parts of the body are being formed. Poor maternal nutrition and severe emotional stress can also endanger the developing organism. As long as they are in good health, teenagers, women in their thirties and forties, and women who have given birth to several children have a high likelihood of problem-free pregnancies.

CHILDBIRTH

It is not surprising that childbirth is often referred to as labor. It is the hardest physical work a woman may ever do. A complex series of hormonal changes initiates the process, which naturally divides into three stages (see Figure 3.10):

1. *Dilation and effacement of the cervix.* This is the longest stage of labor, lasting, on the average, 12 to 14 hours in a first birth and 4 to 6 hours in later births. Contractions of the uterus gradually become more frequent and powerful, causing the *cervix*, or uterine opening, to widen and thin to nothing. As a result, a clear channel from the uterus into the vagina, or birth canal, is created.

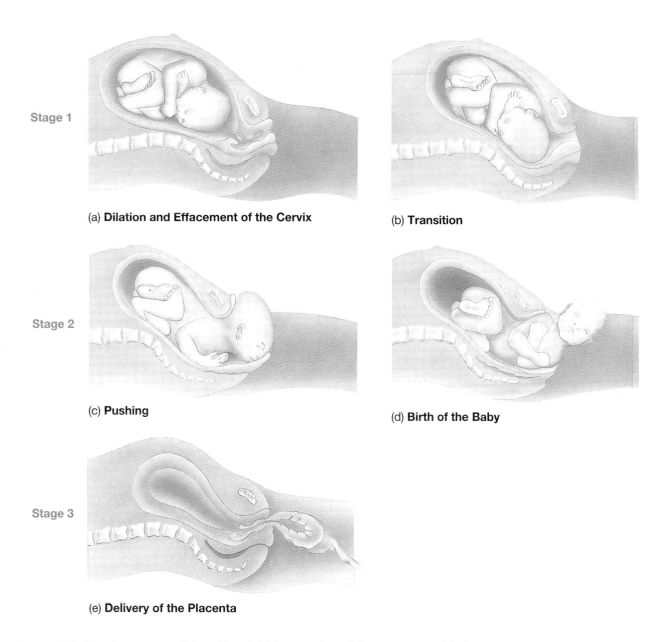

Stage 1

(a) **Dilation and Effacement of the Cervix**

(b) **Transition**

Stage 2

(c) **Pushing**

(d) **Birth of the Baby**

Stage 3

(e) **Delivery of the Placenta**

FIGURE 3.10   The three stages of labor. *Stage 1:* (a) Contractions of the uterus cause dilation and effacement of the cervix; (b) transition is reached when the frequency and strength of the contractions are at their peak and the cervix opens completely. *Stage 2:* (c) The mother pushes with each contraction, forcing the baby down the birth canal, and the head appears; (d) near the end of Stage 2, the shoulders emerge and are followed quickly by the rest of the baby's body. *Stage 3:* (e) With a few final pushes, the placenta is delivered.

2. *Birth of the baby.* Once the cervix is fully open, the baby is ready to be born. This second stage is much shorter than the first, lasting about 50 minutes in a first birth and 20 minutes in later births. Strong contractions of the uterus continue, but they do not do the entire job. The most important factor is a natural urge that the mother feels to squeeze and push with her abdominal muscles. As she does so with each contraction, she forces the baby down and out.

3. *Delivery of the placenta.* Labor comes to an end with a few final contractions and pushes. These cause the placenta to separate from the wall of the uterus and be delivered, a stage that usually lasts about 5 to 10 minutes.

The Baby's Adaptation to Labor and Delivery

So far, we have described the events of childbirth from the outside looking in. Let's consider, for a moment, what the experience must be like for the baby. After being squeezed and pushed for many hours, the infant is forced to leave the warm, protective uterus for a cold, brightly lit external world. The strong contractions expose the head to a great deal of pressure, and they squeeze the placenta and umbilical cord repeatedly. Each time, the baby's supply of oxygen is reduced.

At first glance, these events may strike you as a dangerous ordeal. Fortunately, healthy babies are well equipped to withstand the trauma of childbirth. The force of the contractions causes the infant to produce high levels of stress hormones. Recall that during pregnancy, the effects of maternal stress can endanger the baby. In contrast, during childbirth, the infant's production of stress hormones is adaptive. It helps the baby withstand oxygen deprivation by sending a rich supply of blood to the brain and heart. In addition, it prepares the infant to breathe by causing the lungs to absorb excess liquid and expanding the bronchial tubes (passages leading to the lungs). Finally, stress hormones arouse infants into alertness so they are born wide awake, ready to interact with the surrounding world (Emory & Toomey, 1988; Lagercrantz & Slotkin, 1986).

The Newborn Baby's Appearance

Parents are often surprised at the odd-looking newborn baby, who is a far cry from the storybook image many created in their minds before birth. The average newborn is 20 inches long and $7\frac{1}{2}$ pounds in weight; boys tend to be slightly longer and heavier than girls. Body proportions contribute to the baby's strange appearance. The head is very large compared to the trunk and legs, which are short and bowed. As we will see in later chapters, the combination of a big head (with its well-developed brain) and a small body means that human infants learn quickly in the first few months of life. But unlike most mammals, they cannot get around on their own until much later, during the second half of the first year.

Even though newborn babies may not match the idealized expectations of their parents, some features do make them attractive. Their round faces, chubby cheeks, large foreheads, and big eyes are just those characteristics that make adults feel like picking them up and cuddling them (Berman, 1980; Lorenz, 1943). These features, as we will see in later chapters, are among the many ways in which nature helps get the parent–infant relationship off to a good start.

Assessing the Newborn's Physical Condition: The Apgar Scale

Apgar scale
A rating used to assess the newborn baby's physical condition immediately after birth.

Infants who have difficulty making the transition to life outside the uterus require special assistance at once. To quickly assess the baby's physical condition, doctors and nurses use the **Apgar scale.** As Table 3.8 shows, a rating from 0 to 2 on each of five characteristics is made at 1 and 5 minutes after birth. An Apgar score of 7 or better indicates that the infant is in good physical condition. If the score is between 4 and 6, the baby requires special help in establishing breathing and other vital

TABLE 3.8 *The Apgar Scale*

	SCORE		
SIGN	*0*	*1*	*2*
Heart rate	No heartbeat	Under 100 beats per minute	100 to 140 beats per minute
Respiratory effort	No breathing for 60 seconds	Irregular, shallow breathing	Strong breathing and crying
Reflex irritability (sneezing, coughing, and grimacing)	No response	Weak reflexive response	Strong reflexive response
Muscle tone	Completely limp	Weak movements of arms and legs	Strong movements of arms and legs
*Color**	Blue body, arms, and legs	Body pink with blue arms and legs	Body, arms, and legs completely pink

*Color is the least reliable of the Apgar signs. Vernix, the white cheesy substance that covers the skin, often interferes with the doctor's rating, and the skin tone of nonwhite babies makes it difficult to apply the "pink" criterion. However, newborns of all races can be rated for a pinkish glow that results from the flow of oxygen through body tissues, since skin color is generally lighter at birth than the baby's inherited pigmentation.

SOURCE: Apgar, 1953.

signs. If the score is 3 or below, the infant is in serious danger, and emergency medical attention is needed. Two Apgar ratings are given, since some babies have trouble adjusting at first but are doing well after a few minutes (Apgar, 1953).

APPROACHES TO CHILDBIRTH

Childbirth practices, like other aspects of family life, are molded by the society of which mother and baby are a part. In many village and tribal cultures, expectant mothers are well acquainted with the childbirth process. For example, the Jarara of South America and the Pukapukans of the Pacific Islands treat birth as a vital part of daily life. The Jarara mother gives birth in a passageway or shelter in full view of the entire community, including small children. The Pukapukan girl is so familiar with the events of labor and delivery that she can frequently be seen playing at it. Using a coconut to represent the baby, she stuffs it inside her dress, imitates the mother's pushing, and lets the nut fall at the proper moment. In most nonindustrialized cultures, women are assisted during the birth process, often by being held from behind. Among the Mayans of the Yucatan, the mother leans against the body and arms of a woman called the "head helper," who supports her weight and breathes with her during each contraction (Jordan, 1980; Mead & Newton, 1967).

In large Western nations, childbirth has changed dramatically over the centuries. Before the 1800s, birth usually took place at home and was a family-centered event. Relatives, friends, and children were often present. The nineteenth-century industrial revolution brought greater crowding to cities along with new health problems. Childbirth moved from home to hospital, where the health of mothers and babies could be protected. Once the responsibility for childbirth was placed in the hands of doctors, women's knowledge about it was reduced, and relatives and friends were no longer welcome to participate (Lindell, 1988).

By the 1950s and 1960s, women started to question the medical procedures that came to be used routinely during labor and delivery. Many felt that frequent use of strong drugs and delivery instruments had robbed them of a precious experience and were often not necessary or safe for the baby. Gradually, a new natural

*A*mong the !Kung of Botswana,
Africa, a mother gives birth in a sitting
position, and she is surrounded by
women who encourage and help her.
(SHOSTAK/ANTHRO-PHOTO)

childbirth movement arose in Europe and spread to the United States. Its purpose was to make hospital birth as comfortable and rewarding for mothers as possible. Today, most hospitals carry this theme further by offering birth centers that are family centered in approach and homelike in appearance. And a small but growing number of American women are rejecting institutional birth entirely and choosing to have their babies at home.

Natural, or Prepared, Childbirth

Natural, or **prepared, childbirth** tries to rid mothers of the idea that birth is a painful ordeal that requires extensive medical intervention. Although many different natural childbirth programs exist, all of them draw on methods developed by Grantly Dick-Read (1959) in England and Ferdinand Lamaze (1958) in France. These physicians emphasized that cultural attitudes had taught women to fear the birth experience. An anxious, frightened woman in labor tenses muscles throughout her body, including those in the uterus. This turns the mild pain that sometimes accompanies strong contractions into a great deal of pain.

A typical natural childbirth program consists of three parts:

1. *Classes.* Expectant mothers and fathers attend a series of classes in which they learn about the anatomy and physiology of labor and delivery. Natural childbirth is based on the idea that knowledge about the birth process reduces a mother's fear.
2. *Relaxation and breathing techniques.* Expectant mothers are taught relaxation and breathing exercises aimed at counteracting any pain they might feel during uterine contractions. They also practice creating pleasant visual images in their minds instead of thinking about pain.
3. *Labor coach.* While the mother masters breathing and visualization techniques, the father (or another supportive companion) learns to be a "labor coach." The coach assists the mother by reminding her to relax and breathe,

Natural, or prepared, childbirth
An approach designed to reduce pain and medical intervention and to make childbirth a rewarding experience for parents.

massaging her back, supporting her body during labor and delivery, and offering words of encouragement and affection.

Studies comparing mothers who experience natural childbirth with those who do not reveal that there are many benefits. Mothers' attitudes toward labor and delivery are more positive, and they feel less pain (Lindell, 1988). As a result, they require less medication—usually very little or none at all (Hetherington, 1990). Research suggests that social support may be an important part of the success of natural childbirth techniques. In Guatemalan and American hospitals in which patients were routinely prevented from having friends and relatives with them during childbirth, some mothers were randomly assigned a companion who stayed with them throughout labor, talking to them, holding their hands, and rubbing their backs to promote relaxation. These mothers had fewer birth complications, and their labors were several hours shorter than those of women who did not have supportive companionship. Observations of the Guatemalan mothers in the first hour after delivery showed that those receiving social support were more likely to respond to their babies by talking, smiling, and gently stroking (Kennell et al., 1991; Sosa et al., 1980).

Home Delivery

Home birth has always been popular in certain industrialized nations, such as England, the Netherlands, and Sweden. The number of American women choosing to have their babies at home has increased in recent years, although it is still small, amounting to about 1 percent (Declercq, 1992). These mothers want to recapture the time when birth was an important part of family life. In addition, most want to avoid unnecessary medical procedures and exercise greater control over their own care and that of their babies than hospitals typically permit. Although some home births are attended by doctors, many more are handled by certified nurse-midwives who have degrees in nursing and additional training in childbirth management.

Women who choose home birth want to share the joy of childbirth with family members, avoid unnecessary medical procedures, and exercise greater control over their own care and that of their babies. When assisted by a well-trained doctor or midwife, healthy women can give birth at home safely. (FRANCK LOGUE/STOCK SOUTH)

Is it just as safe to give birth at home as in a hospital? For healthy women who are assisted by a well-trained doctor or midwife, it seems so, since complications rarely occur. In fact, alternative birth settings, such as the home or *freestanding birth centers* (which operate independently of hospitals and offer less in the way of backup medical care), offer low-risk women the advantage of a less costly birth experience without any impact on birth outcomes (Albers & Katz, 1991). However, if attendants are not carefully trained and prepared to handle emergencies, the rate of infant death is high (Schramm, Barnes, & Bakewell, 1987). When mothers are at risk for any kind of complication, the appropriate place for labor and delivery is the hospital, where life-saving treatment is available should it be needed.

Labor and Delivery Medication

Although natural childbirth techniques lessen or eliminate the need for pain-relieving drugs, some form of medication is still used in 80 to 95 percent of births in the United States. *Analgesias* are mild drugs that lessen pain. When given during labor, they are usually intended to help a mother relax. *Anesthesia* is a stronger type of painkiller that blocks sensation. During childbirth, it is generally injected into the spinal column to numb the lower half of the body.

In complicated deliveries, pain-relieving drugs are essential because they permit life-saving medical interventions to be carried out. But when used routinely, they can cause problems. Anesthesia interferes with the mother's ability to feel contractions during the second stage of labor. As a result, she may not push effectively, increasing the likelihood that the baby may have to be pulled from the birth canal with *forceps* (a metal device placed around the infant's head) or a *vacuum extractor* (a plastic suction cup that fits over the top of the head). Both of these instruments involve some risk of injury to the baby (Cunningham, MacDonald, & Gant, 1989; Hanigan et al., 1990).

Labor and delivery medication rapidly crosses the placenta. When given in fairly large doses, it produces a depressed state in the newborn baby that may last for days. The infant is sleepy and withdrawn, sucks poorly during feedings, and is likely to be irritable when awake (Brackbill, McManus, & Woodward, 1985; Brazelton, Nugent, & Lester, 1987). One study found that mothers who received anesthesia viewed their babies as more difficult and less rewarding to care for in the weeks after birth (Murray et al., 1981).

Does the use of medication during childbirth have a lasting impact on the physical and mental development of the child? Some researchers claim so (Brackbill, McManus, & Woodward, 1985), but their findings have been challenged, and contrary results exist (Broman, 1983). Anesthesia may be related to other risk factors that could account for long-term consequences in some studies, and more research is needed to sort out these effects. In the meantime, the negative impact of these drugs on the early infant–mother relationship supports the current trend in the medical profession toward restrained and limited use.

BIRTH COMPLICATIONS

In the preceding sections, we indicated that some babies—in particular, those whose mothers are in poor health, who do not receive good medical care, or who have a history of pregnancy problems—are especially likely to experience birth complications. Insufficient oxygen, a pregnancy that ends too early, and a baby who is born underweight are serious problems that we have mentioned many times. In the following sections, we take a closer look at each of these complications and their impact on later development.

Oxygen Deprivation

113

CHAPTER THREE
———————
BIOLOGICAL FOUNDATIONS,
PRENATAL DEVELOPMENT,
AND BIRTH

A small number of infants are exposed to *anoxia,* or inadequate oxygen supply, during the birth process. Sometimes the problem results from a failure to start breathing immediately after delivery. Although newborns can survive periods without oxygen longer than adults, there is risk of brain damage if breathing is delayed for more than 3 minutes (Stechler & Halton, 1982). At other times, anoxia occurs during labor. Squeezing of the umbilical cord is a common cause, a condition that is especially likely when infants are in **breech position**—turned in such a way that the buttocks or feet would emerge first. Because of this danger, breech babies are often delivered by *Cesarean section,* a surgical procedure in which the doctor makes an incision in the mother's abdomen and lifts the baby out of the uterus. Another cause of oxygen deprivation is *placenta previa,* or premature separation of the placenta, a life-threatening event that requires immediate delivery. Although the reasons for placenta previa are not well understood, teratogens that result in abnormal development of the placenta, such as cigarette smoking, are strongly related to it (Kramer et al., 1991).

Incompatibility between mother and baby in a blood protein called the **Rh factor** can also lead to anoxia. When the mother is Rh negative (lacks the protein) and the father is Rh positive (has the protein), the baby may inherit the father's Rh positive blood type. (Recall from Table 3.2 that Rh positive blood is dominant and Rh negative blood is recessive, so the chances are good that a baby will be Rh positive.) During the third trimester and at the time of birth, some maternal and fetal blood cells usually cross the placenta, generally in small enough amounts to be quite safe. But if even a little of the baby's Rh positive blood passes into the mother's Rh negative bloodstream, she begins to form antibodies to the foreign Rh protein. If these enter the baby's system, they destroy red blood cells, reducing the supply of oxygen. Mental retardation, damage to the heart muscle, and infant death can occur. Since it takes time for the mother to produce antibodies, first-born children are rarely affected. The danger increases with each additional pregnancy. Fortunately, the harmful effects of Rh incompatibility can be prevented in most cases. After the birth of each Rh positive infant, Rh negative mothers are routinely given a vaccine called RhoGam, which prevents the buildup of antibodies (Simkin, Whalley, & Keppler, 1984).

How do children deprived of oxygen during labor and delivery fare as they get older? Longitudinal research shows that they remain behind their agemates in intellectual and motor development throughout early childhood. But by the school years, most catch up in development (Corah et al., 1965; Graham et al., 1962). When problems do persist, the anoxia was usually extreme. Perhaps it was caused by prenatal damage to the baby's respiratory system, or it may have happened because the infant's lungs were not yet mature enough to breathe. For example, babies born more than 6 weeks early commonly have a disorder called *respiratory distress syndrome* (otherwise known as *hyaline membrane disease).* Their tiny lungs are so poorly developed that the air sacs collapse, causing serious breathing difficulties. Today, mechanical ventilators keep many such infants alive. In spite of these measures, some babies suffer permanent brain damage from lack of oxygen, and in other cases their delicate lungs are harmed by the treatment itself (Vohr & Garcia-Coll, 1988). Respiratory distress syndrome is only one of many risks for babies born too soon, as we will see in the following section.

Preterm and Low-Birth-Weight Infants

Babies who arrive 3 weeks or more before the end of a full 38-week pregnancy or who weigh less than $5\frac{1}{2}$ pounds (2,500 grams) have, for many years, been referred to as "premature." A wealth of research indicates that premature babies are at risk for many problems. Birth weight is the best available predictor of infant survival and healthy development. Many newborns who weigh less than $3\frac{1}{3}$ pounds (1,500

Breech position
A position of the baby in the uterus that would cause the buttocks or feet to be delivered first

Rh factor
A protein that, when present in the fetus's blood but not in the mother's, can cause the mother to build up antibodies. If these return to the fetus's system, they destroy red blood cells, reducing the oxygen supply to organs and tissues.

grams) experience difficulties that are not overcome, an effect that becomes stronger as birth weight decreases (Wilcox & Skjoerven, 1992). Frequent illness, inattention, overactivity, and deficits in motor coordination and school learning are some of the problems that extend into the childhood years (McCormick, Gortmaker, & Sobol, 1990; Saigal et al., 1991).

About 1 in 14 infants is born underweight in the United States. Although the problem can strike unexpectedly, it is highest among low-income pregnant women, especially ethnic minorities (Kopp & Kaler, 1989). These mothers, as we indicated earlier in this chapter, are more likely to be undernourished and to be exposed to other harmful environmental influences. In addition, they often do not receive the prenatal care necessary to protect their vulnerable babies.

Prematurity is also common when mothers are carrying twins. Twins are usually born about 3 weeks early, and because of restricted space inside the uterus, they gain less weight than singletons after the 20th week of pregnancy.

PRETERM VERSUS SMALL FOR DATE. Although low-birth-weight infants face many obstacles to healthy development, individual differences exist in how well they do. Over half go on to lead normal lives—even some who weighed only a couple of pounds at birth (Vohr & Garcia-Coll, 1988). To better understand why some of these babies do better than others, researchers have divided them into two groups. The first is called **preterm.** These infants are born several weeks or more before their due date. Although small in size, their weight may still be appropriate for the amount of time they spent in the uterus. The second group is called **small for date.** These babies are below their expected weight when length of the pregnancy is taken into account. Some small-for-date infants are actually full term. Others are preterm infants who are especially underweight.

Of the two types of babies, small-for-date infants usually have more serious problems. During the first year, they are more likely to die, catch infections, and show evidence of brain damage. By middle childhood, they have lower intelligence test scores, are less attentive, and achieve more poorly in school (Teberg, Walther, & Pena, 1988). Small-for-date infants probably experienced inadequate nutrition before birth. Perhaps their mothers did not eat properly, the placenta did not function normally, or the babies themselves had defects that prevented them from growing as they should.

CHARACTERISTICS OF PRETERM INFANTS: CONSEQUENCES FOR CAREGIVING. Imagine a scrawny, thin-skinned infant whose body is only a little larger than the size of your hand. You try to play with the baby by stroking and talking softly, but he is sleepy and unresponsive. When you feed him, he sucks poorly. He is usually irritable during the short, unpredictable periods in which he is awake.

Unfortunately, the appearance and behavior of preterm babies can lead parents to be less sensitive and responsive in caring for them. Compared to full-term infants, preterm babies—especially those who are very ill at birth—are less often held close, touched, and talked to gently. At times, mothers of these infants are overly intrusive, engaging in interfering pokes and verbal commands in an effort to obtain a higher level of response from a baby who is a passive, unrewarding social partner (Patteson & Barnard, 1990). Some parents may step up these intrusive acts when faced with continuing ungratifying infant behavior, which may explain why preterm babies as a group are at risk for child abuse. When these infants are born to isolated, poverty-stricken mothers who have difficulty managing their own lives, then the chances for unfavorable outcomes are increased. In contrast, parents with stable life circumstances and social supports can usually overcome the stresses of caring for a preterm infant. In these cases, even sick preterm babies have a good chance of catching up in development by middle childhood (Cohen & Parmelee, 1983).

These findings suggest that how well preterm infants develop has a great deal to do with the kind of relationship established between parent and child, to which

Preterm

Infants born several weeks or more before their due date.

Small for date

Infants whose birth weight is below normal when length of pregnancy is taken into account.

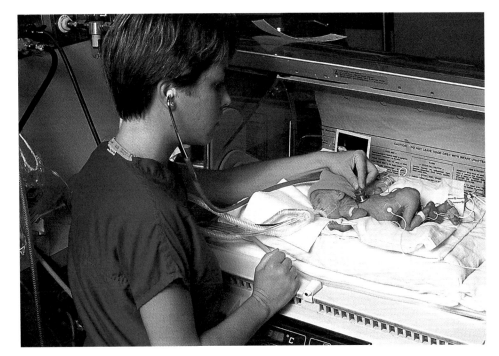

*T*his baby was born many weeks before his due date and breathes with the aid of a respirator. Because he weighs only a few pounds, his survival and development are seriously at risk. (CHARLES CANCELLARE/ PICTURE GROUP)

both partners contribute. If a good relationship between mother and baby can help prevent the negative effects of early birth, then interventions directed at supporting this relationship should help these infants recover.

INTERVENING WITH PRETERM INFANTS. At one time, doctors believed that stimulating a fragile preterm baby could be harmful. Now we know that certain kinds of stimulation in proper doses can promote their development. In some intensive-care nurseries, preterm infants can be seen rocking in suspended hammocks or lying on waterbeds—interventions designed to replace the gentle motion they would have received while being carried in the mother's uterus. Other forms of stimulation have also been used—for example, an attractive mobile or a tape recording of a heart beat, soft music, or the mother's voice. Many studies show that these experiences have important short-term benefits. They promote faster weight gain, more predictable sleep patterns, and greater alertness during the weeks after birth (Cornell & Gottfried, 1976; Schaefer, Hatcher, & Bargelow, 1980).

Touch is an especially important form of stimulation for preterm newborns. In studies of baby animals, touching the skin releases certain brain chemicals that support physical growth—effects that may occur in humans as well (Schanberg & Field, 1987). In one study, preterm infants who were gently massaged several times each day in the hospital gained weight faster and, at the end of the first year, were advanced in mental and motor development over preterm infants not given this stimulation (Field et al., 1986). In developing countries where hospitalization is not always possible, skin-to-skin "kangaroo baby care," in which the preterm infant is tucked between the mother's breasts and peers over the top of her clothing, is being encouraged. The technique is used often in Europe as a supplement to hospital intensive care. It fosters oxygenation of the baby's body, temperature regulation, improved feeding, and infant survival (Anderson, 1991; Whitelaw, 1990).

When effective stimulation helps preterm infants develop, parents are likely to feel good about their infant's growth and interact with the baby more effectively. Interventions that support the parenting side of this relationship generally teach parents about the infant's characteristics and promote caregiving skills. Those that work best include enough sessions so parents can establish a warm relationship with the intervener. Infants whose birth weight is very low or whose

Understanding Birth Complications

In the preceding sections, we discussed a variety of birth complications that threaten children's well-being. Now let's try to put the evidence together. Are there any general principles that might help us understand how infants who survive a traumatic birth are likely to develop? A landmark longitudinal study carried out in Hawaii provides answers to this question.

In 1955, Emmy Werner and Ruth Smith began to follow 670 infants on the island of Kauai who experienced either mild, moderate, or severe birth complications. Each was matched, on the basis of social class and race, with a healthy newborn. The study had two goals: (1) to discover the long-term effects of birth complications; and (2) to find out how family environments influence the child's chances for recovery. Findings revealed that the likelihood of long-term difficulties was increased if birth trauma was severe. At age 18, this group showed ten times the rate of mental retardation, five times the number of mental health problems, and twice the number of physical handicaps as the other children studied. Among mild to moderately stressed children, the best predictor of how well they fared in later years was the quality of their home environments. Those growing up in stable families did almost as well on measures of intelligence and psychological adjustment as those with no birth problems. For these children, the consequences of birth trauma became less and less evident as they matured. In contrast, children exposed to poverty, family disorganization, and mentally ill parents often developed serious learning difficulties, behavior problems, and emotional disturbance during childhood and adolescence (Werner & Smith, 1982).

The Kauai study tells us that as long as birth injuries are not overwhelming, a supportive home environment can restore children's growth. But the most intriguing cases in this study were some exceptions to this overall pattern of findings. One-third of children with *both* fairly serious birth complications and troubled family environments grew into competent adults who fared as well as controls in career attainment and psychological adjustment. Werner and Smith found that these resilient individuals relied on factors outside the family and within themselves to overcome stress. Some had especially attractive personalities that caused them to receive positive responses from relatives, neighbors, and peers. In other cases, a grandparent, aunt, uncle, or baby-sitter established a warm relationship with the child and provided the needed emotional support (Werner, 1989; Werner & Smith, 1992).

The Kauai study reveals that as long as the overall balance of life events tips toward the favorable side, most children with birth problems show great resilience and develop successfully. When negative factors outweigh positive ones, even the sturdiest of newborn babies may become a lifelong casualty.

Brief Review

The hard work of labor takes place in three stages: dilation and effacement of the cervix, birth of the baby, and delivery of the placenta. Stress hormones help the infant withstand the trauma of childbirth. The Apgar scale is used to provide a quick rating of the baby's physical condition immediately after birth. Natural, or prepared, childbirth improves mothers' attitudes toward labor and delivery and reduces the need for medication. Home births are safe for healthy women, provided attendants are well trained. Pain-relieving drugs can cross the placenta, producing a depressed state in the newborn baby. However, long-term effects of medication are not yet established.

Birth complications can threaten children's development. Oxygen deprivation, when extreme, causes lasting brain damage. Preterm and low-birth-weight infants are at risk for many problems. Providing these babies with special stimulation and teaching parents how to care for and interact with them helps restore favorable growth. When newborns with serious complications grow up in favorable social environments, they have a good chance of catching up in development.

HEREDITY, ENVIRONMENT, AND BEHAVIOR: A LOOK AHEAD

Throughout this chapter, we have discussed a wide variety of genetic and early environmental influences, each of which has the power to alter the course of development. When we consider them together, it may seem surprising that any newborn babies arrive intact, but the vast majority do. Over 90 percent of pregnancies in the United States result in normal infants. Born healthy and vigorous, these developing members of the human species soon show wide variation in traits and abilities. Some are outgoing and sociable, whereas others are shy and reserved. By school age, one child loves to read, another is attracted to mathematics, while still a third excels at music or athletics. **Behavior genetics** is a field devoted to discovering the origins of this great diversity in human characteristics. We have already seen that researchers are only beginning to understand the genetic and environmental events preceding birth that affect the child's potential. How, then, do they unravel the roots of the many characteristics emerging after birth that are the focus of the remaining chapters in this book?

All behavior geneticists agree that both heredity and environment are involved in every aspect of development. There is no real controversy on this point because an environment is always needed for genetic information to be expressed (Scarr, 1988). But for polygenic traits (due to many genes) like intelligence and personality, scientists are a long way from knowing the precise hereditary influences involved. They must study the impact of genes on these characteristics indirectly, and the nature–nurture controversy remains unresolved because researchers do not agree on how heredity and environment influence these complex traits.

Some believe it is useful and possible to answer the question of *how much* each factor contributes to differences among children. A second group regards the question of which factor is more important as neither useful nor answerable. These investigators believe heredity and environment do not make separate contributions to behavior. Instead, they are always related, and the real question we

*T*o study the role of heredity in complex human traits, researchers conduct kinship studies in which they compare the characteristics of family members. Sometimes the resemblance between parents and children—both physically and behaviorally—is striking. (SUPERSTOCK)

Behavior genetics

A field of study devoted to uncovering the hereditary and environmental origins of individual differences in human traits and abilities.

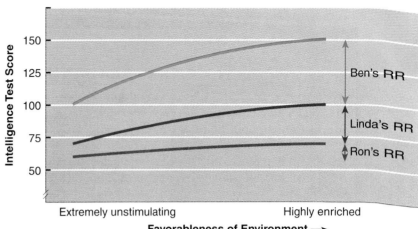

FIGURE 3.14 Intellectual ranges of reaction (RR) for three children in environments that vary from extremely unstimulating to highly enriched. (From I. I. Gottesman, 1963, "Genetic Aspects of Intelligent Behavior." In N. R. Ellis (Ed.), *Handbook of Mental Deficiency*, New York: McGraw-Hill, p. 255. Adapted by permission.)

broad range of environments found in the general population, it is often difficult to generalize heritability and concordance findings to the population as a whole.

Heritability estimates are controversial measures because they can easily be misapplied. For example, high heritabilities have been used to suggest that racial differences in intelligence, such as the poorer performance of black children compared to white children, have a genetic basis (Jensen, 1969, 1985). Yet this line of reasoning is widely regarded as inaccurate. Heritabilities computed on mostly white twin samples do not tell us what is responsible for test score differences between races. We have already seen that there are often large economic and cultural disparities between racial groups. As we will see in Chapter 8, research shows that when black and white children are adopted into economically and culturally similar home environments at an early age, they do not differ in intelligence (Scarr & Weinberg, 1983).

Perhaps the most serious criticism of heritability estimates and concordance rates has to do with their usefulness. Although they are interesting statistics that tell us heredity is undoubtedly involved in complex traits like intelligence and personality, they give us no precise information on how these traits develop or how children might respond when exposed to environments designed to help them develop as far as possible. Researchers who conduct heritability research argue that their studies are a first step. As more evidence accumulates to show that heredity underlies important human characteristics, then scientists can begin to ask better questions—about the specific genes involved, the way they affect development, and how their impact is modified by environmental factors.

The Question of "How?"

According to a second perspective, heredity and environment cannot be divided into separate influences. Instead, behavior is the result of a dynamic interplay between these two forces. How do heredity and environment work together to affect development? Several important concepts shed light on this question.

REACTION RANGE. The first of these ideas is **range of reaction** (Gottesman, 1963). It emphasizes that each person responds to the environment in a unique way because of his or her genetic makeup. Let's explore this idea by taking a look at Figure 3.14. Reaction range can apply to any characteristic; here it is illustrated for intelligence. Notice that when environments vary from extremely unstimulating to highly enriched, Ben's intelligence increases dramatically, Linda's only slightly, and Ron's hardly at all.

Reaction range highlights two important points about the relationship between heredity and environment. First, it shows that because each of us has a

Range of reaction
Each person's unique, genetically determined response to a range of environmental conditions.

unique genetic makeup, we respond quite differently to the same environment. Again, look carefully at Figure 3.14, and notice how a poor environment results in a lower intelligence test score for Ron than Ben. Also, an advantaged environment raises Ben's score far above what is possible for Ron. Second, sometimes different genetic–environmental combinations can make two children look the same! For example, if Ben is raised in an unstimulating environment, his score will be about 100—average for children in general. Linda can also obtain this score, but to do so she must grow up in a very advantaged home. In other words, the concept of range of reaction tells us that children differ in their range of possible responses to the environment. And unique blends of heredity and environment lead to both similarities and differences in behavior.

CANALIZATION. The concept of **canalization** provides another way of understanding how heredity and environment combine. Canalization is the tendency of heredity to restrict the development of some characteristics to just one or a few outcomes. A behavior that is strongly canalized follows a genetically set growth plan, and only strong environmental forces can deflect it from its course (Waddington, 1957). For example, infant perceptual and motor development seems to be strongly canalized, since all normal human babies eventually roll over, reach for objects, sit up, crawl, and walk. It takes extreme conditions to modify these behaviors or cause them not to appear. In contrast, intelligence and personality are less strongly canalized, since they vary much more with changes in the environment. When we look at the kinds of behaviors that are constrained by heredity, we can see that canalization is highly adaptive. Through it, nature ensures that children will develop certain species-typical skills under a wide range of rearing conditions, thereby promoting survival.

Recently, scientists have expanded the notion of canalization to include environmental influences. We now know that environments can also "channel" development, limiting traits that are pliant at the outset to one or a few outcomes (Gottlieb, 1991). For example, when children experience harmful environments early in life, there may be little that later experiences can do to change characteristics (such as intelligence) that were quite flexible to begin with. We have already seen that this is the case for babies who were prenatally exposed to high levels of alcohol, radiation, or anoxia. And later in this book, we will find that it is also true for children who spend many years living in extremely deprived homes and institutions (Turkheimer & Gottesman, 1991).

Using the concept of canalization, we learn that genes restrict the development of some characteristics more than others. And over time, even very flexible behaviors can become fixed and canalized, depending on the environments to which children were exposed.

GENETIC–ENVIRONMENTAL CORRELATION. Nature and nurture work together in still another way. Sandra Scarr and Kathleen McCartney (1983) point out that a major problem in trying to separate heredity and environment is that they are often correlated. According to the concept of **genetic–environmental correlation**, our genes influence the environments to which we are exposed. The way this happens changes with development.

Passive and Evocative Correlation. At younger ages, two types of genetic environmental correlation are common. The first is called *passive* correlation because the child has no control over it. Early on, parents provide environments that are influenced by their own heredity. For example, parents who are good athletes are likely to emphasize outdoor activities and enroll their children in swimming and gymnastics lessons at young ages. Besides getting exposed to an "athletic environment," the children may have inherited their parents' athletic ability. As a result, they are likely to become good athletes for both genetic and environmental reasons.

Canalization
The tendency of heredity to restrict the development of some characteristics to just one or a few outcomes.

Genetic–environmental correlation
The idea that heredity influences the environments to which individuals are exposed.

The second type of genetic–environmental correlation is *evocative.* Children evoke responses from others that are influenced by the child's heredity, and these responses strengthen the child's original style of responding. For example, an active, friendly baby is likely to receive more social stimulation from those around her than a passive, quiet infant. And a cooperative, attentive preschooler will probably receive more patient and sensitive interactions from parents than an inattentive, distractible child.

Active Correlation. At older ages, active genetic–environmental correlation becomes common. As children extend their experiences beyond the immediate family to school, neighborhood, and community and are given the freedom to make more of their own choices, they play an increasingly active role in seeking out environments that fit with their genetic tendencies. The well-coordinated, muscular child spends more time at after-school sports, the musically talented youngster joins the school orchestra and practices his violin, and the intellectually curious child is a familiar patron at her local library.

This tendency to actively choose environments that complement our heredity is called **niche-picking.** Infants and young children cannot do much niche-picking, since adults select environments for them. In contrast, older children and adolescents are much more in charge of their own environments. The niche-picking idea explains why pairs of identical twins reared apart during childhood and later reunited often find, to their great surprise, that they have similar hobbies, food preferences, friendship choices, and vocations (Bouchard et al., 1990). It also helps us understand some curious longitudinal findings indicating that identical twins become somewhat more similar and fraternal twins and adopted siblings less similar in intelligence and personality from infancy to adolescence (Scarr & Weinberg, 1983; Wilson, 1983). The influence of heredity and environment is not constant but changes over time. With age, genetic factors may become more important in determining the environments we experience and choose for ourselves.

A major reason child development researchers are interested in the nature–nurture issue is that they want to find ways to improve environments in order to help children develop as far as possible. The concepts of range of reaction, canalization, and niche-picking remind us that development is best understood as a series of complex exchanges between nature and nurture. When a characteristic is strongly determined by heredity, it can still be modified. However, children cannot be changed in any way we might desire. The success of any attempt to improve development depends on the characteristics we want to change, the genetic makeup of the child, and the type and timing of our intervention.

Niche-picking

A type of genetic–environmental correlation in which individuals actively choose environments that complement their heredity.

CHAPTER SUMMARY

Genetic Foundations

- Each individual's **phenotype,** or directly observable characteristics, is a product of both **genotype** and environment. **Chromosomes,** rodlike structures within the cell nucleus, contain our hereditary endowment. Along their length are **genes,** segments of **DNA** that make us distinctly human and influence our development and characteristics.

- **Gametes,** or sex cells, are produced through the process of cell division known as **meiosis. Crossing over** and independent assortment of chromosomes ensure that each gamete receives a unique set of genes from each parent. Once sperm and ovum unite to form the **zygote,** it starts to develop into a complex human being through cell duplication, or **mitosis.**

- **Identical,** or **monozygotic, twins** develop when a zygote divides in two during the early stages of cell duplication. **Fraternal,** or **dizygotic, twins** result when two ova are released from the mother's ovaries and each is fertilized. If the fertilizing sperm carries an X chromosome, the child will be a girl; if it contains a Y chromosome, a boy will be born.

- **Dominant–recessive** and **codominant** relationships are patterns of inheritance that apply to traits controlled by a single gene. When recessive disorders are **X-linked** (carried on the X chromosome), males are more likely to be affected. Unfavorable genes arise from **mutations,** which can occur spontaneously or be induced by hazardous environmental agents.

- Most relationships between genes and phenotypes are not one-to-one. **Pleiotropism**, the ability of a single gene to affect more than one characteristic, and **modifier genes**, which alter the expression of other genes, are common. Human traits that vary continuously, such as intelligence and personality, are **polygenic,** or influenced by many genes. Since the genetic principles involved are unknown, scientists must study the influence of heredity on these characteristics indirectly.

Chromosomal Abnormalities

- The most common chromosomal abnormality is Down syndrome, which results in physical defects and mental retardation. Effective parenting and early intervention can improve the development of these children.
- Disorders of the **sex chromosomes** are generally milder than defects of the **autosomes.** Contrary to popular belief, males with XYY syndrome are not prone to aggression. Studies of children with triple X, Klinefelter, and Turner syndromes reveal that adding to or subtracting from the usual number of X chromosomes leads to specific intellectual problems. Fragile X syndrome is a major genetic cause of mental retardation.

Reproductive Choices

- **Genetic counseling** helps couples at risk for giving birth to children with hereditary defects decide whether or not to conceive. **Prenatal diagnostic methods** make early detection of abnormalities possible. In some cases, treatment can be initiated before birth. Although donor insemination, in vitro fertilization, and surrogate motherhood permit many barren couples to become parents, these reproductive technologies raise serious legal and ethical concerns.

Prenatal Development

- Prenatal development is usually divided into three phases. The period of the zygote lasts about 2 weeks, from fertilization until the blastocyst becomes deeply implanted into the uterine lining. The period of the **embryo** extends from 2 to 8 weeks, during which the foundations for all body structures are laid down. The period of the **fetus,** lasting until the end of pregnancy, involves a dramatic increase in body size and completion of physical structures. **Age of viability** occurs at the beginning of the final trimester, sometime between 22 and 26 weeks.

Prenatal Environmental Influences

- **Teratogens** are environmental agents that cause damage during the prenatal period. Their effects conform to the sensitive-period concept. The organism is especially vulnerable during embryonic development, since all essential body structures are rapidly emerging. The impact of teratogens differs from one case to the next, due to amount and length of exposure, the genetic makeup of mother and fetus, and the presence or absence of other harmful agents.
- The effects of teratogens are not limited to immediate physical damage. Serious psychological consequences may appear later in development. Drugs, cigarette smoking, alcohol, hormones, radiation, environmental pollution, and certain infectious diseases are teratogens that can endanger the prenatal organism.

- Other maternal factors can either support or complicate prenatal development. When the mother's diet is inadequate, low birth weight and brain damage are major concerns. Severe emotional stress is associated with many pregnancy complications. Its impact can be reduced by providing mothers with social support.
- Maternal age and number of previous births were once thought to be major causes of prenatal problems. Aside from the risk of chromosomal abnormalities in older women, this is not the case. Instead, poor health and environmental risks associated with poverty are the strongest predictors of pregnancy complications.

Childbirth

- Childbirth takes place in three stages, beginning with contractions that open the lower part of the uterus so that the baby can be pushed through the birth canal and ending with delivery of the placenta. During labor, infants produce high levels of stress hormones, which help them withstand oxygen deprivation and arouse them into alertness at birth.
- Newborn babies' large heads and small bodies are odd-looking, but their attractive facial features contribute to adults' desire to pick them up and cuddle them. The **Apgar scale** is used to assess the newborn baby's physical condition at birth.

Approaches to Childbirth

- **Natural**, or **prepared, childbirth** helps reduce stress and pain during labor and delivery. As long as mothers are healthy and assisted by a well-trained doctor or midwife, it is just as safe to give birth at home as in a hospital.
- Pain-relieving drugs are necessary in complicated births. However, when given in large doses, they produce a depressed state in the newborn baby and increase the likelihood of an instrument delivery.

Birth Complications

- Anoxia is a serious birth complication that can damage the brain and other organs. As long as anoxia is not extreme, most affected children catch up in development by the school years.
- Premature births are high among low-income pregnant women and mothers of twins. **Small-for-date** infants usually have longer-lasting problems than **preterm** babies. Some interventions for low-birth-weight infants provide special stimulation in the intensive-care nursery. Others teach parents how to care for and interact with these fragile babies.
- The Kauai study shows that when infants experience birth trauma, a supportive home environment can help restore their growth. Even children with fairly serious birth complications can recover with the help of favorable life events.

Heredity, Environment, and Behavior: A Look Ahead

- **Behavior genetics** is a field devoted to discovering the hereditary and environmental origins of complex characteristics, such as intelligence and personality. Some researchers believe it is useful and possible to determine "how much" each factor contributes to individual differences. These investigators compute **heritability estimates** and **concordance rates** from **kinship studies**.

- Other researchers believe the important question is "how" heredity and environment work together. The concepts of **range of reaction, canalization,** and **genetic–environmental correlation** remind us that development is best understood as a series of complex transactions between nature and nurture.

IMPORTANT TERMS AND CONCEPTS

phenotype (p. 72)
genotype (p. 72)
chromosomes (p. 72)
deoxyribonucleic acid (DNA) (p. 72)
gene (p. 72)
mitosis (p. 74)
gametes (p. 74)
meiosis (p. 74)
crossing over (p. 74)
zygote (p. 74)
identical, or monozygotic, twins (p. 75)
fraternal, or dizygotic, twins (p. 75)
autosomes (p. 76)
sex chromosomes (p. 76)
allele (p. 77)
homozygous (p. 77)
heterozygous (p. 77)
dominant–recessive inheritance (p. 77)
carrier (p. 77)

codominance (p. 80)
mutation (p. 80)
X-linked inheritance (p. 81)
pleiotropism (p. 81)
modifier genes (p. 82)
polygenic inheritance (p. 82)
genetic counseling (p. 86)
prenatal diagnostic methods (p. 86)
amnion (p. 92)
chorion (p. 92)
placenta (p. 92)
umbilical cord (p. 92)
embryo (p. 93)
fetus (p. 94)
vernix (p. 94)
lanugo (p. 95)
age of viability (p. 96)
teratogen (p. 97)

fetal alcohol syndrome (FAS) (p. 100)
fetal alcohol effects (FAE) (p. 100)
Apgar scale (p. 108)
natural, or prepared, childbirth (p. 110)
breech position (p. 113)
Rh factor (p. 113)
preterm (p. 114)
small for date (p. 114)
infant mortality (p. 116)
behavior genetics (p. 119)
heritability estimate (p. 120)
kinship studies (p. 120)
concordance rate (p. 120)
range of reaction (p. 122)
canalization (p. 123)
genetic–environmental
    correlation (p. 123)
niche-picking (p. 124)

C O N N E C T I O N S

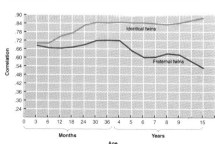

ADAPTIVE VALUE OF REFLEXES. Like breathing and swallowing, some newborn reflexes have survival value. The rooting reflex helps the infant find the mother's nipple. Once the baby locates the nipple, imagine what it would be like if we had to teach the infant the complex lip and tongue movements involved in sucking. If sucking were not automatic, it is unlikely that our species would have survived for a single generation! The swimming reflex helps a baby who is accidentally dropped into a body of water stay afloat, increasing the chances of retrieval by the caregiver.

Other reflexes protect infants from unwanted stimulation. For example, the eye blink reflex helps shield the baby from intense bright light, and the withdrawal reflex is a reaction to unpleasant tactile stimulation. At times, reflexive behavior can reduce infant distress. As any new mother who remembers to bring a pacifier on an outing with her young baby knows, sucking will reduce the mass, uncoordinated activity of a fussy neonate almost immediately.

A few reflexes probably were adaptive during our evolutionary past but no longer serve any special purpose. For example, the Moro or "embracing" reflex is believed to have helped infants cling to their mothers during a time when babies were carried about all day (see photo on page 130). If the baby happened to lose support, the reflex caused the infant to embrace and, along with the powerful grasp reflex (so strong during the first week that it can support the baby's entire weight), regain its hold on the mother's body (Kessen, 1967; Prechtl, 1958).

Finally, several reflexes help parents and babies establish gratifying interaction as soon as possible. An infant who searches for and successfully finds the nipple, sucks easily during feedings, and grasps when her hand is touched encourages parents to respond lovingly and increases their sense of competence as caregivers.

REFLEXES AND THE DEVELOPMENT OF MOTOR SKILLS. Most newborn reflexes disappear during the first 6 months of life, due to a gradual increase in voluntary control over behavior as the brain matures (Touwen, 1984). Currently, researchers disagree about the role reflexes play in the development of voluntary action. Do infant reflexes simply wane before voluntary behavior appears? Or are reflexes an integral and essential prelude to organizing the voluntary skills that come after them?

The fact that babies adapt their reflex actions to changes in stimulation immediately after birth suggests that many reflexes form the basis for complex purposeful behaviors. For example, different finger movements appear in the palmar grasp reflex, depending on how the palm of the hand is stimulated (Touwen, 1978). Similarly, newborn infants quickly adjust the force with which they suck on a nipple, based on how much pressure is required to get the milk (Sameroff, 1968).

A few reflexes that appear to have little purpose may be related to voluntary behavior in subtle ways. For example, the tonic neck reflex may prepare the infant for voluntary reaching. When babies lie on their backs in this "fencing position," they naturally gaze at the hand in front of their eyes. The reflex may encourage them to combine vision with arm movements and, eventually, reach for objects (Knobloch & Pasamanick, 1974).

Certain reflexes drop out in early infancy, but the motor functions involved seem to be renewed later in development. Examples are the palmar grasp, swimming, and stepping responses. In a well-known experiment, babies given daily stimulation of the stepping reflex during the first 2 months not only retained the reflex, but walked on their own several weeks earlier than infants not given this practice (Zelazo, Zelazo, & Kolb, 1972).

Exactly how does early reflexive stimulation contribute to motor control? There are different answers to this question. Philip Zelazo (1983) believes that exercising the stepping reflex promotes development of areas of the cortex that govern voluntary walking. But research by Esther Thelen (1983) provides a more direct explanation. She showed that babies who gained the most weight during the first month of life had the weakest stepping reflex. Also, when the lower part of the infant's body was dipped in water (which lightens the load on the baby's muscles), the reflex reappeared (Thelen, Fisher, & Ridley-Johnson, 1984).

When held upright under the arms, newborn babies show reflexive stepping movements. (INNERVISIONS)

According to Thelen, the stepping reflex drops out because early infant weight gain is not matched by an increase in muscle strength, which permits babies to lift their increasingly heavy legs. But the infant permitted to exercise the stepping reflex builds leg strength early, in the same way that exercise causes an athlete to gain muscle power. Stronger leg muscles, in turn, enable infants to retain the reflex and to stand and walk at an earlier age. Regardless of which position is correct, the work of both Zelazo and Thelen reveals that even though reflexive stepping subsides in many infants, the mechanism responsible for it is used by the brain at a later age.

Do these findings suggest that parents should deliberately exercise newborn stepping and other responses? There is no special reason to do so, since reflexive practice does not produce a child who is a better walker! In the case of the swimming reflex, it is risky to try to build on it. Although young babies placed in a swimming pool will paddle and kick about, they open their mouths and swallow large amounts of water. Consuming too much water lowers the concentration of salt in the baby's blood, which can cause swelling of the brain and seizures. Despite the presence of this remarkable reflex, swimming lessons are best postponed until at least 3 years of age (Micheli, 1985).

THE IMPORTANCE OF ASSESSING NEWBORN REFLEXES. Pediatricians test infant reflexes carefully, especially if the infant has experienced birth trauma, because reflexes provide one way of assessing the health of the baby's nervous system. In brain-damaged infants, reflexes may be weak or absent, or in some cases exaggerated and overly rigid. Brain damage may also be indicated when reflexes persist past the point in development when they should normally disappear. However, individual differences in reflexive responses exist that are not cause for concern. Assessment of newborn reflexes must be combined with other observations of the baby to accurately distinguish normal from abnormal central nervous system functioning (Touwen, 1984).

Newborn States

Throughout the day and night, newborn infants move in and out of six different **states of arousal,** or degrees of sleep and wakefulness, which are described in Table 4.2. During the first month, these states alternate frequently. Quiet alertness is the most fleeting. It usually moves toward fussing and crying relatively quickly. Much to the relief of their fatigued parents, newborns spend the greatest amount of time asleep, taking round-the-clock naps that, on the average, add up to about 16 to 18 hours a day.

Between birth and 2 years, the organization of sleep and wakefulness changes substantially. The decline in total sleep time is not great; the average 2-year-old still needs 12 to 13 hours. Instead, short periods of sleep and wakefulness are gradually put together, and they start to coincide with a night and day schedule. By 4 months, the typical American baby's nightly sleep period resembles that of the parents, in that it is 8 hours long. And over time, infants remain awake for longer daytime periods and need fewer naps—by the second year, only one or two (Berg & Berg, 1987).

These changes in arousal patterns are largely due to brain maturation, but they are affected by the social environment as well. In the United States, night waking is regarded as inconvenient. Parents try hard to get their infants to sleep through the night by offering an evening feeding and putting them down in a separate, quiet room. In doing so, they probably push babies to the limits of their neurological capacities. As the Cultural Influences box on page 135 shows, the practice of isolating infants to promote sleep is rare elsewhere in the world. In non-Western societies, babies typically remain in constant contact with their mothers throughout the day and night, sleeping and waking to nurse at will. For these infants, the average sleep period remains constant, at about 3 hours, from 1

States of arousal
Different degrees of sleep and wakefulness.

TABLE 4.2 Infant States of Arousal

STATE	DESCRIPTION	DAILY DURATION IN NEWBORNS
Regular sleep	The infant is at full rest and shows little or no body activity. The eyelids are closed, no eye movements occur, the face is relaxed, and breathing is slow and regular.	8–9 hours
Irregular sleep	Gentle limb movements, occasional stirring, and facial grimacing occur. Although the eyelids are closed, occasional rapid eye movements can be seen beneath them. Breathing is irregular.	8–9 hours
Drowsiness	The infant is either falling asleep or waking up. The body is less active than in irregular sleep but more active than in regular sleep. The eyes open and close; when open, they have a glazed look. Breathing is even but somewhat faster than in regular sleep.	Varies
Quiet alertness	The infant's body is relatively inactive. The eyes are open and attentive. Breathing is even.	2–3 hours
Waking activity	The infant shows frequent bursts of uncoordinated motor activity. Breathing is very irregular. The face may be relaxed or tense and wrinkled.	2–3 hours
Crying	Waking activity often evolves into crying, which is accompanied by diffuse, vigorous motor activity.	1–2 hours

SOURCE: Wolff, 1966.

to 8 months of age. Only at the end of the first year do they move in the direction of an adultlike sleep–waking schedule (Super & Harkness, 1982).

Although arousal states become more patterned and regular for all infants, striking individual differences in daily rhythms exist that affect parents' attitudes toward and interactions with the baby. A few infants sleep for longer periods at an early age, increasing the rest their parents get and the energy they have for sensitive, responsive care. Babies who cry a great deal require that parents try harder to soothe them. If these efforts are not successful, parents' positive feelings for the infant and sense of competence may suffer. Babies who spend more time in the alert state are likely to receive more social stimulation. And since this state provides opportunities to explore the environment, infants who favor it may have a slight advantage in cognitive development (Moss et al., 1988).

Of the states listed in Table 4.2, the two extremes—sleep and crying—have been of greatest interest to investigators. Each tells us something about normal and abnormal early development.

Rapid-eye-movement (REM) sleep
An "irregular" sleep state in which brain-wave activity is similar to that of the waking state; eyes dart beneath the lids; heart rate, blood pressure, and breathing are uneven; and slight body movements occur.

Non-rapid-eye-movement (NREM) sleep
A "regular" sleep state in which the body is quiet and heart rate, breathing, and brain-wave activity are slow and regular.

SLEEP. A mother and father I know watched one day while their newborn baby slept and wondered why his eyelids and body twitched and his rate of breathing varied, speeding up at some points and slowing down at others. "Is this how babies are supposed to sleep?" they asked, somewhat worried. "Indeed, it is," I responded.

Sleep is made up of at least two states. Irregular, or **rapid-eye-movement (REM) sleep,** is the one these new parents happened to observe. The expression "sleeping like a baby" was probably not meant to describe this state! During REM sleep, the brain and parts of the body are highly active. Electrical brain-wave activity is remarkably similar to that of the waking state. The eyes dart beneath the lids; heart rate, blood pressure, and breathing are uneven; and slight body movements occur. In contrast, during regular, or **non-rapid-eye-movement (NREM) sleep,** the body is quiet, and heart rate, breathing, and brain-wave activity are slow and regular (Dittrichova et al., 1982).

134

While awaiting the birth of a new baby, American middle-class parents typically furnish a special room as the infant's sleeping quarters. Initially, young babies may be placed in a bassinet or cradle in the parents' bedroom for reasons of convenience, but most are moved by 3 to 6 months of age. Many adults in the United States regard this nighttime separation of baby from parent as perfectly natural. Throughout this century, child-rearing advice from experts has strongly encouraged it. For example, Benjamin Spock, in each edition of *Baby and Child Care* from 1945 to the present, states with authority, "I think it is a sensible rule not to take a child into the parents' bed for any reason" (Spock & Rothenberg, 1985, p. 220).

Yet parent–infant "cosleeping" is common around the globe, in industrialized and nonindustrialized societies alike. Japanese children usually lie next to their mothers throughout infancy and early childhood and continue to sleep with a parent or other family member until adolescence (Takahashi, 1990). Among the Mayans of rural Guatemala, mother–infant cosleeping is interrupted only by the birth of a new baby, at which time the older child is moved beside the father or to another bed in the same room (Morelli et al., 1992). Cosleeping is also frequent in some American subcultures. African-American children are more likely than Caucasian-American youngsters to fall asleep with parents and to remain with them for part or all of the night (Lozoff, Wolf, & Davis, 1984). Appalachian children growing up in eastern Kentucky typically sleep with their parents for the first 2 years of life (Abbott, 1992).

Available household space plays a minor role in infant sleeping arrangements. Dominant child-rearing beliefs are much more influential. In one study, researchers interviewed middle-class American mothers and Guatemalan Mayan mothers about their sleeping practices. American mothers frequently mentioned the importance of early independence training, preventing bad habits, and ensuring their own privacy. In contrast, Mayan mothers explained that cosleeping helps build a close parent–child bond, which is necessary for children to learn the ways of people around them. When told that American infants sleep by themselves, Mayan mothers reacted with shock and disbelief, stating that it would be painful for them to leave their babies alone at night (Morelli et al., 1992).

Infant sleeping practices have consequences for other aspects of family life. Sleep problems are not an issue for Mayan parents. Babies doze off in the midst of ongoing social activities, are carried to bed, and nurse on demand without waking the mother. In the United States, getting young children ready for bed often requires an elaborate ritual that consumes a good part of the evening. Many American infants and preschoolers insist on taking security objects to bed with them—a blanket or teddy bear that recaptures the soft, tactile comfort of physical closeness to the mother. In societies in which caregivers are continuously available to babies, children seldom develop these object attachments (Wolf & Lozoff, 1989). Perhaps bedtime struggles, so common in American middle-class homes but rare elsewhere in the world, are related to the stress young children feel when they are required to fall asleep without assistance.

Infant sleeping arrangements, like other parenting practices, are meant to foster culturally valued characteristics in the young. American middle-class parents view babies as dependent beings who must be urged toward independence, and so they usually require them to sleep alone. In contrast, Japanese, Mayan, and Appalachian parents regard young infants as separate beings who need to establish an interdependent relationship with the community to survive.

Like children and adults, newborns alternate between REM and NREM sleep. However, as Figure 4.1 shows, they spend far more time in the REM state than they ever will again throughout their lives. REM sleep accounts for 50 percent of the newborn baby's sleep time. It declines steadily to 20 percent between 3 and 5 years of age, which is about the same percentage it consumes in adulthood.

Another unique feature of the sleep of newborns is that each sleep period begins with a REM cycle; older children and adults do not enter REM until 70 to 100 minutes after falling asleep. By the middle of the first year, infants make the transition to NREM sleep onset, suggesting that they have moved from the primitive sleep organization of the young baby to a more mature sleep organization (Berg & Berg, 1987).

Why do young infants spend so much time in REM sleep? **Autostimulation theory** provides the most widely accepted explanation (Roffwarg, Muzio, & Dement, 1966). In older children and adults, the REM state is associated with dreaming. Babies probably do not dream, at least not in the same way we do. Young infants are believed to have a special need for the stimulation of REM sleep because they spend little time in an alert state, when they can get input from the environment. REM sleep seems to be a way in which the brain stimulates itself. Sleep researchers believe this stimulation is vital for growth of the central nervous

Autostimulation theory
The theory that REM sleep provides stimulation necessary for central nervous system development in young infants.

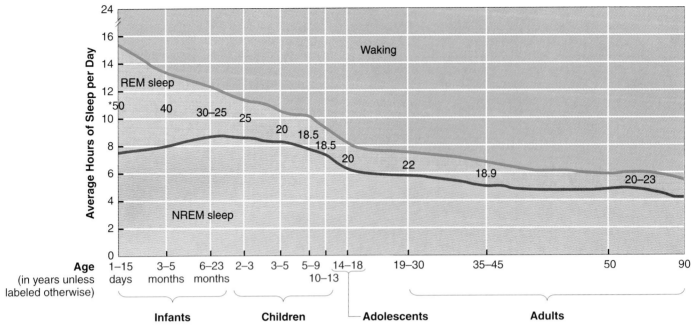

*Percentage REM of total sleep

FIGURE 4.1 Changes in REM sleep, NREM sleep, and the waking state from birth through adulthood. REM sleep declines steadily over the first few years of life. Between 3 and 5 years, it consumes about the same percentage of sleep time as it does in adulthood. In contrast, NREM sleep changes very little over infancy and childhood. It gradually declines in adolescence and adulthood as total sleep time drops off. (Adapted from "Ontogenetic Development of the Human Sleep-Dream Cycle" by H. P. Roffwarg, J. N. Muzio, & W. C. Dement, 1966, *Science, 152*, p. 608. Copyright © 1966 by the AAAS. Revised from original publication by the authors in 1969 on the basis of additional data. Reprinted by permission.)

system. In support of this idea, when newborn babies are encouraged to spend more time awake, their REM sleep declines but their NREM sleep remains unchanged (Boismier, 1977). Also, the percentage of REM sleep is especially great in preterm babies, who are even less able to take advantage of external stimulation than are full-term newborns (Parmelee et al., 1967).

Because the normal sleep behavior of the newborn baby is organized and patterned, observations of sleep states can help identify central nervous system abnormalities. In infants who are brain damaged or who have experienced serious birth trauma, disturbed REM-NREM sleep cycles are often present (Theorell, Prechtl, & Vos, 1974).

CRYING. Crying is the first way that babies communicate, letting parents know they need food, comfort, and stimulation. During the weeks after birth, all infants seem to have some fussy periods during which they are difficult to console. But most of the time, the nature of the cry helps guide parents toward its cause. The baby's cry is a complex auditory stimulus that varies in intensity, from a whimper to a message of all-out distress (Gustafson & Harris, 1990).

Events that cause young infants to cry usually have to do with physical needs. Hunger is the most common cause; but babies may also cry in response to temperature change when undressed, a sudden loud noise, or a painful stimulus. An infant's state often makes a difference in whether the baby will cry in response to a sight or sound. Infants who, when quietly alert, regard a colorful object or the sound of a toy horn with interest and pleasure may react to the same events with a burst of tears when in a state of mild discomfort and diffuse activity (Tennes et al., 1972).

Interestingly, newborn crying can also be caused by the sound of another crying baby. Infants less than a day old cry when they hear a tape recording of another infant's cry, but they do not become distressed at the sound of their own cry. Exactly how young infants make this fine distinction is not understood. Some researchers believe the response reflects an inborn capacity on the part of human beings to react to the suffering of others (Hoffman, 1988; Martin & Clark, 1982).

Adult Responsiveness to Infant Cries. The next time you hear an infant cry, take a moment to observe your own mental and physical reaction. A crying baby stimulates strong feelings of arousal and discomfort in just about anyone—men and women and parents and nonparents alike (Boukydis & Burgess, 1982; Murray, 1985). The powerful effect of the cry is probably innately programmed in all human beings to make sure that babies receive the care and protection they need to survive.

Although parents are not always correct in interpreting the meaning of the baby's cry, experience quickly improves their accuracy (Green, Jones, & Gustafson, 1987). The intensity of the cry along with events that led up to it help parents tell what is wrong. If the baby has not eaten for several hours, it is likely to be hunger. If a period of wakefulness and stimulation preceded the cry, the infant may be tired. A wet diaper, indigestion, or just a desire to be held and cuddled may be the cause. A sharp, piercing cry usually means the baby is in pain. When caregivers hear this sound, they rush to the infant, anxious and worried. Very intense cries are rated as more unpleasant and produce greater physiological arousal in adults, as measured by heart rate and skin conductance (Crowe & Zeskind, 1992). These are adaptive reactions that help ensure an infant in danger will quickly get help.

Soothing a Crying Infant. Even when parents are fairly certain about the cause of the cry, the baby may not always calm down. Fortunately, as Table 4.3 indicates, there are many ways to soothe a crying newborn when feeding and diaper changing do not work. The technique that parents usually try first is lifting the baby to the shoulder; it is also the one that works the best. Being held upright against the parent's gently moving body not only encourages infants to stop crying, but also causes them to become quietly alert and attentive to the environment (Reisman, 1987). Other common soothing methods are offering the baby a pacifier, talking gently or singing, and swaddling (wrapping the baby's body snugly in a blanket). Sometimes a short car ride is helpful. Nestled in a car seat and soothed by the motion and hum of the car motor, babies often fall peacefully asleep.

How quickly and how often should parents respond to their infant's cries? Will reacting promptly and consistently strengthen crying behavior and produce a miniature tyrant? Or will it give infants a sense of confidence that their needs will be met and, over time, reduce fussing and complaining? Available answers to this question are controversial and conflicting. In a well-known study, Sylvia Bell and Mary Ainsworth (1972) found that mothers who delayed or failed to respond to their young baby's cries had infants who cried more at the end of the first year. In addition, these babies developed fewer alternative ways of expressing their desires, such as gestures and vocalizations. The researchers used *ethological theory* to interpret their findings. According to this view, maternal responsiveness is adaptive in that it ensures the infant's basic needs will be met and provides protection from danger. At the same time, it brings baby and mother close together so the mother can respond sensitively to a wide range of infant behaviors and, in the process, encourage the infant to communicate through means other than crying.

Other investigators, however, have challenged Bell and Ainsworth's conclusions. Jacob Gewirtz and Elizabeth Boyd (1977a, 1977b) criticized their methods and, instead, adopted a *behaviorist position.* From this perspective, consistently responding to a crying infant reinforces the crying response and results in a whiny, demanding child. A cross-cultural study carried out in Israel provides support for this position. Infants of Bedouin tribespeople, who believe that babies should never be left to fuss and cry, were compared to home-reared babies as well

TABLE 4.3 *Ways of Soothing a Crying Newborn*	
METHOD	*EXPLANATION*
Lift the baby to the shoulder and rock or walk	This provides a combination of physical contact, upright posture, and motion. It is the most effective soothing technique.
Swaddle the baby	Restricting movement and increasing warmth often soothe a young infant.
Offer a pacifier	Sucking helps babies control their own level of arousal.
Talk softly or play rhythmic sounds	Continuous, monotonous, rhythmic sounds, such as a clock ticking, a fan whirring, or peaceful music, are more effective than intermittent sounds.
Take the baby for a short car ride or walk in a baby carriage; rock the baby in a cradle	Gentle, rhythmic motion of any kind helps lull the baby to sleep.
Massage the baby's body	Stroke the baby's torso and limbs with continuous, gentle motions. This technique is used in some non-Western cultures to relax the baby's muscles.
Combine several of the methods listed above	Stimulating several of the baby's senses at once is often more effective than stimulating only one.
If these methods do not work, permit the baby to cry for a short period of time	Occasionally, a baby responds well to just being put down and will, after a few minutes, fall asleep.

SOURCES: Campos, 1989; Heinl, 1983; Lester, 1985; Reisman, 1987.

as infants raised together in children's houses on Israeli kibbutzim.* Bedouin babies (whose mothers rush to them at the first whimper) fussed and cried the most during the first year, followed by infants living in homes, where there is greater opportunity to respond promptly to a crying baby than on a kibbutz, where babies are cared for in groups (Landau, 1982).

These contrasting theories and findings reveal that there is no easy formula for how parents should respond to their infant's cries. The conditions that prompt infant crying are complex, and parents must make reasoned choices about what to do on the basis of culturally accepted practices, the suspected reason for the cry, its intensity, and the context in which it occurs—for example, in the privacy of the parents' own home or while having dinner at a restaurant. As Figure 4.2 shows, infant crying is greatest during the first 3 months of life, and through most of the first year it peaks in the evenings. Researchers believe that normal difficulties in readjusting the sleep–waking cycle as the central nervous system matures, not parental attention, are responsible for these trends, since they appear in many cultures (St James-Roberts, 1989). Fortunately, crying declines for most babies, and over time it occurs more often for psychological (demands for attention, expressions of frustration) than physical reasons. Both ethological and behaviorist investigators would probably agree that one way parents can lessen older babies' need to cry is to encourage more mature ways of expressing desires.

*A *kibbutz* (plural: kibbutzim) is an Israeli agricultural settlement in which children are reared communally, freeing both parents for full participation in the economic life of the society.

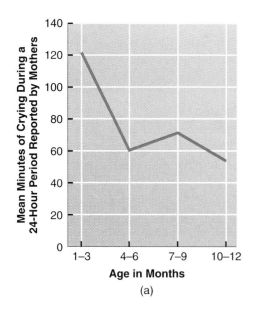

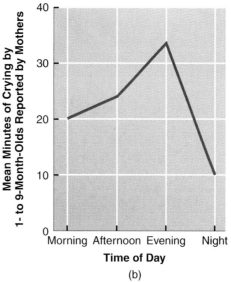

FIGURE 4.2 Crying patterns during the first year of life. A sample of 400 mothers answered questions about how much time their infants spent crying. (a) Crying was greatest during the first 3 months but declined with age. The largest drop occurred after 3 months. (b) During the first 9 months, crying peaked in the evening. (Adapted from St James-Roberts & Halil, 1991.)

Like reflexes and sleep patterns, the infant's cry offers a clue to central nervous system distress. The cries of brain-damaged babies and those who have experienced prenatal and birth complications are often shrill and piercing (Huntington, Hans, & Zeskind, 1990; Lester, 1987). Most parents respond to a sick baby's call for help with extra care and attention. In some cases, however, the cry is so unpleasant and the infant so difficult to soothe that parents become frustrated, resentful, and angry. Research reveals that preterm and sick babies are more likely than healthy infants to be abused by their parents. Often these parents mention a high-pitched, grating cry as one factor that caused them to lose control and harm the baby (Boukydis, 1985; Frodi, 1985).

Neonatal Behavioral Assessment

A variety of instruments permit doctors, nurses, and child development specialists to assess the overall behavioral status of the infant during the newborn period. The most widely used of these tests is T. Berry Brazelton's (1984) **Neonatal Behavioral Assessment Scale (NBAS).** With it, the examiner can look at the baby's reflexes, responsiveness to physical and social stimuli, state changes, and other reactions. Table 4.4 lists some examples of NBAS items.

Neonatal assessment is useful for several reasons. When scores are combined with information from a physical examination, they permit all but a very few cases of severe central nervous system impairment to be diagnosed in the first few weeks of life (Amiel-Tison, 1985). The NBAS and other similar instruments have also helped investigators describe the effects of pregnancy and birth complications on infant behavior (Brazelton, Nugent, & Lester, 1987). In fact, special assessment scales have been developed for use with preterm infants (Als et al., 1980; Korner et al., 1981).

The NBAS has been given to many infants around the world. As a result, researchers have learned a great deal about individual and cultural differences in newborn behavior and how a baby's reactions can be maintained or changed by child-rearing practices. For example, NBAS scores of Asian and Native American babies reveal that they are less irritable than Caucasian infants. Mothers in these cultures often encourage their babies' calm dispositions through swaddling, close physical contact, and nursing at the first signs of discomfort (Chisholm, 1989; Freedman & Freedman, 1969; Murett-Wagstaff & Moore, 1989). In contrast, the poor NBAS scores of undernourished infants born in Zambia, Africa, are quickly changed by the way their mothers care for them. The Zambian mother carries her

Neonatal Behavioral Assessment Scale (NBAS)

A test developed to assess the behavioral status of the infant during the newborn period.

**TABLE 4.4   Sample Items from Brazelton's
Neonatal Behavioral Assessment Scale**

SAMPLE ITEM	DESCRIPTION
Reflexes	See Table 4.1 for examples.
Sensory and motor capacities	
Hearing	The examiner speaks softly into one of the infant's ears. The baby's ability to turn toward the sound is recorded.
Vision	A brightly colored ball is moved horizontally and then vertically before the baby's eyes. The baby's ability to track the ball is recorded.
Alertness	The overall alertness of the baby is rated.
Defensive movements	A small cloth is held lightly over the infant's eyes. The baby's effort to work free of the cloth is recorded.
State changes	
Irritability	The number of times the infant fusses and the kind of stimuli that lead to irritability are recorded.
Cuddliness	The infant's willingness to relax and mold to the examiner's body when held in an alert state is recorded.
Consolability	The effort the examiner must exert to bring the baby from an upset to a quiet state is recorded.
Autonomic reactivity	
Tremulousness	Tremors of the infant's body are rated. If severe, tremulousness indicates central nervous system irritation.
Lability of skin color	Changes in skin color during the examination are noted. A normal newborn shows mild color changes after being undressed, disturbed, or upset, but the original color returns quickly. This reaction is difficult to score in nonwhite babies.

SOURCE: Brazelton, 1984.

baby about on her hip all day, providing a rich variety of sensory stimulation. As a result, by 1 week of age, a once unresponsive newborn has been transformed into an alert, contented baby (Brazelton, Koslowski, & Tronick, 1976).

Can you tell from these examples why a single NBAS score is not a good predictor of later development? Since newborn behavior and parenting styles combine to shape development, changes in NBAS scores over the first week or two of life (rather than a single score) provide the best estimate of the baby's ability to recover from the stress of birth. NBAS "recovery curves" predict intelligence with moderate success well into the preschool years (Brazelton, Nugent, & Lester, 1987).

The NBAS has also been used to help parents get to know their infants. In some hospitals, the examination is given in the presence of parents to teach them about their newborn baby's capacities and unique characteristics. These programs enhance early parent–infant interaction in many types of participants—mothers and fathers, adolescents and adults, low-income and middle-income parents, and full-term and preterm newborns (Brazelton, Nugent, & Lester, 1987; Tedder,

*S*imilar to women in the Zambian
culture, this Inuit mother of Northern
Canada carries her baby about all day,
providing close physical contact and a rich
variety of stimulation. (EASTCOTT/MOMATIAK;
WOODFIN CAMP & ASSOCIATES)

1991). Although lasting effects on development have not been demonstrated, NBAS-based interventions are clearly useful in helping the parent–infant relationship get off to a good start.

Learning Capacities

Learning refers to changes in behavior as the result of experience. Babies come into the world with a built-in set of learning mechanisms that permit them to profit from experience immediately. Infants are capable of two basic forms of learning, which were introduced in Chapter 1: classical and operant conditioning. Now we will discuss them in greater detail. Besides conditioning, infants learn through a natural preference they have for novel stimulation. Finally, one early learning mechanism is likely to surprise you: newborn babies have a remarkable ability to imitate the facial expressions and gestures of adults.

CLASSICAL CONDITIONING. Earlier in this chapter, we discussed a variety of newborn reflexes. These make **classical conditioning** possible in the young infant. In this form of learning, a new stimulus is paired with a stimulus that leads to a reflexive response. Once the baby's nervous system makes the connection between the two stimuli, then the new stimulus by itself produces the behavior.

Recall from Chapter 1 that Russian physiologist Ivan Pavlov first demonstrated classical conditioning in some famous research he conducted with dogs (see pages 17–18). Classical conditioning is of great value to human infants, as well as other animals, because it helps them recognize which events usually occur together in the everyday world. As a result, they can anticipate what is about to happen next, and the environment becomes more orderly and predictable (Rovee-Collier, 1987). Let's take a closer look at the steps of classical conditioning.

Imagine a mother of a new baby, who gently strokes her infant's forehead each time she settles down to nurse the baby. Soon the mother notices that every time the baby's forehead is stroked, he makes active sucking movements. The infant has been classically conditioned. Here is how it happened (see Figure 4.3):

1. Before learning takes place, an **unconditioned stimulus (UCS)** must consistently produce a reflexive, or **unconditioned, response (UCR).** In our example, the stimulus of sweet breast milk (UCS) resulted in sucking (UCR).

Classical conditioning
A form of learning that involves associating a neutral stimulus with a stimulus that leads to a reflexive response.

Unconditioned stimulus (UCS)
In classical conditioning, a stimulus that leads to a reflexive response.

Unconditioned response (UCR)
In classical conditioning, a reflexive response that is produced by an unconditioned stimulus (UCS).

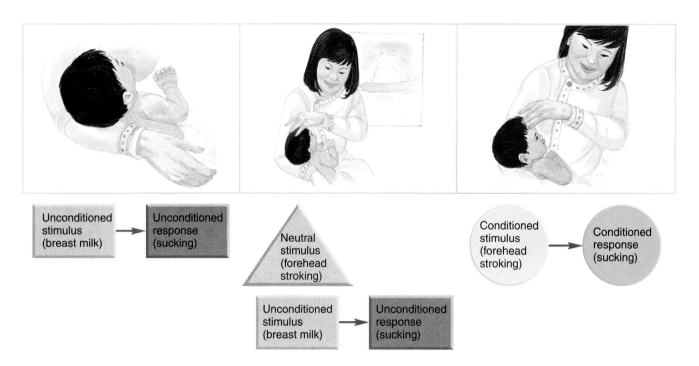

FIGURE 4.3 The steps of classical conditioning. The example here shows how a mother classically conditioned her baby to make sucking movements by stroking his forehead at the beginning of feedings.

2. To produce learning, a neutral stimulus that does not lead to the reflex is presented at about the same time as the UCS. Ideally, the neutral stimulus should occur just before the UCS. The mother stroked the baby's forehead as each nursing period began. Therefore, the stroking (neutral stimulus) was paired with the taste of breast milk (UCS).
3. If learning has occurred, the neutral stimulus by itself produces the reflexive response. The neutral stimulus is then called a **conditioned stimulus (CS),** and the response it elicits is called a **conditioned response (CR).** We know that the baby has been classically conditioned because stroking his forehead outside of the feeding situation (CS) results in sucking (CR).

If the CS is presented alone enough times without being paired with the UCS, the CR will no longer occur. In other words, if the mother strokes the infant's forehead again and again without feeding him, the baby will gradually stop sucking in response to stroking. This is referred to as **extinction.** In a classical conditioning experiment, the occurrence of responses to the CS during the extinction phase shows that learning has taken place.

Although young babies can be classically conditioned, they will not respond to just any pairing of stimuli. To be easily learned, the association between a UCS and a CS must have survival value. Not surprisingly, most CRs of newborns occur in the feeding situation. They are adaptive because they increase the efficiency of food-getting behavior (Blass, Ganchrow, & Steiner, 1984). In fact, babies are so sensitive to stimulus cues surrounding feeding that even the passage of time between meals can serve as an effective CS. Most newborns are fed about every 3 to 4 hours. As the end of this time period approaches (CS), mouthing, sucking, and salivation (CR) increase in frequency and intensity (Rovee-Collier, 1987).

Some responses are very difficult to classically condition in young infants. Fear is one of them. Until the last half of the first year, infants do not have the motor skills to escape unpleasant events. Because they depend on their parents for this kind of protection, they do not have a biological need to form these associa-

Conditioned stimulus (CS)
In classical conditioning, a neutral stimulus that through pairing with an unconditioned stimulus (UCS) leads to a new response (CR).

Conditioned response (CR)
In classical conditioning, an originally reflexive response that is produced by a conditioned stimulus (CS).

Extinction
In classical conditioning, decline of the CR as a result of presenting the CS enough times without the UCS.

tions. But between 8 and 12 months, the conditioning of fear is easily accomplished, as the famous example of little Albert, conditioned by John Watson to withdraw and cry at the sight of a furry white rat, clearly indicates. Return to Chapter 1, page 18, to review this well-known experiment. Then test your knowledge of classical conditioning by identifying the UCS, UCR, CS, and CR in Watson's study. In Chapter 10, we will discuss the development of fear, as well as other emotional reactions, in detail.

Finally, an infant's state often affects classical conditioning. For example, when a baby is highly aroused and crying, the sight of the mother or the sound of her footsteps (CS) predicts relief from discomfort. Under these conditions, infants quickly learn to stop crying and to mouth and suck (CR) in preparation for feeding. However, when the infant is quietly alert, the mother's approach does not have this meaning, and the same response rarely appears (Gekoski, Rovee-Collier, & Carulli-Rabinowitz, 1983). When we look at infant classical conditioning research as a whole, it is clear that babies are not indiscriminate reactors to environmental events. At the very least, the adaptive significance of what is to be learned and the state of the baby are major influences on the range of associations infants will make.

OPERANT CONDITIONING. In classical conditioning, babies build up expectations about stimulus events in the environment, but their behavior does not influence the stimuli that occur. **Operant conditioning** is quite different. In this form of learning, babies act (or operate) on the environment, and stimuli that follow their behavior change the probability that the behavior will occur again. A stimulus that increases the occurrence of a response is called a **reinforcer.** Removing a desirable stimulus or introducing an unpleasant one to decrease the occurrence of a response is called **punishment.**

Operant conditioning of newborn babies has been demonstrated in many studies. Because the young infant can control only a few behaviors, successful operant conditioning is limited to head-turning and sucking responses. For example, newborns quickly learn to turn their heads to the side when this response is followed by a sugar-water reinforcer (Siqueland & Lipsitt, 1966). Young infants also vary their sucking according to the sweetness of the liquid they receive. When water is delivered after a sugar solution, newborns indicate their dislike of the water by reducing their rate of sucking (Lipsitt & Werner, 1981).

Stimulus variety and change are just as reinforcing to young infants as food. Researchers have created special laboratory conditions in which the baby's rate of sucking on a nipple produces a variety of interesting sights and sounds. Newborns will suck faster to see visual designs or to hear music and human voices (Rovee-Collier, 1987). As these findings suggest, operant conditioning has become a powerful tool for finding out what babies can perceive.

As infants get older, operant conditioning expands to include a wider range of stimuli and responses. For example, Carolyn Rovee-Collier places special mobiles over the cribs of 2- to 6-month-olds. When the baby's foot is attached to the mobile with a long cord, it takes only a few minutes for the infant to start kicking vigorously (Rovee-Collier & Hayne, 1987; Shields & Rovee-Collier, 1992). As we will see shortly, this technique has yielded important information about infant memory. And in Chapter 6, we will discover that it has also been used to study babies' ability to categorize stimulus events.

Operant conditioning soon modifies parents' and babies' reactions to each other. As the infant gazes into the adult's eyes, the adult looks and smiles back, and then the infant looks and smiles again. The behavior of each partner reinforces the other, and as a result, both parent and baby continue their pleasurable interaction. As Chapter 10 will reveal, this kind of contingent responsiveness plays an important role in the development of infant–caregiver attachment.

Recall from Chapter 1 that classical and operant conditioning originated with behaviorism, an approach that views the child as a relatively passive responder to environmental stimuli. If you look carefully at the findings just described, you will

Operant conditioning

A form of learning in which a spontaneous behavior is followed by a stimulus that changes the probability that the behavior will occur again.

Reinforcer

In operant conditioning, a stimulus that increases the occurrence of a response.

Punishment

In operant conditioning, removing a desirable stimulus or presenting an unpleasant one to decrease the occurrence of a response.

In **sudden infant death syndrome (SIDS)**, a baby stops breathing, usually during the night, and dies silently without apparent cause. SIDS is the leading cause of infant mortality between 1 and 12 months of age in industrialized nations. It accounts for over one-third of these deaths in the United States (Cotton, 1990; Wilson & Neidich, 1991). The tragedy is especially difficult for parents to bear because of the lack of definite answers as to why SIDS occurs. However, more information about the characteristics of SIDS victims has recently been discovered, and promising hypotheses are being followed up with new research.

Although the precise cause of SIDS is not known, infants who die of it show physical abnormalities from the very beginning. Early medical records of SIDS babies reveal higher rates of prematurity and low birth weight, poor Apgar scores, and limp muscle tone (Buck et al., 1989; Lipsitt, Sturner, & Burke, 1979; Shannon et al., 1987). Abnormal heart rate and respiration, disturbances in sleep-waking activity, and delayed central nervous system development (based on autopsy reports) are also involved (Froggatt et al., 1988; Kinney et al., 1991). At the time of death, over half of babies have a mild respiratory infection. This seems to increase the chances of respiratory failure in an already vulnerable infant (Cotton, 1990).

One hypothesis about the cause of SIDS is that problems in brain functioning prevent these babies from learning how to respond when their survival is threatened—for example, when respiration is suddenly interrupted (Lipsitt, 1990). Between 2 and 4 months of age, when SIDS is most likely to occur, reflexes decline and are replaced by voluntary, learned responses. Respiratory and muscular weak-

nesses of SIDS infants may stop them from acquiring behaviors that replace defensive reflexes. As a result, when breathing difficulties occur during sleep, they do not wake up, shift the position of their bodies, or cry out for help. Instead, they simply give in to oxygen deprivation and death.

In an effort to reduce the occurrence of SIDS, researchers are studying environmental factors associated with it. A baby of a smoking mother is two to three times more likely to die of SIDS than is an infant of a nonsmoker. Prenatal abuse of drugs that depress central nervous system functioning (opiates and barbiturates) increases the risk of SIDS tenfold (Kandall & Gaines, 1991). Other consistent findings are that SIDS babies are more likely to sleep on their stomachs than on their backs, and often they are wrapped very warmly in clothing and blankets (Fleming et al., 1990). Why are these factors associated with SIDS? Scientists think that smoke, depressant drugs, and excessive body warmth (which can be encouraged by putting babies down on their stomachs) strain the respiratory control system in the brain. In an at-risk baby, the respiratory center may stop functioning.

Can simple procedures like quitting smoking, changing an infant's sleeping position, and removing a few bedclothes prevent SIDS? More research is needed to find out for sure. In the meantime, surviving family members require a great deal of help to overcome a sudden and unexpected infant death. Parent support groups, which offer comfort and understanding from others who have experienced the same tragedy, exist in many communities.

---

see that young babies are not passive. Instead, they use any means they can to explore and control their surroundings. In fact, when infants' environments are so disorganized that their behavior does not lead to predictable outcomes, developmental problems, ranging from intellectual retardation to apathy and depression, can result (Cicchetti & Aber, 1986; Seligman, 1975). In addition, as the From Research to Practice box above reveals, deficits in brain functioning may prevent some babies from actively learning certain lifesaving responses; and the absence of such responses may lead to sudden infant death syndrome, a major cause of infant mortality.

Sudden infant death syndrome (SIDS)

Death of a seemingly healthy baby, who stops breathing, usually during the night, without apparent cause.

Habituation

A gradual reduction in the strength of a response as the result of repetitive stimulation.

Dishabituation

Increase in responsiveness after stimulation changes.

HABITUATION AND DISHABITUATION: WINDOW INTO EARLY MEMORY. Take a moment to walk through the rooms of the library, your home, or wherever you happen to be reading this book. What did you notice? Probably those things that are new and different caught your attention first, such as a recently purchased picture on the wall or a piece of furniture that has been moved. At birth, the human brain is set up to be attracted to novelty. **Habituation** refers to a gradual reduction in the strength of a response due to repetitive stimulation. Looking, heart rate, and respiration may all decline, indicating a loss of interest. Once this has occurred, a new stimulus—some kind of change in the environment—causes responsiveness to return to a high level. This recovery is called **dishabituation**. Habituation and dishabituation permit infants to focus their attention on those aspects of the environment they know least about. As a result, learning is more efficient.

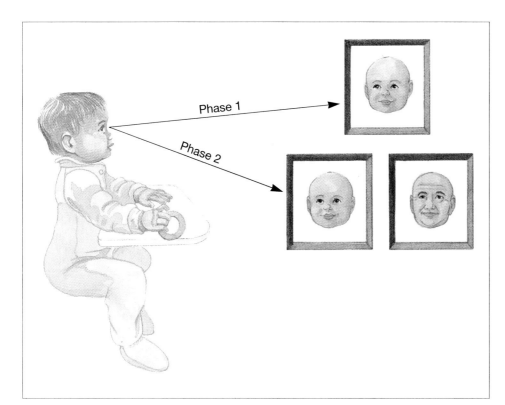

FIGURE 4.4 Example of how the
habituation–dishabituation sequence
can be used to study infant perception
and memory. In Phase 1, infants are
shown (habituated to) a photo of a
baby. In Phase 2, infants are again
shown the baby photo, but this time it
appears alongside a photo of a bald-
headed man. Infants dishabituated to
(spent more time looking at) the photo
of the man, indicating that they
remembered the baby and perceived
the man's face as different from it.
(Adapted from Fagan & Singer, 1979.)

The habituation–dishabituation sequence provides researchers with a mar-
velous window into early memory development. Later in this chapter, we will see
that it is also used to study infant perceptual capacities. Let's look at an example
that illustrates how researchers capitalize on these responses. In one study, habituation and dishabituation were used to find out whether 5- and 6-month-olds
could discriminate two similar photos—one of a baby and the other of a bald-
headed man (see Figure 4.4). In Phase 1 (habituation), infants were shown the
baby photo for a short time. Next, in Phase 2 (dishabituation), the baby photo was
paired with a photo of a bald-headed man. Because infants spent more time looking at the bald-headed man than the baby, the researchers concluded that infants
both remembered the baby face and perceived the man as new and different from
it (Fagan & Singer, 1979).

Habituation–dishabituation research reveals that neonates discriminate and
remember a wide variety of distinct sights, sounds, and smells. Memory for visual
stimuli has been found even in 6-day-old infants born 5 weeks preterm (Werner &
Siqueland, 1978). Very young babies need long exposure times to stimuli to
demonstrate the habituation–dishabituation response. With age, memory processing becomes more efficient. By the middle of the first year, infants require only 5
to 10 seconds of study time for immediate recognition. And gradually, they make
finer distinctions among visual stimuli and remember them longer—at 3 months
for about 24 hours; by the end of the first year for several days; and in the case of
very familiar stimuli, such as a photo of the human face, even weeks (Fagan, 1973;
Martin, 1975).

At this point, let's note that habituation–dishabituation research tells us how long
babies retain a new stimulus in the context of the laboratory, but it underestimates
their ability to remember real-world events they can actively control. Recall Rovee-
Collier's operant conditioning research, in which babies learned to make a mobile
move through foot kicking. In a series of studies, she showed that 2- and 3-month-
olds can remember how to activate the mobile for as long as 2 weeks after they were
first trained (Linde, Morrongiello, & Rovee-Collier, 1985; Rovee-Collier, Patterson, &

Hayne, 1985). Rovee-Collier's findings also highlight a curious feature of infant memory. During the first 6 months of life, it becomes increasingly *context-dependent*. That is, if babies are not tested in the same situation in which they were trained (a crib with the identical patterned bumper), their retention is severely disrupted. According to Rovee-Collier, context-dependent memory is adaptive for infants. It protects early memories from being retrieved in inappropriate situations, where they can be easily modified or extinguished (Rovee-Collier & Shyi, 1992).

Although dishabituation to visual stimuli does not provide a full picture of early memory development, at present, it is the best available infant predictor of later cognitive development. Correlations between it and 3- to 6-year-old IQ consistently range from the .30s to the .60s (Bornstein & Sigman, 1986; Rose, Feldman, & Wallace, 1988, 1992). Researchers believe that the habituation–dishabituation sequence is an especially effective early index of intelligence because it taps basic cognitive processes—attention, memory, and response to novelty—that underlie intelligent behavior at all ages. In Chapter 8, we will describe a new infant intelligence test made up entirely of habituation–dishabituation items.

So far, our discussion has considered only one type of memory—*recognition*. It is the simplest form of remembering because all babies have to do is indicate (by looking or kicking) whether a new stimulus is identical or similar to one previously experienced. *Recall* is a second, more challenging form of memory, since it involves remembering something that is not present. Can infants engage in recall? By the end of the first year, they can, since they find hidden objects and imitate the actions of others hours or days after they first observed the behavior. Recall undergoes much more extended and elaborate development than recognition. We will take it up in more detail in Chapter 7.

NEWBORN IMITATION. For many years, researchers believed that **imitation**—learning by copying the behavior of another person—was beyond the capacity of very young infants. They were not expected to imitate until several months after birth (Bayley, 1969; Piaget, 1945/1951). Then, a growing number of studies began to report that newborns come into the world with the ability to imitate the behavior of their caregivers.

Figure 4.5 shows examples of responses obtained in two of the first studies of newborn imitation (Field et al., 1982; Meltzoff & Moore, 1977). As you can see, babies from 2 days to several weeks old appeared to imitate a wide variety of adult facial expressions. These findings are so extraordinary that it is not surprising they have been challenged. Other researchers who tried to get young babies to imitate were much less successful (see, for example, Abravanel & Sigafoos, 1984; Kaitz et al., 1988). Yet in all of these follow-ups, exposure of newborns to labor and delivery medication could have interfered with this amazing capacity. In one well-controlled investigation, infants born in rural Nepal were tested minutes after a drug-free birth, when they were bright-eyed and alert. They showed clear imitation of two facial expressions: lips widened and lips pursed (Reissland, 1988). Another study of alert newborns found that besides facial expressions, they can imitate head movements as well (Meltzoff & Moore, 1989).

Today, few researchers question the neonate's capacity to imitate. It has been demonstrated in over a dozen investigations. The underlying mechanism responsible for newborn imitation is more controversial. Imitative responses are more difficult to induce in babies 2 to 3 months old than just after birth. Some researchers regard the capacity as little more than a set of *fixed action patterns*—innately triggered, automatic responses to particular stimuli that recede with age, much like a reflex (Kaitz et al., 1988; Reissland, 1988). But Andrew Meltzoff (1990) points out that newborns model a wide variety of facial expressions, and they do so even after short delays—when the adult is no longer demonstrating the behavior. These observations suggest that the capacity is flexible and voluntary. Furthermore, new evidence reveals that imitation does not recede as reflexes do. Babies several months old often do not imitate an adult's behavior right away because they try to

Imitation
Learning by copying the behavior of another person. Also called modeling or observational learning.

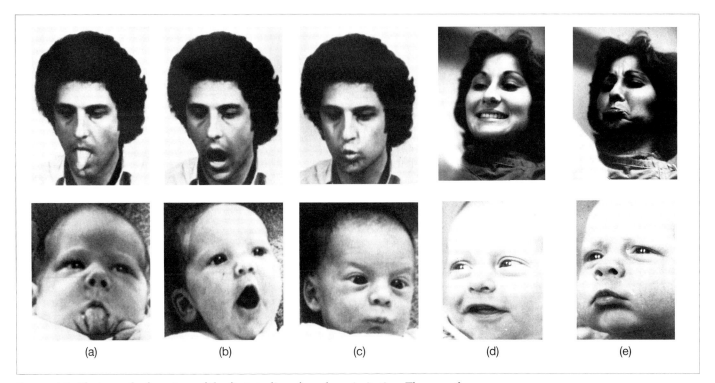

(a)   (b)   (c)   (d)   (e)

FIGURE 4.5 Photographs from two of the first studies of newborn imitation. Those on the left show 2- to 3-week-old infants imitating tongue protrusion (a), mouth opening (b), and lip protrusion (c) of an adult experimenter. Those on the right show 2-day-old infants imitating happy (d) and sad (e) adult facial expressions. (From "Imitation of Facial and Manual Gestures by Human Neonates" by A. N. Meltzoff & M. K. Moore, 1977, *Science, 198*, p. 75; and "Discrimination and Imitation of Facial Expressions by Neonates" by T. M. Field et al., 1982, *Science, 218*, p. 180. Copyright © 1977 and 1982, respectively, by the AAAS. Reprinted by permission.)

play social games of the sort they are used to in face-to-face interaction—smiling, cooing, and waving their arms. When an adult model displays a gesture repeatedly, older babies soon get down to business and imitate (Meltzoff & Moore, 1992).

According to Meltzoff, neonates imitate in much the same way we do—by actively matching body movements they "see" with ones they "feel" themselves make. Later in this chapter, we will encounter evidence that young infants are surprisingly adept at coordinating information across sensory systems. These findings provide additional support for Meltzoff's view of newborn imitation as a deliberate, versatile capacity.

As we will see in Chapter 6, infants' capacity to imitate changes greatly over the first 2 years. But however limited it is at birth, imitation provides the baby with a powerful means of learning. Using imitation, newborns begin to explore their social world, getting to know people by sharing behavioral states with them. In the process, babies notice equivalences between their own actions and those of others, and they start to find out about themselves (see Chapter 11). Furthermore, by capitalizing on imitation, adults can get infants to express desirable behaviors, and once they do, adults can encourage these further. Finally, caregivers take great pleasure in a baby who imitates their facial gestures and actions. Newborn imitation clearly seems to be one of those capacities that helps get the infant's relationship with parents off to a good start.

The newborn baby is equipped with a wide variety of capacities for relating to the surrounding world. Reflexes are the neonate's most obvious organized patterns of behavior. Some, like sucking, have survival value, whereas others, like stepping, form the basis for motor skills that will develop later. Infants move in

Brief Review

and out of six states of arousal that become more organized and predictable with age. Sleep is the dominant state; young infants spend far more time in REM sleep than they will at later ages. A crying baby stimulates strong feelings of discomfort in nearby adults. Fortunately, a crying infant can be soothed in many ways. Neonatal behavioral assessment permits doctors, nurses, and researchers to assess the remarkable capacities of newborn babies.

Infants are marvelously equipped to learn immediately after birth. Through classical conditioning, babies acquire stimulus associations that have survival value. Operant conditioning permits them to control events in the surrounding world. The habituation–dishabituation sequence reveals that even newborns are attracted to novelty and will decrease attention to repetitive stimulation and that recognition memory improves steadily with age. Finally, newborns' amazing ability to imitate the facial expressions and gestures of adults may promote early social interaction with caregivers.

MOTOR DEVELOPMENT IN INFANCY

Virtually all parents eagerly await their infant's mastery of new motor skills. Baby books are filled with proud notations as soon as children hold up their heads, reach for objects, sit by themselves, crawl, and walk alone. Parents' enthusiasm for these achievements makes perfect sense. They are, indeed, milestones of development. With each new motor skill, babies master their bodies and the environment in a new way. For example, sitting alone grants infants an entirely different perspective on the world compared to when they spent much of the day lying on their backs and stomachs. Voluntary reaching permits babies to find out about objects by acting on them. And when infants can move on their own, their opportunities for exploration are multiplied.

Babies' motor achievements have a powerful effect on their social relationships. For example, parents start to restrict the activities of a beginning crawler in ways that were unnecessary when the baby, placed on a blanket, would stay there! New motor skills, such as pointing to and showing toys, permit infants to communicate more effectively. In response, parents devote less time to physical care and more to game playing and verbal requests. Babies' expressions of delight—laughing, smiling, and babbling—as they work on new motor competencies trigger pleasurable reactions in others, which encourage infants' efforts further (Mayes & Zigler, 1992). In this way, motor skills, social competencies, cognition, and language develop together and support one another.

The Organization and Sequence of Motor Development

Gross motor development refers to control over actions that help infants get around in the environment, such as crawling, standing, and walking. In contrast, *fine motor development* has to do with smaller movements, such as reaching and grasping. The Milestones table on the following page shows the average age at which a variety of gross and fine motor skills are achieved during infancy and toddlerhood. Most children follow this sequence fairly closely.

Notice that the table also presents the age ranges during which the majority of infants accomplish each skill. These ranges indicate that although the sequence of motor development is fairly uniform across children, large individual differences exist in the rate at which motor development proceeds. Also, a baby who is a late reacher is not necessarily going to be a late crawler or walker. We would be concerned about a child's development only if many motor skills were seriously delayed.

Look at the table once more, and you will see that there is organization and direction to the infant's motor achievements. First, motor control of the head

MILESTONES
GROSS AND FINE MOTOR DEVELOPMENT
IN THE FIRST TWO YEARS

Motor Skill	Average Age Achieved	Age Range in Which 90 Percent of Infants Achieve the Skill
When held upright, head erect and steady	6 weeks	3 weeks–4 months
When prone, lifts self by arms	2 months	3 weeks–4 months
Rolls from side to back	2 months	3 weeks–5 months
Reaches for dangling ring	3 months	1–5 months
Grasps cube	3 months, 3 weeks	2–7 months
Rolls from back to side	$4\frac{1}{2}$ months	2–7 months
Sits alone	7 months	5–9 months
Crawls	7 months	5–11 months
Pulls to stand	8 months	5–12 months
Plays pat-a-cake	9 months, 3 weeks	7–15 months
Stands alone	11 months	9–16 months
Walks alone	11 months, 3 weeks	9–17 months
Builds tower of two cubes	13 months, 3 weeks	10–19 months
Scribbles vigorously	14 months	10–21 months
Walks up stairs with help	16 months	12–23 months
Jumps in place	23 months, 2 weeks	17–30 months

SOURCE: Bayley, 1969.

NOTE: These milestones represent overall age trends. Individual differences exist in the precise age at which each milestone is attained.

comes before control of the arms and trunk, and control of the arms and trunk is achieved before control of the legs. This head-to-tail sequence is called the **cephalocaudal trend.** Second, motor development proceeds from the center of the body outward, in that head, trunk, and arm control is mastered before coordination of the hands and fingers. This is the **proximodistal trend.** Physical growth during the prenatal period, as well as during infancy and childhood (see Chapter 5), follows these same trends. Because physical and motor development conform to the same general sequence, the cephalocaudal and proximodistal trends are believed to be genetically determined, maturational patterns.

Cephalocaudal trend
An organized pattern of physical growth and motor control that proceeds from head to tail.

Proximodistal trend
An organized pattern of physical growth and motor control that proceeds from the center of the body outward.

*L*ike the Hopi Indians studied by Wayne and Marsena Dennis, this Shoshone baby spends the day tightly bound to a cradle board. The Dennises found that confinement to the cradle board did not hinder the development of walking. They concluded that the emergence of motor skills is largely due to biological maturation. Later studies revealed that both maturation and experience influence the course of motor development. (VICTOR ENGELBERT/PHOTO RESEARCHERS)

Systems of action
In motor development, combinations of previously acquired skills that lead to more advanced ways of exploring and controlling the environment.

Motor Skills as Complex Systems of Action

We must be careful not to think of motor skills as a series of isolated, unrelated accomplishments. Earlier in this century, researchers made this mistake; but today we know that motor development is a matter of acquiring increasingly complex **systems of action**. When motor skills work as a system, separate abilities blend together, each cooperating with others to produce more advanced ways of exploring and controlling the environment. During infancy, new systems of action emerge constantly. For example, control of the head and upper chest are combined into sitting with support. Kicking, rocking on all fours, and reaching are gradually put together into crawling. Then crawling, standing, and stepping are united into walking alone (Hofsten, 1989; Pick, 1989; Thelen, 1989).

The way simple motor acts are reorganized into more effective motor systems is most obvious in the area of fine motor skills. As we will see when we discuss the development of voluntary reaching, the various components—grasping, looking, and moving the arms—at first emerge independently. Then, as babies become increasingly aware of a world of tantalizing things to be explored, they perfect these skills and combine them into successful reaching for objects (Manchester, 1988). Once reaching is accomplished, infants can coordinate it with other actions to produce even more complex skills, such as stacking blocks, putting objects into containers, and eating with a spoon (Connolly & Dagleish, 1989).

Maturation, Experience, and the Development of Motor Skills

What explains the appearance of new motor skills? Over the past half-century, cross-cultural research has suggested some thought-provoking answers. The earliest of these studies, carried out in the 1930s and 1940s, led investigators to the one-sided conclusion that motor development was almost entirely due to biological maturation. For example, Wayne and Marsena Dennis (1940) studied age of walking among the Hopi Indians. Some Hopi mothers bound their infants to cradle-boards throughout the day and night, whereas others had given up this practice. Even though cradle-board babies could not move their arms, trunk, and legs, they walked at the same age as unbound infants—a finding that seemed to suggest that experience was unimportant. But note how comparisons like this pay little attention to subtle experiences that could have affected the motor skill in question. For example, the upright position of the cradle board and the baby's opportunity to move freely when taken off it at night might have made up for lack of activity during the day.

Much later in his career, when Dennis (1960) observed infants raised in very deprived Iranian institutions, he realized that early movement opportunities and a stimulating environment do contribute to motor development. The Iranian babies spent their days lying on their backs in cribs, without toys to play with. Most did not move about on their own until after 2 years of age. When they finally did move, the constant experience of lying on their backs led them to scoot in a sitting position rather than crawl on their hands and knees the way infants raised in more normal situations do. This preference for scooting probably slowed the infants' motor development even further. Babies who scoot come up against furniture with their feet, not their hands. Consequently, they are far less likely to pull themselves to a standing position in preparation for walking. Indeed, only 15 percent of the Iranian orphans walked alone by 3 to 4 years of age.

Refer to the Cultural Influences box on pages 152–153 for additional evidence on how experience affects motor development—this time in Africa and the West Indies. Putting all these findings together, we must conclude that early motor skills, like other aspects of development, are due to complex transactions between nature and nurture. Although heredity ensures that all babies will follow a similar sequence of motor development, early experience can alter this sequence to some degree. And experience can greatly change the rate at which motor milestones are reached.

Fine Motor Development: The Special Case of
Voluntary Reaching

151

CHAPTER FOUR
_____

INFANCY: EARLY LEARNING,
MOTOR SKILLS, AND
PERCEPTUAL CAPACITIES

Of all motor skills, voluntary reaching is believed to play the greatest role in infant cognitive development, since it opens up a whole new way of exploring the environment (Piaget, 1936/1952). By grasping things, turning them over, and seeing what happens when they are released, infants learn a great deal about the sights, sounds, and feel of objects.

The development of reaching and grasping, shown in Figure 4.6, provides an excellent example of how motor skills start out as gross, diffuse activity and move toward mastery of fine movements. When newborns are held in an upright posture, they direct their arms toward an object in front of them. These movements are called **prereaching** because they resemble poorly coordinated swipes or swings. Since newborn babies cannot control their arms or use their eyes to guide their hands, they are rarely successful in contacting the object. Like newborn reflexes, prereaching eventually drops out, around 7 weeks of age. Then, at about 3 months, voluntary reaching appears and gradually improves in accuracy (Bushnell, 1985; Hofsten, 1984). By 5 months, infants sensitively adjust their reaching behavior to object distances. They dramatically reduce their efforts to reach when an object is moved just slightly farther away, from in reach to out of reach (Yonas & Hartman, 1993).

Once infants can reach, they start to modify the nature of their grasp. When the grasp reflex of the newborn period weakens, it is replaced by the **ulnar grasp,** a clumsy motion in which the fingers close against the palm. Around 4 to 5

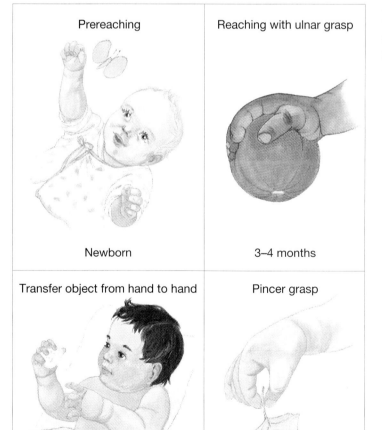

Prereaching | Reaching with ulnar grasp

Newborn | 3–4 months

Transfer object from hand to hand | Pincer grasp

4–5 months | 9 months

FIGURE 4.6 Some milestones of voluntary reaching. The average age at which each skill is attained is given. (Ages from Bayley, 1969; Rochat, 1989.)

Prereaching
The poorly coordinated, primitive reaching movements of newborn babies.

Ulnar grasp
The clumsy grasp of the young infant, in which the fingers close against the palm.

Take a quick survey of several parents you know, asking them these questions: Can young babies profit from training? Should sitting, crawling, and walking be deliberately encouraged? Answers vary widely from culture to culture. Japanese mothers, for example, believe such efforts are unnecessary and unimportant (Caudill, 1973). And among the Zinacanteco Indians of Southern Mexico, rapid motor progress is actively discouraged. Babies who walk before they know enough to keep away from cooking fires and weaving looms are viewed as dangerous to themselves and disruptive to others (Greenfield, 1992). But in other parts of the world, direct stimulation of motor skills is common.

Among the Baganda of Uganda and the Kipsigis of Kenya, babies hold their heads up, sit alone, and walk considerably earlier than North American infants. Infant caregiving customs are believed to be responsible, since babies are advanced only in those motor skills that are trained. As early as 1 month, the Baganda mother begins teaching her infant to sit, since children do not become true members of the Baganda community until they can sit alone properly. Between 1 and 3 months, babies are seated on the adult's lap and held with one arm around the waist. When they are 3 to 4 months old, they are placed on a mat or in a basin, and cloths are wrapped around them for support (Kilbride & Kilbride, 1975). The Kipsigis teach infants in a similar way. Babies are placed in holes dug in the ground, and rolled blankets are used to keep them upright. Walking is promoted by frequently bouncing babies on their feet (Super, 1981).

The West Indians of Jamaica, whose infants are also advanced in head control, sitting, and walking, do not try to train their infants in specific skills. Instead, beginning in the first few weeks of life, babies experience a highly stimulating, formal handling routine. As Figure 4.7 shows, the West Indian mother stretches the baby's arms, legs, and neck, props the infant with cushions to encourage an upright posture, "walks" the baby up her body, and exercises stepping responses. Asked why they use the formal

handling routine, West Indian mothers refer to the traditions of their culture and the need to help babies grow up strong, healthy, and physically attractive (Hopkins & Westra, 1988).

Do these observations mean that mothers everywhere should teach their babies motor skills? The practices described above are meaningful only in particular cultures. Recall that exercising infant reflexes (some of which provide the foundation for later motor skills) has no lasting impact on development. The same is true for a wide variety of motor capacities during the first 2 years of life.

FIGURE 4.7 West Indian mothers use a formal handling routine with their babies. Exercises practiced in the first few months include stretching each arm while suspending the baby (a); holding the infant upside-down by the ankles (b); grasping the baby's head on both sides, lifting upward, and stretching the neck (c); and propping the infant with cushions that are gradually removed as the baby begins to sit independently (d). Later in the first year, the baby is "walked" up the mother's body (e) and encouraged to take steps on the floor while supported (f). (Adapted from "Maternal Handling and Motor Development: An Intracultural Study" by B. Hopkins & T. Westra, 1988, *Genetic, Social and General Psychology Monographs, 14*, pp. 385, 388, 389. Reprinted with permission of the Helen Dwight Reid Educational Foundation. Published by Heldref Publications, 1319 Eighteenth St., N.W., Washington, D. C. 20036-1802. Copyright © 1988.)

months, both hands become coordinated in exploring objects. Babies of this age can hold an object in one hand while the other scans it with the tips of the fingers, and they frequently transfer objects from hand to hand (Rochat, 1989). By the latter part of the first year, infants use the thumb and index finger opposably in a well-coordinated **pincer grasp** (Halverson, 1931). Once the pincer grasp appears, the ability to manipulate objects greatly expands. The 1-year-old can pick up raisins and blades of grass, turn knobs, and open and close small boxes.

By 8 to 11 months of age, reaching and grasping are so well practiced that they are executed smoothly and effortlessly. As a result, attention is released from coordinating the motor skill itself to events that occur before and after obtaining the object. Once reaching is perfected, it can be used to support new cognitive advances, such as those described by Piaget, who observed that infants first begin to search for hidden objects at the end of the first year (Bushnell, 1985).

Pincer grasp
The well-coordinated grasp that emerges at the end of the first year, involving thumb and forefinger opposition.

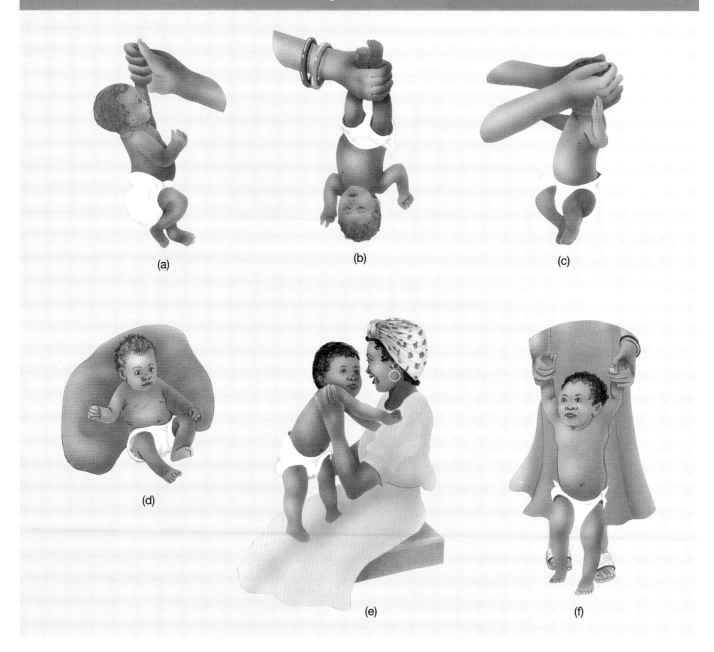

(a)   (b)   (c)

(d)   (e)   (f)

Like other motor milestones, voluntary reaching is affected by early experience. In a well-known study, Burton White and Richard Held (1966) found that institutionalized babies provided with a moderate amount of visual stimulation (at first, simple designs; later, a mobile hung over their cribs) reached for objects 6 to 8 weeks earlier than infants given nothing to look at. A third group of babies provided with massive stimulation (patterned crib bumpers and mobiles at an early age) also reached sooner than unstimulated babies. But this heavy dose of enrichment took its toll. These infants looked away and cried a great deal, and they were not as advanced in reaching as the moderately stimulated group. White and Held's findings remind us that more stimulation is not necessarily better. Trying to push infants beyond their current readiness to handle stimulation can undermine the development of important motor skills.

153

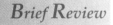

The overall sequence of early motor development follows the cephalocaudal and proximodistal trends. Although the order of motor milestones is similar across children, there are large individual differences in the rate at which motor development proceeds. Each new skill is a matter of developing increasingly complex systems of action. Besides maturation, motor development is affected by movement opportunities, infant-rearing practices, and a generally stimulating environment. Voluntary reaching begins with the uncoordinated prereaching of the newborn baby and gradually evolves into a refined pincer grasp by the end of the first year. Once reaching is well practiced, infants integrate it into increasingly elaborate motor skills and use it to support new cognitive advances.

PERCEPTUAL DEVELOPMENT IN INFANCY

What can infants perceive with the senses at birth, and how does perception change over the first year of life? Researchers have sought answers to these questions for two reasons. The first is the relevance of infant perception to the age-old nature–nurture controversy. Is an adultlike perceptual world given to the infant, or must it be acquired through experience? As we will see shortly, newborns have an impressive array of perceptual capacities. Nevertheless, since improvements occur as the result of both maturation and experience, an appropriate resolution to the nature–nurture debate seems, once again, to lie somewhere between the two extremes. A second reason for interest in infant perception is that it sheds light on other areas of development. For example, because touch, vision, and hearing permit us to interact with other human beings, they are a basic part of emotional and social development. Through hearing, language is learned. And perception provides the foundation for cognitive development, since knowledge about the world is first gathered through the senses.

Studying infant perception is especially challenging because babies cannot describe their experiences. Instead, researchers must find out about their perceptual world by observing the repertoire of behaviors infants do have. Fortunately, the competencies of young babies enable investigators to make use of a variety of responses that vary with stimulation, such as looking, sucking, head turning, facial expressions, and startle reactions. Advances in research technology have also permitted physiological measures, such as changes in respiration and heart rate, to be used. And earlier in this chapter we noted that researchers sometimes take advantage of operant conditioning and the habituation–dishabituation sequence to find out whether infants can make certain perceptual discriminations. We will see many examples of these methods as we explore the baby's sensitivity to touch, taste, smell, sound, and visual stimulation in the following sections.

Touch

In our discussion of preterm infants in Chapter 3, we indicated that touch helps stimulate early physical growth, and, as we will see in Chapter 10, it is important for emotional development as well. Therefore it is not surprising that sensitivity to touch is well developed at birth. Return to the reflexes listed in Table 4.1 on page 131. They reveal that the newborn baby responds to touch, especially around the mouth and on the palms of the hands and soles of the feet. During the prenatal period, these areas, along with the genitals, are the first to become sensitive to touch, followed by other regions of the body (Humphrey, 1978).

Reactions to temperature change are also present at birth. When young infants are undressed, they often express discomfort by crying and becoming more active. Newborn babies are more sensitive to stimuli that are colder than body temperature than to those that are warmer (Humphrey, 1978).

At birth, infants are quite sensitive to pain. If male newborns are circumcised, the procedure is usually done without anesthesia because of the risk of giving pain-relieving drugs to a very young infant. Babies often respond with an intense, high-pitched, stressful cry (Porter, Porges, & Marshall, 1988). In addition, heart rate and blood pressure rise, irritability increases, and the baby's sleep may be disturbed for hours afterward (Anand, Phil, & Hickey, 1987). Recent research aimed at developing safe pain-relieving drugs for newborns promises to ease the stress of such procedures (Blass & Hoffmeyer, 1991). Doctors are beginning to realize that small infants, just like older children and adults, cannot be treated as if they are insensitive to pain.

Sensitivity to touch enhances infants' responsiveness to the environment. In one study, the soft caresses of an experimenter led babies to smile and become increasingly attentive to the adult's face (Stack & Muir, 1992). As soon as infants can grasp objects, touch becomes a major means through which they investigate their world. Watch babies at play, and you will see that they frequently mouth novel objects, running their lips and tongue over the surface, after which they remove the object to take a good look at it. Exploratory mouthing peaks in the middle of the first year and then declines in favor of increasingly elaborate touching with the hands, in which infants turn, poke, and feel the surface of things while knitting their brows and looking intently (Ruff et al., 1992). In Chapter 6, we will see that Piaget regarded this hands-on manipulation of objects, in which touch combines with vision, as essential for early cognitive development.

Taste and Smell

All infants come into the world with the ability to communicate their taste preferences to caregivers. When given a sweet liquid instead of water, newborns use longer sucks with fewer pauses, indicating that they prefer sweetness and try to savor the taste of their favorite food (Crook & Lipsitt, 1976). Facial expressions reveal that infants can distinguish several basic tastes. Much like adults, newborns relax their facial muscles in response to sweetness, purse their lips when the taste is sour, and show a distinct archlike mouth opening when it is bitter (Rosenstein & Oster, 1988; Steiner, 1979). These built-in reactions are important for survival, since (as we will see in Chapter 5) the food that is ideally suited to support the infant's early growth is the sweet-tasting milk from the mother's breast. Salty taste undergoes a different developmental course than sweet, sour, or bitter. At birth, infants are either indifferent to or reject salt solutions in comparison to water. But by 4 months of age, they prefer the salty taste, a change that may prepare them to accept solid foods (Beauchamp, Cowart, & Moran, 1986).

Like taste, the newborn baby's responsiveness to the smell of certain foods is surprisingly similar to that of adults, suggesting that some odor preferences are innate. For example, the smell of bananas or chocolate causes a relaxed, pleasant facial expression, whereas the odor of rotten eggs makes the infant frown (Steiner, 1979). Newborns can also identify the location of an odor and, if it is unpleasant, defend themselves. When a whiff of ammonia is presented to one side of the baby's nostrils, infants less than 6 days old quickly turn their heads in the other direction (Reiser, Yonas, & Wikner, 1976).

In many mammals, the sense of smell plays an important role in eating and protecting the young from predators by helping mothers and babies recognize each other. Although smell is less well developed in human beings than in other mammals, traces of its survival value are still present. In one study, newborns were exposed to the odor of their own mother's breast pad and that of another nursing mother. By 6 days of age, they turned more often in the direction of their own mother's odor (MacFarlane, 1975). The ability to recognize the mother's smell occurs only in breast-fed newborns (Cernoch & Porter, 1985). However, bottle-fed babies prefer the smell of any lactating (milk-producing) woman to the smell of a nonlactating woman. And when given a choice between the smell of the lactating breast and their familiar formula, they once again choose the former (Makin & Porter, 1989; Porter et al., 1992). Neonates seem to have a built-in attraction to the odor of breast milk, which probably helps them locate an appropriate food source and, in the process, learn to identify their own mother.

At birth, babies seem to be quite adept at making taste and odor discriminations. Unfortunately, little is known about how these two senses develop as the result of further brain maturation and experience.

Hearing

Newborn infants can hear a wide variety of sounds, but they are more responsive to some than to others. For example, they prefer complex sounds, such as noises and voices, to pure tones (Bench et al., 1976). In the first few days, infants can already tell the difference between a few sound patterns, such as a series of tones arranged in ascending and descending order. Over the first year, babies organize sounds into increasingly elaborate patterns. If two melodies differing only slightly are played, 1-year-olds can tell that they are not the same (Morrongiello, 1986).

Responsiveness to sound provides support for the young baby's visual and tactile exploration of the environment. Infants as young as 3 days old turn their eyes and head in the general direction of a sound. By 4 months, they can reach fairly accurately toward a sounding object in the dark. The ability to identify the precise location of a sound will improve greatly over the first 6 months and show further gains into the second year (Ashmead et al., 1991; Hillier, Hewitt, & Morrongiello, 1992).

Neonates are particularly sensitive to sounds within the frequency range of the human voice, and they come into the world prepared to respond to the sounds of any human language. Tiny infants can make fine-grained distinctions among a wide variety of speech sounds—"ba" and "ga," "ma" and "na," and the short vowel sounds "a" and "i," to name just a few. In fact, there are only a few speech discriminations that young infants cannot detect, and their ability to perceive sounds not found in their language environment is more precise than an adult's (Aslin, Pisoni, & Jusczyk, 1983). As we will see in Chapter 9, by the middle of the first year, infants start to "screen out" sounds not used in their own language as they listen closely to the speech of those around them (Kuhl et al., 1992). These capacities reveal that the human baby is marvelously equipped for the awesome task of acquiring language.

Listen carefully to yourself the next time you talk to a young baby. You are likely to speak in a high-pitched, expressive voice and use a rising tone at the ends of phrases and sentences. Adults probably communicate this way because they notice that infants are more attentive when they do so. Indeed, newborns prefer human speech with these characteristics (Sullivan & Horowitz, 1983). They will also suck more on a nipple to hear a recording of their mother's voice than that of an unfamiliar woman, and to hear their mother's native tongue as opposed to a foreign language (Mehler et al., 1988; Spence & DeCasper, 1987). These preferences probably developed from hearing the muffled sounds of the mother's voice before birth.

Infants' special responsiveness to their mother's speech probably encourages the mother to talk to the baby. As she does so, both readiness for language and the emotional bond between caregiver and child are strengthened. By 3 months of age, infants pick up information about the feelings of others through hearing. They can distinguish happy- from sad-sounding adult voices (Walker-Andrews & Grolnick, 1983). As we will see later, it will take somewhat more time before babies can discriminate these emotions visually.

Vision

Humans depend on vision more than any other sense for active exploration of the environment. Yet vision is the least mature of the newborn baby's senses. Visual structures in both the eye and brain continue to develop after birth. For example,

(a) **Newborn View**   (b) **Adult View**

FIGURE 4.8 The newborn baby's limited focusing ability and poor visual acuity lead the mother's face, even when viewed from close up, to look much like the fuzzy image in part (a) rather than the clear image in part (b).

the muscles of the *lens*, the part of the eye that permits us to adjust our focus to varying distances of objects, are weak in the neonate (Appleton, Clifton, & Goldberg, 1975). Also, cells in the *retina*, the membrane lining the inside of the eye that captures light and transforms it into messages that are sent to the brain, are not as mature or densely packed as they will be in a few months (Abramov et al., 1982). Furthermore, the *optic nerve* and other pathways that relay these messages along with cells in the *visual cortex* that receive them will not be adultlike for several years (Hickey & Peduzzi, 1987).

Because of these factors, newborn babies cannot focus their eyes very well. In addition, they rarely make full use of the focusing ability they do have because **visual acuity,** or fineness of discrimination, is limited. When you have your vision tested, the doctor estimates how finely you perceive stimuli in comparison to an adult with normal vision. Applying this same index to newborn babies, researchers have found that they see objects at a distance of 20 feet about as well as adults do at 660 feet (Courage & Adams, 1990). In addition, unlike adults (who see nearby objects more clearly), newborn babies see *equally unclearly* across a wide range of distances. As a result, no visual cues are available to help them notice that a near or far object can be sharpened by refocusing the lens (Banks, 1980). Images such as a parent's face, even from close up, look much like the blur shown in Figure 4.8(a).

Newborn infants cannot yet see well, but they actively explore their environment with the limited visual abilities they do have. They scan the visual field for interesting sights and try to track moving objects, although their eye movements are slow and inaccurate (Aslin, 1987; Kremenitzer et al., 1979). The visual system matures rapidly over the first few months of life. By 3 months, infants can focus on objects just as well as adults can. Visual acuity improves steadily throughout infancy. By 6 months, it is about 20/100. At 2 years, it reaches a near-adult level (Courage & Adams, 1990). Scanning and tracking also undergo rapid gains. By 1 month, babies can follow a slowly moving object with a smooth eye movement, a capacity that continues to improve during the first half-year (Aslin, 1987; Hainline, 1985).

An additional aspect of vision that becomes increasingly refined in the early months is color perception. Newborns are sensitive to color, since they prefer to look at colored rather than gray stimuli, but they do not show a definite ability to distinguish particular hues (Adams, 1987). Pathways in the brain that process color information mature rapidly, since babies 1 to 2 months of age can discriminate colors across the entire spectrum (Clavadetscher et al., 1988). By 4 to 5 months, they regard a particular color as the same, even when it varies in brightness (Dannemiller, 1989). Once color sensitivity is well established, habituation–dishabituation research

Visual acuity
Fineness of visual discrimination.

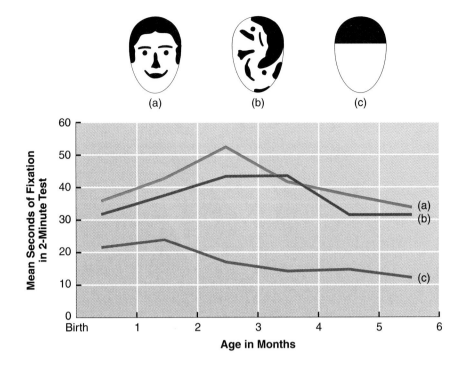

FIGURE 4.11 Early findings on pattern perception. At all ages, including the neonatal period, infants preferred to look at patterned stimuli—a drawing of the human face (a) or one with scrambled facial features (b) rather than a black-and-white oval (c). (From "The Origin of Form Perception" by R. L. Fantz, 1961, *Scientific American, 204*, p. 72. Copyright © 1961 by Scientific American, Inc. All rights reserved.)

Because of their poor vision, very young babies cannot resolve the small features in more complex patterns. To them, the large, bold checkerboard has more contrast, so they prefer to look at it. By 2 months of age, detection of fine-grained detail has improved considerably. As a result, infants become sensitive to the

FIGURE 4.12 The way two checkerboards differing in complexity look to infants in the first few weeks of life. Because of their poor vision, very young infants cannot resolve the fine detail in the more complex checkerboard. It appears blurred, like a gray field. The large, bold checkerboard appears to have more contrast, so babies prefer to look at it. (Adapted from "Infant Visual Perception" by M. S. Banks & P. Salapatek, 1983, in M. M. Haith & J. J. Campos (Eds.), *Handbook of Child Psychology: Vol. 2. Infancy and Developmental Psychobiology*, 4th ed., p. 504. Copyright © 1983 by John Wiley & Sons. Reprinted by permission of John Wiley & Sons, Inc.)

Two checkerboards differing in contrast

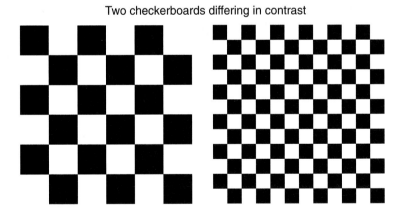

Appearance of checkerboards to very young infants

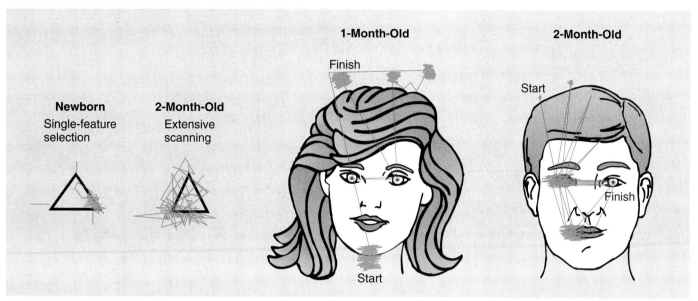

1-Month-Old

2-Month-Old

Newborn
Single-feature
selection

2-Month-Old
Extensive
scanning

Finish

Start

Start

Finish

FIGURE 4.13 Visual scanning of simple and complex patterns by young infants. When scanning a simple triangle, newborns focus only on a single feature, whereas 2-month-olds scan the entire border. When patterns are complex, such as a human face, 1-month-olds limit their scanning to single features on the outskirts of the stimulus, whereas 2-month-olds examine internal features. (From "Pattern Perception in Early Infancy" by P. Salapatek, 1975, in L. B. Cohen & P. Salapatek [Eds.], *Infant Perception: From Sensation to Cognition*, pp. 195, 201. Copyright © 1975 by Academic Press. Reprinted by permission.)

greater contrast in complex patterns and start to spend much more time looking at them (Dodwell, Humphrey, & Muir, 1987).

Combining Pattern Elements. In the early weeks of life, infants respond to the separate parts of a pattern. For example, when shown a triangle or a drawing of the human face, very young babies limit their visual exploration to the outskirts of the stimulus, and they stare at single high-contrast features—one corner of the triangle or the hairline and chin of the face (see Figure 4.13). At about 2 months, when scanning ability and contrast sensitivity have improved, infants inspect the entire border of a geometric shape. And they explore the internal features of complex stimuli like the human face, pausing briefly to look at each salient part (Bronson, 1991; Salapatek, 1975).

Once babies can take in all aspects of a pattern, they combine pattern elements, integrating them into a unified whole. The habituation–dishabituation response can be used to demonstrate this. For example, after habituating to the cross (a) shown in Figure 4.14, infants can be shown two additional patterns. The first (b) involves a change in overall structure. In the second (c), there is no change in structure, only a change in pattern elements. If infants are sensitive to pattern

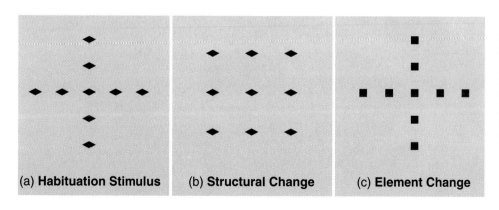

(a) Habituation Stimulus   **(b) Structural Change**   **(c) Element Change**

FIGURE 4.14 Stimuli used to test infants' ability to combine pattern elements. After habituating to pattern (a), 2-month-olds dishabituate to a change in the structure of the pattern (b), not to a change in its elements (c). This indicates that they are sensitive to the overall structure of a pattern. (Adapted from Vurpillot, Ruel, & Castrec, 1977.)

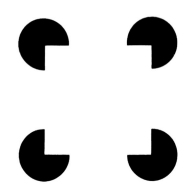

FIGURE 4.15 Subjective boundaries in a visual pattern. Do you perceive a square in the middle of this figure? By 7 months of age, infants do, too. (Adapted from Bertenthal, Campos, & Haith, 1980.)

structure, which of the two stimuli—(b) or (c)—will they look longest at (dishabituate to)? If you chose (b), you are correct. This is precisely how 2- to 3-month-old infants respond (Vurpillot, Ruel, & Castrec, 1977).

Over the first half-year, babies discriminate increasingly complex patterns. By this time, they are so good at detecting pattern organization that they even perceive subjective boundaries that are not really present. For example, look at Figure 4.15. Seven-month-olds perceive a square in the center of this pattern, just as you do (Bertenthal, Campos, & Haith, 1980). Older infants carry this responsiveness to subjective form even further. As Figure 4.16 shows, 9-month-olds can detect the organized, meaningful pattern in a series of moving lights that resemble a person walking, in that they look much longer at this display than they do at upside-down or disorganized versions (Bertenthal et al., 1985). Although 3- to 5-month-olds can tell the difference among these patterns, they do not show a preference for one with both an upright orientation and a humanlike movement pattern (Bertenthal et al., 1987).

By 12 months, infants can extract information about form on the basis of very little information, simply by watching a moving light trace the outline of a shape. In two studies, babies of this age preferred to look at a geometric shape that was different from the one they had just seen outlined by a blinking light. They extracted the shape by combining the light points into an orderly pattern, which they could distinguish from other shapes. Ten-month-olds were unable to make this discrimination (Rose, 1988; Skouteris, McKenzie, & Day, 1992).

Researchers believe that both maturation and experience—development of the visual system combined with exposure to a wide variety of stimuli—underlie infants' increasing ability to detect integrated forms (Proffitt & Bertenthal, 1990). As we saw earlier, visual acuity, scanning, and contrast sensitivity improve greatly during the first few months, and these changes support exploration of complex stimuli (Pipp & Haith, 1984). Also, studies of the development of the visual cortex in animals, along with indirect research on humans, reveal that brain cells respond to specific pattern stimuli, such as vertical, horizontal, and curved lines. Improvements in the sensitivity and organization of these receptors as babies search for regularities in their rich, patterned external world undoubtedly contribute to the detection of pattern organization from ever more subtle cues (Acredolo & Hake, 1982).

Perception of the Human Face. Do newborn babies have an innate capacity to recognize and respond to the human face? Although some early work suggested

FIGURE 4.16 Light displays used to test infants' preference for the motion of a human being walking. (a) Moving lights correspond to the head, shoulder, hip, elbows, wrists, knees, and ankles of a person walking. By 9 months of age, infants prefer this display to (b), an upside-down version, and to (c), a scrambled version. Three- to 5-month-olds can discriminate the three patterns, but they do not show a preference for (a). (From "Converging Operations Revisited: Assessing What Infants Perceive Using Discrimination Measures" by D. R. Proffitt & B. I. Bertenthal, 1990, *Perception & Psychophysics, 47*, p. 5. Reprinted by permission of Psychonomic Society, Inc.)

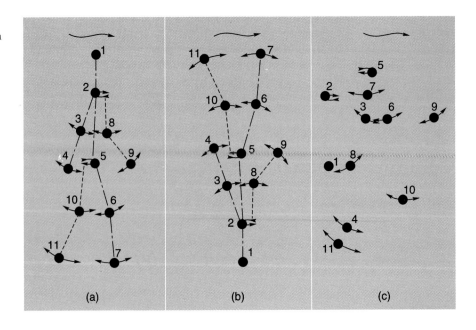

that they do (Fantz, 1961), recent research indicates that they do not. Infants younger than 2 months do not look longer at a drawing of a human face than at a pattern of equal complexity, such as one with scrambled facial features, largely because (as we noted earlier) 1-month-olds do not inspect the internal features of a stimulus.* At 2 to 3 months, when infants explore an entire stimulus, they do look longer at an intact facial pattern than at a scrambled one (Maurer, 1985). Stronger evidence for the emergence of a preference for the human facial configuration comes from findings that 3-month-olds, but not 6-week-olds, look longer at a face than at the same pattern with its contrast reversed (that is, a negative of a face). They show no similar preference when an abstract pattern is paired with its negative (Dannemiller & Stephens, 1988). Infants' recognition of faces does not seem to be a built-in perceptual capacity. Instead, it follows the same developmental course as other aspects of visual perception.

The baby's tendency to search for structure in a patterned stimulus is quickly applied to face perception. By 3 months of age, infants make fine-grained distinctions among the features of different faces. For example, they can tell the difference between the photos of two strangers, even when the faces are moderately similar (Barrera & Maurer, 1981a). Around this time, babies also recognize their mother's face in a photo, since they look longer at it than the face of a stranger (Barrera & Maurer, 1981b). And by 5 months, infants recognize a new photo of a person they had previously seen in a different pose, and they can associate a real face with a color photograph of the same person (Dirks & Gibson, 1977; Fagan, 1976).

As perception of the human face improves, babies recognize and respond more actively to the facial expressions of others. Habituation–dishabituation studies show that between 4 and 7 months, infants can distinguish happy from sad, angry, and fearful faces posed by a single model (Nelson, 1987). Still, researchers believe that babies of this age are not yet discriminating organized emotional patterns. Instead, they are probably reacting to changes in isolated facial features (such as the appearance of bright teeth in a happy pose). Between 7 and 10 months, infants do start to react to emotional expressions as organized wholes. They treat positive faces (happy and surprised) as different from negative ones (sad and fearful), even when these expressions are demonstrated in slightly varying ways by different models (Ludemann, 1991).

Researchers do not yet know how these global distinctions become more refined with age. Also, we must keep in mind that the evidence reviewed so far is based on photographed poses, not the dynamic facial displays that infants see in everyday life. Recent evidence suggests that babies as young as 5 months can discriminate happy and sad emotional patterns in live animated faces. Other distinctions, however, must wait for a later age (Caron, Caron, & MacLean, 1988). As we will see in Chapter 10, infants' sensitivity to facial expressions, although incomplete, supports their earliest social relationships and helps regulate exploration of the environment in adaptive ways.

OBJECT PERCEPTION. Research on pattern perception involves only two-dimensional stimuli, but the environment we live in is made up of stable, three-dimensional objects. Is the perceptual world of infants organized into independently existing objects, much like our own?

Shape and Size Constancy. As we move around the environment and look at objects, the images they cast on our retina are constantly changing in size and shape. To perceive objects as stable and unchanging, we must translate these varying retinal images into a single representation.

---

*Perhaps you are wondering how neonates can display the remarkable imitative capacities described earlier in this chapter if they do not scan the internal features of a face. Recall that the facial expressions in the newborn imitation research were not static poses but live demonstrations. Their dynamic quality probably caused infants to notice them.

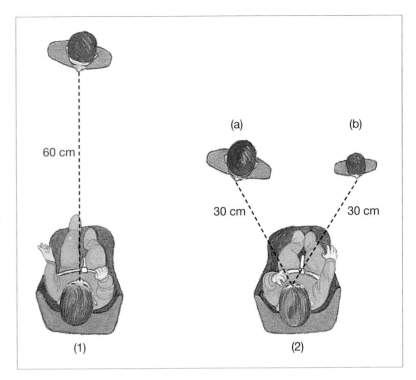

FIGURE 4.17 Testing infants for size constancy. The procedure shown is a simplified version of the one used by McKenzie, Tootell, and Day (1980). (1) Infants were habituated to a large mannequin head 60 cm from their eyes. (2) Then they were tested to see whether they would dishabituate to the same-size mannequin 30 cm away (a) or a smaller mannequin 30 cm away (b). Infants dishabituated to (2b), indicating that they regard objects of the same actual size presented at different distances from their eyes (1 and 2a) as perceptually equivalent.

Perception of an object's shape as stable, despite changes in the shape projected on the retina, is called **shape constancy.** In one study, babies 6 hours to 6 days old were habituated to one of two stimuli: a square or a trapezoid presented at several different slants to the eye. Next, the square and trapezoid were paired together, but both were at slants other than those shown during the habituation phase. Dishabituation was greatest to the novel shape, indicating that newborns had extracted the real shape of the habituation stimulus from diverse images cast on the retina (Slater & Morison, 1985). Shape constancy is present at birth, long before babies have an opportunity to actively rotate objects with their hands and view them from many different angles. It is probably an innate perceptual ability.

Size constancy—perception of an object's size as the same, despite changes in its retinal image size—emerges much later. To test for it, researchers habituated infants to a large mannequin and then determined whether they perceived it as similar to a mannequin of the same size but a different distance away (see Figure 4.17). Under these conditions, 6- to 8-month-olds showed clear evidence of size constancy, and 4-month-olds also did as long as the mannequins were in motion, approaching and receding before the baby's eyes (Day & McKenzie, 1981; McKenzie, Tootell, & Day, 1980). Size constancy seems to depend on depth perception. Recall that infants first become sensitive to kinetic cues for depth, so perhaps it is not surprising that young babies can detect size constancy only when stimuli are moving. Between 4 and 8 months, infants respond to binocular and pictorial depth cues, which may contribute to size constancy with stationary objects around this time (Aslin, 1987).

Perception of Objects as Distinct, Bounded Wholes. Perceptual constancies provide only a partial picture of the extent to which infants perceive a world of independently existing objects. As adults, we distinguish a single object from its surroundings by looking for a regular shape and uniform texture and color. Observations by Piaget (1936/1952) first suggested that young infants do not use these same cues. Piaget dangled a small, attractive object in front of his 6-month-old son Laurent, who eagerly grabbed it. But as soon as it was placed on top of a bigger object, such as a book or pillow, Laurent no longer reached for it. Instead, he reached for the larger, supporting object. Laurent's behavior indicates that he did

Shape constancy
Perception of an object's shape as the same, despite changes in the shape of its retinal image.

Size constancy
Perception of an object's size as the same, despite changes in the size of its retinal image.

not perceive the boundary between two objects created by their different sizes, shapes, and textures. Instead, he treated two objects close together as a single unit.

Recent research supports Piaget's informal observations and also reveals that it is the movement of objects relative to one another and to their background that gradually enables infants to construct a visual world of separate objects. In one series of studies, 5-month-olds were shown two objects, a smaller one in front of a larger one. Sometimes the objects touched each other; at other times they were separated. Also, sometimes the objects were stationary; at other times they moved either independently or together. When objects touched and either stood still or moved in the same direction, infants reached for them as a whole. But when they were separated or moved in opposite directions, infants behaved as if the objects were distinct, and they reached for only one of them (Hofsten & Spelke, 1985; Spelke, Hofsten, & Kestenbaum, 1989).

These findings indicate that at first, motion exerts a stronger effect on infants' identification of an object than do stationary cues, such as shape, texture, and color. Indeed, young babies are fascinated by moving objects. They almost always prefer to look at a moving stimulus instead of an identical stationary one (Slater et al., 1985). As they do so, infants gradually pick up critical information about object characteristics. When an object moves across a background, its various features remain in the same relationship to one another and move together, helping the baby distinguish the object from other units in the visual field. During the second half-year, infants start to rely more on stationary cues to identify objects as separate units.

The Milestones table on page 168 provides an overview of the vast changes that take place in visual perception during the first year. Up to this point, we have considered the sensory systems one by one. Now let's turn to their coordination.

Intermodal Perception

When we take in information from the environment, we often use **intermodal perception.** That is, we combine stimulation from more than one *modality,* or sensory system, at a time. For example, we know that the shape of an object is the same whether we see it or touch it, that lip movements are closely coordinated with the sound of a voice, and that dropping a rigid object on a hard surface will cause a sharp, banging sound.

Are young infants, like adults, capable of intermodal perception, or do they have to learn how to put different types of sensory input together? Although researchers have debated this issue for years, recent evidence reveals that from the start, babies perceive the world in an intermodal fashion (Meltzoff, 1990; Spelke, 1987). Recall that newborns turn in the general direction of a sound, and they reach for objects in a primitive way. These behaviors suggest that infants expect sight, sound, and touch to go together.

By a few weeks after birth, infants show some impressive intermodal associations. In one study, 1-month-old babies were given a pacifier with either a smooth surface or a surface with nubs on it. After exploring it in their mouths, the infants were shown two pacifiers—one smooth and one nubbed. They preferred to look at the shape they had sucked, indicating that they could match touch and visual stimulation without spending months seeing and feeling objects (Meltzoff & Borton, 1979).

Other research reveals that by 4 months, vision and hearing are well coordinated. Lorraine Bahrick (1983) showed infants of this age two films side by side, one with two blocks banging and the other with two sponges being squashed together. At the same time, the sound track for only one of the films (either a sharp banging noise or a soft squashing sound) could be heard. Infants looked at the film that went with the sound track, indicating that they detected a common rhythm in what they saw and heard. In a similar study, 4-month-olds related the shape of an adult's lips to the corresponding vowel sound in speech (Kuhl &

Intermodal perception
Perception that combines information from more than one sensory system.

MILESTONES
VISUAL DEVELOPMENT IN INFANCY

Age	Visual Capacities
Birth–1 month	• Scans single, high-contrast features • Prefers large, bold patterns • Displays shape constancy • Responds to kinetic depth cues
2–3 months	• Has adultlike focusing ability • Perceives colors across entire spectrum • Responds to binocular depth cues • Because of gains in contrast sensitivity, prefers patterns with fine details • Scans internal pattern features • Begins to perceive overall pattern structure
4–5 months	• Organizes colors into categories like those of adults • Shows gains in sensitivity to binocular depth cues • Size constancy emerges • Responds to motion more than features in identifying objects as distinct from their surroundings
6–8 months	• Shows gains in visual acuity, from 20/660 at birth to 20/100 at 6 months • Tracks objects with smooth, efficient eye movements • Detects subjective boundaries in patterns • Responds to features rather than motion in identifying objects as distinct from their surroundings
9–12 months	• Can extract information about a form in the absence of a full image (for example, from a moving light)

NOTE: These milestones represent overall age trends. Individual differences exist in the precise age at which each milestone is attained.

Meltzoff, 1984). And 7-month-olds united emotional expressions across modalities, matching a happy or angry sounding voice with the appropriate face of a speaking person (Soken & Pick, 1992; Walker-Andrews, 1986).

Of course, many intermodal matches, such as the way a train sounds or a teddy bear feels, must be based on experience. But what is so remarkable about intermodal perception is how quickly infants acquire these associations. Most of the time, they need just one exposure to a new situation (Spelke, 1987). In addition, when researchers try to teach intermodal relationships by pairing sights and sounds that do not naturally go together, babies will not learn them (Bahrick, 1988, 1992). Intermodal perception is yet another capacity that helps infants build an orderly, predictable perceptual world.

Understanding Perceptual Development

Now that we have reviewed the development of infant perceptual capacities, these questions arise: How can we put this diverse array of amazing achievements together? Does any general principle account for perceptual development? Eleanor and James Gibson's **differentiation theory** provides widely accepted answers. According to the Gibsons, infants actively search for **invariant features** of the environment—those that remain stable—in a constantly changing percep-

Differentiation theory
The view that perceptual development involves the detection of increasingly fine-grained, invariant features in the environment.

Invariant features
Features that remain stable in a constantly changing perceptual world.

tual world. For example, in pattern perception, at first babies are confronted with a confusing mass of stimulation. But very quickly, they search for features that stand out along the border of a stimulus. Then they explore its internal features, and as they do so, they notice stable relationships among those features. As a result, they detect overall patterns, such as crosses, squares, and faces. The development of intermodal perception also reflects this principle. Again, what babies seem to do is seek out invariant relationships, such as a similar tempo in an object's motion and sound, that unite information across different modalities.

The Gibsons use the word *differentiation* (meaning analyze or break down) to describe their theory because over time, babies make finer and finer distinctions among stimuli. For example, the human face is initially perceived in terms of single, high-contrast features, such as the hairline or chin. Then eyes, nose, and mouth are detected and combined into a pattern. Soon subtle distinctions between one face and another are made, and babies can tell mother, father, and stranger apart. Differentiation also applies to depth and object perception. Notice how in each, sensitivity to motion precedes detection of detailed stationary cues. So one way of understanding perceptual development is to think of it as a built-in tendency to search for order and stability in the surrounding world, a capacity that becomes increasingly fine-tuned with age (Gibson, 1970; Gibson, 1979).

At this point, it is only fair to comment that some researchers believe babies do not just make sense of their world by searching for invariant features. Instead, they impose *meaning* on what they perceive, constructing categories of objects and events in the surrounding environment. We have already seen the glimmerings of this cognitive point of view in some of the evidence reviewed in this chapter. For example, older babies *interpret* a happy voice and face as a source of pleasure and affection and a pattern of blinking lights as a moving human being. We will save our discussion of infant cognition for later chapters, acknowledging for now that the cognitive perspective also has merit in understanding the achievements of infancy. In fact, many researchers combine these two positions, regarding infant development as proceeding from a perceptual to a cognitive emphasis over the first year of life (Mandler, 1992; Salapatek & Cohen, 1987).

Brief Review

Recent research has greatly expanded our understanding of infant perceptual development. Sensitivity to touch, taste, smell, and sound are well developed in the newborn baby. During the first year, infants organize sounds into more complex patterns and become sensitive to the sounds of their own language. Of all the senses, vision is the least mature at birth. Visual acuity, scanning, tracking, and color perception improve during the early months. Depth perception develops as infants detect motion, binocular, and pictorial cues. Gradually, babies move from focusing on the parts of a pattern to perceiving it as an organized whole. Shape constancy is present at birth; size constancy emerges as depth perception improves. At first, infants distinguish objects by attending to their movements; only later do they respond to stationary cues. Young babies have a remarkable ability to combine information across sensory modalities. The Gibsons's differentiation theory provides an overall account of perceptual development.

EARLY DEPRIVATION AND ENRICHMENT: IS INFANCY A SENSITIVE PERIOD OF DEVELOPMENT?

Throughout this chapter, we have discussed how a variety of early experiences affect the development of perceptual and motor skills. In view of the findings already reported, it is not surprising that many investigations have found that warm, stimulating caregiving that is responsive to infants' self-initiated efforts promotes active exploration of the environment and earlier achievement developmental milestones (see, for example, Belsky, Goode, & Most, 1980; Bradley et al., 1989).

The powerful effect of early experience is dramatically apparent in the development of infants who lack the rich, varied stimulation of normal homes. We have already seen that babies reared in deprived institutions are severely retarded in motor development. They also engage in stereotyped, immature play and are overly fearful of new situations that present attractive opportunities for exploration (Collard, 1971). After only a few months, their mental development is far behind that of their home-reared peers (Dennis & Najarian, 1957).

Although these findings indicate that early experience has a profound impact on development, they do not tell us for sure whether infancy is a *sensitive period.* That is, if babies do not experience warm caregiving and appropriate stimulation of their senses in the first year or two of life, will there be lasting deficits from which they cannot fully recover? This question is highly controversial. Some theorists believe that experience operates much like a tape recording that can be made and erased. According to this view, the child's previous adaptations, and the events that led up to them, can be overcome by the quality of the current environment (Kagan, 1980). Other theorists argue that early experience leaves a lasting imprint, combining with current conditions to affect the child's competence (Bowlby, 1980).

For ethical reasons, we cannot deliberately deprive some infants of normal rearing experiences and wait to observe the long-term consequences. However, several natural experiments in which children were victims of deprived early environments but were later exposed to stimulating, sensitive care provide the best available test of whether infancy is a sensitive period of development. A unique feature of these studies is that they allow us to examine the long-lasting effects of early deprivation without the contaminating influence of later deprivation. If the sensitive-period hypothesis is correct, then the effects of deprivation during infancy should persist, even when children are moved into enriched settings.

In one study of this kind, Wayne Dennis (1973) followed the development of children who were placed in a Lebanese orphanage shortly after birth. Through most of the first year, they lay in their cribs and received practically no individual attention from caregivers. Extreme retardation in motor and language development resulted. Many did not sit up until 1 year of age or walk until well into the preschool years. Their IQs between 1 and 6 years were severely depressed, averaging only 53. In 1957, adoption was legalized in Lebanon, and children of a variety of ages left the orphanage for normal homes. By comparing those adopted early (before 2 years of age) with those adopted later, Dennis tested the sensitive-period hypothesis. Findings showed that children adopted before age 2 overcame their earlier retardation, achieving an average IQ of 100 within 2 years. In contrast, those adopted later, although they gained steadily in IQ during childhood, never fully recovered. After 6 to 8 years with their adoptive families, their IQs were only

A deprived early rearing environment can profoundly impair children's development. This poverty-stricken toddler's home life is likely to remain underprivileged throughout her childhood. Even if it does improve, she is unlikely to recover fully from the disadvantages of her first few years. (JOEL GORDON)

in the high 70s. Dennis concluded that environmental improvement by age 2 is necessary for complete recovery of deprived infants.

A more recent study suggests that less severe early deprivation can have lasting consequences as well. Alan Sroufe, Byron Egeland, and Terri Kreutzer (1990) charted the experiences and competencies of a group of low-income children from infancy through middle childhood. Then they looked to see if early measures—attachment of infants to their mothers, exploration and problem solving at age 2, and quality of the home environment during the third year—added anything to later assessments in predicting cognitive, emotional, and social competence in childhood. Each of the early measures remained important. In addition, among children exposed to stresses during the preschool years, those with the greatest capacity for rebound in middle childhood had a history of positive adaptation during infancy (see Figure 4.18).

Unfortunately, most infants reared in underprivileged environments continue to be affected by disadvantaged conditions during their childhood years. Interventions that try to break this pattern by training caregivers to engage in warm, stimulating behaviors with infants are highly effective and have lasting benefits (Andrews et al., 1982; Hunt et al., 1976). One of the most important outcomes of these programs is that passive, apathetic babies become active, alert beings with the capacity to evoke positive interactions from caregivers and initiate stimulating play for themselves.

Finally, it is important to keep in mind that besides impoverished environments, ones that overwhelm children with expectations beyond their current capacities also undermine development. In recent years, expensive early learning centers have sprung up around the United States in which infants are trained with letter and number flash cards and slightly older toddlers are given a full curriculum of reading, math, art, music, gym, and more. There is no evidence that these programs yield smarter, better "super babies" (Siegel, 1987). Instead, as we saw earlier in White and Held's (1966) study of voluntary reaching, trying to prime infants with stimulation for which they are not ready can cause them to withdraw, threatening their spontaneous interest and pleasure in learning. In addition, when such programs promise but do not produce young geniuses, they are likely to lead to disappointed parents who view their children as failures at a very tender age (White, 1990). Thus, they rob infants of a psychologically healthy start on the road to maturity, and they deprive parents of relaxed, pleasurable participation in their children's early growth.

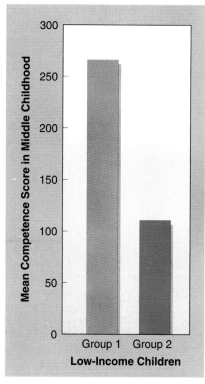

FIGURE 4.18 Is infancy a sensitive period of development? In a recent study, two groups of low-income children were compared. Group 1 had a history of positive adaptation in infancy but then showed poor adaptation during the preschool years. Group 2 showed poor adaptation in both early and later periods. The first group displayed a much greater capacity for rebound in middle childhood, scoring more than twice as high on a measure of overall competence. (Adapted from Sroufe, Egeland, & Kreutzer, 1990.)

CHAPTER SUMMARY

The Organized Newborn

- Infants begin life with remarkable skills for relating to their physical and social worlds. **Reflexes** are the newborn baby's most obvious organized patterns of behavior. Some have survival value, whereas others provide the foundation for voluntary motor skills that will develop later.

- The neonate has a sleep-waking cycle that becomes more organized and patterned with age. Although newborns alternate frequently among various **states of arousal,** they spend most of their time asleep. Sleep consists of at least two states: **rapid-eye-movement (REM)** and **non-rapid-eye-movement (NREM)** sleep. REM sleep time is greater during the newborn period than at any later age. According to **autostimulation theory, (REM)** sleep provides young infants with stimulation essential for central nervous system development.

- A crying baby stimulates strong feelings of discomfort in nearby adults. The intensity of the cry and the events that led up to it help parents figure out what is wrong. Once feeding and diaper changing have been tried, lifting the baby to the shoulder is the most effective soothing technique. Ethological and behaviorist theories disagree on how promptly caregivers should respond to infant cries. A shrill, piercing newborn cry is an indicator of central nervous system distress.

- The most widely used instrument for assessing the behavior of newborn infants is Brazelton's **Neonatal Behavioral Assessment Scale (NBAS).** The NBAS has helped researchers understand individual and cultural differences in newborn behavior. Sometimes it is used to teach parents about their baby's capacities and unique characteristics.

- In **classical conditioning,** a neutral stimulus is paired with an **unconditioned stimulus (UCS)** that produces a reflexive, or **unconditioned, response (UCR).** Once learning has occurred, the neutral stimulus, now called the **conditioned stimulus (CS),** elicits the response, which is called the **conditioned response (CR).** Young infants can be classically conditioned when the pairing of a UCS with a CS has survival value. **Operant conditioning** of infants has been demonstrated in many studies. In addition to food, interesting sights and sounds serve as effective **reinforcers,** increasing the occurrence of a preceding behavior.

- **Habituation–dishabituation** research reveals that at birth, babies are attracted to novelty. Their ability to remember a wide variety of previously experienced stimuli improves over the first year. Newborn infants also have a remarkable capacity to imitate the facial expressions and gestures of adults.

Motor Development in Infancy
- Infants' rapidly emerging motor skills support other aspects of development. Like physical development, motor development follows the **cephalocaudal** and **proximodistal trends.** New motor skills are a matter of combining existing skills into increasingly complex **systems of action.**
- Experience profoundly affects motor development, as shown by research on infants raised in deprived institutions. Stimulation of infant motor skills accounts for cross-cultural differences in motor development. During the first year, infants gradually perfect their reaching and grasping. The poorly coordinated **prereaching** of the newborn period eventually drops out. Once voluntary reaching appears, the clumsy **ulnar grasp** is gradually transformed into a refined **pincer grasp.**

Perceptual Development in Infancy
- The study of infant perception sheds light on the nature–nurture controversy and helps us understand many aspects of psychological development. The senses of touch, taste, smell, and hearing are well developed at birth. Over the first year, babies organize sounds into more complex patterns. Newborns are especially responsive to high-pitched expressive voices, prefer the sound of their mother's voice, and can distinguish almost all sounds in human languages.
- Vision is the least mature of the newborn baby's senses. As the eye and visual centers in the brain mature during the first few months, focusing ability, **visual acuity,** scanning, tracking, and color perception improve rapidly.

- Depth perception helps infants understand the layout of the environment and guides motor activity. Responsiveness to **kinetic depth cues** appears by the end of the first month, followed by sensitivity to **binocular depth cues** between 3 and 6 months. Perception of **pictorial depth cues** emerges last, between 6 and 7 months of age. Experience in moving about independently enhances babies' three-dimensional understanding, including avoidance of edges and drop-offs, such as the deep side of the **visual cliff.**
- **Contrast sensitivity** accounts for infants' early pattern preferences. At first, babies look at the border of a stimulus and at single features. Around 2 months, they explore the internal features of a pattern, and soon they combine pattern elements into a unified whole. Over the first year, infants discriminate increasingly complex patterns. Perception of the human face follows the same sequence of development as sensitivity to other patterned stimuli. Between 7 and 10 months, babies react to emotional expressions as organized wholes.
- Infants gradually build a visual world made up of stable, three-dimensional objects. **Shape constancy** is present at birth; **size constancy** depends on depth perception and first emerges at 4 months of age. The movement of objects relative to one another and their background gradually enables infants to construct a visual world of independently existing objects.
- Young infants have a remarkable, built-in capacity to engage in **intermodal perception.** Although many intermodal associations are learned, infants acquire them quickly, often after just one exposure to a new situation.
- **Differentiation theory** is the most widely accepted account of perceptual development. Over time, infants detect increasingly fine-grained **invariant features** in a constantly changing perceptual world.

Early Deprivation and Enrichment: Is Infancy a Sensitive Period of Development?
- Theorists disagree on whether infancy is a sensitive period in which warm caregiving and appropriate stimulation of the senses have a lasting impact on development. Research indicates that early experience combines with current conditions to affect the child's development. Recovery from a deprived early environment can occur if rearing conditions improve, but it may not be complete.

IMPORTANT TERMS AND CONCEPTS

reflex (p. 130)
states of arousal (p. 133)
rapid-eye-movement (REM) sleep (p. 134)
non-rapid-eye-movement (NREM) sleep (p. 134)
autostimulation theory (p. 135)
Neonatal Behavioral Assessment Scale (NBAS) (p. 139)
classical conditioning (p. 141)
unconditioned stimulus (UCS) (p. 141)
unconditioned response (UCR) (p. 141)
conditioned stimulus (CS) (p. 142)
conditioned response (CR) (p. 142)

extinction (p. 142)
operant conditioning (p. 143)
reinforcer (p. 143)
punishment (p. 143)
sudden infant death syndrome (SIDS) (p. 144)
habituation (p. 144)
dishabituation (p. 144)
imitation (p. 146)
cephalocaudal trend (p. 149)
proximodistal trend (p. 149)
systems of action (p. 150)
prereaching (p. 151)

ulnar grasp (p. 151)
pincer grasp (p. 152)
visual acuity (p. 157)
visual cliff (p. 158)
kinetic depth cues (p. 159)
binocular depth cues (p. 159)
pictorial depth cues (p. 159)
contrast sensitivity (p. 161)
shape constancy (p. 166)
size constancy (p. 166)
intermodal perception (p. 167)
differentiation theory (p. 168)
invariant features (p. 168)

C O N N E C T I O N S

 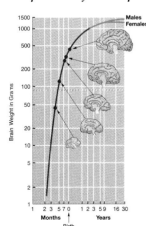

growth, they have pondered this question with respect to **puberty,** the flood of biological events leading to an adult-sized body and sexual maturity at adolescence. When you next have a chance, ask several new parents what they expect their sons and daughters to be like as teenagers. You will probably get answers like these: "Rebellious and uncontrollable." "Full of rages and tempers." "Plagued by one crisis after another." This view, widespread in contemporary American society, dates back to the writings of the eighteenth-century philosopher Jean-Jacques Rousseau, to whom you were introduced in Chapter 1. Rousseau believed that a natural outgrowth of the biological upheaval of puberty was heightened emotionality, conflict, and defiance of adults. Comparing adolescence to a violent storm, he cautioned parents:

> As the roaring of the waves precedes the tempest, so the murmur of rising passions . . . warns us of the approaching danger. A change of temper, frequent outbreaks of anger, a perpetual stirring of the mind, make the child ungovernable. . . . Keep your hand upon the helm or all is lost. (Rousseau, 1762/1955, pp. 172–173)

Although Rousseau's impressions were not based on scientific evidence, they were nevertheless picked up and extended by twentieth-century theorists. The most influential was G. Stanley Hall, whose view of development was grounded in Darwin's theory of evolution (see Chapter 1, page 9). Hall (1904) described adolescence as a cascade of instinctual passions, a phase of growth so turbulent that it resembled the period in which human beings evolved from savages into civilized beings. Without efforts by adults to redirect this sexual fervor into socially useful activities, young people could succumb to a life of decadence and conflict with society.

Were Rousseau and Hall correct in this image of adolescence as a biologically determined, inevitable period of storm and stress? Or do social and cultural factors *combine* with biological change to shape psychological development? In the course of our discussion, we will see what modern research has to say about this issue.

THE COURSE OF PHYSICAL GROWTH

Compared to other animals, primates (including human beings) experience a prolonged period of physical growth. For example, among mice and rats, the time between birth and puberty is only a matter of weeks; it takes no more than 2 percent of the life span. In chimpanzees, who are closest to humans in the evolutionary hierarchy, growth is extended to about 7 years, or one-sixth of the life span. Physical immaturity is even more exaggerated in human beings, who devote about one-fifth of their total years to growing.

Evolutionary reasons for this long period of physical growth are not hard to find. Because physical immaturity ensures that children remain dependent on adults, it provides added time for them to acquire the knowledge and skills necessary for life in a complex social world. In the words of anthropologist Weston LaBarre (1954), "Biologically, it takes more time to become human. Obviously, too, it is the human brain and human learning that gain particular advantages from this biological slow-down" (p. 153).

Changes in Body Size

To parents, the most obvious signs of physical growth are changes in the size of the child's body as a whole. During infancy, these changes are rapid—faster than they will be at any time after birth. By the end of the first year, the infant's height is 50 percent greater than it was at birth; and by 2 years, it is 75 percent greater. Weight shows similar dramatic gains. By 5 months, birth weight has doubled; at 1 year, it has tripled; and at 2 years, it has quadrupled. In fact, if children kept growing at the rate they do during the early months of life, by age 10 they would

Puberty
Biological changes during adolescence that lead to an adult-sized body and sexual maturity.

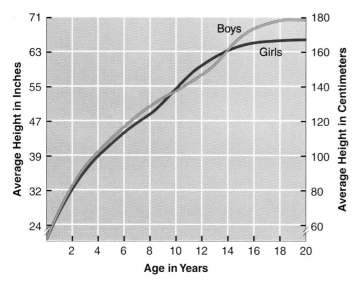

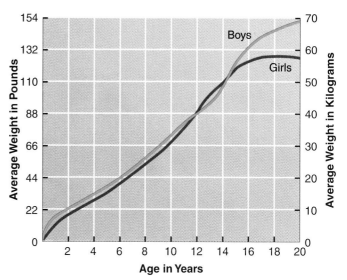

Age in Years

FIGURE 5.1 Height and weight distance curves for males and females, drawn from longitudinal measurements on approximately 175 individuals. (From *Growth and Development: The First Twenty Years in Man* (p. 19) by R. M. Malina, 1975, Minneapolis: Burgess Publishing Company. Copyright © 1975 by Burgess Publishing Company. Adapted by permission.)

be 10 feet tall and weigh over 200 pounds! Fortunately, growth slows in early and middle childhood. Children add about 2 to 3 inches in height and 5 pounds in weight each year. Then, the arrival of puberty brings a sharp acceleration in rate of growth. On the average, adolescents add nearly 10 inches in height and about 40 pounds in weight to reach a mature body size.

Two types of growth curves are used to track these changes in height and weight. The first, shown in Figure 5.1, is a **distance curve**, which plots the average height and weight of a sample of children at each age. It is called a distance curve because it indicates typical yearly progress toward mature body size. The group averages are referred to as *growth norms* and serve as a useful set of standards to

*T*he pubertal growth spurt takes place, on the average, 2 years earlier for girls than for boys. Although these adolescents are the same age, the girl is much taller and more mature looking. (J. GERARD SMITH/MONKMEYER PRESS PHOTO)

Distance curve

A growth curve that plots the average height and weight of a sample of children at each age. Shows typical yearly progress toward mature body size.

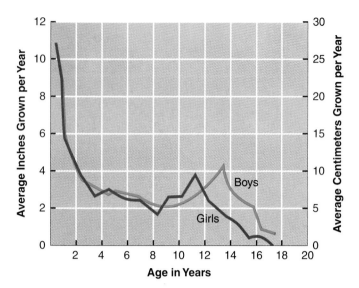

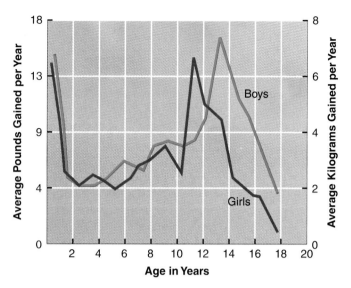

FIGURE 5.2 Height and weight velocity curves for males and females, drawn from longitudinal measurements on approximately 175 individuals. (From *Growth and Development: The First Twenty Years in Man* (p. 20) by R. M. Malina, 1975, Minneapolis: Burgess Publishing Company. Copyright © 1975 by Burgess Publishing Company. Adapted by permission.)

which individual children can be compared. Other information about growth can also be obtained from these curves. Notice how during infancy and childhood, the two sexes are very similar, with the typical girl just slightly shorter and lighter than the typical boy. Around age 11, the girl becomes taller and heavier for a time because her pubertal growth spurt takes place, on the average, 2 years earlier than the boy's. But this advantage is short-lived. At age 14, she is surpassed by the typical boy, whose growth spurt has started, whereas hers is almost finished. Growth in height is complete for most North American and European females by age 16, for males by age $17\frac{1}{2}$ (Tanner, 1990).

A second type of growth curve is the **velocity curve**, depicted in Figure 5.2. It plots the average amount of growth at each yearly interval. As a result, it is much better than the distance curve in revealing the exact timing of growth spurts. Indeed, Figure 5.2 makes plain some growth facts we have already mentioned: rapid but decelerating growth in infancy; a slower, constant rate of growth during childhood; and a sharp increase in growth in early adolescence followed by a swift decrease as the body approaches its adult size.

Since these overall growth trends are derived from group averages, they are deceiving in one respect. Researchers who have carefully tracked height changes of individual children report that rather than steady gains, little growth spurts occur throughout infancy and childhood. In one investigation, infants were followed over the first 21 months of life. They went for periods of 7 to 63 days with no growth and then added as much as a half-inch in a 24-hour period. Almost always, parents described their babies as irritable, restless, and very hungry on the day before the spurt (Lampl, Veldhuis, & Johnson, 1992). A study of Scottish children, who were followed between the ages of 3 and 10, revealed similar but more widely spaced spurts in height. Girls tended to forge ahead at ages $4\frac{1}{2}$, $6\frac{1}{2}$, $8\frac{1}{2}$, and 10, boys slightly later, at $4\frac{1}{2}$, 7, 9, and $10\frac{1}{2}$. In between these spurts were lulls in which growth was slower (Butler, McKie, & Ratcliffe, 1990).

Changes in Body Proportions

As the child's overall size increases, different parts of the body grow at different rates. Recall from Chapter 3 that during the prenatal period, the head develops first from the primitive embryonic disk, followed by the lower portion of the body. During infancy, the head and chest continue to have a growth advantage, but the

Velocity curve
A growth curve that plots the average amount of growth at each yearly interval for a sample of children. Clarifies the timing of growth spurts.

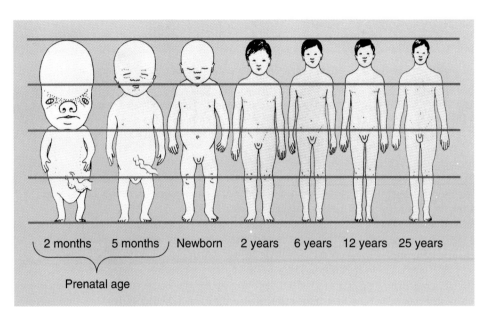

2 months   5 months   Newborn   2 years   6 years   12 years   25 years

Prenatal age

FIGURE 5.3 Changes in body proportions from the early prenatal period to adulthood. This figure illustrates the cephalocaudal trend of physical growth. The head gradually becomes smaller and the legs longer in proportion to the rest of the body.

trunk and legs gradually pick up speed. Do you recognize the familiar *cephalocaudal trend* we discussed in Chapter 4? You can see it depicted in Figure 5.3. Notice that the ratio of leg length to total height is less than 1:4 in the early prenatal period, increases to 1:3 at birth, and is 1:2 by adulthood. Physical growth during infancy and childhood also follows the *proximodistal trend.* It begins at the center of the body and moves outward, with the upper arms growing before the lower arms, which grow before the hands.

Exceptions to these basic growth trends occur during puberty, when growth actually proceeds in the reverse direction. At first, the hands, legs, and feet accelerate, and then the torso, which accounts for most of the adolescent height gain (Wheeler, 1991). This pattern of development explains why young adolescents stop growing out of their shoes and pants before they stop growing out of their jackets. It also helps us understand why early adolescence is regarded as an awkward phase. Because growth is uneven, many young teenagers appear gawky and out of proportion—long legged with giant feet and hands.

Although body proportions of girls and boys are similar in infancy and childhood, major differences that are typical of young adults appear during adolescence. The most obvious are the broadening of the shoulders relative to the hips in boys and the broadening of the hips relative to the shoulders and waist in girls. These differences are caused by the action of sex hormones on skeletal growth. Cells in the hip joints are specialized to respond to the rise in female sex hormones (estrogens), whereas those in the shoulders respond to an increase in male hormones (androgens). Of course, boys also end up much larger than girls, and their legs are longer in relation to the rest of the body. The major reason is that boys benefit from two extra years of preadolescent growth, when the legs are growing the fastest (Tanner, 1990).

Changes in Body Composition

Major changes in the body's muscle-fat makeup take place with age. Body fat (most of which lies just beneath the skin) begins to increase in the last few weeks of prenatal life and continues to do so after birth, reaching a peak at about 9 months of age. This very early rise in "baby fat" helps the small infant keep a constant body temperature. Then, beginning in the second year of life, children become more slender, a trend that continues into middle childhood. At birth, girls have slightly more body fat than boys, a difference that becomes greater over the course of childhood. Around age 8, girls start to add more fat than boys on their

*B*ody proportions and muscle-fat makeup change dramatically between 1 and 5 years. The top-heavy, chubby infant gradually becomes the longer-legged, slender young child. (BOB DAEMMRICH/STOCK BOSTON)

Sex-related differences in motor development are present as early as the preschool years. Boys are slightly advanced over girls in abilities that emphasize force and power. By age 5, they can broad jump a little farther, run a little faster, and throw a ball much farther (about 5 feet beyond the distance covered by girls). Girls have an edge in fine motor skills of drawing and penmanship and in certain gross motor capacities that combine balance and foot movement, such as hopping and skipping. During middle childhood, these differences intensify. For example, a ball thrown by a 12-year-old boy travels, on the average, 43 feet farther than one thrown by a 12-year-old girl. Boys are also more adept at batting, kicking, dribbling, and catching (Cratty, 1986; Roberton, 1984).

Girls are ahead of boys in overall physical maturity, which may be partly responsible for their better balance and precision of movement. Boys' slightly greater muscle mass and (in the case of throwing) longer forearms probably contribute to their skill advantages. But sex-related differences in physical growth during childhood are not large enough to explain boys' superiority in so many gross motor capacities. Instead, adult encouragement and example are powerfully influential. From an early age, baseballs and footballs are purchased for boys; jump ropes, hula hoops, and games of jacks for girls. Although women's participation in athletics has increased since the 1970s, most public sports events continue to be dominated by males, a circumstance that provides few models of outstanding athletic accomplishment for girls (Coakley, 1990).

Parents also hold higher expectations for boys' athletic performance, and children absorb these social messages at an early age. In a recent study of over 800 elementary school pupils, kindergartners through third-graders of both sexes viewed sports in a gender-stereotyped fashion—as much more important for boys. And boys more often stated that it was vital to their parents that they participate in athletics. These attitudes affected children's self-confidence as well as behavior. Girls saw themselves as having less talent at sports, and by sixth grade they devoted less time to athletics than did their male classmates (Eccles & Harold, 1991; Eccles, Jacobs, & Harold, 1990).

Not until puberty do sharp sex-related differences in physical size and muscle strength account for large differences in athletic ability. During adolescence, both sexes gain in gross motor performance, but girls' gains are slow and gradual, leveling off by age 14. In contrast, boys show a dramatic spurt in strength, speed, and endurance that continues through the end of the teenage years. Figure 5.4 illustrates this difference for running speed, broad jump, and throwing distance. Notice how the gender gap widens over time. By midadolescence, very few girls perform as well as the average boy, and practically no boys score as low as the average girl (Beunen et al., 1988).

The fact that the sexes are no longer evenly matched physically may heighten differential encouragement during the teenage years. At school, competence at sports is strongly related to peer admiration among adolescent boys, but it is not an important factor to girls. Look in your local newspaper, and note the much greater attention given to boys' school sports than to girls'. Girls' athletic events rarely attract more than a handful of spectators (Eder & Parker, 1987). By high school, girls' sports participation falls

arms, legs, and trunk, and they do so throughout puberty. In contrast, the arm and leg fat of adolescent boys decreases (Tanner & Whitehouse, 1975).

Muscle grows according to a different pattern than fat, accumulating very slowly throughout infancy and childhood. Then it rises dramatically at adolescence. Although both sexes gain in muscle at puberty, the increase is much greater for boys, who develop larger skeletal muscles and hearts and a greater lung capacity. Also, the number of red blood cells, and therefore the ability to carry oxygen from the lungs to the muscles, increases in boys but not in girls (Katchadourian, 1977). The combined result of these changes is that boys gain far more muscle strength than do girls, a difference that contributes to boys' superior athletic performance during the teenage years. But size and strength cannot account for the childhood advantage of boys in a variety of gross motor skills. As the From Research to Practice box above reveals, beginning in the preschool years, the social environment plays a prominent role.

Skeletal Growth

As we will see in a later section, children of the same age differ markedly in their rates of growth. As a result, researchers have devised methods for measuring progress toward physical maturity. These techniques are useful for studying the

Sphenoid

far short of boys'. According to one recent estimate, about 64 percent of males but only 41 percent of females are active in high school athletics (Berk, 1992b).

Sports do not just improve motor performance. They influence cognitive and social development as well. Interschool and intramural athletics provide important lessons in competition, assertiveness, problem solving, and teamwork. These experiences are less available to females because of the lower status of girls' sports. Clearly, special

steps need to be taken to raise girls' confidence that they can do well at athletics. Educating parents about the minimal differences in school-age boys' and girls' physical capacities and sensitizing them to unfair biases against girls' athletic ability may prove helpful. In addition, greater emphasis on skill training for girls along with increased attention to their athletic achievements is likely to improve their participation and performance.

Yet t
grows fa
from birt
hood, aft
sue (sma
pace thr
at which
to fight
(Shields,
and surv

Individ

Watch s
fer grea
Howeve
small fo
be chec
The
we trav
of the w
shortest

Size in Terms of Percentage of Total Growth

200
18(
16
14
12
1(
8
6
4
2

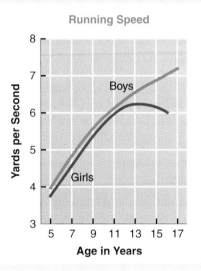

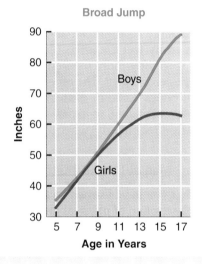

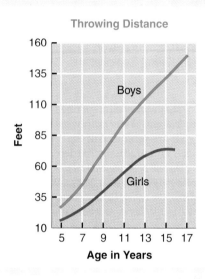

FIGURE 5.4 Age changes in running speed, broad jump, and throwing distance for boys and girls. The gender gap in athletic performance widens during adolescence. (From "Motor Development" by A. Espenschade & H. Eckert, in W. R. Warren & E. R. Buskirk, Eds., *Science and Medicine of Exercise and Sport*, 1974, pp. 329–330. New York: Harper & Row. Adapted by permission of HarperCollins Publishers, Inc.)

causes and consequences of individual differences in physical growth. They also provide rough estimates of children's chronological age in areas of the world where birth dates are not recorded.

SKELETAL AGE. The best way of estimating a child's physical maturity is to use **skeletal age,** a measure of development of the bones of the body. The embryonic skeleton is first formed out of soft, pliable tissue called cartilage. Then, beginning in the sixth week of pregnancy, cartilage cells harden into bone, a very gradual process that continues throughout childhood and adolescence. Once bones have taken on their basic shape, special growth centers called **epiphyses** start to appear just before birth and increase throughout childhood. In the long bones of the body, epiphyses emerge at the two extreme ends of each bone (see Figure 5.5). As growth continues, the epiphyses get thinner and disappear. Once this occurs, no more growth of the bone is possible (Delecki, 1985).

As Figure 5.6 shows, skeletal age can be estimated by X-raying the bones of the body and seeing how many epiphyses there are and the extent to which they are fused. These X-rays are compared to norms established for bone maturity based on large representative samples of children. In the absence of X-rays, dental development offers a clue to rate of skeletal development. A child who gets teeth early is likely to be advanced in physical maturity (Mott, James, & Sperhac, 1990).

Skeletal age
An estimate of physical maturity based on development of the bones of the body.

Epiphyses
Growth centers in the bones where new cartilage cells are produced and gradually harden.

*O*bservations of anthropologist Margaret Mead in Samoa underscored the contribution of social and cultural factors to the wide variability in adolescent adjustment. Today we know that biological and environmental pressures combine to affect adolescent well-being. Still, Mead's work overturned the commonly held belief that adolescence is an inevitable period of storm and stress. (DENNIS BRACK/BLACK STAR)

FIGURE
showin
Cartila;
growth
into bo
lisher fror
Tanner, C
Copyright

FIGUF
skclct
wrist
of the
(From /
Height
Whiteh(
H. Golc
permis:

For
Six
bo

Ge
Cu
chε
grο
ga
ch
mε

Burbank, & Ratner, 1986). But most of the time, adolescence is not absent. A study of 186 tribal and village cultures revealed that almost all had an intervening phase, however brief, between childhood and full assumption of adult roles (Schlegel & Barry, 1991).

In industrialized nations, successful participation in the economic life of society requires many years of education. Consequently, young people face extra years of dependence on parents and a long period in which they are expected to postpone sexual gratification while they master complex systems of knowledge essential to a productive worklife. As a result, adolescence is greatly extended, and teenagers confront a wider array of psychological challenges. A large body of research reveals that puberty is linked to important changes in self-image, mood, and interaction with parents and peers. In the following sections, we will see many examples of how biological and social forces *combine* to affect teenagers' adjustment.

Reactions to Pubertal Changes

How do girls and boys react to the massive physical changes of puberty? Most research aimed at answering this question has focused on girls' feelings about menarche.

GIRLS' REACTIONS TO MENARCHE. Research of a generation or two indicated that menarche was often traumatic and disturbing. For example, one woman, who reached puberty in the 1950s, reported:

> I had no information whatsoever, no hint that anything was going to happen to me. . . . I thought I was on the point of death from internal hemorrhage. . . . What did my highly educated mother do? She read me a furious lecture about what a bad, evil, immoral thing I was to start menstruating at the age of eleven! So young and so vile! Even after thirty years, I can feel the shock of hearing her condemn me for "doing" something I had no idea occurred. (Weideger, 1976, cited in Brooks-Gunn & Reiter, 1990, p. 37)

Recent findings show that girls' reactions to menarche are rarely so unfavorable today. The most common response is "surprise," undoubtedly caused by the sudden onset of the event. Girls often report a mixture of positive and negative emotions—"excited and pleased" as well as "scared and upset." But there are wide individual differences. Some, like this girl, react with joy and elation:

> When I discovered it, I called my mother and she showed me what to do. Then she did something I'll never forget. She told me to come with her and we went to the living room to tell my father. She just looked at me and then at him and said, "Well, your little girl is a young lady now!" My dad gave me a hug and congratulated me and I felt grown-up and proud that I was really a lady at last. That was one of the most exciting days of my life. (Shipman, 1971, p. 331)

As these two accounts suggest, girls' feelings about menarche depend on prior knowledge and support from family members. Both are influenced by social and cultural attitudes toward puberty and sexuality (Greif & Ulman, 1982).

For girls who have no advance information about sexuality, menarche can be shocking and disturbing. Fortunately, the number of girls with no preparation is much smaller today than it was several decades ago. In the 1950s, up to 50 percent were given no prior warning (Shainess, 1961). Today, no more than 10 to 15 percent are uninformed (Brooks-Gunn, 1988b). This shift is probably due to modern parents' greater willingness to discuss sexual matters with their children. Currently, almost all girls get some information from their mothers (Brooks-Gunn & Ruble, 1983). And girls whose fathers are told about pubertal changes adjust especially well. Perhaps a father's involvement reflects a family atmosphere that is highly understanding and accepting of physical and sexual matters (Brooks-Gunn & Ruble, 1980).

182

190

Boys' Reactions to Spermarche. Spermarche is the male pubertal event that is most similar to menarche, but we have much less information about its psychological impact. Available research indicates that like girls' reactions to menarche, boys' responses to spermarche are not intensely negative. Most report mixed feelings. Virtually all boys know about ejaculation ahead of time, but few get any information from parents. Usually they obtain it from reading material (Gaddis & Brooks-Gunn, 1985). In addition, although girls at first keep menarche secret from their peers, within 6 months almost all tell a friend they are menstruating. In contrast, far fewer boys ever tell anyone about spermarche (Brooks-Gunn et al., 1986; Downs & Fuller, 1991). Overall, boys seem to get much less social support for the physical changes of puberty than do girls. This suggests that boys might benefit, especially, from opportunities to ask questions and discuss feelings with a sympathetic male teacher at school.

The Function of Adolescent Initiation Ceremonies. The experience of puberty is affected by the larger cultural context in which boys and girls live. Many tribal and village societies celebrate puberty with a *rite of passage*—a communitywide initiation ceremony that marks an important change in privilege and responsibility. Consequently, these young people know that pubertal changes are honored and valued in their culture. In contrast, Western societies grant little formal recognition to movement from childhood to adolescence or from adolescence to adulthood. Certain religious ceremonies, such as confirmation and the Jewish bar or bat mitzvah, do resemble a rite of passage. But not all young people take part in these rituals, and they usually do not lead to any meaningful change in social status.

Instead, modern adolescents are confronted with many ages at which they are granted partial adult status—for example, an age for starting employment, for driving, for leaving high school, for voting, and for drinking. In some contexts (on the highway and at their place of work), they may be treated like adults. In others (at school and at home), they may still be regarded as children. The absence of a widely accepted marker of physical and social maturity makes the process of becoming an adult especially confusing. Perhaps modern adolescents would benefit from a socially and culturally appropriate substitute to serve the need that simpler societies meet with adolescent initiation rituals (Whisnant & Zegans, 1975).

In this adolescent initiation ceremony, an Apache community celebrates the arrival of puberty in a young girl with an elaborate ritual. (Bill Gillette/Stock Boston)

Pubertal Change, Emotion, and Social Behavior

In the preceding sections, we considered adolescents' reactions to their sexually maturing bodies. Puberty can also affect the young person's emotional state and social behavior. A common belief is that pubertal change has something to do with adolescent moodiness and the desire for greater physical and emotional separation from parents.

ADOLESCENT MOODINESS. Recently, researchers have explored the role of sex hormones in adolescents' emotional reactions. Indeed, higher hormone levels are related to greater moodiness, in the form of anger and irritability for males and anger and depression for females, between 9 and 14 years of age (Brooks-Gunn & Warren, 1989; Nottelmann et al., 1990). But these links are not strong, and we cannot really be sure that a rise in pubertal hormones causes adolescent moodiness.

What else might contribute to the common observation that adolescents are moody creatures? In several studies, the mood fluctuations of children, adolescents, and adults were tracked over a week by having them carry electronic pagers. At random intervals, they were beeped and asked to write down what they were doing, who they were with, and how they felt. As expected, adolescents reported somewhat lower moods than did school-age children and adults (Csikszentmihalyi & Larson, 1984; Larson & Lampman-Petraitis, 1989). But young people whose moods were especially negative were experiencing a greater number of negative life events, such as difficulties in getting along with parents, disciplinary actions at school, and breaking up with a boyfriend or girlfriend. Negative events increased steadily from childhood to adolescence, and teenagers also seemed to react to them with greater emotion than did children (Larson & Ham, 1993).

Furthermore, compared to the moods of adults, adolescents' feelings were less stable. They often varied from cheerful to sad and back again. But teenagers also moved from one situation to another more often, and their mood swings were strongly related to these changes. High points of their days were times spent with friends and in self-chosen leisure and hobby activities. Low points tended to occur in adult-structured settings—class, job, school halls, school library, and church (Csikszentmihalyi & Larson, 1984). Taken together, these findings suggest that situational factors may act in concert with hormonal influences to affect teenagers' moodiness—an explanation consistent with the balanced view of biological and social forces described earlier in this chapter.

PARENT–CHILD RELATIONSHIPS. Parents are quick to notice that as children enter adolescence, their bedroom doors start to close, they often resist spending time with the family, and they become more argumentative. Many studies report that puberty is related to a rise in parent–child conflict. Bickering and standoffs increase as adolescents move toward the peak of the growth spurt and, for girls, just after menarche occurs. During this time, both parents and teenagers report feeling less close to one another (Holmbeck & Hill, 1991; Paikoff & Brooks-Gunn, 1991).

Why should a youngster's more adultlike appearance and sexual maturity trigger these petty disputes between parent and child? Researchers believe the association may have some adaptive value. Among nonhuman primates, the young typically leave the family group around the time of puberty. The same is true in many nonindustrialized cultures (Caine, 1986; Schlegel & Barry, 1991). Departure of young people from the family discourages sexual relations among close blood relatives. But because children in industrialized societies usually remain economically dependent on parents long after they reach puberty, they cannot leave the family. Consequently, a modern substitute for physical departure seems to have emerged—increased psychological distancing between parents and children (Steinberg, 1987).

In later chapters, we will see that adolescents' new powers of reasoning may also contribute to a rise in family tensions. Also, the need for families to redefine relationships as children become physically mature and demand to be treated in adultlike ways may produce a temporary period of conflict. The quarreling that does take place is generally mild. Only a small minority of families experience a serious break in parent–child relationships. In reality, parents and children display both conflict and affection toward one another throughout adolescence. This also makes sense from an evolutionary perspective. Although separation from parents is adaptive, both generations benefit from warm, protective family bonds that last for many years to come (Steinberg, 1990).

The Importance of Early versus Late Maturation

In addition to dramatic physical change, the timing of puberty has a major impact on psychological adjustment. As we will see in the following sections, having physical characteristics that help gain social acceptance can be very comforting to adolescent boys and girls.

EFFECTS OF MATURATIONAL TIMING. Findings of several longitudinal studies indicate that maturational timing acts in opposite directions for boys and girls. Early maturing boys appeared advantaged in many aspects of emotional and social functioning. Both adults and peers viewed them as relaxed, independent, self-confident, and physically attractive. Popular with agemates, they held many leadership positions in school and tended to be athletic stars. In contrast, late maturing boys were not well liked. Peers and adults viewed them as anxious, overly talkative, and attention-seeking in behavior (Clausen, 1975; Jones, 1965; Jones & Bayley, 1950).

Among girls, the impact of early versus late maturation was just the reverse. Early maturing girls had social difficulties. They were below average in popularity, appeared withdrawn and lacking in self-confidence, and held few positions of leadership. Instead, their late maturing counterparts were especially well off. They were regarded as physically attractive, lively, sociable, and leaders at school (Jones & Mussen, 1958).

EXPLAINING MATURATIONAL TIMING EFFECTS. Most research on maturational timing was completed in the 1950s and 1960s, but new studies reveal that the same trends persist today (Brooks-Gunn, 1988a; Petersen, 1985). Two factors seem to account for them: (1) how closely the adolescent's body matches cultural ideals of physical attractiveness; and (2) how well young people "fit in" physically with their peers.

Flip through the pages of your favorite popular magazine, and look at the figures of men and women in the ads. You will see convincing evidence for our society's view of an attractive female as thin and long legged and a good-looking male as tall, broad shouldered, and muscular. The female image is a girlish shape that favors the late developer. The male image is consistent with that of the early maturing boy.

A consistent finding is that early maturing girls have a less positive **body image**—conception of and attitude toward their physical appearance—than do their on-time and late maturing agemates. Among boys, the opposite is true: Early maturation is linked to a positive body image, whereas late maturation predicts dissatisfaction with the physical self (Simmons & Blyth, 1987). Both boys and girls who have physical characteristics regarded by themselves and others as less attractive have a lower sense of self-esteem and are less well liked by peers (Langlois & Stephan, 1981; Lerner & Brackney, 1978). The adoption of society's "beauty is best" stereotype seems to be an important factor in the adjustment of early and late maturing boys and girls.

A second way of explaining differences in adjustment between early and late maturers is in terms of their physical status in relation to agemates. From this perspective, early maturing girls and late maturing boys have difficulty because they fall at the extremes in physical development. Support for this idea comes from evidence that adolescents feel most comfortable with peers who match their own level of biological maturity (Brooks-Gunn et al., 1986; Stattin & Magnusson, 1990).

Body image
Conception of and attitude toward one's physical appearance.

Because few agemates of the same biological status are available, early maturing adolescents of both sexes seek out older companions—a tendency that can lead to some unfavorable consequences. Older peers often encourage early maturing youngsters into activities they find difficult to resist and are not yet ready to handle emotionally, including sexual activity, drug and alcohol use, and minor delinquent acts. Perhaps because of involvements like these, the academic performance of early maturers tends to suffer (Duncan et al., 1985; Stattin & Magnusson, 1990).

Interestingly, school contexts can modify these maturational timing effects. In one study, early maturing sixth-grade girls felt better about themselves when they attended kindergarten through sixth-grade (K–6) rather than kindergarten through eighth-grade (K–8) schools, where they could mix with older adolescents. In the K–6 settings, they were relieved of pressures to adopt behaviors for which they were not ready (Blyth, Simmons, & Zakin, 1985). Similarly, a New Zealand study found that delinquency among early maturing girls was greatly reduced in all-girl schools, which limit opportunities to associate with norm-violating peers (most of whom are boys) (Caspi et al., 1993).

LONG-TERM CONSEQUENCES. Do the effects of early and late maturation persist into adulthood? Longitudinal research reveals some unexpected findings. Among boys, several aspects of adolescent adjustment were still evident well into middle adulthood. At age 38, the social prestige of early maturing males could still be detected in greater social ease and responsible, self-controlled behavior. Similarly, late maturing males, who as adolescents often tried to compensate for their small size through clowning and other antics, remained more impulsive and assertive over the years (Livson & Peskin, 1980).

Beyond these few consistencies, long-term follow-ups show some striking turnabouts in overall well-being. Many early maturing boys and late maturing girls, who had been the focus of admiration in adolescence, became rigid, inflexible, conforming, and somewhat discontented adults. In contrast, late maturing boys and early maturing girls, who were stress-ridden as teenagers, often developed into adults who were independent, flexible, cognitively competent, and satisfied with the direction of their lives (Macfarlane, 1971). How can we explain these remarkable reversals? Perhaps the confidence-inducing adolescence of early maturing boys and late maturing girls does not promote the coping skills needed to solve life's later problems. In contrast, the painful experiences associated with off-time pubertal growth may, in time, contribute to sharpened awareness, clarified goals, and greater stability.

Finally, it is important to note that these long-term outcomes may not hold completely in all cultures. In a Swedish study, achievement difficulties of early maturing girls persisted into young adulthood. They were twice as likely to leave high school after completing the minimum years of compulsory education as their on-time and later maturing counterparts (Stattin & Magnusson, 1990). In countries with highly selective college entrance systems, perhaps it is harder for early maturers to recover from declines in school performance. Clearly, the effects of maturational timing involve a complex blend of biological, immediate social setting, and cultural factors.

Adolescent Sexuality

Virtually all theorists agree that adolescence is an especially important time for the development of sexuality. With the arrival of puberty, hormonal changes—in particular, the production of androgens in young people of both sexes—lead to an increase in sex drive (Udry, 1990). In response, adolescents become very concerned about how to manage sexuality in social relationships, and new cognitive capacities affect their efforts to do so. Yet like the adjustment issues we have already discussed, adolescent sexual attitudes and behavior are heavily influenced by the social context in which the young person is growing up.

THE IMPORTANCE OF CULTURE. Think, for a moment, about when you first learned about the "facts of life" and how you found out about them. In your family, was sex discussed openly or treated with secrecy? Cross-cultural research reveals that exposure to sex, education about it, and efforts to restrict the sexual curiosity of children and adolescents vary widely around the world. At one extreme are a number of Middle Eastern peoples, who are known to kill girls who dishonor their families by losing their virginity before marriage. At the other extreme are several Asian and Pacific Island groups with very permissive sexual attitudes and practices. For example, among the Trobriand Islanders of Melanesia, older companions provide children with explicit instruction in sexual practices. Bachelor houses in which adolescents are expected to engage in sexual experimentation with a variety of partners are maintained (Benedict, 1934b; Ford & Beach, 1951).

For all the publicity granted to the image of a sexually free modern adolescent, you may be surprised to learn that American society falls on the restrictive side of this cultural continuum. Typically, American parents give children little information about sex, discourage them from engaging in sex play, and rarely talk about sex in their presence. When young people become interested in sex, they seek information elsewhere, turning to friends, books, magazines, movies, and television. On prime-time television shows, which adolescents watch the most, premarital sex occurs two to three times each hour and is spontaneous and passionate. Characters are rarely shown taking steps to avoid pregnancy or sexually transmitted disease (Beeghley & Sellers, 1986; Strasburger, 1989).

Think about the messages delivered by these two sets of sources, and you will see that they are contradictory and confusing. On the one hand, adults emphasize that sex at a young age and outside of marriage is wrong. On the other hand, adolescents encounter much in the broader social environment that extols the excitement and romanticism of sex. These mixed messages leave many American teenagers bewildered, poorly informed about sexual facts, and with little sound advice on how to conduct their sex lives responsibly (Gordon & Gilgun, 1987).

ADOLESCENT SEXUAL ATTITUDES AND BEHAVIOR. Although differences exist among subcultural groups, over the past 30 years the sexual attitudes of both adolescents and adults have become more liberal. Compared to a generation ago, more people believe that sexual intercourse before marriage is all right, as long as two people are emotionally committed to one another (Beeghley & Sellers, 1986). Recently, a slight swing back in the direction of conservative sexual beliefs has occurred. A growing number of young people say they are opposed to premarital sex, mentioning both moral and religious values and the risk of sexually transmitted disease (especially AIDS) as reasons (Gallup, 1987).

Trends in sexual activity of adolescents are quite consistent with their beliefs. The rate of premarital sex among young people has risen over time. For example, among high school students, females claiming to have had sexual intercourse grew from 28 percent in 1971 to 48 percent in 1990 (Forrest & Singh, 1990; U.S. Centers for Disease Control, 1992). As Table 5.1 reveals, a substantial minority of boys and girls are sexually active quite early, by ninth grade. The table also indicates that males tend to have their first intercourse earlier than females, and sexual activity is especially high among black adolescents particularly boys.

Yet timing of first intercourse provides us with only a limited picture of adolescent sexual behavior. Most teenagers engage in relatively low levels of sexual activity. The typical 15- to 19-year-old sexually active male—white, black, or Hispanic—has relations with only one girl at a time and spends half the year with no partner at all (Sonenstein, Pleck, & Ku, 1991). When we look closely at adolescent sexual attitudes and behavior, we see that contrary to popular belief, a runaway sexual revolution does not characterize American young people. In fact, the rate of teenage sexual activity in the United States is about the same as in other Western European nations (Jones et al., 1985).

TABLE 5.1 Teenage Sexual Activity Rates by Sex, Ethnic Group, and Grade*

SEX	ETHNIC GROUP			GRADE				TOTAL
	White	Black	Hispanic	9	10	11	12	
Male	56.4	87.8	63.0	48.7	52.5	62.6	76.3	60.8
Female	47.0	60.0	45.0	31.9	42.9	52.7	66.6	48.0
Total	51.6	72.3	53.4	39.6	47.6	57.3	71.9	54.2

*Data reflect the percentage of high school students who report ever having had sexual intercourse.

SOURCE: U.S. Centers for Disease Control, 1992.

CHARACTERISTICS OF SEXUALLY ACTIVE ADOLESCENTS. Teenage sexual activity is linked to a wide range of personal, familial, peer, and educational variables, including early physical maturation, parental separation and divorce, large family size, sexually active friends and older siblings, poor school performance, and lower educational aspirations (Brooks-Gunn & Furstenberg, 1989; Santelli & Beilenson, 1992). Since many of these factors are associated with growing up in a low-income family, it is not surprising that early sexual activity is more common among young people from economically disadvantaged homes. In fact, the high rate of premarital intercourse among black teenagers can largely be accounted for by widespread poverty in the black population (Furstenberg, Brooks-Gunn, & Morgan, 1987).

Unfortunately, nearly half of sexually active American teenagers are at risk for unplanned pregnancy because they do not use contraception at all or use it only occasionally (Santelli & Beilenson, 1992). Why do so many teenagers fail to take precautions? In Chapter 6, we will see that compared to school-age children, adolescents can consider many more possibilities when faced with a problem. But at first, they fail to apply this reasoning to everyday situations. In several studies, teenagers were asked to explain why they did not use birth control. Here are some typical answers:

> You don't say, "Well, I'm going to his house, and he's probably going to try to get to bed with me, so I better make sure I'm prepared." I mean, you don't know it's coming, so how are you to be prepared?
>
> I wouldn't [use contraception] if I was going . . . to have sex casually, you know, like once a month or once every two months. I feel it's more for somebody who has a steady boyfriend. (Kisker, 1985, p. 84)

One reason for responses like these is that advances in *perspective taking*—the capacity to imagine what others may be thinking and feeling (see Chapters 6 and 11)—lead teenagers, for a time, to be extremely concerned about others' opinions of them. Another reason for lack of planning before sex is that intense self-reflection leads many adolescents to believe they are unique and invulnerable to danger. They are likely to conclude that pregnancy only happens to others, not to themselves (Voydanoff & Donnelly, 1990).

Although adolescent cognition has much to do with teenagers' reluctance to use contraception, the social environment also contributes to it. Teenagers who talk openly with their parents about sex are not less sexually active, but they are more likely to use birth control (Brooks-Gunn, 1988b; Moore, Peterson, & Furstenberg, 1986). Unfortunately, many adolescents say they are too scared or embarrassed to ask parents questions about sex or contraception. Although most get some sex education at school, teenagers' knowledge about sex and contraception is often incomplete or just plain wrong. Many do not know where to get birth control counseling and devices (Hayes, 1987). When they do, they tend to be just

*A*dolescence is an especially important time for the development of sexuality. American teenagers receive contradictory and confusing messages from the social environment about the appropriateness of sex. Although the rate of premarital sex has risen among adolescents, most engage in low levels of sexual activity and have only a single partner. (NANCY SHEEHAN/PICTURE CUBE)

as uncomfortable about going to a doctor or family planning clinic as they are about seeking advice from parents (Kisker, 1985).

SEXUAL ORIENTATION. Up to this point, our discussion has focused only on heterosexual behavior. About 1 to 4 percent of young people discover they are lesbian or gay (Billy et al., 1993; Hamer et al., 1993; Kinsey et al., 1953). Adolescence is an equally crucial time for the sexual development of these individuals, and societal attitudes, once again, loom large in how well they fare. Cultures vary as much in their acceptance of homosexuality as they do in their approval of premarital sex. In the United States, homosexuals are stigmatized, as shown by the degrading language often used to describe them (Gordon & Gilgun, 1987). Yet research reveals that homosexuals have no more choice in their sexual orientation than do their heterosexual counterparts.

Although the extent to which homosexuality is due to genetic versus environmental forces remains highly controversial, new evidence indicates that heredity makes an important contribution. Identical twins of both sexes are much more likely than fraternal twins to share a homosexual orientation; the same is true for biological as opposed to adoptive relatives (Bailey & Pillard, 1991; Bailey et al., 1993). Furthermore, male homosexuality tends to be more common on the maternal than paternal side of families. This suggests that it might be X-linked (see Chapter 3). Indeed, a recent gene-mapping study found that among 40 pairs of homosexual brothers, 33 (85.5 percent) had an identical segment of DNA on the X chromosome. One or several genes in that region might predispose males to become homosexual (Hamer et al., 1993).

Yet these findings do not apply to all gay men, since some do not have the genetic marker just described. Family factors are also associated with homosexuality. Looking back on their childhoods, both male and female homosexuals tend to view their same-sex parent as cold and distant (Bell, Weinberg, & Hammersmith, 1981). This does not mean that parents cause their youngsters to become homosexual. Rather, for some children, an early genetic bias away from traditional gender-role behavior may lead them to feel alienated from same-sex parents and peers. A strong desire for affection from people of their own sex may join with biology to push these youngsters in a homosexual direction (Green, 1987). Once again, however, homosexuality does not always develop in this way, since some homosexuals are very comfortable with their gender role and have warm relationships with their parents. Homosexuality probably results from a variety of biological and environmental combinations that are not yet well understood.

A passing attraction to members of the same sex is common during adolescence. About 25 percent of boys and 5 percent of girls have participated in at least one homosexual act by age 15 (Elkind, 1991). In some tribal and village cultures, homosexual behavior among young males is encouraged, as a way of learning about sex and discharging the sex drive (Savin-Williams, 1990). But adolescents in industrialized nations who discover that they have a compelling interest in same-sex partners often experience intense inner conflict. They get little approval for their sexual orientation and feel a profound sense of isolation and loneliness. Almost always, their parents are very upset. Even very open-minded parents respond with considerable pain because they know their youngster will encounter limited acceptance by the larger society. Homosexual adolescents have a special need for caring adults and peers who can help them establish a positive sexual identity and find social acceptance (Gordon & Gilgun, 1987).

Sexually active adolescents, both homosexual and heterosexual, face serious health risks. About 8 to 10 percent of American young people between the ages of 15 and 25 contract sexually transmitted diseases (STDs). If left untreated, sterility and life-threatening complications can result. By far the most serious STD is AIDS. Over one-fifth of cases in the United States originate in adolescence. Drug-abusing and homosexual teenagers account for most of them, but heterosexual spread of the disease is increasing rapidly, especially among females (U.S. Centers for Disease Control, 1993). And for female heterosexuals, there is an added concern: The rate of teenage pregnancy and childbearing in the United States is alarmingly high, an issue we take up in the following section.

TEENAGE PREGNANCY AND CHILDBEARING. Unprotected sexual activity results in more than a million American teenage pregnancies each year, 30,000 to adolescents under age 15. As Figure 5.13 shows, the adolescent pregnancy rate in the United States is twice that of England, Canada, and France, three times that of Sweden, and six times that of the Netherlands. The United States differs from these nations in three important ways: (1) effective sex education reaches fewer teenagers; (2) convenient, low-cost contraceptive services for adolescents are scarce; and (3) many more families live in poverty, which encourages young people to take risks without considering the future implications of their behavior (Jones et al., 1985).

Not all adolescents who conceive give birth to a baby. About 40 percent choose to have an abortion, and 13 percent of teenage pregnancies end in miscarriage (Hayes, 1987). Because the United States has one of the highest adolescent abortion rates of any developed country, the total number of teenage births is actually lower than it was 30 years ago (Vinovskis, 1988). But teenage parenthood is a much greater problem today because modern adolescents are far less likely to marry before childbirth. In 1960, only 15 percent of teenage births were to unmarried females, whereas today, nearly 70 percent are (Children's Defense Fund, 1991a). Increased social acceptance of a young single mother raising a child, along

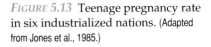
FIGURE 5.13 Teenage pregnancy rate in six industrialized nations. (Adapted from Jones et al., 1985.)

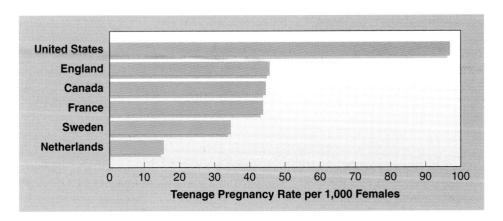

with the belief of many teenage girls that a baby might fill a void in their lives, has meant that only a small number give their infants up for adoption. Each year, about 320,000 unmarried adolescent girls take on the responsibilities of parenthood before they are psychologically mature (Brooks-Gunn & Furstenberg, 1989).

CORRELATES AND CONSEQUENCES OF TEENAGE PREGNANCY. Becoming a parent is challenging and stressful for any person, but it is especially difficult for adolescents, who have not yet established a clear sense of direction for their own lives. As we have already seen, adolescent sexual activity is linked to economic disadvantage. Teenage mothers are many times more likely to be poor than are women who postpone childbearing. A high percentage of out-of-wedlock births are to members of low-income minorities, especially black teenagers. Many of these young people seem to turn to early parenthood as a way to move into adulthood when educational and career avenues are unavailable (Caldas, 1993; Murry, 1992).

Think about these characteristics of teenage parents, and you will quickly see why early childbirth imposes lasting hardships on two generations—adolescent and newborn baby. The lives of pregnant teenagers are often troubled in many ways, and after the baby is born, their circumstances worsen. Only 50 percent of girls who give birth before age 18 finish high school, compared to 96 percent of those who wait to become parents. Both teenage mothers and fathers are likely to be on welfare. If they are employed, their limited education restricts them to unsatisfying, low-paid jobs (Furstenberg, Brooks-Gunn, & Chase-Landsdale, 1989; Mott & Marsiglio, 1985).

In Chapter 3, we saw that poverty-stricken pregnant women are more likely to have inadequate diets and to expose their unborn babies to harmful environmental influences, such as illegal drugs. And many do not receive early prenatal care. These conditions are widespread among pregnant teenagers. As a result, adolescent mothers often experience prenatal and birth complications, and their infants are likely to be born underweight and premature (Makinson, 1985). Children of teenagers are at risk for poor parenting as well. As they get older, many score low on intelligence tests, achieve poorly in school, and engage in disruptive social behavior. Too often, the cycle of adolescent pregnancy is repeated in the next generation. About one-third of girls who have a baby before age 19 were born to teenage mothers (Furstenberg, Levine, & Brooks-Gunn, 1990).

Still, how well adolescent parents and their children fare varies a great deal. Outcomes are more favorable when mothers return to school after giving birth and continue to live in their parents' homes, where child care can be shared with experienced adults. If the teenage mother finishes high school, avoids additional births, and finds a stable marriage partner, long-term disruptions in her own and her child's development are less severe. The small minority of young mothers who fail in all three of these ways face a life of continuing misfortune (Furstenberg, Brooks-Gunn, & Morgan, 1987).

PREVENTION STRATEGIES. Preventing teenage pregnancy and childbearing requires strategies addressing the many factors that underlie early sexual activity and lack of contraceptive use. Informing adolescents about sex and contraception is crucial. Too often, sex education courses are given late in high school (after sexual activity has begun), last no more than a few sessions, and are limited to a catalogue of facts about anatomy and reproduction. Sex education that goes beyond this bare minimum does not encourage early sex, as some opponents claim. It does improve awareness of sexual facts—knowledge that is necessary for responsible sexual behavior (Katchadourian, 1990).

Knowledge, however, is not sufficient to convince adolescents of the importance of postponing sexual activity and practicing contraception. To change teenagers' behavior, sex education must help them build a bridge between what they know and what they do in their everyday lives. Today, a new wave of sex education programs has emerged in which creative discussion and role-playing techniques are being used to teach adolescents the decision-making and social skills they need to resist early and unprotected sex (Barth, Petro, & Leland, 1992; Kirby, 1992).

The most controversial aspect of adolescent pregnancy prevention is a growing movement to provide teenagers with easy access to contraceptives. In some large cities, school-based health clinics offering contraceptive services have been established (Seligmann, 1991). Many Americans argue that placing birth control pills or condoms in the hands of teenagers is equivalent to saying that early sex is okay. Yet in Western Europe, where these clinics are common, teenage sexual activity is no higher than it is in the United States, but pregnancy, childbirth, and abortion rates are much lower (Hayes, 1987; Voydanoff & Donnelly, 1990).

INTERVENING WITH TEENAGE PARENTS. The most difficult and costly way to deal with adolescent parenthood is to wait until after it has happened. Young single mothers need health care for themselves and their children, encouragement to stay in school, job training, instruction in parenting and life-management skills, and high-quality, affordable day care. Currently, new programs that focus on fathers are attempting to increase their financial and emotional commitment to the baby and strengthen the bond between teenage parents (Children's Defense Fund, 1991a; Robinson, 1988). But fathers are very difficult to reach because most either do not admit their paternity or abandon the young mother and baby after a short period of time. At present, the majority of adolescent parents of both sexes do not receive the help they need.

Anorexia Nervosa and Bulimia

A group of adolescents with quite different characteristics than early childbearers also experience serious adjustment difficulties with the advent of puberty. **Anorexia nervosa** is a tragic eating disturbance in which young people starve themselves because of a compulsive fear of getting fat. In all, around 1 million Americans, mostly girls and young women, have the disorder (Brumberg, 1988; Harris, 1991). About 1 percent of middle-class females between the ages of 12 and 25 are affected. It is ironic that in industrialized nations, malnutrition severe enough to interfere with normal adolescent growth occurs most often in affluent homes where food is plentiful, not in poverty-stricken families.

Anorexics have an extremely distorted body image. Even after they have become severely underweight, they conclude that they are fat. Most go on a self-imposed diet so strict that they struggle to avoid eating in response to hunger. To enhance weight loss, anorexics engage in strenuous physical exercise. If family members try to stop them, they seek other ways, such as pacing back and forth in their rooms or getting up in the middle of the night for an energetic workout (Gilbert & DeBlassie, 1984).

The physical consequences of this attempt to reach "perfect" slimness are severe. Anorexics lose between 25 and 50 percent of their body weight and appear painfully thin. Because a normal menstrual cycle requires a body-fat content of about 15 percent, either menarche does not occur or the girl's menstrual periods stop. Malnutrition causes additional physical symptoms—pale skin; brittle, discolored nails; fine dark hairs appearing all over the body; and extreme sensitivity to cold. If allowed to continue, anorexia nervosa can result in shrinking of the heart muscle and kidney failure. About 5 percent of those with the disorder die of it (Harris, 1991).

Anorexia is the combined result of forces within the individual, the family, and the larger culture. We have already seen that the societal image of "thin is beautiful" contributes to the poorer body image of early maturing girls, who are at greatest risk for anorexia (Attie & Brooks-Gunn, 1989). But though almost all adolescent girls go on diets at one time or another, anorexics persist in weight loss to an extreme. Many are perfectionists who have high standards for their own

Anorexia nervosa

An eating disorder in which individuals (usually females) starve themselves because of a compulsive fear of getting fat.

behavior and performance. Typically, these girls are excellent students who are responsible and well behaved—ideal daughters in many respects.

Yet researchers who have studied the family interaction of parents and anorexic daughters have identified problems related to adolescent autonomy that may trigger the compulsive dieting. Often these parents have high expectations for achievement and social acceptance and are overprotective and controlling. Although the daughter tries to meet these demands, inside she is angry at not being recognized as an individual in her own right. Instead of rebelling openly, the anorexic girl expresses her feelings through dieting. Without saying so directly, she tells her parents, "I am a separate person from you, and I can do what I want with my own body!" At the same time, this youngster, who has been so used to having parents make decisions for her, meets the challenges of adolescence with little self-confidence. Starving herself is also a way of avoiding new expectations by returning to a much younger, preadolescent image (Halmi, 1987; Maloney & Kranz, 1991).

Because anorexic girls typically deny that any problem exists, treating the disorder is difficult. Hospitalization is often necessary to prevent life-threatening malnutrition. Family therapy, in which efforts are made to change parent–child interaction and expectations, is the most successful treatment. As a supplementary approach, applied behavior analysis, in which hospitalized anorexics are reinforced for gaining weight with praise, social contact, and opportunities for exercise, is helpful (Gilbert & DeBlassie, 1984). Still, only 30 percent of anorexics fully recover. For many others, eating problems continue in less extreme form.

One-third of anorexics develop **bulimia,** a less severe disorder in which young people (again, mainly girls) engage in binge eating followed by deliberate vomiting, other purging techniques such as heavy doses of laxatives, and strict dieting. However, bulimia is much more common than anorexia nervosa. Only 5 percent of bulimic girls have previously been anorexic (Johnson et al., 1983). Although bulimics share with anorexics a pathological fear of getting fat and a middle-class family background with high expectations, most have quite different personality characteristics. Typically, bulimics are not just impulsive eaters; they also lack self-control in other areas of their lives. Although they tend to be good students and liked by peers, many engage in petty shoplifting and alcohol abuse. Bulimics also differ from anorexics in that they are aware of their abnormal eating habits, feel extremely depressed and guilty about them, and are usually desperate to get help. As a result, bulimia is usually easier to treat through individual and family therapy, support groups, and nutrition education (Harris, 1991).

*A*dolescents with anorexia nervosa have an unrealistic image of their physical appearance. Even after they have become painfully thin, they see themselves as fat. (GEORGE S. ZIMBELL/MONKMEYER PRESS PHOTO)

Puberty is a time of dramatic physical change leading to an adult-sized body and sexual maturity. In contrast to early biologically oriented theories, modern researchers recognize that the psychological impact of pubertal events is a product of both biological and social forces. Typically, girls' emotional reactions to menarche and boys' reactions to spermarche are mixed, although prior knowledge and social support affect their responses. Adolescent moodiness is related to both sex hormone levels and changes in the social environment.

Puberty prompts increased conflict and psychological distancing between parents and children—reactions that appear to be modern substitutes for physical departure from the family in our evolutionary history. The standards and expectations of the culture and peer group lead early maturing boys and late maturing girls to be advantaged in emotional and social adjustment. In contrast, late maturing boys and early maturing girls experience more adjustment difficulties.

American adolescents receive mixed messages from adults and the larger cultural environment about sexual activity. The percentage of sexually active teenagers has increased over time. Homosexual young people face special challenges in establishing a positive sexual identity. Adolescent cognitive processes along with lack of social supports for responsible sexual behavior contribute to high rates of teenage pregnancy, abortion, and premarital childbirth in the United

Brief Review

....

Bulimia

An eating disorder in which individuals (mainly females) go on eating binges followed by deliberate vomiting, other purging techniques such as heavy doses of laxatives, and strict dieting.

States. For many adolescent girls, the cultural ideal of thinness combines with family and psychological problems to produce the serious eating disturbances of anorexia nervosa and bulimia.

DEVELOPMENT OF THE BRAIN

The human brain is the most elaborate and effective living structure on earth today. Yet despite its complexity, at birth the brain is nearer to its adult size than any other organ, and it continues to develop at an astounding pace during the first 2 years of life. To best understand brain growth, we need to look at it from two vantage points. The first is at the microscopic level of individual brain cells. The second is at the larger level of the cerebral cortex, the most complex brain structure and the one responsible for the highly developed intelligence of our species.

Development of Neurons

The human brain has 100 billion to 200 billion **neurons,** or nerve cells, that store and transmit information, many of which have thousands of direct connections with other neurons. Neurons differ from other body cells in that they are not tightly packed together. There are tiny gaps, or **synapses,** between them where fibers from different neurons come close together but do not touch. Neurons release chemicals that cross the synapse, thereby sending messages to one another.

The basic story of brain growth concerns how neurons form this intricate communication system. Each neuron passes through three developmental steps: (1) cell production; (2) cell migration; and (3) cell differentiation (Nowakowski, 1987). In Chapter 3, we indicated that neurons are *produced* in the primitive neural tube of the embryo, from which they *migrate* to form the major parts of the brain. By the end of the second trimester of pregnancy, this process is complete; no more neurons will be generated in the individual's lifetime.

Once neurons are in place, they begin to *differentiate,* establishing their unique functions by extending their fibers to form synaptic connections with neighboring cells. Because developing neurons require space for their axons and dendrites, a surprising aspect of brain growth is that many surrounding neurons die when synapses are formed. Consequently, the peak period of development in any brain area is also marked by the greatest rate of cell death. Fortunately, during embryonic growth, the neural tube produces an excess of neurons—far more than the brain will ever need (Suomi, 1982).

The precise location of each neuron and the direction in which its fibers extend are believed to be genetically determined. But as soon as neurons form connections, a new factor becomes important in their survival: *stimulation.* Neurons that are stimulated by input from the surrounding environment continue to establish new synapses. Those that are seldom stimulated soon die off. This suggests that appropriate stimulation of the child's brain is vital during periods in which the formation of synapses is at its peak (Greenough, Black, & Wallace, 1987).

At this point, you may be wondering: If no more neurons are produced after the prenatal period, what causes the dramatic increase in skull size we mentioned earlier in this chapter? Growth of neural fibers results in some increase in brain weight, but not as much as a second type of cell in the brain. About half the brain's volume is made up of **glial cells**, which do not carry messages. Instead, their most important function is **myelinization,** a process in which neural fibers are coated with an insulating fatty sheath (called myelin) that improves the efficiency of message transfer. Glial cells multiply at a dramatic pace from the fourth month of pregnancy through the second year, after which their rate of production slows down (Spreen et al., 1984). Myelinization is responsible for the rapid gain in overall size

Neurons
Nerve cells that store and transmit information in the brain.

Synapses
The gaps between neurons, across which chemical messages are sent.

Glial cells
Brain cells serving the function of myelinization.

Myelinization
A process in which neural fibers are coated with an insulating fatty sheath (called myelin) that improves the efficiency of message transfer.

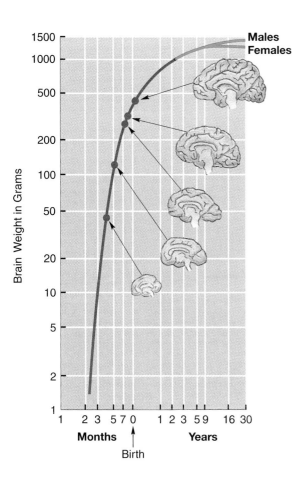

FIGURE 5.14 Increase in weight of the human brain from the prenatal period to adulthood. The rise in brain weight is especially rapid between the fetal period and the child's second birthday (see red line), when glial cells are multiplying at a dramatic pace. As brain weight increases, the cortex becomes more convoluted, or folded. (From *Normal and Abnormal Development of the Human Nervous System* by R. J. Lemire, J. D. Loeser, R. W. Leech, & E. C. Alvord, 1975, New York: Harper & Row, p. 236. Adapted by permission.)

of the brain (see Figure 5.14). By the time the child is 2 years old, the brain is already about 70 percent of its adult weight. At 6 years, it reaches 90 percent.

Development of the Cerebral Cortex

The **cerebral cortex** surrounds the rest of the brain, much like a half-shelled walnut. It is the largest structure of the human brain (accounting for 85 percent of brain weight) and the one responsible for the unique intelligence of our species. The cerebral cortex is also the last brain structure to stop growing. For this reason, it is believed to be much more sensitive to environmental influences than any other part of the brain (Suomi, 1982).

As Figure 5.15 shows, different regions of the cerebral cortex have specific functions, such as receiving information from the senses, instructing the body to move, and thinking. Researchers study the development of these regions by analyzing the chemical makeup and myelinization of the brains of young children who have died. Their findings reveal that the order in which areas of the cortex develop corresponds to the sequence in which various capacities emerge during infancy and childhood. For example, among areas that control body movement, the most advanced at birth is the precentral gyrus (refer again to Figure 5.15). Within it, neurons that control the head, arms, and chest mature ahead of those that control the trunk and legs. Do you recognize a familiar developmental trend? The last portion of the cortex to develop and myelinate is the frontal lobe, which is responsible for thought and consciousness. From age 2 onward, this area functions more effectively, and it continues its growth for years, well into the second and third decades of life (Spreen et al., 1984).

LATERALIZATION OF THE CORTEX. Figure 5.15 shows only one hemisphere, or side, of the cortex. The brain has two hemispheres—left and right. Although they look

Cerebral cortex
The largest structure of the human brain that accounts for the highly developed intelligence of the human species.

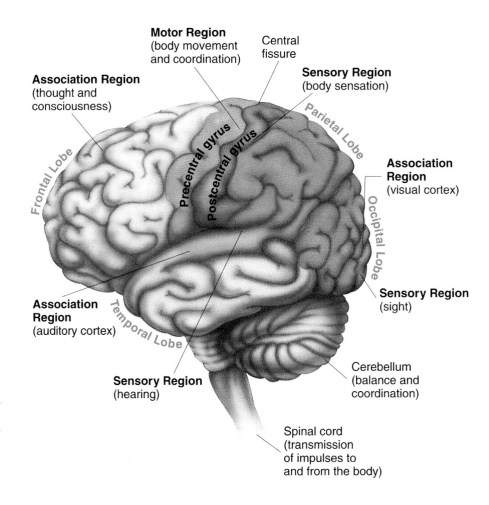

FIGURE 5.15 The left side of the human brain, showing the major structures of the cerebral cortex. The cortex is divided into different lobes, each of which contains a variety of regions with specific functions. *Motor regions* give direct orders to the muscles of the body; *sensory regions* receive direct input from the sense organs; and *association* or *"thought" regions* combine impulses from many other parts of the brain.

Lateralization
Specialization of functions of the two hemispheres of the cortex.

Plasticity
The ability of other parts of the brain to take over functions of damaged regions.

alike, the hemispheres do not have precisely the same functions. Some tasks are done mostly by one and some by the other. For example, each hemisphere receives sensory information from and controls only one side of the body—the one opposite to it.* For most of us, the left hemisphere is responsible for verbal abilities (such as spoken and written language) and positive emotion (for example, joy), whereas the right hemisphere handles spatial abilities (judging distances, reading maps, and recognizing geometric shapes) and negative emotion (such as distress). This pattern may be reversed in left-handed people, but more often, the cortex of left-handers is less clearly specialized than that of right-handers.

Specialization of the two hemispheres is called **lateralization.** Few topics in child development have stimulated more interest than the question of when brain lateralization occurs. The reason researchers are interested in this issue is that they want to know more about brain **plasticity.** A highly plastic cortex is still adaptable because many areas are not yet committed to specific functions. If a part of the brain is damaged, other parts can take over tasks that would have been handled by the damaged region. But once the hemispheres lateralize, damage to a particular region means that the abilities controlled by it will be lost forever.

Researchers used to think that lateralization of the cortex did not begin until after 2 years of age (Lenneberg, 1967). Today we know that this is not the case. Hemispheric specialization is already under way at birth. For example, the majority of neonates favor the right side of the body in their reflexive responses (Grattan et al., 1992). And like adults, most preterm and full-term newborns show greater

*The eyes are an exception. Messages from the right half of each retina go to the left hemisphere; messages from the left half of each retina go to the right hemisphere. Thus, visual information from *both* eyes is received by *both* hemispheres.

electrical brain-wave activity in the left hemisphere while listening to speech sounds. In contrast, the right hemisphere reacts more strongly to nonspeech sounds as well as stimuli (such as a sour-tasting fluid) that cause infants to display negative emotions (Fox & Davidson, 1986; Hahn, 1987).

Although specialization of brain regions begins early in life, it is not yet complete. Dramatic evidence for early plasticity comes from research in which infants had part or all of one hemisphere removed to control violent brain seizures. The remaining hemisphere, whether right or left, took over language and spatial functions as the child matured. But because lateralization had already begun, full recovery did not take place. As these brain-injured infants reached middle childhood and adolescence, they showed many normal abilities, but they had difficulty with very complex verbal and spatial tasks (Goodman & Whitaker, 1985).

Before 1 year of age, the brain is more plastic than at any later time of life, perhaps because many of its synapses have not yet been established (Satz & Bullard-Bates, 1981). Still, the cortex appears to be programmed early on for the hemispheric specialization that is typical of our species. A lateralized brain is certainly adaptive. It permits a wider array of talents to be represented in the two hemispheres than if both sides of the cortex served exactly the same functions.

DEVELOPMENT OF LATERALIZATION: STUDIES OF HANDEDNESS. Even though the hemispheres show early specialization, lateralization increases with age. A growing literature on the development of handedness is providing new insights into the development of lateralization in infancy and childhood.

A strong hand preference reflects the greater capacity of one side of the brain—often referred to as the individual's **dominant cerebral hemisphere**—to carry out skilled motor action. Other abilities located on the dominant side may be superior as well. In support of this idea, for right-handed people, who make up 90 percent of the population, language is housed with hand control in the left hemisphere. For the remaining 10 percent who are left-handed, language is often shared between the hemispheres rather than located in only one. This indicates that the brains of left-handers tend to be less strongly lateralized than those of right-handers (Hiscock & Kinsbourne, 1987). Consistent with this idea, many left-handed individuals are also ambidextrous; that is, although they prefer their left hand, they sometimes use their right hand skillfully as well (McManus et al., 1988).

Is handedness and, along with it, specialization of brain functions hereditary? Although researchers disagree on this issue, certain findings argue against a genetic explanation. Twins—whether identical or fraternal—are more likely than ordinary siblings to display opposite handedness, yet we would expect identical twins to be more alike if heredity played a powerful role. Furthermore, the hand preference of each twin is related to positioning in the uterus (twins usually lie in opposite orientations). According to one theory, lateralization can be traced to prenatal events. New evidence indicates that the way most fetuses lie in the uterus—turned toward the left—may promote greater postural control by the right side of the body (Previc, 1991).

Hand preference shows up early in development—by 5 or 6 months of age (McCormick & Maurer, 1988). However, it is not stable until 2 years, and some intriguing research suggests why. Handedness seems to undergo dips and recoveries that coincide with bursts in language competence. When language forges ahead at a quick pace, it seems to place extra demands on the left hemisphere, resulting in a temporary loss in motor dominance that returns as each new skill—at first babbling, then first words, and finally combining words—becomes well established (Ramsay, 1985; Ramsay & McCune, 1984). Then, in early and middle childhood, hand preference increases, indicating that specialization of brain regions strengthens during this time (McManus et al., 1988).

What about children whose hand use suggests an unusual organization of brain functions? Do these youngsters develop normally? Perhaps you have heard that left-handedness is more frequent among severely retarded and mentally ill

Dominant cerebral hemisphere
The hemisphere of the brain responsible for skilled motor action. The left hemisphere is dominant in right-handed individuals. In left-handed individuals, the right hemisphere may be dominant, or motor and language skills may be shared between the hemispheres.

people than it is in the general population. Although this is true, you also know that when two variables are correlated, this does not mean that one causes the other. Atypical lateralization is probably not responsible for the problems of these individuals. Instead, they may have suffered early brain damage to the left hemisphere, which caused their disabilities and, at the same time, led to a shift in handedness. In support of this idea, left-handedness is associated with a variety of prenatal and birth difficulties that can result in brain damage, including prolonged labor, prematurity, Rh incompatibility, and breech delivery (Coren & Halpern, 1991).

Finally, in considering the evidence on handedness and development, keep in mind that only a small number of left-handers show developmental problems of any kind. In fact, the unusual lateralization of left-handed children may have certain advantages. Left- and mixed-handed youngsters are more likely than their right-handed agemates to develop outstanding verbal and mathematical talents. According to Camilla Benbow (1986), a genetic predisposition for more even distribution of cognitive functions across both hemispheres is responsible for this trend. Still, many left-handed children and adults may be bilateral and ambidextrous for environmental rather than genetic reasons, since they must learn to live in a right-hand biased world.

Other Advances in Brain Development

Besides the cortex, other areas of the brain make strides during infancy and childhood. As we look at these changes, you will see that they have one feature in common. They all involve establishing links among different parts of the brain, increasing the coordinated functioning of the central nervous system. (To see where each of these structures is located, turn back to Figure 5.10 on page 185.)

At the rear and base of the brain is the **cerebellum,** a structure that aids in balance and control of body movement. Fibers linking the cerebellum to the cerebral cortex begin to myelinate after birth, but they do not complete this process until about age 4 (Tanner, 1990). This change undoubtedly contributes to dramatic gains in motor control, so that by the end of the preschool years, children can play a game of hopscotch, pump a playground swing, and throw a ball with a well-organized set of movements.

The **reticular formation,** a structure in the brain stem that maintains alertness and consciousness, myelinates throughout early childhood, continuing its growth into adolescence. Neurons in the reticular formation send out fibers to other areas of the brain. Many go to the frontal lobe of the cortex (McGuinness & Pribram, 1980). Maturation of the reticular formation contributes to gains in sustained, controlled attention that we will discuss in Chapter 7.

A final brain structure that undergoes major changes during early childhood is the **corpus callosum.** It is a large bundle of fibers that connects the two hemispheres so that they can communicate with one another. Myelinization of the corpus callosum does not begin until the end of the first year of life. By 4 to 5 years, its development is fairly advanced (Spreen et al., 1984; Witelson & Kigar, 1988). About this time, children become more proficient at tasks that require transfer of information between the cerebral hemispheres, such as comparing two textured stimuli when each is presented to a different hand (Galin et al., 1979). The corpus callosum continues to mature at a slower rate during middle childhood. More information on how it develops is likely to enhance our understanding of abilities that require collaboration among many parts of the brain, such as abstract thinking and creativity.

Brain Growth Spurts and Sensitive Periods of Development

Earlier we suggested that stimulation of the brain may be critical during periods in which it is growing most rapidly—when formation of synapses is at a peak.

Cerebellum
A brain structure that aids in balance and control of body movements.

Reticular formation
A brain structure that maintains alertness and consciousness.

Corpus callosum
The large bundle of fibers that connects the two hemispheres of the brain.

The existence of sensitive periods in postnatal development of the cortex has been amply demonstrated in studies of animals exposed to extreme forms of sensory deprivation. For example, there seems to be a time when rich and varied visual experiences must occur for the visual centers of the brain to develop normally. If a month-old kitten is deprived of light for as brief a time as 3 or 4 days, these areas of the brain start to degenerate. If the kitten is kept in the dark for as long as 2 months, the damage is permanent (Hubel & Wiesel, 1970). Severe stimulus deprivation also affects overall brain growth. When animals raised as pets are compared to animals reared in isolation, the brains of the pets are heavier and thicker (Greenough, Black, & Wallace, 1987).

Because we cannot ethically expose children to such experiments, researchers interested in identifying sensitive periods for human brain development must rely on less direct evidence. Several investigators have identified intermittent brain growth spurts from infancy into adolescence, based on gains in brain weight and skull size as well as changes in the electrical activity of the cortex (Epstein, 1974a, 1974b, 1980; Thatcher, Walker, & Giudice, 1987). These spurts seem to be related to peaks in children's intelligence test performance and mastery of Piagetian tasks. In infant rhesus monkeys, the ability to search successfully for hidden objects coincides with a dramatic rise in synaptic connections in the frontal lobe of the cortex (Diamond & Goldman-Rakic, 1989; Goldman-Rakic, 1987). Human infants also display changes in brain functioning—more powerful electrical activity in the frontal region—when they master complex object-hiding tasks at the end of the first year (Bell & Fox, 1992).

These findings suggest that formation of synapses may underlie the earliest brain growth spurts. Thinning out of excess neurons, more limited production of synapses, and myelinization may account for the later ones (Fischer, 1987). Exactly how brain development might be supported or disrupted by experience during these periods is still a question for future research. Once we have such information, it will have major implications for child-rearing and educational practices.

Brief Review

The human brain grows faster early in development than any other organ of the body. Neurons develop in a three-step sequence—production, migration, and differentiation—that concludes with the formation of synapses and myelinization. Although the cerebral cortex has already begun to lateralize at birth, it retains considerable plasticity during the first year of life. Hand preference is evident in infancy and strengthens over early childhood, a sign of increasing brain lateralization. Left-handedness is sometimes associated with developmental abnormalities; however, the majority of left-handed children show no problems of any kind. The cerebellum, the reticular formation, and the corpus callosum undergo considerable development during early childhood, contributing to connections between different parts of the brain. Research supports the existence of intermittent brain growth spurts from infancy into adolescence. Each may be a sensitive period during which appropriate stimulation is required for optimal development of human intelligence.

FACTORS AFFECTING PHYSICAL GROWTH

Physical growth, like other aspects of development, results from the continuous and complex interplay between heredity and environment. In the following sections, we take a closer look at this familiar theme. We will see that in addition to genetic makeup, nutrition, relative freedom from disease, and emotional well-being affect the body's development. And, as the Social Issues box on page 208 reveals, environmental pollutants pose a serious threat to the healthy growth of many children.

Five-year-old Desonia lives in an old, dilapidated tenement in a slum area of a large American city. Layers of paint applied over the years can be seen flaking off the inside walls and the back porch. The oldest paint chips are lead based. As an infant and young preschooler, Desonia picked them up and put them in her mouth. The slightly sweet taste of the leaded flakes encouraged her to nibble more. Soon Desonia became listless, apathetic, and irritable. Her appetite dropped off, her stomach hurt, and she vomited frequently. When Desonia complained of constant headaches, began to walk with an awkward gait, and experienced repeated convulsions (involuntary muscle contractions), her parents realized that she had more than a passing illness. At a nearby public-health clinic, Desonia's blood was analyzed and her bones X-rayed. The tests showed that she had severe lead poisoning, a condition that results in permanent brain damage and (if allowed to persist) early death (Friedman & Weinberger, 1990; Veerula & Noah, 1990).

Despite years of public education, many parents remain unaware of the consequences of exposure to lead paint. In the United States, as many as 800,000 preschool children are believed to have dangerously high levels of lead in their bodies (American Academy of Pediatrics, 1987). Although inner-city youngsters growing up in deteriorated housing are at greatest risk, the problem is not limited to low-income families. Children of advantaged parents who purchase and restore old homes (built before 1950) can also be affected.

Severe lead poisoning has declined over the past two decades in the United States, following passage of laws restricting use of lead-based paint. But lead already present in homes is difficult to remove. As a result, many children continue to receive low doses that result in lasting cognitive and behavioral impairments. In one study, young children with varying degrees of low-level lead exposure were followed over an 11-year period. The more lead in their bodies during the early years of life, the lower their IQ scores and the more likely they were to have a wide variety of academic difficulties during the school years, including problems with reading, vocabulary, fine motor coordination, and sustained attention. During adolescence, they earned poorer grades than their agemates, and they were seven times more likely to drop out of high school (Needleman et al., 1979, 1990).

Childhood lead poisoning has been called "the silent epidemic of American cities" (Fee, 1990, p. 570). Communities should require that lead-based paint be removed from older housing before children become residents. Until children's environments can be made safe, health professionals need to educate parents of all social classes about the hazards of lead exposure. High-risk children should be tested regularly, and if the lead concentration in their blood is too high, treated immediately. Recent evidence suggests that the effects of moderate lead exposure are partially reversible. In one study, the greater the reduction in children's blood lead level, the more their IQ scores rose over the following 6 months (Ruff et al., 1993).

Heredity

Since identical twins are much more alike in body size than are fraternal twins, we know that heredity is an important factor in physical growth. However, this resemblance depends on when infant twins are measured. At birth, the differences in lengths and weights of identical twins are actually greater than those of fraternal twins. The reason is that identical twins share the same placenta, and one baby usually manages to get more nourishment. As long as negative environmental factors are not severe, the smaller baby recovers and swings back to her genetically determined path of growth within a few months (Wilson, 1976). This tendency is called **catch-up growth,**[*] and it persists throughout childhood and adolescence.

Genes control growth by influencing the body's production of and sensitivity to hormones. Sometimes mutations disrupt this process, leading to deviations in physical size. For example, return to Tables 3.2 and 3.3 on pages 78–79 to review the impact of hereditary defects on physical growth. Occasionally, a mutation becomes widespread in a population. Consider the Efe of Zaire, an African people who typically grow to an adult height of less than 5 feet. During early childhood, the growth of Efe children tapers off to a greater extent than that of other preschoolers because their bodies are less responsive to growth hormone (GH). By age 5, the average Efe child is shorter than over 97 percent of 5-year-olds in the United States (Bailey, 1990).

Catch-up growth
Physical growth that returns to its genetically determined path after being delayed by environmental factors.

*Notice the resemblance of *catch-up growth* to the term *canalization*, which we discussed in Chapter 3, page 123. Body growth is a strongly canalized process.

When environmental conditions are adequate, height and rate of physical maturity (as measured by skeletal age and timing of menarche) are strongly influenced by heredity. For example, identical twins generally reach menarche within a month or two of each other, whereas fraternal twins differ by about 12 months (Tanner, 1990). Body weight is also affected by hereditary makeup, since the weights of adopted children correlate more strongly with those of their biological than adoptive parents (Stunkard, Foch, & Hrubec, 1986). Nevertheless, reaching genetic potential in any aspect of physical growth depends on appropriate environmental support, and good nutrition is essential.

PHYSICAL GROWTH

Nutrition

Table 5.2 shows the many substances required for normal growth and daily functioning of the human body. Proteins, fats, and carbohydrates are the three basic components of the diet. Proteins are essential for growth, maintenance, and repair of body tissues; carbohydrates supply the primary fuel to meet the body's energy needs; and fats contribute to energy reserves and insulate the body against heat loss. We also need minerals, such as calcium for bone tissue and iron to support the oxygen-carrying power of red blood cells. Vitamins are critical as well, such as A for sight and D for skeletal growth. As extensive as it is, this list of essential nutrients is probably not exhaustive. Some substances are not included because they are not yet established as essential for humans.

AGE-RELATED NUTRITIONAL NEEDS. Nutrition is important at any time during development, but it is especially critical during infancy because of rapid brain and

TABLE 5.2 Essential Human Nutrients

Proteins

Fats

Carbohydrates

Water

Minerals

Calcium	Iron	Cobalt
Phosphorus	Zinc	Chromium
Potassium	Selenium	Fluorine
Sulfer	Manganese	Silicon
Sodium	Copper	Vanadium
Chlorine	Iodine	Nickel
Magnesium	Molybdenum	Tin

Vitamins

A	Riboflavin
D	Niacin
E	Pyroxidine
K	Pantothenic acid
Ascorbic acid	Folacin
Thiamin	B_{12}

Biotin

SOURCE: From "The Causes of Malnutrition" by F. E. Johnston, 1980, in L. S. Greene & F. E. Johnston (Eds.), *Social and Biological Predictors of Nutritional Status, Physical Growth, and Neurological Development*, p. 2. New York: Academic Press. Copyright © 1980 by Academic Press. Reprinted by permission.

TABLE 5.3 Nutritional and Health Advantages of Breast Milk	
ADVANTAGE	DESCRIPTION
Correct balance of fat and protein	Compared to the milk of other mammals, human milk is higher in fat and lower in protein. This balance, as well as the unique proteins and fats contained in human milk, is ideal for a rapidly myelinating nervous system.
Nutritional completeness	A mother who breast-feeds need not add other foods to her infant's diet until the baby is 6 months old. The milks of all mammals are low in iron, but the iron contained in breast milk is much more easily absorbed by the baby's system. Consequently, bottle-fed infants need iron-fortified formula.
Protection against disease	Through breast-feeding, antibodies are transferred from mother to child. As a result, breast-fed babies have far fewer respiratory and intestinal illnesses and allergic reactions than do bottle-fed infants.
Digestability	Since breast-fed babies have a different kind of bacteria growing in their intestines than do bottle-fed infants, they rarely become constipated or have diarrhea.

SOURCE: American Academy of Pediatrics, 1984.

*B*reast-feeding is especially important in developing countries, where infants are at risk for malnutrition and early death due to widespread poverty. This Huastec baby of southern Mexico is likely to grow normally during the first year because his mother decided to breast-feed. (JEAN GERARD SIDANER/ PHOTO RESEARCHERS)

body growth. Pound for pound, a young baby's energy needs are twice as great as those of an adult. This is because 25 percent of the infant's total caloric intake is devoted to growth, and extra calories are needed to keep rapidly developing organs of the body functioning properly (Pipes, 1989).

Babies do not just need enough food. They need the right kind of food. In early infancy, breast-feeding is especially suited to their needs, and bottled formulas try to imitate it. Table 5.3 summarizes the major nutritional and health advantages of breast milk. Because of these benefits, breast-fed babies in poverty-stricken regions of the world are much less likely to be malnourished and 6 to 14 times more likely to survive the first year of life. Too often, bottle-fed infants in developing countries are given low-grade nutrients, such as rice water or highly diluted cow's and goat's milk. When formula is available, it is generally contaminated due to poor sanitation (Grant, 1992).

Partly as a result of the natural childbirth movement, over the past two decades, breast-feeding has become more common in industrialized nations, especially among well-educated, middle-class women. Today, over 60 percent of American mothers breast-feed their babies (National Center for Health Statistics, 1991). However, breast-feeding is not for everyone. Some mothers simply do not like it, or they are embarrassed by it. Occasionally, medical reasons prevent a mother from nursing. If she is taking certain drugs, they can be transmitted to the baby through the milk. If she has a serious viral or bacterial disease, such as AIDS or tuberculosis, she runs the risk of infecting her baby (Seltzer & Benjamin, 1990). As we will see in Chapter 10, emotional well-being is affected by the warmth and sensitivity of caregiving, not by the type of milk offered. Breast- and bottle-fed youngsters show no differences in psychological development (Fergusson, Horwood, & Shannon, 1987).

By 6 months of age, infants require the nutritional diversity of solid foods, and around 1 year, their diets should include all the basic food groups (Mott, James, & Sperhac, 1990). At about age 2, there is often a dramatic change in the quantity and variety of foods that children will eat. Many who as toddlers tried anything and everything become picky eaters. This decline in appetite is normal. It occurs because growth has slowed. And preschoolers' wariness of new foods may be adaptive. Young children are still learning which items are safe to eat and which are not. By sticking to familiar foods, they are less likely to swallow dangerous substances when adults are not around to protect them (Rozin, 1990).

Once puberty arrives, rapid body growth leads to a dramatic rise in food intake. This increase in nutritional requirements comes at a time when the eating habits of many young people are the poorest. Of all age groups, adolescents are the most likely to consume empty calories. As a result, about 75 percent of North American teenagers suffer from iron deficiency, the most common nutritional problem of adolescence. Most teenagers also do not get enough calcium, and they tend to be deficient in riboflavin (vitamin B$_2$) and magnesium, both of which support metabolism (Malina, 1990). Adolescents' poor diets do not have serious consequences if they are merely a temporary response to peer influences and a busy schedule, but they can be harmful if they extend a lifelong pattern of poor nutrition.

MALNUTRITION. In developing countries where food resources are limited, malnutrition is widespread. Recent evidence indicates that 40 to 60 percent of the world's children do not get enough to eat (Lozoff, 1989). Among the 4 to 7 percent who are severely affected, malnutrition leads to two dietary diseases: marasmus and kwashiorkor.

Marasmus is a wasted condition of the body that usually appears in the first year of life. It is caused by a diet that is low in all essential nutrients. The disease often occurs when a baby's mother is severely malnourished. As a result, she cannot produce enough breast milk, and bottle-feeding is also inadequate. Her starving baby becomes painfully thin and is in danger of dying.

Unlike marasmus, **kwashiorkor** is not the result of general starvation. Instead, it is due to an unbalanced diet, one that is very low in protein. Kwashiorkor usually strikes after weaning, between 1 and 3 years of age. It is common in areas of the world where children get just enough calories from starchy foods, but protein resources are scarce. The body responds by breaking down its own protein reserves. Soon the child's belly enlarges, the feet swell, the hair begins to fall out, and a rash appears on the skin. A once bright-eyed, curious youngster becomes irritable and listless.

Children who manage to survive these extreme forms of malnutrition grow to be smaller in all body dimensions (Galler, Ramsey, & Solimano, 1985a). In addition, their brains are seriously affected. One long-term study of marasmic children revealed that an improved diet led to some catch-up growth in height, but the children failed to catch up in head size (Stoch et al., 1982). The malnutrition probably interfered with myelinization, causing a permanent loss in brain weight. By the time these youngsters reach middle childhood, they score low on intelligence tests, show poor fine motor coordination, and have difficulty paying attention in school (Galler, Ramsey, & Solimano, 1985b; Galler et al., 1984).

Recall from our discussion of prenatal malnutrition in Chapter 3 that poverty and stressful living conditions make the impact of poor diet even worse. The passivity and irritability of malnourished children reduce their ability to evoke sensitive caregiving from parents whose lives are already severely disrupted. For this reason, interventions for malnourished children must improve the family situation as well as the child's nutrition. Even better are efforts at prevention—providing food supplements and medical care to at-risk mothers and children before the effects of malnutrition run their course.

In Chapter 3, we noted that prenatal malnutrition is not confined to developing countries. The same is true for malnutrition after birth. A recent survey revealed that over 12 percent of children in the United States go to bed hungry (Food Research and Action Center, 1991). Although few of these children have marasmus or kwashiorkor, their physical growth and ability to learn in school are

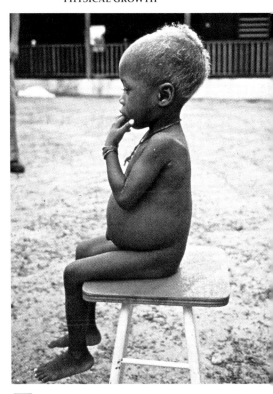

*T*he swollen abdomen and listless behavior of this child are classic symptoms of kwashiorkor, a nutritional illness that results from a diet very low in protein. (CNRI/PHOTOTAKE)

Marasmus

A disease usually appearing in the first year of life that is caused by a diet low in all essential nutrients. Leads to a wasted condition of the body.

Kwashiorkor

A disease usually appearing between 1 and 3 years of age that is caused by a diet low in protein. Symptoms include an enlarged belly, swollen feet, hair loss, skin rash, and irritable, listless behavior.

still affected. Malnutrition is clearly a national and international crisis—one of the most serious problems confronting the human species today.

OBESITY. Approximately 27 percent of American children suffer from **obesity,** a greater than 20 percent increase over average body weight, based on the child's age, sex, and physical build (Gortmaker et al., 1987). Overweight and obesity are growing problems in industrialized nations like the United States. Childhood obesity has climbed steadily since the 1960s, with over 80 percent of affected youngsters retaining their overweight status as adults (Dietz, Bandini, & Gortmaker, 1990; Muecke et al., 1992). These children have serious emotional and social difficulties and are at risk for lifelong health problems. High blood pressure and cholesterol levels along with respiratory abnormalities, symptoms that are powerful predictors of heart disease and early death, begin to appear in the early school years (Taitz, 1983; Unger, Kreeger, & Christoffel, 1990). Childhood obesity is a complex physical disorder with many contributing factors.

CAUSES OF OBESITY. All children are not equally at risk for becoming overweight. Fat children tend to have fat parents, and concordance for obesity is greater in identical than fraternal twins. These findings suggest that heredity has some effect. But similarity among family members is not strong enough to imply that genetics accounts for any more than a susceptibility to obesity (Dietz, Bandini, & Gortmaker, 1990). One indication that environment is powerfully important is the consistent relation between social class and overweight. Low-income youngsters in industrialized nations are not just at greater risk for malnutrition. They are also more likely to be obese (Garn & Clark, 1976). Among the factors responsible are lack of knowledge about healthy diet; a tendency to buy high-fat, low-cost foods; and family stress, which prompts overeating in some individuals.

Animal research reveals that overfeeding rats early in development causes their bodies to produce too many fat cells, which act to maintain the overweight condition (Knittle & Hirsch, 1968; Winick & Noble, 1966). Does this same biological factor operate in human beings? Research indicates that only a slight correlation exists between fatness in infancy and obesity at older ages. As yet, there is no evidence that a well-nourished human baby—even a very chubby one—can accumulate too many fat cells (Roche, 1981).

In instances in which fatness in infancy does extend into childhood, parental feeding practices seem to mediate the relationship. Some mothers interpret almost all the discomforts of their children as a desire for food. They anxiously overfeed their babies and fail to help them learn the difference between hunger and other physical and emotional discomforts (Weil, 1975). Parents of older obese children can be seen using food as a reward and as a way to relieve the child's anxiety (Bruch, 1970). When food is used to reinforce other behaviors, children start to value the treat itself as well as other similar foods (Birch, 1987). In families in which these practices are common, high-calorie treats gradually come to symbolize warmth, comfort, and relief of tension.

Perhaps because of these feeding experiences, obese children soon develop maladaptive eating habits. Research shows that they are more responsive to external stimuli associated with food—taste, sight, smell, and time of day—and less responsive to internal hunger cues than are normal-weight individuals. This difference is present in middle childhood and may develop even earlier (Ballard et al., 1980; Constanzo & Woody, 1979). Overweight individuals also eat faster and chew their food less thoroughly, a behavior pattern that appears in overweight children as early as 18 months of age (Drabman et al., 1979).

Fat children do not just eat more; they are less physically active than their normal-weight peers. This inactivity is both cause and consequence of their overweight condition. Recent evidence indicates that the rise in childhood obesity in the United States over the past 30 years is in part due to television viewing. Next

Obesity is an emotionally painful and physically debilitating disorder. This boy has difficulty keeping up with his agemates in a gunnysack race. Because of peer rejection, fat children often lead lonely lives. (BOB DAEMMRICH/STOCK BOSTON)

Obesity
A greater than 20 percent increase over average body weight, based on the child's age, sex, and physical build.

to already existing obesity, time spent in front of the TV set is the best predictor of future obesity among school-age children (Dietz & Gortmaker, 1985; Gortmaker, Dietz, & Cheung, 1990). Television greatly reduces the time that children devote to physical exercise. At the same time, TV ads encourage them to eat fattening, unhealthy snacks—soft drinks, sweets, and salty chips and popcorn (Carruth, Goldberg, & Skinner, 1991).

Psychological Consequences of Obesity. Unfortunately, physical attractiveness is a powerful predictor of social acceptance. Both children and adults rate obese youngsters as less likeable than children with a wide range of physical disabilities (Brenner & Hinsdale, 1978; Lerner & Schroeder, 1971). By middle childhood, obese children have a low sense of self-esteem, report feeling more depressed, and display more behavior problems than do their peers. A vicious cycle emerges in which unhappiness and overeating contribute to one another, and the child remains overweight (Banis et al., 1988).

Treating Obesity. Obesity is best treated in childhood, before the harmful behaviors that sustain it become well established. Yet childhood obesity is difficult to treat because it is a family disorder. A recent study comparing several treatment approaches found that the most effective intervention was family-based and focused on changing behaviors. Both parent and child revised eating patterns, exercised daily, and reinforced each other with praise and points for progress, which they exchanged for special activities and times together (Epstein et al., 1987). A follow-up after 5 years showed that children maintained their weight loss more effectively than did adults. This finding underscores the importance of intervening with obese children at an early age (Epstein et al., 1990).

Infectious Diseases

Among well-nourished youngsters, ordinary childhood illnesses have no effect on physical growth. But when children are poorly fed, disease interacts with malnutrition in a vicious spiral, and the consequences can be severe.

In developing nations where a large proportion of the population live in poverty, illnesses such as measles and chicken pox (which typically do not appear until after age 3 in industrialized nations) occur in infancy and take the form of severe illnesses. In these countries, many children do not receive a program of immunizations. In addition, poor diet depresses the body's immune system, making children far more susceptible to disease (Eveleth & Tanner, 1990; Salomon, Mata, & Gordon, 1968). Disease, in turn, is a major cause of malnutrition and, through it, affects physical growth. Illness reduces appetite, and it limits the body's ability to absorb foods that children do eat.

In industrialized nations, childhood diseases have declined dramatically during the past half-century, largely due to widespread immunization of infants and young children. Although the majority of preschoolers in the United States are immunized, a growing minority do not receive full protection until 5 or 6 years of age, when it is required for school entry. As a result, cases of preventable disease have risen in recent years (Cutts et al., 1992).

Figure 5.16 compares preschool immunization rates in the United States with those of a variety of European nations. How is it that European countries manage to score so well, whereas the United States does poorly? In earlier chapters, we noted that because of lack of medical insurance, many families in the United States do not have access to the health care they need. Yet in other industrialized nations, health care is regarded as a fundamental human right, no different from the right to education. As a result, medical insurance is government-sponsored and available to all citizens, and children receive a free or low-cost regimen of health checkups and immunizations beginning in early infancy (Williams, 1990).

Widespread, government-sponsored immunization of infants and young children is a cost-effective means of supporting healthy growth by dramatically reducing the incidence of childhood disease.
(JIM SELBY/PHOTO RESEARCHERS)

214

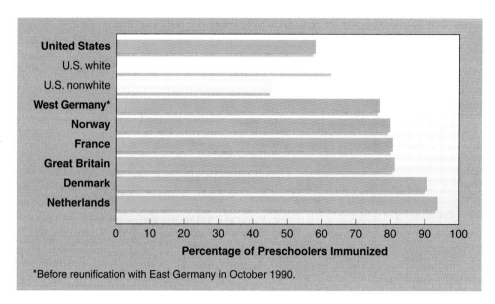

FIGURE 5.16 Immunization rates for preschool children in the United States and European nations, based on the most recent cross-national data. Children were immunized for diphtheria, tetanus, pertussis (whooping cough), measles, and polio. The low immunization rate for U.S. racial minority children is of special concern, since their overall poorer health makes them more vulnerable to complications when disease strikes. Notice that immunization of U.S. white preschoolers also falls below the figures for other countries. (Adapted from Williams, 1990.)

Inorganic failure to thrive

A growth disorder usually present by 18 months of age that is caused by lack of affection and stimulation.

Deprivation dwarfism

A growth disorder observed between 2 and 15 years of age. Characterized by substantially below average stature, weight that is usually appropriate for height, immature skeletal age, and decreased GH secretion. Caused by emotional deprivation.

Emotional Well-Being

We are not used to thinking of love and stimulation as necessary for healthy physical growth, but they are just as vital as food. Two serious growth disorders are the result of lack of affection and attention.

Inorganic failure to thrive is usually present by 18 months of age. Infants who have it show all the signs of marasmus, described earlier in this chapter. However, no organic (or biological) cause for the baby's wasted appearance can be found. Enough food is offered, and the infant does not have a serious illness. The behavior of babies with failure to thrive provides a strong clue to its diagnosis. In addition to apathy and withdrawal, these infants keep their eyes on nearby adults, anxiously watching their every move. They rarely smile when the mother comes near or cuddle when picked up (Leonard, Rhymes, & Solnit, 1986; Oates, 1984).

The family circumstances surrounding failure to thrive help explain these typical reactions. During feeding, diaper changing, and play sessions, mothers of these infants seem cold and distant, at other times impatient and hostile (Drotar et al., 1990; Haynes et al., 1983). In response, babies try to protect themselves by keeping track of the threatening adult's whereabouts and, when she approaches, avoiding her gaze. In one study, the breakdown in mother–infant interaction leading to failure to thrive was already evident in the first few days after birth. Mothers whose infants later developed the disorder spent less time looking at their babies and terminated interaction more quickly than did mothers of controls, and feeding problems appeared soon after delivery (Vietze et al., 1980). When treated early, through intensive family therapy or placement in a caring foster home, failure-to-thrive infants show quick catch-up growth. But if the problem is not corrected in infancy, some children remain small and display lasting cognitive and emotional difficulties (Altemeier et al., 1984; Drotar & Sturm, 1988).

Deprivation dwarfism appears later than failure to thrive, usually between 2 and 15 years. Its most striking features are substantially below average stature, decreased GH secretion, and immature skeletal age. Children with the disorder do not look malnourished; their weight is usually appropriate for their height. Researchers believe that severe emotional deprivation affects communication between the hypothalamus and pituitary gland, resulting in stunted growth. When such children are removed from their emotionally inadequate environments, their GH levels quickly return to normal, and they grow rapidly. But if treatment is delayed until later in development, the dwarfism can be permanent (Oates, Peacock, & Forrest, 1985).

Caregiving problems associated with these growth disorders are often grounded in poverty and family disorganization, which place parents under severe stress. With their own emotional resources depleted, parents have little energy available to meet the psychological needs of their children. However, failure to thrive and deprivation dwarfism do not occur just among the poor. They sometimes appear in economically advantaged families when marital conflict or other pressures cause parents to behave insensitively and destructively toward their children (Gagan, 1984).

The study of growth disorders highlights important influences on physical growth that are not readily apparent when we observe the healthy, normally developing child. In the case of failure to thrive and deprivation dwarfism, we become consciously aware of the close connection between sensitive, loving care and how children grow.

CHAPTER SUMMARY

The Course of Physical Growth

- Compared to other species, human beings experience a prolonged period of physical growth. **Distance** and **velocity curves** show the overall pattern of change: Gains in height and weight are rapid during infancy, slow and steady during middle childhood, and rapid again during **puberty.**

- In childhood, physical growth follows cephalocaudal and proximodistal trends. During puberty, growth actually proceeds in the reverse direction, and sex-related differences in body proportions appear. Body fat is laid down quickly during the first 9 months, then rapidly again at adolescence for girls. In contrast, muscle development is slow and gradual until puberty, when it rises dramatically, especially for boys.

- **Skeletal age,** a measure based on the number of **epiphyses** and the extent to which they are fused, is the best way to estimate the child's overall physical maturity. Girls are advanced over boys, a gap that widens over infancy and childhood. At birth, infants have six **fontanels,** which permit skull bones to expand as the brain grows.

- Physical growth is an asynchronous process. The **general growth curve** refers to change in overall body size. Other systems of the body, such as the brain, the genitals, and the lymph tissue, have their own unique timetables of maturation.

- Large individual and group differences in body growth exist that are the combined result of heredity and environment. **Secular trends in physical growth** have occurred in industrialized nations. Because of improved health and nutrition, many children are growing larger and reaching physical maturity earlier than their ancestors.

- Physical growth is controlled by hormones released by the **pituitary gland,** located at the base of the brain near the **hypothalamus,** which initiates and regulates pituitary secretions. **Growth hormone (GH)** affects the development of almost all body tissues. **Thyroxine,** released by the thyroid gland, influences brain growth and body size. Sexual maturation is controlled by the sex hormones—**estrogens** and **androgens.**

Puberty: The Physical Transition to Adulthood

- Accompanying rapid changes in body size and proportions at puberty are changes in **primary** and **secondary sexual characteristics. Menarche** (first menstruation) occurs relatively late in the girl's sequence of pubertal events, after the peak in the height spurt. In the following year, growth of the breasts and pubic and underarm hair are completed. As the boy's body and sex organs enlarge and pubic and underarm hair appear, **spermarche** (first ejaculation) and deepening of the voice take place. These events are followed by growth of facial and body hair.

The Psychological Impact of Pubertal Events

- Recent research shows that puberty is not a biologically determined, inevitable period of storm and stress. Instead, adolescent adjustment varies widely and is a product of both biological and social forces.

- Girls generally react to menarche with surprise and mixed emotions, but whether their feelings lean in a positive or negative direction depends on advance information and support from family members. Boys usually know ahead of time about spermarche, but they receive less social support for the physical changes of puberty than do girls.

- Besides hormone levels, situational changes are associated with adolescent moodiness. Puberty is accompanied by an increase in mild conflict and psychological distancing between parent and child.

- Timing of puberty influences psychological adjustment. Early maturing boys and late maturing girls, whose appearance closely matches cultural standards of physical attractiveness, have a more positive **body image,** feel more self-confident, and hold more positions of leadership. In contrast, early maturing girls and late maturing boys, who fit in least well physically with peers, experience emotional and social difficulties.

- The hormonal changes of puberty lead to an increase in sex drive, but social factors affect how teenagers manage their sexuality. Compared to most cultures, the United States is fairly restrictive in its attitude toward adolescent sex.

Sexual attitudes of adults and adolescents have become more liberal in recent years, and the rate of teenage sexual activity has risen.

- Nearly half of sexually active American teenagers do not practice contraception regularly. Adolescent cognitive processes and a lack of social support for responsible sexual behavior underlie this trend.
- About 1 to 4 percent of young people discover they are lesbian or gay. Although heredity makes an important contribution, homosexuality probably results from a variety of biological and environmental combinations that are not yet well understood. Lesbian and gay teenagers face special problems in establishing a positive sexual identity.
- Adolescent pregnancy, abortion, and childbearing are higher in the United States than in many industrialized nations. Teenage parenthood is often associated with dropping out of school and poverty, circumstances that risk the well-being of both adolescent and newborn child. Improved sex education and contraceptive services for adolescents reduce teenage pregnancy and childbearing.
- Girls who reach puberty early, who are dissatisfied with their body images, and who grow up in economically advantaged homes are at risk for eating disorders. **Anorexia nervosa** tends to appear in girls who have perfectionist personalities and overprotective and controlling parents. The impulsive eating and purging of bulimia is associated with lack of self-control in other areas of life.

Development of the Brain
- The human brain achieves its peak period of growth earlier than other organs. During infancy, **neurons** form **synapses** at a rapid rate. Stimulation determines which neurons will survive and which will die off. **Glial cells,** which are responsible for **myelinization,** multiply dramatically through the second year and result in large gains in brain weight.
- **Lateralization** refers to specialization of the hemispheres of the **cerebral cortex.** In early infancy, before many regions

have taken on specialized roles, there is high brain **plasticity.** However, some brain specialization already exists at birth.
- Hand preference reflects the individual's **dominant cerebral hemisphere.** It first appears in infancy and gradually increases, indicating that lateralization strengthens during early and middle childhood. Although left-handedness is more frequent among children with developmental problems, the great majority of left-handed children show no abnormalities of any kind.
- During infancy and early childhood, connections are established among different brain structures. Fibers linking the **cerebellum** to the cerebral cortex myelinate, enhancing children's balance and motor control. The **reticular formation,** responsible for alertness and consciousness, and the **corpus callosum**, which connects the two cerebral hemispheres, also develop rapidly.
- Research suggests that growth spurts in the human cortex occur intermittently from infancy into adolescence. These may be sensitive periods in which appropriate stimulation is necessary for full development of human intelligence.

Factors Affecting Physical Growth
- Twin and adoption studies reveal that heredity contributes to children's height, weight, and rate of physical maturation. Good nutrition is crucial for children to reach their full growth potential. Breast-feeding is especially suited to infants' growth needs. As growth slows in early childhood, appetite declines. It rises sharply during puberty.
- The importance of nutrition is tragically evident in the dietary diseases of **marasmus** and **kwashiorkor,** which affect large numbers of children in developing countries. In industrialized nations, **obesity** is a nutritional problem with severe health and psychological consequences.
- Infectious disease can combine with poor nutrition to undermine healthy physical development. **Inorganic failure to thrive** and **deprivation dwarfism** illustrate the importance of affection and stimulation for normal human growth.

IMPORTANT TERMS AND CONCEPTS

puberty (p. 176)
distance curve (p. 177)
velocity curve (p. 178)
skeletal age (p. 181)
epiphyses (p. 181)
fontanels (p. 182)
general growth curve (p. 182)
secular trends in physical growth (p. 184)
pituitary gland (p. 185)
hypothalamus (p. 185)
growth hormone (GH) (p. 185)
thyroxine (p. 186)
estrogens (p. 186)

androgens (p. 186)
primary sexual characteristics (p. 187)
secondary sexual characteristics (p. 187)
menarche (p. 188)
spermarche (p. 189)
body image (p. 193)
anorexia nervosa (p. 200)
bulimia (p. 201)
neurons (p. 202)
synapses (p. 202)
glial cells (p. 202)
myelinization (p. 202)
cerebral cortex (p. 203)

lateralization (p. 204)
plasticity (p. 204)
dominant cerebral hemisphere (p. 205)
cerebellum (p. 206)
reticular formation (p. 206)
corpus callosum (p. 206)
catch-up growth (p. 208)
marasmus (p. 211)
kwashiorkor (p. 211)
obesity (p. 212)
inorganic failure to thrive (p. 214)
deprivation dwarfism (p. 214)

CONNECTIONS

 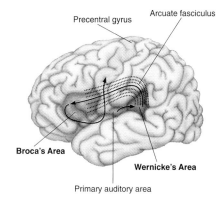

♦ **Kitagawa Utamaro,** *Frau mit Kinder neben Nahkastchen*
(Woman with Child by Sewing Box)

Edo period, c. 1790–1795. Color woodcut, Oban—format 37 x 24.7 cm.

Museum fur Ostasiatische Kunst, Berlin

Cognitive Development: Piagetian and Vygotskian Perspectives

Cognition refers to the inner processes and products of the mind that lead to "knowing." It includes all mental activity—remembering, symbolizing, categorizing, problem solving, creating, fantasizing, and even dreaming. Indeed, we could easily expand this list, since mental processes make their way into virtually everything human beings do (Flavell, 1985).

Among the great contributions of the Swiss theorist Jean Piaget was his view of human cognition as a complex set of diverse components that develop in a richly interwoven fashion. Piaget's *cognitive-developmental* stage theory stands as one of the three dominant twentieth-century positions on cognitive development (see Chapter 1). The other two are Lev Semanovich Vygotsky's *sociocultural theory,* which we consider alongside Piaget's perspective, and *information processing,* which we examine in Chapter 7.

The theories of Piaget and Vygotsky form a natural counterpoint. Both men were born in 1896, although they lived and worked in widely separated parts of the world—Piaget in Switzerland, Vygotsky in Russia. In their earliest investigations, each addressed the same puzzling issue in similarly titled volumes: the role of language in cognitive development. Do children first master ideas and then translate them into words? Or does the capacity for language open new cognitive doors, enabling children to think in more advanced ways?

In *The Language and Thought of the Child,* Piaget (1923/1926) claimed that language was relatively unimportant in spurring the young child's thinking forward. Instead, he argued, major cognitive advances take place as children act directly on the physical world, discover the shortcomings of their current ways of thinking, and revise them to create a better fit with external reality.

A few years later, the bold young Vygotsky (1934/1986) challenged this conclusion. In *Thought and Language,* he claimed that human mental activity is the result of *social,* not independent, learning. According to Vygotsky, as children master challenging everyday tasks, they engage in cooperative dialogues with adults and more expert peers, who assist them in their efforts. During these interactions, cognitive processes that are adaptive in a particular culture are socially transferred to children. Since language is the primary means through which humans exchange social meanings, Vygotsky viewed it as crucial for cognitive change. Indeed, Vygotsky regarded the acquisition of language as the most significant moment in children's development (Blanck, 1990).

On the basis of this brief description, do you find it difficult to decide between Piaget's and Vygotsky's perspectives? Before we can evaluate the work of these two giants of cognitive development, we must become thoroughly acquainted with each theory and the research it has stimulated.

PIAGET'S COGNITIVE-DEVELOPMENTAL THEORY

Piaget conceived of human cognition as a network of mental structures created by an active organism constantly striving to make sense of experience. This view was revolutionary when it first reached the United States in the middle of the twentieth century. It represented a dramatic break with the then dominant perspective of behaviorism, which steered clear of any constructs of mind and regarded the child as passively shaped by external forces (Beilin, 1992). By the 1960s, Piaget's ideas were embraced by American researchers with enthusiasm. His vision of the child as an intrinsically motivated learner, the variety of tasks he devised to assess cognitive development, and the relevance of his theory for education made it especially attractive.

Piaget received his early training in biology and philosophy. As a young boy, he spent his afternoons at the Museum of Natural History in Neufchatel, where he became intensely interested in how the shell structures of mollusks, which populate the lakes of Switzerland, are uniquely adapted to the animals' habitat. During his teenage years, Piaget's godfather introduced him to an area of philosophy called *epistemology,* which is concerned with the analysis of various forms of knowledge. Shortly after completing his Ph.D. in zoology, Piaget applied his background in science and philosophy to the construction of a biological account of the origins of knowledge (Piaget, 1952a). As a result, his theory of cognitive development came to have a distinctly biological flavor.

Key Piagetian Concepts

According to Piaget, just as the body has physical structures that enable it to adapt to the environment, so the mind builds psychological structures—organized ways of making sense of experience—that permit it to adapt to the external world. In the development of these structures, children are intensely active. They select and interpret experience in terms of their current structures, and they also modify those structures so that they take into account more subtle aspects of the surrounding world. For Piaget, each child's mental reality is his or her own unique construction. But since all of us possess the same biological equipment for acting on and interpreting experience, the course of cognitive development is the same for all human beings.

Piaget believed that children move through four stages of development—sensorimotor, preoperational, concrete operational, and formal operational—during which the exploratory behaviors of infants are transformed into the abstract, logical intelligence of adolescence and adulthood. To appreciate his view of how such vast change occurs, we must examine a set of important concepts. These convey Piaget's ideas about *what changes with development*, and *how cognitive change takes place*.

*A*ccording to Piaget's theory, at first schemes are motor action patterns. As this 1-year-old takes apart, bangs, and drops these nesting cups, she discovers that her movements have predictable effects on objects and that objects influence one another in regular ways. (Erika Stone)

WHAT CHANGES WITH DEVELOPMENT. According to Piaget, specific *psychological structures*, or **schemes,** change with age. At first, schemes are motor action patterns. For example, watch a 6-month-old baby grasp and release objects, and you will see that the "dropping scheme" is fairly rigid; the infant simply lets go of a rattle or teething ring in her hand. But by 18 months, the "dropping scheme" has become much more deliberate and creative. Given an opportunity, a baby of this age is likely to toss all sorts of objects down the basement stairs, throwing some up in the air, bouncing others off walls, releasing some gently and others with all the force her little body can muster. Soon, schemes will move from an action-based level to a mental level. When this happens, the child will not just act on objects. She will show evidence of thinking before she acts (Ginsburg & Opper, 1988). This change, as we will see later, marks the transition from sensorimotor to preoperational thought.

Piaget believed that all schemes are spontaneously exercised; children have a natural tendency to use them repeatedly. For example, an infant who has just mastered voluntary reaching is likely to apply the new scheme to a wide variety of objects. And preschoolers often engage in tireless practice of representational schemes by demanding that the same story be read to them over and over again. As schemes are exercised, they come into contact with new information. Gradually, children notice the gap between their current schemes and external reality, and they try to reduce this discrepancy.

HOW COGNITIVE CHANGE TAKES PLACE. To explain how schemes change, Piaget identified two important intellectual *functions:* adaptation and organization. The basic properties of these functions remain the same throughout life, despite the wide variety of schemes they create.

Adaptation. **Adaptation** involves building schemes through direct interaction with the environment. It is made up of two complementary processes: **assimilation** and **accommodation**. Piaget (1936/1952b) borrowed these terms directly from the field of biological growth. When we eat to support our body's cells, we *assimilate* food and make it like ourselves. At the same time, we must *accommodate* to what we eat, adjusting our digestion to the special properties of each food.

Cognitive adaptation works in much the same way. During *assimilation*, we interpret the external world in terms of our current schemes. For example, the infant who puts a variety of objects in his mouth is assimilating them all into his sensorimotor sucking scheme. And the preschooler who sees her first camel at the zoo and calls out, "Horse!" has sifted through her collection of schemes until she finds one that resembles the strange-looking creature. In *accommodation,* we adjust old schemes or create new ones after noticing that our current thinking does not capture the environment completely. The baby who begins to suck differently on the edge of a blanket than on a nipple has started to modify the sucking scheme. And the preschooler who calls a camel a "lumpy horse" has noticed that certain characteristics of camels are not like horses and revised her "horse scheme" accordingly.

Scheme
In Piaget's theory, a specific structure, or organized way of making sense of experience, that changes with age.

Adaptation
In Piaget's theory, the process of building schemes through direct interaction with the environment. Made up of two complementary activities: assimilation and accommodation.

Assimilation
That part of adaptation in which the external world is interpreted in terms of current schemes.

Accommodation
That part of adaptation in which old schemes are created and new ones adjusted to produce a better fit with the environment.

221

So far, we have referred to assimilation and accommodation as separate activities, but Piaget regarded them as always working together. That is, in every interchange with the environment, we interpret information using our existing structures, and we also refine them to achieve a better fit with experience. But the balance between assimilation and accommodation varies from one time period to another. When children are not changing very much, they assimilate more than they accommodate. Piaget called this a state of cognitive *equilibrium,* implying a steady, comfortable condition. During times of rapid cognitive change, however, children are in a state of *disequilibrium,* or cognitive discomfort. They realize that new information does not match their current schemes, so they shift away from assimilation toward accommodation. Once they have modified their schemes, they move back toward assimilation, exercising their newly changed structures until they are ready to be modified again.

Piaget used the term **equilibration** to sum up this back-and-forth movement between equilibrium and disequilibrium throughout development. Each time equilibration occurs, more effective schemes are produced. Because children take in a wider range of aspects of the environment, there is less and less to throw them out of balance (Piaget, 1985). Consequently, the times of greatest accommodation are the earliest ones, and (as we will soon see) the sensorimotor stage is Piaget's most complex period of development.

Organization. Schemes also change through a second process called **organization.** It takes place internally, apart from direct contact with the environment. Once children form new cognitive structures, they start to rearrange them, linking them with other schemes so they are part of a strongly interconnected cognitive system. For example, eventually the baby will relate "grasping," "sucking," "dropping," and "throwing" to his developing understanding of "nearness" and "farness." And the preschooler will construct a separate "camel scheme," but it will be connected by similarities and differences to her understanding of horses and other animals. According to Piaget, schemes reach a true state of equilibrium when they become part of a broad network of structures that can be jointly applied to the surrounding world (Flavell, 1963; Piaget, 1936/1952b).

The Piagetian Notion of Stage

Each of Piaget's four stages groups together similar qualitative changes in many schemes that occur during the same time period of development (Tanner & Inhelder, 1956). As a result, his stage sequence has two important characteristics. First, it is *invariant,* which means that the stages always emerge in a fixed order; no stages can be skipped. Second, the stages are *universal;* they are assumed to describe the cognitive development of children everywhere (Piaget, Inhelder, & Szeminska, 1948/1960).

Notice how Piaget's assumption of an invariant, universal stage sequence grants maturation a strong role in his theory. Yet although he viewed the order of development as genetically determined, he emphasized that many factors—both hereditary and environmental—affect the speed with which individual children move through the stages (Piaget, 1926/1928). In fact, Piaget regarded maturation and experience as making joint and inseparable contributions to development, since children cannot progress through the stages without opportunities to exercise their schemes in a rich and varied external world.

As we examine Piaget's stages in greater detail in the following sections, we will describe development as he saw it, noting research that supports his observations. Then, for each stage, we will consider recent findings that seriously challenge his ideas. Before we begin, you may find it useful to return to Table 1.4 on page 21, which provides an overview of Piaget's sequence of development.

Equilibration

In Piaget's theory, back-and-forth movement between cognitive equilibrium and disequilibrium throughout development, which leads to more effective schemes.

Organization

In Piaget's theory, the internal rearrangement and linking together of schemes so that they form a strongly interconnected cognitive system.

In Piaget's theory, children actively build psychological structures, or schemes, as they manipulate and explore their world. Two processes, adaptation (which combines assimilation and accommodation) and organization, account for changes in schemes. Through equilibration, schemes develop a more effective match with external reality. According to Piaget, children develop through a series of four invariant, universal cognitive stages.

THE SENSORIMOTOR STAGE (BIRTH TO 2 YEARS)

The difference between the newborn baby and the 2-year-old child is so vast that the **sensorimotor stage** is divided into six substages. Piaget's observations of his own three children served as the basis for this description of development. Piaget watched carefully and also presented his son and two daughters with little tasks (such as hidden objects) that helped reveal their understanding of the world. Nevertheless, the fact that Piaget's research on infant cognition was based on such a limited sample caused many investigators to question the validity of his sensorimotor stage. It is now widely agreed that Piaget underestimated the cognitive competence of young babies.

Sensorimotor Learning Mechanisms

According to Piaget, at birth infants know so little about the world that they cannot purposefully explore it. This presents a problem for young babies, since they need some way of adapting their first schemes. The **circular reaction** provides a special means of doing so. It involves stumbling onto a new experience caused by the baby's own motor activity. The reaction is "circular" because the infant tries to repeat the event again and again. As a result, a sensorimotor response that first occurred by chance becomes strengthened into a new scheme. For example, imagine a 2-month-old, who accidentally makes a smacking noise when finishing a feeding. The baby finds the sound intriguing, so she tries to repeat it until, after a few days, she becomes quite expert at smacking her lips.

During the first 2 years, the circular reaction changes in several ways. At first, it is centered around the infant's own body. Later, it turns outward, toward manipulation of objects. Finally, it becomes experimental and creative, aimed at producing novel effects in the environment. Piaget considered these revisions in the circular reaction so important that he named the sensorimotor substages after them.

Two additional capacities—*play* and *imitation*—first appear during the sensorimotor stage. They also serve as important mechanisms for solidifying old schemes and creating new ones. Piaget viewed play as the purest form of assimilation—practicing already acquired schemes just for the pleasure of doing so. (Later we will see that other theorists, including Vygotsky, regard this definition as too narrow.) In contrast, imitation emphasizes accommodation, since it involves copying behaviors that are not yet in the child's repertoire. According to Piaget, what infants and children play at and imitate provides excellent indicators of their advancing cognitive capacities.

The Sensorimotor Substages

As we examine Piaget's six sensorimotor substages, you may find it helpful to refer to the Milestones table on page 224, which provides a summary of each.

SUBSTAGE 1: REFLEXIVE SCHEMES (BIRTH TO 1 MONTH). Piaget regarded newborn reflexes as the building blocks of sensorimotor intelligence. As we will see in Substage 2, sucking, grasping, and looking quickly change as they are applied to

Sensorimotor stage
Piaget's first stage, during which infants "think" with their eyes, ears, hands, and other sensorimotor equipment. Spans the first 2 years of life.

Circular reaction
In Piaget's theory, a means of building schemes in which infants try to repeat a chance event caused by their own motor activity.

MILESTONES
COGNITIVE DEVELOPMENT DURING PIAGET'S SENSORIMOTOR STAGE

Sensorimotor Substage	Typical Adaptive Behaviors	Object Permanence	Play	Imitation
1. **Reflexive schemes (birth–1 month)**	• Newborn reflexes	• None	• None	• None; however, research on newborn imitation disputes this (see Chapter 4)
2. **Primary circular reactions (1–4 months)**	• Simple motor habits centered around the infant's own body; limited anticipation of events	• None; however, habituation–dishabituation research reveals that the beginnings of object permanence are present by $3\frac{1}{2}$ months	• Beginnings of playful exercise of schemes for their own sake	• Beginnings of imitation; believed by Piaget to be limited to copying another person's imitation of the infant's behavior
3. **Secondary circular reactions (4–8 months)**	• Actions aimed at repeating interesting effects in the surrounding world; however, operant-conditioning research suggests that secondary circular reactions are present during the first month (see Chapter 4)	• Ability to retrieve a partially hidden object	• Same as Substage 2	• Spontaneous imitation of another's actions, but only if the infant has practiced the behavior many times
4. **Coordination of secondary circular reactions (8–12 months)**	• Intentional or goal-directed action sequences; improved anticipation of events	• Ability to retrieve a hidden object from the first location in which it is hidden	• Playful exercise of "means" in means-end behavior sequences	• Imitation of behaviors slightly different from ones the infant usually performs
5. **Tertiary circular reactions (12–18 months)**	• Exploration of the properties of objects by acting on them in novel ways	• Ability to search in several locations for a hidden object	• More varied and experimental sensorimotor play	• Imitation of unfamiliar behaviors
6. **Mental representation (18 months–2 years)**	• Internal images of absent objects and past events	• Ability to find an object that has been moved while out of sight	• Beginnings of make-believe play	• Deferred imitation; however, recent evidence indicates that it appears as early as Substage 4

Note: These milestones represent overall age trends. Individual differences exist in the precise age at which each milestone is attained.

the environment. But at first, infants apply reflexive behaviors rather indiscriminately, to whatever stimulus comes in contact with their lips or the palms of their hands. In one amusing example, a mother reported to me that her 2-week-old daughter lay on the bed next to her father while he took a nap. Suddenly, he awoke with a start. The baby had latched on and begun to suck on his back!

Piaget believed that at birth, infants are totally egocentric beings. *Egocentrism*—the inability to distinguish one's own cognitive perspective from the perspectives of others—reappears in several forms across his stages. **Sensorimotor egocentrism** involves a merging of the self with the surrounding world, an absence of the understanding that the self is an object in a world of objects. It declines over the sensorimotor period, as infants gradually discover that their own actions are separate from external reality (Piaget, 1936/1952b).

SUBSTAGE 2: PRIMARY CIRCULAR REACTIONS—THE FIRST LEARNED ADAPTATIONS (1 TO 4 MONTHS). In this substage, infants start to gain voluntary control over their actions by repeating chance behaviors that lead to satisfying results. Consequently, they develop some simple motor habits, such as sucking their thumbs and opening and closing their hands. Babies in this substage also begin to vary their behavior in response to environmental demands. For example, they open their mouths differently to a nipple than to a spoon. Young infants also show a limited ability to anticipate events. A hungry 3-month-old is likely to stop crying as soon as his mother enters the room and moves toward the crib—an event signaling that feeding time is near.

Piaget called the first circular reactions *primary,* and he regarded them as quite limited. Notice how, in the examples just given, infants' adaptations are oriented toward their own bodies and motivated by basic needs. According to Piaget, babies of this age are not yet very concerned with the effect of their actions on the external world. Therefore, the infant of a few months of age is still a very egocentric being.

Piaget believed that play and imitation first emerge in Substage 2. Young babies can be seen exercising simple motor habits playfully, smiling gleefully as they repeat a newly developed action. According to Piaget, the first efforts at imitation are limited to copying someone else's imitation of the baby's own actions. However, recall from Chapter 4 that neonates can imitate an adult's facial expressions and gestures. So imitation seems to be one of the areas in which Piaget misjudged the young baby's competence.

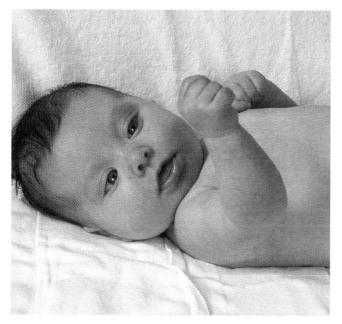

*D*uring Piaget's Substage 2, infants' adaptations are oriented toward their own bodies. This young baby carefully watches the movements of her hands, a primary circular reaction that helps her gain voluntary control over behavior. (ERIKA STONE)

Sensorimotor egocentrism
A form of egocentrism present in infancy that involves a merging of the self with the surrounding world, an absence of the understanding that the self is an object in a world of objects.

SUBSTAGE 3: SECONDARY CIRCULAR REACTIONS—MAKING INTERESTING SIGHTS LAST (4 TO 8 MONTHS). Think back to our discussion of motor development in Chapter 4. Between 4 and 8 months, infants sit up and become skilled at reaching for, grasping, and manipulating objects. These motor achievements play a major role in turning babies' attention outward toward the environment. Using the secondary circular reaction, they try to repeat interesting sights and sounds that are caused by their own actions. In the following illustration, notice how Piaget's 4-month-old son Laurent gradually builds the sensorimotor scheme of "hitting" over a 10-day period:

> At 4 months 7 days [Laurent] looks at a letter opener tangled in the strings of a doll hung in front of him. He tries to grasp (a scheme he already knows) the doll or the letter opener but each time, his attempts only result in his knocking the objects (so they swing out of his reach). . . . At 4 months 15 days, with another doll hung in front of him, Laurent tries to grasp it, then shakes himself to make it swing, knocks it accidentally, and then tries simply to hit it . . . . At 4 months 18 days, Laurent hits my hands without trying to grasp them, but he started by simply waving his arms around, and only afterwards went on to hit my hands. The next day, finally, Laurent immediately hits a doll hung in front of him. The [hitting] scheme is now completely differentiated [from grasping]. (Piaget, 1936/1952b, pp. 167–168)

Although they are a great improvement over the previous substage, secondary circular reactions provide infants with only a narrow means for influencing the environment. When an exciting event does occur (such as Laurent hitting the doll), babies do not yet explore the object that gave rise to it. Instead, they simply repeat a newly acquired action with respect to an object over and over again, in a fairly single-minded fashion.

Improved control over their own behavior permits infants of this substage to imitate the behaviors of others more effectively. However, babies under 8 months imitate only those actions that they themselves have practiced many times. They cannot adapt flexibly and quickly, copying behaviors that are novel and unfamiliar (Kaye & Marcus, 1981). Therefore, although 4- to 8-month-olds enjoy watching an adult demonstrate a game of pat-a-cake or peek-a-boo, they are not yet able to participate.

SUBSTAGE 4: COORDINATION OF SECONDARY CIRCULAR REACTIONS (8 TO 12 MONTHS). Now infants start to organize schemes. They combine secondary circular reactions into new, more complex action sequences. As a result, two landmark cognitive changes take place.

First, infants can engage in **intentional, or goal-directed, behavior**. Before this substage, actions that led to new schemes had a random, hit-or-miss quality to them—*accidentally* bringing the thumb to the mouth or *happening* to hit the doll hung over the crib. But by 8 months, infants have had enough practice with a variety of schemes that they coordinate them deliberately to solve sensorimotor problems. The clearest example is provided by Piaget's object-hiding tasks, in which he shows the baby an attractive toy and then hides it behind his hand or under a cover. Infants of this substage can find the object. In doing so, they coordinate two schemes: "pushing" aside the obstacle and "grasping" the toy. Piaget regarded these means-end action sequences as the first truly intelligent behavior and the foundation for all later problem solving.

The fact that infants can retrieve hidden objects reveals that they have begun to attain a second cognitive milestone: **object permanence,** the understanding that objects continue to exist when out of sight. But awareness of object permanence is not yet complete. If an object is moved from one hiding place (A) to another (B), babies will search for it only in the first hiding place (A). Because 8- to 12-month-olds make this **AB search error,** Piaget concluded that they do not have a clear image of the object as persisting when hidden from view.

Substage 4 brings several additional advances. First, infants can anticipate events more effectively, and using their new capacity for intentional behavior,

Intentional, or goal-directed, behavior
A sequence of actions in which schemes are deliberately combined to solve a problem.

Object permanence
The understanding that objects continue to exist when they are out of sight.

AB search error
The error made by 8- to 12-month-olds after an object is moved from hiding place A to hiding place B. Infants in Piaget's Substage 4 search for it only in the first hiding place (A).

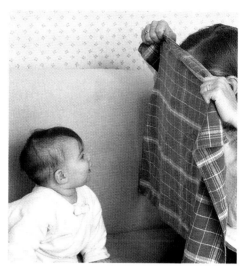

As infants master the nuances of object permanence, they delight in hiding-and-finding games such as peek-a-boo. (LAURA DWIGHT/PETER ARNOLD, INC.)

they sometimes try to change those experiences. For example, a baby of this age might crawl after his mother when she puts on her coat, whimpering and hanging on to keep her from leaving. Second, now babies imitate behaviors that are slightly different from those they usually perform. After watching someone else, they try to stir with a spoon, push a toy car, or drop raisins in a cup. Once again, they draw on their capacity for intentional behavior—purposefully modifying schemes to fit an observed action (Piaget, 1945/1951).

Finally, play extends to practicing the means in babies' new means-end action sequences. On one occasion, Piaget's son began by pushing an obstacle aside to obtain a toy but ended up ignoring the toy and instead pushing the obstacle (Piaget's hand or a piece of cardboard) again and again for fun (Piaget, 1945/1951).

SUBSTAGE 5: TERTIARY CIRCULAR REACTIONS—DISCOVERING NEW MEANS THROUGH ACTIVE EXPERIMENTATION (12 TO 18 MONTHS). At this substage, the circular reaction—now called *tertiary*—becomes experimental and creative. Toddlers do not just repeat behaviors that lead to familiar results. They *repeat with variation*, provoking new outcomes. Recall the example on page 221 of the child dropping objects down the basement steps, trying this, then that, and then another action in a deliberately exploratory approach. Because 12- to 18-month-olds deal with the world in this way, they are far better sensorimotor problem solvers than they were before. For example, they can figure out how to fit a shape through a hole in a container by turning and twisting it until it falls through, and they can use a stick to obtain a toy that is out of reach.

According to Piaget, this new capacity to experiment leads to a more advanced understanding of object permanence. Older infants look in not just one, but several locations to find a hidden toy. Thus, they no longer make the AB search error. Their more flexible action patterns also permit them to imitate many more behaviors, such as stacking blocks, scribbling on paper, and making funny faces. And once babies vary their actions with respect to objects, they clearly distinguish themselves from the surrounding world. As a result, sensorimotor egocentrism disappears.

SUBSTAGE 6: MENTAL REPRESENTATION—INVENTING NEW MEANS THROUGH MENTAL COMBINATIONS (18 MONTHS TO 2 YEARS). Substage 5 is the last truly sensorimotor stage. Substage 6 brings with it the ability to make **mental representations** of reality—internal images of absent objects and past events. As a result, children can solve problems through symbolic means instead of trial-and-error behavior. One sign of this new capacity is that children arrive at solutions to sensorimotor problems suddenly, suggesting that they experiment with actions inside their heads.

Mental representation
An internal image of an absent object or a past event.

Faced with her doll carriage stuck against the wall, Piaget's daughter Lucienne paused for a moment, as if to "think," and then immediately went to the other side to push it in the reverse direction. Had she been in Substage 5, she would have bumped and pulled it in a random fashion until it was free to move again.

With the capacity to represent, toddlers arrive at a more advanced understanding of object permanence—that objects can move or be moved when out of sight. Try the following object-hiding task with an 18- to 24-month-old as well as a younger child: Put a small toy inside a box and the box under a cover. Then, while the box is out of sight, dump the toy out and show the toddler the empty box. The Substage 6 child finds the hidden toy easily. Younger infants are baffled by this situation.

Representation also brings with it the capacity for **deferred imitation**—the ability to remember and copy the behavior of models who are not immediately present. A famous example is Piaget's daughter Jacqueline's imitation of another child's temper tantrum:

> Jacqueline had a visit from a little boy . . . who, in the course of the afternoon, got into a terrible temper. He screamed as he tried to get out of a playpen and pushed it backwards, stamping his feet. Jacqueline stood watching him in amazement. . . . The next day, she herself screamed in her playpen and tried to move it, stamping her foot lightly several times in succession. (Piaget, 1936/1952b, p. 63)

Finally, the emergence of representation leads to a major change in the nature of play. At the end of the sensorimotor period, children engage in **make-believe play,** in which they reenact familiar activities, such as pretending to eat, go to sleep, or drive a car. As the sensorimotor period draws to a close, mental symbols quickly become major instruments of thinking.

Recent Research on Sensorimotor Development

Over the past 20 years, many researchers have tried to confirm Piaget's observations of sensorimotor development. Their findings show that infants display certain cognitive capacities much sooner than Piaget believed. Earlier we noted the challenge posed by studies of newborn imitation, and you have already read about other conflicting evidence as well. Think back to the operant-conditioning research reviewed in Chapter 4 (page 143). Recall that newborns will suck vigorously on a nipple that produces a variety of interesting sights and sounds, a behavior that closely resembles Piaget's secondary circular reaction. It appears that infants try to explore and control the external world before 4 to 8 months. In fact, they do so as soon as they are born.

Piaget may have underestimated infant capacities because he did not have the sophisticated experimental techniques for studying early cognitive development that are available today (Flavell, 1985). As we consider recent research on sensorimotor development, we will see that operant conditioning and the habituation–dishabituation response have been used ingeniously to find out what the young baby knows.

OBJECT PERMANENCE. Before 8 months, do babies really believe that an object spirited out of sight no longer exists? It appears not. In a series of studies in which babies did not have to engage in active search, Renee Baillargeon (1987; Baillargeon & DeVos, 1991) found evidence for object permanence as early as $3\frac{1}{2}$ months of age! In one study, infants were habituated to both a short and a tall smiley faced carrot, each of which passed behind a screen on alternate trials (see Figure 6.1a). Then, using a screen with a large window in its upper half, the experimenter presented two test events, again on alternate trials. The first was a *possible event,* in which the short carrot (which was shorter than the window's lower edge) passed behind the screen and reappeared on the other side (Figure 6.1b). The second was an *impossible event,* in which the tall carrot passed behind the screen, did not appear in the window (although it was taller than the window's lower edge), and then miraculously emerged intact on the other side (Figure 6.1c). Young

Deferred imitation
The ability to remember and copy the behavior of models who are not immediately present.

Make-believe play
A type of play in which children pretend, acting out everyday and imaginary activities.

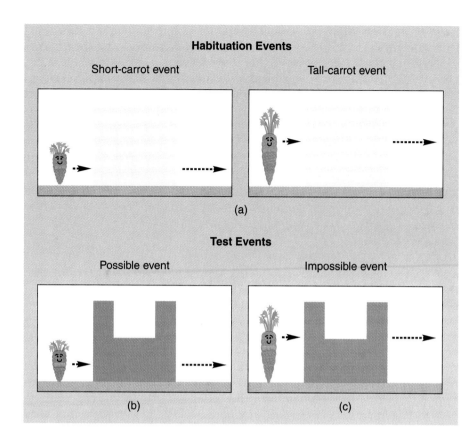

Habituation Events

Short-carrot event

Tall-carrot event

(a)

Test Events

Possible event

Impossible event

(b)

(c)

Figure 6.1 Study in which infants were tested for object permanence using the habituation–dishabituation response. (a) First, infants were habituated to two events: a short carrot and a tall carrot moving behind a yellow screen, on alternate trials. Then two test events were presented, in which the color of the screen was changed to blue to help the infant notice that it now had a window. (b) In the possible event, the short carrot (which was shorter than the window's lower edge) moved behind the blue screen and reappeared on the other side. (c) In the impossible event, the tall carrot (which was taller than the window's lower edge) moved behind the screen, did not appear in the window, but then emerged intact on the other side. Infants as young as $3\frac{1}{2}$ months dishabituated to the impossible event, suggesting that they understood object permanence. (Adapted from "Object Permanence in Young Infants: Further Evidence" by R. Baillargeon & J. DeVos, 1991, *Child Development, 62*, p. 1230. © The Society for Research in Child Development, Inc. Reprinted by permission.)

infants dishabituated to, or looked with much greater interest and surprise at, the impossible event, indicating that they are aware of the continued existence of objects that are hidden from view.

If $3\frac{1}{2}$-month-olds grasp the idea of object permanence, then what explains Piaget's finding that much older infants (who are quite capable of voluntary reaching) do not try to search for hidden objects? One explanation is that just as Piaget's theory suggests, they cannot yet coordinate the separate means-end schemes—pushing aside the obstacle and grasping the object—necessary to retrieve a hidden toy. In other words, what they *know* about object permanence is not yet evident in their searching behavior (Baillargeon et al., 1990).

Once 8- to 12-month-olds actively search for hidden objects, they make the AB search error. For some years, researchers thought babies had trouble remembering an object's new location after it was hidden in more than one place. But recent findings reveal that 8-month-olds are quite good at remembering the last location in which an object was hidden (Baillargeon, DeVos, & Graber, 1989). Why don't they search in the right place when given an opportunity? Once again, before 12 months, infants seem to have difficulty translating what they know about an object moving from one place to another into a successful search strategy. This ability to integrate knowledge with action may depend on rapid maturation of the cortex at the end of the first year (see Chapter 5, page 207).

MENTAL REPRESENTATION. In Piaget's theory, infants lead purely sensorimotor lives; they cannot represent experience until about 18 months of age. Yet new studies of deferred imitation and categorization reveal that the transition to mental representation takes place much earlier than Piaget predicted.

Deferred Imitation. Piaget studied imitation by noting when his own three children demonstrated it in their everyday behavior. Under these conditions, a great deal has to be known about the infant's daily life to be sure that deferred imitation has occurred. Also, some babies might be capable of deferred imitation but have very few opportunities to display it.

Recently, Andrew Meltzoff (1988c) brought 9-month-olds into a laboratory and deliberately tried to induce deferred imitation. The babies were shown three novel toys: an L-shaped piece of wood that could be bent, a box with a button that could be pushed, and a plastic egg filled with metal nuts that could be shaken. When tested after a 24-hour delay, infants who saw these actions modeled were far more likely to reproduce them than were babies exposed to the objects but not shown how they work.

Meltzoff's findings show that deferred imitation, a form of representation, is present almost a year before Piaget expected it to be. Also, his research reveals that 9-month-olds can keep not just one, but several actions in mind at the same time. By 14 months, toddlers use deferred imitation skillfully to enrich their range of sensorimotor schemes. They can retain as many as six modeled behaviors over a 1-week period (Meltzoff, 1988b).

The Beginnings of Categorization. Young babies' ability to categorize objects and events is also incompatible with a strictly sensorimotor approach to experience in which mental representation is absent. Recall the operant-conditioning research in which infants kicked to make a mobile move that was attached to their foot by a long cord (see Chapter 4, page 143). By creatively varying the mobile stimuli, Carolyn Rovee-Collier has shown that the beginnings of categorization are present in the early months of life. In one study, 3-month-olds kicked a mobile made of a uniform set of stimuli—small blocks, all with the letter A on them. After a delay, kicking returned to a high level only if the babies were given a mobile whose elements were labeled with the same form (the letter A). If the form was changed (from A's to 2's), infants no longer kicked vigorously. While learning to make the mobile move, the babies had *mentally* grouped together its physical features, associating the kicking response with the category "A" and, at later testing, distinguishing it from the category "2" (Hayne, Rovee-Collier, & Perris, 1987).

Habituation–dishabituation research has also been used to study early categorization. For example, infants can be shown a series of pictures belonging to one category (such as hot dog, piece of bread, slice of salami). Then the experimenter observes whether they look longer at, or dishabituate to, a picture that is not a member of the category (chair) than one that is (apple). The findings of such studies reveal that 9- to 12-month-olds structure objects into an impressive array of categories—food items, birds, stuffed animals, vehicles, and more (Oakes, Madole, & Cohen, 1991; Roberts, 1988; Ross, 1980; Sherman, 1985). Besides organizing the physical world, infants of this age also categorize their emotional and social worlds. They sort people into males and females (Francis & McCroy, 1983), have begun to distinguish emotional expressions, and can discriminate the natural movements of people from other motions (see Chapter 4, page 164).

In the second year, children become active categorizers during their play. In a recent study, the emergence of object-sorting behavior was carefully observed (Gopnik & Meltzoff, 1987a). Twelve-month-olds merely touched objects that belong together, without grouping them. A little later, single-category grouping occurred. For example, when given four balls and four boxes, 16-month-olds put all the balls together but not the boxes. And finally, around 18 months, children could sort the objects exhaustively into two classes.

When we combine these capacities with other achievements of the first 2 years that we will discuss in later chapters—for example, that events taking place before 10 to 11 months can be recalled up to a year and a half later (see Chapter 7) and that around 1 year, infants start to communicate with symbolic gestures (see Chapter 9)—it seems clear that mental representation is not the culmination of sensorimotor development. Instead, sensorimotor and symbolic schemes appear to be developing concurrently over the course of infancy (Mandler, 1992a, 1992b).

EVALUATION OF THE SENSORIMOTOR STAGE. In view of the evidence just discussed, how should we evaluate the accuracy of Piaget's sensorimotor stage? Clearly,

*T*his 3-month-old infant discovered that by kicking, she could shake a mobile made of small blocks with the letter A on them. After a delay, the baby continued to kick vigorously only if the mobile she saw was labeled with the same form (the letter A). She did not kick when given a mobile with a different form (the number 2). The infant's behavior shows that she groups similar stimuli into categories and can distinguish the category A from the category 2. (COURTESY OF CAROLYN ROVEE-COLLIER, RUTGERS UNIVERSITY)

important cognitive capacities emerge in preliminary form long before Piaget expected them to do so. At the same time, when these capacities first appear, they may not be secure enough to make a large difference in the baby's understanding of the world or to serve as the foundation for new knowledge. Piaget's substages do mark the full-blown achievement of many infant cognitive milestones, if not their first appearance. Follow-up research consistently shows that infants anticipate events, actively search for hidden objects, flexibly vary the circular reaction, and engage in make-believe within the general time frame that Piaget said they do (Corman & Escalona, 1969; Užgiris & Hunt, 1975).

The disagreements between Piaget's observations and those of recent research raise more questions about *how* early development takes place than *what* infants achieve during the first 2 years. Consistent with Piaget's ideas, motor activity does facilitate the construction of some forms of knowledge. For example, in Chapter 4, we indicated that babies who are experienced crawlers are better at finding hidden objects and perceiving depth on the visual cliff. But it is likely that infants do not need to construct all aspects of their world through motor action. The beginnings of some schemes, such as object permanence and imitation, may be prewired into the human brain from the start. Other important schemes may develop through purely perceptual learning—by looking and listening—rather than through acting directly on the world. Recently, Jean Mandler (1992a, 1992b) has argued that babies develop their first categories through an innate process of perceptual analysis in which they detect commonalities in the features and movements of objects and translate these into simplified images of experience.

Finally, infants do not develop in the neat stepwise fashion implied by Piaget's theory, in which a variety of skills change together as each new substage is attained. Instead, many sensorimotor capacities emerge separately and gradually. For example, a baby at one level of progress on imitation is likely to be at quite another on object permanence (Harris, 1983). This finding, along with the early emergence of representation, is among a rapidly accumulating body of evidence that questions Piaget's stagewise view of development.

Brief Review

The vast changes that take place during the sensorimotor stage are divided into six substages. The circular reaction, a special means that infants use to adapt schemes, is first oriented toward the infants' own body, then turns outward to the surrounding world, and finally becomes experimental and creative. During the last three substages, infants make strides in intentional behavior and understanding object permanence. By the final substage, they start to represent reality, display deferred imitation, and engage in make-believe play. Recent evidence reveals that secondary circular reactions, object permanence, deferred imitation, and categorization are present much earlier than Piaget assumed. These findings raise questions about his claim that infants construct all aspects of their world through motor activity and that early cognitive development is best characterized as a purely sensorimotor stage.

THE PREOPERATIONAL STAGE (2 TO 7 YEARS)

As children move from the sensorimotor to the **preoperational stage,** the most obvious change is an extraordinary increase in representational activity. Although infants have some ability to represent their world, between the ages of 2 and 7, this capacity blossoms.

Language and Thought

As we will see in Chapter 9, around the end of the second and beginning of the third year, tremendous strides in language take place. Piaget acknowledged that

Preoperational stage
Piaget's second stage, in which rapid development of representation takes place. However, thought is not yet logical. Spans the years from 2 to 7.

language is our most flexible means of mental representation. By detaching thought from action, it permits cognition to be far more efficient than it was during the sensorimotor stage. When we think in words, we overcome the limits of immediate time and space. We can deal with the past, present, and future all at once, creating larger, interconnected images of reality (Miller, 1989).

Yet despite the power of language, Piaget did not regard it as responsible for more advanced forms of cognition. Instead, he believed that sensorimotor activity leads to internal images of experience, which children then label with words (Piaget, 1936/1952b). Some evidence is certainly consistent with this idea. For example, children's first words have a strong sensorimotor basis. They usually refer to objects that move or to familiar actions (see Chapter 9). Also, certain early words are linked to specific nonverbal cognitive achievements. Use of disappearance terms, like "all gone," occurs at about the same time as mastery of advanced object-permanence problems. And success and failure expressions, such as "there!" and "uh-oh," appear when children can solve sensorimotor problems suddenly, in Piaget's Substage 6. Finally, a sharp spurt in vocabulary between 18 months and 2 years coincides with the ability to sort objects into several categories (Gopnik & Meltzoff, 1987b). This "naming explosion" probably builds on infants' diverse preverbal categories, which become more elaborate by the end of the second year.

Still, Piaget's theory does not tell us exactly how sensorimotor schemes are transformed into images, and then into categories, to which words are eventually attached (Mandler, 1992b). And, as we have already suggested in the introduction to this chapter, Piaget may have misjudged the power of language to spur children's cognition forward. For example, we will see later that whereas language development is supported by early categories, learning names for things may, in turn, enhance conceptual skills.

Make-Believe Play

Make-believe play provides another excellent example of the development of representation during the preoperational stage. Like language, it increases dramatically during early childhood. Piaget believed that through pretending, children practice and strengthen newly acquired symbolic schemes. Drawing on Piaget's ideas, several investigators have traced changes in make-believe during early childhood.

CHANGES IN MAKE-BELIEVE. Compare an 18-month-old's pretending with that of a 2- to 3-year-old. You are likely to see examples of three important changes, each of which reflects the preschool child's growing symbolic mastery.

First, make-believe becomes increasingly detached from the real-life conditions associated with it. At first, toddlers use only realistic objects—for example, a toy telephone to talk into or a cup to drink from. Around age 2, they use less real-

During the preschool years, make-believe play blossoms. This child uses objects as active agents in a complex play scene. (M. SILUK/THE IMAGE WORKS)

istic toys, such as a block for a telephone receiver, more frequently. Sometime during the third year, children can imagine objects and events without any support from the real world. This indicates that children's representations are becoming more flexible, since a play symbol no longer has to resemble the object it denotes (Bretherton et al., 1984; Corrigan, 1987).

Second, the way in which the "child as self" participates in play changes with age. When make-believe first appears, it is directed toward the self; that is, children pretend to feed or wash only themselves. A short time later, pretend actions are directed toward other objects, as when the child feeds a doll. And early in the third year, objects are used as active agents. The child becomes a detached participant who makes a doll feed itself or a parent doll feed a baby doll. This sequence reveals that make-believe gradually becomes less self-centered, as children realize that agents and recipients of pretend actions can be independent of themselves (Corrigan, 1987; Ungerer et al., 1981).

Finally, over time, play includes increasingly complex scheme combinations. For example, the toddler can pretend to drink from a cup but does not yet combine pouring and drinking. Later on, children coordinate pretend schemes, especially in **sociodramatic play,** the make-believe with others that first appears around age $2\frac{1}{2}$ (Corrigan, 1987). By age 4 to 5, children build effectively on one another's play themes, create and coordinate several roles in an elaborate plot, and have a sophisticated understanding of story lines (Göncü, 1993).

FUNCTIONS AND CONSEQUENCES OF MAKE-BELIEVE. Piaget clearly captured an important aspect of make-believe when he emphasized the opportunities it affords for exercising symbolic schemes. He also noted its emotionally integrative function, a feature emphasized in psychoanalytic theory. An anxiety-provoking event, such as a visit to the doctor's office or discipline by a parent, is likely to be revisited in the young child's play, but with roles reversed so that the child is in command and compensates for the unpleasant experience (Erikson, 1950; Piaget, 1945/1951). In addition, Piaget commented that pretend allows children to become familiar with social role possibilities. In cultures around the world, young children act out family scenes and highly visible occupations—police officer, doctor, and nurse in Western nations; rabbit hunter and potter among the Hopi Indians; and hut builder and spear maker among the Baka of West Africa (Garvey, 1990). In this way, play provides young children with important insights into the link between self and wider society.

Nevertheless, today Piaget's view of make-believe as mere practice of symbolic schemes is regarded as too limited. Research indicates that play not only

These 4-year-olds coordinate several make-believe roles with the assistance of a very cooperative family pet. Their enjoyment of sociodramatic play contributes to cognitive, emotional, and social development. (TOM MCCARTHY/STOCK SOUTH)

Sociodramatic play
The make-believe play with others that first appears around age $2\frac{1}{2}$.

reflects, but also contributes to children's cognitive and social skills (Singer & Singer, 1990). Sociodramatic play has been studied most thoroughly. In contrast to social nonpretend activities (such as drawing or putting puzzles together), during social pretend, preschoolers' interactions last longer, show more involvement, draw larger numbers of children into the activity, and are more cooperative (Connolly, Doyle, & Reznick, 1988). When we consider these findings, it is not surprising that preschoolers who spend more time at sociodramatic play are advanced in cognitive development, show an enhanced ability to understand the feelings of others, and are seen as more socially competent by their teachers (Burns & Brainerd, 1979; Connolly & Doyle, 1984). Young children who especially enjoy pretending also score higher on tests of imagination and creativity (Dansky, 1980; Pepler & Ross, 1981).

These findings offer strong justification for play as a central part of preschool and day-care programs and the daily life of the preschool child. Later we will return to the origins and consequences of make-believe from an alternative perspective—Vygotsky's.

Pictorial Representation

Children's drawings are another important mode of symbolic expression. Even the scrawls of toddlers, which seem to be little more than tangles of lines, are often "experiments in representation" (Winner, 1986, pp. 25–26). At first, children's artistic efforts take the form of gestures rather than pictures. For example, one 18-month-old took her crayon and hopped it around the page, explaining as she made a series of dots, "Rabbit goes hop-hop." By age 3, scribbles start to become pictures. Often this happens after children make a gesture with the crayon, notice that they have drawn a recognizable shape, and then decide to label it.

A major milestone in children's drawing occurs when they begin to use lines to represent the boundaries of objects. This permits them to draw their first picture of a person by age 3 or 4. Look at the variations of stick figures on the left in Figure 6.2. This tadpole image is a universal one in which the limits of the preschooler's fine motor skills reduce the figure to the simplest form that still looks like a human being (Gardner, 1980; Winner, 1986).

Unlike many adults, young children do not demand that a drawing be realistic. But as cognitive and fine motor skills improve, they learn to desire greater realism. As a result, they create more complex drawings, like the one shown on the right in Figure 6.2, made by a 6-year-old child. Still, children of this age are not very particular about mirroring reality. The perceptual distortions help make their pictures look fanciful and inventive. Not until about age 9 do children figure out how to represent depth in their drawings (Nicholls & Kennedy, 1992). Accomplished artists, who also try to depict reality freely, must often work hard to do deliberately what they did without effort as 5- and 6-year-olds.

Limitations of Preoperational Thought

Aside from the development of representation, Piaget described preschool children in terms of what they *cannot*, rather than *can*, understand (Beilin, 1992). The very name of the stage—*pre*operational—indicates that Piaget compared preschoolers to older, more capable concrete operational children. As a result, he discovered little of a positive nature about the young child's thinking. Later, when we take up new research on preoperational thought, we will see that Piaget underestimated the cognitive competencies of early childhood, just as he did with infancy.

To appreciate the characteristics of the preoperational stage, you will need to master some concepts Piaget used to describe children's thought. These are summarized in Table 6.1. As you look over these characteristics, you will see that for Piaget, **operations**—mental representations of actions that obey logical rules—are where cognitive development is headed. In the preoperational stage, children are

Operations
In Piaget's theory, mental representations of actions that obey logical rules.

FIGURE 6.2 Examples of young children's drawings. The universal tadpolelike form that children use to draw their first picture of a person is shown on the left. The tadpole soon becomes an anchor for greater detail, as arms, fingers, toes, and facial features sprout from the basic shape. By the end of the preschool years, children produce more complex, differentiated pictures, like the one on the right, drawn by a 6-year-old child. (Tadpole drawings from *Artful Scribbles: The Significance of Children's Drawings* by H. Gardner, 1980, p. 64. Copyright © by Howard Gardner. Reprinted by permission of Basic Books, a division of HarperCollins Publishers, Inc. Six-year-old's picture from "Where Pelicans Kiss Seals" by E. Winner, August 1986, *Psychology Today*, 20(8), p. 35. Reprinted by permission of the author.)

not capable of operations. Instead, their thinking is rigid, limited to one aspect of a situation at a time, and strongly influenced by the way things appear at the moment. As a result, when judged by adult standards, preoperational reasoning often seems distorted and incorrect.

EGOCENTRISM AND ANIMISM. According to Piaget, the most serious deficiency of this stage, the one that underlies all others, is **preoperational egocentrism**. Now, with the emergence of new representational capacities, egocentrism appears in a different form. Preoperational children are egocentric with respect to their symbolic viewpoints. That is, they are unaware of viewpoints other than their own, and they believe that everyone else perceives, thinks, and feels the same way they do (Piaget, 1950).

Piaget's most convincing demonstration of egocentrism involves his *three-mountains problem* (see Figure 6.3). A child is permitted to walk around a display of three mountains of different heights arranged on a table. Then the child stands on one side, and a doll is placed at various locations around the display. The child must choose a photograph that shows what the display looks like from the doll's perspective. Below the age of 6 or 7, most children simply select the photo that shows the mountains from their own point of view (Piaget & Inhelder, 1948/1956).

Egocentrism, Piaget pointed out, is responsible for preoperational children's **animistic thinking**—the belief that inanimate objects have lifelike qualities, such as thoughts, wishes, feelings, and intentions, just like themselves (Piaget, 1926/1930). The 3-year-old who charmingly explains that the sun is angry at the clouds and has chased them away is demonstrating this kind of reasoning.

Piaget argued that egocentrism leads to the rigidity and illogical nature of preoperational thought. Young children's thinking proceeds so strongly from their own point of view that they do not accommodate, or revise their schemes, in response to feedback from the physical and social world. Egocentric thought is not reflective thought, which critically examines itself. But to fully appreciate

Preoperational egocentrism
A form of egocentrism present during the preoperational stage involving the inability to distinguish the symbolic viewpoints of others from one's own.

Animistic thinking
The belief that inanimate objects have lifelike qualities, such as thoughts, wishes, feelings, and intentions.

235

TABLE 6.1 *Major Characteristics of Piaget's Preoperational Stage*

CHARACTERISTIC	DESCRIPTION	EXAMPLE
Egocentrism	Preoperational children assume that others perceive, think, and feel just the way they do. According to Piaget, this belief underlies all other limitations of the preoperational stage.	Three-year-old Josie turned on the TV in the living room while her father ate breakfast in the kitchen. "What's that boy doing?" called Josie while pointing to the screen, failing to realize that her father couldn't see the TV from where he was sitting.
Animistic thinking	Preoperational children regard inanimate objects as having lifelike qualities, just like the self.	Josie and her parents watched the sunset after spending a day at the seashore. As the sun started to sink below the horizon and the sky darkened, Josie remarked, "That sunshine's getting very sleepy."
Perception-bound thought	Preoperational children make judgments based on the immediate, perceptual appearance of objects.	Josie's mother handed her a large glass half full of lemonade and her brother a small glass filled to the top. "Fill mine up like Billie's so I'll have just as much," said Josie.
Centration	Preoperational children tend to center on one aspect of a situation to the neglect of other important features.	At preschool, it was Hallie's fourth birthday. Although Amy was only 3, Josie announced, "Amy's older 'cause she's taller," centering on height as a measure of age.
States versus transformations	Preoperational children focus on momentary states, failing to consider dynamic trans-formations between them. As a result, they have difficulty relating beginning and ending states in a situation.	Josie saw her little cousin Susie, whom she had played with several times before, dressed up in a bathing suit and cap. "What's that baby's name?" Josie asked. Later, when Susie had her shirt and shorts on, Josie said, "Oh, it's Susie again."
Irreversibility	Preoperational children cannot think through a series of steps in a problem and then go backward, mentally returning to the starting point.	Josie's mother tried to explain, "When Susie puts on a bathing suit, she's still the same person." But Josie insisted that the bathing-suit baby was not Susie. She failed to imagine Susie changing from her shorts and shirt into her suit and then back again.
Transductive reasoning	Preoperational children reason from particular event to particular event rather than in an appropriately causal fashion.	"Why does it get dark at night?" the teacher asked the children at preschool one day. "Because we go to bed," responded Josie.
Lack of hierarchical classification	Preoperational children have difficulty grouping objects into hierarchies of classes and subclasses.	Josie's teacher gave her some paper shapes to sort—red and blue squares and circles. Josie put all the red ones in one pile and the blue ones in another, but she had difficulty separating the groups further, by shape.

these shortcomings of the preoperational stage, let's consider some additional tasks that Piaget presented to children.

Conservation
The understanding that certain physical characteristics of objects remain the same, even when their outward appearance changes.

INABILITY TO CONSERVE. Piaget's most important tasks are the conservation prob-lems. **Conservation** refers to the idea that certain physical characteristics of objects remain the same even when their outward appearance changes. A typical example is the conservation-of-liquid problem. The child is presented with two identical tall glasses of water and asked if they contain equal amounts. Once the child agrees, the water in one glass is poured into a short, wide container, changing the

FIGURE 6.3 Piaget's three-mountains problem. Each mountain is distinguished by its color and by its summit. One has a red cross, another a small house, and the third a snow-capped peak. Children at the preoperational stage are egocentric. They cannot select a picture that shows the mountains from the doll's perspective. Instead, they simply choose the photo that shows their own vantage point.

appearance of the water but not its amount. Then the child is asked whether the amount of water is still the same or whether it has changed. Preoperational children think the quantity of water is no longer the same. They explain their reasoning in ways like this: "There is less now because the water is way down here" (that is, its level is so low in the short, wide container) or "There is more water now because it is all spread out." In Figure 6.4, you will find other conservation tasks you can try with children.

Preoperational children's inability to conserve highlights several related aspects of their thinking. First, their understanding is **perception-bound.** They are easily distracted by the concrete, perceptual appearance of objects (it *looks* like there is less water in the short, wide container, so there *must be* less water). Second, their thinking is *centered,* or characterized by **centration**. In other words, they focus on one aspect of a situation and neglect other important features. In the case of conservation of liquid, the child centers on the height of the water in the two containers, failing to realize that all changes in height are compensated by changes in width. Third, children of this stage focus on *momentary states* rather than *dynamic transformations* between them. For example, in the conservation-of-liquid problem, they treat the initial and final states of the water as completely unrelated events. This tendency to emphasize **states versus transformations** is dramatically illustrated by another problem Piaget presented to children. A bar is allowed to fall freely from an upright position to a horizontal one. Then the child is asked either to draw or to select a picture that shows what happened. Preoperational children focus only on the beginning and ending states, ignoring the bar's intermediate path of movement.

The most important illogical feature of preoperational thought is *irreversibility.* **Reversibility,** the opposite of this concept, characterizes every logical operation. It refers to the ability to mentally go through a series of steps and then reverse direction, returning to the starting point. In the case of conservation of liquid, the preoperational child fails to see how the existence of the same amount of liquid is ensured by imagining it being poured back into its original container.

TRANSDUCTIVE REASONING. Reversible thinking is flexible and well organized. Because preoperational children are not capable of it, Piaget concluded that their causal reasoning often consists of disconnected facts and contradictions. He called young children's incorrect explanations **transductive reasoning,** which means reasoning from particular to particular. In other words, preschoolers simply link together two events that occur close in time and space in a cause-and-effect fashion.

Perception-bound
Being easily distracted by the concrete, perceptual appearance of objects.

Centration
The tendency to focus on one aspect of a situation and neglect other important features.

States versus transformations
The tendency to treat the initial and final states in a problem as completely unrelated.

Reversibility
The ability to mentally go through a series of steps and then reverse direction, returning to the starting point.

Transductive reasoning
Reasoning from one particular event to another particular event, instead of from general to particular or particular to general.

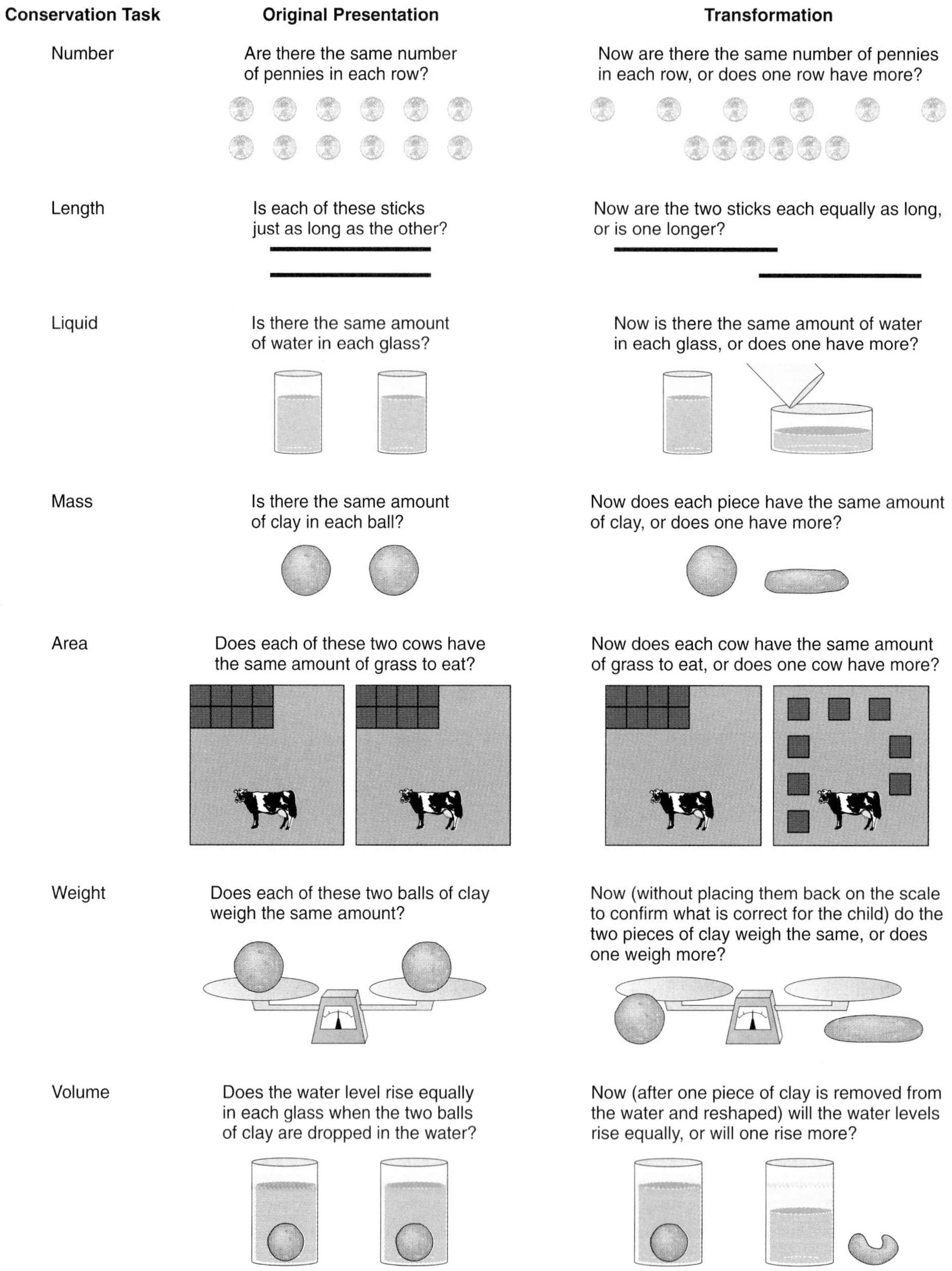

Conservation Task	Original Presentation	Transformation
Number	Are there the same number of pennies in each row?	Now are there the same number of pennies in each row, or does one row have more?
Length	Is each of these sticks just as long as the other?	Now are the two sticks each equally as long, or is one longer?
Liquid	Is there the same amount of water in each glass?	Now is there the same amount of water in each glass, or does one have more?
Mass	Is there the same amount of clay in each ball?	Now does each piece have the same amount of clay, or does one have more?
Area	Does each of these two cows have the same amount of grass to eat?	Now does each cow have the same amount of grass to eat, or does one cow have more?
Weight	Does each of these two balls of clay weigh the same amount?	Now (without placing them back on the scale to confirm what is correct for the child) do the two pieces of clay weigh the same, or does one weigh more?
Volume	Does the water level rise equally in each glass when the two balls of clay are dropped in the water?	Now (after one piece of clay is removed from the water and reshaped) will the water levels rise equally, or will one rise more?

FIGURE 6.4 Some Piagetian conservation tasks. Children at the preoperational stage cannot yet conserve. These tasks are mastered gradually over the concrete operational period. Children in Western nations typically acquire conservation of number, length, liquid, and mass sometime between 6 and 7 years; area and weight between 8 and 10 years; and volume between 10 and 12 years.

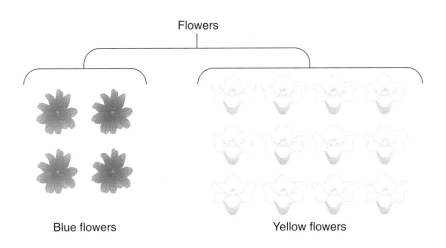

Flowers

Blue flowers   Yellow flowers

FIGURE 6.5 A Piagetian class-inclusion problem. Children are shown 16 flowers, 4 of which are blue and 12 of which are yellow. Asked whether there are more yellow flowers or more flowers, the preoperational child responds, "More yellow flowers," failing to realize that both yellow and blue flowers are included in the category of "flowers."

Sometimes this leads to some fantastic connections, as in the following interview Piaget conducted with a young child about why the clouds move:

> You have already seen the clouds moving along? What makes them move?—*When we move along, they move along too.*—Can you make them move?—*Everybody can, when they walk.*—When I walk and you are still, do they move?—*Yes.*—And at night, when everyone is asleep, do they move?—*Yes.*—But you tell me that they move when somebody walks.—*They always move. The cats, when they walk, and then the dogs, they make the clouds move along.* (Piaget, 1926/1929, p. 62)

LACK OF HIERARCHICAL CLASSIFICATION. During the preoperational stage, children also have difficulty with **hierarchical classification**. That is, they cannot yet organize objects into hierarchies of classes and subclasses on the basis of similarities and differences between the groups. Piaget illustrated this with his famous *class-inclusion problem.* Children are shown a set of common objects, such as 16 flowers, most of which are yellow and a few of which are blue (see Figure 6.5). When asked whether there are more yellow flowers or more flowers, preoperational children respond confidently, "More yellow flowers!" Their approach to the problem shows a tendency to center on the overriding perceptual feature of yellow and an inability to think reversibly by moving from the whole class (flowers) to the parts (yellow and blue) and back again.

SUMMING UP PREOPERATIONAL THOUGHT. How can we combine the diverse characteristics of the preoperational stage into a unified description of what Piaget believed the young child's thought to be like? John Flavell, a well-known Piagetian scholar, suggests that Piaget viewed all these traits as expressions of a single, underlying orientation. Taken together, they reveal that preoperational thought

> bears the impress of its sensory-motor origins. . . . It is extremely concrete . . . concerned more with immobile, eye-catching configurations than with more subtle, less obvious components . . . it is unconcerned with proof or logical justification and, in general, unaware of the effect of its communication on others. In short, in more respects than not, it resembles sensory-motor action which has simply been transposed to a new (symbolic) arena of operation. (Flavell, 1963, p. 162)

Recent Research on Preoperational Thought

Over the past two decades, Piaget's account of a cognitively deficient preschool child has been seriously challenged. If researchers give his tasks in just the way he originally designed them, indeed they find that preschoolers perform poorly. But a close look at Piagetian problems reveals that many contain unfamiliar elements or too many pieces of information for young children to handle at once. As a

Hierarchical classification
The organization of objects into classes and subclasses on the basis of similarities and differences between the groups.

result, preschoolers' responses often do not reflect their true abilities. Piaget also missed many naturally occurring instances of preschoolers' effective reasoning. Let's look at some examples to illustrate these points.

EGOCENTRISM AND ANIMISM. Are young children really so egocentric that they believe a person standing in a different location in a room sees the same thing they see? Although children's responses to Piaget's three-mountains task suggest that the answer is "yes," more recent studies say "no." When researchers change the nature of the visual display to include familiar objects and use methods other than picture selection (which is difficult even for 10-year-olds), 4-year-olds show clear awareness of others' vantage points (Borke, 1975; Newcombe & Huttenlocher, 1992).

Nonegocentric responses also appear in young children's everyday interactions with people. For example, preschoolers adapt their speech to fit the needs of their listeners. Four-year-olds use shorter, simpler expressions when talking to 2-year-olds than to agemates or adults (Gelman & Shatz, 1978). Also, in describing objects, children do not use such words as "big" and "little" in a rigid, egocentric fashion. Instead, they *adjust* their descriptions, taking account of context. By age 3, children judge a 2-inch shoe as small when seen by itself (because it is much smaller than most shoes) but as big when asked about its appropriateness for a very tiny 5-inch doll (Gelman & Ebeling, 1989). These flexible communicative skills challenge Piaget's description of young children as strongly egocentric.

Recent studies also indicate that Piaget overestimated preschoolers' animistic beliefs because he asked children about objects with which they have little direct experience, such as the clouds, sun, and moon. Children as young as 3 rarely think that very familiar inanimate objects, like rocks and crayons, are alive. They do make errors when questioned about certain vehicles, such as trains and airplanes. But these objects appear to be self-moving, a characteristic of almost all living things. And they also have some lifelike features—for example, headlights that resemble eyes (Dolgin & Behrend, 1984; Massey & Gelman, 1988; Richards & Siegler, 1986). Children's responses result from incomplete knowledge about some objects, not from a rigid belief that inanimate objects are alive.

ILLOGICAL CHARACTERISTICS OF THOUGHT. Many studies have reexamined the illogical characteristics that Piaget saw in the preoperational stage. Results show that when preschoolers are given tasks that are simplified and made relevant to their everyday lives, they do better than Piaget might have expected.

For example, when a conservation-of-number task is scaled down to include only three items instead of six or seven, 3-year-olds perform well (Gelman, 1972). And when preschoolers are asked carefully worded questions about what happens to substances (such as sugar) after they are dissolved in water, they display some surprisingly sophisticated understandings. Most 3- to 5-year-olds know that the substance is conserved—that it continues to exist, can be tasted, and makes the liquid heavier, even though it is invisible in the water. And the majority of 5-year-olds reconcile the apparent contradiction between invisibility and continued existence by indicating that particles too tiny to be seen are in the water (Au, Sidle, & Rollins, 1993; Rosen & Rozin, 1993).

Preschoolers' ability to notice and reason about transformations is also evident on other problems. In one study, children were shown "picture stories" of familiar experiences. In some, an object went from its basic state to a changed condition. For example, a cup became a wet cup. In others, it returned from its changed condition to its basic state. That is, a wet cup became a (dry) cup. Children were asked to pick an item from three choices (in this case, water, drying-up cloth, or feather) that caused the object to change. Most 3-year-olds had difficulty: they picked water for both transformations. But 4-year-olds did well. They selected the appropriate intermediate objects and reasoned effectively in either direction, from basic states to changed conditions and back again (Das Gupta & Bryant, 1989). This suggests that by age 4, preschoolers notice transformations, reverse their thinking, and understand causality in familiar contexts.

Indeed, a close look at 3- and 4-year-olds' conversations reveals that they use causal terms, such as "if–then" and "because," with the same degree of accuracy as do adults (McCabe & Peterson, 1988). Transductive reasoning seems to occur only when children grapple with unfamiliar topics. Otherwise, they base their causal inferences on several adultlike principles. For example, preschoolers know that physical events are determined by other physical events, that causes occur before (not after) effects, and that an event is more likely to be causal if it consistently (rather than unpredictably) precedes another event. Over the preschool years, these ideas strengthen; 5-year-olds see them as necessary to infer causality (Bullock, 1985; Bullock, Gelman, & Baillargeon, 1982). Although young children cannot yet consider the complex interplay of forces that adolescents and adults can, they often analyze their experiences accurately in terms of basic cause-and-effect relations.

CATEGORIZATION. Even though preschoolers have difficulty with Piagetian class-inclusion tasks, their everyday knowledge is organized into nested categories at an early age. Earlier we saw that even infants categorize, grouping together objects with similar physical features. By the second year, children have formed a variety of global categories consisting of objects that do not necessarily look alike but that are *the same kind of thing.* For example, between $1\frac{1}{2}$ and $2\frac{1}{2}$ years, children treat kitchen utensils, bathroom objects, animals, vehicles, plants, and furniture as distinct categories (Bauer & Mandler, 1989b; Mandler & Bauer, 1988; Mandler, Bauer, & McDonough, 1991). Consider these object groupings, and you will see that they provide yet another challenge to Piaget's assumption that young children's thinking is always perception-bound. In forming them, perceptual similarity cannot play a primary role. For example, the category of "kitchen utensils" includes objects that differ widely in appearance but that go together because of their common function and place of use.

Over the early preschool years, these global categories differentiate. Children form many *basic-level categories*—ones at an intermediate level of generality, such as "chairs," "tables," "dressers," and "beds." Language development may build on as well as facilitate these new categorical discriminations. A recent study revealed that 18-month-olds who use more object names in their everyday speech score higher on basic-level object-sorting tasks (Gopnik & Meltzoff, 1992). Perhaps the very act of naming helps young children recognize that all things can be classified. As a result, they detect more refined categories in the world of objects. In support of this idea, Korean children learn a language that emphasizes verbs rather than nouns, and object names are often omitted from sentences. They develop object-grouping skills later than do their English-speaking counterparts (Gopnik & Choi, 1990).

By 3 to 4 years, preschoolers can easily move back and forth between basic-level and *superordinate-level categories,* such as "furniture." They also break down the basic-level categories into *subcategories,* such as "rocking chairs" and "desk chairs" (Mervis, 1987; Mervis & Crisafi, 1982). Young children's category systems are not yet very complex, and concrete operational reasoning facilitates their development (Ricco, 1989). But the capacity to classify hierarchically is present in early childhood.

APPEARANCE VERSUS REALITY. So far, we have seen that young children show some remarkably advanced reasoning when presented with familiar situations and simplified problems. Yet new studies also reveal that in certain situations, preschoolers are easily tricked by the outward appearance of things, just as Piaget suggested.

John Flavell and his colleagues took a close look at children's ability to distinguish appearance from reality. They presented children with objects that were disguised in various ways and asked what the items were, "really and truly." At age 3, children had some ability to separate the way an object appeared to feel from the way it truly felt. For example, they understood that even though an ice cube did not feel cold to their gloved finger, it "really and truly" was cold (Flavell, Green, & Flavell, 1989). But preschoolers were easily tricked by sights and sounds. When asked whether a white piece of paper placed behind a blue filter is "really and truly blue" or whether a can that sounds like a baby crying when turned over is "really and truly a baby," they often responded "yes!" Not until 6 to 7 years did children do well on these tasks (Flavell, Green, & Flavell, 1987).

How do children go about mastering distinctions between appearance and reality? Make-believe play may be important. Children can tell the difference between pretend play and real experiences long before they answer many appearance–reality problems correctly (DiLalla & Watson, 1988; Woolley & Wellman, 1990). During make-believe, they integrate a wide variety of objects into their make-believe themes. Often we hear them say such things as, "Pretend this block is a telephone," or "Let's use this block for a house." Experiencing the contrast between everyday and playful use of objects may help children refine their understanding of what is real and what is unreal in the surrounding world.

EVALUATION OF THE PREOPERATIONAL STAGE. How can we make sense of the contradictions between Piaget's conclusions and the findings of recent research? The evidence as a whole indicates that Piaget was partly wrong and partly right about young children's cognitive capacities. When given simple tasks based on familiar experiences, preschoolers show the beginnings of logical operations long before the concrete operational stage. But their reasoning is not as well developed as that of school-age children, since they fail Piaget's three-mountains, conservation, and class-inclusion tasks and have difficulty separating appearance from reality.

The fact that preschoolers have some logical understanding suggests that the attainment of logical operations is a gradual process. Operational thought is not absent at one point in time and suddenly present at another. Instead, children demonstrate mature reasoning at an early age, although it is incomplete. Evidence that preschool children can be trained to perform well on Piagetian problems, such as conservation and class inclusion, supports this idea (Beilin, 1978; McCabe & Siegel, 1987). It makes sense that children who possess part of a capacity will benefit from training, unlike those with no understanding at all. In addition, a variety of training methods are effective, including language-based techniques, such as social interaction with more capable peers, adult instruction that points out contradictions in children's logic, and efforts to help children remember the component parts of a problem.

Nevertheless, training of concrete operational skills is not equally effective for all children. Three-year-olds, for example, can be trained, but they do not improve as much as 4-year-olds, and the effects of training young preschoolers rarely generalize to new tasks (Field, 1981; Siegler, 1981). These findings suggest, in line with Piaget's theory, that children with the least mature schemes try to accommodate to new information, but they cannot do so as well as older youngsters with more developed cognitive structures.

Still, the idea that logical operations develop gradually poses yet another challenge to Piaget's stage concept, which assumes sudden and abrupt change toward logical reasoning around 7 years of age (Gelman & Baillargeon, 1983). Although they still have a great deal of developing to do, new research shows that the minds of young children are considerably more coherent and organized than Piaget thought they were.

Brief Review

During Piaget's preoperational stage, mental representation flourishes, as indicated by children's language, make-believe play, and drawings and paintings. Aside from representation, Piaget's theory emphasizes the young child's cognitive limitations. Egocentrism underlies a variety of illogical features of preoperational thought, including animism, an inability to pass conservation tasks, transductive reasoning, and lack of hierarchical classification. Recent research reveals that when tasks are simplified and made relevant to children's everyday experiences, preschoolers show the beginnings of logical reasoning. These findings indicate that operational thought is not absent during early childhood, and they challenge Piaget's notion of stage.

TABLE 6.2 *Major Characteristics of the Concrete Operational Stage*

CHARACTERISTIC	DESCRIPTION	EXAMPLE
Conservation	Concrete operational children recognize that certain physical characteristics of objects remain the same even when their outward appearance changes.	After spilling 10 pennies stacked on her desk all over the floor, Lizzie bent down to search for them. "I know there have to be ten," she said to herself, "because that's how many I put in that little pile on my desk yesterday."
Decentration	Concrete operational children coordinate several important features of a task rather than centering on only the perceptually dominant one.	After getting two glasses of lemonade from the kitchen, one for her brother and one for herself, Lizzie remarked, "Don't worry, I gave you just as much. My glass is tall but thin. Yours is short but wide."
Reversibility	Concrete operational children can think through the steps in a problem and then go backward, returning to the starting point.	Lizzie understands that addition and subtraction are reversible operations. In other words, when you add 7 plus 8 to get 15, then this tells you that 15 minus 8 must be 7.
Hierarchical classification	Concrete operational children can flexibly group and regroup objects into hierarchies of classes and subclasses.	Lizzie discussed how to display her rock collection with her friend Marina. Marina suggested, "You could divide them up by size and then by color. Or you could use shape and color."
Seriation	Concrete operational children are guided by an overall plan when arranging items in a series.	Lizzie decided to arrange her rocks by size. She quickly lined up all 20 rocks in a row, selecting the smallest and then the next smallest from the pile, until the arrangement was complete.
Transitive inference	Concrete operational children can seriate mentally. After comparing A with B and B with C, they can infer the relationship between A and C.	"I saw Tina's new lunch box, and it's bigger than mine," Marina said while eating her sandwich with Lizzie one day. "Well, it must be bigger than mine, too, because look—my box isn't even as big as yours," said Lizzie.
Spatial operations	Concrete operational children conserve distance; understand the relations among distance, time, and speed; and create organized cognitive maps of familiar environments.	Lizzie realizes that a truck blocking the sidewalk does not change the distance to the end of her street. She also knows that if she runs faster than Marina for the same amount of time, she will travel farther. And she can draw a map that depicts the route from her house to Marina's house with major landmarks along the way.
Horizontal décalage	Logical concepts are mastered gradually over the course of middle childhood.	Lizzie understood conservation of number and liquid before she mastered conservation of area and weight.

THE CONCRETE OPERATIONAL STAGE (7 TO 11 YEARS)

Concrete operational stage
Piaget's third stage, during which thought is logical, flexible, and organized in its application to concrete information. However, the capacity for abstract thinking is not yet present. Spans the years from 7 to 11.

Piaget viewed the **concrete operational stage**, which spans the years from 7 to 11, as a major turning point in cognitive development. When children attain it, their thought more closely resembles that of adults than that of the sensorimotor and preoperational child (Piaget & Inhelder, 1967/1969). According to Piaget, concrete operational reasoning is far more logical, flexible, and organized than cognition was during the preschool period. Table 6.2 summarizes the major characteristics of this stage.

Operational Thought

Concrete operations are evident in the school-age child's performance on a wide variety of Piagetian tasks. In the following sections, we examine the major attainments of this period.

CONSERVATION. Piaget regarded *conservation* as the single most important achievement of the concrete operational stage, since it provides clear evidence of *operations*. In conservation of liquid, for example, concrete operational children state that the amount of liquid has not changed, and they are likely to explain in ways like this: "The water's shorter but it's also wider. If you pour it back, you'll see that it's the same amount." Notice how in this response, the child coordinates several aspects of the task rather than centering on only one, as a preschooler would do. In other words, during middle childhood, children are capable of *decentration;* they recognize that a change in one aspect of the water (its height) is compensated for by a change in another aspect (its width). This explanation also illustrates *reversibility*—the capacity to imagine the water being returned to the original container as proof of conservation.

HIERARCHICAL CLASSIFICATION. By the end of middle childhood, operational thought permits children to categorize more effectively, and they pass Piaget's class-inclusion problem (Achenbach & Weisz, 1975; Hodges & French, 1988). You can see evidence for this in children's play activities. Collections of all kinds of objects become common during the school years. At age 10, one boy I know spent hours sorting and resorting his large box of baseball cards. At times he grouped them by league and team membership, at other times by playing position and batting average. He could separate the players into a variety of classes and subclasses and flexibly rearrange them. This understanding is beyond the grasp of most preschoolers, who typically insist that a set of objects can be sorted in only one way.

SERIATION. The ability to order items along a quantitative dimension, such as length or weight, is called **seriation.** To test for it, Piaget asked children to arrange sticks of different lengths from shortest to longest. Older preschoolers can form the series, but they do so haphazardly. They put the sticks in a row but make many errors and take a long time to correct them. In contrast, 6- to 7-year-olds are guided by an orderly plan. They create the series efficiently by beginning with the smallest stick, then moving to the next smallest, and so on, until the ordering is complete.

The concrete operational child's improved grasp of quantitative arrangements is also evident in a more challenging seriation problem—one that requires children to seriate mentally. This ability is called **transitive inference.** In a well-known transitive-inference problem, Piaget showed children pairings of differently colored sticks. From observing that stick A is longer than stick B and stick B is longer than stick C, children must make the mental inference that A is longer than C. Not until age 7 or 8 do children perform well on this task (Chapman & Lindenberger, 1988; Piaget, 1967).

Piaget referred to the abilities we have considered so far—conservation, hierarchical classification, and seriation—as *logico-arithmetic operations.* He thought they were responsible for the school-age child's increased facility with quantitative tasks. As we will see in Chapter 7 when we consider the development of mathematical reasoning, preschoolers have some impressive numerical skills, including the ability to count small arrays and add and subtract small sets of items. But most mathematical knowledge is acquired after early childhood. Elementary school children do have a more quantitative, measurement-oriented approach to many tasks than do preschoolers (Fuson, 1988).

SPATIAL OPERATIONS. In addition to logico-arithmetic operations, the concrete operational child also masters a variety of *spatial operations.* These deal with distance and spatial relationships among objects.

*A*n improved ability to categorize underlies children's interest in collecting objects during middle childhood. This boy enjoys sorting his rock collection into an elaborate structure of classes and subclasses. (BLAIR SEITZ/PHOTO RESEARCHERS)

Seriation
The ability to order items along a quantitative dimension, such as length or weight.

Transitive inference
The ability to seriate—or arrange items along a quantitative dimension—mentally.

Distance, Time, and Speed. Piaget found that comprehension of distance improves during middle childhood, as a special conservation task reveals. To administer this problem, make two small trees out of modeling clay and place them apart on a table. Next, put a block or thick piece of cardboard between the trees. Then ask the child whether the trees are nearer together, farther apart, or still the same distance apart. Preschoolers say the distance has become smaller. They do not seem to realize that a filled space has the same value as an empty space (Piaget, Inhelder, & Szeminska, 1948/1960). By the early school years, children grasp this idea easily. Four-year-olds can conserve distance when questioned about a very familiar scene or when a path is marked between two objects, which helps them represent the distance. However, their understanding is not as solid and complete as that of the school-age child (Fabricius & Wellman, 1993; Miller & Baillargeon, 1990).

According to Piaget (1946/1970), concrete operational thinking permits children to combine distance with other physical concepts, such as time and speed. He reported that children first master the positive relationships between speed and distance (the faster you travel, the farther you go) and time and distance (the longer you travel, the farther you go). Only later do they understand the negative relationship between speed and time (the faster you travel, the less time it takes to get to your destination). More recent research confirms Piaget's predictions. Children grasp these associations successively between first and third grade (Acredolo, Adams, & Schmid, 1984).

Cognitive Maps. School-age children's more advanced understanding of space can also be seen in their drawings of familiar environments, such as their neighborhood or school. At age 6, children can create a fairly accurate picture of where their desk is located in relation to the door, windows, and chalkboard of the classroom. With age, they can draw larger spaces—for example, the classroom in relation to the main office, the gymnasium, and the playground. These mental representations of large-scale environments are called **cognitive maps**. They require considerable perspective-taking skill, since the entire space cannot be seen at once. Instead, children must infer the overall layout by relating the separate parts to one another.

Many studies support Piaget's assumption that children's cognitive maps undergo important changes from early to middle childhood (Piaget & Inhelder, 1948/1956). Preschoolers' maps display *landmarks,* but they are fragmented and disorganized. The more effective thinking of the school years permits 6- and 7-year-olds to arrange landmarks along an *organized route of travel,* such as the path they usually walk from home to school. However, the relationship of routes to one another has not yet been mastered. By the end of middle childhood, children form an *overall configuration of a large-scale space* in which landmarks and routes are interrelated (Newcombe, 1982; Siegel, 1981).

Once again, however, the ability to represent spatial layouts does not emerge suddenly. Research indicates that children as young as 3 can use a simple map to navigate their way through a space they have never seen before (Uttal & Wellman, 1989). However, preschoolers cannot yet create an organized map of their own. "Map literacy" improves greatly during middle childhood (Liben & Downs, 1986; Spencer, Blades, & Morsley, 1989).

Limitations of Concrete Operational Thought

Because of their improved ability to conserve, classify, seriate, and deal with spatial concepts, school-age children are far more capable problem solvers than they were during the preschool years. But concrete operational thinking suffers from one important limitation. Children think in an organized, logical fashion only when dealing with concrete information they can directly perceive. Their mental

Cognitive maps
Mental representations of large-scale environments.

operations work poorly when applied to abstract ideas—ones not directly apparent in the real world.

Children's solutions to transitive-inference problems provide a good illustration. When shown pairs of sticks of unequal length, 9-year-olds easily figure out that if stick A is longer than stick B and stick B is longer than stick C, then stick A is longer than stick C. But when given an entirely hypothetical version of this task, such as "Susan is taller than Sally and Sally is taller than Mary. Who is the tallest?" they have great difficulty. Not until age 11 or 12 can children solve this problem easily.

The fact that logical thought is at first tied to immediate situations helps account for a special feature of concrete operational reasoning. Perhaps you have already noticed that school-age children do not master all of Piaget's concrete operational tasks at once. Instead, they do so in a step-by-step fashion. For example, they usually grasp conservation problems in a certain order: first number; then length, mass, and liquid; and finally area and weight (Brainerd, 1978). Piaget used the term **horizontal décalage** (meaning development within a stage) to describe this gradual mastery of logical concepts. The horizontal décalage is another indication of the concrete operational child's difficulty with abstractions. School-age children do not come up with general logical principles and then apply them to all relevant situations. Instead, they seem to work out the logic of each problem they encounter separately.

Recent Research on Concrete Operational Thought

According to Piaget, brain maturation combined with experience in a rich and varied external world should lead children everywhere to reach the concrete operational stage. He did not believe that operational thinking depends on particular kinds of experiences. Yet recent evidence indicates that specific cultural practices have a great deal to do with children's mastery of Piagetian tasks (Rogoff, 1990).

A large body of evidence shows that conservation is often delayed in non-Western societies. For example, among the Hausa of Nigeria, who live in small agricultural settlements and rarely send their children to school, even the most basic conservation tasks—number, length, and liquid—are not understood until age 11 or later (Fahrmeier, 1978). This suggests that for children to master conservation and other Piagetian concepts, they must take part in everyday activities that promote this way of thinking. Many children in Western nations, for example, have learned to think of fairness in terms of equal distribution—a value emphasized by their culture. They have many opportunities to divide materials, such as

*I*n non-Western societies, conservation is often delayed. The everyday activities of this Nigerian girl may not promote the kind of reasoning required to pass Piagetian conservation tasks. Compared to her Western counterparts, she probably has fewer opportunities to see the same quantity arranged in different ways. (M. BERTINETTI/PHOTO RESEARCHERS)

Horizontal décalage
Development within a Piagetian stage. Gradual mastery of logical concepts during the concrete operational stage provides an example.

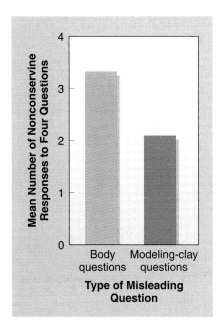

FIGURE 6.6 College students' responses to misleading questions about conservation of weight. Misleading questions often led to nonconserving responses from these well-educated adults, especially when they referred to the student's body. (Adapted from Winer, Craig, and Weinbaum, 1992.)

crayons and Halloween treats, equally among themselves and their friends. Because they often see the same quantity arranged in different ways, they grasp conservation early. But in cultures where these experiences are rare, conservation is unlikely to appear at the expected age (Light & Perrett-Clermont, 1989).

In addition to specific experiences, the phrasing of questions and the objects to which they refer can have a profound effect on Piagetian task performance. In a recent study, researchers asked college students misleading questions about conservation of weight. Sometimes the question referred to the student's body ("When do you weigh more, when you are walking or running?") and sometimes it referred to an external object ("When did the modeling clay weigh more, when it was a ball or when it was in the shape of a sausage?"). As Figure 6.6 reveals, misleading questions led to many nonconserving responses, especially when they referred to the student's body. Interestingly, those students who were asked to explain their answers and who had heard of Piaget were less likely to be tricked by the misleading questions (Winer, Craig, & Weinbaum, 1992).

Taken together, these findings reveal that concrete operations are not always used, even by adults! Instead, people seem to have at least two modes of thinking that are evoked in different situations: one that is person-centered and intuitive, and one that is object-centered and logically consistent. This is troublesome for Piaget's theory, since it indicates that concrete operational reasoning may not be a form of logic that emerges universally during middle childhood and, once present, overrides less mature ways of thinking. Instead, it may be a product of direct training, context, and cultural conditions (Gellatly, 1987; Light & Perrett-Clermont, 1989; Robert, 1989).

Brief Review

During the concrete operational stage, thought is more logical, flexible, and organized than it was during the preschool years. The ability to conserve indicates that children can decenter and reverse their thinking. School-age children also have an improved grasp of classification, seriation, and spatial concepts. However, they cannot yet think abstractly. Recent research indicates that concrete operational reasoning is often delayed in non-Western societies, and it is strongly subject to situational conditions. These findings indicate that it may not be a natural form of thinking that emerges spontaneously and universally in middle childhood, as Piaget believed.

TABLE 6.3 *Major Characteristics of the Formal Operational Stage*

CHARACTERISTIC	DESCRIPTION	EXAMPLE
Hypothetico-deductive reasoning	When faced with a problem, formal operational adolescents think of all possible factors that could affect the outcome, even those not immediately suggested by the concrete features of the situation. Then they try them out in a step-by-step fashion to find out which ones work in the real world.	In biology class, Louis had to determine which of two fertilizers was best for growing African violets. Louis thought, "The kind of fertilizer might not be the only factor that's important. Its concentration and how often the plant is fed might also make a difference." So Louis planned an experiment in which each fertilizer would be applied in several strengths and according to different feeding schedules. He made sure to design the experiment so he could determine the separate effects of each factor on plant growth.
Propositional thought	Formal operational adolescents can evaluate the logic of statements by reflecting on the statements themselves. They do not need to consider them against real-world circumstances.	Louis was given the following propositional task and asked to indicate whether the conclusion was true, false, or uncertain: Premise 1: All animals are purple. Premise 2: A frobe is purple. Conclusion: A frobe is an animal. Louis concluded, correctly, that whether a frobe is an animal is uncertain. "A frobe might be an animal," he answered, "but it might also be a purple thing that is not an animal."

THE FORMAL OPERATIONAL STAGE
(11 YEARS AND OLDER)

According to Piaget, the capacity for abstract thinking begins around age 11. At the **formal operational stage,** the adolescent reasons much like a scientist searching for solutions in the laboratory. Concrete operational children can only "operate on reality," but formal operational adolescents can "operate on operations." In other words, concrete things and events are no longer required as objects of thought (Inhelder & Piaget, 1955/1958). Instead, adolescents can come up with new, more general logical rules through internal reflection. Table 6.3 summarizes two major features of the formal operational stage.

Hypothetico-Deductive Reasoning

At adolescence, young people first become capable of **hypothetico-deductive reasoning.** When faced with a problem, they start with a *general theory* of all possible factors that might affect an outcome and deduce from it specific hypotheses (or predictions) about what might happen. Then they test these hypotheses in an orderly fashion to see which ones work in the real world. Notice how this form of problem solving begins with possibility and proceeds to reality. In contrast, concrete operational children start with reality—with the most obvious predictions about a situation. When these are not confirmed, they cannot think of alternatives and fail to solve the problem.

Adolescents' performance on Piaget's famous pendulum problem illustrates this new hypothetico-deductive approach. Suppose we present several school-age children and adolescents with strings of different lengths, objects of different weights to attach to the strings, and a bar from which to hang the strings. Then we

Formal operational stage
Piaget's final stage, in which adolescents develop the capacity for abstract, scientific thinking. Begins around age 11.

Hypothetico-deductive reasoning
A formal operational problem-solving strategy in which adolescents begin with a general theory of all possible factors that could affect an outcome in a problem and deduce specific hypotheses, which they test in an orderly fashion.

*D*uring the formal operational stage, adolescents solve problems by thinking of all possible hypotheses that could occur in a situation. Then they test these predictions systematically to see which ones apply in the real world. (BACHMANN/THE IMAGE WORKS)

ask each of them to figure out what influences the speed with which a pendulum swings through its arc.

Formal operational adolescents come up with four hypotheses: (1) the length of the string; (2) the weight of the object hung on it; (3) how high the object is raised before it is released; and (4) how forcefully the object is pushed. Then, by varying one factor at a time while holding all others constant, they try out each of these possibilities. Eventually they discover that only string length makes a difference.

In contrast, concrete operational children's experimentation is unsystematic. They cannot separate out the effects of each variable. For example, they may test for the effect of string length without holding weight constant by comparing a short, light pendulum with a long, heavy one. Also, they fail to notice variables that are not immediately suggested by the concrete materials of the task—the height from which the pendulum is released and the forcefulness with which it is pushed.

Propositional Thought

A second important characteristic of the formal operational stage is **propositional thought.** Adolescents can evaluate the logic of propositions (verbal statements) without referring to real-world circumstances. In contrast, concrete operational children can evaluate the logic of statements only by considering them against concrete evidence in the real world.

In one study of propositional reasoning, an experimenter showed children and adolescents a pile of poker chips and indicated that some statements would be made about them. The subject was asked to tell whether each statement was true, false, or uncertain. In one condition, the experimenter hid a chip in her hand and then asked the subject to evaluate the following propositions:

> "Either the chip in my hand is green or it is not green."
> "The chip in my hand is green and it is not green."

In another condition, the experimenter held either a red or a green chip in full view and made the same statements.

School-age children focused on the concrete properties of the poker chips rather than on the logic of the statements. As a result, they replied that they were

Propositional thought
A type of formal operational reasoning in which adolescents evaluate the logic of verbal statements without referring to real-world circumstances.

*I*n Piaget's formal operational stage, adolescents engage in propositional thought. As he discusses an algebraic equation with his teacher, this 14-year-old shows that he can reason with symbols that do not necessarily represent objects in the real world. (JOHN LEI/STOCK BOSTON)

uncertain to both statements when the chip was hidden from view. When it was visible, they judged both statements to be true if the chip was green and false if it was red. In contrast, adolescents analyzed the logic of the statements as propositions. They understood that the "either–or" statement is always true and the "and" statement is always false, regardless of the poker chip's color (Osherson & Markman, 1975).

Although Piaget believed that language did not play a central role in spurring cognition forward in childhood, he acknowledged that it plays a larger part during adolescence. Abstract thought requires language-based systems of representation that do not stand for real things, such as those that exist in higher mathematics. Around age 14 or 15, high school students start to use these systems in algebra and geometry. Formal operational thought also involves verbal reasoning about abstract concepts (Brainerd, 1978). Adolescents demonstrate their capacity to think in this way when they ponder the relation among time, space, and matter in physics and wonder about justice and freedom in philosophy.

Formal Operational Egocentrism

Adolescents' capacity to think abstractly, combined with the physical changes they are undergoing, means that they start to think more about themselves. Piaget believed that the arrival of this stage is accompanied by **formal operational egocentrism**: the inability to distinguish the abstract perspectives of self and others (Inhelder & Piaget, 1955/1958). As teenagers imagine what others must be thinking, two distorted images of the relation between self and other appear.

The first is called the **imaginary audience.** Young teenagers regard themselves as always on stage. They are convinced that they are the focus of everyone else's attention and concern (Elkind & Bowen, 1979). As a result, they become extremely self-conscious, often going to great lengths to avoid embarrassment. The imaginary audience helps us understand the long hours adolescents spend in the bathroom inspecting every detail of their appearance as they envision the response of the rest of the world. It also accounts for their sensitivity to public criticism. To teenagers, who believe that everyone around them is monitoring their performance, a critical remark from a parent or teacher can be a mortifying event.

A second cognitive distortion is the **personal fable.** Because teenagers are so sure that others are observing and thinking about them, they develop an inflated opinion of their own importance. They start to feel that they are special and unique. Many adolescents view themselves as reaching great heights of glory as well as

Formal operational egocentrism
A form of egocentrism present during the formal operational stage involving an inability to distinguish the abstract perspectives of self and other.

Imaginary audience
Adolescents' belief that they are the focus of everyone else's attention and concern.

Personal fable
Adolescents' belief that they are special and unique. Leads them to conclude that others cannot possibly understand their thoughts and feelings and that they are invulnerable to danger.

sinking to unusual depths of despair. As one teenager wrote in her diary, "My parents' lives are so ordinary, so stuck in a rut. Mine will be different. I'll realize my hopes and ambitions." The personal fable also contributes to adolescent risk-taking. Teenagers who have sex without contraceptives or weave in and out of traffic at 80 miles an hour are generally convinced of their uniqueness and invulnerability.

Consistent with Piaget's theory, the imaginary audience and personal fable are strongest during the transition to formal operations. They gradually decline over the adolescent years (Enright, Lapsley, & Shukla, 1979; Lapsley et al., 1988). Nevertheless, some experts believe that these distorted visions of the self may not represent a return to egocentrism. Instead, they may be an outgrowth of advances in perspective taking, which cause young teenagers to be very concerned with what others think (Lapsley et al., 1986). Adolescents may also cling to the idea that others are preoccupied with their appearance and behavior for emotional reasons. Doing so helps them maintain a hold on important relationships as they struggle to separate from parents and establish an independent sense of self (Lapsley, 1990).

Recent Research on Formal Operational Thought

Many researchers have conducted follow-up studies of formal operational thought, asking questions similar to those we discussed with respect to earlier stages: Is there evidence that abstract reasoning appears sooner than Piaget expected? Do all individuals reach formal operations during the teenage years?

ARE YOUNG CHILDREN CAPABLE OF ABSTRACT REASONING? School-age children show the glimmerings of abstract reasoning, but they are not as competent as adolescents and adults. For example, training improves performance on hypothetico-deductive tasks like the pendulum problem. But the effects of training last longer and generalize more easily to new tasks with a high school or college student than with a school-age child (Greenbowe et al., 1981; Kuhn, Ho, & Adams, 1979).

Similarly, young children's capacity for propositional thought is quite limited. For example, they have great difficulty reasoning from premises that contradict reality or their own beliefs. Consider the following set of statements: "If dogs are bigger than elephants and elephants are bigger than mice, then dogs are bigger than mice." Children younger than 10 judge this reasoning to be false, since all the relations specified do not occur in real life (Moshman & Franks, 1986).

Furthermore, in instances in which school-age children respond correctly to propositional tasks, their success seems to be due to an "atmosphere effect." Positive statements are always answered with "yes" and negative statements are always answered with "no," even though this strategy often violates the most basic rules of logic (Markovits, Schleifer, & Fortier, 1989). For example, when given the following premises (one of which is negative), school-age children usually draw an incorrect conclusion:

> Premise 1: If there is a knife, then there is a fork.
> Premise 2: There is not a knife.
> Question: Is there a fork?
> Wrong conclusion: No, there is not a fork. (Kodroff & Roberge, 1975)

Around age 11, young people in Western nations show an improved ability to analyze the logic of a series of propositions, regardless of whether statements are positive, negative, or consistent with their own values. As Piaget's theory indicates, propositional thought improves steadily over the adolescent years (Markovits & Vachon, 1989, 1990).

DO ALL INDIVIDUALS REACH THE FORMAL OPERATIONAL STAGE? Try giving the knife-and-fork task to some of your friends and see how well they do. You are likely to find that even well-educated adults have difficulty with abstract reasoning! About 40 to 60 percent of college students fail Piaget's formal operational problems (Keating, 1979).

Why is it that so many college students, and adults in general, are not fully formal operational? The reason is that people are most likely to think abstractly in situations in which they have had extensive experience. This is supported by evidence that taking college courses leads to improvements in formal reasoning related to course content. For example, math and science prompts gains in propositional thought, social science in methodological and statistical reasoning (Lehman & Nisbett, 1990). Consider these findings carefully, and you will see that formal operational thought, like the concrete stage that preceded it, appears to be a gradual development. And rather than emerging in all contexts at once, it is situation- and task-specific.

Finally, in many village and tribal cultures, formal operational reasoning does not appear at all (Gellatly, 1987; Scribner, 1977). Piaget acknowledged that because of lack of opportunity to solve hypothetical problems, abstract thought might not appear in some societies. Still, these findings raise questions similar to those discussed earlier. Is the highest stage really an outgrowth of children's independent efforts to make sense of their world? Or is it a culturally transmitted way of thinking that is specific to literate societies and taught in school? This issue, along with others, has prompted many investigators to doubt the overall validity of Piaget's theory.

LARGER QUESTIONS ABOUT THE VALIDITY OF PIAGET'S THEORY

Piaget awakened psychologists and educators to a view of children as active knowledge seekers who undergo complex cognitive changes. Yet a wealth of research reveals that his theory has important shortcomings.

Problems of Clarity and Accuracy

Some of Piaget's ideas are not clearly spelled out. Think, for a moment, about Piaget's explanation of cognitive change—in particular, equilibration and its attendant processes of adaptation and organization. Just what the child does to equilibrate seems vague and imprecise. As an example of this problem, recall our description of organization, the notion that the structures of each stage form a coherent whole. Piaget is not very explicit about how the diverse achievements of each stage—for example, conservation, hierarchical classification, seriation, and spatial concepts during concrete operations—are bound together by a single, underlying form of thought (Flavell, 1982).

Throughout this chapter, we have noted that several of Piaget's ideas are now regarded as either incorrect or only partially correct. For example, Piaget's belief that infants and young children must act on the environment to revise their cognitive structures is too narrow a notion of how learning takes place. As we will see when we turn to Vygotsky's sociocultural theory, cognitive development is not always self-generating, and left to their own devices, children may not always notice those aspects of a situation that are needed for an improved understanding. In addition, many efforts to verify Piaget's account of the timetable of development have not been successful. As Flavell (1992) states:

> The recent trend in the field has been to highlight the cognitive competencies of young children . . . , the cognitive shortcomings of adults, and the cognitive inconsistencies of both, effectively pushing from both ends of childhood towards the middle and blurring the differences between the two groups. (p. 1000)

Are There Stages of Cognitive Development?

This brings us to the most controversial question about Piaget's theory: Does cognitive development actually take place in stages? Throughout this chapter, we have seen that many cognitive changes proceed slowly and gradually. Few abilities are absent during one period and then suddenly present in another. Also, there seem to be few periods of cognitive equilibrium. Instead, within each stage, children seem to be constantly modifying structures and acquiring new skills.

Today virtually all experts agree that children's cognition is not as broadly stagelike as Piaget believed. At the same time, contemporary researchers disagree on how general or specific cognitive development actually is (Flavell, 1992; Siegler, 1991). Some theorists deny the existence of any stagewise change. They believe that children gradually work out their understanding of each type of task separately. Their thought processes are regarded as basically the same at all ages—just present to a greater or lesser extent (Gelman & Baillargeon, 1983). These assumptions form the basis of a major competing approach to Piaget's theory—information processing, which we take up in Chapter 7.

Other experts think that the stage notion is still valid, but it must be modified. For example, in Chapter 7 we will also consider the work of some neo-Piagetians, who combine Piaget's stage approach with the information-processing emphasis on task-specific change (Case, 1992; Fischer & Farrar, 1987). These theorists believe that Piaget's strict stage definition needs to be transformed into a less tightly knit concept, one in which a related set of competencies develops over an extended time period, depending on both biological maturity and specific experiences. Flavell (1985) retains the stage idea because he finds it hard to believe that the child's cognition is so completely variable across tasks that it has no coherence. As he notes, "Perhaps what the field needs is another genius like Piaget to show us how, and to what extent, all those cognitive-developmental strands within the growing child are really knotted together" (p. 297).

PIAGET AND EDUCATION

Piaget's theory has had a major impact on education, especially at the preschool and early elementary school levels. Three educational principles have served as the foundation for a variety of Piagetian-based curricula developed over the past 30 years:

1. *An emphasis on discovery learning.* In a Piagetian classroom, children are encouraged to discover for themselves through spontaneous interaction with the environment. Instead of presenting ready-made knowledge verbally, teachers provide a rich variety of activities designed to promote exploration and discovery and permit children to choose freely among them.

2. *Sensitivity to children's readiness to learn.* A Piagetian classroom does not try to speed up development. Instead, Piaget believed that appropriate learning experiences build on children's current level of thinking. Teachers watch and listen to their pupils, introducing experiences that permit them to practice new schemes and that are likely to challenge incorrect ways of viewing the world. But new skills are not imposed before children indicate they are interested or ready, since this leads to superficial memorization of adult formulas rather than true understanding (Johnson & Hooper, 1982).

3. *Acceptance of individual differences.* Piaget's theory assumes that all children go through the same sequence of development, but they do so at different rates. Therefore, teachers must make a special effort to arrange activities for individuals and small groups rather than for the total class (Ginsburg & Opper, 1988). In addition, teachers evaluate educational progress by comparing each child to his or her own previous development. They are less interested in how children measure up to normative standards or the average performance of same-age peers (Gray, 1978).

Educational applications of Piaget's theory, like his stages, have been criticized. Perhaps the greatest challenge has to do with his insistence that young children learn only through acting on the environment (Hooper & DeFrain, 1980).

Nevertheless, Piaget's influence on education has been powerful and long-lasting. He gave teachers new ways to observe, understand, and enhance young children's development and offered strong theoretical justification for child-oriented approaches to classroom teaching and learning.

Brief Review

In Piaget's formal operational stage, the capacity for abstraction appears, as indicated by hypothetico-deductive reasoning and propositional thought. New cognitive powers lead to formal operational egocentrism, in the form of the imaginary audience and personal fable. Adolescents and adults are most likely to display abstract thinking in areas in which they have had extensive experience. In village and tribal cultures, it does not appear at all. Major criticisms of Piaget's theory include the vagueness of his ideas about cognitive change, inaccuracies in his account of the timetable of development, and evidence that children's cognition is not as broadly stagelike as he assumed. Piaget's theory has had a powerful influence on education, promoting discovery learning, sensitivity to children's readiness to learn, and acceptance of individual differences.

VYGOTSKY'S SOCIOCULTURAL THEORY

According to Piaget, the most important source of cognition is the child himself—a busy, self-motivated explorer who forms ideas and tests them against the world, without external pressure. Vygotsky also believed that children are active seekers of knowledge, but he did not view them as solitary agents. Instead, he constructed a theory in which the child and the social environment collaborate to mold cognition in culturally adaptive ways.

Early events in Vygotsky's life contributed to his vision of human cognition as inherently social and language based. As a young boy in Russia, he was instructed at home by a private tutor, who conducted lessons using the Socratic dialogue—an interactive, question-and-answer approach that challenged current conceptions to promote heightened understanding. By the time Vygotsky entered the University of Moscow, his primary interest was a verbal field—literature. Upon graduation, he was first a teacher. Only later did he turn to psychology (Blanck, 1990; Kozulin, 1990).

Vygotsky died of tuberculosis when he was only 37 years old. Although he wrote prolifically, he had little more than a decade to formulate his ideas. Consequently, his theory is not as completely specified as that of Piaget. Nevertheless, the field of child development is currently experiencing a burst of interest in Vygotsky's sociocultural perspective. The major reason for his appeal seems to lie in his rejection of an individualistic view of the developing child in favor of a socially formed mind (Wertsch & Tulviste, 1992).

According to Vygotsky, infants are endowed with basic perceptual, attentional, and memory capacities that are shared with other animals. These undergo a natural course of development during the first 2 years through simple and direct contact with the environment. But once children become capable of mental representation, especially through language, their ability to participate in social dialogues surrounding culturally important tasks is enhanced. Soon young children start to communicate with themselves in much the same way that they converse with others. As a result, basic mental capacities are transformed into uniquely human, higher cognitive processes. Let's see how this happens, as we explore the Piagetian–Vygotskian controversy introduced at the beginning of this chapter in greater detail.

Piaget versus Vygotsky: Children's Private Speech

Watch preschoolers as they go about their daily activities, and you will see that they frequently talk out loud to themselves as they play and explore the environ-

*D*uring the preschool years, children frequently talk to themselves as they play and explore the environment. Research supports Vygotsky's theory that children use private speech to guide their behavior when faced with challenging tasks. With age, private speech is transformed into silent, inner speech, or verbal thought. (ELIZABETH CREWS)

ment. For example, as a 5-year-old worked a puzzle at preschool one day, I heard him say, "Where's the red piece? I need the red one. Now a blue one. No, it doesn't fit. Try it here." On another occasion, while sitting next to another child, he blurted out, "It broke," without explaining what or when.

Piaget (1923/1926) called these utterances *egocentric speech*, a term expressing his belief that they reflect the preoperational child's inability to imagine the perspectives of others. For this reason, Piaget said, young children's talk is often "talk for self" in which they run off thoughts in whatever form they happen to occur, regardless of whether they are understandable to a listener. Piaget believed that cognitive maturity and certain social experiences—namely, disagreements with peers—eventually bring an end to egocentric speech. Through arguments with agemates, children repeatedly see that others hold viewpoints different from their own. As a result, egocentric speech declines and is replaced by social speech, in which children adapt what they say to their listeners.

Vygotsky (1934/1986) voiced a powerful objection to Piaget's conclusion that young children's language is egocentric and nonsocial. He reasoned that children speak to themselves for self-guidance and self-direction. Because language helps children think about their own behavior and select courses of action, Vygotsky regarded it as the foundation for complex cognitive skills, such as controlled, sustained attention; deliberate memorization and recall; categorization; planning; problem solving; and self-reflection. As children get older and tasks become easier, their self-directed speech declines and is internalized as silent, inner speech—the verbal dialogues we carry on with ourselves while thinking and acting in everyday situations.

Over the past two decades, researchers have carried out many studies to determine which of these two views is correct. Almost all the findings have sided with Vygotsky. As a result, children's speech-to-self is now referred to as **private speech** instead of egocentric speech. Research shows that children use more of it when tasks are difficult, after they make errors, or when they are confused about how to proceed (Berk, 1992a). Also, just as Vygotsky predicted, with age private speech goes underground, changing from utterances spoken out loud into whispers and silent lip movements (Berk & Landau, 1993; Frauenglass & Diaz, 1985). Finally, children who use private speech freely when faced with difficult tasks are more attentive and involved and show greater improvement in performance than their less talkative agemates (Behrend, Rosengren, & Perlmutter, 1992; Bivens & Berk, 1990).

If private speech is a central force in cognitive development, where does it come from? Vygotsky's answer to this question highlights the social origins of cognition, his main difference of opinion with Piaget.

Private speech
Self-directed speech that children use to plan and guide their own behavior.

*T*his mother assists her young son in making a music box work. By presenting a task within the child's zone of proximal development and fine-tuning her support to fit his momentary needs, she promotes intersubjectivity and provides an effective scaffold for learning. (ERIKA STONE)

The Social Origins of Cognitive Development

Vygotsky (1930–1935/1978) believed that all higher cognitive processes have their origins in social interaction. Through joint activities with more mature members of society, children come to master activities and think in ways that have meaning in their culture. A special concept, the **zone of proximal** (or potential) **development,** explains how this happens. It refers to a range of tasks that the child cannot yet handle alone but can accomplish with the help of adults and more skilled peers. As children engage in cooperative dialogues with more mature partners, they take the language of these dialogues, make it part of their private speech, and use this speech to organize their independent efforts in the same way.

Although Vygotsky was not very explicit about the features of these dialogues that promote transfer of cognitive processes to children, contemporary researchers believe that at least two characteristics are important. The first is **intersubjectivity.** It refers to the process whereby two participants who begin a task with different understandings arrive at a shared understanding (Newson & Newson, 1975). Intersubjectivity creates a common ground for communication as each partner adjusts to the perspective of the other. Adults try to promote it when they translate their own insights in ways that are within the child's grasp. For example, an adult might point out the links between a new task and ones the child already knows. As the child stretches to understand the interpretation, she is drawn into a more mature approach to the situation (Rogoff, 1990).

A second feature of social experience that fosters children's development is **scaffolding** (Bruner, 1983; Wood, 1989). It refers to a changing quality of social support over the course of a teaching session. Adults who offer an effective scaffold for children's independent mastery adjust the assistance they provide to fit the child's current level of performance. When the child has little notion of how to proceed, the adult uses direct instruction, breaking the task down into manageable units and calling the child's attention to specific features. As the child's competence increases, effective scaffolders gradually and sensitively withdraw support in accord with the child's self-regulatory efforts and success cues.

Is there evidence to support these ideas on the social origins of cognitive development? Research shows that as early as the first few months, caregivers

Zone of proximal development
In Vygotsky's theory, a range of tasks that the child cannot yet handle alone but can do with the help of more skilled partners.

Intersubjectivity
A process whereby two participants who begin a task with different understandings arrive at a shared understanding.

Scaffolding
A changing quality of support over a teaching session in which adults adjust the assistance they provide to fit the child's current level of performance. Direct instruction is offered when a task is new; less help is provided as competence increases.

One of my husband Ken's shared activities with our two sons when they were young was to bake pineapple upside-down cake, a favorite treat. I remember well one Sunday afternoon when a cake was in the making. Little Peter, then 21 months old, stood on a chair at the kitchen sink, busy pouring water from one cup to another.

"He's in the way, Dad!" complained 4-year-old David, trying to pull Peter away from the sink.

"Maybe if we let him help, he'll give us some room," Ken suggested. As David stirred the batter, Ken poured some into a small bowl for Peter, moved his chair to the side of the sink, and handed him a spoon.

"Here's how you do it, Petey," instructed David, with an air of superiority. Peter watched as David stirred, then tried to copy his motion. When it was time to pour the batter, Ken helped Peter tip the small bowl so its contents flowed into the pan.

"Time to bake it," said Ken.

"Bake it, bake it," repeated Peter, as he watched Ken slip the pan into the oven.

Several hours later, we observed one of Peter's earliest instances of make-believe play. He got his pail from the sandbox and after filling it with a handful of sand, carried it into the kitchen and put it down on the floor in front of the oven. "Bake it, bake it," Peter called to Ken. Together, father and son lifted the pretend cake inside the oven.

Historically, the emergence of make-believe was studied in isolation from the social environment in which it usually occurs. Until recently, most researchers observed young children while playing alone. Probably for this reason, Piaget and his followers concluded that toddlers discover make-believe independently, as soon as they are capable of representational schemes. Vygotsky's theory has challenged this view. He believed that society provides children with opportunities to represent culturally meaningful activities in play. Make-believe, like other mental functions, grows out of interactions with others (Smolucha, 1992). In the example just described, Peter's capacity to represent daily events was extended when Ken drew him into the baking task and helped him act it out in play.

New research supports the idea that early make-believe is the combined result of children's readiness to engage in it and social experiences that promote it. In several recent studies, researchers compared toddlers' solitary play with their play while interacting with their mothers. In each case, toddlers engaged in more than twice as much make-believe when mothers were involved. In addition, caregiver support led early make-believe to move toward a more advanced level (Fiese, 1990; Slade, 1987; Zukow, 1986). For example, when adults actively took part, toddlers were more likely to combine representational schemes into more complex sequences, as Peter did when he put the sand in the bucket ("making the batter"), carried it into the kitchen, and (with Ken's help) put it in the oven ("baking the cake").

In many cultures, adults do not spend much time playing with young children. Instead, older siblings fill in by letting toddlers join in their play and by modeling appropriate actions (Zukow, 1989). Notice how in the episode described here, David showed Peter how to stir the batter, and Peter was quickly drawn into the baking activity.

Make-believe is a major means through which children extend their cognitive skills and learn about important activities in their culture. Vygotsky's theory, and the findings that support it, tell us that providing a stimulating environment is only part of what is necessary to promote early cognitive development. In addition, young children must be invited and encouraged by their elders to become active participants in the social world around them.

Once children can pretend, Vygotsky (1930–1935/1978) believed that through their play they create their own zones of proximal development. He wrote, "In play a child is always above his average age, above his daily behavior; in play it is as though he were a head taller than himself" (p. 102). Much evidence fits with Vygotsky's conclusion. Preschoolers' thinking about the pretend world seems to be more flexible and advanced than their thinking about the real world as they reason imaginatively about characters, events, and places (Lillard, 1993; Rubin, Fein, & Vandenberg, 1983).

---

and babies engage in finely tuned emotional communication (see Chapter 10) and joint gazing at objects—forms of intersubjectivity that are related to advanced play, language, and problem-solving skills during the second year (Belsky, Goode, & Most, 1980; Frankel & Bates, 1990; Tamis-LeMonda & Bornstein, 1989). In early childhood, mothers who are effective scaffolders in teaching their children to solve a challenging puzzle have youngsters who use more private speech and who are more successful when asked to do a similar puzzle by themselves (Behrend, Rosengren, & Perlmutter, 1992; Berk & Spuhl, 1992).

Finally, as the From Research to Practice box above reveals, the social support of a more skilled partner also fosters the development of make-believe play. According to Vygotsky (1930–1935/1978), make-believe is a unique context that encourages children to try out a wide variety of challenging skills.

VYGOTSKY AND EDUCATION

Vygotsky's theory offers new visions of teaching and learning—ones that empha-size the importance of social context and collaboration. Today, educators are eager to use his ideas to enhance children's development.

Piagetian and Vygotskian classrooms clearly have features in common, such as opportunities for active participation and acceptance of individual differences. But a Vygotskian classroom goes beyond self-initiated discovery. Instead, it promotes *assisted discovery.* Teachers guide children's learning with explanations, demonstra-tions, and verbal prompts, carefully tailoring their efforts to each child's zone of proximal development. Assisted discovery is also promoted by *peer collaboration.* Pupils who vary in ability work in groups, teaching and assisting one another.

The Social Issues box on the following page summarizes a recent large-scale experiment in elementary education, grounded in sociocultural theory, that has been remarkably successful in helping low-income ethnic minority children learn. In the following sections, we examine two additional Vygotskian-based educational innovations, each of which incorporates assisted discovery and peer collaboration.

Reciprocal Teaching

Reciprocal teaching is a method of instruction designed to improve reading com-prehension in children who are at risk for academic difficulties or who are already experiencing difficulties (Palincsar & Brown, 1984). Recently, the approach has been adapted to other subject-matter areas as well, such as scientific problem solv-ing (Palincsar, 1992). A collaborative learning group is formed in which a teacher and two to four pupils take turns leading dialogues on the content of a text pas-sage. Within the dialogues, group members flexibly apply four cognitive strate-gies: questioning, summarizing, clarifying, and predicting.

Once group members have read the passage, a dialogue leader (at first the teacher, later a pupil) begins by asking *questions* about its content. Pupils pose answers, raise additional questions, and in case of disagreement, reread the text. Next, the leader *summarizes* the passage, and discussion takes place to achieve consensus on the summary. Then a period occurs in which participants *clarify* ideas that are ambiguous or unfamiliar to any group members. Finally, the leader encourages pupils to *predict* upcoming content based on prior knowledge and clues in the passage (Palincsar & Klenk, 1992).

Over the past decade, hundreds of elementary and junior high school pupils have participated in reciprocal teaching. Such children show substantial gains in reading comprehension compared to controls exposed to alternative instructional strategies with the same reading materials (Lysynchuk, Pressley, & Vye, 1990). Notice how reciprocal teaching creates a zone of proximal development in which children, with the aid of teachers and peers, gradually assume more responsibility for the task. Reciprocal teaching also keeps reading activities whole rather than breaking them down into isolated skills removed from the complexities of real text passages (Engliert & Palincsar, 1991). In line with Vygotsky's theory, the method ensures that children learn within a culturally meaningful context that is applicable to their everyday lives.

Reciprocal teaching

A method of teaching based on Vygotsky's theory in which a teacher and two to four pupils form a collaborative learning group. Dialogues occur that create a zone of proximal development in which reading comprehension improves.

Cooperative Learning

Although reciprocal teaching uses peer collaboration, a teacher is present to guide it, helping to ensure its success. According to Vygotsky (1930–1935/1978), more knowledgeable peers can also lead children's learning forward, as long as they adjust the help they provide to fit the less mature child's zone of proximal develop-ment. Recall that Piaget, too, thought that peer interaction could contribute to cog-nitive change. In fact, he regarded discussion with agemates as more valuable than discussion with adults, since a child might superficially accept an adult's perspec-

The Kamehameha Elementary Education Program (KEEP) is an educational experiment grounded in Vygotsky's sociocultural theory that is designed to foster high achievement as well as independence, positive social relationships, and excitement about learning. The zone of proximal development serves as the foundation for KEEP's theory of instruction. To motivate development, KEEP integrates a variety of strategies that have traditionally belonged to other theories into supportive teacher-pupil dialogues:

- *Modeling,* to introduce children to unfamiliar skills
- *Instructing,* to direct children toward the next specific act they need to learn in order to move through the zone of proximal development
- *Verbal feedback* (or reinforcement), to let children know how well they are progressing in relation to reasonable standards of performance
- *Questioning,* to encourage children to think about the task
- *Explaining,* to provide strategies and knowledge necessary for thinking in new ways

These techniques are applied in activity settings specially designed to enhance opportunities for teacher–child and child–child communication. In each setting, children work on a project that ensures that their learning will be active and directed toward a meaningful goal. For example, they might read a story and engage in lively discussion about its meaning or draw a map of the playground to promote understanding of geography. Sometimes activity settings include the whole class. More often, they involve small groups that foster cooperative learning and permit teachers to stay in touch with how well each child is doing. The precise organization of each KEEP classroom is adjusted to fit the unique learning styles of its pupils, creating culturally responsive environments. For example, depending on pupil makeup, activity setting discourse might reflect the lively paced interactive style of native Hawaiians or the patient turn-taking of the Navajo (Gallimore & Tharp, 1990; Tharp & Gallimore, 1988).

Thousands of low-income minority children have attended KEEP classrooms in the public schools of Hawaii, on a Navajo reservation in Arizona, and in Los Angeles. So far, research suggests that the approach is highly effective in helping children who typically achieve poorly learn. In KEEP schools, minority pupils performed at their expected

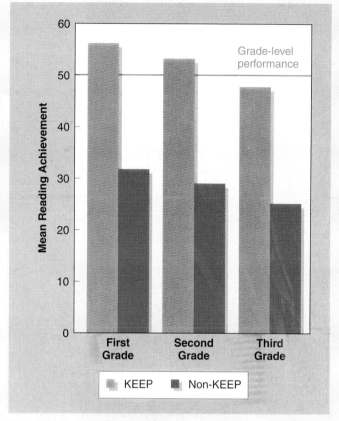

FIGURE 6.7   Reading achievement of KEEP-instructed and traditionally instructed first- through third-grade low-income minority pupils. The KEEP children performed at grade level; the non-KEEP pupils performed substantially below grade level. (Adapted from *Rousing Minds to Life: Teaching, Learning, and Schooling in Social Context* by R. G. Tharp & R. Gallimore, 1988, New York: Cambridge University Press, p. 116. Adapted by permission.)

grade level in reading achievement, much better than children of the same background enrolled in traditional schools (see Figure 6.7). Classroom observations also showed that KEEP pupils participated actively in class discussion, used elaborate language structures, frequently supported one another's learning, and were more attentive and involved than were non-KEEP controls (Tharp & Gallimore, 1988). As the KEEP model becomes more widely applied, perhaps it will prove successful with all types of children because of its comprehensive goals and effort to meet the learning needs of a wide range of pupils.

---

tive without critically examining it, out of an unquestioning belief in the adult's authority. Piaget also asserted that clashing viewpoints—arguments jarring the young child into noticing a peer's point of view—were necessary for peer interaction to stimulate movement toward logical thought (Tudge & Rogoff, 1987).

Today, peer collaboration is used in many classrooms, but evidence is mounting that it is successful only under certain conditions. A crucial factor is **cooperative learning**—structuring the peer group so that students work together toward

Cooperative learning
A learning environment structured into groups of peers who work together toward a common goal.

*C*onsistent with Vygotsky's theory, the success of peer collaboration depends on cooperative learning. When peers work toward a common goal by resolving differences of opinion, sharing responsibility, and engaging in cooperative dialogues, cognitive development is enhanced. (TONY FREEMAN/PHOTOEDIT)

a common goal. Conflict and disagreement do not seem to be as important in fostering development as the extent to which peers achieve intersubjectivity—by resolving differences of opinion, sharing responsibility, and engaging in cooperative dialogues (Forman, 1987; Nastasi, Clements, & Battista, 1990; Perlmutter et al., 1989; Tudge, 1992). And in line with Vygotsky's theory, children's planning and problem solving improve most when their peer partner is an "expert"—especially capable at the task (Azmitia, 1988; Radziszewska & Rogoff, 1988). These findings indicate that teachers need to group together children with varied abilities and provide guidelines for group interaction in order to reap the full benefits of peer collaboration.

EVALUATION OF VYGOTSKY'S THEORY

Piaget and Vygotsky shared the belief that children arrive at knowledge through actively participating in the world around them. Yet in granting social experience a fundamental role in cognitive development, Vygotsky's theory is unique in helping us understand the wide variation in cognitive skills across cultures. Unlike Piaget, who emphasized universal cognitive change, Vygotsky's theory leads us to expect highly variable development, depending on the child's specific cultural experiences. For example, the reading, writing, and mathematical activities of children who go to school in literate societies generate cognitive capacities that differ from those in preliterate cultures. Yet the elaborate spatial skills of Australian aborigines, whose food-gathering missions require that they find their way through barren desert regions, or the proportional reasoning of Brazilian fishermen, promoted by their navigational experiences, are no less advanced (Carraher, Schliemann, & Carraher, 1988; Kearins, 1981). Instead, each is a unique form of thinking demanded by the particular settings that make up a culture's way of life (Tulviste, 1991).

Vygotsky's theory, like Piaget's, has not gone unchallenged. Although Vygotsky acknowledged the role of diverse symbol systems (such as pictures, maps, and algebraic expressions) in mediating the development of higher cognitive processes, he elevated language to highest importance. Yet as Barbara Rogoff (1990) points out, finely tuned, scaffolded instruction may not be the only means, or even the most important means, through which thought develops in some cultures. For example, the young child inducted into sailing a canoe in Micronesia may learn more from direct observation and practice than from joint participation with and verbal guidance by adults. It is possible that the type of assistance offered varies greatly from one culture to the next, depending on the tasks that must be mastered for success in each society. So we are reminded once again that children learn in many ways, and as yet, no single theory provides a complete account of cognitive development.

Finally, recall that Vygotsky stated that the natural and cultural lines of development join, forming a single developmental pathway. But in focusing on the cultural line, he said little about the natural line—far less than did Piaget or information processing, to which we now turn. Consequently, we cannot tell from Vygotsky's theory exactly how elementary processes contribute to higher mental processes derived from social experience (Wertsch & Tulviste, 1992). It is intriguing to speculate about the broader theory that might exist today had these two giants of cognitive development had the chance to meet and weave together their extraordinary accomplishments.

CHAPTER SUMMARY

Piaget's Cognitive-Developmental Theory
- Influenced by his background in biology, Piaget viewed cognitive development as an adaptive process. By acting directly on the environment, children move through four stages in which internal structures achieve a better fit with external reality.
- In Piaget's theory, psychological structures, or **schemes,** change in two ways. The first is through **adaptation,** which is made up of two complementary processes: **assimilation** and **accommodation.** The second is through **organization,** the internal rearrangement of schemes so that they form a strongly interconnected cognitive system. Piaget's assumed that the stages are invariant and universal.

The Sensorimotor Stage (Birth to 2 Years)
- Piaget's **sensorimotor stage** is divided into six substages. Through the **circular reaction,** the newborn baby's reflexes are gradually transformed into the more flexible action patterns of the older infant, and **sensorimotor egocentrism** declines. During Substage 4, infants develop **intentional,** or **goal-directed, behavior** and begin to understand **object permanence.** By Substage 6, they become capable of **mental representation,** as shown by sudden solutions to sensorimotor problems, **deferred imitation,** and **make-believe play.**
- Today, it is widely recognized that Piaget underestimated the capacities of young infants. Secondary circular reactions, object permanence, and representation, in the form of deferred imitation and categorization, are present earlier than Piaget believed. It is possible that infants do not have to construct all aspects of their cognitive world through motor activity. Some schemes may be there from the start, and others may develop through purely perceptual learning.

The Preoperational Stage (2 to 7 Years)
- Rapid advances in mental representation, including language, make-believe play, and pictorial representation, mark the beginning of the **preoperational stage.** With age, make-believe becomes increasingly complex, evolving into **sociodramatic play** with others. Preschoolers' make-believe not only reflects, but contributes to cognitive development.

- Aside from representation, Piaget described the young child in terms of deficits rather than strengths. The most serious deficiency is **preoperational egocentrism,** an inability to distinguish the perspectives of others from one's own. It leads to a variety of illogical features of thought. According to Piaget, preschoolers engage in **animistic thinking,** and their cognitions are **perception-bound, centered,** focused on **states rather than transformations,** and **irreversible.** In addition, preoperational children engage in **transductive reasoning** rather than truly causal reasoning. Because of these difficulties, they fail **conservation** and **hierarchical classification** tasks.
- When young children are given simplified problems relevant to their everyday lives, their performance appears much more mature. This indicates that logical thought develops gradually over the preschool years, a finding that challenges Piaget's concept of stage.

The Concrete Operational Stage (7 to 11 Years)
- During the **concrete operational stage,** thought is far more logical and organized than it was during the preschool years. The ability to conserve indicates that children can decenter and reverse their thinking. In addition, they are better at hierarchical classification, **seriation,** and **transitive inference.** School-age youngsters have an improved understanding of distance, and they can combine it with other concepts, such as time and speed. **Cognitive maps** become more organized and accurate during middle childhood.
- Concrete operational thought is limited in that children can reason logically only about concrete, tangible information; they have difficulty with abstractions. Piaget used the term **horizontal décalage** to describe the school-age child's gradual mastery of logical concepts, such as conservation.
- Recent evidence indicates that specific cultural practices, the phrasing of questions, and the objects to which they refer can have a profound effect on Piagetian task performance. Concrete operations may not be a natural form of logical that emerges universally in middle childhood. Instead, it may be a product of direct training, context, and cultural conditions.

The Formal Operational Stage
(11 Years and Older)

- In Piaget's **formal operational stage,** abstract thinking appears. Adolescents engage in **hypothetico-deductive reasoning.** When faced with a problem, they think of all possibilities, including ones that are not obvious, and test them against reality in an orderly fashion. **Propositional thought** also develops. Young people can evaluate the logic of verbal statements without considering them against real-world circumstances.

- Early in this stage, **formal operational egocentrism** appears. Adolescents have difficulty distinguishing the abstract perspectives of self and other. As a result, two distorted images of the relation between self and other appear: the **imaginary audience** and **personal fable.**

- Recent research reveals school-age children display the beginnings of abstract reasoning, but they are not as competent as adolescents and adults. In addition, many college students and adults are not fully formal operational, and formal thought does not appear at all in many village and tribal cultures. These findings indicate that Piaget's highest stage is reached gradually rather than abruptly and is affected by specific learning experiences.

Larger Questions About the Validity
of Piaget's Theory

- A wealth of research reveals that Piaget's theory has important shortcomings. Some ideas, such as his explanation of cognitive change, are not clearly spelled out. Others, such as the timetable of development, are not entirely accurate. The most hotly debated question is whether cognitive development actually takes place in stages.

Piaget and Education

- Piaget's theory has had a lasting impact on educational programs for young children. A Piagetian classroom promotes discovery learning, sensitivity to children's readiness to learn, and acceptance of individual differences.

Vygotsky's Sociocultural Theory

- In contrast to Piaget, who viewed children as solitary agents, Vygotsky constructed a theory in which the child and the social environment collaborate to mold cognition in culturally adaptive ways. Once children become capable of mental representation, especially through language, the natural line of mental development begins to be transformed by the social line.

- Whereas Piaget believed that language does not play a major role in cognitive development, Vygotsky regarded it as the foundation for all higher cognitive processes. As children and more skilled partners engage in cooperative dialogues surrounding tasks within the **zone of proximal development,** children incorporate the language of these dialogues into their **private speech** and use it to organize their independent efforts in the same way. **Intersubjectivity** and **scaffolding** are features of social interaction that promote transfer of cognitive processes to children.

Vygotsky and Education

- A Vygotskian classroom emphasizes assisted discovery in the form of verbal guidance from teachers and peer collaboration. Vygotskian-based educational innovations include **reciprocal teaching** and **cooperative learning.**

Evaluation of Vygotsky's Theory

- Vygotsky's theory helps us understand the wide variation in cognitive skills across cultures. However, verbal dialogues that scaffold children's efforts may not be the only means, or even the most important means, through which thought develops in some cultures. Piaget emphasized the natural line, Vygotsky the cultural line of development. A broader theory might exist today had these two contemporaries had the chance to meet and integrate their ideas.

IMPORTANT TERMS AND CONCEPTS

scheme (p. 221)
adaptation (p. 221)
assimilation (p. 221)
accommodation (p. 221)
equilibration (p. 222)
organization (p. 222)
sensorimotor stage (p. 223)
circular reaction (p. 223)
sensorimotor egocentrism (p. 225)
intentional, or goal-
    directed, behavior (p. 226)
object permanence (p. 226)
AB search error (p. 226)
mental representation (p. 227)
deferred imitation (p. 228)

make-believe play (p. 228)
preoperational stage (p. 231)
sociodramatic play (p. 233)
operations (p. 234)
preoperational egocentrism (p. 235)
animistic thinking (p. 235)
conservation (p. 236)
perception-bound (p. 237)
centration (p. 237)
states versus transformations (p. 237)
reversibility (p. 237)
transductive reasoning (p. 237)
hierarchical classification (p. 239)
concrete operational stage (p. 243)
seriation (p. 244)

transitive inference (p. 244)
cognitive maps (p. 245)
horizontal décalage (p. 246)
formal operational stage (p. 248)
hypothetico-deductive reasoning (p. 248)
propositional thought (p. 249)
formal operational egocentrism (p. 250)
imaginary audience (p. 250)
personal fable (p. 250)
private speech (p. 255)
zone of proximal development (p. 256)
intersubjectivity (p. 256)
scaffolding (p. 256)
reciprocal teaching (p. 258)
cooperative learning (p. 259)

C O N N E C T I O N S

If you are interested in . . .	Turn to . . .	To learn about . . .
Play 	Chapter 11, p. 437	Make-believe play and the child's theory of mind
	Chapter 15, pp. 602–604	Social and cognitive maturity of play during the preschool years
	Chapter 15, p. 606	Influence of play materials on peer sociability
	Chapter 15, pp. 626–627	Influence of television on imaginative play
Influence of Piaget on child development research  Jean Piaget	Chapter 4, pp. 166–167	Infant perception of objects as distinct, bounded wholes
	Chapter 7, pp. 271–272	Combining Piagetian and information-processing approaches to cognitive development
	Chapter 7, pp. 285–286	A constructivist approach to information processing
	Chapter 8, pp. 318–319	Piagetian-based intelligence tests
	Chapter 11, pp. 435–436	Emergence of self-recognition
	Chapter 11, pp. 455–460	Development of perspective taking
	Chapter 12, pp. 481–485	Piaget's theory of moral development
	Chapter 13, pp. 537–539	Emergence of gender-role identity
Vygotsky's sociocultural theory   Lev Vygotsky	Chapter 1, pp. 28–29	Cross-cultural research and Vygotsky's sociocultural theory
	Chapter 7, pp. 291–292	Self-regulation of cognitive performance
	Chapter 10, pp. 400–401	Language and emotional self-regulation
	Chapter 12, pp. 502–505	Language, self-control, and moral self-regulation
	Chapter 15, pp. 606–607	Mixed-age interaction and children's development
	Chapter 15, p. 630	Computers and cognitive development

♦ **Walter Ufer,** *Her Treasury Jar*
Private Collection/Nefsky/Art Resource

Cognitive Development:
An Information-Processing Perspective

T he information-processing view of cognition rose to the forefront of the field of child development partly as a reaction to the inadequacies of Piaget's theory. Unlike the Piagetian perspective, information processing does not offer a single, unified theory of children's thinking. Instead, it is an approach followed by researchers studying a wide variety of aspects of cognition. Their goal is to find out how children and adults operate on different kinds of information, coding, transforming, and organizing it as it makes its way through the cognitive system.

This chapter provides an overview of the information processing perspective. First, we review general and developmental models of the human cognitive system that have served as major forces in research. Next, we turn to three basic operations that enter into all of human thinking: perception, attention, and memory. We also consider how children's growing knowledge of the world and awareness of their own mental activities affect these basic operations.

As we examine each of these topics, we will return to a theme that surfaced many times in Chapter 6: the role of cultural context and task demands in cognitive performance. Consider the experience of one researcher, who interviewed Kpelle farmers of Liberia about how they would sort a set of 20 familiar objects as an aid to remembering them. Members of this preliterate society arranged the objects by function. For example, they placed a knife with an orange and a hoe with a potato rather than putting all the tools in one pile and the food items in another, as the researcher expected them to do (Glick, 1975). Puzzled that Kpelle adults would approach this task much like young children in Western nations, the researcher asked for an explanation. Many Kpelle replied that a wise person would do it that way. In exasperation, the researcher finally blurted out, "How would a fool do it?" Right away, he got the kinds of object groupings he had been looking for!

The Kpelle study suggests that societal definitions of skilled performance can mold information processing in certain directions. In this chapter, we pay special attention to how schooling, with its emphasis on literacy, mathematics, scientific reasoning, and retention of discrete pieces of information, channels cognition in culturally specific ways. Although information-processing theorists are especially interested in internal, self-generated changes that take place with age, they also want to find out how external influences—from teaching techniques to cultural values—affect the way children and adults approach various tasks. Our discussion concludes with an evaluation of the strengths and weaknesses of information processing as a framework for understanding cognitive development.

THE INFORMATION-PROCESSING APPROACH

Most information-processing theorists view the mind as a complex, symbol-manipulating system through which information flows, operating much like a digital computer. Information from the environment is *encoded*, or taken in by the system and retained in symbolic form. Then a variety of internal processes operate on it, *recoding it*, or revising its symbolic structure into a more effective representation, and then *decoding* it, or interpreting its meaning by comparing and combining it with other information in the system. When these cognitive operations are complete, output, in the form of a task solution, occurs.

Consider this brief description of information processing, and perhaps you can see why researchers have found the computer analogy of human mental functioning so attractive. It shares with Piaget's theory a view of the mind as an active processor of information. But beyond this, the computer model offers clarity and precision in a way that many Piagetian concepts do not. Using computerlike diagrams and flowcharts, investigators can map the exact series of steps children and adults execute when faced with a task or problem. Some do so in such detail that the same mental operations can be programmed into a computer. Then computer simulations are used to test predictions about how children and adults approach a variety of tasks (Siegler, 1983).

Other information-processing investigators do not rely on computer simulations to test their ideas. Instead, they draw from a wealth of other methods, such as tracking eye movements, analyzing error patterns, and examining self-reports of mental processes. But all hold in common a strong commitment to explicit models of cognitive functioning, each component of which must be thoroughly tested with research (Klahr, 1992; Kuhn, 1992).

GENERAL MODELS OF INFORMATION PROCESSING

Store model

Atkinson and Shiffrin's model of mental functioning, which views information as being held in three parts of the system for processing: the sensory register, short-term memory, and long-term memory.

How do information-processing researchers conceive of the human mental system? Two major models have influenced research on children's thinking.

Atkinson and Shiffrin's Store Model

The most widely known computerlike model of mental functioning is Atkinson and Shiffrin's (1968) **store model**. As Figure 7.1 shows, it is called a store model

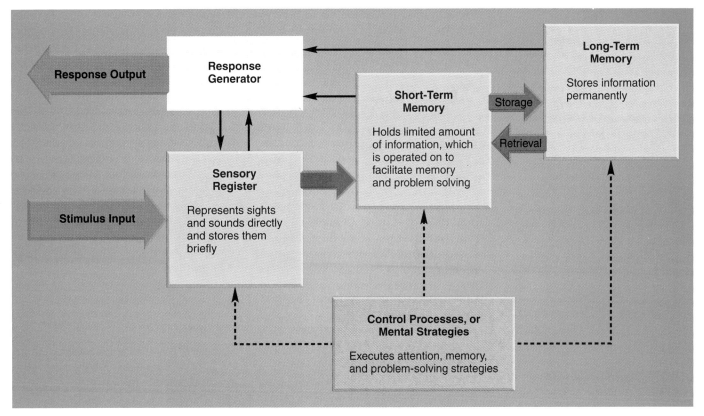

FIGURE 7.1 Atkinson and Shiffrin's model of the human information-processing system. (Adapted from "Storage and Retrieval Processes in Long-Term Memory" by R. M. Shiffrin & R. C. Atkinson, 1969, *Psychological Review, 76,* p. 180. Copyright © 1969 by the American Psychological Association. Adapted by permission.)

because information is assumed to be held, or stored, in three parts of the system for processing: the sensory register, short-term memory, and long-term memory. Atkinson and Shiffrin regard these stores as inborn and universal among all human beings. You can think of them as the *hardware* of the mental system. Each is limited in the speed with which it can process information. In addition, the sensory register and short-term memory are limited in capacity. They can hold on to only a certain amount of information for a brief period until it fades away entirely.

As information flows through each store, it can be operated on and transformed using **control processes,** or **mental strategies**—the *software* of the system. When we use strategies to manipulate input in various ways, we increase the efficiency of thinking as well as the chances that information will be retained for later use. According to Atkinson and Shiffrin, control processes are not innate; they are learned, and individuals differ in how well they use them. To understand these ideas more clearly, let's take a brief look at each component of Atkinson and Shiffrin's model.

COMPONENTS OF THE STORE MODEL. First, information enters the **sensory register.** Here, sights and sounds are represented directly, but they cannot be held for long. For example, take a moment to look around, and then close your eyes. An image of what you saw persists briefly, but then it decays or disappears, unless you use control processes, or mental strategies, to preserve it. For example, you can *attend* to some details more carefully than others, thereby increasing the chances that the selected input will transfer to the next step of the information-processing system.

The second way station of the mind is **short-term memory.** This is the central processing unit, the conscious part of our mental system, where we actively operate on a limited amount of information. For example, if you are studying this book effectively, you are constantly applying mental strategies, manipulating

Control processes, or mental strategies
Procedures that operate on and transform information, increasing the efficiency of thinking and the chances that information will be retained.

Sensory register
In Atkinson and Shiffrin's store model, the first part of the mental system through which information flows, where sights and sounds are represented directly but held only briefly.

Short-term memory
In Atkinson and Shiffrin's store model, the central processing unit of the mental system, where information is consciously operated on using control processes, or mental strategies.

267

input to ensure that it will be retained and available to solve problems. Perhaps you are attending to certain information that seems most important. Or you may be using a variety of memory strategies, such as taking notes, repeating information to yourself, or grouping pieces of information together, as the Kpelle farmers were asked to do in the study described at the beginning of this chapter.

Think, for a moment, about why you apply strategies to retain information in short-term memory. The sensory register, although also limited, can take in a wide panorama of information. But when input reaches the short-term store, a bottleneck occurs. Once the limited number of slots in short-term memory is occupied, either new information cannot enter the system, or if it does, it will push out existing information. However, the capacity limit of short-term memory is not a matter of physical pieces of information, but of *meaningful chunks*. Therefore, by connecting separate pieces through strategy use, you can increase your memory capacity. And the longer information is retained in the system, the greater the chances that it will be transferred to the third, and largest, storage bin of the system.

Unlike the sensory register and working memory, the capacity of **long-term memory**, our permanent knowledge base, is limitless. In fact, so much input is stored in long-term memory that we sometimes have problems with *retrieval*, or getting information back from the system. To aid retrieval, we apply strategies in long-term memory just as we do in short-term memory. For example, consider how information in your long-term memory is arranged. According to Atkinson and Shiffrin (1968), it is categorized according to a master plan based on contents, much like a "library shelving system which is based upon the contents of books" (p. 181). When information is filed in this way, it can be retrieved quite easily by following the same network of associations that was used to store it in the first place.

RESEARCH TESTING THE STORE APPROACH. Much evidence is consistent with Atkinson and Shiffrin's store model (Siegler, 1983). For example, the well-known **serial-position effect** that occurs when you try to memorize a list of items supports the distinction between short- and long-term memory. Items in the middle are less likely to be remembered than those at the beginning or the end. However, over time, items at the end decay from memory, whereas those at the beginning continue to be retained. Researchers believe this happens because items learned last are held only temporarily in short-term memory, whereas those learned first have had enough time to transfer to the long-term store.

In one study, researchers found this same effect as early as 7 months of age. Babies were shown three photos of women's faces. Then each infant was assigned to a condition in which the first, middle, or last photo was paired with a new photo. Memory for the original photo was determined by measuring the extent to which the babies dishabituated to, or spent more time looking at, the new photo. As Figure 7.2 shows, when babies were tested immediately, the first and last photos were remembered much more effectively than the middle photo. After a 1-minute delay, memory for the last photo declined, and at 5 minutes it disappeared (Cornell & Bergstrom, 1983). These findings are consistent with Atkinson and Shiffrin's assumption that separate short- and long-term memory stores are fundamental to the human information-processing system.

Other findings have raised questions about the store model. The capacity limits of the sensory register and short-term memory have been found to vary widely from study to study. For example, retention of visual information in the sensory register ranges from 250 milliseconds to 25 seconds. And the short-term store, once thought to be limited to 7 slots, actually varies from 2 to 20 (Siegler, 1983). Difficulties in identifying the precise size of these "hardware units" have led some researchers to doubt their existence and turn toward a levels-of-processing view.

The Levels-of-Processing Model

The **levels-of-processing model** abandons the idea of a series of containers with fixed limits on how much information can be grasped at once. Instead, it assumes

Long-term memory
In Atkinson and Shiffrin's store model, the part of the mental system that contains our permanent knowledge base.

Serial-position effect
In memory tasks involving lists of items, the tendency to remember ones at the beginning and end better than those in the middle.

Levels-of-processing model
A model of mental functioning in which retention of information depends on the depth to which it is analyzed. Attentional resources determine processing capacity.

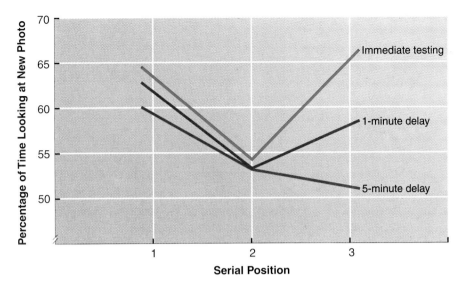

FIGURE 7.2 Serial-position findings in a study of 7-month-old infants. In the immediate testing condition, photos in the first and last serial positions were remembered best. After delays of 1 and 5 minutes, memory for the last photo declined and disappeared, respectively. (Adapted from Cornell & Bergstrom, 1983.)

that retention depends on the depth to which information is processed by the system. For example, we could encode a written word superficially, according to its *perceptual features,* by noticing whether it is printed in capital or lowercase letters. At a slightly deeper level, we could encode the word by attending to its *phonemic features,* or how it sounds. In this instance, we might repeat the word aloud to ourselves, or rhyme it with another word, several times. At the deepest level of processing, we would encode the word according to its meaning, or *semantic features,* by relating it to other information already in our systems (Craik & Lockhart, 1972). In the levels-of-processing model, information that is analyzed shallowly decays quickly and is soon forgotten. In contrast, information interpreted meaningfully and linked to existing knowledge is retained much longer (Craik & Tulving, 1975).

According to the levels-of-processing view, the difficulty we experience in trying to handle many pieces of information at once is not due to a fixed-size memory container. Instead, it has to do with the extent to which we can distribute our attention across several activities at once. As a result, the limited-slot idea of short-term memory is replaced by the concept of **working memory**. It refers to the conscious pool of attentional resources from which our information-processing activities draw (Baddeley, 1992). The amount of attention a person must allocate to a task depends on how well learned, or automatic, the cognitive processes required by it happen to be. Unskilled individuals must devote more attention. As a result, resources are drawn away from other activities they might engage in at the same time. In contrast, automatic cognitive processes demand little or no attentional capacity, and individuals can engage in other tasks simultaneously (Klatzky, 1984).

Let's use an example to illustrate this idea. Consider two children, one a novice and the other an expert bicycle rider. The attention of the novice is entirely consumed by efforts to steer, control the pedals, and maintain balance. Indeed, parents are best off insisting that this child practice in traffic-free areas, since little or no attentional resources remain for other cognitive activities, such as watching out for cars and pedestrians. In contrast, the practiced bicyclist rides easily around the neighborhood, delivering papers, chewing gum, and carrying on a conversation with a nearby rider at the same time.

Research on the Store versus Levels-of-Processing Models

When applied to development, the store and levels-of-processing models emphasize somewhat different features. The store approach suggests that both the hardware of the system (size of the information containers) and the software (control

Working memory
In the levels-of-processing model, the conscious pool of attentional resources from which our information-processing activities draw.

*C*hildren gradually learn to
supplement their limited-capacity
cognitive systems with external aids to
processing. This child uses a calendar
to keep track of how many days remain
before an important event.
(ROBERT BRENNER/PHOTOEDIT)

processes) change with age. That is, what develops may be both a bigger computer and a wider array of effective programs, or strategies. In contrast, the levels-of-processing model assumes that all changes have to do with software, or the functioning of the system. In other words, many cognitive processes become less capacity-consuming as the result of years of practice with strategies, which eventually leads to more efficient use of available space (Siegler, 1983).

Research we will review throughout this chapter indicates that without a doubt, use of control processes improves with age. Children gradually acquire a variety of strategies for conserving space within the limited-capacity systems they have. They also learn how to supplement their limited systems with external aids to processing, employing calendars, notebooks, libraries, and even computers to enhance their ability to retain information (Flavell, 1985).

Does the structural hardware of the system also expand? There is disagreement on this issue, but recent evidence on speed of processing suggests that overall capacity does increase. Robert Kail (1988, 1991) gave individuals between 7 and 22 years of age a variety of basic cognitive tasks in which they had to respond as quickly as possible. For example, in a visual search task, subjects were shown a single digit and asked to signal if it was among a set of digits that appeared on a screen. In a mental rotation task, they were given pairs of letters in any of six different orientations and asked to decide whether the letters were identical or mirror images. And in a mental addition task, subjects were presented with addition problems and answers, and they had to indicate whether or not the solution was correct.

As Figure 7.3 reveals, Kail found that processing time decreased with age for all tasks. But even more important, the rate of change was the same across many activities—a fairly rapid decline that trailed off around 12 years of age. This pattern was also evident when subjects performed perceptual–motor tasks, such as releasing a button or tapping as fast as possible—activities that do not rely heavily on mental strategies (Kail, 1991). According to Kail, similarity in development of processing speed across such a diverse array of tasks implies an age-related gain in basic information-processing resources. This permits the cognitive systems of older children to hold on to more information at once. As a result, they can scan it more quickly and generate faster responses in a wide range of situations.

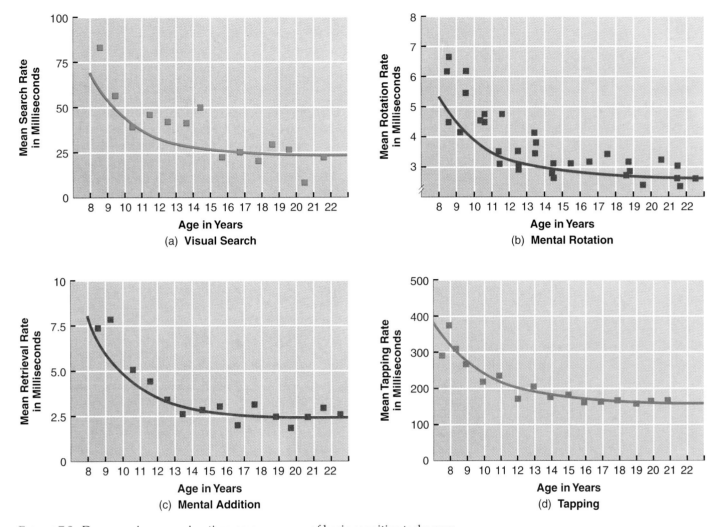

FIGURE 7.3 Decreases in processing time across a range of basic cognitive tasks over childhood and adolescence. That the rate of decline is so uniform across activities suggests that the overall capacity, or size, of the information-processing system is expanding. (Parts a–c from "Developmental Functions for Speeds of Cognitive Processes" by R. Kail, 1988, *Journal of Experimental Child Psychology, 45,* p. 361. Copyright © 1988 by Academic Press. Reprinted by permission of the publisher and author; part d from "Processing Time Declines Exponentially During Childhood and Adolescence" by R. Kail, 1991, *Developmental Psychology, 27,* p. 265. Copyright © 1991 by the American Psychological Association. Adapted by permission.)

In sum, although the precise capacity limits of the cognitive system are hard to pin down, *both* its hardware and its software seem to change over the course of childhood. As we turn now to developmental models of information processing, we will see efforts to integrate these two aspects—the first emphasizing brain maturation, the second experience in transforming information—into an overall picture of how the cognitive system changes with age.

DEVELOPMENTAL MODELS OF INFORMATION PROCESSING

The store and levels-of-processing models are *general* approaches to information processing. Neither makes precise statements about how children's thinking changes with age. However, several *developmental* models that have attracted widespread attention exist (Case, 1985, 1992; Fischer & Pipp, 1984; Halford, 1990). To create an overall vision of development, each uses Piaget's theory as a starting point, reinterpreting it within an information-processing framework. Consequently, these theories are often termed *neo-Piagetian*. Let's take a brief look at two of them: Case's M-space and Fischer's skill theory.

Case's M-Space

Robbie Case (1985, 1992) views cognitive development as a matter of increases in information-processing capacity that result from more efficient strategy use. Piagetian schemes, in Case's theory, constitute the child's mental strategies. With age, a computerlike construct called **mental space,** or **M-space**—a notion similar to working memory—expands. Increases in M-space are due to three factors. The first is *brain maturation.* Myelinization (see Chapter 5) improves the speed of neural processing and, thereby, the efficiency of thought. Second, *exercise of strategies* contributes. As schemes are repeatedly practiced, they become more automatic and require less attentional capacity, freeing up extra M-space for the child to work on combining old schemes and generating new ones. Once the schemes of a Piagetian stage become sufficiently automatized, enough M-space is available to consolidate them into an improved representational form. As a result, children acquire *central conceptual structures,* networks of concepts and relations that permit them to think about a wide range of situations in more advanced ways. These structures are a third way in which M-space expands, since they lead to more efficient ways of interpreting experience and solving problems (Case & Griffin, 1990). When children acquire them, they move up to a new stage of development.

Case's theory also offers an information-processing account of horizontal décalage—that many Piagetian milestones, such as conservation, appear in specific situations at different times rather than being mastered all at once. Case assumes that different forms of the same logical insight vary in the processing demands they make of the child. Therefore, each successive Piagetian task requires more M-space for mastery.

Think back to the various Piagetian tasks we discussed in Chapter 6. A notable feature of them is that at each new stage of development, a greater number of features must be held in memory and combined to reach a correct solution. Children's ability to pass more advanced Piagetian tasks is correlated with their *digit span*—the number of discrete digits they can recall from a list, often used to assess the limits of working memory (Case, 1977, 1978). This finding is consistent with Case's suggestion that combining schemes in more complex problem solving is accompanied by an expansion of a central processing resource pool (M-space) with development.

Fischer's Skill Theory

Kurt Fischer's **skill theory** also reformulates Piaget's stages but places more emphasis on children's specific experiences than does Case. According to Fischer, a *skill* is a Piagetian scheme applied to a particular task or set of tasks. How broadly applicable a skill is depends on brain maturation and the range of environments to which the child has been exposed (Fischer & Farrar, 1987; Fischer & Pipp, 1984). To understand how these two factors work together, let's look at some concepts Fischer uses to describe skill development.

Each child has an *optimal level of skill performance,* or upper limit of processing capacity, that cannot be exceeded without further brain maturation. Fischer identifies three optimal skill levels that correspond to Piaget's stages: sensorimotor actions, representations, and abstractions. However, children (and adults) seldom function optimally, because using the most advanced skills possible depends on extensive support from the environment. Therefore, within each level, an extended period of skill learning takes place in which the child acquires new competencies on specific tasks, integrates them with others, and gradually transforms them into more general, higher-order skills.

For example, a 5-year-old who cannot yet conserve liquid may have some isolated skills, such as (1) after water is poured from a tall into a short glass, the

Mental space, or M-space
In Case's theory, a construct similar to working memory. It expands with brain maturation, exercise of strategies, and formation of central conceptual structures, which permit the child to move up to a new Piagetian stage.

Skill theory
Fischer's theory, in which each Piagetian stage is viewed as an extended period of skill learning in which the child acquires new competencies on specific tasks, integrates them with others, and gradually transforms them into more general, higher-order skills. As a result, the child moves up to a new Piagetian stage.

height of the water level is reduced; and (2) after water is poured from a thin into a wide glass, the width of the water increases. But until the child has had enough experience transferring liquids from one container to another, she cannot combine these two separate skills into a conserving response. Once a more advanced skill is mastered in a particular situation, it can be transferred to other similar situations. In our example, conservation can then be applied to mass or weight. Eventually the child coordinates several task-specific skills into a new broadly applicable principle. When this happens, cognition moves to a higher level of functioning—in this case, from representation to abstraction.

In the theories of both Case and Fischer, each major advance in thinking coincides with a dramatic increase in working memory. Although more evidence is needed to support this idea, many researchers agree that surmounting memory limits is a crucial factor in cognitive development. These neo-Piagetian approaches are also unique in offering an integrated picture of how basic capacity, strategies, and learning interact to produce development (Siegler, 1991).

General or Modular Mind?

Note how Case and Fischer have woven a widespread observation into their theories—that development is uneven across tasks. At the same time, both theorists believe that overall gains in processing capacity take place, granting older children the potential for complex skills not possible at younger ages.

Tension between these two facets of development currently pervades information-processing research. The models described in the preceding sections regard the mind as a *general, or all-purpose,* computing device whose basic capacities undergo periodic change. But other investigators disagree. They see the mind as a *modular* device, each aspect of which has its own capacities, structures, and timetable of development (Fodor, 1983). The modular view predicts widely varying competence across tasks and domains of knowledge, such as verbal, mathematical, scientific, and social. The variation is due partly to children's experiences

*I*nformation-processing researchers differ sharply in whether they view the mind as a general, all-purpose or a modular device. Some believe that the same underlying processing capacities govern children's performance on the social and verbal tasks depicted above. Any unevenness in development can be explained by variations in experience across domains. Others argue that each aspect of development has its own capacities, structures, and timetable, which are imposed by maturation. (*LEFT:* TOM MCCARTHY/THE PICTURE CUBE; *RIGHT:* SYBIL SHACKMAN/MONKMEYER PRESS PHOTO)

in each area, but modular theorists also think maturation imposes distinct limits on what children of different ages can attain in each domain.

Which of these views best fits the evidence? Currently, there is research to support both! Case and his collaborators have shown that as long as the complexity of tasks in different domains is carefully controlled, children approach numerical, spatial, and social-reasoning problems in similar ways. This suggests a common underlying pattern of development (Case et al., 1992; Marini & Case, 1989). At the same time, other researchers have presented evidence that children's ways of thinking about their physical and social worlds are unique and not transferable from one domain to the next (Carey & Gelman, 1991; Keil, 1989; Wellman & Gelman, 1992). For this reason, they believe that development within each must be charted separately.

A final group of investigators argues that both general and domain-specific development take place. A future challenge will be to discover just how they interact and influence one another (Ceci, 1989; Sternberg, 1989). In this chapter, we consider research representing both views. We begin with work that stems from the general perspective—children's encoding of information, memory strategies, and awareness of their own mental activities. Then we turn to domains of academic learning that have recently become the subject of intensive research.

Brief Review

Information-processing researchers are committed to explicit models of cognitive functioning that map the precise steps children and adults use when faced with a task or problem. Two general models of information processing have influenced research on children's cognition. Atkinson and Shiffrin's store model regards the limited capacity of our mental systems as due to fixed-size sensory and short-term memory stores. In contrast, the levels-of-processing view emphasizes allocation of attention as responsible for processing limitations. Two developmental models—Case's M-space and Fischer's skill theory—reinterpret Piaget's stages in information-processing terms. Each accounts for unevenness in development across tasks as well as broad cognitive changes. Whether the mind is best viewed in general or modular terms is a major controversy in information-processing research.

SENSORY PROCESSING

How do children encode information perceived with the senses? Is the development of sensory processing a matter of noticing increasingly subtle aspects of objective reality? Or do children structure their own experience by imposing ever deeper layers of meaning on what they perceive? As we look closely at these competing views, you will discover that we have already visited each in previous chapters.

Differentiation Theory

Eleanor and James Gibson's **differentiation theory** is a major perspective on the processing of sensory information. Recall from Chapter 4 that as the result of brain maturation and repeated exposure to stimulation, infants become more skilled at detecting *invariant features*—stable aspects of an object or pattern that distinguish it from other stimuli. Differentiation theory regards the external world as bringing order to perceptual experience. As children explore the environment, they naturally detect more fine-grained features of it.

In Chapter 4, we noted that the initial sensory-processing task for infants involves locating objects in space. Once babies do so, they start to identify objects according to their distinctive features. During childhood, this process of detecting the detailed structure of stimulation continues (Gibson & Spelke, 1983). Eleanor Gibson (1970) has applied differentiation theory to the way children discriminate graphic forms as they learn to read, since written symbols contain especially subtle and challenging distinctive features.

Differentiation theory
The view that processing sensory information involves detecting increasingly fine-grained, invariant features in the environment.

At first, preschoolers become sensitive to global distinctions among written symbols. By age 3 or 4, they can discriminate letters and numbers from scribbling and pictures, although they cannot yet identify many individual graphic forms. How do children distinguish particular letters? To find out, Gibson and her colleagues asked children whether pairs of letters were the same or different and noted how long it took them to make each judgment. Using this information, the researchers constructed treelike "confusion matrices" showing which letters are most often mistaken for one another. The matrix in Figure 7.4 reveals a clear pattern of increasing differentiation. Among a set of 9 letters, children first separated curved from straight forms. Then, within the curved set, round letters (C and G) were split from nonround letters (P and R); within the straight set, square letters (E and F) were distinguished from diagonals (M, N, and W). Finally, diagonals were differentiated (Gibson, Schapiro, & Yonas, 1968).

That children find letters with diagonals especially hard to discriminate fits quite well with other findings. In one study, researchers showed 3- to 8-year-olds the pairs of forms in Figure 7.5. All the children easily discriminated the first and third pairs, involving vertical versus horizontal and right-side-up versus upside-down comparisons. But practically no child under age $6\frac{1}{2}$ could tell the difference between the diagonals in the second pair. Also, the right-left distinction in the fourth pair was quite difficult (Rudel & Teuber, 1963).

Does this last comparison remind you of young children's tendency to confuse letters that are mirror images, such as *b* and *d* and *p* and *q*? Until age 7 or 8, they reverse such letters frequently in their handwriting. One reason is that before children learn to read, they do not find it especially useful to notice the difference between mirror-image forms. In everyday life, left-right reversals occur only when objects are twin aspects of the same thing. For example, two cups, one with a handle on the left and one with a handle on the right, are the same to preschoolers. In contrast, children easily discriminate a cup turned upside-down, one placed right side up, and one turned on its side, since they have many daily experiences in which objects must be placed right side up to be used effectively (Bornstein, 1988). Research reveals that the ability to tune into mirror images, as well as scan a printed line carefully from left to right, depends in part on experience with reading materials (Casey, 1986). In other words, the very activity of learning to read helps children notice the distinctive features of letterlike forms.

Of course, becoming a skilled reader entails much more than letter discrimination. Children must combine what they perceive on the printed page with a variety of information-processing activities, including sustained attention, memory, comprehension, and inference making. But perceptual skills do seem to be essential, since children with advanced visual abilities read at higher levels (Fisher, Bornstein, & Gross, 1985; Kavale, 1982). We will return to reading development in a later section.

Enrichment Theory

In differentiation theory, children become better at noticing the structure already present in the surrounding world. In contrast, **enrichment theory** places the locus of perceptual organization inside the individual. According to this view, sensory processing is a matter of using cognitive schemes to interpret incoming information. As schemes are refined with age, perceptual intake from the environment is enriched accordingly. For example, a young child's experience with the family cat leads him to build, at first, a scheme for a furry, four-legged, meowing object. Gradually, this image is elaborated to include the slinkiness of the cat's movement, the peacefulness of its sleep, and the contentment of its purr. Each time more information is included in the cat scheme, the child's apprehension of the object is enhanced.

Notice how in viewing sensory processing as a matter of mental interpretation of events, enrichment theory has a distinctly Piagetian flavor. However, some

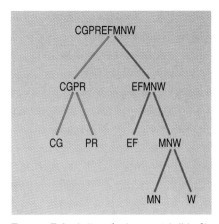

FIGURE 7.4 A "confusion matrix" indicating how children discriminate letters according to their distinctive features. (From "The Development of Perception as an Adaptive Process" by E. J. Gibson, 1970, *American Scientist, 58*, p. 106. Reprinted by permission.)

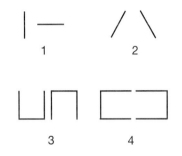

FIGURE 7.5 Pairs of forms 3- to 8-year-olds were asked to discriminate. Children found the diagonals in pair 2 and the left-right mirror image in pair 4 difficult to tell apart. (From "Discrimination of Direction of Line in Children" by R. G. Rudel & H. L. Teuber, 1963, *Journal of Comparative and Physiological Psychology, 56*, p. 893. Copyright © 1993 by the American Psychological Association. Reprinted by permission.)

Enrichment theory
The view that sensory processing involves using cognitive schemes to interpret incoming information.

*A*ccording to differentiation theory, the early phase
of learning to read involves increasingly fine-grained
detection of the invariant features of graphic forms.
(GEORGE GOODWIN/MONKMEYER PRESS PHOTO)

Notice how in viewing sensory processing as a matter of mental interpretation of events, enrichment theory has a distinctly Piagetian flavor. However, some
information-processing investigators agree with it as well (Fischer & Bidell, 1991;
Klahr, Langley, & Neches, 1987; Neisser, 1967). The enrichment position helps
remind us of the fine line that exists between perception and cognition. And when
we consider both differentiation and enrichment positions together, we are provided with a more complete picture. Both the nature of stimulation and the individual's approach to it are influential during each phase of information processing. This is a point we will return to many times in this chapter.

ATTENTIONAL PROCESSING

Attention is fundamental to human thinking, since it determines the sources of
information that will be considered in any task or problem. Parents and teachers are
quick to notice that young children spend only short times involved in tasks, have
difficulty focusing on details, and are easily distracted. Attention improves greatly
over the course of childhood, becoming more controlled, adaptable, and planful.

Control

Watch young children at play, and you are likely to see that attention becomes
more focused and sustained with age. In a recent study, infants and preschoolers
were seated at a table with age-appropriate toys. Concentrated involvement rose
steadily between 1 and 4 years. Infants' and older children's patterns of attention
also differed. After playing for a short time, babies tended to habituate. Their loss
of interest suggested that their attention was externally controlled by the physical
properties of the toys. In contrast, preschoolers became increasingly attentive as
the play session progressed. Their capacity to engage in complex play seemed to
support focused engagement with objects (Ruff & Lawson, 1990). Nevertheless,
even 5- and 6-year-olds do not remain attentive for very long. When observed
during free play at preschool, the average time they spend in a single activity is
about 7 minutes (Stodolsky, 1974).

As sustained attention improves, children become better at deliberately focusing on just those aspects of a situation that are relevant to their task goals, ignor-

ing other sources of information. Researchers study this increasing selectivity of attention by introducing irrelevant stimuli into a task. Then they see how well children attend to its central elements (Lane & Pearson, 1982). In a typical experiment of this kind, school-age children and adults were asked to sort decks of cards as fast as possible on the basis of shapes appearing on each card—for example, circles in one pile and squares in another. Some decks contained no irrelevant information. Others included either one or two irrelevant stimuli, such as lines running across the shapes or stars appearing above or below them. Children's ability to ignore unnecessary information was determined by seeing how much longer it took them to sort decks with irrelevant stimuli. As Figure 7.6 indicates, the ability to keep attention on central features of the task improved sharply between 6 and 9 years of age (Strutt, Anderson, & Well, 1975).

Adaptability

Older children are also more adaptable; they flexibly adjust their attention to the momentary requirements of situations. For example, in judging whether pairs of stimuli are the same or different, sixth-graders quickly shift their basis of judgment (from size to shape to color) when asked to do so. Second-graders have trouble with this type of task (Pick & Frankel, 1974).

Older children are also better at adapting their attention to changes in their own learning. When given lists of items to learn and allowed to select half for further study, first-graders do not choose systematically. But by third grade, children show a strong tendency to select those they had previously missed (Masur, McIntyre, & Flavell, 1973). When learning more complex information, such as prose passages, the ability to allocate attention on the basis of previous performance continues to improve into the college years (Brown, Smiley, & Lawton, 1978).

Planfulness

By the end of early childhood, attention also becomes more planful, as children's visual search behavior in familiar environments reveals. In one study, researchers had 3- to 5-year-olds look for a lost object in their preschool play yard. Each child was taken through the setting by an experimenter, who stopped at eight locations along the way to play a game (see Figure 7.7). In the third location, the adult took

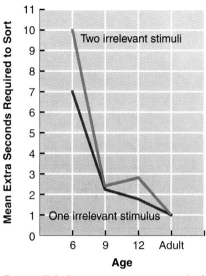

FIGURE 7.6 Improvement in control of attention over the elementary school years. School-age children and adults were asked to sort decks of cards on the basis of shapes that appeared on each card. Six-year-olds took much longer to sort when the decks contained irrelevant stimuli (lines and stars) than when they did not. By age 9, sorting speed was only slightly affected by the presence of irrelevant information. (Adapted from "A Developmental Study of the Effects of Irrelevant Information on Speeded Classification" by G. F. Strutt, D. R. Anderson, & A. D. Well, 1975, *Journal of Experimental Child Psychology, 20,* p. 132. Copyright © 1975 by Academic Press. Adapted by permission.)

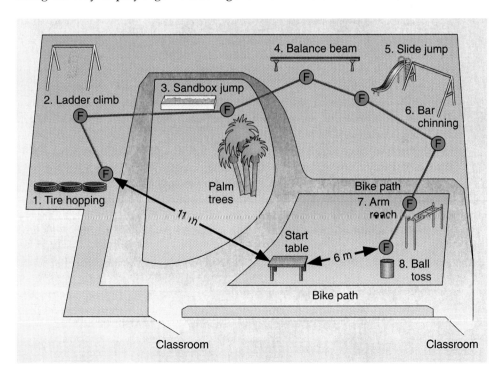

FIGURE 7.7 Layout of the playground in a study of children's visual search behavior. The children played games at eight locations. Each location was marked by a flag (F) displaying a picture of the game played there. Red yarn stretching between the flags defined the path from locations 1 to 8, so children could easily retrace their steps during the search phase of the study. (From "Development of Search Procedures in Real-Life Spatial Environments" by H. M. Wellman, S. C. Somerville, & R. J. Haake, 1979, *Developmental Psychology, 15,* p. 532. Copyright © 1979 by the American Psychological Association. Reprinted by permission of the author.)

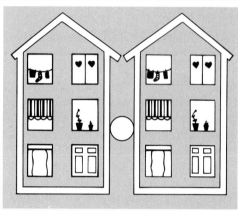

FIGURE 7.8 Pairs of houses children were asked to judge as the same or different. Preschoolers' eye movements showed that they did not examine all stimulus features systematically. As a result, they frequently judged different houses to be the same. In contrast, 6- to 9-year-olds used an exhaustive search strategy in which they compared the details of the houses window to window. (From "The Development of Scanning Strategies and Their Relation to Visual Differentiation" by E. Vurpillot, 1968, *Journal of Experimental Child Psychology, 6,* p. 634. Copyright © 1968 by Academic Press. Reprinted by permission.)

could not find it at location 3, they gave up or searched outside the "critical area" (the path between location 3, where the picture was taken, and location 7, where the camera was discovered missing). In contrast, older preschoolers were more likely to confine their search to the critical area and visit each possible location, searching systematically and exhaustively (Wellman, Somerville, & Haake, 1979).

Still, preschoolers' planful attentional strategies have a long way to go before they are very mature. When asked to compare detailed pictures like those in Figure 7.8, school-age children search much more thoroughly for similarities and differences (Vurpillot, 1968). And on complex tasks, they make decisions about what to do first and what to do next in a more orderly fashion. For example, when researchers gave 5- to 9-year-olds lists of 25 items to obtain from a play grocery store, older children took time to scan the store before starting on a shopping trip. They also followed shorter routes through the aisles (Gauvain & Rogoff, 1989).

Why does attention improve so rapidly from early to middle childhood? Brain maturation and the demands of school tasks may be jointly responsible. The attentional strategies we have discussed are certainly critical for successful school performance, and individual differences in sustained attention are fairly stable over time (Campbell et al., 1986; Ruff et al., 1990). Unfortunately, some children have great difficulty paying attention during the school years. See the From Research to Practice box on the following page for a discussion of the serious learning and behavior problems of these attention-deficit hyperactivity disordered children.

Brief Review

According to differentiation theory, the external world brings order to perceptual experience; sensory processing involves noticing increasingly fine-grained, invariant properties of objects and patterns. Differentiation theory accounts for how children go about discriminating subtle features of written symbols. In contrast, enrichment theory views sensory processing as a matter of using cognitive schemes to interpret incoming information. As schemes are refined, per-

While the other fifth-graders worked quietly at their desks, Calvin squirmed in his seat, dropped his pencil, looked out the window, fiddled with his shoelaces, and talked out. "Hey Joey," he yelled to a classmate over the top of several desks, "wanna play ball after school?" Joey didn't answer. He and the other children weren't eager to play with Calvin. Out on the playground, Calvin was a poor listener and failed to follow the rules of the game. When up at bat, he had difficulty taking turns. In the outfield, he tossed his mitt up in the air and looked elsewhere when the ball came his way. Calvin's desk at school and his room at home were a chaotic mess. He often lost pencils, books, and other materials necessary for completing assignments.

Calvin is one of 3 to 5 percent of school-age children with **attention-deficit hyperactivity disorder (ADHD)** (American Psychiatric Association, 1987). Although boys are diagnosed 5 to 10 times more often than girls, recent evidence suggests that just as many girls may suffer from the disorder. Girls are less likely to be identified because their symptoms are usually not as flagrant (Hynd et al., 1991).

Children with ADHD have great difficulty staying on task for more than a few minutes. In addition, they often act impulsively, ignoring social rules and lashing out with hostility when frustrated. Many (but not all) are hyperactive. They charge through their days with excessive motor activity, leaving parents and teachers frazzled and other children annoyed. Not surprisingly, children with ADHD have few friends; their behaviors lead them to be soundly rejected by their classmates (Henker & Whalen, 1989).

The intelligence of these youngsters is normal, and they show no signs of serious emotional disturbance. Instead, attentional difficulties are at the heart of their problems. They do poorly on laboratory tasks requiring sustained attention, and they find it hard to ignore irrelevant information (Douglas, 1983; Landau, Milich, & Lorch, 1992). Although some outgrow these difficulties, most continue to have trouble concentrating and finding friends into adolescence and adulthood.

ADHD does not have a single cause. Heredity seems to play an important role, since the disorder runs in families, and identical twins share it more often than do fraternal twins. Also, an adoptive child who is inattentive and hyperactive is likely to have a biological parent (but not an adoptive parent) with similar symptoms (Alberts-Corush,

Firestone, & Goodman, 1986; Biederman et al., 1990; O'Connor et al., 1980).

At the same time, ADHD is associated with a variety of environmental factors. These children are somewhat more likely to come from homes in which marriages are unhappy and family stress is high (Whalen, 1983). Also, recall from earlier chapters that prenatal teratogens as well as childhood lead exposure are linked to later attentional problems. Dietary causes, such as food additives and sugar, have been suggested, but there is little evidence that these play important roles (Hynd et al., 1991).

Calvin's doctor eventually prescribed stimulant medication, the most common treatment for ADHD. As long as dosage is carefully regulated, these drugs reduce activity level and improve attention, academic performance, and peer relations for 70 percent of children who take them (Barkley, 1990). Researchers do not know precisely why stimulants are helpful. Some speculate that they change the chemical balance in brain regions that inhibit impulsiveness and hyperactivity. Others believe that children with ADHD are chronically underaroused. That is, normal levels of stimulation do not engage their attention, so they seek excitement everywhere. Stimulant drugs may work because they have an alerting effect on the brain. As a result, they decrease the child's need to engage in off-task and self-stimulating behaviors.

Although stimulant medication is relatively safe, its impact is only short term. Drugs cannot teach children ways of compensating for inattention and impulsivity (Whalen & Henker, 1991). Combining medication with interventions that model and reinforce appropriate academic and social behavior seems to be the most effective approach to treatment (Hynd et al., 1991). Teachers can also create conditions in classrooms that support these pupils' special learning needs. Short work periods followed by a chance to get up and move around help them concentrate. Finally, family intervention is particularly important. Inattentive, overactive children strain the patience of parents, who are likely to react punitively and inconsistently in return—a child-rearing style that strengthens inappropriate behavior. Breaking this cycle is as important for children with ADHD as it is for the defiant, aggressive youngsters we will discuss in Chapter 12. In fact, 50 percent of the time these two sets of behavior problems occur together (Henker & Whalen, 1989).

---

ceptual intake from the environment is enhanced. From this perspective, the locus of perceptual organization lies within the individual.

Attention improves greatly over the course of childhood. During the preschool years, children show gains in focused, sustained attention during play. Over middle childhood, the ability to attend to relevant information and ignore irrelevant stimuli in a task improves. Older children are also better at adapting attention to momentary requirements of situations and deciding what to do first and what to do next in a planful, orderly fashion.

Attention-deficit hyperactivity disorder (ADHD)

A childhood disorder involving inattentiveness, impulsivity, and excessive motor activity. Often leads to academic failure and social problems.

SHORT-TERM OR WORKING MEMORY

As attention improves with age, so do **memory strategies,** deliberate mental activities we use to increase the likelihood of holding information in short-term memory and transferring it to our long-term knowledge base. As we will see in the following sections, although memory strategies start to emerge during the preschool years, they are not very successful at first. Around the time children enter elementary school, these techniques take a giant leap forward (Kail, 1990).

Strategies for Storing Information

Researchers have studied the development of three strategies that enhance memory for new information: rehearsal, organization, and elaboration.

REHEARSAL. The next time you look up a new phone number that you need to retain until you have a chance to dial it, take note of your own behavior. You will probably repeat the information to yourself, a memory strategy called **rehearsal**. Preschoolers show the beginnings of rehearsal. When asked to remember a set of familiar toys, they name, look at, and manipulate them more and play with them less than when not instructed to remember them. However, naming the toys has little effect on memory until about 6 years of age (Baker-Ward, Ornstein, & Holden, 1984). Furthermore, when young children are given less familiar materials, they rarely rehearse. In a well-known study, researchers presented 6- and 10-year-olds with pictures of objects to remember. Many more older than younger children audibly repeated the objects' names or moved their lips, and those who rehearsed recalled far more objects (Keeney, Canizzo, & Flavell, 1967).

Why are young children not very adept at rehearsal? Is the problem a **production deficiency,** a failure to use the strategy in situations where it could be helpful? Or is it a **control deficiency,** an inability to execute the strategy effectively even when it is used? Look closely at the findings we have reviewed so far, and you will see that *both* problems are involved. Let's explore some additional evidence that supports this conclusion.

Studies in which nonrehearsing children have been taught to rehearse highlight an early production deficiency. Training improves recall on the task at hand substantially. But when given an opportunity to rehearse later without prompting, most trained children abandon the strategy (Hagen, Hargrove, & Ross, 1973; Keeney, Canizzo, & Flavell, 1967). So although young children can be taught to rehearse, they fail to use the strategy in new situations or maintain it over time.

When children first rehearse spontaneously, a control deficiency is evident, since their efforts are not very successful. Eight-year-olds commonly repeat items one-by-one. For example, given a list beginning with "desk, man, yard, cat," most say "cat, cat, cat" after hearing the word "cat." In contrast, older children combine previously presented words with the newest item. After hearing "cat," they say "desk, man, yard, cat," an approach that greatly improves recall (Kunzinger, 1985; Ornstein, Naus, & Liberty, 1975). With age, children also become better at varying the strategy to fit the material to be learned. For example, 9- and 10-year-olds tend to rehearse repeatedly when given a random list of numbers (such as 5, 7, 3, 4, 6) but only once or not at all when given a serially ordered list (4, 5, 6, 7, 8), since they can rely on counting to retain it. In contrast, 5- and 6-year-olds are less effective in adjusting rehearsal efforts to fit with list characteristics. They often fail to take note of a list's features before deciding how to memorize (McGilly & Siegler, 1990).

The preschool child's minimal use of rehearsal and the young elementary school child's less effective execution of it reveal that the development of rehearsal skill is a gradual process. When a strategy is new, children have difficulty applying it successfully (Wellman, 1988b). After much time and practice, the strategy becomes less of an effort and more automatic, and it can be used skillfully and adaptively in a wide range of situations.

Memory strategies

Deliberate mental activities that improve the likelihood of retaining information in short-term memory and transferring it to the long-term knowledge base.

Rehearsal

The memory strategy of repeating information.

Production deficiency

The failure to use a mental strategy in situations where it could be helpful.

Control deficiency

The inability to execute a mental strategy effectively.

ORGANIZATION. If in trying to remember the phone number mentioned in the preceding section, you group digits into meaningful chunks, you are using a second memory strategy, called **organization**. It causes recall to improve dramatically.

Like rehearsal, the beginnings of organization can be seen in very young children. For example, when circumstances permit, they use *spatial organization* to aid their memories. In a study of 2- to 5-year-olds, an adult placed either an M&M or a wooden peg in each of 12 identical containers and handed them one by one to the child, who was asked to remember where the candy was hidden. By age 4, children put the candy containers in one place on the table and the peg containers in another, a strategy that almost always led to perfect recall (DeLoache & Todd, 1988). But preschoolers do not yet use *semantic organization*—grouping objects or words into meaningful categories—to aid recall. With intensive instruction they can be taught to do so, but training does not always improve their memory performance (Carr & Schneider, 1991; Lange & Pierce, 1992).

Once children semantically organize to retain information, the quality of their organizational strategies improves with age. Before age 9 or 10, children divide their lists into a greater number of categories and change their groupings from one trial to the next (Moely, 1977). Also, they tend to link items together by function. For example, consider the following items:

hat	carrot	head	rabbit
feet	monkey	banana	shoes

A 7- to 8-year-old is likely to say "hat-head," "feet-shoes," and "monkey-banana." In contrast, older children and adults group these items into clothing, body parts, animals, and food. The first approach is probably not a deliberate attempt to organize, since it appears to depend on *involuntary associations* between items. In other words, when asked to think of something that goes with "hat," we are more likely to say "head" than "shoes" because hat and head go together in everyday experience (Bjorklund & Jacobs, 1985; Frankel & Rollins, 1985).

These findings suggest that the first organizational efforts take place quite automatically, without much awareness on the part of the child. Indeed, unless items are highly familiar and strongly associated, children age 8 and younger do not group them at all (Best & Ornstein, 1986). As with rehearsal, organization requires more attentional resources on the part of younger than older children (Bjorklund & Harnishfeger, 1987). But grouping by associative relations may support the development of categorical organization. Once children engage in an automatic grouping process, they may notice it and begin to apply more mature forms of relating items together. As they do so, they start to use organization to aid memory under less favorable task conditions (Bjorklund, 1987).

ELABORATION. Sometimes information cannot be categorized easily. For example, suppose "fish" and "pipe" are among a list of words you need to learn. If to retain them, you imagine a fish smoking a pipe, you used a memory strategy called **elaboration**. It involves creating a relationship, or shared meaning, between two or more pieces of information that are not members of the same category.

Compared to other strategies, elaboration is a late-developing skill that rarely appears before age 11. Once individuals discover this memory technique, they find it so effective that it tends to replace other strategies (Schneider & Pressley, 1989). The very reason elaboration is so successful helps explain why it is late to emerge as a spontaneous strategy. It requires a great deal of mental effort to execute. To use elaboration, we must translate items into images and think of a relationship between them. Children's working memories must expand before they can carry out these activities simultaneously (Pressley et al., 1987).

Perhaps for this reason, teaching children under age 11 to elaborate is not very successful. When they do try to use the strategy, they usually produce static images, such as, "The dog had a car." In contrast, adolescents and adults generate active images that are more memorable, as in "The dog raced the car through

CHAPTER SEVEN
COGNITIVE DEVELOPMENT:
AN INFORMATION-PROCESSING
PERSPECTIVE

Organization
The memory strategy of grouping information into meaningful chunks.

Elaboration
The memory strategy of creating a relation between two or more items that are not members of the same category.

town" (Reese, 1977). Increased knowledge of ways items can be combined in memory undoubtedly contributes to the older individual's more successful use of elaboration (Pressley, 1982).

Environmental Contexts and Memory Strategies

In most of the laboratory studies we have reviewed so far, children were asked to learn discrete bits of information, and memorizing was the only goal of their activity. In everyday life, people rarely engage in retaining listlike material. Rather, they participate in a variety of daily activities that produce excellent memory as a natural by-product of the activity itself (Rogoff, 1990). In a study illustrating this idea, 4- and 5-year-olds were told either to play with a set of toys or to remember them. The play condition produced far better recall. Rather than just naming or touching objects, children instructed to play engaged in many spontaneous organizations that helped them recall. These included functional use of objects (pretending to eat a banana or putting a shoe on a doll) and narrating their activities, as in "I'm squeezing this lemon" or "Fly away in this helicopter, doggie" (Newman, 1990).

These findings help explain why the Kpelle farmers, described at the beginning of this chapter, viewed functional grouping as "the wise way" to organize familiar objects. Much like young children, people in non-Western cultures who have no formal schooling do not spontaneously use or benefit from instruction in memory strategies. They consistently do poorly when asked to learn material presented as isolated units, devoid of the structuring imposed by the way things appear and are used in their everyday lives (Cole & Scribner, 1977; Rogoff & Mistry, 1985). Both young children and nonschooled people may seldom use the memorizing techniques we have discussed because they see little reason to remember information for its own sake.

In contrast, deliberate memorization is common in school, and academic tasks requiring list learning provide children with a great deal of motivation to use memory strategies. In fact, Western children may receive so much practice in acquiring discrete bits of information that they apply memory strategies inappropriately when trying to recall information embedded in meaningful contexts. For example, 9-year-old Guatemalan Mayan children do slightly better than American children when told to remember the placement of 40 familiar objects in a play scene (see Figure 7.9). Under these conditions, many American youngsters try to

As these Guatemalan Mayan boys discuss the intricacies of effective kite-flying, they demonstrate a keen memory for information embedded in meaningful contexts. Yet when given a list-memory task of the kind American children often perform in school, they do poorly.
(ULRIKE WELSCH/PHOTO RESEARCHERS)

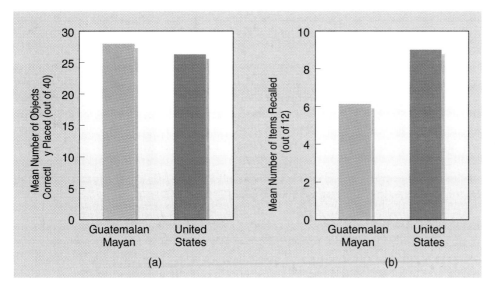

FIGURE 7.9 Comparison of 9-year-old Guatemalan Mayan and American children's memory for (a) placement of objects in a familiar play scene and (b) a word list. Mayan children did slightly better when asked to recall information in a meaningful context. American children were advantaged on a list-learning task. (Adapted from Kagan et al., 1979; Rogoff & Waddell, 1982.)

rehearse object names when it is more effective to keep track of spatial relations (Rogoff & Waddell, 1982). The skill shown by Mayan children in remembering contextually organized information contrasts sharply with their poor performance on list-memory tasks (Kagan et al., 1979).

Looked at in this way, the development of memory strategies is not just a matter of a more competent information-processing system. It is also a product of task demands and cultural circumstances.

Brief Review

Production and control deficiencies characterize young children's use of memory strategies. Preschoolers seldom engage in deliberate efforts to improve their memory, nor do they show lasting gains from training. During the early years of formal schooling, children acquire greater competence in rehearsal and organization. Elaboration emerges later, after age 11. The need to learn isolated bits of information, a typical requirement of schooling in Western nations, influences the development of memory strategies.

LONG-TERM MEMORY

So far, we have discussed strategies for putting information into memory. Once it enters our long-term knowledge base, it must be *retrieved,* or recovered, to be used again. In the following sections, we consider how children retrieve information from long-term memory. Then we turn to their expanding long-term knowledge base and its impact on memory performance.

Retrieval of Information

Information can be retrieved from memory in three ways: through recognition, recall, and reconstruction. As we discuss the development of these approaches to remembering, we will also take up an intriguing, universal memory problem: our inability to recollect experiences that occurred during the first few years of our lives.

RECOGNITION. Noticing that a stimulus is identical or similar to one previously experienced is called **recognition**. It is the simplest form of retrieval, since the material to be remembered is fully present during testing to serve as its own retrieval cue. As the habituation research we discussed in Chapter 4 shows, even young infants are capable of recognition. The ability to recognize a larger number of stimuli over longer delays improves steadily from infancy through early childhood. By age 4,

Recognition
A type of memory that involves noticing whether a stimulus is identical or similar to one previously experienced.

recognition memory is highly accurate. After viewing a series of 80 pictures, children of this age correctly discriminated 90 percent from pictures not in the original set (Brown & Campione, 1972).

Because recognition appears so early in life and preschoolers' performance approaches that of adults on many tasks, it is probably a fairly automatic process that does not depend on a deliberate search of long-term memory. Nevertheless, the ability of older individuals to apply strategies during storage, such as systematic scanning of visual stimuli and rehearsal, increases the number of items later recognized, especially when they are complex and unfamiliar (Mandler & Robinson, 1978; Nelson & Kosslyn, 1976). Also, growth in general knowledge undoubtedly supports gains in recognition memory. With age, children encounter fewer stimuli with which they have no experience (Perlmutter, 1984).

RECALL. In contrast to recognition, **recall** is more difficult, since it involves remembering a stimulus that is not present. Perhaps there are only a few cues to what it is, or none at all beyond the original context in which it was learned. Therefore, to recall, you must generate a mental representation of the absent stimulus.

The beginnings of recall appear before 1 year of age as long as memories are strongly cued. Think back to our discussion of deferred imitation in Chapter 6. Its presence at 9 months is good evidence for recall. In other instances, researchers have asked parents to keep diary accounts of their babies' memories. Many examples of recall for people, places, and objects appear in the records. The following diary entry of a 7-month-old's memory of his father is an example:

> My husband called from work and I let him talk to Rob. (Rob) looked puzzled for a while and then he turned and looked at the door. Rob thought of the only time he hears his dad's voice when he knows Dad isn't home is when his Dad just got home. He heard his dad's voice and based on past experiences, he reasoned that his dad must be home, so he looked at the door. (Ashmead & Perlmutter, 1980, p. 4)

In other studies, children between 2 and 3 years recalled events many months and even years earlier, from a time before they had learned to talk (Fivush, Gray, & Fromhoff, 1987; Myers, Clifton, & Clarkson, 1987). However, what is recalled about an event that happened long ago is only a portion of what can potentially be remembered. In one longitudinal study, sixth-graders were asked to tell what happened when they went to an archaeological museum in kindergarten. They said much less about the experience than when they were asked the same question 6 weeks after the museum trip actually occurred. But in response to fairly specific external retrieval cues, including photos of the actual event, sixth-graders

*R*ecall *improves dramatically with age. When provided with specific external retrieval cues, such as photos, older children even show surprisingly accurate memory for events that occurred many years earlier.* (JEFF GREENBERG/THE PICTURE CUBE)

Recall
A type of memory that involves remembering a stimulus that is not present.

remembered a great deal. And in some respects, their recall was more accurate. For example, they inferred that adults had hidden artifacts in a sandbox for them to find, whereas in kindergarten they simply recalled digging for relics (Hudson & Fivush, 1991).

When younger and older children are asked to recall information after an identical time lapse, older children's recall is considerably more accurate and complete. In fact, compared to recognition, recall shows much greater improvement with age (Perlmutter, 1984). The reason is that older individuals are much better at strategic processing. During the elementary school years, semantic organization of the knowledge base increases. Children develop more consistent and stable categories, which they arrange into more elaborate hierarchies. When stimuli are deeply processed at encoding so they are connected with other information in long-term memory, then a wide variety of *internal* retrieval cues can be used to recall them later.

THE MYSTERY OF INFANTILE AMNESIA. A puzzling question arises from the findings we have reviewed so far: If babies are capable of both recognition and recall and young preschoolers can remember events that happened during infancy, then what explains **infantile amnesia**—the fact that practically none of us can retrieve experiences that happened to us before age 3? Forgetting cannot be due to the passage of time, since we can recall many events that occurred long ago, particularly when they are cued. And Sigmund Freud's (1905/1953) well-known explanation—that our early memories are so charged with themes of infantile sexuality that we have pushed them back into the unconscious—also remains unsupported. People who undergo intensive psychotherapy in an effort to understand their early lives are still unable to retrieve these experiences (White & Pillemer, 1979).

At present, there are several plausible explanations of infantile amnesia. One possibility is that brain maturation during early childhood accounts for it. Growth of the frontal lobes of the cortex along with other structures may be necessary before experiences can be stored in ways that permit them to be retrieved many years later (Boyer & Diamond, 1992; Nadel & Zola-Morgan, 1984).

A second hypothesis suggests that two levels of memory exist, one that operates unconsciously and automatically, another that is conscious and intentional. Infants' memories may be largely of the first kind, children's and adults' memories of the second; but the second system cannot access events stored by the first. In support of this idea, 9-year-olds shown pictures of their preschool classmates react physiologically in ways consistent with remembering, even when they do not consciously recall the child (Newcombe, Fox, & Prime, 1989, as cited by Siegler, 1991).

A final, related idea is that infants encode information in ways that are incompatible with approaches to retrieval at later ages. For example, adults often use verbal means for storing information; infants' processing is nonverbal. Time of the day and season of the year are meaningful memory cues to adults but not to infants. Again, this incompatibility probably prevents older individuals from retrieving their earliest experiences (Neisser, 1967; Siegler, 1991).

Currently, none of these theories is fully substantiated. Infantile amnesia is still a mystery to modern researchers.

RECONSTRUCTION. Read the following passage about George, a convict who has escaped from prison. Then close your book and try to write the story down or tell it to a friend:

> George was alone. He knew they would soon be here. They were not far behind him when he left the village, hungry and cold. He dared not stop for food or shelter for fear of falling into the hands of his pursuers. There were many of them; they were strong and he was weak. George could hear the noise as the uniformed band beat its way through the trees not far behind him. The sense of their presence was everywhere. His

Infantile amnesia
The inability of older children and adults to remember experiences that happened before age 3.

spine tingled with fear. Eagerly he awaited the darkness. In darkness he would find safety. (Brown et al., 1977, p. 1456)

Now compare your version with the original. Is it a faithful reproduction?

When people are given complex, meaningful material to remember, condensations, additions, and distortions appear that are not just the result of memory failure. Instead, they are due to a radical transformation of the information. This suggests that we do not always copy material into the system at storage and faithfully reproduce it at retrieval. Instead, much information we encounter in our daily lives, such as written and spoken language, is selected and interpreted in terms of our existing knowledge. And once the material is transformed, we often have difficulty distinguishing it from the original (Bartlett, 1932; Paris & Lindauer, 1977). Perhaps you noticed that this *constructivist approach* to information processing is quite consistent with Piaget's ideas. He believed that information cannot be imposed ready-made on the child. Instead, it is built by the mind through the functions of adaptation and organization.

Constructive processing can take place during any phase of information processing. It can occur during storage. In fact, the memory strategies of organization and elaboration are within the province of constructive memory, since both require us to generate relationships among stimuli. Yet earlier we saw that young children rarely use these strategies. Constructive processing can also involve **reconstruction** of information while it is in the system or being retrieved. Do children reconstruct stored information? The answer is clearly yes.

Children's reconstructive processing has been studied by asking them to recall prose material. Like adults, when children retell a story, they condense, integrate, and add information. For example, by age 6 or 7, children recall the important features of a story and forget the unimportant ones, combine information into more tightly knit units, and reorder the sequence of events to make it more logical (Barclay & Reid, 1974; Bischofshausen, 1985; Christie & Schumacher, 1975; Mandler, 1984). And they often report information that fits with the meaning of a passage but that was not really presented. For example, after elementary school pupils listened to the story of George, the escaped convict, the following statements appeared in their reconstructions:

All the prison guards were chasing him.

He climbed over the prison walls.

He was running so the police would be so far away that their dogs would not catch his trail. (Brown et al., 1977, p. 1459)

In revising the information in meaningful ways, children provide themselves with a wealth of helpful retrieval cues that can be used during recall. By the early elementary school years, children's memory for prose material resembles that of adults in its emphasis on reconstruction of information.

Between ages 4 and 12, reconstruction goes further as the ability to draw inferences about actors and actions within a story improves (Paris & Lindauer, 1977). For example, preschoolers easily draw inferences when story statements concern the physical causes of events. When given the sentence, "As Jennifer was walking to the store, she turned a somersault and lost her dollar," 4-year-olds infer how Jennifer lost her money. But not until the early to mid-elementary school years can children make inferences about psychological causes, as in the following sentence: "As Jennifer was walking to the store, she became very excited and lost her dollar." Young children have a much fuller understanding of physical than psychological causation, a difference that affects their ability to infer relationships (Thompson & Myers, 1985).

Since inference making is so important for comprehending and recalling complex information, are there ways to facilitate it? Think back to our discussion of reciprocal teaching in Chapter 6. Discussions aimed at clarifying and predicting future prose content require pupils to make inferences—one reason this method has been so successful.

Reconstruction

A memory process in which complex, meaningful material is reinterpreted in terms of existing knowledge.

(a)

(b)

FIGURE 7.10 Partial picture (a) and complete picture (b) used to illustrate the sentence "The workman dug a hole in the ground" in a study of children's inferential processing. Use of illustrations can help children draw inferences that serve as helpful retrieval cues for prose passages. (From "Partial Picture Effects on Children's Memory for Sentences Containing Implicit Information" by G. E. Miller & M. Pressley, 1987, *Journal of Experimental Child Psychology, 43*, p. 303. Copyright © 1987 by Academic Press. Reprinted by permission.)

Illustrations can also help children infer connections in text passages. In one study, 6- and 7-year-olds were read sentences like this: "The workman dug a hole in the ground." As each sentence was presented, some children viewed a "partial picture" that suggested, but did not depict, the instrument used (see Figure 7.10a). Later, when the experimenter cued sentence recall by naming each inferred instrument (in this case, "shovel"), the "partial picture" group remembered just as much as a group that saw "complete pictures" (see Figure 7.10b). And both groups recalled nearly twice as much as children who saw no pictures at all (Miller & Pressley, 1987). These findings suggest that well-designed illustrations can enhance prose memory by encouraging inferential processing.

Knowledge and Memory Performance

At several points during our discussion, we suggested that children's expanding knowledge base may promote improved memory. Many researchers believe that cognitive development is largely a matter of acquiring **domain-specific knowledge**—knowledge of a specific content area that makes new, related information more meaningful so it is easier to store and retrieve (Bjorklund, 1987; Mandler, 1983; Siegler, 1983).

Indeed, much research supports this idea. The more children and adults know about a content area, the more they can encode and hold in working memory (Harris et al., 1990; Huttenlocher & Burke, 1976). Knowing more about a topic also improves strategy use. In one study, a 5-year-old learned and applied a new alphabetic strategy for recalling people's names far more easily when the to-be-retrieved items were her classmates' names rather than the names of strangers (Chi, 1982).

If children's growing knowledge base accounts for better memory performance, then in areas in which children are more knowledgeable than adults, they should show better recall. To test this idea, Michelene Chi (1978) looked at how well third- through eighth-grade chess experts could remember complex chessboard arrangements. The children were compared to adults who knew how to play chess but were not especially knowledgeable. Just as expected, the children could reproduce the chessboard configurations considerably better than the adults

Domain-specific knowledge
Knowledge of a specific content area that makes new, related information more meaningful so it is easier to store and retrieve.

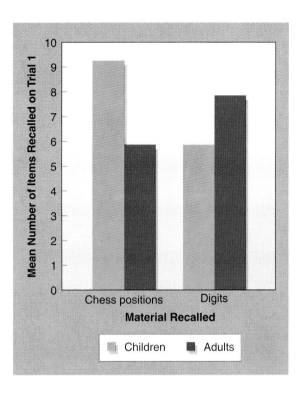

FIGURE 7.11 Performance of skilled child chess players and adults on two tasks: memory for complex chessboard arrangements and numerical digits. The child chess experts recalled more on the chess task, the adults on the digit task. These findings show that size of the knowledge base contributes to memory performance. (Adapted from Chi, 1978.)

could. These findings cannot be explained by the selection of very bright youngsters with exceptional memories. On a standard digit-span task in which the same subjects had to recall a list of numbers, the adults did better than the children. The children showed superior memory only in the domain of knowledge in which they were expert (see Figure 7.11).

In Chi's study of chess-playing children, better memory was largely attributed to a greater quantity of knowledge. Experts also have a more elaborately structured knowledge base that permits them to apply organizational strategies more adeptly and to retrieve familiar items automatically. To illustrate this idea, Wolfgang Schneider and David Bjorklund (1992) classified elementary school children as experts or novices in knowledge of soccer. Then both groups were given lists of soccer and nonsoccer items to learn. As in Chi's study, experts remembered far more items on the soccer list (but not on the nonsoccer list) than did nonexperts. In observing how fourth-graders studied soccer items, the researchers found that both groups used organizational strategies. But experts were more likely to apply these strategies during retrieval (as indicated by clustering of items during recall). And within each category searched, experts remembered more items.

Although knowledge clearly plays a major role in memory development, it may have to be quite broad and well structured before it can facilitate memory performance. A brief series of lessons designed to increase knowledge in a particular area does not affect children's ability to recall information in that domain (DeMarie-Dreblow, 1991). Until children have enough knowledge and have time to connect it into stable, well-formed hierarchies, they may not be able to apply it to new memory problems (Chi & Ceci, 1987).

Finally, we must keep in mind that knowledge is not the only factor involved in strategic memory processing. Children who are expert in a particular area, whether it be chess, math, social studies, or spelling, are usually highly motivated. Faced with new material, they say to themselves, "What can I do to clarify the meaning of this information so I can learn it more easily?" As a result, they not only acquire knowledge more quickly, but they actively use what they know to add more. Research reveals that academically successful and unsuccessful students differ in just this way. Poor students fail to approach memory tasks by asking how previously stored information can clarify new information. This, in turn, interferes with the development of a broad knowledge base (Bransford et al., 1981; Brown et al., 1983). Looked at in this way, knowledge acquisition and memory strategies are intimately related and support one another.

Scripts: Basic Building Blocks of Structured Knowledge

Think back to research we have discussed in this chapter and in Chapter 6 on children's ability to categorize. It shows that a structured long-term knowledge base begins to form as early as the preschool years. How do children begin to build a coherent network of knowledge, and in what ways does it change with age?

Our vast, intricately organized general knowledge system, which for purposes of clarity we now refer to as **semantic memory,** must grow out of the young child's **episodic memory,** or memory for many personally experienced events (Tulving, 1972). How semantic memory emerges from a foundation of specific, real-world experiences is considered by some researchers to be one of the most puzzling questions about memory development (Nelson & Brown, 1978).

Like adults, preschoolers remember familiar experiences in terms of **scripts,** general representations of what occurs and when it occurs in a particular situation. For very young children, scripts begin as a structure of main acts. For example, when asked to tell what happens when you go to a restaurant, a 3-year-old might say, "You go in, get the food, eat, and then pay." Although children's first scripts contain only a few acts, as long as events in a situation take place in a logical order, they are almost always recalled in correct sequence (Fivush, Kuebli, & Clubb, 1992). This is true even for 1- and 2-year-olds, who cannot yet verbally describe events but who act them out with toys (Bauer & Mandler, 1989a, 1992). With age, children can form a script on the basis of fewer repetitions of an event (Farrar & Goodman, 1992). Their scripts also become more elaborate, as in the following restaurant account given by a 5-year-old child: "You go in. You can sit in the booths or at a table. Then you tell the waitress what you want. You eat. If you want dessert, you can have some. Then you pay and go home" (Fivush, 1984; Nelson & Gruendel, 1981).

Scripts are a special form of reconstructive memory, and they provide yet another example of continuity in memory processing from early childhood to adulthood. When we experience repeated events, we fuse them into the same script representation. Then any specific instance of a scripted experience becomes hard to recall. For example, unless it was out of the ordinary, you probably cannot remember exactly what you had for dinner 2 days ago. The same is true for young children. By the second day of kindergarten, 5-year-olds have difficulty recalling specific events that occurred on the first day of class, although they can describe what happened in general terms (Fivush, 1984; Hudson, 1988).

Once held in long-term memory, a script can be used to predict what will happen on similar occasions in the future. In this way, scripts serve as a basic means through which children (and adults) organize and interpret everyday experiences. For example, young children rely on scripts when listening to and telling stories. They recall more events from stories that are based on familiar event sequences than on unfamiliar ones (Hudson & Nelson, 1983). Children also apply script structures to the stories they act out in play. Listen carefully to preschoolers' make-believe. You will hear scripts reflected in their dialogues when they pretend to put the baby to bed, go on a trip, or play school (Nelson & Gruendel, 1981).

According to Katherine Nelson, scripts may be the developmental link between early episodic memory and a semantically organized long-term memory store (Nelson & Brown, 1978; Nelson & Gruendel, 1981). In one study, 3- and 4-year-olds remembered script-related items (such as peanut butter, bologna, cheese—foods often eaten at lunchtime) in clustered form and recalled them more easily than a typical categorical list (toast, cheese, ice cream—foods) (Lucariello & Nelson, 1985). It appears that relationships among items are first understood in

*L*ike adults, young children remember familiar experiences in terms of scripts. After going to the grocery store with his father many times, this boy is unlikely to recall the details of a particular shopping trip. But he will be able to describe what typically happens when you go shopping, and his account will become more elaborate with age. Scripts help us organize and interpret our everyday experiences.
(Tony Freeman/PhotoEdit)

Semantic memory
The vast, intricately organized knowledge system in long-term memory.

Episodic memory
Memory for personally experienced events.

Scripts
General representations of what occurs and when it occurs in a particular situation.

When child abuse and neglect, divorce, and other civil and criminal cases reach the courtroom, children are often called on to serve as witnesses. Having to provide such testimony can be difficult and traumatic. Almost always, children must report on events that were highly stressful. In doing so, they may have to speak against a parent or other relative toward whom they feel a strong sense of loyalty. In some family disputes, they may fear punishment for telling the truth. In addition, child witnesses are confronted with a strange and unfamiliar situation—at the very least an interview in the judge's chambers, and at most an open courtroom with judge, jury, and spectators and the possibility of unsympathetic cross-examination. Not surprisingly, there is considerable debate about the accuracy of children's recall under these conditions.

In most states, it is rare for children under age 5 to be asked to testify, whereas those 6 years and older often are. Children between ages 10 and 14 are generally assumed competent to appear in court (Saywitz, 1987). These guidelines make good sense in view of what we know about memory development. Compared to preschoolers, school-age children are better able to give detailed descriptions of past experiences and make accurate inferences about others' motives and intentions. Also, older children are more resistant to misleading and suggestive questions of the sort asked by attorneys when they probe for more information or, in cross-examination, try to influence the content of the child's response. However, when properly questioned, even preschoolers can recount episodes they have witnessed with considerable accuracy. And they are highly resistant to leading questions that imply physical or sexual abuse when it did not occur (Rudy & Goodman, 1991; Saywitz et al., 1991).

Does high stress at the time an event takes place seriously distort children's recall? According to some theorists, stress narrows attention, causing a sharp decline in memory performance. But others argue that the arousal associated with stress fosters more detailed and persistent memory (Christianson, 1992). Researchers have examined this question by studying children's recall of naturally occurring stressful events for which complete records can be obtained. In one investigation, observers rated 3- to 6-year-olds' degree of stress during an inoculation at the doctor's office. Several days later, the children were asked questions about the experience. Their memory was just as detailed as that of children who underwent a nonstressful procedure. And highly upset children, who cried intensely, actually showed better recall and were less suggestible than their less stressed counterparts (Goodman et al., 1991). These findings indicate that children's memory for a traumatic event involving their own bodies (of the kind that occurs in abuse cases) can be highly accurate. Nevertheless, research also shows that negative affect can impair young children's processing of events taking place in the wider field by interfering with encoding of information (Bugental et al., 1992).

Furthermore, when children are interviewed in a frightening courtroom setting, their ability to report past events completely and accurately is often reduced (Goodman et al., 1992). To ease the trauma of providing evidence, legal officials can use special interviewing methods, such as puppets who ask questions and through which the child answers. In some communities, "court schools" exist in which children are prepared for trial through visits to legal chambers and opportunities to role-play courtroom activities. As part of this process, children can be encouraged to admit not knowing an answer rather than guessing or going along with what an adult appears to expect (Cole & Loftus, 1987).

If a child is likely to experience severe distress as a result of appearing in court, then procedures exist for modifying typical courtroom practices. Children can testify over closed-circuit TV or behind a screen where they do not have to face the defendant. When it is not wise for the child to participate directly, expert witnesses can provide testimony that reports on the child's emotional condition and that contains important elements of the child's story (Bulkley, 1989).

terms of familiar events within an organized script framework. Once children develop an array of script sequences, objects that share the same function but occur in different scripts (eating toast for breakfast, peanut butter for lunch) may be joined together in a single, more typical semantic category (food).

The accuracy and completeness of children's episodic and reconstructive memory has recently taken on special applied significance. Increasingly, children are being called on to testify in court cases in which their recollections play a critical role in legal decisions affecting their own welfare. How reliable are children's memories under these conditions? See the Social Issues box above for a discussion of this topic.

Brief Review

During infancy, retrieval changes from recognition of previously experienced stimuli to include recall in the presence of salient retrieval cues. Over childhood and adolescence, recall improves steadily as the knowledge base becomes better organized and memory strategies are applied more effectively. Children, like adults, often recall complex, meaningful information in reconstructed form. Reconstructive processing improves as the ability to draw inferences expands, a change that permits children to better understand and recall prose material.

Growth in size and structure of the knowledge base has a major impact on memory performance. Like adults, young children remember everyday experiences in terms of scripts—general representations that become more elaborate with age. Scripts may serve as the developmental link between memory for personal experiences and our semantically organized, general knowledge system.

METACOGNITION

Throughout this chapter, we have mentioned many ways in which cognitive processing becomes more reflective and deliberate with age. These trends suggest that another form of knowledge we have not yet considered may influence how well children remember and solve problems. **Metacognition** refers to awareness and understanding of various aspects of thought. To work most effectively, the information-processing system must arrive at such realizations as, "I'd better write that phone number down or I'll forget it"; and "This paragraph is complicated; I'll have to read it again to grasp the author's point."

But for metacognitive knowledge to be helpful, children must apply it on a moment-by-moment basis. They must constantly monitor what they do, calling on what they know about thinking to overcome difficulties. In the following sections, we consider these higher-level, "executive" aspects of information processing.

Metacognitive Knowledge

With age, metacognitive knowledge expands in three ways. Children become increasingly concious of cognitive capacities, of strategies for processing information, and of task variables that facilitate or impede performance.

KNOWLEDGE OF COGNITIVE CAPACITIES. Listen closely to the conversations of young children, and you will find evidence that awareness of mental activity emerges remarkably early. Such words as "think," "remember," and "pretend" are among the first verbs to appear in children's vocabularies. After age $2\frac{1}{2}$, they use them appropriately to refer to internal states, as when they say, "It's not real, I was just pretending" or "I thought the socks were in the drawer, 'cept they weren't" (Wellman, 1985, p. 176).

Piaget (1926/1930) first suggested that young children have difficulty distinguishing between mental events and external reality. They separate these realms quite well in everyday language, as the examples just given reveal. But when questioned about subtle distinctions, they show confusion. For example, 4-year-olds believe that if you get an answer right, then you "knew" and "remembered," but if you get it wrong, then you "guessed" or "forgot" (Miscione et al., 1978; Moore, Bryant, & Furrow, 1989). They do not realize that the meaning of these terms depends on people's *certainty about their knowledge,* not objective performance. Furthermore, young preschoolers are not yet aware that what they know about an object depends on the sensory modality through which it is perceived. Before age 4 to 5, many say that a puppet can tell that a ball is blue by feeling it or that a sponge is wet by looking at it (O'Neill, Astington, & Flavell, 1992). Finally, prior to age 6, children think that all events must be directly observed to be known. They do not understand that *mental inferences* can be a source of knowledge (Sodian & Wimmer, 1987).

Even though their grasp of cognitive activities is incomplete, young children realize that the mind is a limited-capacity device, and both internal and external factors affect its functioning. Three- and 4-year-olds know that noise, lack of inter-

Metacognition
Awareness and understanding of various aspects of thought that affect performance.

est, and thinking about other things can interfere with attention to a task (Miller & Zalenski, 1982). And by age 5, most children understand that information briefly presented or that must be retained for a long time is more likely to be forgotten (Kreutzer, Leonard, & Flavell, 1975). Nevertheless, school-age youngsters have a more complete grasp of the impact of psychological factors on performance. For example, they recognize that doing well on a task depends on focusing attention—concentrating, wanting to do it, and not being tempted by anything else (Miller & Bigi, 1979).

How, then, should we describe the difference between the young child's understanding of cognitive capacities and that of the older child? Preschoolers know that we have an internal mental life, but they seem to view the mind as a passive container of information. Below age 4 or 5, they believe that physical experience with the environment determines mental experience. In contrast, older children regard the mind as an active, constructive agent that selects and transforms information and affects how the world is perceived (Pillow, 1988b; Wellman, 1988a). Look again at the findings we have discussed, and note how they illustrate this change.

*S*chool-age children show improved metacognitive knowledge. This child is aware that writing down a phone message is a very effective strategy for overcoming the limits of memory capacity. (FRANK SITEMAN/THE PICTURE CUBE)

KNOWLEDGE OF STRATEGIES AND TASK VARIABLES. Consistent with their more active view of the mind, school-age children are far more conscious of strategies for processing information than are preschoolers. By third grade, awareness of memory strategies is sophisticated. Children realize that in studying material for later recall, it is helpful to devote most effort to items you know least well. And when asked, they show that they know quite a bit about effective memory strategies. Witness this 8-year-old's response to the question of what she would do to remember a phone number:

> Say the number is 663-8854. Then what I'd do is—say that my number is 663, so I won't have to remember that really. And then I would think now I've got to remember 88. Now I'm 8 years old, so I can remember, say, my age two times. Then I say how old my brother is, and how old he was last year. And that's how I'd usually remember that phone number. [Is that how you would most often remember a phone number?] Well, usually I write it down. (Kreutzer, Leonard, & Flavell, 1975, p. 11)

Older children also have a more complete understanding of task variables that affect performance. Kindergartners are aware of a few factors that make a memory task easy or hard—for example, the number of items, their familiarity, how much study time is available, and whether they must recognize or recall them (Speer & Flavell, 1979; Wellman, 1977). But by the mid-elementary school years, children are aware of much more—for example, that a list of semantically related items is easier to remember than unrelated items and that recalling prose material word for word is more difficult than paraphrasing it (Kreutzer, Leonard, & Flavell, 1975; Tenney, 1975).

Once children become conscious of the many factors that influence mental activity, they combine them into an integrated understanding. School-age children take account of *interactions* among variables—how age and motivation of the learner, effective use of strategies, and nature and difficulty of the task work together to affect cognitive performance (Wellman, 1985). In this way, metacognition truly becomes comprehensive in middle childhood.

Self-Regulation

Although knowledge of mental activity expands, many studies report that it is only weakly related to task performance (Byrd & Gholson, 1985; Flavell, 1976; Moynahan, 1973). This suggests that school-age children have difficulty with the second aspect of metacognition mentioned earlier: putting what they know into action. They are not yet good at **self-regulation,** the process of continuously monitoring progress toward a goal, checking outcomes, and redirecting unsuccessful efforts.

One way self-regulation can be assessed is by looking at children's **comprehension monitoring,** or sensitivity to how well they understand a spoken or written message. In one study, fourth- and sixth-graders listened to short essays containing missing or inconsistent information, as in the following passage:

> Janet decided to play some records. She looked through all the songs and picked out her favorite. It was a song called "As Time Goes By." She said to herself, "I haven't played this one in a long time. She played it quietly so she would not disturb her family. She was out of practice so it sounded funny sometimes.* Janet sang along with the music. She knew some of the words and she hummed the rest. The last verse of the song was the part she liked the best. After that song was finished she played another one. [*Sentence is inconsistent with Janet playing records.] (Beal, 1990, p. 249)

Sixth-graders detected more text problems than fourth-graders, a finding confirmed by other research. In fact, school-age children even fail to notice gaps and contradictions in prose that they produce themselves—a major reason they rarely revise their writing (Fitzgerald, 1987). Their self-regulatory difficulties do not stem from an inability to adequately repair the text. Once problems are pointed out, they are quite good at correcting them (Beal, 1990).

Current evidence indicates that self-regulation of cognitive performance develops slowly over the childhood years. This is not surprising, since monitoring learning outcomes is a cognitively demanding activity, requiring constant evaluation of effort and progress. By adolescence, self-regulation is a strong predictor of academic success. Students who do well in school know when they possess a skill and when they do not. If they run up against obstacles, such as poor study conditions, a confusing text passage, or an unclear class lecture, they take steps to organize the learning environment, review the material, or seek other sources of support. This active, purposeful approach contrasts sharply with the passive orientation of students who do poorly (Borkowski et al., 1990; Zimmerman, 1990).

Parents and teachers can foster children's self-regulatory skills by pointing out the special demands of tasks, encouraging the use of strategies, and emphasizing the value of self-correction. As adults ask children questions and help them monitor their own behavior in circumstances where they are likely to encounter difficulties, children can internalize these procedures and make them part of their own self-regulatory skills.

Think about these practical suggestions for fostering self-regulation. Do they resemble Vygotsky's theory about the self-guiding role of private speech, which we discussed in Chapter 6? The ideas are much the same, since Vygotsky emphasized that the self-regulatory function of children's speech-to-self has its origins in dialogues with others. In fact, Vygotsky's theory has been a source of inspiration for *metacognitive training*. Many studies show that providing children with instructions to check and monitor their progress toward a goal has a substantial impact on their learning (Pressley & Ghatala, 1990). In addition, training that goes beyond demonstrating an effective strategy to emphasizing why it is effective enhances children's use of it in new situations (Fabricius & Cavalier, 1989; Moely et al., 1986). When adults tell children *why* and not just *what* to do, they provide a rationale for future action. Then children learn not only how to get a particular task done, but what to do when faced with new problems (Brown et al., 1983).

In later chapters, we will return to the topic of self-regulation, since it also has a major influence on emotional and social development. And as we turn now to development within academic skill areas, notice how the importance of self-regulation is ever-present. But before we consider these domains of learning, you may find to helpful to review the Milestones table on page 294, which summarizes the diverse changes in general information processing that we have discussed.

Self-regulation

The process of continuously monitoring progress toward a goal, checking outcomes, and redirecting unsuccessful efforts.

Comprehension monitoring

Sensitivity to how well one understands a spoken or written message.

MILESTONES
DEVELOPMENT OF GENERAL INFORMATION PROCESSING

Age	Basic Capacities	Strategies	Knowledge	Metacognition
Birth–5 years	•Organization of the mental system into sensory register, short-term memory, and long-term memory is adultlike. •Many basic capacities are present, including attention, recognition, recall, and reconstruction.  •Overall capacity, or size, of the system increases.	•Sensory processing moves from locating objects in space to discriminating their fine-grained, distinctive features. •Attention becomes more focused and sustained. •Beginnings of memory strategies are present, but they are seldom used spontaneously and have little effect on performance.	•Knowledge expands and shows adultlike organization in areas of expertise. •Familar events are remembered in terms of scripts, which become more elaborate with age.	•Consciousness of mental activity emerges. •Differentiation among a variety of mental acts occurs, including knowing, remembering, guessing, and forgetting. •Awareness of a limited-capacity mental system is present, but preschoolers view it as a passive container of information.
6–10 years	•Overall capacity, or size, of the system continues to increase.	•Discrimination of distinctive features in sensory processing improves. •Attention becomes more controlled, adaptable, and planful. •Memory strategies of rehearsal and semantic organization are executed more effectively. •Capacity to draw inferences in reconstructive processing expands.	•Knowledge continues to expand and become more intricately organized, which facilitates strategy use and retrieval.	•Knowledge of the impact of psychological factors on performance, including focusing attention and applying memory strategies, increases. •Knowledge of the impact of task variables on performance increases and is integrated with other factors. •Self-regulation improves slowly.
11 years–adulthood	•Overall capacity, or size, of the system continues to increase, but at a slower pace than in childhood.	•Memory strategy of elaboration appears and improves.	•Knowledge continues to expand and become better organized.	•Metacognitive knowledge and self-regulation continue to improve.

Note: These milestones represent overall age trends. Individual differences exist in the precise age at which each milestone is attained.

C hildren's metacognitive knowledge changes from a passive to an active view of mental functioning as awareness of a wider array of cognitive capacities, strategies, and task variables expands. Self-regulation develops slowly over the childhood years; children do not always apply their metacognitive understanding. Teaching children self-regulatory skills can have broad effects on their learning.

APPLICATIONS OF INFORMATION PROCESSING TO ACADEMIC LEARNING

Over the past decade, interest in the development of information processing has been extended to children's mastery of academic skills. A rapidly growing body of research focuses on learning in different subject-matter areas. Because paths to competence vary across knowledge domains, each area has been studied separately. Nevertheless, the research has features in common. First, investigators identify the cognitive capacities and strategies necessary for skilled performance, try to trace their development, and pinpoint the ways in which good and poor learners differ. Then using this information, they design and test instructional procedures to improve children's learning. In the following sections, we discuss a sampling of these efforts in reading, mathematics, and scientific reasoning.

Reading

As Table 7.1 shows, while reading we execute many skills simultaneously, taxing all aspects of our information-processing systems. We must perceive single letters and letter combinations, translate them into speech sounds, learn to recognize the visual appearance of many common words, hold chunks of text in working memory while interpreting their meaning, and combine the meanings of various parts of a text passage into an understandable whole. In fact, reading is such a demanding process that if one or more skills are poorly developed, they will compete for attentional resources in our limited memories, and reading performance will decline (Frederiksen & Warren, 1987; Perfetti, 1988).

How do children go about identifying written words when first learning to read? Robert Siegler (1986) has devised and tested a *model of strategy choice,* which shows that children rely on several strategies, choosing adaptively among them. Automatic retrieval is the most efficient technique, and each time children encounter a new word, they may try it. But if a particular combination of letters is not strongly associated with any words they know, children resort to backup

---

TABLE 7.1 *Cognitive Components of Skilled Reading*

LOWER-LEVEL SKILLS	HIGHER-LEVEL SKILLS
• Perceptual encoding of single letters and letter combinations	• Locating meanings of written words in long-term memory
• Decoding single letters and letter combinations into speech sounds	• Combining word meanings into clauses and sentences
• Sight recognition of common words, to reduce time-consuming decoding	• Using prose context to refine word, clause, and sentence meanings
• Holding chunks of text in working memory for higher-level processing	• Combining sentence meanings into higher-order relations
	• Using previous knowledge to draw inferences about text meaning
	• Engaging in comprehension monitoring to check processing accuracy

SOURCES: Frederiksen & Warren, 1987; Perfetti, 1988.

*P*arents who read to their young
children provide vital preparation for
the complex task of independent
reading. (STEPHEN MARKS)

strategies, such as sounding out the word or asking for help. With practice, the appearance of each word becomes more strongly associated with its identity in long-term memory. When this happens, children gradually give up capacity-consuming backup strategies in favor of rapid retrieval. As we will see shortly, Siegler's model of strategy choice is broadly applicable. It describes how children make adaptive strategy choices that strike a balance between speed and accuracy on a diverse array of tasks.

Currently, psychologists and educators are engaged in a "great debate" about how to teach beginning reading. On one side are those who take a **whole-language approach** to reading instruction. They argue that reading should be taught to young children in a way that parallels natural language learning. From the very beginning, children should be exposed to text in its complete form—stories, poems, letters, posters, and lists—so they can appreciate the communicative function of written language. According to these experts, as long as reading is kept whole and meaningful, children will be motivated to discover the specific skills they need as they gain experience with the printed word (Goodman, 1986; Watson, 1989). On the other side of the debate are those who advocate a **basic-skills approach.** According to this view, children should be given simplified text materials. At first, they should be coached on phonics—the basic rules for translating written symbols into sounds. Only later, after they have mastered these skills, should they get complex reading material (Rayner & Pollatsek, 1989; Samuels, 1985).

Research does not yet show clear-cut superiority for either of these approaches (McKenna, Robinson, & Miller, 1990). In fact, a third, more moderate group of experts believes that children learn best when they receive a balanced mixture of both (Barr, 1991). Learning the basics   relations between letters and sounds—enables children to decipher words they have never seen before. As this process becomes more automatic, it releases children's attention to the higher-level activities involved in comprehending the text's meaning. But if practice in basic skills is overemphasized, children may lose sight of the goal of reading—understanding. Many teachers report cases of pupils who can read aloud fluently but who comprehend very little. These children might have been spared serious reading problems if they had received meaning-based instruction that included attention to basic skills.

Reading development begins long before formal schooling. It builds on a broad foundation of spoken language, experience with literacy materials, and understanding of the world. Parents who converse with their preschoolers, take

Whole-language approach

An approach to beginning reading instruction that parallels children's natural language learning and keeps reading materials whole and meaningful.

Basic-skills approach

An approach to beginning reading instruction that emphasizes training in phonics—the basic rules for translating written symbols into sounds—and simplified reading materials.

them on outings, and expose them to print in everyday life have youngsters who arrive at school with both general and literacy-related knowledge that eases the difficulty of early text processing (McGee & Richgels, 1990). Reading to young children seems to be especially important. It is related to preschoolers' understanding of the purpose and features of written symbols and to later success in school (Crain-Thoreson & Dale, 1992; Wells, 1985).

Mathematics

Mathematical reasoning, like reading, builds on a foundation of informally acquired knowledge. By 4 months, infants have a primitive sense of number. Habituation–dishabituation research shows that they can discriminate one from two objects and two from three (Strauss & Curtis, 1984). At 7 months, babies can even recognize the same small quantity when it is presented in different sensory modalities (vision and sound) (Starkey, Spelke, & Gelman, 1983).

In the early preschool years, children start to attach verbal labels (such as lots, little, big, and small) to different amounts and sizes. And between ages 2 and 3, many begin to count. However, counting at first is little more than a memorized routine. Often numbers are recited in an unbroken string like this: "Onetwothreefourfivesix!" Or children repeat a few number words while vaguely pointing toward objects they have seen others count (Fuson, 1988).

Very soon, however, counting strategies become more precise. Most 3-year-olds have established an accurate one-to-one correspondence between a short sequence of number words and the items they represent (Gelman & Gallistel, 1986). Sometime between ages 3 and 4, they grasp the vital principle of _cardinality_. They understand that the last word in a counting sequence indicates the quantity of items in a set. They also know that if two groups of objects match up (for example, every jar has its own spoon or every doll its own cup), then each set contains the same number of items (Becker, 1989; Fuson, 1988; Sophian, 1988).*

Mastery of cardinality quickly increases the efficiency of children's counting. By the late preschool years, children no longer need to start a counting sequence with the number "one." Instead, knowing that there are six items in one pile and some additional ones in another, they begin with the number "six" and _count on_ to determine the total quantity. Eventually, they generalize this strategy and _count down_ to find out how many items remain after some are taken away. Once these strategies are mastered, children start to manipulate numbers without requiring that countable objects be physically present (Fuson, 1988). At this point, counting on fingers becomes an intermediate step on the way to automatic performance of basic arithmetic operations. By age 8 or 9, children naturally apply their additive understanding to multiplication, first approaching it as a kind of repeated addition (Nesher, 1988).

Cross-cultural evidence suggests that the basic arithmetic knowledge just described emerges universally around the world (Resnick, 1989; Saxe, Guberman, & Gearhart, 1987). However, children may acquire it at different rates, depending on the extent to which informal counting experiences are available in their everyday lives. In homes and preschools where adults provide many occasions and requests for quantification, children construct these basic concepts sooner. Then they are solidly available as supports for the wide variety of mathematical skills that are taught in school.

Once children reach school, how do they acquire basic math facts that will permit them to solve more advanced problems efficiently? As with word identification in reading, Siegler studied this process in mathematics, applying his model of strategy choice (Siegler & Jenkins, 1989; Siegler & Shrager, 1984). Again, he discovered that children use diverse strategies adaptively. For example, when given

_C_ounting on fingers is an early, spontaneous strategy that children use to learn basic math facts. As they repeatedly use this technique and others, answers become more strongly associated with problems, and children give up the strategy in favor of automatic retrieval. (ELIZABETH ZUCKERMAN/PHOTOEDIT)

_____

*As Piaget's conservation-of-number task reveals, at first, preschoolers' understanding of cardinality is fragile. It is easily overcome by the appearance of a set of objects. However, the findings reported here indicate that young children understand much more about numbers than Piaget assumed.

the problem 5 + 3, children typically try to retrieve the answer automatically. If this does not work, they resort to backup procedures. They may count from one, put up three fingers on one hand and five on the other but recognize the total without counting, apply the count-on strategy described earlier, or sometimes guess. As children apply backup strategies, they receive feedback about the speed and accuracy with which each works on particular problems. This information influences their later choices. Gradually, children start to emphasize strategies that result in correct and quicker solutions. In the process, answers become more strongly associated with problems, and children move toward the most efficient technique—automatic retrieval.

Return for a moment to the description of children's identification of written words on pages 295–296, and note the similarity between strategy choice and discovery of efficient procedures in both reading and math. Siegler (1989) reports similar findings for other domains as well, including time telling, spelling, and memory tasks. His research suggests a common approach to acquiring new knowledge in which diverse strategies are tried and the most successful ones survive, even though the specific strategies and information learned vary widely across domains. As Siegler comments, "(S)trategy choices are made through a general choice process that operates on task-specific representations" (p. 1). Notice how this conclusion supports the view that the mind has both general and domain-specific properties, which interact to produce cognitive change.

Arguments about how to teach mathematics resemble the positions discussed earlier in the area of reading. Extensive speeded practice to promote automatic retrieval is pitted against "number sense," or understanding. Further research is likely to show that some blend of these two approaches is most beneficial. In the case of basic number facts, Siegler (1988) found that compared to good students, poor students move too quickly toward trying to retrieve answers automatically. Their responses are often wrong because they have not used backup strategies accurately and long enough to build strong associations between problems and correct solutions. This suggests that teaching pupils how to apply backup strategies successfully and encouraging them to take time to do so is vital for promoting successful math fact retrieval.

A similar picture emerges when we look at pupils who experience difficulties with more complex skills, such as carrying in addition, borrowing in subtraction, and operating with decimals and fractions. Often these youngsters apply a method that is close to what they have been taught but that yields a wrong answer. Their mistakes indicate that they have tried to memorize a procedure but do not understand the basis for it (Resnick, 1989). For example, look at the following subtraction errors:

$$
\begin{array}{r}
427 \\
-138 \\
\hline
311
\end{array}
\qquad
\begin{array}{r}
^6\!\not{7}\,0\,0\,^1\!2 \\
-544\ 5 \\
\hline
144\ 7
\end{array}
$$

In the first problem, the child consistently subtracts a smaller from a larger digit, regardless of which is on top. In the second, columns with zeros are repeatedly skipped in a borrowing operation, and whenever there is a zero on top, the bottom digit is written as the answer. Researchers believe that an overemphasis on drill-oriented math that discourages children from using their naturally acquired counting strategies to grasp new skills underlies these difficulties (Fuson, 1988; Resnick, 1989).

Cross-cultural evidence suggests that American math instruction may have gone too far in emphasizing computational drill over numerical understanding. As we will see in greater detail in Chapter 15, children in Asian nations are ahead of American pupils in mathematical development at all levels of schooling. As the Cultural Influences box on the following page illustrates, they receive a variety of supports for acquiring mathematical knowledge that are not available to American

Elementary school pupils in the United States find multidigit addition and subtraction problems requiring trades between columns to be very difficult. Results of a recent national assessment of math achievement revealed that half of third-graders gave wrong answers to a three-digit subtraction problem of this kind (Kouba et al., 1988). Many American children try to solve such problems by rote, without grasping crucial aspects of the procedure. They seem to have a confused, single-digit conception of multidigit numbers. For example, they tend to view the 3 in 5,386 as being just 3 rather than 300. As a result, when they carry to or borrow from this column, they are likely to compute the value incorrectly.

Korean 7- and 8-year-olds, by contrast, are highly accurate at multidigit addition and subtraction. What accounts for their superior performance? To find out, Karen Fuson and Youngshim Kwon (1992) asked Korean second- and third-graders to solve a set of two- and three-digit problems, observed their methods, and asked questions about their knowledge. The performance of the children was excellent. For example, even though second-graders had not yet received formal instruction on three-digit problems, their scores were nearly perfect in addition. In subtraction, they solved 78 percent of three-digit problems correctly.

Quantitative understanding of multidigit numbers was clearly responsible for the Korean pupils' exceptional competence. Almost all identified the tens' and hundreds' columns correctly as they described how to solve problems. And no Korean child viewed a "1" mark signaling trading to the tens column as "one," as American children typically do. Instead, they clearly identified it as "ten." Especially remarkable were third-graders' clear explanations of how to perform complex multistep trading operations that stump their American agemates. Here are two examples:

400
− 165
235

I borrowed one hundred. And I gave nine tens to the tens' column and the remainder, ten, to the ones' column.

As four becomes three, the zero in the tens' column becomes nine and the zero in the ones' column becomes ten. (Fuson & Kwon, 1992, p. 502)

In fact, most Korean third-graders no longer wrote extra marks when solving problems like this one. They could handle intricate trading procedures mentally.

Fuson and Kwon point to several cultural, language-based, and instructional factors that account for the sharp skill advantage of Korean over American pupils. First, use of the metric system in Korea, which presents one, ten, hundred, and thousand values in all areas of measurement, helps children think in ways consistent with place value. Second, English words for two-digit numbers (such as twelve and thirteen) are irregular and do not convey the idea of tens and ones. The structure of Korean number words ("ten two," "ten three") makes this composition obvious. Third, Korean teachers use phrases that explicitly describe the trading operation. Instead of carrying, they say "raise up," and instead of borrowing, they say "bring down." Fourth, textbooks in Korea do a much better job of helping children discriminate place values. Hundreds', tens', and ones' columns have separate color codes, and pictures depicting their relative sizes are often linked to addition and subtraction problems (Fuson, 1992). Finally, multidigit problems are introduced earlier in Korean schools. American pupils spend more time on problems requiring no trading, increasing the chances that they will apply single-digit concepts inappropriately to multidigit numbers.

In sum, what appears at first glance to be the same cognitive task is actually quite different for American than Korean pupils. Fuson and Kwon's findings highlight several ways in which adults might ease children's mastery of numerical concepts in the United States.

children. The result is deeper processing—the formation of secure numerical concepts that provide a firm foundation for mastery of new skills.

Scientific Reasoning

What does it mean to think scientifically? In Chapter 1, we addressed this question (see page 3). The heart of scientific reasoning is the coordination of theories with evidence. A scientist can clearly describe the theory that he or she favors, knows what evidence is needed to support it and what would refute it, and can explain how pitting evidence against available theories led to the acceptance of one theory as opposed to others.

Deanna Kuhn and her collaborators (1988) have conducted extensive investigations into the development of scientific reasoning. Third-, sixth-, and ninth-graders, adults of mixed educational backgrounds, and professional scientists were provided with evidence, sometimes consistent and sometimes conflicting with theories. This was followed by questions about the validity of each theory. In one problem, subjects were asked to theorize about which of several features of sports balls, such as size, color, or surface texture, influences the quality of a player's serve. Then they were told about the theory of Mr. (or Ms.) S, who believed that size of the ball was important, and the theory of Mr. (or Ms.) C, who believed that color made a difference. Next, the interviewer presented evidence by placing balls with certain characteristics in two baskets labeled "good serve" and "bad serve."

Kuhn found that third- and sixth-graders, and older subjects to a lesser degree, reason in ways that are very different from scientists. The youngest subjects had the greatest difficulty coordinating theories with evidence. When evidence contradicted their preferred theory, they sometimes made slight but inadequate adjustments in the theory, without conscious awareness that they had done so. More often, children ignored conflicting evidence or misinterpreted it in ways consistent with their theory. Their willingness to distort evidence in this way is dramatically illustrated by Allen, a third-grader, who judged that size was causal (with large balls producing good serves and small balls bad serves). When shown incomplete evidence—a single, large light-colored ball in the "good serve" basket and no balls in the "bad serve" basket—Allen insisted that it proved Mr. S's theory (which was also his own) to be correct. Asked to explain, he stated flatly, "Because this ball is big. . . . the color doesn't really matter" (Kuhn, 1989, p. 677).

These findings reveal that children have special difficulty discriminating theory from evidence. Instead of regarding pieces of evidence as separate from and bearing on a theory, they blend the two into a single representation of "the way things are." What are the cognitive skills that support scientific reasoning? According to Kuhn (1989), metacognition—thinking about thought—is most important. Individuals must represent the theory as an object of thought rather than a mirror image of reality. And they must also set aside their own preference for the theory and consider what the evidence says about it as their sole basis for judgment.

How does the development of skill in coordinating theory with evidence take place? Education clearly makes a difference, since the performance of older subjects in Kuhn's research was strongly influenced by years of schooling. But even at advanced levels of education, scientific reasoning is rarely taught directly. Instead, in virtually all subject-matter areas, individuals receive practice in setting aside their own experiences and beliefs to infer conclusions that follow from information given. Many experiences of this kind probably foster scientific reasoning (Kuhn, Amsel, & O'Loughlin, 1988).

This suggests that the same skills might develop in contexts that offer children repeated opportunities to match theories against evidence. In a study that examined this idea, the reasoning strategies of fifth- and sixth-graders were followed over eight sessions as they experimented with a microcomputer racetrack. The children were asked to determine which of five factors affected the speed of race cars: engine size, wheel size, presence of tail fins, presence of a muffler, or color. An adult showed them how they could design road tests with the computer to test predictions (Schauble, 1990).

Children's strategies were very disorganized. Although they were given logbooks to record plans and comparisons, few used them. No child worked out an overall approach to the problem ahead of time. Many of their comparisons of features did not permit valid conclusions. And children often judged evidence to be consistent with their own prior theories when it was not. Nevertheless, performance improved steadily (even though at the end of the study it was still far from perfect). For each road test, children were asked to state a plan, and after they ran a comparison, they had to draw a conclusion and justify it. As Figure 7.12 shows, the percentage of high-level plans, valid comparisons, and appropriate conclusions and justifications increased. Continuous opportunities to pit theory against evidence encouraged children to reflect on their current strategies, revise them, and think more scientifically.

Perhaps you noticed that the capacity to coordinate theory with evidence shares features with Piaget's formal operational stage. Kuhn's work shows that scientific

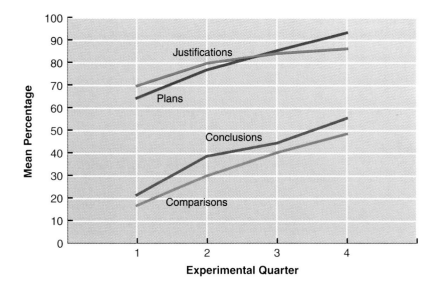

FIGURE 7.12 Changes over time in fifth- and sixth-graders' scientific reasoning on a microcomputer racetrack problem. High-level plans, valid comparisons, and appropriate conclusions and justifications increased with repeated practice in pitting theory against evidence. Still, at the end of the 8-week study, scientific reasoning was far from perfect. (From "Belief Revision in Children: The Role of Prior Knowledge and Strategies for Generating Evidence" by L. Schauble, 1990, *Journal of Experimental Child Psychology*, *49*, p. 46. Copyright © 1990 by Academic Press. Reprinted by permission.)

reasoning becomes more common during adolescence, just as Piaget assumed. It also depends on the metacognitive skills to which Piaget referred when he spoke of "operating on operations" (see Chapter 6, page 248). Nevertheless, recent findings indicate that scientific reasoning is not the result of an abrupt, stagewise change in general capacity. Instead, it develops gradually out of specific experiences that require individuals to match theories against evidence. Identifying tasks and contexts that promote scientific reasoning opens the door to instructional interventions that support its development. In all of these ways, the new wave of research on scientific thinking skills reflects core tenets of the information-processing perspective.

Brief Review

R ecently, information-processing researchers have turned their attention to children's academic learning. Efficient reading requires simultaneous execution of many lower-level and higher-level skills. It builds on a firm foundation of general and literacy-related knowledge acquired during the preschool years. Similarly, young children's spontaneously constructed number concepts and counting strategies serve as the basis for mathematics taught in school. Siegler's model of strategy choice explains how children use diverse strategies adaptively to master basic knowledge in academic domains. In both reading and math, instruction that provides balanced attention to basic skills and understanding seems most beneficial. Tasks that offer repeated practice in coordinating theory with evidence promote metacognitive skills necessary for scientific reasoning.

EVALUATION OF THE
INFORMATION-PROCESSING APPROACH

A major strength of the information-processing approach is its explicitness and precision in breaking down complex cognitive performance into its components. Information processing has provided a wealth of detailed evidence on how younger versus older, and more skilled versus less skilled individuals perceive, attend to, memorize, and solve problems. Compared to Piaget's theory, it also offers a more precise account of cognitive change. Because information-processing researchers view thinking as a collection of separate skills rather than a single entity, they rely on many mechanisms to explain development. The most important ones are summarized in Table 7.2. As you review them, think back to research discussed in this chapter that illustrates the role of each. Finally, information processing is beginning to clarify which aspects of cognitive development are domain-specific, which are general, and how they work together. In doing so, it is

TABLE 7.2 Mechanisms of Cognitive Change from the Information-Processing Perspective

MECHANISM	DESCRIPTION
Overall processing capacity	Size of the mental system increases as a result of brain maturation.
Processing efficiency	Speed of basic operations increases, consuming less capacity in working memory and freeing up resources for other mental activities.
Encoding information	Encoding, in the form of sensory processing and attention, becomes more detailed and selective.
Strategy execution	Strategies become more effective, improving storage, representation, and retrieval of information.
Knowledge	Amount and structure of domain-specific knowledge increases, easing strategy use and retrieval.
Metacognition	Awareness and understanding of cognitive processes expands and self-regulation improves, leading strategies to be applied in a wider range of situations.

SOURCE: Kuhn, 1992.

contributing to our understanding of academic learning and to instructional methods that enhance school performance.

Nevertheless, the information-processing perspective has several limitations that prevent it from serving as a complete account of cognitive development. The first, ironically, stems from its central strength: by analyzing cognition into its components, information processing has had difficulty putting them back together into a broad comprehensive theory. For this reason, many child development specialists resist abandoning Piaget's view in favor of it. In fact, efforts to build general theories of development within an information-processing framework, such as Case's M-space and Fischer's skill theory, have succeeded only by retaining essential features of Piaget's stage sequence.

Furthermore, the computer metaphor, although bringing precision to research on the human mind, has drawbacks. Computer models of cognitive processing, though complex in their own right, do not reflect the richness of many real-life learning experiences. For example, they tell us little about aspects of cognition that are not linear and logical, such as imagination and creativity (Greeno, 1989). In addition, computers cannot feel, and they do not have desires, interests, and intentions. Although they interact with other machines through networks and modems, they cannot form friendships, take another person's perspective, or adopt moral and social values. Perhaps because of the narrowness of the computer metaphor, information processing has not yet told us much about the links between cognition and other areas of development. Currently, researchers are intensely interested in whether information processing can enhance our understanding of how children think about their social world. We will see some examples of this new emphasis in later chapters. But it is still true that extensions of Piaget's theory prevail when it comes to research on children's social and moral development.

Despite its shortcomings, the information-processing approach holds great promise for the future. New breakthroughs in understanding the joint operation of mechanisms of cognitive development, specifying the processing capacities of infants and toddlers (who remain understudied), and designing instructional methods that support children's learning are likely to take place in the years to come.

CHAPTER SUMMARY

The Information-Processing Approach

- The information-processing approach views the mind as a complex, symbol-manipulating system that operates much like a computer. The computer analogy helps researchers analyze thought into separate components, each of which can be studied thoroughly to yield a detailed understanding of what children and adults do when faced with a task or problem.

General Models of Information Processing

- Atkinson and Shiffrin's **store model** assumes that information moves through three parts of the mental system, where **control processes,** or **mental strategies,** operate on it so that it can be retained and used efficiently. The **sensory register** and **short-term memory** are limited in capacity. **Long-term memory,** which contains our permanent knowledge base, is limitless. The **serial-position effect** supports the distinction between short- and long-term memory.
- According to the **levels-of-processing model,** retention depends on the depth to which information is processed by the system. Instead of a short-term memory store, our limited cognitive capacity is due to **working memory,** a conscious pool of attentional resources from which our information-processing activities draw. As tasks become well learned, or automatic, they consume less attention, and resources are freed for other activities.

Developmental Models of Information Processing

- Several developmental models that reinterpret Piaget's theory within an information-processing framework have attracted widespread attention. According to Case, development involves the expansion of **mental space,** or **M-space,** a computerlike construct similar to working memory. Brain maturation and automaticity of schemes due to practice release extra M-space for the child to combine old schemes and generate new ones. When schemes are consolidated into central conceptual structures, M-space increases further, and the child moves up to a new Piagetian stage.
- Fischer's **skill theory** emphasizes that each child has an optimal skill level that depends on brain maturation and corresponds to a Piagetian stage. Within each skill level, progress depends on the opportunities to practice schemes in a wide range of situations and integrate them into higher-order skills.
- Both Case and Fischer believe the mind undergoes general changes with age. Currently, theorists disagree on whether the human mental system is a general or a modular computing device.

Sensory Processing

- According to **differentiation theory,** development of sensory processing involves the detection of increasingly fine-grained, invariant features in the external world. **Enrichment theory,** a competing viewpoint, regards perceptual organization as located inside the individual. As cognitive schemes are refined, perceptual intake from the environment is enriched accordingly.

Attentional Processing

- With age, children sustain attention for longer periods of time and select stimuli on the basis of their relevance to task goals. Older children are better at adapting attention to the momentary requirements of situations. Attention also becomes more planful, as children's visual search behavior reveals.

Short-Term or Working Memory

- Although the beginnings of **memory strategies** can be seen during the preschool years, young children rarely engage in **rehearsal** or **organization** when given unfamiliar materials. Both **production** and **control deficiencies** underlie the early use of memory strategies. **Elaboration** is a late-developing memory skill that rarely appears before age 11.
- Like young children, people in non-Western cultures who have no formal schooling do not spontaneously use or benefit from instruction in memory strategies. Tasks requiring children to memorize unrelated pieces of information in school promote deliberate memory strategies in middle childhood.

Long-Term Memory

- **Recognition,** the simplest form of retrieval, is a fairly automatic process that is highly accurate by the preschool years. In contrast, **recall,** or remembering an absent stimulus, is more difficult and shows much greater improvement with age. **Infantile amnesia** may be due to changes in brain functioning and memory processing during the first few years of life.
- Even young children engage in **reconstruction** when remembering complex, meaningful material. Over middle childhood, the ability to draw inferences from prose material expands.
- Gains in the size and structure of **domain-specific knowledge** enhance memory performance by making new, related information easier to store and retrieve. However, children differ not only in what they know, but in how well they use their knowledge to acquire new information. Knowledge and memory strategies support one another.
- Like adults, young children remember familiar experiences in terms of scripts—general representations of what occurs and when it occurs in a particular situation. Scripts may be the developmental link in the transition from episodic to semantic memory.

Metacognition

- **Metacognition**—awareness and understanding of cognitive capacities, strategies, and task variables—changes from a passive to an active view of mental functioning in middle childhood. **Self-regulation**—using metacognitive knowledge to monitor performance—develops slowly over the childhood years. Instruction in self-regulation helps children generalize effective strategies to new situations.

Applications of Information Processing to Academic Learning

- Skilled reading involves executing many lower- and higher-level skills simultaneously, taxing all aspects of the information-processing system. Experts disagree on whether a **whole-language approach** or **basic-skills approach** should be used to teach beginning reading. A balanced mixture of both is probably most effective. Reading builds on general and literacy-related knowledge acquired before formal schooling.
- Children develop counting strategies and construct basic mathematical concepts during the preschool years. Siegler's model of strategy choice explains how children use diverse strategies adaptively to learn basic math facts, identify written words in reading, and acquire knowledge in other domains. As with reading, instruction that combines practice in basic skills with conceptual understanding seems best in mathematics.
- Children (and to a lesser degree, adolescents and adults) have difficulty coordinating theories with evidence. Tasks that offer repeated practice in pitting theories against evidence promote the metacognitive skills necessary for scientific reasoning.

Evaluation of the Information-Processing Approach

- A major strength of the information-processing approach is its explicitness and precision in breaking down cognition into separate elements so each can be studied thoroughly. So far, information processing has not led to a broad, comprehensive theory or told us much about the links between cognition and other areas of development.

IMPORTANT TERMS AND CONCEPTS

store model (p. 266)
control processes, or mental strategies (p. 267)
sensory register (p. 267)
short-term memory (p. 267)
long-term memory (p. 268)
serial-position effect (p. 268)
levels-of-processing model (p. 268)
working memory (p. 269)
mental space, or M-space (p. 272)
skill theory (p. 272)
differentiation theory (p. 274)

enrichment theory (p. 275)
attention-deficit hyperactivity disorder (ADHD) (p. 279)
memory strategies (p. 280)
rehearsal (p. 280)
production deficiency (p. 280)
control deficiency (p. 280)
organization (p. 281)
elaboration (p. 281)
recognition (p. 283)
recall (p. 284)

infantile amnesia (p. 285)
reconstruction (p. 286)
domain-specific knowledge (p. 287)
semantic memory (p. 289)
episodic memory (p. 289)
scripts (p. 289)
metacognition (p. 291)
self-regulation (p. 293)
comprehension monitoring (p. 293)
whole-language approach (p. 296)
basic-skills approach (p. 296)

CONNECTIONS

The **psychometric approach** to cognitive development is the basis for the wide variety of intelligence tests available for assessing children's mental abilities. As Nora's testing of Jermaine illustrates, compared to Piagetian and information-processing views, the psychometric perspective is far more product-oriented than process-oriented. For the most part, it focuses on outcomes and results—*how many* and *what kinds* of questions children can answer correctly at different ages. *How* children arrive at solutions to problems is emphasized less. Researchers interested in intelligence testing ask such questions as, What factors, or dimensions, make up intelligence, and how do they change with age? How can cognitive development be measured so that scores are useful for predicting future academic achievement, career attainment, and other aspects of intellectual success? To what extent do children of the same age differ in intelligence, and what factors explain these differences?

As we examine these issues, we will quickly become immersed in the IQ nature–nurture debate, waged over the course of this century. We will look closely at genetic and environmental influences on intelligence as well as the controversy over whether intelligence tests yield biased estimates of the abilities of low-income ethnic minority children like Jermaine. Our discussion concludes by moving "beyond IQ" to the development of creativity and special talents. Although these traits are among the most highly valued human characteristics, they are not represented on current intelligence tests for children.

███████████

DEFINITIONS OF INTELLIGENCE

Take a moment to jot down a list of behaviors you view as typical of people who are highly intelligent. Did you come up with just one or two characteristics or a great many? When Robert Sternberg (1982) asked nearly 500 laypeople to complete a similar exercise, he found that their responses were surprisingly similar to the views of experts. Both regard intelligence as a complex construct made up of verbal ability, practical problem solving, and social competence. These findings indicate that most people do not think of intelligence as a single ability. Instead, their definitions include a variety of attributes.

Now try another exercise. This time, list five traits you regard as characterizing intelligent 6-month-olds, 2-year-olds, 10-year-olds, and adults. The problem of defining children's intelligence is especially challenging, since behaviors that reflect intelligent behavior change with age. When students in an introductory psychology course were given this task, their descriptions differed greatly from one developmental period to the next. As Table 8.1 reveals, sensorimotor responsiveness became less important, whereas problem solving and reasoning became more important, in much the same way that Piaget suggested intelligence changes with age. Furthermore, after infancy, college students stressed the role of verbal and symbolic knowledge, an emphasis that fits with both Piagetian and information-processing views (Siegler & Richards, 1980).

The researchers also asked college students to estimate correlations among the mental abilities mentioned for each age. Students thought there would be some close connections, but they predicted considerable distinctiveness as well. As we will see in the following sections, scientific theories underlying the measurement of intelligence reveal this same tension between a single, overarching ability versus a collection of only loosely related skills.

Alfred Binet: A Holistic View

The social and educational climate of the late nineteenth and early twentieth centuries led to the rise of the intelligence testing movement. Perhaps the most important influence was the beginning of universal public education in Europe

Psychometric approach

An approach to cognitive development that focuses on the construction of tests to assess mental abilities.

6-MONTH-OLDS	2-YEAR-OLDS	10-YEAR-OLDS	ADULTS
1. Recognition of people and objects	1. Verbal ability	1. Verbal ability	1. Reasoning
2. Motor coordination	2. Learning ability	2, 3, 4. Learning ability; problem solving; reasoning (all three tied)	2. Verbal ability
3. Alertness	3. Awareness of people and environment		3. Problem solving
4. Awareness of environment	4. Motor coordination		4. Learning ability
5. Verbalization	5. Curiosity	5. Creativity	5. Creativity

SOURCE: From *College Students' Prototypes of Children's Intelligence* by R. S. Siegler & D. D. Richards, 1980. Paper presented at the annual meeting of the American Psychological Association, New York. Adapted by permission of the author.

and the United States. Once schools opened their doors to children of all social classes, not just society's privileged, educators called for methods that would help them identify pupils who could not profit from regular classroom instruction. The first successful intelligence test, completed by French psychologist Alfred Binet and his colleague Theodore Simon in 1905, responded to this need.

Binet was asked by the French Ministry of Instruction to develop an objective method for identifying retarded pupils who required assignment to special classes. Other researchers had tried to assess intelligence using simple laboratory measures of sensory responsiveness and reaction time (Cattell, 1890; Galton, 1883). Binet believed that very different kinds of test items were needed—ones that did not dissect intelligence into elementary processes, but instead required individuals to apply complex functions involved in intelligent behavior, such as memory, good judgment, and abstraction. Consequently, Binet and Simon devised a test of "general mental ability" that included a variety of verbal and nonverbal reasoning tasks. Their test was also the first *developmental approach* to test construction. Items varied in difficulty, and each was classified according to the age at which a typical child could first pass it (Brody, 1992).

The Binet test was so successful in predicting school performance that it became the basis for new intelligence tests developed in other countries. In 1916, Lewis Terman at Stanford University adapted it for use with American schoolchildren. Since then, the American version has been known as the Stanford-Binet Intelligence Scale. The Stanford-Binet has been revised several times over this century. Later we will see that it no longer provides just a single, holistic measure of intelligence. Nevertheless, many of its items continue to resemble those on Binet's original scale.

The Factor Analysts: A Multifaceted View

As intelligence tests became more widely used, psychologists and educators became increasingly aware that a single score might not adequately represent human mental functioning. As Figure 8.1 shows, a wide variety of tasks typically appear on intelligence tests for children. Researchers seeking clearer definitions of intelligence had to confront the important issue of whether it really is a holistic trait or a collection of many different abilities.

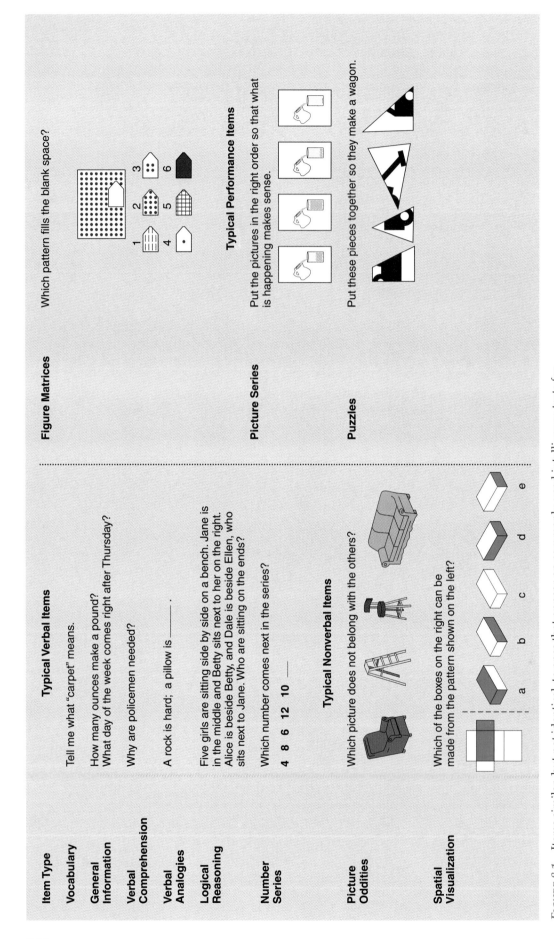

Item Type	Typical Verbal Items		Figure Matrices	Which pattern fills the blank space?
Vocabulary	Tell me what "carpet" means.			
General Information	How many ounces make a pound? What day of the week comes right after Thursday?			
Verbal Comprehension	Why are policemen needed?			
Verbal Analogies	A rock is hard; a pillow is ———.			
Logical Reasoning	Five girls are sitting side by side on a bench. Jane is in the middle and Betty sits next to her on the right. Alice is beside Betty, and Dale is beside Ellen, who sits next to Jane. Who are sitting on the ends?			
Number Series	Which number comes next in the series? 4 8 6 12 10 ———		**Picture Series**	Put the pictures in the right order so that what is happening makes sense.
	Typical Nonverbal Items		**Puzzles**	Put these pieces together so they make a wagon.
Picture Oddities	Which picture does not belong with the others?			
Spatial Visualization	Which of the boxes on the right can be made from the pattern shown on the left?			

FIGURE 8.1. Items similar, but not identical, to ones that appear on commonly used intelligence tests for children. In contrast to verbal items, nonverbal items do not require reading or direct use of language. Performance items are also nonverbal, but they require the child to draw or construct something rather than merely give a correct answer. (Logical reasoning, picture oddities, spatial visualization, and figure matrices items are adapted with the permission of The Free Press, a Division of Macmillan, Inc., from *Bias in Mental Testing* by Arthur R. Jensen, pp. 150, 154, 157, and 160. Copyright © 1980 by Arthur R. Jensen.)

To resolve this dilemma, a special technique was used to analyze the performances of individuals on intelligence tests. **Factor analysis** is a complicated statistical procedure in which scores on many separate items are combined into a few factors, which substitute for the separate scores. Then the researcher gives each factor a name, based on common characteristics of items that are closely correlated with the factor. For example, if vocabulary, verbal comprehension, and verbal analogies items all correlate highly with the same factor, it might be labeled "verbal ability." Using this method, many efforts were made to identify the mental abilities that contribute to successful performance on intelligence tests.

EARLY FACTOR ANALYSTS. The first influential factor analyst was British psychologist Charles Spearman (1927), who found that all the test items he examined correlated to some degree with one another. Therefore, Spearman proposed the existence of a common underlying **general factor,** or what he termed **"g."** At the same time, he noticed that test items were not perfectly correlated. In other words, they varied in the extent to which they tapped "g." Consequently, he suggested that each item also measured a **specific factor,** called **"s,"** that was unique to the task. Spearman's identification of "g" and "s" led his view of mental abilities to be called the *two-factor theory of intelligence.*

According to Spearman, "g" was central and supreme, and he was especially interested in its psychological characteristics. With further study, Spearman concluded that "g" represented some kind of abstract reasoning power. Test items that required individuals to form relationships and apply general principles seemed to be the strongest correlates of "g," and they were also the best predictors of intellectual performance outside the testing situation.

Louis Thurstone (1938), an American contemporary of Spearman, soon took issue with his emphasis on "g." Instead, Thurstone argued, separate intellectual abilities that are unrelated to one another exist. Thurstone gave over 50 intelligence tests to a large number of college students, and their scores produced seven clear factors. As a result, he concluded that intelligence consists of seven distinct **primary mental abilities:** verbal meaning, perceptual speed, reasoning, number, rote memory, word fluency, and spatial visualization.

Spearman's and Thurstone's findings represent two different ways of thinking about intelligence. Today, each is supported by research and accounts for part of the story. Later we will see that many modern test designers reconcile these two views by proposing a *hierarchical model* of mental abilities. At the highest level is "g," assumed to be present in all specialized factors. These factors, in turn, are measured by subtests, or groups of related items. Subtest scores provide information about a child's strengths and weaknesses, and they can also be combined into an overall index of general intelligence (Brody, 1992).

MODERN FACTOR ANALYSTS. Several important modern mental-ability theorists have extended the efforts of the early factor analysts. One of the most influential is J. P. Guilford (1967, 1985, 1988), who rejected the existence of "g" and instead proposed a complex, three-dimensional **structure-of-intellect model** (see Figure 8.2). According to Guilford, every intellectual task can be classified according to (1) its content, (2) the mental operation involved, and (3) the product resulting from the operation. For example, think back to the similarities task Nora gave Jermaine, described at the beginning of this chapter. In Guilford's system, it would be classified as semantic (content), evaluation (operation), and relations (product). By combining the three dimensions in all possible ways, the structure-of-intellect model generates a total of 180 separate ability factors.

In addition to its large number of mental abilities, Guilford's model has other unusual features. Its "behavioral" content category acknowledges that a separate social intelligence exists, involving sensitivity to the mental states of others. In addition, Guilford added tests of creative thinking to his factor analytic studies. He concluded that an essential operation for creativity is *divergent production*—the

Factor analysis
A complicated statistical procedure that combines scores from many separate test items into a few factors, which substitute for the separate scores. Used to identify mental abilities that contribute to performance on intelligence tests.

General factor, or "g"
In Spearman's theory of intelligence, a common factor representing abstract reasoning power that underlies a wide variety of test items.

Specific factor, or "s"
In Spearman's theory of intelligence, a mental-ability factor that is unique to a particular task.

Primary mental abilities
In Thurstone's theory of intelligence, seven distinct mental abilities identified through factor analysis (verbal meaning, perceptual speed, reasoning, number, rote memory, word fluency, and spatial visualization).

Structure-of-intellect model
Guilford's 180-factor model of intelligence, which classifies each intellectual task according to three dimensions: content, mental operation, and product.

Contents

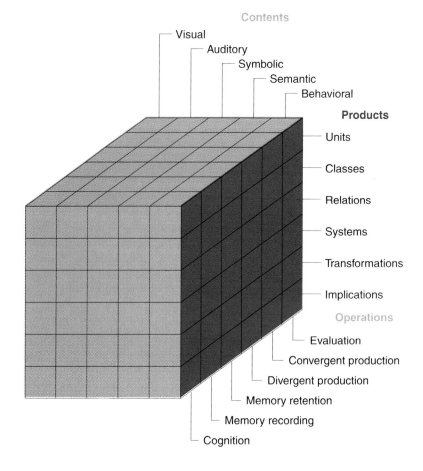

FIGURE 8.2 Guilford's structure-of-intellect model.
(From "Some Changes in the Structure-of-Intellect Model" by J. P. Guilford,
1988, *Educational and Psychological Measurement, 48*, p. 3. Reprinted by
permission.)

fluent generation of a wide variety of alternatives, as reflected in the question, "Think of as many meanings for the word 'bolt' as you can." In contrast, *convergent production* is noncreative. It involves arriving at a single correct answer, as in the question, "Bolt most nearly means: (a) to paint, (b) to sing, (c) to run, (d) to hang." According to Guilford, creative thinking is also flexible thinking. It requires a ready ability to switch categories of thought, an aspect represented by the product *transformations.* As we will see at the end of this chapter, tests commonly used to assess children's creativity are based on Guilford's ideas.

Although Guilford's model of mental abilities is the most comprehensive available, other researchers have not obtained clear factor analytic support for it. Consequently, they question whether such an extensive list of factors accurately represents human intelligence. Recently, Guilford suggested that his 180 factors could be reduced to a smaller number of higher-order mental abilities. However, evidence for this hierarchical version of his theory is also limited (Brody, 1992).

Raymond B. Cattell's (1971, 1987) approach to defining intelligence differs sharply from Guilford's, as it accepts "g"and divides it into only two factors. **Crystallized intelligence** depends on culturally loaded, fact-oriented information. Tasks highly correlated with it include vocabulary, general information, and arithmetic problems. In contrast, **fluid intelligence** requires very little specific knowledge. It involves the ability to see complex relationships and solve problems, as in the number series, spatial visualization, and figure matrix items shown in Figure 8.1.

Among children who are similar in cultural and educational background, crystallized and fluid intelligence are highly correlated, and it is difficult to distinguish them. In these instances, the strong relationship is probably due to the fact that children who are high in fluid intelligence acquire specific information with greater ease. But when children who differ greatly in cultural and educational

Crystallized intelligence

In Cattell's theory, a form of intelligence that depends on culturally loaded, fact-oriented information.

Fluid intelligence

In Cattell's theory, a form of intelligence that requires very little specific knowledge but involves the ability to see complex relationships and solve problems.

experiences are tested, the two abilities are easier to identify; children with the same fluid capacity may perform quite differently on tests that emphasize crystallized tasks. As these findings suggest, Cattell's theory has important implications for the issue of cultural bias in intelligence testing. We will see later that efforts to devise culture-fair tests usually emphasize fluid over crystallized items.

RECENT ADVANCES IN DEFINING INTELLIGENCE

Although factor analysis has been the major approach to defining mental abilities, many researchers believe its usefulness will remain limited unless it is combined with other theoretical approaches to the study of human cognition. Factor analysts have been criticized for devoting too much attention to identifying factors and too little to clarifying the cognitive processes that underlie them. Once we understand exactly what separates individuals who can solve certain mental test items from those who cannot, we will know much more about why a particular child does well or poorly and what skills must be worked on to improve performance.

Combining Psychometric and Information-Processing Approaches

To overcome the limitations of factor analysis, some researchers have combined psychometric and information-processing approaches. These investigators conduct **componential analyses** of children's test scores by correlating them with laboratory measures designed to assess the speed and effectiveness of information processing. In this way, they hope to provide process-oriented explanations of mental test performance.

*T*his boy solves a math problem with the help of a special set of small blocks. Children who apply strategies adaptively, using backup procedures when they cannot recall an answer rather than guessing, develop the capacity for fast, accurate retrieval and score higher on intelligence tests. (STEPHEN MARKS)

Which information-processing components have turned out to be good predictors of intelligence? Many studies reveal that basic efficiency of thinking is correlated with the "g" factor. For example, simple reaction time and the quickness with which individuals can discriminate two stimuli are moderately related to general intelligence (Jensen, 1987; Kranzler & Jensen, 1989). Although these findings appear to suggest that individuals whose nervous systems function more efficiently have an edge when it comes to complex intellectual skills, rapid responding is not the only processing correlate of mental test performance. Strategy use also makes a difference, and it may explain some of the association between response speed and intelligence.

In a recent study, researchers used Siegler's model of strategy choice (see Chapter 7, pages 295–296) to see if the way 4- to 6-year-olds apply strategies to simple addition problems is related to mental test scores. Adaptive strategy users—children who retrieved answers accurately, used backup techniques (such as counting) when they could not recall a math fact, and seldom guessed—did considerably better on a measure of general intelligence and on subtests of mathematical and spatial abilities than their less adaptive agemates (Geary & Burlingham-Dubree, 1989). As we saw in Chapter 7, children who apply strategies adaptively develop the capacity for fast, accurate retrieval in a skill area—an ability that seems to carry over to performance on intelligence test items.

Componential research has also highlighted cognitive processes that appear unrelated to test performance but that children can rely on to compensate for tested mental ability. Recent evidence suggests that certain aspects of metacognition—awareness of problem-solving strategies and organizational and planning skills—are not good predictors of general intelligence (Casey et al., 1991; Kreitler & Kreitler, 1987). In one study, fourth- and fifth-graders who were average in mental ability but high in metacognitive knowledge about problem solving did far better on Piagetian formal operational tasks (such as the pendulum problem) than highly intelligent classmates who knew little about effective problem-solving techniques (Swanson, 1990).

Componential analysis

A research procedure aimed at clarifying the cognitive processes responsible for intelligence test scores by correlating them with laboratory measures designed to assess the speed and effectiveness of information processing.

As these findings illustrate, componential analyses are beginning to isolate specific cognitive skills on which training might be especially helpful to some children. Nevertheless, the componential approach has one major shortcoming. It attributes intelligence entirely to causes within the child. Yet throughout Chapter 7, we showed that cultural and situational factors profoundly affect children's cognitive skills. Recently, Robert Sternberg expanded the componential approach into a comprehensive theory that views intelligence as a product of both internal and external forces.

Sternberg's Triarchic Theory

Sternberg's (1985, 1988) **triarchic theory of intelligence** is made up of three interacting subtheories (see Figure 8.3). The first, the *componential subtheory*, spells out the information-processing skills that underlie intelligent behavior. You are already familiar with its main elements—metacognition, strategy application, and knowledge acquisition—from reading Chapter 7.

According to Sternberg, children's use of these components is not just a matter of internal capacity. It is also a function of the conditions under which intelligence is assessed. The *experiential subtheory* states that highly intelligent individuals, compared to less intelligent ones, process information more skillfully in novel situations. When given a relatively new task, the bright person learns rapidly, making strategies automatic so working memory is freed for more complex aspects of the situation.

Think, for a moment, about the implications of this idea for measuring children's intelligence. To accurately compare children in brightness—in ability to deal with novelty and learn efficiently—all children would need to be presented with equally unfamiliar test items. Otherwise, some children will appear more intelligent than others simply because of their past experiences, not because they are really more cognitively skilled. These children start with the unfair advantage of prior practice on the tasks.

This point brings us to the third part of Sternberg's model, his *contextual subtheory*. It proposes that intelligent people skillfully *adapt* their information-processing skills to fit with their personal desires and the demands of their everyday

FIGURE 8.3 Sternberg's triarchic theory of intelligence.

Triarchic theory of intelligence
Sternberg's theory, which states that information-processing skills, prior experience with tasks, and contextual (or cultural) factors interact to determine intelligent behavior.

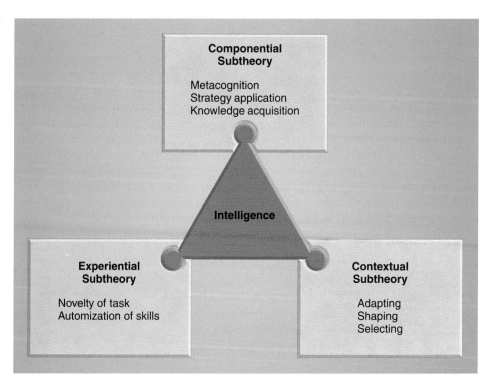

*B*ecause of his cultural background, this Guatemalan Mayan boy is likely to find the demands of intelligence testing to be strange and confusing. Yet he displays sophisticated abilities in everyday life. (DAVID ALLEN HARVEY/WOODFIN CAMP & ASSOCIATES)

worlds. When they cannot adapt to a situation, they try to *shape*, or change, it to meet their needs. If they cannot shape it, they *select* new contexts that are consistent with their goals. The contextual subtheory emphasizes that intelligent behavior is never culture-free. Because of their backgrounds, some children come to value behaviors required for success on intelligence tests, and they easily adapt to the tasks and testing conditions. Others with different life histories misinterpret the testing context or reject it entirely because it does not suit their needs. Yet such children may display very sophisticated abilities in daily life—for example, telling stories, engaging in elaborate artistic activities, accomplishing athletic feats, or interacting skillfully with other people (Sternberg, 1988).

Sternberg's theory emphasizes the complexity of intelligent behavior and the wide variety of human mental skills. Like Cattell's distinction between crystallized and fluid intelligence, Sternberg's ideas are relevant to the controversy surrounding cultural bias in intelligence testing, a topic we return to later in this chapter.

Gardner's Theory of Multiple Intelligences

Howard Gardner's (1983) **theory of multiple intelligences** provides yet another view of how information-processing skills underlie intelligent behavior. But unlike the componential approach, it does not begin with existing mental tests and try to isolate the processing elements required to succeed on them. Instead, Gardner believes intelligence should be defined in terms of distinct sets of processing operations that permit individuals to solve problems, create products, and discover new knowledge in a diverse array of culturally valued activities. Accordingly, Gardner dismisses the idea of a single overarching mental ability, or "g," and proposes seven independent intelligences, which are described in Table 8.2.

Gardner acknowledges that if tests were available to assess all of these abilities, factor analysis should yield low correlations among them. But he regards neurological support for their separateness as more persuasive. Research indicating that damage to a certain part of the adult brain influences only one ability (such as linguistic or spatial) while sparing others suggests that the affected ability is independent. The existence of prodigies, who show precocious development in only one area, such as language, music, or mathematics, also fits with Gardner's belief in distinct abilities.

Finally, Gardner argues that each intelligence has a unique biological potential, a distinct course of development, and different expert, or "end-state" performances. At the same time, he stresses that a lengthy process of education is required to trans-

Theory of multiple intelligences Gardner's theory, which identifies seven distinct intelligences on the basis of distinct sets of processing operations applied in culturally meaningful activities (linguistic, logico-mathematical, musical, spatial, bodily-kinesthetic, interpersonal, and intrapersonal).

TABLE 8.2 *Gardner's Multiple Intelligences*

INTELLIGENCE	PROCESSING OPERATIONS	END-STATE PERFORMANCE POSSIBILITIES
Linguistic	Sensitivity to the sounds, rhythms, and meanings of words and the different functions of language	Poet, journalist
Logico-mathematical	Sensitivity to, and capacity to detect, logical or numerical patterns; ability to handle long chains of logical reasoning	Mathematician, scientist
Musical	Ability to produce and appreciate pitch, rhythm (or melody), and aesthetic-sounding tones; understanding of the forms of musical expressiveness	Violinist, composer
Spatial	Ability to perceive the visual-spatial world accurately, to perform transformations on these perceptions, and to re-create aspects of visual experience in the absence of relevant stimuli	Sculptor, navigator
Bodily-kinesthetic	Ability to use the body skillfully for expressive as well as goal-directed purposes; ability to handle objects skillfully	Dancer, athlete
Interpersonal	Ability to detect and respond appropriately to the moods, temperaments, motivations, and intentions of others	Therapist, salesperson
Intrapersonal	Ability to discriminate complex inner feelings and to use them to guide one's own behavior; knowledge of one's own strengths, weaknesses, desires, and intelligences	Person with detailed, accurate self-knowledge

SOURCES: Gardner, 1983; Gardner & Hatch, 1989.

form any raw intellectual potential into a mature social role. This means that cultural values and learning opportunities have a great deal to do with the extent to which a child's strengths are realized and the ways in which they are expressed.

Does Gardner's theory remind you of the modular view of the mind we discussed in Chapter 7? Indeed, he is sympathetic to this position. Gardner's work has been especially helpful in efforts to understand and nurture children's special talents, a topic we will take up at the end of this chapter. At the same time, reservations have been raised about his theory. Neurological support for the independence of his intelligences is weak. Logico-mathematical ability, in particular, seems to be governed by many brain regions, not just one. Similarly, exceptionally gifted individuals whose abilities are broad rather than limited to a particular domain exist (Feldman & Goldsmith, 1991). Finally, current mental tests do tap several of Gardner's intelligences (linguistic, logico-mathematical, and spatial), and evidence for "g" suggests that they have common features.

In sum, Gardner's list of abilities has yet to be firmly grounded in research. Nevertheless, his ideas have been powerful enough to reawaken the debate over a unitary versus multifaceted human intelligence. Still, without clear evidence in favor of one side or the other, most test designers (as we will see in the following sections) strike a balance between these two views.

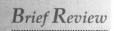

Brief Review

Binet and Simon's first successful intelligence test provided a single score designed to identify children who required assignment to special school classes. Factor analysts sought answers to the question of whether intelligence is a holistic trait or a collection of many different abilities. Their findings led to the identification of a general factor, or "g," as well as a wide variety of distinct mental abilities. Recently, researchers have combined the psychometric and information-processing approaches, conducting componential analyses aimed at uncovering the processing skills that predict mental test scores. Sternberg has expanded this approach into a triarchic theory that considers intelligence to be the combined result of processing skills, experience with tasks, and contextual (or cultural) influences. According to Gardner's theory of multiple intelligences, seven distinct domains of ability, each defined by unique processing operations, represent the diversity of human intelligence. ....

FIGURE 8.4 "Unisex" child in the Stanford-Binet Intelligence Scale, designed to reduce gender bias in the test. (From *The Stanford-Binet Intelligence Scale: Fourth Edition, Guide for Administering and Scoring* by R. L. Thorndike, E. P. Hagen, & J. M. Sattler, 1986, Chicago: Riverside Publishing. Reprinted by permission.)

REPRESENTATIVE INTELLIGENCE TESTS FOR CHILDREN

A wide variety of tests are currently available to assess children's intelligence. Those that pupils take every 2 or 3 years in their classrooms are *group-administered tests.* They permit many children to be tested at once and require very little training of teachers who give them. Group tests are useful for instructional planning and identifying pupils who require more extensive evaluation with *individually administered tests.* Unlike group tests, individual tests demand considerable training and experience to give well. The examiner not only considers the child's answers but also carefully observes the child's behavior, noting such reactions as attentiveness to and interest in the tasks and wariness of the adult. These observations provide insights into whether the test score is accurate or underestimates the child's ability. Two individual tests—the Stanford-Binet and the Wechsler—are most often used to identify highly intelligent children and diagnose those with learning problems.

The Stanford-Binet Intelligence Scale

The **Stanford-Binet Intelligence Scale,** the modern descendant of Binet's first successful test, is appropriate for individuals between 2 and 18 years of age. Translated and adopted throughout the world, it has often served as the yardstick against which other intelligence tests have been measured. Unlike earlier editions, the 1986 revision measures both general intelligence and four intellectual factors: verbal reasoning, quantitative reasoning, spatial reasoning, and short-term memory (Thorndike, Hagen, & Sattler, 1986). Within these factors are 15 subtests that permit a detailed analysis of each child's mental abilities. The verbal and quantitative factors emphasize crystallized intelligence (culturally loaded, fact-oriented information), such as the child's knowledge of vocabulary and comprehension of sentences. In contrast, the spatial-reasoning factor taps fluid intelligence. It is believed to be less culturally biased because it requires little in the way of specific information.

Like many current tests, the Stanford-Binet is designed to be sensitive to ethnic minority children and children with physical disabilities and to reduce gender bias. Pictures of children from different racial groups, a child in a wheelchair, and "unisex" figures that can be interpreted as male or female are included (see Figure 8.4).

Nevertheless, the new Stanford-Binet has been criticized on several grounds. Its model of mental ability, which blends the theories of Spearman and Cattell, has been difficult to verify with factor analysis. Another serious drawback is that the test takes an especially long time to give—up to 2 hours for some children (Sattler, 1988).

The Wechsler Intelligence Scale for Children

The **Wechsler Intelligence Scale for Children–III (WISC–III)** is the third edition of a widely used test for 6- through 16-year-olds. A downward extension of it— the *Wechsler Preschool and Primary Scale of Intelligence–Revised (WPPSI–R)* is appropriate for children 3 through 8 (Wechsler, 1989, 1991). The Wechsler tests offered both a measure of general intelligence and a variety of separate factor scores long

Stanford-Binet Intelligence Scale

An individually administered intelligence test that is the modern descendent of Alfred Binet's first successful test for children. Measures general intelligence and four factors: verbal reasoning, quantitative reasoning, spatial reasoning, and short-term memory.

Wechsler Intelligence Scale for Children–III (WISC–III)

An individually administered intelligence test that includes a measure of both general intelligence and a variety of verbal and performance scores.

before the Stanford-Binet. As a result, over the past two decades, psychologists and educators have come to prefer the WISC and the WPPSI for individual assessment of children.

Both the WISC–III and the WPPSI–R measure two broad intellectual factors: verbal and performance. Each contains 6 subtests, yielding 12 separate scores in all. Performance items (look back at Figure 8.1 on page 310 for examples) require the child to arrange materials rather than talk to the examiner. Consequently, these tests provided one of the first means through which non–English-speaking children and children with speech and language disorders could demonstrate their intellectual strengths.

The Wechsler tests were also the first to be standardized on children representing the total population of the United States, including racial and ethnic minorities. Their broadly representative standardization samples have served as models for many other tests, including the recent version of the Stanford-Binet.

Other Intelligence Tests

Although the Stanford-Binet and Wechsler scales are the most well-known intelligence tests, others based on alternative approaches do exist. Perhaps the most innovative is the **Kaufman Assessment Battery for Children (K-ABC).** It is the first major test to be grounded in information-processing theory. Published in 1983, the K-ABC measures the intelligence of children from ages $2\frac{1}{2}$ through 12 on the basis of two broad types of information-processing skills. The first, *simultaneous processing,* demands that children integrate a variety of stimuli at the same time, as when they are asked to label an incomplete picture or recall the placement of objects on a page presented only briefly. The second, *sequential processing,* refers to problems that require children to think in a step-by-step fashion. Examples include repeating a series of digits or hand movements presented by the examiner.

The K-ABC makes a special effort to respond to the needs of culturally different children through its unusually flexible administration procedures. If a child fails one of the first three items on any subtest, the examiner is permitted to "teach the task." The tester can use alternative wording and gestures and may even communicate in a language other than English (Kaufman & Kaufman, 1983).

Like the most recent Stanford-Binet, the K-ABC is not without critics. Some point out that the test samples a narrow range of information-processing skills and that there is little research support for the simultaneous/sequential processing distinction (Conoley, 1990; Sternberg, 1984a). Nevertheless, the K-ABC is responsive to a new trend to define intelligence in terms of cognitive processes, and it is likely to inspire new tests that draw on information-processing models.

In the 1960s and 1970s, researchers became interested in whether Piaget's theory could be applied to the measurement of individual differences in intelligence. Several tests for school-age children that include conservation and classification problems were devised (Goldschmid & Bentler, 1968; Humphreys, Rich, & Davey, 1985). Performance on these measures correlates well with traditional mental test scores and academic achievement. But Piagetian scales have not caught hold strongly, largely because they do not sample as wide a range of mental abilities as the Stanford-Binet, Wechsler, and Kaufman tests. Piaget's theory has had a somewhat greater impact in the area of infant assessment, as we will see in the following section.

Kaufman Assessment Battery for Children (K-ABC)

An individually administered intelligence test that measures two broad types of information-processing skills: simultaneous and sequential processing. The first major test to be grounded in information-processing theory.

INFANT INTELLIGENCE TESTS. Accurately measuring the intelligence of infants is an especially challenging task. Unlike children, babies cannot answer questions or follow directions. All we can do is present them with stimuli, coax them to respond, and observe their behavior. In addition, infants are not necessarily cooperative subjects. They are likely to become distracted, fatigued, or bored during testing. Some tests depend heavily on information supplied by parents to compensate for the uncertain behavior of these young test-takers.

Most infant measures consist largely of perceptual and motor responses. For example, the 1969 edition of the *Bayley Scales of Infant Development,* a commonly used infant test, was inspired by the early normative work of Arnold Gesell (see Chapter 1, pages 10–11). It consists of two parts: (1) the Mental Scale, which includes such items as turning to a sound, looking for a fallen object, building a tower of cubes, and naming pictures; and (2) the Motor Scale, which assesses fine and gross motor skills, such as grasping, sitting, drinking from a cup, and jumping (Bayley, 1969). Despite careful construction, infant tests emphasizing these types of items are poor predictors of intelligence during the childhood years, at least for samples of normal babies. The consistency of this finding has led researchers to conclude that infant perceptual and motor behaviors do not represent the same aspects of intelligence assessed in childhood.

In an effort to increase its predictive validity, the Bayley test has just been extensively revised. Its new version includes items that emphasize infant memory, problem solving, categorization, and other complex cognitive skills—responses that, as we will see in a moment, are far more likely to correlate with later mental test scores (The Psychological Corporation, 1993). Nevertheless, traditional infant tests do show some predictability for very low-scoring babies (Honzik, 1983). As a result, they continue to be used for *screening*—helping to identify for further observation and intervention infants who have a high likelihood of experiencing future developmental problems (Lewis & Sullivan, 1985).

Recall from Chapter 4 that dishabituation to visual stimuli is the best available infant correlate of childhood intelligence. Unlike typical infant test items, it seems to tap aspects of cognitive processing (attention, memory, and response to novelty) that are important in the verbal, conceptual, and problem-solving skills assessed at later ages. Recently, a new test made up entirely of habituation–dishabituation items, the *Fagan Test of Infant Intelligence,* was constructed. To take it, the infant sits on the mother's lap and views a series of pictures. After exposure to each one, looking time toward a novel picture that is paired with the familiar one is recorded. Scores on the Fagan test are moderately correlated with IQ during the preschool years. In addition, the Fagan test is highly effective in identifying babies who (without intervention) will soon show serious delays in mental development (Fagan & Montie, 1988; Fagan, Shepherd, & Knevel, 1991).

For many years, infant tests based on Piaget's theory have been available. For example, Uzgiris and Hunt's (1975) *Infant Psychological Development Scale* contains eight subtests, each of which assesses an important sensorimotor milestone, such as imitation and object permanence. Like the habituation–dishabituation response, object permanence is a better predictor of preschool intelligence than traditional infant tests, perhaps because it, too, reflects a basic cognitive process—problem solving (Wachs, 1975).

THE COMPUTATION AND DISTRIBUTION OF IQ SCORES

Once an intelligence test has been given, the examiner computes a raw score on the basis of the child's answers. It must be converted to an **intelligence quotient (IQ)** that permits the child's performance to be compared to the performances of other individuals.

The Traditional IQ Score

In the original Stanford-Binet scale, IQs were obtained by converting the raw score to a **mental age (MA),** which indicates the age at which children, on the average, obtain that score. For example, if the average raw score of 8-year-olds is

Intelligence quotient (IQ)

A score that permits an individual's performance on an intelligence test to be compared to the performances of other individuals.

Mental age (MA)

A measure of performance on an intelligence test that indicates the age at which children, on the average, obtain that score.

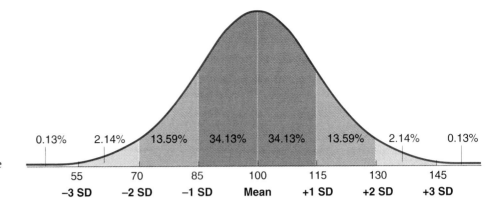

FIGURE 8.5 The normal curve, with the baseline scaled in both IQ and standard deviation (SD) units. Areas under the curve are given in percentages. By summing the percentages to the left of an individual's IQ, we can obtain a percentile rank, which refers to the proportion of people of the same age that the individual scored better than on the test.

40, then a raw score of 40 is equivalent to a mental age of 8. An IQ can then be computed by dividing the child's mental age by his chronological age (CA) and multiplying by 100:

$$IQ = \frac{MA}{CA} \times 100$$

Notice how the formula considers children with IQs of 100 to be average in mental development, since they perform as expected for their chronological age. Those with IQs above 100 are advanced in mental development, since their raw scores are like those of older children. And children with IQs below 100 are behind in mental development for a similar reason.

Although the mental age approach provides a convenient way of comparing children's test scores, it has two major drawbacks. First, it encourages people who are not familiar with the basis of the score to conclude that an 8-year-old with a mental age of 12 is like a 12-year-old in all respects. Yet expecting this child to keep up with children 4 years older in academic and social situations would be unreasonable (Sattler, 1988). Second, intellectual development is much more rapid among younger than older children. The difference in mental ability between a 2- and a 3-year-old is far greater than it is between a 10- and an 11-year-old, but an IQ based on mental age does not take this into account. For these reasons, a different approach to computing IQ is generally used today.

The Modern IQ Score

The modern method of arriving at an IQ directly compares a child's raw score to the scores of children of the same chronological age. It is called a **deviation IQ** because it is based on the degree to which a child's performance deviates from the average of same-age children. When a test is constructed, it is given to a large, representative sample of individuals. Performances at each age level form a *normal*, or *bell-shaped, curve* in which most scores fall near the center (the mean or average) and progressively fewer fall out toward the extremes. Two important features of the normal curve are its *mean*, or the average score, and its *standard deviation*, which provides a measure of the average variability, or "spread-out-ness," of the scores from the mean.

Deviation IQ

An IQ score based on the degree to which a child's performance deviates from the average of same-age children.

Most intelligence tests convert their raw scores so that the mean is set at 100 and the standard deviation at 15. As Figure 8.5 shows, knowing the mean and standard deviation, we can determine the percentage of individuals at each age who fall above or below a certain score. Then, when we speak of a particular IQ, we know exactly what it means. For example, as Table 8.3 makes clear, a child with an IQ of 100 does better than 50 percent of same-age children. A child with an IQ of 85 does better than only 16 percent of her agemates, whereas a child with an IQ of 130 outperforms 98 percent of them. Look at Figure 8.5 once more, and

TABLE 8.3 *Meaning of Different IQ Scores*

SCORE	PERCENTILE RANK *Child does better than . . . percent of same-age children*	
70	2	
85	16	
100 (average IQ)	50	
115	84	
130	98	

notice how most scores cluster near the mean. The IQs of the great majority of the population (95.5 percent) fall between 70 and 130, with only a few people achieving very high or very low scores.

Intelligence tests for children typically measure overall intelligence as well as a variety of separate factors. The Stanford-Binet and Wechsler scales are the most commonly used individually administered tests. The Kaufman Assessment Battery for Children is the first major test to be grounded in information-processing theory. Each of these tests includes features that respond to the special needs of ethnic minority children. Traditional infant tests, which consist largely of perceptual and motor responses, predict childhood intelligence poorly. Because tests of recognition memory and object permanence tap basic cognitive processes, they are better predictors. Modern test designers have replaced the mental age approach to computing IQ with the deviation IQ, which permits a direct comparison of a child's performance with a representative sample of same-age children.

Brief Review

WHAT AND HOW WELL DO
INTELLIGENCE TESTS PREDICT?

Already we have seen that infant perceptual and motor tasks are poor predictors of later intellectual performance. But what about the more frequently given childhood tests? Psychologists and educators who use test scores to make decisions about the educational placement of children assume that they are good indicators of future intelligence and scholastic performance. How well does IQ actually fare as a predictive measure?

Stability of IQ Scores

Stability refers to how effectively IQ predicts itself from one age to the next. Do children who obtain a particular IQ at 3 or 4 years perform about the same during elementary school and again when tested in high school? To answer this question, researchers rely on longitudinal studies in which the same children have been tested repeatedly over many ages.

CORRELATIONAL STABILITY. One way of examining the stability of IQ is to correlate scores obtained from repeated testings. This tells us whether children who score low or high in comparison to their agemates at one point in time continue to do so later. Examining these correlations, researchers have identified two generalizations about the stability of IQ:

1. *The older the child at time of first testing, the better the prediction of later IQ.* For example, in one longitudinal study, the correlation between scores at 2 and 5 years was only .32. It rose to .70 between ages 5 and 8, and .85 between 9 and 12 (Honzik, Macfarlane, & Allen, 1948). Preschool IQs do not predict school-age scores as well as later measures, but after age 6, there is good stability, with many correlations in the .70s and .80s. Relationships between two testings obtained in the adolescent years are as high as the .80s and .90s (Humphreys, 1989; Sontag, Baker, & Nelson, 1958).

2. *The closer in time two testings are, the stronger the relationship between the scores.* For example, a 4-year-old IQ correlates with a 5-year score at .72, but prediction drops by age 6 to .62. By age 18, it has declined to .42 (Honzik, Macfarlane, & Allen, 1948).

Taken together, these findings indicate that before 5 or 6 years, IQ is largely a measure of present ability, not a dependable, enduring measure. Why do preschool scores predict less well than later scores? One frequently cited reason is similar to the one we discussed with respect to infant tests: differences in the nature of test items. Concrete knowledge tends to be tested at younger ages, abstract problem solving later on. Success on the first may require different skills than success on the second (Siegler & Richards, 1982). Another explanation is that during early periods of rapid development, one child may spurt ahead of another and reach a plateau, whereas a second child, moving along slowly and steadily from behind, may catch up with and eventually overtake the first. Because children frequently change places with one another in a distribution during periods of rapid change, all measures of developmental progress, including height and weight, are less stable and predictable at these times. IQ seems to be no exception.

STABILITY OF ABSOLUTE SCORES. So far, we have looked at IQ stability in terms of how well children maintain their relative standing among agemates over time. We can also view stability in absolute terms by examining each child's profile of IQ scores on a series of repeated testings. Take a moment to look back at the examples of age-related changes in IQ scores we discussed in Chapter 2 (page 59). The evidence reveals that the majority of children experience substantial IQ fluctuations over childhood and adolescence—in most cases, 10 to 20 points, and sometimes much more (Honzik, Macfarlane, & Allen, 1948).

Recall, also, that children who changed the most tended to have orderly profiles in which scores either increased or decreased with age. A close look at the characteristics and life experiences of these children highlights factors that may be responsible for these IQ variations. Gainers were more independent and competitive about doing well in school. In addition, their parents took greater interest in their intellectual accomplishments, applied greater pressure to succeed, and used rational, democratic discipline. In contrast, decliners tended to have parents who made little effort to stimulate them and who showed extremes in child rearing, using either very severe or very lax discipline (McCall, Appelbaum, & Hogarty, 1973; Sontag, Baker, & Nelson, 1958).

When ethnic minority children who live in poverty are selected for special study, many show IQ declines. Although both genetic and environmental factors contribute to children's IQ profiles (Cardon et al., 1992), environment seems to be the overriding factor in the case of poverty-stricken youngsters. Their decreasing scores have been attributed to the **cumulative deficit hypothesis**. It suggests that the effects of underprivileged rearing conditions worsen the longer children remain in them. As a result, early cognitive deficits lead to more deficits that become harder to overcome as children get older (Klineberg, 1963). This idea has

Cumulative deficit hypothesis
A view that attributes the age-related decline in IQ among poverty-stricken ethnic minority children to the compounding effects of underprivileged rearing conditions.

served as the basis for many early intervention programs, which are intensive efforts to offset these declines.

What evidence exists to support the cumulative deficit? In a study of African-American children growing up under severely depressed conditions in the rural South, older siblings consistently obtained lower IQs than their younger brothers and sisters. But no such relation appeared for less disadvantaged African-American children living in California (Jensen, 1974). This finding is consistent with a cumulative deficit rather than a genetically determined IQ profile. To fit with a genetic explanation, *both* the southern and California-reared groups should have displayed age-related IQ declines.

In sum, many children show substantial changes in the absolute value of IQ that are the combined result of personal characteristics, child-rearing practices, and the quality of their living environments. Nevertheless, once IQ becomes reasonably stable in a correlational sense, it predicts a variety of outcomes, as we will see in the following sections.

IQ as a Predictor of Scholastic Performance

Thousands of studies reveal that intelligence tests have accomplished their goal of predicting academic achievement. Correlations range from .40 to .70 and are typically around .50 (Brody, 1992). Children with higher IQs also get better grades and stay in school longer. As early as age 7, IQ is moderately correlated with adult educational attainment (McCall, 1977).

Why is IQ an effective predictor of scholastic performance? Researchers differ in how they answer this question. Some believe IQ and achievement both depend on the same abstract reasoning processes that underlie Spearman's "g." A child well endowed with "g" is better able to acquire knowledge and skills taught in school. That IQ correlates best with achievement in the more abstract school subjects, such as English, mathematics, and science, is consistent with this interpretation (Jensen, 1980).

Other researchers argue that intelligence and achievement both sample from the same pool of culturally specific information. From this point of view, an intelligence test is partly an achievement test, and a child's past experiences affect performance on both measures (Zigler & Seitz, 1982). Support for this view comes from evidence that crystallized intelligence (which reflects acquired knowledge) does a much better job of predicting academic achievement than does its fluid counterpart (Kaufman, Kamphaus, & Kaufman, 1985).

A wealth of research indicates that IQ scores are effective predictors of scholastic performance. Researchers disagree, however, on the underlying basis of this relationship. (DENNIS MACDONALD/ THE PICTURE CUBE)

It is widely accepted that intelligence affects achievement in school, but how important is schooling in the development of intelligence? Stephen Ceci (1990, 1991) reviewed hundreds of studies addressing this question. Taken together, they suggest that events taking place in classrooms have a profound effect on mental test performance.

Consider, first, the small but consistent drop in IQ that takes place over the summer months, especially among low-income children, whose summer activities least resemble school tasks. For advantaged children, whose vacation pursuits (such as academic-type camps) are often like those of school, the summer decline does not occur (Heyns, 1978).

Research dating back to the early part of this century reveals that irregular school attendance has an even greater impact on IQ. In one study, test scores of children growing up in "hollows" of the Blue Ridge Mountains were compared. All were descendants of Scottish-Irish and English immigrants, whose families had lived in the hollows for generations. One hollow was located at the foot of the mountains and had schools in session 9 months of the year. In the other more isolated hollows, schooling was irregular. Children's IQs varied substantially with level of schooling available. Those who received the most had a 10- to 30-point advantage (Sherman & Key, 1932).

Delayed entry into school is similarly related to test scores. In the Netherlands during World War II, many schools were closed as a result of the Nazi occupation. The IQs of children who started school several years late dropped about 7 points (DeGroot, 1951). Similar findings come from a study of children of Indian settlers in South Africa, whose schooling was postponed up to 4 years because their villages did not have teachers. Compared to Indian children in nearby villages who attended school, they showed a loss of 5 IQ points per year (Ramphal, 1962).

Dropping out of school also has a detrimental effect on IQ. In a Swedish study, a large random sample of 13-year-old boys were given intelligence tests. At age 18, they were retested as part of the country's national military registration. The impact of dropping out was determined by comparing children who were similar in IQ, social class, and school grades at age 13. Each year of high school not completed amounted to a loss of 1.8 IQ points, up to a maximum of 8 points for all 4 years of high school (Härnqvist, 1968).

Although many factors contribute to individual differences in mental test performance, amount of schooling clearly emerges as a major force. Ceci (1991) believes that schooling influences IQ in at least three ways: (1) by teaching children factual knowledge relevant to test questions; (2) by promoting information-processing skills, such as memory strategies and categorization, that are tapped by test items; and (3) by encouraging attitudes and values that foster successful test performance, such as listening carefully to an adult's questions, answering under time pressure, and trying hard.

As you can probably imagine, researchers who believe heredity plays a crucial role in individual differences in IQ prefer the first of these explanations. Those who favor the power of environment prefer the second. Since the IQ–achievement correlation is stronger among identical than fraternal twins, heredity does seem to be important (Thompson, Detterman, & Plomin, 1991). But children's experiences also contribute. For example, findings reviewed in the Cultural Influences box above indicate that IQ not only predicts future achievement but is itself increased by years of schooling! Clearly, the relationship between intelligence and achievement is complex and determined by multiple factors.

Finally, although IQ predicts achievement better than any other tested measure, notice that the correlation is far from perfect. Other factors, such as motivation and personality characteristics that lead some children to try hard and want to do well in school, are just as important in accounting for individual differences in scholastic performance (Zigler & Seitz, 1982).

IQ as a Predictor of Occupational Attainment

Psychologists and educators would probably be less concerned with IQ scores if they were unrelated to long-term indicators of life success. But research indicates that childhood IQ predicts adult occupational attainment just about as well as it correlates with academic achievement. By second grade, pupils with the highest IQs are those who are most likely to enter prestigious professions, such as medicine, science, law, and engineering (McCall, 1977). Furthermore, IQ is related to how successful a person is likely to be within an occupation. Employees who score higher on mental tests tend to receive higher job competence ratings from supervisors in a wide range of occupations (Hunter & Hunter, 1984).

Once again, however, we must keep in mind that the relationship between IQ and occupational attainment is far from perfect. Factors related to family background, such as parental encouragement, modeling of career success, and connections in the world of work, also predict occupational choice and attainment (Grotevant & Cooper, 1988). Furthermore, years of schooling is a stronger predictor of occupational success than is IQ (Featherman, 1980). And we have already seen that IQ and schooling appear to be mutually influential.

Finally, personal variables also figure prominently in career achievement. In 1923, Lewis Terman initiated a longitudinal study of over 1,500 children with IQs above 135, who were followed well into mature adulthood. By middle age, more than 86 percent of the men in the sample had entered high-status professional and business occupations, a higher percentage than would have been expected for a random sample of individuals from similar home backgrounds (Terman & Oden, 1959).* But not all were professionally successful. Looking closely at those who fared best compared to those who fared worst, Terman found that their IQs were similar, averaging around 150. But the highly successful group appeared to have "a special drive to succeed, a need to achieve, that had been with them from grammar school onward" (Goleman, 1980, p. 31). They also experienced more intellectually stimulating home lives and a lower rate of family disruption due to parental divorce—factors that may have contributed to their achievement-oriented style.

In sum, vocational achievement seems to be a complex function of intelligence, education, motivation, family influences, and special opportunity. At present, no clear evidence indicates that IQ is more important than any of these other factors.

IQ as a Predictor of Psychological Adjustment

Is IQ so influential that it predicts indicators of life success beyond school and the workplace, such as emotional and social adjustment? During middle childhood, children with higher IQs tend to be better liked by their agemates (Hartup, 1983). But the reasons for this association are not clear. A child's social competence is also related to child-rearing practices, health, physical appearance, and personality, all of which are correlated with IQ.

Another way of exploring the relationship between IQ and psychological adjustment is to look at the mental test performance of children who are clearly poorly adjusted, such as highly aggressive children who engage in norm-violating acts. Chronic delinquents do tend to have lower IQs, but the association is weak, and researchers believe that IQ probably does not play a causal role (Hirschi & Hindelang, 1977). Instead, the troubled family lives of these youngsters appear to increase the chances of slow mental development and poor school performance. Young people who fail repeatedly in school are likely to conclude that traditional routes to occupational success will be closed to them. Consequently, they may seek alternative sources of reward, turning to antisocial peer groups and criminal behavior (Patterson, DeBaryshe, & Ramsey, 1989).

Finally, many adjustment disorders, such as high anxiety, fearfulness, social withdrawal, and depression, are unrelated to mental test scores (Graham, 1979). When we look at the evidence as a whole, we must conclude that a high IQ offers little guarantee of happiness and life satisfaction. And its imperfect prediction of other indicators of success, such as scholastic performance and occupational attainment, provides strong justification for never relying on IQ alone to forecast a child's future or make important educational placement decisions.

*Born in the early part of this century during an era quite different from our own, nearly half of the women in Terman's sample became housewives. However, of those who had professional careers, there were examples of outstanding accomplishments. Among them were scientists (one of whom contributed to the development of the polio vaccine), several novelists and journalists, and highly successful businesswomen (Terman & Oden, 1959).

Research consistently shows that IQ is an effective predictor of scholastic performance and occupational attainment. It is also linked to some aspects of psychological adjustment. However, in each instance, a wide variety of personal, familial, and experiential factors may intervene in the relationship. Although a high IQ does offer certain advantages, IQ alone tells us little that is definite about a child's chances for future success.

RACIAL, ETHNIC, AND SOCIAL-CLASS DIFFERENCES IN IQ

When we compare individuals in terms of academic achievement, years of education, and the status of their occupations, it quickly becomes clear that certain sectors of the population are advantaged over others. In searching for the roots of these disparities, researchers have compared the IQ scores of racial, ethnic, and social-class groups. Their findings are responsible for sparking the IQ nature–nurture debate. If group differences in IQ exist, then either there must be genetic differences between rich and poor and black and white children, or children with disadvantaged backgrounds must have fewer opportunities to acquire the skills needed for successful test performance.

In the 1970s, the IQ nature–nurture controversy escalated, after psychologist Arthur Jensen (1969) published a controversial article in the *Harvard Educational Review,* entitled "How Much Can We Boost IQ and Scholastic Achievement?" Jensen's answer to this question was "not much." He argued that heredity is largely responsible for individual, racial, and social-class differences in IQ, a position he continues to maintain (Jensen, 1980, 1985).

Jensen's work received widespread public attention. It was followed by an outpouring of responses and research studies. In addition, there were ethical challenges from scientists deeply concerned that his conclusions would be used inappropriately to fuel social prejudices. Today, the controversy has died down. Most researchers have come to the reasoned conclusion that both genetic and environmental factors make important contributions to individual and group differences in IQ. Furthermore (as we indicated in Chapter 3), the two factors are often difficult to disentangle. But before we consider the evidence on this issue, let's look at group differences in IQ scores, since they are at the heart of the controversy.

Differences in General Intelligence

American black children score, on the average, 15 points below American white children on measures of general intelligence (Brody, 1992). A smaller social-class

What are the origins of racial and social-class differences in intelligence? Research aimed at answering this question has been the subject of heated controversy. (MARY KATE DENNY/PHOTOEDIT)

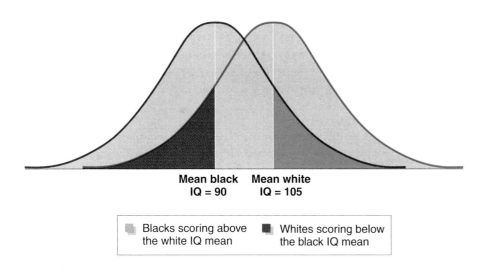

Mean black
IQ = 90

Mean white
IQ = 105

Blacks scoring above the white IQ mean

Whites scoring below the black IQ mean

FIGURE 8.6 IQ score distributions for black and white children. The means represent approximate values obtained in studies of children reared by their biological parents.

difference also exists. In one large-scale study, low-income children scored 9 points below middle-income children (Jensen & Figueroa, 1975). Since 44 percent of African-American children live in poverty compared to nearly 22 percent of all children in the United States, a reasonable question is whether social class fully accounts for the black-white IQ difference. It accounts for some but not all of it. When black and white children are matched on family income, the black-white IQ gap is reduced by only a third (Jencks, 1972).

No racial differences exist on infant measures of dishabituation to visual stimuli that are good predictors of later IQ (Fagan & Singer, 1983). But before the third year of life, African-American children lag behind their white counterparts on other mental tests, a difference that persists into adulthood (Brody, 1992). Still, we must keep in mind that there is great variability in IQ within each race and social class. For example, as Figure 8.6 shows, the IQ distributions of blacks and whites overlap greatly. About 16 percent of blacks score above the white mean, and the same percentage of whites score below the black mean. In fact, race and social class account for only about one-fourth of the total variation in IQ (Jensen, 1980). Nevertheless, these group differences are large enough and serious enough that they cannot be ignored.

Differences in Specific Mental Abilities

Are racial and social-class differences limited to certain kinds of mental abilities? Arthur Jensen (1985, 1988) believes so. In his **Level I–Level II theory,** Jensen distinguishes two kinds of intelligence. Level I refers to items emphasizing short-term and rote memory, such as digit span and recall of basic arithmetic facts. In contrast, Level II involves abstract reasoning and problem solving—items strongly correlated with Spearman's "g," such as vocabulary, verbal comprehension, spatial visualization, and figure matrices. (Turn back to Figure 8.1 on page 310 to review examples of these items.)

According to Jensen, black-white and social-class differences in IQ are largely due to Level II abilities; the groups are about the same in Level I intelligence (Jensen, 1985, 1988; Naglleri & Jensen, 1987). Furthermore, Jensen indicated that among Level II abilities, black children do worst on the least culturally loaded, fluid-type items (such as figure matrices) and best on crystallized tasks (such as vocabulary). Therefore, he argued, black-white IQ differences cannot be caused by cultural bias in the tests. Jensen's conclusion—that blacks are least well endowed with higher-order, abstract forms of intelligence—intensified public outcries about the racist implications of his work.

Is there support for Jensen's Level I–Level II theory? In reviewing a large number of studies, one researcher judged that most were consistent with it

Level I–Level II theory
Jensen's controversial theory, which states that racial and social-class differences in IQ are due to genetic differences in higher-order, abstract forms of intelligence (Level II) rather than basic memory skills (Level I).

(Vernon, 1981, 1987). But others have not been able to confirm the theory. For example, Nathan Brody (1987) found that test items strongly correlated with "g" did not always produce the largest black-white IQ differences. A second group of researchers reported that both Level I and Level II scores declined similarly with social class (Stankov, Horn, & Roy, 1980).

These findings suggest that "g" contributes to racial and social-class differences in IQ, but it is not the only basis for them. At present, the evidence on specific mental abilities is not clear enough to favor either a genetic or cultural-bias explanation. To explore the basis for individual and group differences in IQ, we must turn to a very different set of evidence.

EXPLAINING INDIVIDUAL AND GROUP DIFFERENCES IN IQ

Over the past two decades, researchers have conducted hundreds of studies aimed at uncovering the origins of racial, social-class, and individual differences in mental abilities. The research falls into three broad classes: (1) investigations addressing the importance of heredity; (2) those that look at whether IQ scores are biased measures of low-income and minority children's true abilities; and (3) those that examine the quality of children's home environments as a major influence on their mental test performance.

Genetic Influences

Recall from Chapter 3 that behavioral geneticists examine the relative contributions of heredity and environment to complex human characteristics by conducting *kinship studies,* in which they compare individuals of differing degrees of genetic relationship to one another. Let's look closely at what they have discovered about genetic influences on IQ.

HERITABILITY OF INTELLIGENCE. In Chapter 3, we introduced the most common method for studying the role of heredity in IQ—the *heritability estimate.* To briefly review, first the IQs of pairs of family members who vary in the extent to which they share genes in common are correlated. Then, using a complicated statistical procedure, the correlations are compared to arrive at an index of heritability, ranging from 0 to 1, that indicates the proportion of variation among individuals due to genetic factors.

Let's begin our consideration of the importance of heredity by looking closely at the correlations on which heritability estimates are based. Thomas Bouchard and Matt McGue (1981) summarized worldwide findings on the IQs of kinship pairs. The correlations, listed in Table 8.4, clearly show that the greater the genetic similarity between family members, the more they resemble one another in IQ. In fact, two of the correlations reveal that heredity is, without question, partially responsible for individual differences in mental test performance. The correlation for identical twins reared apart (.72) is much higher than for fraternal twins reared together in the same household (.60).

When researchers look at how these kinship correlations change with age, they find additional support for the importance of heredity. As Figure 8.7 shows, when a sample of twins was followed from infancy into adolescence, the correlations for identicals gradually increased and those for fraternals decreased (Wilson, 1983). Do these trends remind you of the *niche-picking* idea we discussed in Chapter 3? Common rearing experiences support the similarity of fraternal twins during childhood. But as they get older and are released from the influence of their families, each fraternal twin follows a course of development, or finds a niche, that fits with his or her unique genetic makeup. As a result, their IQ scores diverge. In contrast, the genetic likeness of identical twins leads them to seek out similar niches in adolescence. Consequently, their IQ resemblance is even greater

TABLE 8.4 *Worldwide Summary of IQ Correlations Between Kinship Pairs*

KINSHIP PAIR	AVERAGE WEIGHTED CORRELATION	TOTAL NUMBER OF KINSHIP PAIRS INCLUDED	NUMBER OF STUDIES
Identical twins reared together	.86	4,672	34
Identical twins reared apart	.72	65	3
Fraternal twins reared together	.60	5,546	41
Biological siblings reared together	.47	26,473	69
Biological siblings reared apart	.24	203	2
Parent–biological child living together	.42	8,433	32
Parent–biological child living apart	.22*	814	4
Nonbiological siblings (adopted–natural pairings)	.29	345	5
Nonbiological siblings (adopted–adopted pairings)	.34	369	6
Parent–adopted child	.19	1,397	6

*This correlation is lower than the values obtained in three recent adoption studies, which reported correlations of .31, .37, and .43 (Horn, 1983; Phillips & Fulker, 1989; Scarr & Weinberg, 1983).

SOURCE: From "Familial Studies of Intelligence: A Review" by T. J. Bouchard, Jr., & M. McGue, 1981, *Science, 212,* p. 1056. Copyright © 1981 by the AAAS. Reprinted by permission.

than it was during childhood. Other similar studies agree that the contribution of heredity to intelligence strengthens with development (DeFries, Plomin, & LaBuda, 1987; Loehlin, Horn, & Willerman, 1989).

Although kinship studies highlight the importance of heredity, a careful review of all the correlations in Table 8.4 reveals that its role is only moderate. For example, the correlation for identical twins reared apart (.72) is considerably lower than when they are reared together (.86), a difference that points to the importance

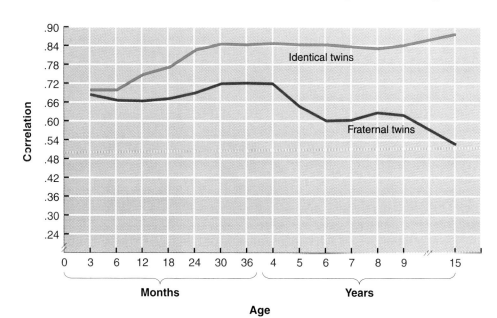

FIGURE 8.7 Age-related changes in IQ correlations for a sample of identical and fraternal twins. (From "The Louisville Twin Study: Developmental Synchronies in Behavior" by R. S. Wilson, 1983, *Child Development, 54,* p. 311. © The Society for Research in Child Development, Inc. Reprinted by permission.)

of environment. Other comparisons that stress the role of environment include the stronger correlation for fraternal twins than ordinary siblings (due to twins' more similar rearing conditions); the stronger correlation for siblings reared together than apart; and the stronger correlation for parents and biological children living together than apart. Finally, parents and adopted children, as well as unrelated siblings, show low positive correlations, again providing support for the effects of common rearing conditions.

As we indicated in Chapter 3, heritability estimates are usually computed using correlations for identical and fraternal twins. Typical values arrived at over the past 20 years range from .30 to .70 (Bouchard et al., 1990; McGue & Bouchard, 1989). The true value is believed to be about .50, which means that half the variation in IQ is due to individual differences in heredity (Scarr & Kidd, 1983). This is a much more modest estimate than the value of .80 arrived at by Jensen as part of his controversial 1969 article.

Furthermore, we noted in Chapter 3 that even this moderate value may be too high, since twins reared together often experience very similar overall environments. And even when they are reared apart, they are often placed in foster and adoptive homes that are advantaged and alike in many ways. When the range of environments to which twins are exposed is restricted, heritabilities underestimate the role of environment and overestimate the role of heredity. So although heritability research offers convincing evidence that genetic factors contribute to IQ, disagreement persists over how large the role of heredity really is (Ceci, 1990).

DO HERITABILITY ESTIMATES EXPLAIN RACIAL AND SOCIAL-CLASS DIFFERENCES IN IQ? Despite the limitations of the heritability estimate, Jensen (1969, 1973) relied on it to support the argument that racial and social-class differences in IQ have a strong genetic basis. This line of reasoning is widely regarded as inappropriate. Although heritability estimates computed *within* black and white populations are similar, they provide no direct evidence about what is responsible for *between-group* differences in IQ (Brody, 1992; Plomin, 1990).

In a well-known example, Richard Lewontin (1976) showed that using within-group heritabilities to explain between group-differences is like comparing different seeds in different soil. Suppose we take a handful of "white" corn seeds (which vary in genetic makeup) and plant them in the same pot with a rich supply of fertilizer designed to promote plant growth. Then we take a handful of "black" seeds and grow them under quite different conditions, in a pot with half as much fertilizer. We find that although the plants in each group vary in height, the "white" seeds, on the average, grow taller than the "black" seeds. *Within* each group, individual differences in plant height are largely due to heredity, since growth environments of all plants were much the same. But the *between-group* difference is probably environmental, since the fertilizer given to the "black" seeds was far less plentiful.

To be sure of this conclusion, we could design a second study in which we expose the "black" seeds to a full supply of fertilizer and see if they reach an average height that equals that of the "white" seeds. If they do, then we would have more powerful evidence that environment is responsible for the previous group difference. In the next section, we will see that researchers have conducted natural experiments of this kind by studying the IQs of children adopted into homes very different from their family of origin.

ADOPTION RESEARCH. Adoption studies provide a wider range of information than the twin evidence on heritability we have considered so far. Correlations of children with their biological and adoptive family members can be examined for the relative importance of heredity and environment. Even more important, researchers can gain insight into how malleable IQ is by looking at changes in the absolute value of test scores as the result of growing up in an advantaged family.

One of the earliest and best-known of these investigations was carried out nearly a half-century ago by Marie Skodak and Harold Skeels (1949). They repeatedly tested the intelligence of 100 children who had been placed in adoptive homes before 6 months of age. Although the biological parents were largely low income, the adoptive parents were well above average in earnings and education. Children's scores remained above the population mean throughout middle childhood and into adolescence, suggesting that IQ is highly malleable! Nevertheless, children's IQs still showed substantial correlation with the scores of their biological mothers, providing support for the influence of heredity.

Skodak and Skeels's groundbreaking study suffered from one important limitation. *Selective placement* of adoptees took place. That is, children with the best-off biological parents tended to be placed with the most advantaged adoptive families. When this occurs, genetic and environmental influences on children's IQ scores cannot be separated completely.

But more recent adoption research, in which selective placement was judged to be minimal, agrees with Skodak and Skeels's findings. The Texas Adoption Project resulted from the discovery of a large private adoption agency that had routinely given IQ tests to unwed mothers staying in its residence until they gave birth. Children of two extreme groups of mothers—those with IQs below 95 and those with IQs above 120—were chosen for special study. As Figure 8.8 shows, when tested in middle childhood, both groups scored above average in IQ. But children of the low-IQ biological mothers did not do nearly as well as children of brighter mothers who were placed in similar adoptive families (Horn, 1983; Willerman, 1979). And when correlations were examined, adopted children showed an increasing tendency to resemble their biological mothers as they grew older and a decreasing tendency to be similar to their adoptive parents (Loehlin, Horn, & Willerman, 1989). In sum, adoption research shows that *both* environment *and* heredity contribute significantly to IQ.

The fact that adopted children have consistently been found to score above average in IQ suggests that the social-class difference in intelligence has a substantial environmental component. But concluding that it is entirely due to environment is probably too extreme. Although children of low-IQ biological mothers adopted into middle-class families attain above-average IQs, they generally score somewhat lower than their adoptive parents' natural children, with whom they share equally privileged rearing conditions. In addition, adoption studies repeatedly reveal stronger correlations between the IQ scores of biological than adoptive relatives (Horn, 1983; Plomin & DeFries, 1983; Scarr & Weinberg, 1983). On the basis of these findings, several researchers have concluded that the social class–IQ relationship is partly genetic in origin (Bouchard & Segal, 1985; Scarr & Weinberg, 1978).

What about the black-white IQ gap? In this case, adoption research shows that it is environmental; it cannot be assigned to racially linked, inferior genes. See the Cultural Influences box on page 332 for a description of this important research.

Cultural Background and Test Bias

A controversial question raised about racial and ethnic differences in IQ has to do with whether they are an artifact of test content and administration procedures. If a test samples culturally specific knowledge and skills that not all groups of children have had an equal opportunity to learn, then is it a fair measure of the intelligence of all children?

This question has been the subject of heated debate. Some experts reject the idea that intelligence tests are biased, claiming that they were intended to represent important aspects of success in the common culture. According to this perspective, since current mental tests predict scholastic performance equally well for majority and minority children, they are fair measures for both groups (Barrett & Depinet, 1991; Jensen, 1980; Oakland & Parmelee, 1985). Others take a broader view of test bias. They believe that lack of prior exposure to test content, language customs, and motivational concerns lead IQ scores to underestimate the abilities of low-income minority children (Ceci, 1990; Sternberg, 1988; Zigler & Seitz, 1982). To evaluate this position, let's look at each of these factors.

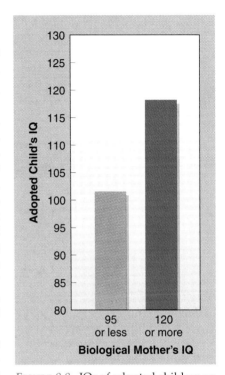

FIGURE 8.8 IQs of adopted children as a function of biological mothers' IQ in the Texas Adoption Project. In this study, selective placement was not great enough to account for the large difference in performance between the two groups. (Adapted from Willerman, 1979.)

Two transracial adoption studies, both focusing on the development of black children growing up in white middle-class homes, provide evidence on the origins of IQ differences between black and white children. If Jensen's claim that black children are limited in potential is correct, then IQs of black adoptees should remain considerably below those of other children growing up in advantaged white families. If black children are as well equipped genetically as white children, then their IQs should rise when they are reared by white parents "in the culture of the tests and schools."

Sandra Scarr and Richard Weinberg (1976, 1983) gave IQ tests during childhood and adolescence to over one hundred transracially adopted black children. Two-thirds were placed during the first year of life, one-third after 12 months of age. The white adoptive parents had high-average to superior IQs, were well above average in occupational status and income, and had 4 to 5 more years of education than the children's biological parents. When tested in childhood, the adoptees attained an average IQ of 106, considerably above the general population mean. The scores of those who had been adopted within the first 12 months were even higher. They averaged 110, 20 points above the mean of children growing up in low-income black communities. The researchers concluded that heredity cannot account for black children's typically depressed intelligence test scores.

A second transracial study lends insight into cultural experiences that contributed to Scarr and Weinberg's findings. Elsie Moore (1986) compared the test-taking behavior and parent–child interaction of two groups of black adoptees: one growing up in white and the other growing up in black middle-class families. Tested between 7 and 10 years of age, the traditionally adopted children did well, attaining a mean IQ of 104. But scores of their transracially adopted counterparts were much higher, averaging 117.

Consistent with their superior scores, the transracially adopted group approached the test with attitudes and strategies conducive to success. They were more task-involved and persistent, and their responses were more elaborate. When they did not know an answer, they rarely attributed failure to their own inability. The transracially adopted group's greater test-taking confidence was, in turn, related to their mothers' special support of problem-solving behavior. When asked to teach their children a difficult task, the white mothers displayed more encouragement and enthusiasm for their children's efforts.

These findings indicate that rearing environment, not hereditary endowment, accounts for the black-white IQ gap. However, the researchers were careful to point out that their findings are not an endorsement for widespread adoption of black children into white homes. Instead, they call for more research on ways in which ethnically different families promote a diverse array of cognitive skills.

PRIOR EXPOSURE TO TEST CONTENT. Many researchers argue that IQ scores are affected by specific information acquired as part of middle-class upbringing. Unfortunately, efforts to make tests fairer to minorities, either by basing them on more familiar content or by eliminating crystallized items and using only fluid tasks, has not raised the scores of these children very much (Kaplan, 1985). For example, *Raven Progressive Matrices* is one of the most commonly used culture-fair tests of fluid intelligence. To see a typical item, look back at the figure matrix task in Figure 8.1. Yet low-income minority children continue to perform more poorly on the Raven test, and others like it, than their white middle-class agemates (Jensen, 1980).

Nevertheless, it is possible that high scores on fluid tests depend on subtle learning opportunities. In one study, children's performance on a spatial reasoning subscale of the WISC was related to the extent to which they had played a popular but expensive game that (like the test items) required them to arrange blocks to duplicate a design as quickly as possible (Dirks, 1982). Low-income minority children, who often grow up in more "people-oriented" than "object-oriented" homes, may lack experiences with games and objects that promote certain intellectual skills. In line with this possibility, when a large, ethnically diverse sample of parents were asked about characteristics important to their idea of an intelligent first-grader, Anglo-Americans valued cognitive traits over noncognitive ones. In contrast, ethnic minorities (Cambodian, Filipino, Vietnamese, and Mexican immigrants) saw noncognitive attributes—motivation, self-management, and social skills—as equally or more important than cognitive skills. Mexican parents, especially, highly valued the social component of intelligence (Okagaki & Sternberg, 1993).

*M*iddle-income children grow up in more "object-oriented" homes, low-income ethnic minority children in more "people-oriented" homes. The many opportunities this middle-class boy has to play with construction toys give him an advantage on tests of spatial reasoning.
(MIRO VINTONIV/STOCK BOSTON)

Finally, recall the evidence presented earlier in this chapter that the more time children spend in school, the higher their IQ scores. It also supports the conclusion that exposure to specific information resembling the content of intelligence tests affects performance on a wide range of mental-ability tasks (Ceci, 1991).

LANGUAGE CUSTOMS. Ethnic minority families often foster unique language skills that do not match the expectations of most classrooms and testing situations. Shirley Brice Heath (1982, 1989), an anthropologist who spent many hours observing in low-income black homes in a southeastern American city, found that adults asked black children very different kinds of questions than is typical in white middle-class families. From an early age, white parents ask knowledge-training questions, such as "What color is it?" and "What's this story about?" that resemble the questioning style of tests and classrooms. In contrast, the black parents asked only "real" questions—ones that they themselves did not know the answer to. Often these were analogy questions ("What's that like?") or story-starter questions ("Didja hear Miss Sally this morning?") that called for elaborate responses about whole events and had no single right answer. The black children developed complex verbal skills at home, such as storytelling and exchanging quick-witted remarks. But these worked poorly when they got to school. The children were confused by the questions they encountered in classrooms and often withdrew into silence.

When faced with the strangeness of the testing situation, the minority child may look to the examiner for cues about how to respond. Yet most intelligence tests permit tasks to be presented in only one way, and they allow no feedback. Consequently, minority children may simply give the first answer that comes to mind, not one that truly represents what they know. Turn back to the beginning of this chapter and review Jermaine's responses to Nora's questions. Jermaine appeared to repeat his first answer because he had trouble figuring out the task's meaning, not because he was unable to classify objects. Had Nora prompted him to look at the questions in a different way, his performance might have been better (Miller-Jones, 1989).

MOTIVATIONAL CONCERNS. When tested by an unfamiliar adult, children from poverty backgrounds often reply "I don't know" to the simplest of questions, including "What's your name?" The response does not reflect lack of ability. Instead, it is due to wariness of the examiner and the testing situation. As a result, the fearful child behaves in ways aimed at minimizing interaction and terminating the unpleasant experience as quickly as possible (Zigler & Finn-Stevenson, 1992). Besides discomfort in the presence of strangers, many low-income minority children do not define testing conditions in achievement terms. They may be more concerned with attention and approval from the adult than answering as many questions correctly as possible (Zigler & Seitz, 1982).

Research indicates that IQs improve when testing conditions are modified so that the minority child has a chance to become familiar with the examiner, is praised frequently, and is given easier items after incorrect responses to minimize the emotional consequences of failure. In the most impressive of these studies, preschoolers from poverty-stricken backgrounds who experienced a short play period with the examiner or who were tested a second time showed gains of 10 points. In contrast, the scores of middle-class children increased by only 3 points (Zigler, Abelson, & Seitz, 1973).

Although these procedures ease adjustment of young children to the testing situation, many low-income minority children suffer from more deep-seated motivational difficulties. As they experience repeated academic failure, they are likely to develop a self-defeating style marked by withdrawal, disengagement, and reduced effort that severely affects their approach to tests and school tasks. Recent evidence indicates a growing discrepancy over the school years between high- and low-achieving children in their motivation to excel on standardized tests (Paris et al., 1991). As a result, IQs may become especially inaccurate indicators of these youngsters' learning potential at older ages.

Overcoming Test Bias

Although not all experts agree, today there is greater acknowledgment that IQ scores can underestimate the intelligence of culturally different children. A special concern exists about incorrectly labeling minority children as slow learners and assigning them to remedial classes, which are far less stimulating than regular school experiences. Because of this danger, precautions are advised when evaluating children for the purpose of educational placement. Besides test scores, assessments of children's adaptive behavior—their ability to cope with the demands of their everyday environments—should be obtained (Landesman & Ramey, 1989). The child who does poorly on an IQ test yet plays a complex game on the playground, figures out how to rewire a broken TV, or cares for younger siblings responsibly is unlikely to be mentally deficient.

In addition, test designers have become increasingly aware of the importance of using culturally relevant procedures and materials to test minority children. Current efforts to do so have produced some impressive results. For example, steps taken to increase test fairness in construction of the K-ABC (see page 318) cut the typical black-white IQ gap in half and nearly equalized the scores of Hispanic and white youngsters (Kaufman, Kamphaus, & Kaufman, 1985).

A few researchers advocate that new tests move even further in this direction. For example, Dalton Miller-Jones (1989) points out that minority children are often capable of the cognitive operations called for by test items. But because they are used to thinking in other ways in daily life, they may not access the required operation immediately. He recommends that assessment procedures permit examiners to probe for the reasoning behind a child's response. Then answers can be evaluated in light of the range of cognitive processes emphasized in the child's ethnic group.

Miller-Jones's proposal requires that we understand much more than we currently do about the impact of cultural contexts on cognitive development. Until we have such knowledge, should we suspend the use of intelligence tests in schools? Most regard this solution as unacceptable, since important educational decisions would be based only on subjective impressions—a policy that actually increases the discriminatory placement of minority children (Reschly, 1981).

Intelligence tests are useful as long as they are interpreted carefully by examiners who are sensitive to the impact of culture on test performance. And despite their limitations, IQ scores continue to be valid measures of school learning potential for the majority of Western children.

Home Environment and IQ

Racial, ethnic, and social-class differences are not the only important IQ variations with environmental explanations. As we indicated earlier, children of the *same* ethnic and social-class background also vary in IQ. Many studies support the conclusion that home environmental factors contribute to these differences.

Researchers divide home influences into two broad types. The first, called **shared environmental influences**, are factors that pervade the general atmosphere of the home and, therefore, affect all children living in it to the same extent. The availability of stimulating toys and books and modeling by parents of intellectual activities are good examples. The second type, **nonshared environmental influences,** refers to factors that make siblings *different* from one another. Examples include unique treatment by parents, birth order and spacing, as well as certain events, such as moving to a new neighborhood, that affect one sibling more than another. Let's see what research says about each of these classes of environmental events.

SHARED ENVIRONMENTAL INFLUENCES. To assess the impact of home environment on intelligence, Robert Bradley, Bettye Caldwell, and Richard Elardo developed the **Home Observation for Measurement of the Environment (HOME)**, a checklist for gathering information about the quality of children's home lives through observation and parental interview (Bradley & Caldwell, 1979; Bradley et al., 1988; Elardo, Bradley, & Caldwell, 1975). Separate infancy, preschool, and middle childhood versions exist. Table 8.5 shows the subscales measured by each.

Evidence on HOME confirms the findings of many years of research—that stimulation provided by parents is linked to mental development. All infant and preschool subscales are moderately correlated with IQ, although the most important ones change with age. In infancy, organization of the physical environment and variety in daily stimulation show strongest relationships with mental test scores. During the preschool years, warmth, stimulation of language and academic behavior, and provision of appropriate play materials are the best predictors (Bradley & Caldwell, 1976; Elardo, Bradley, & Caldwell, 1975, 1977). Furthermore, high HOME scores during infancy are associated with IQ gains between 1 and 3 years, whereas low HOME scores predict declines as large as 15 to 20 points (Bradley et al., 1989). The strength of the association between HOME and IQ declines in middle childhood, perhaps because older children spend longer periods of time in other settings, such as school. Nevertheless, the relationship is still present (Luster & Dubow, 1992).*

When home environments within different social class and ethnic groups are examined, the findings are much the same. A stimulating physical environment, encouragement of achievement, and affection are repeatedly linked to IQ, no matter what the child's background (Bradley & Caldwell, 1981, 1982; Bradley et al., 1989; Luster & Dubow, 1992). In fact, HOME scores are more effective predictors of children's mental development than are global ratings of family status, such as social class and parent education.

At the same time, we must be careful about interpreting these correlational findings, since they tell us nothing definite about causation. In all the studies

Shared environmental influences
Environmental influences that pervade the general atmosphere of the home and affect all children living in it to the same extent.

Nonshared environmental influences
Environmental influences that make children living in the same family different from one another.

Home Observation for Measurement of the Environment (HOME)
A checklist for gathering information about the quality of children's home lives through observation and parental interviews. Infancy, preschool, and middle childhood versions exist.

*Because the middle childhood version of HOME is new, we do not yet know which of its subscales predict IQ most effectively. In one study, two were especially strong predictors of academic achievement: provision for active stimulation (for example, encouraging hobbies, trips to the library, and organizational memberships) and family participation in stimulating experiences (visiting friends or relatives, attending musical or theater performances) (Bradley, Caldwell, & Rock, 1988).

rivalry with a sibling are examples. The most important nonshared influences may be of this kind. To understand their role in mental development, we need more intensive studies of children growing up in the same family than have been accomplished to date (Brody, 1992; McCall, 1983).

Brief Review

The existence of racial, ethnic, and social-class differences in intelligence test performance has sparked the IQ nature–nurture debate. Heritability estimates indicate that genetic factors account for about half of the variation among individuals in mental test scores. However, heritabilities cannot explain racial and social-class differences in IQ. Adoption research reveals that IQ is highly malleable. At the same time, heredity remains important, since adopted children's scores are more strongly correlated with the IQs of their biological than adoptive relatives.

Researchers who view mental tests as biased point to test content, language customs, and motivational concerns that can lead IQs to underestimate the intelligence of low-income and ethnic minority children. Supplementing IQs with measures of adaptive behavior and adjusting testing procedures to take cultural differences into account are ways of reducing test bias. A stimulating home environment and parental warmth and encouragement of achievement consistently predict higher mental test scores. Factors considered by the confluence model, such as birth order and spacing, also predict IQ, but they are not very powerful.

EARLY INTERVENTION AND INTELLECTUAL DEVELOPMENT

In the 1960s, during a decade in which the United States launched a "war on poverty," a wide variety of early intervention programs for economically disadvantaged preschoolers were initiated. They were based on the assumption that learning problems were best treated early, before the beginning of formal schooling, as well as the hope that early enrichment would offset the declines in IQ and achievement common among children from low-income and ethnic minority backgrounds.

Many intervention programs continue to exist today. The most widespread is **Project Head Start,** initiated by the federal government in 1965. A typical Head Start program provides children with a year or two of preschool education before they enter school, along with nutritional and medical services. In addition, parent involvement is a central part of the Head Start philosophy. Parents serve on policy councils and contribute to program planning. They also work directly with children in classrooms, attend special programs on parenting and child development, and receive services directed at their own social, emotional, and vocational needs. Currently, over 1,300 Head Start centers located around the country enroll about 720,000 children (Children's Defense Fund, 1993).

The Impact of Early Intervention

Two decades of research on the long-term benefits of early intervention have played a major role in the survival of Head Start. But the first widely publicized evaluation seriously threatened the program's continuation. It reported that Head Start had only minimal effects on children's intelligence and school achievement (Cicerelli, Evans, & Schiller, 1969). The study was criticized immediately. Carried out a year or more after children had completed Head Start, it suffered from inadequate matching of program and control children and poor sampling of the variety of Head Start interventions available at the time (Smith & Bissell, 1970). Still, many people were convinced by these conclusions. The findings became an important part of Jensen's (1969) argument that the low IQs of poor children were largely hereditary and could not be changed very much.

Project Head Start

A federal program that provides low-income children with a year or two of preschool education before school entry and that encourages parent involvement in children's development.

Economically disadvantaged preschoolers who experience the comprehensive early intervention of Head Start show greater short-term gains in IQ than do similar children who attend other types of preschools or no preschool at all. Although the IQ advantage washes out over time, early intervention has a lasting impact on children's ability to meet basic educational requirements during elementary and secondary school. (J. CHENET/WOODFIN CAMP & ASSOCIATES)

Fortunately, new studies of high-quality university-based early interventions were conducted in which powerful longitudinal designs replaced the questionable approach of the first evaluation. The most important of these was coordinated by the Consortium for Longitudinal Studies, a group of investigators who combined data from seven interventions. Results showed that children who attended programs scored higher in IQ and achievement than controls during the first 2 to 3 years of elementary school. After that time, differences in test scores declined. Nevertheless, children who received intervention remained ahead on measures of real-life school adjustment into adolescence. As Figure 8.10 shows, they were less likely to be placed in special-education classes or retained in grade, and a greater number graduated from high school. There were also lasting benefits in attitudes and motivation. Children who attended programs were more likely to give achievement-related reasons (such as school or job accomplishments) for being proud of themselves, and their mothers held higher vocational aspirations for them (Lazar & Darlington, 1982; Royce, Darlington, & Murray, 1983). A separate report on the long-term outcomes of one program suggested benefits lasting into young adulthood. It was associated with a reduction in delinquency and teenage pregnancy and a greater likelihood of employment (Berrueta-Clement et al., 1984).

Evaluations of Head Start

Do these findings on outstanding university-based programs generalize to Head Start centers located in American communities? Although some studies report only minimal benefits, new evidence reveals that they are biased by one very important factor: Because not all poor children can be served, Head Start typically enrolls the most disadvantaged preschoolers. Controls to whom they are compared often do not come from such extremely impoverished families (Schnur, Brooks-Gunn, & Shipman, 1992).

A recent investigation of Head Start programs in two large cities took this into account. It also looked carefully at the effectiveness of Head Start by comparing it to other preschool alternatives as well as to no preschool at all. Results showed that Head Start children, compared to "other preschool" and "no preschool" groups, had less educated mothers, came from more crowded households, and

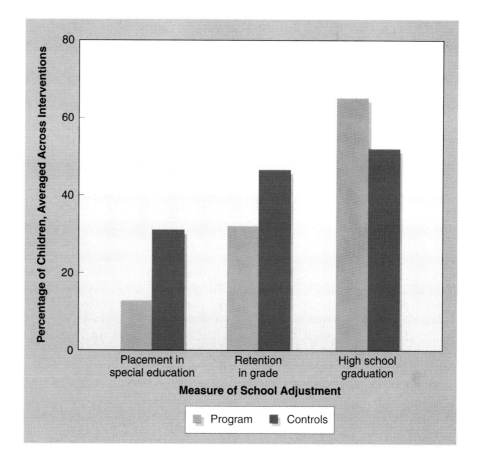

FIGURE 8.10 Benefits of early intervention programs. Low-income children who received intervention fared better than controls on real-life indicators of school adjustment. (Adapted from Royce, Darlington, & Murray, 1983.)

were more likely to be growing up in single-parent homes. Before entering the program, they scored well below the other groups on mental tests. Yet at the end of a year's intervention, Head Start children showed *greater gains* than both comparison groups (Lee, Brooks-Gunn, & Schnur, 1988). Furthermore, when African-American children, who comprised a majority of the sample, were followed up 1 to 2 years after Head Start, gains on several cognitive measures were sustained, although they were no longer as great as they had been immediately after the program (Lee et al., 1990).

A consistent finding of research on Head Start and other preschool interventions is that almost all children experience an eventual **washout effect.** In other words, improvements in IQ and achievement do not last for more than a few years (McKey et al., 1985). This is not surprising, since poverty-stricken children typically attend underfunded, poorer quality schools, especially when they live in urban areas (Kozol, 1991; Wilson, 1987). Their elementary school experiences may cancel out earlier gains. This suggests that to be most effective, interventions need to be supplemented with high-quality educational supports through the school years (Ramey & Ramey, 1990). More intensive programs that start earlier might also produce more enduring gains. Indeed, this is what is suggested by another intervention effort, the Carolina Abecedarian Project, which you can read about in the Social Issues box on the following page.

Despite declining test scores, Head Start graduates (like those of university-based programs) show an improved ability to meet basic educational requirements during elementary and secondary school (Schweinhart & Weikart, 1986). Although researchers are not sure how these effects are achieved, one possibility is that they are largely the result of changes in the attitudes, behaviors, and life circumstances of parents, who create better rearing environments for their children. Consequently, new interventions are being conceived as *two-generation* models.

Washout effect
The loss of IQ and achievement gains resulting from early intervention within a few years after the program ends.

In the 1970s, an experiment was begun to find out if educational enrichment starting at a very early age could prevent the declines in mental development that affect children born into extreme poverty. The Carolina Abecedarian Project identified over a hundred infants at serious risk for school failure, based on parent education and income, a history of poor school achievement among older siblings, and other family problems. Shortly after birth, the babies were randomly assigned to either a treatment or a control group.

Between 3 weeks and 3 months of age, infants in the treatment group were enrolled in a full-time, year-round day-care program, where they remained until they entered kindergarten. During the first 3 years, the children received stimulation aimed at promoting motor, cognitive, language, and social skills. After age 3, the goals of the program expanded to include prereading and math concepts. At all ages, special emphasis was placed on adult–child communication. Teachers were trained to engage in informative, helpful, and nondirective interaction with the children, who were talked to and read to daily. Both treatment and control children received nutrition and health services. The primary difference between them was the day-care experience, designed to support the treatment group's mental development.

Intelligence test scores were gathered on the children regularly, and (as Figure 8.11 indicates) during infancy the performance of the two groups began to diverge. Treatment children scored higher than controls throughout the preschool years (Ramey & Campbell, 1984). Although the high-risk backgrounds of both groups led their IQs to decline over middle childhood, follow-up testing at ages 8 and 12 revealed that treatment children maintained their IQ advantage over controls. In addition, at age 12, treatment youngsters were achieving considerably better, especially in reading, writing, and general knowledge (Campbell & Ramey, 1991; Martin, Ramey, & Ramey, 1990). These findings suggest that providing children with continuous, high-quality enrichment from infancy through the preschool years is an effective way to reduce the devastating impact of poverty on children's mental development.

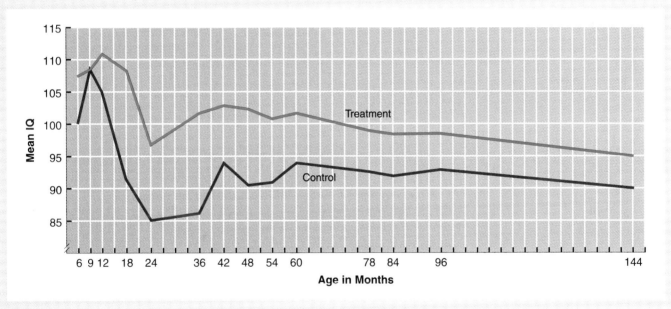

FIGURE 8.11 IQ scores of treatment and control children from 6 months to 12 years in the Carolina Abecedarian Project. (From *The Carolina Abecedarian Project* by F. A. Campbell & C. T. Ramey, 1991, in M. Burchinal (Chair), *Early Experience and Children's Competencies: New Findings from Four Longitudinal Studies.* Symposium presented at the biennial meeting of the Society for Research in Child Development, Seattle, WA. Reprinted by permission of the authors.)

A Two-Generation Program Strategy

A typical parent component of early intervention emphasizes teaching parenting skills and providing other supports that encourage parents to act as supplementary intervenors for their child. Researchers believe these efforts may not be enough (White, Taylor, & Moss, 1992). By expanding intervention to include developmental goals for *both* parents and children, program benefits might be extended. A parent helped to move out of poverty with education, vocational training, and other social services is likely to show improved psychological well-being and greater interest in planning for the future. When combined with child-centered intervention, these gains may translate into lasting changes in parenting behavior and exceptionally strong, long-term benefits for children (Collins, 1993).

Currently, a variety of two-generation models are being tried—several in conjunction with Head Start (Smith, 1991). Although the approach is too new to have yielded much research, one pioneering effort, Project Redirection, provides cause for optimism. In it, teenage mothers received a variety of services for themselves and their babies, including education, employment, family planning, life management, parent education, and child health care. A 5-year follow-up revealed that participants obtained higher HOME scores, were less likely to be on welfare, and had higher family earnings than controls receiving less intensive intervention. In addition, program children were more likely to have enrolled in Head Start, and they had higher verbal IQs (Polit, Quint, & Riccio, 1988).

The Future of Early Intervention

Although over one-fifth of American preschoolers are eligible for Head Start by virtue of their poverty level, at present the program serves less than one-third of these children (Children's Defense Fund, 1992b). Yet Head Start and other interventions like it are highly cost-effective. Program expenses are far less than the funds required to provide special education, treat delinquency, and support welfare dependency. Because of its demonstrated returns to society, a move is currently under way to expand Head Start to reach all eligible 3- and 4-year-olds by 1996 (Collins, 1993).

Nevertheless, the distance in IQ and school achievement between Head Start graduates and their more advantaged peers remains considerable. As early intervention becomes more widespread, there is a need to find ways of increasing and sustaining the short-term cognitive gains that result from 1- and 2-year programs. The research we have considered indicates that more intensive, longer-lasting efforts that focus on the development of both parents and children offer hope of reaching these goals.

BEYOND IQ: INTELLECTUALLY GIFTED CHILDREN

At the beginning of this chapter, we indicated that the concept of intelligence, to experts and laypeople alike, means much more than mental abilities that predict success in school. Today, educators recognize that **gifted** children—those who display exceptional intellectual strengths—have diverse characteristics. Some are high-IQ youngsters with scores above 130—the standard definition of giftedness based on intelligence test performance (Horowitz & O'Brien, 1986). High-IQ children, as we have seen, are particularly quick at academic work. They have keen memories and an exceptional capacity to analyze a challenging problem and move toward a correct solution. Yet over the past two decades, recognition that intelligence tests do not sample the entire range of human mental skills has led to an expanded conception of giftedness in public schools.

Creativity

Besides high IQ, high *creativity* can result in a child being designated as gifted. In adults, creativity generally involves unusual achievement at some culturally meaningful activity, such as writing, music, painting, science, or mathematics (Sternberg & Davidson, 1986; Wallach, 1985). Of course, children are not yet mature enough to make such outstanding contributions. Therefore, in childhood, creativity has taken on a more restricted definition that has its origins in Guilford's distinction between convergent and divergent production. **Convergent thinking,** with its emphasis on arriving at a single correct answer to a problem, is the type of cognition emphasized on intelligence tests. **Divergent thinking,** in

Giftedness
Exceptional intellectual ability. Includes high IQ, creativity, and specialized talent.

Convergent thinking
The generation of a single correct answer to a problem. Type of cognition emphasized on intelligence tests.

Divergent thinking
The generation of multiple and unusual possibilities when faced with a task or problem. Associated with creativity.

FIGURE 8.12 Responses of a highly creative 8-year-old to a figural measure of creativity. This child was asked to make as many pictures as she could from the circles on the page. The titles she gave her drawings, from left to right, are as follows: "dracula," "one-eyed monster," "pumpkin," "hula-hoop," "poster," "wheelchair," "earth," "moon," "planet," "movie camera," "sad face," "picture," "stoplight," "beach ball," "the letter O," "car," "glasses." (Test form copyright © 1980 by Scholastic Testing Service, Inc. Reprinted by permission of Scholastic Testing Service, Inc., from *The Torrance Tests of Creative Thinking* by E. P. Torrance.)

contrast, refers to the generation of multiple and unusual possibilities when faced with a task or problem.

Both verbal and figural tests of divergent thinking exist. A verbal measure might ask children to name as many uses for common objects (such as a newspaper) as they can. A figural measure might ask them to come up with as many drawings based on a circular motif as possible (Torrance, 1980). Responses can be scored for the number of ideas generated as well as their originality. For example, saying that a newspaper can be used "as handgrips for a bicycle" would be more unusual than saying it can be used "to clean things." Figure 8.12 displays the responses of a highly creative 8-year-old to a figural creativity test. Divergent thinking, as well as other indicators of creativity (such as outstanding adult accomplishment), is only weakly related to IQ, a finding that underscores the importance of looking beyond performance on traditional mental tests when identifying gifted children (Kogan, 1983; Reis, 1989).

Comparisons of identical and fraternal twins reveal that the contribution of heredity to individual differences in divergent thinking is extremely weak (Pezzullo, Thorsen, & Madaus, 1972). This suggests that creativity may be especially sensitive to encouragement by parents and teachers. Studies of the home environments of creative children reveal that their parents value nonconformity, emphasize intellectual curiosity, and are highly accepting of their youngster's individual characteristics. Children who score high on measures of divergent thinking are, in turn, broad in their interests, attracted by complexity, and relatively unconcerned about conventional social norms (Albert & Runco, 1986; Wallach, 1985).

Complementing these home background findings, research suggests that the fact- and memory-oriented emphasis of many school classrooms may inhibit divergent thinking. In one study, kindergartners responded with a higher proportion of original responses to creativity tasks than did individuals from second grade into the adult years (Moran et al., 1983). The researchers concluded that the answer-centered approach of most school tasks may make pupils cautious about expressing unusual ideas. Consistent with this interpretation, first- through third-graders attending classrooms that provide greater freedom and choice in learning activities score higher in divergent thinking (Thomas & Berk, 1981).

A wealth of evidence indicates that the venturesome thinking measured by tests of divergent thinking can be encouraged. Many successful techniques have been identified, including modeling of a fluent style of responding and instructing students in generating a wide range of ideas (Runco, 1990). Because of its imaginative quality, make-believe play is especially facilitating. Whether young children engage in it spontaneously or it is induced by an adult, make-believe is related to enhanced performance on divergent-thinking tasks (Dansky, 1980; Pepler & Ross, 1981).

Nevertheless, some researchers question whether promoting divergent thinking is a worthwhile goal. At best, it has turned out to be an imperfect predictor of real-life creative accomplishment (Kogan, 1983; Wallach, 1985). Partly for this reason, many investigators have turned their attention away from general measures of creativity toward the assessment of talent in childhood.

Talent

*S*pecialized talents are rooted in native ability, but they also depend on long-term, systematic instruction. This talented girl profits from apprenticeship in science under a dedicated, highly skilled mentor. (FRANK SITEMAN/THE PICTURE CUBE)

Modern definitions of giftedness have been extended to include *specialized talent*. There is clear evidence that outstanding performances in particular areas, such as literature, mathematics, science, art, athletics, and leadership, have roots in specialized skills that first appear in childhood (Gardner, 1983; Gardner & Hatch, 1989). Recently, researchers have begun to study the unique cognitive processing skills of talented children. Findings reveal that they encode relevant information especially rapidly and are highly adept at combining and comparing it with existing knowledge—capacities that permit many new insights (Shaughnessy, 1990; Sternberg & Davidson, 1986). But the difference between a talented youngster and a less exceptional child is not just cognitive. It is also emotional and motivational. Almost always, a love for the subject and a powerful desire to master it are involved (Sternberg, 1984b).

Although native ability and unusual dedication play a clear role in the development of talent, these traits are not sufficient. They must be nurtured in a favorable social environment (Albert & Runco, 1986). Studies of talented children as well as highly accomplished adult musicians, mathematicians, and athletes point to the importance of systematic instruction from an early age, apprenticeship under inspiring teachers, and deeply committed parents who assist with children's learning (Bloom, 1985; Feldman & Goldsmith, 1991). These findings suggest that the most effective way to foster creativity is to provide talented pupils with training aimed at helping them reach the limits of a particular field and then move beyond.

Educating Gifted Children

Teaching gifted children with a wide range of capacities is a monumental task. Enrichment activities in regular classrooms and pullout programs in which bright youngsters are gathered together for special instruction have been common ways of serving the gifted for decades. Yet these approaches are of limited value, since they usually provide the same experience to all pupils without considering each child's unique talents and skills.

Current trends in gifted education place greater emphasis on building each child's special abilities. One approach is to provide accelerated learning opportunities in which gifted pupils are given fast-paced instruction in a subject or are advanced to a higher grade. Acceleration is a controversial practice because of concerns that bright pupils might suffer socially if they are placed with older pupils. Yet when children are carefully selected on the basis of their maturity, acceleration is highly successful. Longitudinal studies indicate that accelerated pupils continue to be socially well adjusted while demonstrating outstanding academic accomplishments (Brody & Benbow, 1987).

Other innovative techniques include special after-school or Saturday programs that bring children with similar talents together or mentorships in which a highly skilled adult tutors a gifted pupil in a relevant field (Kornhaber, Krechevsky, & Gardner, 1991; Reis, 1989). In some states, Governor's Schools provide advanced instruction in both academic and artistic subjects. As yet, we know little about which of these approaches works best for children of different ages and talents. But one clear benefit of them is that practices designed to stimulate complex problem solving and creativity in the gifted are beginning to spill over into regular classrooms.

Recently, Gardner's theory of multiple intelligences has served as the basis for several model programs that provide domain-specific enrichment to all pupils. A wide variety of meaningful activities, each designed to tap a specific intelligence or set of intelligences, serve as contexts for assessing strengths and weaknesses as well as teaching new skills. For example, linguistic intelligence might be fostered and evaluated through storytelling or playwriting; spatial intelligence through drawing, sculpting, or taking apart and reassembling objects; and kinesthetic intelligence through dance or pantomime (Ramos-Ford & Gardner, 1990).

Evidence is still needed on how effectively these programs nurture children's talents. But so far, they have succeeded in one way—by highlighting the special strengths of some pupils who previously had been considered unexceptional or even at risk for school failure (Gardner & Hatch, 1989). Consequently, they may be especially useful in identifying talented minority children, who are underrepresented in school programs for the gifted (Ford & Harris, 1990). How best to maximize the creative resources of the coming generation—the future poet and scientist as well as the everyday citizen—is a challenging task for future research.

CHAPTER SUMMARY

Definitions of Intelligence

- The **psychometric approach** to cognitive development is the basis for the wide variety of intelligence tests used to assess individual differences in children's mental abilities. In the early 1900s, Alfred Binet developed the first successful test, which provided a single, holistic measure of intelligence.

- **Factor analysis** soon emerged as a major means for determining whether intelligence is a single trait or a collection of many different abilities. The research of Spearman and Thurstone led to two schools of thought. The first regarded test items as having in common one **general factor**, or **"g."** The second viewed intelligence as a set of distinct **primary mental abilities.**

- Modern factor analysts have extended the work of Spearman and Thurstone. Guilford's **structure-of-intellect model** defines a total of 180 separate abilities, several of which acknowledge the existence of social intelligence and creativity. Cattell's distinction between **fluid** and **crystallized intelligence** has influenced many attempts to create culture-fair tests.

Recent Advances in Defining Intelligence

- To provide process-oriented explanations of mental test performance, some researchers conduct **componential analyses** of children's scores by correlating them with laboratory measures of information processing. So far, findings reveal that basic efficiency of thinking and adaptive strategy use are related to measures of general intelligence. Sternberg's **triarchic theory of intelligence** extends these efforts. It views intelligence as a complex interaction of information-processing skills, specific experiences, and contextual (or cultural) influences.

- According to Gardner's **theory of multiple intelligences,** mental abilities should be defined in terms of unique sets of processing operations applied in culturally meaningful activities. His list of seven distinct intelligences has been particularly influential in efforts to understand and nurture children's special talents.

Representative Intelligence Tests for Children

- The **Stanford-Binet Intelligence Scale** and the **Wechsler Intelligence Scale for Children–III** are most often used to identify highly intelligent children and diagnose those with learning problems. The **Kaufman Assessment Battery for Children** is the first major test to be grounded in information-processing theory. Each of these tests provides an overall IQ as well as a profile of subtest scores.

- Traditional infant tests, which consist largely of perceptual and motor responses, predict childhood IQ poorly. The Fagan Test of Infant Intelligence, made up entirely of habituation–dishabituation items, taps basic aspects of cognitive processing and is the best available infant predictor of childhood IQ. Measures of object permanence also correlate better with preschool intelligence than do traditional infant tests.

The Computation and Distribution of IQ Scores
- Modern test designers have abandoned the **mental age (MA)** approach to computing IQ in favor of the **deviation IQ.** It compares a child's raw score to the performance of a large representative sample of same-age children.

What and How Well Do Intelligence Tests Predict?
- IQs obtained after age 6 show substantial correlational stability. Nevertheless, most children display considerable age-related change in the absolute value of their scores. Poverty-stricken ethnic minority children often experience declines due to a **cumulative deficit,** or the compounding effects of underprivileged rearing conditions.
- IQ is an effective predictor of scholastic performance, occupational attainment, and certain aspects of psychological adjustment. However, the underlying causes of these correlational findings are complex. Besides IQ, home background, personality, motivation, and education contribute substantially to academic and life success.

Racial, Ethnic, and Social-Class Differences in IQ
- Black and low-income children score lower on intelligence tests than do white and middle-income children, findings responsible for kindling the IQ nature–nurture debate. Jensen's **Level I–Level II theory** attributes the poorer scores of these children largely to a genetic deficiency in higher-order, abstract forms of ability. However, his theory has been challenged by subsequent research.

Explaining Individual and Group Differences in IQ
- Heritability estimates support a moderate role for heredity in accounting for individual differences in IQ. However, they cannot be used to explain racial, ethnic, and social-class differences in test scores.
- Adoption studies indicate that advantaged rearing conditions can raise the absolute value of children's IQs substantially. At the same time, adopted children's scores correlate more strongly with those of their biological than adoptive relatives, providing support for the influence of heredity.

Research on black children reared in white middle-class homes reveals that the black-white IQ gap is environmentally determined.
- Experts disagree on whether intelligence tests yield biased measures of the mental abilities of low-income minority children. IQ predicts academic achievement equally well for majority and minority children. However, lack of familiarity with test content, language customs, and motivational factors can lead test scores to underestimate minority children's intelligence.
- Besides heredity, **shared** and **nonshared environmental influences** contribute to individual differences in intelligence. Research with the **Home Observation for Measurement of the Environment (HOME)** indicates that overall quality of the home environment consistently predicts IQ. Although the HOME–IQ relationship is partly mediated by heredity, a stimulating family environment does promote higher mental test scores. Factors considered by the **confluence model,** such as birth order and spacing, are also linked to IQ. However, these relationships are weak, and the confluence model has received only mixed support.

Early Intervention and Intellectual Development
- Research on high-quality university-based early interventions as well as **Head Start** programs located in American communities shows that immediate IQ gains **wash out** with time. However, lasting benefits occur in school adjustment and ability to meet basic educational requirements.
- To induce larger and longer-lasting cognitive gains, early intervention needs to start earlier, last longer, and be more intensive. Two-generation program strategies are currently being tried to see if they lead to more powerful long-term outcomes.

Beyond IQ: Intellectually Gifted Children
- **Giftedness** includes high IQ, high creativity, and exceptional talent. **Convergent thinking** is the type of cognition emphasized on intelligence tests. Children who score high in **divergent thinking,** a common measure of creativity, usually come from homes in which nonconformity and intellectual curiosity are valued. Research suggests that the fact-oriented emphasis of traditional classrooms may dampen divergent thinking.
- Because divergent thinking is an imperfect predictor of real-life creative accomplishment, many investigators have turned to the study of specialized talent. A combination of exceptional ability, dedication, and intense and highly supportive instruction contributes to the development of talent.

IMPORTANT TERMS AND CONCEPTS

psychometric approach (p. 308)
factor analysis (p. 311)
general factor, or "g" (p. 311)
specific factor, or "s" (p. 311)
primary mental abilities (p. 311)
structure-of-intellect model (p. 311)
crystallized intelligence (p. 312)
fluid intelligence (p. 312)
componential analysis (p. 313)
triarchic theory of intelligence (p. 314)
theory of multiple intelligences (p. 315)

Stanford-Binet Intelligence Scale (p. 317)
Wechsler Intelligence Scale for
    Children–III (WISC–III) (p. 317)
Kaufman Assessment Battery for Children
    (K-ABC) (p. 318)
intelligence quotient (IQ) (p. 319)
mental age (MA) (p. 319)
deviation IQ (p. 320)
cumulative deficit hypothesis (p. 322)
Level I–Level II theory (p. 327)
shared environmental influences (p. 335)

nonshared environmental
    influences (p. 335)
Home Observation for Measurement of
    the Environment (HOME) (p. 335)
confluence model (p. 337)
Project Head Start (p. 338)
washout effect (p. 340)
giftedness (p. 342)
convergent thinking (p. 342)
divergent thinking (p. 342)

C O N N E C T I O N S

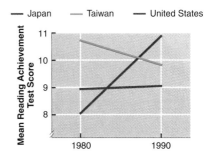

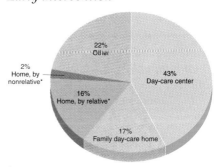

* "Home" refers to either the child's home or the caregiver's home.

"There's a beehive at Uncle Joe's farm, so we could get some there," suggests Connie.

"We won't be seeing Uncle Joe until next summer," explains Connie's mother. "I'll get a jar at the store while you're at nursery school."

....

Language—the most awesome of universal human achievements—develops with extraordinary speed over the early childhood years. At age 1, Mark uses single words to name familiar objects and convey his desires. Three-year-old Susan already grasps some subtle conventions of human communication. Although her father's message is phrased as a question, she knows that he intends it to be a command and willingly complies by closing the door. In her report of the accomplished act, Susan combines words into meaningful sentences she has never heard before. Even her mistakes, such as "shutted," attest to her active, rule-oriented approach to language. Four-year-old Connie produces longer utterances and more sophisticated language structures. In making topic-relevant comments in a short exchange with her mother, Connie shows that she is a skilled conversational partner.

Children's amazing linguistic accomplishments raise some of the most puzzling questions about development. How are a vast vocabulary and an intricate grammatical system acquired in such a short time? Is language a separate capacity, or is it simply one aspect of our general cognitive ability? Without exposure to a rich verbal environment, will young children invent their own language? Do all children acquire language in the same way, or are there individual and cultural differences?

To explore these questions, we follow the common practice of dividing language into four components. By examining each separately, we can more fully appreciate the diverse skills children must master to become competent communicators. Our discussion of development opens with the fiery theoretical debate of the 1950s between behaviorist B. F. Skinner and linguist Noam Chomsky, which inspired the burst of research since that time. Then we turn to infant preparatory skills that set the stage for the child's first words during the second year of life. Next, for each component of language, we first describe *what* develops and then treat the more controversial question of *how* children acquire so much in so little time. We conclude with the challenges and benefits of bilingualism—mastering two languages—in childhood.

COMPONENTS OF LANGUAGE

When children learn language, exactly what is it that they must learn? Language consists of several subsystems that have to do with sound, meaning, overall structure, and everyday use. Knowing language entails mastering each of these aspects and combining them into a flexible communicative system.

The first component, **phonology**, refers to the sounds of language. If you have ever visited a foreign country in which you did not know the language, you probably wondered how anyone could analyze the rapid flow of speech sounds into organized strings of words. Yet in English, you easily apply an intricate set of rules to comprehend and produce complicated sound patterns. How you acquired this ability is the story of phonological development.

Semantics involves vocabulary, or the way underlying concepts are expressed in words and word combinations. As we will see later, when young children first use a word, it often does not mean the same thing as it does to an adult. To build a versatile vocabulary, preschoolers must refine the meanings of thousands of words and connect them into elaborate networks of related terms. With age, children not only use many words correctly but become consciously aware of what they mean. As a result, they can define and experiment with words in imaginative ways.

Phonology
The component of language concerned with understanding and producing speech sounds.

Semantics
The component of language concerned with understanding the meaning of words and word combinations.

To engage in effective verbal communication, children must combine four components of language that have to do with sound, meaning, overall structure, and everyday use. (JULIE O'NEIL/ THE PICTURE CUBE)

Once mastery of vocabulary is progressing, children begin to combine words and modify them in meaningful ways. Knowledge of **grammar** consists of two main parts: *syntax,* the rules by which words are arranged into sentences; and *morphology,* the use of grammatical markers that indicate number, tense, case, person, gender, active or passive voice, and other meanings (the "-s" and "-ed" endings are examples in English).

Finally, **pragmatics** refers to the communicative side of language. To interact effectively, children must learn to take turns, maintain topic relevance, and communicate clearly. They must also figure out how to use gestures, tone of voice, and the context in which an utterance is spoken to clarify its meaning. Pragmatics also involves *sociolinguistic knowledge,* since society dictates how language should be spoken. To be successful communicators, children must acquire certain interaction rituals, such as verbal greetings and leave takings. They must also adjust their speech to mark important social relationships, such as differences in age and status.

As we take up each of the four aspects of language, you will see that they are really interdependent. Acquisition of each one facilitates mastery of the others.

THEORIES OF LANGUAGE DEVELOPMENT

During the first half of this century, research on language development was primarily descriptive—aimed at establishing norms of development. The first studies identified milestones that applied to children around the globe: all babbled around 6 months, said their first words at about 1 year, combined words at the end of the second year, and were in command of a vast vocabulary and most grammatical constructions by 4 to 5 years of age. The regularity of these achievements suggested a process largely governed by maturation. Yet at the same time, language seemed to be learned, since without exposure to a spoken language, children who were born deaf or who were severely neglected did not acquire verbal communication. This apparent contradiction set the stage for a nature–nurture debate as intense as any that has been waged in the field of child development. By the end of the 1950s, two major figures had taken opposite sides in the controversy.

The Behaviorist Perspective

In his book *Verbal Behavior,* published in 1957, B. F. Skinner concluded that language, just like any other behavior, is learned as adults apply the principles of *operant conditioning* to their children's verbalizations. As the baby makes sounds,

Grammar
The component of language concerned with syntax, the rules by which words are arranged into sentences, and morphology, the use of grammatical markers that indicate number, tense, case, person, gender, and other meanings.

Pragmatics
The component of language concerned with how to engage in effective and appropriate communication with others.

parents reinforce those that are most like words with smiles, hugs, and speech in return. For example, at 12 months, my older son David could often be heard babbling something like this: "book-a-book-a-dook-a-dook-a-book-a-nook-a-book-aaa." One day, I held up his picture book while he babbled away and said, "Book!" Very soon, David was saying "book-aaa" in the presence of books.

Although operant conditioning has been used to account for children's verbal behavior, other behaviorists have used *classical conditioning* to explain children's ability to respond appropriately to the language they hear (Staats, 1971). For example, when a mother says "milk" just before or while feeding her baby, the infant associates the word with the food stimulus. Very soon, the word elicits a response similar to the one produced by the milk itself.

Finally, *imitation* has also been added to behaviorist accounts, to explain how children rapidly pick up complex verbal behaviors, such as whole phrases and sentences (Whitehurst & Vasta, 1975). And imitation can combine with reinforcement to promote language learning, as when a parent coaxes, "Say 'I want a cookie'" and delivers praise and a treat after the child responds correctly.

As these examples indicate, conditioning and imitation seem to play some role in early language learning. At the same time, only a few researchers cling to the behaviorist perspective today (see, for example, Moerk, 1992; Whitehurst & Valdez-Menchaca, 1988). Think, for a moment, about the process of language development that we have described. Adults must engage in intensive language tutoring—continuously modeling and reinforcing so that by age 6, children have an extensive vocabulary and produce an enormous number of complex sentences. This seems like a physically impossible task, even for the most conscientious parents. Furthermore, we have already seen that children create novel utterances that could not have been copied from or reinforced by others, such as Susan's use of "shutted" at the beginning of this chapter. This suggests that instead of learning specific sentences, young children develop a working knowledge of grammatical rules that they use to understand and produce language.

Nevertheless, the ideas of Skinner and other behaviorists should not be dismissed entirely. Throughout this chapter, we will see many examples of how adult responsiveness and example support children's language learning even though they do not fully explain it. Behaviorist principles are also extremely valuable to speech and language therapists in their efforts to help children with serious language delays and disabilities overcome their problems (Whitehurst et al., 1989).

The Nativist Perspective

Linguist Noam Chomsky's (1957) book *Syntactic Structures,* along with his critical review of Skinner's theory, first convinced the scientific community that children assume much responsibility for their own language learning. In contrast to behaviorism, Chomsky (1959) argued that internal mental structures are at the heart of our capacity to interpret and generate language. His alternative theory is a nativist account that regards language as a biologically based, uniquely human accomplishment.

Focusing on children's grammatical achievements, Chomsky reasoned that the rules for sentence organization are too complex to be directly taught to or discovered by cognitively immature young children. Instead, humans are born with a **language acquisition device (LAD),** a biologically based, innate system for picking up language that needs only to be triggered by verbal input from the environment. The LAD permits children, as soon as they have acquired sufficient vocabulary, to combine words into grammatically consistent, novel utterances and to understand the meaning of sentences they hear.

How can a single LAD account for children's mastery of diverse languages around the world? According to Chomsky (1976), within the LAD is a *universal grammar,* a built-in storehouse of rules that apply to all human languages. Young children use this knowledge to decipher important grammatical categories and relationships in any language to which they are exposed. In proposing a universal grammar, Chomsky's theory emphasizes features the world's languages have in

Language acquisition device (LAD)

In Chomsky's theory, a biologically based, innate system for picking up language that permits children, as soon as they have acquired sufficient vocabulary, to combine words into grammatically consistent utterances and to understand the meaning of sentences they hear.

Can instances be found in which children develop complex language systems with only minimal language input? If so, this evidence would serve as strong support for Chomsky's idea that human beings are born with a biological program for language development.

In a series of studies, Susan Goldin-Meadow reported that deaf preschoolers who had not been taught sign language spontaneously produced a gestural communication system strikingly similar to hearing children's verbal language (Goldin-Meadow & Morford, 1985; Goldin-Meadow & Mylander, 1983). However, critics claim that the deaf children's competencies might have resulted from subtle gestural exchanges with their parents (Bohannon & Warren-Leubecker, 1989).

The study of *creoles* offers an alternative test of the nativist perspective. Creoles are languages that arise rapidly from *pidgins*, which are minimally developed "emergency" tongues that result when several language communities migrate to the same area and no dominant language exists to support interaction among them. In 1876, large numbers of immigrants from China, Japan, Korea, the Philippines, Puerto Rico, and Portugal came to Hawaii to work in the sugar industry. The multilingual population quickly outnumbered other residents—English speakers and native Hawaiians alike. Out of this melting pot, Hawaiian Pidgin English emerged, a communication system with a small vocabulary and narrow range of grammatical options that permitted new immigrants to "get by" in everyday life. Pidgin English, however, was so limited in its possibilities and applied so unsystematically that it may have offered young children too little language input from which to learn. Yet within 20 to 30 years, a new complex language, Hawaiian Creole English, which borrowed vocabulary from its pidgin and foreign-language predecessors, became widespread. How could this remarkable linguistic achievement have occurred?

Derek Bickerton (1981, 1984) concludes that the next generation of children must have invented the language, relying on innate mechanisms. Support for this conclusion is of two kinds. First, the structure of creole languages is similar around the world, suggesting that a common genetic program underlies them. Second, creole grammar resembles the linguistic structures children first use when acquiring any language and their incorrect hypotheses about complex grammatical forms. For example, expressions like "He no bite you" and "Where he put the toy?" are perfectly correct in Hawaiian Creole English. According to Bickerton:

> The child does not, initially, "learn language." As he develops, the genetic program for language which is his hominid inheritance unrolls exactly as does the genetic program that determines his increase in size (and) muscular control. . . . "Learning" consists of adapting this program, revising it, adjusting it to fit the realities of the cultural language he happens to encounter. Without such a program, the simplest of cultural languages would be quite unlearnable. . . . (1981, pp. 296–297)

According to Bickerton, the child's biological language is always there, under the surface, ready to reemerge when cultural language is shattered. However, no one has yet been able to observe the language development of first-generation creole children directly. Some researchers claim that without such evidence, we cannot be entirely sure that adult input plays little role in the creation of creole (Bohannon, MacWhinney, & Snow, 1990).

common. It assumes that the wide variation that exists in their structural properties can be reduced to the same underlying set of rules. Furthermore, since the LAD is specifically suited for language processing, sophisticated cognitive capacities are not required to master the structure of language. Instead, children do so spontaneously with only limited language exposure. Therefore, in sharp contrast to the behaviorist view, the nativist perspective regards deliberate training by parents as unnecessary for language development. Instead, the LAD ensures that language will be acquired early and swiftly, despite its inherent complexity.

SUPPORT FOR THE NATIVIST PERSPECTIVE. Are children biologically primed to acquire language? Research reviewed in the Cultural Influences box above, which suggests that children have a remarkable ability to invent new language systems, provides some of the most powerful support for this perspective. And three additional sets of evidence—efforts to teach nonhuman primates language systems, localization of language functions in the human brain, and investigations into whether a sensitive period exists for language development—are also consistent with Chomsky's view that humans are prepared for language in a specialized way. Let's look at each in turn.

Can Great Apes Acquire Language? Is the ability to master a grammatically complex language system a uniquely human attribute? To find out, many

*N*im, a chimp taught American Sign Language, built a vocabulary of more than one hundred signs over several years of training. In addition, his two-sign combinations, such as "groom me," "hug Nim," and "Nim book," were similar to those of human toddlers. But for sign strings longer than two, Nim's productions showed little resemblance to human grammar. (SUSAN KUKLIN/PHOTO RESEARCHERS)

attempts have been made to teach language to chimpanzees, who are closest to humans in the evolutionary hierarchy. In some instances, researchers have created artificial languages for this purpose, such as plastic tokens that can be manipulated to represent sentences or computer consoles that generate strings of visual symbols (Premack, 1976; Rumbaugh, 1977). In other cases, chimps have been trained in American Sign Language, a gestural communication system used by the deaf that is as elaborate as any spoken language (Gardner & Gardner, 1969; Terrace et al., 1980).

Clearly, great apes have some capacity for symbolic communication. For example, in the wild, young chimpanzees and orangutans use intentional gestures, such as cupping their hands to request food from their mothers, that precede spoken language in human children (Bard, 1992; Ghiglieri, 1988). Nevertheless, the ability of apes to acquire a humanlike language system appears to be quite limited. Many months and sometimes years of training and reinforcement are necessary to get them to master a basic vocabulary. And although their two-sign combinations resemble the two-word utterances of human toddlers, there is no convincing evidence that chimpanzees can master complex grammatical forms. Sign strings longer than two generally do not conform to a rule-based structure (Berko Gleason, 1989). For example, one chimp named Nim either repeated information or combined words nonsensically in his 3- and 4-word utterances. "Eat Nim eat" and "Play me Nim play" are typical examples (Berko Gleason, 1989; Terrace et al., 1980).

Still, these findings do not tell us for sure that humans are endowed with a specialized language capacity. Perhaps cognitive abilities or social and motivational factors account for the linguistic gap between chimpanzees and humans. Furthermore, not all species of apes have been studied as extensively as the common chimp, the subject of the research just described. Recently, Sue Savage-Rumbaugh and her collaborators (1990, 1993) began to investigate pygmy chimps, who are more socially skilled and adept at observational learning than are common chimps. The researchers also used a new instructional approach in which they encouraged these chimps to comprehend a wide range of expressions before requiring that they produce language—a form of acquisition resembling that of human children. Results revealed more rapid vocabulary development and better comprehension of novel sentences than ever before attained by nonhuman primates. Nevertheless, even pygmy chimps require several extra years of experience to attain the basic grammatical understandings of human 2- to 3-year-olds. And other evidence lends additional weight to the nativist argument.

Language Areas in the Brain. Humans have evolved specialized regions in the brain that support language skills. Recall from Chapter 5 that for most individuals, language is housed in the left hemisphere of the cortex. Within it are two well-

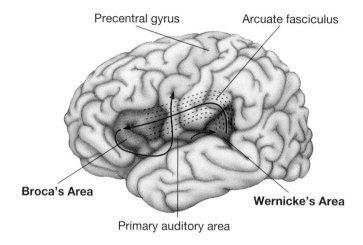

FIGURE 9.1 Two structures in the left hemisphere of the cortex responsible for language processing. *Broca's area* controls language production by creating a detailed program for articulation, which it sends to the face area of the *precentral gyrus* (responsible for motor control). Damage to Broca's area disrupts production but not comprehension of speech. *Wernicke's area* interprets language by receiving impulses from the *primary auditory area* (where sensations from the ears are sent). Damage to Wernicke's area results in speech laced with nonsense words and difficulty comprehending the speech of others. Wernicke's area communicates with Broca's area through a bundle of nerve fibers called the *arcuate fasciculus.*

established language structures (see Figure 9.1). **Broca's area,** located in the frontal lobe, controls language production. Damage to it results in a specific *aphasia,* or communication disorder, in which the person has good comprehension but has trouble speaking. In contrast, **Wernicke's area,** located in the temporal lobe, is responsible for interpreting language. When it is damaged, speech is fluent and grammatical, but it contains many nonsense words. Comprehension of others' speech is also impaired (Maratsos, 1989).

Furthermore, when children experience widespread injury to the left hemisphere, grammar is the language function most likely to be permanently damaged. Under these conditions, phonology and semantics seem to be taken over by the right hemisphere. This finding certainly fits with the idea that an LAD-like structure for grammatical processing exists in a specific part of the brain (Curtiss, 1989).

Is There a Sensitive Period for Language Development? Recall from Chapter 5 that the brain, although already lateralized at birth, becomes increasingly specialized during childhood. Erik Lenneberg (1967) first proposed that children must acquire language during the age span of brain lateralization, which he believed to be complete by puberty. If this idea is correct, it would provide further support for the nativist position that language development has unique biological properties.

To test this sensitive-period idea, researchers have tracked the recovery of severely abused children who experienced little human contact in childhood. The most recent thorough study is of Genie, a child isolated at 20 months in the back room of her parents' house and not discovered until she was $13\frac{1}{2}$ years old.* Genie's early environment was linguistically and emotionally impoverished. No one was permitted to talk to her, and she was beaten when she made any noise. Over several years of training with dedicated caregivers, Genie's language developed, but not nearly to the same extent as that of normal children. Although she eventually acquired a large vocabulary and good comprehension of everyday conversation, her grammatical abilities (like those of the brain-damaged youngsters mentioned in the preceding section) were limited. Genie's case, along with findings on several other similar children, fits with Lenneberg's hypothesis that language learning is optimal during the period of brain lateralization (Curtiss, 1977, 1989).

What about acquiring a second language? Is this task harder during adolescence and adulthood, after a sensitive period for language development is passed? Once again, research indicates that this is the case. Compared to children, adolescents and adults make faster initial progress when they move to a foreign country and must learn a new language (Snow & Hoefnagel-Höhle, 1978). But their ultimate

Broca's area

A language structure located in the frontal lobe of the cerebral cortex that controls language production.

Wernicke's area

A language structure located in the temporal lobe of the cerebral cortex that is responsible for interpreting language.

---

*Medical records of Genie's early infancy suggest that she was an alert, responsive baby. Her motor development was normal, and she said her first words just before her confinement, after which all language disappeared. Therefore, mental retardation is an unlikely explanation for the course of her development.

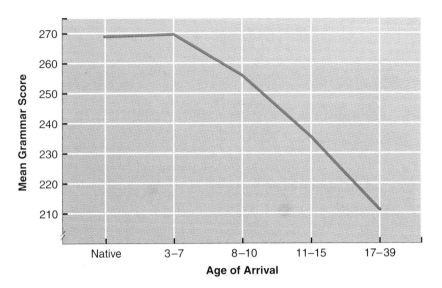

FIGURE 9.2 Relationship between age of arrival of Chinese and Korean immigrants in the United States and performance on a test of English grammar. Individuals who began learning English in childhood attained the competence of native speakers. With increasing age through adolescence, scores declined. (From "Critical Period Effects in Second Language Learning: The Influence of Maturational State on the Acquisition of English as a Second Language" by J. S. Johnson & E. L. Newport, 1989, *Cognitive Psychology*, 21, p. 79. Copyright © 1989 by Academic Press. Reprinted by permission.)

attainment is not as high. For example, in a study of Chinese and Korean adults who had immigrated to the United States at varying ages, those who began mastering English between 3 and 7 years scored as well as native speakers on a test of grammatical knowledge (see Figure 9.2). As age of arrival in the United States increased through adolescence, test scores gradually declined. Similar outcomes occur among deaf adults who learned American Sign Language at different ages (Johnson & Newport, 1989; Newport, 1991).

LIMITATIONS OF THE NATIVIST PERSPECTIVE. Chomsky's theory has had a major impact on current views of language development. It is now widely accepted that a uniquely human biological predisposition plays a powerful role in language learning. Still, Chomsky's account of development has been challenged on several grounds.

First, comparisons among languages reveal vastly different grammatical systems. Chomsky (1981) as well as others have attempted to specify an underlying universal grammar, but as yet a single set of rules that encompasses all languages has not been identified. Even simple grammatical distinctions, such as the use of *the* versus *a*, are made in quite different ways around the world. For example, several African languages rely on tone patterns to designate these articles. In Japanese and Chinese, they are inferred entirely from sentence context. In Finnish, *en* is attached to the front of a word to signify *the*, to the back of a word to signify *a*. Critics of Chomsky's theory doubt the existence of a universal grammar that can account for such varied approaches to conveying the same grammatical forms (Maratsos, 1989).

Second, Chomsky's assumption that grammatical knowledge is innately determined does not fit with certain observations of language development. Although extraordinary strides are made during preschool years, children's acquistion of many sentence constructions is not immediate but steady and gradual. Complete mastery of some forms (such as the passive voice) is not achieved until well into middle childhood, and very subtle aspects of grammar continue to be refined into the adult years (Horgan, 1978; Menyuk, 1977). This suggests that more learning and discovery are involved in grammatical development than Chomsky assumed.

Finally, dissatisfaction with Chomsky's theory has also arisen from its lack of comprehensiveness. For example, in focusing on language structure at the sentence level, it cannot explain how children weave statements together into connected discourse and develop strategies for sustaining meaningful conversations. Perhaps because Chomsky did not dwell on the pragmatic side of language, his theory grants little importance to the quality of language input and social experience in supporting language development (McLean & Snyder-McLean, 1978).

Furthermore, we have already noted that the nativist perspective does not regard children's cognitive capacities as important. Yet in our discussion of Piaget's theory in Chapter 6, we saw that attainment of cognitive milestones is involved in children's early vocabulary growth. And later in this chapter, we will encounter evidence that cognitive development has at least some effect on children's ability to detect grammatical structure as well.

The Interactionist Perspective

In recent years, new theories of language development have arisen, emphasizing interactions between inner predispositions and environmental inputs, replacing the dichotomy that grew out of the Skinner–Chomsky debate. Although several interactionist models exist, virtually all stress the social context of language learning. An active child, well endowed for acquiring language, observes and engages in social exchanges with others. Out of this experience, the child builds a communication system that relates the form and content of language to its social meaning. According to this view, native capacity, a strong desire to interact with others, and a rich linguistic and social environment combine to assist children in discovering the functions and regularities of language (Bohannon & Warren-Leubecker, 1989).

Although all interactionists regard the child as an active communicative being, debate continues over the precise nature of children's innate abilities. Some theorists accept a modified view of Chomsky's position, which states that although children are primed to make sense of language, they formulate and refine hypotheses about its structure based on input they receive (Slobin, 1985; Wexler & Culicover, 1980). Other theorists are impressed by the remarkable cognitive capacities of infants and preschoolers that we discussed in earlier chapters. They believe children make sense of their complex language environments by applying powerful analytic tools of a general cognitive kind rather than ones that are specifically tuned to language (Bates, 1993; Bates & MacWhinney, 1987; Nelson, 1989).

As we chart the course of language development, we will describe some of these new views, but we must keep in mind that none are completely verified yet. Indeed, even interactionist theories have not escaped the critical eye of modern researchers. Because interactionists assume that language competence grows out of communicative experience, we should not be able to find children who show large disparities between pragmatics and other aspects of language skill. Yet recall that Genie's development was quite uneven in this respect. And studies of severely retarded youngsters reveal that their semantic and conversational skills often lag considerably behind their grammatical achievements, which may be more innately determined (Curtiss, 1989).

Consequently, today there is increasing acknowledgment that biology, cognition, and social experience may operate in different balances with respect to each component of language. And to complicate matters further, the relative contributions of these factors may change with age (Owens, 1992). Research on children's language continues to face many theoretical puzzles. We still know much more about the course of language development than precisely how language acquisition takes place (Rice, 1989).

Brief Review

In mastering language, children acquire four components—phonology, semantics, grammar, and pragmatics—that they combine into a flexible communication system. Three theories provide different accounts of how children develop language. According to Skinner and other behaviorists, language is learned through conditioning and imitation. However, these principles cannot account for the speed of early language development or children's novel, rule-based utterances. In contrast, Chomsky's nativist view regards children as biologically equipped with a language acquisition devise (LAD) that supports rapid early mastery of the structure of language. Although much evidence supports a biological contribution to language development, Chomsky's theory fails to explain many aspects of language learning. Interactionist theories offer a compromise between these two views, stressing that innate abilities and social contexts combine to promote language development.

....

PRELINGUISTIC DEVELOPMENT: GETTING READY TO TALK

From the very beginning, infants are prepared to acquire language. During the first year of life, inborn capabilities, cognitive and social milestones, and environmental supports pave the way for the onset of verbal communication.

Receptivity to Language

Recall from Chapter 4 that neonates are especially sensitive to the pitch range of the human voice and find speech to be more pleasing than other sounds. In addition, they have an astonishing ability to make fine-grained distinctions among the sounds of virtually any human language. Because this skill may help them crack the phonological code of their native tongue, let's look at it more closely.

As adults, we analyze the speech stream into **phonemes,** or sound categories—the smallest speech units we can perceive, such as the difference between the consonant sounds in "pa" and "ba." Phonemes are not the same across all languages. For example, "ra" and "la" are separate sounds to English speakers, but Japanese individuals hear them as the same. Similarly, an English speaker has trouble perceiving the difference between the two "p" sounds used in the Thai language. This tendency to perceive as identical a range of sounds that belong to the same phonemic class is called **categorical speech perception**. Like children and adults, 1-month-olds are capable of it. But unlike older individuals, they are sensitive to a much wider range of categories than exists in their own language environment (Werker, 1989).

Do these findings indicate that infants are born with a special speech decoder that permits them to analyze the sound stream of any language to which they are exposed? Probably not, since babies look for well-defined boundaries in both speech and nonspeech sounds. Speech is simply easier to separate into units than other sound stimuli (Aslin, Pisoni, & Jusczyk, 1983). Within the first few days after birth, babies distinguish and prefer the overall sound pattern of their native tongue from that of other languages (Mehler et al., 1988). As infants continue to listen actively to the talk of people around them, they learn to focus on meaningful sound variations. By 6 months of age, long before they are ready to talk, babies start to organize speech into the phonemic categories of their own language. In other words, they stop responding to sound distinctions that are not useful in their language community (Kuhl et al., 1992).

In the second half of the first year, babies focus on larger speech units that are critical to making sense of what they hear. They start to detect the phrase units of their native language. In one study, researchers recorded two versions of a mother telling a story. In the first, she spoke naturally, with pauses occurring between clauses, like this: "Cinderella lived in a great big house [pause], but it was sort of dark [pause] because she had this mean stepmother." In the second version, the mother inserted pauses in unnatural places—in the middle of clauses: "Cinderella lived in a great big house, but it was [pause] sort of dark because she had [pause] this mean stepmother." Like adults, 7- to 10-month-olds clearly preferred speech with natural breaks (Hirsh-Pasek et al., 1987).

How do infants manage to isolate meaningful sounds and grammatically relevant phrases in a complex speech stream at such an early age? Their built-in tendency to search for invariant features in a constantly changing perceptual world is undoubtedly at the heart of these remarkable achievements (see Chapter 4). At the same time, special features of adult talk to young language learners assist babies

Phoneme
The smallest speech unit that can be distinguished perceptually.

Categorical speech perception
The tendency to perceive a range of sounds that belong to the same phonemic class as identical.

with this task. Adults in many countries speak to infants and toddlers in **motherese**—a form of language made up of short sentences with high-pitched, exaggerated intonation, clear pronunciation, and distinct pauses between speech segments (Fernald et al., 1989; Newport, Gleitman, & Gleitman, 1977).

Why do adults use motherese? They do not seem to be deliberately trying to teach infants to talk, since many of the same speech qualities appear when they communicate with foreigners. Motherese probably arises from an unconscious desire to keep a young child's attention and ease the task of understanding, and it works effectively in these ways. From birth on, infants prefer to listen to motherese over other kinds of adult talk. When they hear it, they respond with visual focus, positive affect, and (at older ages) vocalizations that are similar in pitch and intonation (Cooper & Aslin, 1990; Masataka, 1992).

Furthermore, parents constantly fine-tune motherese, adjusting the length and content of their utterances to fit with children's needs. For example, in a recent study of "baby talk" in four cultures, Argentinean, French, Japanese, and American mothers tended to speak to 5-month-olds in affect-laden ways, emphasizing greetings, repeated sounds, and terms of endearment. At 13 months, when toddlers began to understand as well as respond, a greater percentage of maternal speech in each culture was information-laden—concerned with giving directions, asking questions, and describing what was happening at the moment (Bornstein et al., 1992). Research indicates that the more effectively parents modify speech complexity over the first year, the better their children's language comprehension at 18 months of age (Murray, Johnson, & Peters, 1990).

T *his Nepalese mother speaks to her baby daughter in short, clearly pronounced sentences with high-pitched, exaggerated intonation. Adults in many countries use this form of language, called* motherese, *with infants and toddlers. It eases the task of early language learning.* (DAVID AUSTEN/STOCK BOSTON)

First Speech Sounds

Around 2 months, babies begin to make vowel-like noises, called **cooing** because of their pleasant "oo" quality. Gradually, consonants are added, and around 6 months **babbling** appears, in which infants repeat consonant–vowel combinations in long strings, such as "babababababa" and "nananananana."

The timing of early babbling seems to be due to maturation, since babies everywhere (even those who are deaf) start babbling at about the same age and produce a similar range of early sounds (Stoel-Gammon & Otomo, 1986). However, for babbling to develop further, infants must be exposed to human speech. Around 7 months, babbling starts to include the sounds of mature spoken languages. However, if a baby's hearing is impaired, these speechlike sounds are far less frequent, and in the case of deaf infants, they are totally absent (Oller & Eilers, 1988). But babbling is not restricted to the spoken modality. When deaf infants are exposed to sign language from birth, they babble manually in much the same way hearing infants do through speech (Petitto & Marentette, 1991).

Although language input is necessary for babbling to be sustained, maturation continues to affect its development through the second half of the first year. Adults cannot change a baby's babbled sounds through reinforcement and modeling, although they can, to some extent, influence the overall amount of babbling (Dodd, 1972). Also, the development of babbling follows a universal pattern. At first, infants produce a limited number of sounds that expand to a much broader range by 12 months of age. Babbling continues for 4 or 5 months after infants say their first words (Locke, 1989; Thevenin et al., 1985).

Nevertheless, a careful look at babbling reveals that infants are applying the knowledge they have gained from many months of listening to their native tongue. By 1 year of age, intonation patterns of the babbling stream resemble those of the child's language community (Levitt & Wang, 1991). As a result, babbling often seems like conversational speech without intelligible words. In addition, as infants get ready to talk, they babble the consonant and vowel sounds of their own language with increasing frequency, some of which are transferred to their first words (Boysson-Bardies & Vihman, 1991; Levitt & Utmann, 1992). Finally, watch an older baby babble, and you are likely to see that certain patterns

Motherese
The form of language adopted by adults when speaking to infants and toddlers that is made up of short sentences with high-pitched, exaggerated intonation, clear pronunciation, and distinct pauses between speech segments.

Cooing
Pleasant vowel-like noises made by infants beginning around 2 months of age.

Babbling
Repetition of consonant–vowel combinations in long strings, beginning around 6 months of age.

of sounds appear in particular contexts—for example, when manipulating objects, looking at books, and walking upright (Blake & Boysson-Bardies, 1992).

These features of babbling indicate that it paves the way for language in at least two ways. First, babbling permits speech sounds to be exercised in a preparatory way for early words. And second, links between babbled sounds and contexts suggest that these early vocalizations are meaningful from the baby's perspective. Through babbling, infants seem to experiment with the semantic function of language before they speak in more conventional ways.

Becoming a Communicator

At birth, infants are already prepared for some aspects of conversational behavior. For example, newborn babies can initiate interaction by making eye contact and terminate it by looking away. Around 4 months, they start to gaze in the same direction adults are looking, and adults follow the baby's line of vision as well. When this happens, parents often comment on what the infant sees. In this way, the environment is labeled for the baby. Researchers believe this kind of joint attention may be quite important for early language development. Infants who experience it often tend to talk earlier and show faster vocabulary development (Dunham & Dunham, 1992; Tomasello, 1990).

By 3 months, the beginnings of conversational turn-taking can be seen. The baby vocalizes, the caregiver vocalizes in return, waits for a response, and vocalizes again. In Western cultures, these vocal exchanges are common, but the adult is largely responsible for sustaining them (Schaffer, 1979). Several months later, turn-taking games, such as pat-a-cake and peek-a-boo, appear. At first, the parent starts the game and the infant is an amused observer. But by 12 months, infants become active participants, exchanging roles with the parent. As they do so, they practice the turn-taking pattern of human conversation, and they also hear words paired with the actions they perform (Ratner & Bruner, 1978).

At the end of the first year, as infants become capable of intentional behavior, they use two forms of preverbal gestures to influence the behavior of others. The first is the **protodeclarative**, in which the baby touches an object, holds it up, or points to it while looking at others to make sure they notice. In the second, the **protoimperative,** the infant gets another person to do something by pointing, reaching, and often making sounds at the same time (Bates, 1979). Over time, some of these gestures become explicitly representational—much like those that appear in children's early make-believe play (see Chapter 6). For example, a 1- to 2-year-old might sniff to refer to flowers, lift her arms over her head to indicate big, and flap her arms to refer to a butterfly. In this way, gestural communication provides yet another context in which young children learn about the functions of language—that meanings can be symbolized and conveyed to others (Acredolo & Goodwyn, 1990).

Early in the second year, turn-taking and children's gestural communication come together, especially in situations in which children's messages do not communicate clearly. For example, witness the following efforts by a 14-month-old to get his mother to give him a sponge from the kitchen counter:

> *Jordan:* (Vocalizes repeatedly until his mother turns around.)
> *Mother:* (Turns around to look at him.)
> *Jordan:* (Points to one of the objects on the counter.)
> *Mother:* Do you want this? (Holds up milk container.)
> *Jordan:* (Shakes his head "no.") (Vocalizes, continues to point.)
> *Mother:* Do you want this? (Holds up jelly jar.)
> *Jordan:* (Shakes his head "no.") (Continues to point.) (Two more offer–rejection pairs.)
> *Mother:* This? (Picks up sponge.)
> *Jordan:* (Leans back in highchair, puts arms down, tension leaves body.)
> *Mother:* (Hands Jordan sponge.) (Golinkoff, 1983, pp. 58–59)

*T*his infant uses the protodeclarative, a preverbal gesture in which he points to communicate something about these flowers. Soon words will be uttered along with these gestures, which will diminish as the child makes the transition to verbal communication. (STAN RIES/PICTURE CUBE)

Protodeclarative

A preverbal gesture through which infants make an assertion about an object by touching it, holding it up, or pointing to it.

Protoimperative

A preverbal gesture in which infants point, reach, and make sounds to get another person to do something.

Soon, words are uttered along with the gestures that made up the infant's preverbal communicative acts. Then the gestures diminish as children discover that words are more easily understood by others and as parents encourage their youngster's first meaningful verbalizations (Goldin-Meadow & Morford, 1985).

A final note: Throughout our discussion, we have stressed that progress toward spoken language is encouraged by caregivers who involve infants in dialoguelike exchanges. Recently, questions have been raised about how necessary these early interactive experiences are. In some societies, such as the Kaluli of Papua New Guinea and the people of Western Samoa, adults rarely treat infants as communicative partners and never play social games with them. Not until infants crawl and walk do sibling caregivers take charge, talk directly to babies, and respond to their vocalizations. Yet Kaluli and Samoan children acquire language within the normal time frame of development (Ochs, 1988; Schieffelin & Ochs, 1987). These findings suggest that adult molding of infant communication may not be essential. But when it occurs, it clearly supports the transition from the preverbal phase to the much longer, linguistic period of childhood.

Brief Review

During infancy, biological predispositions, cognitive development, and a responsive social environment join together to prepare the child for language. Neonates have a built-in capacity to detect a wide variety of sound categories in human speech. By the middle of the first year, they become increasingly sensitive to the phonemes and phrase structure of their native tongue. Cooing begins at about 2 months, babbling around 6 months. By 1 year, babbling reflects the intonation and sound patterns of the native language, and infants use preverbal gestures to influence the behavior of others. When adults use motherese, engage infants in turn-taking exchanges, and respond to babies' preverbal gestures, they support the transition to verbal communication.

PHONOLOGICAL DEVELOPMENT

Think about the sounds you might hear if you listened in on a 1- or 2-year-old trying out her first handful of words. You probably imagined an assortment of interesting pronunciations, such as "nana" for banana, "oap" for soap, and "weddy" for ready, as well as some puzzling productions that the child uses like words but that do not resemble adult forms. For "translations" of these, you have to ask the child's parent. Phonological development is a complex process that depends on the child's ability to attend to the sound sequences of speech, produce sounds voluntarily, and combine them into understandable words and phrases. Between 1 and 4 years of age, children make considerable progress at this task (Ingram, 1986).

Experts in phonology view children mastering the pronunciation of their language as young problem solvers. In trying to figure out how to talk like people around them, they adopt a variety of temporary strategies for producing sounds that bring adult words within their current range of physical and cognitive capabilities (Menn, 1989). Let's look at how they do so.

The Early Phase

Children's first words are limited by the small number of sounds they can control. The easiest sound sequences start with consonants, end with vowels, and include repeated syllables, as in "mama," "dada," "bye-bye," and "nigh-nigh" (for night-night). In other instances, young speakers may use the same sound to represent a variety of words, a feature that makes their speech hard to understand. For example, one toddler substituted "bat" for as many as 12 different words, including "bad," "bark," "bent," and "bite" (Ingram, 1986).

we consider these findings as a whole, early vocabulary development appears to support the interactionist's emphasis on the combined impact of children's inner predispositions and linguistic and social worlds.

TYPES OF WORDS. Look back at Table 9.2, and you will see that three types of words—object, action, and state—are the most common in young children's vocabularies. Careful study of each provides researchers with important information about the course of semantic development (Clark, 1983).

Object and Action Words. Although children differ in the first words they choose to learn, virtually all early language learners have far more object than action words in their beginning vocabularies (Gentner, 1982; Nelson, 1973). If actions are an especially important means through which infants find out about their world, then why this early emphasis on naming objects?

The major reason seems to be that concepts referred to by nouns are especially salient to young children because they are perceptually distinct, bounded wholes. As a result, when children start to talk, all they need to do is match objects with their appropriate labels. In contrast, verbs are cognitively more complex in that they require an understanding of the *relationship* between objects and actions (Gentner, 1982). Nevertheless, characteristics of the linguistic environment have some effect on toddlers' relative use of object and action words. For example, the structure of English emphasizes nouns more than do some non-Western languages. In Japanese and Korean, nouns are often omitted entirely from adult sentences, and verbs are stressed. In line with this difference, Japanese and Korean toddlers acquire action words earlier than their English-speaking counterparts do (Choi, 1991; Clancy, 1985).

When English-speaking children first refer to actions, they often use a variety of words to represent them. For example, a toddler might use a noun, such as "door," or a preposition, such as "out," to convey the idea that she wants to open something. As their vocabularies expand at the end of the second and the beginning of the third year, children use many more words to refer to actions that for adults are verbs (Clark, 1983).

State Words. Between 2 and $2\frac{1}{2}$ years, children's state (or modifier) words expand to include labels for attributes of objects, such as size and color ("big," "red") as well as possession ("my toy," "Mommy purse"). Words referring to the functions of objects appear soon after (for example, "dump truck," "pickup truck") (Nelson, 1976).

Children's acquisition of new words reflects their mastery of underlying concepts. With respect to state words referring to an object's location, "in" is acquired first, followed by "on" and then "under." (NANCY SHEEHAN)

When state words are related in meaning, general distinctions (which are cognitively easier) appear first. For example, among words referring to the size of objects, children acquire "big–small" first, followed by "tall–short," "high–low," and "long–short," and finally "wide–narrow" and "deep–shallow." The same is true for temporal terms, which modify actions. Between ages 3 and 5, children first master "now" versus "then" and "before" versus "after," followed by "today" versus "yesterday" and "tomorrow" (Clark, 1983; Stevenson & Pollitt, 1987).

State words referring to the location and movement of objects provide additional examples of how cognition influences vocabulary development. Below age 2, children can easily imitate an adult's action in putting an object "in" or "on" another object, but they have trouble imitating the placement of one object "under" another. These terms appear in children's vocabularies in just this order, with all three achieved around $2\frac{1}{2}$ years of age (Clark, 1973). With respect to motion words, those that describe an object's source ("out," "off") and path of movement ("up," "down") appear before ones that refer to the place an object comes to rest ("here," "there"). The reason is that describing the end point of an object's motion demands that children grasp the relationship between all three concepts—where an object started, how it moved, and where it ended (Stockman & Vaughn-Cooke, 1992).

State terms serve a vital communicative function. Because they refer to the qualities of objects and actions, children can use them to express many more concepts than they could previously. As more of these words are mastered, preschoolers' language becomes increasingly flexible.

UNDEREXTENSIONS AND OVEREXTENSIONS. When young children first learn new words, they often do not use them in just the way we do. Sometimes they apply the word too narrowly, an error called **underextension**. For example, at 16 months, my younger son used the word "bear" only to refer to a special teddy bear to which he had become attached. A more common error between 1 and $2\frac{1}{2}$ years of age is **overextension**—applying the word to a wider collection of objects and events than is appropriate. For example, a toddler might use the word "car" to refer to a great many objects, including buses, trains, trucks, and fire engines.

Overextensions are yet another illustration of very young children's sensitivity to categorical relations. Children do not overextend words randomly. Instead, they apply them to a class of similar referents—for example, using "dog" to refer to a variety of furry, four-legged animals, or "open" to mean opening a door, peeling fruit, and undoing shoe laces (Behrend, 1988; Clark, 1983). Furthermore, children overextend many more words in production than they do in comprehension. That is, a 2-year-old may refer to trucks, trains, and bikes as "cars" but point to these objects correctly when given their names in a comprehension task (Clark, 1978; Rescorla, 1980). This suggests that children sometimes overextend deliberately because they have difficulty remembering the right word or have not yet acquired a suitable word. From this perspective, overextension is a strategy young children use to stretch their limited vocabularies to the utmost. As vocabularies expand, overextensions gradually disappear.

WORD COINAGES AND METAPHORS. To fill in for words they have not yet learned, young children apply their vocabulary in other creative ways. As early as age 2, they coin new words based on ones they already know. At first, children operate on whole words, as in the technique of compounding. For example, a child might say "break-machine" for a machine that breaks things and "plant-man" for a gardener. Later they convert verbs into nouns and nouns into verbs, as in one child's use of "needle it" to mend something. Soon after, children discover more specialized word coinage techniques, such as adding -*er* to identify the doer of a particular action—for example, "crayoner" for a child using crayons instead of paints. Children give up coined words as soon as they acquire conventional labels for their intended meanings (Clark & Hecht, 1982). Still, their ability to invent these

Underextension

An early vocabulary error in which a word is applied too narrowly, to a smaller number of objects or events than is appropriate.

Overextension

An early vocabulary error in which a word is applied too broadly, to a wider collection of objects and events than is appropriate.

expressions is evidence for a remarkable, rule-governed approach to language at an early age.

Yet another way that preschoolers extend language meanings is through metaphor. Some very clever ones appear in their everyday language. For example, one 3-year-old used the expression "fire engine in my tummy" to describe a recent stomachache (Winner, 1988). Not surprisingly, the metaphors young preschoolers use and understand are based largely on concrete, sensory comparisons, such as "clouds are pillows" and "leaves are dancers." Once their vocabulary and knowledge of the world expand, they start to appreciate ones based on nonsensory comparisons as well, such as, "Friends are like magnets" (Karadsheh, 1991; Keil, 1986). Metaphors permit children to communicate in especially vivid and memorable ways. And sometimes they are the only means we have to convey what we want to say.

Later Semantic Development

Because the average 6-year-old's vocabulary is already quite large, parents and teachers are less aware of gains that take place during middle childhood and adolescence. Between the start of elementary school and young adulthood, vocabulary more than doubles, eventually exceeding 30,000 words. In addition, as we saw in Chapter 7, the knowledge base that underlies school-age children's vocabulary becomes better organized and hierarchically arranged. This permits them to use words more precisely and think about them differently than they did at younger ages.

If you look carefully at children's word definitions, you will see examples of this change. Five- and 6-year-olds give very concrete descriptions that refer to functions or appearance—for example, knife: "when you're cutting carrots"; bicycle: "it's got wheels, a chain, and handlebars." By the end of elementary school, their definitions emphasize more general, socially shared information. Synonyms and explanations of categorical relationships appear—for example, knife: "Something you could cut with. A saw is like a knife. It could also be a weapon" (Litowitz, 1977; Wehren, De Lisi, & Arnold, 1981). This advance reflects the older child's ability to deal with word meanings on an entirely verbal plane. Fifth- and sixth-graders no longer need to be shown what a word refers to in order to understand it. They can add new words to their vocabulary simply by being given a definition (Dickinson, 1984).

School-age children's more reflective, analytical approach to language permits them to appreciate the multiple meanings of words. For example, they recognize that many words, such as "sharp" or "cool," have psychological as well as physical meanings: "What a cool shirt!" or "That movie was really neat!" This grasp of double meanings permits 8- to 10-year-olds to comprehend more subtle metaphors than they could at earlier ages, such as "sharp as a tack," "spilling the beans," and "left high and dry" (Waggoner & Palermo, 1989; Winner, 1988). It also leads to a change in children's humor. In middle childhood, riddles and puns requiring children to go back and forth between different meanings of the same key word are common:

"Hey, did you take a bath?" "No! Why, is one missing?"

"Order! Order in the court!" "Ham and cheese on rye, your honor?"

"Why did the old man tiptoe past the medicine cabinet?" "Because he didn't want to wake up the sleeping pills."

Preschoolers may laugh at these statements because they are nonsensical. But they cannot tell a good riddle or pun, nor do they understand why these jokes are funny (McGhee, 1979).

Finally, adolescents' capacity for abstract reasoning permits them to grasp words rarely used at younger ages, such as "counterintuitive," "incredible," "revolutionize," and "philosophy." In addition, teenagers can understand subtle nonliteral word meanings. As a result, they become masters of irony and sarcasm

(Winner, 1988). "Don't have a major brain explosion," one 16-year-old commented to his sister one evening when she complained about having to write an essay for school. And on another occasion, when his mother fixed a dish for dinner that he disliked, he quipped, "Oh boy, my favorite!" Young children sometimes realize that a sarcastic remark is insincere if it is said in a very exaggerated, mocking tone of voice. But adolescents and adults need only notice the discrepancy between the statement and its context to grasp the intended meaning (Capelli, Nakagawa, & Madden, 1990).

New Ideas About How Semantic Development Takes Place

Research shows that adult feedback facilitates semantic development. When adults go beyond correcting and provide an explanation ("That's not a car. It's a truck. See, it has a place to put things in."), toddlers are more likely to move toward conventional word meanings (Chapman, Leonard, & Mervis, 1986). Still, there is no way that adults can tell children exactly what concept each new word picks out. For example, if an adult points to a dog and calls it a "doggie," it is not clear whether the word refers to four-legged animals, the dog's shaggy ears, the shape of its wagging tail, or its barking sound. Therefore, a major role in vocabulary development must be played by the child's cognitive processing.

New research indicates that a special part of working memory, a *phonological store* that permits us to retain speech-based information, supports young children's fast mapping. The more rapidly 4-year-olds can repeat back nonsense words to an experimenter (a measure of phonological memory skill), the greater their vocabulary growth over the following year. This suggests that a child with good phonological memory produces traces of new words that are clear and persistent enough to increase their chances of being transferred to long-term memory and linked with relevant concepts. But phonological memory does not provide a full account of word learning. After age 5, its ability to predict vocabulary growth breaks down. By then, the causal relationship reverses: Children's semantic knowledge influences how quickly they form phonological traces and acquire new words (Gathercole et al., 1992). And even at younger ages, there is good evidence that children rely heavily on words they already know to figure out the meanings of new ones.

Recently, Eve Clark (1988, 1990) proposed an explanation of semantic development called **lexical contrast theory**. It assumes that two principles govern vocabulary growth. The first is *conventionality*, children's natural desire to acquire words and word meanings of their language community. The second is *contrast*, which explains how new word meanings are added. According to Clark, children assume that the meaning of each word they hear is unique. Therefore, when they hear a new label, they immediately try to figure out its meaning by contrasting it with words currently in their vocabulary.

Many researchers have criticized Clark for not being specific about the hypotheses young children use to determine new word meanings (Gathercole, 1987; Golinkoff et al., 1992). Ellen Markman (1989, 1992) makes a stronger claim about children's early word learning. She believes that in the early phases of vocabulary growth, children adopt a **principle of mutual exclusivity.** That is, they assume that words mark entirely separate (nonoverlapping) categories. The principle of mutual exclusivity works well as long as available referents are perceptually very distinct. For example, when 2-year-olds are told the names of two very different novel objects (a clip and a horn), they assign each label correctly, to the whole object and not to a part of it. And they almost never call the horn a "clip" or the clip a "horn" on later occasions (Waxman & Senghas, 1992).

But mutual exclusivity cannot account for what young children do when adults call a single object by more than one name. Under these conditions, preschoolers are just as systematic in inferring word meanings. They assume the new word refers either to a higher- or lower-order category or to particular attributes, such as the

Lexical contrast theory
A theory that attributes semantic development to two principles: conventionality, children's natural desire to acquire the words and word meanings of their language community; and contrast, children's discovery of meanings by contrasting new words with ones currently in their vocabulary.

Principle of mutual exclusivity
The assumption by children in the early stages of vocabulary growth that words mark entirely separate (nonoverlapping) categories.

object's shape, color, or proper name (Hall, 1991; Waxman & Hatch, 1992). For example, in a study in which 2-year-olds were given a new word for an object for which they already had a label ("fep" for dog), they took the new word to mean a subset of the original category (a certain kind of dog) (Taylor & Gelman, 1988, 1989). The researchers concluded that young children's tendency to contrast novel with familiar labels helps them build their first concept hierarchies.

In sum, children seem to rely on a variety of strategies to guide early word learning, all of which are not yet clearly specified. We still have much to discover about the processes responsible for the phenomenal pace of semantic development.

Brief Review

Semantic development takes place with extraordinary speed as preschoolers fast map thousands of words into their vocabularies. Although individual differences exist, object words are emphasized first; action and state words increase later. Errors of underextension and overextension gradually decline as preschoolers enlarge and refine their vocabularies. During middle childhood, understanding of word meanings becomes more flexible and precise. Adolescents acquire many abstract words and grasp subtle nonliteral word meanings. Adult feedback assists with word learning, but a major role is played by the child's cognitive processing. Lexical contrast theory is a recent controversial account of how semantic development takes place.

·····························

GRAMMATICAL DEVELOPMENT

Grammar requires that children use more than one word in a single utterance. In studying grammatical development, researchers have puzzled over the following questions: Does the very young child use a consistent grammar, and if so, is it like that of the adult? Is grammatical learning special, or does it depend on more general cognitive processes? And what is the role of adult teaching—in particular, corrective feedback for errors—in acquiring grammar? Perhaps you already noticed that these questions have been prompted by Chomsky's theory. If a nativist account is plausible, then grammar should appear early, and the role of adult input should be minimal. We will consider evidence on these issues as we chart the course of grammatical development.

First Word Combinations

Sometime between $1\frac{1}{2}$ and $2\frac{1}{2}$ years, first sentences appear. Children combine two words, such as "Mommy shoe," "go car," and "more cookie." Children's two-word utterances have been called **telegraphic speech**. Like a telegram, they focus on high-content words and leave out smaller, less important ones, such as "can," "the," and "to." In addition, word endings like "-s" and "-ed" are not yet present. However, keep in mind that telegraphic speech characterizes children learning languages that emphasize word order, like English and French. In languages where word order is flexible and small grammatical markers are stressed, children's first sentences include them from the start (de Villiers & de Villiers, 1992; Slobin, 1985). Furthermore, although English-speaking 2-year-olds omit these tiny grammatical elements from their own speech, they detect them in adult utterances (Gerken, Landau, & Remez, 1990). Once again, comprehension is ahead of production.

Even though the two-word utterance is limited in form, children the world over use it flexibly to express a wide variety of meanings (see Table 9.3). In doing so, are children already applying a consistent grammar? At least to some extent they are, since children rarely engage in gross violations of the structure of their language. For example, English-speaking children usually say "Daddy eat" rather than "eat daddy" and "my chair" rather than "chair my" (Bloom, 1990). This suggests that young children have some sensitivity to word-order rules.

Telegraphic speech
Children's two-word utterances that, like a telegram, leave out smaller and less important words.

TABLE 9.3   Common Meanings Expressed by Children's Two-Word Utterances

MEANING	EXAMPLE
Agent–action	"Tommy hit"
Action–object	"Give cookie"
Agent–object	"Mommy truck" (meaning Mommy push the truck)
Action–location	"Put table" (meaning put X on the table)
Entity–location	"Daddy outside"
Possessor–possession	"My truck"
Attribution–entity	"Big ball"
Demonstrative–entity	"That doggie"
Notice–noticed object	"Hi mommy," "Hi truck"
Recurrence	"More milk"
Nonexistence–nonexistent or disappeared object	"No shirt," "No more milk"

SOURCE: Brown, 1973.

Yet considerable controversy exists over the extent to which children at the two-word stage grasp the grammatical categories of their language. According to some investigators, a full adultlike grammar lies behind these two-word sentences, since children often use the same construction to express different underlying propositions. For example, a child might say "Mommy cookie" when he sees his mother eating a cookie and use the same phrase on another occasion to indicate that he wants his mother to give him a cookie. Perhaps the more elaborate structure is present in the child's mind, but an inability to remember and produce a longer word string prevents him from displaying it (Bloom, 1970).

Other researchers disagree, arguing that two-word sentences are based on a very limited fundamental structure that is different from the grammar of adults (Maratsos & Chalkley, 1980; Radford, 1988). For example, Jonathan, a child studied by Martin Braine (1976), produced several actor–action combinations, such as "Mommy sit," "Daddy sleep," and "Daddy work." However, these utterances did not reflect a general understanding of subject–verb relations, since Jonathan used the structure only in specific situations—when a person was moving from one place to another (such as his father going to bed or leaving for work). Also, many creative combinations that children produce during the two-word period do not conform to adult grammatical restrictions. For example, Andrew, another child studied by Braine, said "more hot" and "more read." He clearly applied a rule—"more + X"—in generating these utterances. But the combinations he created are not acceptable in English grammar.

These findings suggest that in first combining words, children are preoccupied with figuring out the meanings of words and using their limited vocabularies in whatever way possible to get their thoughts across to others (Maratsos, 1983). Some of their expressions match adult rules, whereas others seem to reflect their own hypotheses about particular word combinations (Owens, 1992). However, as we will see in the next section, it does not take long for children to grasp the basic structure of their language.

From Two-Word Utterances to Complex Speech

Between 2 and 3 years of age, three-word sentences appear. In English-speaking children, they conform to a relatively fixed word order: subject–verb–object. Although at one time this sequence was thought to be a universal grammatical structure and to represent a natural order of thoughts, we now know that this is not the case. Instead, young children adopt the word orders of the adult speech to which they are exposed (de Villiers & de Villiers, 1992). For example, for "It is broken," a German 2-year-old says, "Kaputt is der" (literally translated as "Broken is it"). Yet German children find their native tongue no more difficult to learn than do children born into English-speaking homes.

THE DEVELOPMENT OF GRAMMATICAL MORPHEMES. As children move beyond two-word utterances, they clearly appreciate the formal grammatical categories of their language. In a study in which the utterances of young preschoolers were carefully examined, by $2\frac{1}{2}$ years, words clearly obeyed the regularities of adult English usage. Children created sentences in which adjectives, articles, nouns, noun phrases, prepositions, and prepositional phrases appeared in the same structural format as adults generate them (Valian, 1986).

At about the same time, a grammatical explosion takes place. Children add **grammatical morphemes***—small markers that change the meaning of sentences, as in "John's dog" and "he *is* eating." A striking finding is that these morphemes are acquired in a highly regular order by English-speaking 2- and 3-year-olds (Brown, 1973; de Villiers & de Villiers, 1973; Kuczaj, 1977). The sequence is shown in Table 9.4. Nevertheless, children do not use these morphemes consistently for months or even years after they first appear (de Villiers & de Villiers, 1992; Maratsos, 1983).

Why does this regular order of development occur? Since adults' use of grammatical morphemes is unrelated to children's learning, language input cannot be responsible (Pinker, 1981). Instead, two characteristics of the morphemes themselves play important roles. The first is *structural complexity*. For example, adding the endings "-ing" or "-s" is structurally less complex than using various forms of the verb "to be." In these, the child has to take account of different forms that express tense and make the verb agree with the subject (for example, "I am coming" versus "They are coming"). Second, grammatical morphemes differ in *semantic complexity*, or the number and difficulty of the meanings they express. For example, adding "-s" to a word requires only one semantic distinction—the difference between one and more than one. In contrast, using the various forms of "to be" involves many more, including an understanding of person, number, and time of occurrence (Brown, 1973).

Research on children acquiring different languages illustrates the impact of both factors. For example, children learning English, Italian, and Turkish acquire morphemes that denote location (in English, these would be prepositions, such as "in" and "on") sooner than children learning Serbo-Croatian, in which expressing location is structurally more complex (Johnston & Slobin, 1979). At the same time, semantic complexity is clearly involved, since across languages, there is considerable similarity in the order in which children acquire grammatical morphemes with the same meaning (Slobin, 1982).

Grammatical morphemes
Small markers that change the meaning of sentences, as in "John's dog" and "he *is* eating."

Overregularization
Application of regular grammatical rules to words that are exceptions.

OVERREGULARIZATION. Look again at Table 9.4, and you will see that some morphemes with irregular forms are acquired before those with regular forms. For example, children use past tense irregular verbs, such as "ran" and "broke," before they acquire the regular "-ed" ending. But once children grasp a regular morphological rule, they extend it to words that are exceptions, a type of error called **overregularization**. "My toy car breaked," "I runned faster than you," and

*A *morpheme* is the smallest meaningful unit of speech (in contrast to a phoneme, which is the smallest perceptible unit of speech sound).

TABLE 9.4 Order of Acquisition of English Grammatical Morphemes

MORPHEME	EXAMPLE
1. Verb present progressive ending (-ing)	"He singing."
2. Preposition "on"	"On horsie."
3. Preposition "in"	"In wagon."
4. Noun plural (-s)	"Cats."
5. Verb irregular past tense	"He ran." "It broke."
6. Noun possessive	"Daddy's hat."
7. Verb uncontractible "be" form used with adjective, preposition, or noun phrase	"Are kitties sleepy?"
8. Articles "a" and "the"	"A cookie." "The bunny."
9. Verb regular past tense ending (-ed)	"He kicked it."
10. Verb present tense, third person singular regular ending (-s)	"He likes it."
11. Verb present tense, third person singular irregular ending	"She has [from have] a cookie." "He does [from do] a good job."
12. Auxiliary verb uncontractible "be" forms	"Are you eating?"
13. Verb contractible "be" forms used with adjective, preposition, or noun phrase	"He's inside." "They're sleepy."
14. Auxiliary verb contractible "be" forms	"He's coming." "Doggie's eating."

SOURCE: Brown, 1973.

"We each have two foots" are expressions that begin to appear between 2 and 3 years of age. Overregularization occurs only occasionally—on the average, in 4.9 percent of instances in which children use irregular verbs, a rate that remains constant into middle childhood. Therefore, it does not reflect a grammatical defect that must be unlearned. Instead, it shows that children apply grammatical rules creatively, since they do not hear mature speakers use these overregularized forms (Marcus et al., 1992).

Additional evidence for the creative use of morphological rules comes from a classic study by Jean Berko (1958). She showed children pictures of unusual objects and actions that were given labels, such as "wug" for a birdlike creature and "rick" for a swinging motion. The labels occurred in sentences that Berko asked children to complete. Preschoolers easily added correct grammatical morphemes to many novel verbs. For example, they completed the sentences in Figure 9.4 with the expressions "wugs" and "ricked."

At this point, you may be wondering: Why do children use some correct irregular forms before they start to overregularize? In all languages, irregular forms are assigned to important, frequently used words. Since young children hear them often, they probably learn these instances by rote memory. But when they grasp a morphological rule, they apply it broadly, making their language more orderly than it actually is. Sometimes children even impose the rule on well-learned exceptions—for example, when they say "ated" or "felled" (Bybee & Slobin, 1982; Kuczaj, 1977). At other times, children's memory for an irregular morpheme may

FIGURE 9.4 Two examples from
Berko's "wug test." (From "The Child's
Learning of English Morphology" by J. Berko, 1958,
Word, 14, pp. 154–155. Reprinted by permission.)

fail. Then they call on the rule to generate the form, and overregularization results (Marcus et al., 1992).

The Development of Complex Grammatical Forms

Once children master the auxiliary verb "to be," the door is open to a variety of new expressions. In English, auxiliary verbs play important roles in many sentence structures that are variations on the basic subject–verb–object form. Negatives and questions are examples.

NEGATIVES. Three types of negation exist, which appear in children's speech in the following order: (1) *nonexistence,* in which the child remarks on the absence of something, such as "no cookie" or "all gone crackers"; (2) *rejection,* in which the child expresses opposition to something, such as "no take bath"; and (3) *denial,* in which the child denies the truthfulness of something, such as "That not my kitty" (Bloom, 1970; Clancy, 1985).

As these examples illustrate, before age 3, children tend to use the rule "no + utterance" to express nonexistence and rejection, but they use an internal form of negation to express denial. Their early constructions probably result from listening to parental speech. When parents express nonexistence or rejection, they often put "no" at the beginning of the sentence, as in "No more cookies" or "No, you can't have another cracker." Around 3 to $3\frac{1}{2}$ years, children add auxiliary verbs to their sentences and become sensitive to the way they combine with negatives. As a result, appropriate grammatical constructions of all three kinds appear, such as, "There aren't any more cookies" (nonexistence), "I don't want a bath" (rejection), and "That isn't my kitty" (denial) (Tager-Flusberg, 1989).

QUESTIONS. Like negatives, questions first appear during the early preschool years and show an orderly pattern of development. English-speaking children can use rising intonation to convert an utterance into a yes/no question, as in "Mommy baking cookies?" As a result, they produce them earlier than children learning languages in which the structure of yes–no questions is more complex (Bowerman, 1973).

Correct question form requires that children invert the subject and auxiliary verb. In the case of *wh- questions*—ones that begin with "what," "where," "which," "who," "when," "why," and "how"—the *wh-* word must also be placed at the

*L*ike *English-speaking children, this Korean boy will master yes/no questions before* wh- *questions, which are both semantically and structurally more difficult.* (FUJIFOTOS/THE IMAGE WORKS)

beginning of the sentence. When first creating questions, English-speaking children cling to the subject–verb–object word order that is so basic to the English language. As a result, they do not make the inversion. A 2-year-old is likely to say, "What you doing?" and "Where Daddy going?" A little later, children include the auxiliary without inverting, as in "What you are doing?" Finally, they can apply all the rules for producing a question. In languages as different as English, Korean, and Tamil (spoken in India), correct question form appears first for yes/no questions and later for *wh-* questions, which are both semantically and structurally more difficult (Clancy, 1989; Vaidyanathan, 1988).

OTHER COMPLEX CONSTRUCTIONS. Between ages 3 and 6, children begin to use increasingly complex grammatical forms. First, conjunctions appear connecting whole sentences ("Mom picked me up, *and* we went to the park") and verb phrases ("I got up *and* ate breakfast") (Bloom et al., 1980). Later, children produce embedded sentences ("I think he will come"), tag questions ("Dad's going to be home soon, isn't he?"), indirect object–direct object structures ("He showed his friend the present"), and passive sentences ("The dog was patted by the girl"). As the preschool years draw to a close, children use most of the grammatical structures of their native language competently (Tager-Flusberg, 1989).

Later Grammatical Development

Although preschoolers have an impressive mastery of grammar, development is not yet complete. During the school years, children's grasp of some constructions improves. The passive voice is one example. At all ages, children produce more abbreviated passives ("It got broken" or "They got lost") than full passives ("The glass was broken by Mary"). However, full passives are rarely used by 3- to 6-year olds. They increase steadily during middle childhood and early adolescence (Horgan, 1978).

Older children also apply their understanding of the passive voice to a wider range of nouns and verbs. Preschoolers comprehend the passive best when the subject of the sentence is an animate being and the verb is an action word ("The boy is kissed by the girl"). Over the school years, the passive form extends to inanimate subjects, such as drum or hat, and experiential verbs, such as like or know (Lempert, 1989; Pinker, Lebeaux, & Frost, 1987). What accounts for this developmental trend? Recall that action is salient to young children in mastering vocabulary, a bias that may also influence their early acquisition of grammatical rules. But learning is also affected by input from the environment. Preschoolers rarely hear adults use experiential passives in everyday life, yet when exposed to them in the laboratory, they willingly integrate them into their own speech (de Villiers, 1984; Gordon & Chafetz, 1990).

Another grammatical achievement of middle childhood is a grasp of infinitive phrases, such as the difference between "John is eager to please" and "John is easy to please." Carol Chomsky (1969) tested children's understanding of this construction by blindfolding a doll and asking, "Is the doll *easy or hard to see?*" Results showed that 5-year-olds always equate the grammatical subject—"doll" in this instance—with the agent role. That is, they respond "hard to see" as if they understand the question to mean something like, "Is the doll able to see?" Between ages 5 and 10, children gradually separate subject from agent in these kinds of sentences (Karmiloff-Smith, 1979).

Like vocabulary, later grammatical achievements are fostered by children's cognitive development and improved ability to analyze and reflect on language. Older children can deal with more complex relationships and are more attentive to subtle linguistic cues. These capacities play major roles in helping them understand the most intricate grammatical forms (Wallach, 1984).

New Ideas About How Grammatical Development Takes Place

In view of the complexity of what is learned, preschoolers' mastery of most of the grammar of their language is truly astounding. Currently, there are various conjectures about how this early learning takes place.

STRATEGIES FOR ACQUIRING GRAMMAR. Evidence that grammatical development is an extended rather than sudden process has raised questions about Chomsky's strict nativist account. Some experts have concluded that grammar is largely a product of general cognitive development, or children's tendency to search the environment for consistencies and patterns of all sorts (Bates & MacWhinney, 1987; Bever, 1982; Maratsos, 1983; Nelson, 1989). Yet among these theorists, there is intense debate about how the structure of language is created.

According to one view, young children rely on the semantic properties of words to figure out basic grammatical regularities—an approach called the **semantic bootstrapping hypothesis**. For example, children might begin by grouping together words with "object qualities" as nouns and words with "action qualities" as verbs and then merge these semantic categories with observations they make about how particular words are used in sentences (Bates & MacWhinney, 1987; Matthei, 1987; Pinker, 1984). Others take the view that children form grammatical categories through direct observations of the structure of language. That is, they notice which words appear in the same positions in sentences, take the same morphological endings, and are similarly combined with other words and, over time, group them into the same grammatical class (Braine, 1987; Maratsos & Chalkley, 1980). It is also possible that some complex combination of semantic and structural analysis leads children to acquire the grammar of their language (Maratsos, 1983).

Still other theorists, while also focusing on processing mechanisms, agree with the essence of Chomsky's position that they are specially tuned for language learning. For example, Dan Slobin (1985) proposes that children do not start with an innate knowledge of grammatical rules, as Chomsky believed. However, they do have a special **language-making capacity (LMC)**—a set of procedures for analyzing the language they hear that supports the discovery of grammatical regularities. Studying the development of children acquiring over 40 different languages, Slobin found common patterns suggesting that a basic set of strategies exists. Nevertheless, controversy continues over whether there is a universal, built-in language-processing device or whether children in different parts of world

Semantic bootstrapping hypothesis

A hypothesis that states that young children rely on the semantic properties of words to figure out basic grammatical regularities.

Language-making capacity (LMC)

According to Slobin's theory, a built-in set of procedures for analyzing language that supports the discovery of grammatical regularities.

develop unique strategies that are influenced by the specific language that they hear (Bowerman, 1989; de Villiers & de Villiers, 1992).

ENVIRONMENTAL SUPPORT FOR GRAMMATICAL DEVELOPMENT. Besides inherent capacities, researchers have been interested in what aspects of linguistic input to children might make the task of grammatical mastery easier. Research consistently shows that although adults correct children's semantics, they rarely provide direct feedback about grammaticality (de Villiers & de Villiers, 1992). For example, an early study reported that when a child said, "There's an animal farmhouse," the parent quickly explained that the building was really a lighthouse. In contrast, the statement "Her curling my hair" was met with an approving response because the parent was, in fact, curling the child's hair (Brown & Hanlon, 1970). These findings confirm that young children must figure out the intricacies of grammar largely on their own.

Nevertheless, adults could be offering subtle, indirect feedback about grammatical errors through two techniques, which they generally use in combination: **expansions** and **recasts**. For example, a parent hearing a child say, "I gotted new red shoes," might respond, "Yes, you got a pair of new red shoes," *expanding* the complexity of the child's statement as well as *recasting* its incorrect features into appropriate form. Parents and nonparents alike are far more likely to respond in these ways after children make errors. When sentences are well formed, adults tend to either continue the topic of conversation or repeat exactly what the child just said (Bohannon & Stanowicz, 1988; Penner, 1987). Furthermore, children often imitate adult recasts of their errors, but they rarely imitate adult repetitions of their correct speech (Bohannon & Symons, 1988). Notice how expansions and recasts highlight the precise difference between a missing grammatical structure in the child's utterance and an adult sentence containing it. Mothers who frequently reformulate children's utterances in these ways have preschoolers who make especially rapid progress in language development (Cross, 1978; Farrar, 1990; Nelson et al., 1984).

However, the impact of such feedback has been challenged. Critics argue that it is not provided to all children in all cultures. And even when it is given, it may not be offered frequently enough and across a broad enough range of mistakes to serve as an important source of grammatical development (Marcus, 1993; Valian, 1993). In sum, virtually all investigators agree that young children are amazing processors of linguistic structure. But the extent to which factors in the language environment help them correct errors and take the next grammatical step forward remains a hotly contested issue in child language research.

Children are active, rule-oriented learners whose earliest word combinations begin to reflect the grammar of their native tongue. As children move beyond two-word utterances, they add grammatical morphemes in a regular order influenced by the semantic and structural complexity of the forms to be learned. By age 6, children have mastered most of the grammar of their native tongue. Certain complex forms, however, continue to be refined in middle childhood. Powerful processing strategies are largely responsible for young children's grammatical achievements, but researchers disagree on whether they are of a general cognitive kind or especially tuned to language. Adult feedback may support children's mastery of grammar, but its impact continues to be debated. We still have much to discover about the ingredients of grammatical development and how they work together.

Brief Review

PRAGMATIC DEVELOPMENT

Besides phonology, vocabulary, and grammar, children must learn to use language effectively in social contexts. For a conversation to go well, participants must take turns, stay on the same topic, state their messages clearly, and conform

Expansions
Adult responses that elaborate on a child's utterance, increasing its complexity.

Recasts
Adult responses that restructure a child's incorrect speech into appropriate form.

to cultural rules that govern how individuals are supposed to interact. During the preschool years, children make considerable headway in mastering the pragmatics of language.

Acquiring Conversational Skills

At the beginning of early childhood, children are already skilled conversationalists. In face-to-face interaction with peers, they take turns, make eye contact, respond appropriately to their partner's remarks, and maintain a topic over time (Garvey, 1974; Podrouzek & Furrow, 1988). Nevertheless, certain conversational strategies that help sustain interaction are added at later ages. One of these is the **turnabout,** in which the speaker not only comments on what has just been said but also adds a request to get the partner to respond again. Turnabouts increase over the preschool years. Very young children may not use them because they cannot yet generate many words in each turn (Goelman, 1986). Between ages 5 and 9, more advanced conversational strategies appear, such as **shading,** in which a change of topic is initiated gradually rather than abruptly by modifying the focus of discussion (Wanska & Bedrosian, 1985).

Effective conversation also depends on understanding the **illocutionary intent** of utterances—that is, what a speaker *means to say,* regardless of whether the form of the utterance is perfectly consistent with it. For example, the statement, "Would you like to make cookies?" can be a request for information, an offer to provide an activity, or a directive to do something, depending on its context. By age 3, children comprehend a variety of utterances as requests for action even when they are not directly expressed that way, such as "I need a pencil" or "Why don't you tickle me?" (Garvey, 1974). During middle childhood, illocutionary knowledge develops further. For example, in the context of having forgotten to do his chore of taking the garbage out, an 8-year-old understands that his mother's statement, "The garbage is beginning to smell," really means, "Take the garbage out!" Appreciating form-intention pairings like this one requires children to make subtle inferences between content and utterance that are beyond preschoolers' cognitive capacities (Ackerman, 1978).

Still, surprisingly advanced conversational abilities are present at a very early age, and they probably grow out of early interactive experiences with adults and siblings. In fact, conversational give-and-take with skilled speakers seems to be an especially important context for all aspects of early language development. Opportunities to interact with adults, either at home or in preschool, are consistently related to general measures of language progress (Byrne & Hayden, 1980; McCartney, 1984). See the From Research to Practice box on the following page for additional evidence on the role of adult and sibling conversations in young children's pragmatic development.

Learning to Communicate Clearly

Effective communication requires the ability to produce clear verbal messages as well as recognize when messages we receive are unclear so we can ask for more information. These aspects of language are called **referential communication skills.**

Laboratory tasks designed to assess children's ability to communicate clearly typically present them with challenging situations in which they must describe one object among a group of very similar objects to a listener. For example, in one study, 3- to 10-year-olds were shown several eight-object arrays. In each, objects were similar in size, shape, and color. Children were asked to indicate which object they liked best as a birthday present for an imaginary friend. Most 3-year-olds gave ambiguous descriptions. When asked for clarification, they relied heavily on gestures, such as pointing. The ability to send clear messages improved steadily with age (Deutsch & Pechmann, 1982).

Turnabout
A conversational strategy in which the speaker not only comments on what has just been said but also adds a request to get the partner to respond again.

Shading
A conversational strategy in which a change of topic is initiated gradually by modifying the focus of discussion.

Illocutionary intent
What a speaker means to say, regardless of whether the form of the utterance is perfectly consistent with it.

Referential communication skills
The ability to produce clear verbal messages and to recognize when the meaning of others' messages is unclear.

Most research on the role of social interaction in language development has focused on mother–child pairs. Later-born children, however, typically spend their first few years in the presence of siblings. Only on rare occasions do these youngsters have the attention of a parent all to themselves.

Consistent with the confluence model we discussed in Chapter 8 (see page 337), several studies report that the presence of another child reduces the quantity and quality of parent–child interaction. Mothers of more than one child address each with fewer utterances, use more commands, and provide fewer comments and questions—factors thought to account for the slower early vocabulary growth of twins and, to a lesser extent, later-born children (Jones & Adamson, 1987; Tomasello, Mannle, & Kruger, 1986).

But vocabulary is only one aspect of language development. Research suggests that participating in multichild family interaction may have certain positive consequences. Recently, Michelle Barton and Michael Tomasello (1991) brought 19- to 25-month-old toddlers, their mothers, and their 3- to 5-year-old siblings into a laboratory and asked them to play with some novel toys. Even the youngest toddlers closely monitored the actions of their mothers and siblings, frequently establishing joint attentional focus with them. When they did so, toddlers were especially likely to join in interaction, sparking elaborate verbal exchanges. As Figure 9.5 shows, mother–toddler–sibling conversations

M*other–toddler–sibling interaction seems to offer a unique context for enhancing the pragmatics of language. The younger child in this family may become especially skilled at joining in conversations and adapting his speech to the needs of his listeners.* (ROBERT E. SCHWERZEL / STOCK BOSTON)

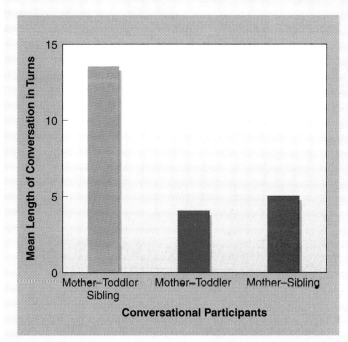

FIGURE 9.5 Average number of turns in mother–toddler–sibling conversations compared to mother–toddler and mother–sibling conversations. When all three interacted together, conversations almost tripled in length, and each participant took more turns. (Adapted from Barton & Tomasello, 1991.)

were almost three times longer than either mother–toddler or mother–sibling conversations. When all three interacted together, each participant took more turns.

Mother–toddler–sibling interaction seems to offer a unique context for acquiring the pragmatics of language. For example, successfully joining an ongoing conversation requires a toddler to understand the other speakers' topic and think of a way to add to it rather than just stating whatever comes to mind. Furthermore, as toddlers listen to the conversations of others, they are exposed to models that may be especially important for certain language skills, such as how to use personal pronouns ("I" versus "you") and refer to people not present (Forrester, 1988; Oshima-Takane, 1988). Finally, communicating with siblings requires children to adapt their utterances to partners who may be far less willing than caregivers to give in to their wishes.

In sum, young children appear to profit in different ways from single and multichild language learning environments, and both are important for development. Although homes with older siblings may reduce adult sensitivity to individual children, they provide a rich variety of linguistic stimulation that helps children learn to use language for social purposes.

*C*ontext affects young children's *referential communication skills. When talking on the telephone, this 3-year-old is likely to have trouble communicating clearly because he lacks the supports available in face-to-face interaction, such as visual access to his partner's reaction and to objects that are topics of conversation.* (TONY FREEMAN/PHOTOEDIT)

Speech registers
Language adaptations to social expectations.

These findings may remind you of Piaget's notion of *egocentric speech*—that young children have difficulty taking the perspective of others and communicating in a way that meets their needs (see Chapter 6). However, when preschoolers engage in face-to-face interaction with familiar people or are given simpler communication tasks, they show little evidence of egocentrism. Instead, they adjust their speech to the needs of their listeners quite competently (Warren-Leubecker & Bohannon, 1989). This suggests that context has much to do with the clarity of young children's messages. Over time, children become more adept at communicating clearly in unfamiliar, highly demanding situations in which their partners do not provide the supports typical in everyday conversation—acknowledging effective statements, pointing out inconsistencies, and prompting alternative explanations (Lloyd, Boada, & Forns, 1992; Warren & Tate, 1992).

Children's ability to evaluate the adequacy of messages they receive also improves with age. Around age 3, preschoolers start to ask others to clarify ambiguous messages (Revelle, Karabenick, & Wellman, 1981). At first, children recognize when a message provides a poor description of a concrete object (Ackerman, 1993). Only later do they become good at telling when a message is inconsistent with something said earlier. Detection of this kind of difficulty requires the listener to retrieve previous discourse from memory and match it against currently spoken information. It depends on the *comprehension monitoring* skills we discussed in Chapter 7 and is a late developing achievement, improving gradually during middle childhood and adolescence (Sonnenschein, 1986a).

Sociolinguistic Understanding

Language adaptations to social expectations are called **speech registers**. As early as the preschool years, children are sensitive to them. In one study, 4- to 7-year-olds were asked to act out different roles with hand puppets. Even the youngest children showed that they understood the stereotypic features of different social positions. They used more commands when playing socially dominant and male roles, such as teacher, doctor, and father, and more politeness routines and indirect requests when playing less dominant and feminine roles, such as pupil, patient, and mother (Anderson, 1984).

Speech adjustments based on familiarity and age also appear during the preschool and early elementary school years. Children give fuller explanations to an unfamiliar listener than to someone with whom they share common experiences, such as a friend or family member (Sonnenschein, 1986b). They also simplify their speech when talking to a very young child (see Chapter 6, page 240). These abilities are refined in middle childhood. For example, when communicating with an unfamiliar listener or a 2-year-old, fourth-graders include more redundant information than do first-graders. Older children apply their more advanced referential communication skills to their speech-register adjustments, taking extra steps to accommodate the needs of their listeners (Sonnenschein, 1988).

The importance of register adjustments is reflected in how often parents teach social routines as part of the child's first communicative acts. Infants are encouraged to wave "bye-bye" before they can grasp the meaning of the gesture. By age 2, when children fail to say "please," "thank you," or "hi" and "good-bye," parents usually demand an appropriate response (Berko Gleason, 1977). In some cultures, much greater emphasis is placed on tutoring young children in social routines than in language per se. For example, Kaluli mothers of New Guinea model socially appropriate statements, terminating their utterance with the word *ellema* (say it). If the child is too young to imitate, the mother may pitch her voice up and repeat the routine, as if the infant or toddler were speaking (Schieffelin & Ochs, 1987).

Parents everywhere seem to realize that a child can get by in the world without perfectly correct pronunciation, grammar, and a large vocabulary. But failing to use socially acceptable speech can lead to scorn and rejection, causing a child's message not to be received at all (Greif & Berko Gleason, 1980).

During early and middle childhood, children acquire a variety of pragmatic devices that permit them to engage in more sustained and effective conversation with others. Over this same period, referential communication in unfamiliar, highly demanding situations improves. Sensitivity to speech registers is present during the preschool years. Parents the world over realize the importance of socially appropriate communication and tutor children in social routines from an early age.

DEVELOPMENT OF METALINGUISTIC AWARENESS

In previous sections, we noted several times that older children's more reflective and analytical approach to language is involved in later linguistic achievements. The ability to think about language as a system is called **metalinguistic awareness.** Researchers have been especially interested in when it emerges and the role it plays in a variety of language-related accomplishments.

The beginnings of metalinguistic awareness are already present in early childhood. For example, by age 4, children are aware that word labels are arbitrary and not part of the objects to which they refer. When asked whether an object could be called by a different name in a new language, they respond "yes." Four-year-olds can also make some conscious syntactic judgments—for example, that a puppet who says "nose your touch" or "dog the pat" is saying his sentences backward. These early metalinguistic understandings are good predictors of vocabulary and grammatical development during the preschool years (Smith & Tager-Flusberg, 1982).

Nevertheless, young children view language primarily as a means of communication, and they seldom treat it as an object of thought. Full flowering of metalinguistic skills does not take place until middle childhood. For example, around age 8, children can divide spoken words into phonemes (Tunmer & Nesdale, 1982). They can also judge the grammatical correctness of a sentence even if its meaning is false or senseless, whereas preschoolers cannot (Bialystok, 1986). School-age children's metalinguistic knowledge is also evident in their improved ability to define words and appreciate their multiple meanings in puns, riddles, and metaphors—skills that continue to be refined into adolescence (McGhee-Bidlack, 1991; Winner, 1988).

Metalinguistic awareness emerges as language use becomes more automatic, freeing children from the immediate linguistic context so they can attend to how messages are communicated. By the early school years, a variety of metalinguistic skills are related to better reading achievement (Ehri, 1979). This makes sense, since to map printed text onto oral language, children must have some conscious knowledge of the structure of spoken language. However, researchers are not yet sure which metalinguistic abilities are most important. Once more is known, training in metalinguistic skills might turn out to be an especially effective means of encouraging reading progress.

As we will see in the final section of this chapter, bilingual children are advanced in metalinguistic awareness (as well as other cognitive skills). But before we conclude with this topic, turn to the Milestones table on pages 382–383, which provides an overview of the many aspects of language development we have discussed throughout this chapter.

BILINGUALISM: LEARNING TWO LANGUAGES IN CHILDHOOD

Most American children speak only one language, their native tongue of English. Yet throughout the United States and the world, many children grow up bilingual. They learn two languages, and sometimes more than two, during the child-

Metalinguistic awareness
The ability to think about language as a system.

381

MILESTONES
LANGUAGE DEVELOPMENT

Age	Phonology	Semantics	Grammar	Pragmatics	Metalinguistic Awareness
Birth–1 year	• Categorical speech perception is present. • Speech sounds become organized into phonemic categories of native language. • Intonation and sound patterns of babbling begin to resemble those of native language.	• Preference for sound pattern of native language is present. • Certain patterns of babbled sounds appear in particular contexts. • Preverbal gestures develop.	• Sensitivity to natural phrase units develops.	• Joint attention with caregiver is established. • Ability to engage in vocal exchanges with caregiver develops. • Participation in turn-taking games improves.	• Not present
1–2 years	• Systematic strategies to simplify word pronunciation appear.	• First words are produced; vocabulary builds to several hundred words. • Object words are emphasized first; action and state words follow soon after. • Word coinages appear.	• Two-word utterances, in the form of telegraphic speech, appear. • A beginning appreciation of grammatical rules is present. • First grammatical morphemes are added.	• Conversational turn-taking and topic maintenance are present.	• Not present
3–5 years	• Pronunciation improves greatly.	• Word coinage forms expand. • Metaphors based on concrete, sensory comparisons appear.	• Sentences clearly reflect an appreciation of adult grammatical categories. • Grammatical morphemes continue to be added in a regular order. • Many complex grammatical structures are added.	• Conversational strategies that help sustain interaction, such as the turnabout, appear. • Understanding of illocutionary intent is present. • Ability to adjust speech in accord with social expectations develops.	• The beginnings of metalinguistic awareness emerge. "Nose your touch!" "That's backwards!"

hood years. Current estimates indicate that 2.5 million American school-age children speak a language other than English at home. This figure is expected to double by the year 2000 (Hakuta & Garcia, 1989).

Children can become bilingual in two ways: (1) by acquiring both languages at the same time in early childhood, or (2) by learning a second language after mastering the first. Children of bilingual parents who teach both languages in the early years show no special problems with language development. For a time, they appear to develop more slowly because they mix the two languages. But this is not an indication of linguistic confusion, since bilingual parents do not maintain strict language separation either. Instead, it reflects the young child's desire to use

Age	Phonology	Semantics	Grammar	Pragmatics	Metalinguistic Awareness
6–10 years	• Pronunciations signaling subtle differences in meaning are mastered.	• At school entry, vocabulary includes about 14,000 words. • Meanings of words are grasped on the basis of definitions. • Appreciation of multiple meanings of words leads to expanded understanding of metaphors and humor.	• A few complex grammatical structures, such as the passive voice and infinitive phrases, continue to be refined.	• Advanced conversational strategies, such as shading, appear. • Understanding of illocutionary intent expands. • Referential communication in unfamiliar, highly demanding contexts improves.	• Metalinguistic awareness develops rapidly.
11 years– adulthood	• Changes in syllabic stress after certain difficult words take on endings are mastered.	• Vocabulary builds to about 30,000 words. • Many abstract words are added to vocabulary. • Understanding of subtle nonliteral word meanings, as in irony and sarcasm, improves.	• Refinement of complex grammatical structures continues.	• Referential communication—especially detection of unclear messages received—continues to improve.	• Metalinguistic awareness continues to be refined.

Note: These milestones represent overall age trends. Individual differences exist in the precise age at which each milestone is attained.

any means available to communicate (Goodz, 1989). These bilingual youngsters acquire normal native ability in the language of their surrounding community and good to native ability in the second language, depending on their exposure to it. When children acquire a second language after they already speak a first language, it generally takes about a year to become as fluent in the second language as native-speaking agemates (Reich, 1986).

Until recently, a commonly held belief among Americans was that childhood bilingualism led to cognitive and linguistic deficits as well as a sense of personal rootlessness, since the bilingual child was thought to identify only weakly with mainstream American culture. This negative attitude has been fueled by racial and

*S*everal million American school-age
children speak a language other than
English in their homes and neighborhoods.
Research shows that bilingualism enhances
many cognitive and linguistic skills.
(CHET SEYMOUR/THE PICTURE CUBE)

SOCIAL ISSUES Bilingual Education in the United States

V incente, a 7-year-old boy who recently immigrated
from Mexico to the United States, attends a bilingual
education classroom in a large American city. His teacher,
Serena, is fluent in both Spanish and English. At the beginning of the year, Serena instructed Vincente and his classmates in their native tongue. As the children mixed with
English-speaking youngsters at school and in the community, they quickly picked up English phrases, such as, "My
name is . . . ," "I wanna," and "Show me." Serena reinforced her pupil's first efforts to speak English, helping
them feel confident about communicating in a second language. Gradually, she introduced more English into classroom learning experiences. At the same time, she continued
to strengthen the children's native language and culture.

Vincente is enrolled in one of a variety of bilingual education programs serving the growing number of American
children with limited proficiency in English. Although state
and federal funding for bilingual education has increased in
recent years, it reaches less than 10 percent of children in
need (Children's Defense Fund, 1992b). Furthermore, the
question of how Vincente and other children like him
should be taught in school continues to be hotly debated.

On one side of the controversy are those who believe
that language minority children should be instructed only
in English. According to this view, time spent communicating in the child's native tongue subtracts from English language achievement, which is crucial for success in the
world of school and work. On the other side are educators
like Serena, who are committed to truly bilingual education—developing Vincente's native language while fostering his mastery of English. Supporters of this view believe
that instruction in the native tongue lets minority children
know that their heritage is respected (McGroarty, 1992). In
addition, by avoiding abrupt submersion in an English-
speaking environment, bilingual education prevents *semi-*

lingualism, or inadequate proficiency in both languages.
When minority children experience a gradual loss of the
first language as a result of being taught the second, they
end up limited in both languages for a period of time, a circumstance that leads to serious academic difficulties.
Semilingualism is one factor believed to contribute to the
high rates of school failure and dropout among low-income
Hispanic youngsters, who make up nearly 50 percent of the
American language minority population (August & Garcia,
1988; Ruiz, 1988).

At present, public opinion sides with the first of these
two viewpoints. Many states have passed laws declaring
English to be their official language, creating conditions in
which schools have no obligation to teach minority pupils
in languages other than English. Yet research underscores
the value of instruction in the child's native tongue. In
classrooms where both languages are integrated into the
curriculum, minority children are more involved in learning, participate more actively in class discussions, and
acquire the second language more easily. In contrast, when
teachers speak only in a language their pupils can barely
understand, children display frustration, boredom, and
withdrawal (Cazden, 1984; Wong-Fillmore et al., 1985).

Some researchers have pointed out a curious paradox
in American educational practice. Although minority children are encouraged to become English monolinguals,
instruction in foreign languages is highly valued for middle-class native English-speaking pupils (Hakuta & Garcia,
1989). Recently, a few schools have experimented with a
new form of bilingual education designed to benefit both
groups. In these programs, limited-English-proficient and
fluent-English-speaking children are assigned in equal
numbers to the same classroom, and instruction is directed
at helping all achieve competence in English and a second
language.

ethnic prejudices, since bilingualism in the United States is strongly associated with low-income minority status (Diaz, 1983). A large body of research now shows that bilingualism has a positive impact on development. Children who are fluent in two languages do better than monolingual controls on tests of analytical reasoning, concept formation, and cognitive flexibility (Hakuta, Ferdman, & Diaz, 1987). And, as we mentioned earlier, their metalinguistic skills are particularly well developed. They are more aware that words are arbitrary symbols, more conscious of language structure and detail, and better at noticing errors of grammar and meaning in spoken and written prose—capacities that enhance their reading achievement (Galambos & Goldin-Meadow, 1990; Ricciardelli, 1992).

The advantages of bilingualism provide strong justification for bilingual education programs in American schools. The Social Issues box on page 384 describes the current controversy over bilingual education in the United States. As you will see, bilingual children rarely receive support for their native language in classrooms. Yet bilingualism provides one of the best examples of how language, once learned, becomes an important tool of the mind and fosters cognitive development. In fact, the goals of schooling could reasonably be broadened to include helping all children become bilingual, thereby fostering the cognitive, language, and cultural enrichment of the entire nation (Hakuta, 1986; Ruiz, 1988).

CHAPTER SUMMARY

Components of Language
- Language consists of four subsystems: **phonology, semantics, grammar,** and **pragmatics.** In becoming competent speakers of their native tongue, children must master each component and combine them into a flexible communication system.

Theories of Language Development
- Three theories provide different accounts of language development. According to the behaviorist perspective, language, like other behaviors, is learned through conditioning and imitation. Behaviorism has difficulty accounting for the speed of language progress and for children's novel, rule-based utterances. However, it has had a lasting impact on efforts to help children with serious language delays and disabilities.
- Chomsky's nativist perspective proposes that humans are born with a **language acquisition device (LAD)** that permits children, as soon as they have acquired sufficient vocabulary, to speak in a grammatically consistent fashion and understand the language they hear. Evidence indicating that a complex language system is unique to humans, that language functions are housed in specific regions of the brain, and that a sensitive period for language development exists is consistent with nativist theory. However, vast diversity among the world languages and children's gradual acquisition of many constructions has raised questions about Chomsky's assumption of a universal grammar within the LAD ensuring built-in knowledge of grammatical rules.
- In recent years, interactionist theories have arisen, stressing that innate abilities and social contexts combine to promote language development. Today, there is increasing acknowledgment that biology, cognition, and social experience may operate in different balances with respect to each component of language. Grammar may be more innately determined than other aspects of linguistic skill.

Prelinguistic Development: Getting Ready to Talk
- Infants are specially prepared for language learning. Newborn babies are capable of **categorical speech perception** and are sensitive to a much wider range of **phonemes** than are children and adults. By 6 months, infants focus more intently on the sound categories of their own language. In the second half of the first year, they start to detect its phrase units. The special features of **motherese** ease the young child's task of making sense of language.
- Infants begin to **coo** at about 2 months and **babble** around 6 months. Over the first year, the range of babbled sounds expands. Then, as infants get ready to talk, the intonation and sound patterns of babbling start to resemble those of the child's language community. Also, certain patterns of babbles appear in particular contexts, suggesting that infants are experimenting with the semantic function of language.
- The beginnings of conversational behavior can be seen in the first few months as infants and caregivers establish joint attention, and the adult comments on what the baby sees. Turn-taking is present in early vocal exchanges, and by the end of the first year, babies become active participants in turn-taking games. Around this time, they start to use two preverbal gestures, the **protodeclarative** and **protoimperative,** to influence the behavior of others. Soon, words are uttered and gestures diminish as children make the transition to verbal communication.

Phonological Development
- The first words children say are influenced partly by what they can pronounce. When learning to talk, children apply systematic phonological strategies to simplify adult pronunciations.
- Pronunciation improves greatly over the preschool years as the vocal tract matures and children engage in active problem solving. Certain accent patterns that signal subtle differences in meaning are not mastered until late childhood and adolescence.

Semantic Development

- Vocabulary increases at an extraordinary pace during early childhood, an accomplishment that is even more awesome when we consider that children's language **comprehension** develops ahead of **production**. To build an extensive vocabulary quickly, children engage in **fast mapping**.
- Striking individual differences in rate and form of semantic development exist. Girls show faster early vocabulary growth than boys, and reserved, cautious toddlers may wait for a time before beginning to speak. Most toddlers use a **referential style** of language learning. A smaller number who use an **expressive style** have vocabularies that grow more slowly.
- Early vocabularies emphasize object words; action and state words appear soon after, an order influenced by cognitive development. When first learning new words, children make errors of **underextension** and **overextension**. Word coinages and metaphors permit children to expand the range of meanings they can express through language.
- In middle childhood, children can grasp word meanings from definitions, and comprehension of metaphor and humor expands. Adolescents' ability to reason abstractly leads to a wider vocabulary and appreciation of subtle meanings, as in irony and sarcasm.
- A special part of working memory, a phonological store that permits us to retain speech-based information, supports vocabulary growth in early childhood. According to **lexical contrast theory,** children figure out the meaning of new words by contrasting them with ones they already know. The **principle of mutual exclusivity** explains children's acquisition of some, but not all, early words.

Grammatical Development

- Between $1\frac{1}{2}$ and $2\frac{1}{2}$ years, children combine two words to express a variety of meanings. These first sentences have been called **telegraphic speech**, since they leave out smaller, less important words. Early word combinations do not always follow adult grammatical rules.
- As children move beyond two-word utterances, a grammatical explosion takes place. Their speech conforms to the formal grammatical categories of their language, and they add **grammatical morphemes** in a consistent order that is a product of both structural and semantic complexity. Once children acquire a regular morphological rule, they occasionally **overregularize,** or extend it to words that are exceptions. New expressions based on auxiliary verbs, such as negatives and questions, are soon mastered.
- Between the ages of 3 and 6, a variety of complex constructions are added. Still, certain forms, such as the passive voice and infinitive phrases, continue to be refined in middle childhood.
- Debate continues over how children acquire most of the grammar of their native tongue during early childhood. Some experts believe grammar is a product of general cognitive development. Others agree with the essence of Chomsky's theory that children are specially tuned for language learning. According to one view, children have a **language-making capacity (LMC)** that supports the discovery of grammatical regularities. Adults provide children with indirect feedback about grammatical errors, in the form of **expansions** and **recasts**. However, the impact of such feedback on grammatical development has been challenged.

Pragmatic Development

- Even young children are effective conversationalists, although strategies that help sustain interaction, such as the **turnabout** and **shading,** are added in early and middle childhood. During this time, children's understanding of **illocutionary intent** improves, and they also acquire more effective **referential communication skills**. Preschoolers are sensitive to **speech registers**. Parents tutor children in social routines at an early age, emphasizing the importance of adapting language to social expectations.

Development of Metalinguistic Awareness

- Although preschoolers show the beginnings of **metalinguistic awareness**, major advances do not take place until middle childhood. By the early school years, metalinguistic skills are good predictors of reading achievement.

Bilingualism: Learning Two Languages in Childhood

- Historically, Americans have held negative attitudes toward childhood bilingualism, a view that has been fueled by racial and ethnic prejudices. A large body of research

IMPORTANT TERMS AND CONCEPTS

phonology (p. 350)
semantics (p. 350)
grammar (p. 351)
pragmatics (p. 351)
language acquisition device (LAD) (p. 352)
Broca's area (p. 355)
Wernicke's area (p. 355)
phoneme (p. 358)
categorical speech perception (p. 358)
motherese (p. 359)
cooing (p. 359)
babbling (p. 359)

protodeclarative (p. 360)
protoimperative (p. 360)
comprehension (p. 363)
production (p. 363)
fast mapping (p. 365)
referential style (p. 365)
expressive style (p. 365)
underextension (p. 367)
overextension (p. 367)
lexical contrast theory (p. 369)
principle of mutual exclusivity (p. 370)
telegraphic speech (p. 370)

grammatical morphemes (p. 372)
overregularization (p. 372)
semantic bootstrapping hypothesis (p. 376)
language-making capacity (LMC) (p. 376)
expansions (p. 377)
recasts (p. 377)
turnabout (p. 378)
shading (p. 378)
illocutionary intent (p. 378)
referential communication skills (p. 378)
speech registers (p. 380)
metalinguistic awareness (p. 381)

C O N N E C T I O N S

engrossed in play. During the hour, Brenda displayed a whole new range of emotional reactions, including embarrassment at seeing chocolate on her chin in a mirror and pride as I remarked on the tall tower she had built out of blocks.

In this chapter, we turn to the child's emotions, a topic that has captured the attention of researchers from virtually every major theoretical persuasion. Although the emotional side of development was overshadowed by cognition for several decades, new excitement surrounds the topic today. A large body of research indicates that emotions play a central role in all aspects of human experience.

Our discussion brings together several lines of evidence. We begin with major theories that provide contrasting views of the role of emotions in development and everyday life. Then we chart changes in emotional expressiveness and understanding with age. As we do so, we will account for Zack, Emily, and Brenda's expanding range of emotional capacities. Next, our attention turns to temperament—individual differences in style of emotional responding. We will consider both biological and environmental contributions to these differences as well as their consequences for future development. Finally, we take up attachment to the caregiver, the child's first affectional tie that emerges during infancy. We will see how the feelings of security that grow out of this important bond provide a vital source of support for the child's exploration, sense of independence, and expanding social relationships.

THEORIES OF EMOTIONAL DEVELOPMENT

Three major viewpoints—behaviorism and social learning theory, cognitive-developmental discrepancy theory, and the more recent functionalist approach—have guided research on emotional development. Although the functionalist perspective has gained in popularity because of its broad explanatory power, each viewpoint has made lasting contributions to our understanding of children's emotions.

Behaviorism and Social Learning Theory

From the beginning of this century, behaviorists accorded emotional reactions an important role in children's development. According to John Watson, three innate emotions are present at birth: fear, induced by loud noises or loss of support; rage, prompted by restriction of body movements; and love, evoked by touching and caressing. As we indicated in Chapter 1, one of Watson's major findings was that emotional reactions to new stimuli, such as 9-month-old Albert's fearful reaction to a furry white rat, could be learned through *classical conditioning*. Watson concluded that all affective responses to objects and people were learned in this way (Watson & Raynor, 1920). In the 1960s, *operant conditioning* became an influential account of children's emotions as several researchers showed that infant smiling, vocalizing, and crying could be changed through caregivers' use of reinforcement and punishment (Etzel & Gewirtz, 1967; Rheingold, Gewirtz, & Ross, 1959).

Social learning theory emphasizes *modeling* of others' emotional reactions as another important means through which children associate feelings with particular situations. In recent years, Albert Bandura (1986, 1989) has expanded this view, adding a cognitive component to traditional social learning theory. According to Bandura, as children's representational ability improves, they can engage in *emotional self-arousal* by thinking about their own affectively charged past experiences or ones they have seen happen to others.

Although some emotional reactions are acquired through conditioning and modeling, behaviorist and social learning accounts are limited. They cannot explain why certain responses emerge spontaneously, without having been learned. For example, recall how Zack accepted unfamiliar adults, whereas Emily and Brenda

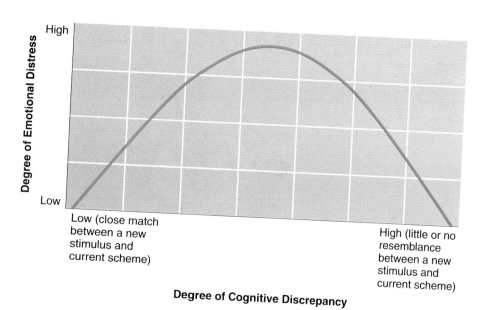

ety, whi
on mem
dren's re
tion at
from th
things l
them—
a few (I
Un
the rela
and his
half-ye
their w
dren's
happir
reflect
ment j
tive st
but fo
reacte
pullin
ing re
were
of ma

EMOT
as sn
erful
ior. F
by 3
resp
(Coh
studi
eithe
expr
agai
turn
& Ti

for
of a
glai
tha
res}
de\

EM
be\
sp\
shi
pe
ter
Lι
ex
in
in
th

were wary of them. As we will see later in this chapter, fear of strangers typically appears during the second half of the first year, despite the fact that infants previously responded positively to unfamiliar people, who continue to smile at and offer toys to the baby. Throughout this chapter, we will see that children often react emotionally in ways that cannot be accounted for by basic learning mechanisms.

Cognitive-Developmental Discrepancy Theory

Instead of viewing emotions as central forces in development, cognitive-developmental theorists regard them as by-products of cognitive processing. The first to take this position was Donald Hebb (1946, 1949), whose **discrepancy theory** of emotional development explained how distress reactions came to be elicited by novel stimuli. According to Hebb, when children encounter a new stimulus, they compare it to a scheme, or internal representation, of a familiar object. The similarity between the novel stimulus and the child's scheme determines the emotional response. Little discrepancy produces very mild distress, but as the discrepancy increases, the child's distress reaction intensifies. When the discrepancy is very great, the stimulus can no longer be assimilated, and the distress reaction declines. As Figure 10.1 shows, Hebb's theory predicts an inverted U-shaped relationship between cognitive discrepancy and emotional distress.

Later, other researchers modified Hebb's theory, suggesting that it could explain a wide variety of emotional reactions (Kagan, Kearsley, & Zelazo, 1978; McCall & McGhee, 1977). For example, they argued that the positive emotions of interest and happiness are due to a moderate discrepancy between a current scheme and a new event. As the stimulus becomes more unusual, the child's reaction turns to anxiety and fear.

Discrepancy theory is especially effective in accounting for children's interest in and exploration of their physical world. Many studies show that infants look longer at visual stimuli that are moderately discrepant from ones they know well. For example, 10-week-old babies first shown a picture of an arrow in one orientation (↕) attend more to new arrows that are somewhat different (↗) rather than very different (↔) from the first stimulus (McCall, Kennedy, & Appelbaum, 1977). Also, recall the study by White and Held (1966) discussed in Chapter 4, in which newborns exposed to massive stimulation (mobiles and patterned crib bumpers) were irritable and unhappy, whereas those given a moderate amount of stimulation were curious and attentive. These findings also fit the predictions of discrepancy theory. Finally, discrepancy theory explains why young children often play happily with new toys but ignore familiar ones. It helps us understand why many

Discrepancy theory

A theory of emotional development in which a child's reaction to a novel stimulus is determined by the degree of similarity between the stimulus and a scheme of a familiar object, to which the stimulus is compared.

D

dren
phys
betu
he re
his e
Goo

baby's pangs of hunger and her feeding practices are accompanied by sensitive, loving care, the baby builds a sense of trust that his needs will be met (Erikson, 1950). As a result, the infant feels confident about separating from her for brief periods of time to explore the environment. Eventually, the child forms a permanent, positive inner image of the mother that can be relied on for emotional support during brief absences.

Compared to behaviorism, the psychoanalytic approach provides a much richer view of the attachment bond, regarding it as critical for exploration of the environment, cognitive mastery, and emotional security. Psychoanalytic theories also recognize that deep affectional bonds, once formed, can endure over separations from loved individuals.

Despite its strengths, the psychoanalytic perspective has been criticized on two grounds. First, because it builds on Freud's oral stage, it (like the drive-reduction model) overemphasizes the importance of feeding in the development of attachment. Second, although psychoanalytic theory has much to say about the mother's contribution to the attachment relationship, it grants far less importance to the infant's characteristics and behavior. As we will see in the following section, ethological theory is unique in emphasizing that babies are biologically prepared to contribute actively to ties established with their caregivers.

Bowlby's Ethological Theory

Today, **ethological theory of attachment** is the most widely accepted view of the infant's emotional tie to the caregiver. Recall from Chapter 1 that according to ethology, many human behaviors have evolved over the history of our species because they promote survival. John Bowlby (1969), who first applied this idea to the infant–caregiver bond, was originally a psychoanalyst. As you will see shortly, his theory retains a number of psychoanalytic features. At the same time, Bowlby was inspired by Konrad Lorenz's studies of imprinting in baby geese (see Chapter 1). He believed that the human baby, like the young of other animal species, is endowed with a set of built-in behaviors that help keep the parent nearby, increasing the chances that the infant will be protected from danger. Contact with the parent also ensures that the baby will be fed, but Bowlby was careful to point out that feeding is not the basis for attachment. Instead, the attachment bond has strong biological roots. It can best be understood within an evolutionary framework in which survival of the species is of utmost importance.

Although ethological theory was stimulated by evidence on imprinting, it cannot serve as an adequate account of human attachment. In contrast to the imprinted gosling, whose time for development is short, human infants have a long period of immaturity and an extraordinary capacity for learning. As a result, the infant's relationship to the parent is not fixed but changes over time. According to Bowlby, it begins as a set of innate signals that call the adult to the baby's side. Over time, a true affectional bond develops, which is supported by new emotional and cognitive capacities as well as a history of sensitive, responsive care. The development of attachment takes place in four phases:

1. *The preattachment phase* (birth to 6 weeks). A variety of built-in signals—grasping, smiling, crying, and gazing into the adult's eyes—help bring newborn babies into close contact with other humans. Once the adult responds, infants encourage her to remain nearby, since they are comforted when picked up, stroked, and talked to softly. In addition, they often protest when put down from the arms of the caregiver (Schaffer & Emerson, 1964). Babies of this age can recognize their own mother's smell and voice (see Chapter 4). However, they are not yet attached to her, since they do not mind being left with an unfamiliar adult.

2. *The "attachment-in-the-making" phase* (6 weeks to 6–8 months). During this phase, infants start to respond differently to a familiar caregiver than to a stranger. For example, the baby smiles, laughs, and babbles more freely when interacting with the mother and quiets more quickly when she picks him up. As infants engage in face-to-face interaction with the parent and experience relief from distress, they

Ethological theory of attachment
A theory formulated by Bowlby, which views the infant's emotional tie to the familiar caregiver as an evolved response that promotes survival.

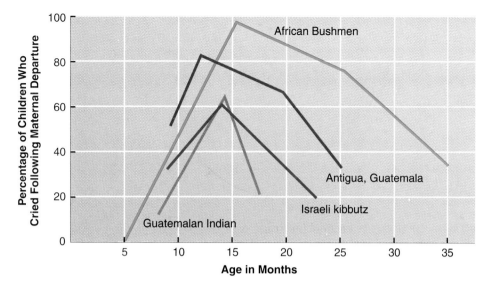

FIGURE 10.5 Development of separation anxiety. In cultures around the world, separation anxiety emerges in the second half of the first year, increasing until about 15 months and then declining. (From *Infancy: Its Place in Human Development* by J. Kagan, R. B. Kearsley, & P. R. Zelazo, 1978, Cambridge, MA: Harvard University Press, p. 107. Copyright © 1978 by the President and Fellows of Harvard College. All rights reserved. Reprinted by permission.)

learn that their own actions affect the behavior of those around them. As a result, they begin to develop an expectation that the caregiver will respond when signaled. But babies still do not protest when separated from the parent, despite the fact that they can recognize and distinguish her from unfamiliar people.

3. *The phase of "clear-cut" attachment* (6–8 months to 18 months–2 years). Now attachment to the familiar caregiver is evident. Babies of this period show **separation anxiety**, in that they become very upset when the adult on whom they have come to rely leaves. Separation anxiety appears universally around the world after 6 months of age, increasing until about 15 months (see Figure 10.5). Its appearance suggests that infants have a clear understanding that the parent continues to exist when not in view. Consistent with this idea, babies who have not yet mastered Piagetian object permanence usually do not become anxious when separated from their mothers (Lester et al., 1974).

Besides protesting the parent's departure, older infants and toddlers act more deliberately to maintain her presence. They approach, follow, and climb on her in preference to others. And they use her as a secure base from which to explore, venturing into the environment and then returning for emotional support, as we indicated earlier in this chapter.

4. *Formation of a reciprocal relationship* (18 months to 2 years and on). By the end of the second year, rapid growth in representation and language permits toddlers to understand some of the factors that influence the parent's coming and going and to predict her return. As a result, separation protest declines. Now children start to negotiate with the caregiver, using requests and persuasion to alter her goals rather than crawling after and clinging to her.

Understanding and trying to modify the mother's goals requires a beginning ability to see things from another's perspective. Children start to develop this capacity during the early preschool years, but parents can foster it by clarifying their goals to children. In one study, mothers who explained to their 2-year-olds that they were leaving and would return soon and who also suggested something for the child to do in the meantime ("Build me a house with Tinkertoys while I'm gone") had children who took the separation well. In contrast, 2-year-olds whose mothers "slipped out" without giving advance warning were likely to become very upset (Weinraub & Lewis, 1977). Explanations that match the child's level of understanding work best. Short descriptions of where the parent is going and when she will return are most effective. Lengthy ones delivered long before departure actually heighten separation anxiety (Adams & Passman, 1981).

According to Bowlby (1980), out of their experiences during these four phases, children construct an enduring affectional tie to the caregiver. Once firmly established, it bridges time and distance, and preschoolers no longer need to engage in behaviors that maintain the nearness of the caregiver as insistently as

Separation anxiety
An infant's distress reaction to the departure of the familiar caregiver.

TABLE 10.3 Episodes in the Strange Situation

EPISODE	EVENTS	ATTACHMENT BEHAVIORS OBSERVED
1	Experimenter introduces parent and baby to playroom and then leaves.	
2	Parent is seated while baby plays with toys.	Parent as a secure base
3	Stranger enters, is seated, and talks to parent.	Reaction to unfamiliar adult
4	Parent leaves room. Stranger responds to baby and offers comfort if upset.	Separation anxiety
5	Parent returns, greets baby, and if necessary offers comfort. Stranger leaves room.	Reaction to reunion
6	Parent leaves room.	Separation anxiety
7	Stranger enters room and offers comfort.	Ability to be soothed by stranger
8	Parent returns, greets baby, if necessary offers comfort, and tries to reinterest baby in toys.	Reaction to reunion

NOTE: Episode 1 lasts about 30 seconds; the remaining episodes each last about 3 minutes. Separation episodes are cut short if the baby becomes very upset. Reunion episodes are extended if the baby needs more time to calm down and return to play.

SOURCE: Ainsworth et al., 1978.

they did before. This inner representation of the parent–child bond becomes a vital part of personality. It serves as an **internal working model,** or set of expectations concerning the availability of attachment figures, their likelihood of providing support during times of stress, and the self's interaction with those figures, that affect all future close relationships—through childhood and adolescence and into adult life (Bretherton, 1992).

Measuring the Security of Attachment

Although virtually all family-reared babies become attached to a familiar caregiver by the second year, the quality of this relationship differs greatly from child to child. Some infants appear especially relaxed and secure in the presence of the caregiver; they know they can count on her for protection and support. Others seem more anxious and uncertain. Researchers have developed special methods for assessing attachment security so they can study the factors that influence it and its impact on later development.

The **Strange Situation** is the most widely used technique for measuring the quality of attachment between 1 and 2 years of age. In designing it, Mary Ainsworth and her colleagues (1978) reasoned that if the development of attachment has gone along well, infants and toddlers should use the parent as a secure base from which to explore an unfamiliar playroom. In addition, when the parent leaves for a brief period of time, the child should show separation anxiety, and an unfamiliar adult should be less comforting than the parent. As summarized in Table 10.3, the Strange Situation takes the baby through eight short episodes in which brief separations from and reunions with the parent take place.

Observing the responses of infants to these episodes, researchers have identified a secure attachment pattern and three patterns of insecurity (Ainsworth et al., 1978; Main & Solomon, 1990). They are as follows:

- **Secure attachment.** These infants use the parent as a secure base. When separated, they may or may not cry, but if they do, it is due to the parent's

Internal working model
A set of expectations derived from early caregiving experiences concerning the availability of attachment figures, their likelihood of providing support during times of stress, and the self's interaction with those figures that affect all future close relationships.

Strange Situation
A procedure involving short separations from and reunions with the parent that assesses the quality of the attachment bond.

Secure attachment
The quality of attachment characterizing infants who are distressed by parental separation and easily comforted by the parent when she returns.

418

*A*fter a short separation, this securely attached infant seeks physical contact with his mother and is easily comforted by her presence. (CRAIG HAMMELL/THE STOCK MARKET)

absence, since they show a strong preference for her over the stranger. When the parent returns, they actively seek contact, and their crying is reduced immediately. About 65 percent of American babies show this pattern.

- **Avoidant attachment.** These infants seem unresponsive to the parent when she is present. When she leaves, they are usually not distressed, and they react to the stranger in much the same way as the parent. During reunion, they avoid or are slow to greet the parent, and when picked up, they often fail to cling. About 20 percent of American babies show this pattern.
- **Resistant attachment.** Before separation, these infants seek closeness to the parent and often fail to explore. When she returns, they display angry, resistive behavior, sometimes hitting and pushing. In addition, many continue to cry after being picked up and cannot be comforted easily. This pattern is found in about 10 to 15 percent of American infants.
- **Disorganized/disoriented attachment**. This recently discovered pattern seems to reflect the greatest insecurity. At reunion, these infants show a variety of confused, contradictory behaviors. For example, they might look away while being held by the parent or approach her with flat, depressed affect. Most of these babies communicate their disorientation and apprehension with a dazed facial expression. A few cry out unexpectedly after having calmed down or display odd, frozen postures. About 5 to 10 percent of American infants show this pattern.

Infants' reactions in the Strange Situation closely resemble their use of the parent as a secure base and their response to separation in the home environment (Blanchard & Main, 1979; Vaughn & Waters, 1990). For this reason, the procedure is a powerful tool for assessing attachment security.

Stability of Attachment and Cultural Variations

For middle-class infants experiencing stable life conditions, quality of attachment to the caregiver is highly stable over the second year of life (Owen et al., 1984; Waters, 1978). In fact, recent evidence summarized in Table 10.4 reveals that such children continue to respond to the parent in a similar fashion when reobserved in a laboratory reunion episode several years later, at age 6 (Main & Cassidy, 1988). However, when families experience major life changes, such as a shift in employment or marital status, the quality of attachment often changes—sometimes positively and at other times negatively (Thompson, Lamb, & Estes, 1982; Vaughn et al., 1989). This is an expected outcome, since family transitions affect parent–child interaction, which, in turn, influences the attachment bond.

Avoidant attachment
The quality of insecure attachment characterizing infants who are usually not distressed by parental separation and who avoid the parent when she returns.

Resistant attachment
The quality of insecure attachment characterizing infants who remain close to the parent before departure and display angry, resistive behavior when she returns.

Disorganized/disoriented attachment
The quality of insecure attachment characterizing infants who respond in a confused, contradictory fashion when reunited with the parent.

ATTACHMENT CLASSIFICATION IN INFANCY	SIXTH-YEAR BEHAVIOR WHEN REUNITED WITH MOTHER*
Secure	This child is relaxed throughout the reunion and either initiates pleasurable interaction or responds positively to the parent's initiations. Typically, the child seeks closeness or physical contact without seeming dependent.
Avoidant	This child keeps his or her distance from the parent, looking and speaking as little as possible by remaining occupied with toys or activities.
Resistant	This child shows exaggerated intimacy with the parent in movements, posture, and tone of voice. At the same time, the child displays avoidance (for example, by talking to the parent with back turned) as well as hostility and sometimes fear or sadness.
Disorganized/disoriented	This child tries to direct and control the parent's behavior, assuming a role that is more appropriate for a parent. In some cases, the child does so by humiliating or rejecting the parent, with such statements as, "I told you, keep quiet!" or "Don't bother me!" In other cases, the child is overly solicitous or nervously cheerful at reunion, jumping, skipping, and clapping hands.

*Correspondences between attachment classification in infancy and sixth-year behavior when reunited with mother held for 84 percent of a sample of 40 middle-class children.

SOURCE: Main & Cassidy, 1988.

Nevertheless, cross-cultural evidence indicates that Strange Situation behavior may have to be interpreted differently in other cultures. For example, German infants show considerably more avoidant attachment than American babies do. However, German parents encourage their infants to be nonclingy and independent, so the baby's behavior may be an intended outcome of cultural beliefs and practices (Grossmann et al., 1985). An unusually high number of Japanese infants display a resistant response, but once again, the reaction may not represent true insecurity. Japanese mothers rarely leave their babies in the care of unfamiliar people, so the Strange Situation probably creates far greater stress for them than it does for infants who frequently experience maternal separations (Miyake, Chen, & Campos, 1985; Takahashi, 1990). Despite these cultural variations, the secure pattern is still the most common attachment classification in all societies studied to date (van IJzendoorn & Kroonenberg, 1988).

Factors That Affect Attachment Security

A variety of factors might be expected to affect attachment security. First, simply having an opportunity to establish a close relationship with one or a few caregivers should be critical. Second, because it assures the infant that the caregiver will respond to his signals and needs, sensitive parenting should lead to greater attachment security. Third, since infants actively contribute to the attachment relationship, an infant's characteristics should make a difference in how well it proceeds. And finally, because children and parents are embedded in larger contexts, family circumstances should influence attachment quality. In the following sections we examine each of these factors.

MATERNAL DEPRIVATION. The powerful impact of the baby's affectional tie to the caregiver is most evident when it is absent. In a series of landmark studies, René Spitz (1945, 1946) observed institutionalized babies who had been given up by their mothers between the third month and the end of the first year. The infants were placed on a large ward where they shared a nurse with at least seven other babies. In contrast to the happy, outgoing behavior they had shown before separation, they wept and withdrew from their surroundings, lost weight, and had difficulty sleeping. If a caregiver whom the baby could get to know did not replace the mother, the depression deepened rapidly.

According to Spitz, institutionalized infants experienced emotional difficulties not because they were separated from their mothers, but because they were prevented from forming a bond with one or a few adults. A more recent study of maternally deprived children supports this conclusion. Researchers followed the development of infants reared in an institution that offered a good caregiver/child ratio and a rich selection of books and toys. However, staff turnover was so rapid that the average child had a total of 50 different caregivers by the age of $4\frac{1}{2}$! Many of these children became "late adoptees" who were placed in homes after age 4. Since most developed deep ties with their adoptive parents, this study indicates that a first attachment bond can develop as late as 4 to 6 years of age. But throughout childhood and adolescence, these youngsters were more likely to display emotional and social problems, including an excessive desire for adult attention, "overfriendliness" to unfamiliar adults and peers, and difficulties in establishing friendships (Hodges & Tizard, 1989; Tizard & Hodges, 1978; Tizard & Rees, 1975). Although follow-ups into adulthood are necessary to be sure, these results leave open the possibility that fully normal development depends on establishing close bonds with caregivers during the first few years of life.

QUALITY OF CAREGIVING. Even when infants experience the closeness of one or a few caregivers, parental behavior that is insensitive to their needs should lead to insecure attachment. To test this idea, researchers have related various aspects of maternal caregiving to the quality of the attachment bond. The findings of many studies reveal that securely attached infants have mothers who respond promptly to infant signals and handle their babies tenderly and carefully. In contrast, insecurely attached infants have mothers who dislike physical contact, handle them awkwardly, and behave in a "routine," overstimulating, or angry and forceful manner when meeting the baby's needs (Ainsworth et al., 1978; Belsky, Rovine, & Taylor, 1984; Isabella, 1993; Kiser et al., 1986).

Exactly what is it that mothers of securely attached babies do to support their infant's feelings of trust? In one study, mother–infant interaction was videotaped and carefully coded for each partner's behavior. Findings indicated that a special form of communication called **interactional synchrony** separated the experiences of secure from insecure babies (Isabella & Belsky, 1991). Interactional synchrony is best described as a sensitively tuned "emotional dance" in which the caregiver reacts to infant signals in a well-timed, appropriate fashion. In addition, both partners match emotional states, especially the positive ones (Stern, 1985).

But more research is needed to document the link between interactional synchrony and secure attachment. Other research reveals that only 30 percent of the time are exchanges between mothers and their babies perfectly "in sync" with one another. The remaining 70 percent of the time, interactive errors occur (Tronick, 1989; Tronick, Cohn, & Shea, 1986). Perhaps warm, sensitive caregivers and their babies become especially skilled at repairing these errors and returning to a synchronous state. For example, if the mother is momentarily distracted, her infant is likely to whimper and look away. This prompts the mother to turn back to the baby with a direct gaze, a smile, and a comforting sound. Nevertheless, finely tuned, coordinated interaction does not characterize mother–infant interaction everywhere. Among the Gusii of Kenya, mothers rarely cuddle, hug, and interact playfully with their babies, although they are very responsive to their infants' needs (LeVine & LeVine, 1988). This suggests that secure attachment depends on attentive caregiving, but its association with moment-by-moment contingent interaction is probably culturally specific (MacDonald, 1992).

When caregiving is extremely inadequate, it is a powerful predictor of disruptions in attachment. Child abuse and neglect (topics we will consider in Chapter 14) are associated with all three forms of attachment insecurity. Among maltreated

Interactional synchrony
A sensitively tuned "emotional dance" in which the caregiver responds to infant signals in a well-timed, appropriate fashion and both partners match emotional states, especially the positive ones.

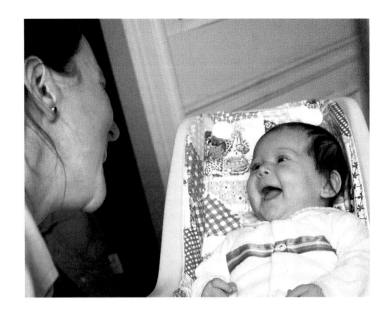

*T*his mother and baby engage in a sensitively tuned form of communication called interactional synchrony in which they match emotional states, especially the positive ones. Interactional synchrony may support the development of secure attachment, but it does not characterize mother–infant interaction in all cultures. (JULIE O'NEIL/THE PICTURE CUBE)

infants, the most worrisome classification—disorganized/disoriented attachment—is especially high (Carlson et al., 1989). Infants of depressed mothers also show the uncertain behaviors of this pattern, mixing closeness, resistance, and avoidance while looking very sad and depressed themselves (Lyons-Ruth et al., 1990; Radke-Yarrow et al., 1985).

INFANT CHARACTERISTICS. Since attachment is the result of a *relationship* that builds between two partners, infant characteristics should affect how easily it is established. Indeed, there is good evidence that this is the case. In Chapter 3, we saw that prematurity, birth complications, and newborn illness make caregiving more taxing for parents. In poverty-stricken, stressed families, these infant conditions are linked to attachment insecurity (Wille, 1991). But when parents have the time and patience to care for a baby with special needs and the infant is not very sick, at-risk newborns fare quite well in attachment security (Easterbrooks, 1989).

Infants also vary considerably in temperament, but the precise role that temperament plays in the development of secure attachment has been intensely debated. Some researchers believe that temperament is largely responsible for the way babies respond in the Strange Situation. They believe, for example, that babies who are irritable and fearful may simply react to brief separations with intense anxiety, regardless of the parent's sensitivity to the baby (Kagan, 1989). Although a few studies report relationships between proneness to distress in early infancy and later insecure attachment, overall the relationship is weak and inconsistent (Izard et al., 1991; Mangelsdorf et al., 1990; Thompson, Connell, & Bridges, 1988; Vaughn et al., 1989, 1992). This suggests that Strange Situation behavior is not just a reflection of the baby's temperamental style.

Other findings argue against the primacy of temperament as well. First, quality of attachment to the mother and the father is often similar, a resemblance that could be due to parents' tendency to react in the same way to their baby's temperamental characteristics (Fox, Kimmerly, & Schafer, 1991; Rosen & Rothbaum, 1993). Nevertheless, a substantial number of infants establish distinct attachment relationships with each parent and with their substitute caregivers (Goossens & van IJzendoorn, 1990). If infant temperament were the overriding determinant of attachment quality, we would expect attachment classification to be more constant across attachment figures than it is.

Second, the findings of several investigations suggest that when infant irritability is linked to attachment insecurity, caregiving conditions mediate the relationship. For example, in one study, newborn irritability predicted attachment insecurity only for those babies whose mothers reported that they had few social

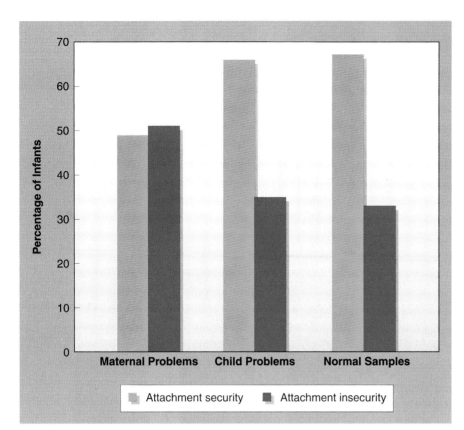

FIGURE 10.6 Comparison of the effects of maternal and child problem behaviors on the attachment bond. Maternal problems were associated with a sharp rise in attachment insecurity. In contrast, child problems had little impact on the rate of attachment security and insecurity, which resembled that of normal samples. (Adapted from van IJzendoorn et al., 1992.)

supports in the form of help from husbands, relatives, and friends (Crockenberg, 1981). And in another study, distress-prone infants who became insecurely attached were especially likely to have mothers with rigid, controlling personalities who probably had difficulty altering their immediate plans to comfort a baby who often fussed and cried (Mangelsdorf et al., 1990).

Finally, additional evidence that caregiving can override the impact of infant characteristics comes from a study comparing the effects of maternal and child problem behaviors on the attachment bond. Combining data from over 34 studies including more than a thousand mother–infant pairs, the researchers found that maternal problems—such as mental illness, teenage parenthood, and child maltreatment—were associated with a sharp rise in attachment insecurity. In contrast, child problems—ranging from prematurity and developmental delays to serious physical disabilities and psychological disorders—had little impact on attachment quality (see Figure 10.6). Instead, the occurrence of security and insecurity resembled that of normal samples (van IJzendoorn et al., 1992).

A major reason that temperament and other child characteristics do not show strong relationships with attachment security may be that their influence depends on goodness-of-fit. From this perspective, many attributes of children can lead to secure attachment as long as the caregiver modifies her behavior to fit the needs of the baby (Sroufe, 1985). But when a mother's capacity to do so is limited—for example, by her own personality or by stressful living conditions—then infants with difficult temperaments and problem behaviors are at greater risk for attachment insecurity. In sum, the reason maternal sensitivity is an effective predictor of the quality of the attachment bond is that the very concept of sensitive caregiving implies a mother who adjusts her caregiving to suit the unique characteristics of her baby.

FAMILY CIRCUMSTANCES. We have already indicated, in this and previous chapters, that quality of caregiving can be fully understood only in terms of the larger social environment in which parent and child are embedded. In this respect, several factors influence parental contributions to attachment security. In families where there is

TABLE 10.5 Relationship of Mothers' Internal Working Models to Infant Attachment Security

TYPE OF MATERNAL WORKING MODEL	DESCRIPTION	INFANT ATTACHMENT CLASSIFICATION*
Autonomous/secure	These mothers show objectivity and balance in discussing their childhood experiences, whether they were positive or negative. They neither idealize their parents nor feel angry about the past. Their explanations are coherent and believable.	Secure
Dismissing	These mothers devalue the importance of their attachment relationships. They tend to idealize their parents without being able to recall specific experiences. What they do recall is discussed intellectually, with little emotion.	Avoidant
Overinvolved	These mothers talk about their childhood experiences with highly charged emotion, sometimes expressing anger toward their parents. They appear overwhelmed and confused about their early attachments and cannot discuss them coherently.	Resistant

*Correspondences between type of maternal working model and infant attachment classification held for 70 to 80 percent of mother–infant pairs.

SOURCE: Main & Goldwyn, in press.

stress and instability, insensitive parenting and insecure attachment are especially high. However, the availability of social supports, especially a good marital relationship and the spouse's assistance in caregiving, reduces stress and predicts greater attachment security (Howes & Markman, 1989; Pianta, Sroufe, & Egeland, 1989).

Unfortunately, not all parents have access to supportive family ties. In one study of poverty-stricken depressed and abusive mothers, home visitors provided an accepting, trustworthy relationship, offered help in making use of community resources, and modeled and reinforced more effective caregiving over a 9- to 18-month period. Compared to controls, home-visited babies scored 10 points higher in mental development and were twice as likely to be securely attached. The longer lasting the intervention, the more involved high-risk mothers were with their babies (Lyons-Ruth et al., 1990).

Parents bring to the family context a long history of attachment experiences, out of which they construct internal working models that they apply to the bonds established with their babies. To assess parents' "state of mind" with respect to attachment, Carol George, Nancy Kaplan, and Mary Main (1985) devised the Adult Attachment Interview. It asks adults for childhood memories of attachment experiences along with an evaluation of those memories. How parents interpret their experiences, as opposed to the positive or negative nature of the events themselves, provides an overall impression of the adult's working model. Three types of attachment representations, summarized in Table 10.5, have been identified.

Quality of maternal working models is clearly related to infant attachment security—results replicated in studies carried out in the United States, Germany, Great Britain, and the Netherlands (Fonagy, Steele, & Steele, 1991; Grossmann et al., 1988; Main & Goldwyn, in press; van IJzendoorn et al., 1991). Autonomous/secure mothers typically have secure infants, dismissing mothers avoidant infants, and overinvolved mothers resistant infants—correspondences that hold for 70 to 80 percent of mother–infant pairs (Crowell & Feldman, 1988, 1991; Haft & Slade, 1989). Fathers' responses to the Adult Attachment Interview are less clearly related to infant attachment than are mothers' responses, perhaps because fathers typically spend less time with infants (Main & Goldwyn, in press; van IJzendoorn et al., 1991). Nevertheless, the quality of fathers' marital and parental relationships predicts their attitudes toward their babies. This suggests that working models also provide an important foundation for infant–father emotional ties (Cox et al., 1989; Cox et al., 1992).

These findings indicate, in line with both psychoanalytic and ethological theories, that parents' childhood experiences are transferred to the next generation by way of their internal working models of attachment relationships. This does not mean that adults with unhappy upbringings are destined to become insensitive parents. Instead, the way parents *view* their childhoods—their ability to integrate new information into their working models, to come to terms with negative events, and to look back on their own parents in an understanding, forgiving way—appears to be much more influential in how they rear their children than the actual history of care they received.

Multiple Attachments: The Father's Special Role

We have already indicated that babies develop attachments to a variety of familiar people—not just mothers, but fathers, siblings, grandparents, and substitute caregivers as well. Although Bowlby (1969) made room for multiple attachments in his theory, he believed that infants are predisposed to direct their attachment behaviors to a single attachment figure, especially when they are distressed. Observations of infants support this idea. When an anxious, unhappy 1-year-old is permitted to choose between the mother and father as a source of comfort and security, the infant usually chooses the mother (Lamb, 1976). This preference declines over the second year of life until, around 18 months, it is no longer present. And when babies are not distressed, they approach, touch, ask to be held, vocalize, and smile equally to both parents (Clarke-Stewart, 1978).

Fathers are salient figures in the lives of babies, beginning to build relationships with them shortly after birth. Observations of and interviews with fathers reveal that they respond to the arrival of their baby in much the same way as mothers. Most are elated and describe a feeling state called **engrossment,** a term that captures the involvement and interest fathers display toward their newborn child (Greenberg & Morris, 1974). Regardless of their social class or whether they participated in childbirth classes, fathers touch, look at, talk to, and kiss their newborn babies just as much as mothers do (Parke & Tinsley, 1981).

Like mothers', fathers' sensitive caregiving predicts secure attachment—an effect that becomes stronger the more time they spend with their babies (Cox et al., 1992). But as infancy progresses, mothers and fathers from a variety of cultures—Australia, Israel, India, Italy, Japan, and the United States—relate to babies in different ways. Mothers devote more time to physical care and expressing affection. In contrast, fathers spend more time in playful interaction (Lamb, 1987; Roopnarine et al., 1990). Also, when mothers and fathers play with babies, their behaviors tend to be different. Mothers more often provide toys, talk to infants, and initiate conventional games like pat-a-cake and peek-a-boo. In contrast, fathers tend to engage in more exciting, highly physical bouncing and lifting games, especially with their infant sons (Yogman, 1981). In view of these differences, it is not surprising that babies tend to look to their mothers when distressed and to their fathers for playful stimulation.

However, this picture of "mother as caregiver" and "father as playmate" is changing in some families as a result of the revised work status of women. Employed mothers tend to engage in more playful stimulation of their babies than do unemployed mothers, and their husbands are somewhat more involved in caregiving (Cox et al., 1992). When fathers are the primary caregivers, they usually retain their arousing play style in addition to looking after the baby's physical well-being (Lamb & Oppenheim, 1989). Such highly involved fathers are less gender-stereotyped in their beliefs, have sympathetic, friendly personalities, and regard parenthood as an especially enriching experience (Lamb, 1987; Levy-Shiff & Israelashvili, 1988).

Engrossment
The father's experience of elation and emotional involvement following the birth of his child.

*W*hen playing with their
babies, especially sons, fathers
tend to engage in highly physical,
bouncing and lifting games.
(STEVE STARR/STOCK BOSTON)

A warm marital bond supports both parents' involvement with babies, but cross-cultural evidence suggests that it is particularly important for fathers. Among the Aka hunters and gatherers of Central Africa, fathers devote more time to infant care than in any other known society. The relationship between Aka husband and wife is unusually cooperative and intimate. Throughout the day, they share hunting, food preparation, and social activities. The more they are together, the greater the Aka father's interaction with his baby (Hewlett, 1992b).

Research on fathers as attachment figures reminds us of the complex, multidimensional nature of the infant's social world. No evidence exists to support the commonly held assumption that women are biologically prepared to be more effective caregivers than are men.

Attachment and Later Development

According to psychoanalytic and ethological theories, the inner feelings of affection and security that result from a healthy attachment relationship support all aspects of psychological development. Consistent with this view, research indicates that quality of attachment to the mother in infancy is related to cognitive and social development in early and middle childhood.

In one longitudinal study, securely attached infants showed more elaborate make-believe play and greater enthusiasm, flexibility, and persistence in problem solving by 2 years of age. At age 4, these children were rated by their preschool teachers as high in self-esteem, socially competent, cooperative, autonomous, popular, and empathic. In contrast, their avoidantly attached peers were viewed as isolated and disconnected, whereas those who were resistantly attached were regarded as disruptive and difficult. Studied again at age 11 while attending a summer camp, children who were secure as infants had more favorable relationships with peers, were more likely to form close friendships, and were judged as more socially skilled by their counselors (Elicker, Englund, & Sroufe, 1992; Matas, Arend, & Sroufe, 1978; Sroufe, 1983).

Other studies report similar relationships between infant attachment security and childhood play, problem solving, and social competence (Frankel & Bates,

The consistency of these findings has been taken by some to mean that secure attachment in infancy causes increased cognitive and social competence during later years. Yet more evidence is needed before we can be certain of this conclusion. It is possible that differences in development are largely due to continuity in child rearing rather than the quality of early attachment per se (Lamb et al., 1985). In line with this view, parents who care for their infants in a sensitive, responsive fashion are more likely to provide effective support and guidance as their children move on to the challenges of school and peer relations (Booth, Rose-Krasnor, & Rubin, 1991). And among infants who experience major changes in family and caregiving conditions, early attachment security is not an effective predictor of later development (Erickson, Sroufe, & Egeland, 1985).

Finally, earlier in this chapter we saw that infants deprived of a familiar caregiver showed long-term adjustment difficulties. But similar outcomes do not always occur for infants who do become attached but for whom the relationship is less than ideal. In some studies, insecurely attached infants became preschoolers with severe adjustment problems; in others, they did not (Bates & Bayles, 1988; Fagot & Kavanaugh, 1990; Lyons-Ruth, Alpern, & Repacholi, 1993). Clearly, more research is needed to determine how attachment security combines with other forces to affect children's internal working models and the course of future development.

C ompared to behaviorist and psychoanalytic perspectives, ethological theory of attachment provides a more effective explanation of the development of attachment. According to this view, infants are biologically prepared to contribute to the attachment bond, which evolved to promote survival. In early infancy, babies' innate signals keep the parent nearby. By 6 to 8 months, separation anxiety and use of the caregiver as a secure base indicate that a true attachment has formed. Representation and language help older children tolerate brief separations from the parent.

Brief Review

The Strange Situation is the most widely used technique for measuring the quality of the infant–caregiver relationship. Caregiving that is responsive to babies' needs supports the development of secure attachment; insensitive caregiving is linked to attachment insecurity. Infant illness and irritable and fearful temperamental styles make attachment security harder to achieve, but good parenting can override the impact of infant characteristics. Family conditions, including stress, instability, and parents' own attachment experiences as reflected in their internal working models, also contribute to attachment quality. Mothers more often relate to their babies through physical care and expressing affection, fathers through highly active play. Secure infant–mother attachment predicts cognitive and social competence at later ages, but continuity of caregiving may be largely responsible for this association.

ATTACHMENT AND SOCIAL CHANGE: MATERNAL EMPLOYMENT AND DAY CARE

Over the past two decades, women have entered the labor force in record numbers. By the early 1990s, 53 percent of mothers with an infant under age 1 and almost 60 percent with a child under age 3 were employed (Children's Defense Fund, 1992b). In response to this trend, researchers and laypeople alike have raised questions about the impact of day care and daily separations of infant from mother on the attachment bond.

The Social Issues box on page 428 reviews the current controversy over whether maternal employment and day care threaten the emotional security of young children. Although research is still in its early stages, the weight of current evidence suggests that quality of substitute care and family conditions, rather than day care itself, may be the important factors. This conclusion is strengthened by the findings

Recent studies indicate that American infants placed in full-time day care before 12 months of age are more likely than home-reared babies to display insecure attachment—especially avoidance—in the Strange Situation. Does this mean that babies who experience daily separations from their employed mothers and early placement in day care are at risk for developmental problems? Some researchers think so (Belsky & Braungart, 1991; Sroufe, 1988), whereas others disagree (Clarke-Stewart, 1989; Scarr, Phillips, & McCartney, 1990). Yet a close look at the evidence reveals that we should be extremely cautious about concluding that day care is harmful to infants.

First, the rate of attachment insecurity among day-care infants is only slightly higher than that of non-day-care infants (36 versus 29 percent), and it is similar to the overall figure reported for children in industrialized countries around the world (Lamb, Sternberg, & Prodromidis, 1992). In fact, most infants of employed mothers are securely attached. This suggests that the early emotional development of day-care children is within normal range.

Second, we have seen that family conditions affect attachment security. Many employed women find the pressures of handling two full-time jobs (work and motherhood) stressful. Some respond less sensitively to their babies because they are fatigued and harried, thereby risk-

ing the infant's security (Owen & Cox, 1988). Other employed mothers probably value and encourage their infant's independence. In these cases, avoidance in the Strange Situation may represent healthy autonomy rather than insecurity (Clarke-Stewart, 1989).

Finally, poor-quality day care may contribute to the slightly higher rate of attachment insecurity among infants of employed mothers. In one study, babies classified as insecurely attached to both mother and caregiver tended to be placed in day-care environments with many children and few adults, where their bids for attention were frequently ignored (Howes et al., 1988).

Taken together, research suggests that a small number of infants may be at risk for attachment insecurity due to inadequate day care and the joint pressures of full-time employment and parenthood experienced by their mothers. However, using this as evidence to justify a reduction in infant day-care services is inappropriate. When family incomes are limited or mothers who want to work are forced to stay at home, children's emotional security is not promoted (Hock & DeMeis, 1987). Instead, it makes sense to increase the availability of high-quality day care and to educate parents about the vital role of sensitive caregiving in early emotional development.

of research in Sweden, where day care is nationally regulated and liberally funded to ensure its high quality. Swedish children who entered day care before their first birthday received higher teacher ratings on cognitive, emotional, and social competence at ages 8 and 13 than did children who started day care later or experienced no day care at all (Andersson, 1989, 1992).

In contrast to most Western European countries, the quality of American day care is cause for deep concern. Standards are set by the states, and they vary greatly across the nation. In some places, caregivers need not have any special training in child development, and one adult is permitted to care for as many as 8 to 12 babies at once. Large numbers of infants and toddlers everywhere attend unlicensed day-care homes, where no one checks to see that even minimum health and safety standards are met (Zigler & Gilman, 1993). Children who enter poor-quality day care during the first year of life and remain there over the preschool years are rated by teachers as distractible, low in task involvement, and inconsiderate of others when they reach kindergarten (Howes, 1990).

Unfortunately, children most likely to receive inadequate day care come from low-income families. Their parents cannot afford to pay for the kind of services they need. As a result, these children receive a double dose of vulnerability, both at home and in the day-care environment. Table 10.6 lists signs of high-quality care that can be used in choosing a day-care setting for an infant or toddler. Of course, for parents to make this choice, there must be enough good day care available. Recognizing that American day care is in a state of crisis, Congress recently allocated modest funding to upgrade its quality and assist parents—especially those with low incomes—in paying for it through tax relief (Jacobs & Davies, 1991). This is a hopeful sign, since good day care supports the development of all children, and it can serve as effective early intervention for children whose development is at risk, much like the programs we discussed in Chapter 8. We will return to maternal employment and day care in Chapter 14, when we consider their consequences for development during childhood and adolescence in greater detail.

TABLE 10.6 Signs of High-Quality Day Care for Infants and Toddlers

PROGRAM CHARACTERISTICS	SIGNS OF QUALITY
Physical setting	Indoor environment is clean, in good repair, well lit, and well ventilated. Fenced outdoor play space is available. Setting does not appear overcrowded when children are present.
Toys and equipment	Play materials are appropriate for infants and toddlers and stored on low shelves within easy reach. Cribs, high chairs, infant seats, and child-sized tables and chairs are available. Outdoor equipment includes small riding toys, swings, slide, and sandbox.
Caregiver/child ratio	In day-care centers, caregiver/child ratio is no greater than 1 to 4. Group size (number of children in one room) is no greater than 8 infants with 2 caregivers and 12 toddlers with 3 caregivers. In family day-care homes, caregiver is responsible for no more than 6 children; within this group, no more than 2 are infants and toddlers. Staffing is consistent, so infants and toddlers can form relationships with particular caregivers.
Daily activities	Daily schedule includes times for active play, quiet play, naps, snacks, and meals. It is flexible rather than rigid, to meet the needs of individual children. Atmosphere is warm and supportive, and children are never left unsupervised.
Caregiver training	Caregiver has at least some training in child development, first aid, and safety.
Relationships with parents	Parents are welcome anytime. Caregivers talk frequently with parents about children's behavior and development.
Licensing and accreditation	Day-care setting, whether a center or home, is licensed by the state. Accreditation by the National Academy of Early Childhood Programs or the National Association for Family Day Care is evidence of especially high-quality day care.

CHAPTER SUMMARY

Theories of Emotional Development

- Three theoretical viewpoints have enhanced our understanding of emotional development. Although some emotional reactions are acquired through conditioning and modeling, behaviorism and social learning theory cannot explain why certain responses emerge spontaneously, without having been learned. Cognitive-developmental **discrepancy theory** is helpful in accounting for children's interest in and exploration of their physical world, but it has difficulty explaining their reactions to people. The **functionalist approach,** which emphasizes that emotions are central, adaptive forces in all aspects of human activity, including cognitive processing, social behavior, and physical health, has the broadest explanatory power.

Development of the Expression of Discrete Emotions

- Signs of almost all the **basic emotions** are present in infancy, each of which becomes more recognizable with age. Happiness strengthens the parent–child bond and reflects as well as supports cognitive and physical mastery. The **social smile** appears between 6 and 10 weeks, laughter around 3 to 4 months.
- Anger and fear, especially in the form of **stranger anxiety,** increase in the second half of the first year as infants become better able to evaluate objects and events. These emotions

have special adaptive value as infants' motor capacities improve. Once fear develops, infants start to use the familiar caregiver as a **secure base** from which to explore.

- At the end of the second year, self-awareness and socialization experiences provide the foundation for **self-conscious emotions,** such as shame, embarrassment, and pride. Self-conscious emotions become more internally governed with age.
- **Emotional self-regulation**—the ability to adjust emotional arousal to a comfortable level of intensity—emerges from the early infant–caregiver relationship. As motor, cognitive, and language development proceed, children gradually acquire a diverse array of self-regulatory strategies and flexibly adjust them to situational demands. During the preschool years, children start to conform to the **emotional display rules** of their culture. In middle childhood, they become consciously aware of these rules.

Understanding and Responding to the Emotions of Others

- As infants develop the capacity to meaningfully interpret emotional expressions, they actively seek emotional information from others. **Social referencing** appears at the end of the first year. Preschoolers have an impressive understanding of the causes, consequences, and behavioral signs of emotion. The capacity to consider multiple sources of information in interpreting others' feelings develops during middle childhood. Older children also realize that people can experience mixed emotions.

- The development of **empathy** involves a complex interaction of cognition and affect. As self-awareness emerges, 1-year-olds show empathy for the first time. Gains in language, emotional understanding, and perspective taking support an increase in empathic reactions over the childhood years. Parents who display empathic concern and who set clear limits on children's display of inappropriate emotions foster the development of empathy. Empathy is an important motivator of **prosocial, or altruistic, behavior.**

Temperament and Development

- Children differ greatly in **temperament,** or style of emotional responding. Three temperamental patterns—the **easy child,** the **difficult child,** and the **slow-to-warm-up child**—were identified in the New York Longitudinal Study.
- Temperament is most often assessed through parental self-reports, although behavior ratings by others familiar with the child and direct observations are also used. Researchers are beginning to identify physiological reactions that are markers of temperament. For example, heart rate and electrical activity in the frontal region of the cerebral cortex distinguish **inhibited** from **uninhibited children.**
- Kinship studies reveal that temperament is modestly heritable. They also suggest that nonshared environmental influences are more important than shared influences in contributing to temperament, although not all researchers agree. Racial and ethnic differences in temperament appear to be due to the combined influence of heredity and cultural variations in child rearing.
- Temperament is consistently related to cognitive performance and social behavior throughout childhood. The **goodness-of-fit model** describes how temperament and environmental pressures combine to affect the course of development.

Development of Attachment

- The development of **attachment** has been the subject of intense theoretical debate. Although **drive-reduction, operant-conditioning,** and psychoanalytic explanations exist, the most widely accepted view is **ethological theory of attachment.** It regards babies as biologically prepared to contribute actively to ties established with their caregivers, which promote survival.
- In early infancy, a set of built-in behaviors encourages the parent to remain close to the baby. Around 6 to 8 months, **separation anxiety** and use of the parent as a secure base indicate that a true attachment bond has formed. As representation and language develop, preschoolers better understand the parent's goals, and separation anxiety declines. Out of early caregiving experiences, children construct an **internal working model** that serves as a guide for all future close relationships.
- The **Strange Situation** is the most widely used technique for measuring the quality of attachment between 1 and 2 years of age. Four attachment classifications have been identified: **secure, avoidant, resistant,** and **disorganized/disoriented.** Cultural conditions must be considered in interpreting reactions in the Strange Situation.
- A variety of factors affect the development of attachment. Infants deprived of affectional ties with one or a few adults show lasting emotional and social problems. Sensitive, responsive caregiving promotes secure attachment; insensitive caregiving is linked to attachment insecurity. Even ill and temperamentally irritable and fearful infants are likely to become securely attached if parents adapt their caregiving to suit the baby's needs. Family conditions, including stress, instability, and parents' own history of attachment experiences, influence the security of the infant–caregiver bond.
- Besides attachments to mothers, infants develop strong ties to fathers. When interacting with babies, mothers devote more time to physical care and expressing affection, fathers to stimulating, playful interaction. Secure attachment during infancy predicts cognitive and social competence in early and middle childhood. However, continuity of child rearing may be responsible.

Attachment and Social Change: Maternal Employment and Day Care

- Maternal employment and day care are associated with a slight risk of attachment insecurity among American infants. However, this relationship seems to be due to poor-quality day care and stressful conditions in some families with employed mothers.

IMPORTANT TERMS AND CONCEPTS

discrepancy theory (p. 391)
functionalist approach (p. 392)
Type A behavior pattern (p. 394)
basic emotions (p. 395)
social smile (p. 396)
stranger anxiety (p. 398)
secure base (p. 398)
self-conscious emotions (p. 399)
emotional self-regulation (p. 400)
emotional display rules (p. 401)
social referencing (p. 402)
empathy (p. 404)
prosocial, or altruistic, behavior (p. 404)

temperament (p. 407)
easy child (p. 407)
difficult child (p. 407)
slow-to-warm-up child (p. 407)
inhibited child (p. 409)
uninhibited child (p. 409)
goodness-of-fit model (p. 413)
attachment (p. 414)
drive-reduction model of
    attachment (p. 415)
operant-conditioning model of
    attachment (p. 415)

ethological theory of
    attachment (p. 416)
separation anxiety (p. 417)
internal working model (p. 418)
Strange Situation (p. 418)
secure attachment (p. 418)
avoidant attachment (p. 419)
resistant attachment (p. 419)
disorganized/disoriented
    attachment (p. 419)
interactional synchrony (p. 421)
engrossment (p. 425)

C O N N E C T I O N S

people's behavior—from *simple, one-sided explanations* to *complex interacting relationships* that take into account both person and situational variables. Finally, social cognition moves toward a *metacognitive level of understanding*. As children get older, their thinking is no longer limited to social reality. They also think about their own and other people's social thoughts.

Although nonsocial and social cognition share many features, they differ in important respects. Consider, for a moment, how much easier it is to predict the motions of physical objects, such as a rolling ball, than the actions of people. Movements of things can be fully understood from the physical forces that act on them. In contrast, the behavior of people is not simply the result of others' actions toward them. It is also determined by inner states that cannot be observed directly.

In view of this complexity, we might expect social cognition to develop more slowly than nonsocial cognition. Yet surprisingly, it does not. We will see that children demonstrate some sophisticated understandings at early ages, even though others take a long time to develop. Unique features of social experience probably help children make early sense of its complexity. First, the fact that people are animated beings and objects of deep emotional investment makes them especially interesting to think about. Second, social experience continually presents children with discrepancies between behaviors they expect and those that occur, which prompts them to revise their thoughts about social concerns. Finally, children and the people with whom they interact are all human beings, with the same basic nervous system and a shared background of experiences. This means that interpreting behavior from the self's point of view often helps us understand others' actions. When it does not, humans are equipped with a unique capacity— *perspective taking*—that permits them to imagine what another's thoughts and feelings might be. Perspective taking is so important for psychological development that we have already mentioned it many times in earlier parts of this book, and we will devote considerable attention to it in this chapter.

Our discussion is organized around three aspects of social-cognitive development: thinking about the self, thinking about other people, and thinking about relationships between people. Perhaps you have noticed that we have already considered some social-cognitive topics in previous chapters. Good examples are referential communication skills in Chapter 9 and emotional understanding in Chapter 10. Children's sense of morality is another important social-cognitive topic, but research on it is so extensive that it merits a chapter of its own. We will consider the development of moral reasoning in Chapter 12.

THINKING ABOUT THE SELF

Virtually all investigators agree that two distinct aspects of the self, first identified by philosopher William James (1890/1963) over a century ago, emerge and become more refined with age. The first is the "I," or *existential self*. It includes the following realizations: that the self is separate from the surrounding world, can act on and gain a sense of control over its environment, has a private, inner life not accessible to others, and maintains a continuous existence over time. The second facet of the self is the "me," a *reflective observer* that treats the self as an object of knowledge and evaluation by sizing up its diverse attributes. Self-understanding begins with the dawning of self-awareness in the second year of life and gradually evolves into a rich, multifaceted view of the self's characteristics and capacities over childhood and adolescence. As we trace the blossoming of this increasingly elaborate and organized image of the self, we will see that the "I" and the "me" are intimately intertwined and influence each other.

Social cognition

Thinking about the self, other people, and social relationships.

This infant notices the correspondence between his own movements and the movements of the image in the mirror, a cue that helps him figure out that the grinning baby is really himself. (PAUL DAMIEN/TONY STONE WORLDWIDE)

Emergence of Self-Recognition

Self-recognition refers to perception of the self as a separate being, distinct from people and objects in the surrounding world. As early as the first few months of life, infants smile and return friendly behaviors to their reflection in a mirror. At what age do they realize that the charming baby gazing and grinning back is really the self?

To answer this question, researchers have conducted clever laboratory observations in which they expose infants and toddlers to images of themselves in mirrors, on videotapes, and in still photographs. In one study, 9- to 24-month-olds were placed in front of a mirror. Then, under the pretext of wiping the baby's face, each mother was asked to dab red dye on her infant's nose. Younger infants touched the mirror, as if the red mark had nothing to do with any aspect of themselves. But by 15 months, children began to rub their strange-looking little red noses, a response that rose steadily until age 2 (Lewis & Brooks-Gunn, 1979). In addition, some toddlers entertain themselves by acting silly or coy in front of the mirror—actions that also signify the beginnings of self-recognition (Bullock & Lutkenhaus, 1990).

At first, babies react to *contingency cues* when presented with their own moving image. A "live" video playback of their actions prompted 9- to 12-month-olds to play a kind of peek-a-boo game in which they moved their head, body, or hand in and out of the camera's view, a pattern of behavior that increased with age. By the middle of the second year, toddlers respond to *featural cues*, which have to do with their unique visual appearance. They behave differently when shown a film of another child rather than one of themselves—smiling, moving toward, and attending more closely to the unfamiliar toddler but imitating and trying contingent play with the self. Around age 2, recognition of the self is well established. Children look and smile more at a photo of themselves than one of another child. And almost all use their name or a personal pronoun ("I" or "me") to label their own image or refer to themselves (Lewis & Brooks-Gunn, 1979).

How do toddlers develop an awareness of the self's existence? As yet, little evidence is available to answer this question. Many theorists believe that the beginnings of self lie in infants' developing *sense of agency*—recognition that their own actions cause objects and people to react in predictable ways. Parents who encourage babies to explore the environment and who respond to their signals consistently and sensitively help them construct a sense of agency. Then, as infants act on the environment, they notice different effects that may help them sort out self from other people and objects. For example, batting a mobile and seeing it swing in a

Self-recognition
Perception of the self as a separate being, distinct from people and objects in the surrounding world.

*T*he struggle between these 2-year-olds
over an attractive toy is a sign of
developing selfhood. At first, children often
assert their sense of self by becoming more
possessive about objects. The ability to
distinguish self from other also permits
young children to learn how to resolve
disputes and share. (CREWS/THE IMAGE WORKS)

Categorical self
Early classification of the self
according to salient ways in which
people differ, such as age, sex, and
physical characteristics.

Theory of mind
A coherent understanding of
people as mental beings with a
rich inner life accessible to
themselves and not to others.

pattern different from the infant's own actions informs the baby about the relation
between self and the physical world. Smiling and vocalizing at a caregiver who
smiles and vocalizes back helps specify the relation between self and the social
world. And watching the movement of one's own hand provides still another kind
of feedback—one under much more direct control than other people or objects. The
contrast among these experiences may help infants build an image of self as separate from external reality (Case, 1991; Lewis, 1991; Lewis & Brooks-Gunn, 1979).

Self-awareness quickly becomes a central part of children's emotional and
social lives. At first, children's sense of self is so bound up with particular possessions and actions that they spend much time asserting their rights to objects. In
one study, 2-year-olds' ability to distinguish between self and other was assessed.
Then each child was observed interacting with a peer in a laboratory playroom.
The stronger the children's self-definitions, the more possessive they were about
objects, claiming them as "Mine!" This was despite the fact that the playroom contained duplicates of many toys (Levine, 1983). These findings suggest that rather
than being a sign of selfishness, early struggles over objects are a sign of developing selfhood, an effort to clarify boundaries between self and other.

Besides prompting children's first disagreements, the ability to distinguish
self from other supports the emergence of a wide variety of emotional and social
skills. In Chapter 10, we saw that self-conscious emotions depend on self-awareness. Toddlers who pass the mirror self-recognition task are more likely to display
empathy, prosocial behavior, and imitative play with peers (Asendorpf &
Baudonniére, 1993; Bischof-Köhler, 1991). The ability to distinguish self from
other also permits children to cooperate for the first time in playing games, solving simple problems, and resolving disputes over objects (Brownell & Carriger,
1990; Caplan et al., 1991).

Once children become self-aware, they use their representational and language
capacities to relate themselves to other people, in much the same way that they
group together physical objects (see Chapter 6). Between 18 and 30 months, children
develop a **categorical self** as they classify themselves and others according to salient
ways in which people differ, such as age ("baby," "boy," or "man"), sex ("boy" versus "girl" and "woman" versus "man"), physical characteristics ("big," "strong"),
and even goodness and badness ("I good girl." "Tommy mean!"). They also start to
refer to the self's competencies ("Did it!" "I can't") (Dunn, 1987; Stipek, Gralinski, &
Kopp, 1990). These are the first steps toward developing a psychological self—a
major achievement of the childhood years.

Young Children's Theory of Mind

As children think more about themselves and others, they begin to form a naive
theory of mind—a coherent understanding of people as mental beings with a rich
inner life accessible to themselves and not to others. Recall from Chapter 7 that
after age $2\frac{1}{2}$, children refer to mental states, such as "want," "think," and "pretend,"
frequently and appropriately in everyday language. Although they confuse certain
mental terms and tend to view the mind as a passive container of information
rather than an active interpreter of experience (see page 272), young preschoolers
are clearly aware of an *inner self* of private thoughts and imaginings.

What is the young child's view of the inner self like, and how does it change
with age? Investigators are interested in answering this question because ideas
about the mind are powerful tools in predicting and explaining our own and others' everyday behavior. Just as we cannot make sense of the physical world without a grasp of time, space, and the permanence of objects, so we cannot understand the social world without a theory of mind.

Research reveals that 2-year-olds have only a primitive grasp of the distinction
between mental life and behavior. They think that people always behave in ways
consistent with their desires and do not understand that a person's beliefs affect his
actions (Wellman & Woolley, 1990). According to Henry Wellman (1990), from age

3 or 4 on, children's ideas about how the mind works are differentiated, organized, and accurate enough to qualify as a theory. Older preschoolers know that both *beliefs* and *desires* determine *actions,* and they understand the relationship among these three constructs. Wellman labels their theory of mind a **belief-desire theory**— a conception of mentality that closely resembles the everyday psychology of adults.

DEVELOPMENT OF BELIEF-DESIRE REASONING. To explore the emergence of belief-desire reasoning, researchers have presented children with stories about actors desiring or not desiring an outcome and believing or not believing it would happen. Then the outcome either happens or does not happen. Here is one example:

> Lisa wants it to be sunny today because she wants to play on her new swingset. But, Lisa thinks it's going to rain today. She thinks it's going to rain because she heard the weather man say it might rain. Look, it rains. (Wellman & Banerjee, 1991, p. 194)

Children are asked to indicate how Lisa would feel—happy or unhappy (a desire-related emotion) and surprised or unsurprised (a belief-related emotion). Both 3- and 4-year-olds easily give the appropriate desire-related feeling. They know that Lisa will be happy if she gets the weather she wants and unhappy if she does not (Hadwin & Perner, 1991; Wellman & Bartsch, 1988). And when the interviewing method is changed to clarify the meaning of emotional terms (preschoolers often confuse surprise with happiness), even 3-year-olds display some awareness that surprise occurs in situations that violate prior beliefs, a response that becomes consistent around age 4 (Wellman & Banerjee, 1991).

A more dramatic illustration of belief-desire reasoning comes from games in which preschoolers are asked to mislead an adult. By age 4, children realize that people can hold *false beliefs* that combine with desire to determine behavior (Harris, 1991; Perner, 1991). In one study, $2\frac{1}{2}$- to 4-year-olds were asked to hide the driver of a toy truck underneath one of five cups in a sandbox so that an adult, who happened to be out of the room, could not find it. An experimenter alerted the child to the fact that the truck, after delivering the driver to the cup, left telltale tracks in the sand as a sign of where it had been. Most 2- and 3-year-olds needed explicit prompts to hide the evidence—smoothing over the tracks and returning the truck to its starting place. In contrast, 4-year-olds thought of doing these things on their own. They were also more likely to trick the adult by laying false tracks or giving incorrect information about where the driver was hidden (Sodian et al., 1991). Other research confirms that children's understanding of the role of false belief in guiding their own and others' actions strengthens between ages 4 and 5 (Astington & Gopnik, 1991; Lewis & Osborne, 1990; Siegal & Beattie, 1992; Wimmer & Hartl, 1991).

Preschoolers' mastery of false belief is a remarkable achievement. It indicates that they can make genuine psychological predictions based on awareness of mental states, which they understand can differ from reality. Is this early grasp of mentality unique to children growing up in industrialized nations, where adults frequently explain behavior in terms of inner beliefs and desires? A recent study of the Baka, a hunting and gathering people living in Cameroon, West Africa, found that children's understanding of false belief develops at the same age as in the United States (Avis & Harris, 1991). That belief-desire reasoning shows a similar timetable of development in such different cultures strengthens the possibility that it is a universal feature of early childhood development.

WHERE DOES A THEORY OF MIND ORIGINATE? How do children manage to develop a theory of mind at such a young age? There are various speculations. Like self-recognition, perhaps belief-desire reasoning originates in infants' sense of agency, which leads them to infer that actions have an internal cause (Poulin-Dubois & Shultz, 1988). Make-believe play may also foster an early grasp of mentality. As children observe themselves using one object to represent another, they notice that the mind can change what objects mean. These experiences may trigger an awareness of belief in determining behavior (Leslie, 1988). Imitation may also provide an

Belief-desire theory
The theory of mind that emerges around age 3 to 4 in which both beliefs and desires determine behavior and that closely resembles the everyday psychology of adults.

important foundation for thinking about the mind. When imitating another's body movements, infants use their capacity for intermodal perception (see Chapter 4) to match behaviors they observe with those they feel themselves make. Their primitive plan to imitate an action, located inside the body, has much of the character of mental states. At the same time, imitation teaches infants that other people are like themselves. Perhaps this prompts them to conclude that others are also mental beings (Meltzoff & Gopnik, 1993).

Many researchers believe children are biologically prepared to develop a theory of mind, in much the same way they are primed to acquire language. The importance of an early grasp of mental states for normal development is tragically illustrated by children with *infantile autism*, who are indifferent to other people, display poor knowledge of social rules, and show delayed or absent language development. Recent evidence suggests that autistic individuals suffer from a specific impairment in mentalistic reasoning and in the early capacities believed to underlie it. Autistic subjects fail tasks that require an understanding of others' cognitive states, and their vocabularies rarely contain such words as "believe," "think," "know," and "pretend." In addition, their ability to imitate and engage in make-believe play is limited. Yet other cognitive skills—especially those that involve the physical world—are intact (Baron-Cohen, 1991; Tager-Flusberg, 1992).

These findings support the assumption that the normal human brain is specially tuned to develop a belief-desire theory. Nevertheless, investigators disagree on the extent to which this early understanding is due to maturation or social experiences common to most young children—a controversy that awaits additional research (Astington & Gopnik, 1991).

At older ages, children distinguish more clearly among different cognitive and emotional states (see Chapters 7 and 10) and between their own mental state and that of others, as we will see when we take up the development of perspective taking in a later section. Theorizing about the mind is a long developmental process, and we will add to our understanding of it throughout this chapter.

Development of Self-Concept

As children develop an appreciation of their inner mental world, they think more intently about themselves. During early childhood, they start to construct a **self-concept,** or set of beliefs about their own characteristics. Studies in which children have been asked to describe themselves indicate that preschoolers' self-concepts are largely based on concrete characteristics, such as names, physical appearance, possessions, and typical behaviors. For example, in one investigation of 3- to 5-year-olds, the most frequently mentioned attributes were typical actions, such as "I go to school," "I can wash my hair by myself," and "I help mommy" (Keller, Ford, & Meacham, 1978). These findings indicate, in agreement with Piaget and other theorists, that acting on the environment and finding out what one can do provide an especially important early basis for self-definition (Damon & Hart, 1988; Erikson, 1950; Piaget, 1954).

But preschoolers' understanding of themselves is not limited to observable attributes. When questioned in a way that evokes descriptions of commonly experienced emotions and attitudes, children as young as $3\frac{1}{2}$ demonstrate that they have a rudimentary understanding of their unique psychological characteristics. For example, they describe themselves in ways like this: "I'm happy when I play with my friends" or "I don't like being with grown-ups" (Eder, 1989). And when read statements and asked to tell whether they are true of themselves (a much easier task than producing a self-description), $3\frac{1}{2}$-year-olds often respond consistently. For example, a preschooler who says that she "doesn't push in front of other people in line" is also likely to indicate that she "feels like being quiet when angry" and "usually does what Mommy or the teacher says," as if she implicitly recognizes that she is high in self-control (Eder, 1990).

Self-concept
A set of beliefs about one's own characteristics.

Over time, children seem to organize these statements about internal states and behaviors into dispositional conceptions that they are aware of and can verbalize to others. Between ages 8 and 11, a major shift takes place in children's self-descriptions, which begin to mention personality traits. Look at the following examples, and you will see evidence for this change.

A boy, age 7: I am 7 and I have hazel brown hair and my hobby is stamp collecting. I am good at football and I am quite good at sums and my favourite game is football and I love school and I like reading books and my favourite car is an Austin. (Livesley & Bromley, 1973, p. 237)

A girl age 11½: My name is A. I'm a human being. I'm a girl. I'm a truthful person. I'm not pretty. I do so-so in my studies. I'm a very good cellist. I'm a very good pianist. I'm a little bit tall for my age. I like several boys. I like several girls. I'm old-fashioned. I play tennis. I am a very good swimmer. I try to be helpful. I'm always ready to be friends with anybody. Mostly I'm good, but I lose my temper. I'm not well-liked by some girls and boys. I don't know if I'm liked by boys or not. (Montemayor & Eisen, 1977, pp. 317–318)

A girl almost age 13: I have a fairly quick temper and it doesn't take much to rouse me. I can be a little bit sympathetic to the people I like, but to the poor people I dislike my temper can be shown quite easily. I'm not thoroughly honest, I can tell a white lie here and there when it's necessary, but I am trying my hardest to redeem myself, as after experience I've found it's not worth it. If I cannot get my way with various people I walk away and most likely never talk to that person again. I take an interest in other people and I like to hear about their problems as more than likely they can help me solve my own. My friends are used to me now and I don't really worry them. I worry a bit after I have just yelled somebody out and more than likely I am the first to apologize. (Livesley & Bromley, 1973, p. 239)

Notice how action remains an important feature of self-concept, but in a different way than during the preschool years. Older children emphasize typical behaviors less and competencies more, as in: "I am quite good at sums" or "I'm a very good cellist" (Damon & Hart, 1988). In addition, the number of psychological attributes increases with age. At first, children mention overall qualities—"smart," "honest," "friendly," "truthful," and "able to control my temper." When these general ideas about the self are firmly in place, adolescents start to qualify them: "I have a *fairly* quick temper," "I'm *not thoroughly* honest." This trend reflects an understanding that psychological qualities often change from one situation to the next (Barenboim, 1977). Finally, adolescents' self-descriptions place somewhat greater emphasis on social virtues, such as being considerate and cooperative, which reflects their greater concern with being liked and viewed positively by others (Rosenberg, 1979).

*A*cting on the world is an especially important source of self-definition to preschoolers. When questioned about his self-concept, this child is likely to describe typical behaviors, such as "I can comb my hair by myself." He may also mention commonly experienced emotions and attitudes, indicating that he has a beginning appreciation of his unique psychological characteristics. (BRENT JONES/STOCK BOSTON)

Influences on Self-Concept

What factors are responsible for these revisions in self-concept? Cognitive development certainly affects the changing *structure* of the self. School-age children, as we saw in Chapter 6, are better at coordinating several aspects of a situation and reasoning about their physical world. They also show an improved ability to relate separate observations in the social realm, combining typical experiences and behaviors into stable personality traits (Harter, 1983; Paget & Kritt, 1986).

The *content* of the developing self-concept, however, is largely derived from interaction with others. Early in this century, sociologists C. H. Cooley (1902) and George Herbert Mead (1934) described the self as a blend of what we imagine important people in our lives think of us. Mead called this reflected or social self the **generalized other**. He indicated that a well-organized, psychological self develops when children can comprehend the attitudes others take toward them. Mead's ideas indicate that *perspective-taking skills*—in particular, an improved ability to imagine what other people are thinking—are a crucial factor in the development of self-concept. Indeed, as we will see later in this chapter, perspective taking improves greatly

Generalized other
A blend of what we imagine important people in our lives think of us; determines the content of self-concept.

*D*uring the school years, children's self-concepts expand to include feedback from a wider range of people as they spend more time in settings beyond the home. Girl scouting and its associated qualities of friendliness, helpfulness, and kindness are probably important aspects of the self-definitions of these two girls. (JOEL GORDON)

over middle childhood and adolescence. Consequently, older children are better at reading the messages they receive from others and incorporating these into their self-definitions (Rosenberg, 1979). Consistent with the operation of the generalized other, both teacher and peer appraisals of fourth graders' competence are strong predictors of the adjustments they make in their self-concepts over the course of the school year (Cole, 1991).

During middle childhood, children look to more people for information about themselves as they enter a wider range of settings in school and community. This is reflected in school-age children's frequent reference to social groups, such as scouting and athletic leagues, in their self-descriptions (Livesley & Bromley, 1973). Gradually, as children move into adolescence, their sources of self-definition become more selective. Although parents remain influential, between ages 8 and 15, peers become more important. And over time, self-concept becomes increasingly vested in the feedback children receive from their close friends (Rosenberg, 1979).

Finally, it is important to note that the changes we have described are based entirely on interviews with American and Western European children. The little cross-cultural research available suggests that development of self-concept does not follow the same path in all societies. In small village and tribal cultures, the self and social group are not differentiated so completely. Recently, William Damon and Daniel Hart (1988) compared the self-descriptions of children in an isolated Puerto Rican fishing village with those of children in a small American town. Puerto Rican children more often characterized themselves as "polite," "nice," "respectful," and "obedient" and justified these social traits by noting the positive reactions they evoke from family members and friends. In contrast, American children more often mentioned individualistic traits, such as interests, preferences, and cognitive and social skills. In characterizing themselves, children from complex cultures seem to be more egoistic and competitive, those from simpler cultures more concerned with the welfare of others—a finding that underscores the powerful impact of the social environment on the makeup of self-concept.

Self-Esteem: The Evaluative Side of Self-Concept

So far, we have focused on how the general structure and content of self-concept change with age. Another component of self-concept is **self-esteem,** the judgments we make about our own worth and the feelings associated with those judgments.

Self-esteem
An aspect of self-concept that involves judgments about one's own worth and the feelings associated with those judgments.

According to Morris Rosenberg (1979), "a person with high self-esteem is fundamentally satisfied with the type of person he is, yet he may acknowledge his faults while hoping to overcome them" (p. 31). High self-esteem implies a realistic evaluation of the self's characteristics and competencies, coupled with an attitude of self-acceptance and self-respect.

Self-esteem ranks among the most important aspects of children's social-cognitive development. Children's evaluations of their own competencies affect their emotional experiences and future behavior in similar situations as well as their long-term psychological adjustment. Research reveals that as soon as a categorical self with features that can be judged positively or negatively is in place, children start to become self-evaluative beings. Around age 2, they call a parent's attention to an achievement, such as completing a puzzle, by pointing and saying something like, "Look, Mom!" In addition, 2-year-olds are likely to smile when they succeed at a task set for them by an adult and look away or frown when they fail (Stipek, Recchia, & McClintic, 1992). Furthermore, recall from Chapter 10 that by age 3, self-conscious emotions of pride and shame are clearly linked to self-evaluation (see page 399). Self-esteem originates early in life, and (as we will see in the next section) its structure becomes increasingly elaborate over the childhood years.

ONE SELF-ESTEEM OR MANY? Take a moment to think about your own self-esteem. Besides a global appraisal of your worth as a person, you have a variety of separate self-judgments concerning how well you perform in different settings and activities. As early as the preschool years, children distinguish how they feel about various aspects of the self. In fact, children seem to develop an array of separate self-esteems first, only later integrating them into an overall impression. According to Susan Harter (1983, 1990), before middle childhood, children do not have a general sense of self-worth, since they have not yet constructed a coherent psychological picture of themselves.

Researchers have studied the multifaceted nature of self-esteem in the same way that they have explored the question of whether there is one intelligence or many: by applying *factor analysis** to children's ratings of themselves on many characteristics. For example, Harter (1982, 1986) asked children to indicate the extent to which a variety of statements, such as "I am good at homework," "I'm usually the one chosen for games," and "Most kids like me," are true of themselves. Her findings reveal that before age 7, children distinguish how well others like them (social acceptance) from how "good" they are at doing things (competence). And when procedures are specially adapted for young children—for example, by questioning them individually and showing pictures of what each statement means—their sense of self-worth appears even more differentiated (Marsh, Craven, & Debus, 1991).

By 7 to 8 years, children have formed at least three separate self-esteems—academic, physical, and social—that become more refined with age. For example, academic self-worth divides into performance in different school subjects, social self-worth into peer and parental relationships (Marsh, 1990). Furthermore, school-age children combine their separate self-evaluations into a general appraisal of themselves—an overall sense of self-worth (Harter, 1990). Consequently, during middle childhood, self-esteem takes on the hierarchical structure shown in Figure 11.1.

With the arrival of adolescence, several new dimensions of self-esteem are added—close friendship, romantic appeal, and job competence—that reflect salient concerns of this period. Furthermore, the hierarchical structure of self-esteem is reflected even more clearly in factor-analytic studies, and it is similar for young people of different social classes and ethnic groups (Cauce, 1987; Harter, 1990; Marsh, 1989a; Marsh & Gouvernet, 1989).

*If you need to review the meaning of factor analysis, return to Chapter 8, page 311.

*S*elf-esteem rises during adolescence. Most young people have an optimistic outlook on life and are proud of their new competencies. (STEPHEN MARKS)

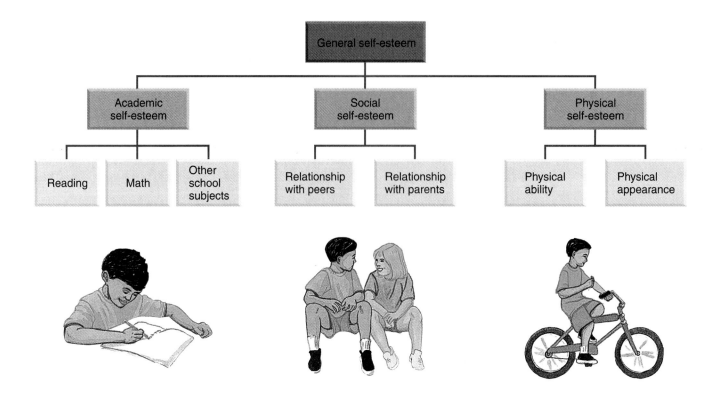

FIGURE 11.1 Hierarchical structure of self-esteem in middle childhood. From their experiences in different settings, children form at least three separate self-esteems—academic, social, and physical. These differentiate into a variety of subareas and combine to form an overall sense of self-worth. (From "Self-Concept: Validation of Construct Interpretations" by R. Shavelson, J. J. Hubner, & J. C. Stanton, 1976, *Review of Educational Research, 46*, 407–441. Adapted by permission.)

CHANGES IN LEVEL OF SELF-ESTEEM. Once self-esteem is established, does it remain stable or does it fluctuate? Many studies show that self-esteem is very high during early childhood. Then it drops over the first few years of elementary school as children start to make **social comparisons**—that is, judge their abilities, behavior, appearance, and other characteristics in relation to those of others (Marsh et al., 1984; Stipek & MacIver, 1989). In one investigation, kindergartners through third-graders rated their own and each of their classmates' "smartness" at school. Pupils in all grades could give estimates of classmates' abilities that were similar to those teachers gave. But the self-ratings of kindergartners and first-graders were overly favorable and unrelated to teacher or peer judgments. Not until second grade did pupil self-ratings resemble the opinions of others (Stipek, 1981). In another study, second-graders could make use of their own score along with the scores of several peers in judging their own task performance, but younger pupils could not (Ruble et al., 1980). Once children enter school, they receive frequent feedback about themselves in relation to their classmates. In addition, they become cognitively better able to make sense of such information. As a result, self-esteem adjusts to a more realistic level that matches the opinions of others as well as objective performance.

Typically, the drop in self-esteem is not great enough to be harmful. In fact, from fourth grade on, self-esteem rises for the majority of young people (Nottelmann, 1987; Wallace, Cunningham, & Del Monte, 1984). The only exceptions to this trend are a temporary decline in self-worth associated with the transition to junior high school and, occasionally, to high school. Entry into a new school, accompanied by

Social comparisons

Judgments of abilities, behavior, appearance, and other characteristics in relation to those of others.

442

new expectations by teachers and peers, may interfere with adolescents' ability to make realistic judgments about their behavior and performance for a period of time.

This steady increase in self-esteem is yet another reason that modern researchers question the widespread assumption discussed in Chapter 5—that adolescence is a time of emotional turmoil. To the contrary, the rise in self-worth suggests that for most young people, becoming an adolescent leads to feelings of pride and self-confidence (Powers, Hauser, & Kilner, 1989). This is true not just in the United States, but around the world. A study of self-esteem in 10 industrialized countries showed that the majority of teenagers had an optimistic outlook on life, a positive attitude toward school and work, and faith in their ability to cope with life's problems (Offer, 1988).

Influences on Self-Esteem

Up to this point, we have discussed general trends in the development of self-esteem. There are also wide individual differences that are strongly correlated with everyday behavior. For example, academic self-esteem predicts children's school achievement as well as their willingness to try hard at challenging tasks (Marsh, Smith, & Barnes, 1985). Children with high social self-esteem are consistently better liked by their peers (Harter, 1982). And as we saw in Chapter 5, boys come to believe they have more athletic talent than do girls, and they are also more advanced in a variety of physical skills.

Because self-esteem is so powerfully related to behavior, researchers have been intensely interested in finding out which social influences cause it to be high for some children and low for others. If ways can be found to improve children's sense of self-worth, then many aspects of child development might be enhanced as well.

CULTURE. Cultural forces have a profound impact on self-esteem. For example, in Chapter 5 we noted that during adolescence, early maturing girls and late maturing boys tend to feel poorly about themselves—outcomes influenced by cultural standards of physical beauty. Gender-stereotyped expectations for physical attractiveness and achievement have an especially detrimental effect on the self-esteem of girls. Beginning in adolescence, they score substantially lower than boys in overall sense of self-worth—partly because girls worry more about their appearance and partly because they feel more insecure about their abilities (Simmons & Blyth, 1987).

Furthermore, the strong role of social comparison in self-esteem does not characterize children everywhere. Puerto Rican fishing village children, discussed earlier in this chapter, almost never make statements referring to social comparisons. Yet among American children, such statements are common, both in self-descriptions ("I'm better at kickball than any other kid in my class") and in everyday conversations ("Hey, how many math problems did you get right?") (Damon & Hart, 1988; Ruble, 1987). An even greater emphasis on social comparison may underlie the consistent finding that Taiwanese children score lower in self-esteem than American children, despite their higher academic achievement (Chiu, 1992–1993; Stigler, Smith, & Mao, 1985). In Taiwanese classrooms, competition is tough and achievement pressure is high. Because so much stress is placed on school performance, Taiwanese children have fewer opportunities than American children to feel successful in other ways.

CHILD-REARING PRACTICES. Child-rearing practices are consistently related to self-esteem. Children with parents who are warm and responsive and who provide reasonable expectations for behavior feel especially good about themselves (Baumrind, 1971, 1991; Bishop & Ingersoll, 1989; Coopersmith, 1967). If you think carefully about this finding, you will see that it makes perfect sense. Warm, positive parenting lets children know they are accepted as competent, worthwhile human beings. And firm but appropriate expectations, backed up with explanations, seem to help children make sensible choices and evaluate their own behavior against reasonable standards. In contrast, highly coercive parenting communicates a sense of inadequacy to children. It suggests that their behavior needs to be controlled by adults because they are ineffective in managing it themselves.

Although parental acceptance and maturity demands are undoubtedly important ingredients of high self-esteem, we must keep in mind that these findings are correlational. We cannot really separate the extent to which child-rearing styles are causes of or reactions to children's characteristics and behavior. Research focusing on the precise content of adults' messages to children has been far more successful at isolating factors that affect children's sense of self-worth. Let's see how these communicative forces mold children's evaluations of themselves in achievement contexts.

Development of Achievement-Related Attributions

Attributions are our common, everyday explanations for the causes of behavior—the answers we provide to the question, "Why did I [or another person] do that?" We group the causes of our own and others' behavior into two broad categories: *external, environmental causes* and *internal, psychological causes.* Then we further divide the category of psychological causes into two types: *ability* and *effort.* In assigning a cause, we use certain rules. If a behavior occurs for many people but only in a single situation (the whole class gets A's on Mrs. Apple's French test), we conclude that it is externally caused (the test was easy). In contrast, if an individual displays a behavior in many situations (Sally always gets A's on French tests), we judge the behavior to be internally caused—by ability, effort, or both.

In Chapter 8, we showed that although intelligence predicts school achievement, the relationship is far from perfect. Differences among children in **achievement motivation**—the tendency to persist at challenging tasks—explain why some less intelligent pupils do better in school than their more intelligent classmates and why children who are equal in ability often respond differently in achievement situations (Dweck & Elliott, 1983). Because achievement motivation inspires us to acquire new knowledge and skills and increases the self's competence, it is highly valued in all human societies (Fyans et al., 1983). Today, researchers regard achievement-related attributions as the main reason some children are competent learners who display initiative when faced with obstacles to success, whereas others give up easily when their task goals are not immediately achieved.

EMERGENCE OF ACHIEVEMENT-RELATED ATTRIBUTIONS. Infants start to engage in competence-increasing activities almost as soon as they enter the world. In earlier chapters, we showed that young babies express great pleasure at acquiring a new skill—satisfaction that reinforces their efforts and motivates similar behavior in the future. Because infants lack the cognitive capacities necessary for self-evaluation, they do not reflect on the implications of their achievements. Instead, they are naturally driven toward mastery of activities that support their development. Achievement motivation is believed to have roots in this early drive (White, 1959).

By the end of the second year, children turn to adults for evaluations of their accomplishments, and they react to approval and disapproval with expressions of pride and shame. In the process, they pick up information about the meaning of competence in their culture (Stipek, Recchia, & McClintic, 1992). And around age 3, they begin making attributions about their successes and failures. These attributions affect their expectancies of success, and expectancies, in turn, influence the extent to which children try hard in the future.

Many studies show that preschoolers are "learning optimists" who rate their own ability as very high, often underestimate task difficulty, and hold positive expectancies of success. When asked to react to a situation in which one person does worse on a task than another, young children indicate that the lower-scoring person can still succeed if she keeps on trying, and they believe that a smart person is one who expends more effort (Nicholls, 1978). This does not mean that when working on a task, preschoolers never get frustrated or angry. Casual obser-

*M*ost preschoolers have a high sense of self-esteem, a quality that encourages them to persist at new tasks during a period in which many new skills must be mastered.
(MIRO VINTONIV/STOCK BOSTON)

Attributions
Common, everyday explanations for the causes of behavior.

Achievement motivation
The tendency to persist at challenging tasks.

vation reveals that, indeed, they do. But most young children recover easily from these experiences, and their attributions support a continuation of the initiative they displayed during infancy (Dweck & Elliott, 1983).

One reason that young children's attributions are so optimistic is that cognitively, they cannot yet separate effort and ability in explaining their successes and failures. Instead, they view all good things as going together: A person who tries hard is also a smart person who is going to succeed (Kun, 1977; Nicholls, 1978). Belief in their own capacities is also supported by the patience and encouragement of adults, who typically praise much more than they criticize preschoolers in achievement situations. Most parents realize that young children are developing rapidly in a multitude of ways. They know that a child who has trouble riding a tricycle or cutting with scissors at age 3 is likely to be able to do so a short time later. Preschoolers, too, are aware that they are growing bigger and stronger, and most recognize that failure on one occasion often translates into success on another.

Nevertheless, even a little disapproval can undermine a young child's enthusiasm for learning. Although preschoolers do not grasp the difference between ability and effort, they have formed general notions of goodness and badness that they apply to success and failure experiences. In one study, kindergartners were told stories about a child who works hard on a task (such as drawing a picture) but makes a small error and receives criticism from the teacher. To help children relate the stories to themselves, they were asked to act them out with toys and assume the role of the main character. Kindergartners who downgraded their products in response to criticism were more likely to express negative emotion, say they would no longer participate in the activity, and generalize their feelings to new tasks. In addition, they tended to see themselves as bad and deserving of negative feedback. Finally, such children were more likely to report that their parents would berate them for making the mistake that happened in the story (Heyman, Dweck, & Cain, 1992).

Clearly, some 5- and 6-year-olds already take small failures as an indication of their general unworthiness and have difficulty coping with negative outcomes (Dweck, 1991). They show early signs of maladaptive achievement behaviors that, as we will see in the next section, become more common as performance evaluations increase.

MASTERY-ORIENTED VERSUS LEARNED-HELPLESS CHILDREN. During middle childhood, children distinguish ability and effort, and they take more information into account in explaining their performance (Chapman & Skinner, 1989; Dweck & Leggett, 1988). Yet school-age children vary greatly in the extent to which they account for their successes and failures in healthy and adaptive ways. Children who are high in achievement motivation develop **mastery-oriented attributions**. They believe their successes are due to ability—a characteristic they can improve through trying hard and can count on in the future when faced with new challenges. And when failure occurs, mastery-oriented children attribute it to factors about themselves or the environment that can be changed or controlled, such as insufficient effort or a very difficult task. So regardless of whether these children succeed or fail, they take an industrious, persistent, and enthusiastic approach to learning.

Unfortunately, other children, who develop **learned helplessness**, hold far less flattering explanations for their performance. They attribute their failures, not their successes, to ability. And on occasions in which they do succeed, they are likely to conclude that external factors, such as luck, are responsible. Furthermore, unlike their mastery-oriented counterparts, learned-helpless children have come to believe that ability is a fixed characteristic of the self that cannot be changed. They do not think competence can be improved by trying hard. So when a task is difficult, these children experience an anxious loss of control. They quickly give up, saying "I can't do this," before they have really tried (Elliott & Dweck, 1988).

Over time, the ability of learned-helpless children ceases to predict their performance. Indeed, many are very bright pupils who have concluded that they are

*R*epeated negative evaluations about their ability can cause children to develop learned helplessness—low expectancies of success and debilitating anxiety when faced with challenging tasks. This learned-helpless boy is overwhelmed by a poor grade. He seems to have concluded that there is little he can do to improve his performance. (MACDONALD PHOTOGRAPHY/ENVISION)

Mastery-oriented attributions
Attributions that credit success to high ability and failure to insufficient effort. Leads to high expectancies of success and a willingness to approach challenging tasks.

Learned helplessness
Attributions that credit success to luck and failure to low ability. Leads to low expectancies of success and anxious loss of control in the face of challenging tasks.

445

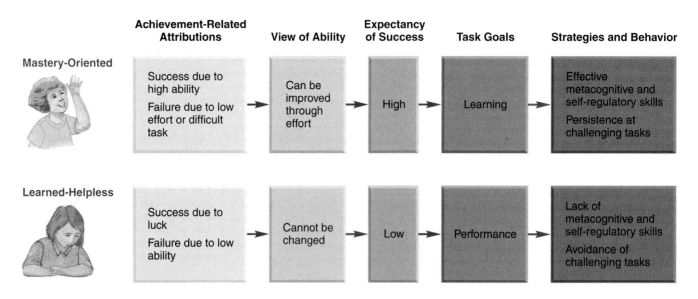

	Achievement-Related Attributions	View of Ability	Expectancy of Success	Task Goals	Strategies and Behavior
Mastery-Oriented	Success due to high ability Failure due to low effort or difficult task	Can be improved through effort	High	Learning	Effective metacognitive and self-regulatory skills Persistence at challenging tasks
Learned-Helpless	Success due to luck Failure due to low ability	Cannot be changed	Low	Performance	Lack of metacognitive and self-regulatory skills Avoidance of challenging tasks

FIGURE 11.2 Consequences of mastery-oriented and learned-helpless attributional styles.

incompetent (Phillips, 1987; Wagner & Phillips, 1992). Because they fail to make the connection between prior knowledge and what they can do, learned-helpless children do not develop the metacognitive and self-regulatory skills that are necessary for high achievement (see Chapter 7). Lack of effective learning strategies, reduced persistence, and a sense of being controlled by external forces sustain one another in a vicious cycle (Carr, Borkowski, & Maxwell, 1991; Heyman & Dweck, 1992).

Attributional styles affect the goals children pursue in learning situations. Mastery-oriented children focus on *learning goals*—increasing ability through effort and seeking information on how to do so. In contrast, the interests of learned-helpless children are much narrower. They focus on *performance goals*—obtaining positive and avoiding negative judgments of their fragile sense of ability. To protect themselves from painful feelings of failure, learned-helpless children soon begin to select less challenging tasks and, eventually, less challenging courses and even less demanding careers. As Figure 11.2 shows, learned helplessness prevents children from pursuing tasks they are capable of mastering and from realizing their potential.

INFLUENCES ON ACHIEVEMENT-RELATED ATTRIBUTIONS. What accounts for the very different attributions of mastery-oriented and learned-helpless children? The messages they receive from parents and teachers play a key role. Children who display a learned-helpless style tend to have parents who set unusually high standards yet believe their child is not very capable and has to work harder to succeed (Parsons, Adler, & Kaczala, 1982; Phillips, 1987).

Experimental research confirms the powerful impact of adult feedback on children's attributional styles. In one study, children were led to believe their ability to do a task was either high or low. Then they were given one of two types of task instructions: a message that emphasized a performance goal ("You'll be graded by experts on this task") or a message that highlighted a learning goal ("This task sharpens the mind and will help you with your studies"). Children who were told they had low ability and for whom a performance goal was emphasized responded to mistakes in a learned-helpless fashion—by giving up, displaying negative affect, and remarking on their lack of talent. In contrast, children encouraged to pursue a learning goal behaved in a mastery-oriented fashion, persisting in attempts to find solutions regardless of their perceived ability (Elliott & Dweck, 1988).

The achievement motivation of certain children is especially likely to be undermined by adult feedback. Girls more often than boys blame their ability for poor performance. Girls also tend to receive messages from teachers and parents that their ability is at fault when they do not do well (Phillips & Zimmerman, 1990). Low-income ethnic minority children are also vulnerable to learned help-lessness. In most studies comparing teacher communication with black and white pupils, black children received less favorable feedback (Aaron & Powell, 1982; Hillman & Davenport, 1978; Irvine, 1986). Also, when ethnic minority children observe that adults in their own family are not rewarded by society for their achievement efforts, they may give up themselves. Many African-American children may come to believe that even if they do try in school, social prejudice will prevent them from succeeding in the end (Ogbu, 1988).

Finally, cultural values for achievement affect the likelihood that children will develop learned helplessness. Compared to Americans, Chinese and Japanese parents and teachers believe that success in school depends much more on effort than innate ability. Even though Asian children's overall self-esteem may be lower than that of American children, the mastery-oriented style fostered in their homes and schools contributes to their high academic achievement (Stevenson & Lee, 1990). We will return to these intriguing cultural differences when we consider the topic of schooling in Chapter 15.

ATTRIBUTION RETRAINING. Attribution research suggests that even adults who are, on the whole, warm and supportive may send subtle messages to children that undermine their competence. **Attribution retraining** is an effective approach to intervention that encourages learned-helpless children to believe that they can overcome failure if only they exert more effort. Most often, children are asked to work on tasks that are hard enough so that some failure experiences are bound to occur. Then they get repeated feedback that helps them revise their attributions, such as, "You can do it if you try harder." Children are also taught to view their successes as due to both ability and effort rather than chance factors by giving them additional feedback after they succeed, such as, "You're really good at this" or "You really tried hard on that one" (Dweck, 1975; Schunk, 1983). Another approach is to encourage these low-effort children to focus less on grades and more on mastering the task for its own sake (Stipek & Kowalski, 1989). Finally, learned-helpless children may need instruction in metacognitive and self-regulatory strategies to make up for learning lost in this area because of their debilitating attributional style (Borkowski et al., 1990).

To work well, attribution retraining is best begun in middle childhood, before children's views of themselves become hard to change. An even better approach is for parents and teachers to prevent learned helplessness before it happens by carefully considering the feedback they give to children. Finally, extra measures need to be taken to support mastery-oriented attributions on the part of girls and ethnic minority children—by providing models of adult success and ensuring equality of opportunity in society at large.

Constructing an Identity

During adolescence, thinking about the self extends further, as the following short essay written by a 17-year-old girl in response to the question "Who Am I?" indicates:

> I am a human being. I am a girl. I am an individual. I don't know who I am. I am a Pisces. I am a moody person. I am an indecisive person. I am a very curious person. I am not an individual. I am a loner. I am an American (God help me). I am a Democrat. I am a liberal person. I am a radical. I am a conservative. I am a pseudoliberal. I am an atheist. I am not a classifiable person (i.e., I don't want to be). (Montemayor & Eisen, 1977, p. 318)

This statement illustrates the quest for **identity,** first recognized by psychoanalyst Erik Erikson (1950, 1968) as the major personality achievement of adolescence and

Attribution retraining
An approach to intervention in which attributions of learned-helpless children are modified through feedback that encourages them to believe in themselves and persist in the face of task difficulty.

Identity
A well-organized conception of the self made up of values, beliefs, and goals to which the individual is solidly committed.

as a critical step toward becoming a productive, happy adult. Constructing an identity involves defining who you are, what you value, and the directions you choose to pursue in life. This search for self is the driving force behind many new commitments—to a sexual orientation (see Chapter 5), to a vocation, and to ethical, political, religious, and cultural ideals.

Erikson regarded successful psychosocial outcomes in infancy and childhood as paving the way toward a positive identity formation. (Return to Chapter 1, page 17, to review Erikson's stages.) Although the seeds of identity are planted early, not until adolescence do young people become absorbed in this task. According to Erikson, in complex societies, teenagers experience an *identity crisis*—a temporary period of confusion and distress as they experiment with alternatives before settling on a set of values and goals. During this period, what adolescents once took for granted they question. Through a process of inner soul-searching, they sift through characteristics that defined the self in childhood and combine them with new commitments. Then they mold these into a solid inner core that provides a sense of sameness as they move through different roles in daily life.

Although current theorists agree with Erikson that questioning of the self's values, plans, and priorities is necessary for a mature identity, they no longer refer to this process as a *crisis* (Baumeister, 1990). The term suggests a sudden, intense upheaval of the self. For some young people, identity development is traumatic and disturbing, but for most it is not. *Exploration* better describes the typical adolescent's experience. Identity formation usually proceeds in a very gradual, uneventful way. The many daily choices teenagers make—"whom to date, whether or not to break up, having intercourse, taking drugs, going to college or working, which college, what major, studying or playing, being politically active"—and the reasons for them are gradually put together into an organized self-structure (Marcia, 1980, p. 161).

Erikson described the negative outcome of the adolescent period as *identity diffusion*. Some young people appear shallow and directionless, either because earlier conflicts have been resolved negatively or society restricts their choices to ones that do not match their abilities and desires. As a result, they are unprepared for the psychological challenges of adulthood. Is there research to support Erikson's ideas about identity development? In the following sections, we will see that adolescents go about the task of defining the self in ways that closely match Erikson's description.

PATHS TO IDENTITY. Using a clinical interviewing procedure, researchers have grouped adolescents into four categories, called identity statuses, which show the progress they have made toward forming a mature identity (Grotevant & Cooper, 1981). Table 11.1 summarizes these identity statuses: **identity achievement, moratorium, identity foreclosure,** and **identity diffusion.**

Adolescents often shift from one status to another until identity is attained. Both cross-sectional and longitudinal research reveals that young adolescents often start out as identity diffused and foreclosed and gradually move toward moratorium and identity achievement (see Figure 11.3) (Archer, 1982; Meilman, 1979). College triggers increased exploration as young people are exposed to new career options and life-styles. Most teenagers who go to work right after high school graduation settle on a self-definition earlier than do college-bound youths (Munro & Adams, 1977). But those who find it difficult to realize their occupational goals because of lack of training or vocational choices are at risk for identity diffusion (Archer, 1989b).

At one time, it was thought that adolescent females postponed the task of establishing an identity until later life and, instead, focused their energies on Erikson's sixth stage, intimacy development. We now know that this is not the case. Girls do show more sophisticated reasoning in identity areas related to intimacy, such as sexuality and family/career priorities. In this respect, they are actually ahead of boys in identity development. Otherwise, the process and timing of identity formation are the same for boys and girls (Archer, 1989a).

Identity achievement

The identity status of individuals who have explored and committed themselves to self-chosen values and goals.

Moratorium

The identity status of individuals who are exploring alternatives in an effort to find values and goals to guide their life.

Identity foreclosure

The identity status of individuals who have accepted ready-made values and goals that authority figures have chosen for them.

Identity diffusion

The identity status of individuals who do not have firm commitments to values and goals and are not actively trying to reach them.

TABLE 11.1 *The Four Identity Statuses*

IDENTITY STATUS	DESCRIPTION	SAMPLE RESPONSE TO IDENTITY INTERVIEW
Identity achievement	Having already explored alternatives, identity achieved individuals are committed to a clearly formulated set of self-chosen values and goals. They feel a sense of psychological well-being, of sameness through time, and of knowing where they are going.	When asked how willing she would be to give up going into her chosen occupation if something better came along, the adolescent responds, "I might, but I doubt it. I've thought long and hard about law as a career. I'm pretty certain it's for me."
Moratorium	Moratorium means delay or holding pattern. These individuals have not yet made definite commitments. They are in the process of exploration—gathering information and trying out activities, with the desire to find values and goals to guide their life.	When asked if he had ever had doubts about his religious beliefs, the adolescent answers, "Yes, I guess I'm going through that right now. I just don't see how there can be a god and yet so much evil in the world."
Identity foreclosure	Identity foreclosed individuals have committed themselves to values and goals without taking time to explore alternatives. Instead, they accept a ready-made identity that authority figures (usually parents but sometimes teachers, religious leaders, or romantic partners) have chosen for them.	When asked if she had ever reconsidered her religious beliefs, the adolescent states, "No, not really, our family is pretty much in agreement on these things."
Identity diffusion	Identity diffused individuals lack clear direction. They are not committed to values and goals, nor are they actively trying to reach them. They may have never explored alternatives, or they may have tried to do so but found the task too threatening and overwhelming.	When asked about his attitude toward nontraditional gender roles, the adolescent responds, "Oh, I don't know. It doesn't make much difference to me. I can take it or leave it."

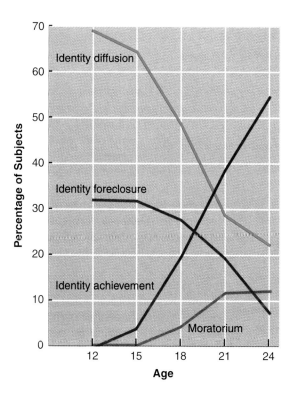

FIGURE 11.3 Percentages of young people between ages 12 and 24 in each of the four identity statuses, based on cross-sectional data. At first, most adolescents are identity foreclosed or diffused. With age, a shift toward moratorium and identity achievement takes place. (Adapted from Meilman, 1979.)

anything with certainty are more often identity diffused or in a state of moratorium. Adolescents who have come to appreciate that rational criteria can be used to choose among alternative visions are likely to have joined the ranks of the identity achieved (Boyes & Chandler, 1992).

Recall that infants who develop a healthy sense of agency have parents who provide both emotional support and freedom to explore. A similar link between parenting and identity exists at adolescence. When the family serves as a "secure base" from which teenagers can confidently move out into the wider world, identity development is enhanced. Adolescents who feel attached to their parents but who are also free to voice their own opinions tend to be identity achieved or in a state of moratorium (Grotevant & Cooper, 1985; Lapsley, Rice, & FitzGerald, 1990). Foreclosed teenagers usually have close bonds with parents, but they lack opportunities for healthy separation. And diffused young people report the lowest levels of warm, open communication at home (Papini, Micka, & Barnett, 1989).

Identity development also depends on schools and communities that provide young people with rich and varied opportunities for exploration. Erikson (1968) noted that it is "the inability to settle on an occupational identity which most disturbs young people" (p. 132). Classrooms that promote high-level thinking, extracurricular and community activities that enable teenagers to take on responsible roles, and vocational training programs that immerse young people in the real world of adult work foster identity achievement. A chance to talk with adults and older peers who have worked through identity questions can also help young people resolve doubts about identity-related matters (Waterman, 1989).

Finally, the larger cultural context and historical time period affect identity development. Among modern adolescents, exploration and commitment take place earlier in the identity domains of vocational choice and gender-role preference than in religious and political values. Yet a generation ago, when the Vietnam War divided Americans and disrupted the lives of thousands of young people, the political beliefs of American youths took shape sooner (Archer, 1989b; Waterman, 1985). Societal forces are also responsible for the special problems ethnic minority adolescents face in forming a secure personal identity, as the Cultural Influences box on the following page describes.

Brief Review

By the end of the second year, self-recognition is well established and underlies children's first struggles with peers over objects, prosocial acts, and formation of a categorical self. Early in the preschool years, children become aware of an inner self of private thoughts and imaginings. By age 4, they have formed a sophisticated theory of mind in which they understand the relationship of belief and desire to behavior. Self-concept evolves from an appreciation of typical emotions, attitudes, and observable characteristics to an emphasis on stable personality traits in middle childhood. At the same time, self-esteem differentiates, becomes hierarchically organized, and declines as school-age children begin to make social comparisons and evaluate their performance at different activities. From fourth grade on, self-esteem rises for the majority of young people. Adult communication patterns affect children's attributions for success and failure in achievement contexts and their willingness to persist at challenging tasks.

Erikson first recognized identity—the formation of a coherent set of values and life plans—as the major personality achievement of adolescence. Four identity statuses describe the degree of progress adolescents have made toward forming a mature identity. Identity achievement and moratorium are adaptive statuses associated with positive personality characteristics. Teenagers in a long-term state of identity foreclosure or diffusion tend to have adjustment difficulties. Realization that rational procedures can be used to choose among competing beliefs and values, parents who provide emotional support and freedom to explore, schools and communities that are rich in opportunities, and societies that permit young people from all backgrounds to realize their personal goals foster identity development.

Most American white adolescents are aware of their cultural ancestry, but it is usually not a matter of intense concern for them. Since the values of their home lives are consistent with mainstream American culture, ethnicity does not prompt intense identity exploration (Rotheram-Borus, 1989).

But for teenagers who are members of minority groups, ethnicity is a central part of the quest for identity, and it presents difficult, sometimes overwhelming challenges. Different skin colors, native languages, and neighborhoods set minority youths apart and increase the prejudices to which they are exposed. As they develop cognitively and become more sensitive to feedback from the social environment, they become painfully aware that they are targets of discrimination and inequality. This discovery complicates their efforts to develop a sense of cultural belonging and a set of personally meaningful life goals. One African-American journalist, looking back on his adolescence, remarked, "If you were black, you didn't quite measure up. . . . you didn't see any black people doing certain things, and you couldn't rationalize it. I mean, you don't think it out but you say, 'Well, it must mean that white people are better than we are. Smarter, brighter—whatever' " (Monroe, Goldman, & Smith, 1988, pp. 98–99).

Minority youths often feel caught between the standards of the larger society and the traditions of their culture of origin. Some respond by rejecting aspects of their ethnic background. In one study, Asian-American 15- to 17-year-olds were more likely than African-Americans and Hispanics to hold negative attitudes toward their subcultural group. Perhaps the absence of a social movement stressing ethnic pride of the kind available to African-American and Hispanic teenagers underlies this finding. Asian-American young people in this study had trouble naming well-known personalities who might serve as ethnic role models (Phinney, 1989). Some Asian parents are overly restrictive of their children out of fear that assimilation into the larger society will undermine cultural traditions, and their teenagers rebel. One Southeast Asian refugee described his daughter's behavior: "She complains about going to the Lao temple on the weekend and instead joined a youth group in a neighborhood Christian Church. She refused to wear traditional dress on the Lao New Year. The girl is setting a very bad example for her younger sisters and brothers" (Nidorf, 1985, pp. 422–423).

Other minority teenagers react to years of shattered self-esteem, school failure, and barriers to success in the American mainstream by defining themselves in contrast to majority values. A Mexican-American teenager who had given up on school commented, "Mexicans don't have a chance to go on to college and make something of themselves." Another, responding to the question of what it takes to be a successful adult, mentioned "being on the streets" and "knowing what's happening." He pointed to his uncle, leader of a local gang, as an example (Matute-Bianchi, 1986, pp. 250–251).

The challenges minority youths face in blending mainstream with ethnic-group values are also apparent in the experiences of academically successful African-American

These Mexican-American girls dress in traditional costume and perform traditional Mexican dances at a fiesta in a large Texas city. When minority youths encounter respect for their cultural heritage in schools and communities, they are more likely to retain ethnic values and customs as an important part of their identities. (BOB DAEMMRICH/THE IMAGE WORKS)

adolescents. To avoid being labeled white by their peers, they frequently try to conceal their abilities and accomplishments (Clark, 1991). Because it is painful and confusing, many minority high school students dodge the task of forming an ethnic identity. As many as 50 percent are diffused or foreclosed on ethnic-identity issues (Phinney, 1989).

How can society help minority adolescents resolve identity conflicts constructively? A variety of efforts are relevant, including reducing poverty, promoting effective parenting, and ensuring that schools respect minority youths' ethnic heritage and unique learning styles. Minority adolescents who are ethnic-identity achieved—who have explored and adopted values from both their primary culture and the dominant culture—tend to be achieved in other areas of identity as well. They also have a higher sense of self-esteem, feel a greater sense of mastery over the environment, and show more positive family and peer relations (Phinney, 1989; Phinney & Alipuria, 1990). These findings support the notion that promoting the ethnic identity of minority youths enhances many aspects of emotional and social adjustment.

Finally, lack of concern by many white adolescents with their own ethnic origins (other than American) implies a view of the social world that is out of touch with the pluralistic nature of American society. The racial and ethnic distinctions with which most of us are familiar (African-American, Asian-American, Caucasian, Hispanic, Native American) oversimplify the rich cultural diversity of the American populace (Spencer & Dornbusch, 1990). Interventions that increase the multicultural sensitivity of white teenagers lead to greater awareness of their own ethnic heritage. And majority adolescents who are secure in their own ethnic identity are less likely to hold negative stereotypes of their minority peers (Rosenthal, 1987; Rotheram-Borus, in press).

453

Children's understanding of other people—their descriptions of others' personalities and inferences about their behavior and mental states—has much in common with their developing understanding of themselves. In the following sections, we will see that this facet of social cognition also becomes increasingly differentiated and well organized with age.

Person Perception

Person perception concerns how we size up people with whom we are familiar in everyday life. To study it, researchers use methods similar to those that focus on children's self-concepts: asking them to describe people they know, such as "Can you tell me what kind of person _____ is?"

Like their self-descriptions, below age 8, children's descriptions of others focus on commonly experienced emotions and attitudes, concrete activities, and behaviors. Over time, children discover consistencies in the actions of people they know and begin to mention personality traits (Barenboim, 1977; Eder, 1989). At first, these references are closely tied to behavior and consist of implied dispositions, such as "He is always fighting with people" or "She steals and lies" (Peevers & Secord, 1973). Later, children mention traits directly, but they are vague and stereotyped—for example, "good," "nice," or "acts smart." Gradually, sharper descriptions appear, such as "honest," "trustworthy," "generous," "polite," and "selfish" (Livesley & Bromley, 1973).

About the time they begin comparing themselves to others, children start to make comparisons between people. These also change from concrete to abstract. At first, children cast comparisons in behavioral terms: "Billy runs a lot faster than Jason." Around age 10 to 12, after children have had sufficient experience inferring personality traits, they integrate these into social comparisons: "Paul's a lot more considerate than thick-headed Del" (Barenboim, 1981, p. 133).

During adolescence, as abstract thinking becomes better established, inferences about others' personalities are drawn together into organized character sketches (Livesley & Bromley, 1973; O'Mahoney, 1989). As a result, between ages 14 and 16, teenagers present much richer accounts of people they know that combine physical traits, typical behaviors, and inner dispositions. Adolescents also recognize that their own experiences with a person, and therefore their impressions, may differ from the opinions of other people (Barenboim, 1977).

Understanding Intentions

Besides getting to know others as personalities, children must learn how to interpret their behavior. Making behavior meaningful and deciding how to react to it often depend on distinguishing actions that are deliberate and intentional from those that are accidental. By age 2, preschoolers already have intentions on their minds. In everyday conversations, they say "gonna," "hafta," and "wanna" to announce actions they are about to perform (Brown, 1973). Think back to our discussion of children's theory of mind, and you will find further evidence for an early appreciation that intention, or desire, underlies action. Preschoolers often rely on this grasp of purposefulness to defend themselves. After being scolded for bumping into a playmate or spilling a glass of milk, they exclaim, "It was an accident!" or "I didn't do it on purpose!" (Shultz, 1980).

By 2½ to 3 years, this understanding extends to others. Preschoolers become sensitive to behavioral cues that help them tell if another person is acting intentionally. At first, they focus on the person's statements. If a person says he is going

Person perception
The way individuals size up people with whom they are familiar in everyday life.

to do something and then does it, 3-year-olds judge the behavior as deliberate. If statements and actions do not match, then the behavior was not intended (Astington, 1991). By the end of the preschool years, children focus on a much wider range of information to judge intentionality. For example, 5-year-olds note whether a person is concentrating on what she is doing, whether her action leads to positive or negative outcomes (negative ones are usually not intended), and whether some external cause can account for the person's behavior (Smith, 1978).

The intentional acts humans are capable of extend beyond the ones we have considered so far. We can intentionally pretend to engage in unintentional behavior, like falling over an object or bumping into someone. We can also deliberately refrain from acting but pretend that our lack of response was unintentional, by saying something like "I forgot all about it!" Researchers are just beginning to find out how children come to understand these deceptive forms of intentional behavior. Between 5 and 9 years of age, children rely increasingly on a *verbal–nonverbal consistency rule* to evaluate the sincerity of others' stated intentions. For example, older children understand quite well that telling another person you like something when you look neutral or unhappy probably means you are not telling the truth (Rotenberg, Simourd, & Moore, 1989). The ability to detect more subtle efforts to conceal intentions depends on awareness of fine-grained features of a situation as well as sophisticated perspective-taking skills, a topic we examine in the next section.

Finally, children differ in how accurately they interpret others' intentions. Those who get along well with adults and peers make these judgments easily. In contrast, highly aggressive children show striking biases in inferring intentions; they often see hostility where it does not exist. As the From Research to Practice box on page 456 reveals, such children require special help in learning how to evaluate and respond appropriately to others' behavior.

Development of Perspective Taking

In this and previous chapters we have emphasized that **perspective taking**—the capacity to imagine what other people may be thinking and feeling—is important for a wide variety of social-cognitive achievements, including referential communication skills (Chapter 9), understanding others' emotions (Chapter 10), self-concept and self-esteem, person perception, and inferring intentions. Recall that Piaget regarded egocentrism—preschoolers' inability to take the viewpoint of another—as the major feature responsible for the immaturity of their thought, in both the physical and social domains. But we have also seen much evidence that young children are not as egocentric as Piaget believed. Indeed, they show some capacity for perspective taking as soon as they separate self from others in the second year of life. Nevertheless, Piaget's ideas inspired a wealth of research on children's capacity to take the perspective of others, which improves steadily over childhood and adolescence.

SELMAN'S STAGES OF PERSPECTIVE TAKING. Robert Selman developed a five-stage model of major changes in perspective-taking skill. He asked preschool through adolescent-age youngsters to respond to social dilemmas in which the characters have differing information and opinions about an event. Here is one example:

> Holly is an 8-year-old girl who likes to climb trees. She is the best tree climber in the neighborhood. One day while climbing down from a tall tree she falls off the bottom branch but does not hurt herself. Her father sees her fall. He is upset and asks her to promise not to climb trees anymore. Holly promises.
>
> Later that day, Holly and her friends meet Sean. Sean's kitten is caught up in a tree and cannot get down. Something has to be done right away or the kitten may fall. Holly is the only one who climbs trees well enough to reach the kitten and get it down, but she remembers her promise to her father. (Selman & Byrne, 1974, p. 805)

Perspective taking
The capacity to imagine what other people may be thinking and feeling.

The inferences children make about others' intentions powerfully affect their responses in social situations. For example, if Bobby's knocking down the block tower is viewed as a deliberately hostile action, his peers are likely to be angry and retaliate with aggression. If his destroying the block tower is seen as accidental or prosocial (an effort to help clean up the room), other children are unlikely to seek revenge.

Since children often respond with hostility when they regard others' behavior as threatening, Kenneth Dodge hypothesized that highly aggressive children may behave as they do because of biased social cognition—perceiving hostile intentions in situations where they do not exist. The findings of much research are consistent with this idea (Dodge, 1985; Dodge & Tomlin, 1987; Quiggle et al., 1992).

In one study, Dodge (1980) told aggressive and nonaggressive boys of elementary school age that they could win a prize for putting together a puzzle and that another (fictitious) boy was working on a similar puzzle in an adjoining room. When each subject was partly finished, the experimenter borrowed his puzzle to show it to the other boy. Moments later, the subject heard his puzzle crashing apart, along with one of three taped messages: a *hostile condition*, in which the other boy said he did not want the subject to win a prize; a *prosocial condition*, in which the boy said he would help the subject get more done, but as he put another piece in, he accidentally knocked the puzzle over; and an *ambiguous condition*, in which the puzzle could be heard breaking apart, but the intentions of the boy were not clear. Then the experimenter returned with the subject's destroyed puzzle as well as the other child's partly finished one.

Both groups responded to the hostile condition with retaliatory aggression—by messing up the other boy's puzzle. However, in the ambiguous condition, aggressive boys were far more likely to display hostility than their nonaggressive counterparts. And other research shows that aggressive children sometimes lash out in the face of prosocial and accidental cues as well—conditions in which nonaggressive children seldom do (Dodge, 1985; Dodge & Somberg, 1987).

What factors in the backgrounds of highly aggressive children lead them to interpret others' intentions inaccurately? Harsh discipline appears to be important. Dodge and his colleagues showed that preschoolers whose parents punish with slaps, spankings, and other harmful acts were more likely to give aggressive solutions to social problems in which an actor's intention is benign or unclear. Furthermore, children with this biased style of processing intentions engaged in more aggressive acts when observed in kindergarten the following year (Dodge, Bates, & Pettit, 1990; Weiss et al., 1992).

Primed to interpret others' actions in a hostile fashion, aggressive children behave in combative ways that lead their peers to respond in kind. By the end of middle childhood, normal peers hold biased views of the intentions of highly aggressive children, perceiving malice even when their intent is benign because of the aggressive child's long history of belligerent behavior (Dodge & Frame, 1983).

Dodge's work suggests that interventions aimed at teaching aggressive children to interpret the behaviors of others accurately may help reduce their hostility. Once aggressive children begin to change, peers need to be taught to view them differently so that their past reputations no longer provoke reactions that sustain their overly hostile view of the world. Finally, noncoercive child rearing fosters accurate appraisals of others' intentions and nonaggressive approaches to solving social problems—a point we will return to in later chapters.

After the dilemma is presented, children answer questions that highlight their ability to interpret the story from varying points of view, such as:

Does Sean know why Holly cannot decide whether or not to climb the tree?

What will Holly's father think? Will he understand if she climbs the tree?

Does Holly think she will be punished for climbing the tree? Should she be punished for doing so?

Table 11.2 summarizes Selman's five stages of perspective taking. As you can see, children gradually include a wider range of information in their understanding of others' viewpoints. At first, they have only a limited idea of what other people might be thinking and feeling. Over time, they become more conscious of the fact that people can interpret the same event in different ways. Soon, children can "step in another person's shoes" and reflect on how that person might regard their own thoughts, feelings, and behavior. Finally, they can examine the relationship between two people's perspectives simultaneously, at first from the vantage point of a disinterested spectator and later by making reference to societal values.

RESEARCH CONFIRMING SELMAN'S DEVELOPMENTAL SEQUENCE. As Table 11.3 indicates, cross-sectional findings on Selman's dilemmas show that maturity of perspective

TABLE 11.2 Selman's Stages of Perspective Taking

STAGE OF PERSPECTIVE TAKING	APPROXIMATE AGE RANGE	DESCRIPTION	TYPICAL RESPONSE TO "HOLLY" DILEMMA
Level 0: *Undifferentiated*	3–6 years	Children recognize that self and other can have different thoughts and feelings, but they frequently confuse the two.	The child predicts Holly will save the kitten because she does not want it to get hurt and believes Holly's father will feel just as she does about her climbing the tree: "Happy, he likes kittens."
Level 1: *Social-Informational*	4–9 years	Children understand that different perspectives may result because people have access to different information.	When asked how Holly's father will react when he finds out she climbed the tree, the child responds, "If he didn't know anything about the kitten, he would be angry. But if Holly shows him the kitten, he might change his mind."
Level 2: *Self-Reflective*	7–12 years	Children can "step in another person's shoes" and view their own thoughts, feelings, and behavior from the other person's perspective. They also recognize that others can do the same.	When asked whether Holly thinks she will be punished, the child says, "No. Holly knows that her father will understand why she climbed the tree." This response assumes that Holly's point of view is influenced by her father being able to "step in her shoes" and understand why she saved the kitten.
Level 3: *Third-Party*	10–15 years	Children can step outside a two-person situation and imagine how the self and other are viewed from the point of view of a third, impartial party.	When asked whether Holly should be punished, the child says, "No, because Holly thought it was important to save the kitten. But she also knows that her father told her not to climb the tree. So she'd only think she shouldn't be punished if she could get her father to understand why she had to climb the tree." This response steps outside the immediate situation to view both Holly's and her father's perspective simultaneously.
Level 4: *Societal*	14 years–adult	Individuals understand that third-party perspective taking can be influenced by one or more systems of larger societal values.	When asked if Holly should be punished, the individual responds, "No. The value of humane treatment of animals justifies Holly's action. Her father's appreciation of this value will lead him not to punish her."

SOURCES: Selman, 1976; Selman & Byrne, 1974.

taking rises steadily with age. Also, longitudinal research reveals gradual movement to the next higher stage over 2 to 5 years, with no individuals skipping stages and practically none moving back to a previous stage (Gurucharri & Selman, 1982; Selman, 1980). These findings provide strong support for Selman's assumption that his stages form an age-related, invariant sequence.

LEVEL	AGE 4	AGE 6	AGE 8	AGE 10	AGE 13	AGE 16	ADULT
0	80	10	0	0	0	0	0
1	20	90	40	20	7	0	0
2	0	0	50	60	50	21	0
3	0	0	10	20	36	58	0
4	—	—	—	—	7	21	100

SOURCE: From "A Structural-Developmental Analysis of Levels of Role Taking in Middle Childhood" by R. L. Selman & D. F. Byrne, 1974, *Child Development, 45,* 803–806. © The Society for Research in Child Development, Inc. Reprinted by permission. Additional data from "The Development of Role Taking in Adolescence" by D. F. Byrne, 1973, unpublished doctoral dissertation, Harvard University.

Cognitive Development and Perspective Taking. Selman's stages are also related to nonsocial-cognitive milestones—findings that offer additional support for his developmental progression. Individuals who fail Piaget's concrete operational tasks tend to be at Selman's Level 0; those who pass concrete but not formal operational tasks tend to be at Levels 1 and 2; and those who are increasingly formal operational tend to be at Levels 3 and 4 (Keating & Clark, 1980; Krebs & Gillmore, 1982). Furthermore, each set of Piagetian tasks tends to be mastered somewhat earlier than its related perspective-taking level (Walker, 1980). This suggests that Piagetian milestones are a *necessary but not sufficient condition* for the attainment of Selman's perspective-taking stages. Additional social-cognitive capacities are required, and researchers are just beginning to discover which ones are involved, as we will see in the following section.

Perspective-Taking Games. Besides responses to social dilemmas, "games and the delights of deception" offer ideal opportunities to study perspective taking (Selman, 1980, p. 49). According to several researchers, preschoolers' limited perspective-taking skills are largely due to their passive view of the mind—their assumption that what a person knows is the result of simply observing rather than actively interpreting experience (Chandler, 1988; Pillow, 1988a). In agreement with this idea, 4-year-olds understand quite clearly that because of greater experience, children and adults know more than babies do. Nevertheless, when asked to play a special "privileged information game" that challenges their perspective-taking capacities, these same preschoolers run into difficulty.

In one study, an experimenter showed 4- to 6-year-olds pictures of objects and then covered them in such a way that either a nondescript part or an identifiable part of the object was left showing (see Figure 11.5). Next, children were asked whether two observers—a baby and a child—who had never seen the full pictures could recognize the objects from the incomplete versions. Four-year-olds often said that an observer could tell what the object was from a nondescript part. They made little allowance for another's difficulty in inferring the meaning of a tiny part without having seen the full picture. And although 4-year-olds were well aware that children are more knowledgeable than babies, they did not apply this understanding to the perspective-taking game. They thought a baby would be able to recognize pictures of nondescript and identifiable object parts just as easily as an older child, even when the objects (a horse or teeter-totter) were unfamiliar to infants. Not until age 6 did children realize that simply seeing a picture does not determine a person's view of it. Instead, what the observer brings to the situation in terms of prior experience and knowledge affects their ability to interpret it (Taylor, Cartwright, & Bowden, 1991). Around 6 to 8 years, children understand

Identifiable horse   Nondescript horse

FIGURE 11.5 In viewing each of these pictures for the first time, can a baby or a child tell that the object depicted is a horse? In a recent study, 4-year-olds thought that both observers could recognize the horse, even from a nondescript part. Not until age 6 did they realize that prior experience (having seen the full picture) as well as greater knowledge (being older and familiar with horses) affects an individual's ability to interpret the pictures. (Adapted from Taylor, Cartwright, & Bowden, 1991.)

that besides knowledge, people's beliefs and expectations can also lead to quite different views of new information (Pillow, 1991).

Other gamelike tasks have focused on **recursive thought,** the self-embedded form of perspective taking that involves thinking about what another person is thinking. Selman's stages suggest that the capacity to think recursively (Levels 3 and 4) improves over the adolescent years, a trend that is supported by research. Patricia Miller, Frank Kessel, and John Flavell (1970) asked first- through sixth-graders to describe cartoon drawings showing one- and two-loop recursive thought (see Figure 11.6). By sixth grade, only 50 percent of children had mastered one-loop

One-loop recursion
"The boy is thinking that he is thinking about himself."

Two-loop recursion
"The boy is thinking that the girl is thinking of the father thinking of the mother."

FIGURE 11.6 Cartoon drawings depicting recursive thought. Not until midadolescence do young people master the complexities of this self-embedded form of perspective taking. (From "Thinking About People Thinking About People Thinking About . . . : A Study of Social Cognitive Development" by P. H. Miller, F. S. Kessel, & J. H. Flavell, 1970, *Child Development, 41,* p. 616. © The Society for Research in Child Development, Inc. Reprinted by permission.)

Recursive thought
The self-embedded form of perspective taking that involves thinking about what another person is thinking.

recursions, and two-loop recursions were rare. Not until midadolescence do young people master the complexities of recursive understanding (Flavell et al., 1968).

Recursive thought is a feature of perspective taking that makes human interaction truly reciprocal. People often call on it to clear up misunderstandings, as when they say, "I thought you would think I was just kidding when I said that." Recursive thinking is also involved in our attempts to disguise our real thoughts and feelings, when we reason in ways like this: "He'll think I'm jealous if I tell him I don't like his new car, so I'll pretend I do" (Perner, 1988). Finally, the capacity to think recursively contributes to the intense self-focusing and concern with the imaginary audience typical of early adolescence (see Chapter 6). As Miller, Kessel, and Flavell (1970) point out, "Often to their pain, adolescents are much more gifted at this sort of wondering than first graders are" (p. 623).

PERSPECTIVE TAKING AND SOCIAL BEHAVIOR. Children's developing perspective-taking skills help them get along with other people. When we anticipate another person's point of view, social relationships become more predictable. Each individual can plan actions with some knowledge of what the other person is likely to do in return. In addition, when children recognize that other people may have thoughts and feelings different from their own, they can respond to the momentary needs of others more effectively. It is not surprising that perspective taking is related to a wide variety of social skills. Good perspective takers are more likely to display empathy and compassion, and they are better at thinking of effective ways to handle difficult social situations (Eisenberg et al., 1987; Marsh, Serafica, & Barenboim, 1981). For these reasons, they tend to be especially well liked by peers (LeMare & Rubin, 1987; Rubin & Maioni, 1975).

Nevertheless, some contradictory relationships between perspective taking and social behavior exist, which suggest that the association is complex and influenced by other factors. Perspective-taking tasks that are good predictors of prosocial behavior typically require children to understand another person's feeling state (Iannotti, 1985). Taking the emotional perspective of another person encourages children to empathize—a response that increases the chances that children will act on their awareness. In contrast, perspective-taking tasks that require children to imagine what an opponent is thinking in a competitive game or that describe the experiences of different characters in a story often do not predict prosocial acts and sometimes are linked to disruptive behavior (Kurdek, 1978). This suggests that depending on the context in which perspective taking is assessed, children who are skilled at it may be as adept at guarding their own interests as they are at cooperating with and helping others. In fact, a few mildly antisocial acts, such as knowing how to needle your sister to "get her goat," sometimes make use of masterful perspective-taking skills.

Young people who display extremes of antisocial behavior are often delayed in the development of perspective taking. Chronic delinquents have great difficulty imagining the thoughts and feelings of others (Chandler, 1973; Lee & Prentice, 1988). As a result, they often mistreat adults and peers without experiencing the guilt and remorse that is engendered by awareness of another's point of view (MacQuiddy, Maise, & Hamilton, 1987). Because deficits in perspective taking may sustain hostile behavior, researchers have experimented with ways of inducing sensitivity to others' viewpoints to lessen antisocial acts and encourage prosocial responding.

TRAINING PERSPECTIVE-TAKING SKILLS. Interventions that encourage troubled adolescents to act out real-world roles can promote perspective taking. In one study, girls assigned to a residential treatment center because of repeated antisocial acts role-played situations in which they encountered difficulties in everyday life over a 15-session period. Compared to a control-group experiencing a fitness program, girls who participated in role-playing improved in awareness of others' viewpoints, ability to analyze interpersonal problems, empathy, and acceptance of individual differences. These gains translated into greater prosocial behavior during classroom observations (Chalmers & Townsend, 1990). A similar intervention for antisocial boys also led to more effective perspective taking and a reduction in antisocial acts (Chandler, 1973). That social behavior is enhanced after a relatively brief perspective-taking training program provides further support for the central role of this social-cognitive skill in effective human interaction.

Brief Review

L ike self-concept, person perception shifts from a focus on concrete activities and behaviors to an emphasis on personality traits in middle childhood. During adolescence, inferences about others' psychological characteristics are drawn together into organized character sketches. The ability to infer intentions from others' behavior emerges during the preschool years and becomes refined in middle childhood. Perspective taking undergoes vast changes from early childhood into adolescence. It begins with limited awareness of others' thoughts and feelings and evolves into advanced recursive and societal perspective-taking capacities. The development of perspective taking builds on Piagetian nonsocial cognitive milestones and children's awareness that the mind actively interprets experience. Perspective taking is related to a wide variety of social skills.

THINKING ABOUT RELATIONS BETWEEN PEOPLE

As children develop, they apply their insights into the inner psychological worlds of themselves and others to an understanding of relations between people. A relatively recent emphasis in social-cognitive research has to do with how children reason about friendship and interpersonal conflict.

Understanding Friendship

To an adult, friendship is not a one-sided relationship. You can like someone without being a friend to that person, since your liking may not be returned. Instead, friendship is a mutual relationship involving companionship, sharing, understanding of thoughts and feelings, and caring for and comforting one another in times of need. In addition, mature friendships endure over time and survive occasional conflicts.

Children's ideas about friendship do not start out this way. Researchers have interviewed children of different ages, asking them to name a best friend, explain why that person is a friend, and indicate what they expect of a close friend. In addition, children sometimes respond to dilemmas about friendship that tap motives for friendship formation, characteristics of friendship, ways in which good friends solve conflicts, and how and why friendships break up. From children's answers, several theories of the development of friendship understanding have emerged. All emphasize that friendship begins as a concrete relationship based on pleasurable activity and evolves into a more abstract relationship based on mutual consideration and psychological satisfaction (Damon, 1977; Selman, 1980; Youniss, 1980). William Damon has combined the work of other investigators into a three-stage sequence.

LEVEL 1: FRIENDSHIP AS A HANDY PLAYMATE* (ABOUT 4 TO 7 YEARS). Interviews with preschoolers show that they already understand something about the uniqueness of friendship. They know that a friend is someone "who likes you," with whom you spend a lot of time playing, and with whom you share toys. As yet, there is little sense of appreciating another person's personality traits, since (as we saw earlier) young children are only beginning to size up themselves and others in terms of unique psychological characteristics.

*I have provided titles for each of the stages to help you remember them.

Because friendship is viewed concretely, in terms of play and exchange of material goods, young children regard it as easily begun—for example, by meeting in the neighborhood and saying "Hi." However, friendship does not yet have a long-term, enduring quality. Level 1 children say that a friendship can dissolve when one partner refuses to share, hits, or is not available to play. The following answer of a 5-year-old boy to the question "What makes a good friend?" sums up the young child's view of friendship: "Boys play with boys, trucks play with trucks, dogs play with dogs." When the interviewer probed, "Why does that make them good friends?" the child answered, "Because they do the same things" (Selman, 1980, p. 136).

LEVEL 2: FRIENDSHIP AS MUTUAL TRUST AND ASSISTANCE (ABOUT 8 TO 10 YEARS). During middle childhood, children's concepts of friendship become more complex and psychologically based. Look closely at the responses of this 8-year-old to questions about what makes a best friend:

> Who's your best friend? *Shelly.* Why is Shelly your best friend? *Because she helps me when I'm sad, and she shares....* What makes Shelly so special? *I've known her longer, I sit next to her and got to know her better....* How come you like Shelly better than anyone else? *She's done the most for me. She never disagrees, she never eats in front of me, she never walks away when I'm crying, and she helps me on my homework....* How do you get someone to like you? ... *If you're nice to [your friends], they'll be nice to you.* (Damon, 1988, pp. 80–81)

As these statements show, friendship is no longer just a matter of engaging in the same activities. Instead, it is a mutually agreed on relationship in which children like each other's personal qualities and respond to one another's needs and desires. Since friendship is a matter of both children wanting to be together, getting it started takes more time and effort than it did at earlier ages. And once a friendship is formed, trust becomes its defining feature. School-age children state that a good friendship is based on acts of kindness that signify each person can be counted on to support the other. Consequently, events that break up a friendship are quite different than they were during the preschool years. Older children regard violations of trust, such as not helping when others need help, breaking promises, and gossiping behind the other's back, as serious breaches of friendship. And once a rift occurs, it cannot be patched up as easily as it could at younger ages—by playing nicely after a conflict. Instead, apologies and explanations for violating friendship expectations are necessary (Damon, 1977; Selman, 1980).

During middle childhood, children's concepts of friendship become more psychologically based. These girls enjoy being together because they like each other's personal qualities. Mutual trust is a defining feature of their friendship. Each child counts on the other to provide support and assistance. (JERRY HOWARD/STOCK BOSTON)

LEVEL 3: FRIENDSHIP AS INTIMACY AND LOYALTY (11 TO 15 YEARS AND OLDER). By early adolescence, friendship takes on greater depth. When asked to comment on the meaning of friendship, teenagers stress two characteristics. The first, and most important, is *intimacy*. Adolescents seek psychological closeness and mutual understanding from their friends. Second, more than younger children, teenagers want their friends to be *loyal*—to stick up for them and not to leave them for somebody else (Berndt & Perry, 1990).

Because friendship has this depth dimension to it, adolescents regard it as a relationship formed over a long period of time by "getting to know someone." In addition, friends are viewed as important in relieving psychological distress, such as loneliness, sadness, and fear. And because true mutual understanding implies forgiveness, only an extreme falling out can lead Level 3 relationships to dissolve. Here is how one teenager described his best friendship:

> *Well, you need someone you can tell anything to, all kinds of things that you don't want to spread around. That's why you're someone's friend.* Is that why Jimmy is your friend? Because he can keep a secret? *Yes, and we like the same kinds of things. We speak the same language. My mother says we're two peas in a pod. . . .* Do you ever get mad at Jimmy? *Not really.* What if he did something that got you really mad? *He'd still be my best friend. I'd tell him what he did wrong and maybe he'd understand. I could be wrong too, it depends.* (Damon, 1977, p. 163)

RESEARCH ON CHILDREN'S DEVELOPING UNDERSTANDING OF FRIENDSHIP. Both cross-sectional and longitudinal research confirm the sequence of friendship understanding just described (Bigelow, 1977; Bigelow & LaGaipa, 1975; Keller & Wood, 1989). Also, virtually every study shows that even after a psychological appreciation of friendship emerges, early concepts, such as sharing common activities, are not abandoned. Instead, they are integrated into more mature concepts. Furthermore, friendship reasoning is related to advances in perspective taking (Selman, 1981). We would certainly expect this to be the case, since a more advanced appreciation of friendship implies greater awareness of others' thoughts and feelings.

ARE CHILDREN'S CONCEPTS OF FRIENDSHIP RELATED TO FEATURES OF THEIR REAL FRIENDSHIPS? If social cognition plays a vital role in everyday behavior, then children's developing ideas about friendship should predict changes in the qualities of their real friendships. There is good evidence that this is the case.

Stability of Friendships. First, we would expect greater friendship stability as mutual trust and loyalty become more important in children's expectations of their friends. In one study, friendship choices of first-, fourth-, and eighth-graders were gathered in the fall and spring of the school year. Friendships did become more stable from first to fourth grade, but no change occurred from fourth to eighth grade. The researchers discovered that eighth-graders permitted a larger number of friendships to dissolve and were very selective about adding new friends (Berndt & Hoyle, 1985). Two factors seem to be responsible for this trend. First, friendships become more exclusive with age, especially for girls, because (as we will see shortly) they typically demand greater closeness in the relationship than do boys. Second, as children approach puberty, varying rates of development and new interests lead to a period of change in choice of friends (Berndt, 1986, 1988).

Although friendship stability does increase with age, children's friendships are remarkably stable at all ages. Even during the preschool years, two-thirds of children who identify one another as friends do so again 4 to 6 months later (Gershman & Hayes, 1983). However, lasting friendships at younger ages are more a function of the constancy of social environments, such as preschool and neighborhood, than of social cognition. In one study, preschoolers maintained friendships over a summer vacation only when parents made special arrangements for children to play together (Schaivo & Solomon, 1981).

Interaction Between Friends. Second, a more mature understanding of friendship might lead older children to behave with more mutual responsiveness and emotional sensitivity toward friends. Actually, interactions among friends have a unique quality at all ages. Preschoolers give twice as much reinforcement, in the form of greetings, praise, and compliance, to children whom they identify as friends, and they also receive more from them. Friends are also more emotionally expressive—talking, laughing, and looking at each other more often than nonfriends (Hartup, 1983). Apparently, spontaneity and intimacy characterize friendships very early, although children are not able to verbalize that these qualities are essential to a good friendship until much later.

Prosocial behavior toward friends does increase with age. When working on a task together, fourth-grade friends help and share more than first-grade friends do (Berndt, 1981). Cooperation and generosity between friends continue to rise into adolescence. One study found that fifth- and sixth-graders who had close friendships did better on an emotional perspective-taking task, and they behaved in a more caring way toward others in general (McGuire & Weisz, 1982). Many prosocial behaviors may emerge first in the context of friendship and then generalize to other people.

School-age friends do not just behave more prosocially. They also freely compete with each other to a greater extent than nonfriends. Since children regard friendship as based on equality, they seem especially concerned about losing a contest to a friend (Berndt, 1988). Also, when children hold differing opinions, friends are more likely to voice them than are nonfriends (Nelson & Aboud, 1985). As early as middle childhood, friends seem to be secure enough in their approval of one another to risk being direct about their opinions. As a result, friendship probably provides an important context in which children learn to tolerate argument, disagreement, and criticism.

Resemblance Between Friends. Finally, the value adolescents attach to feeling especially "in sync" with their close friends would lead us to expect friendship pairs to become increasingly similar in attitudes and values at older ages. Actually, the attributes on which friends are most alike throughout childhood and

*I*n schools and neighborhoods where interracial contact is common, many children form close cross-race friendships. (TONY FREEMAN/PHOTOEDIT)

adolescence are race, sex,* and social class. But by adolescence, friends also resemble one another in psychological characteristics, such as educational aspirations, political beliefs, and willingness to try drugs and engage in minor lawbreaking acts (Epstein, 1983a). Perhaps teenagers choose companions like themselves to increase the supportiveness of friendship. Once they do so, adolescent friends influence each other. Best friends become more alike in attitudes and values over time (Kandel, 1978a).

Still, similarity between friends is partly due to the way the social world is organized. Most children and adolescents live in neighborhoods that are fairly homogeneous in terms of race, income, and belief systems. In one study of friendships in an integrated junior high school, over 50 percent of seventh- to ninth-graders reported at least one close cross-race school friend. But these friendships seldom extended to out-of-school contexts unless adolescents lived in integrated neighborhoods where interracial contact was common (DuBois & Hirsch, 1990).

SEX-RELATED DIFFERENCES IN FRIENDSHIPS. Ask several girls and boys age 10 or older to describe their close friendships, and you are likely to find a consistent difference. Emotional closeness and trust are more common in girls' talk about friends than in boys' (Buhrmester & Furman, 1987; Bukowski & Kramer, 1986). This does not mean that boys rarely form close friendship ties. They often do, but the quality of their friendships is more variable. In one survey of high school students, 45 percent of boys described their best friendships as highly intimate; 35 percent said they were guarded in communication. In contrast, 65 percent of girls reported very intimate best friendships, whereas only 5 percent had relationships that were distant and superficial (Youniss & Smollar, 1986). The intimacy of boys' friendships is related to their gender-role identity. Boys who identify strongly with the traditional masculine role are less likely to form close friendships than those who are more flexible in their gender-related preferences (Jones & Dembo, 1989).

DEVELOPMENTAL CONSEQUENCES OF FRIENDSHIPS. Although young people who are well adjusted to begin with are better able to form and sustain close peer ties, warm supportive friendships further their development. The reasons are several:

1. *Close friendships provide opportunities to develop a wide variety of social-cognitive skills.* Through open, honest communication, friends become sensitive to each other's strengths and weaknesses, needs and desires. They get to know themselves and their partners especially well, a process that supports the development of self-concept, perspective taking, identity, and intimate ties beyond the family.
2. *Close friendships provide support in dealing with the stresses of everyday life.* Because friendship enhances sensitivity to and concern for another, it increases the likelihood of empathy and prosocial behavior. Adolescents with supportive friendships report fewer daily hassles and more "uplifts" than do others (Kanner et al., 1987). As a result, anxiety and loneliness are reduced while self-esteem and sense of well-being are fostered.
3. *Close friendships can improve attitudes toward school.* Young people with satisfying friendships tend to do well in school. The link between friendship and academic performance depends, of course, on the extent to which each friend values achievement (Epstein, 1983b). But overall, close friendship ties promote good school adjustment in both middle- and low-income students. When teenagers enjoy interacting with friends at school, perhaps they begin to view all aspects of school life more positively (Savin-Williams & Berndt, 1990).

*Although interaction between boys and girls increases during adolescence, stable friendships continue to be limited to members of the same sex. In one survey of nearly 2,000 high school students between the ages of 13 and 18, 91 percent reported that their best friend was of their own sex (Kandel, 1978b).

In sum, friendships provide children and adolescents with invaluable contexts in which they can form new attachments and develop a deep understanding of another person. As a result, they may be as vital for development as early family relationships. Several decades ago, psychiatrist Harry Stack Sullivan (1953) wrote about the significance of childhood friendships:

> If you will look very closely at one of your children when he finally finds a chum—somewhere between eight-and-a-half and ten—you will discover something very different in the relationship—namely, that your child begins to develop a real sensitivity to what matters to another person. And this is not in the sense of "what should I do to get what I want," but instead "what should I do to contribute to the happiness or to support the prestige and feeling of worthwhileness of my chum." So far as I have been able to discover, nothing remotely like this appears before. . . . Thus the developmental epoch of preadolescence is marked by the coming of integrating tendencies which, when they are completely developed, we call love. . . . (pp. 245–246)

Recent research on the development of friendship confirms Sullivan's vision.

Understanding Conflict: Social Problem Solving

Children, even when they are best friends, sometimes come into conflict with one another. Recall that Piaget (1923/1926) granted social conflict an important role in development. He believed that arguments and disagreements help children notice others' viewpoints, which leads to a decline in egocentrism. In Chapter 6, we noted that resolution of conflict, rather than conflict per se, encourages development. Indeed, even preschoolers seem to handle most of their quarrels constructively. Observations show that only rarely do conflicts lead to intensely hostile encounters. Instead, arguments, refusals, denials, and opposition are much more common. Furthermore, conflicts are not very frequent when compared to children's friendly, cooperative interactions (Hay, 1984). And when conflicts do occur, they are usually brief and settled by children themselves (Bakeman & Brownlee, 1982; O'Keefe & Benoit, 1982).

Despite their infrequency and brevity, peer conflicts are important. Watch children work out their disputes over play objects ("That's mine!" "I had it first!"), entry into and control over play activities ("I'm on your team, Jerry." "No you're not!"), and disagreements over facts, ideas, and beliefs ("I'm taller than he is." "No, you aren't!"). You will see that they take these matters quite seriously. Recent research reveals that social conflicts offer children invaluable learning opportunities in **social problem solving**. In their efforts to resolve conflicts effectively—in ways that are both acceptable to others and beneficial to the self—children must bring together a variety of social-cognitive skills. These include encoding and interpreting social cues, generating alternative strategies for reaching a goal, evaluating the effectiveness of each strategy in preparation for choosing one, and enacting it.

Kenneth Dodge (1985) regards social problem solving as a special, interpersonal form of the more general problem-solving process. He organizes the steps of social problem solving into the sequence shown in Figure 11.7. Notice how this flowchart takes an *information-processing approach* to social cognition. It clarifies the exact series of steps a child might use in grappling with a social problem and arriving at a solution. Once this is known, then specific processing deficits can be identified, and treatment programs can be tailored to meet children's individual needs.

Researchers are especially interested in social problem solving because of its profound impact on social competence. Well-adjusted children who get along with peers interpret social cues accurately and have a repertoire of effective strategies that they apply adaptively. In contrast, maladjusted children who are disliked by peers, either because they are highly aggressive or because they are anxious and withdrawn, have great difficulty solving social problems (Dodge, 1985; Vitaro & Pelletier, 1991). When social problem-solving skills improve, both chil-

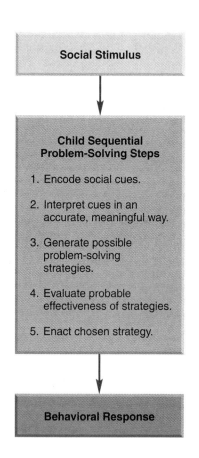

FIGURE 11.7 A social problem-solving flowchart. (Adapted from Dodge, 1985.)

Social problem solving
Resolving social conflicts in ways that are both acceptable to others and beneficial to the self.

dren and adolescents show gains in academic, emotional, and social adjustment (Dubow et al., 1991; Elias et al., 1986).

DEVELOPMENT OF SOCIAL PROBLEM SOLVING. George Spivack and Myrna Shure (1974, 1985) conducted pioneering research on social problem solving, stimulating the large body of research that exists today. Focusing on strategy generation, they asked young children to think of as many ways as they could to deal with hypothetical conflicts, such as wanting to play with a toy someone else has. Their findings, as well as the results of more recent studies, show that the ability to generate a variety of solutions to social conflicts increases over the preschool and early school years (Dubow & Tisak, 1989; Rubin & Krasnor, 1985).

Besides quantity of strategies, the quality of strategies generated by children improves with age. During middle childhood, younger children, as well as children with especially poor peer relations, describe strategies that impulsively meet their needs, such as grabbing, hitting, or ordering another child to obey. Older children and those with good peer relations assert their needs in ways that also consider the needs of others. They rely on friendly persuasion and compromise, sometimes suggesting that a conflict might be solved by creating new mutual goals. In doing so, they recognize that solutions to immediate problems have an important bearing on the future of the relationship (Downey & Walker, 1989; Selman & Demorest, 1984; Yeates, Schultz, & Selman, 1991).

Other researchers have expanded the study of social problem solving in an effort to find out at what other points, besides strategy generation, children with poor peer relations have difficulty. In one study, Dodge and his collaborators (1986) assessed school-age children's skillfulness at each of the five problem-solving steps in Figure 11.7. A videotape dramatized a problem involving entry into a play group. In the first scene, two children played a board game, and the researchers measured each subject's ability to *encode and interpret social cues* about the video characters' willingness to let the subject join the game. Then, subjects generated strategies for joining the game, and their responses were coded in the following ways:

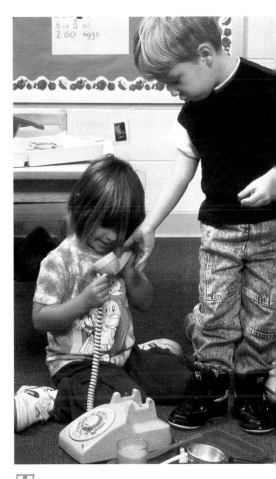

*T*his preschooler confronts a common social problem: He wants to play with a toy that another child has. With age, he will think of more effective strategies for solving the problem, and his tendency to react impulsively, by grabbing, is likely to decline. (JIM PICKERELL)

- *Competent:* Polite requests to play and other friendly comments.
- *Aggressive:* Threats, physical force, and barging in without asking.
- *Self-centered:* Statements about the self, such as "Hey, I know how to play that!"
- *Passive:* Shy, hovering responses, such as waiting and "hanging around."
- *Appeals to authority:* For example, "The teacher said I could play."

Next, subjects viewed five more scenes in which a child tried to enter the game using each of these strategies, and they engaged in *strategy evaluation* by indicating whether or not the technique would succeed. Finally, subjects participated in *strategy enactment* by demonstrating a way of joining the game.

In a separate session, the investigators assessed children's actual social competence by having them gain entry into a real peer-group activity in the laboratory. Results showed that all five social problem-solving skills were related to children's performance. Each social-cognitive measure also predicted how effectively children joined play activities while being observed on their school playground. In sum, children's processing of social information in a hypothetical situation was highly effective in explaining their behavior in similar everyday social contexts.

TRAINING SOCIAL PROBLEM SOLVING. Intervening with children who are poor social problem solvers is especially important. Besides improving peer relations, effective social problem solving can provide children with a sense of mastery and self-worth in the face of stressful life events. It reduces the risk of adjustment difficulties in children from low-income and troubled families (Downey & Walker, 1989; Pettit, Dodge, & Brown, 1988).

MILESTONES
SOCIAL-COGNITIVE DEVELOPMENT

Age	Thinking About the Self	Thinking About Other People	Thinking About Relations Between People
1–2 years	• Self-recognition emerges and becomes well established. • By age 2, a categorical self develops. • Self-evaluative statements appear.	• By age 2, ability to categorize people according to salient characteristics develops. • Beginnings of perspective taking emerge.	
3–5 years	• A belief-desire theory of mind emerges. • Self-concept emphasizes observable characteristics and commonly experienced emotions and attitudes. • Self-esteem is typically high and consists of at least two dimensions: social acceptance and competence. • Achievement-related attributions appear.	• Person perception emphasizes observable characteristics and commonly experienced emotions and attitudes. • Inferring others' intentions from behavioral cues improves. • Perspective taking is limited; children assume that what people observe determines their perspective.	• Friendship is viewed concretely, in terms of play and exchange of material goods. • Variety of social problem-solving strategies expands.
6–10 years	• Self-concept emphasizes personality traits. • Self-esteem becomes hierarchically organized: at least three dimensions (academic, physical, and social) are present, which differentiate into subareas and are combined into an overall impression. • Self-esteem declines as children start to make social comparisons, then rises. • Achievement-related attributions differentiate into ability and effort.	• Person perception emphasizes personality traits and social comparisons. "Peter is nicer than you!" • Understanding deceptive forms of intentional behavior improves. • Perspective taking expands; children understand that people can interpret the same event in different ways.	• Friendship emphasizes mutual trust and assistance. • Quality of social problem-solving strategies improves.
11 years–adulthood	• New aspects of self-esteem are added (close friendship, romantic appeal, and job competence). • Self-esteem continues to rise. • Identity develops.	• Person perception consists of organized character sketches. • Recursive and societal perspective taking develop.	• Friendship emphasizes intimacy and loyalty.

Note: These milestones represent overall age trends. Individual differences exist in the precise age at which each milestone is attained.

Spivack and Shure (1974) devised a well-known and widely applied social problem-solving training program. For several months, preschoolers and kindergartners participate in daily sessions in which puppets act out social problems and children discuss ways to resolve them. In addition, teachers intervene as conflicts arise in the classroom, pointing out consequences of children's behavior and suggesting alternative strategies. In several studies, trained pupils, in contrast to untrained controls, improved in both social reasoning and teacher-rated adjustment—gains still evident months after the program ended (Feis & Simons, 1985; Ridley & Vaughn, 1982). Older elementary school children benefit from similar interventions (Stiefvater, Kurdek, & Allik, 1986).

At present, researchers are not sure which ingredients of social problem-solving training are most effective. Some evidence suggests that practice in strategy enactment needs to accompany social-cognitive training. When children have had many opportunities to engage in maladaptive behaviors, repeated practice of new techniques may be necessary to overcome their habitual responses (Mize & Ladd, 1988). Also, current programs have not been tailored to fit the social-cognitive deficits of particular children. But it is in precisely these ways that the information-processing approach to social problem solving promises to make a unique contribution.

On a final note, social-cognitive training is not the only means for helping children with poor social competence. In Chapter 15, we will take up other approaches, including reinforcement, modeling, and direct teaching of social skills. The Milestones table on page 468 provides an overview of the changes in social cognition we have considered in this chapter.

CHAPTER SUMMARY

- The development of **social cognition** deals with how children's understanding of themselves, other people, and relationships between people changes with age.

Thinking About the Self
- Reactions of infants to images of themselves indicate that **self-recognition** is well established by the end of the second year. The emergence of representational and language capacities permits toddlers to construct a **categorical self** as they classify themselves and others on the basis of salient characteristics, such as age, sex, and physical characteristics. Self-awareness provides the foundation for early struggles over objects as well as cooperation and prosocial behavior.

- During the preschool years, children form a naive **theory of mind,** an understanding of themselves and others as mental beings with a rich inner world of private thoughts and imaginings. Around age 3 to 4, this theory becomes a **belief-desire theory** that closely resembles the everyday psychology of adults. Early emergence of a theory of mind may be supported by infants' sense of agency as well as make-believe play and imitation. Many researchers believe that the normal human brain is biologically prepared to develop a belief-desire theory.

- During the preschool years, children begin to construct a **self-concept,** or set of beliefs about their own characteristics. In middle childhood, self-concept changes from an appreciation of typical emotions, attitudes, and observable characteristics to an emphasis on personality traits, a transformation supported by cognitive development and perspective-taking skills. Children's self-concepts tend to

emphasize individualistic traits in complex cultures, social traits in simpler cultures.

- **Self-esteem,** the judgments we make about our own worth, differentiates, becomes hierarchically organized, and declines over the first few years of elementary school as children start to make **social comparisons.** Except for a temporary drop associated with school transition, self-esteem rises from fourth grade on. For most young people, becoming an adolescent leads to feelings of pride and self-confidence. Self-esteem is influenced by cultural forces. Child-rearing practices that are warm and responsive and that provide reasonable expectations for mature behavior are consistently related to high self-esteem.

- Research on achievement-related **attributions** has identified adult communication styles that affect children's self-esteem and **achievement motivation.** Children with **mastery-oriented attributions** credit their successes to high ability and their failures to insufficient effort. In contrast, those with **learned helplessness** attribute their successes to luck and failures to low ability. Children who receive negative feedback about their ability and pressure to focus on performance goals develop the learned-helpless pattern. **Attribution retraining** has succeeded in improving the self-evaluations and task performance of learned-helpless children.

- Erikson first recognized **identity**—the construction of a solid self-definition consisting of self-chosen values and goals—as the major personality achievement of adolescence. In complex societies, a period of exploration is necessary to form a personally meaningful identity.

- **Identity achievement** and **moratorium** are psychologically healthy identity statuses. **Identity foreclosure** and **identity**

diffusion are related to adjustment difficulties. Adolescents who recognize that rational criteria can be used to choose among beliefs and values and who feel attached to parents but free to disagree are likely to be advanced in identity development. Schools and communities that provide young people with rich and varied options for exploration support the search for identity.

Thinking About Other People

- Like self-concept, **person perception** places greater emphasis on personality traits and becomes more differentiated and organized with age. Over the preschool years, children become increasingly skilled at distinguishing intentional from unintentional acts. During middle childhood, they begin to detect deceptive forms of intentional behavior.
- **Perspective taking** improves greatly from childhood to adolescence, as Selman's five-stage sequence indicates. Mastery of Piagetian tasks and a view of the mind as an active interpreter of experience are related to advances in perspective taking. During adolescence, **recursive thought** is mastered.
- The ability to understand the viewpoints of others contributes to a wide variety of social skills. Young people who display extremes of antisocial behavior are often

greatly delayed in the development of perspective taking. Interventions that train perspective-taking skills by having troubled adolescents role-play interpersonal problems result in improvements in social cognition and behavior.

Thinking About Relations Between People

- Children's understanding of friendship evolves from a concrete relationship based on sharing activities and material goods to more abstract conceptions based on mutual trust and intimacy. In line with this change, children's real friendships are characterized by greater stability, prosocial responding, and similarity in attitudes and values with age. Girls emphasize emotional closeness and trust in their friendships more than boys do. Close friendships foster a wide variety of social–cognitive skills, provide support in dealing with everyday stresses, and can improve attitudes toward school.
- With age, children become better at resolving conflict through **social problem solving**. All components of the social problem-solving process—encoding and interpreting social cues and generating, evaluating, and enacting strategies—predict social competence. Training in social problem solving leads to gains in psychological adjustment for both preschool and school-age children.

IMPORTANT TERMS AND CONCEPTS

social cognition (p. 434)
self-recognition (p. 435)
categorical self (p. 436)
theory of mind (p. 436)
belief-desire theory (p. 437)
self-concept (p. 438)
generalized other (p. 439)
self-esteem (p. 440)

social comparisons (p. 442)
attributions (p. 444)
achievement motivation (p. 444)
mastery-oriented attributions (p. 445)
learned helplessness (p. 445)
attribution retraining (p. 447)
identity (p. 447)
identity achievement (p. 448)

moratorium (p. 448)
identity foreclosure (p. 448)
identity diffusion (p. 448)
person perception (p. 454)
perspective taking (p. 455)
recursive thought (p. 459)
social problem solving (p. 466)

C O N N E C T I O N S

If you are interested in . . .	Turn to . . .	To learn about . . .
Self-understanding	Chapter 5, pp. 190–191	Adolescent reactions to pubertal changes
	Chapter 5, p. 198	Sexual identity of homosexual adolescents
	Chapter 6, pp. 225, 235, pp. 250–251	Egocentrism in Piaget's theory
	Chapter 7, pp. 291–292	Metacognitive knowledge
	Chapter 10, pp. 403–404	Emotional understanding in childhood
	Chapter 13, pp. 536–541	Gender-role identity
Perspective taking	Chapter 5, p. 196	Perspective taking and sexually active teenagers' use of contraceptives
	Chapter 6, p. 245	Perspective taking and children's cognitive maps
	Chapter 6, p. 255	Peer interaction and perspective taking in Piaget's theory
	Chapter 6, p. 256	Intersubjectivity, perspective taking, and transfer of cognitive skills to children
	Chapter 10, p. 404	Perspective taking and empathy
	Chapter 12, pp. 490–491	Perspective taking and moral understanding
	Chapter 13, p. 540	Perspective taking and gender-role identity in adolescence
	Chapter 15, p. 604	Perspective taking and peer sociability in middle childhood
Aggression in childhood	Chapter 7, p. 279	Attention-deficit hyperactivity disorder and aggression
	Chapter 12, pp. 507–513	Development of aggression
	Chapter 15, p. 610	Peer rejection and aggression
	Chapter 15, p. 611	Bullies and their victims
	Chapter 15, p. 615	Dominance hierarchies and control of peer-group aggression
	Chapter 15, p. 616	Peer reinforcement of aggressive behavior
	Chapter 15, p. 624	Television and aggression

*S*chool-age children's notions of
authority are not limited to unquestioning
respect for the power of adults, as Piaget
assumed. This safety-patrol member is
regarded as a legitimate authority by his
peers because he holds an important
position and is especially knowledgeable
about traffic-safety matters. (JOEL GORDON)

REASONING ABOUT AUTHORITY. New evidence on young children's understanding of authority reveals that they do not regard adults with the unquestioning respect Piaget assumed. Later in this chapter, we will see that preschoolers judge certain acts, such as hitting and stealing, to be wrong regardless of the opinions of authorities. When asked to explain why they think these behaviors should be prohibited, even 3- and 4-year-olds express concerns about harming or otherwise violating the welfare of other people rather than obeying the dictates of adults (Nucci & Turiel, 1978; Smetana, 1981, 1985).

By the early school years, children have formed complex, differentiated notions about the legitimacy of authority figures. In one study, kindergartners through sixth-graders were asked questions designed to assess their view of how broad a school principal's authority should be. Pupils of all ages did not conceive of an authority as having general powers that apply across all situations. Most rejected a principal's right to set rules or issue directives in settings other than his own school, a response that strengthened with age. However, when an act (fighting) could harm another person, children made an exception: They thought a principal should intervene and stop the behavior if it occurred in an out-of-school public context (a city park). But most did not extend this right to a private context (the child's home) (Laupa & Turiel, 1993).

Furthermore, adult status is not required for school-age children to accept someone as an authority. Peers are also regarded as legitimate authorities when they hold certain positions (such as safety-patrol member) or are particularly knowledgeable in a skill area (Laupa, 1991; Laupa & Turiel, 1986). Clearly, young children's concepts of authority do not focus solely on power and status. Instead, several factors are coordinated at a much earlier age than Piaget anticipated—the attributes of the individual, the type of behavior to be controlled, and the context in which it occurs.

STAGEWISE PROGRESSION. An additional point about Piaget's theory is that the characteristics associated with each stage do not correlate very highly, as we would expect if each represented a general, unifying organization of moral judgment. As Thomas Lickona (1976) puts it, "The child's moral thought, as it unfolds in Piagetian interviews, is not all of a piece but more of a patchwork of diverse parts" (p. 240). But in fairness, Piaget (1932/1965) observed the mixture of heteronomous and autonomous reasoning in the responses of many children and recommended that the two moralities be viewed as fluid, overlapping "phases" (p. 317) rather than tightly knit stages.

Finally, moral development is currently regarded as a more extended process than Piaget believed. In fact, Kohlberg's theory, to which we now turn, identifies three stages beyond the first appearance of autonomous morality. Over the past two decades, Piaget's ground-breaking work has been supplanted by Kohlberg's more comprehensive six-stage sequence. Nevertheless, it is clear that Kohlberg's theory is a direct continuation of the research Piaget began—the search for universal stages of moral development and the study of how moral understanding is intimately tied to cognitive growth (Lickona, 1976).

Kohlberg's Extension of Piaget's Theory

Like Piaget, Kohlberg used a clinical interviewing procedure to study moral development, but he based his stage sequence on situations quite different from Piaget's stories. Whereas Piaget asked children to judge the naughtiness of a character who had already decided on a moral course of action, Kohlberg presented subjects with **moral dilemmas** and asked them to decide both what the main actor should do and why. Perhaps as a result, he obtained a clearer picture of the reasoning on which moral decisions are based. Today, Kohlberg's clinical interviewing procedure is widely used to assess moral understanding. Two more efficient, questionnaire approaches have also been devised: the Defining Issues Test and the Sociomoral Reflection Measure–Short Form.

THE CLINICAL INTERVIEW. Each of Kohlberg's dilemmas presents a genuine crisis that pits one moral value against another. The best known of these is the "Heinz dilemma," which asks subjects to choose between the value of obeying the law (not stealing) and the value of human life (saving a dying person):

> In Europe, a woman was near death from cancer. There was one drug the doctors thought might save her. A druggist in the same town had discovered it, but he was charging ten times what the drug cost him to make. The sick woman's husband, Heinz, went to everyone he knew to borrow the money, but he could only get together half of what it cost. The druggist refused to sell it cheaper or let Heinz pay later. So Heinz got desperate and broke into the man's store to steal the drug for his wife. Should Heinz have done that? Why or why not? (paraphrased from Colby et al., 1983, p. 77)

Kohlberg emphasized that it is the *structure* of the answer—the way an individual reasons about the dilemma—and not the *content* of the response (whether to steal or not to steal) that determines moral maturity. Individuals who believe Heinz should take the drug and those who think he should not can be found at each of Kohlberg's first four stages. To bring out the structure of moral understanding, the interview is lengthy and free-ranging. After a dilemma is presented, follow-up questions elicit views on such issues as obedience to laws and authority figures and understanding of higher moral values, such as respect for human life. In the Heinz dilemma, the interviewer would ask: "If Heinz does not love his wife, should he still steal the drug for her?" "Why or why not?" "Is it important for people to do everything they can to save another's life?" "Why?" "It is against the law for Heinz to steal. Does that make it morally wrong?" "Why or why not?"

Although structure is the primary consideration for determining an individual's moral progress, at the highest two stages content is also relevant. Morally mature individuals do not just agree on why certain actions are justified. They also agree on what people ought to do when faced with a moral dilemma. Given a choice between obeying the law and preserving individual rights, the most advanced moral thinkers support individual rights (in the Heinz dilemma, stealing the drug to save a life). As we look at development in Kohlberg's scheme, we will see that moral reasoning and content are at first independent, but eventually they are integrated into a coherent ethical system (Kohlberg, Levine, & Hewer, 1983). Does this remind you of adolescents' efforts to formulate a sound, well-organized set of personal values in identity development, discussed in Chapter

Moral dilemma
A conflict situation presented to subjects, who are asked to decide both what the main actor should do and why. Used to assess the development of moral reasoning.

TABLE 12.1 "Heinz Dilemma" Issue Statements from the Defining Issues Test (DIT)

WHICH ISSUES ARE MOST IMPORTANT IN MAKING A DECISION ABOUT WHAT HEINZ SHOULD DO?*

1. Whether a community's laws are going to be upheld.

2. Is Heinz willing to risk getting shot as a burglar or going to jail for the chance that stealing the drug might help?

3. Isn't it only natural for a loving husband to care so much for his wife that he'd steal?

4. What values are going to be the basis for governing how people act toward each other?

5. Whether the law in this case is getting in the way of the most basic claim of any member of society.

NOTE: 1. Stage 4. 2. Stage 2. 3. Stage 3. 4. Stage 6. 5. Stage 5.

SOURCE: From *Revised Manual for the Defining Issues Test* by J. R. Rest, 1979, Minneapolis: Moral Research Projects. Reprinted by permission of the author.

11? According to some theorists, the development of identity and moral understanding are part of the same process (Davidson & Youniss, 1991; Marcia, 1988).

THE DEFINING ISSUES TEST. A less time-consuming method for assessing moral maturity is James Rest's **Defining Issues Test (DIT).** It asks individuals to read a series of dilemmas and rate the importance of "moral issue" statements in deciding on a course of action. Each statement captures the essence of moral understanding at a particular stage in Kohlberg's scheme. By scoring the ratings, the researcher can identify a stage of reasoning as well as the relative importance attached to "principled morality," or Kohlberg's highest level. Some DIT issue statements related to the Heinz dilemma are given in Table 12.1. Which ones seem most important to you in deciding what Heinz should do? The note at the bottom of the table gives the stage of reasoning represented by each statement.

Individuals typically appear more advanced in moral development on the DIT than in Kohlberg's clinical interview (Rest, 1979a). This is not surprising, since Kohlberg's method asks subjects to produce moral reasoning, whereas the DIT requires only that they recognize and rate their preferences for stage-linked statements. Recall from Chapter 7 that recognition is a far less demanding process than active generation of a response. Otherwise, the DIT yields findings similar to clinical interviewing scores. As a result, it is used often in moral reasoning research.

THE SOCIOMORAL REFLECTION MEASURE–SHORT FORM. The most recent method for assessing moral understanding is the **Sociomoral Reflection Measure–Short Form (SRM–SF).** Like Kohlberg's clinical interview and the DIT, the SRM–SF asks subjects to evaluate the importance of moral values. Also like the clinical interview (but unlike the DIT), it requires subjects to produce moral reasoning. Here are four of its eleven questions:

> Let's say a friend of yours needs help and may even die, and you're the only person who can save him or her. How important is it for a person (without losing his or her own life) to save the life of a friend?
>
> What about saving the life of anyone? How important is it for a person (without losing his or her own life) to save the life of a stranger?
>
> How important is it for people not to take things that belong to other people?
>
> How important is it for people to obey the law? (Gibbs, Basinger, & Fuller, 1992, pp. 151–152)

Defining Issues Test (DIT)

A questionnaire for assessing moral understanding in which subjects read a series of moral dilemmas and rate the importance of "moral issue" statements representing each of Kohlberg's stages in deciding on a course of action.

Sociomoral Reflection Measure–Short Form (SRM–SF)

A questionnaire for assessing moral understanding in which subjects rate the importance of moral values addressed by brief, dilemma-inspired questions and explain their ratings. Does not require subjects to read and think about lengthy moral dilemmas.

After reading each question, subjects rate the importance of the value it addresses (as "very important," "important," or "not important") and write a brief explanation of their rating. The explanations are coded for thinking that reflects Kohlberg's stages.

The SRM–SF is even less time-consuming to administer than the DIT because it does not require subjects to read and think about lengthy moral dilemmas. Instead, they merely answer brief, dilemma-inspired questions and justify their response. Nevertheless, scores on the SRM–SF correlate well with those obtained from clinical interviews (Gibbs, Basinger, & Fuller, 1992). Apparently, moral understanding can be measured without using dilemmas—a discovery that is likely to ease the task of conducting moral development research.

KOHLBERG'S STAGES OF MORAL UNDERSTANDING. Kohlberg organized his six stages into three general levels and made strong statements about the properties of this sequence. First, he regarded the stages as *invariant* and *universal*—a sequence of steps that people everywhere move through in a fixed order. Second, he viewed each new stage as a more *equilibrated* way of making and justifying moral judgments. That is, each successive stage builds on the reasoning of the preceding stage, resulting in a more logically consistent and morally adequate concept of justice. Finally, each stage was believed to form an *organized whole*—a qualitatively distinct pattern of moral reasoning that a person applies across a wide range of situations (Colby & Kohlberg, 1987; Walker, 1988). Recall from Chapter 6 that these characteristics are the very ones Piaget used to describe his cognitive stages.

Furthermore, Kohlberg believed that moral understanding is promoted by the same factors that Piaget thought were important for cognitive development: *disequilibrium*, or actively grappling with moral issues and noticing weaknesses in one's current thinking; and *gains in perspective taking*, which permit individuals to resolve moral conflicts in more complex and effective ways. As we examine Kohlberg's developmental sequence and illustrate it with responses to the Heinz dilemma, look for changes in cognition and perspective taking that each stage assumes.

The Preconventional Level. At the **preconventional level,** morality is externally controlled. As in Piaget's heteronomous stage, children accept the rules of authority figures, and actions are judged by their consequences. Behaviors that result in punishment are viewed as bad, and those that lead to rewards are seen as good.

- *Stage 1: The punishment and obedience orientation.* Children at this stage find it difficult to consider two points of view in a moral dilemma. As a result, they ignore people's intentions and instead focus on fear of authority and avoidance of punishment as reasons for behaving morally.

   Pro-stealing: "If you let your wife die, you will get in trouble. You'll be blamed for not spending the money to help her, and there'll be an investigation of you and the druggist for your wife's death." (Kohlberg, 1969, p. 381)

   Anti-stealing: "You shouldn't steal the drug because you'll be caught and sent to jail if you do. If you do get away, your conscience would bother you thinking how the police would catch up with you any minute." (Kohlberg, 1969, p. 381)

- *Stage 2: The instrumental purpose orientation.* Awareness that people can have different perspectives in a moral dilemma appears, but this understanding is, at first, very concrete. Individuals view right action as what satisfies their personal needs, and they believe others also act out of self-interest. Reciprocity is understood as equal exchange of favors—"you do this for me and I'll do that for you."

   Pro-stealing: "The druggist can do what he wants and Heinz can do what he wants to do. . . . But if Heinz decides to risk jail to save his wife, it's his life he's risking; he can do what he wants with it. And the same goes for the druggist; it's up to him to decide what he wants to do." (Rest, 1979a, p. 26)

   Anti-stealing: "(Heinz) is running more risk than it's worth unless he's so crazy about her he can't live without her. Neither of them will enjoy life if she's an invalid." (Rest, 1979a, p. 27)

Preconventional level
Kohlberg's first level of moral development, in which moral understanding is based on rewards, punishment, and the power of authority figures.

The Conventional Level. At the **conventional level,** individuals continue to regard conformity to social rules as important, but not for reasons of self-interest. They believe that actively maintaining the current social system is important for ensuring positive human relationships and societal order.

- *Stage 3: The "good boy–good girl" orientation, or the morality of interpersonal cooperation.* The desire to obey rules because they promote social harmony first appears in the context of close personal ties. Stage 3 individuals want to maintain the affection and approval of friends and relatives by being a "good person"—trustworthy, loyal, respectful, helpful, and nice. The capacity to view a two-person relationship from the vantage point of an impartial, outside observer supports this new approach to morality. At this stage, the individual understands reciprocity in terms of the Golden Rule.

  Pro-stealing: "No one will think you're bad if you steal the drug, but your family will think you're an inhuman husband if you don't. If you let your wife die, you'll never be able to look anyone in the face again." (Kohlberg, 1969, p. 381)

  Anti-stealing: "It isn't just the druggist who will think you're a criminal, everyone else will too. After you steal it, you'll feel bad thinking how you brought dishonor on your family and yourself; you won't be able to face anyone again." (Kohlberg, 1969, p. 381)

- *Stage 4: The social-order-maintaining orientation.* At this stage, the individual takes into account a larger perspective—that of societal laws. Moral choices no longer depend on close ties to others. Instead, rules must be enforced in the same evenhanded fashion for everyone, and each member of society has a personal duty to uphold them. The Stage 4 individual believes laws cannot be disobeyed under any circumstances because they are vital for ensuring societal order.

  Pro-stealing: "He should steal it. Heinz has a duty to protect his wife's life; it's a vow he took in marriage. But it's wrong to steal, so he would have to take the drug with the idea of paying the druggist for it and accepting the penalty for breaking the law later."

  Anti-stealing: "It's a natural thing for Heinz to want to save his wife, but it's still always wrong to steal. You have to follow the rules regardless of how you feel or regardless of the special circumstances. Even if his wife is dying, it's still his duty as a citizen to obey the law. No one else is allowed to steal, why should he be? If everyone starts breaking the law in a jam, there'd be no civilization, just crime and violence." (Rest, 1979a, p. 30)

The Postconventional or Principled Level. Individuals at the **postconventional level** move beyond unquestioning support for the rules and laws of their own society. They define morality in terms of abstract principles and values that apply to all situations and societies.

- *Stage 5: The social-contract orientation.* At Stage 5, individuals regard laws and rules as flexible instruments for furthering human purposes. They can imagine alternatives to their social order, and they emphasize fair procedures for interpreting and changing the law when there is a good reason to do so. When laws are consistent with individual rights and the interests of the majority, each person follows them because of a social-contract orientation—free and willing participation in the system because it brings about more good for people than if it did not exist.

  Pro-stealing: "Although there is a law against stealing, the law wasn't meant to violate a person's right to life. Taking the drug does violate the law, but Heinz is justified in stealing in this instance. If Heinz is prosecuted for stealing, the law needs to be reinterpreted to take into account situations in which it goes against people's natural right to keep on living."

Conventional level
Kohlberg's second level of moral development, in which moral understanding is based on conforming to social rules to ensure positive human relationships and societal order.

Postconventional level
Kohlberg's highest level of moral development, in which individuals define morality in terms of abstract principles and values that apply to all situations and societies.

- *Stage 6: The universal ethical principle orientation.* At this highest stage, right action is defined by self-chosen ethical principles of conscience that are valid for all humanity, regardless of law and social agreement. These values are abstract, not concrete moral rules like the Ten Commandments. Stage 6 individuals typically mention such principles as equal consideration of the claims of all human beings and respect for the worth and dignity of each person.

    Pro-stealing: "If Heinz does not do everything he can to save his wife, then he is putting some value higher than the value of life. It doesn't make sense to put respect for property above respect for life itself. [People] could live together without private property at all. Respect for human life and personality is absolute and accordingly [people] have a mutual duty to save one another from dying." (Rest, 1979a, p. 37)

Research on Kohlberg's Stages

Is there support for Kohlberg's developmental sequence? If his theory is correct, movement through the stages should be related to age, cognitive development, and gains in perspective taking. Also, moral development should conform to the strict stage properties that Kohlberg assumed.

AGE-RELATED CHANGE AND INVARIANT STAGES. A wealth of cross-sectional research reveals that progress through Kohlberg's stages is strongly related to age (Rest, 1986). But longitudinal studies provide the most convincing evidence for Kohlberg's developmental sequence. The most extensive of these is a 20-year continuation of Kohlberg's first study of adolescent boys in which 58 of the 84 original subjects were reinterviewed at regular 3- to 4-year intervals. Like cross-sectional findings, the correlation between age and moral maturity was strong, at .78. In addition, the stages formed an invariant developmental sequence. Almost all subjects moved through them in the predicted order, without skipping steps or returning to less mature reasoning once a stage had been attained (Colby et al., 1983). Other longitudinal findings also confirm the invariance of Kohlberg's stages (Rest, 1986; Snarey, Reimer, & Kohlberg, 1985; Walker, 1989; Walker & Taylor, 1991b).

A striking feature of age trends in moral reasoning is that development is very slow and gradual. Figure 12.1 shows the extent to which subjects used each stage of moral reasoning between ages 10 and 36 in the longitudinal study just described. Notice how Stages 1 and 2 decrease in early adolescence, whereas Stage 3 increases through midadolescence and then declines. Stage 4 rises over the teenage years

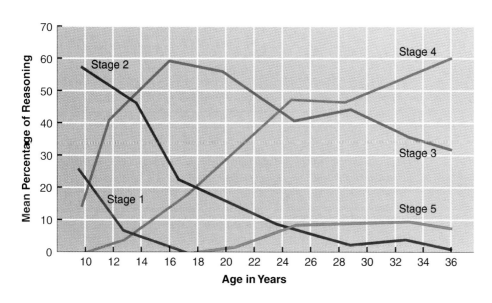

FIGURE 12.1 Mean percentage of moral reasoning at each stage for each age level in the 20-year longitudinal follow-up of Kohlberg's first study of adolescent boys. (From "A Longitudinal Study of Moral Judgment," by A. Colby, L. Kohlberg, J. Gibbs, & M. Lieberman, 1983, *Monographs of the Society for Research in Child Development, 48,* (1–2, Serial No. 200), p. 46. © The Society for Research in Child Development, Inc. Reprinted by permission.)

until, by early adulthood, it is the typical response. Few people move beyond it to Stage 5. In fact, postconventional morality is so rare that there is no clear evidence that Kohlberg's Stage 6 actually follows Stage 5. The highest stage of moral development is still a matter of speculation.

ARE KOHLBERG'S STAGES ORGANIZED WHOLES? As you read the Heinz dilemma, you probably came up with your own solution to it. Now, try to think of a moral problem you recently faced in everyday life. How did you solve it? Did your reasoning fall at the same stage as your thinking about Heinz and his dying wife? If each of Kohlberg's stages forms an organized whole, then individuals should use the same level of moral reasoning across many tasks and situations.

When Kohlberg's interviewing procedure is used, most individuals do show fairly uniform reasoning from one moral dilemma to another (Walker, 1988). But Kohlberg's scoring procedure tends to minimize variability in subjects' responses. Alternative scoring approaches produce greater diversity in moral thought (Gibbs, Basinger, & Fuller, 1992; Rest, 1983).

Furthermore, when methods used to elicit moral reasoning are varied, quality of thinking changes as well. We have already mentioned that the DIT produces more advanced moral judgments than Kohlberg's clinical interview. Varying aspects of the dilemmas has a profound effect as well. When subjects generate real-life moral problems of their own, they tend to fall at a lower stage than on hypothetical dilemmas (Trevethan & Walker, 1989). Perhaps real-life problems elicit moral reasoning below a person's actual capacity because they bring out the many practical considerations involved in an actual moral conflict. Consistent with this idea, moral responses also become less mature when dilemmas highlight the possibility of punishment for the main actor—for example, stating that if Heinz decides to steal the drug, he will "be caught for sure and sent to prison" (Sobesky, 1983, p. 578). Emphasizing punishment increases subjects' concern with self-interest, a major preconventional basis of morality.

The influence of situational factors on moral judgment suggests that like Piaget's cognitive stages, Kohlberg's moral stages are best viewed in terms of a loose rather than strict concept of stage. Rather than developing in a neat stepwise fashion, each individual seems to draw on a range of moral responses that vary with context. With age, this range shifts upward as less mature moral reasoning is gradually replaced by more advanced moral thought (Rest, 1979a). Apparently, Piaget was right to think of less mature and more mature moralities as overlapping phases.

COGNITIVE PREREQUISITES FOR MORAL REASONING. Moral maturity, whether based on Piaget's or Kohlberg's theories, is positively correlated with IQ, performance on Piagetian cognitive tasks, and perspective-taking skill (Kurdek, 1980; Lickona, 1976; Rest, 1979a). However, Kohlberg (1969, 1976) believed that moral development depends on cognition and perspective taking in a very specific way. He argued that each moral stage requires certain cognitive and perspective-taking capacities, but these are not enough to ensure moral advances. In addition, reorganization of thought unique to the moral domain is necessary. In other words, Kohlberg hypothesized that cognitive and perspective-taking attainments are *necessary but not sufficient conditions* for each of the moral stages.

Recall from Chapter 11 that the "necessary but not sufficient" criterion also applies to the relation between Piaget's cognitive and Selman's perspective-taking stages, so Kohlberg's hypothesis is an expansion of this idea. Although no single study has examined all of the stage relationships in Table 12.2, research shows that cognitive, perspective-taking, and moral development are related in ways consistent with Kohlberg's predictions (Krebs & Gillmore, 1982; Selman, 1976). For example, in a study of fourth- through seventh-graders, with only one exception all children at Stage 3 moral reasoning scored at either a higher stage or the matching stage of cognition and perspective taking (Walker, 1980). Furthermore, attempts to increase moral reasoning reveal that it cannot be stimulated beyond

TABLE 12.2 The Relation Between Kohlberg's Moral, Piaget's Cognitive, and Selman's Perspective-Taking Stages

KOHLBERG'S MORAL STAGE	DESCRIPTION	PIAGET'S COGNITIVE STAGE	SELMAN'S PERSPECTIVE-TAKING STAGE
Punishment and obedience orientation	Fear of authority and avoidance of punishment are reasons for behaving morally.	Preoperational, early concrete operational	Social-informational
Instrumental purpose orientation	Satisfying personal needs determines moral choice.	Concrete operational	Self-reflective
"Good boy–good girl" orientation	Maintaining the affection and approval of friends and relatives motivates good behavior.	Early formal operational	Third-party
Social-order-maintaining orientation	A duty to uphold laws and rules for their own sake justifies moral conformity.	Formal operational	Societal
Social-contract orientation	Fair procedures for changing laws to protect individual rights and the needs of the majority are emphasized.		
Universal ethical principle orientation	Abstract universal principles that are valid for all humanity guide moral decision making.		

the stage for which an individual has the appropriate cognitive prerequisites (Arbuthnot et al., 1983; Walker & Richards, 1979).

Environmental Influences on Moral Reasoning

What other factors besides the attainment of Piaget's and Selman's stages might promote moral maturity? Earlier we mentioned Kohlberg's belief that actively grappling with moral issues is vital for moral change. As we will see in the following sections, many environmental factors are related to moral understanding, including peer interaction, child-rearing practices, schooling, and aspects of culture.

The weakness of this research is one we have mentioned many times before: Correlational studies cannot tell us for sure that an important cause of moral reasoning has been isolated. Fortunately, in some cases, experiments that manipulate the experience in question have been conducted, demonstrating its role in moral development. Furthermore, a growing body of evidence suggests that the way these experiences work is by inducing disequilibrium—presenting young people with cognitive challenges, which stimulate them to think about moral problems in more complex ways.

PEER INTERACTION. Research relating peer experiences to progress through Kohlberg's stages supports Piaget's belief that interaction with agemates promotes moral understanding. Maturity of moral reasoning is correlated with peer popularity, participation in social organizations, and service in leadership roles (Enright & Sutterfield, 1980; Harris, Mussen, & Rutherford, 1976). Studies conducted in Africa underline the importance of exposure to diverse peer value systems for stimulating

*I*ntense, animated discussions about
moral issues in which peers confront,
critique, and attempt to clarify one
another's statements lead to gains in moral
understanding. (STEPHEN MARKS)

moral thought. Kenyan and Nigerian students enrolled in ethnically and racially
mixed high schools and colleges were advanced in moral development compared
to those enrolled in homogeneous settings (Edwards, 1978; Maqsud, 1977).

Peer experiences have provided the framework for many interventions aimed
at improving moral understanding. A major feature of most of them is peer discussion and role-playing of moral problems. A study by Moshe Blatt and
Lawrence Kohlberg (1975) yielded particularly impressive findings. After participating in either teacher- or student-led classroom discussions of moral dilemmas
for one semester, many sixth- and tenth-graders moved partially or totally to the
next moral stage, a change not found in pupils who did not receive the intervention. A year later, these differences were still evident. Other peer discussion interventions have also produced gains in moral reasoning, although in most instances
the change is slight.

Which aspects of peer discussion stimulate moral development? Several
researchers have tackled this question by conducting fine-grained analyses of peer
dialogues, comparing those that produce stage change with those that lead to little or no change. In one study, college students who confronted, critiqued, and
attempted to clarify one another's statements gained in moral maturity. In contrast, nongainers made assertions, told personal anecdotes, or expressed confusion about the task (Berkowitz & Gibbs, 1983). In another study, small friendship
groups of university students participated in weekly interaction sessions. Some
discussed hypothetical moral dilemmas, whereas others played games designed
to stir up actual moral problems—for example, a game called "Ghetto" in which
citizens confront a corrupt staff person who represents "the system." In the
games, students engaged in more intense expressions of disagreement. During
discussions, interactions tended to be emotionally controlled, intellectual
responses to conflict. Games facilitated moral reasoning far more effectively than
did discussions (Haan, Aerts, & Cooper, 1985).

Taken together, these findings indicate that cognitively probing, emotionally
involved exchanges between peers are especially effective in stimulating moral
understanding. Finally, because moral development is a gradual process, it usually
takes many peer interaction sessions over weeks or months to produce moral change.

CHILD-REARING PRACTICES. Child-rearing practices associated with mature moral
reasoning reflect rational, democratic processes. Lawrence Walker and John
Taylor (1991a) assessed level of moral reasoning and interaction styles of mothers
and fathers as they discussed moral dilemmas with their first- through tenth-
grade children. Parents who created a supportive atmosphere by listening sensi-

tively, asking clarifying questions, presenting higher-level reasoning, and using praise and humor had children who gained most in moral understanding when interviewed 2 years later. In contrast, parents who lectured, used threats, or made sarcastic remarks had children who changed little or not at all. These effects were especially strong when families discussed a child-generated rather than hypothetical moral dilemma. Because the child's moral problem was directly relevant to parents' and children's lives, it probably provoked discussion that better resembled day-to-day family interaction.

Other research reveals that parents who use low levels of power assertion and high levels of warmth and inductive discipline and who encourage participation in family decision making have morally mature children (Parikh, 1980; Saltzstein, 1976). In sum, the kind of parent who facilitates moral understanding is verbal, rational, and affectionate and promotes a cooperative style of family life (Edwards, 1981).

SCHOOLING. Years of schooling completed is one of the most powerful predictors of moral development. In one study, adolescents graduating from high school were followed over a 10-year period. Some did not go to college (the "low" education group), others went for a short time (the "moderate" education group), and still others graduated from college (the "high" education group). As Figure 12.2 shows, college graduates continued to gain in moral maturity, those with some college leveled off after they left college, and those with no college education declined (Rest & Narvaez, 1991). Moral reasoning seems to advance regularly only as long as a person remains in school.

Why does schooling make such a difference in moral maturity? There could be many reasons, including exposure to morally relevant subject matter and opportunities to interact with teachers and peers about moral concerns. Kohlberg (1984) suggested that higher education is an especially important arena for moral development because it introduces young people to social issues that extend beyond familiar, face-to-face relationships to entire political or cultural groups. Consistent with this idea, college students who report more academic perspective-taking opportunities (for example, classes that emphasize open discussion of opinions) and who indicate that they have become more aware of social diversity tend to be more advanced in moral reasoning (Mason & Gibbs, 1993).

The question of how best to foster moral development in schools has been the focus of much research and debate. To find out more about Kohlberg's approach to moral education, turn to the From Research to Practice box on page 495.

Years of schooling is a powerful predictor of moral maturity. The social diversity of many college campuses, which introduces young people to issues that involve entire political and cultural groups, probably contributes to gains in moral reasoning. (GRANITSAS/THE IMAGE WORKS)

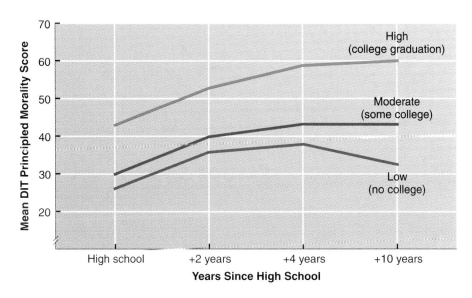

FIGURE 12.2 Relationship of level of schooling completed to principled morality score on the Defining Issues Test (DIT) in a 10-year longitudinal follow-up of high school graduates. (From "The College Experience and Moral Development" by J. R. Rest & D. Narvaez, 1991, in W. M. Kurtines & J. L. Gewirtz, Eds., *Handbook of Moral Behavior and Development*, Vol. 2, Hillsdale, NJ: Lawrence Erlbaum Associates, p. 235. Adapted by permission.)

*Y*oung people growing up on Israeli kibbutzim receive training in the governance of their society at an early age. As a result, they understand the role of societal laws and rules in resolving moral conflict and are advanced in moral reasoning. (LOUIS GOLDMAN/PHOTO RESEARCHERS)

CULTURE. Cross-cultural research reveals that individuals in technologically advanced, urban cultures move through Kohlberg's stages more rapidly and advance to higher levels than do individuals in nonindustrialized, village societies. Stages 4 and above are not reached by members of isolated peasant communities, whereas they are attained by high school- and college-educated adolescents and adults in developed nations (Snarey & Keljo, 1991).

Why these cultural differences exist is a matter of considerable debate. One explanation addresses the role of societal institutions in advanced moral understanding. In traditional village cultures, moral cooperation is based on direct relations between people. Yet Stage 4 to 6 reasoning depends on understanding the role of laws and government institutions in resolving moral conflict (Kohlberg, 1969). In support of this view, in cultures where young people participate in the institutions of their society at early ages, moral reasoning is advanced. For example, on *kibbutzim,* small but technologically complex agricultural settlements in Israel, children receive training in the governance of their community beginning in middle childhood. By third grade, they mention more concerns about societal laws and rules when discussing moral conflicts than do Israeli city-reared or American children (Fuchs et al., 1986). During adolescence and adulthood, a greater percentage of kibbutz than American individuals reach Kohlberg's Stages 4 and 5 (Snarey, Reimer, & Kohlberg, 1985).

A second possible reason for cultural variation in moral understanding is that Kohlberg's dilemmas are not well suited to certain cultures. Some researchers note that in non-Western societies, people occasionally respond in ways that are not easily scorable in Kohlberg's scheme. Recall from Chapter 11 that self-concepts in simpler cultures are less individualistic and more communal than they are in Western nations. This very difference seems to characterize moral reasoning as well (Reid, 1990). In village societies, moral statements that portray the individual as vitally connected to the social group through a deep sense of community responsibility are common. For example, one New Guinea village leader placed the blame for the Heinz dilemma on the entire social group, stating, "If I were the

494

Kohlberg's theory has been the dominant force in moral education for the past quarter-century (Sockett, 1992). His ideas changed over the course of his career, reflecting the tension between two major approaches to moral education. At first, Kohlberg rejected teaching moral content, or a ready-made "bag of virtues." Instead, he stressed improving moral reasoning through discussion of moral dilemmas. Already we have seen that teacher-led peer dialogues about hypothetical moral problems do lead to more mature moral reasoning. But Kohlberg came to question the ability of these interventions to change moral thinking and behavior in everyday life. Eventually he concluded that teaching moral content—kindness, honesty, fairness, and truthfulness—is necessary and compatible with his theory, as long as educators use a rational approach to rule making (Power, Higgins, & Kohlberg, 1989).

Kohlberg enlarged his concept of moral education to include training in moral content, reasoning, and behavior through the **just community,** a small society within a school in which teachers and students practice a democratic way of life. A central feature of the program is the weekly community meeting, in which the entire group gathers to create and refine school policy. Once rules are made, teachers do not stand back; they help students build a commitment to them. For example, at one meeting in a just community school, the group agreed not to allow smoking during a field trip to a movie. Yet as soon as the lights dimmed, several students lit up. The teachers stopped the film and led a short discussion about the importance of upholding agreements. Morality is also fostered through the teaching of subject matter. Students identify moral dilemmas in literature and evaluate and justify courses of action. In social studies, they consider questions of human rights and good citizenship. And in science, they address such moral problems as environmental pollution and nuclear arms.

Do just community programs make a difference in the moral lives of students? When effectively implemented, they can be highly successful. As the moral atmosphere of the school takes shape, students usually express a strong commitment to it. Here is a typical comment of a just community participant: "(Our school) is a real community. People have rights and can bring up issues of concern . . . and people listen to what you have to say, and therefore make you feel like a real person" (Power, Higgins, & Kohlberg, 1989, p. 190). Preliminary research indicates that advances in moral maturity from one year to the next were much greater in just community settings than in traditional or other alternative high schools. And adolescents who felt the strongest sense of community showed the greatest moral stage gains (Higgins, 1991; Power, Higgins, & Kohlberg, 1989).

According to Kohlberg, to understand and feel justice, adolescents have to be both justly treated and called on to act justly. This requires an educational democracy—a school in which everyone has a voice and in which the worth of rules is judged by their fairness to all involved (Sockett, 1992).

---

judge, I would give him only light punishment because he asked everybody for help but nobody helped him" (Tietjen & Walker, 1985, p. 990).

These findings raise the question of whether Kohlberg's highest stages represent a culturally specific rather than universal way of thinking—one limited to Western societies that emphasize individual rights and an appeal to an inner, private conscience. One way to explore this issue is to examine the development of moral reasoning in societies that are just as complex as Western nations but guided by very different philosophical traditions. Turn to the Cultural Influences box on page 496 for research carried out in India that sheds additional light on the cross-cultural validity of Kohlberg's theory.

Are There Sex-Related Differences in Moral Reasoning?

The debate over the universality of Kohlberg's stages has also been extended to gender. Carol Gilligan (1982) is the most well-known figure among those who have argued that Kohlberg's theory does not adequately represent the morality of females. She believes that feminine morality emphasizes an "ethic of care," but Kohlberg's system devalues it. Return to the description of Kohlberg's stages on pages 487–489 and notice how Stage 3 is based on interpersonal obligations. In contrast, Stages 4 to 6 stress justice—an abstract, rational commitment to moral ideals that according to Gilligan, tends to be encouraged in males. In her view, a concern for others is a *different*, not less valid basis for moral judgment than a focus on impersonal rights.

Just community
Kohlberg's approach to moral education, in which a small society of teachers and students practice a democratic way of life.

Was Kohlberg correct that an abstract sense of justice exists that humans everywhere would attain if exposed to adequate educational and social experiences? To investigate this issue, Jyotsna Vasudev and Raymond Hummel (1987) studied the development of moral reasoning in India—a country that is as structurally complex as any Western society and that has a class of adults sufficiently well educated to attain Kohlberg's postconventional level. Yet India's traditions, religions, and philosophies are based on unique moral concepts not found in Western nations. Consequently, the study of moral development among Indian subjects offers an ideal opportunity to test the universality of Kohlberg's theory.

Moral reasoning interviews were conducted with urban middle-class subjects from 11 to over 50 years of age whose religious affiliation was either Hindu, Jain, or Sikh—a group of similar theologies emphasizing nonviolence and the interrelatedness of all forms of life. Consistent with research on Western samples, Indian subjects displayed Kohlberg's age-related sequence of moral understanding, with all three levels represented and 20 percent of adults giving postconventional responses. These findings support Kohlberg's assumption that principled morality is not just a Western phenomenon.

At the same time, themes emerged in Indian subjects' reasoning that did not fit with Kohlberg's stages. For example, an emphasis on collective solutions to moral dilemmas rather than appeals to private conscience appeared among the most morally mature individuals. The Heinz dilemma was especially meaningful to these respondents, who related it to pressing problems of the Indian population. Yet they resisted choosing a course of action, explaining that a moral solution should not be the burden of a single individual but of the entire society. As one woman explained:

> The problems that Heinz is up against are not individual problems that are afflicting 1 or 2 Heinzes of the world. These are social problems. Forget Heinz in Europe, just come to India and you are speaking of the same thing with 60% of the people living below the poverty line. In fact, Heinz's story is being repeated all around us all the time with wives dying, with children dying, and there is no money to save them. . . . So Heinz in his individual capacity—yes, okay, steal the drug, but it's not going to make any difference on a larger scale; and if his wife dies it is not going to make any difference on a larger scale. I don't think in the final analysis a solution can be worked out on an individual basis. . . . It will probably have to be tackled on a macro level. (Vasudev & Hummel, 1987, p. 110)

The collective solutions given by Indian subjects resemble those of Israeli kibbutz and Communist Chinese samples—also not represented in Kohlberg's system (Snarey, Reimer, & Kohlberg, 1985; Walker & Moran, 1991). Kohlberg's justice morality taps an important universal dimension of human moral reasoning. Yet it does not describe the whole domain of morality in every culture. From a cross-cultural perspective, both commonalities and diversity exist in principled moral thought.

Many studies have tested Gilligan's claim that Kohlberg's approach underestimates the moral maturity of females, and most do not support it (Walker, 1991). On hypothetical dilemmas as well as everyday moral problems, adolescent and adult females do not fall behind males in development. Also, themes of justice and caring appear in the responses of both sexes, and when girls do raise interpersonal concerns, they are not downscored in Kohlberg's system (Kahn, 1992; Thoma, 1986; Walker, 1989). These findings suggest that although Kohlberg emphasized justice rather than caring as the highest of moral ideals, his theory does include both sets of values.

Still, Gilligan's claim that research on moral development has been limited by too much attention to rights and justice (a "masculine" ideal) and too little attention to care and responsiveness (a "feminine" ideal) is a powerful one. Some evidence shows that although the morality of males and females taps both orientations, females do tend to stress care, or empathic perspective taking, whereas males either stress justice or use justice and care equally (Galotti, Kozberg, & Farmer, 1991; Gibbs, Arnold, & Burkhart, 1984; Gilligan & Attanucci, 1989). The difference in emphasis appears most often when subjects discuss real-life rather than hypothetical dilemmas. Consequently, it may be largely a function of men's and women's daily lives. In support of this idea, one study found that restricting moral problems to child-rearing concerns eliminated gender differences in reasoning between mothers and fathers. As the researchers noted, men "only needed to have their attention drawn to an important part of their lives to manifest the care concerns already abundantly present" (Clopton & Sorell, 1993, p. 99).

Although current evidence indicates that justice and caring are not gender-specific moralities, Gilligan's work has had the effect of broadening conceptions of the highly moral person. Mary Brabeck (1983) notes:

> When Gilligan and Kohlberg's theories are taken together, the moral person is seen as one whose moral choices reflect reasoned and deliberate judgments that ensure justice be accorded each person while maintaining a passionate concern for the well-being and care of each individual. Justice and care are then joined . . . and the need for autonomy and for interconnection are united in an enlarged and more adequate conception of morality. (p. 289)

Moral Reasoning and Behavior

A central assumption of the cognitive-developmental perspective is that moral understanding should affect moral motivation. As young people grasp the underlying moral "logic" of human social cooperation, they are upset when this logic is violated. As a result, they gradually realize that behaving in line with the way one thinks is an important part of creating and maintaining a just social world (Rest, 1983). On the basis of this idea, Kohlberg predicted a very specific relationship between moral thought and behavior: The two should come closer together as individuals move toward the higher stages of moral understanding (Blasi, 1990).

Consistent with Kohlberg's prediction, advanced moral reasoning is related to many aspects of social behavior (Blasi, 1980). Higher-stage individuals more often engage in prosocial acts, such as helping, sharing, and defending victims of injustice (Gibbs et al., 1986). They are also more honest. For example, they are less likely to cheat on assignments and tests in school (Harris, Mussen, & Rutherford, 1976).

Yet even though a clear connection between moral thought and action exists, it is important to keep in mind that it is only moderate. We have already seen that moral behavior is also influenced by noncognitive factors, including the emotions of empathy and guilt and a long history of experiences that affect moral choice and decision making. Researchers have yet to discover how all these complex facets of morality work together (Blasi, 1983).

Further Questions About Kohlberg's Theory

Although there is much support for Kohlberg's theory, it continues to face some challenges. The most important of these concern the relationship of moral structure to content, Kohlberg's conception of moral maturity, and the appropriateness of his stages for characterizing the moral reasoning of young children.

Kohlberg's emphasis on structure rather than content to assess moral development has troubled many researchers. Although he acknowledged that these two aspects merge at the postconventional level into a mature vision of morality, the relation between structure and content at the first four stages is less clear. Progress through these stages hardly seems to be of much consequence unless it also brings about more valid moral commitments. To fully verify Kohlberg's theory, current researchers need to clarify how each advance in moral structure leads to improvements in moral content, or particular kinds of moral choice (Lapsley, Enright, & Serlin, 1989; Walker, 1989).

A related controversy has to do with Kohlberg's belief that moral maturity is not achieved until the postconventional level. Yet if people had to reach Stages 5 and 6 to be considered truly morally mature, few individuals anywhere would measure up! Recall that postconventional morality is attained only in industrialized societies by a highly educated, elite few. John Gibbs (1991) questions the appropriateness of the term "conventional level," pointing out that the reasoning to which it refers already entails moral maturity. Stages 3 and 4 require vital moral constructions—an understanding of mutual trust as the basis for obligations between people and of widely accepted moral standards as necessary for the continuation of society. Gibbs believes that "postconventional morality" should not be viewed as the level against which others are judged immature. Instead, he regards such reasoning as a reflective, philosophical orientation beyond the realm of spontaneous, everyday moral thought.

Finally, Kohlberg's stages largely describe changes in moral reasoning during adolescence and adulthood. They tell us little about moral understanding in early and middle childhood. Indeed, Kohlberg's moral dilemmas are remote from the experiences of most young children and may not be clearly understood by them. When children are given moral problems related to their everyday lives, their responses indicate that Kohlberg's preconventional level, much like Piaget's heteronomous morality, underestimates their moral reasoning. We take a close look at this evidence in the following sections.

Brief Review

According to Kohlberg's three-level, six-stage theory, morality changes from concrete, externally oriented reasoning to more abstract, principled justifications for moral choices. Each moral stage builds on cognitive and perspective-taking capacities. Research suggests a powerful role for environmental contexts in the development of moral understanding. Advanced moral reasoning is not attained unless supports exist on many levels, including family, peers, schooling, and wider society. Although Kohlberg's theory emphasizes a morality of justice rather than a morality of care, it does not underestimate the moral maturity of females. As individuals advance through Kohlberg's stages, moral reasoning becomes better related to behavior. Recent challenges to Kohlberg's theory question its assumptions about the relation of moral structure to content, its definition of moral maturity, and its view of the moral reasoning of young children.

MORAL REASONING OF YOUNG CHILDREN

Researchers using moral dilemmas specifically designed for children have addressed three facets of their moral understanding: (1) their ability to distinguish moral rules from social conventions; (2) their ideas about fair distribution of rewards; and (3) their prosocial reasoning—how they choose between self-interest and meeting the needs of others. Besides being relevant to children's real-life experiences, the moral problems used in these studies differ from Kohlberg's in that the role of laws and the possibility of punishment are deemphasized. When dilemmas are formulated in these ways, young children reveal some surprisingly advanced moral judgments.

Moral versus Social-Conventional Understanding

Piaget and Kohlberg regarded the young child's moral understanding as superficial and externally motivated. Yet as early as age 3, children have a beginning grasp of justice. Many studies reveal that preschool and young grade-school children distinguish *moral rules*, which protect people's rights and welfare, from *social conventions*, arbitrary customs such as dress styles, table manners, and rituals of social interaction (Nucci, 1981; Nucci & Turiel, 1978; Smetana, 1981, 1985). In one study, 2- and 3-year-olds were interviewed about drawings depicting familiar moral and social conventional transgressions. For example, a moral picture showed a child stealing an agemate's apple; a social-conventional picture showed a child eating ice cream with fingers. By 34 months, children viewed moral transgressions as more generalizably wrong (not okay regardless of the setting in which they are committed). And by 42 months, they indicated that moral (but not social-conventional) violations would still be wrong if an adult did not see them and no rules existed to prohibit them (Smetana & Braeges, 1990).

How do young children come to make these distinctions? According to Elliott Turiel (1983), not through parental instruction, since adults insist that children conform to social conventions just as often as they press for obedience to moral rules. Instead, children actively make sense of their experiences in both types of situations. They observe that people respond differently to violations of moral rules than breaks with social convention. When a moral offense occurs, children react emotionally, describe their own injury or loss, tell another child to stop, or retaliate. And an adult who intervenes is likely to call attention to the rights and feelings of the victim. In contrast, children often do not respond to violations of social convention. And in these situations, adults tend to demand obedience without explanation, as when they state, "Say the magic word!" or "Don't eat with your fingers" (Smetana, 1989; Turiel, Smetana, & Killen, 1991).

Turiel makes a strong case for early emergence of distinct moral and social-conventional domains of understanding. Yet the very criticism of Kohlberg's theory mentioned earlier—that it overemphasizes individual rights—has also been leveled at the moral–social-conventional distinction (Witherell & Edwards, 1991). Although non-Western children also separate morality from social convention, the dichotomy is often less sharp. For example, 8- to 10-year-old Hindu children agree with their American counterparts that breaking promises, destroying another person's property, and kicking harmless animals are morally wrong. At the same time, they regard food and politeness transgressions, such as eating chicken the day after a father's death or calling parents by their first names, as far more serious than selfish behavior or even family violence (Shweder, Mahapatra, & Miller, 1990). In India, as in many developing countries, culturally specific practices that strike Western outsiders as arbitrary customs often have profound moral and religious significance.

Clearly, children grapple with the distinction between moral rules and social conventions at a remarkably early age. Yet the boundary drawn between them varies considerably and is a joint product of cognitive development and social experience. We are reminded, once again, that there are both cultural universals and diversity in moral thought.

Distributive Justice

In everyday life, children frequently experience situations that involve **distributive justice**—beliefs about how to divide up resources fairly. Heated discussions often take place over how much weekly allowance is to be given to siblings of different ages, who has to sit where in the family car on a long trip, and in what way an eight-slice pizza is to be shared by six hungry playmates. William Damon (1977, 1988) has studied changing concepts of distributive justice over early and

These five children have figured out how to divide up two pizzas fairly among themselves. Already, they have a well-developed sense of distributive justice. (JEFF DUNN/THE PICTURE CUBE)

Distributive justice
Beliefs about how to divide up material goods fairly.

TABLE 12.3 Damon's Sequence of Distributive Justice Reasoning

BASIS OF REASONING	AGE	DESCRIPTION
Equality	5–6 years	Fairness involves strictly equal distribution of goods. Special considerations like merit and need are not taken into account.
Merit	6–7 years	Fairness is based on deservingness. Children recognize that some people should get more because they have worked harder.
Benevolence	8 years	Fairness includes giving special consideration to those who are disadvantaged. More should be given to those who are in need.

SOURCE: Damon, 1977, 1988.

middle childhood by asking children to resolve dilemmas like the ones just mentioned. His developmental sequence is supported by both cross-sectional and longitudinal evidence (Enright et al., 1984; Enright, Franklin, & Manheim, 1980).

Even 4-year-olds recognize the importance of sharing, but their reasons for doing so often seem contradictory and self-serving. When asked why they gave some of their toys to a playmate, preschoolers typically say something like this: "I shared because if I didn't, she wouldn't play with me"; or "I let her have some, but most are for me because I'm older."

As children enter middle childhood, they start to express more mature notions of distributive justice (see Table 12.3). At first, their ideas of fairness are based on *equality.* Children in the early school grades are intent on making sure that each person gets the same amount of a treasured resource, such as money, turns in a game, or a delicious treat.*

A short time later, children start to view fairness in terms of *merit.* Extra rewards should be given to someone who has worked especially hard or otherwise performed in an exceptional way. Finally, around 8 years, children can reason on the basis of *benevolence.* They recognize that special consideration should be given to those in a condition of disadvantage, like the needy or the handicapped. Children of this age say that an extra amount might be given to a child who cannot produce as much or does not get any allowance from his parents. They also adapt their basis of fairness to fit the situation—for example, relying more on equality when allocating votes in an election and more on merit and benevolence when distributing material goods (Sigelman & Waitzman, 1991).

According to Damon (1988), parental advice and encouragement support these developing standards of justice, but the give-and-take of peer interaction is especially important. Peer disagreements, along with efforts to resolve them, make children more sensitive to others' perspectives, and this supports their developing ideas of fairness (Kruger, 1992). Advanced distributive justice reasoning, in turn, is associated with more effective social problem solving and a greater willingness to help and share with others (Blotner & Bearison, 1984; McNamee & Peterson, 1986).

Research on children's concepts of distributive justice indicates that they construct complex notions of fairness much earlier than Piaget and Kohlberg believed. In fact, fear of punishment and respect for authority do not even appear as themes

*Recall from Chapter 6 that in some cultures, equal sharing of goods among children is not common, and conservation is greatly delayed (see pages 246–247). It is possible that Damon's sequence of distributive justice reasoning does not represent children's concepts of fairness in all societies.

in children's distributive justice rationales. Because Damon's dilemmas minimize the relevance of these factors to moral choice, they permit some impressively mature moral reasoning to rise to the surface.

Prosocial Reasoning

Return for a moment to Kohlberg's Heinz dilemma, and notice how to help his wife, Heinz has no choice but to break the law and steal. In most everyday situations in which children must decide whether to act prosocially, the cost is not disobeying the law or an authority figure. Instead, it is not satisfying one's own wants or needs. Nancy Eisenberg asked preschoolers through twelfth-graders to respond to prosocial dilemmas in which the primary sacrifice in aiding another person is giving up personal desires. Here is a typical one given to younger children:

> One day a girl named Mary was going to a friend's birthday party. On her way she saw a girl who had fallen down and hurt her leg. The girl asked Mary to go to her house and get her parents so the parents could come and take her to the doctor. But if Mary did run and get the child's parents, she would be late for the birthday party and miss the ice cream, cake, and all the games. What should Mary do? Why? (Eisenberg, 1982, p. 231)

Conducting both cross-sectional and longitudinal research, Eisenberg found that responses formed the age-related sequence summarized in Table 12.4 (Eisenberg, Lennon, & Roth, 1983; Eisenberg et al., 1987, 1991; Eisenberg-Berg, 1979; Eisenberg-Berg & Roth, 1980).

Notice how Eisenberg's developmental levels resemble Kohlberg's stages. For example, her hedonistic, pragmatic orientation is like Kohlberg's Stage 2, her approval-focused orientation is like Kohlberg's Stage 3, and her internalized values orientation includes forms of reasoning that seem to match Kohlberg's Stages 4 to 6. But several features of Eisenberg's findings depart from Kohlberg's. Once again, punishment- and authority-oriented reasoning is absent from children's responses.

TABLE 12.4 Eisenberg's Levels of Prosocial Reasoning

LEVEL	APPROXIMATE AGE	DESCRIPTION
Hedonistic, pragmatic orientation	Preschool, early elementary school	Right behavior satisfies one's own needs. Reasons for helping or not helping refer to gains for the self—for example, "I wouldn't help because I might be hungry."
"Needs of others" orientation	Preschool, elementary school	Concern for the physical, material, and psychological needs of others is expressed in simple terms, without clear evidence of perspective taking or empathic feeling—for example, "He needs it."
Stereotyped, approval-focused orientation	Elementary school and secondary school	Stereotyped images of good and bad people and concern for approval justify behavior—for example, "He'd like him more if he helped."
Empathic orientation	Later elementary school and secondary school	Reasoning reflects an emphasis on perspective taking and empathic feeling for the other person—for example, "I'd feel bad if I didn't help because he'd be in pain."
Internalized values orientation	Small minority of secondary school students, no elementary school pupils	Justifications for moral choice are based on internalized values, norms, desire to maintain contractual obligations, and belief in the dignity, rights, and equality of all individuals—for example, "I would feel bad if I didn't help because I'd know that I didn't live up to my values."

SOURCE: Eisenberg, 1982.

Also, children's prosocial understanding is clearly advanced when compared to the timing of Kohlberg's stages.

Finally, prosocial dilemmas bring out a form of moral reasoning that Eisenberg calls "empathic." By the late elementary school years, children realize that empathy is an important motivator of prosocial behavior. In one study, 9- and 10-year-olds who empathized easily advanced to higher levels of prosocial understanding during early adolescence (Eisenberg et al., 1987). According to Eisenberg, empathic feelings may encourage more mature prosocial thought and strengthen its realization in everyday behavior. In line with this idea, young people at the highest prosocial levels do tend to respond more altruistically than those who are less advanced (Eisenberg-Berg, 1979; Eisenberg-Berg & Hand, 1979; Eisenberg et al., 1991). Eisenberg is one researcher who has made a start at putting the cognitive, affective, and behavioral components of morality together.

The research reviewed in the preceding sections reveals that moral understanding in childhood is a rich, diverse phenomenon not completely described by any single theory. Children's responses to a wide range of moral problems, including ones that focus on justice, fair distribution, and prosocial behavior, are needed to comprehensively represent the development of moral thought.

Brief Review

When children are asked to reason about moral problems in which the role of laws and the possibility of punishment are deemphasized, they display moral judgments that are considerably more advanced than predicted by Piaget and Kohlberg. Even preschoolers have a beginning grasp of justice in that they distinguish moral rules from social conventions. During middle childhood, children's notions of how to divide up resources fairly become more differentiated and adapted to the requirements of situations. Prosocial moral dilemmas yield earlier attainment of advanced forms of moral reasoning than Kohlberg's sequence suggests.

DEVELOPMENT OF SELF-CONTROL

The study of moral reasoning tells us what people think they would do and why when faced with a moral problem. But we have already indicated that people's good intentions often fall short. Whether children and adults act in accord with their beliefs depends in part on characteristics we call will power, firm resolve, or, put more simply, **self-control.** Self-control in the moral domain involves inhibiting an impulse to engage in behavior that violates a moral standard. Sometimes it is called resistance to temptation. In the first part of this chapter, we noted that inductive discipline and models who demonstrate as well as verbalize self-controlled behavior foster children's self-control. But these practices become effective only when children develop the ability to resist temptation. When and how does the child's capacity for self-control develop?

Beginnings of Self-Control

The beginnings of self-control are supported by cognitive achievements of the second year that we discussed in earlier chapters. To behave in a self-controlled fashion, children must have some ability to think of themselves as separate, autonomous beings who can direct their own actions. And they must also have the representational and memory capacities to internalize a caregiver's directive and apply it to their own behavior (Kopp, 1987).

As these abilities mature, the first glimmerings of self-control appear in the form of **compliance.** Between 12 and 18 months, children start to show clear awareness of caregivers' wishes and expectations and can voluntarily obey simple requests and commands (Kaler & Kopp, 1990; Luria, 1961). And, as every parent

Self-control

Inhibiting an impulse to engage in behavior that violates a moral standard.

Compliance

Voluntary obedience to requests and commands.

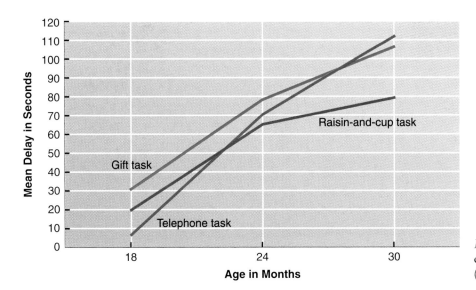

FIGURE 12.3 Age changes in delay of gratification between 18 and 30 months of age.
(Adapted from Vaughn, Kopp, & Krakow, 1984.)

knows, they can also decide to do just the opposite! One way toddlers assert their emerging sense of autonomy is by resisting adult directives. But among those who experience warm, sensitive caregiving and reasonable expectations for mature behavior, opposition is far less common than compliance (Crockenberg & Litman, 1990). For most toddlers, resistance is gradually transformed into polite refusals and skilled efforts to negotiate compromises with parents over the preschool years (Kuczynski et al., 1987; Kuczynski & Kochanska, 1990).

Parents are usually delighted at toddlers' newfound ability to comply, since it indicates that they are ready to learn the rules of social life. Nevertheless, control of the child's actions during the second year depends heavily on prompts from caregivers (Kopp, 1987). According to Vygotsky (1934/1986), children cannot guide their own behavior until they incorporate adult standards into their own speech and use it to instruct the self. Recall from Chapter 6 that this self-directed form of language is called *private speech.* The development of compliance quickly leads to toddlers' first consciencelike verbalizations—for example, correcting the self by saying "no, can't" before touching a light socket, jumping on the sofa, or taking candy from a forbidden dish (Kochanska, 1993).

Researchers typically study self-control by creating situations in the laboratory much like the ones just mentioned. Notice how each calls for **delay of gratification**—waiting for a more appropriate time and place to engage in a tempting act or obtain a desired object. In one study, 18-, 24-, and 30-month-old children were given three delay-of-gratification tasks. In the first, they were asked not to touch an interesting toy telephone that was within arm's reach. In the second, raisins were hidden under cups, and they were instructed to wait until the experimenter said it was all right to pick up a cup and eat a raisin. In the third, they were told not to open a gift until the experimenter had finished her work. As Figure 12.3 shows, on all three problems the ability to delay gratification increased substantially between 18 and 30 months. Furthermore, by 30 months, clear individual differences in the capacity for self-control were present. Consistent with Vygotsky's theory, the single best predictor of them was language development (Vaughn, Kopp, & Krakow, 1984).

Children's ability to engage in socially approved behaviors and to inhibit undesirable behaviors leads caregiver expectations to increase. Recently, Heidi Gralinski and Claire Kopp (1993) asked mothers to indicate which things they require or encourage their young children to do and which things they insist they not do between 13 and 30 months of age. As Figure 12.4 reveals, rules expanded from a narrow focus on safety, property, and respect for others to a broader emphasis on the realities of living in a social world. Gradually, mothers placed more emphasis on issues related to family routines, self-care, and independence until, at 30 months,

Delay of gratification
Waiting for a more appropriate time and place to engage in a tempting act or obtain a desired object.

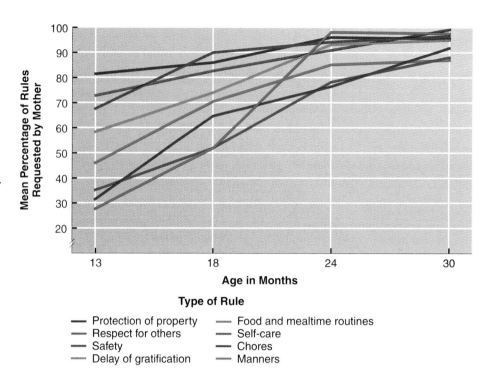

FIGURE 12.4 Percentage of eight types of rules mothers reported asking of their 13- to 30-month-old children. Mothers emphasized safety, property, and respect rules early. As children's capacity for self-control increased over this age period, mothers introduced a wider array of rule expectations related to the realities of living in a social world. (From "Everyday Rules for Behavior: Mothers' Requests to Young Children" by J. H. Gralinski & C. B. Kopp, 1993, *Developmental Psychology, 29*, p. 579. Copyright © 1993 by the American Psychological Association. Reprinted by permission.)

all rules were stressed to the same degree. If you compare these trends with the gains depicted in Figure 12.3, you will see that overall, mothers' expectations dovetail nicely with children's emerging capacity for self-control.

Development of Self-Control in Childhood and Adolescence

Although the capacity for self-control is in place by the third year, it is not complete. Cognitive development—in particular, improvements in attention and mental representation—permits children to use a variety of effective self-instructional strategies for resisting temptation. As a result, delay of gratification undergoes steady improvement during childhood and adolescence (Mischel, Shoda, & Rodriguez, 1989).

STRATEGIES FOR SELF-CONTROL. Walter Mischel (1974) has studied exactly what children think and say to themselves that promotes gains in resistance to temptation. In several studies, preschoolers were shown two rewards: a highly desirable one that they would have to wait for and a less desirable one that they could have anytime during the waiting period. Informal observations revealed that allocation of attention was especially important in the ability to delay gratification. Rather than focusing on the rewards, the most self-controlled preschoolers used any technique they could think of to divert themselves from the desired objects, including covering their eyes, inventing games with their hands and feet, singing, and even trying to go to sleep!

In everyday situations, preschoolers find it difficult to keep their minds off tempting activities and objects for very long. When their thoughts do turn to an enticing but prohibited goal, the way children mentally represent it has much to do with their success at self-control. Mischel found that teaching children to transform the stimulus in ways that deemphasize its arousing qualities is highly effective in promoting delay of gratification. In one study, some preschoolers were told to think about marshmallows imaginatively as "white and puffy clouds." Others were asked to focus on their realistic, "sweet and chewy properties." Children in the stimulus-transforming, imaginative condition waited much longer before eating the marshmallow reward (Mischel & Baker, 1975).

The development of self-control is well under way by the time children enter school, where they are frequently required to delay gratification. Standing in line is a common event in the lives of these pupils, who have developed strategies for waiting patiently. (JIM PICKERELL)

In the study just described, an experimenter taught young children to use delay-enhancing strategies. How good are they at thinking up these techniques on their own? Research shows that when an adult refrains from giving preschoolers instructions in how to resist temptation, their ability to wait in delay-of-gratification tasks declines considerably. In contrast, first- and second-graders do just as well regardless of whether an adult provides them with strategies or not (Toner & Smith, 1977). These findings indicate that not until the early elementary school years are children very good at thinking up their own strategies for resisting temptation. By this time, self-control has been transformed into a flexible capacity for *moral self-regulation*—the ability to monitor one's own conduct, constantly adjusting it as circumstances present opportunities to violate inner standards (Bandura, 1991; Kopp, 1987).

KNOWLEDGE OF STRATEGIES. In Chapter 7, we indicated that metacognitive knowledge, or awareness of strategies, plays an important role in the development of self-regulation. When 3- to 11-year-olds were interviewed to find out how much they knew about situational conditions and self-instructions likely to help them do well on a delay-of-gratification task, preschoolers thought of only a few tactics, such as "Close two eyes" and "Talk to the wall." Sometimes they mentioned ineffective techniques, such as looking at the rewards "because it makes me feel good," thereby defeating their own efforts at self-control (Mischel & Mischel, 1983).

Over middle childhood, children suggested an increasingly broad array of successful strategies and explained why they worked by referring to their arousal-reducing properties. But not until the late elementary school years did they mention techniques involving transformations of rewards or their own arousal states. For example, one 11-year-old recommended saying, "the marshmallows are filled with an evil spell." Another said he would tell himself, "I hate marshmallows, I can't stand them. But when the grown-up gets back, I'll tell myself 'I love marshmallows' and eat it" (Mischel & Mischel, 1983, p. 609).

Perhaps awareness of the importance of transforming ideation appears so late in development because it requires the abstract, hypothetical reasoning powers of formal operational thought. But once this advanced metacognitive understanding emerges, it facilitates moral self-regulation. In a study of older children with social adjustment difficulties attending a special summer camp, those who knew that an abstract representation of a reward would help them delay used more effective strategies and were able to wait longer in the presence of tempting objects. Furthermore, their self-regulatory skills generalized to everyday life. Children who performed well in a laboratory delay situation were rated as getting along better with peers throughout the summer (Rodriguez, Mischel, & Shoda, 1989).

MILESTONES

MORAL DEVELOPMENT

Age	Moral Internalization	Moral Construction	Self-Control
1½–2 years	• Concern with deviations from standards first appears. • Modeling of a wide variety of prosocial acts begins. 		• Compliance and delay of gratification emerge.
3–6 years	• Guilt reactions to transgressions first appear. • By the end of this period, internalization of many prosocial standards and prohibitions has occurred.	• Sensitivity to intentions in making moral judgments is present. • Complex, differentiated notions about the legitimacy of authority figures are formed. • Distinction between moral rules and social conventions develops. • Distributive justice and prosocial moral reasoning are self-serving. • At the end of this period, distributive justice is based on equality.	• Delay of gratification improves. • Adult-provided strategies assist with self-control; children can generate only a few strategies on their own. • Self-control is transformed into a flexible capacity for moral self-regulation.
7–11 years	• Internalization of societal norms continues.	• Preconventional responses to Kohlberg's hypothetical moral dilemmas, focusing on rewards, punishment, and the power of authority figures, are common. • Distributive justice reasoning includes merit and, eventually, benevolence; the basis of fairness is adapted to the situation. • Prosocial moral reasoning reflects concern with others' needs and approval. 	• Generation of self-control strategies increases in variety. • Awareness of effective self-control strategies and why they work expands.
12 years–adulthood		• Conventional responses to Kohlberg's hypothetical moral dilemmas, emphasizing human relationships and societal order, increase. • Moral thought and action become integrated as individuals move toward Kohlberg's higher stages. • Postconventional responses to Kohlberg's hypothetical moral dilemmas, reflecting abstract principles and values, appear among a few highly educated individuals in Western cultures. • Prosocial moral reasoning reflects empathic feelings, norms, and abstract values. 	• Moral self-regulation continues to improve.

Note: These milestones represent overall age trends. Individual differences exist in the precise age at which each milestone is attained. Also, see Chapter 10, page 406, for additional milestones related to morally relevant emotions of empathy and guilt.

INDIVIDUAL DIFFERENCES. Longitudinal research reveals modest stability in children's capacity to manage their behavior in a morally relevant fashion. Mischel and his collaborators found that 4-year-olds able to wait longer in delay-of-gratification tasks were especially adept as adolescents in applying metacognitive and self-regulatory skills to their behavior. Their parents saw them as more verbally fluent and responsive to reason; as better at concentrating and planning ahead; and as coping with stress more maturely. When applying to college, those who had been self-controlled preschoolers scored somewhat higher on the Scholastic Aptitude Test (SAT), although they were no more intelligent than children less able to resist temptation (Mischel, Shoda, & Peake, 1988; Shoda, Mischel, & Peake, 1990). Other studies following children over many years report similar findings (Funder, Block, & Block, 1983).

Researchers believe these enduring individual differences are the combined result of temperamental characteristics and child-rearing practices (Kochanska, 1993). Consistent with this idea, impulsive children, who often act without thinking and are hot-tempered when they do not get their way, show deficits in moral self-regulation. In a recent study, toddlers rated high in impulsivity had a weaker internalized conscience when studied again at 8 to 10 years of age, in that they responded with fewer expressions of guilt and reparation to stories involving transgressions (Kochanska, 1991). In Chapter 10, we noted that a mismatch between a child's temperamental style and parenting practices can undermine psychological adjustment for many years to come. As we will see in the final section of this chapter, when temperamentally vulnerable children are exposed to highly power-assertive, inconsistent discipline, they display long-term, serious problems in observing standards of conduct. But before we turn to the topic of aggression, you may find it helpful to review the moral changes we have discussed throughout this chapter, which are summarized in the Milestones table on page 506.

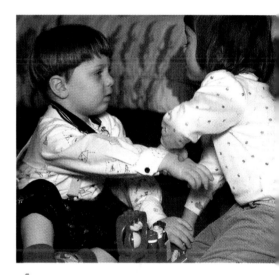

*A*n occasional expression of aggression is normal among young children. These preschoolers display instrumental aggression as they struggle over an attractive toy. Instrumental aggression declines with age as children learn how to compromise and share. (RITA MANNINI/PHOTO RESEARCHERS)

THE OTHER SIDE OF SELF-CONTROL: DEVELOPMENT OF AGGRESSION

Beginning in late infancy, all children display aggression from time to time, and as opportunities to interact with siblings and peers increase, aggressive outbursts occur more often. But recall from Chapter 11 that conflicts between young children are far less frequent than friendly, cooperative interaction. An occasional aggressive act is normal and to be expected, and these encounters often become important learning experiences as adults intervene and teach children alternative ways of satisfying desires. Nevertheless, as early as the preschool years, some children show abnormally high rates of aggression. They lash out with verbal insults and physical assaults in situations that appear to involve little or no provocation. Allowed to continue, their belligerent behavior can lead to lasting deficits in moral development and self-control and to an antisocial life-style. To understand this process, let's see how aggression develops during childhood and adolescence.

Emergence of Aggression

During the second half of the first year, infants develop the cognitive capacity to identify sources of anger and frustration and the motor skills to lash out at them (see Chapter 10). As a result, two forms of aggression emerge. The most common is **instrumental aggression.** In this form, children are not deliberately hostile. Instead, they want an object, privilege, or space, and in trying to get it, they push, shout at, or otherwise attack a person who is in the way. The other type, **hostile aggression,** is meant to hurt, as when the child hits, insults, or tattles on a playmate with no other aim in mind than to injure the other person.

Instrumental aggression
Aggression aimed at obtaining an object, privilege, or space with no deliberate intent to harm another person.

Hostile aggression
Aggression intended to harm another person.

Both the form of aggression and the way it is expressed change with age. In a classic study, mothers were asked to keep records of their children's angry outbursts. Physical aggression was gradually replaced by verbal aggression over the preschool years (Goodenough, 1931). Rapid language development contributes to this change, but it is also due to adults' and peers' strong negative reactions to pushing, hitting, and biting (Parke & Slaby, 1983). In another study, aggressive acts of 4- to 7-year-olds were recorded at school. Instrumental aggression declined over this age period, whereas hostile, person-oriented outbursts increased. An interesting finding was that tattling, criticism, and ridicule seldom provoked aggression in 4- and 5-year-olds but often did in 6- and 7-year-olds (Hartup, 1974). Older children seem better able to "read" malicious behavior in others and, as a result, more often respond with a hostile retaliation.

Although children of both sexes show this general pattern of development, on the average boys are more aggressive than girls, a trend that appears in many cultures around the world (Whiting & Edwards, 1988). In Chapter 13, when we take up sex-related differences in aggression in greater detail, we will see that biological factors—in particular, male sex hormones, or androgens—are influential. In humans, androgens contribute to boys' higher rate of physical activity, which seems to increase their opportunities for aggressive encounters (Parsons, 1982). At the same time, the development of gender roles is important. As soon as 2-year-olds become dimly aware of gender stereotypes—that males and females are expected to behave differently—aggression drops off in girls but is maintained in boys (Fagot & Leinbach, 1989; Fagot, Leinbach, & Hagen, 1986). Then, parents' tendency to discipline boys more harshly magnifies this effect.

From middle childhood on, aggression is a highly stable personality characteristic, especially among males (Cairns et al., 1989). In a longitudinal investigation that spanned 22 years, very aggressive 8-year-olds became 30-year-olds who were more likely to score high in aggressive inclinations on a personality test, use severe punishment with their children, and be convicted of criminal offenses (see

FIGURE 12.5 Relationship of childhood aggression to criminal behavior in adulthood for males and females. (From "Stability of Aggression Over Time and Generations" by L. R. Huesmann, L. D. Eron, M. M. Lefkowitz, & L. O. Walder, 1984, *Developmental Psychology, 20,* p. 1125. Copyright © 1984 by the American Psychological Association. Reprinted by permission.)

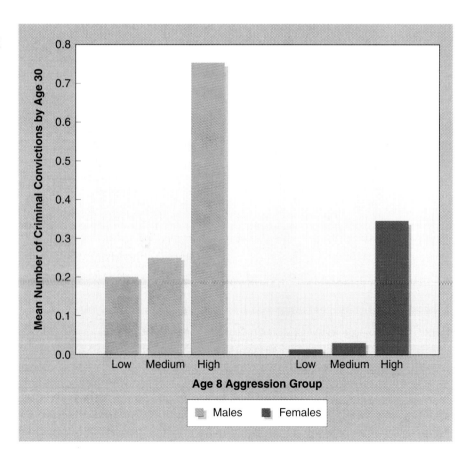

Figure 12.5). In this study, the researchers also tracked the aggressive tendencies of the subjects' family members and found strong continuity across generations. Highly aggressive children were more likely to have parents and grandparents who were antisocial themselves and whose behavior problems were apparent in their own childhoods (Huesmann et al., 1984).

In recent years, researchers have made considerable progress in identifying individual and environmental factors that sustain aggressive behavior. Although some children—especially those who are impulsive and overactive—are clearly at risk for high aggression, a large body of evidence indicates that whether or not they become so depends on child-rearing conditions (Landau & McAninch, 1993). Strife-ridden families, poor parenting practices, and exposure to televised violence are strongly linked to children's antisocial acts. In this chapter, we focus on family influences, reserving the topic of television for Chapter 15.

The Family as Training Ground for Aggressive Behavior

The same child-rearing practices that undermine the development of moral internalization and self-control are correlated with aggression. Love withdrawal, power assertion, physical punishment, and inconsistent discipline are linked to antisocial behavior from early childhood through adolescence, in children of both sexes (Parke & Slaby, 1983). Parents who use these tactics fail to teach acceptable alternatives, serve as aggressive models, and frustrate their children's need for nurturance so that they vent their anger on others. These ineffective and destructive techniques are often found together in the same family, compounding their harmful consequences (Olweus, 1980).

Home observations of aggressive children reveal that anger and punitiveness quickly spread from one family member to another, creating a conflict-ridden family atmosphere and an "out-of-control" child (Holden & Ritchie, 1991; Patterson, DeBaryshe, & Ramsey, 1989). As Figure 12.6 shows, the pattern begins with coercive parental discipline, which is made more likely by stressful life experiences, the parent's own personality, or a temperamentally difficult child. Once the parent threatens, criticizes, and punishes, then the child whines, yells, and refuses until the parent finds the child's behavior to be too much and "gives in." The sequence is likely to be repeated, since at the end of each exchange, both parent and child get relief for

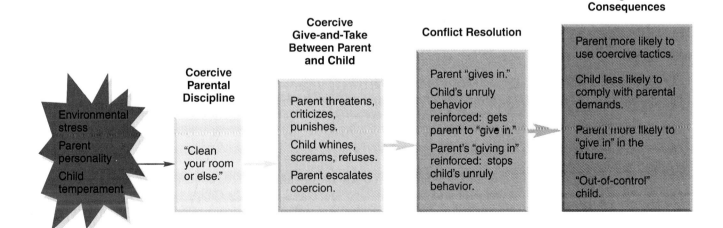

FIGURE 12.6 Coercive interaction pattern that induces and sustains aggression among family members.

Helping Children and Parents Control Aggression

Help for aggressive children must break the cycle of hostilities between family members and promote effective ways of understanding and relating to others. Interventions with preschool and school-age children have been most successful. Once antisocial patterns persist into adolescence, so many factors act to sustain them that treatment is far more difficult (Kazdin, 1987).

CATHARSIS: AN UNSUCCESSFUL STRATEGY. In the past, a widely held belief was that **cathartic treatment** could reduce aggressive behavior. The idea was originally inspired by psychoanalytic theory, which assumed that aggressive urges gradually build up and, unless drained off, result in hostile outbursts. The cathartic approach involves offering safe opportunities to engage in aggression, such as a session with a punching bag. Another technique is to provide passive exposure to the aggression of others. Violent television and reading materials are assumed to discharge hostility as children identify with aggressive characters and experience their behavior indirectly.

From what we have said about modeling in this and other chapters, are you doubtful about the success of cathartic treatment? If so, you are correct. It has received little research support. In fact, it can heighten aggressive tendencies (Liebert & Sprafkin, 1988; Mallick & McCandless, 1966).

COACHING, MODELING, AND REINFORCING ALTERNATIVE BEHAVIORS. Procedures based on social learning theory have been devised to interrupt destructive family interaction. Gerald Patterson (1982) has designed a successful parent-training program of this kind. A therapist provides modeling and coaching in child discipline by observing the parent's inept practices, demonstrating alternatives, and insisting that the parent practice them. Parents learn not to give in to an acting-out child and not to escalate forceful attempts to control misbehavior. In addition, they are taught to pair commands with reasons and to replace verbal insults and spankings with more effective strategies, such as time out and withdrawal of privileges. Research reveals that after only a few weeks of such training, antisocial behavior declined and parents began to view their children more positively—gains still evident a year later (Patterson & Fleishman, 1979; Patterson et al., 1975).

On the child's side, interventions that teach alternative ways of resolving conflict that are incompatible with aggression are helpful. Sessions in which children model and role-play cooperation and sharing and see that these behaviors lead to rewarding social outcomes reduce aggression and increase positive social behavior (Zahavi & Asher, 1978). Once aggressive children begin to change, parents need to be reminded to give them attention and approval for their prosocial acts (Patterson, 1982). The coercive cycles of parents and aggressive children are so pervasive that these children often get punished when they do behave appropriately!

SOCIAL-COGNITIVE INTERVENTIONS. The social-cognitive deficits of aggressive children prevent them from experiencing empathy to another person's pain and suffering—an important inhibitor of aggressive behavior. Furthermore, since aggressive children have few opportunities to witness family members acting in sensitive, caring ways, they miss early experiences that are vital for promoting empathic responding (see Chapter 10). In such children, empathy may have to be directly taught. In one program, sessions in which children practiced identifying others' feelings and expressing their own reduced hostility among peers and increased cooperation, helping, and generosity (Feshbach & Feshbach, 1982). Empathy training necessarily involves taking the perspectives of others. In Chapter 11, we showed that the antisocial acts of delinquent and troubled adolescents could be reduced through a role-playing intervention that improved perspective taking. Perhaps this intervention worked so well because it promoted empathic responding, which served as a deterrent to aggressive behavior.

Cathartic treatment
A form of treatment for aggressive behavior that assumes hostile impulses can be drained off through opportunities to engage in aggression or through passive exposure to the aggression of others. Has received little research support.

COMPREHENSIVE APPROACHES. According to some researchers, effective treatment for antisocial children and youths needs to be multifaceted, encompassing social understanding, relating to others, and self-control. Although only a few such efforts have been tried, their success supports the power of a comprehensive approach. In one program addressing both social-cognitive deficits and self-control difficulties of aggressive adolescents, participants improved in social problem-solving skills, reduced their endorsement of beliefs supporting aggression, and were rated as less impulsive and aggressive compared to controls (Guerra & Slaby, 1990). In another intervention, teacher-nominated antisocial youths who discussed moral dilemmas over a 4-month period and who also received training in listening, communicating, and caring for one another showed gains in moral judgment and behavior (including improved grades, school attendance, and conduct) that persisted for at least a year after treatment (Arbuthnot & Gordon, 1986; see also Leeman, Gibbs, & Fuller, 1993).

Yet even these multidimensional treatments can fall short if children remain embedded in hostile home lives, antisocial peer groups, and violent neighborhood settings. Intensive efforts to create nonaggressive environments—at the family, community, and cultural levels—are needed to support the interventions just described and to ensure optimal development of all children. We will return to this theme several times in later chapters.

CHAPTER SUMMARY

Morality as Rooted in Human Nature

- The biological perspective on moral development is represented by a controversial field called **sociobiology.** It assumes that morality is grounded in the genetic heritage of our species, perhaps through prewired emotional reactions. Although human morality cannot be fully explained in this way, the biological perspective reminds us of the adaptive significance of moral behavior.

Morality as the Adoption of Societal Norms

- Psychoanalytic and social learning theories regard moral development as a matter of **internalization:** the adoption of preexisting, ready-made standards of conduct as one's own.

- According to Freud, morality emerges with the resolution of the Oedipus and Electra conflicts during the phallic stage of development. Fear of punishment and loss of parental love lead children to form a **superego** through **identification** with the same-sex parent and to redirect hostile impulses toward the self in the form of guilt.

- Although guilt is an important motivator of moral action, Freud's interpretation of it is no longer widely accepted. In contrast to Freudian predictions, power assertion and love withdrawal do not foster conscience development. Instead, **induction** is far more effective. Recent psychoanalytic ideas place greater emphasis on a positive parent–child relationship and earlier beginnings of morality. However, they retain continuity with Freud's theory in regarding emotion as the basis for moral development.

- Social learning theory views moral behavior as acquired in the same way as other responses: through modeling and reinforcement. Young children readily imitate morally relevant behaviors, including resistance to temptation, if models make their efforts explicit by verbalizing them. Effective models are warm and powerful and practice what they preach. Harsh punishment does not promote moral internalization and socially desirable behavior. Instead, it provides children with aggressive models, leads them to avoid the punishing adult, and can spiral into serious abuse.

Morality as Social Understanding

- In contrast to psychoanalytic and social learning theories, the cognitive-developmental perspective assumes that morality develops through **construction**—actively thinking about right and wrong in situations in which social conflicts arise.

- Piaget's work was the original inspiration for the cognitive-developmental perspective. He identified two stages of moral understanding: **heteronomous morality,** in which children view moral rules in terms of **realism** and as fixed dictates of authority figures; and **autonomous morality,** in which children use **reciprocity** as a standard of fairness and regard rules as flexible, socially agreed-on principles. Although Piaget's theory describes the general direction of moral development, it underestimates the moral capacities of young children.

- Piaget's work inspired Kohlberg's expanded theory. Kohlberg presented subjects with **moral dilemmas** that required them to both choose and justify a course of action. As a result, he identified three levels of moral understanding, each of which contains two stages: the **preconventional level,** in which morality is viewed as controlled by rewards, punishments, and the power of authority figures; the **conventional level,** in which conformity to social rules is regarded as necessary to preserve positive human relationships and societal order; and the **postconventional level,** in which individuals define morality in terms of abstract principles and values that apply to all situations and societies. Besides Kohlberg's clinical interview, two efficient, questionnaire approaches for assessing moral understanding have been devised: the **Defining Issues Test (DIT)** and the **Sociomoral Reflection Measure–Short Form (SRM–SF).**

- Kohlberg's stages are strongly related to age and form an invariant sequence. However, the influence of situational factors on moral judgment suggests that moral development fits a less tightly organized stage conception than Kohlberg assumed. Piaget's cognitive and Selman's perspective-taking stages are necessary but not sufficient conditions for each advance in moral reasoning. Many experiences contribute to maturity of moral thought, including peer interaction; warm, rational child-rearing practices; and years of schooling.
- Cross-cultural research indicates that a certain level of societal complexity is required for Kohlberg's highest stages. At the same time, his theory does not encompass the full range of moral reasoning in all cultures. Although Kohlberg's theory does not underestimate the moral maturity of females, it emphasizes justice rather than caring as the most central moral ideal. Maturity of moral reasoning is moderately related to a wide variety of moral behaviors.

Moral Reasoning of Young Children
- Kohlberg's theory, like Piaget's, underestimates young children's moral understanding. As early as age 3, children have a beginning grasp of justice in that they distinguish moral rules from social conventions. However, this dichotomy is often less pronounced in non-Western cultures. Research on **distributive justice** and prosocial reasoning reveals that when moral dilemmas deemphasize the role of laws and the possibility of punishment, children display some surprisingly sophisticated moral judgments.

Development of Self-Control
- The emergence of **self-control** is supported by self-awareness and representational and memory capacities of the second year. The first glimmerings of self-control appear in the form of **compliance.** Researchers typically study self-control by creating situations in the laboratory that call for **delay of gratification.** The ability to delay increases steadily over the third year. Language development—in particular, use of self-directed speech to guide behavior—is believed to be involved.
- During the preschool years, children profit from adult-provided self-control strategies. Over middle childhood, they produce an increasing variety of strategies themselves and become consciously aware of which ones work well and why. Modest stability in moral self-regulation from childhood to adolescence is believed to result from the combined influence of temperament and child-rearing practices.

The Other Side of Self-Control: Development of Aggression
- Aggression first appears in late infancy. Over the preschool years, physical forms are replaced by verbal forms, and **instrumental aggression** declines, whereas **hostile aggression** increases. Beginning in middle childhood, aggression is a highly stable characteristic, particularly among boys.
- Although impulsive, overactive children are at risk for high aggression, whether or not they become so depends on child-rearing conditions. Strife-ridden family environments and power-assertive, inconsistent discipline promote self-perpetuating cycles of aggressive behavior. Children who are products of these family processes develop social-cognitive deficits and distortions that add to the long-term maintenance of aggression.
- Among interventions designed to reduce aggression, **cathartic treatment** has been shown to be unsuccessful. Procedures based on social learning theory that interrupt destructive family processes by training parents in child discipline and teaching children alternative ways of resolving conflict work well in middle childhood. Social-cognitive interventions, including empathy and perspective-taking training, are also beneficial. Comprehensive interventions addressing the multiple factors that sustain antisocial behavior may be the most effective approach to treatment.

IMPORTANT TERMS AND CONCEPTS

sociobiology (p. 474)
internalization (p. 475)
superego (p. 475)
identification (p. 475)
induction (p. 476)
time out (p. 479)
construction (p. 481)
heteronomous morality (p. 482)
realism (p. 482)

immanent justice (p. 482)
autonomous morality (p. 482)
reciprocity (p. 483)
moral dilemma (p. 485)
Defining Issues Test (DIT) (p. 486)
Sociomoral Reflection Measure–Short
    Form (SRM–SF) (p. 486)
preconventional level (p. 487)
conventional level (p. 488)

postconventional level (p. 488)
just community (p. 495)
distributive justice (p. 499)
self-control (p. 502)
compliance (p. 502)
delay of gratification (p. 503)
instrumental aggression (p. 507)
hostile aggression (p. 507)
cathartic treatment (p. 512)

CONNECTIONS

The activity choices and behaviors of these young children reveal that they have already adopted many of the gender-linked standards of their cultural community. Jenny, Karen, and Rachel used dresses, dolls, and household props to act out a stereotypically feminine scene of nurturance. In contrast, Nathan, Tommy, and David's play is active, competitive, and masculine in theme. And already, these preschoolers interact more often with children of their own sex than of the opposite sex.

What causes young children's play and social preferences to become so strongly gender typed, and how do these attitudes and behaviors change with age? Do societal expectations affect the way children think about themselves as masculine and feminine beings, thereby limiting their potential? To what extent do widely held beliefs about the characteristics of males and females reflect reality? Is it true that the average boy is aggressive, competitive, and good at spatial and mathematical skills, whereas the average girl is passive, nurturant, and good at verbal skills? How large are differences between the sexes, and in what ways do biological and environmental factors contribute to them? These are the central questions asked by researchers who study gender typing, and we will answer each of them in this chapter.

Perhaps more than any other area of child development, the study of gender typing has responded to societal change. Largely because of progress in the area of women's rights, over the past 25 years, major shifts have occurred in how sex-related differences are regarded. Until the early 1970s, the adoption of gender-typed behavior was viewed as a desirable goal of child rearing and essential for healthy psychological adjustment. Today, many people recognize that some gender-typed characteristics, such as extreme aggressiveness and competitiveness on the part of males and passivity and conformity on the part of females, are serious threats to mental health (Huston, 1983; Ruble, 1988).

Consistent with this realization, theoretical revision marks the study of gender typing. At one time, psychoanalytic theory offered an influential account of how children acquired "masculine" and "feminine" traits. According to Freud (1925/1961), these attitudes and behaviors were adopted in the same way as other societal standards—through identification with the same-sex parent during the preschool years. Today we know that interactions with opposite-sex parents, siblings, teachers, and peers, along with examples of gender-appropriate behavior in the surrounding culture, also play powerful roles. Furthermore, recent research shows that gender typing begins earlier and lasts much longer than Freud believed, continuing into adolescence and even adulthood. Finally, Freud's theory, as well as Erikson's (1950) extension of it, regards gender typing as a natural outcome of biological differences between the sexes. Although debate continues over this assumption, firm commitment to it has not been helpful in the quest to discover how children might be released from gender-based definitions of appropriate behavior. As a result, most researchers have abandoned the psychoanalytic approach in favor of other perspectives.

Social learning theory, with its emphasis on modeling and reinforcement, and cognitive-developmental theory, with its focus on children as active thinkers about their social world, are major current approaches to gender typing. However, neither is sufficient by itself. We will see that a recent information-processing view, *gender schema theory,* combines elements of both these views to explain how children acquire gender-typed knowledge and behavior.

Along with new theories have come new terms. Considerable controversy surrounds the labels *sex* and *gender*. Some researchers use these words interchangeably. Others apply them in a way that makes causal assumptions—*sex* to refer to biologically based differences and *gender* to socially influenced characteristics. Still others object to this convention because our understanding of many differences is still evolving. Also, it perpetuates too strong a dichotomy between nature and nurture (Unger & Crawford, 1993). I use another system that avoids these problems. *Sex-related* refers to comparisons between males and females that do not involve any causal inference; we simply say that a difference exists. In contrast, *gender* is used when judgments are being made about either biological or environmental causes (Deaux, 1993).

Throughout this chapter, you will encounter a variety of additional terms. Two of these involve the public face of gender in society. **Gender stereotypes** are widely held beliefs about characteristics deemed appropriate for males and females. **Gender roles** are the reflection of these stereotypes in everyday behavior (Rosen & Rekers, 1980; Ruble & Ruble, 1982). **Gender-role identity** is the private face of gender. It refers to perception of the self as relatively masculine or feminine in characteristics, abilities, and behaviors. Finally, **gender typing**, a term already mentioned, is the process of developing gender-linked beliefs, gender roles, and a gender-role identity (Huston, 1983). As we explore this process, you will see that it is complex and multiply determined. Biological, cognitive, and social factors are involved.

GENDER STEREOTYPES AND GENDER ROLES

Gender stereotypes have appeared in religious, philosophical, and literary works for centuries. For example, in ancient times, Aristotle wrote:

> Woman is more compassionate than man and has a greater propensity to tears. She is, also, more envious, more querulous, more slanderous, and more contentious. Farther still, the female is more dispirited, more despondent, more impudent and more given to falsehood than the male. . . . But the male . . . is more disposed to give assistance in danger, and is more courageous than the female. (cited in Miles, 1935, p. 700)

Although the past three decades have brought a new level of awareness about the wide range of roles possible for each gender, strong beliefs about differences between males and females remain. In the 1960s, researchers began to ask people what personality characteristics they consider typical of men and women. Widespread agreement emerged in many studies. **Instrumental traits**, reflecting competence, rationality, and assertiveness, were regarded as masculine; **expressive traits**, emphasizing warmth, caring, and sensitivity, were viewed as feminine (Ruble & Ruble, 1982). During the 1970s and 1980s, a period of intense political activism over gender equality, these stereotypes remained essentially the same. For example, Table 13.1 lists characteristics that college students of the 1980s identified as masculine and feminine. The findings are very similar to those of a similar study carried out 15 years earlier (Rosenkrantz et al., 1968; Ruble, 1983). Furthermore, cross-cultural research on respondents from 30 nations reveals that the instrumental–expressive dichotomy is a widely held stereotype around the world (Williams & Best, 1982).

Besides personality traits, other components of gender stereotyping exist. These include physical characteristics (tall, strong, and sturdy for men; soft, dainty, and graceful for women), occupations (truck driver, insurance agent, and chemist for men; elementary school teacher, secretary, and nurse for women), and activities or behaviors (good at fixing things and leader in groups for men; good at child care and decorating the home for women) (Biernat, 1991b; Deaux & Lewis, 1984). The variety of attributes consistently identified as masculine or feminine, their broad acceptance, and their stability over time suggest that gender stereotypes are deeply ingrained patterns of thinking. When do children become aware of them, and what implications do they have for gender-role adoption?

Gender Stereotyping in Early Childhood

Recall from Chapter 11 that around age 2, children label their own sex and that of other people, using such words as "boy" versus "girl" and "woman" versus "man." As soon as these categories are established, children start to sort out what

Gender stereotypes
Widely held beliefs about characteristics deemed appropriate for males and females.

Gender roles
The reflection of gender stereotypes in everyday behavior.

Gender-role identity
Perception of the self as relatively masculine or feminine in characteristics, abilities, and behaviors.

Gender typing
The process of developing gender roles and a gender-role identity.

Instrumental traits
Masculine-stereotyped personality traits that reflect competence, rationality, and assertiveness.

Expressive traits
Feminine-stereotyped personality traits that reflect warmth, caring, and sensitivity.

TABLE 13.1 Some Characteristics Regarded as Stereotypically Masculine and Feminine in College Students in the 1980s	
MASCULINE CHARACTERISTICS	FEMININE CHARACTERISTICS
Independent	Emotional
Aggressive	Home-oriented
Skilled in business	Kind
Mechanical aptitude	Cries easily
Outspoken	Creative
Acts as a leader	Considerate
Self-confident	Devotes self to others
Takes a stand	Needs approval
Ambitious	Gentle
Not easily influenced	Aware of others' feelings
Dominant	Excitable in a major crisis
Active	Expresses tender feelings
Makes decisions easily	Enjoys art and music
Doesn't give up easily	Tactful
Stands up under pressure	Feelings hurt easily
Likes math and science	Neat
Competitive	Likes children
Adventurous	Understanding

SOURCE: Ruble, 1983.

they mean in terms of activities and behaviors. As a result, a wide variety of gender stereotypes are mastered.

Preschoolers associate many toys, articles of clothing, tools, household items, games, occupations, and even colors (pink and blue) with one sex as opposed to the other (Huston, 1983; Picariello, Greenberg, & Pillemer, 1990; Weinraub et al., 1984). In a study illustrating the range of gender stereotypes acquired at an early age, chil-

*B*y age 1½, gender-stereotyped game and toy choices are present, becoming increasingly consistent with age. Already, these 3-year-olds play in highly gender-stereotyped ways.
(LEFT, ERIKA STONE/PHOTO RESEARCHERS; RIGHT, STEPHEN MARKS)

dren as young as $2\frac{1}{2}$ were shown pictures of boys and girls. As each was presented, the experimenter described it by making a statement about a gender-stereotyped behavior, physical characteristic, activity, or future role—for example, "I can hit you," "I look nice," "I like to play ball," and "When I grow up, I'll be a nurse." Children of both sexes indicated that girls "like to play with dolls," "talk a lot," "never hit," say "I need some help," and later on as grown-ups will "clean the house" and "be a nurse." They also believed that boys "like to help father," say "I can hit you," and as future adults will "be boss" and "mow the grass" (Kuhn, Nash, & Brucken, 1978).

Even before children can label their own sex and match up statements and objects with male and female figures, their play suggests that they already have some implicit knowledge about "gender-appropriate" activities. By $1\frac{1}{2}$ years, gender-stereotyped game and toy choices are present in both laboratory and naturalistic settings (Caldera, Huston, & O'Brien, 1989; Fagot, 1978; Fagot, Leinbach, & Hagan, 1986). Between ages 1 and 3, these preferences become highly consistent for both boys and girls (O'Brien & Huston, 1985).

A striking feature of preschoolers' gender stereotypes is that they operate like blanket rules rather than flexible guidelines. In several studies, researchers labeled a target child as a boy or girl and then provided either gender-typical or gender-atypical information about the target's characteristics. Next, children were asked to rate the target on additional gender-stereotypic attributes. Preschoolers typically relied on only the gender label in making these judgments, ignoring the specific information. For example, when told, "Tommy is a boy. Tommy's best friend is a girl, and Tommy likes to play house," children under age 6 nevertheless said that Tommy would much prefer to play with cars and train engines than sewing machines and dolls (Berndt & Heller, 1986; Biernat, 1991b; Martin, 1989).

The rigidity of preschoolers' gender stereotypes helps us understand some commonly observed everyday behaviors. Shown a picture of a Scottish bagpiper wearing a kilt, a 4-year-old is likely to state, "Men don't wear skirts!" At preschool, children can be heard exclaiming that girls don't drive fire engines and can't be police officers and boys don't take care of babies and can't be the teacher. These one-sided judgments are a joint product of gender stereotyping in the environment, young children's cognitive immaturity (in particular, their difficulty integrating several conflicting sources of information), and their limited understanding of the biological basis of male and female. As we will see later, concrete observable characteristics—activities, toys, occupations, hairstyles, and clothing—are the defining features of gender for the majority of 3- to 5-year-olds. Most have not yet learned that genital characteristics override social cues in determining a person's sex.

Gender Stereotyping in Middle Childhood and Adolescence

By age 5, gender stereotyping of activities and occupations is well established. During middle childhood and adolescence, knowledge of stereotypes strengthens in the less obvious areas of personality traits and achievement. At the same time, older children begin to realize that gender-stereotypic attributes are *associated*, not *defining* features of gender. As a result, beliefs about the characteristics and capacities of males and females become more flexible.

PERSONALITY TRAITS. To assess stereotyping of personality traits, researchers ask children to assign "masculine" adjectives (such as tough, rational, and cruel) and "feminine" adjectives (such as gentle, affectionate, and dependent) to either a male or female stimulus figure. Recall from Chapter 11 that not until middle childhood are children good at sizing up people in terms of psychological dispositions. This same finding carries over to awareness of gender stereotypes.

Research carried out in many countries, including England, Canada, France, Germany, India, Korea, the Netherlands, and the United States, reveals that stereotyping of personality traits increases steadily over the elementary school years, becoming adultlike around age 11 (Beere, 1990; Best et al., 1977). A large Canadian study examined the pattern of children's trait learning and found that the stereotypes acquired first reflected "own-sex favoritism." Kindergartners through second-graders had greatest knowledge of traits that portrayed their own gender in a positive light. Once trait stereotyping was well under way, elementary school pupils were most familiar with "positive feminine" traits and "negative masculine" traits (Serbin, Powlishta, & Gulko, 1993). In addition to learning specific stereotypes, children seemed to pick up a widely held general impression—that of girls as "sugar and spice and everything nice" and boys as "snakes and snails and puppy dog tails."

ACHIEVEMENT AREAS. Shortly after entering elementary school, children figure out which academic subjects and skill areas are "masculine" and which are "feminine." Throughout the school years, they regard reading, art, and music as more for girls and mathematics, athletics, and mechanical skills as more for boys (Eccles, Jacobs, & Harold, 1990; Huston, 1983; Stein, 1971; Stein & Smithells, 1969). These stereotypes can also be found in other cultures. When elementary school pupils in the United States, Japan, and Taiwan were asked to name the school subject they liked best, girls were more likely to choose reading and boys mathematics in all three countries. Asked to predict how well they would do in the two subjects once they reached high school, boys thought they would do better in mathematics than did girls. In contrast, no sex-related difference in favor of girls emerged in predictions about reading (Lummis & Stevenson, 1990).

Other more subtle forms of achievement stereotyping appear during middle childhood. Recall our discussion of achievement-related attributions in Chapter 11, which indicated that attributing failure to ability as opposed to effort undermines achievement motivation. Elementary school pupils tend to explain the failures of females, particularly in "cross-gender" activities, as due to ability. In contrast, they interpret corresponding male failures more generously, in terms of insufficient effort or learning opportunities (Nemerowicz, 1979).

Furthermore, by the mid-elementary school years, children have acquired a more general stereotype of achievement as a "masculine" norm. In one study, third- through twelfth-graders were told stories about a woman (Anne) and a man (John) who either succeeded or failed in medical school. Then they rated how nice each was under both conditions. Boys and girls of all ages indicated that Anne was somewhat less nice than John when both succeeded. However, John was much less nice than Anne when they both failed. Although children and adolescents are biased in favor of a male who succeeds, they seem to evaluate a male who fails to reach an important achievement goal especially negatively (Hawkins & Pingree, 1978).

TOWARD GREATER FLEXIBILITY. Clearly, school-age children and adolescents are knowledgeable about a wide variety of gender stereotypes. But awareness of gender-typical attributes does not mean that older children always approve of these distinctions. During middle childhood, a more open-minded view of what males and females can and should do also emerges (Serbin & Sprafkin, 1986; Trautner et al., 1989).

Look back at how gender stereotyping was assessed in the studies described earlier, and you will see that virtually all used a forced-choice technique in which children had to assign a characteristic to either one gender or the other. In some instances, researchers have also asked whether a personality trait might be appropriate for *both* genders—a response that provides a measure of stereotype flexibility. In the Canadian study mentioned earlier, stereotype knowledge and flexibility were assessed, and as Figure 13.1 reveals, both increased from kindergarten to sixth grade (Serbin, Powlishta, & Gulko, 1993). In another study, school-age children's flexible appreciation of activity and occupational stereotypes paralleled their expanding appreciation of social conventions—that many social practices are arbitrary rules arrived at by group consensus, not fixed immutable laws (Carter & Patterson, 1982).

As gender stereotypes become more flexible and children develop the cognitive capacity to integrate conflicting social cues, they no longer rely on only a gender

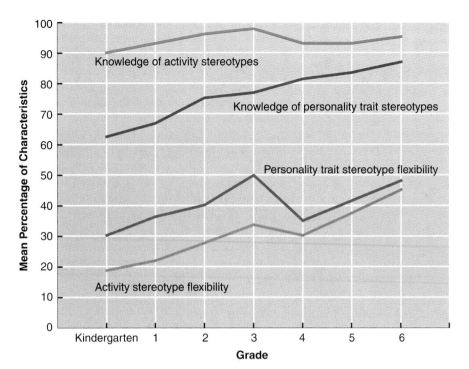

FIGURE 13.1 Grade changes in knowledge and flexibility of gender stereotypes in a cross-sectional study of over 500 Canadian school-age children. (From "The Development of Sex Typing in Middle Childhood" by L. A. Serbin, K. K. Powlishta, & J. Gulko, 1993, *Monographs of the Society for Research in Child Development, 58* (2, Serial No. 232), p. 35. © The Society for Research in Child Development, Inc. Adapted by permission.)

label to predict what a person will be like. They also take into account the individual's unique characteristics. Unlike preschoolers, when school-age children and adolescents are told about a target child named Tommy who likes to play house, they notice both the child's sex and his interest. Realizing that many attributes are shared by boys and girls, older subjects say that Tommy would probably enjoy several other "cross-gender" activities and some gender-typical ones as well (Biernat, 1991b; Martin, 1989).

This decline in rigidity of stereotypes is also reflected in children's answers to the question, "Why do you think boys and girls are different/do different things?" Between 6 and 18 years, responses focus less on physical explanations ("Boys have different things in their innards than girls") and more on socialization experiences ("We do different things because it is the way we have been brought up") (Smith & Russell, 1984; Ullian, 1976).

Individual and Group Differences in Gender Stereotyping

Almost all children acquire extensive knowledge of gender stereotypes by middle childhood, following the overall pattern just described. But while they are developing, children differ widely in the makeup of their understanding. Research shows that the various components of gender stereotyping—activities, behaviors, occupations, and personality traits—do not correlate highly (Deaux & Lewis, 1984; Serbin, Powlishta, & Gulko, 1993). This suggests that gender typing is not a unitary aspect of development. Instead, it is more like "an intricate puzzle that the child pieces together in a rather idiosyncratic way" (Hort, Leinbach, & Fagot, 1991, p. 196). To build a coherent notion of gender, children must assemble many elements, including gender labels, a diverse array of stereotypes, and evaluations of the appropriateness of each. The precise pattern in which they acquire the pieces, the rate at which they do so, and the flexibility of their beliefs vary greatly from child to child (Signorella, 1987).

Group differences in gender stereotyping also exist. The strongest of these is between boys and girls. A large body of research reveals that boys hold more gender-stereotypic views. In toddlerhood, they play more often with "gender-consistent" toys, a difference that persists through the preschool years (Bussey & Bandura, 1992; O'Brien & Huston, 1985). By middle childhood and adolescence, boys make more stereotyped judgments on all the components of stereotyping (Archer, 1984; Cummings & Taebel, 1980; Fenema & Sherman, 1977; Kleinke & Nicholson, 1979; Raymond & Benbow, 1986). In addition, they are less flexible in their view of occupational stereotypes, and they are more likely to devalue the achievements of females and to attribute sex-related differences to physical rather than social causes (Etaugh & Rose, 1975; Nemerowicz, 1979; Smith & Russell, 1984). However, in a few recent studies, boys and girls did not always differ in these ways (Biernat, 1991a; Serbin, Powlishta, & Gulko, 1993). One heartening possibility is that boys, especially, are beginning to view gender roles as encompassing a wider variety of possibilities than was previously the case.

Research including ethnic minorities indicates that black children hold less stereotyped views of females than do white children (Bardwell, Cochran, & Walker, 1986; Kleinke & Nicholson, 1979). Perhaps this finding is due to aspects of African-American family life. For example, more black than white women with children under 18 are employed (U.S. Bureau of the Census, 1992). This means that African-American children are more likely to have mothers whose lives reflect less traditional gender roles.

Finally, although no social-class differences in gender stereotyping are present in childhood, middle-class individuals tend to hold more flexible gender-stereotyped views than their lower-class counterparts in adolescence and adulthood (Canter & Ageton, 1984; Lackey, 1989; Serbin, Powlishta, & Gulko, 1993). Years of schooling along with a wider array of options in life may contribute to this difference.

Gender Stereotyping and Gender-Role Adoption

Do children's gender-stereotyped patterns of thinking influence gender-role adoption, thereby restricting their experiences and potential? The evidence on this issue is mixed. Gender-typed preferences and behaviors increase sharply over the preschool years—the same period in which children rapidly acquire a wide variety of stereotypes. In addition, boys, who make more stereotypical judgments, show greater conformity to their gender role than do girls (Edelbrock & Sugawara, 1978; Huston, 1983).

But these parallel patterns of development do not tell us for sure that stereotyping shapes children's behavior. Indeed, research suggests that the relationship is not that clear-cut. Knowledge of gender stereotypes is related only weakly to gender-role adoption. In other words, children well versed in gender-related expectations are not necessarily highly gender typed in everyday life (Coker, 1984; Downs & Langlois, 1988; Serbin, Powlishta, & Gulko, 1993; Weinraub et al., 1984).

Why might this be the case? First, some gender-role preferences, such as the desire to play with "gender-appropriate" toys and same-sex playmates, are acquired before children know much about stereotypes (Blakemore, LaRue, & Olejnik, 1979; Perry, White, & Perry, 1984). Second, we have already seen that children master the components of gender-stereotyped knowledge in diverse ways, each of which may have different implications for their behavior. Finally, by middle childhood, virtually all children know a great deal about gender stereotypes—knowledge so universal that it cannot predict variation in gender-role adoption.

According to Aletha Huston (1983), gender-typed knowledge and behavior may develop along different lines during the preschool years, perhaps becoming integrated in middle childhood. In support of this idea, stereotype flexibility rather than knowledge per se is a moderately effective predictor of gender-role adoption during the school years. Children who believe that many stereotyped expectations are appropriate for both sexes are more likely to cross gender lines in the activities, playmates, and occupational roles they choose for themselves (Serbin, Powlishta, & Gulko, 1993; Signorella, Bigler, & Liben, 1993).

The impact of stereotypes on behavior is likely to become more powerful as children incorporate these ideas into their gender-role identities—self-perceptions about what they can and should do at play, in school, and as future participants in society. But the development of gender-role identity is a topic we treat later in this chapter. For now, let's turn to various influences that promote children's gender-typed beliefs and behavior.

During the preschool years, children acquire a wide variety of gender stereotypes about activities, behaviors, and occupations. Less obvious stereotypes involving personality traits and achievement areas are added in middle childhood. At the same time, a more flexible view of stereotyped characteristics emerges. Children master the components of gender stereotyping in diverse ways, and the flexibility of their beliefs varies considerably. Group differences in stereotyping also exist. In most studies, boys' judgments are more stereotyped than girls', and black children hold less stereotyped views of females than do white children. Social-class differences in stereotyping do not emerge until adolescence. School-age children with a flexible appreciation of gender stereotypes are less gender typed in their preferences and behavior.

Brief Review

BIOLOGICAL AND ENVIRONMENTAL INFLUENCES ON GENDER STEREOTYPING AND GENDER-ROLE ADOPTION

According to social learning theorists, direct teaching is the way gender-stereotyped knowledge and behaviors are transmitted to children. We will see shortly that much research is consistent with this point of view. Nevertheless, some people argue that biological makeup leads each sex to be uniquely suited to fill particular roles and that most societies do little more than encourage gender differences that are genetically based. Is there evidence to support this idea?

The Case for Biology

Although practically no modern theorist would claim that "biology is destiny," serious questions about biological influences on gender typing remain (Ruble, 1988). Two sources of evidence have been used to support the role of biology: (1) cross-cultural similarities in gender stereotypes and gender-role adoption; and (2) the influence of hormones on gender-role behavior. Let's examine each in turn.

HOW MUCH CROSS-CULTURAL SIMILARITY EXISTS IN GENDER TYPING? Earlier in this chapter, we noted that the instrumental–expressive dichotomy is reflected in the gender stereotyping of many national groups. Although this finding fits with the assumption that social influences simply build on genetically determined differences between the sexes, we must be cautious in drawing this conclusion.

A close look at cross-cultural findings reveals that most societies promote instrumental traits in males and expressive traits in females, but great diversity exists in the *magnitude* of this difference (Hendrix & Johnson, 1985; Whiting & Edwards, 1988b). Consider Nyansongo, a small agricultural settlement in Kenya. Nyansongo mothers, who work 4 to 5 hours a day in the gardens, assign the care of young children, the tending of the cooking fire, and the washing of dishes to older siblings. Since children of both sexes perform these duties, girls are relieved of total responsibility for "feminine" tasks and have more time to interact with agemates. Their greater freedom and independence leads them to score higher than girls of other village and tribal cultures in dominance, assertiveness, and playful roughhousing. In contrast, boys' caregiving responsibilities mean that they often display help-giving and emotional support (Whiting & Edwards, 1988a). Among industrialized nations, Sweden is widely recognized as a society in which traditional gender beliefs and behaviors are considerably reduced (see the Cultural Influences box on page 526).

Of all nations in the world, Sweden is unique in its valuing of gender equality and its social programs that translate this commitment into action. Over a century ago, Sweden's ruling political party adopted equality as a central tenet. One social class was not to exploit another, nor one gender another. In the 1960s, Sweden's expanding economy required that women enter the labor force in large numbers. When the question arose as to who would help sustain family life, the Swedish populace called on the principle of equality and answered: fathers, just like mothers.

The Swedish "equal roles family model" maintains that husband and wife should have the same opportunity to pursue a career and be equally responsible for housework and child care. To support this goal, day-care centers had to be made available outside the home. Otherwise, a class of less privileged women might be exploited for caregiving and domestic work—an outcome that would contradict the principle of equality. And since full-time employment for both parents often strains a family with young children, Sweden mandated that mothers and fathers with children under age 8 could reduce the length of their working day to 6 hours, with a corresponding reduction in pay but not in benefits (Sandqvist, 1992).

According to several indicators, Sweden's family model is highly successful. Maternal employment is extremely high; over 80 percent of mothers with infants and preschoolers work outside the home. Day-care centers are numerous, of high quality, and heavily subsidized by the government. And although Swedish fathers do not yet share housework and child care equally with mothers, they are more involved than fathers in North America and other Western European nations. In one international study of 40 countries, Swedish men rated themselves lowest in "masculine" traits. On most, they fell at about the same level as Swedish women, and on some, below them (Hofstede, 1980). These findings provide further evidence that gender roles in Sweden are less differentiated than elsewhere.

Has Sweden's progressive family policy affected the gender beliefs and behaviors of its youths? A study of Swedish and American adolescents found that the "masculine" role was more highly valued than the "feminine" role in both countries. However, this difference was less pronounced in Sweden, where young people regarded each gender as a blend of instrumental and expressive traits. And although Swedish adolescents more often aspired to stereotyped occupations than did their American counterparts, Swedish girls felt considerably better about their gender—a difference that might be due to greater equalization in men's and women's pay scales and a widespread attitude in Sweden that "feminine" work is important to society. Finally, compared to American adolescents, Swedish young people more often viewed gender roles as a matter of learned tasks and domains of expertise rather than inborn personality traits or sets of rights and duties (Intons-Peterson, 1988).

Traditional gender typing is not completely eradicated in Sweden. But great progress has been made as a result of steadfastly pursuing a program of equal opportunity for males and females for several decades.

Furthermore, cultural reversals of traditional gender typing exist. Over half a century ago, anthropologist Margaret Mead (1935/1963) conducted a classic study of three tribal societies in New Guinea. Among the Arapesh, both men and women were cooperative and nurturant; among the Mundugumore, both sexes were ruthless and aggressive; and among the Tchambuli, women were dominant and assertive whereas men were passive and dependent.

These examples indicate that experience can have a profound impact on gender typing. Nevertheless, it can still be argued that deviations from traditional gender roles are more the exception than the rule. Biological pressures may still be operating, appearing in behavior as long as cultural pressures against them are not extreme. Because cross-cultural findings are inconclusive, scientists have turned to a more direct test of the importance of biology—research on the impact of sex hormones on gender-role adoption.

SEX HORMONES AND GENDER-ROLE ADOPTION. In Chapters 3 and 5, we discussed how genetic makeup, mediated by hormones, regulates sexual development and body growth in males and females. Sex hormones also affect brain development and neural activity in many animal species, and they do so in humans as well (Hines & Green, 1991). Are hormones, which so pervasively affect body structures, also important in gender-role adoption?

Activity Level and Preference for Same-Sex Peers. Experiments with animals reveal that exposure to sex hormones during certain sensitive periods does affect

*B*eginning in the preschool years, children seek out playmates of their own sex. Sex hormones are believed to influence children's play styles, leading to calm, gentle actions among girls and rough, noisy movements among boys. Then preschoolers naturally choose same-sex partners who share their interests and behaviors.
(LEFT, JEFF GREENBERG/PHOTOEDIT; RIGHT, STEPHEN MARKS)

behavior. For example, prenatally administered androgens (male sex hormones) increase active play in both male and female mammals. Androgens also promote male-typical sexual behavior and aggression and suppress maternal caregiving in a wide variety of species (Bardin & Catterall, 1981; Meany, Stewart, & Beatty, 1985; Quadagno, Briscoe, & Quadagno, 1977).

Eleanor Maccoby (1988, 1990a) argues that at least some of these hormonal effects extend to humans. In the introduction to this chapter, we noted that as early as the preschool years, children seek out playmates of their own sex—a preference that has been observed in a wide variety of cultures and many mammalian species (Meany, Stewart, & Beatty, 1985; Whiting & Edwards, 1988a). At age 4, children already spend three times as much time with same-sex than opposite-sex playmates. By age 6, this ratio has climbed to 11 to 1 (Maccoby & Jacklin, 1987). Throughout the school years, children continue to show a strong preference for same-sex peers, a trend that declines in adolescence when puberty triggers an interest in the opposite sex (Hayden-Thomson, Rubin, & Hymel, 1987; Serbin, Powlishta, & Gulko, 1993).

Why is sex segregation so widespread and persistent? According to Maccoby, early on, hormones affect play styles, leading to rough, noisy movements among boys and calm, gentle actions among girls. Then, as children begin to interact with peers, they naturally choose same-sex partners whose interests and behaviors are compatible with their own. By age 2, girls already appear overwhelmed by boys' rambunctious behavior. When paired with a boy in a laboratory play session, the girl stands idly by while he explores the toys (Jacklin & Maccoby, 1978). A similar reaction occurs in nonhuman primates. When a male juvenile initiates rough, physical play, male peers join in, whereas females withdraw (Meany, Stewart, & Beatty, 1985).

Exceptional Human Sexual Development. For ethical reasons, we cannot experimentally manipulate hormones in humans to be sure they affect activity level and choice of play partners in these ways. But cases do exist in which hormone levels varied naturally or were modified for medical reasons. John Money, Anke Ehrhardt, and their collaborators conducted research on children with *adrenogenital syndrome (AGS)*, a disorder in which prenatal exposure to unusually high levels of androgens or androgenlike hormones occurred. In some AGS subjects, a genetic defect caused the adrenal system to malfunction. In others, the mother was given a synthetic hormone during pregnancy to prevent miscarriage.

Although physical development of AGS boys remains unaffected, girls are usually born with masculinized external genitals. Most of those in Money and Ehrhardt's studies underwent surgical correction in infancy or childhood; a few experienced it in later life. Also, those with genetic AGS were given continuous drug therapy to correct the hormone imbalance (Ehrhardt & Baker, 1974; Ehrhardt, Epstein, & Money, 1968; Money & Ehrhardt, 1972).

Interviewing AGS subjects and their family members, Money and Ehrhardt found that the girls displayed "masculine" gender-role behavior. They preferred boys as playmates; liked cars, trucks, and blocks better than dolls; were uninterested in fantasizing about traditional feminine roles (such as bride and mother); and were less concerned with matters of physical appearance (clothing, jewelry, and hairstyle) than non-AGS girls. Also, both boys and girls with AGS showed higher activity levels, as indicated by greater participation in active sports and outdoor games. The researchers concluded that prenatal androgen exposure is a biological factor that supports "masculine" gender-role behavior.

Critics, however, point out that Money and Ehrhardt cannot rule out the contribution of subtle environmental pressures to the differences found. For example, genital abnormalities, in some cases not corrected until well beyond infancy, may have caused family members to perceive affected girls as boyish and unfeminine and to treat them accordingly (Huston, 1983; Quadagno, Briscoe, & Quadagno, 1977). Furthermore, in the course of their medical treatment, girls with genetic AGS were probably told that as adults they might have difficulty conceiving a child. Perhaps they showed little interest in marriage and motherhood because they were unsure of these possibilities in their own lives. In fact, a careful look at Money and Ehrhardt's (1972) cases reveals that girls with nongenetic AGS, who after surgery required no further medical intervention, were not especially disinterested in traditional feminine roles.

Furthermore, research on individuals reared as members of the opposite sex because they had ambiguous genitals indicates that in most cases, gender typing is consistent with sex of rearing, regardless of genetic sex (Baker, 1980; Money, 1985). In instances in which these individuals do decide to switch gender roles, they usually move from "feminine" to "masculine"—to the gender associated with more highly valued characteristics. Consider some striking findings on genetic males born with female-looking genitals because of a prenatal androgen deficiency. In four villages in the Dominican Republic, where this defect is common, all but one of those reared as a girl changed to a masculine gender role in adolescence and young adulthood (Imperato-McGinley et al., 1979). Although the researchers inferred from this finding that "androgens make a strong and definite contribution to gender typing" (p. 1236), additional research questions this conclusion. Among the Sambia of Papua New Guinea, sexually ambiguous males reared as females switched gender roles only in response to social pressures—when it became clear that they could not fulfill their cultural destiny of bearing children (Herdt & Davidson, 1988).

Studies of individuals exposed to high levels of prenatal androgens but without genital effects yield mixed results. Some report a rise in "masculine" attributes, including activity level, independence, self-confidence, and preference for aggressive solutions to social problems (Ehrhardt, 1975; Reinisch, 1981). But many others show no clear effects (Hines, 1982).

Taken together, research on the impact of sex hormones suggests that they may affect some aspects of gender typing. The most uniform finding involves activity level, which may lead to a preference for same-sex peers and certain "gender-appropriate" toys (Berenbaum & Hines, 1992). Since other behavioral outcomes are neither large nor consistent, biological makeup probably plays little role. Finally, it is important to keep in mind that even biological factors can be modified by experience. For example, in animal research, social dominance and environmental stress increase androgen production (Macrides, Bartke, & Dalterio, 1975; Rose, Holaday, & Bernstein, 1976).

A wealth of evidence reveals that environmental factors provide powerful support for gender-role development. As we will see in the following sections, adults view boys and girls differently, and they treat them differently. In addition, children's social contexts—home, school, and community—provide them with many opportunities to observe people behaving in ways consistent with gender stereotypes. And as soon as children enter the world of the peer group, their agemates encourage conformity to gender roles.

PERCEPTIONS AND EXPECTATIONS OF ADULTS. When adults are asked to observe neutrally dressed infants who are labeled as either boy or girl, they "see" qualities that fit with the baby's artificially assigned sex. In research of this kind, adults tend to rate infants' physical features and (to a lesser extent) their personality traits in a gender-stereotyped fashion (Stern & Karraker, 1989; Vogel et al., 1991). Among new parents, these gender-biased perceptions seem to be even stronger. In one study, mothers and fathers were interviewed 24 hours after the birth of their first child. Although male and female newborns did not differ in length, weight, or Apgar scores, parents perceived them differently. They rated sons as firmer, larger featured, better coordinated, more alert, stronger, and hardier and daughters as softer, finer featured, more delicate, more awkward, and more inattentive (Rubin, Provenzano, & Luria, 1974).

During childhood and adolescence, parents continue to hold different perceptions and expectations of their sons and daughters. They persist in interpreting children's behavior in stereotyped ways, want their preschoolers to play with "gender-appropriate" toys, and say that boys and girls should be raised differently. For example, when asked about their child-rearing values, parents tend to emphasize achievement, competitiveness, and control of emotion as important for boys. In contrast, they regard warmth, "ladylike" behavior, and close supervision of activities as important for girls. These differences have changed very little over the past several decades (Block, 1983; Brooks-Gunn, 1986; McGuire, 1988).

TREATMENT BY PARENTS. Do adults actually treat children in accord with their stereotypical beliefs? A combined analysis of 172 studies reported that on the whole, differences in the way parents socialize boys and girls are not large (Lytton & Romney, 1991). However, this does not mean that parental treatment is unimportant. It simply says that if we sum across age periods and behaviors, we find only a few clear trends. When the evidence is examined closely, consistent age effects emerge. Younger children receive more direct training in gender roles than do older children—a finding that is not surprising, since gender typing takes place especially rapidly during early childhood (Fagot & Hagan, 1991). And wide variation from study to study suggests that some parents practice differential treatment much more intensely than do others.

Infancy and Early Childhood. In infancy and early childhood, parents encourage a diverse array of "gender-appropriate" play activities and behaviors. As early as the first few months of life—before children can express their own preferences—parents begin to create different environments for boys and girls. Bedrooms are decorated with distinct colors and motifs. Guns, cars, tools, and footballs are purchased for boys; dolls, tea sets, jewelry, and jump ropes for girls. A child who makes a special request for a birthday or Christmas present is far more likely to receive it if it is a "gender-consistent" toy (Etaugh & Liss, 1992; Pomerleau et al., 1990; Robinson & Morris, 1986).

Parents also actively reinforce gender-role conformity in young children. For example, they react more positively when a young son as opposed to a daughter plays with cars and trucks, demands attention, runs and climbs, or tries to take toys from others. In contrast, they more often direct play activities, provide help, discuss emotions, and encourage assistance with household tasks when interacting with a daughter (Dunn, Bretherton, & Munn, 1987; Fagot, 1978; Fagot & Hagan, 1991). Early in development, then, parents provide experiences that encourage assertiveness, exploration, and engagement with the physical world in boys and imitation, dependency, and social orientation in girls (Block, 1983).

Middle Childhood. During middle childhood, issues of achievement become more salient to parents as children's skills expand. Observations of mothers and fathers interacting with their school-age children in teaching situations reveal that they demand greater independence from boys than girls. For example, when a child requests help, parents more often ignore or refuse to respond to a son, whereas they offer help right away to a daughter (Rothbart & Rothbart, 1976). And the way parents provide help to each sex differs. They behave in a more mastery-oriented fashion with sons, setting higher standards and pointing out important features of the task. In contrast, they frequently stray from task goals to joke and play with daughters (Block, Block, & Harrington, 1975). Furthermore, during a conversation, parents often interrupt daughters but permit sons to finish their statements, subtly delivering the message that what a boy has to say is more important (Greif, 1979).

Parents also hold gender-differentiated perceptions of and expectations for children's competencies in various school subjects. In longitudinal research on over 2,100 families with school-age children, Jacqueline Eccles, Janet Jacobs, and Rena Harold (1990) found that parents rated daughters as more competent in English than sons; the reverse was true for mathematics and sports. These beliefs were stronger than actual skill differences among the children. In fact, boys and girls in this sample performed equally well in the two academic areas, based on grades and achievement-test scores. What else besides overt performance influenced parents' judgments? The researchers discovered that parents' stereotypes about the abilities of males and females played a significant role. The more parents endorsed the idea of gender-specific abilities, the more likely they were to believe that their child was naturally talented in a gender-typical field and would find "opposite-gender" pursuits to be difficult. These judgments, in turn, influenced children's self-perceptions of ability, the effort they devoted to mastering particular skills, and their later performance (Eccles et al., 1989; Jacobs, 1991). The researchers speculated that this chain of events is likely to affect the occupations that males and females seek out and qualify for. As the Social Issues box on the following page reveals, gender segregation continues to exist in many vocational domains.

Differential treatment by parents extends to the freedom granted children in their everyday lives. During middle childhood, boys are allowed to range farther

_T_his Lapp boy of Norway wanders far from home as he tends his family's sled reindeer. The freedom he is granted promotes independence and self-reliance. Because his sisters are given household tasks, they spend much more time under the watchful eye of adults. (BRYAN AND CHERRY ALEXANDER)

Over the past two decades, high school boys' vocational preferences have remained strongly gender-stereotyped, whereas girls have expressed increasing interest in occupations traditionally held by men (Sandberg et al., 1991). Nevertheless, women's progress in entering and excelling at male-dominated professions has been slow. As Table 13.2 shows, the percentage of women engineers, lawyers, and doctors increased between 1972 and 1991 in the United States, but it falls far short of equal representation. Women remain heavily concentrated in the less well paid, traditionally feminine professions of literature, social work, education, and nursing (U.S. Bureau of the Census, 1992). In virtually all fields, their achievements lag behind those of men, who write more books, make more discoveries, hold more positions of leadership, and produce more works of art (Reis, 1991).

As we will see in the final section of this chapter, ability cannot account for these dramatic sex-related differences. Instead, gender-stereotyped messages from the social environment play a key role. Although girls' grades are higher than those of boys during the first few years of school, they reach adolescence less confident of their abilities. During the last two years of high school, the proportion of girls in gifted programs drops off (Read, 1991; Reis, 1991). When high school students were asked what discouraged them from continuing in gifted programs, parental and peer pressures and attitudes of teachers and counselors ranked high on girls' lists (Read, 1991). Some parents still regard professional accomplishment as unnecessary for girls and as risking their chances for marriage and motherhood. At times, counselors advise girls not to enroll in advanced math and science courses for similar reasons. And there is evidence that high school teachers tend to view bright male students as more capable than their female counterparts (Blaubergs, 1980; Grau, 1985). Once communicated, these beliefs can be reinforced by peers.

During college, the career aspirations of academically talented females decline further. In one longitudinal study, high school valedictorians were followed over a 10-year period—through college and into the work world. By their sophomore year, young women showed a decline in estimates of their intelligence, whereas young men did not. Women also shifted their expectations toward less demanding careers because of concerns about combining work with motherhood and unresolved questions about their ability. Even though female valedictorians outperformed their male counterparts in college courses, they achieved at lower levels after career entry (Arnold & Denny, 1985). Another longitudinal study reported similar findings. Educational aspirations of mathematically talented females declined considerably during college, as did the number majoring in the sciences (Benbow & Arjimand, 1990).

These findings reveal a pressing need for programs that sensitize parents, teachers, and school counselors to the special problems girls face in developing and maintaining high career aspirations. Research shows that academically talented girls' aspirations rise in response to career guidance that encourages them to set high goals—ones that match their abilities, interests, and values (Kerr, 1983). Those who continue to achieve have three experiences in common: a college environment that values and supports the accomplishments of females, frequent interaction with faculty and professionals in their chosen fields, and the opportunity to test their abilities in a nurturing environment (Arnold & Denny, 1985). Finally, models of women who combine work with motherhood are important. Many girls are surprised to learn that married women scientists with children achieve just as much professionally as their single female colleagues do (Cole & Zuckerman, 1987).

TABLE 13.2 *Percentage of Females in Various Professions, 1972, 1983, 1991*

PROFESSION	YEAR		
	1972	*1983*	*1991*
Engineering	0.8	5.8	8.2
Law	3.8	15.8	19.0
Medicine	9.3	15.8	20.1
Writing, art, entertainment	31.7	42.7	46.7
Social work	55.1	64.3	68.0
Elementary and secondary education	70.0	70.9	74.3
Higher education	28.0	36.3	40.8
Library, museum curatorship	81.6	84.4	83.0
Nursing	92.6	95.8	94.8

SOURCE: U.S. Bureau of the Census, 1992.

from home without adult supervision (Newson & Newson, 1976). Assignment of chores reflects this same trend. In many cultures, girls are given tasks, such as food preparation, cleaning, and baby-sitting, that keep them close to home, whereas boys are given responsibilities that take them into the surrounding world, such as yard work and errands (Whiting & Edwards, 1988a). As we noted earlier, when cultural circumstances require children to perform "cross-gender" chores (as is the case in Nyansongo), the range of behaviors practiced expands.

Although these findings might be taken to suggest that girls in Western cultures be granted more freedom and boys assigned more gender-atypical tasks, the consequences of doing so are not so straightforward. Recent evidence shows that when fathers hold stereotypical views and their sons engage in "feminine" housework, boys experience strain in the father–child relationship, feel stressed by their responsibilities, and judge themselves to be less competent (McHale et al., 1990). In contrast, a match between parental values and nontraditional child-rearing practices leads to benefits for children. In one study, 6-year-olds growing up in countercultural families that were highly committed to gender equality were compared to agemates living in conventional homes or experiencing other countercultural alternatives (for example, communes emphasizing spiritual and pronature values but not gender equality). Children in gender countercultural homes were less likely to classify objects and occupations in stereotypical ways, and girls more often aspired to nontraditional careers (Weisner & Wilson-Mitchell, 1990).

Mothers versus Fathers. In most aspects of differential treatment of boys and girls, fathers are the ones who discriminate the most. For example, in Chapter 10 we saw that fathers tend to engage in more physically stimulating play with their infant sons than daughters, whereas mothers tend to play in a quieter way with infants of both sexes. In childhood, fathers more than mothers encourage "gender-appropriate" activities, and they place more pressure to achieve on sons than on daughters (Jacklin & Maccoby, 1983; Lytton & Romney, 1991).

Parents also seem especially committed to ensuring the gender typing of children of their own sex. While mothers go on shopping trips and bake cookies with their daughters, fathers play catch, help coach the Saturday morning soccer game, and go fishing with their sons. This same-sex-child bias is another aspect of gender-role training that is more pronounced for fathers. When asked whether certain aspects of child rearing are the domain of one parent rather than the other, parents of boys indicated that fathers have a special responsibility to serve as a role model and play companion to their sons (Fagot, 1974).

TREATMENT BY TEACHERS. Besides parents, teachers encourage children to conform to traditional gender roles. In most classrooms, obedience is valued and assertiveness is discouraged. Research shows that preschool and elementary school teachers positively reinforce pupils of both sexes for "feminine" rather than "masculine" play and instructional activities (Brophy & Good, 1974; Etaugh, Collins, & Gerson, 1975; Oettingen, 1985). Surprisingly, experienced male teachers do so as much as female teachers (Fagot, 1985a; Robinson & Canaday, 1978). This "feminine bias" is believed to promote discomfort for boys in school, but it may be equally or even more harmful for girls, who willingly conform with possible long-term negative consequences for their sense of independence and self-esteem (Huston, 1983).

Teachers also act in ways that maintain and even extend gender roles taught at home. In preschool, they contribute to "gender-appropriate" activity preferences by calling on boys rather than girls to demonstrate how to use a new masculine-stereotyped item (Serbin, Connor, & Iler, 1979). They also react to children's social behaviors in terms of gender stereotypes. In one study, researchers observed teachers' interactions with very young children who were participants in toddler play groups. The teachers attended to boys' assertive behaviors (such as grabbing a toy or pushing a child) by talking to them, giving them a new toy, or physically moving them. When girls engaged in these behaviors, they were ignored. In contrast, girls' gestures, gentle touches, and talking were responded to more often than the same behaviors in boys. Children of both sexes were similar in their styles of interacting at the start of the play groups. But when observed again 9 months later, the boys had become more assertive, and the girls talked to teachers more (Fagot et al., 1985).

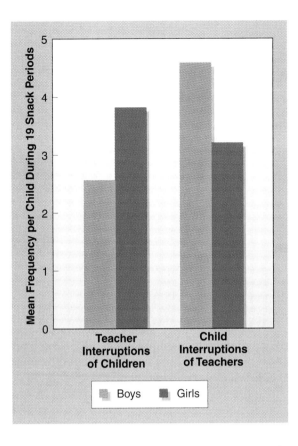

FIGURE 13.2 Interruptions by teachers of children and by children of teachers at snack time in preschool. Children were observed in groups of two boys and two girls at a table with a female teacher. (Adapted from Hendrick & Stange, 1991.)

At older ages, teachers discourage aggression and other forms of misbehavior in all children, but they do so more frequently and forcefully in boys (Etaugh & Harlow, 1975; Serbin et al., 1973). Teachers' greater scolding and disapproval of boys seems to result from an expectation that boys will misbehave more often than girls—a belief based partly on boys' actual behavior and partly on gender stereotypes (Huston, 1983). At the same time, preschool teachers follow parents' lead in interrupting girls more often than boys during conversation, thereby promoting boys' social dominance and girls' passivity. By age 4, children react in kind (see Figure 13.2). Boys interrupt their female teachers more often than girls do (Hendrick & Stange, 1991).

Just as teachers can promote gender typing, they can also do the opposite by modifying the way they communicate with children. For example, when teachers introduce new materials in a non–gender-biased fashion, praise all pupils for independence and persistence, and ignore attention-seeking and dependency, children's activity choices and behavior change accordingly (Serbin, Connor, & Citron, 1978; Serbin, Connor, & Iler, 1979). However, girls are more responsive to these interventions than boys are. And most of the time, changes in children's behavior are short lived. As soon as the usual interaction patterns resume in the classroom, children return to their prior ways of responding. Like nontraditional families, schools that are successful in modifying gender typing have clearly articulated philosophies about gender equality that pervade all aspects of classroom life (Berk & Lewis, 1977; Bianchi & Bakeman, 1978).

OBSERVATIONAL LEARNING. In addition to direct pressures from adults, numerous gender-typed models are available in children's environments. Although American society has changed to some degree, children come in contact with many real people who conform to traditional gender-role expectations. As Aletha Huston (1983) points out:

> The average child sees women cooking, cleaning, and sewing; working in "female" jobs such as clerical, secretarial, sales, teaching, nursing; choosing to dance, sew, or play bridge for recreation; and achieving in artistic or literary areas more often than in

science and engineering. That same child sees men mowing the lawn, washing the car, or doing household repairs; working in "male" occupations . . . choosing team sports, fishing, and nights with "the boys" for recreation; and achieving in math, science, and technical areas more often than in poetry or art. In school, the teachers of young children are women; the teachers of older students and the administrators with power are usually men. . . . Hence, although there are some individual differences, most children are exposed continually in their own environments to models of [gender-stereotyped] activities, interests, and roles. (pp. 420–421)

Reflections of gender in the media are also stereotyped. As we will see in Chapter 15, the way males and females are represented in television programs has changed very little in recent years (Signorielli, 1989). Also, analyses of the content of children's storybooks and textbooks reveal that they continue to portray males and females stereotypically. Boys and men outnumber girls and women as main characters, and males take center stage in most of the exciting and adventurous plot activities. Females, when they do appear as important characters, are often engaged in housekeeping and caring for children. The availability of gender-equitable reading materials for children is increasing, but school texts at the high school level have been especially slow to change (Noddings, 1992).

When children are exposed to nonstereotyped models, they are less traditional in their beliefs and behaviors. Children who see their parents cross traditional gender lines on a daily basis—mothers who are employed and fathers who take over household and child-care responsibilities—are less stereotyped in their views of men and women (Carlson, 1984; Levy, 1989; Selkow, 1984; Weinraub et al., 1984). Girls with career-oriented mothers show special benefits. They more often engage in typically masculine activities (such as physically active play), have higher educational aspirations, and hold nontraditional vocational goals (Hoffman, 1989; Tauber, 1979). Finally, among children of divorced parents, boys in father-absent homes and girls in mother-absent homes are less gender typed, perhaps because they have fewer opportunities to observe traditional gender roles than they would in a two-parent household (Brenes, Eisenberg, & Helmstadter, 1985; Santrock & Warshak, 1979).

PEERS. Earlier we noted that children's preference for same-sex peers is widespread and probably biologically influenced. But once formed, sex-segregated peer associations become powerful environments for strengthening traditional beliefs and behaviors.

Observations of preschoolers reveal that by age 3, same-sex peers positively reinforce one another for "gender-appropriate" play by praising, approving, imitating, or joining in the activity of an agemate (Fagot & Patterson, 1969; Langlois & Downs, 1980). In contrast, when preschoolers display "gender-inappropriate" play—for example, when boys play with dolls or girls with woodworking tools—they are criticized and rebuffed. Peer rejection is greater for boys who frequently engage in "cross-gender" behavior. Their male peers ignore them even when they do enter "masculine" activities (Fagot, 1977).

Boys and girls also develop different styles of social influence in sex-segregated peer groups. To get their way with male peers, boys more often rely on commands, threats, and physical force. In contrast, girls learn to emphasize polite requests and persuasion. These tactics succeed with other girls but not with boys, who start to ignore girls' gentle tactics by school entry (Borja-Alvarez, Zarbatany, & Pepper, 1991; Charlesworth & Dzur, 1987; Leaper, 1991). Consequently, an additional reason that girls may stop interacting with boys is that they do not find it very rewarding to communicate with an unresponsive social partner (Maccoby, 1988, 1990a).

Although children prefer same-sex playmates, mixed-sex interaction does occur, and adults can promote it. When teachers comment approvingly, interaction between boys and girls is sustained on a short-term basis (Serbin, Tonick, & Sternglanz, 1977). Also, recall from Chapter 2 that changing the design of the preschool classroom by joining gender-typed activity areas (blocks and housekeeping) increases mixed-sex play (see page 45). Interaction between boys and girls is encouraged on a long-term basis in classrooms in which teaching nonstereotyped values is an important part of the school curriculum (Lockheed, 1986).

Some researchers believe that fostering mixed-sex interaction is a vital means for broadening developmental possibilities for both boys and girls (Lloyd & Smith, 1985). However, to be successful, interventions may also need to modify the styles of social influence acquired by children in their same-sex peer relations. Otherwise, boys are likely to dominate and girls to react passively, thereby strengthening traditional gender roles and the stereotypes each sex holds of the other (Lockheed & Harris, 1984).

SIBLINGS. Growing up with siblings of the same or opposite sex also affects gender typing. But compared to peer influences, sibling effects are more complex because their impact depends on birth order and family size (Wagner, Schubert, & Schubert, 1993).

If sibling effects operated just like peer influences, we would expect a family of same-sex siblings to promote traditional gender roles and a family of mixed-sex siblings to do just the opposite. In an observational study of the play behaviors of 4- to 9-year-olds in their homes, the activities of same-sex siblings were highly "gender appropriate." But among opposite-sex siblings, play choices were determined by the sex of the older child. In fact, this effect was so strong that boys with older sisters actually played "house" and "dolls" as much as pairs of sisters did. In contrast, boys with older brothers never engaged in these "feminine" pursuits (Stoneman, Brody, & MacKinnon, 1986).

But curiously, other research contradicts these findings. For example, when 8- and 9-year-olds were videotaped playing with toys in a laboratory, play with "opposite-gender" toys was more common among children whose siblings were all of their own sex (Tauber, 1979). Several other studies also report that individuals with same-sex siblings are less stereotyped in their interests and personality characteristics than are those from mixed-sex families (Grotevant, 1978; Leventhal, 1970).

How can these conflicting results be explained? Recall from Chapter 10 that an important *nonshared family environmental influence* on personality development is that siblings often strive to be different from one another. This effect is strongest when children are of the same sex and come from large families. A close look at the

*W*hen siblings are the same sex, they are more likely to be assigned "cross-gender" chores. This father encourages his daughters to help with yard work—a responsibility typically reserved for boys. (MacDonald Photos/Envision)

research just described reveals that studies reporting a *modeling and reinforcement effect* (an increase in gender typing among same-sex siblings) were limited to children from small, two-child families. In contrast, those reporting a *differentiation effect* included children from large families. In homes with many children, a younger child may not emulate an older sibling out of a need to stand out as unique.

In addition, parents may sometimes relax pressures toward gender typing when their children are all of the same sex. Consistent with this idea, mothers are more willing to give their child an "opposite-gender" toy as a gift if the child's older sibling is of the same sex (Stoneman, Brody, & MacKinnon, 1986). Also, in all-girl and all-boy families, children are more likely to be assigned "cross-gender" chores because no "gender-appropriate" child is available to do the job. Therefore, families in which siblings are all of the same sex may provide some special opportunities to step out of traditional gender roles.

Brief Review

Cross-cultural similarities in gender typing are not consistent enough to support a strong role for biology. Prenatally administered androgens promote a variety of "masculine" behaviors in animal species. Studies of children with adrenogenital syndrome (AGS) suggest similar (but more limited) effects in humans that are difficult to separate from environmental influences. Beginning in infancy, adults view boys and girls differently, and they treat them differently. Parents actively promote "gender-appropriate" play activities and behaviors in young children. During middle childhood, they demand greater independence from boys in achievement situations, hold gender-stereotyped beliefs about children's abilities in school subjects, and grant boys more freedom in their everyday lives. Adoption of traditional gender roles receives further support from teachers, same-sex peers, and models in the surrounding environment. Sibling effects on gender typing are jointly influenced by sex of siblings, birth order, and family size.

GENDER-ROLE IDENTITY

Besides biological and environmental influences, another factor eventually comes to influence gender typing: *gender-role identity*, a person's perception of the self as relatively masculine or feminine in characteristics. By middle childhood, researchers can measure gender-role identity by asking children to rate themselves on personality traits, since at that time, self-concepts begin to emphasize psychological attributes over concrete behaviors (see Chapter 11). Table 13.3 shows some sample items from a gender-role identity questionnaire designed for school-age children, who are asked to evaluate each statement on a four-point scale, from "very true of me" to "not at all true of me" (Boldizar, 1991). Similar methods for assessing gender-role identity are used with adults (Bem, 1974; Spence, Helmreich, & Stapp, 1975).

Individuals differ considerably in the way they respond to these questionnaires. A child or adult with a "masculine" identity scores high on traditionally masculine items (such as self-sufficient, ambitious, and forceful) and low on traditionally feminine ones (such as affectionate, soft spoken, and cheerful). Someone with a "feminine" identity does just the reverse. Although the majority of individuals view themselves in gender-typed terms, a substantial minority (especially females) have a type of gender-role identity called **androgyny.** They score high on both masculine and feminine personality characteristics (Bem, 1974; Boldizar, 1991).

Research indicates that gender-role identity is a good predictor of psychological adjustment. Masculine and androgynous children and adults have a higher sense of self-esteem, whereas feminine individuals often think poorly of themselves (Alpert-Gillis & Connell, 1989; Boldizar, 1991). In line with their flexible self-definitions, androgynous individuals are more adaptable in behavior—for example, able to show masculine independence or feminine sensitivity, depend-

Androgyny

A type of gender-role identity in which the person scores high on both masculine and feminine personality characteristics.

TABLE 13.3 Sample Items from a Gender-Role Identity Questionnaire for School-Age Children

PERSONALITY TRAIT	ITEM
Masculine	
Self-sufficient	I can take care of myself.
Ambitious	I'm willing to work hard to get what I want.
Forceful	I can get most people to do what I want them to do most of the time.
Assertive	It's easy for me to tell people what I think, even when I know they will probably disagree with me.
Competitive	When I play games, I really like to win.
Feminine	
Affectionate	When I like someone, I do nice things for them to show them how I feel.
Soft-spoken	I usually speak softly.
Cheerful	I am a cheerful person.
Sympathetic	It makes me feel bad when someone else is feeling bad.
Yielding	When there's a disagreement, I usually give in and let others have their way.

SOURCE: From "Assessing Sex Typing and Androgyny in Children: The Children's Sex Role Inventory" by J. P. Boldizar, 1991, *Developmental Psychology, 27*, p. 509. Copyright © 1991 by the American Psychological Association. Reprinted by permission.

ing on the situation (Bem, 1975; Taylor & Hall, 1982). And they show greater maturity of moral judgment than individuals with other gender-role orientations (Bem, 1977; Block, 1973; Spence, Helmreich, & Stapp, 1975).

However, a close look at these findings reveals that the masculine component of androgyny is largely responsible for the superior psychological health of androgynous females over those with traditional identities (Taylor & Hall, 1982; Whitley, 1983). Feminine women seem to have adjustment difficulties because many of their traits are not highly valued by society. Nevertheless, the existence of an androgynous identity demonstrates that masculinity and femininity are not opposites, as many people believe. It is possible for children to acquire a mixture of positive qualities traditionally associated with each gender—an orientation that may best help them realize their potential. And in a future society in which feminine characteristics are socially rewarded to the same extent as masculine ones, androgyny may very well represent the ideal personality.

Emergence of Gender-Role Identity

How do children develop gender-role identities that consist of varying mixtures of masculine and feminine characteristics? Both social learning and cognitive-developmental answers to this question exist.

According to social learning theory, *behavior comes before self-perceptions.* Preschoolers first acquire gender-typed responses through modeling and reinforcement. Only later do they organize these behaviors into society's gender-role

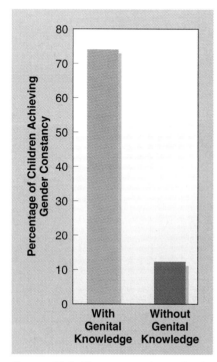

FIGURE 13.3 Percentage of preschoolers with and without genital knowledge who achieved gender constancy in a study of 3- to 5-year-olds. (Adapted from Bem, 1989.)

Gender constancy

The understanding that sex remains the same even if clothing, hairstyle, and play activities change.

Gender labeling

Kohlberg's first stage of gender understanding, in which preschoolers can label the sex of themselves and others correctly.

Gender stability

Kohlberg's second stage of gender understanding, in which preschoolers have a partial understanding of the permanence of sex; they grasp its stability over time.

Gender consistency

Kohlberg's final stage of gender understanding, in which children master gender constancy.

expectations, which they accept as appropriate for themselves. In contrast, cognitive-developmental theory emphasizes that *self-perceptions come before behavior.* Over the preschool years, children first acquire a cognitive appreciation of the permanence of their sex. They develop **gender constancy,** the understanding that sex remains the same even if clothing, hairstyle, and play activities change. Once formed, children use this idea to guide their actions, and a preference for gender-typed activities appears.

Social learning and cognitive-developmental theories lead to strikingly different predictions about gender-role development. But before we look at what research has to say about the accuracy of each, let's trace the development of gender constancy during the preschool years.

DEVELOPMENT OF GENDER CONSTANCY. Lawrence Kohlberg (1966) first proposed that before age 6 or 7, children cannot maintain the constancy of their gender, just as they cannot pass Piagetian conservation problems. Only gradually do they attain this understanding, by moving through three stages of development:

1. **Gender labeling.** During the early preschool years, children can label their own sex and that of others correctly. But when asked such questions as, "When you (a girl) grow up, could you ever be a daddy?" or "Could you be a boy if you wanted to?" young children freely answer yes (Slaby & Frey, 1975). In addition, when shown a doll whose hairstyle and clothing are transformed before their eyes, children indicate that the doll's sex is no longer the same (Marcus & Overton, 1978; McConaghy, 1979).
2. **Gender stability.** At this stage, children have a partial understanding of the permanence of sex. They grasp its stability over time. But even though they know that male and female babies will eventually become boys and girls and men and women, they continue to insist, as they did at younger ages, that changing hairstyle, clothing, or "gender-appropriate" activities will lead a person to switch sexes as well (Fagot, 1985b; Slaby & Frey, 1975).
3. **Gender consistency.** During the late preschool and early school years, children become certain of the *situational consistency* of their sex (Marcus & Overton, 1978; Siegal & Robinson, 1987). They know that sex remains constant even if a person decides to dress in "opposite-gender" clothes or engage in nontraditional activities (Emmerich, 1981; McConaghy, 1979).

Many studies confirm that gender constancy emerges in the sequence just described. In addition, mastery of gender constancy is associated with attainment of conservation, as Kohlberg assumed (De Lisi & Gallagher, 1991; Marcus & Overton, 1978). Yet research shows that cognitive immaturity is not the only reason for preschoolers' poor performance on gender-constancy tasks. It also results from limited social experience—in particular, lack of opportunity to learn about genital differences between the sexes. In many households in Western societies, young children do not see members of the opposite sex naked. Therefore, they distinguish males and females using the only information they do have—the way each gender dresses and behaves. In a study in which preschoolers' genital knowledge was assessed, most 3- to 5-year-olds who knew about genital characteristics also understood gender constancy (see Figure 13.3). In contrast, those who had not yet acquired genital information typically failed the gender-constancy task (Bem, 1989).

HOW WELL DOES GENDER CONSTANCY PREDICT GENDER-ROLE ADOPTION? Is cognitive-developmental theory correct that gender constancy is primarily responsible for children's gender-typed behavior? From findings discussed earlier in this chapter, perhaps you have already concluded that evidence for this assumption is weak. Long before most preschoolers appreciate the permanence of their sex, they show a wide variety of gender-typed responses and are especially attentive to same-sex models (Bussey & Bandura, 1984). "Gender-appropriate" behavior appears so early in the preschool years that modeling and reinforcement must account for its initial appearance. In line with social learning theory, a recent cross-sectional study found that preschoolers first acquired "gender-consistent" play behavior and clear awareness of peer disapproval of "cross-gender" activities. Only later, around age 4, did they apply these social standards to themselves, anticipating feeling good for play with "gender-appropriate" toys and bad for play with "gender-inappropriate" toys. Once these self-evaluative reactions were established, children seemed to rely on them to regulate their own actions. Gender-linked self-evaluations were effective predictors of gender-typed activities in a laboratory play session (Bussey & Bandura, 1992).

Although gender constancy does not initiate gender-role conformity, the cognitive changes that lead up to it do seem to facilitate gender typing. In one longitudinal study, children who reached the stage of gender labeling early (before 27 months) showed especially rapid development of "gender-appropriate" play preferences between $1\frac{1}{2}$ and $2\frac{1}{2}$ years of age. In this and other research, early gender labelers were also more knowledgeable about gender stereotypes than their late-labeling peers (Fagot & Leinbach, 1989; Fagot, Leinbach, & O'Boyle, 1992). In another study, preschoolers' understanding of gender stability was related to their knowledge of stereotypes, preference for same-sex playmates, and choice of "gender-consistent" toys (Martin & Little, 1990). These findings suggest that as soon as children acquire basic gender categories, they use them as the basis for acquiring gender-relevant information and modifying their own behavior.

If a complete understanding of gender constancy is not necessary for gender-role adoption, then just what is its function in children's development? Considerable debate surrounds this issue. Some researchers believe gender constancy strengthens children's gender typing. According to this view, when a new concept is formed, it should spark increased information seeking and attempts to behave in ways consistent with it (Ruble & Frey, 1991; Stangor & Ruble, 1989). Other researchers think gender constancy may free children to experiment with "opposite-gender" choices. From this perspective, children who have not attained gender constancy may engage in "gender-appropriate" behavior because they believe that doing so is what makes them a boy or girl. Once gender constancy is achieved, children understand that their sex remains the same regardless of their gender-role preferences. As a result, nontraditional behaviors become less threatening (Bem, 1989; Huston, 1983).

At present, research testing these hypotheses is conflicting. Some studies report that gender constancy leads to a rise in "gender-appropriate" activity choices (Eaton, Von Bargen, & Keats, 1981; Frey & Ruble, 1992; Stangor & Ruble, 1989). Others find that it predicts greater gender-stereotype flexibility (Ullian, 1976; Urberg, 1979). And yet a third set of findings indicates that gender constancy has no impact whatsoever on preschoolers' already well-developed gender-role preferences (Bussey & Bandura, 1992; Carter & Levy, 1988; Levy & Carter, 1989; Martin & Little, 1990). Whichever position is correct, the impact of gender constancy on children's gender typing is not great. As we will see in the following section, gender-role adoption is more powerfully affected by children's beliefs about how tight the connection needs to be between their own gender and behavior (Maccoby, 1990b).

Gender-Role Identity During Middle Childhood and Adolescence

During middle childhood, boys' and girls' gender-role identities follow different paths of development. Self-ratings on personality traits reveal that from third to sixth grade, boys strengthen their identification with the "masculine" role. In contrast, girls' identification with feminine characteristics declines. Although girls' overall orientation still leans toward the feminine side, they are clearly the more androgynous of the sexes (Boldizar, 1991; Serbin, Powlishta, & Gulko, 1993). In early adolescence, the gender-role identities of both sexes become more traditional

During middle childhood, girls feel freer than boys to engage in "opposite-sex" activities. These girls participate in a team sport typically reserved for boys and men. (TONY FREEMAN/PHOTOEDIT)

for a period of time. Then, by the mid- to late-adolescent years, a move back in the direction of androgyny occurs, a trend that is stronger for girls than boys (Huston & Alvarez, 1990; Leahy & Eiter, 1980).

Children's activity preferences and behaviors follow a similar pattern. Unlike boys, girls do not increase their preference for gender-typed activities in middle childhood. Instead, they experiment with a wider range of options. Besides cooking, sewing, and baby-sitting, they join organized sports teams, take up science projects, and build forts in the backyard (Huston-Stein & Higgins-Trenk, 1978). Then a temporary return to gender-stereotyped interests occurs in early adolescence that eventually becomes less pronounced (Leahy & Eiter, 1980; Stoddart & Turiel, 1985).

These changes are due to a mixture of social and cognitive forces. We have already seen that society attaches greater prestige to "masculine" characteristics. Girls undoubtedly become aware of this as they grow older. As a result, in middle childhood they start to identify with "masculine" traits and are attracted to some typically masculine activities. Messages from adults and agemates are also influential. A girl can act like a "tomboy" with little disapproval from parents and peers, but a boy who behaves like a "sissy" is likely to be ridiculed and rejected.

In early adolescence, puberty magnifies differences in appearance between boys and girls, causing teenagers to spend more time thinking about themselves in gender-linked ways. And when adolescents start to date, they often become more gender typed as a way of increasing their attractiveness to the opposite sex (Crockett, 1990). Finally, gains in perspective taking lead young teenagers to be very preoccupied with what others think, which adds to gender-role conformity. As young people move toward establishing a mature personal identity, they become less concerned with others' opinions of them and more involved in finding meaningful values to include in their self-definitions (see Chapter 11). As a result, highly stereotypic self-perceptions decline.

INDIVIDUAL DIFFERENCES. Although gender-role identity follows the general path of development just described, individual differences exist at all ages, and they are moderately related to gender-role behavior. A more masculine and less feminine identity is associated with a higher sense of overall academic competence as well as better performance on spatial and mathematical tasks (Boldizar, 1991; Newcombe & Dubas, 1992; Signorella & Jamison, 1986). Although girls with feminine orientations are more popular with agemates, masculine-oriented children of both sexes are more assertive and less dependent (Hall & Halberstadt, 1980). At present, androgynous children are not especially advantaged in any of these areas.

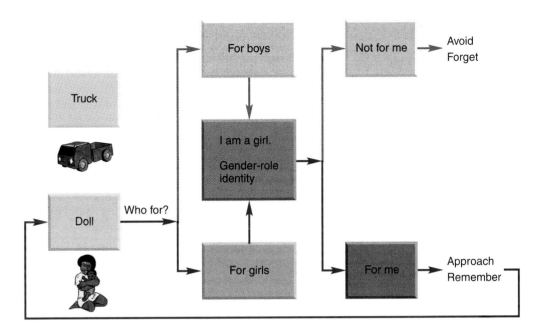

FIGURE 13.4 Effect of gender schemas on gender-typed preferences and behaviors. This girl's network of gender schemas leads her to approach and explore "feminine" toys, such as dolls, and to avoid "masculine" ones, such as trucks. (From "A Schematic Processing Model of Sex Typing and Stereotyping in Children" by C. L. Martin & C. F. Halverson, Jr., 1981, *Child Development, 52*, p. 1121. © The Society for Research in Child Development, Inc. Adapted by permission.)

Instead, a gender-role identity that leans toward the masculine side seems to be the key factor in predicting positive cognitive and social outcomes for children.

Since these relationships are correlational, we cannot really tell whether masculine and feminine self-perceptions *arise from particular behaviors* (as social learning theory assumes) or *serve as guides for behavior* (as cognitive-developmental theory predicts). According to recent theory and research, the answer is *both*, as we will see in the following section.

Gender Schema Theory: A New Approach to Gender-Role Identity

Gender schema theory is an information-processing approach to gender typing that combines social learning and cognitive-developmental features. It also integrates the various elements of the gender-typing process—stereotyping, gender-role identity, and gender-role adoption—into a unified picture of how masculine and feminine orientations emerge and are often strongly maintained (Bem, 1981, 1983; Martin & Halverson, 1981, 1987).

According to gender schema theory, at an early age, children respond to instruction from others, picking up gender-typed preferences and behaviors. At the same time, they start to organize these experiences into *gender schemas*, or masculine and feminine categories, that they use to interpret their world. As soon as children can label their own sex, they start to select gender schemas that are consistent with it, applying those categories to themselves. As a result, self-perceptions become gender typed and serve as additional gender schemas that children use to process information and guide their own behavior.

Figure 13.4 shows how this network of gender schemas strengthens gender-typed preferences and behaviors. Let's take the example of a child who has been taught that "dolls are for girls" and "trucks are for boys" and who also knows that she is a girl. Our child uses this information to make decisions about how to behave. Because her schemas lead her to conclude that "dolls are for me," when

Gender schema theory
An information-processing approach to gender typing that combines social learning and cognitive-developmental features to explain how environmental pressures and children's cognitions work together to affect stereotyping, gender-role identity, and gender-role adoption.

TABLE 13.4 Current Sex-Related Differences in Mental Abilities and Personality Traits

CHARACTERISTIC	SEX-RELATED DIFFERENCE*
Verbal abilities	Girls show faster early language development and are advantaged in reading achievement throughout the school years.
Spatial abilities	Boys outperform girls in spatial abilities by middle childhood, a difference that persists throughout the life span. However, the difference is evident only on certain types of spatial tasks.
Mathematical abilities	Beginning in adolescence, boys do better than girls on tests of mathematical reasoning. The difference is especially pronounced among high-achieving pupils. Many more boys perform exceptionally well in math.
School achievement	Girls get better grades than boys in all academic subjects from kindergarten through third grade, after which the difference disappears. By junior high school, boys start to show an advantage in mathematics.
Achievement motivation	Sex-related differences in achievement motivation are linked to type of task. Boys perceive themselves as more competent and have higher expectancies of success in "masculine" achievement areas, such as mathematics, sports, and mechanical skills. Girls have higher expectancies and set higher standards for themselves in "feminine" areas, such as English and art.
Emotional sensitivity	As early as the preschool years, girls are more effective senders and receivers of emotional information. Girls also score higher on self-report measures of empathy, although only between 1 and 2 years are they more empathic in real-life situations.
Fear, timidity, and anxiety	Girls are more fearful and timid than boys, a difference that is present as early as the first year of life. In school, girls are more anxious about failure and expend more energy trying to avoid it. In contrast, boys are greater risk-takers. This difference is reflected in boys' higher injury rates at every age between 2 and 18 years.
Compliance and dependency	Beginning in the preschool years, girls are more compliant than boys in response to directives from either adults or peers. They also engage in more help-seeking from adults and score higher in dependency on personality tests. In contrast, boys are more dominant and assertive.
Activity level	Boys are more active than girls.
Aggression	Beginning in the preschool years, boys are more aggressive than girls, but the difference is small during childhood. In adolescence, boys are far more likely to become involved in antisocial behavior and violent crime.
Developmental problems	Many types of developmental problems are more common among boys, including speech and language disorders, reading disabilities, and behavior problems such as hyperactivity, hostile acting-out behavior, and emotional and social immaturity. More boys than girls are born with genetic defects and mental retardation.

*During childhood, all differences listed are small; gender accounts for no more than 5 percent of individual differences among children.

SOURCES: Benbow & Stanley, 1980; Eisenberg & Lennon, 1983; Feingold, 1988; Friedman, 1989; Hall, 1978; Hall & Halberstadt, 1981; Hyde, 1984; Hyde & Linn, 1988; Linn & Hyde, 1989; Prior et al., 1993; Reznick et al., 1989; Zahn-Waxler et al., 1992.

Jacklin's review did underestimate sex-related differences, particularly in the realm of personality. However, even though more differences have since been confirmed, a repeated conclusion of new studies is that the disparities between boys and girls are quite small. Gender accounts for no more than 5 percent of individual differences among children in any characteristic, leaving most to be explained by other factors (Deaux, 1985).* Also, some differences have changed over time. For example, during the past several decades, the gender gap has narrowed in all areas of mental ability in which differences have been identified, except for upper-level mathematics, where boys' advantage has remained constant (Feingold, 1988; Friedman, 1989; Linn & Hyde, 1989). This trend is a reminder that sex-related differences are not fixed for all time. The general picture of how boys and girls differ may not be the same in the twenty-first century as it is today.

Mental Abilities

Sex-related differences in mental abilities remain consistent with the findings of Maccoby and Jacklin—favoring girls in verbal skills and boys in spatial and mathematical skills. Many researchers believe heredity is involved in the verbal and spatial disparities, and they have attempted to identify the specific biological processes responsible. But no biological factor operates in an experiential vacuum. In the case of each type of intellectual ability, we will see that environment plays an important role.

VERBAL ABILITIES. Early in development, girls are ahead in language progress. They begin to talk earlier and show faster vocabulary growth during the second year, after which boys catch up (see Chapter 9). Throughout the school years, girls attain higher scores on reading achievement tests and account for a lower percentage of children referred for remedial reading instruction (Halpern, 1986; Lummis & Stevenson, 1990; Mullis et al., 1991). However, girls' advantage on tests of general verbal ability has declined considerably since the 1970s. At present, it is so small that researchers judge it to be negligible (Feingold, 1988; Hyde & Linn, 1988).

Girls' more rapid early language development is difficult to explain in purely environmental terms. The most common biological explanation is their faster rate of physical maturation. In animals as well as humans, androgens appear to slow the development of the left cerebral hemisphere, where language functions are housed for most people (see Chapter 5). The left side of the cortex is slightly smaller and functionally less mature in males than females (Diamond et al., 1983; Shucard et al., 1981).

However, girls' superior reading performance is probably due to experience, since by school entry their advantage in language has long since disappeared. Earlier in this chapter, we showed that children think of reading as a feminine subject, that parents rate daughters as more competent at it, and that schools are feminine-biased settings in which boys' greater activity level and noncompliance lead them to be targets of teacher disapproval. Consistent with this idea, girls' tendency to learn to read more quickly is reduced or eliminated in countries where reading and early school learning are regarded as well suited to the male gender role (e.g., Preston, 1962).

SPATIAL ABILITIES. Spatial skills involve the ability to mentally manipulate visual information. The male advantage in spatial performance is small (Linn & Hyde, 1989). However, since sex-related differences in spatial abilities have implications for math and science education and entry into scientific careers, they have commanded a great deal of research attention.

*Although this estimate is very small and means that the distributions of boys' and girls' scores on every ability and personality characteristic overlap considerably, researchers still regard a difference of this size as meaningful. For example, even if gender accounted for only 4 to 5 percent of individual differences, this would amount to 60 percent of one group but only 40 percent of the other scoring above the mean on the attribute in question.

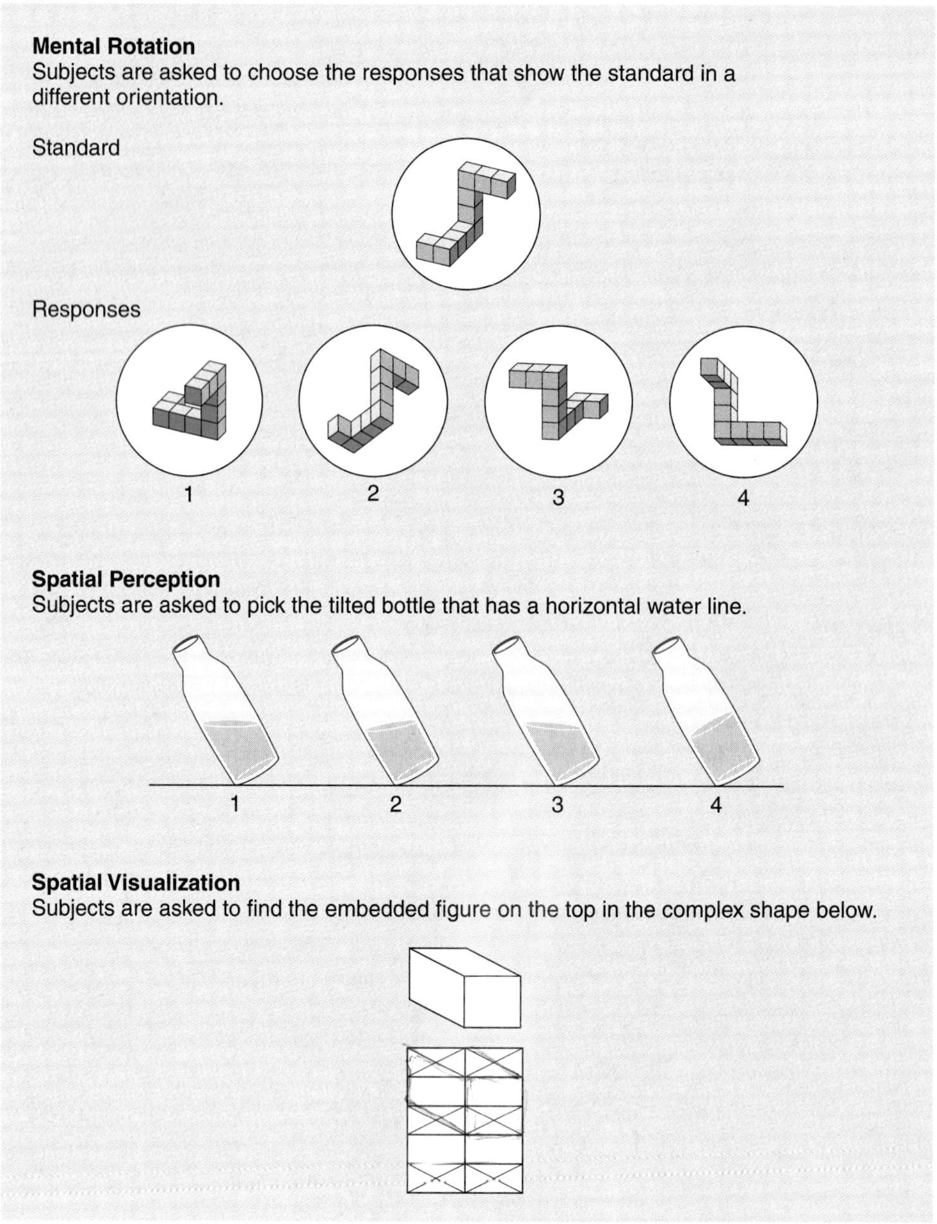

Mental Rotation
Subjects are asked to choose the responses that show the standard in a different orientation.

Standard

Responses

1   2   3   4

Spatial Perception
Subjects are asked to pick the tilted bottle that has a horizontal water line.

1   2   3   4

Spatial Visualization
Subjects are asked to find the embedded figure on the top in the complex shape below.

FIGURE 13.5 Types of spatial tasks on which the performance of males and females has been compared. (From "Emergence and Characterization of Sex Differences in Spatial Ability: A Meta-Analysis" by M. C. Linn & A. C. Petersen, 1985, *Child Development, 56,* pp. 1482, 1483, 1485. © The Society for Research in Child Development, Inc. Reprinted by permission.)

The study of spatial skills is complicated by the fact that a variety of spatial tasks exist (see Figure 13.5). The gender gap is strongest for *mental rotation tasks,* in which subjects must rotate a three-dimensional figure rapidly and accurately inside their heads. In addition, males do better on *spatial perception tasks,* in which people must determine spatial relationships based on the orientation of their own bodies. Sex-related differences in *spatial visualization tasks* involving complex mental manipulation of spatially presented material are less clear. Many strategies can be used to solve these problems. Although males may solve them with spatial manipulations, perhaps females come up with other equally effective cognitive strategies and, for this reason, do just as well (Linn & Petersen, 1985).

Sex-related differences in spatial abilities are clearly evident by middle childhood and persist throughout the life span (Johnson & Meade, 1987; Kerns & Berenbaum, 1991; Linn & Petersen, 1985). The pattern is consistent enough to suggest a biological mediator. Although many controversial hypotheses about the biological mechanisms involved have been suggested, recent research has focused on two of them:

1. *The brain lateralization/maturation rate hypothesis.* Deborah Waber's (1976) theory of how brain lateralization and maturation rate work together to produce

disparities between males and females in mental abilities has been the subject of intense research scrutiny in recent years. Waber hypothesized that girls' faster rate of physical maturation leads to earlier specialization of the left hemisphere. This enhances verbal skills, which develop quickly during the first few years of life. In contrast, boys' slower maturation rate is believed to promote stronger right-hemispheric specialization during adolescence, a pattern believed to enhance later-emerging spatial abilities.

As yet, research testing Waber's theory offers only limited support. Some studies report a slight advantage in spatial skills for late maturing adolescents (Gilger & Ho, 1989; Newcombe & Dubas, 1987). Others, however, find no relationship between maturation rate and mental abilities (Newcombe, Dubas, & Baenninger, 1989). Furthermore, even when late maturers outperform early maturers on spatial tasks, they do not always show evidence of greater right-hemispheric specialization (Bruder et al., 1987; Newcombe & Dubas, 1992).

2. *The prenatal androgen hormone hypothesis.* A second hypothesis is that prenatal exposure to androgen hormones accounts for the male advantage in spatial abilities. In one study, adolescents who had experienced elevated androgen levels due to a genetic disorder did better on a battery of spatial tasks than did their unaffected siblings and cousins, who served as controls (Resnick et al., 1986). Additional research indicates that individuals with severe prenatal deficiencies of either male or female hormones have difficulty with spatial skills (Hier & Crowley, 1982; Netley, 1986).* And one study—this time of prenatal androgen variation within normal range— found a link with spatial ability at age 4, but only for girls and in the opposite direction expected: The greater the hormone exposure, the lower the spatial score (Finegan, Niccols, & Sitarenios, 1992). These findings suggest that prenatal hormones may affect spatial skills, but they do not operate according to a straightforward rule. Some investigators believe hormones may exert their influence by interacting with brain lateralization and maturation rate, but a great deal of work needs to be done to sort out these complex relationships.

Although less attention has been devoted to the impact of environment on sex-related differences in spatial abilities, several studies suggest that experience can widen or reduce the gender gap. Boys' early play activities may contribute to their advantage, since children who play with manipulative, "masculine" toys do better on spatial tasks (Dirks, 1982; Fagot & Littman, 1976). Also, girls' limited exposure to certain scientific principles may sometimes prevent them from demonstrating their spatial competencies. In a study in which female college students were given information about a relevant physical rule before solving the spatial perception problem in Figure 13.5, their performance equaled that of males (Liben & Golbeck, 1984). Finally, on spatial rotation tasks for which sex-related differences are largest, females differ only in speed, not accuracy, and training improves their scores substantially (Linn & Petersen, 1985; Lohman, 1988). Perhaps females' greater anxiety about failing in achievement situations contributes to their longer solution time, although less efficient mental strategies may also play a role.

MATHEMATICAL ABILITIES. The male advantage in mathematics is clearly evident by high school, although among highly gifted youngsters, it is present earlier—by age 13. When all students are considered, the size of the difference is small. But among the most capable, the gender gap is considerable. In a series of studies, Camilla Benbow and Julian Stanley (1980, 1983) examined the mathematical performance of thousands of high-achieving seventh- and eighth-grade pupils invited to take the Scholastic Aptitude Test long before they needed to do so for college admission. Year after year, the boys outscored the girls on the mathematics subtest. Twice as many boys as girls had scores above 500; 13 times as many scored over 700. Sex-related differences in mathematics do not occur on all kinds of test items. Boys and girls perform equally well on tests of basic math knowledge, and girls do

*C*hildren who play with manipulative, "masculine" toys do better on spatial tasks. Providing girls with opportunities to engage in construction activities may reduce the gender gap in spatial abilities. (JEFF GREENBERG/PHOTO RESEARCHERS)

* In Chapter 3, we indicated that Turner syndrome girls, who are missing an X chromosome, have trouble with spatial tasks. They are deficient in female sex hormones.

better in computational skills. The difference appears on tests of mathematical reasoning, primarily in solving complex word problems (Friedman, 1989; Hyde, Fenema, & Lamon, 1990).

Some researchers believe the gender gap in mathematics, particularly at the high end of the distribution, is biologically based. Although several hypotheses about the biological processes involved exist (including sex hormones and brain lateralization), none have been verified (Benbow, 1988). One common assumption is that sex-related differences in mathematical abilities are rooted in boys' superior spatial skills. If this is true, then children's spatial and mathematical scores should be positively correlated, but research reveals inconsistent relationships. And in some studies, verbal skills are just as effective as spatial skills in predicting math achievement (Linn & Petersen, 1985; Parsons, 1982).

Although evidence for the role of heredity is weak, support for the importance of environment has become increasingly strong. The mathematics gender gap is related to pupil attitudes and self-esteem. Earlier in this chapter, we noted that long before sex-related differences in math achievement are present, children view math as a masculine subject and parents believe boys are better at it. Furthermore, girls' tendency to attribute their academic failures to low ability (rather than insufficient effort) reduces their self-confidence and promotes high anxiety in achievement situations (see Chapter 11). Girls display this learned-helpless style particularly strongly in mathematics (Stipek, 1984). Over time, girls start to regard math as less useful for their future lives and are more likely than boys to stop taking math courses when they are not mandatory. The end result of this chain of events is that girls—even those who are highly talented academically—are handicapped in developing abstract mathematical concepts and problem solving (Linn & Hyde, 1989; Marsh, 1989b).

Personality Traits

Sex-related differences in personality traits exist that are in line with gender stereotypes. Those most often studied include emotional sensitivity, compliance and dependency, and aggression.

EMOTIONAL SENSITIVITY. Females are stereotyped as the more emotionally sensitive of the sexes. Recent reviews of many studies indicate that, in fact, females send and receive emotional messages more effectively than do males. The difference, although small, appears early. When asked to make judgments of others' emotional states using nonverbal cues, girls perform better than boys beginning in the preschool years (Hall, 1978). Girls also express feelings more freely through facial and body gestures (Hall & Halberstadt, 1981). Furthermore, as early as age 2, they use more emotion words in their conversations with others (Dunn, Bretherton, & Munn, 1987).

It would be reasonable to expect these differences to extend to empathic responding, but so far the evidence is mixed. On self-report measures of empathy, girls and women consistently score higher than boys and men. But when observed for behavioral signs that they are empathizing with the distress of a nearby person, 1- to 2-year-old girls display greater concern than do boys, but preschool- through adolescent-age youngsters show no difference (Eisenberg & Lennon, 1983; Zahn-Waxler et al., 1992; Zahn-Waxler, Robinson, & Emde, 1992).

As with other attributes, both biological and environmental explanations for sex-related differences in emotional sensitivity exist. One possibility is that females are genetically prewired to be more emotionally sensitive as a way of ensuring that they will be well prepared for the caregiving role. Against this interpretation is a growing body of evidence that girls are not naturally more nurturant than boys. Before age 5, boys and girls spend equal amounts of time talking to and playing with a baby in either laboratory or natural environments (Berman, 1986; Fogel et al., 1987). In middle childhood, boys' willingness to relate to infants declines, but they

*G*irls' greater emotional sensitivity is probably environmentally determined, since boys are just as caring and affectionate in certain situations—for example, when interacting with a cherished pet.
(LARRY LAWFER/THE PICTURE CUBE)

continue to respond with just as much care and affection to pets and elderly relatives (Melson & Fogel, 1988). Furthermore, sex-related differences in emotional sensitivity are not present in adulthood when parents interact with their own babies. In Chapter 10, we saw that fathers are very affectionate with their infants and are just as competent caregivers as mothers. And in Chapter 4, we noted that men and women react in a similar fashion to the sound of a crying baby.

Cultural expectations that girls be warm and expressive and boys be distant and controlled seem largely responsible for the gender gap in emotional sensitivity. In infancy, mothers respond more often to a baby girl's cries of distress than to a boy's (Malatesta et al., 1986; Malatesta & Haviland, 1982). And during childhood, parents place much greater pressure on girls to be kind, considerate, and compassionate (Zahn-Waxler, Cole, & Barrett, 1991). In addition, when talking about past experiences with their preschool children, both mothers and fathers use a greater number and variety of emotion words and are more willing to discuss sadness with their daughters than their sons (Fivush, 1991; Kuebli & Fivush, 1992). Taken together, these findings suggest that girls are given far more encouragement to express and reflect on feelings than are boys.

COMPLIANCE AND DEPENDENCY. Beginning in the preschool years, girls are more compliant than boys, both to adult and peer demands. Girls also seek help and information from adults more often and score higher in dependency on personality tests (Block, 1976; Jacklin & Maccoby, 1978). There is widespread agreement that these patterns of behavior are learned, and they have much to do with activity environments in which boys and girls spend their time.

From an early age, girls are encouraged to participate in adult-structured activities at home and in preschool. In contrast, boys are attracted to activities in which adults are minimally involved or entirely absent. As a result, boys and girls engage in very different social behaviors. Compliance and bids for help and attention appear more often in adult-structured contexts, whereas assertiveness, leadership, and creative use of materials occur more often in unstructured pursuits (Carpenter, 1983). Ideally, boys and girls should experience a balanced array of activities to develop both the capacity to lead and assert as well as comply with others' directives. In one study, the assertive and compliant tendencies of preschoolers of both sexes were easily modified by assigning them to classroom activities that differed in degree of adult structure (Carpenter, Huston, & Holt, 1986).

AGGRESSION. Aggression has attracted *behaviour* more research attention than any other sex-related difference. In Chapter 12, we noted that boys are more aggressive than girls in many cultures. The findings are consistent in study after study: Beginning in the preschool years, boys engage in more physical and verbal aggression, and by adolescence, boys are ten times more likely to be involved in antisocial behavior and violent crime (U.S. Department of Justice, 1992).

Nevertheless, the gender gap in aggression is small in childhood, accounting for only 5 percent of individual differences (Hyde, 1984). Also, it tends to appear in particular situations. Physically aggressive acts are especially frequent in boys' interactions with other boys; they occur less often in mixed-sex interaction (Barrett, 1979; Maccoby & Jacklin, 1980). And boys are far more likely than girls to retaliate with aggression when they are physically attacked (Darvill & Cheyne, 1981).

In early adolescence, boys continue to rely on direct confrontation when provoked by a peer. In contrast, girls' aggressive acts become increasingly indirect and concealed. In one longitudinal study extending from fourth grade through junior high, children were asked at yearly intervals to describe two recent conflicts with agemates, one same-sex and one opposite-sex. As Figure 13.6 shows, by seventh grade, the percentage of girls reporting same-sex disputes involving social alienation—malicious gossip, rumor-spreading, and exclusion—rose dramatically. Boys never mentioned these kinds of conflicts! Unlike direct attacks, these hidden social cruelties make it difficult for victims to identify the perpetrator and retaliate. Consequently, they permit girls to behave aggressively while avoiding

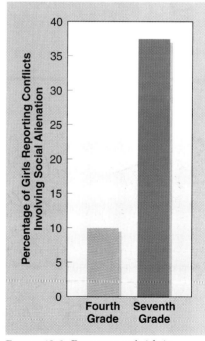

FIGURE 13.6 Percentage of girls in fourth and seventh grade reporting conflicts involving social alienation (malicious gossip, rumor-spreading, and exclusion) with same-sex peers. Findings for boys are not shown because they never mentioned these kinds of conflicts. (Adapted from Cairns et al., 1989.)

open conflict, which violates the "feminine" gender role. Because girls' aggression goes underground in this way, it becomes difficult to observe at older ages. Since most research focuses on physical and verbal assaults, it probably underestimates girls' aggressiveness by early adolescence.

Biological Influences. Because greater aggression by males is present early in life, generalizes across cultures, and is found in many animal species, almost all researchers agree that biology must be involved. Earlier we mentioned that androgen hormones are related to aggression in animals; they are also believed to play a role in humans. But think back for a moment to our discussion of children with adrenogenital syndrome. Although they were exposed to abnormally high levels of androgens during the prenatal period, they were not more aggressive (although they did show higher activity levels). This suggests that in humans, only a *predisposition* for aggression results from androgen exposure. Researchers currently believe that the impact of male sex hormones is indirect. They affect certain behaviors that, when combined with environmental influences, lead to a higher likelihood of aggressive outcomes.

One possibility is that prenatal androgens promote physical activity, which may or may not be translated into aggression, depending on child-rearing conditions. For example, a very active child who participates in activities that involve aggression, such as water fights, boxing matches, and tackle football, is likely to become more aggressive than a child who participates in nonaggressive pursuits, such as track, baseball, or swimming. One study lends support to this idea. Third- and fourth-graders indicated their own activity preferences and nominated the most aggressive pupils in their class in fall of the school year and 1 year later. Girls showed little attraction to aggressive activities, and their choices did not predict later behavior. But for boys who were neither high nor low in aggression at the beginning of the study, activity preferences had a strong impact. Those who liked activities involving aggressive acts were viewed by peers as much higher in aggression the following year (Bullock & Merrill, 1980).

Another hypothesis is that prenatal hormones influence brain functioning in ways that affect children's emotional reactions. According to this view, hormone levels might induce more frequent displays of excitement, anger, or anxiety, which have an increased likelihood of resulting in aggression in the presence of certain environmental conditions. Indeed, there is evidence that early hormone levels (measured at birth from umbilical cord blood samples) predict excited emotional states for boys during the first 2 years of life, although no relationships exist for girls (Marcus et al., 1985).

Besides the prenatal period, adolescence is a second phase in which hormonal changes have implications for aggressive behavior. Adolescent boys who are high in androgens report more sadness and anxiety, and they also display more aggressive traits, such as hostile reactions to threatening acts from peers, low tolerance for frustration, and rebellious and delinquent behavior (Nottelmann et al., 1987; Olweus, 1980; Susman et al., 1987). In one study, higher estrogens and androgens were linked to more frequent expressions of anger by adolescent girls in a laboratory discussion session with their parents (Inoff-Germain et al., 1988).

Although much more research is needed, the evidence we have so far suggests that there are multiple pathways between hormones and aggression, that each involves a complex series of steps, and that each may vary with the sex and age of the child. It is also clear that whether hormonally induced responses, such as activity level or emotional state, are channeled into aggressive acts depends on environmental conditions.

Environmental Influences. In Chapter 12, we showed how strife-ridden families and coercive child-rearing practices promote aggressive behavior. For several reasons, boys are more likely to be affected by these interaction patterns than girls. Parents more often use physical punishment with boys, which encourages them to adopt the same tactics in their own relationships. In contrast, inductive discipline, which promotes self-control and empathy, is used more often with girls (Block, 1978). In addition, parents are less likely to interpret fighting as aggressive when it occurs among boys (Condry & Ross, 1985). The stereotype reflected in the familiar saying "Boys will be boys" may lead many adults to overlook male hostility unless it is extreme. This sets up conditions in which it is encouraged, or at least tolerated. In view of these findings, it is not surprising that school-age boys expect less parental disapproval and report feeling less guilty for aggressive acts than do girls (Perry, Perry, & Weiss, 1989).

Furthermore, arguing between husband and wife, although stimulating aggression among all family members, seems to have a greater effect on boys. In a study in which 2-year-olds overheard angry verbal exchanges between adults while playing with a familiar peer in a laboratory, girls tended to show fearful, withdrawing reactions, such as freezing in place and covering or hiding their faces. In contrast, boys engaged in more aggression, lashing out at their playmates (Cummings, Iannotti, & Zahn-Waxler, 1985). During the school years, boys report feeling more hostile than do girls after observing angry exchanges between adults (Cummings et al., 1989).

Putting together all of the evidence, we can see that boys have a higher likelihood of becoming embroiled in circumstances that serve as training ground for aggressive and antisocial behavior. Biological predispositions and encouragement from the social environment, acting in complex combination, are responsible.

Brief Review

Boys and girls differ in a variety of mental abilities and personality traits. Girls show more rapid early language development and higher reading achievement and are more emotionally sensitive, compliant, and dependent. Boys are advantaged in spatial and mathematical skills and are more aggressive. However, these disparities are small and in the case of mental abilities, have declined considerably over the last several decades. Although biological factors are involved in some differences, they make it only slightly easier for one sex to acquire certain attributes. Both boys and girls can learn all of them, and families, schools, and peers affect the size of each difference. Finally, in view of the many ways in which it is possible for human beings to vary, our overall conclusion must be that males and females are much more alike in developmental potential than they are different from each other.

DEVELOPING NON-GENDER-STEREOTYPED CHILDREN

The Milestones table on page 552 provides an overview of changes in gender typing considered in this chapter. We have seen that children's developmental possibilities can be seriously limited by persistent gender stereotypes in their culture. Although many researchers and laypeople recognize the importance of rearing children who feel free to express their human qualities without fear of violating gender-role expectations, no easy recipe exists for accomplishing this difficult task. It needs to be tackled on many fronts—in the home, at school, and in the wider society.

Throughout our discussion, we have mentioned ways in which gender stereotyping and gender-role adoption can be reduced. But even children who are fortunate enough to grow up in homes and schools that minimize stereotyping will eventually encounter it in the media and in what men and women typically do in the surrounding community. Until societal values change, children need early experiences that repeatedly counteract their readiness to absorb our culture's extensive network of gender-linked associations.

Sandra Bem (1983, 1984) suggests that parents and teachers make a special effort to delay young children's learning of gender-stereotyped messages. Adults can begin by eliminating traditional gender roles from their own behavior and

Age	Gender Stereotyping and Gender-Role Adoption	Gender-Role Identity	Sex-Related Differences in Mental Abilities and Personality Traits
1½–5 years	• "Gender-appropriate" play activities emerge and become highly consistent. • Gender stereotyping of activities, occupations, and behaviors develops. • Preference for same-sex peers emerges and increases.	• Gender constancy develops in a three-stage sequence over the preschool years: gender labeling, gender stability, and gender consistency. • By the end of this period, gender-linked self-evaluations form.	• Girls show more rapid language development during the second year, after which boys catch up. • Girls' greater emotional sensitivity emerges and persists into adulthood. • Girls' greater compliance and dependency is evident. • Boys' greater verbal and physical aggression emerges and persists into adulthood.
6–11 years	• Knowledge of gender stereotypes strengthens, especially in areas of personality traits and achievement. • Gender stereotyping becomes more flexible. • Girls experiment with "opposite-gender" activities; boys' preference for "masculine" pursuits increases.	• "Masculine" gender-role identity strengthens among boys; girls' gender-role identity becomes more androgynous.	• Girls are ahead in reading achievement throughout the school years. • Boys' advantage in spatial abilities emerges and persists throughout the life span. • Boys' greater verbal and physical aggression is sustained; by the end of this age period, girls show a rise in aggressive acts involving social alienation (gossip, rumor-spreading, and exclusion).
12–20 years	• Traditional gender-role conformity increases in early adolescence and gradually declines. • Preference for same-sex peers becomes less pronounced after puberty.	• Gender-role identities of both sexes become more traditional in early adolescence, a trend that gradually declines, especially among girls.	• Boys' advantage in mathematical reasoning emerges. 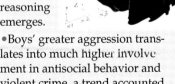 • Boys' greater aggression translates into much higher involvement in antisocial behavior and violent crime, a trend accounted for by a small number of adolescents.

Note: These milestones represent overall age trends. Individual differences exist in the precise age at which each milestone is attained and in the extent of gender typing.

from the alternatives they provide for children. For example, mothers and fathers can take turns making dinner, bathing children, and driving the family car, and they can provide sons and daughters with both trucks and dolls and pink and blue clothing. Teachers can make sure that all children spend some time each day in adult-structured and unstructured activities. Also, efforts can be made to shield children from media presentations that indicate males and females differ in what they can do.

At the same time, parents can teach young children that anatomy and reproduction are the only characteristics that determine a person's sex. Because many preschoolers do not understand this idea, they mistakenly assume that arbitrary cultural practices are the basis of gender. By encouraging children to construct their first gender-linked associations on the basis of biology, parents can capitalize on preschoolers' tendency to view rules and categories rigidly. Once young children grasp that sex is narrowly determined by genital characteristics, then they should be less likely to define it in terms of dress, activities, and behavior (Bem, 1984).

Once children notice the wide array of gender stereotypes in their society, parents and teachers can point out exceptions. For example, they can arrange for children to see males and females pursuing nontraditional careers. And they can reason with children, explaining that interests and skills, not sex, should determine a person's occupation. Furthermore, older children can be told about the historical roots and current consequences of gender equalities in our society—why, for example, there has never been a female president, why few fathers stay home with their children, and why stereotyped views of men and women are hard to change (Bem, 1984). As these efforts help children build concepts of themselves and their social world that are not limited by a masculine–feminine dichotomy, they contribute to the transformation of societal values. And they bring us closer to a time when people will be released from the constraints of traditional gender roles.

CHAPTER SUMMARY

Gender Stereotypes and Gender Roles

- Despite progress in the area of women's rights, over the past several decades, gender stereotypes have remained essentially the same. **Instrumental traits** continue to be regarded as masculine, **expressive traits** as feminine—a dichotomy that is widely held around the world. Stereotyping of physical characteristics, occupations, and activities is also common.

- Children begin to acquire **gender stereotypes** and **gender roles** early in the preschool years. By middle childhood, they are aware of many stereotypes, including activities, occupations, personality traits, and achievement areas. Preschoolers' understanding of gender stereotypes is rigid and inflexible. Over the elementary school years, children develop a more open-minded view of what males and females can and should do.

- Individual and group differences in children's gender-stereotype knowledge and flexibility exist. Children acquire the components of gender stereotyping in different patterns and to different degrees. Boys hold more stereotyped views than girls, white children more than black children. Although social-class differences do not exist in childhood, middle-class adolescents hold more flexible views than do their lower-class counterparts.

- Awareness of gender stereotypes is only weakly related to gender-role adoption. Stereotype flexibility, however, is a moderately good predictor of children's willingness to cross gender lines during the school years.

Biological and Environmental Influences on Gender Stereotyping and Gender-Role Adoption

- Cross-cultural similarities in gender stereotypes and gender-role adoption have been used to support the role of biology in **gender typing.** However, great diversity exists in the extent to which cultures endorse the instrumental–expressive dichotomy, and cases of traditional gender-role reversal exist.

- Prenatal androgen levels may underlie sex-related differences in activity level, which, in turn, promote children's preference for same-sex playmates. Research on children with adrenogenital syndrome (AGS) supports this conclusion. However, other "masculine" gender-role behaviors of AGS children may be due to environmental pressures. In instances in which children are reared as members of the opposite sex because of ambiguous genitals, gender typing is usually consistent with sex of rearing, regardless of genetic sex.

- Beginning in infancy, parents hold gender-stereotyped perceptions and expectations of boys and girls and create different environments for them. By the preschool years, parents reinforce their children for many "gender-appropriate" play activities and behaviors. During middle childhood, they demand greater independence from boys in achievement situations, hold gender-stereotyped beliefs about children's abilities in various school subjects, and allow boys more freedom in their everyday lives. Fathers differentiate between boys and girls more than mothers do. Also, each parent takes special responsibility for the gender typing of the same-sex child.

- Teachers also encourage gender-typical behaviors and activities, and children have many opportunities to observe traditional gender roles in the surrounding environment. When interacting with children of their own sex, boys and girls receive further reinforcement for "gender-appropriate" play and develop different styles of social influence. Sibling influences on gender typing vary with birth order and family size. In small, two-child families, younger children tend to imitate the gender-role behavior of their older sibling. In large families, same-sex siblings often strive to be different from one another. As a result, they are likely to be less stereotyped in their interests and personality characteristics.

Gender-Role Identity

- Researchers measure **gender-role identity** by asking children and adults to rate themselves on "masculine" and "feminine" personality traits. Although most people have traditional identities, some are **androgynous,** scoring high on both masculine and feminine characteristics. At present, the masculine component of androgyny is largely responsible for its association with superior psychological adjustment.
- According to social learning theory, preschoolers first acquire gender-typed responses through modeling and reinforcement and only later organize them into cognitions about themselves. Cognitive-developmental theory suggests that **gender constancy** must be achieved before children can develop gender-typed behavior.
- Children master gender constancy by moving through three stages: **gender labeling, gender stability,** and **gender consistency.** Understanding of gender constancy is associated with attainment of conservation and opportunities to learn about genital differences between the sexes. In contrast to cognitive-developmental predictions, "gender-appropriate" behavior is acquired long before gender constancy. However, gender labeling and gender stability, along with gender-linked self-evaluations, appear to facilitate gender-role adoption.
- During middle childhood, boys strengthen their identification with the "masculine" role, whereas girls become more androgynous. In early adolescence, the gender-role identi-

ties of both sexes become more traditional, a trend that gradually becomes less pronounced.

- **Gender schema theory** is an information-processing approach to gender typing that combines social learning and cognitive-developmental features. As children learn gender-typed preferences and behaviors, they form masculine and feminine categories, or gender schemas, that they apply to themselves and use to interpret their world. Schema-consistent information is attended to and approached, whereas schema-inconsistent information is ignored, misinterpreted, or actively rejected. As a result, children learn much more about "gender-appropriate" than "gender-inappropriate" activities and behaviors.

To What Extent Do Boys and Girls Really Differ in Gender-Stereotyped Attributes?

- Girls are advanced in early language development and in reading achievement and are more emotionally sensitive, compliant, and dependent. Boys do better at spatial and mathematical skills and are more aggressive. However, in all instances the differences are small.
- Biological factors may underlie sex-related differences in language development and spatial abilities, but the precise biological processes involved have not yet been identified. Adult encouragement and learning opportunities contribute importantly to differences in reading and spatial and mathematical skills. Girls' greater emotional sensitivity, compliance, and dependency are largely due to gender-stereotyped expectations and child-rearing practices.
- Prenatal and pubertal hormones appear to contribute to greater aggression in males. However, hormones probably exert their effects indirectly, by affecting activity level or emotional reactions that when combined with certain child-rearing conditions, increase the likelihood of aggressive behavior. Parents are more likely to use physical punishment with boys and to overlook their aggressive behavior. In addition, boys seem to react with greater hostility than do girls to strife-ridden family atmospheres.

Developing Non-Gender-Stereotyped Children

- Parents and teachers can counteract young children's readiness to absorb gender-linked associations by delaying access to gender stereotypes and emphasizing that anatomy and reproduction, not dress, activities, and behavior, determine a person's sex. Once children notice gender stereotypes, adults can point out exceptions and discuss the arbitrariness of gender inequalities in society.

IMPORTANT TERMS AND CONCEPTS

gender stereotypes (p. 519)
gender roles (p. 519)
gender-role identity (p. 519)
gender typing (p. 519)

instrumental traits (p. 519)
expressive traits (p. 519)
androgyny (p. 536)
gender constancy (p. 538)

gender labeling (p. 538)
gender stability (p. 538)
gender consistency (p. 538)
gender schema theory (p. 541)

C O N N E C T I O N S

 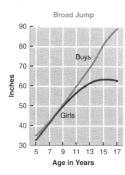

Although some functions have been taken over by or are shared with other institutions, three important ones—reproduction, socialization, and emotional support—remain primarily the province of the family. These functions are especially concerned with children, since they include giving birth to, rearing, and nurturing the young. Researchers interested in finding out how modern families fulfill these functions take a **social systems perspective**, viewing the family as a complex set of interacting relationships influenced by the larger social context.

THE FAMILY AS A SOCIAL SYSTEM

The social systems perspective on family functioning grew out of researchers' efforts to describe and explain the complex patterns of interaction that take place among family members. As we review its features, you will see that it has much in common with Bronfenbrenner's (1979, 1989) ecological systems theory, discussed in Chapter 1.

When child development specialists first began to study the family in the middle part of this century, they investigated in a very limited way. Most research focused on the mother–child relationship and emphasized one-way effects of maternal treatment on children's behavior. Today, family systems theorists recognize that children are not mechanically shaped by the inputs of others. You already know from earlier chapters that *bidirectional* influences exist in which the behaviors of each family member affect those of others. The very term *family system* implies that the responses of all family members are interrelated (Kantor & Lehr, 1975; Minuchin, 1988). These system influences operate both *directly* and *indirectly*.

Direct and Indirect Influences

Recently I witnessed the followed two episodes as I passed through the checkout counter at the supermarket:

> Little Danny stood next to tempting rows of candy as his mother lifted groceries from the cart onto the counter. "Pleeeease, can I have it, Mom?" begged Danny, holding up a large package of bubble gum. "Do you have a dollar? Just one?"
>
> "No, not today," his mother answered softly. "Remember, we picked out your special cereal. That's what I need the dollar for." Danny's mother handed him the cereal while gently taking the bubble gum from his hand and returning it to the shelf. "Here, let's pay the man," she said, as she lifted Danny into the empty grocery cart where he could see the checkout counter.

> Three-year-old Meg sat in the cart while her mother transferred groceries to the counter. Meg turned around, grabbed a bunch of bananas, and started to pull them apart.
>
> "Stop it, Meg!" shouted her mom, who snatched the bananas from Meg's hand. Meg reached for a chocolate bar from a nearby shelf while her mother wrote the check. "Meg, how many times have I told you, DON'T TOUCH!" Loosening the candy from Meg's tight little grip, Meg's mother slapped her hand. Meg's face turned red with anger as she began to wail. "Keep this up, and you'll get it when we get home," threatened Meg's mom as they left the store.

These observations fit with a wealth of research on the family system. Many studies show that when parents (like Danny's mom) are firm but patient, children tend to comply with their requests. And when children cooperate, their parents are likely to be warm and gentle in the future. In contrast, parents (like Meg's mom) who discipline with harshness and impatience have children who refuse and rebel. And because children's misbehavior is stressful for parents, they may increase their use of punishment, leading to more unruliness by the child. In these examples, the behavior of one family member helps sustain a form of interaction in another that either promotes or undermines children's well-being.

The impact of family relationships on child development becomes even more complicated when we consider that interaction between any two members is

Social systems perspective
A view of the family as a complex set of interacting relationships influenced by the larger social context.

affected by others present in the setting. Recall from Chapter 1 that Bronfenbrenner called these indirect influences the effect of *third parties.* Researchers have become intensely interested in how a range of relationships—mother with father, parent with sibling, grandparent with parent—modifies the child's direct experiences in the family.

Third parties can serve as effective supports for children's development, or they can undermine children's well-being. For example, when the parents' marital relationship is warm and considerate, mothers and fathers praise and stimulate their children more and nag and scold them less. In contrast, when a marriage is tense and hostile, parents are likely to criticize and punish (Cox et al., 1989; Howes & Markman, 1989; Simons et al., 1992). Disputes between parents over child-rearing issues seem to be particularly harmful. They are linked to a rise in child behavior problems over and above the increase associated with non-child-related marital difficulties (Jouriles et al., 1991).

Yet even when children's adjustment is strained by arguments between their parents, other family members may help restore effective interaction. Grandparents are a case in point. They can promote children's development in many ways—both directly, by responding warmly to the child, and indirectly, by providing parents with child-rearing advice, models of child-rearing skill, and even financial assistance (Cherlin & Furstenberg, 1986). Of course, like any indirect influence, grandparents' involvement can sometimes have adverse effects. Later in this chapter, we will see that when quarrelsome relations exist between grandparents and a divorced custodial parent, children may suffer.

To make matters even more complicated, the social systems perspective views the interplay of forces within the family as constantly adapting to changes in its members (Kantor & Lehr, 1975). Individuals continue to develop throughout the life span. As a result, interaction is not static, but shifts across time. For example, as children acquire new skills, parents adjust the way they treat their more competent youngsters. Then changes in child rearing pave the way for new achievements and further modifications in family relationships. In fact, no other social unit is required to adjust to such vast changes in its members as is the family.

The Family System in Context

The social systems perspective, as we noted earlier, views the family as affected by larger social contexts. Connections to the community—in terms of *formal organizations,* such as school, workplace, day-care center, and church or synagogue, as well as *informal social networks* of relatives, friends, and neighbors—affect parent–child relationships. For example, child adjustment problems, particularly those that appear early in development, last a long time, and are related to parental conflict, are more common in urban than rural settings. Although population density and poverty contribute to this finding, fragmented communication networks are also responsible. Psychological disturbance is highest in inner-city areas in which families move often, parks and playgrounds are in disarray, community centers providing leisure-time activities do not exist, and telephones and visits among friends and neighbors are rare. In contrast, when family ties to the community are strong—as indicated by regular church attendance and frequent contact with friends and relatives—family stress and child adjustment problems are reduced (Garbarino & Sherman, 1980; Werner & Smith, 1982).

Why do ties to the community reduce family stress and enhance child development? There are several reasons. First, social support offers interpersonal acceptance. A neighbor or relative who listens sympathetically and tries to relieve a parent's concern enhances self-esteem. The parent, in turn, is likely to behave more sensitively toward her children. In one study of families experiencing economic strain, social networks influenced parenting indirectly by reducing mothers' feelings of depression (Simons et al., 1993). Second, social networks provide parents with opportunities to exchange valuable information, goods, and services.

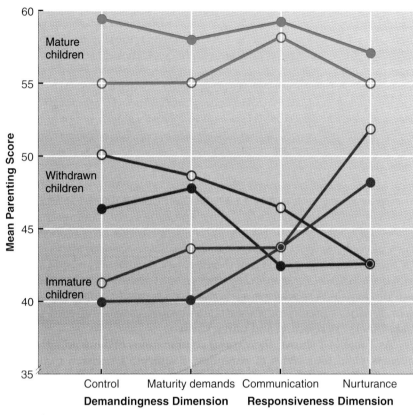

FIGURE 14.1 Relationship of demandingness and responsiveness to preschoolers' competence. Parenting was observed at home and in a structured laboratory situation in which parents were asked to teach and play with their children. Psychologists rated children's competence after observing them for several months at nursery school. Notice how parenting scores for the "mature" children are high in both demandingness and responsiveness, reflecting the authoritative style. (From "Child Care Practices Anteceding Three Patterns of Preschool Behavior" by D. Baumrind, 1967, *Genetic Psychology Monographs, 75*, p. 73. Reprinted with permission of the Helen Dwight Reid Educational Foundation. Published by Heldref Publications, 4000 Albermarle Street, N.W., Washington, D.C. 20016. Copyright © 1967.)

● Parenting score based on structured laboratory observations
○ Parenting score based on home observations

particularly high in independence and desire to master new tasks and boys in friendliness and cooperativeness (Baumrind & Black, 1967). Recent evidence confirms a positive association between authoritative parenting and emotional and social skills during the preschool years (Denham, Renwick, & Holt, 1991).

Researchers who have examined the correlates of authoritative parenting at older ages also report that it is linked to many aspects of competence. These include high self-esteem, social and moral maturity, involvement in school learning, and academic achievement in high school (Block, 1971; Dornbusch et al., 1987; Lamborn et al., 1991; Steinberg, Elman, & Mounts, 1989; Steinberg et al., 1992).

AUTHORITARIAN CHILD REARING. Parents who use an **authoritarian style** are also demanding, but they place such a high value on conformity that they are unresponsive—even outright rejecting—when children are unwilling to obey. "Do it because I say so!" is the attitude of these parents. As a result, they engage in very little give-and-take with children, who are expected to accept an adult's word for what is right in an unquestioning manner. If the child does not, authoritarian parents resort to force and punishment. The authoritarian style is clearly biased in favor of parents' needs; children's self-expression and independence are suppressed.

Baumrind found that preschoolers with authoritarian parents were anxious, withdrawn, and unhappy (see Figure 14.1). When interacting with peers, they tended to react with hostility when frustrated (Baumrind, 1967). Boys, especially, were high in anger and defiance. Girls were dependent and lacking in exploration, and they retreated from challenging tasks (Baumrind, 1971).

In adolescence, young people with authoritarian parents continue to be less well adjusted than those exposed to an authoritative style. Nevertheless, teenagers used to authoritarian child rearing do better in school and are less likely to engage in antisocial acts than those with undemanding parents—that is, who use either of the two styles we are about to discuss (Baumrind, 1991; Lamborn et al., 1991).

Authoritarian style

A parenting style that is demanding but low in responsiveness to children's rights and needs. Conformity and obedience are valued over open communication.

PERMISSIVE CHILD REARING. The **permissive style** of child rearing is nurturant and accepting, but it avoids making demands or imposing controls of any kind. Permissive parents allow children to make many of their own decisions at an age when they are not yet capable of doing so. They can eat meals and go to bed when they feel like it and watch as much television as they want. They do not have to learn good manners or do any household chores. And they are permitted to interrupt and annoy others without any parental restraint. Although some permissive parents truly believe this approach to child rearing is best, many others lack confidence in their ability to influence their child's behavior and are disorganized and ineffective in running their households.

As Figure 14.1 indicates, Baumrind (1967) found that children of permissive parents were very immature. They had difficulty controlling their impulses and were disobedient and rebellious when asked to do something that conflicted with their momentary desires. They were also overly demanding and dependent on adults, and they showed less persistence on tasks at preschool than children of parents who exerted more control. The link between permissive parenting and dependent, nonachieving behavior was especially strong for boys (Baumrind, 1971).

In adolescence, parental indulgence continues to be related to poor self-control. Permissively reared teenagers are less involved in school learning and use drugs more frequently than do teenagers whose parents communicate clear standards for behavior (Baumrind, 1991; Lamborn et al., 1991).

UNINVOLVED CHILD REARING. Undemanding parenting combined with indifferent or rejecting behavior constitutes the **uninvolved style**. Uninvolved parents show little commitment to caregiving beyond the minimum effort required to feed and clothe their child. Often these parents are so overwhelmed by the many pressures and stresses in their lives that they have little time and energy to spare for children. As a result, they cope with the demands of parenting by doing what they can to avoid inconvenience. They may respond to the child's demands for easily accessible objects, but any efforts that involve long-term goals, such as establishing and enforcing rules about homework and acceptable social behavior, are weak and fleeting (Maccoby & Martin, 1983).

At its extreme, uninvolved parenting is a form of child maltreatment called *neglect.* Especially when it begins early, it disrupts virtually all aspects of development. Emotionally detached, depressed mothers who show little interest in their babies have children who soon show deficits in many domains, including attachment, cognition, play, and emotional and social skills (Egeland & Sroufe, 1981; Radke-Yarrow et al., 1985). By age 3, the low warmth and control that result from parental depression are consistently related to aggressive, acting-out behavior (Miller et al., 1993). Even when parental disengagement is less pronounced, the development of children is impaired. In one longitudinal study, preschoolers whose mothers were uninvolved as opposed to responsive during the first few years were noncompliant and demanding. Asked to wait while the mother filled out a questionnaire, these children tugged and pulled at her clothing, grabbed her pencil, and sometimes kicked and hit (Martin, 1981).

Uninvolved parenting also works poorly at older ages. Research in Finland and the United States shows that parents who rarely have conversations with their adolescents, take little interest in their life at school, and are seldom aware of their whereabouts have youngsters who are low in tolerance for frustration and emotional control, do poorly in school, lack long-term goals, and are prone to engage in delinquent acts (Baumrind, 1991; Lamborn et al., 1991; Pulkkinen, 1982).

What Makes the Authoritative Style So Effective?

The authoritative style predicts positive cognitive, emotional, and social outcomes so consistently that Baumrind believes it causes superior development. But like other correlational findings, these results are open to different interpretations.

Permissive style

A parenting style that is responsive but undemanding. An overly tolerant approach to child rearing.

Uninvolved style

A parenting style that is both undemanding and unresponsive. Reflects minimal commitment to child rearing.

According to Catherine Lewis (1981), perhaps parents of mature children use demanding tactics because their youngsters have cooperative, obedient dispositions, not because firm control is an essential ingredient of effective parenting. But Baumrind (1983) points out that many children of authoritative parents do not submit willingly to adult directives. Resistance by children occurred often in the authoritative homes she studied, but parents handled it patiently and rationally. They neither gave in to children's unreasonable demands nor responded harshly and arbitrarily. Baumrind emphasizes that not just firm control, but *rational and reasonable* use of firm control, facilitates children's competence.

Nevertheless, children's characteristics contribute to the ease with which parents can apply the authoritative style. Recall from Chapter 10 that temperamentally difficult children are more likely to receive coercive discipline. And when children resist, some parents respond inconsistently, at first by being punitive and later by giving in, thereby reinforcing the child's unruly behavior. Children of parents who go back and forth between authoritarian and uninvolved styles are especially aggressive and irresponsible and do very poorly in school (see Chapter 12). Over time, the relationship between parenting and children's characteristics probably becomes increasingly bidirectional. An impulsive, noncompliant child makes it very hard for parents to be firm, rational, and consistent, but child-rearing practices can strengthen or reduce difficult behavior (Maccoby & Martin, 1983).

Why does an authoritative style support children's competence and help bring the recalcitrant behavior of poorly socialized children under control? There are several reasons. First, control that appears fair and reasonable to the child, not arbitrary, is far more likely to be complied with and internalized. Second, nurturant parents who are secure in the standards they hold for their children provide models of caring concern as well as confident, assertive behavior. They are also more effective reinforcing agents, praising children for striving to meet their expectations and making good use of disapproval, which works best when applied by an adult who has been warm and caring. Finally, authoritative parents make demands that fit with children's ability to take responsibility for their own behavior. As a result, these parents let children know that they are competent individuals who can do things successfully for themselves, and high self-esteem and mature, independent behavior are fostered (Kuczynski et al., 1987).

Adapting Child Rearing to Children's Development

Since authoritative parents continually adapt to children's growing competence, their practices change with age. In the following sections, we will see that a gradual lessening of direct control supports children's development, as long as it is built on continuing parental warmth and involvement in child rearing.

PARENTING IN MIDDLE CHILDHOOD: COREGULATION. During middle childhood, the amount of time children spend with parents declines dramatically. In a study in which parents kept diaries of family activities, they reported spending less than half as much time in caregiving, teaching, reading, and playing with 5- to 12-year-olds as they did with preschoolers (Hill & Stafford, 1980). The school-age child's growing independence means that parents must deal with new issues—for example, how to promote responsible behavior and constructive use of leisure time, whether children's friends are good influences, and how to deal with problems at school (Maccoby, 1984a).

Although parents face a new set of concerns, child rearing becomes easier for those who established an authoritative style during the early years (Maccoby, 1984b). Reasoning works more effectively with school-age children because of their greater capacity for logical thinking. Of course, older children sometimes use their cognitive skills to bargain and negotiate—behaviors that can try parents' patience. But parents can appeal to their child's better developed sense of self-esteem, humor, and morality to resolve these difficulties. Perhaps because parents and children have, over time, learned how to resolve conflicts, coercive discipline declines over middle childhood (Maccoby, 1984a).

As children demonstrate that they can take on new responsibilities, parents gradually shift control to the child. This does not mean that they let go entirely. Instead, effective parents of school-age children engage in **coregulation,** a transitional form of supervision in which they exercise general oversight while permitting children to be in charge of moment-by-moment decision making. Coregulation supports and protects school-age children, who are not yet ready for total independence. At the same time, it prepares them for adolescence, when they will make many important decisions themselves.

Coregulation grows out of a cooperative relation between parent and child—one based on mutual respect. Here is a summary of its critical ingredients:

> The parental tasks . . . are threefold. First, [parents] must monitor, guide, and support their children at a distance—that is, when their children are out of their presence; second, they must effectively use the times when direct contact does occur; and third, they must strengthen in their children the abilities that will allow them to monitor their own behavior, to adopt acceptable standards of [good] conduct, to avoid undue risks, and to know when they need parental support and guidance. Children must be willing to inform parents of their whereabouts, activities, and problems so that parents can mediate and guide when necessary. (Maccoby, 1984a, pp. 191–192)

School-age children often press for greater independence, but most know how much they need their parents' continuing support. In one study, fourth-graders described parents as the most influential people in their lives. They often turned to mothers and fathers for affection, advice, enhancement of self-worth, and assistance with everyday problems (Furman & Buhrmester, 1992).

PARENTING IN ADOLESCENCE: FOSTERING AUTONOMY. During adolescence, young people in complex societies deal with the need to choose from many options by seeking **autonomy**—establishing themselves as separate, self-governing individuals. Autonomy extends beyond school-age children's capacity to regulate their own behavior in the absence of parental monitoring. It has a vital *emotional component*—relying more on oneself and less on parents for support and guidance. And it also has an important *behavioral component*—making decisions independently by carefully weighing one's own judgment and the suggestions of others to arrive at a well-reasoned course of action (Hill & Holmbeck, 1986; Steinberg & Silverberg, 1986). If you look carefully at the concept of autonomy, you will see that it is closely related to the quest for identity. Research suggests that adolescents who successfully establish personally meaningful values and life goals are autonomous. They have given up childish dependence on parents for a more mature, responsible relationship (Frank, Pirsch, & Wright, 1990).

Autonomy receives support from a variety of changes within the adolescent. In Chapter 5, we saw that puberty triggers psychological distancing from parents. In addition, as young people look more mature, they are granted more independence and responsibility. Cognitive development also paves the way toward autonomy. Abstract thinking permits teenagers to solve problems in more mature ways and to foresee the consequences of their actions more clearly. How can parents foster this readiness for autonomy? Controversy surrounds this question.

Take a moment to think back to Erikson's psychosocial theory, discussed in Chapter 1. Like identity, autonomy is a concern that returns at various points during the life cycle. Recall that it is a central task of toddlerhood, and it resurfaces again at adolescence, when social expectations demand a new level of self-reliance. According to several psychoanalytic theorists, adolescent autonomy is promoted by emotional detachment—less warmth and closeness, which helps free the young person from a childish view of parents as perfect, all-powerful protectors (Bloom, 1980; Blos, 1979; Freud, 1958). A study of 2,400 adolescents, however, revealed that autonomy can be arrived at in different ways. When young people reported feeling autonomous yet characterized their relationship with parents as

Coregulation

A transitional form of supervision in which parents exercise general oversight while permitting children to be in charge of moment-by-moment decision making.

Autonomy

A sense of oneself as a separate, self-governing individual. An important developmental task of adolescence that is closely related to the quest for identity.

*A*dolescent autonomy is effectively achieved in the context of warm parenting. This mother supports her daughter's desire to try new experiences, relaxing control in accord with the adolescent's readiness to take on new responsibilities without threatening the parent–child bond. (KOPSTEIN/MONKMEYER PRESS PHOTO)

unsupportive, they actually showed poor psychological adjustment. But autonomy achieved in the context of warm, supportive parent–child ties carried advantages. It was associated with high self-esteem, self-reliance, and work orientation as well as academic competence (Lamborn & Steinberg, 1993).

Other research also indicates that mature autonomy is fostered by close, not distant, family ties, whereas tense family relationships signify problems, not positive adolescent development (Hill & Holmbeck, 1986; Kandel & Lesser, 1972). These findings suggest that the task for parents and teenagers is not one of just separating. Instead, parents need to gradually relax control in accord with the adolescent's readiness for more freedom without threatening the parent–child bond. An authoritative style begun in childhood encourages this process. Authoritative parents meet the challenges of adolescence by establishing guidelines that are flexible, open to discussion, and implemented in an atmosphere of concern and fairness. It is not hard for them to explain the basis of their decisions, solicit and consider carefully the adolescent's input, and gradually modify their rules as the young person moves closer to adulthood (Steinberg, 1990, 1993). If you return to Chapter 11, you will see that this very blend of connection and independence promotes identity development as well.

Social-Class and Ethnic Variations in Child Rearing

Research examining parenting in over 180 societies reveals that a style that is responsive but moderately demanding is the most common pattern around the world. Many cultures seem to have discovered for themselves the link between authoritative parenting and healthy psychological development (Rohner & Rohner, 1981). Nevertheless, in the United States and other Western nations, consistent differences in child rearing exist that are linked to social class and ethnicity.

SOCIAL CLASS. When asked about qualities they would like to encourage in their children, parents who work in skilled and semiskilled manual occupations (for example, machinists, truck drivers, and custodians) tend to place a high value on external characteristics, such as obedience, neatness, and cleanliness. In contrast, parents in white-collar and professional occupations tend to emphasize inner psychological traits, such as curiosity, happiness, and self-control. These differences in values are reflected in parenting behaviors. Middle-class parents talk to and stimulate their babies more and grant them greater freedom to explore. When their children are older, they use more explanations, verbal praise, and inductive discipline. In contrast, lower-class parents are more likely to be restrictive. Because they think that infants can easily be spoiled, they often limit the amount of rocking and cuddling they do (Luster, Rhoades, & Haas, 1989). Later on, commands, such as "You do that because I told you to," as well as criticism and physical punishment occur more often in low-income households (Laosa, 1981).

Social-class differences in child rearing can be understood in terms of different life conditions in low-income and middle-income families. Low-income parents often feel a sense of powerlessness and lack of influence in relationships beyond the home. For example, at work they must obey the rules of others in positions of power and authority. When they get home, their parent–child interaction seems to duplicate these experiences, only with them in the authority roles. In contrast, middle-class parents have a greater sense of control over their own lives. At work, they are used to making independent decisions and convincing others of their point of view. At home, they teach these same skills to their children. The values and behaviors required for success in the world of work are believed to affect parents' ideas about traits important to train in their children, who are expected to enter similar work roles in the future (Kohn, 1979).

Education also contributes to social-class differences in child rearing. Middle-class parents' interest in verbal stimulation and in fostering the development of children's inner characteristics is supported by years of schooling, during which they observed models of adult–child verbal instruction, acquired advanced verbal skills, and learned to think about abstract, subjective ideas. In a study carried out in Mexico, where female school enrollment has recently increased, the more years of education a mother had, the more she stimulated her young child through face-to-face conversation (Richman, Miller, & LeVine, 1992).

Furthermore, the greater economic security of middle-class parents frees them from the burden of having to worry about making ends meet on a daily basis. As a result, they can devote more energy and attention to their own inner characteristics and those of their children. And they can also provide many more experiences—from toys to special outings to after-school lessons—that encourage these characteristics (Hoffman, 1984).

POVERTY. When families become so low income that they slip into poverty, then effective parenting and children's development are seriously threatened. Shirley Brice Heath (1990), an anthropologist who has spent many years studying children and families of poverty, describes the case of Zinnia Mae, who grew up in Trackton, a close-knit black community located in a small southeastern American city. As unemployment struck Trackton in the 1980s and citizens moved away, 16-year-old Zinnia Mae caught a ride to Atlanta. Two years later, Heath visited her there. By then, Zinnia Mae was the mother of three children—a 16-month-old daughter named Donna and 2-month-old twin boys. She had moved into a high-rise public housing project, one of eight concrete buildings surrounding a dirt plot scattered with broken swings, seesaws, and benches.

Each of Zinnia Mae's days was much the same. She watched TV and talked with her girlfriends on the phone. The children had only one set meal (breakfast) and otherwise ate whenever they were hungry or bored. Their play space was limited to the living-room sofa and a mattress on the floor. Toys consisted of scraps of a blanket, spoons and food cartons, a small rubber ball, a few plastic cars, and a roller skate abandoned in the building. Zinnia Mae's most frequent words were, "I'm so tired." She worried about how to get papers to the welfare office and where to find a baby-sitter so she could go to the laundry or grocery.

At Heath's request, Zinnia Mae agreed to tape record her interactions with her children over a 2-year period. In 500 hours of tape (other than simple directions or questions about what the children were doing), Zinnia Mae started a conversation with Donna and the boys only 18 times. Cut off from community ties

*H*omelessness in the United States has risen over the past decade. Families like this one travel from place to place in search of employment and a safe and secure place to live. At night, they sleep in the family car. Because of constant stresses, homeless children are usually behind in development, have frequent health problems, and show poor psychological adjustment. (RICK BROWNE/STOCK BOSTON)

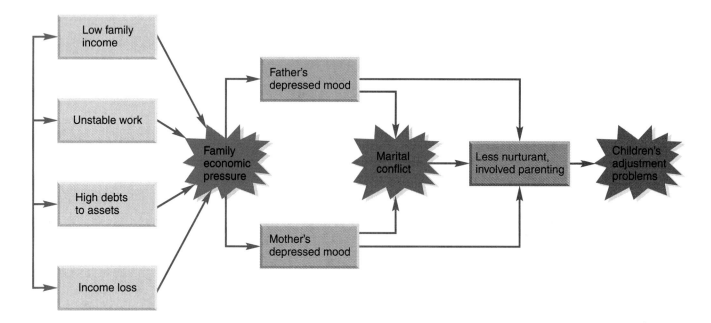

FIGURE 14.2 Pathway from family economic pressure to children's adjustment. When stresses pile up, parents become demoralized. Their depressed mood prompts a rise in marital conflict and a decline in nurturant, involved parenting. Disrupted parenting, in turn, leads to children's adjustment problems. In a recent study of seventh-grade boys, some of whose parents were experiencing severe financial difficulties, this sequence of events was confirmed. (Adapted from "A Family Process Model of Economic Hardship and Adjustment of Early Adolescent Boys" by R. D. Conger, K. J. Conger, G. H. Elder, Jr., F. O. Lorenz, R. L. Simons, & L. B. Whitbeck, 1992, *Child Development, 63*, p. 528. © The Society for Research in Child Development, Inc. Reprinted by permission.)

and preoccupied with day-to-day survival, Zinnia Mae found it difficult to join in activities with her children. As a result, Donna and her brothers experienced a barren, understimulating home life—one very different from the family and community in which Zinnia Mae herself had grown up.

The constant stresses that accompany poverty gradually weaken the family system. Poor families experience many daily hassles—bills to pay, the car breaking down, loss of welfare and unemployment payments, something stolen from the house, to name just a few. When daily crises arise, parents become depressed, irritable, and distracted, marital conflict rises, parenting becomes less nurturant and involved, and children's development suffers (Compas et al., 1989; Patterson, 1988). This sequence of events, summarized in Figure 14.2, was recently tested and confirmed in a study of seventh-grade boys, some of whose parents experienced job instability and declining income (Conger et al., 1992). Negative outcomes for children are especially severe in single-parent families, in families living in poor housing located in dangerous neighborhoods, and in homeless families—circumstances that make everyday existence even more difficult (McLoyd, 1990; Patterson, 1991; Rafferty & Shinn, 1991).

ETHNICITY. Ethnic groups often have distinct child-rearing beliefs and practices. Some involve variations in demandingness that appear to be adaptive when viewed in light of cultural values and the context in which parent and child are situated. For example, compared to Caucasian-Americans, Chinese adults describe their own parenting techniques and those they experienced as children as more controlling (Berndt et al., 1993; Chao, 1982). As Figure 14.3 shows, this greater emphasis on control continues to characterize Chinese parents who have immigrated to the United States. It seems to reflect deeply engrained Confucian values stressing strict discipline and respect for elders that have survived rapid social change and migration to a new country (Lin & Fu, 1990). Although wide variation

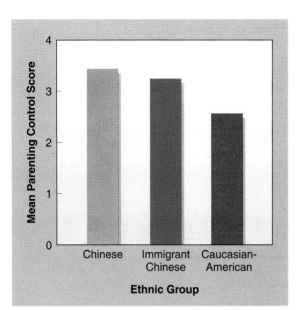

FIGURE 14.3 Self-reported emphasis on control by Chinese, immigrant Chinese, and Caucasian-American parents. In this study, mothers and fathers who were living in Taiwan, who had immigrated from Taiwan to the United States, and who were Caucasian-American citizens were asked to rate their parenting styles. Both groups of Chinese parents emphasized control to a greater extent than did Caucasian-American parents. (Adapted from Lin & Fu, 1990.)

among African-American families exists, some research suggests black mothers tend to rely on an adult-centered approach in which they expect immediate obedience from children. This trend is stronger for mothers who are younger, less educated, less involved in organized religion, and rearing their children alone (Kelley, Power, & Wimbush, 1992). Strict demands for compliance, however, make sense under certain conditions. When parents have few social supports and live in dangerous neighborhoods, forceful discipline may be necessary to protect children from becoming victims of crime or involved in antisocial activities (Ogbu, 1985).

The family structure and child-rearing customs of certain ethnic minorities buffer the stress and disorganization that result from living in poverty. A case in point is the African-American family, which has managed to survive generations of extreme economic deprivation and racism. A far greater percentage of American black than white children live in poverty, and a greater percentage also experience the strain of parental divorce, widowhood, and out-of-wedlock teenage pregnancy (Children's Defense Fund, 1992b; Wilson, 1986). As the Cultural Influences box on page 572 indicates, the African cultural tradition of **extended family households,** in which one or more adult relatives live with the parent-child **nuclear family unit**, is a vital feature of African-American family life that has enabled its members to survive and, in some instances, overcome highly adverse social conditions. Active and involved extended families also characterize other ethnic minorities, such as Asian-American, Native American, and Hispanic groups (Harrison et al., 1990). The study of these families illustrates the remarkable ability of the family unit to mobilize its cultural traditions to support its members under circumstances of high life stress.

Child-rearing practices can be organized along two dimensions: demandingness and responsiveness. When combined, these characteristics yield four styles of parenting: authoritative, authoritarian, permissive, and uninvolved. The authoritative style is linked to many aspects of competence, whereas children experiencing uninvolved child rearing fare least well. Because authoritative parents make reasonable demands and are highly responsive to children's needs, they easily adapt to children's changing capacities. During middle childhood, effective parents engage in coregulation, a transitional form of supervision in which they exercise general oversight while granting children more decision-making power. In adolescence, warm, supportive parenting in which control is gradually relaxed in accord with adolescents' readiness for greater freedom fosters mature autonomy and positive adjustment.

The authoritative style is the most common pattern of child rearing around the world. Nevertheless, consistent social-class differences exist; low-income parents

Brief Review

Extended family household
A household in which parent and child live with one or more adult relatives.

Nuclear family unit
The part of the family that consists of parents and their children.

The African-American extended family can be traced to the African heritage of most black Americans. In many African societies, newly married couples do not start their own households. Instead, they marry into a large extended family that assists its members with all aspects of daily life. This tradition of a broad network of kinship ties traveled to the United States during the period of slavery. Since then, it has served as a protective shield against the destructive impact of poverty and racial prejudice on African-American family life (McLoyd, 1990; Wilson, 1989). Today, more black than white adults have relatives other than their own children living in the same household. African-American parents also see more kin during the week and perceive them as more important figures in their lives, respecting the advice of relatives and caring deeply about what they think is important (Wilson, 1986).

By providing emotional support and sharing income and essential resources, the African-American extended family helps reduce the stress of poverty and single parenthood. In addition, extended-family members often help with the rearing of children (Pearson et al., 1990). The presence of grandmothers in the households of many African-American teenagers and their infants protects babies from the negative influence of an overwhelmed and inexperienced mother. In one study, black grandmothers displayed more sensitive interaction with the babies of their teenage daughters than did the teenage mothers themselves. The grandmothers also provided basic information about infant development to these young mothers (Stevens, 1984). Furthermore, black adolescent mothers living in extended families are more likely to complete high school and get a job and less likely to be on welfare than mothers living on their own—factors that return to benefit children's well-being (Furstenberg & Crawford, 1978).

Among older children, extended family living is associated with more positive adult–child interaction, better school achievement, and improved psychological adjustment (Wilson & Tolson, 1985). In families with adolescents, kinship support increases the likelihood of authoritative parenting, which, in turn, is related to self-reliance, emotional well-being, and reduced delinquency (Taylor, Casten, & Flickinger, 1993).

Finally, the African-American extended family plays an important role in transmitting black cultural values to children. Compared to African-American nuclear families, extended-family arrangements place more emphasis on

*S*trong bonds with extended-family members have helped to protect the development of many African-American children growing up under conditions of poverty and single parenthood. (KAREN KASMAUSKI/WOODFIN CAMP & ASSOCIATES)

cooperation and moral and religious values (Tolson & Wilson, 1990). Older black adults, such as grandparents and great grandparents, are also more likely to possess a strong ethnic identity and to regard educating children about their African heritage as an important part of socialization (Thornton & Taylor, 1988). These influences strengthen family bonds, protect children's development, and increase the chances that the extended-family life-style will carry over to the next generation.

tend to be more coercive, whereas middle-income parents use more explanations and inductive discipline. The constant stresses that accompany poverty undermine effective parenting and children's development. Ethnic variations in child rearing exist that can be understood in terms of cultural values and the context in which the family is situated.

Over the past several decades, rapid transitions in family life have taken place in Western industrialized nations—trends that have been particularly marked in the United States. A smaller family size due to a declining birth rate, a rise in marital breakup and single-parent households, and increased participation in the labor market by mothers with children of all ages have reshaped the modern family system. Today, the traditional family form of male breadwinner and female homemaker characterizes only a small minority of American families. In 1950, 60 percent of families fit this pattern; today, less than 7 percent do (Kain, 1990).

In the following sections, we discuss these changes in the American family, emphasizing how each affects family relationships and, ultimately, children's development. In reading about these shifts in family life, you may begin to wonder, as many people do, whether the institution of the family is in a state of crisis. Anxiety over family disintegration is not new to our times. Family transitions have always existed; they are simply more numerous and visible today than in the past. Modern families are not so much fragmented as they are more pluralistic than ever before (Hareven, 1982). Still, rapid social change has intensified pressures on the family. Throughout our discussion, we will see examples of the need for social policies that strengthen kin and community supports, which have sustained the family for centuries.

From Large to Small Families

In the mid-1950s, the peak of the post–World War II baby boom, the average number of children in an American family was 3.8. After that time, the birth rate declined steadily, until it reached 1.8 children per family in the early 1970s, where it remains today. Compared to several decades ago, there are many more one- and two-child families, as well as more couples opting to have no children (Glick, 1990). Some experts project that the birth rate will drop even further by the early part of the twenty-first century.

Family size has declined in the United States for several reasons. Improved contraception along with legalized abortion make the current period one of greater choice with respect to having children. Also, many more women are experiencing the economic and personal rewards of a career. A family size of one or two children is certainly more compatible with a woman's decision to divide her energies between work and family. Furthermore, more couples are delaying the birth of their first child until they are well established professionally and secure economically (see Chapter 3). Adults who postpone parenthood are likely to have fewer children (Hofferth, 1984). Finally, marital instability is another reason contemporary families are smaller. More couples today get divorced before their childbearing plans are complete.

FAMILY SIZE AND PARENT–CHILD INTERACTION. Overall, a smaller family size has positive effects on parent–child interaction. Parents who have fewer children are more patient and use less punishment. They also have more time to devote to each child's activities, schoolwork, and other special needs. Together, these findings may account for the fact that children who grow up in smaller families have somewhat higher intelligence test scores, do better in school, and have a higher sense of self-esteem. Children's problem behavior also varies with family size. Parents of only one or two children sometimes pressure their youngsters too much. As a result, anxiety is more common in small families. In contrast, coercive discipline and reduced supervision probably contribute to higher rates of antisocial behavior and delinquency in families with many children (Wagner, Schubert, & Schubert, 1985).

However, these findings require an important qualification. Large families are usually less well off economically than smaller ones are. Factors associated with

The People's Republic of China has 21 percent of the world's population but only 7 percent of its fertile land. In the late 1970s, the Central Committee of the Communist Party concluded that quality of life for China's citizens would not improve without drastic efforts to control its swelling population. In 1979, it implemented a one-child family policy, which was strictly enforced in urban areas and strongly encouraged in rural regions. As a result, a profound generational change occurred. Although the majority of adults of childbearing age had siblings, most of their children did not. By 1985, 86 percent of babies born in Beijing and 91 percent born in Shanghai were only children (Gu, Poston, & Shu, 1987).

Critics of the policy complained that it might ruin the character of the Chinese people. In a culture where kinship relations form the basis of daily life, media reports predicted that parents and grandparents would engage in pampering and spoiling, causing children to behave like "little emperors" (Falbo, 1992). Researchers soon began to investigate the development of China's new generation of children.

Toni Falbo and Dudly Poston (1993) have carried out the most comprehensive study of the characteristics of Chinese only and non-only children to date. They selected a representative sample of 4,000 third- and sixth-graders, 1,000 from each of four provinces, each geographically distinct and containing a highly diverse population. The older pupils had been born before implementation of the one-child family policy, the younger pupils afterward. All took verbal and mathematical achievement tests. Parent, teacher, peer, and self-ratings on a variety of attributes provided a measure of personality, which was specially designed to tap the "little emperor" syndrome—whether children were selfish, dependent, uncooperative, and disrespectful of their elders. Finally, children's height and weight were measured to see if the new policy was associated with improved physical development.

Much like findings in Western nations, Chinese only children were advanced in academic achievement. In three of the four provinces, they outscored non-only children in verbal skills. Although differences were less clear in math, only children never scored lower than first and last borns, and they usually did better than at least one of these groups. Only children had few distinguishing personality characteristics. And in two of the provinces, they were physically larger than their classmates. The economic benefits parents received from limiting family size may have resulted in better nutrition and health care for children.

Chinese only children seem to be developing as well or better than their counterparts with siblings. Why are so many Chinese adults convinced that only children are "little emperors?" When rapid social change takes place, people used to different conditions may regard the new lifestyle as a threat to the social order. In the case of the one-child family policy, they may incorrectly assume that lack of siblings is the cause of children's difficulties, failing to consider that the large number of only children in China today guarantees that they will dominate *both* success and failure groups.

This mural reminds citizens that limiting family size is a basic national policy in the People's Republic of China. In urban areas, the majority of couples have no more than one child. (OWEN FRANKEN/STOCK BOSTON)

Only Children

Without a chance to experience the closeness and conflicts of sibling relationships, are children born into one-child families disadvantaged in development? Many people think so. Parents of only children often report that relatives and friends pres-

TABLE 14.2 *Advantages and Disadvantages of a One-Child Family*

	ADVANTAGES	DISADVANTAGES
Mentioned by parents	Having time to pursue one's own interests and career Less financial pressure Not having to worry about "playing favorites" among children	Walking a "tightrope" between healthy attention and overindulgence Having only one chance to "make good" as a parent Being left childless in case of the child's death
Mentioned by children	Avoiding sibling rivalry Having more privacy Enjoying greater affluence Having a closer parent–child relationship	Not getting to experience the closeness of a sibling relationship Feeling too much pressure from parents to succeed Having no one to help care for parents when they get old

Source: Hawke & Knox, 1978.

sure them to have a second, believing that an only child is destined to be spoiled, self-centered, and selfish. This stereotype has been strengthened by the child-rearing advice of experts, which can be traced as far back as 1907, when G. Stanley Hall remarked, "Being an only child is a disease in itself" (Fenton, 1928, p. 547).

A great deal of research in Western nations indicates that sibling relationships bring many benefits, but they are not essential for normal development. Only children are as well adjusted as other children, and they are advantaged in some respects. A review of over 500 studies revealed that children growing up in one-child families score higher in self-esteem and achievement motivation than do other children. Consequently, they do better in school and attain higher levels of education (Falbo, 1992). One reason for these trends may be that only children have somewhat closer relationships with their parents, who exert more pressure for mastery and accomplishment. As long as these demands are not unreasonable, they seem to have positive effects on development (Claudy, 1984; Falbo & Polit, 1986).

Are these findings restricted to Western industrialized countries, where family size is a matter of individual choice? The People's Republic of China has a rigid family policy in which urban couples are given strong economic incentives to have no more than one child. Because they are limited to a single offspring, are Chinese parents rearing the new generation of children with indulgence, making Hall's pronouncement a reality? Refer to the Cultural Influences box on the preceding page and you will see that Chinese only children differ very little from their Western counterparts.

Nevertheless, the one-child family has both pros and cons, as does every family life-style. In a survey in which only children and their parents were asked what they liked and disliked about living in a single-child family, each mentioned a set of advantages and disadvantages, which are summarized in Table 14.2. The list is useful for Western parents to consider when deciding how many children would best fit their own personal and family life plans.

Divorce

Parental separation and divorce are extremely common in the lives of American children. Between 1960 and 1980, the divorce rate in the United States tripled and then stabilized. Currently, it is the highest in the world, nearly doubling that of the second-ranked country, Sweden. Over 1 million American children experience the separation and divorce of their parents each year. At any given time, about one-fourth of the child population lives in single-parent households. Although the large majority (85 percent) reside with their mothers, the number in father-headed

577

TABLE 14.3 Factors Related to Children's Adjustment to Divorce

FACTOR	DESCRIPTION
Custodial parent's psychological health	A mature, well-adjusted parent is better able to handle stress, shield the child from conflict, and engage in authoritative parenting.
Child characteristics	
Age	Preschool and early elementary school children often blame themselves and show intense separation anxiety. Older children may also react strongly by engaging in disruptive, antisocial acts. However, some display unusually mature, responsible behavior.
Temperament	Children with difficult temperaments are less able to withstand stress and show longer-lasting difficulties.
Sex	Boys in mother-custody households experience more severe and longer-lasting problems than do girls.
Social supports	The ability of divorced parents to set aside their hostilities, contact with the noncustodial parent, and positive relationships with extended family members, teachers, and friends lead to improved outcomes for children.

households has increased over the past decade, from 9 to 15 percent (Meyer & Garasky, 1993).

Children spend an average of 5 years in a single-parent home, or almost a third of their total childhood. For many, divorce eventually leads to new family relationships. About two-thirds of divorced parents marry a second time. Half of these children eventually experience a third major change in their family lives—the end of their parents' second marriage (Furstenberg & Cherlin, 1991; Glick, 1990).

These figures reveal that divorce is not a single event in the lives of parents and children. Instead, it is a transition that leads to a variety of new living arrangements, accompanied by changes in housing, income, and family roles and responsibilities (Wallerstein, 1991). Since the 1960s, many studies have reported that marital breakup is quite stressful for children. But research also reveals great variation in how children respond. Among the factors that make a difference are the custodial parent's psychological well-being, the child's characteristics, and social supports within the family and surrounding community. Our knowledge has been enhanced by several longitudinal studies that have tracked children over many years as well as a large number of short-term investigations. As we look at evidence on the impact of divorce, you may find it helpful to refer to the summary in Table 14.3.

IMMEDIATE CONSEQUENCES. The period surrounding divorce is often accompanied by a rise in family conflict as parents try to settle disputes over finances, personal belongings, and child custody. Once one parent moves out, additional events threaten the parent–child relationship. Mother-headed households typically experience a sharp drop in income. Many divorced women lack the education and experience needed for well-paid jobs. Furthermore, half of those supposed to receive child support from the absent father get less than the full amount or none at all (Children's Defense Fund, 1992b). Divorced mothers often have to move to new housing for economic reasons, reducing supportive ties to neighbors and friends. When those who were homemakers must find immediate employment, young children are likely to experience inadequate child care while the mother is away and a distracted, unavailable parent while she is at home (Hetherington, Stanley-Hagan, & Anderson, 1989; Nelson, 1993).

These life circumstances often lead to a highly disorganized family situation called "minimal parenting" (Wallerstein & Kelly, 1980). Predictable events and routines—scheduled mealtimes and bedtimes, household chores, and joint parent–child activities—usually disintegrate. As children react with distress and anger to their less secure home lives, discipline may become harsh and inconsistent as mothers try to recapture control of their upset youngsters. Fathers usually spend more time with children immediately after divorce, but often this contact decreases over time. When fathers see their children only occasionally, they are inclined to be permissive and indulgent. This often conflicts with the mother's style of parenting and makes her task of managing the child on a day-to-day basis even more difficult (Furstenberg & Nord, 1985; Hetherington, Cox, & Cox, 1982).

In view of these changes, it is not surprising that children experience painful emotional reactions following divorce. But the intensity of their feelings and the way these are expressed vary with children's age, temperament, and sex.

Children's Age. The cognitive immaturity of preschool and early school-age children makes it difficult for them to grasp the reasons behind their parents' separation. Because they often blame themselves and take the marital breakup as a sign that they could be abandoned by both parents, younger children are often profoundly upset. They may whine and cling, displaying intense separation anxiety. Preschoolers are especially likely to fantasize that their parents will get back together (Wallerstein, 1983; Wallerstein, Corbin, & Lewis, 1988).

Older children are better able to understand the reasons behind their parents' divorce. They recognize that strong differences of opinion, incompatible personalities, and lack of caring for one another are responsible (Neal, 1983). The ability to accurately assign blame may reduce some of the pain children feel. Still, many school-age and adolescent youngsters react strongly to the end of their parents' marriage. Particularly when family conflict is high, they are likely to display adjustment difficulties (Borrine et al., 1991; Forehand et al., 1991). Undesirable peer activities that provide an escape from unpleasant home lives, such as running away, truancy, and delinquent behavior, are common (Doherty & Needle, 1991; Dornbusch et al., 1985).

However, not all older children react this way. For some—especially the oldest child in the family—divorce can trigger more mature behavior. They may willingly take on extra burdens, such as household tasks, care and protection of younger siblings, and emotional support of a depressed, anxious mother. But if these demands are too great, older children may eventually become resentful and withdraw from the family into some of the more destructive behavior patterns just described (Hetherington, Stanley-Hagan, & Anderson, 1989; Wallerstein & Kelly, 1980).

Children's Temperament and Sex. In earlier chapters, we noted that temperament can either reduce or increase children's risk for maladjustment. When temperamentally difficult children are exposed to stressful life events and inadequate parenting, their problems are likely to be compounded. In contrast, easy children are less often targets of parental impatience and anger and are also better able to cope with adversity when it hits (Garmezy, 1983; Rutter, 1987).

These findings help us understand sex-related differences in children's response to divorce. Girls sometimes show internalizing reactions, such as crying, self-criticism, and withdrawal. More often, they display some demanding, attention-getting behavior. But in mother-custody families, boys experience more serious adjustment difficulties. Recall from Chapter 13 that boys are more active, assertive, and noncompliant than girls to begin with. These behaviors escalate when boys encounter parental conflict and inconsistent discipline (Hetherington, Cox, & Cox, 1982). Longitudinal research in Great Britain and the United States reveals that many sons of divorcing couples were impulsive and undercontrolled long before the marital breakup—behaviors that may have contributed to as well as been caused by their parents' marital problems. As a result, these boys entered the period of family turmoil surrounding divorce with a reduced capacity to cope with family stress (Block, Block, & Gjerde, 1988; Cherlin et al., 1991; Hetherington, 1991).

Perhaps because their behavior is so unruly, boys of divorcing parents receive less emotional support and are viewed more negatively by mothers, teachers, and peers. Furthermore, the coercive cycles of interaction that boys often establish with their divorced mothers soon spread to sibling relations. In mother-custody families with sons, quarreling, teasing, hitting, and other negative behaviors toward siblings increase (Baldwin & Skinner, 1989; MacKinnon, 1989; Zaslow, 1989). These outcomes compound boys' difficulties. Children of both sexes show declines in achievement during the aftermath of divorce, but school problems are greater for boys (Guidubaldi & Cleminshaw, 1985).

Long-Term Consequences. The majority of children show improved adjustment by 2 years after divorce. Yet a significant number continue to have serious difficulties for many years. Because they are more often exposed to ineffective child rearing, boys and children with difficult temperaments are especially likely to experience lasting emotional problems (Hetherington & Clingempeel, 1992). Among girls, the most consistent long-term consequences have to do with heterosexual behavior—a rise in sexual activity at adolescence, short-lived sexual relationships in early adulthood, and lack of self-confidence in associations with men (Kalter et al., 1985; Wallerstein & Corbin, 1989).

The overriding factor in positive adjustment following divorce is effective parenting—in particular, how well the custodial parent handles stress, shields the child from family conflict, and engages in authoritative parenting (Buchanan, Maccoby, & Dornbusch, 1991; Hetherington, 1991). Contact with noncustodial fathers is also important. For girls, a good father–child relationship appears to contribute to healthy heterosexual development. For boys, it seems to play a critical role in overall psychological well-being. In fact, several studies reveal that outcomes for sons are better when the father is the custodial parent (Camara & Resnick, 1988; Santrock & Warshak, 1986). Fathers are more likely than mothers to praise a boy's good behavior and less likely to ignore his disruptiveness (Hetherington, Cox, & Cox, 1982). The father's image of greater power and authority may also help him obtain more compliance from a son. Furthermore, boys whose fathers maintain frequent contact have more opportunities to identify with and adopt their father's self-controlled behavior.

Contact with noncustodial fathers is important in children's adjustment to divorce. This divorced father and his daughter enjoy an especially warm relationship during visitation periods—a circumstance that will contribute to her long-term adjustment. (DAVID YOUNG-WOLFF/PHOTOEDIT)

Although divorce is painful for children, there is clear evidence that those who remain in a stressed, intact family are more poorly adjusted than those who have weathered the stormy transition to a single-parent family and are living in low-conflict households (Block, Block, & Gjerde, 1988; Hetherington, Cox, & Cox, 1982; Long & Forehand, 1987). Children whose divorcing parents put aside their disagreements and support each other in their parenting roles have the best chance of growing up competent, stable, and happy. When parental cooperation is not possible, caring extended family members and friends can reduce the likelihood that divorce will result in long-term disruption (Hetherington, Stanley-Hagan, & Anderson, 1989).

Schools can also make a difference. Cognitive and social outcomes are improved if preschool and school-age children attend classrooms in which teachers provide consistent structure and create a democratic atmosphere in which warmth is combined with reasonable demands for mature behavior (Hetherington, Cox, & Cox, 1982; Peres & Pasternack, 1991). Note that these are the very ingredients of good parenting associated with favorable adjustment in intact families. Children of divorce clearly benefit from a nurturant, predictable school environment when these experiences are not available at home.

HELPING CHILDREN AND FAMILIES ADJUST TO DIVORCE. Awareness that divorce is highly stressful for parents and children has led to community-based services aimed at helping them through this difficult time. Parents Without Partners is a national organization with a membership of 180,000. It provides publications, telephone referrals,

Before the 1970s, grandparents did not have the right to petition the courts for visitation privileges with their grandchildren after parental separation and divorce. Legally mandated visitation was reserved for parents, who regulated grandparents' access to children. Although grandparent visitation cases occasionally reached the courts, judges were wary about granting these requests. They recognized that intense conflict between parents and grandparents lay behind most petitions and that it was not in the best interests of children to embroil them in intergenerational disputes (Derdeyn, 1985).

In recent years, a rising population of older Americans has led to a broadening of grandparents' rights. Interest groups representing senior citizens have convinced state legislators to support the grandparent–grandchild relationship during an era in which a high rate of marital breakup has threatened extended family ties. Today, all 50 states permit grandparents to seek legal visitation judgments (Thompson et al., 1989). The new policy is also motivated by a well-intentioned desire on the part of lawmakers to

foster children's access to social supports within the family and widespread belief in the specialness of the grandparent–grandchild relationship. As we saw earlier in this chapter, grandparents can promote children's development in many ways—both directly, through their relationship with the child, and indirectly, by providing parents with child-rearing advice, models of child-rearing skill, and financial assistance.

Nevertheless, serious questions have been raised about legalizing children's ties to their grandparents. The most significant factor in how children's development is affected by interaction with grandparents is the quality of the grandparents' relationship with the children's parents. If it is positive, children are likely to benefit. But courtroom battles that turn parents and grandparents into adversaries may close the door to gains that would otherwise result from frequent grandparent–grandchild contact. In sum, available research suggests that the courts should exercise considerable restraint in awarding grandparent visitation rights in divorce cases (Thompson et al., 1989).

and programs through local chapters designed to relieve the problems of single parents. Support groups for children are also available, often sponsored by churches, synagogues, schools, and mental health agencies, in which fears and concerns are shared and coping skills are taught. Evaluations of the effectiveness of these programs suggest that they can reduce stress and promote improved communication among family members (Emery, 1988).

Another recently developed intervention is **divorce mediation**. It consists of a series of meetings between divorcing adults and a trained professional, who tries to help them settle disputes, such as property division and child custody. Its purpose is to avoid legal battles that intensify family conflict. In some states, divorce mediation is voluntary. In others, it must be attempted before a case is heard by a judge. Research reveals that it increases out-of-court settlements, compliance with agreements, and feelings of well-being among divorcing parents. Because it reduces family hostilities, divorce mediation probably benefits children, although little research has addressed this issue directly (Emery & Wyer, 1987).

A relatively new child-custody option tries to keep both parents involved with children. In **joint custody**, the court grants the mother and father equal say in important decisions about the child's upbringing. Joint custody eliminates the "winner" and "loser" resolution to child-custody disputes that sometimes reduces the "loser's" willingness to spend time with the children. Nevertheless, it is a highly controversial practice, and many experts have raised questions about it. Joint custody results in a variety of living arrangements. In most instances, children reside with one parent and see the other on a fixed schedule, much like the typical sole-custody situation. In other cases, parents share physical custody, and children must move between homes weekly, monthly, or yearly. Sometimes these transitions require a shift not just in residence, but also in school and peers. As a result, they introduce a new kind of instability that may be especially hard on some children (Johnston, Kline, & Tschann, 1989). The success of joint custody requires a cooperative relationship between divorcing parents. If they continue to quarrel, it prolongs children's exposure to a hostile family atmosphere (Furstenberg & Cherlin, 1991). See the Social Issues box above for an additional legal practice that poses similar risks to children's well-being.

Divorce mediation

A series of meetings between divorcing adults and a trained professional, who tries to help them settle disputes. Aimed at avoiding legal battles that intensify family conflict.

Joint custody

A child-custody arrangement following divorce in which the court grants both parents equal say in important decisions about the child's upbringing.

581

Finally, for many single-parent families, child support from the absent parent is necessary to relieve financial strain. In response to a recent federal law, all states have established procedures for withholding wages from parents who fail to make these court-ordered payments. Although child support is usually not enough to lift a single-parent family out of poverty, it can ease its burdens substantially (Children's Defense Fund, 1992b).

Remarriage

Life in a single-parent home is often a temporary condition. Many parents remarry within a few years, merging parent, stepparent, and children into a new family structure called the **blended, or reconstituted, family.** For some children, this expanded family network is a positive turn of events that brings with it greater adult attention. But for most, it presents difficult adjustments (Bray, 1988; Hetherington, Cox, & Cox, 1985). Stepparents often use different child-rearing practices than the child is used to, and having to switch to new rules and expectations can be stressful (Lutz, 1983). In addition, children often regard steprelatives as "intruders" into the family. Indeed, their arrival does change interaction with the natural parent. But how well children adapt is, once again, related to the overall quality of family functioning. This varies depending on which parent remarries as well as on the age and sex of the child. As we will see, older children and girls seem to have the hardest time (see Table 14.4).

MOTHER/STEPFATHER FAMILIES. The most frequent form of blended family is a mother/stepfather arrangement, since mothers generally retain custody of the child. Under these conditions, boys usually adjust quickly. They welcome a stepfather who is warm and involved and who offers relief from the coercive cycles of interaction that tend to build with their divorced mothers. Mothers' friction with sons also declines for other reasons—greater economic security, another adult to share household tasks, and an end to loneliness. One study found that less than 2 years after remarriage, boys living in mother/stepfather households were doing almost as well as those in nondivorced families (Hetherington, Cox, & Cox, 1985). In contrast, girls adapt less favorably when custodial mothers remarry. Stepfathers disrupt the close ties many girls established with their mothers in a single-parent family, and girls

Blended, or reconstituted, family
A family structure resulting from remarriage of a divorced parent that includes parent, child, and new steprelatives.

TABLE 14.4 Factors Related to Children's Adjustment to Remarriage

FACTOR	DESCRIPTION
Form of blended family	Children living in father/stepmother families display more adjustment difficulties than those in mother/stepfather families, perhaps because father-custody children start out with more problems.
Child characteristics Age	Adolescents find it harder to adjust, perhaps because remarriage makes it more difficult for them to deal with their own sexuality and establish autonomy. Also, compared to children, they are more aware of the impact of remarriage on their own lives.
Sex	Girls display more severe reactions than do boys because of interruptions in close bonds with custodial parents and greater conflict with stepmothers.
Repeated marital transitions	The more marital transitions experienced, the greater the possibility of severe and long-lasting adjustment difficulties.
Social supports	See Table 14.3.

often react to the new arrangement with "sulky, resistant, ignoring, critical behavior" (Hetherington, 1989, p. 7; Vuchinich et al., 1991).

Note, however, that age affects these findings. Early adolescents of both sexes find it harder to adjust to blended families and often display high levels of disruptive and antisocial behavior (Hetherington & Clingempeel, 1992; Hobart, 1987). Young teenagers are in the midst of dealing with their own budding sexuality and establishing autonomy. The presence of a stepparent may make these tasks more difficult (Hetherington, 1991). Furthermore, because adolescents are more aware of the impact of remarriage on their own lives, they may challenge some aspects of it that children simply accept, creating more relationship issues with their steprelatives.

FATHER/STEPMOTHER FAMILIES. Although only a few studies have focused on father/stepmother families, research consistently reveals more confusion for children under these conditions. In the case of noncustodial fathers, remarriage often leads to reduced contact. They tend to withdraw from their "previous" families, more so if they have daughters rather than sons (Hetherington, Cox, & Cox, 1982). When fathers have custody, children typically react negatively to remarriage. One reason is that children living with fathers often start out with more problems. Perhaps the biological mother could no longer handle the unruly child (usually a boy), so the father and his new wife are faced with a youngster who has serious behavior problems. In other instances, the father is granted custody because of a very close relationship with the child, and his remarriage disrupts this bond (Brand, Clingempeel, & Bowen-Woodward, 1988).

Girls, especially, have a hard time getting along with their stepmothers (Hobart & Brown, 1988). Sometimes (as just mentioned) this occurs because the girl's relationship with her father is threatened by the remarriage. In addition, girls often become entangled in loyalty conflicts between their two mother figures. Noncustodial mothers (unlike fathers) are likely to maintain regular contact with children, but frequent visits by mothers are associated with less favorable stepmother–stepdaughter relations. The longer girls live in father/stepmother households, the more positive their interaction with stepmothers becomes. With time and patience they do adjust, and eventually girls benefit from the support of a second mother figure (Brand, Clingempeel, & Bowen-Woodward, 1988).

REPEATED MARITAL TRANSITIONS. Although children often respond intensely to parental remarriage, once they become convinced of their parents' continuing love and support, behavior problems subside. Unfortunately, many children do not have a chance to settle into a happy blended family, since the divorce rate for second marriages is higher than for first marriages. In a recent study of fourth-grade boys, the more marital transitions children experienced, the more severe and prolonged their adjustment difficulties (see Figure 14.4). Furthermore, parents with poor child-rearing skills and antisocial tendencies (as indicated by arrest records, drug use, and personality tests) were particularly likely to undergo several divorces and remarriages. In the process, they exposed their children to recurring episodes of high family conflict and inconsistent parenting (Capaldi & Patterson, 1991). When marital transitions pile up, they become part of a cluster of negative life events that severely disrupt children's development.

Maternal Employment

For many years, divorce has been associated with a high rate of maternal employment, due to financial strains experienced by mothers responsible for maintaining their own families. But over the last several decades, women of all sectors of the population—not just those who are single and poor—have gone to work in increasing numbers. The most dramatic change in labor-force participation has occurred among mothers in two-parent families. The percentage with children

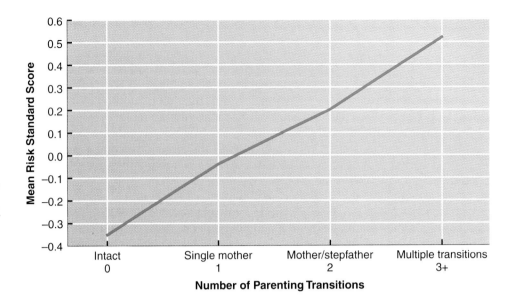

FIGURE 14.4 Boys' risk for poor adjustment by number of parenting transitions. The greater the number of transitions, the higher the risk score. Risk was determined by averaging seven adjustment measures: antisocial behavior, drug use, deviant peer associations, peer rejection, poor academic skills, low self-esteem, and depression. (Adapted from "Relation of Parental Transitions to Boys' Adjustment Problems: I. A Linear Hypothesis. II. Mothers at Risk for Transitions and Unskilled Parenting" by D. M. Capaldi & G. R. Patterson, 1991, *Developmental Psychology, 27*, p. 494. Copyright © 1991 by the American Psychological Association. Reprinted by permission.)

under age 18 who are employed has more than doubled since 1960, from 28 to 67 percent. Today, for children of any age in either one- or two-parent families, more than 50 percent of their mothers work (U.S. Bureau of the Census, 1992).

In Chapter 10, we discussed the impact of maternal employment on infant–mother attachment and concluded that for babies, the consequences depend on the quality of day care and the continuing parent–child relationship. This same conclusion applies to development during later years. In addition, many studies agree that a host of factors—the mother's work satisfaction, the support she receives from her husband, the child's sex, and the social class of the family—have a bearing on whether children show benefits or problems from growing up in an employed-mother family.

MATERNAL EMPLOYMENT AND CHILD DEVELOPMENT. As long as mothers want to work, like their jobs, and have found satisfactory child-care arrangements, employment is associated with greater life satisfaction for both low-income and middle-income mothers (Goldberg & Easterbrooks, 1988; Gove & Zeiss, 1987). Children of mothers who enjoy working and remain committed to parenting show especially positive adjustment—a higher sense of self-esteem, more positive family and peer relations, less gender-stereotyped beliefs, and better grades in school (Hoffman, 1989; Williams & Radin, 1993). These benefits undoubtedly result from parenting practices. Employed mothers who value their parenting role are more likely to use authoritative child rearing (Greenberger & Goldberg, 1989). They schedule special times to devote to their children and also encourage greater responsibility and independence—factors that promote favorable cognitive and social development.

A modest increase in fathers' involvement in child-care and household duties also accompanies maternal employment, and it seems to facilitate a variety of aspects of children's development (Zaslow, Rabinovich, & Suwalsky, 1991). In a longitudinal study of maternal employment, fathers' early involvement in child care was positively related to intelligence, academic achievement, and mature social behavior for both sons and daughters (Gottfried, 1991). Furthermore, fathers' participation is one of the routes through which children of employed mothers acquire gender-stereotype flexibility (Baruch & Barnett, 1986; Williams, Radin, & Allegro, 1992).

But there are some qualifiers to these encouraging findings. First, outcomes associated with maternal employment are more positive for daughters than sons. Girls, especially, profit from the image of female competence. Daughters of employed mothers have higher educational aspirations and, in college, are more likely to choose nontraditional careers, such as law, medicine, and physics (Hoffman, 1974). In contrast, boys in low-income homes are sometimes adversely affected. They tend to admire their fathers less and to interact more negatively with them. These findings are probably due to a lingering belief in lower-class homes that when a mother works, the father has failed in his provider role (Hoffman, 1989).

Beyond these sex and social-class differences, several other factors make a difference in how children adjust to maternal employment. Women continue to hold less prestigious jobs than men, and they earn less than men in comparable occupations. Because these factors affect income and morale, they are likely to influence how mothers feel and behave with children at the end of the working day. Furthermore, when employment places heavy demands on the mother's schedule, children are at risk for ineffective parenting. Working long hours and spending little time with school-age children are associated with less favorable outcomes, both cognitively and socially (Moorehouse, 1991). In contrast, part-time employment seems to have benefits for children of all ages, probably because it permits mothers to meet the needs of youngsters with a wide range of characteristics (Alvarez, 1985; Williams & Radin, 1993).

SUPPORT FOR EMPLOYED MOTHERS AND THEIR FAMILIES. The research we have reviewed indicates that as long as mothers have the necessary supports to engage in effective parenting, maternal employment offers children many advantages. In dual-earner families, the husband's willingness to share responsibilities is crucial. Although men assist to a greater extent than they did in decades past, women still shoulder most household and child-care tasks (Robinson, 1988). If the father helps very little or not at all, the mother carries a double load, at home and at work, leading to fatigue, distress, and reduced time and energy for children.

Besides fathers, work settings, communities, and government policies can help employed mothers in their child-rearing roles. Part-time employment and liberal paid maternity and paternity leaves (including time off when children are ill) would help many women juggle the demands of work and child rearing. Although these workplace supports are widely available in Western Europe and Canada, at present only unpaid employment leave is mandated by U.S. federal law (see Chapter 1, page 37). Finally, high-quality day care is vital for parents' peace of mind and children's healthy development, as we will see in the following section.

*A*s long as this mother enjoys her job, remains committed to parenting, and finds satisfactory child-care arrangements, her baby is likely to develop into a child with high self-esteem, positive family and peer relations, flexible beliefs about gender, and good grades in school. (THOMAS S. ENGLAND/ PHOTO RESEARCHERS)

Day Care

Even more than infants and toddlers, preschoolers spend considerable time away from their parents in day-care settings. Figure 14.5 shows the varied ways in which American 3- and 4-year-olds are cared for while their parents are at work, based on a recent national survey. About 35 percent spend most of these hours in either their own home or another home, cared for by a relative or nonrelative. The largest proportion—43 percent—attend day-care centers. Out-of-home care is especially common during the preschool years because organized child-care facilities generally specialize in preschoolers; fewer accommodate infants or provide before- and after-school care for 5- to 13-year-olds. Figure 14.5 also reflects the tremendous shortage of affordable day care in the United States. Twenty-two percent of employed mothers of 3- and 4-year-olds get by without any day-care arrangements, a figure that rises to 34 percent and 51 percent for infants and school-age children, respectively (Lombardi, 1993; Willer et al., 1991).

Since day-care centers are easiest for researchers to study, most investigations have focused on them. In recent years, more research has accumulated on children's experiences in *family day-care homes*, in which a neighborhood woman looks after a small group of children in her own home. However, these studies are still

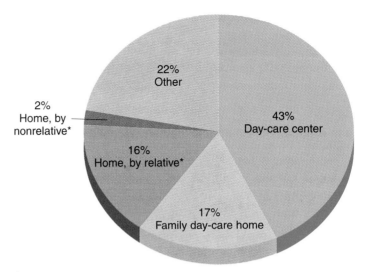

* "Home" refers to either the child's home or the caregiver's home.

FIGURE 14.5 Who's minding America's preschoolers? The chart refers to settings in which 3- and 4-year-olds spend most time while their parents are at work. The "other" category consists mostly of children cared for by their mothers during working hours. Over one-fourth of 3- and 4-year-olds experience more than one type of child care, a fact not reflected in the chart. (Adapted from *The Demand and Supply of Child Care in 1990: Joint Findings from the National Child Care Survey 1990 and A Profile of Child Care Settings* by B. Willer, S. L. Hofferth, E. E. Kisker, P. Divine-Hawkins, E. Farquhar, & F. B. Glantz, 1991, Washington, D.C.: National Association for the Education of Young Children. Reprinted by permission.)

few in number. And at present, we know practically nothing about how the millions of children watched by relatives or baby-sitters or whose parents try to work and care for them at the same time respond to these arrangements.

DAY CARE AND CHILD DEVELOPMENT. The first investigations of day care, carried out in the 1960s and 1970s, compared preschoolers enrolled in high-quality, university-sponsored centers with non–day-care children of the same social class. Although the environments sampled were limited to model programs, the research responded to public concerns that children would suffer from long hours in group-care situations. With respect to cognitive development, middle-class children in day care did not differ from controls. And in some studies of low-income children, enriched day-care experiences were associated with improved performance. For these youngsters, good day care seemed to serve as effective early intervention, reducing the impact of an underprivileged home life. Several studies also indicated that children in high-quality day care were advantaged in sociability with peers (Belsky & Steinberg, 1978; Caldwell, 1993).

Once research had established that day care need not be harmful and could be beneficial, researchers turned to the study of day-care programs in ordinary communities, comparing children's experiences and development in environments that differed widely in quality. The National Day Care Study, which included over 60 day-care centers serving low-income children in three large cities, and The National Day Care Home Study, involving several hundred family day-care homes serving a diverse urban population, were the first large-scale community-based investigations (Divine-Hawkins, 1981; Ruopp et al., 1979). The goals of both were to determine the relationship of such dimensions of quality as group size (number of children in a single space), caregiver/child ratio, and caregiver educational preparation. In each study, caregivers' behavior toward children was observed. Also, tests of cognitive and language development were given in the fall and spring of the year.

Findings were remarkably consistent. In both center and home environments, group size and caregiver/child ratio influenced caregivers' style of interaction. As the number of children decreased (to around 2 to 4 in family day-care homes and to about 14 preschoolers with at least 2 caregivers in day-care centers), adults spent less time commanding and correcting and more time in verbally stimulating interaction. Furthermore, caregivers trained in child development, early childhood education, or a related field were more verbally stimulating as well as responsive to children's needs. Finally, in the center study, smaller group size and greater caregiver education predicted large gains in cognitive and language development over a year's time.

Recent research has replicated as well as extended these findings. In a large study of day-care centers in two states, group size and caregiver/child ratio were related to an even broader array of classroom processes, including caregiver warmth, attention, stimulation, and provision of a rich variety of developmentally appropriate activities. These experiences, in turn, fostered secure attachment to caregivers and greater involvement with peers, which together predicted socially competent behavior (Howes, Phillips, & Whitebook, 1992). Furthermore, caregiver responsiveness and spacious, well-equipped environments and activities that meet the needs of preschoolers have been repeatedly linked to enhanced cognitive, language, and social skills for both low-income and middle-income preschoolers (Howes, 1988b; McCartney, 1984; Phillips, McCartney, & Scarr, 1987; Scarr et al., 1993).

Table 14.5 summarizes the characteristics of high-quality day care for preschool children, based on current findings. When these ingredients are absent, the well-being of children from all walks of life is undermined. Furthermore, research indicates that parents who enroll their preschoolers in low-quality day care tend to lead stressful lives and use inappropriate child-rearing techniques—factors that, when combined, pose an especially serious risk to children's development (Howes, 1990).

DAY-CARE POLICIES IN THE UNITED STATES AND OTHER WESTERN NATIONS. As we noted in Chapter 10, the overall state of American day care is alarmingly inadequate. Since no federal standards exist, day-care quality varies greatly from state to state. Many caregivers have little or no specialized education for teaching young children, and in some states, 1 adult is permitted to supervise as many as 12 to 15 preschoolers. From 75 to 90 percent of family day-care homes are unlicensed and therefore not monitored for quality of care. Salaries of caregivers typically fall below the poverty line, with few if any fringe benefits. As a result, over 40 percent leave their jobs annually (Willer et al., 1991; Zigler & Gilman, 1993). Tax relief to help American parents pay for day care has increased in recent years (see Chapters 1 and 10), but many continue to have difficulty affording it. At current rates, more than 25 percent of the annual earnings of a minimum-wage worker with one young child are consumed by day-care fees (Maynard & McGinnis, 1993). Although publicly funded centers for low-income families exist, they fall far short of the need. In some places, waiting lists have swelled into the thousands (Children's Defense Fund, 1992b).

In Western Europe, government-supported day care for all 2½- to 3-year-olds up to the age of compulsory schooling is widely available. The need for places for infants and toddlers is not as great as in the United States because of generous parental leave policies following the birth of a child. Furthermore, caregivers are usually paid on the same scale as elementary school teachers, and they receive health insurance and other benefits just like any other citizen. Standards for group size, caregiver/child ratios, and caregiver educational preparation (factors shown by research to be critical markers of quality) are rigorously set and enforced. Center-based care is the most common form in Western Europe, but many governments also support family day care by paying caregivers directly, providing training for them, and inspecting their homes for health and safety. Since programs are heavily subsidized, parents pay only a small income-related fee, usually less than 10 percent of the average woman's wages (Kamerman, 1993; Scarr et al., 1993).

TABLE 14.5 Signs of High-Quality Day Care for Preschool Children

PROGRAM CHARACTERISTICS	SIGNS OF QUALITY
Physical setting	Indoor environment is clean, in good repair, and well ventilated. Classroom space is divided into richly equipped activity areas, including make-believe play, blocks, science, math, games and puzzles, books, art, and music. Fenced outdoor play space is equipped with swings, climbing equipment, tricycles, and sandbox.
Group size	In day-care centers, no more than 16 to 18 preschoolers with 2 teachers.
Caregiver/child ratio	In day-care centers, teacher is responsible for no more than 8 children. In day-care homes, caregiver is responsible for no more than 6 children.
Daily activities	Most of the time, children work individually or in small groups. Children select many of their own activities and learn through experiences relevant to their own lives. Caregivers facilitate children's involvement, accept individual differences, and adjust expectations to children's developing capacities.
Caregiver education	Caregiver has college-level specialized educational preparation in early childhood development, early childhood education, or a related field.
Relationships with parents	Parents are encouraged to observe and participate. Caregivers talk frequently with parents about children's behavior and development.
Licensing and accreditation	Day-care setting, whether a center or home, is licensed by the state. Accreditation by the National Academy of Early Childhood Programs or the National Association for Family Day Care is evidence of especially high-quality day care.

SOURCE: National Association for the Education of Young Children, 1984.

Day care is a legal right and nearly as accessible as public schooling in Western European countries. It is one element in a wide array of policies designed to attract mothers back to the labor force after the child's first year while ensuring family well-being and fostering children's development. Because the United States does not yet have a national day-care policy, it lags far behind other Western industrialized nations in supply, quality, and affordability of day-care services.

Self-Care

Care for school-age children while their parents are at work also has important implications for development. In recent years, much public concern has been voiced about the estimated 2.4 million 5- to 13-year-olds in the United States who regularly look after themselves during after-school hours (Cain & Hofferth, 1989). Although many return home to an empty house, others "hang out" with peers in the neighborhood or in nearby shopping malls during late afternoons and evenings. The status of these **self-care children** has sparked much debate, since current evidence reveals inconsistent findings. Some studies report that they suffer

Self-care children
Children who look after themselves during after-school hours.

from low self-esteem, fearfulness, antisocial behavior, and poor academic achievement, whereas others show no such effects (Padilla & Landreth, 1989). However, most research has failed to take into account the type of self-care arrangement.

When investigators look closely at how self-care children spend their time and what their family circumstances are like, trends are much clearer. Interviewing fifth- through eighth-grade children about their after-school experiences, Lawrence Steinberg (1986) found that children who had a history of authoritative parenting, were monitored from a distance by telephone calls, and had regular after-school chores appeared responsible and well adjusted. In contrast, those left to their own devices were more likely to bend to peer pressure and engage in antisocial behavior. Amount of self-care also makes a difference. One study found that eighth-graders in self-care for more than 11 hours per week were twice as likely to be frequent users of illegal drugs than were agemates who never cared for themselves. Perhaps a great deal of time in self-care is a sign of weak parental control and monitoring—factors consistently linked to poor adjustment (Richardson et al., 1989). Finally, children from single-parent, poverty-stricken homes who care for themselves are at greater risk for antisocial behavior than are those in after-school programs. Nevertheless, self-care for these children is no worse than returning home to an overwhelmed, psychologically unavailable mother who offers her child little emotional support (Vandell & Ramanan, 1991).

Parents need to consider children's maturity carefully before deciding on self-care. Before age 8 or 9, children should not be left unsupervised because it is doubtful that they have the cognitive and social skills to deal with emergencies (Galambos & Maggs, 1991; Peterson, 1989). Unfortunately, when children express discomfort with the self-care arrangement, are not mature enough to handle it, or could benefit from an after-school program because of an underprivileged home life, many parents have no alternative. Organized day care for school-age children is rare in American communities. Furthermore, enrolling a child in a low-quality after-school program may do more harm than good. One study found that third-graders who attended crowded day-care centers with inadequately trained staff fared worse in academic achievement and social competence than children who reported to a sitter or took care of themselves (Vandell & Corasaniti, 1988). High-quality day care is vital for children's well-being at all ages, even during middle childhood.

R apid transitions in family life have taken place in Western industrialized nations. The recent trend toward a smaller family size is associated with more favorable child development. Nevertheless, most children continue to grow up with at least one brother or sister. By the end of the younger child's first year, siblings have become salient social partners. Although unequal treatment by parents promotes sibling rivalry, sibling relationships serve as important sources of companionship, emotional support, and assistance and contribute to many aspects of social competence. Nevertheless, only children are just as well adjusted as children with siblings, and they are advantaged in academic achievement and educational attainment.

Brief Review

Large numbers of American children experience the divorce of their parents. Although many adjust well by 2 years after the divorce, boys and temperamentally difficult children are likely to display lasting emotional problems. Effective parenting is the most important factor in helping children adapt to life in a single-parent family. When parents remarry, children living in father/stepmother families, and daughters especially, display more adjustment difficulties.

Maternal employment is related to high self-esteem, reduced gender stereotyping, and mature social behavior. However, these outcomes vary with children's sex and social class, the demands of the mother's job, and the father's participation in child rearing. High-quality day care fosters cognitive, language, and social skills among low-income and middle-income children. Unfortunately, much day care in the United States is substandard and poses serious risks to children's development.

VULNERABLE FAMILIES: CHILD MALTREATMENT

Families, as we indicated in the first part of this chapter, contribute to the mainte-nance of society by serving as contexts in which children are loved, protected, and encouraged to develop into competent, caring adults. Throughout our discussion of family transitions, we encountered examples of the many factors, both within and outside the family, that contribute to parents' capacity to be warm, consistent, and appropriately demanding. As we turn now to the topic of child maltreatment, we will see that when these vital supports for effective child rearing break down, children as well as their parents can suffer terribly.

Incidence and Definitions

Child maltreatment is as old as the history of humankind, but only recently has there been widespread acceptance that the problem exists, research aimed at understanding it, and programs directed at helping maltreated children and their families. Perhaps this increase in public and professional concern is due to the fact that child maltreatment is especially common in large industrialized nations (Gelles & Cornell, 1983). It occurs so often in the United States that a recent gov-ernment committee called it a "national emergency." A total of 2.7 million cases were reported to juvenile authorities in 1991, an increase of 165 percent over the previous decade (Children's Defense Fund, 1992b). The true figure is surely much higher, since most cases, including ones in which children suffer serious physical injury, go unreported.

Child maltreatment takes the following forms:

1. *Physical abuse.* Assaults on children that produce pain, cuts, welts, bruises, burns, broken bones, and other injuries.
2. *Sexual abuse.* Sexual comments, fondling, intercourse, and other forms of exploitation.
3. *Physical neglect.* Living conditions in which children do not receive enough food, clothing, medical attention, or supervision.
4. *Emotional neglect.* Failure of caregivers to meet children's needs for affection and emotional support.
5. *Psychological abuse.* Actions that seriously damage children's emotional, social, or cognitive functioning.

Although all experts recognize that these five types exist, they do not agree on the range of adult behaviors and how frequent and intense they must be to be called maltreatment. Consensus on a definition is important, since if we cannot define abuse and neglect, we are hampered in studying their origins and impact on chil-dren and designing effective interventions (Zuraivin, 1991). The greatest problems arise in the case of subtle, ambiguous behaviors. For example, some experts regard psychological abuse, in which children are ridiculed, humiliated, rejected, scape-goated, or terrorized by an adult, as the most frequent and destructive form, since it accompanies most other types (Grusec & Walters, 1991). Yet definitions of psycho-logical abuse are especially complex and serious in their consequences for children and families. If they are too narrow and include only the most severe instances of mental cruelty, they allow many harmful actions toward children to continue unchecked and untreated. If they are too lenient, they can result in arbitrary, disrup-tive legal intrusions into family life (Melton & Thompson, 1987).

Origins of Child Maltreatment

When child maltreatment first became a topic of research in the early 1960s, it was viewed as rooted in adult psychological disturbance. The first studies indicated that adults who abused or neglected their children usually had a history of mal-

Until recently, child sexual abuse was viewed as a rare occurrence. When children came forward with it, adults often thought that they had fantasized the experience, and their claims were not taken seriously. In the 1970s, efforts by professionals along with widespread media attention caused child sexual abuse to be recognized as a serious national problem. Although over 200,000 cases are reported each year, this statistic greatly underestimates the actual number, since affected children feel frightened, confused, and guilty and are usually pressured into silence (Hartman & Burgess, 1989).

Sexual abuse is committed against children of both sexes, but more often against girls than boys. Its incidence is highest in middle childhood, but it also occurs at younger and older ages. Few children experience only a single episode. For some, the abuse begins early in life and continues for many years (Finkelhor, 1984; Gomez-Schwartz, Horowitz, & Cardarelli, 1990). Generally, the abuser is male—a parent or someone whom the parent knows well. Often it is a father, stepfather, or live-in boyfriend, somewhat less often, an uncle or older brother. In a few instances, mothers are the offenders, more often with sons than daughters. If a nonrelative is responsible, it is usually someone the child has come to know and trust (Alter-Reid et al., 1986; Pierce & Pierce, 1985).

In the overwhelming majority of cases, the abuse is serious. Children are subjected to intercourse, oral-genital contact, fondling, and forced stimulation of the adult. Abusers make the child comply in a variety of distasteful ways, including deception, bribery, verbal intimidation, and physical force (Gomez-Schwartz, Horowitz, & Cardarelli, 1990). You may be wondering how any adult—especially, a parent or close relative—could possibly violate a child sexually. Many offenders deny their own responsibility. They blame the abuse on the willing participation of a seductive youngster. Yet children are not capable of making a deliberate, informed decision to enter into a sexual relationship! Even at older ages, they are not free to say yes or no (Finkelhor, 1984). Instead, abusers tend to have characteristics that predispose them toward sexual exploitation. They have great difficulty controlling their impulses, may suffer from psychological disorders, and are often addicted to alcohol and drugs. Furthermore, they tend to pick out victims who are unlikely to defend themselves—children who are physically weak, emotionally deprived, and socially isolated (Faller, 1990).

Reported cases of child sexual abuse are strongly linked to poverty, marital instability, and resulting weakening of family ties. Children who live in homes where there is a history of constantly changing characters—repeated marriages, separations, and new partners—are especially vulnerable. But community surveys reveal that middle-class children in relatively stable homes are also victims. Economically advantaged families are simply more likely to escape detection (Gomez-Schwartz, Horowitz, & Cardarelli, 1990).

The adjustment problems of child sexual abuse victims are severe. Depression, low self-esteem, mistrust of adults, feelings of anger and hostility, and difficulties in getting along with peers are common. Younger children often react with sleep difficulties, loss of appetite, and generalized fearfulness. Adolescents sometimes run away or show suicidal reactions (Haugaard & Reppucci, 1988; Watkins & Bentovim, 1992). Abuse that is committed by a relative, involves force, and continues for a long time is associated with greater long-term harm (Beitchman et al., 1992).

Sexually abused children frequently display sexual knowledge and behavior beyond that which is appropriate for their age. They have learned from their abusers that sexual overtures are acceptable ways to get attention and rewards. As they move toward young adulthood, they tend to be promiscuous and to enter into unhealthy relationships. Females are likely to choose husbands who abuse both them and their children (Faller, 1990). As mothers, they often show poor parenting skills, abusing and neglecting their own children (Pianta, Egeland, & Erickson, 1989). In this way, the harmful impact of sexual abuse is transmitted to the next generation.

Treating victims of child sexual abuse is difficult. Once the abuse is revealed, the reactions of family members—anxiety about harm to the child, anger toward the abuser, and sometimes hostility toward the victim for telling—can increase children's distress. Since sexual abuse typically appears in the midst of other serious family problems, long-term therapy with both children and parents is usually necessary (Gomez-Schwartz, Horowitz, & Cardarelli, 1990).

The best way to reduce the suffering of child sexual abuse victims is to prevent it from continuing. Children's testimony, as we noted in Chapter 7, is currently being taken more seriously by the courts. In schools, sex education programs can help children recognize inappropriate sexual advances and encourage them to report these actions. Finally, educating teachers, caregivers, and other adults who work with children about the signs and symptoms of sexual abuse can help ensure that victimized children are identified early and receive the help they need.

treatment in their own childhoods, unrealistic expectations that children would satisfy their own unmet emotional needs, and poor control of aggressive impulses (Kempe et al., 1962; Spinetta & Rigler, 1972). (See the Social Issues box above for a discussion of child sexual abuse, which was not recognized as a serious social problem until the 1970s.)

TABLE 14.6 Factors Related to Child Maltreatment

FACTOR	DESCRIPTION
Parent characteristics	Psychological disturbance; substance abuse; history of abuse as a child; belief in harsh, physical discipline; desire to satisfy unmet emotional needs through the child; unreasonable expectations for child behavior; young age (most under 30); low educational level
Child characteristics	Premature or very sick baby; difficult temperament; inattentiveness and overactivity; other developmental problems
Family characteristics	Low income; poverty; homelessness; marital instability; social isolation; physical abuse of mother by husband or boyfriend; frequent moves; large, closely spaced families; overcrowded living conditions; disorganized household; lack of steady employment; other signs of high life stress
Community	Characterized by social isolation; few parks, day-care centers, preschool programs, recreation centers, and churches to serve as family supports
Culture	Approval of physical force and violence as ways to solve problems

SOURCES: Pianta, Egeland, & Erickson, 1989; Simons et al., 1991; Zigler & Hall, 1989.

It soon became clear that although child maltreatment was more common among disturbed parents, a single "abusive personality type" did not exist. Sometimes, even "normal" parents harmed their children! Also, parents who were abused as children did not always repeat the cycle with their own youngsters (Hunter & Kilstrom, 1979; Simons et al., 1991). For help in understanding child maltreatment, researchers turned to the social systems perspective on family functioning. They discovered that child abuse and neglect are affected by many interacting variables—at the family, community, and cultural levels. Table 14.6 summarizes factors associated with child maltreatment. The more that are present, the greater the chances that abuse or neglect will occur. Let's examine each set of influences in turn.

THE FAMILY. Within the family, parent and child often contribute jointly to child maltreatment. Certain children have an increased likelihood of becoming targets of abuse. These include premature or very sick babies and children who are temperamentally difficult, inattentive or overactive, or who have other developmental problems. But whether such children are actually maltreated depends on characteristics of parents (Pianta, Egeland, & Erickson, 1989). In one study, temperamentally difficult children had mothers who believed they could do little to control their child's behavior. Instead, they attributed the child's unruliness to a stubborn or bad disposition, an interpretation that led them to move quickly toward physical force when the child misbehaved (Bugental, Blue, & Cruzcosa, 1989). Furthermore, although many abusive parents hold high expectations for their child's development, they do not provide the necessary encouragement that assists children in meeting these goals. Consequently, their children are disappointments. Abusive parents typically express little pleasure in parenthood and satisfaction with and affection for their child (Trickett et al., 1991).

Once child abuse gets started, it quickly becomes part of a self-sustaining family pattern. The small irritations to which abusive parents react—a fussy baby, a preschooler who knocks over a glass of milk, or a child who will not mind immediately—soon become bigger ones. Then the harshness of parental behavior increases as well. By the preschool years, abusive and neglectful parents seldom interact with their children. When they do, communication is almost always negative (Trickett & Kuczynski, 1986). Maltreated children, in turn, engage in especially high rates of misbehavior, gradually developing serious learning and adjustment problems, including difficulties with peers, academic failure, depression, noncompliant acting-out behavior, substance abuse, and delinquency (Hotaling et al., 1988; Salzinger et al., 1993; Simons, Conger, & Whitbeck, 1988; Sternberg et al., 1993). These outcomes contribute to further mistreatment.

Most parents, however, have enough self-control not to respond to their children's misbehavior with abuse, and not all children with developmental problems are mistreated. Other factors must combine with these conditions to prompt an extreme parental response. Research reveals that unmanageable parental stress is strongly associated with all forms of maltreatment. Such factors as low income, unemployment, marital conflict, overcrowded living conditions, frequent moves, and extreme household disorganization are common in abusive homes. These conditions increase the chances that parents will be so overwhelmed that they cannot meet basic child-rearing responsibilities or will vent their frustrations by lashing out at their children (Pianta, Egeland, & Erickson, 1989).

THE COMMUNITY. The majority of abusive parents are isolated from both formal and informal social supports in their communities. There are at least two causes of this social isolation. First, because of their own life histories, many of these parents have learned to mistrust and avoid others. They do not have the skills necessary for establishing and maintaining positive relationships with friends and relatives (Polansky et al., 1985). Second, abusive parents are more likely to live in neighborhoods that provide few links between family and community, such as parks, day-care centers, preschool programs, recreation centers, and churches (Garbarino & Sherman, 1980). For these reasons, they lack "lifelines" to others and have no one to turn to for help during particularly stressful times.

THE LARGER CULTURE. One final set of factors—cultural values, laws, and customs—profoundly affects the chances that child maltreatment will occur when parents feel overburdened. Societies that view force and violence as appropriate ways to solve problems set the stage for child abuse. These conditions exist in the United States. Although all 50 states have laws designed to protect children from maltreatment, strong support still exists for the use of physical force in parent–child relations. For example, during the past 25 years, the U.S. Supreme Court has twice upheld the right of school officials to use corporal punishment to discipline children. Crime rates have risen in American cities, and television sets beam graphic displays of violence into family living rooms. In view of the widespread acceptance of violent behavior in American culture, it is not surprising that most parents use slaps and spankings at one time or another to discipline their children. In countries where physical punishment is not accepted, such as Luxembourg and Sweden, child abuse is rare (Zigler & Hall, 1989).

Preventing Child Maltreatment

Since child maltreatment is embedded within families, communities, and society as a whole, efforts to prevent it must be directed at each of these levels. Many approaches have been suggested. These include interventions that teach high-risk parents effective child-rearing and disciplinary strategies, high school child development courses that include direct experience with children, and broad social programs that have as their goal full employment and better economic conditions for low-income families (Rosenberg & Reppucci, 1985).

We have already seen that providing social supports to families is very effective in easing parental stress. It is not surprising that this approach sharply

you idiot!
you idiot!
you idiot!
you idiot!
you idiot!
you idiot!
you idiot!
you idiot!
y

**Children learn
by repetition.**

You don't have to hit
to hurt.

San Francisco
Child Abuse Council
(415) 668-0494

*Public-service announcements help prevent
child abuse by educating people about the
problem and informing them where to seek
help. This poster reminds adults that
degrading remarks can hit as hard as a fist.*
(COURTESY SAN FRANCISCO CHILD ABUSE COUNCIL)

reduces child maltreatment. Research indicates that social support is the major
distinguishing factor between mothers who repeat their own histories of abuse
with their children and those who do not. Mothers who break the intergenerational cycle are more likely to have received affection and comfort from a nonabusive adult in their own childhoods, to have entered into therapy at some time during their lives, and to have established a satisfying relationship with a mate
(Egeland, Jacobvitz, & Sroufe, 1988). Parents Anonymous, a national organization
that has as its main goal helping child-abusing parents learn constructive parenting practices, does so largely through providing social supports to families. Each
of its local chapters offers self-help group meetings, daily telephone calls, and regular home visits to relieve social isolation and teach child-rearing skills.

Crisis intervention services also exist in many communities. Nurseries offer
temporary child care when parents feel they are about to lose control, and telephone hotlines offer immediate help to parents under stress and refer them to
appropriate community agencies when long-term assistance is warranted.

Other preventive approaches include announcements in newspapers and magazines and on television and radio that are designed to educate people about child
maltreatment and tell them where to seek help (Rosenberg & Reppucci, 1985).
Besides these efforts, changes in the overall attitudes and practices of American culture are needed. Many experts believe that child maltreatment cannot be eliminated
as long as violence is widespread and corporal punishment continues to be
regarded as an acceptable child-rearing alternative (Gil, 1987; Zigler & Hall, 1989).

Although more cases reach the courts than in decades past, child maltreatment remains a crime that is difficult to prove. Most of the time, the only witnesses are the child victims themselves or other loyal family members. Even in
court cases in which the evidence is strong, judges hesitate to impose the ultimate
safeguard against further harm: permanent removal of the child from the family.

There are several reasons for this reluctant posture. First, in American society,
government intervention into family life is viewed as a last resort, to be used only
when there is near certainty that a child will be denied basic care and protection.
Second, despite destructive family relationships, maltreated children and their
parents are usually attached to one another. Most of the time, neither desires separation. Finally, the American legal system tends to regard children as parental
property rather than as human beings in their own right, and this has also stood
in the way of court-ordered protection (Hart & Brassard, 1987).

Even with intensive treatment, some adults persist in their abusive acts. An estimated 1,383 children (half of them under 1 year of age) died from abuse or neglect in 1991, more than in each of the 6 previous years in which such data were collected (Children's Defense Fund, 1992b). In cases where parents are unlikely to change their behavior, taking the drastic step of separating parent from child and legally terminating parental rights is the only reasonable course of action.

Child maltreatment is a distressing and horrifying topic. When we consider how often it occurs in the United States, a society that claims to place a high value on the dignity and worth of the individual, it is even more appalling. Yet there is reason to be optimistic. Great strides have been made in understanding and preventing child maltreatment over the last several decades. Although we still have a long way to go, the situation for abused and neglected children is far better now than it has been at any time in history (Kempe & Kempe, 1984).

CHAPTER SUMMARY

Evolutionary Origins

- The human family can be traced to our hunting-and-gathering ancestors. When bipedalism evolved and arms were freed to carry things, our ancestors found it easier to cooperate and share, especially in providing food for the young. A single male became committed to a female and their joint offspring, a relationship that enhanced survival.

Functions of the Family

- Besides promoting the survival of its own members, the family performs essential functions for society. In complex societies, these are largely restricted to reproduction, socialization, and emotional support.

The Family as a Social System

- Modern researchers view the family from a **social systems perspective**—as a complex set of interacting relationships affected by the larger social context. Bidirectional influences exist in which the behaviors of each family member affect those of others. Connections to the community—through formal organizations and informal social networks—promote effective family interaction and enhance children's development.

Socialization Within the Family

- Two broad dimensions, demandingness and responsiveness, describe individual differences in the way parents go about the task of socialization. When combined, they yield four styles of parenting. The **authoritative style**, which is both demanding and responsive, promotes cognitive, emotional, and social competence from early childhood into adolescence. The **authoritarian style**, which is high in demandingness but low in responsiveness, is associated with anxious, withdrawn, dependent child behavior. The **permissive style** is responsive but undemanding; children who experience it typically show poor self-control and achievement. Finally, the **uninvolved style** is low in both demandingness and responsiveness. It disrupts virtually all aspects of development.

- As children get older, a gradual lessening of control supports development, as long as parental warmth and involvement in child rearing are maintained. In middle childhood, effective parents engage in **coregulation,** exerting general oversight while permitting children to be in charge of moment-by-moment decision making. During adolescence, mature **autonomy** is fostered by parenting that grants young people independence in accord with their readiness for it while maintaining close family ties.

- The authoritative style is the most common form of child rearing in many cultures around the world. Nevertheless, in many societies, differences in child rearing are linked to social class and ethnicity. Effective parenting, along with children's development, is seriously undermined by the stress and disorganization of living in poverty. **Extended family households,** in which one or more adult relatives live with the parent–child **nuclear family unit,** are common among ethnic minorities and protect children's development under conditions of high life stress.

Family Transitions

- Over the past several decades, rapid transitions in family life have taken place in Western industrialized nations. The trend toward smaller families has positive consequences for parent–child interaction and children's development. Nevertheless, most children still grow up with at least one sibling. Because of their emotional intensity and frequency of interaction, sibling relationships promote many aspects of social competence. Unequal parental treatment increases sibling rivalry. During adolescence, sibling relationships become less intense, but attachment to siblings remains strong for most young people.

- Contrary to popular belief, sibling relationships are not essential for normal development. Only children are as well adjusted as children with siblings, and they are advantaged in school achievement and educational attainment.

- Divorce is extremely common in the lives of American children. Although painful emotional reactions usually accompany the period surrounding divorce, children with difficult temperaments and boys in mother-custody homes react more strongly and are more likely to show lasting adjustment problems. The most consistent long-term effects for girls involve heterosexual behavior in adolescence and young adulthood. The overriding factor in positive adjustment following divorce is good parenting. Contact with the noncustodial parent is also important. Because **divorce mediation** helps parents resolve their disputes, it can reduce children's exposure to conflict. **Joint custody** is a controversial practice that requires a cooperative relationship between divorcing parents to be successful.

- When divorced parents remarry, children must adapt to a **blended,** or **reconstituted, family**, a transition that is often difficult. How well children do varies depending on which parent remarries and on the age and sex of the child. Boys usually adjust well in mother/stepfather families. In contrast, children in father/stepmother families, especially girls, display the greatest problems. Because repeated marital transitions expose children to recurring episodes of family conflict and inconsistent parenting, they severely disrupt development.

- As long as mothers enjoy their work and remain committed to parenting, maternal employment is associated with favorable consequences for children, including a higher sense of self-esteem, more positive family and peer relations, and less gender-stereotyped beliefs. However, outcomes are more positive for daughters than sons, and boys in low-income homes sometimes show adverse effects. The father's willingness to share household and child-rearing responsibilities along with workplace supports, such as part-time employment and generous parental leave, help mothers juggle the multiple demands of work and child rearing.

- American children experience a diverse array of day-care arrangements while their parents are at work. Center-based care is the most common form during the preschool years. Research indicates that when group size is small, caregiver/child ratios are generous, and caregivers are well educated, they communicate in more stimulating and responsive ways and provide developmentally appropriate activities. As a result, many aspects of child development are fostered. The United States lags far behind other Western nations in supply, quality, and affordability of day-care services.

- During middle childhood, millions of children look after themselves during after-school hours. When **self-care children** have a history of authoritative parenting and are monitored from a distance, they fare well. In contrast, children left to their own devices are at risk for antisocial behavior. High-quality organized day care for school-age children is not widely available in the United States.

Vulnerable Families: Child Maltreatment
- Child maltreatment is related to factors within the family, community, and larger culture. Certain characteristics of children, such as prematurity or a difficult temperament, combined with unmanageable parental stress and isolation from supportive ties to the community increase the chances that maltreatment will occur. When a society approves of force and violence as appropriate means for solving problems, child abuse is promoted.

IMPORTANT TERMS AND CONCEPTS

social systems perspective (p. 560)
authoritative style (p. 563)
authoritarian style (p. 564)
permissive style (p. 565)
uninvolved style (p. 565)

coregulation (p. 567)
autonomy (p. 567)
extended family household (p. 571)
nuclear family unit (p. 571)

divorce mediation (p. 581)
joint custody (p. 581)
blended, or reconstituted, family (p. 582)
self-care children (p. 588)

CONNECTIONS

CHAPTER
15

◆ **Edvard Munch,** *Two Girls with Blue Aprons*
1904–1905, Munch Museet, Oslo/Erich Lessing/Art Resource

Peers, Media, and Schooling

Four 6-year-old pupils are gathered around one of the computers in their first-grade classroom, using Logo, a flexible computer language in which numerical instructions yield geometric shapes, to draw a snowman on the screen. As John assumes control of the keyboard, the children consider how large to make the snowman's hat. Their conversation is richly woven with ideas and joint efforts at problem solving:

> Kevin: Small.
> John: Two. [referring to units specifying size in Logo]
> Andrew: Shh, listen to what Cathie says. What number?
> Cathie: I don't know. John, I think you should decide. It's your hat.
> Kevin: Should take four.
> Cathie: I think that would be too big, wouldn't it?
> Kevin: You've never took four before.
> Andrew: Do three . . . It'll be too big.

> John: I say two.
> Cathie: If you say two, put in two, John. Put in two. [John draws the square.] That's fine, isn't it?
> [Now the children decide on a length for the brim.]
> Andrew: Two . . . One . . .
> John: Try one.
> Kevin: And then do another one?
> Cathie: Well, it's got to go to the corner, and one past . . .
> John: Right, two. . . . Will I go forward? (Hughes & Macleod, 1986, pp. 197–198)

In creating the snowman, these young children cooperate to reach a common goal, generate alternative strategies for solution, extend their knowledge of mathematical estimation, and begin to master a technology that plays a central role in the economic and leisure life of their society. Their cognitive and social competencies illustrate the importance of three contexts for development. Beginning at an early age, socialization in the family is supplemented by experiences in the wider world of peers, media, and school.

In all human societies, children spend many hours in one another's company. In no culture are they reared entirely by adults. In Chapter 11, we saw how one special type of peer relationship, friendship, contributes uniquely to development. In this chapter, we take a broader look at how peer sociability changes with age, the many factors that support it, and its profound significance for psychological adjustment. Next we turn to television and computers, reviewing what is known about the effects of these captivating electronic devices on children's cognitive and social skills. Finally, our discussion addresses the school, an institution established to assist the family in transmitting culturally valued knowledge to the next generation. We consider how physical settings, educational philosophies, quality of teacher–pupil interaction, and the ability mix of pupils affect educational experiences in classrooms. We conclude the chapter with an evaluation of the success of American schools in equipping young people to keep pace with their counterparts in other industrialized nations and in preparing them for productive work lives.

THE IMPORTANCE OF PEER RELATIONS

How critical are peer relations for development, and what way do they add to children's experiences with caring adults? To find out for sure, we would need to study a group of children reared only by parents, comparing their competencies to children growing up under typical conditions. These circumstances rarely occur naturally and are unethical to arrange experimentally among humans. But scientists have conducted such studies with nonhuman primates, and their findings lend insight into the function of peer experiences. Harry Harlow (1969) reported that maternally reared rhesus monkeys with no peer contact display a broad array of social problems, including immature play, excessive aggression and fearfulness, and less effective cooperation among group members at maturity. Harlow concluded that although peer bonds are usually not as intense as attachments to parents, their impact on social competence is considerable.

Parent and peer associations seem to complement one another. The parent–child bond emphasizes caregiving and affection, providing children with the security to venture into the world of peers. Peer interaction, in turn, consists mainly of play and socializing, permitting children to expand the social skills they have begun to acquire within the family (Hartup & Moore, 1990). In addition, peer relations are flexible enough so that they can fill in, at least to some extent, for the early parent–child bond. In a special type of investigation called **peer-only rearing,** researchers reared rhesus monkey infants in groups without adults.

Peer-only rearing
A type of study in which nonhuman primates are reared together from birth without adults.

When given a choice between their preferred peer (the one they most often sought closeness to during rearing), a familiar peer, and an unfamiliar peer, peer-only reared monkeys spent most time near the preferred peer. In addition, the preferred peer served as an effective source of security in a novel cage, reducing the distress of peer-only reared subjects more effectively than did other agemates (Higley et al., 1992).

Nevertheless, peer-only reared monkeys do not fare as well in development as their counterparts with typical parental and peer upbringing. In the study just described, monkeys who experienced a warm mother–child bond prior to peer exposure were playful and curious when placed in a novel setting with their preferred peer. In contrast, peer-only reared monkeys spent much of their time either clinging to or hovering near their preferred agemate, constantly seeking reassurance. Perhaps for this reason, peer-only reared monkeys display some behavior problems as they get older, including increased dominant and submissive (as opposed to friendly) interaction with unfamiliar agemates, reduced exploration, and deficient sexual behavior (Goy & Goldfoot, 1974). Nevertheless, within their familiar peer group, peer-only reared monkeys do develop socially competent behavior, and they are far better off than monkeys reared in isolation (Suomi & Harlow, 1978).

Can these findings be generalized to human children? A unique parallel to the peer-only rearing research just described suggests that in large measure, they can. In the 1940s, Anna Freud and Sophie Dann (1951) studied six young German-Jewish orphans whose parents were murdered in the Nazi gas chambers shortly after the children's birth. They remained together in a concentration camp for several years, without close ties to adults. When World War II ended, the children were brought to England and cared for in a country house until they could adjust to their new surroundings. Observations revealed that each orphan was passionately attached to other members of the group, becoming upset when separated, even for brief moments. Their behavior was also intensely prosocial; they freely shared, comforted, and offered assistance to one another. At the same time, the children showed many anxious symptoms, including intense thumb sucking, restlessness, immature forms of play, and periods of aggression toward as well as complete dependency on their caregivers. As they gradually built trusting relationships with adults, the children's play, language, and exploration developed rapidly. In sum, peers serve as vital sources of security in threatening situations and contribute to many aspects of development. But they do so more effectively when they are preceded by a warm, supportive relationship with a caregiver.

As we turn now to the development of peer sociability, a word of caution is in order. Strictly speaking, the term *peer* means equal in rank or standing. Most of the research we will discuss bears the mark of this definition, since it focuses on children who are close in age. Investigators have emphasized the study of agemates because observing children is easiest in age-graded settings, such as daycare centers, schools, and summer camps. Yet in the neighborhood, where children's activities are harder to track, more than half their contacts are with children who differ by at least a year in age (Barker & Wright, 1955; Ellis, Rogoff, & Cromer, 1981). And in cultures where children are not segregated by age for schooling and recreation, cross-age interaction is even more common (Weisner & Gallimore, 1977; Whiting & Edwards, 1988) We will consider what is known about mixed-age peer interaction as our discussion proceeds. But it is important to note that the heavy research focus on agemates limits what we currently know about the diversity of children's peer experiences.

DEVELOPMENT OF PEER SOCIABILITY

Peer sociability begins early in cultures where children experience regular contact with one another during the first year of life. Observations of infant playmates indicate that signs of peer interaction are already present. Gradually, these evolve into the more complex, better coordinated social exchanges of the childhood and adolescent years. The development of peer sociability is supported by and contributes to important cognitive, language, and emotional milestones that we discussed in previous chapters (Brownell, 1986).

Infant and Toddler Beginnings

When pairs of infants are brought together in a laboratory, looking accompanied by touching is present at 3 to 4 months, peer-directed smiles and babbles by 6 months. These isolated social acts increase until by the second half of the first year, an occasional reciprocal exchange occurs in which babies smile, laugh, gesture, or otherwise imitate each other's behavior (Eckerman & Whatley, 1977; Vandell, Wilson, & Buchanan, 1980).

Between 1 and 2 years, peer social behavior develops further. Isolated acts decline, and coordinated interaction occurs more often. Older toddlers also combine several behaviors, such as looking, vocalizing, gesturing, and smiling, into a single social act (Bronson, 1981). By age 2, when both the mother and a peer are present, attempts to engage the peer in play occur more often than initiations to the mother (Eckerman, Whatley, & Kutz, 1975).

Nevertheless, we must be careful not to exaggerate infants' and toddlers' social capacities. Even in laboratory playrooms where these young playmates have little else to capture their attention, peer social contacts do not occur often, and sustained interaction is rare. Furthermore, the rise in reciprocal exchanges that occurs by the end of the second year consists largely of imitations of the other child's actions, such as jumping, chasing, or banging a toy. Not until age 2 to $2\frac{1}{2}$ do children frequently use words to affect a peer's behavior, as when they say "Let's play chase," or engage in complementary roles, such as feeding a doll that another child is holding (Eckerman, Davis, & Didow, 1989; Howes & Matheson, 1992).

But peer sociability is present in the first 2 years, and research suggests that it is supported by the early infant–caregiver relationship. From interacting with sensitive, responsive adults, babies learn how to send and interpret emotional signals in their first peer associations (Jacobson et al., 1986; Parke et al., 1988). Consistent with this idea, infants who experience a warm parental relationship engage in more extended peer social exchanges (Vandell & Wilson, 1987). These children, in turn, display more socially competent behavior during the preschool years (Howes, 1988a; Howes & Matheson, 1992; Howes & Stewart, 1987).

The Preschool Years

Between ages 2 and 5, the amount and quality of peer interaction changes greatly. In the early part of this century, Mildred Parten (1932) observed young children in nursery school and noticed a dramatic rise with age in joint, interactive play. She concluded that social development proceeds in a three-step sequence. It begins with **nonsocial activity**—unoccupied, onlooker behavior and solitary play. Then it shifts to a form of limited social participation called **parallel play,** in which a child plays near other children with similar materials but does not try to influence their behavior. At the highest level, preschoolers engage in two forms of true social interaction. The first is **associative play,** in which children engage in separate activities, but they interact by exchanging toys and commenting on one another's behavior. The second is **cooperative play**—a more advanced type of interaction in which children orient toward a common goal, such as acting out a make-believe theme or working on the same product, for example, a sand castle or painting.

Recent longitudinal research indicates that these play forms typically emerge in the order suggested by Parten, but they do not form a developmental sequence in which later-appearing ones replace earlier ones (Howes & Matheson, 1992). Instead, all types coexist during the preschool years (see Table 15.1). Furthermore, although

Nonsocial activity
Unoccupied, onlooker behavior and solitary play.

Parallel play
A form of limited social participation in which the child plays near other children with similar materials but does not interact with them.

Associative play
A form of true social participation in which children are engaged in separate activities, but they interact by exchanging toys and commenting on one another's behavior.

Cooperative play
A form of true social participation in which children's actions are directed toward a common goal.

*T*hese children are engaged in parallel play. Although they sit side by side and use similar materials, they do not try to influence one another's behavior. Parallel play remains frequent and stable over the preschool years. (GEORGE GOODWIN/ MONKMEYER PRESS PHOTO)

nonsocial activity does decline with age, it is still the most frequent form of behavior among 3- to 4-year-olds. Even among kindergartners it continues to take up as much as a third of children's free play time. Also, solitary and parallel play remain fairly stable from 3 to 6 years, and together, these categories account for as much of the young child's play as highly social, cooperative interaction. Social development during the preschool years is not just a matter of eliminating nonsocial and partially social activity from the child's behavior.

We now understand that it is the *type*, rather than the amount, of solitary and parallel play that changes during early childhood. In a detailed study of preschoolers' play behavior, researchers rated the *cognitive maturity* of nonsocial, parallel, and cooperative play by applying the categories shown in Table 15.2. Within each of Parten's play types, 5-year-olds engaged in more cognitively mature behavior than did 4-year-olds (Rubin, Watson, & Jambor, 1978).

These findings are helpful in responding to the concerns of some parents, who wonder if a young child who spends large amounts of time playing alone is developing normally. Only certain kinds of nonsocial activity—aimless wandering and functional play involving immature, repetitive motor action—are cause for concern during the preschool years. Most nonsocial play of preschoolers is not

TABLE 15.1 Changes in Parten's Social Play Types from Preschool to Kindergarten Age

PLAY TYPE	PRESCHOOL (3–4 YEARS)	KINDERGARTEN (5–6 YEARS)
Nonsocial activity	41%	34%
Unoccupied, onlooker behavior	(19%)	(14%)
Solitary play	(22%)	(20%)
Parallel play	22%	23%
Cooperative play	37%	43%

SOURCES: Preschool percentages are averages of those reported by Barnes (1971); Rubin, Maioni, and Hornung (1976); Rubin, Watson, and Jambor (1978); and Smith (1978). Kindergarten figures are averages of those reported by Barnes (1971) and Rubin, Watson, and Jambor (1978).

Brief Review

Second, well-known peers (much like familiar caregivers) provide young children with a sense of security. As a result, they explore and interact with greater freedom and enthusiasm.

Experiments with rhesus monkeys reveal that peer interaction is a vital source of social competence and can, to some extent, fill in for the early parent–child bond. However, peer interaction supports development more effectively if it is preceded by a warm relationship with a caregiver.

Peer sociability begins in infancy as isolated smiles, gestures, and babbles evolve into coordinated interaction over the first 2 years. During the preschool years, cooperative play increases, but solitary and parallel play are also common. Within each of these play types, children's activities become more cognitively complex with age. In middle childhood and adolescence, gains in communication skills and greater awareness of social norms contribute to advances in peer interaction. Rough-and-tumble play increases in middle childhood. In our evolutionary past, it may have been important for the development of fighting skill.

Parents influence young children's peer relations by arranging peer-play activities and teaching and modeling effective social skills. Situational factors are also important. Richly equipped play environments, nonspecific toys, and same-age, familiar peers promote highly positive, cooperative child–child interaction. Cross-age contact permits older children to practice prosocial skills and younger children to learn from the expertise of more mature partners.

PEER ACCEPTANCE

As we all know from our own childhoods, some children are more desirable peer companions than others. Peer acceptance refers to likability—the extent to which a child is viewed by agemates as a worthy social partner. Researchers usually assess it with self-report instruments called **sociometric techniques.** For example, children may be asked to nominate several peers in their class whom they especially like or dislike, to indicate for all possible pairs of classmates which one they prefer to play with, or to rate each peer on a scale from "like very much" to "like very little" (Asher & Hymel, 1981). Children as young as 4 years of age can answer these questions reliably (Hymel, 1983).

Sociometric techniques yield four different categories of social acceptance: **popular children,** who get many positive votes; **rejected children,** who are actively disliked; **controversial children,** who get a large number of positive and negative votes; and **neglected children,** who are seldom chosen, either positively or negatively. About two-thirds of pupils in a typical elementary school classroom fit one of these categories. The remaining one-third are average in peer acceptance; they do not receive extreme scores (Coie, Dodge, & Coppotelli, 1982).

Peer acceptance is a powerful predictor of current as well as later psychological adjustment. Rejected children, especially, are unhappy, alienated, poorly achieving children with a low sense of self-esteem. Both teachers and parents view them as having a wide range of emotional and social problems (Achenbach & Edelbrock, 1981; French & Waas, 1985). Peer rejection during middle childhood is also strongly associated with poor school performance, dropping out, antisocial behavior, and delinquency in adolescence and criminality in young adulthood (Morison & Masten, 1991; Ollendick et al., 1992; Parker & Asher, 1987). In contrast, research on the long-term outcomes of neglected peer status suggests that it carries much less risk of long-term psychological difficulties. And at present, we have little evidence on how controversial children, who are both liked and disliked, fare in the long run.

Although poor peer acceptance predicts a wide variety of later life problems and certainly may contribute to them, keep in mind that the evidence just described

Sociometric techniques
Self-report measures that ask peers to evaluate one another's likability.

Popular children
Children who get many positive votes on sociometric measures of peer acceptance.

Rejected children
Children who are actively disliked and get many negative votes on sociometric measures of peer acceptance.

Controversial children
Children who get a large number of positive and negative votes on sociometric measures of peer acceptance.

Neglected children
Children who are seldom chosen, either positively or negatively, on sociometric measures of peer acceptance.

is correlational. Therefore, peer relations may not be a major causal factor. Instead, they may be linked to psychological adjustment through other prior influences, such as children's personality characteristics, parenting practices, or some combination of the two. Indeed, warm support, explanations, and encouragement tend to characterize the child-rearing experiences of popular children, high life stress and ineffective, power-assertive discipline the home lives of rejected children (Dekovic & Janssens, 1992; Dishion, 1990; Hart, Ladd, & Burleson, 1990; Putallaz & Heflin, 1990). At the same time, we will see that popular and rejected youngsters' styles of interaction prompt very different reactions from agemates, which probably compound the impact of family influences. In the following sections, we consider factors in the peer situation that increase the chances that a child will fall into one rather than another peer acceptance category.

Origins of Acceptance in the Peer Situation

What leads one child to be liked, a second to be disliked, and a third to evoke neither positive nor negative reactions from peers? To explore this question, researchers have correlated many child characteristics with sociometric scores. They have also conducted short-term longitudinal research to isolate the behavioral causes of different types of peer acceptance. But before we turn to these findings, let's look at the significance of an important nonbehavioral attribute for children's popularity: their physical appearance.

PHYSICAL APPEARANCE. In Chapter 5, we indicated that physical attractiveness has an important bearing on peer acceptance. Recall that children and adolescents who deviate from society's ideal standards of physical beauty as a result of obesity or pubertal timing are less well accepted by peers.

Although the strong preference in our culture for a lithesome female body and a muscular male physique is probably learned (see Chapter 5), partiality for facial features emerges so early that it may be built in. Three- to 6-month-old infants look longer at faces judged attractive as opposed to unattractive by adults, regardless of the age, race, and sex of the model (Langlois et al., 1991). By 12 months, they vary their behavior in response to attractiveness, showing more positive affect and involved play and less withdrawal toward an attractive as opposed to unattractive unfamiliar adult (Langlois, Roggman, & Rieser-Danner, 1990). Furthermore, individuals of a wide variety of cultural and racial groups are in remarkable agreement on what constitutes facial attractiveness: a "typical" facial configuration, one that results when many human faces are averaged together (Cunningham, 1986; Langlois & Roggman, 1990).

During early and middle childhood, children hold different social expectations of attractive and unattractive agemates. When asked to guess the characteristics of unfamiliar peers from their photographs, they attribute friendliness, smartness, and niceness to those who are good-looking and aggressiveness and other negative behaviors to those who are unattractive (Adams & Crane, 1980; Langlois & Stephan, 1977). Attractiveness is also associated with popularity and behavior ratings among children who know each other well, although these relationships are stronger for girls than boys (Langlois & Styczynski, 1979).

Do children derive their opinions about attractive and unattractive agemates from the way they actually behave or from stereotypes held by adults? To investigate this question, Judith Langlois and Chris Downs (1979) assigned preschoolers to the following same-age, same-sex pairs: two attractive children, two unattractive children, and one attractive and one unattractive child. Then they observed each pair in a laboratory play session. No differences based on attractiveness were present at age 3. But by age 5, unattractive children more often aggressed against their partners than attractive children did. These findings indicate that unattractive children actually display some of the negative behaviors peers attribute to them. However, differences did not appear until the end of the preschool years, so it is possible that unattractive children responded as they did because of others' prior reactions to their physical appearance.

Teachers and parents hold the same "beauty is best" bias shown by peers in their expectations of children (Adams, 1978; Ritts, Patterson, & Tubbs, 1992). In one study, the stronger the bias held by a mother against unattractive children, the more likely her child was to prefer the handsomer of two agemates as a play partner (Adams & Crane, 1980). The evidence as a whole indicates that beginning early in life, a preference for attractive over unattractive children translates into differential treatment by adults and peers. Then children may respond in kind to the way they are treated, thereby sustaining the opinions of those with whom they come in contact.

SOCIAL BEHAVIOR. Already we have suggested that social behavior plays a powerful role in peer acceptance. A wealth of research indicates that popular, rejected, controversial, and neglected children interact with agemates in distinct ways.

Popularity is consistently associated with cooperative, friendly social behavior. Well-liked children are especially effective social problem solvers who communicate with peers in sensitive, mature ways (Newcomb, Bukowski, & Pattee, 1993). When they do not understand another child's reaction, they are likely to ask for an explanation (Rubin, 1972). If they disagree with a play partner in a game, they go beyond voicing their displeasure; they suggest what the other child could do instead. When they want to enter an ongoing play group, they adapt their behavior to the flow of peer activity (Gottman, Gonso, & Rasmussen, 1975; Ladd & Price, 1987). In view of these findings, it is not surprising that popular children are described by their classmates as kind, trustworthy companions who possess leadership qualities (Carlson, Lahey, & Neeper, 1984; Parkhurst & Asher, 1992).

Rejected children, in contrast, display a wide range of negative social behaviors. But recent evidence indicates that not all of these disliked children look the same. At least two subtypes exist (Rubin, LeMare, & Lollis, 1990). **Rejected-aggressive children,** the largest subgroup, show severe conduct problems—high rates of conflict, hostility, and hyperactive, inattentive, and impulsive behavior. They are also deficient in several social-cognitive skills that we discussed in Chapter 11. For example, they are more likely than other children to misinterpret the innocent behaviors of others as hostile, to be poor social problem solvers, and to blame others for their social difficulties (Crick & Ladd, 1993; Rubin & Daniels-Bierness, 1983; Waas, 1988). In contrast, **rejected-withdrawn children**, a smaller subgroup, are passive and socially awkward. Teachers and peers view them as insensitive, socially incompetent, and rarely engaging in prosocial behavior. Rejected-withdrawn children, especially, feel lonely, hold negative expectations for how peers will treat them, and are very concerned about being scorned and attacked (Bierman, Smoot, & Aumiller, 1993; Parkhurst & Asher, 1992; Rabiner, Keane, & MacKinnon-Lewis, 1993). Indeed, because of their inept, submissive style of interaction, these children are at risk for abuse at the hands of bullies (see the From Research to Practice box on the following page).

Consistent with the mixed peer opinion they engender, controversial children display a blend of positive and negative social behaviors. Like rejected-aggressive children, they are hostile and disruptive, yet they also engage in positive, prosocial acts (Parkhurst & Asher, 1992). As a result, they are salient individuals to their classmates and, much like popular children, are regarded as leaders (Coie, Dodge, & Coppotelli, 1982). Even though they are disliked by some peers, controversial children have some qualities that protect them from social exclusion. As a result, they appear to be relatively happy and comfortable with their peer relationships (Newcomb, Bukowski, & Pattee, 1993; Parkhurst & Asher, 1992).

Neglected children fall at the opposite extreme of controversial children, engaging in low rates of peer interaction of all kinds. They often choose to play alone; classmates regard them as shy children who do not call attention to themselves. Nevertheless, a surprising finding is that neglected children, once thought

Rejected-aggressive children
A subgroup of rejected children who engage in high rates of conflict, hostility, and hyperactive, inattentive, and impulsive behavior.

Rejected-withdrawn children
A subgroup of rejected children who are passive and socially awkward.

Follow the activities of aggressive children over a school day, and you will see that they reserve their hostilities for a small number of peers who consistently serve in the role of victims. What is it about these children that invites and sustains attacks against them? Answers to this question are important, since efforts to reduce victimized children's chances of being targeted for abuse would help to control peer aggression.

In one of the most comprehensive studies of the aggressor–victim relationship, Dan Olweus (1978, 1984) asked Swedish teachers to nominate adolescent male bullies, their "whipping boys," and well-adjusted classmates. Then judgments of each group's characteristics were obtained from teachers, mothers, peers, and the boys themselves. Compared to bullies and well-adjusted adolescents, whipping boys were chronically anxious (at home and at school), low in self-esteem, ostracized by peers, physically weak, and afraid to defend themselves.

These findings suggest that victimized children might be attacked more than others because they are perceived as weak and likely to provide their aggressors with rewarding consequences. Indeed, research on younger children indicates that this is the case. In an observational study of preschoolers, frequently victimized children often reinforced their attackers by giving in to their demands, crying, assuming defensive postures, and failing to fight back (Patterson, Littman, & Bricker, 1967). Victimized preschoolers also have histories of resistant attachment to their caregivers that may contribute to their radiation of anxious vulnerability (Troy & Sroufe, 1987).

Victim status tends to be stable over time. By elementary school, about 1 child in 10 is severely harassed by aggressive agemates, and peers view these victims differently. David Perry, Jean Williard, and Louise Perry (1990) had fourth- through seventh-graders identify aggressive and victimized classmates. Then they selected several victimized children with extreme scores along with nonvictimized controls to serve as stimuli for further peer reaction. While imagining aggressing toward these targets, children were asked to indicate the likelihood of and value they attached to certain outcomes. Their responses revealed that they expected victimized children to give up desirable objects, show signs of distress, and fail to retaliate far more often than controls. In addition, children attached greater importance to retrieving objects, felt less discomfort at the prospect of causing pain and suffering, and were less alarmed at the possibility of retaliation when thinking about victims than nonvictims. These reactions were especially strong for boys and aggressive children. In sum, peers not only expect to succeed at attacking a victimized child but also exaggerate the importance of doing so while minimizing harmful consequences.

Aggression and victimization are not polar opposites. In two studies, some of the most extreme victims were also among the most aggressive (Olweus, 1978; Perry, Kusel, & Perry, 1988). They often picked fights, got others into trouble, and were easily angered. Perhaps these children foolishly provoke stronger agemates, who then prevail over them. Although both aggressive and victimized children are rejected by peers, these highly aggressive–highly abused youngsters are the most despised, placing them at severe risk for maladjustment.

Interventions that change victimized children's negative opinions of themselves and that teach them to respond in nonreinforcing ways to their attackers (for example, with assertiveness and humor to teasing) are vital. Nevertheless, the findings just described should not be taken to imply that victimized children are to blame for their abuse. Instead, the responsibility lies with bullies who brutally taunt and assault them and adults who supervise children's interactions.

to be in need of treatment, are usually well adjusted. They are not less socially skilled than their average counterparts (Newcomb, Bukowski, & Pattee, 1993; Parkhurst & Asher, 1992). Instead, these are the children who enjoy solitary activities, mentioned earlier in this chapter. Despite their low rates of social interaction, they do not report feeling especially lonely or unhappy about their social life (Crick & Ladd, 1993). Their neglected status probably reflects their lack of visibility to agemates.

Are the distinct patterns of social behavior just described actually responsible for variations in peer acceptance? Longitudinal research suggests that they are. Kenneth Dodge (1983) brought groups of unacquainted second-grade boys together for a series of play sessions, observed their behavior, and had them make sociometric ratings at the end of the study. Much like the findings just described, boys who came to be popular were friendly and cooperative, those who came to be rejected behaved antisocially, and those who developed a controversial status engaged in both prosocial and antisocial acts. Neglected boys showed some inappropriate social behaviors, but they were rarely aggressive. In a similar study,

John Coie and Janet Kupersmidt (1983) reported that many children who were neglected by familiar classmates broke away from their usual pattern of playing alone and became more sociable. The fact that neglected children can behave in a positive, outgoing manner in new situations may be one reason that, as a group, they are well adjusted.

Helping Rejected Children

A variety of interventions aimed at improving the peer relations and psychological adjustment of rejected children have been developed. Most are based on social learning theory and involve coaching, modeling, and reinforcement of positive social skills, such as how to begin interacting with a peer, cooperate in play, and respond to another child with friendly emotion and approval. Several of these programs have produced gains in social competence and peer acceptance that were still present from several weeks to a year later (Bierman, 1986; Ladd, 1981; Mize & Ladd, 1990).

Some researchers believe that these interventions might be made more effective by combining them with other treatments. Often rejected children are poor students, and their low academic self-esteem magnifies their negative reactions to teachers and classmates. Intensive academic tutoring has been shown to improve their school achievement and social acceptance (Coie & Krehbiel, 1984). In addition, techniques designed to reduce the high levels of antisocial behavior of rejected-aggressive children are helpful. In one study, including verbal prohibitions against antisocial acts and negative consequences for engaging in them in a social-skills coaching program led to better social acceptance than a program that focused only on teaching positive social behavior (Bierman, Miller, & Stabb, 1987).

Social-cognitive interventions, such as training in perspective taking and modifying expectancies for social success, have also produced favorable outcomes. In one study, rejected children (who, after many rebuffs, become pessimistic about their ability to be liked by peers) were led to anticipate social success before joining a group of unfamiliar peers. Children who received the induction were better liked, and girls actually behaved more competently (Rabiner & Coie, 1989). Rejected children seem to make better use of the social skills they do have when they believe that peers will accept them.

Finally, we have seen that the problems rejected children experience may originate, at least in part, within the family. Therefore, interventions that focus on the individual child may not be sufficient. If the quality of parent–child interaction is not changed, rejected children may soon return to their old behavior patterns. The most successful approach to treatment may involve replacing coercive cycles with effective parenting techniques (see Chapter 12) in addition to promoting improved peer relations.

Brief Review

Peer acceptance is a powerful predictor of long-term psychological adjustment. Rejected children, especially, display serious academic and behavior problems. Physical attractiveness is related to likability. Differential treatment of physically attractive and unattractive children may affect the way they behave, thereby sustaining peer opinion. Children's social behavior is a major determinant of peer acceptance. Popular children interact in a cooperative, friendly fashion; rejected children behave antisocially and ineptly; and controversial children display a mixture of positive and negative social behaviors. Although neglected children engage in low rates of peer interaction, they are usually socially competent and well adjusted. Interventions that train social skills, provide academic tutoring, reduce antisocial behavior, and change social cognitions lead to improved social acceptance of rejected children.

PEER GROUPS

If you watch children in the schoolyard or neighborhood, you will see that groups of three to a dozen or more often gather. The organization of these collectives changes greatly with age. Younger children "behave simply as a number of independent persons, each mainly concerned with his own immediate ends" (Isaacs, 1933, p. 213). By the end of middle childhood, children display a strong desire for group belongingness. Together, they generate unique values and standards for behavior. They also create a social structure of leaders and followers that ensures group goals will be met. When these characteristics are present, a **peer group** is formed (Hartup, 1983).

In Chapter 11, we saw how friendships in middle childhood and adolescence contribute to the development of trust and sensitivity. Children's experiences in peer groups also provide a unique context for social learning—one in which children practice cooperation, leadership, and followership and develop a sense of loyalty to collective goals. Through these experiences, children experiment with and learn much about the functioning of social organizations.

Peer Group Formation

A classic study by Muzafer Sherif and his colleagues (1961), called the Robbers Cave experiment, illustrates how peer groups form, their main features, and the functions they serve in children's lives. Fifth-grade boys were brought to a summer campground called Robbers Cave, divided into two clusters of 11 members each, and removed to separate campsites. Although friendships quickly developed, a strong group structure did not emerge until the camp staff arranged activities that required cooperation and interdependence. Backpacking trips into the woods and opportunities to improve swimming and athletic areas led the campers to create a division of labor. Soon several boys with superior skills took on greater status—one for his cooking, another for his athletic ability, and a third for his entertaining personality. Over time, a clear ranking of leaders and followers emerged.

As the group structure took shape, the boys at each campsite developed distinct notions of appropriate behavior and ways of doing things. For example, one group generated a "norm of toughness." They engaged in rowdiness and swearing, suppressed any signs of pain when injured, and refused treatment for cuts and scratches. In contrast, a "norm of good behavior" arose in the other group. These boys used clean language and behaved politely and considerately. At each campsite, group members coined nicknames for one another and used special language styles. Eventually the groups took names for themselves: the Rattlers and the Eagles. The boys in each group took pride in its accomplishments and displayed a strong group identity.

The next phase of Sherif's study showed that a group's norms and social structures develop further, based on its relationship with "outsiders." The camp counselors arranged for the Rattlers and Eagles to "discover" one another and scheduled a tournament of competitive games. The solidarity of each group quickly deteriorated as members blamed each other for defeat. Sparked by intergroup rivalry, a new set of leaders and normative behaviors appeared. Among the Rattlers, a large bully whose aggressiveness had been suppressed during the early period of group formation emerged as a hero. Members hurled insults and retaliated against the outgroup, with each successful attack intensifying group solidarity. Over time, the Rattlers and Eagles stereotyped each other as nasty and sneaky, reactions that further magnified the social distance between the groups.

In the final phase of the study, the camp staff tried to create friendly interaction between the groups. Joint recreational activities, however, were disasters, providing opportunities for each group to continue berating the other. But once the counselors planned events with *superordinate goals*, intergroup hostility began

Peer group
Peers who form a social unit by generating unique values and standards of behavior and a social structure of leaders and followers.

to subside. In one instance, the water supply "broke down," and in another, a truck preparing to get food for the hungry campers "stalled." As a result, all the campers joined forces to solve common problems, negative stereotyping declined, and new friendships emerged that cut across group lines.

The Robbers Cave experiment reveals that peer groups form when individuals perceive that others share similar goals. Norms and social structures emerge and change in the service of common motivations. Although racial and ethnic differences often promote prejudice and stereotyping, Sherif's study shows that hatred by an in-group of an out-group can occur without them. Competition for highly desired resources is enough to produce deep-seated intergroup hostilities. Superordinate goals can reduce intergroup hatred and promote positive attitudes and relationships. Now let's look more closely at two features that Sherif's study indicates are essential for peer group cohesion: group norms and social structures.

Group Norms

Group norms are especially evident during the teenage years, when peer groups become more tightly knit and exclusive. Adolescent peer groups are organized around **cliques,** small groups of about five to seven members who are good friends and, therefore, usually alike in age, race, and social class (see Chapter 11). In early adolescence, cliques are limited to same-sex members, but by the midadolescent years, mixed-sex groups become common. The cliques within a typical high school can be identified by their interests. Once formed, they often develop dress codes, ways of speaking, and behaviors that separate them from one another and from the adult world.

Sometimes several cliques with similar norms form a larger, more loosely organized group called a **crowd.** Unlike the more intimate clique, membership in a crowd is based on reputation and stereotype. Whereas the clique serves as the main context for direct interaction, the crowd grants the adolescent an identity within the larger social structure of the school. For example, here is a description of the norms of several highly visible crowds in one high school:

> *Sporties* . . . are adolescents of both sexes who engage in sports, who attend sports activities, and who drink beer. *Workers* are students who have jobs, who are motivated to accumulate money, who own cars, and whose social lives revolve mostly around the automobile. *Crispies* are students who use drugs on other than a one-time basis, who are the best football players, and who do not work very hard at school. *Musicians* are students who spend much time in the music room, who attend or assist with performance activities of one type or another, and who drink alcoholic beverages. *Debaters* are those who read a lot, get good grades, participate in clubs focused on intellectual activities and who drink Pepsi-Cola at their parties. (Hartup, 1983, p. 146)

What influences the assortment of teenagers into cliques and crowds with particular normative characteristics? Longitudinal research in which adolescent values and peer associates have been tracked over time reveals that both family and peer influences are important. When teenagers join a clique, they select one that is compatible with their current values. Then new norms generated by the group modify their original beliefs and behaviors. A study of 4,000 sixth- through eleventh-graders illustrates this process. Subjects were surveyed about their smoking behavior and that of their parents and peers. Then the same questions were asked again 1 year later. Compared to their nonsmoking counterparts, adolescents who took up smoking during the year of the study were more likely to have both parents and peer associates who smoked (Chassin et al., 1986). Many norms generated by the peer group seem to be extensions of ones acquired at home.

In early adolescence, as interest in dating increases, boys' and girls' cliques come together. The merger takes place slowly. At junior high school dances and parties, clusters of boys and girls can be seen standing on opposite sides of the room, watching but seldom interacting. As mixed-sex cliques form and "hang out" together, they provide a supportive context for boys and girls to get to know each other, offering models for how to interact with the opposite sex and opportunities to

Clique
A small group of about five to seven members who are good friends.

Crowd
A large, loosely organized group consisting of several cliques with similar normative characteristics.

*T*hese teenage girls have a unique dress code, speak to each other in distinct ways, and engage in behaviors that separate them from other cliques and the adult world. Cliques serve as the main context for peer interaction during adolescence, permitting young people to acquire new social skills and experiment with values and roles in the absence of adult monitoring. (ROGER DOLLARHIDE/MONKMEYER PRESS PHOTO)

do so without having to be intimate. Gradually, the larger group divides into couples, several of whom spend time together, going to parties and movies. By late adolescence, boys and girls feel comfortable enough about approaching each other directly that the mixed-sex clique is no longer needed and disappears (Dunphy, 1963; Padgham & Blyth, 1990).

Just as cliques gradually decline in importance, so do crowds. As adolescents formulate their own personal values and goals, they no longer feel a strong need to wear a "badge" that broadcasts, through dress, language, and preferred activities, who they are. Nevertheless, both cliques and crowds serve vital functions during the teenage years. The clique provides a context for acquiring new social skills and for experimenting with values and roles in the absence of adult monitoring. The crowd offers adolescents the security of a temporary identity as they separate from the family and begin to construct a coherent sense of self (Brown, 1990).

Group Social Structures

In all groups, members differ in power or status, an arrangement that fosters division of responsibilities and smooth, cooperative interaction. Group norms and social structures are related. Leaders are generally the major norm-setters, and the ideas of high-status peers are usually sufficient to alter the group's opinion (Fine, 1980). How do leaders and followers emerge in children's groups?

Ethological research reveals that group social structures are sometimes based on toughness or assertiveness. A **dominance hierarchy** is a stable ordering of individuals that predicts who will win when conflict arises between group members. Observations of arguments, threats, and physical attacks between children reveal a consistent lineup of winners and losers as early as the preschool years. This hierarchy becomes increasingly stable during middle childhood and adolescence, especially among boys (Pettit et al., 1990; Savin-Williams, 1979).

Like dominance relations among animals, those among human children serve the adaptive function of limiting aggression among group members. Once a dominance hierarchy is clearly established, hostility is rare. When it occurs, it is very restrained, often taking the form of playful verbal insults that can be accepted cheerfully by the target (Fine, 1980). This gradual replacement of friendly insults for more direct hostility may help children and adolescents learn how to control their aggressive impulses.

Dominance hierarchy
A stable ordering of group members that predicts who will win under conditions of conflict.

Think back to the Robbers Cave study, and you will see that group structures are not always a matter of the largest and strongest children rising to the top. When group goals involve the conquest of "outsiders," then a structure based on dominance is likely to emerge, as it did when the Rattlers and Eagles played competitive games. At other times, many personal qualities become relevant. During adolescence, group structures depend less on size and strength and more on talents that support important normative activities, such as knowing what to do on a camp-out, being a skilled athlete or effective debater, or behaving sociably (Savin-Williams, 1980). Since adolescent peer groups vary widely in their normative concerns, social power accrues to different young people in different situations (Hartup, 1983).

PEER RELATIONS AND SOCIALIZATION

We have seen that peer interaction contributes to a wide variety of skills that help children and adolescents adapt successfully to their social worlds. Just how do peers socialize one another? As we will see in the following sections, they use some of the same techniques that parents do: reinforcement, modeling, and direct pressures to conform to certain expectations.

Peer Reinforcement and Modeling

Children's responses to one another serve as reinforcers, modifying the extent to which they display certain behaviors. Turn back to Chapter 13, pages 534–535, to review how peers reinforce traditional gender-role behavior. Peer reinforcement clearly begins early, and it increases with age. Children often use it for positive ends. Preschoolers value the positive, prosocial behaviors of their agemates. Children who engage in attentive, approving, and affectionate social acts are likely to receive similar behaviors in return (Charlesworth & Hartup, 1967; Leiter, 1977).

However, children are just as receptive to peer reinforcement for antisocial responses as they are for prosocial behavior. In the From Research to Practice box on page 611, we showed that the hostile acts of bullies are repeatedly reinforced by the passivity of their victims. Children who retaliate—for example, by hitting back or holding on to a desired toy—and who succeed at getting an aggressor to retreat punish that child's actions. At the same time, their own behavior is rewarded. A striking finding of observational research on preschoolers is a steady increase in aggressive behavior on the part of initially nonaggressive children who counterattack in the face of peer hostility (Patterson, Littman, & Bricker, 1967). Peer feedback is an important means through which children's aggression is enhanced as well as controlled, and even mild-mannered children can learn to behave aggressively from being targets of hostile attacks.

Besides dispensing reinforcers, peers provide one another with models of a broad array of social behaviors. Peer imitation is common throughout the preschool years, but by middle childhood it declines (Grusec & Abramovitch, 1982). Recall from Chapter 12 that once children internalize the rules of social life, they no longer need to rely so heavily on observations of others for information about how to behave. Although children will copy each other's negative behaviors, those whose parents have guided them toward socially acceptable standards of conduct can resist these influences, and they serve as prosocial models for others (Toner, Parke, & Yussen, 1978).

The powerful effects of peer reinforcement and modeling have led researchers to experiment with peers as agents of behavior change. Socially competent children can be trained to encourage improved social skills in less competent peers, and both show gains in social maturity as a result (Strain, 1977). Peers can also tutor less knowledgeable children at school, teaching, modeling and reinforcing academic skills. Carefully planned peer tutoring programs in which tutors are trained and supervised by adult teachers promote self-esteem and learning in both tutors and tutees. Peer tutoring is especially effective with low-income ethnic minority pupils, many of whom achieve poorly in school (Bargh & Schul, 1980; Strickland & Ascher, 1992).

Peer Conformity

Conformity to peer pressure is greater during adolescence than in childhood or young adulthood—a finding that is not surprising when we consider how much time teenagers spend together. But contrary to popular belief, adolescence is not a period in which young people blindly do whatever their peers ask. Peer conformity is a complex process that varies with the adolescent's age and need for social approval and with the situation.

In one study of nearly 400 junior and senior high students, adolescents reported that they felt greatest pressure to conform to the most obvious behaviors of their peers: dressing and grooming like everyone else and participating in social activities, such as dating and going to parties and school dances (see Figure 15.1). Peer pressure to engage in proadult behavior, such as getting good grades and cooperating with parents, was also strong. Although pressure toward misconduct rose in early adolescence, compared to other areas it was low. Many teenagers said that their friends actively discouraged antisocial acts. These findings show that peer and parental pressures often act in concert, toward *desirable* ends! Finally, peer pressures were only modestly related to teenagers' actual values and behaviors. Clearly, these young people did not always follow the dictates of peers (Brown, Lohr, & McClenahan, 1986).

Perhaps because of greater concern with what their friends think of them, early adolescents are more likely than younger or older individuals to give in to peer pressure, especially when it comes to antisocial behavior (Brown, Clasen, & Eicher, 1986). Yet when parents and peers disagree, even young teenagers do not consistently rebel against their families. Instead, parents and peers differ in their spheres of greatest influence. Parents have more impact on teenagers' basic life

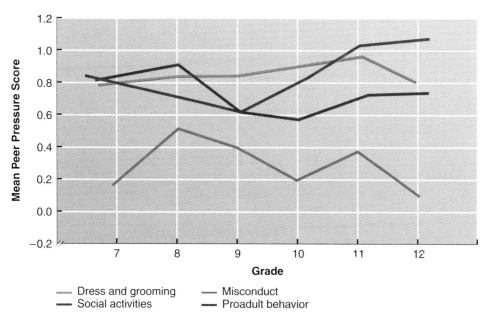

FIGURE 15.1 Grade changes in perceived peer pressure in four areas of behavior in a cross-sectional study of junior and senior high school students. Overall, teenagers felt greatest pressure to conform to dress and grooming styles and social activities. Pressure to engage in proadult behavior was also high. Although peer pressure toward misconduct peaked in early adolescence, it was relatively low. (From "Early Adolescents' Perceptions of Peer Pressure" by B. B. Brown, M. J. Lohr, & E. L. McClenahan, 1986, *Journal of Early Adolescence, 6*, p. 147. Reprinted by permission.)

In the United States, teenage alcohol and drug use is pervasive—higher than in any other industrialized nation (Newcomb & Bentler, 1989). By age 14, 42 percent of young people have already tried cigarette smoking, 50 percent have tried drinking, and 23 percent have tried at least one illegal drug (usually marijuana). By the end of high school, 15 percent are regular cigarette users, 32 percent have engaged in heavy drinking at least once, and over 57 percent have experimented with illegal drugs. Of these, about a third have tried at least one highly addictive and toxic substance, such as amphetamines, cocaine, phencyclidine (PCP), or heroin (U.S. Department of Health and Human Services, 1990, 1991).

Surprisingly, these high figures represent a decline in adolescent alcohol and drug use since 1985 (see Figure 15.2). Why do so many young people subject themselves to the health risks associated with these substances? Part of the reason is cultural. Modern adolescents live in a drug-

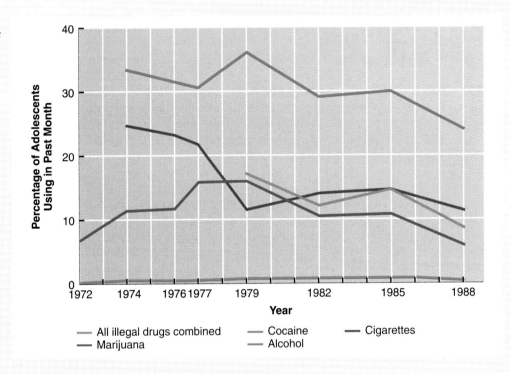

FIGURE 15.2 Percentage of 12- to 17-year-olds reporting use of alcohol, cigarettes, and illegal drugs in the past month, 1972–1988. (From U.S. Department of Heath and Human Services, 1990.)

values and educational plans (Kandel & Lesser, 1972; Sebald, 1986). Peers are more influential in short-term, day-to-day matters, such as type of dress, taste in music, and choice of friends. Adolescents' personal characteristics also made a difference. Young people who feel competent and worthwhile are less likely to fall in line behind peers who engage in undesirable behavior, such as early sexual activity, delinquency, and frequent drug use (see the Social Issues box above). Finally, authoritative parenting, which encourages high self-esteem, social and moral maturity, and a positive view of parents, is related to greater resistance to unfavorable peer pressure (Baumrind, 1991).

Before we turn to the impact of media on children, you may find it helpful to examine the Milestones table on page 620, which summarizes the development of peer relations.

Brief Review

By the end of middle childhood, peer groups form, through which children and adolescents learn much about the functioning of social organizations. Group norms foster a sense of belongingness. Group social structures lead to a dependent society. For example, they see adults using caffeine to wake up in the morning, cigarettes to cope with daily hassles, a drink to calm down in the evening, and additional remedies to relieve stress and other symptoms (Horan & Straus, 1987).

For most adolescents, drug use simply reflects their intense curiosity about "adultlike" behaviors. A recent longitudinal study revealed that the majority of subjects dabbled in alcohol as well as tobacco and marijuana when they became teenagers. These experimenters were not headed for a life of decadence and addiction, as many adults believe. Instead, they were psychologically healthy, sociable, inquisitive young people who were actually better adjusted throughout their childhoods than abstainers—teenagers who never used drugs at all. In a society in which substance use is commonplace, it appears that some involvement with drugs is normal and to be expected (Shedler & Block, 1990).

Yet adolescent drug experimentation should not be taken lightly. Because most drugs impair perception and thought processes, a single heavy dose can lead to permanent injury or death. And a worrisome minority of teenagers move from substance use to abuse—taking drugs regularly, requiring increasing amounts to achieve the same effect, and finding themselves unable to stop (Newcomb & Bentler, 1989). Four percent of high school seniors are daily drinkers, and almost as many indicate that they took an illegal drug on a daily basis over the past month (U.S. Department of Health and Human Services, 1991).

In contrast to experimenters, drug abusers are seriously troubled adolescents who are inclined to express their unhappiness through impulsive, antisocial behavior (Shedler & Block, 1990). Peer encouragement—friends who use drugs, urge the adolescent to do so, and provide access

to illegal substances—is the most consistent predictor of early abuse, but it does not occur in isolation. Other predisposing factors include a low-income background, family mental health problems, parental drug use, poor school performance, and such psychological traits as low self-esteem, anxiety, depression, lack of close relationships, and attraction to deviant behaviors. The more of these risk factors that combine, the more likely an adolescent is to become a heavy user of alcohol, cigarettes, and marijuana and to move in the direction of addiction to hard drugs (Bentler, 1992; Newcomb, Maddahian, & Bentler, 1986).

School-based programs that go beyond conveying information to teach skills for resisting peer pressure and communities that offer substitute activities, such as drug-free video arcades, dances, and sports events, are helpful in reducing drug experimentation. Efforts like these may be partly responsible for the recent decrease in adolescent substance use. But some drug taking seems to be inevitable. Weekend on-call transportation services that any young person can contact for a safe ride home, with no questions asked, help prevent teenagers from endangering themselves and others when they do experiment.

Drug abuse, as we have seen, occurs for quite different reasons than does occasional use. Therefore, different strategies are needed to deal with it. Hospitalization is often a necessary and even lifesaving first step. Once the young person is weaned from the drug, long-term therapy to treat low self-esteem, anxiety, and impulsiveness, and academic and vocational training to improve life success and satisfaction are generally needed. Not much is known about the best way to treat adolescent drug abuse. Even the most comprehensive programs have relapse rates that are alarmingly high—from 35 to 70 percent (Newcomb & Bentler, 1989).

division of responsibility and offer practice in leader and follower roles. Adolescent peer groups are organized around cliques, small groups of good friends, and crowds, large, loosely organized groups based on reputation and stereotype. The clique provides a setting in which adolescents learn social skills and try out new values and roles. The crowd offers a temporary identity as teenagers work on constructing their own. During adolescence, group structures depend less on dominance and more on characteristics that support a group's normative activities.

Children socialize one another through reinforcement, modeling, and direct pressures to conform to peer expectations. The powerful effects of peer reinforcement and modeling have inspired social skills and tutoring programs in which peers serve as agents of behavior change. Conformity to peer pressure rises in adolescence, but teenagers do not mindlessly "follow the crowd." Peers have a more powerful impact on everyday matters of dress and social behavior, parents on basic life values and educational plans.

Age	Peer Sociability	Peer Groups	Peer Socialization
Birth–2 years	• Isolated social acts increase over the first year and are gradually replaced by coordinated interaction.		• At the end of this period, peer modeling and reinforcement are evident.
2½–6 years	• At the beginning of this period, children first use words to affect a peer's behavior. • Parallel play appears, remains stable from 3 to 6 years, and becomes more cognitively mature. • Cooperative play increases—especially sociodramatic play, the most mature form. • Rough-and-tumble play emerges.	• Collectives of children gather in the neighborhood, but they show little desire for group belonging. • Dominance hierarchies emerge.	• Peer modeling and reinforcement increase.
7–11 years	• Gains in peer communication skills take place, including improvements in interpreting and responding to the emotions and intentions of others. • Peer interaction becomes more prosocial, and aggression (in the form of physical attacks) declines. • Rough-and-tumble play becomes increasingly common.	• At the end of this period, peer groups with distinct norms and social structures emerge. • Dominance hierarchies become increasingly stable.	• As children internalize social rules, peer modeling declines.
12–20 years	• Peer interaction becomes more cooperative. • More time is spent with peers than any other social partners.	• Peer groups become more tightly knit and exclusive, organized around cliques. • Sometimes several cliques with similar normative characteristics combine, forming a crowd.	• Conformity to peer pressure increases and gradually declines.

Note: These milestones represent overall age trends. Individual differences exist in the precise age at which each milestone is attained.

TELEVISION

Exposure to television is almost universal in the United States and other Western industrialized nations. Ninety-eight percent of American homes have at least one television set, over 50 percent have two or more, and a TV set is switched on in a typical household for an average of 7.1 hours per day. Although the popularity of television is widespread, there is good reason to be concerned about its effects on children and youths. In an unusual investigation, residents of a small Canadian town were studied just before TV reception became available in their community and then 2 years later. School-age children showed a drop in reading ability and creative thinking, a rise in gender-stereotyped beliefs, and an increase in verbal and physical aggression during play. In addition, the arrival of television was related to a sharp drop in community participation by adolescents and adults (Williams, 1986).

Worrisome findings like these have been reported in hundreds of studies over the past four decades. But they are not an inherent part of the medium itself. Instead, they result from the way it is used in our society. As our discussion proceeds, we will see that television has as much potential for good as for ill. If the content of TV programming were improved and adults capitalized on it to enhance children's interest in their everyday worlds, television could be a powerful, cost-effective means of strengthening cognitive, emotional, and social development.

How Much Television Do Children View?

The amount of time children spend in front of television sets is extraordinary. The average American child watches over 3 hours per day, clocking in a total of 25 hours in a single week (Nielsen, 1990). When we consider how much time the set is on during weekends, school holidays, and summer vacations, children spend more time watching television than they do in any other waking activity, including going to school and interacting with family members or peers. Even toddlers are surprisingly committed viewers. One study found that children under age 2 were exposed to an average of 2 hours of TV per day (Hollenbeck, 1978).

Children differ in their attraction to television. As Figure 15.3 indicates, age makes a difference. Viewing time rises over the preschool years, shows a slight dip around school entry, and then increases in early adolescence, after which it declines. Boys watch slightly more TV than do girls from the preschool years on (Huston et al., 1990). And at all ages, children with lower IQs, who come from low-income families, and who are members of poverty-stricken ethnic minorities tend to watch the most (Huston, Watkins, & Kunkel, 1989). Excessive TV viewing

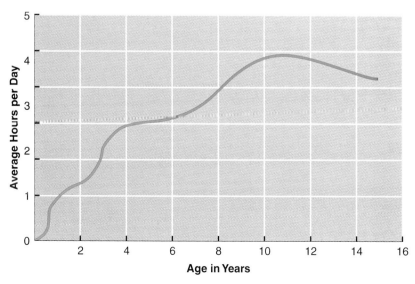

FIGURE 15.3 Estimated average hours of television viewing by age, based on research conducted over the past 20 years. (Reprinted with permission from *The Early Window: Effects of Television on Children and Youth* (3rd ed.) by R. M. Liebert & J. Sprafkin, 1988, p. 5. New York: Pergamon Books Ltd.)

is also associated with adjustment problems, such as family and peer difficulties and less trusting perceptions of other people (Liebert, 1986; Singer, Singer, & Rapaczynski, 1984).

Development of Television Literacy

As early as the second year, children start to learn from TV. In a laboratory study in which a videotaped adult produced a simple action on a novel toy, 14-month-olds who saw the action engaged in it more often than did controls exposed to an adult who did not display it (see Figure 15.4). And when presented with the toy after a 24-hour delay, these young subjects showed deferred imitation, indicating that they remembered the action. Even very young children can make sense of televised images, relating what they see to their own behavior (Meltzoff, 1988a).

When watching actual TV programs, children are confronted with a rapid stream of people, objects, places, words, and sounds. Television, or film, has its

FIGURE 15.4 A 14-month-old imitating a televised action. (a) The adult pulls apart the novel toy. Notice how the toddler leans forward and carefully studies the action. (b) The toddler is given the toy. (c) The toddler pulls apart the toy, imitating the behavior of the adult. These findings indicate that infants can imitate and learn from what they see on TV at a far earlier age than was previously thought possible. (Courtesy of A. N. Meltzoff. Reprinted by permission.)

(a)

(b)

(c)

own specialized code of conveying information. Researchers liken the task of cracking this code to that of learning to read, calling it **television literacy** (Anderson & Smith, 1984). Although the symbolic learning required to understand television is not as great as that demanded by reading, it is still considerable. Television literacy has two parts. The first involves understanding the *form* of the message. Children must master the meaning of a variety of visual and auditory effects, such as camera zooms, panoramic views, fadeouts, split screens, instant replays, and sound effects. Second, they must process the *content* of the message, constructing an accurate story line by integrating scenes, character behavior, and dialogue into a meaningful whole. These two parts are really interdependent, since television form provides essential cues to a program's content.

During early and middle childhood, children are captivated by TV's salient perceptual features. When a program contains quickly paced character movement, special effects, loud music, nonhuman speech, or children's voices, they become highly attentive. At other times, they look away, play with toys, or talk to others in the same room (Rice, Huston, & Wright, 1982; Wright et al., 1984). While involved in other activities, preschoolers follow the TV sound track. They turn back to the set when they hear cartoon characters and puppets speaking and certain words, such as "Big Bird" and "cookie," that signal the content is likely to be interesting and meaningful to them (Alwitt et al., 1980).

Clearly, young children are selective and strategic processors of televised information, but how much do they really understand? According to research, not a great deal. Before age 8, children have difficulty integrating separate scenes into a continuous story line. As a result, they often do not relate a TV character's behavior to prior intentions and later consequences (Collins, Berndt, & Hess, 1974; Collins et al., 1978). Other TV forms are confusing as well, such as fades, which signal the passage of time, and instant replays, which preschoolers take as repeated events (Anderson & Smith, 1984; Rice, Huston, & Wright, 1986). Furthermore, young children find it hard to distinguish real-life from fantasized televised material. Because they have little knowledge of how a TV works, they generally believe that puppets and cartoon characters are alive and real (Quarfoth, 1979).

Cognitive development and experience in watching TV lead to gains in television literacy (Greenfield, 1984; Salomon, 1979). Understanding of cinematic forms and memory for information important to plot comprehension increase sharply from middle childhood to adolescence. In addition, older children can draw inferences about televised material. For example, fifth- to eighth-graders recognize that a character who at first seems like a "good guy" but who unexpectedly behaves callously and aggressively is really a double-dealing "bad guy" in the end. In contrast, younger children find it difficult to reconcile their initially positive expectations with the character's eventual bad behavior. Consequently, they evaluate the character and his actions much more favorably (Collins, 1983).

In sum, preschool and early school-age children assimilate televised information piecemeal, assume that much of it is realistic, and are unable to critically evaluate it. These factors increase the chances that they will imitate and believe what they see on the screen. Let's take a close look at the impact of TV on children's social learning.

Television and Social Learning

Since the 1950s, researchers and public citizens have been concerned about the attitudes and behaviors that television cultivates in child and adolescent viewers. Most studies have focused on the implications of TV violence for the development of antisocial conduct. Still others have addressed the power of TV to teach undesirable gender, racial, and ethnic stereotypes. In addition, a growing body of evidence illustrates TV's as yet untapped potential to contribute to children's cognitive and social competence.

Television literacy
The task of learning television's specialized symbolic code of conveying information.

*A*lthough television has the potential to support development, too often it teaches that aggression is an acceptable way to solve problems. Viewing violent TV is consistently linked to antisocial behavior in children and adolescents. (MARY KATE DENNY/PHOTOEDIT)

AGGRESSION. Most American television—82 percent of all programs broadcast—contains at least some violence. In children's programming, the incidence is especially high: 32 violent acts per hour, a rate that is greater than that of adult prime-time shows. It is estimated that the average child will witness 8,000 made-for-TV murders before finishing elementary school. Of all TV fare, children's cartoons are the most violent (Waters, 1993).

Reviewers of thousands of studies have concluded that television violence increases aggressive acts in children and adolescents (Dorr & Kovaric, 1980; Friedrich-Cofer & Huston, 1986; Hearold, 1986; Liebert & Sprafkin, 1988). Their case is strengthened by the fact that research using a wide variety of research designs, methods, and subjects has yielded similar findings. In addition, the relationship between TV violence and aggression remains the same after many factors that might otherwise account for it are controlled, such as IQ, social class, school achievement, and child-rearing practices (Friedrich-Cofer & Huston, 1986; Parke & Slaby, 1983).

Violent programming not only creates short-term difficulties in family and peer relations, but has long-term effects as well. Longitudinal research reveals that highly aggressive children have a greater appetite for violent TV. As they watch more, they become increasingly likely to resort to hostile ways of solving problems, a spiraling pattern of learning that contributes to serious antisocial acts by adolescence and young adulthood (Friedrich-Cofer & Huston, 1986). In the most extensive longitudinal study conducted to date, boys who watched many violent programs at age 8 were more likely to be rated by peers as highly aggressive at age 19 and to have committed serious criminal acts by age 30 (see Figure 15.5) (Huesmann, 1986; Lefkowitz et al., 1972).

Television violence also "hardens" children to aggression, making them more willing to tolerate it in others. In one study, fifth-graders watched either an aggressive detective show or a nonaggressive baseball game. Then each subject was left "in charge" of two younger children (who were supposedly playing in a nearby room and could be watched on a video monitor) and told to notify the experimenter if anything went wrong. A prepared film showed the younger children becoming increasingly hostile toward each other and destructive of property. Subjects who had seen the aggressive film took much longer to seek help, and many tolerated all but the most violent acts among their charges (Drabman & Thomas, 1976).

Furthermore, compared to light viewers, heavy viewers of violent TV believe that there is much more violence and danger in society (Gerbner et al., 1979; Singer, Singer, & Rapaczynski, 1984). These findings suggest that violent television modifies children's attitudes toward social reality so they increasingly match what they see on TV. Children begin to think of the world as a mean and scary place where aggressive acts are a widespread and acceptable means for solving problems.

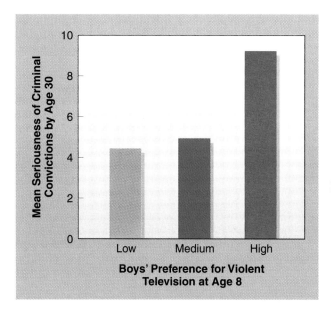

FIGURE 15.5 Relationship between boys' violent television viewing at age 8 and seriousness of criminal convictions at age 30. (From "Psychological Processes Promoting the Relation Between Exposure to Media Violence and Aggressive Behavior by the Viewer" by L. R. Huesmann, 1986, *Journal of Social Issues, 42*, p. 129. Reprinted by permission.)

GENDER, RACIAL, AND ETHNIC STEREOTYPES. Television conveys stereotypes that are common in American society. Although African-Americans are better represented on TV than they once were, too often they are segregated from whites in child- and adult-oriented programs. Other racial and ethnic minorities rarely appear, and when they do, they tend to be depicted negatively, as villains or victims of violence (Gerbner et al., 1986). Similarly, women appear less often than men as main characters, and they are usually cast in "feminine" roles, such as wife, mother, nurse, teacher, or secretary (Macklin & Kolbe, 1984). Even formal features of TV sometimes reflect gender stereotypes. For example, TV toy commercials aimed at boys have more scene shifts, rapid cuts, blaring music, and sound effects, conveying a masculine image of "fast, sharp, and loud." Those aimed at girls emphasize camera fades and background music, conveying a "feminine" image of "gradual, soft, and fuzzy." By first grade, children can tell from these features whether an ad is meant for boys or girls (Huston et al., 1984).

Are children's attitudes toward other people affected by TV's stereotyped portrayals? Much like the association between televised violence and aggressive behavior, a bidirectional relationship between TV viewing and gender stereotyping may exist. Research suggests that adolescents who hold strong gender-stereotyped beliefs are especially attracted to TV programs with stereotyped characters (Friedrich-Cofer et al., 1978). At the same time, television viewing is linked to gains in gender stereotyping over time (Kimball, 1986; Morgan, 1982). Little evidence exists on TV's impact on racial and ethnic stereotypes. In one study, children were shown cartoons that portrayed African-Americans either positively or negatively. Substantial changes in white children's beliefs that matched program content occurred after only a single viewing session. The beliefs of black children became more favorable regardless of which program they viewed. Apparently, the mere presence of African-American TV characters was enough to make their attitudes more positive (Graves, 1975).

CONSUMERISM. Television commercials directed at children "work" by increasing product sales. In the aisles of grocery and toy stores, young children can be seen asking their parents for advertised products. Adult refusals often result in arguments (Atkin, 1978). Although children can distinguish a TV program from a commercial as early as 3 years of age, below age 8 they seldom grasp the selling purpose of the ad. They think commercials are well-intentioned efforts by film makers to be helpful to viewers (Levin, Petros, & Petrella, 1982). Around age 8 or 9, most children understand that commercials are meant to persuade, and by age 11, they realize that advertisers will resort to clever techniques to sell their products. As a result, children become increasingly skeptical of the truthfulness of commercial messages (Ward, Wackman, & Wartella, 1977).

Nevertheless, even older children and adolescents find many commercials alluring. In a study of 8- to 14-year-old boys, celebrity endorsement of a racing toy made the product more attractive, and live racetrack images led to exaggerated estimates of the toy's positive features (Ross et al., 1984). Sugary foods make up about 80 percent of advertising aimed at children. When parents give in to children's demands, young TV viewers come to prefer these snacks and are convinced by TV messages that they are healthy (Atkin, Reeves, & Gibson, 1979; Gorn & Goldberg, 1982). The ease with which television advertising can manipulate children's beliefs and preferences has raised questions about whether child-directed commercials, especially those aimed at young children, constitute fair and ethical practice by the broadcasting industry (Huston, Watkins, & Kunkel, 1989).

PROSOCIAL BEHAVIOR. Many TV programs include acts of cooperating, helping, and comforting. A large-scale review of research on prosocial television leaves little doubt that it can increase children's prosocial behavior (Hearold, 1986). But the evidence also highlights some important qualifications to TV's prosocial impact. Almost all the findings are short term and limited to situations quite similar to those shown on TV (Liebert & Sprafkin, 1988). In addition, television programs often mix prosocial and antisocial intentions and behavior. Recall that young children have difficulty integrating these elements. As a result, they usually attend to the characters' aggressions and miss the prosocial message, and their antisocial behavior rises accordingly. These findings reveal that prosocial TV has positive effects only when it is free of violent content (Collins, Berndt, & Hess, 1974; Liss, Reinhardt, & Fredriksen, 1983).

Finally, parents who use authoritative child rearing rather than commands and physical force have children who watch more prosocial programs (Abelman, 1985). Consequently, children from families that already promote social and moral maturity probably benefit most from prosocial television.

Television, Academic Learning, and Imagination

Since the early days of television, educators have been interested in its potential for strengthening school performance, especially among low-income children who enter kindergarten behind their middle-class peers. "Sesame Street," the most popular educational program for young children, was created for public television with this goal in mind. Its founders believed that by using fast-paced action, lively sound effects, and humorous characters to stress letter and number recognition, counting, vocabulary, and basic concepts, they could enhance children's academic development. Today, half of 2- to 5-year-olds in the United States regularly watch "Sesame Street," and it is broadcast in more than 40 countries around the world (Liebert & Sprafkin, 1988).

Research shows that "Sesame Street" works well as an academic tutor. During the program's first year, researchers evaluated its effectiveness on a diverse sample of 950 preschoolers. As Figure 15.6 shows, the more children watched, the more they gained on tests designed to measure the program's learning goals (Ball & Bogatz, 1970). A second study revealed that when regular viewers from urban disadvantaged families entered first grade, teachers rated them as better prepared for school than their light-viewing counterparts (Bogatz & Ball, 1972). Recent findings are consistent with these early evaluations. For example, "Sesame Street" viewing is positively related to vocabulary development among preschoolers varying widely in social class (Rice et al., 1990).

In other respects, however, the rapid-paced format of "Sesame Street" and other children's programs has been criticized. It has not earned high marks in the area of imagination and creativity. Longitudinal research reveals that more TV viewing at ages 3 and 4 is associated with less elaborate make-believe play in

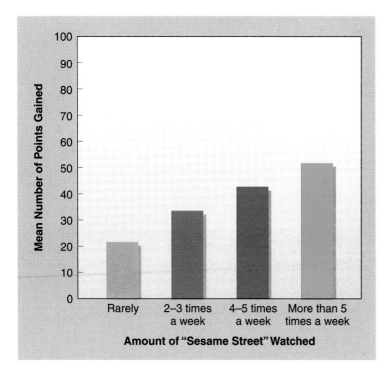

FIGURE 15.6 Relationship between amount of "Sesame Street" viewing and preschoolers' gains on tests of basic academic knowledge. (From Ball & Bogatz, 1970.)

older preschoolers and lower creativity scores in elementary school children (Singer & Singer, 1981, 1983). In experiments designed to see which kinds of TV programs promote imaginative play, gains occurred only for slow-paced, nonviolent material with a clear story line, not for rapid-paced, disconnected bits of information (Huston-Stein et al., 1981; Tower et al., 1979).

Some experts argue that because television presents such complete data to the senses, in heavy doses it encourages reduced mental effort and shallow information processing. Too much television also takes up time children would otherwise spend in activities that require sustained concentration and active thinking, such as reading, playing, and interacting with adults and peers (Singer & Singer, 1990). However, television can support cognitive development as long as children's viewing is not excessive and programs are specially designed to take into account their developmental needs.

Improving Children's Television

Improving children's television is an especially challenging task. Over time, high-quality programming has dropped off and advertising has risen as commercial broadcasting stations have tried to reach larger audiences and boost profits. Public broadcasting and cable TV offer some excellent programs for children. But government funding for public television has declined during the past two decades, and cable (which depends on user fees) is less available to low-income families. Furthermore, there are fewer restrictions today than there once were on program content and advertising for children. For example, in the past, characters in children's programs were not permitted to sell products. Today they often do— a strategy that greatly increases children's desire to buy. In addition, the amount of time that can be devoted to commercials during child-oriented TV is no longer limited (Huston, Watkins, & Kunkel, 1989).

Professional organizations and citizens groups, such as Action for Children's Television, a 20,000-member association, have pressed for government regulation of TV. Many would like to see networks required to provide a certain amount of educational programming for children. And some believe it would be best to ban child-directed advertising. But the First Amendment right to free speech has made

TABLE 15.3 Parental Strategies for Regulating Children's TV Viewing

STRATEGY	DESCRIPTION
Limit TV viewing	Avoid using TV as a baby-sitter. Provide clear rules that limit what children can watch—for example, an hour a day and only certain programs—and stick to the rules.
Refrain from using TV as a reinforcer	Do not use television to reward or punish children, a practice that increases its attractiveness.
Encourage child-appropriate viewing	Encourage children to watch programs that are child-appropriate and informative.
Explain televised information to children	As much as possible, watch with children, helping them understand what they see. When adults express disapproval of on-screen behavior, raise questions about the realism of televised information, and encourage children to discuss it, they teach children to evaluate TV content rather than accept it uncritically.
Link televised content to everyday learning experiences	Build on TV programs in constructive ways, encouraging children to move away from the set into active engagement with their surroundings. For example, a program on animals might spark a trip to the zoo, a visit to the library for books about animals, or new ways of observing and caring for the family pet.
Model good viewing practices	Avoid excess television viewing, especially violent programs, yourself. Parental viewing patterns influence children's viewing patterns.
Use authoritative child rearing	Respond to children with warmth and reasonable demands for mature behavior. Children who experience these practices prefer programs with prosocial content and are less attracted to violent TV.

SOURCES: Abelman, 1985; Dorr, Kovaric, & Doubleday, 1989; St. Peters et al., 1991.

the federal government reluctant to place limits on television content. And broadcasters, whose profits are at risk, are certainly against restriction (Liebert & Sprafkin, 1988).

Until children's television does improve, parents need to be educated about the dangers of excessive TV viewing, and children need to be taught critical viewing skills. Table 15.3 lists some strategies that parents can use to regulate their children's viewing and protect them from the impact of harmful TV.

COMPUTERS

Invention of the microcomputer chip in the 1970s made it possible for the general public to have ready access to computer technology. Today, microcomputers are a familiar fixture in the everyday lives of children and adolescents, offering a wide range of entertainment and learning tools. By 1990, over 97 percent of American public schools had integrated computers into their instructional programs. And as computer technology became increasingly affordable, the number of American homes with at least one computer increased from 750,000 in 1981 to 22 million in 1990 (U.S. Bureau of the Census, 1992).

Computers provide learning environments that are cognitively stimulating and socially interactive. Special steps are needed to ensure that girls and minority pupils have equal access to them. Without teacher intervention, boys can dominate computers in classrooms. (ARTHUR TILLEY/UNIPHOTO)

Children and adolescents are fascinated by computers. They generally prefer them to television, perhaps because computers combine the visual and auditory liveliness of TV with an active, participatory role for the user. As one child commented, "It's fun because you get to control it. TV controls itself" (Greenfield, 1984, p. 128). What is the impact of this interactive medium on the human mind and the world we live in? Many researchers believe that one way to answer this question is to study how computers affect children—their impact on cognitive development, academic achievement, everyday activities, and social behavior.

Advantages of Computers

Most research on computers and child development has been carried out in classrooms, where computer use can be easily observed. The findings reveal that computers can have rich educational and social benefits. Children as young as 3 years of age like computer activities and can type in simple commands on a standard keyboard. Yet they do not find the computer so captivating that it diverts them from other worthwhile play activities (Campbell & Schwartz, 1986). Furthermore, preschool and elementary school pupils prefer to use computers socially. Small groups often gather around the machine, and children take turns as well as help one another figure out next steps, as illustrated in the vignette at the beginning of this chapter. Children are far more likely to collaborate when working with the computer than with paper and pencil (Clements, Nastasi, & Swaminathan, 1993; Kull, 1986). The common belief that computers channel children into solitary pursuits is unfounded.

What do children learn from computers? This depends on what they do with them. Three major uses of computers in classrooms are computer-assisted instruction, word processing, and programming.

COMPUTER-ASSISTED INSTRUCTION. In **computer-assisted instruction (CAI)**, children acquire new knowledge and practice academic skills with the help of learning software. The unique features of many CAI programs make them effective and absorbing ways to learn. For example, pupils can begin at points that match their current level of mastery, and programs are often written to intervene when children's responses indicate that special help is needed. Also, multiple communication modes of text, graphics, animation, voice, and music enhance children's attention and interest. Most CAI programs provide drill and practice on basic academic skills. A few emphasize rote memorization less and discovery learning, reasoning, and problem solving more. For example, in one, children operate a lemonade stand and learn about economic principles of cost, profit, supply, and demand in a familiar context.

Computer-assisted instruction (CAI)
Use of computers to transmit new knowledge and practice academic skills.

Reviews of hundreds of studies reveal that as long as children use them regularly over a period of several months, drill-and-practice programs are highly successful in improving reading and mathematics skills during the early elementary school years (Clements & Nastasi, 1992; Hess & McGarvey, 1987; Lepper & Gurtner, 1989). The individualization and repetition offered by drill-and-practice software is especially beneficial for pupils with learning difficulties (Niemiec & Walberg, 1987). However, these applications tap only a small part of the computer's instructional potential and children's cognitive capacities. When drill-and-practice activities are overemphasized, they can subtract from children's opportunities to learn through active, meaningful experimentation (Clements, Nastasi, & Swaminathan, 1993).

WORD PROCESSING. In word processing, the computer does not instruct. Instead, it serves as a tool for writing and editing text material. Children can use word processing programs as soon as they begin to read and write. When the computer becomes part of the language arts curriculum, it permits children to write freely and try out letters and words without having to grapple with handwriting at the same time. In addition, children can plan and revise the text's meaning and style as well as check their spelling. As a result, they worry less about making mistakes, and the written products they produce tend to be longer and of higher quality (Clements & Nastasi, 1992; Levin, Boruta, & Vasconellos, 1983).

In the early stages of learning to write, word processing is especially effective in encouraging better written prose, but it is not as helpful with the mechanics of writing. For example, first-graders learn to spell more accurately when they write by hand than when they type (Cunningham & Stanovich, 1990). This suggests that word processing should not replace the traditional mode of writing instruction. Instead, it is best used to build on and enhance it.

PROGRAMMING. Programming offers children the highest degree of control over the computer, since they must tell it what to do. Specially designed computer languages, such as Logo, are available to introduce children to programming skills. Research shows that computer programming leads to improvements in concept formation, problem solving, and creativity (Clements, 1991; Clements & Nastasi, 1992; Degelman et al., 1986). Also, since children must detect errors in their programs to get them to work, programming helps them reflect on their own thought processes. Several studies report gains in metacognition and self-regulation as a result of a programming experience (Clements, 1986, 1990; Miller & Emihovich, 1986). Finally, children who know how to program are more aware of the uses of computers and how they function (Pea & Kurland, 1984). As a result, they are better prepared to participate in a society in which computers are becoming increasingly important in everyday life.

In the studies just mentioned, teachers were always available to encourage and support children's efforts. They questioned, prompted, and modeled, providing a vital scaffold for mastery of programming skills. Furthermore, in open-ended programming contexts like Logo, children are especially likely to formulate and solve problems collaboratively, to appear highly motivated, and to display positive attitudes toward learning (Clements & Nastasi, 1992). Consistent with Vygotsky's theory, social interaction surrounding challenging tasks in the computer environment appears especially well suited for fostering a wide variety of higher cognitive processes.

As Figure 15.7 indicates, drill-and-practice software accounts for the majority of elementary school pupils' classroom computer use, whereas word processing and programming activities become increasingly common in junior high and high school. Yet the research we have reviewed indicates that with the right kind of software and adult assistance, elementary school pupils can use the computer in remarkably sophisticated ways. In the process, they reap intellectual as well as social benefits.

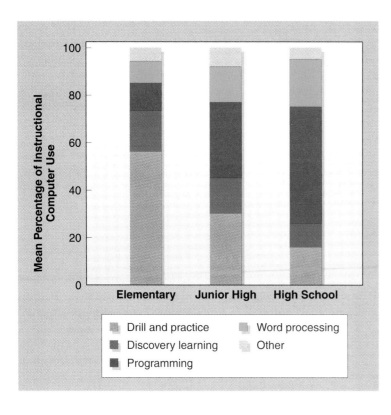

FIGURE 15.7 Classroom instructional use of computers by level of schooling, based on a survey of teachers in 2,331 American schools. Drill-and-practice software is emphasized at the elementary school level. It declines in favor of word processing and programming in junior high and high school. (Adapted from Becker & Sterling, 1987.)

Concerns About Computers

Although computers provide children with many learning advantages, they raise serious concerns as well. Computers appear most often in the homes and schools of economically well-off pupils. Furthermore, high-IQ pupils are attracted to problem-solving software and dislike the frequent feedback of drill-and-practice programs. In contrast, lower-IQ pupils like computer activities with lively animation and graphics and are uncomfortable with the lack of structure in problem-solving software (although with adult and peer support, they benefit from it) (Clements, Nastasi, & Swaminathan, 1993). As a result, some experts believe that computers are widening the gap in intellectual skills that already exists between lower- and middle-income children (Laboratory of Comparative Human Cognition, 1989).

Furthermore, by the end of middle childhood, boys spend much more time with computers than do girls, both in and out of school. Traditional gender-role expectations have led adults to encourage this difference. Parents of sons are twice as likely as parents of daughters to install a computer in the home. Even when girls have ready access to computers, much of the software available is unappealing to them because it emphasizes themes of war, violence, and male-dominated sports (Lepper, 1985). Girls' reduced involvement with computers may contribute to sex-related differences in math achievement and interest in scientific careers that emerge by adolescence (see Chapter 13). Yet girls' tendency to retreat from computers can be overcome. When teachers present computers in the context of cooperative rather than competitive learning and software is designed with the interests of girls in mind, they become enthusiastic users (Hawkins & Sheingold, 1986; Linn, 1985).

Finally, video games account for most out-of-school, recreational use of computers by children and adolescents, especially boys. Many parents are seriously concerned about the allure of these fast-paced electronic amusements, fearing that their youngsters will become overly involved as well as more aggressive because of the games' highly violent content. At present, however, we do not know if video games are as detrimental to children's well-being as televised violence (Delphi Communication Sciences, 1990).

Amer: A merican children spend more time watching TV than they do in any other waking activity. Before age 8, children have difficulty processing televised information accurately. Heavy TV viewing promotes aggressive behavior; gender, racial, and ethnic stereotypes; and a naive belief in the truthfulness of advertising. Although the right kind of televised content can encourage prosocial behavior, academic skills, and imaginative thinking, the positive potential of the TV medium remains largely untapped.

Computers have become increasingly common in the lives of children. At school, children often collaborate on computer activities. Computer-assisted instruction, word processing, and programming each offer unique educational benefits. Nevertheless, the advantages of computers are more accessible to children who are economically well off, high in IQ, and male.

SCHOOLING

Unlike the informal world of peer relations, the school is a formal institution designed to transmit knowledge and skills children need to become productive members of society. Children spend many hours in school—6 hours a day, 5 days a week, 36 weeks of the year—totaling, altogether, about 15,000 hours by high school graduation. In earlier chapters, we noted that schools are vital forces in children's development, affecting their modes of remembering, reasoning, problem solving, and social and moral understanding. How do schools exert such a powerful impact? Research looking at schools as complex social systems—their physical environments, educational philosophies, teacher–pupil interaction patterns, and the larger cultural context in which they are embedded—provides important insights into this question.

Physical Environments

The physical plants of all schools are similar: Each has classrooms, hallways, a playground, and a lunchroom. But they are also different. Schools vary in how classrooms are furnished and arranged and in how many pupils are enrolled—factors that make an important difference in children's life at school.

CLASSROOM SEATING ARRANGEMENTS. Teachers' room arrangements often reflect their educational philosophies. The familiar row-and-column seating plan usually indicates a traditional approach to classroom learning, circles and clusters of desks a more open orientation—two philosophies we will take up shortly. Therefore, it is difficult to study room arrangements apart from the teacher's instructional program, but a few researchers have isolated the impact of physical setting. As Figure 15.8 shows, when children are seated in rows and columns, pupil location affects participation: Teachers interact the most with children seated "front and center" (Adams, 1969). Although sociable children tend to choose central desks and shy children desks on the outskirts of the classroom, the seating effect is not simply the result of pupil personality. When sociable pupils sit away from the center, their participation declines (Koneya, 1976).

Do these findings mean that teachers should locate quiet pupils in central desks, where they will be more likely to be noticed and to participate in class discussions? Doing so could lead to considerable anxiety for shy children. A better approach might be to rearrange the entire seating plan so that participation of all pupils is enhanced. In an experiment in which three seating arrangements—row-and-column, large circle, and small clusters of desks—were compared, the circular configuration worked best in promoting participation and attention during class discussion. The cluster arrangement ranked second, and the row-and-column seating plan produced more pupil withdrawal and off-task behavior than either of the other conditions (Rosenfield, Lambert, & Black, 1985).

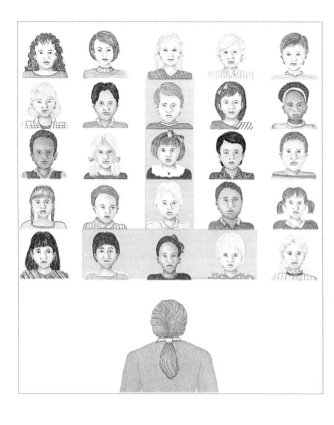

FIGURE 15.8 Area associated with highest pupil participation rates in the row-and-column classroom seating arrangement. (Adapted from Adams, 1969.)

CLASS AND STUDENT BODY SIZE. Is there an optimal class size that fosters effective pupil learning? Reviews of research indicate that as classes drop below 15 or 20 pupils, academic achievement improves. Above this threshold, however, class size has little impact on children's performance (Cooper, 1989; Glass et al., 1982). A recent experiment confirmed this conclusion. Kindergartners in 76 elementary schools were randomly assigned to three class types: small (15 to 20 pupils), regular (22 to 25 pupils), and regular plus aide (22 to 25 pupils with the assistance of a full-time teacher's aide), arrangements that continued into first grade. Small-class pupils scored higher in reading and math achievement during both years of the study, an effect that was particularly strong for minority pupils. The presence of a teacher's aide in regular-size classes also enhanced achievement, but not as much as assignment to a small class (Finn & Achilles, 1990).

Why is small class size beneficial? Teachers of fewer children spend less time disciplining and more time granting pupils individual attention—factors that may be responsible for the achievement gains just mentioned (Cahan et al., 1983). In addition, when class size is small, both teachers and pupils are more satisfied with their life at school (Smith & Glass, 1980).

By the time students reach junior high and high school, they no longer spend most of their time in a single, self-contained classroom. Instead, they move from one class to the next and have access to many activities outside regular academic instruction. As a result, the relevant physical context becomes the school as a whole. One feature of the general school environment that is consistently related to adolescents' behavior is student body size. A greater percentage of students in small high schools than in large ones are actively involved in the extracurricular life of their schools. Schools of 500 to 700 students or less promote personalized conditions because there are fewer people to ensure that clubs, sports events, and social activities will function. As a result, young people enter a greater number and variety of activities and hold more positions of responsibility and leadership. In contrast, plenty of people are available to fill activity slots in large schools, so only a small elite can be genuinely active (Barker & Gump, 1964; Lindsay, 1984).

In view of these findings, it is not surprising that adolescents in small schools report a greater sense of personal responsibility, competence, and challenge from their extracurricular experiences. This is true even for "marginal" students—those with low IQs, academic difficulties, and poverty-stricken backgrounds—who otherwise display little commitment to school life (Willems, 1967). A special advantage of small schools is that potential dropouts are far more likely to join in activities, gain recognition for their abilities, and remain until graduation. Small schools are not associated with gains in achievement, but the experiences they offer are equally important. Longitudinal research reveals that the sense of social obligation engendered in small high schools carries over to community participation in adult life (Berk, 1992b).

Educational Philosophies

Each teacher brings to the classroom an educational philosophy that plays a major role in children's learning experiences. Two philosophical approaches have been studied extensively. They differ in what children are taught, the way they are believed to learn, the extent to which decision making rests with teacher or child, and how pupil progress is evaluated.

In a **traditional classroom**, the goal of instruction is to transmit culturally valued knowledge and standards of conduct. The teacher is the sole authority for information, rules, and decision making and does most of the talking. Pupils are relatively passive in the learning process and spend most of their time at their desks—listening, responding when called on, and completing teacher-assigned tasks. Their progress is evaluated by how well they keep pace with a common set of expectations for everyone in their grade. As a result, children are compared to one another and to normative standards for academic achievement.

In an **open classroom**, acquiring culturally valued knowledge is important, but not to the exclusion of other goals. Emotional and social development as well as academic progress is emphasized. In addition, children are viewed as active agents in their own development. The teacher assumes a flexible authority role, sharing decision making with pupils, who learn at their own pace. Children are evaluated by considering their progress in relation to their own prior development. How well they compare to same-age pupils is less important. A glance inside the door of an open classroom reveals richly equipped learning centers, small groups of pupils working on tasks they choose themselves, and a teacher who moves from one area to another, guiding and supporting in response to children's individual needs (Minuchin & Shapiro, 1983).

Over the past 30 years, the pendulum in American education has swung back and forth between these two approaches. In the 1960s and early 1970s, open education gained in popularity, inspired by Piaget's view of children as active, motivated learners. Then, as high school students' scores on the Scholastic Aptitude Test (SAT) declined over the 1970s, a "back to basics" movement arose. As a result, classrooms returned to traditional, teacher-directed instruction, a style still prevalent today.

The combined results of many studies reveal that open classrooms are highly successful in promoting autonomous learning, respect for individual differences, and pupil interest and involvement. Children in open classrooms are more independent; they express less need for approval than their traditionally instructed counterparts. In addition, pupils exposed to open education cooperate more effectively when working on common tasks, and sociometric techniques reveal fewer extremes of popularity and rejection. In these environments, children with a wide range of characteristics are accepted, and pupils interact more often with peers who differ from themselves in sex and race. Finally, children in open classrooms like school better than those in traditional classrooms, and their attitudes toward school become increasingly positive as they spend more time in the setting (Hedges, Giaconia, & Gage, 1981; Horwitz, 1979; Walberg, 1986).

Open classrooms are clearly associated with a variety of emotional and social advantages, but they do not lead to better academic achievement. When differ-

Traditional classroom

Classroom based on an educational philosophy that emphasizes transmission of culturally valued knowledge and standards of conduct. The teacher is the sole authority, pupils are relatively passive in the learning process, and progress is evaluated by how well pupils keep pace with a common set of expectations for everyone in their grade.

Open classroom

Classroom based on an educational philosophy that values emotional and social development in addition to academic progress. The teacher assumes a flexible authority role, pupils are active in the learning process, and children are evaluated by considering their progress in relation to their own prior development.

ences do appear, open education pupils generally perform slightly below those in traditional classrooms. One careful review of research revealed that open programs placing greatest emphasis on child-directed learning and individualized evaluation of pupil progress were especially effective in fostering high self-esteem and positive attitudes toward school, but they sacrificed achievement to some degree (Giaconia & Hedges, 1982). Studies of nongraded classrooms—mixed-age settings that vary in whether they adopt traditional or open educational goals— yield similar findings. When nongraded programs combine pupils who are at the same level of academic progress for teacher-directed learning, achievement scores tend to be higher than in regular, graded classrooms. When nongraded settings emphasize self-paced pupil learning, their impact on achievement is much less consistent (Gutiérrez & Slavin, 1992). Apparently, direct teaching, especially when it matches pupils' current instructional level, is best suited for spurring academic achievement forward.

Although much research has focused on the traditional–open dichotomy, it actually oversimplifies the real world of classroom philosophical differences. In several studies, some classrooms could not be identified as either traditional or open, but instead fell somewhere in between (Aitken, Bennett, & Hesketh, 1981; Minuchin et al., 1969). This suggests that more precise distinctions among educational philosophies are needed to enhance our understanding of how classroom environments affect development. Perhaps a balanced mixture of traditional and open education will turn out to promote high achievement as well as emotional and social well-being. Turn back to Chapter 6, page 259, to reread the description of the Kamehameha Elementary Education Project (KEEP), a philosophical approach based on Vygotsky's sociocultural theory that represents this intermediate point of view. KEEP has been remarkably successful in fostering both achievement and enthusiasm for learning among ethnic minority pupils.

School Transitions

Besides the physical environment and educational philosophy, an additional structural feature of schooling has important implications for pupils' academic performance and adjustment: the timing of transitions from one school level to the next. Many American 5- and 6-year-olds are already accustomed to school-like settings, since they have attended preschool and day-care centers. Still, entering kindergarten is a major milestone. Parents take pride in their children's readiness for greater independence and responsibility. At the same time, they worry about how well prepared their youngsters are for a more earnest approach to learning. Children, in turn, must accommodate to new physical settings, adult authorities, daily schedules, peer companions, and academic challenges.

EARLY ADJUSTMENT TO SCHOOL. In a study of factors that predict effective transition to kindergarten, Gary Ladd and Joseph Price (1987) gathered observational and interview data on children at the end of preschool and during their kindergarten year. Both child and setting characteristics ensuring supportive ties to peers were major contributors to favorable school adjustment. Children who displayed positive social behaviors in preschool, such as cooperative play and friendly interaction with a wide range of agemates, seemed to transfer these skills to the kindergarten setting. They were better liked by peers and rated by teachers as more involved in classroom life. The presence of preschool friends in kindergarten also enhanced adaptation. Perhaps familiar agemates served as a secure base from which to develop new ties, thereby enhancing children's peer acceptance and feelings of comfort in the classroom. Finally, children who retained more out-of-school peer relationships viewed school more favorably after kindergarten entry. The continuity of these nonschool ties may have provided children with a greater sense of stability in their otherwise changing social environments.

special concern is that an **educational self-fulfilling prophecy*** can be set in motion. In other words, pupils may adopt teachers' positive or negative views and start to live up to them.

In the 1960s, Robert Rosenthal and Lenore Jacobson (1968) conducted a famous experiment in which they tested this hypothesis. First, pupils in an elementary school took an IQ test, and teachers were falsely informed that test results could identify children expected to "bloom," or show an intellectual growth spurt, during the following months. Each teacher was provided with a list of "bloomers" in her class (children randomly chosen by the researchers). Then the IQ test was given again at the end of the school year. Results indicated that first- and second-graders for whom teachers expected gains actually showed them. But no self-fulfilling prophecy effects appeared among third- through sixth-graders.

Rosenthal and Jacobson's study was soon criticized on methodological grounds, and many other investigations failed to confirm its findings. Later, it became clear that teachers, especially those who are self-confident and experienced, will reject experimenter-provided expectancies if they do not match their firsthand observations (Carter et al., 1987). Research that has done most to advance our understanding of self-fulfilling prophecies focuses on teachers' *naturally formed expectancies*, their impact on teacher–pupil interaction, and their consequences for children's learning. Findings reveal that although teachers interact differently with high and low achievers, in most cases their behavior is a reality-based response to pupils' learning needs and does not cause children to do better or worse in school. But sometimes teachers do harbor unfair judgments of children. Unfortunately, they are usually biased in a negative direction, resulting in more unfavorable classroom experiences and achievement than would otherwise occur (Brophy, 1983).

Self-fulfilling prophecies interact in complex ways with teacher and pupil characteristics. When teachers emphasize competition and frequently make public comparisons among pupils, children are especially aware of teacher opinion, increasing the likelihood that it can affect their performance (Weinstein et al., 1987). Furthermore, teachers who regard low-achieving pupils as limited by ability rather than effort or learning opportunities are likely to provide them with little encouragement for mastering challenging tasks. And when teachers have a strong fear of losing control of their class, they are especially likely to initiate negative self-fulfilling prophecies. They do so by avoiding public communication with disruptive, low-achieving pupils and giving them feedback that is abrupt, inconsistent, and not based on the quality of their work (Cooper, 1979). Withdrawn children may also be prime candidates for biased teacher expectancies. Since they rarely approach teachers, they provide little information about what they are like as learners. This makes it easier for teachers who hold inappropriate expectancies to sustain them (Brophy, 1983).

TEACHERS' REACTIONS TO CHILDREN'S ETHNIC AND SOCIAL-CLASS BACKGROUNDS. The American school has often been described as a white, middle-class institution in which the social attitudes of the larger society prevail. Indeed, teachers sometimes respond in stereotyped ways to low-income and ethnic minority pupils, making them especially susceptible to negative self-fulfilling prophecies. In Chapter 11, we noted that black children often receive less favorable feedback from teachers than do white children, a circumstance that undermines their achievement motivation. One study found that as early as the preschool years, teachers provided less verbal stimulation in classes of low-income than middle-income children (Quay & Jarrett, 1986).

Recall from Chapter 8 that ethnic minority children often have unique language customs, knowledge, and skills that differ sharply from those valued at school. Teachers who are unaware of this fact may interpret the minority pupil's

Educational self-fulfilling prophecy
The idea that pupils may adopt teachers' positive or negative attitudes toward them and start to live up to these views.

---

*Most research on self-fulfilling prophecies focuses on the teacher–pupil relationship, but the effect can occur in other social contexts, such as parent–child and peer interaction. Try to think of other findings we have discussed in this and earlier chapters that can be viewed as self-fulfilling prophecies.

behavior as uncooperative when it is not. For this reason, it is vital that teachers understand the values and practices that culturally different children bring to the classroom. Then they can adjust learning experiences to take account of the child's background, and negative self-fulfilling prophecies with serious consequences for the school performance of minority children can be avoided.

Ability Grouping

In many schools, pupils are *ability grouped* or *tracked* into classes in which children of similar achievement levels are taught together. The practice is designed to ease teachers' task of having to meet a wide range of academic needs in the same learning environment. Yet teachers' treatment of different ability groups may be an especially powerful source of self-fulfilling prophecies. In low-ability groups, pupils receive more drill on basic facts and skills, a slower learning pace, and less time on academic work. Gradually, children in low groups show a drop in self-esteem, are viewed by themselves and others as "not smart," and limit their friendship choices to children within their own group. Not surprisingly, ability grouping widens the gap between high and low achievers (Slavin, 1987). At least into the early years of secondary school, mixed-ability classes are desirable. Research suggests that they do not stifle the more able students, and they have intellectual and social benefits for poorly performing youngsters (Oakes, Gamoran, & Page, 1992).

By the time adolescents enter high school, some tracking is unavoidable because certain aspects of instruction must dovetail with the young person's future educational and career plans. In the United States, high school students are counseled into a college preparatory, vocational, or general education sequence. Unfortunately, educational inequalities of earlier years tend to be perpetuated. Low-income minority students are assigned in large numbers to noncollege tracks. One study found that a good student from a disadvantaged family had only half as much chance of ending up in an academically oriented program as a student of equal ability from a middle-class background (Vanfossen, Jones, & Spade, 1987).

High school students are separated into academic and vocational tracks in virtually all industrialized nations. But the American system differs from those of Western Europe, Japan, and China in important respects. In most of those countries, students take a national examination to determine their placement in high school. The outcome usually fixes future possibilities for the young person. In the United States, educational decisions are more fluid. Students who are not assigned to a college preparatory track or who do poorly in high school can still get a college education. But by the adolescent years, social-class differences in quality of education and academic achievement have already sorted American students more drastically than is the case in other countries. In the end, many young people do not benefit from this more open system. Compared to other developed nations, the United States has a higher percentage of high school dropouts and adolescents with very limited academic skills (Hamilton, 1990; Rohlen, 1983).

Teaching Pupils with Special Needs

So far, we have seen that effective teachers flexibly adjust their teaching strategies to accommodate pupils with a wide range of abilities and characteristics. These adjustments, however, are especially challenging when children have learning difficulties. Over the past two decades, extra steps have been taken to create appropriate learning environments for these pupils. The Individuals with Disabilities Education Act (Public Law 101-475), first passed in 1975 and revised in 1990, mandates that schools place children who require special supports for learning in the "least restrictive" environments that meet their educational needs. The goal of the law was to better prepare pupils for participation in society by providing educational experiences as similar as possible to those of the majority.

According to PL 101-475, school districts must offer an array of options for special-needs children. Among these are separate schools, self-contained classrooms in regular school buildings, and integration into classes serving pupils without disabilities. **Mainstreaming** is a term that refers to this last alternative. PL 101-475 recognizes that regular classroom placement is not appropriate for all children and does not require it. But since passage of the law, a rapid increase in mainstreaming has occurred. Some mainstreamed pupils are *mildly mentally retarded*—children whose IQs fall between 55 and 70 and who also show problems in adaptive behavior (Grossman, 1983). But most are pupils with **learning disabilities**—those with a specific learning disorder (for example, in reading, writing, or math computation) that results in poor school achievement. Learning disabled pupils are average or above-average in IQ, and their problems cannot be traced to any obvious physical handicap, emotional problem, or environmental disadvantage. Instead, faulty brain functioning is believed to underlie their difficulties (Hammill, 1990). Some of the disorders run in families, suggesting that they are at least partly genetic (Pennington & Smith, 1988). In most instances, the cause is unknown.

Does mainstreaming accomplish its dual goal of providing more appropriate academic experiences and integrated participation in classroom life? At present, research findings are not positive on either of these points. Achievement differences between mainstreamed pupils and those taught in self-contained classrooms are not great (MacMillan, Keogh, & Jones, 1986). Furthermore, mainstreamed children are often rejected by peers. Those who are mentally retarded are overwhelmed by the social skills of their classmates; they cannot interact quickly or adeptly in a conversation or game. And the processing deficits of some children with learning disabilities also lead to problems in social awareness and responsiveness (Hartup, 1983; Rourke, 1988). As a result, these children report considerable dissatisfaction with their peer experiences and intense feelings of loneliness (Taylor, Asher, & Williams, 1987).

Does this mean that mainstreaming is not a good way to serve children with special learning needs? This extreme conclusion is not warranted. Many regular classroom teachers do not have the training or the time to give these pupils all the help they need. Often these children do best when they receive instruction in a *resource room* for part of the day and in the regular classroom for the remainder. In the resource room, a special-education teacher works with pupils individually and in small groups. Then, depending on their abilities, children are mainstreamed for different subjects and amounts of time. This flexible approach makes it more likely that the unique academic needs of each child will be served (Keogh, 1988; Lerner, 1989).

Once children enter the regular classroom, teachers must make a special effort to promote peer acceptance. When instruction is carefully individualized and teachers minimize comparisons with higher-achieving classmates, mainstreamed pupils show gains in self-esteem and achievement (Madden & Slavin, 1983). Also, cooperative learning experiences in which a mainstreamed child and several classmates work together on the same task have been found to promote friendly interaction and improved social acceptance (Nastasi & Clements, 1991). Finally, teachers can prepare children for the arrival of a special-needs pupil. Under these conditions, mainstreaming may lead to gains in emotional sensitivity, perspective taking, and prosocial behavior among classmates that break down social barriers and promote early integration of individuals with disabilities into the mainstream of American life.

Mainstreaming
The integration of pupils with learning difficulties into regular classrooms for all or part of the school day.

Learning disabilities
Specific learning disorders (for example, in reading, writing, or math computation) that result in poor school achievement, despite an average or above-average IQ.

Brief Review

Schools are powerful forces in children's development. The physical environment—the way classrooms are arranged and how many pupils are enrolled—affects participation and academic achievement. Pupils who attend open classrooms are more independent, tolerant of individual differences, and positive about their school experience; those in traditional classrooms are slightly advantaged in achievement. School transitions create new adjustment problems. Supportive ties to peers ease entry into kindergarten. The earlier school transition takes place in adolescence, the more likely it is to depress psychological well-being, especially among girls. Teachers who are effective classroom managers and who provide cognitively stimulating activities enhance children's involvement and academic performance. Educational self-fulfilling prophecies are likely to occur when teachers emphasize competition and comparisons among pupils, have difficulty controlling the class, and engage in ability grouping. Disruptive, low-achieving pupils, withdrawn children, and low-income, ethnic minority pupils are especially susceptible. To be effective, mainstreaming must be carefully tailored to meet the academic and social needs of children with learning difficulties.

HOW WELL EDUCATED ARE AMERICAN YOUNG PEOPLE?

Our discussion of schooling has focused largely on what teachers can do in classrooms to support the education of children and adolescents. Yet many factors, both within and outside schools, affect children's learning. Societal values, school resources, quality of teaching, and parental encouragement all play important roles. Nowhere are these multiple influences more apparent than when schooling is examined in cross-cultural perspective.

Cross-National Research on Academic Achievement

American students consistently fare poorly when their achievement is compared to students in other industrialized nations. In international studies of mathematics and science achievement, young people from Asian nations have been among the top performers, whereas Americans have scored no better than at the mean and often at the bottom of the pack (Husén, 1967; International Education Association, 1988; McKnight et al., 1987). For example, in one survey of the math achievement of eighth- and twelfth-graders in 15 nations, American students fell at about the international average in computational skills but well below it in complex problem solving. Among college-bound students about to complete high school, the United States ranked among the poorest-scoring nations in overall performance (see Table 15.4).

These trends emerge early in development. In a series of large-scale studies, Harold Stevenson, Shin-Ying Lee, and James Stigler carefully examined the achievement of elementary school children in Japan, Taiwan, and the United States. In one investigation, nearly 1,500 first- and fifth-graders were selected to represent children in three metropolitan areas: Sendai (Japan), Taipei (Taiwan), and Minneapolis. Math and reading achievement were measured with tests based on content common to all three locations. In addition, the researchers observed in classrooms and interviewed the children as well as their parents and teachers. Findings revealed that Asian children were far ahead of their American counterparts in math achievement at the beginning of elementary school, a difference that became stronger with increasing grade level. Less extreme gaps occurred in reading, in which Taiwanese children scored highest, Japanese children lowest, and American children in between (Stevenson, 1992; Stevenson & Lee, 1990).

Pupils in the investigation just described were tested in 1980. Over the following decade, the researchers returned to the three sites to look for possible changes in students' performance. In 1984 and 1990, as many of the first-graders who could be located were restudied, when they reached fifth- and eleventh-grade, respectively. To supplement this longitudinal sample, in 1990, several thousand

TABLE 15.4 *Mathematics Achievement of College-Bound High School Seniors in 15 Nations*

NATION (ranked in order of performance)	MEAN PERCENTAGE CORRECT ON ACHIEVEMENT TESTS*
Hong Kong	74
Japan	70
Finland	61
England and Wales	60
Sweden	58
New Zealand	55
Belgium (Flemish)	52
Canada (Ontario)	51
Belgium (French)	48
Israel	46
Scotland	43
United States	40
Canada (British Columbia)	38
Thailand	35
Hungary	32

*The percentage is an average of each nation's performance on the following six achievement tests: sets and relations, number systems, algebra, geometry, elementary functions and calculus, and probability and statistics.

SOURCE: McKnight et al., 1987.

fifth- and eleventh-graders were given achievement tests in each city. As Figure 15.10(a) shows, from 1980 to 1990, Japanese and Taiwanese fifth-graders remained ahead of Americans in math achievement, and the gap between Taiwanese and American pupils widened. Furthermore, American pupils fell behind both groups of Asian pupils in reading achievement, while Japanese pupils took the lead (see Figure 15.10b). Finally, longitudinal trends in Figure 15.10(c) reveal that the math achievement status of American students did not improve as they moved from first to eleventh grade (Stevenson, Chen, & Lee, 1993; Stevenson & Stigler, 1992).

Why do American students fall so far behind their Asian counterparts in academic accomplishments? A common assumption is that Asian pupils are high achievers because they are "smarter," but this is not true. They do not do better on intelligence tests than their American agemates (Stevenson et al., 1985). Instead, as the Cultural Influences box on page 646 explains, a wide variety of social forces combine to foster a much stronger commitment to learning in Asian families and schools.

National Assessments of Educational Progress

Periodic assessments of the academic competence of American youths confirm the worrisome picture of cross-cultural research. The Nation's Report Card summarizes the reading, writing, math, and science achievement of nationally represen-

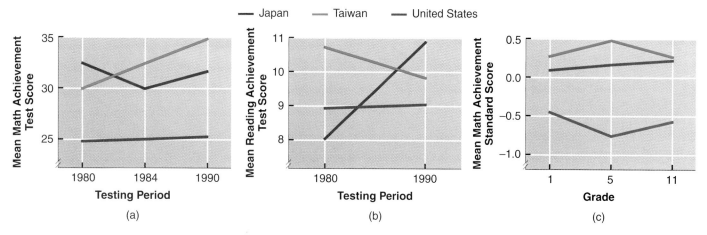

FIGURE 15.10 Math and reading achievement at three testing periods in Japan, Taiwan, and the United States. (a) From 1980 to 1990, Japanese fifth graders maintained their lead over American fifth graders in math achievement, and the gap between Taiwanese and American children steadily increased. (b) American fifth graders fell behind both Asian groups in reading achievement. Japanese fifth graders, who scored lowest in 1980, ranked first in 1990. (c) A longitudinal follow-up of first graders when they reached fifth and eleventh grades revealed that the math achievement status of American students did not improve. (From "Mathematics Achievement of Chinese, Japanese, and American Children: Ten Years Later" by H. W. Stevenson, C. Chen, & S-Y. Lee, 1993, *Science, 259*, p. 54. Copyright © 1993 by the AAAS.)

tative samples of 9-, 13-, and 17-year-olds every 4 years. Its findings reveal that although over 90 percent of American students master basic literacy and math skills by age 13, their accomplishments at the end of high school are disappointing. For example, in 1990 the average performance of 17-year-olds did not reach a level in reading that permitted them to understand and explain moderately complicated information. In math, it did not move beyond an intermediate level of skill required to read simple graphs and solve basic algebraic equations. Results on writing and scientific reasoning were least encouraging. Only 68 percent of 17-year-olds could prepare a clear paragraph for a job application. Only 43 percent showed some specialized knowledge of scientific principles and an understanding of experimental design (Mullis et al., 1991).

Additional information in the Nation's Report Card highlights several causes of these disappointing outcomes. Consistent with findings we have discussed in previous chapters, a stimulating home environment was related to better academic performance. But schooling also played a major role, since quality of classroom instruction was clearly associated with achievement. For example, amount of homework assigned was positively correlated with performance. By the 1980s, teachers were giving more homework than they did in previous years. Still, as many as 30 percent of high school students reported less than 1 hour per night, and 6 percent had none. In math, the cognitive level of most classroom teaching matched the low level of pupil performance. Math instruction rarely moved beyond memorizing basic facts and rules (Dossey et al., 1988).

By the turn of the twenty-first century, many more jobs in the United States will demand high levels of literacy and technical knowledge. School reforms are currently under way, aimed at helping young people master the language, math, and science skills necessary to meet these work-force needs. Effective educational change, however, must take into account the life background and future goals of students. Toughening academic standards will improve the competence of college-bound youths from advantaged homes. But it is likely to further discourage many low-income, poorly achieving young people, who can only fall farther behind under these conditions (Parrish, 1991). As we will see next, besides strengthening aca-

Why do American pupils achieve poorly in comparison to their counterparts in many other industrialized nations, whereas Asian pupils consistently perform well? Research examining societal, school, and family conditions in Japan, Taiwan, and the United States provides some answers.

1. *Cultural valuing of academic achievement.* In Japan and Taiwan, natural resources are limited. Progress in science and technology is essential for economic well-being. Since a well-educated work force is necessary to meet this goal, children's mastery of academic skills is vital. In the United States, attitudes toward academic achievement are far less unified. Many Americans believe it is more important to encourage children to feel good about themselves and to explore various areas of knowledge than to perform well in school.

2. *Emphasis on effort.* Japanese and Taiwanese parents and teachers believe that all children have the potential to master challenging academic tasks if they work hard enough. In contrast, many more of their American counterparts regard native ability as the key to academic success (Stevenson, 1992). These differences in attitude may contribute to the fact that American parents are less inclined to encourage activities at home that might enhance school performance. Japanese and Taiwanese children spend more free time reading and playing academic-related games than do children in the United States (Stevenson & Lee, 1990).

3. *Involvement of parents in education.* Asian parents devote many hours to helping their children with homework. American parents spend very little and, at least while their children are in elementary school, do not regard homework as especially important. Overall, American parents are far more satisfied with the quality of their children's education, hold lower standards for their children's academic performance, and are less concerned about how well their youngsters are doing in school, even after having been told about the weak performance of the United States on an international scale (Stevenson, Chen, & Lee, 1993; Stevenson & Lee, 1990).

4. *High-quality education for all.* Unlike American teachers, Japanese and Taiwanese teachers do not make early educational decisions on the basis of achievement. There are no separate ability groups or tracks in elementary school. Instead, all pupils receive the same nationally mandated high-quality curriculum. Academic lessons are particularly well organized and presented in ways that capture children's attention. Topics in mathematics are treated in greater depth, and there is less repetition of material taught the previous year (Stevenson & Lee, 1990). In the United States, wide variation in quality of schooling exists. Low-income, ethnic minority children have a much higher likelihood of attending underequipped schools offering poor-quality instruction than do their middle-income counterparts.

5. *More time devoted to instruction.* In Japan and Taiwan, the school year is over 50 days longer than in the United States, and much more time is devoted to academic pursuits, especially mathematics. However, Asian schools are

*J*apanese children achieve considerably better than their American counterparts for a variety of reasons. A longer school day permits frequent alternation of academic instruction with pleasurable activity. This approach probably makes learning easier and more enjoyable. (EIJI MIYAZAWA/BLACK STAR PUBLISHING COMPANY)

not regimented, austere places, as many Americans believe. Instead, an 8-hour school day means extra recesses and a longer lunch period, with plenty of time for play and social interaction (Stevenson, 1992).

6. *Communication between teachers and parents.* Japanese and Taiwanese teachers get to know their pupils especially well. They teach the same children for two or three years and make visits to the home once or twice a year. Continuous communication between teachers and parents takes place with the aid of small notebooks that children carry back and forth every day and in which messages about assignments, academic performance, and behavior are written. No such formalized system of frequent teacher–parent communication exists in the United States (Stevenson & Lee, 1990).

Do Japanese and Taiwanese young people pay a price for the pressure placed on them to succeed? By high school, academic work often displaces other experiences, since Asian students must pass a highly competitive entrance exam to gain admission to college. But they do not report feeling more anxious about school than their American counterparts—in fact, less so (Stevenson, Chen, & Lee, 1993). Although the educational system of one society cannot simply be transplanted to cure the ills of another, awareness of the ingredients of Asian success has prompted Americans to rethink current educational practices.

demic instruction, special efforts are needed in the area of vocational education to help non-college-bound youths prepare for productive work roles.

Making the Transition from School to Work

Approximately 25 percent of American adolescents graduate from high school without plans to go to college. Although they have a much better chance of finding employment than those who drop out, non–college-bound youths have fewer work opportunities than they did several decades ago. More than one-fourth of high school graduates younger than 20 who do not continue their education are unemployed. When they do find work, most are limited to low-paid, unskilled jobs. In addition, they have few alternatives to turn to for vocational counseling and job placement as they make the transition from school to work (Bailey, 1993; Hamilton, 1990).

American employers prefer to hire young adults, regarding the recent high school graduate as insufficiently prepared for a demanding, skilled occupation. Indeed, there is some truth to this conclusion. During high school, almost half of American adolescents are employed—a greater percentage than in any other developed country. But most of these are middle-class students in pursuit of spending money rather than vocational training. Low-income teenagers who need to contribute to family income find it harder to get jobs (Children's Defense Fund, 1992b). Furthermore, the jobs adolescents hold are limited to low-level repetitive tasks that provide little contact with adult supervisors and do not prepare them for well-paid careers. A heavy commitment to such jobs is actually harmful. High school students who work more than 15 hours a week have poorer school attendance, lower grades, and less time for extracurricular activities. They also report more drug and alcohol use and feel more distant from their parents. And perhaps because of the menial nature of their jobs, employed teenagers tend to become cynical about work life. Many admit to having stolen from their employers (Greenberger & Steinberg, 1986; Steinberg & Dornbusch, 1991).

When work experiences are specially designed to meet educational and vocational goals, outcomes are very different. Work-study programs are related to positive school and work attitudes, improved achievement, and lower dropout rates among teenagers whose low-income backgrounds and weak academic skills make them especially vulnerable to unemployment (Owens, 1982; Steinberg, 1984). Yet high-quality vocational preparation for American adolescents who do not go to college is scarce. Unlike Western European nations, the United States has no widespread training system to prepare its youths for business and industrial occupations or manual trades. The federal government does support some job-training programs, but most are too short to make a difference in the lives of poorly skilled adolescents, who need intensive training and academic remediation before they are ready to enter the job market. And at present, these programs serve only a small minority of young people who need assistance (Children's Defense Fund, 1992b).

Inspired by successful programs in Western Europe, youth apprenticeship strategies that coordinate on-the-job training with classroom instruction are being considered as an important dimension of educational reform in the United States. The Cultural Influences box on page 648 describes Germany's highly successful apprenticeship system. Bringing together the worlds of schooling and work offers many benefits. These include helping non–college-bound adolescents establish productive lives right after graduation; motivating at-risk youths, who learn more effectively when basic skills are linked to everyday experiences; and contributing to the nation's economic growth (Bailey, 1993; Hamilton, 1993).

Nevertheless, implementing an apprenticeship system poses major challenges. Among these are overcoming the reluctance of employers to assume part of the responsibility for youth vocational training; creating institutional structures that ensure cooperation between schools and businesses; and finding ways to prevent

Rolf, an 18-year-old German vocational student, is an apprentice at Brandt, a large industrial firm known worldwide for its high-quality products. Like many German companies, Brandt has a well-developed apprenticeship program that includes a full-time professional training staff, a suite of classrooms, and a lab equipped with the latest learning aids. Apprentices move through more than 10 major divisions in the company that are carefully selected to meet their learning needs. Rolf has worked in purchasing, inventory, production, personnel, marketing, sales, and finance. Now in cost accounting, he assists Herr Stein, his supervisor, in designing a computerized inventory-control system. Rolf draws a flowchart of the new system under the direction of Herr Stein, who explains that each part of the diagram will contain a set of procedures to be built into a computer program.

Rolf is involved in complex and challenging projects, guided by caring mentors who love their work and want to teach it to others. Two days a week, he attends the *Berufsschule,* a part-time vocational school. On the job, Rolf applies a wide range of academic skills, including reading, writing, problem solving, and logical thinking. His classroom learning is directly relevant to his daily life (Hamilton, 1990).

Germany has the most successful apprenticeship system in the world for preparing young people to enter modern business and industry. More than 60 percent of adolescents participate in it, making it the most common form of secondary education. German adolescents who do not go to the *Gymnasium* (college preparatory high school) usually complete full-time schooling by age 15 or 16, but education remains compulsory until age 18. They fill the 2-year gap with part-time vocational schooling combined with apprenticeship. Students are trained for a wide range of occupations—more than 400, leading to over 20,000 specialized careers. Each apprenticeship is jointly planned by educators and employers. Apprentices who complete training and pass a qualifying examination are certified as skilled workers and earn union-set wages for that occupation. Businesses provide financial support for the program because they know it guarantees a competent, dedicated work force (Hamilton, 1990, 1993).

The German apprenticeship system offers a smooth and rewarding path from school to career for young people who do not enter higher education. More than half of all apprentices are hired by the firms in which they were trained. Most others find jobs in the same occupation. For those who change careers, the apprentice certificate is a powerful credential. Employers view successful apprentices as responsible and capable workers and are willing to invest in further training to adapt the individual's skills to other occupations. As a result, German adolescents establish themselves in well-paid careers with security and advancement possibilities between the ages of 18 and 20 (Hamilton, 1990). Their opportunities contrast sharply with the limited vocational options of American high school graduates.

underprivileged youths from being concentrated in the lowest skilled apprenticeship placements, a circumstance that would perpetuate current social inequalities (Bailey, 1993; Hamilton, 1993). Pilot apprenticeship projects along with new research are currently under way, in an effort to surmount these difficulties and break down the dichotomy that exists between learning and working in the United States.

A Final Note

Our discussion ends on a note of concern mixed with hopefulness about the quality of American schools. Education defines a society's ability to compete in a complex world economy, make new discoveries, transmit a common cultural identity to each new generation, and enjoy an enriched quality of life. Success in improving American schools is crucial for the optimal development of children and the future of the nation as a whole. The American educational system has risen to challenges before; today it provides basic education to a larger percentage of its population than any other country in the world. Already, school systems throughout the country have responded to the current educational crisis with some needed reforms. The greater attention and scrutiny being directed at American education is an encouraging sign. It reflects the firm desire of educators and concerned citizens to rebuild an educational system capable of guiding American children toward a prosperous and civilized adulthood in a rapidly changing world.

The Importance of Peer Relations

- Research with nonhuman primates suggests that parent and peer relations complement one another. The parent–child bond provides children with the security to venture forth into the world of peers. Peer interaction, in turn, permits children to expand the social skills they have begun to acquire within the family. Studies of **peer-only rearing** reveal that peer relations can, to some extent, fill in for the early parent–child bond. However, peer-only reared monkeys do not fare as well in development as their counterparts with typical parental and peer upbringing.

Development of Peer Sociability

- Peer sociability begins in infancy with isolated social acts that are gradually replaced by coordinated exchanges in the second year of life. During the preschool years, interactive play with peers increases. According to Parten, **nonsocial activity** shifts to **parallel play** and then to **associative** and **cooperative play.** However, research indicates that these play forms do not form a developmental sequence in which later-appearing ones replace earlier ones. Instead, all coexist among preschoolers. Sociodramatic play becomes especially frequent and enhances cognitive, emotional, and social skills.
- During middle childhood, peer interaction is more sensitively tuned to others' perspectives and increasingly governed by prosocial norms. In addition, **rough-and-tumble play** becomes more common. In our evolutionary past, this friendly chasing and play-fighting may have been important for the development of fighting skill. In adolescence, peers show greater skill at working on tasks cooperatively.

Influences on Peer Sociability

- Parents influence young children's peer relations by creating opportunities for agemates to get together, offering advice and guidance about how to interact with playmates, and modeling effective social skills.
- Situational factors affect peer sociability. When play materials and space are in short supply, negative interactions increase. Same-age and familiar peers encourage more intense and cooperative exchanges. Mixed-age interaction provides older children with practice in prosocial behavior and younger children with opportunities to learn from their older companions.

Peer Acceptance

- **Sociometric techniques** are used to distinguish four types of peer acceptance: **popular children,** who are liked by many agemates; **rejected children,** who are actively disliked; **controversial children,** who are both liked and disliked; and **neglected children,** who are seldom chosen, either positively or negatively. Rejected children often experience lasting adjustment difficulties.
- Physical attractiveness is related to peer acceptance. Attractive and unattractive children may respond in kind to the way they are treated, sustaining peer opinion.
- The most powerful predictor of peer acceptance is social behavior. Popular children are socially skilled and communicate with agemates in mature, sensitive ways. At least two subtypes of peer rejection exist. **Rejected-aggressive children** are hostile, hyperactive, inattentive, and impulsive, whereas **rejected-withdrawn children** are passive and socially awkward. Controversial children display a blend of positive and negative social behaviors. Although neglected children often choose to play by themselves, they are socially competent and well adjusted.
- Interventions that improve the peer acceptance of rejected children include coaching in social skills, academic remediation, and social-cognitive interventions that enhance perspective taking and expectancies for social success.

Peer Groups

- By the end of middle childhood, **peer groups** with unique norms and social structures of leaders and followers emerge. In adolescence, tightly organized peer groups called **cliques** become common. Sometimes several cliques form a larger, more loosely organized group called a **crowd** that grants the adolescent an identity within the larger social structure of the school. Teenagers' choice of a peer group results from a blend of family and peer influences.
- Group social structures sometimes consist of **dominance hierarchies,** which serve the adaptive function of limiting aggression among group members. During adolescence, dominance becomes less important, and leadership is often based on talents that support important normative activities of the peer group.

Peer Relations and Socialization

- Peers serve as socialization agents through reinforcement, modeling, and direct pressures to conform to social behaviors. Peer conformity is strongest during early adolescence. However, peers seldom demand total conformity, and most peer pressures do not conflict with important adult values.

Television

- Children spend more time watching TV than in any other waking activity. Heavy viewers tend to have lower IQs, come from low-income families, and have adjustment problems. Cognitive development and experience in watching TV gradually lead to gains in **television literacy** during middle childhood and adolescence.
- Televised violence is related to short- and long-term increases in aggressive behavior and makes children more willing to tolerate aggression in others. TV also conveys stereotypes that affect children's beliefs about gender, racial, and ethnic groups. Children are easily manipulated by TV commercials. Not until age 8 or 9 do they understand the selling purpose of the ads.
- Television can foster prosocial behavior as long as it is free of violent content. Appropriately designed programs also have the potential for promoting academic learning and imagination.

Computers

- Computers can have rich cognitive and social benefits. In classrooms, pupils often use computers collaboratively. During the early elementary school years, **computer-**

basic emotions. Emotions that can be directly inferred from facial expressions, such as happiness, interest, surprise, fear, anger, sadness, and disgust.

basic-skills approach. An approach to beginning reading instruction that emphasizes training in phonics—the basic rules for translating written symbols into sounds—and simplified reading materials. Distinguished from *whole language approach.*

behavior genetics. A field of study devoted to uncovering the hereditary and environmental origins of individual differences in human traits and abilities.

behaviorism. An approach that views directly observable events—stimuli and responses—as the appropriate focus of study and the development of behavior as taking place through classical and operant conditioning.

belief-desire theory. The theory of mind that emerges around age 3 to 4 in which both beliefs and desires determine behavior and that closely resembles the everyday psychology of adults.

biased sampling. Failure to select subjects who are representative of the population of interest in a study.

binocular depth cues. Depth cues that rely on each eye receiving a slightly different view of the visual field; the brain blends the two images, creating three dimensionality.

blended, or reconstituted, family. A family structure resulting from remarriage of a divorced parent that includes parent, child, and new steprelatives.

body image. Conception of and attitude toward one's physical appearance.

breech position. A position of the baby in the uterus that would cause the buttocks or feet to be delivered first.

Broca's area. A language structure located in the frontal lobe of the cerebral cortex that controls language production.

bulimia. An eating disorder in which individuals (mainly females) go on eating binges followed by deliberate vomiting, other purging techniques such as heavy doses of laxatives, and strict dieting.

C

canalization. The tendency of heredity to restrict the development of some characteristics to just one or a few outcomes.

carrier. A heterozygous individual who can pass a recessive gene to his or her children.

catch-up growth. Physical growth that returns to its genetically determined path after being delayed by environmental factors.

categorical self. Early classification of the self according to salient ways in which people differ, such as age, sex, and physical characteristics.

categorical speech perception. The tendency to perceive a range of sounds that belong to the same phonemic class as identical.

cathartic treatment. A form of treatment for aggressive behavior that assumes hostile impulses can be drained off through opportunities to engage in aggression or through passive exposure to the aggression of others. Has received little research support.

centration. The tendency to focus on one aspect of a situation and neglect other important features. A characteristic of Piaget's preoperational stage.

cephalocaudal trend. An organized pattern of physical growth that proceeds from head to tail.

cerebellum. A brain structure that aids in balance and control of body movements.

cerebral cortex. The largest structure of the human brain that accounts for the highly developed intelligence of the human species. Surrounds the rest of the brain, much like a half-shelled walnut.

child development. A field of study devoted to understanding all aspects of human growth from conception through adolescence.

chorion. The outer membrane that forms a protective covering around the prenatal organism. It sends out tiny fingerlike villi, from which the placenta begins to emerge.

chromosomes. Rodlike structures in the cell nucleus that store and transmit genetic information.

circular reaction. In Piaget's theory, a means of building schemes in which infants try to repeat a chance event caused by their own motor activity.

classical conditioning. A form of learning that involves associating a neutral stimulus with a stimulus that leads to a reflexive response.

clinical interview. A method in which the researcher uses flexible, open-ended questions to probe for the subject's point of view.

clinical method. A method in which the researcher attempts to understand the unique individual child by combining interview data, observations, and sometimes test scores.

clique. A small group of about 5 to 7 members who are either close or good friends.

codominance. A pattern of inheritance in which both alleles, in a heterozygous combination, are expressed.

cognitive maps. Mental representations of large-scale environments.

cognitive-developmental theory. An approach introduced by Piaget that views the child as actively building psychological structures and cognitive development as taking place in stages.

cohort effects. The effects of cultural-historical change on the accuracy of findings: Children born in one period of time are influenced by particular cultural and historical conditions.

compliance. Voluntary obedience to requests and commands.

componential analysis. A research procedure aimed at clarifying the cognitive processes responsible for intelligence test scores by correlating them with laboratory measures designed to assess the speed and effectiveness of information processing.

comprehension. In language development, the words and word combinations that children understand. Distinguished from *production.*

comprehension monitoring. Sensitivity to how well one understands a spoken or written message.

computer-assisted instruction (CAI). Use of computers to transmit new knowledge and practice academic skills.

concordance rate. The percentage of instances in which both members of a twin pair show a trait when it is present in one pair member. Used to study the role of heredity in traits that can be judged as either present or absent, such as emotional and behavior disorders.

concrete operational stage. Piaget's third stage, during which thought is logical, flexible, and organized in its application to concrete information. However, the capacity for abstract thinking is not yet present. Spans the years from 7 to 11.

conditioned response (CR). In classical conditioning, an originally reflexive response that is produced by a conditioned stimulus (CS).

conditioned stimulus (CS). In classical conditioning, a neutral stimulus that through pairing with an unconditioned stimulus (UCS) leads to a new response (CR).

confluence model. A view that regards mental development as a function of family size, birth order, and spacing—factors that affect the quality of the environment each child experiences within the family.

conservation. In Piaget's theory, the understanding that certain physical characteristics of objects remain the same, even when their outward appearance changes.

construction. The process of moral development in which children actively attend to and weigh multiple aspects of situations in which social conflicts arise and derive new moral insights.

continuous development. A view that regards development as a cumulative process of adding on more of the same types of skills that were there to begin with. Distinguished from *discontinuous development.*

contrast sensitivity. A general principle accounting for early pattern preferences, which states that if babies can detect a difference in contrast between two patterns, they will prefer the one with more contrast.

control deficiency. The inability to execute a mental strategy effectively.

control processes, or mental strategies. In information processing, procedures that operate on and transform information, increasing the efficiency of thinking as well as the chances that information will be retained.

controversial children. Children who get a large number of positive and negative votes on sociometric measures of peer acceptance. Distinguished from *popular, neglected,* and *rejected children.*

conventional level. Kohlberg's second level of moral development, in which moral understanding is based on conforming to social rules to ensure positive human relationships and societal order.

convergent thinking. The generation of a single correct answer to a problem. Type of cognition emphasized on intelligence tests. Distinguished from *divergent thinking.*

cooing. Pleasant vowel-like noises made by infants beginning around 2 months of age.

cooperative learning. A learning environment structured into groups of peers who work together toward a common goal.

cooperative play. A form of true social participation in which children's actions are directed toward a common goal. Distinguished from *nonsocial activity, parallel play,* and *associative play.*

coregulation. A transitional form of supervision in which parents exercise general oversight while permitting children to be in charge of moment-by-moment decision making.

corpus callosum. The large bundle of fibers that connects the two hemispheres of the brain.

correlation coefficient. A number, ranging from +1.00 to –1.00, that describes how two measures, or variables, are related to one another. The size of the number shows the strength of the relationship. The sign of the number (+ or –) refers to the direction of the relationship.

correlational design. A research design in which the investigator gathers information without altering subjects' experiences and examines relationships between variables. Does not permit inferences about cause and effect.

cross-sectional design. A research design in which groups of subjects of different ages are studied at the same point in time. Distinguished from *longitudinal design.*

crossing over. Exchange of genes between chromosomes next to each other during meiosis.

crowd. A large, loosely organized group consisting of several cliques with similar normative characteristics.

crystallized intelligence. In Cattell's theory, a form of intelligence that depends on culturally loaded, fact-oriented information. Distinguished from *fluid intelligence.*

cumulative deficit hypothesis. A view that attributes the age-related decline in IQ among poverty-stricken ethnic minority children to the compounding effects of underprivileged rearing conditions.

D

debriefing. Providing a full account and justification of research activities to subjects who participated in a study in which deception was used.

deferred imitation. The ability to remember and copy the behavior of models who are not immediately present.

Defining Issues Test (DIT). A questionnaire for assessing moral understanding in which subjects read a series of moral dilemmas and rate the importance of "moral issue" statements representing each of Kohlberg's stages in deciding on a course of action.

delay of gratification. Waiting for a more appropriate time and place to engage in a tempting act or obtain a desired object.

deoxyribonucleic acid (DNA). Long, double-stranded molecules that make up chromosomes, segments of which are genes.

dependent variable. The variable the researcher expects to be influenced by the independent variable in an experiment.

deprivation dwarfism. A growth disorder observed between 2 and 15 years of age. Characterized by substantially below average stature, weight that is usually appropriate for height, immature skeletal age, and decreased GH secretion. Caused by emotional deprivation.

developmental psychology. A branch of psychology devoted to understanding all changes that human beings experience throughout the life span.

deviation IQ. An IQ score based on the degree to which a child's performance deviates from the average of same-age children.

differentiation theory. The view that perceptual development involves the detection of increasingly fine-grained, invariant features in the environment.

difficult child. A child whose temperament is such that he or she has irregular daily routines, is slow to accept new experiences, and tends to react negatively and intensely. Distinguished from *easy child* and *slow-to-warm-up child.*

discontinuous development. A view in which new and different modes of interpreting and responding to the world emerge at particular time periods. Assumes that development takes place in stages. Distinguished from *continuous development.*

discrepancy theory. A theory of emotional development in which a child's reaction to a novel stimulus is determined by the degree of similarity between the stimulus and a scheme of a familiar object, to which the stimulus is compared.

dishabituation. Increase in responsiveness after stimulation changes.

disorganized/disoriented attachment. The quality of insecure attachment characterizing infants who respond in a confused, contradictory fashion when reunited with the parent. Distinguished from *secure, avoidant,* and *resistant attachment.*

distance curve. A growth curve that plots the average height and weight of a sample of children at each age. Shows typical yearly progress toward maturity.

distributive justice. Beliefs about how to divide up material goods fairly.

divergent thinking. The generation of multiple and unusual possibilities when faced with a task or problem. Associated with creativity. Distinguished from *convergent thinking.*

divorce mediation. A series of meetings between divorcing adults and a trained professional, who tries to help them settle disputes. Aimed at avoiding legal battles that intensify family conflict.

dizygotic twins. See fraternal twins.

domain-specific knowledge. Knowledge of a specific content area that makes new, related information more meaningful so it is easier to store and retrieve.

dominance hierarchy. A stable ordering of group members that predicts who will win under conditions of conflict.

dominant cerebral hemisphere. The hemisphere of the brain responsible for skilled motor action. The left hemisphere is dominant in right-handed individuals. In left-handed individuals, the right hemisphere may be dominant, or motor and language skills may be shared between the hemispheres.

dominant–recessive inheritance. A pattern of inheritance in which, under heterozygous conditions, the influence of only one allele is apparent.

drive-reduction model of attachment. A behaviorist view that regards the mother's satisfaction of the baby's hunger (primary drive) as the basis for the infant's preference for her (secondary drive).

E

easy child. A child whose temperament is such that he or she quickly establishes regular routines in infancy, is generally cheerful, and adapts easily to new experiences. Distinguished from *difficult child* and *slow-to-warm-up child.*

ecological systems theory. Bronfenbrenner's approach, which views the child as developing within a complex system of relationships affected by multiple levels of the environment, from immediate settings of family and school to broad cultural values and programs.

educational self-fulfilling prophecy. The idea that pupils may adopt teachers' positive or negative attitudes toward them and start to live up to these views.

ego. In Freud's theory, the rational part of personality that reconciles the demands of the id, the superego, and the external world.

elaboration. The memory strategy of creating a relation between two or more items that are not members of the same category.

embryo. The prenatal organism from 2 to 8 weeks after conception, during which time the foundations of all body structures and internal organs are laid down.

emotional display rules. Rules that specify when and where it is culturally appropriate to express emotions.

emotional self-regulation. Strategies for adjusting our emotional state to a comfortable level of intensity so we can remain productively engaged in our surroundings.

empathy. The ability to understand the feelings of others and respond with complementary emotions.

engrossment. The father's experience of elation and emotional involvement following the birth of his child.

enrichment theory. The view that sensory processing involves using cognitive schemes to interpret incoming information.

epiphyses. Growth centers in the bones where new cartilage cells are produced and gradually harden.

episodic memory. Memory for personally experienced events.

equilibration. In Piaget's theory, back-and-forth movement between cognitive equilibrium and disequilibrium throughout development, which leads to more effective schemes. Describes how assimilation and accommodation work together to produce cognitive change.

estrogens. Hormones produced chiefly by the ovaries that cause the breasts, uterus, and vagina to mature and the body to take on feminine proportions during puberty.

ethnography. A method in which the researcher attempts to understand the unique values and social processes of a culture or a distinct social group by living with its members and taking field notes for an extended period of time.

ethological theory of attachment. A theory formulated by Bowlby, which views the infant's emotional tie to the familiar caregiver as an evolved response that promotes survival.

ethology. An approach concerned with the adaptive, or survival, value of behavior and its evolutionary history.

event sampling. An observational procedure in which the researcher records all instances of a particular event or behavior during a specified time period.

exosystem. In ecological systems theory, settings that do not contain children but that affect their experiences in immediate settings. Examples are parents' workplaces and health and welfare services in the community.

expansions. Adult responses that elaborate on a child's utterance, increasing its complexity.

experimental design. A research design in which the investigator randomly assigns subjects to treatment conditions. Since the researcher directly manipulates changes in an independent variable and observes their effects on a dependent variable, the design permits inferences about cause and effect.

expressive style. A style of early language learning in which toddlers use language mainly to talk about the feelings and needs of themselves and other people. Initial vocabulary emphasizes pronouns and social formulas. Distinguished from *referential style.*

expressive traits. Feminine-stereotyped personality traits that reflect warmth, caring, and sensitivity.

extended family household. A household in which parent and child live with one or more adult relatives.

extinction. In classical conditioning, decline of the conditioned response (CR) as a result of presenting the conditioned stimulus (CS) enough times without the unconditioned stimulus (UCS).

F

factor analysis. A complicated statistical procedure that combines scores from many separate test items into a few factors, which substitute for the separate scores. Used to identify mental abilities that contribute to performance on intelligence tests.

fast mapping. Connecting a new word with an underlying concept after only a brief encounter. Explains how children manage to add new words to their vocabularies at such a rapid rate.

fetal alcohol effects (FAE). The condition of children who display some but not all of the defects of fetal alcohol syndrome. Usually their mothers drank alcohol in smaller quantities during pregnancy.

fetal alcohol syndrome (FAS). A pattern of defects that results when pregnant women consume large amounts of alcohol during most or all of pregnancy. Includes mental retardation, slow physical growth, and facial abnormalities.

fetus. The prenatal organism from the beginning of the 3rd month to the end of pregnancy, during which time completion of body structures and dramatic growth in size takes place.

field experiment. A research design in which subjects are randomly assigned to treatment conditions in natural settings.

fluid intelligence. In Cattell's theory, a form of intelligence that requires very little specific knowledge but involves the ability to see complex relationships and solve problems. Distinguished from *crystallized intelligence.*

fontanels. Six soft spots that separate the bones of the skull at birth.

formal operational egocentrism. A form of egocentrism present during the formal operational stage involving an inability to distinguish the abstract perspectives of self and other.

formal operational stage. Piaget's final stage, in which adolescents develop the capacity for abstract, scientific thinking. Begins around age 11.

fraternal, or dizygotic, twins. Twins resulting from the release and fertilization of two ova. They are genetically no more alike than ordinary siblings. Distinguished from *identical,* or *monozygotic, twins.*

functionalist approach. A theoretical perspective that regards emotions as central, adaptive forces in all aspects of human activity.

G

gametes. Human sperm and ova, which contain half as many chromosomes as a regular body cell.

gender consistency. Kohlberg's final stage of gender understanding, in which children master gender constancy.

gender constancy. The understanding that sex remains the same even if clothing, hairstyle, and play activities change.

gender labeling. Kohlberg's first stage of gender understanding, in which preschoolers can label the sex of themselves and others correctly.

gender-role identity. Perception of the self as relatively masculine or feminine in characteristics, abilities, and behaviors.

gender roles. The reflection of gender stereotypes in everyday behavior.

gender schema theory. An information-processing approach to gender typing that combines social learning and cognitive-developmental features to explain how environmental pressures and children's cognitions work together to affect stereotyping, gender-role identity, and gender-role adoption.

gender stability. Kohlberg's second stage of gender understanding, in which preschoolers have a partial understanding of the permanence of sex; they grasp its stability over time.

gender stereotypes. Widely held beliefs about characteristics deemed appropriate for males and females.

gender typing. The process of developing gender roles and a gender-role identity.

gene. A segment of a DNA molecule that contains genetic instructions.

general factor, or "g." In Spearman's theory of intelligence, a common factor representing abstract reasoning power that underlies a wide variety of test items.

general growth curve. Curve that represents overall changes in body size—rapid growth during infancy, slower gains in early and middle childhood, and rapid growth once more during adolescence.

generalized other. A blend of what we imagine important people in our lives think of us; determines the content of self-concept.

genetic counseling. Counseling that helps couples assess the likelihood of giving birth to a baby with a hereditary disorder.

genetic–environmental correlation. The idea that heredity influences the environments to which individuals are exposed.

genotype. The genetic makeup of the individual.

giftedness. Exceptional intellectual ability. Includes high IQ, creativity, and specialized talent.

glial cells. Brain cells serving the function of myelinization.

goodness-of-fit model. Thomas and Chess's model, which states that when the child's temperament and environmental pressures are in harmony, or achieve a "good fit," development is optimal. When dissonance, or a "poor fit," between temperament and environment exists, maladjustment and distorted development occur.

grammar. The component of language concerned with syntax, the rules by which words are arranged into sentences, and morphology, the use of grammatical markers that indicate number, tense, case, person, gender, and other meanings.

grammatical morphemes. Small markers that change the meaning of sentences, as in "John's dog" and "he *is* eating."

growth hormone (GH). A pituitary hormone that affects the development of almost all body tissues, except the central nervous system and genitals.

H

habituation. A gradual reduction in the strength of a response as the result of repetitive stimulation.

heritability estimate. A statistic that measures the extent to which individual differences in complex traits, such as intelligence and personality, are due to genetic factors.

heteronomous morality. Piaget's first stage of moral development, in which children view moral rules as having a permanent existence, as unchangeable, and as requiring strict obedience.

heterozygous. Having two different alleles at the same place on a pair of chromosomes. Distinguished from *homozygous.*

hierarchical classification. The organization of objects into classes and subclasses on the basis of similarities and differences between the groups.

Home Observation for Measurement of the Environment (HOME). A checklist for gathering information about the quality of children's home lives through observation and parental interview.

homozygous. Having two identical alleles at the same place on a pair of chromosomes. Distinguished from *heterozygous.*

horizontal décalage. Development within a Piagetian stage. Gradual mastery of logical concepts during the concrete operational stage provides an example.

hostile aggression. Aggression intended to harm another individual. Distinguished from *instrumental aggression.*

human development. An interdisciplinary field of study devoted to understanding all changes human beings experience throughout the life span.

hypothalamus. A structure located at the base of the brain that initiates and regulates pituitary secretions.

hypothesis. A prediction about behavior drawn from a theory.

hypothetico-deductive reasoning. A formal operational problem-solving strategy in which adolescents begin with a general theory of all possible factors that could affect an outcome in a problem and deduce specific hypotheses, which they test in an orderly fashion.

I

id. In Freud's theory, the part of the personality that is the source of basic biological needs and desires.

identical, or monozygotic, twins. Twins that result when a zygote, during the early stages of cell duplication, divides in two. They have the same genetic makeup. Distinguished from *fraternal,* or *dizygotic, twins.*

identification. In Freud's theory, the process leading to formation of the superego in which children take the same-sex parent's characteristics into their personality.

identity achievement. The identity status of individuals who have explored and committed themselves to self-chosen values and goals. Distinguished from *moratorium, identity foreclosure,* and *identity diffusion.*

identity diffusion. The identity status of individuals who do not have firm commitments to values and goals and are not actively trying to reach them. Distinguished from *identity achievement, moratorium,* and *identity foreclosure.*

identity foreclosure. The identity status of individuals who have accepted ready-made values and goals that authority figures have chosen for them. Distinguished from *identity achievement, moratorium,* and *identity diffusion.*

identity. A well-organized conception of the self made up of values, beliefs, and goals to which the individual is solidly committed.

illocutionary intent. What a speaker means to say, regardless of whether the form of the utterance is perfectly consistent with it.

imaginary audience. Adolescents' belief that they are the focus of everyone else's attention and concern.

imitation. Learning by copying the behavior of another person. Also called *modeling* or *observational learning.*

immanent justice. The belief that wrongdoing inevitably leads to punishment. Characterizes Piaget's stage of heteronomous morality.

independent variable. The variable manipulated by the researcher in an experiment by randomly assigning subjects to treatment conditions.

induction. A type of discipline in which the effects of the child's misbehavior on others are communicated to the child.

infant mortality. The number of deaths in the first year of life per 1,000 live births.

infantile amnesia. The inability of older children and adults to remember experiences that happened before age 3.

information processing. An approach that views the human mind as a symbol-manipulating system through which information flows and that regards cognitive development as a continuous process.

informed consent. The right of individuals, including children, to have explained to them, in language they can understand, all aspects of a research study that may affect their willingness to participate.

inhibited child. A child who withdraws and displays negative emotion to novel stimuli. Distinguished from *uninhibited child.*

inorganic failure to thrive. A growth disorder usually present by 18 months of age that is caused by lack of affection and stimulation.

instrumental aggression. Aggression aimed at obtaining an object, privilege, or space with no deliberate intent to harm another person. Distinguished from *hostile aggression.*

instrumental traits. Masculine-stereotyped personality traits that reflect competence, rationality, and assertiveness.

intelligence quotient, or IQ. A score that permits an individual's performance on an intelligence test to be compared to the performances of other individuals.

intentional, or goal directed, behavior. A sequence of actions in which schemes are deliberately combined to solve a problem.

interactional synchrony. A sensitively timed "emotional dance," in which the caregiver responds to infant signals in a well-timed, appropriate fashion and both partners match emotional states, especially the positive ones.

intermodal perception. Perception that combines information from more than one sensory system.

internal working model. A set of expectations derived from early caregiving experiences concerning the availability of attachment figures, their likelihood of providing support during times of stress, and the self's interactions with those figures that affect all future close relationships.

internalization. The process of moral development in which children adopt preexisting, ready-made standards for right action as their own.

intersubjectivity. A process whereby two participants who begin a task with different understandings arrive at a shared understanding.

invariant features. In differentiation theory of perceptual development, features that remain stable in a constantly changing perceptual world.

J

joint custody. A child-custody arrangement following divorce in which the court grants both parents equal say in important decisions about the child's upbringing.

just community. Kohlberg's approach to moral education, in which a small society of teachers and students practice a democratic way of life.

K

Kaufman Assessment Battery for Children (K-ABC). An individually administered intelligence test that measures two broad types of information-processing skills: simultaneous and sequential processing. The first major test to be grounded in information-processing theory.

kinetic depth cues. Depth cues created by movements of the body or of objects in the environment.

kinship studies. Studies comparing the characteristics of family members to determine the importance of heredity in complex human characteristics.

kwashiorkor. A disease usually appearing between 1 and 3 years of age that is caused by a diet low in protein. Symptoms include an enlarged belly, swollen feet, hair loss, skin rash, and irritable and listless behavior.

L

laboratory experiment. An experiment conducted in the laboratory, which permits the maximum possible control over treatment conditions.

language acquisition device (LAD). In Chomsky's theory, a biologically based, innate system for picking up language that permits children, as soon as they have acquired sufficient vocabulary, to combine words into grammatically consistent utterances and to understand the meaning of the sentences they hear.

language making capacity (LMC). According to Slobin's theory, a built-in set of procedures for analyzing language that supports the discovery of grammatical regularities.

lanugo. A white, downy hair that covers the entire body of the fetus, helping the vernix stick to the skin.

lateralization. Specialization of functions of the two hemispheres of the cortex.

learned helplessness. Attributions that credit success to luck and failure to low ability. Leads to low expectancies of success

and anxious loss of control in the face of challenging tasks. Distinguished from *mastery-oriented attributions.*

learning disabilities. Specific learning disorders (for example, in reading, writing, or math computation) that result in poor school achievement, despite an average or above average IQ. Believed to be due to faulty brain functioning.

Level I–Level II theory. Jensen's controversial theory, which states that racial and social-class differences in IQ are due to genetic differences in higher-order, abstract forms of intelligence (Level II) rather than basic memory skills (Level I).

levels-of-processing model. A model of mental functioning in which retention of information depends on the depth to which it is analyzed. Attentional resources determine processing capacity.

lexical contrast theory. A theory that attributes semantic development to two principles: conventionality, children's natural desire to acquire the words and word meanings of their language community; and contrast, children's discovery of meanings by contrasting new words with ones currently in their vocabulary.

long-term memory. In Atkinson and Shiffrin's store model of mental functioning, the part of the mental system that contains our permanent knowledge base.

longitudinal design. A research design in which one group of subjects is studied repeatedly at different ages. Distinguished from *cross-sectional design.*

longitudinal-sequential design. A research design with both longitudinal and cross-sectional components in which groups of subjects born in different years are followed over time.

M

macrosystem. In ecological systems theory, the values, laws, and customs of a culture that influence experiences and interactions at lower levels of the environment.

mainstreaming. The integration of pupils with learning disabilities into regular classrooms for all or part of the school day.

make-believe play. A type of play in which children pretend, acting out everyday and imaginary activities.

marasmus. A disease usually appearing in the first year of life that is caused by a diet low in all essential nutrients. Leads to a wasted condition of the body.

mastery-oriented attributions. Attributions that credit success to high ability and failure to insufficient effort. Leads to high expectancies of success and a willingness to approach challenging tasks. Distinguished from *learned helplessness.*

matching. A procedure for assigning subjects with similar characteristics in equal numbers to treatment conditions in an experiment. Ensures that groups will be equivalent on factors likely to distort the results.

maturation. A genetically determined, naturally unfolding course of growth.

mechanistic theories. Theories that regard the child as a passive reactor to environmental inputs. Distinguished from *organismic theories.*

meiosis. The process of cell division through which gametes are formed and in which the number of chromosomes in each cell is halved.

memory strategies. Deliberate mental activities that improve the likelihood of remembering.

menarche. First menstruation.

mental age (MA). A measure of performance on an intelligence test that indicates the age at which children, on the average, obtain that score.

mental representation. An internal image of an absent object or a past event.

mental space, or M-space. In Case's neo-Piagetian theory of cognitive development, a construct similar to working memory. It expands with brain maturation, exercise of strategies, and formation of central conceptual structures, which permit the child to move up to a new Piagetian stage.

mesosystem. In ecological systems theory, connections among children's immediate settings.

metacognition. Awareness and understanding of various aspects of thought that affect performance.

metalinguistic awareness. The ability to think about language as a system.

microgenetic design. A research design in which change is tracked from the time it begins until it stabilizes, as subjects master an everyday or novel task.

microsystem. In ecological systems theory, the activities and interaction patterns in the child's immediate surroundings.

mitosis. The process of cell duplication, in which each new cell receives an exact copy of the original chromosomes.

modifier genes. Genes that modify the effect of another gene on a characteristic by either enhancing or diluting its effects.

monozygotic twins. See identical twins.

moral dilemma. A conflict situation presented to subjects, who are asked to decide both what the main actor should do and why. Used to assess the development of moral reasoning.

moratorium. The identity status of individuals who are exploring alternatives in an effort to find values and goals to guide their life. Distinguished from *identity achievement, identity diffusion,* and *identity foreclosure.*

motherese. The form of language adopted by adults when speaking to infants and toddlers that is made up of short sentences with high-pitched, exaggerated intonation, clear pronunciation, and distinct pauses between speech segments.

mutation. A sudden but permanent change in a segment of DNA.

myelinization. A process in which neural fibers are coated with an insulating fatty sheath (called myelin) that improves the efficiency of message transfer.

N

natural experiment. A research design in which the investigator studies already existing treatments in natural settings by carefully selecting groups of subjects with similar characteristics.

natural, or prepared, childbirth. An approach designed to reduce pain and medical intervention and to make childbirth a rewarding experience for parents.

naturalistic observation. A method in which the researcher goes into the natural environment to observe the behavior of interest. Distinguished from *structured observation.*

nature-nurture controversy. Disagreement among theorists about whether genetic or environmental factors are the most important determinants of development and behavior.

neglected children. Children who are seldom chosen, either positively or negatively, on sociometric measures of peer acceptance. Distinguished from *popular, rejected,* and *controversial children.*

Neonatal Behavioral Assessment Scale (NBAS). A test developed by Brazelton to assess the behavior of the infant during the newborn period. Considers reflexes, responsiveness to physical and social stimuli, state changes, and other reactions.

neurons. Nerve cells that store and transmit information in the brain.

niche-picking. A type of genetic-environmental correlation in which individuals actively choose environments that complement their heredity.

noble savage. Rousseau's view of the child as naturally endowed with an innate plan for orderly, healthy growth.

non-rapid-eye-movement (NREM) sleep. A "regular" sleep state in which the body is quiet and heart rate, breathing, and brain wave activity are slow and regular. Distinguished from *rapid-eye-movement (REM) sleep.*

nonshared environmental influences. Environmental influences that make children living in the same family different from one another. Distinguished from *shared environmental influences.*

nonsocial activity. Unoccupied, onlooker behavior and solitary play. Distinguished from *parallel, associative,* and *cooperative play.*

normative approach. An approach in which age-related averages are computed to represent the typical child's development.

nuclear family unit. The part of the family that consists of parents and their children.

O

obesity. A greater than 20 percent increase over average body weight, based on the child's age, sex, and physical build.

object permanence. The understanding that objects continue to exist when they are out of sight.

observer bias. The tendency of observers who are aware of the purposes of a study to see and record what is expected rather than subjects' actual behaviors.

observer influence. The tendency of subjects to react to the presence of an observer and behave in unnatural ways.

open classroom. Classroom based on the educational philosophy that values emotional and social development in addition to academic progress. The teacher assumes a flexible authority role, pupils are active in the learning process, and children are evaluated by considering their progress in relation to their own prior development. Distinguished from *traditional classroom.*

operant conditioning. A form of learning in which a spontaneous behavior is followed by a stimulus that changes the probability that the behavior will occur again.

operant-conditioning model of attachment. A behaviorist view that regards the mother's contingent reinforcement of the baby's social behavior as the basis for the infant's preference for her.

operations. In Piaget's theory, mental representations of actions that obey logical rules.

organismic theories. Theories that assume the existence of psychological structures inside the child that underlie and control development. Distinguished from *mechanistic theories.*

organization. In Piaget's theory, the internal rearrangement and linking together of schemes so that they form a strongly interconnected cognitive system. In information processing, the memory strategy of grouping related information into meaningful chunks.

overextension. An early vocabulary error in which a word is applied too broadly, to a wider collection of objects and events than is appropriate. Distinguished from *underextension.*

overregularization. Application of regular grammatical rules to words that are exceptions. For example, saying "mouses" instead of "mice."

P

parallel play. A form of limited social participation in which the child plays near other children with similar materials but does not interact with them. Distinguished from *nonsocial activity, associative play,* and *cooperative play.*

peer group. Peers who form a social unit by generating unique values and standards of behavior and a social structure of leaders and followers.

peer-only rearing. A type of study in which nonhuman primates are reared together from birth without adults.

perception-bound. Being easily distracted by the concrete, perceptual appearance of objects. A characteristic of Piaget's preoperational stage.

permissive style. A parenting style that is responsive but undemanding. An overly tolerant approach to parenting. Distinguished from *authoritative, authoritarian,* and *uninvolved styles.*

person perception. The way individuals size up people with whom they are familiar in everyday life.

personal fable. Adolescents' belief that they are special and unique. Leads them to conclude that others cannot possibly understand their thoughts and feelings and that they are invulnerable to danger.

perspective taking. The capacity to imagine what other people may be thinking and feeling.

phenotype. The individual's physical and behavioral characteristics, which are determined by both genetic and environmental factors.

phoneme. The smallest speech unit that can be distinguished perceptually.

phonology. The component of language concerned with understanding and producing speech sounds.

pictorial depth cues. Depth cues artists use to make a painting look three-dimensional, such as receding lines, texture changes, and overlapping objects.

pincer grasp. The well-coordinated grasp emerging at the end of the first year, involving thumb and forefinger opposition.

pituitary gland. A gland located at the base of the brain that releases hormones affecting physical growth.

placenta. The organ that separates the mother's bloodstream from the embryo or fetal bloodstream but permits exchange of nutrients and waste products.

plasticity. The ability of other parts of the brain to take over functions of damaged regions.

pleiotropism. The influence of a single gene on more than one characteristic.

polygenic inheritance. A pattern of inheritance in which many genes determine a characteristic.

popular children. Children who get many positive votes on sociometric measures of peer acceptance. Distinguished from *rejected, controversial,* and *neglected children.*

postconventional level. Kohlberg's highest level of moral development, in which individuals define morality in terms of abstract principles and values that apply to all situations and societies.

practice effects. Changes in subjects' natural responses as a result of repeated testing.

pragmatics. The component of language concerned with how to engage in effective and appropriate communication with others.

preconventional level. Kohlberg's first level of moral development, in which moral understanding is based on rewards, punishments, and the power of authority figures.

preformationism. Medieval view of the child as a miniature adult.

prenatal diagnostic methods. Medical procedures that permit detection of problems before birth. Includes amniocentesis, chorionic villi biopsy, ultrasound, fetoscopy, and maternal blood analysis.

preoperational egocentrism. A form of egocentrism present during Piaget's preoperational stage involving the inability to distinguish the symbolic viewpoints of others from one's own.

preoperational stage. Piaget's second stage, in which rapid development of representation takes place. However, thought is not yet logical. Spans the years from 2 to 7.

prereaching. The poorly coordinated, primitive reaching movements of newborn babies.

preterm. Infants born several weeks or more before their due date. Although small in size, their weight may still be appropriate for the time they spent in the uterus.

primary mental abilities. In Thurstone's theory of intelligence, seven distinct mental abilities identified through factor analysis (verbal meaning, perceptual speed, reasoning, number, rote memory, word fluency, and spatial visualization).

primary sexual characteristics. Physical features that involve the reproductive organs directly (ovaries, uterus, and vagina in females; penis, scrotum, and testes in males).

principle of mutual exclusivity. The assumption by children in the early stages of vocabulary growth that words mark entirely separate (nonoverlapping) categories.

private speech. Self-directed speech that children use to plan and guide their own behavior.

production. In language development, the words and word combinations that children use. Distinguished from *comprehension.*

production deficiency. The failure to use a mental strategy in situations where it could be helpful.

Project Head Start. A federal program providing low-income children with a year of preschool education before school entry and that encourages parent involvement in children's development.

propositional thought. A type of formal operational reasoning in which adolescents evaluate the logic of verbal statements without referring to real-world circumstances.

prosocial, or altruistic, behavior. Actions that benefit another person without any expected reward for oneself.

protection from harm. The right of research participants to be protected from physical or psychological harm.

protodeclarative. A preverbal gesture though which infants make an assertion about an object by touching it, holding it up, or pointing to it.

protoimperative. A preverbal gesture in which infants point, reach, and make sounds to get another person to do something.

proximodistal trend. An organized pattern of physical growth that proceeds from the center of the body outward.

psychoanalytic perspective. An approach to personality development introduced by Freud that assumes children move through a series of stages in which they confront conflicts between biological drives and social expectations. The way these conflicts are resolved determines psychological adjustment.

psychometric approach. An approach to cognitive development that focuses on the construction of tests to assess mental abilities.

psychosexual theory. Freud's theory, which emphasizes that how parents manage children's sexual and aggressive drives during the first few years is crucial for healthy personality development.

psychosocial theory. Erikson's theory, which emphasizes that the demands of society at each Freudian stage not only promote the development of a unique personality, but also ensure that individuals acquire attitudes and skills that help them become active, contributing members of their society.

puberty. Biological changes during adolescence that lead to an adult-sized body and sexual maturity.

public policy. Laws and government programs designed to improve current conditions.

punishment. In operant conditioning, removing a desirable stimulus or presenting an unpleasant one to decrease the occurrence of a response.

R

random assignment. An evenhanded procedure for assigning subjects to treatment groups, such as drawing numbers out of a hat or flipping a coin. Increases the chances that subjects' characteristics will be equally distributed across treatment conditions in an experiment.

range of reaction. Each person's unique, genetically determined response to a range of environmental conditions.

rapid-eye-movement (REM) sleep. An "irregular" sleep state in which brain-wave activity is similar to that of the waking state; eyes dart beneath the lids, heart rate, blood pressure, and breathing are uneven; and slight body movements occur. Distinguished from *rapid-eye-movement (REM) sleep.*

realism. A view of rules as external features of reality rather than subjective, internal principles. Characterizes Piaget's heteronomous stage.

recall. A type of memory that involves remembering a stimulus that is not present. Distinguished from *recognition.*

recasts. Adult responses that restructure a child's incorrect speech into appropriate form.

reciprocal teaching. A method of teaching based on Vygotsky's theory in which a teacher and two to four pupils form a collaborative learning group. Dialogues occur that create a zone of proximal development in which reading comprehension improves.

reciprocity. A standard of fairness in which individuals express the same concern for the welfare of others as they do for themselves.

recognition. A type of memory that involves noticing whether a stimulus is identical or similar to one previously experienced. Distinguished from *recall.*

reconstruction. A memory process in which complex, meaningful material is reinterpreted in terms of existing knowledge.

recursive thought. The self-embedded form of perspective taking that involves thinking about what another person is thinking.

referential communication skills. The ability to produce clear verbal messages and to recognize when the meaning of others' messages is unclear.

referential style. A style of early language learning in which toddlers use language mainly to label objects. Distinguished from *expressive style.*

reflex. An inborn, automatic response to a particular form of stimulation.

rehearsal. The memory strategy of repeating information.

reinforcer. In operant conditioning, a stimulus that increases the occurrence of a response.

rejected children. Children who are actively disliked and get many negative votes on sociometric measures of peer acceptance. Distinguished from *popular, controversial,* and *neglected children.*

rejected-aggressive children. A subgroup of rejected children who engage in high rates of conflict, hostility, and hyperactive, inattentive, and impulsive behavior. Distinguished from *rejected-withdrawn children.*

rejected-withdrawn children. A subgroup of rejected children who are passive and socially awkward. Distinguished from *rejected-aggressive children.*

reliability. The consistency, or repeatability, of measures of subjects' behavior.

resistant attachment. The quality of insecure attachment characterizing infants who remain close to the parent before departure and display angry, resistive behavior when she returns. Distinguished from *secure, avoidant,* and *disorganized/disoriented attachment.*

reticular formation. A brain structure that maintains alertness and consciousness.

reversibility. The ability to mentally go through a series of steps in a problem and then reverse direction, returning to the starting point. In Piaget's theory, part of every logical operation.

Rh factor. A protein that, when present in the fetus's blood but not in the mother's, can cause the mother to build up antibodies. If these return to the fetus's system, they destroy red blood cells, reducing the oxygen supply to organs and tissues.

rough-and-tumble play. A form of peer interaction involving friendly chasing and play-fighting that, in our evolutionary past, may have been important for the development of fighting skill.

rubella. Three-day German measles. Causes a wide variety of prenatal abnormalities, especially when it strikes during the embryonic period.

S

scaffolding. A changing quality of support over a teaching session in which adults adjust the assistance they provide to fit the child's current level of performance. Direct instruction is offered when a task is new; less help is provided as competence increases.

scheme. In Piaget's theory, a specific structure, or organized way of making sense of experience, that changes with age.

scripts. General representations of what occurs and when it occurs in a particular situation. A basic means through which children (and adults) organize and interpret everyday experiences.

secondary sexual characteristics. Features visible on the outside of the body that serve as signs of sexual maturity but do not involve the reproductive organs (for example, breast development in females, appearance of underarm and pubic hair in both sexes).

secular trends in physical growth. Changes in body size and rate of growth from one generation to the next.

secure attachment. The quality of attachment characterizing infants who are distressed by parental separation and easily comforted by the parent when she returns. Distinguished from *resistant, avoidant,* and *disorganized/disoriented attachment.*

secure base. The use of the familiar caregiver as a base from which the infant confidently explores the environment and returns for emotional support.

self-care children. Children who look after themselves during after-school hours.

self-concept. A set of beliefs about one's own characteristics.

self-conscious emotions. Emotions that involve injury to or enhancement of the sense of self. Examples are shame, embarrassment, guilt, envy, and pride.

self-control. Inhibiting an impulse to engage in behavior that violates a moral standard.

self-esteem. An aspect of self-concept that involves judgments about one's own worth and the feelings associated with those judgments.

self-recognition. Perception of the self as a separate being, distinct from people and objects in the surrounding world.

self-regulation. The process of continuously monitoring progress toward a goal, checking outcomes, and redirecting unsuccessful efforts.

semantic bootstrapping hypothesis. A hypothesis that states that young children rely on the semantic properties of words to figure out basic grammatical regularities.

semantic memory. The vast, intricately organized knowledge system in long-term memory.

semantics. The component of language concerned with understanding the meaning of words and word combinations.

sensitive period. A time span that is optimal for certain capacities to emerge and in which the individual is especially responsive to environmental influences.

sensorimotor egocentrism. A form of egocentrism present in infancy that involves merging the self with the surrounding world, an absence of the understanding that the self is an object in a world of objects.

sensorimotor stage. Piaget's first stage, during which infants and toddlers "think" with their eyes, ears, hands, and other sensorimotor equipment. Spans the first 2 years of life.

sensory register. In Atkinson and Shiffrin's store model of mental functioning, the first part of the mental system through which information flows, where sights and sounds are represented directly but held only briefly.

separation anxiety. An infant's distressed reaction to the departure of the familiar caregiver.

serial-position effect. In memory task involving lists of items, the tendency to remember ones at the beginning and end better than those in the middle.

seriation. The ability to arrange items along a quantitative dimension, such as length or weight.

sex chromosomes. The 23rd pair of chromosomes, which determines the sex of the child. In females, called XX; in males, called XY.

shading. A conversational strategy in which a change of topic is initiated gradually by modifying the focus of discussion.

shape constancy. Perception of an object's shape as the same, despite changes in the shape of its retinal image.

shared environmental influences. Environmental influences that pervade the general atmosphere of the home and affect all children living in it to the same extent. Distinguished from *nonshared environmental influences.*

short-term memory. In Atkinson and Shiffrin's store model of mental functioning, the central processing unit of the mental system, where information is consciously operated on using control processes, or mental strategies.

size constancy. Perception of an object's size as the same, despite changes in the size of its retinal image.

skeletal age. An estimate of physical maturity based on development of the bones of the body.

skill theory. Fischer's neo-Pagetian theory of cognitive development, in which each Piagetian stage is viewed as an extended period of skill learning in which the child acquires new competencies on specific tasks, integrates them with others, and gradually transforms them into more general, higher-order skills. As a result, the child moves up to a new Piagetian stage.

slow-to-warm-up child. A child whose temperament is such that he or she is inactive, shows mild, low-key reactions to environmental stimuli, is negative in mood, and adjusts slowly to new experiences. Distinguished from *easy child* and *difficult child.*

small for date. Infants whose birth weight is below normal when length of pregnancy is taken into account. May be full term or *preterm.*

social cognition. Thinking about the self, other people, and social relationships.

social comparisons. Judgments of abilities, behavior, appearance, and other characteristics in relation to those of others.

social learning theory. An approach that emphasizes the role of modeling, or observational learning, in the development of behavior.

social policy. Any planned set of actions directed at solving a social problem or attaining a social goal.

social problem solving. Resolving social conflicts in ways that are both acceptable to others and beneficial to the self.

social referencing. Relying on another person's emotional reaction to appraise an uncertain situation.

social smile. The smile evoked by the stimulus of the human face. First appears between 6 and 10 weeks.

social systems perspective. A view of the family as a complex set of interacting relationships influenced by the larger social context.

sociobiology. A field that assumes many complex social behaviors, including morally relevant prosocial acts, are rooted in our genetic heritage and have evolved because of their survival value.

sociocultural theory. Vygotsky's theory, in which children acquire the ways of thinking and behaving that make up a community's culture through cooperative dialogues with more knowledgeable members of that society.

sociodramatic play. The make-believe play with others that first appears around age $2\frac{1}{2}$.

sociometric techniques. Self-report measures that ask peers to evaluate one another's likability.

Sociomoral Reflection Measure–Short Form (SRM–SF). A questionnaire for assessing moral understanding in which subjects rate the importance of moral values addressed by brief, dilemma-inspired questions and explain their ratings. Does not require subjects to read and think about lengthy moral dilemmas.

specific factor, or "s." In Spearman's theory of intelligence, a mental-ability factor that is unique to a particular task.

specimen record. An observational procedure in which the researcher records a description of the subject's entire stream of behavior for a specified time period.

speech registers. Language adaptations to social expectations.

spermarche. First ejaculation of seminal fluid.

stage. A qualitative change in thinking, feeling, and behaving that characterizes a particular time period of development.

Stanford-Binet Intelligence Scale. An individually administered intelligence test that is the modern descendent of Alfred Binet's first successful test for children. Measures overall IQ and four factors: verbal reasoning, quantitative reasoning, spatial reasoning, and short-term memory.

states of arousal. Different degrees of sleep and wakefulness.

states versus transformations. The tendency to treat the initial and final states in a problem as completely unrelated. A characteristic of Piaget's preoperational stage.

store model. Atkinson and Shiffrin's model of mental functioning, which views information as being held in three parts of the system for processing: the sensory register, short-term memory, and long-term memory.

Strange Situation. A procedure involving short separations from and reunions with the parent that assesses the quality of the attachment bond.

stranger anxiety. The infant's expression of fear in response to unfamiliar adults. Appears in many babies after 7 months of age.

structure-of-intellect model. Guilford's 180-factor model of intelligence, which classifies each intellectual task according to three dimensions: content, mental operation, and product.

structured interview. A method in which the researcher asks each subject the same questions in the same way.

structured observation. A method in which the researcher sets up a cue for the behavior of interest and observes that behavior in a laboratory. Distinguished from *naturalistic observation*.

sudden infant death syndrome (SIDS). Death of a seemingly healthy baby, who stops breathing, usually during the night, without apparent cause.

superego. In Freud's theory, the part of the personality that is the seat of conscience and is often in conflict with the id's desires.

synapses. Gaps between neurons, across which chemical messages are sent.

systems of action. In motor development, combinations of previously acquired skills to produce a more advanced skill.

T

tabula rasa. Locke's view of the child as a blank slate whose character is shaped by experience.

telegraphic speech. Children's two-word utterances that, like a telegram, leave out smaller and less important words.

television literacy. The task of learning television's specialized symbolic code of conveying information.

temperament. Stable individual differences in quality and intensity of emotional reaction.

teratogen. Any environmental agent that causes damage during the prenatal period.

theory. An orderly, integrated set of statements that describes, explains, and predicts behavior.

theory of mind. A coherent understanding of people as mental beings with a rich inner life accessible to themselves and not to others.

theory of multiple intelligences. Gardner's theory, which identifies seven distinct intelligences on the basis of distinct sets of processing operations applied in culturally meaningful activities (linguistic, logico-mathematical, musical, spatial, bodily-kinesthetic, interpersonal, and intrapersonal).

thyroxine. A hormone released by the thyroid gland that is necessary for central nervous system development and body growth.

time out. A form of mild punishment in which children are removed from the immediate setting until they are ready to act appropriately.

time sampling. An observational procedure in which the researcher records whether or not certain behaviors occur during a sample of short time intervals.

traditional classroom. Classroom based on an educational philosophy that emphasizes transmission of culturally valued knowledge and standards of conduct. The teacher is the sole authority, pupils are relatively passive in the learning process, and progress is evaluated by how well pupils keep pace with a common set of expectations for everyone in their grade.

transductive reasoning. Reasoning from one particular event to another particular event, instead of from general to particular or particular to general. A characteristic of Piaget's preoperational stage.

transitive inference. The ability to seriate—or arrange items along a quantitative dimension—mentally.

triarchic theory of intelligence. Sternberg's theory, which states that information-processing skills, prior experience with tasks, and contextual (or cultural) factors interact to determine intelligent behavior.

turnabout. A conversational strategy in which the speaker not only comments on what has just been said but also adds a request to get the partner to respond again.

Type A behavior pattern. A behavior pattern characterized by excessive competitiveness, impatience, restlessness, and irritability. Associated with high blood pressure and cholesterol levels as well as heart disease in adulthood.

U

ulnar grasp. The clumsy grasp of the young infant, in which the fingers close against the palm.

umbilical cord. The long cord connecting the prenatal organism to the placenta that delivers nutrients and removes waste products.

unconditioned response (UCR). In classical conditioning, a reflexive response that is produced by an unconditioned stimulus (UCS).

unconditioned stimulus (UCS). In classical conditioning, a stimulus that leads to a reflexive response.

underextension. An early vocabulary error in which a word is applied too narrowly, to a smaller number of objects and events than is appropriate. Distinguished from *overextension*.

uninhibited child. A child who approaches and displays positive emotion to novel stimuli. Distinguished from *inhibited child*.

uninvolved style. A parenting style that is both undemanding and unresponsive. Reflects minimal commitment to child rearing. Distinguished from *authoritative*, *authoritarian*, and *permissive styles*.

V

validity. The extent to which measures in a research study accurately reflect what the investigator intended to measure.

velocity curve. A growth curve that plots the average amount of growth at each yearly interval for a sample of children. Clarifies the timing of growth spurts.

vernix. A white, cheeselike substance covering the fetus and preventing the skin from chapping due to constant exposure to the amniotic fluid.

visual acuity. Fineness of visual discrimination.

visual cliff. An apparatus used to study depth perception in infants. Consists of a glass-covered table and a central platform, from which babies are encouraged to crawl. Patterns placed beneath the glass create the appearance of a shallow and deep side.

W

washout effect. The loss of IQ and achievement gains resulting from early intervention within a few years after the program ends.

Wechsler Intelligence Scale for Children–III (WISC–III). An individually administered intelligence test that includes both an overall IQ and a variety of verbal and performance scores.

Wernicke's area. A language structure located in the temporal lobe of the cerebral cortex that is responsible for interpreting language.

whole-language approach. An approach to beginning reading instruction that parallels children's natural language learning and keeps reading materials whole and meaningful. Distinguished from *basic skills approach*.

working memory. In the levels-of-processing model of mental functioning, the conscious pool of attentional resources from which our information-processing activities draw.

X

X-linked inheritance. A pattern of inheritance in which a recessive gene is carried on the X chromosome. Males are more likely to be affected.

Z

zone of proximal development. In Vygotsky's theory, a range of tasks that the child cannot yet handle alone but can do with the help of more skilled partners.

zygote. The union of sperm and ovum at conception.

References

A

Aaron, R., & Powell, G. (1982). Feedback practices as a function of teacher and pupil race during reading groups instruction. *Journal of Negro Education, 51,* 50–59.

Aaronson, L. S., & MacNee, C. L. (1989). Tobacco, alcohol, and caffeine use during pregnancy. *Journal of Obstetrics, Gynecology, and Neonatal Nursing, 18,* 279–287.

Abbott, S. (1992). Holding on and pushing away: Comparative perspectives on an eastern Kentucky child-rearing practice. *Ethos, 20,* 33–65.

Abelman, R. (1985). Styles of parental disciplinary practices as a mediator of children's learning from prosocial television portrayals. *Child Study Journal, 15,* 131–145.

Abramov, I., Gordon, J., Hendrickson, A., Hainline, L., Dobson, V., & La Bossiere, E. (1982). The retina of the newborn infant. *Science, 217,* 265–267.

Abramovitch, R., Freedman, J. L., Thoden, K., & Nikolich, C. (1991). Children's capacity to consent to participation in psychological research: Some empirical findings. *Child Development, 62,* 1100–1109.

Abravanel, E., & Sigafoos, A. D. (1984). Exploring the presence of imitation during early infancy. *Child Development, 55,* 381–392.

Achenbach, T. M. (1978). *Research in developmental psychology: Concepts, strategies, methods.* New York: Free Press.

Achenbach, T. M., & Edelbrock, C. S. (1981). Behavioral problems and competencies reported by parents of normal and disturbed children aged 4 through 16. *Monographs of the Society for Research in Child Development, 46* (1, Serial No. 188).

Achenbach, T. M., Phares, V., Howell, C. T., Rauh, V. A., & Nurcombe, B. (1990). Seven-year outcome of the Vermont intervention program for low-birthweight infants. *Child Development, 61,* 1672–1681.

Achenbach, T. M., & Weisz, J. R. (1975). A longitudinal study of developmental synchrony between conceptual identity, seriation, and transitivity of color, number, and length. *Child Development, 46,* 840–848.

Ackerman, B. P. (1978). Children's understanding of speech acts in unconventional frames. *Child Development, 49,* 311–318.

Ackerman, B. P. (1993). Children's understanding of the speaker's meaning in referential communication. *Journal of Experimental Child Psychology, 55,* 56–86.

Ackerman, S. H., Keller, S. E., Schleifer, S. J., Shindledecker, R. D., Camerino, M., Hofer, M. A., Weiner, H., & Stein, M. (1988). Premature maternal separation and lymphocyte function. *Brain and Behavior Immunology, 2,* 161–165.

Acredolo, C., Adams, A., & Schmid, J. (1984). On the understanding of the relationships between speed, duration, and distance. *Child Development, 55,* 2151–2159.

Acredolo, L. P., & Goodwyn, S. W. (1990). Sign language in babies: The significance of symbolic gesturing for understanding language development. In R. Vasta (Ed.), *Annals of child development* (Vol. 7, pp. 1–42). Greenwich, CT: JAI Press.

Acredolo, L. P., & Hake, J. L. (1982). Infant perception. In B. B. Wolman (Ed.), *Handbook of developmental psychology* (pp. 244–283). Englewood Cliffs, NJ: Prentice-Hall.

Adams, G. R. (1978). Racial membership and physical attractiveness effects on preschool teachers' expectations. *Child Study Journal, 8,* 29–41.

Adams, G. R., Abraham, K. G., & Markstrom, C. A. (1987). The relations among identity development, self-consciousness, and self-focusing during middle and late adolescence. *Developmental Psychology, 23,* 292–297.

Adams, G. R., & Crane, P. (1980). An assessment of parents' and teachers' expectations of preschool children's social preference for attractive or unattractive children and adults. *Child Development, 51,* 224–231.

Adams, R. E., & Passman, R. H. (1981). The effects of preparing two-year-olds for brief separations from their mothers. *Child Development, 52,* 1068–1070.

Adams, R. J. (1987). An evaluation of color preference in early infancy. *Infant Behavior and Development, 10,* 143–150.

Adams, R. S. (1969). Location as a feature of instructional interaction. *Merrill-Palmer Quarterly, 15,* 309–321.

Adcock, A. G., Nagy, S. N., & Simpson, J. A. (1991). Selected risk factors in adolescent suicide attempts. *Adolescence, 26,* 817–828.

Ainsworth, M. D. S., Blehar, M., Waters, E., & Wall, S. (1978). *Patterns of attachment.* Hillsdale, NJ: Erlbaum.

Aitken, M., Bennett, S. N., & Hesketh, J. (1981). Teaching styles and pupil progress: A re-analysis. *British Journal of Educational Psychology, 51,* 187–196.

Albers, L. L., & Katz, V. L. (1991). Birth setting for low-risk pregnancies. *Journal of Nurse-Midwifery, 36,* 215–220.

Albert, R. S., & Runco, M. A. (1986). The achievement of eminence: A model based on a longitudinal study of exceptionally gifted boys and their families. In R. J. Sternberg & J. E. Davidson (Eds.), *Conceptions of giftedness* (pp. 332–357). New York: Cambridge University Press.

Alberts-Corush, J., Firestone, P., & Goodman, J. T. (1986). Attention and impulsivity characteristics of the biological and adoptive parents of hyperactive and normal control children. *American Journal of Orthopsychiatry, 56,* 413–423.

Ales, K. L., Druzin, M. L., & Santini, D. L. (1990). Impact of advanced maternal age on the outcome of pregnancy. *Surgery, Gynecology & Obstetrics, 171,* 209–216.

Alessandri, S. M., Sullivan, M. W., & Lewis, M. (1990). Violation of expectancy and frustration in early infancy. *Developmental Psychology, 26,* 738–744.

Allen, L. F., Palomares, R. S., DeForest, P., Sprinkle, B., & Reynolds, C. R. (1991). The effects of intrauterine cocaine exposure: Transient or teratogenic? *Archives of Clinical Neuropsychology, 6,* 133–146.

Alpert-Gillis, L. J., & Connell, J. P. (1989). Gender and sex-role influences on children's self-esteem. *Journal of Personality, 57,* 97–114.

Als, H., Lester, B. M., Tronick, E., & Brazelton, T. B. (1980). Toward a research instrument for the assessment of preterm infants' behavior (APIB). In H. E. Fitzgerald, B. M. Lester, & M. W. Yogman (Eds.), *Theory and research in behavioral pediatrics* (Vol. 1, pp. 35–63). New York: Plenum.

Altemeier, W. A., O'Connor, S. M., Sherrod, K. B., & Vietze, P. M. (1984). Prospective study of antecedents for nonorganic failure to thrive. *Journal of Pediatrics, 106,* 360–365.

Alter-Reid, K., Gibbs, M. S., Lachenmeyer, J. R., Sigal, J., & Massoth, N. A. (1986). Sexual abuse of children: A review of empirical findings. *Clinical Psychology Review, 6,* 249–266.

Altshuler, J. L., & Ruble, D. N. (1989). Developmental changes in children's awareness of strategies for coping with uncontrollable stress. *Child Development, 60,* 1337–1349.

Alvarez, W. F. (1985). The meaning of maternal employment for mothers and their perceptions of their three-year-old children. *Child Development, 56,* 350–360.

Alwitt, L. F., Anderson, D. R., Lorch, E. P., & Levin, S. R. (1980). Preschool children's visual attention to attributes of television. *Human Communication Research, 7,* 52–67.

American Academy of Pediatrics. (1984). Report of the task force on the assessment of the scientific evidence relating to infant-feeding practices and infant health. *Pediatrics, 74,* 579–762.

American Academy of Pediatrics. (1987). Statement on childhood lead poisoning. *Pediatrics, 79,* 457–465.

American Academy of Pediatrics. (1992). Preventive health care for young children: Findings from a 10-country study and directions for United States policy. *Pediatrics, 83,* 983–997.

American Medical Association. (1992, December). *Report to the Consumer Product Safety Commission on infant walkers.* Nashville, TN: Author.

American Psychiatric Association. (1987). *Diagnostic and statistical manual of mental disorders* (3rd ed., rev.). Washington, DC: Author.

American Psychological Association. (1982). *Ethical principles in the conduct of research with human participants.* Washington, DC: Author.

Amiel-Tison, C. (1985). Pediatric contribution to the present knowledge on the neurobehavioral status of infants at birth. In J. Mehler & R. Fox (Eds.), *Neonate cognition: Beyond the blooming buzzing confusion* (pp. 365–380). Hillsdale, NJ: Erlbaum.

Anand, K. J. S., Phil, D., & Hickey, P. R. (1987). Pain and its effects in the human neonate and fetus. *New England Journal of Medicine, 317,* 1321–1329.

Anderson, D. R., & Smith, R. (1984). Young children's TV viewing: The problem of cognitive continuity. In F. J. Morrison, C. Lord, & D. P. Keating (Eds.), *Applied developmental psychology* (Vol. 1, pp. 115–163). Orlando, FL: Academic Press.

Anderson, E. S. (1984). The acquisition of sociolinguistic knowledge: Some evidence from children's verbal role play. *Western Journal of Speech Communication, 48,* 125–144.

Anderson, G. C. (1991). Current knowledge about skin-to-skin (kangaroo) care for preterm infants. *Journal of Perinatology, 11,* 216–226.

Andersson, B-E. (1989). Effects of public day care—A longitudinal study. *Child Development, 60,* 857–866.

Andersson, B-E. (1992). Effects of day-care on cognitive and socioemotional competence of thirteen-year-old Swedish schoolchildren. *Child Development, 63,* 20–36.

Andrews, L. B. (1987). Ethical and legal aspects of in-vitro fertilization and artificial insemination by donor. *Urologic Clinics of North America, 14,* 633–643.

Andrews, S. R., Blumenthal, J. B., Johnson, D. L., Kahn, A. J., Ferguson, C. J., Lasater, T. M., Malone, P. E., & Wallace, D. B. (1982). The skills of mothering: A study of parent child development centers. *Monographs of the Society for Research in Child Development, 47* (6, Serial No. 198).

Antonarakis, S. E. (1992). The meiotic stage of nondisjunction in trisomy 21: Determination by using DNA polymorphisms. *American Journal of Human Genetics, 50,* 544–550.

Apgar, V. (1953). A proposal for a new method of evaluation in the newborn infant. *Current Research in Anesthesia and Analgesia, 32,* 260–267.

Appleton, T., Clifton, R., & Goldberg, S. (1975). The development of behavioral competence in infancy. In F. D. Horowitz (Ed.), *Review of child development research* (Vol. 4, pp. 101–186). Chicago: University of Chicago Press.

Arbuthnot, J., & Gordon, D. A. (1986). Behavioral and cognitive effects of a moral reasoning development intervention for high-risk behavior-disordered adolescents. *Journal of Consulting and Clinical Psychology, 85,* 1275–1301.

Arbuthnot, J., Sparling, Y., Faust, D., & Kee, W. (1983). Logical and moral development in preadolescent children. *Psychological Reports, 52,* 209–210.

Archer, C. J. (1984). Children's attitudes toward sex-role division in adult occupational roles. *Sex Roles, 10,* 1–10.

Archer, S. L. (1982). The lower age boundaries of identity development. *Child Development, 53,* 1551–1556.

Archer, S. L. (1989a). Gender differences in identity development: Issues of process, domain, and timing. *Journal of Adolescence, 2,* 117–138.

Archer, S. L. (1989b). The status of identity: Reflections on the need for intervention. *Journal of Adolescence, 12,* 345–359.

Archer, S. L., & Waterman, A. S. (1990). Varieties of identity diffusions and foreclosures: An exploration of subcategories of the identity statuses. *Journal of Adolescent Research, 5,* 96–111.

Aries, P. (1962). *Centuries of childhood.* New York: Random House.

Arnold, K., & Denny, T. (1985). *The lives of academic achievers: The career aspirations of male and female high school valedictorians and salutatorians.* Paper presented at the annual meeting of the American Educational Research Association, Chicago.

Aronfreed, J. (1968). *Conduct and conscience.* New York: Academic Press.

Arsenio, W. F., & Kramer, R. (1992). Victimizers and their victims: Children's conceptions of the mixed emotional consequences of moral transgressions. *Child Development, 63,* 915–927.

Arterberry, M. E., & Yonas, A. (1988). Infants' sensitivity to kinetic information for three-dimensional object shape. *Perception & Psychophysics, 44,* 1–6.

Arterberry, M., Yonas, A., & Bensen, A. S. (1989). Self-produced locomotion and the development of responsiveness to linear perspective and texture gradients. *Developmental Psychology, 25,* 976–982.

Asendorpf, J. B., & Baudonnière, P-M. (1993). Self-awareness and other-awareness: Mirror self-recognition and synchronic imitation among unfamiliar peers. *Developmental Psychology, 29,* 88–95.

Asher, S. R., & Hymel, S. (1981). Children's social competence in peer relations: Sociometric and behavioral assessment. In J. D. Wine & M. D. Smye (Eds.), *Social competence* (pp. 125–157). New York: Guilford.

Ashmead, D. H., Davis, D. L., Whalen, T., & Odom, R. D. (1991). Sound localization and sensitivity to interaural time differences in human infants. *Child Development, 62,* 1211–1226.

Ashmead, D. H., & Perlmutter, M. (1980). Infant memory in everyday life. In M. Perlmutter (Ed.), *New directions for child development* (Vol. 10, pp. 1–16). San Francisco: Jossey-Bass.

Ashton, G. C., & Borecki, I. B. (1987). Further evidence for a gene influencing spatial ability. *Behavior Genetics, 17,* 243–256.

Aslin, R. N. (1987). Visual and auditory development in infancy. In J. D. Osofsky (Ed.), *Handbook of infant development* (2nd ed., pp. 5–97). New York: Wiley.

Aslin, R. N., Pisoni, D. B., & Jusczyk, P. W. (1983). Auditory development and speech perception in infancy. In M. M. Haith & J. J. Campos (Eds.), *Handbook of child psychology: Vol. 2. Infancy and developmental psychobiology* (4th ed., pp. 573–687). New York: Wiley.

Astington, J. W. (1988). Children's understanding of the speech act of promising. *Journal of Child Language, 15,* 157–173.

Astington, J. W. (1991). Intention in the child's theory of mind. In C. Moore & D. Frye (Eds.), *Children's theories of mind* (pp. 157–172). Hillsdale, NJ: Erlbaum.

Astington, J. W., & Gopnik, A. (1991). Theoretical explanations of children's understanding of the mind. *British Journal of Developmental Psychology, 9,* 7–31.

Astley, S. J., Clarren, S. K., Little, R. E., Sampson, P. D., & Daling, J. R. (1992). Analysis of facial shape in children gestationally exposed to marijuana, alcohol, and/or cocaine. *Pediatrics, 89,* 67–77.

Atkin, C. (1978). Observation of parent-child interaction in supermarket decision making. *Journal of Marketing, 42,* 41–45.

Atkin, C., Reeves, B., & Gibson, W. (1979). *Effects of television food advertising on children.* Paper presented at the meeting of the Association for Education in Journalism, Houston, TX.

Atkinson, R. C., & Shiffrin, R. M. (1968). Human memory: A proposed system and its control processes. In K. W. Spence & J. T. Spence (Eds.), *Advances in the psychology of learning and motivation* (Vol. 2, pp. 90–195). New York: Academic Press.

Atkinson-King, K. (1973). Children's acquisition of phonological stress contrasts. *UCLA Working Papers in Phonetics, 25.*

Attie, I., & Brooks-Gunn, J. (1989). Development of eating problems in adolescent girls: A longitudinal study. *Developmental Psychology, 25,* 70–79.

Au, T. K., Sidle, A. L., & Rollins, K. B. (1993). Developing an intuitive understanding of conservation and contamination: Invisible particles as a plausible mechanism. *Developmental Psychology, 29,* 286–299.

August, D., & Garcia, E. E. (1988). *Language minority education in the United States.* Springfield, IL: Charles C. Thomas.

Avis, J., & Harris, P. (1991). Belief-desire reasoning among Baka children: Evidence for a universal conception of mind. *Child Development, 62,* 460–467.

Azmitia, M. (1988). Peer interaction and problem solving: When are two heads better than one? *Child Development, 59,* 87–96.

Azmitia, M., & Hesser, J. (1993). Why siblings are important agents of cognitive development: A comparison of siblings and peers. *Child Development, 64,* 430–444.

B

Baddeley, A. (1992). Working memory. *Science, 255,* 556–559.

Bahrick, L. E. (1983). Infants' perception of substance and temporal synchrony in multimodal events. *Infant Behavior and Development, 6,* 429–451.

Bahrick, L. E. (1988). Intermodal learning in infancy: Learning on the basis of two kinds of invariant relations in audible and visible events. *Child Development, 59,* 197–209.

Bahrick, L. E. (1992). Infants' perceptual differentiation of amodal and modality-specific audio-visual relations. *Journal of Experimental Child Psychology, 53,* 180–199.

Bai, D. L., & Bertenthal, B. L. (1992). Locomotor status and the development of spatial search skills. *Child Development, 63,* 215–226.

Bailey, J. M., & Pillard, R. C. (1991). A genetic study of male sexual orientation. *Archives of General Psychiatry, 43,* 808–812.

Bailey, J. M., Pillard, R. C., Neale, M. C., & Agyei, Y. (1993). Heritable factors influence sexual orientation in women. *Archives of General Psychiatry, 50,* 217–223.

Bailey, R. C. (1990). Growth of African pygmies in early childhood. *New England Journal of Medicine, 323,* 1146.

Bailey, T. (1993). Can youth apprenticeship thrive in the United States? *Educational Researcher, 22*(3), 4–10.

Baillargeon, R. (1987). Object permanence in 3.5- and 4.5-month-old infants. *Developmental Psychology, 23,* 655–664.

Baillargeon, R., & DeVos, J. (1991). Object permanence in young infants: Further evidence. *Child Development, 62,* 1227–1246.

Baillargeon, R., DeVos, J., & Graber, M. (1989). Location memory in 8-month-old infants in a non-search AB task: Further evidence. *Cognitive Development, 4,* 345–367.

Baillargeon, R., Graber, M., DeVos, J., & Black, J. (1990). Why do young infants fail to search for hidden objects? *Cognition, 36,* 255–284.

Baird, P., & Sadovnick, A. D. (1987). Life expectancy in Down syndrome. *Journal of Pediatrics, 110,* 849–854.

Bakeman, R., Adamson, L. B., Konner, M., & Barr, R. G. (1990). !Kung infancy: The social context of object exploration. *Child Development, 61,* 794–809.

Bakeman, R., & Brownlee, J. R. (1982). Social rules governing object conflicts in toddlers and preschoolers. In K. H. Rubin & H. S. Ross (Eds.), *Peer relationships and social skills in childhood* (pp. 99–111). New York: Springer-Verlag.

Baker, S. W. (1980). Biological influences on human sex and gender. *Signs: Journal of Women in Culture and Society, 6,* 80–96.

Baker-Ward, L., Ornstein, P. A., & Holden, D. J. (1984). The expression of memorization in early childhood. *Journal of Experimental Child Psychology, 37,* 555–575.

Baldwin, D. V., & Skinner, M. L. (1989). Structural model for antisocial behavior: Generalization to single-mother families. *Developmental Psychology, 25,* 45–50.

Baldwin, J. M. (1895). *Mental development in the child and the race: Methods and processes.* New York: Macmillan.

Baldwin, J. M. (1897). *Social and ethnical interpretations in mental development: A study in social psychology.* New York: Macmillan.

Ball, S., & Bogatz, G. (1970). *The first year of "Sesame Street": An evaluation.* Princeton, NJ: Educational Testing Service.

Ballard, B. D., Gipson, M. T., Guttenberg, W., & Ramsey, K. (1980). Palatability of food as a factor influencing obese and normal-weight children's eating habits. *Behavior Research and Therapy, 18,* 598–600.

Bancroft, J., Axworthy, D., & Ratcliffe, S. (1982). The personality and psycho-sexual development of boys with 47 XXY chromosome constitution. *Journal of Child Psychology and Psychiatry, 23,* 169–180.

Band, E. B., & Weisz, J. R. (1988). How to feel better when it feels bad: Children's perspectives on coping with everyday stress. *Developmental Psychology, 24,* 247–253.

Bandura, A. (1967). Behavioral psychotherapy. *Scientific American, 216,* 78–86.

Bandura, A. (1977). *Social learning theory.* Englewood Cliffs, NJ: Prentice-Hall.

Bandura, A. (1986). *Social foundations of thought and action: A social cognitive theory.* Englewood Cliffs, NJ: Prentice-Hall.

Bandura, A. (1989). Social cognitive theory. In R. Vasta (Ed.), *Annals of child development* (Vol. 6, pp. 1–60). Greenwich, CT: JAI Press.

Bandura, A. (1991). Social cognitive theory of moral thought and action. In W. M. Kurtines & J. L. Gewirtz (Eds.), *Handbook of moral behavior and development* (Vol. 1, pp. 45–103). Hillsdale, NJ: Erlbaum.

Banis, H. T., Varni, J. W., Wallander, J. L., Korsch, B. M., Jay, S. M., Adler, R., Garcia-Temple, E., & Negrete, V. (1988). Psychological and social adjustment of obese children and their families. *Child: Care, Health, and Development, 14,* 157–173.

Banks, M. S. (1980). The development of visual accommodation during early infancy. *Child Development, 51,* 646–666.

Banks, M. S., & Ginsburg, A. P. (1985). Early visual preferences: A review and new theoretical treatment. In H. W. Reese (Ed.), *Advances in child development and behavior* (Vol. 19, pp. 207–246). New York: Academic Press.

Banks, M. S., & Salapatek, P. (1981). Infant pattern vision: A new approach based on the contrast sensitivity function. *Journal of Experimental Child Psychology, 31,* 1–45.

Banks, M. S., & Salapatek, P. (1983). Infant visual perception. In M. M. Haith & J. J. Campos (Eds.), *Handbook of child psychology: Vol. 2. Infancy and developmental psychobiology* (4th ed., pp. 436–571). New York: Wiley.

Barclay, J. R., & Reid, M. (1974). Semantic integration in children's recall of discourse. *Developmental Psychology, 10,* 277–281.

Bard, K. A. (1992). Intentional behavior and intentional communication in young free-ranging orangutans. *Child Development, 63,* 1186–1197.

Bardin, C. W., & Catterall, J. F. (1981). Testosterone: A major determinant of extragenital sexual dimorphism. *Science, 211,* 1285–1293.

Bardwell, J. R., Cochran, S. W., & Walker, S. (1986). Relationship of parental education, race, and gender to sex role stereotyping in five-year-old kindergartners. *Sex Roles, 15,* 275–281.

Barenboim, C. (1977). Developmental changes in the interpersonal cognitive system from middle childhood to adolescence. *Child Development, 48,* 1467–1474.

Barenboim, C. (1981). The development of person perception in childhood and adolescence: From behavioral comparisons to psychological constructs to psychological comparisons. *Child Development, 52,* 129–144.

Bargh, J. A., & Schul, Y. (1980). On the cognitive benefits of peer teaching. *Journal of Educational Psychology, 72,* 593–604.

Barker, R. G., & Gump, P. V. (1964). *Big school, small school: High school size and student behavior.* Stanford, CA: Stanford University Press.

Barker, R. G., & Wright, H. F. (1955). *Midwest and its children.* New York: Harper & Row.

Barkley, R. A. (1990). *Attention deficit hyperactivity disorder: A handbook for diagnosis and treatment.* New York: Guilford.

Barnes, D. M. (1989). Fragile X syndrome and its puzzling genetics. *Science, 243,* 171–172.

Barnes, K. E. (1971). Preschool play norms: A replication. *Developmental Psychology, 5,* 99–103.

Baron-Cohen, S. (1991). Do people with autism understand what causes emotion? *Child Development, 62,* 385–395.

Barr, H. M., & Streissguth, A. P. (1991). Caffeine use during pregnancy and child outcome: A 7-year prospective study. *Neurotoxicology and Teratology, 13,* 441–448.

Barr, H. M., Streissguth, A. P., Darby, B. L., & Sampson, P. D. (1990). Prenatal exposure to alcohol, caffeine, tobacco, and aspirin: Effects on fine and gross motor performance in 4-year-old children. *Developmental Psychology, 26,* 339–348.

Barr, R. (1991, May). Toward a balanced perspective on beginning reading. *Educational Researcher, 20* (4), 30–32.

Barrera, M. E., & Maurer, D. (1981a). Discrimination of strangers by the three-month-old. *Child Development, 52,* 559–563.

Barrera, M. E., & Maurer, D. (1981b). Recognition of mother's photographed face by the three-month-old infant. *Child Development, 52,* 714–716.

Barrett, D. E. (1979). A naturalistic study of sex differences in children's aggression. *Merrill-Palmer Quarterly, 25,* 193–203.

Barrett, D. E., & Yarrow, M. R. (1977). Prosocial behavior, social inferential ability, and assertiveness in children. *Child Development, 48,* 475–481.

Barrett, G. V., & Depinet, R. L. (1991). A reconsideration of testing for competence rather than for intelligence. *American Psychologist, 46,* 1012–1024.

Barrett, K. C., & Campos, J. J. (1987). Perspectives on emotional development II: A functionalist approach to emotions. In J. D. Osofsky (Ed.), *Handbook of infant development* (2nd ed., pp. 555–578). New York: Wiley.

Barth, R. P., Petro, J. V., & Leland, N. (1992). Preventing adolescent pregnancy with social and cognitive skills. *Journal of Adolescent Research, 7,* 208–232.

Bartlett, F. C. (1932). *Remembering.* Cambridge: Cambridge University Press.

Barton, M. E., & Tomasello, M. (1991). Joint attention and conversation in mother–infant–sibling triads. *Child Development, 62,* 517–529.

Baruch, G. K., & Barnett, R. C. (1986). Fathers' participation in family work and children's sex-role attitudes. *Child Development, 57,* 1210–1223.

Bates, E. (1979). *The emergence of symbols: Cognition and communication in infancy.* New York: Academic Press.

Bates, E. (1993, March). *Nature, nurture, and language.* Invited address presented at the biennial meeting of the Society for Research in Child Development, New Orleans.

Bates, E., Bretherton, I., & Snyder, L. (1988). *From first words to grammar.* New York: Cambridge University Press.

Bates, E., & MacWhinney, B. (1987). Competition, variation, and language learning. In B. MacWhinney (Ed.), *Mechanisms of language acquisition* (pp. 157–193). Hillsdale, NJ: Erlbaum.

Bates, J. E. (1987). Temperament in infancy. In J. D. Osofsky (Ed.), *Handbook of infant development* (2nd ed., pp. 1101–1149). New York: Wiley.

Bates, J. E., & Bayles, K. (1988). Attachment and the development of behavior problems. In J. Belsky & T. Nexworski (Eds.), *Clinical implications of attachment* (pp. 253–294). Hillsdale, NJ: Erlbaum.

Bates, J. E., Freeland, C. A. B., & Lounsbury, M. C. (1979). Measurement of infant difficultness. *Child Development, 50,* 794–803.

Baudonnière, P-M. (1988). Evolution in mode of social exchange in 2-, 3-, and 4-year-old peers. *European Bulletin of Cognitive Psychology, 8,* 241–263.

Bauer, P. J., & Mandler, J. M. (1989a). One thing follows another: Effects of temporal structure on 1- to 2-year-olds' recall of events. *Developmental Psychology, 25,* 197–206.

Bauer, P. J., & Mandler, J. M. (1989b). Taxonomies and triads: Conceptual organization in one- to two-year-olds. *Cognitive Psychology, 21,* 156–184.

Bauer, P. J., & Mandler, J. M. (1992). Putting the horse before the cart: The use of temporal order in recall of events by one-year-old children. *Developmental Psychology, 28,* 441–452.

Baumeister, R. F. (1990). Identity crisis. In R. M. Lerner, A. C. Petersen, & J. Brooks-Gunn (Eds.), *The encyclopedia of adolescence* (Vol. 1, pp. 518–521). New York: Garland.

Baumrind, D. (1967). Child care practices anteceding three patterns of preschool behavior. *Genetic Psychology Monographs, 75,* 43–88.

Baumrind, D. (1971). Current patterns of parental authority. *Developmental Psychology Monograph, 4* (No. 1, Pt. 2).

Baumrind, D. (1983). Rejoinder to Lewis's reinterpretation of parental firm control effects: Are authoritative families really harmonious? *Psychological Bulletin, 94,* 132–142.

Baumrind, D. (1991). The influence of parenting style on adolescent competence and substance use. *Journal of Early Adolescence, 11,* 56–95.

Baumrind, D., & Black, A. E. (1967). Socialization practices associated with dimensions of competence in preschool boys and girls. *Child Development, 38,* 291–327.

Bayley, N. (1969). *Bayley Scales of Infant Development.* New York: Psychological Corporation.

Beal, C. R. (1990). The development of text evaluation and revision skills. *Child Development, 61,* 247–258.

Beauchamp, G. K., Cowart, B. J., & Moran, M. (1986). Developmental changes in salt acceptability in human infants. *Developmental Psychobiology, 19,* 17–25.

Becker, H. J., & Sterling, C. W. (1987). Equity in school computer use: National data and neglected considerations. *Journal of Educational Computing Research, 3,* 289–311.

Becker, J. (1989). Preschoolers' use of number words to denote one-to-one correspondence. *Child Development, 60,* 1147–1157.

Beeghley, L., & Sellers, C. (1986). Adolescents and sex: A structural theory of premarital sex in the United States. *Deviant Behavior, 7,* 313–336.

Beere, C. A. (1990). *Gender roles: A handbook of tests and measures.* New York: Greenwood Press.

Behrend, D. A. (1988). Overextensions in early language comprehension: Evidence from a signal detection approach. *Journal of Child Language, 15,* 63–75.

Behrend, D. A., Rosengren, K. S., & Perlmutter, M. (1992). The relation between private speech and parental interactive style. In R. M. Diaz & L. E. Berk (Eds.), *Private speech: From social interaction to self-regulation* (pp. 85–100). Hillsdale, NJ: Erlbaum.

Behrman, R. E., & Vaughan, V. C. (1987). *Nelson textbook of pediatrics* (13th ed.). Philadelphia: Saunders.

Beilin, H. (1978). Inducing conservation through training. In G. Steiner (Ed.), *Psychology of the twentieth century* (Vol. 7, pp. 260–289). Munich: Kindler.

Beilin, H. (1992). Piaget's enduring contribution to developmental psychology. *Developmental Psychology, 28,* 191–204.

Beitchman, J. H., Zucker, K. J., Hood, J. E., daCosta, G. A., Akman, D., & Cassavia, E. (1992). A review of the long-term effects of child sexual abuse. *Child Abuse & Neglect, 16,* 101–118.

Belkin, L. (1992, July 28). Childless couples hang on to last hope, despite law. *The New York Times,* pp. B1–B2.

Bell, A., Weinberg, M., & Hammersmith, S. (1981). *Sexual Preference: Its development in men and women.* Bloomington, IN: Indiana University Press.

Bell, M. A., & Fox, N. A. (1992). The relations between frontal brain electrical activity and cognitive development during infancy. *Child Development, 63,* 1142–1163.

Bell, S. M., & Ainsworth, M. D. S. (1972). Infant crying and maternal responsiveness. *Child Development, 43,* 1171–1190.

Bell-Dolan, D. J., Foster, S. L., & Sikora, D. M. (1989). Effects of sociometric testing on children's behavior and loneliness in school. *Developmental Psychology, 25,* 306–311.

Bellinger, D., Leviton, A., Waternaux, C., Needleman, H., & Rabinowitz, M. (1987). Longitudinal analysis of prenatal and postnatal lead exposure and early cognitive development. *New England Journal of Medicine, 316,* 1037–1043.

Belmont, L., & Marolla, F. A. (1973). Birth order, family size, and intelligence. *Science, 182,* 1096–1101.

Belsky, J., & Braungart, J. M. (1991). Are insecure-avoidant infants with extensive day-care experience less stressed by and more independent in the Strange Situation? *Child Development, 62,* 567–571.

Belsky, J., Fish, M., & Isabella, R. (1991). Continuity and discontinuity in infant negative and positive emotionality: Family antecedents and attachment consequences. *Developmental Psychology, 27,* 421–431.

Belsky, J., Goode, M., & Most, R. (1980). Maternal stimulation and infant exploratory competence: Cross-sectional, correlational and experimental analyses. *Child Development, 51,* 1168–1178.

Belsky, J., Rovine, M., & Taylor, D. G. (1984). The Pennsylvania infant and family development project, III. The origins of individual differences in infant-mother attachment: Maternal and infant contributions. *Child Development, 55,* 718–728.

Belsky, J., & Steinberg, L. (1978). The effects of day care: A critical review. *Child Development, 49,* 929–949.

Bem, S. L. (1974). The measurement of psychological androgyny. *Journal of Consulting and Clinical Psychology, 42,* 155–162.

Bem, S. L. (1975). Sex role adaptability: One consequence of psychological androgyny. *Journal of Personality and Social Psychology, 31,* 634–643.

Bem, S. L. (1977). On the utility of alternative procedures for assessing psychological androgyny. *Journal of Consulting and Clinical Psychology, 45,* 196–205.

Bem, S. L. (1981). Gender schema theory: A cognitive account of sex typing. *Psychological Review, 88,* 354–364.

Bem, S. L. (1983). Gender schema theory and its implications for child development: Raising gender aschematic children in a gender-schematic society. *Signs: Journal of Women in Culture and Society, 8,* 598–616.

Bem, S. L. (1984). Androgyny and gender schema theory: A conceptual and empirical integration. In R. A. Dienstbier & T. B. Sonderegger (Eds.), *Nebraska Symposium on Motivation* (Vol. 34, pp. 179–226). Lincoln: University of Nebraska Press.

Bem, S. L. (1989). Genital knowledge and gender constancy in preschool children. *Child Development, 60,* 649–662.

Benacerraf, B. R., Green, M. F., Saltzman, D. H., Barss, V. A., Penso, C. A., Nadel, A. S., Heffner, L. J., Stryker, J. M., Sandstrom, M. M., & Frigoletto, F. D., Jr. (1988). Early amniocentesis for prenatal cytogenetic evaluation. *Radiology, 169,* 709–710.

Benbow, C. P. (1986). Physiological correlates of extreme intellectual precocity. *Neuropsychologia, 24,* 719–725.

Benbow, C. P. (1988). Sex differences in mathematical reasoning ability in intellectually talented preadolescents: Their nature, effects, and possible causes. *Behavioral and Brain Science, 11,* 169–232.

Benbow, C. P., & Arjimand, O. (1990). Predictors of high academic achievement in mathematics and science by mathematically talented students: A longitudinal study. *Journal of Educational Psychology, 82,* 430–441.

Benbow, C. P., & Stanley, J. C. (1980). Sex differences in mathematical ability: Fact or artifact? *Science, 210,* 1262–1264.

Benbow, C. P., & Stanley, J. C. (1983). Sex differences in mathematical reasoning: More facts. *Science, 222,* 1029–1031.

Bench, R. J., Collyer, Y., Mentz, L., & Wilson, I. (1976). Studies in infant behavioural audiometry: I. Neonates. *Audiology, 15,* 85–105.

Benedict, R. (1934a). Anthropology and the abnormal. *Journal of Genetic Psychology, 10,* 59–82.

Benedict, R. (1934b). *Patterns of culture.* Boston: Houghton Mifflin.

Bentler, P. M. (1992). Etiologies and consequences of adolescent drug use: Implications for prevention. *Journal of Addictive Diseases, 11,* 47–61.

Berenbaum, S. A., & Hines, M. A. (1992). Early androgens are related to childhood sex-typed toy preferences. *Psychological Science, 3,* 203–206.

Berg, W. K., & Berg, K. M. (1987). Psychophysiological development in infancy: State, startle, and attention. In J. Osofsky (Ed.), *Handbook of infant development* (2nd ed., pp. 238–317). New York: Wiley.

Bergman, L. R., & Magnusson, D. (1986). Type A behavior: A longitudinal study from childhood to adulthood. *Psychosomatic Medicine, 48,* 134–142.

Berk, L. E. (1985). Relationship of caregiver education to child-oriented attitudes, job satisfaction, and behaviors toward children. *Child Care Quarterly, 14,* 103–129.

Berk, L. E. (1992a). Children's private speech: An overview of theory and the status of research. In R. M. Diaz & L. E. Berk (Eds.), *Private speech: From social interaction to self-regulation* (pp. 17–53). Hillsdale, NJ: Erlbaum.

Berk, L. E. (1992b). The extracurriculum. In P. W. Jackson (Ed.), *Handbook of research on curriculum* (pp. 1002–1043). New York: Macmillan.

Berk, L. E., & Landau, S. (1993). Private speech of learning disabled and normally achieving children in classroom academic and laboratory contexts. *Child Development, 64,* 556–571.

Berk, L. E., & Lewis, N. G. (1977). Sex role and social behavior in four school environments. *Elementary School Journal, 77,* 205–217.

Berk, L. E., & Spuhl, S. (1992, September). *Maternal teaching, private speech, and task performance.* Paper presented at the First International Conference on Sociocultural Research, Madrid, Spain.

Berko Gleason, J. (1977). Talking to children: Some notes on feedback. In C. E. Snow & A. Ferguson (Eds.), *Talking to children: Language acquisition and input* (pp. 199–205). Cambridge: Cambridge University Press.

Berko Gleason, J. (1989). Studying language development. In J. Berko Gleason (Ed.), *The development of language* (2nd ed., pp. 1–34). Columbus, OH: Merrill.

Berko, J. (1958). The child's learning of English morphology. *Word, 14,* 150–177.

Berkowitz, M. W., & Gibbs, J. C. (1983). Measuring the developmental features of moral discussion. *Merrill-Palmer Quarterly, 29,* 399–410.

Berman, P. (1980). Are women more responsive than men to the young? A review of developmental and situational variables. *Psychological Bulletin, 88,* 668–695.

Berman, P. W. (1986). Young children's responses to babies: Do they foreshadow differences between maternal and paternal styles? In A. Fogel & G. F. Melson (Eds.), *Origins of nurturance* (pp. 25–51). Hillsdale, NJ: Erlbaum.

Berndt, T. J. (1981). The effects of friendship on prosocial intentions and behavior between friends. *Developmental Psychology, 17,* 408–416.

Berndt, T. J. (1986). Children's comments about their friendships. In M. Perlmutter (Ed.), *Cognitive perspectives on children's social and behavioral development* (pp. 189–212). Hillsdale, NJ: Erlbaum.

Berndt, T. J. (1988). The nature and significance of children's friendships. In R. Vasta (Ed.), *Annals of child development* (Vol. 5, pp. 155–186). Greenwich, CT: JAI Press.

Berndt, T. J., Cheung, P. C., Lau, S., Hau, K-T., & Lew, W. J. F. (1993). Perceptions of parenting in mainland China, Taiwan, and Hong Kong: Sex differences and societal differences. *Developmental Psychology, 29,* 156–164.

Berndt, T. J., & Heller, K. A. (1986). Gender stereotypes and social inferences: A developmental study. *Journal of Personality and Social Psychology, 50,* 889–898.

Berndt, T. J., & Hoyle, S. G. (1985). Stability and change in childhood and adolescent friendships. *Developmental Psychology, 21,* 1007–1015.

Berndt, T. J., & Perry, T. B. (1990). Distinctive features and effects of early adolescent friendships. In R. Montemayor, G. R. Adams, & T. P. Gullotta (Eds.), *From childhood to adolescence: A transitional period?* (pp. 269–287). Newbury Park, CA: Sage.

Berrueta-Clement, J. R., Schweinhart, L. J., Barnett, W. S., Epstein, A. S., & Weikart, D. P. (1984). Changed lives: The effects of the Perry Preschool Program on youths through age 19. *Monographs of the High/Scope Research Foundation, 8.*

Bertenthal, B. I., & Campos, J. J. (1987). New directions in the study of early experience. *Child Development, 58,* 560–567.

Bertenthal, B. I., Campos, J. J., & Barrett, K. (1984). Self-produced locomotion: An organizer of emotional, cognitive, and social development in infancy. In R. Emde & R. Harmon (Eds.), *Continuities and discontinuities in development* (pp. 174–210). New York: Plenum.

Bertenthal, B. I., Campos, J. J., & Haith, M. (1980). Development of visual organization: The perception of subjective contours. *Child Development, 51,* 1077–1080.

Bertenthal, B. I., Proffitt, D. R., Kramer, S. J., & Spetner, N. B. (1987). Infants' encoding of kinetic displays varying in relative coherence. *Developmental Psychology, 23,* 171–178.

Bertenthal, B. I., Proffitt, D. R., Spetner, N. B., & Thomas, M. A. (1985). The development of infant sensitivity to biomechanical motions. *Child Development, 56*, 531–543.

Best, D. L., & Ornstein, P. A. (1986). Children's generation and communication of mnemonic organizational strategies. *Developmental Psychology, 22*, 845–853.

Best, D. L., Williams, J. E., Cloud, J. M., Davis, S. W., Robertson, L. S., Edwards, J. R., Giles, H., & Fowles, J. (1977). Development of sex-trait stereotypes among young children in the United States, England, and Ireland. *Child Development, 48*, 1375–1384.

Beunen, G. P., Malina, R. M., Van't Hof, M. A., Simons, J., Ostyn, M., Renson, R., & Van Gerven, D. (1988). *Adolescent growth and motor performance.* Champaign, IL: Human Kinetics.

Bever, T. G. (1982). Some implications of the nonspecific bases of language. In E. Wanner & L. R. Gleitman (Ed.), *Language acquisition: The state of the art* (pp. 429–449). Cambridge: Cambridge University Press.

Bhavnagri, N., & Parke, R. D. (1991). Parents as direct facilitators of children's peer relationships: Effects of age of child and sex of parent. *Journal of Social and Personal Relationships, 8*, 423–440.

Bialystok, E. (1986). Factors in the growth of linguistic awareness. *Child Development, 57*, 498–510.

Bianchi, B. D., & Bakeman, R. (1978). Sex-typed affiliation preferences observed in preschoolers: Traditional and open school differences. *Child Development, 49*, 910–912.

Bickerton, D. (1981). *Roots of language.* Ann Arbor, MI: Karoma.

Bickerton, D. (1984). The language bioprogram hypothesis. *Behavioral and Brain Sciences, 7*, 178–188.

Biederman, J., Faraone, S. V., Keenan, K., Knee, D., & Tsuang, M. T. (1990). Family-genetic and psychosocial risk factors in DSM-III attention deficit disorder. *Journal of the American Academy of Child and Adolescent Psychiatry, 29*, 526–533.

Bierman, K. L. (1986). Process of change during social skills training with preadolescents and its relation to treatment outcome. *Child Development, 57*, 230–240.

Bierman, K. L., Miller, C. L., & Stabb, S. D. (1987). Improving the social behavior and peer acceptance of rejected boys: Effects of social skill training with instructions and prohibitions. *Journal of Consulting and Clinical Psychology, 55*, 194–200.

Bierman, K. L., Smoot, D. L., & Aumiller, K. (1993). Characteristics of aggressive-rejected, aggressive (nonrejected), and rejected (nonaggressive) boys. *Child Development, 64*, 139–151.

Biernat, M. (1991a). A multi-component, developmental analysis of sex-typing. *Sex Roles, 24*, 567–586.

Biernat, M. (1991b). Gender stereotypes and the relationship between masculinity and femininity: A developmental analysis. *Journal of Personality and Social Psychology, 61*, 351–365.

Bigelow, B. J. (1977). Children's friendship expectations: A cognitive-developmental study. *Child Development, 48*, 246–253.

Bigelow, B. J., & LaGaipa, J. J. (1975). Children's written descriptions of friendship: A multidimensional analysis. *Developmental Psychology, 11*, 857–858.

Bigler, R. S., & Liben, L. S. (1992). Cognitive mechanisms in children's gender stereotyping: Theoretical and educational implications of a cognitive-based intervention. *Child Development, 63*, 1351–1363.

Billy, J. O. G., Tanfer, K., Grady, W. R., & Klepinger, D. H. (1993). The sexual behavior of men in the United States. *Family Planning Perspectives, 25*, 52–60.

Birch, L. L. (1987). Children's food preferences: Developmental patterns and environmental influences. In R. Vasta (Ed.), *Annals of child development* (Vol. 4, pp. 131–170). Greenwich, CT: JAI Press.

Birnholz, J. C., & Benacerraf, B. R. (1983). The development of human fetal hearing. *Science, 222*, 516–518.

Bischof-Köhler, D. (1991). The development of empathy in infants. In M. E. Lamb & H. Keller (Eds.), *Infant development: Perspectives from German-speaking countries* (pp. 1–33). Hillsdale, NJ: Erlbaum.

Bischofshausen, S. (1985). Developmental differences in schema dependency for temporally ordered story events. *Journal of Psycholinguistic Research, 14*, 543–556.

Bishop, S. M., & Ingersoll, G. M. (1989). Effects of marital conflict and family structure on the self-concepts of pre- and early adolescents. *Journal of Youth and Adolescence, 18*, 25–38.

Bivens, J. A., & Berk, L. E. (1990). A longitudinal study of the development of elementary school children's private speech. *Merrill-Palmer Quarterly, 36*, 443–463.

Bjorklund, D. F. (1987). How age changes in knowledge base contribute to the development of children's memory: An interpretive review. *Developmental Review, 7*, 93–130.

Bjorklund, D. F., & Harnishfeger, K. K. (1987). Developmental differences in the mental effort requirements for the use of an organizational strategy in free recall. *Journal of Experimental Child Psychology, 44*, 109–125.

Bjorklund, D. F., & Jacobs, J. W. (1985). Associative and categorical processes in children's memory: The role of automaticity in the development of organization in free recall. *Journal of Experimental Child Psychology, 39*, 599–617.

Blake, J., & Boysson-Bardies, B. de (1992). Patterns in babbling: A cross-linguistic study. *Journal of Child Language, 19*, 51–74.

Blakemore, J. E. O., LaRue, A. A., & Olejnik, A. B. (1979). Sex-appropriate toy preference and the ability to conceptualize toys as sex-role related. *Developmental Psychology, 15*, 339–340.

Blanchard, M., & Main, M. (1979). Avoidance of the attachment figure and social-emotional adjustment in day-care infants. *Developmental Psychology, 15*, 445–446.

Blanck, G. (1990). Vygotsky: The man and his cause. In L. C. Moll (Ed.), *Vygotsky and education* (pp. 31–58). New York: Cambridge University Press.

Blaney, P. H. (1986). Affect and memory: A review. *Psychological Bulletin, 98*, 229–246.

Blasi, A. (1980). Bridging moral cognition and moral action: A critical review of the literature. *Psychological Bulletin, 88*, 593–637.

Blasi, A. (1983). Moral cognition and moral action: A theoretical perspective. *Developmental Review, 3*, 178–210.

Blasi, A. (1990). Kohlberg's theory and moral motivation. In D. Schrader (Ed.), *New directions for child development* (No. 47, pp. 51–57). San Francisco: Jossey-Bass.

Blass, E. M., Ganchrow, J. R., & Steiner, J. E. (1984). Classical conditioning in newborn humans 2–48 hours of age. *Infant Behavior and Development, 7*, 223–235.

Blass, F. M., & Hoffmeyer, L. B. (1991). Sucrose as an analgesic for newborn infants. *Pediatrics, 87*, 215–218.

Blatt, M., & Kohlberg, L. (1975). The effects of classroom moral discussion upon children's level of moral judgment. *Journal of Moral Education, 4*, 129–161.

Blaubergs, M. S. (1980, March). Sex-role stereotyping and gifted girls' experience and education. *Roeper Review, 2*(3), 13–15.

Block, J. (1971). *Lives through time.* Berkeley, CA: Bancroft Books.

Block, J. H. (1973). Conceptions of sex role: Some cross-cultural and longitudinal perspectives. *American Psychologist, 28*, 512–526.

Block, J. H. (1976). Issues, problems, and pitfalls in assessing sex differences: A critical review of "The Psychology of Sex Differences." *Merrill-Palmer Quarterly, 22,* 283–308.

Block, J. H. (1978). Another look at sex differentiation in the socialization behaviors of mothers and fathers. In J. Sherman & F. L. Denmark (Eds.), *Psychology of women: Future directions for research* (pp. 29–87). New York: Psychological Dimensions.

Block, J. H. (1983). Differential premises arising from differential socialization of the sexes: Some conjectures. *Child Development, 54,* 1335–1354.

Block, J. H., Block, J., & Harrington, D. (1975). *Sex role typing and instrumental behavior: A developmental study.* Paper presented at the annual meeting of the Society for Research in Child Development, Denver.

Block, J., Block, J. H., & Gjerde, P. F. (1988). Parental functioning and home environment in families of divorce: Prospective and concurrent analyses. *Journal of the American Academy of Child and Adolescent Psychiatry, 27,* 207–213.

Bloom, B. S. (Ed.). (1985). *Developing talent in young people.* New York: Ballantine.

Bloom, L. (1970). *Language development: Form and function in emerging grammars.* Cambridge, MA: MIT Press.

Bloom, L. (1990). Developments in expression: Affect and speech. In N. Stein & T. Trabasso (Eds.), *Psychological and biological approaches to emotion* (pp. 215–245). Hillsdale, NJ: Erlbaum.

Bloom, L., Lahey, M., Liften, K., & Fiess, K. (1980). Complex sentences: Acquisition of syntactic connections and the semantic relations they encode. *Journal of Child Language, 7,* 235–256.

Bloom, M. V. (1980). *Adolescent-parent separation.* New York: Gardner.

Bloom, P. (1990). Syntactic distinctions in child language. *Journal of Child Language, 17,* 343–355.

Blos, P. (1979). *The adolescent passage.* New York: International Universities Press.

Blotner, R., & Bearison, D. J. (1984). Developmental consistencies in socio-moral knowledge: Justice reasoning and altruistic behavior. *Merrill-Palmer Quarterly, 30,* 349–367.

Blurton Jones, N. (1972). Categories of child-child interaction. In N. Blurton Jones (Ed.), *Ethological studies of child behaviour* (pp. 97–127). Cambridge: Cambridge University Press.

Blyth, D., Hill, J., & Thiel, K. (1982). Early adolescents' significant others: Grade and gender differences in perceived relationships with familial and nonfamilial adults and young people. *Journal of Youth and Adolescence, 11,* 425–450.

Blyth, D. A., Simmons, R. G., & Zakin, D. F. (1985). Satisfaction with body image for early adolescent females: The impact of pubertal timing within different school environments. *Journal of Youth and Adolescence, 14,* 207–225.

Bobak, I. M., Jensen, M. D., & Zalar, M. K. (1989). *Maternity and gynecologic care.* St. Louis: Mosby.

Bodurtha, J., Tams, L., & Jackson-Cook, C. (1992). Prenatal genetic counseling: What is fragile X? *Virginia Medical Quarterly, 119,* 97–98.

Boer, F., Goedhart, A. W., & Treffers, P. D. A. (1992). Siblings and their parents. In F. Boer & J. Dunn (Eds.), *Children's sibling relationships* (pp. 41–54). Hillsdale, NJ: Erlbaum.

Bogatz, G. A., & Ball, S. (1972). *The second year of "Sesame Street": A continuing evaluation.* Princeton, NJ: Educational Testing Service.

Bohannon, J., & Symons, V. (1988, April). *Conversational conditions of children's imitation.* Paper presented at the biennial Conference on Human Development, Charleston, SC.

Bohannon, J. N., III, MacWhinney, B., & Snow, C. (1990). No negative evidence revisited: Beyond learnability or who has to prove what to whom. *Developmental Psychology, 26,* 221–226.

Bohannon, J. N., III, & Stanowicz, L. (1988). The issue of negative evidence: Adult responses to children's language errors. *Developmental Psychology, 24,* 684–689.

Bohannon, J. N., III, & Warren-Leubecker, A. (1989). Theoretical approaches to language acquisition. In J. Berko Gleason (Ed.), *The development of language* (2nd ed., pp. 167–223). Columbus, OH: Merrill.

Boismier, J. D. (1977). Visual stimulation and wake-sleep behavior in human neonates. *Developmental Psychobiology, 10,* 219–227.

Boldizar, J. P. (1991). Assessing sex typing and androgyny in children: The children's sex role inventory. *Developmental Psychology, 27,* 505–515.

Boldizar, J. P., Perry, D. G., & Perry, L. C. (1989). Outcome values and aggression. *Child Development, 60,* 571–579.

Bonvillian, J., Nelson, K. E., & Charrow, V. (1976). Language and language-related skills in deaf and hearing children. *Sign Language Studies, 12,* 211–250.

Booth, C. L., Rose-Krasnor, L., & Rubin, K. H. (1991). Relating preschoolers' social competence and their mothers' parenting behaviors to early attachment security and high-risk status. *Journal of Social and Personal Relationships, 8,* 363–382.

Borghraef, M., Fryns, J. P., Dielkens, A., Pyck, K., & van den Berghe, H. (1987). Fragile (X) syndrome: A study of the psychological profile of 23 prepubertal patients. *Clinical Genetics, 32,* 179–186.

Borja-Alvarez, T., Zarbatany, L., & Pepper, S. (1991). Contributions of male and female guests and hosts to peer group entry. *Child Development, 62,* 1079–1090.

Borke, H. (1975). Piaget's mountains revisited: Changes in the egocentric landscape. *Developmental Psychology, 11,* 240–243.

Borkowski, J. G., Carr, M., Rellinger, E., & Pressley, M. (1990). Self-regulated cognition: Interdependence of metacognition, attributions, and self-esteem. In B. Jones & L. Idol (Eds.), *Dimensions of thinking and cognitive instruction* (pp. 53–92). Hillsdale, NJ: Erlbaum.

Bornstein, M. H. (1988). Perceptual development across the life cycle. In M. H. Bornstein & M. E. Lamb (Eds.), *Developmental psychology: An advanced textbook* (pp. 151–204). Hillsdale, NJ: Erlbaum.

Bornstein, M. H. (1989). Sensitive periods in development: Structural characteristics and causal interpretations. *Psychological Bulletin, 105,* 179–197.

Bornstein, M. H., Kessen, W., & Weiskopf, S. (1976). The categories of hue in infancy. *Science, 191,* 201–202.

Bornstein, M. H., & Lamb, M. E. (1992). *Development in infancy: An introduction* (3rd ed.). New York: McGraw-Hill.

Bornstein, M. H., & Sigman, M. D. (1986). Continuity in mental development from infancy. *Child Development, 57,* 251–274.

Bornstein, M. H., Tal, J., Rahn, C., Galperín, C. Z., Pêcheux, M., Lamour, M., Toda, S., Azuma, H., Ogino, M., & Tamis-LeMonda, C. S. (1992). Functional analysis of the contents of maternal speech to infants of 5 and 13 months in four cultures: Argentina, France, Japan, and the United States. *Developmental Psychology, 28,* 593–603.

Borrine, M. L., Handal, P. J., Brown, N. Y., & Searight, H. R. (1991). Family conflict and adolescent adjustment in intact, divorced, and blended families. *Journal of Consulting and Clinical Psychology, 59,* 753–755.

Borstelmann, L. J. (1983). Children before psychology: Ideas about children from antiquity to the late 1800s. In W. Kessen (Ed.), *Handbook of child psychology: Vol. 1. History, theory, and methods* (4th ed., pp. 1–40). New York: Wiley.

Bouchard, T. J., Jr., Lykken, D. T., McGue, M., Segal, N. L., & Tellegen, A. (1990). Sources of human psychological differences: The Minnesota Study of Twins Reared Apart. *Science, 250,* 223–228.

Bouchard, T. J., Jr., & McGue, M. (1981). Familial studies of intelligence: A review. *Science, 212,* 1055–1058.

Bouchard, T. J., Jr., & Segal, N. L. (1985). Environment and IQ. In B. B. Wolman (Ed.), *Handbook of intelligence* (pp. 391–464). New York: Wiley.

Boukydis, C. F. Z. (1985). Perception of infant crying as an interpersonal event. In B. M. Lester & C. F. Z. Boukydis (Eds.), *Infant crying* (pp. 187–215). New York: Plenum.

Boukydis, C. F. Z., & Burgess, R. L. (1982). Adult physiological response to infant cries: Effects of temperament of infant, parental status and gender. *Child Development, 53,* 1291–1298.

Bower, G. (1981). Mood and memory. *American Psychologist, 36,* 128–148.

Bowerman, M. (1973). *Early syntactic development: A cross-linguistic study with special reference to Finnish.* Cambridge: Cambridge University Press.

Bowerman, M. (1989). Learning a semantic system: What role do cognitive predispositions play? In M. Rice & R. Schiefelbusch (Eds.), *The teachability of language* (pp. 133–170). Baltimore: Paul H. Brookes.

Bowlby, J. (1969). *Attachment and loss: Vol. 1. Attachment.* New York: Basic Books.

Bowlby, J. (1980). *Attachment and loss: Vol. 3. Loss.* New York: Basic Books.

Boyer, K., & Diamond, A. (1992). Development of memory for temporal order in infants and young children. In A. Diamond (Ed.), *Development and neural bases of higher cognitive function* (pp. 267–317). New York: New York Academy of Sciences.

Boyes, M. C., & Chandler, M. (1992). Cognitive development, epistemic doubt, and identity formation in adolescence. *Journal of Youth and Adolescence, 21,* 277–304.

Boysson-Bardies, B. de, & Vihman, M. M. (1991). Adaptation to language: Evidence from babbling and first words in four languages. *Language, 67,* 297–319.

Brabeck, M. (1983). Moral judgment: Theory and research on differences between males and females. *Developmental Review, 3,* 274–291.

Brackbill, Y., McManus, K., & Woodward, L. (1985). *Medication in maternity: Infant exposure and maternal information.* Ann Arbor: University of Michigan Press.

Brackbill, Y., & Nichols, P. L. (1982). A test of the confluence model of intellectual development. *Developmental Psychology, 18,* 192–198.

Bradley, R. H., & Caldwell, B. M. (1976). The relation of infants' home environments to mental test performance at fifty-four months: A follow-up study. *Child Development, 47,* 1172–1174.

Bradley, R. H., & Caldwell, B. M. (1979). Home Observation for Measurement of the Environment: A revision of the preschool scale. *American Journal of Mental Deficiency, 84,* 235–244.

Bradley, R. H., & Caldwell, B. M. (1981). The HOME Inventory: A validation of the preschool scale for black children. *Child Development, 52,* 708–710.

Bradley, R. H., & Caldwell, B. M. (1982). The consistency of the home environment and its relation to child development. *International Journal of Behavioral Development, 5,* 445–465.

Bradley, R. H., Caldwell, B. M., & Elardo, R. (1979). Home environment and cognitive development in the first 2 years: A cross-lagged panel analysis. *Developmental Psychology, 15,* 246–250.

Bradley, R. H., Caldwell, B. M., & Rock, S. L. (1988). Home environment and school performance: A ten-year follow-up and examination of three models of environmental action. *Child Development, 59,* 852–867.

Bradley, R. H., Caldwell, B. M., Rock, S. L., Hamrick, H. M., & Harris, P. (1988). Home Observation for Measurement of the Environment: Development of a home inventory for use with families having children 6 to 10 years old. *Contemporary Educational Psychology, 13,* 58–71.

Bradley, R. H., Caldwell, B. M., Rock, S. L., Ramey, C. T., Barnard, K. E., Gray, C., Hammond M. A., Mitchell, S., Gottfried, A., Siegel, L., & Johnson, D. L. (1989). Home environment and cognitive development in the first 3 years of life: A collaborative study involving six sites and three ethnic groups in North America. *Developmental Psychology, 25,* 217–235.

Braine, M. D. S. (1976). Children's first word combinations. *Monographs of the Society for Research in Child Development, 41* (1, Serial No. 164).

Braine, M. D. S. (1987). What is learned in acquiring word classes—A step toward an acquisition theory. In B. MacWhinney (Ed.), *Mechanisms of language acquisition* (pp. 65–87). Hillsdale, NJ: Erlbaum.

Brainerd, C. J. (1978). *Piaget's theory of intelligence.* Englewood Cliffs, NJ: Prentice-Hall.

Brand, E., Clingempeel, W. E., & Bowen-Woodward, K. (1988). Family relationships and children's psychological adjustment in stepmother and stepfather families: Findings and conclusions from the Philadelphia Stepfamily Research Project. In E. M. Hetherington & J. D. Arasteh (Eds.), *Impact of divorce, single parenting, and stepparenting on children* (pp. 299–324). Hillsdale, NJ: Erlbaum.

Bransford, J. D., Stein, B. S., Shelton, T. S., & Owings, R. A. (1981). Cognition and adaptation: The importance of learning to learn. In J. Harvey (Ed.), *Cognition, social behavior, and the environment* (pp. 93–110). Hillsdale, NJ: Erlbaum.

Braungart, J. M., Fulker, D. W., & Plomin, R. (1992). Genetic mediation of the home environment during infancy: A sibling adoption study of the HOME. *Developmental Psychology, 28,* 1048–1055.

Braungart, J. M., Plomin, R., DeFries, J. C., & Fulker, D. W. (1992). Genetic influence on tester-rated infant temperament as assessed by Bayley's Infant Behavior Record: Nonadoptive and adoptive siblings and twins. *Developmental Psychology, 28,* 40–47.

Bray, J. H. (1988). Children's development during early remarriage. In E. M. Hetherington & J. D. Arasteh (Ed.), *Impact of divorce, single parenting, and stepparenting on children* (pp. 279–298). Hillsdale, NJ: Erlbaum.

Brazelton, T. B. (1984). *Neonatal Behavioral Assessment Scale.* Philadelphia: Lippincott.

Brazelton, T. B., Koslowski, B., & Tronick, E. (1976). Neonatal behavior among urban Zambians and Americans. *Journal of the American Academy of Child Psychiatry, 15,* 97–107.

Brazelton, T. B., Nugent, J. K., & Lester, B. M. (1987). Neonatal Behavioral Assessment Scale. In J. D. Osofsky (Ed.), *Handbook of infant development* (2nd ed., pp. 780–817). New York: Wiley.

Brenes, M. E., Eisenberg, N., & Helmstadter, G. C. (1985). Sex role development of preschoolers from two-parent and one-parent families. *Merrill-Palmer Quarterly, 31,* 33–46.

Brennan, W. M., Ames, E. W., & Moore, R. W. (1966). Age differences in infants' attention to patterns of different complexities. *Science, 151,* 354–356.

Brenner, D., & Hinsdale, G. (1978). Body build stereotypes and self-identification in three age groups of females. *Adolescence, 13,* 551–562.

Bretherton, I. (1992). The origins of attachment theory: John Bowlby and Mary Ainsworth. *Developmental Psychology, 28,* 759–775.

Bretherton, I., Fritz, J., Zahn-Waxler, C., & Ridgeway, D. (1986). Learning to talk about emotions: A functionalist perspective. *Child Development, 57,* 529–548.

Bretherton, I., O'Connell, B., Shore, C., & Bates, E. (1984). The effect of contextual variation on symbolic play: Development from 20 to 28 months. In I. Bretherton (Ed.), *Symbolic play and the development of social understanding* (pp. 271–298). New York: Academic Press.

Broberg, A., Lamb, M. E., & Hwang, P. (1990). Inhibition: Its stability and correlates in 16- to 40-month-old children. *Child Development, 61,* 1153–1163.

Brody, G. H., Graziano, W. G., & Musser, L. M. (1983). Familiarity and children's behavior in same-age and mixed-age peer groups. *Developmental Psychology, 19,* 568–576.

Brody, G. H., Stoneman, Z., & Burke, M. (1987). Child temperaments, maternal differential behavior, and sibling relationships. *Developmental Psychology, 23,* 354–362.

Brody, G. H., Stoneman, Z., & McCoy, J. K. (1992). Associations of maternal and paternal direct and differential behavior with sibling relationships: Contemporaneous and longitudinal analyses. *Child Development, 63,* 82–92.

Brody, G. H., Stoneman, Z., McCoy, J. K., & Forehand, R. (1992). Contemporaneous and longitudinal associations of sibling conflict with family relationship assessments and family discussions about sibling problems. *Child Development, 63,* 391–400.

Brody, L. E., & Benbow, C. P. (1987). Accelerative strategies: How effective are they for the gifted? *Gifted Child Quarterly, 3,* 105–110.

Brody, N. (1987). Jensen, Gottfredson, and the black-white difference in intelligence test scores. *Behavioral and Brain Sciences, 10,* 507–508.

Brody, N. (1992). *Intelligence* (2nd ed.). San Diego: Academic Press.

Broman, S. H. (1983). Obstetric medications. In C. C. Brown (Ed.), *Childhood learning disabilities and prenatal risk* (pp. 56–64). New York: Johnson & Johnson.

Bronfenbrenner, U. (1979). *The ecology of human development: Experiments by nature and design.* Cambridge, MA: Harvard University Press.

Bronfenbrenner, U. (1989). Ecological systems theory. In R. Vasta (Ed.), *Annals of child development* (Vol. 6, pp. 187–251). Greenwich, CT: JAI Press.

Bronfenbrenner, U., & Crouter, A. C. (1983). The evolution of environmental models in developmental research. In W. Kessen (Ed.), *Handbook of child psychology: Vol. 1. History, theory and methods* (pp. 357–476). New York: Wiley.

Bronson, G. W. (1991). Infant differences in rate of visual encoding. *Child Development, 62,* 44–54.

Bronson, W. C. (1981). *Toddlers' behaviors with agemates: Issues of interaction, cognition, and affect.* Norwood, NJ: Ablex.

Brooks, J., & Lewis, M. (1976). Infants' responses to strangers: Midget, adult, and child. *Child Development, 47,* 323–332.

Brooks-Gunn, J. (1986). The relationship of maternal beliefs about sex typing to maternal and young children's behavior. *Sex Roles, 14,* 21–35.

Brooks-Gunn, J. (1988a). Antecedents and consequences of variations in girls' maturational timing. *Journal of Adolescent Health Care, 9,* 365–373.

Brooks-Gunn, J. (1988b). The impact of puberty and sexual activity upon the health and education of adolescent girls and boys. *Peabody Journal of Education, 64,* 88–113.

Brooks-Gunn, J., & Furstenberg, F. F., Jr. (1989). Adolescent sexual behavior. *American Psychologist, 44,* 249–257.

Brooks-Gunn, J., & Reiter, E. O. (1990). The role of pubertal processes in the early adolescent transition. In S. Feldman & G. Elliott (Eds.), *At the threshold: The developing adolescent* (pp. 16–53). Cambridge, MA: Harvard University Press.

Brooks-Gunn, J., & Ruble, D. N. (1980). Menarche: The interaction of physiology, cultural, and social factors. In A. J. Dan, E. A. Graham, & C. P. Beecher (Eds.), *The menstrual cycle: A synthesis of interdisciplinary research* (pp. 141–159). New York: Springer-Verlag.

Brooks-Gunn, J., & Ruble, D. N. (1983). The experience of menarche from a developmental perspective. In J. Brooks-Gunn & A. C. Peterson (Eds.), *Girls at puberty* (pp. 155–177). New York: Plenum.

Brooks-Gunn, J., & Warren, M. P. (1989). Biological and social contributions to negative affect in young adolescent girls. *Child Development, 60,* 40–55.

Brooks-Gunn, J., Warren, M. P., Samelson, M., & Fox, R. (1986). Physical similarity of and disclosure of menarcheal status to friends: Effects of grade and pubertal status. *Journal of Early Adolescence, 6,* 3–14.

Brophy, J. E. (1983). Research on the self-fulfilling prophecy and teacher expectations. *Journal of Educational Psychology, 75,* 631–661.

Brophy, J. E., & Evertson, C. (1976). *Learning from teaching: A developmental perspective.* Boston: Allyn and Bacon.

Brophy, J. E., & Good, T. L. (1974). *Teacher–student relationships: Causes and consequences.* New York: Holt, Rinehart and Winston.

Brophy, J. E., & Good, T. L. (1986). Teacher behavior and student achievement. In M. C. Wittrock (Ed.), *Handbook of research on teaching* (3rd ed., pp. 328–375). New York: Macmillan.

Brown, A. L., Bransford, J. D., Ferrara, R. A., & Campione, J. C. (1983). Learning, remembering and understanding. In J. H. Flavell & E. M. Markman (Eds.), *Handbook of child psychology: Vol. 3. Cognitive development* (4th ed., pp. 77–166). New York: Wiley.

Brown, A. L., & Campione, J. C. (1972). Recognition memory for perceptually similar pictures in preschool children. *Journal of Experimental Psychology, 95,* 55–62.

Brown, A. L., Smiley, S. S., Day, J. D., Townsend, M., & Lawton, S.Q.C. (1977). Intrusion of a thematic idea in children's recall of prose. *Child Development, 48,* 1454–1466.

Brown, A. L., Smiley, S. S., & Lawton, S. Q. C. (1978). The effects of experience on the selection of suitable retrieval cues for studying texts. *Child Development, 49,* 829–835.

Brown, B. (1990). Peer groups. In S. Feldman & G. Elliott (Eds.), *At the threshold: The developing adolescent* (pp. 171–196). Cambridge, MA: Cambridge University Press.

Brown, B. B., Clasen, D., & Eicher, S. (1986). Perceptions of peer pressure, peer conformity dispositions, and self-reported behavior among adolescents. *Developmental Psychology, 22,* 521–530.

Brown, B. B., Lohr, M. J., & McClenahan, E. L. (1986). Early adolescents' perceptions of peer pressure. *Journal of Early Adolescence, 6,* 139–154.

Brown, J. R., & Dunn, J. (1992). Talk with your mother or your sibling? Developmental changes in early family conversations about feelings. *Child Development, 63,* 336–349.

Brown, R. (1973). *A first language: The early stages.* Cambridge, MA: Harvard University Press.

Brown, R., & Hanlon, C. (1970). Derivational complexity and order of acquisition in child speech. In J. R. Hayes (Ed.), *Cognition and the development of language* (pp. 11–53). New York: Wiley.

Brownell, C. A. (1986). Convergent developments: Cognitive-developmental correlates of growth in infant/toddler peer skills. *Child Development, 57,* 275–286.

Brownell, C. A., & Carriger, M. S. (1990). Changes in cooperation and self-other differentiation during the second year. *Child Development, 61,* 1164–1174.

Bruch, H. (1970). Juvenile obesity: Its courses and outcome. In C. V. Rowlan (Ed.), *Anorexia and obesity* (pp. 231–254). Boston: Little, Brown.

Bruder, G. E., Meyer-Bahlburg, H. F. L., Squire, J. M., & Ehrhardt, A. A. (1987). Dichotic listening following idiopathic precocious puberty: Speech processing capacity and temporal efficiency. *Brain and Language, 31,* 267–275.

Brumberg, J. J. (1988). *Fasting girls.* Cambridge, MA: Harvard University Press.

Bruner, J. S. (1983). *Child's talk: Learning to use language.* Oxford: Oxford University Press.

Bryant, B. K. (1982). An index of empathy for children and adolescents. *Child Development, 53,* 413–425.

Buchanan, C. M., Maccoby, E. E., & Dornbusch, S. M. (1991). Caught between parents: Adolescents' experience in divorced homes. *Child Development, 62,* 1008–1029.

Buck, G. M., Cookfair, D. L., Michalek, A. M., Nasca, P. C., Standfast, S. J., Sever, L. E., & Kramer, A. A. (1989). Intrauterine growth retardation and risk of sudden infant death syndrome (SIDS). *American Journal of Epidemiology, 129,* 874–884.

Bugental, D. B., Blue, J., Cortez, V., Fleck, K., & Rodriquez, A. (1992). Influences of witnessed affect on information processing in children. *Child Development, 63,* 774–786.

Bugental, D. B., Blue, J., & Cruzcosa, M. (1989). Perceived control over caregiving outcomes: Implications for child abuse. *Developmental Psychology, 25,* 532–539.

Buhrmester, D., & Furman, W. (1987). The development of companionship and intimacy. *Child Development, 58,* 1101–1115.

Buhrmester, D., & Furman, W. (1990). Perceptions of sibling relationships during middle childhood and adolescence. *Child Development, 61,* 1387–1398.

Bukowski, W. M., & Kramer, T. L. (1986). Judgments of the features of friendship among early adolescent boys and girls. *Journal of Early Adolescence, 6,* 331–338.

Bulatao, R. A., & Arnold, F. (1977). *Relationships between the value and cost of children and fertility: Cross-cultural evidence.* Paper presented at the General Conference of the International Union for the Scientific Study of Population, Mexico City.

Bulkley, J. A. (1989). The impact of new child witness research on sexual abuse prosecutions. In S. J. Ceci, D. F. Ross, & M. P. Toglia (Eds.), *Perspectives on children's testimony* (pp. 208–229). New York: Springer-Verlag.

Bullock, D., & Merrill, L. (1980). The impact of personal preference on consistency through time: The case of childhood aggression. *Child Development, 51,* 808–814.

Bullock, M. (1985). Causal reasoning and developmental change over the preschool years. *Human Development, 28,* 169–191.

Bullock, M., Gelman, R., & Baillargeon, R. (1982). The development of causal reasoning. In W. J. Friedman (Ed.), *The developmental psychology of time* (pp. 209–254). New York: Academic Press.

Bullock, M., & Lutkenhaus, P. (1990). Who am I? The development of self-understanding in toddlers. *Merrill-Palmer Quarterly, 36,* 217–238.

Burns, S. M., & Brainerd, C. J. (1979). Effects of constructive and dramatic play on perspective taking in very young children. *Developmental Psychology, 15,* 512–521.

Burton, B. K. (1992). Limb anomalies associated with chorionic villus sampling. *Obstetrics and Gynecology, 79* (Pt. 1), 726–730.

Bushnell, E.W. (1985). The decline of visually guided reaching during infancy. *Infant Behavior and Development, 8,* 139–155.

Buss, A. H., & Plomin, R. (1984). *Temperament: Early developing personality traits.* Hillsdale, NJ: Erlbaum.

Bussey, K. (1992). Lying and truthfulness: Children's definitions, standards, and evaluative reactions. *Child Development, 63,* 129–137.

Bussey, K., & Bandura, A. (1984). Influence of gender constancy and social power on sex-linked modeling. *Journal of Personality and Social Psychology, 47,* 1292–1302.

Bussey, K., & Bandura, A. (1992). Self-regulatory mechanisms governing gender development. *Child Development, 63,* 1236–1250.

Butler, G. E., McKie, M., & Ratcliffe, S. G. (1990). The cyclical nature of prepubertal growth. *Annals of Human Biology, 17,* 177–198.

Bybee, J., & Slobin, D. (1982). Rules and schemes in the development and use of the English past tense. *Language, 58,* 265–289.

Byrd, D. M., & Gholson, B. (1985). Reading, memory, and metacognition. *Journal of Educational Psychology, 77,* 428–436.

Byrne, M. C. (1973). The development of role taking in adolescence. *Dissertation Abstracts International, 34* 56478. (University Microfilms No. 74-11, 314).

Byrne, M. C., & Hayden, E. (1980). *Topic maintenance and topic establishment in mother-child dialogue.* Paper presented at the meeting of the American Speech and Hearing Association, Detroit, MI.

C

Cahan, L. S., Filby, N. N., McCutcheon, G., & Kyle, D. W. (1983). *Class size and instruction.* New York: Longman.

Cain, V. S., & Hofferth, S. L. (1989). Parental choice of self-care for school-age children. *Journal of Marriage and the Family, 51,* 65–77.

Caine, N. (1986). Behavior during puberty and adolescence. In G. Mitchell & J. Erwin (Eds.), *Comparative primate biology: Vol. 2A. Behavior, conservation, and ecology* (pp. 327–361). New York: Alan R. Liss.

Cairns, R. B. (1983). The emergence of developmental psychology. In W. Kessen (Ed.), *Handbook of child psychology: Vol. 1. History, theory, and methods* (4th ed., pp. 41–102). New York: Wiley.

Cairns, R. B. (1992). The making of a developmental science: The contributions and intellectual heritage of James Mark Baldwin. *Developmental Psychology, 28*, 17–24.

Cairns, R. B., Cairns, B. D., Neckerman, H. J., Ferguson, L. L., & Gariépy, J-L. (1989). Growth and aggression: 1. Childhood to early adolescence. *Developmental Psychology, 25*, 320–330.

Caldas, S. J. (1993). Current theoretical perspectives on adolescent pregnancy and childbearing in the United States. *Journal of Adolescent Research, 8*, 4–20.

Caldera, Y. M., Huston, A. C., & O'Brien, M. (1989). Social interactions and play patterns of parents and toddlers with feminine, masculine, and neutral toys. *Child Development, 60*, 70–76.

Caldwell, B. M. (1993). Impact of day care on the child. *Pediatrics, 91*, 225–228.

Camara, K. A., & Resnick, G. (1988). Interparental conflict and cooperation: Factors moderating children's post-divorce adjustment. In E. M. Hetherington & J. D. Arasteh (Ed.), *Impact of divorce, single parenting, and stepparenting on children* (pp. 169–195). Hillsdale, NJ: Erlbaum.

Camarata, S., & Leonard, L. B. (1986). Young children pronounce object words more accurately than action words. *Journal of Child Language, 13*, 51–65.

Campbell, F. A., & Ramey, C. T. (1991). *The Carolina Abecedarian Project.* In M. Burchinal (Chair), Early experience and children's competencies: New findings from four, longitudinal studies. Symposium presented at the biennial meeting of the Society for Research in Child Development, Seattle, WA.

Campbell, P. F., & Schwartz, S. S. (1986). Microcomputers in the preschool: Children, parents, and teachers. In P. Campbell & G. Fein (Eds.), *Young children and microcomputers* (pp. 45–60). Englewood Cliffs, NJ: Prentice-Hall.

Campbell, S. B., Ewing, E. J., Breaux, A. M., & Szumowski, E. K. (1986). Parent referred problem 3-year-olds: Follow-up at school entry. *Journal of Child Psychology and Psychiatry, 27*, 473–488.

Campos, J. J., & Bertenthal, B. I. (1989). Locomotion and psychological development. In F. Morrison, K. Lord, & D. Keating (Eds.), *Applied developmental psychology* (Vol. 3, pp. 229–258). New York: Academic Press.

Campos, J. J., Caplovitz, K. B., Lamb, M. E., Goldsmith, H. H., Stenberg, C. (1983). Socioemotional development. In M. M. Haith & J. J. Campos (Eds.), *Handbook of child psychology: Vol. 3. Infancy and developmental psychobiology* (pp. 783–915). New York: Wiley.

Campos, R. G. (1989). Soothing pain-elicited distress in infants with swaddling and pacifiers. *Child Development, 60*, 781–792.

Camras, L. A., Oster, H., Campos, J. J., Miyake, K., & Bradshaw, D. (1992). Japanese and American infants' responses to arm restraint. *Developmental Psychology, 28*, 578–583.

Camras, L. A., & Sachs, V. B. (1991). Social referencing and caretaker expressive behavior in a day care setting. *Infant Behavior and Development, 14*, 27–36.

Canter, R. J., & Ageton, S. S. (1984). The epidemiology of adolescent sex-role attitudes. *Sex Roles, 11*, 657–676.

Capaldi, D. M., & Patterson, G. R. (1991). Relation of parental transitions to boys' adjustment problems: I. A linear hypothesis. II. Mothers at risk for transitions and unskilled parenting. *Developmental Psychology, 27*, 489–504.

Capelli, C. A., Nakagawa, N., & Madden, C. M. (1990). How children understand sarcasm: The role of context and intonation. *Child Development, 61*, 1824–1841.

Caplan, M., Vespo, J., Pedersen, J., & Hay, D. F. (1991). Conflict and its resolution in small groups of one- and two-year-olds. *Child Development, 62*, 1513–1524.

Capron, A. M. (1991). Whose child is this? *Hastings Center Report, 21*(6), 37–38.

Cardon, L. R., Fulker, D. W., DeFries, J. C., & Plomin, R. (1992). Continuity and change in general cognitive ability from 1 to 7 years of age. *Developmental Psychology, 28*, 64–73.

Carey, S. (1978). The child as word learner. In M. Halle, G. Miller, & J. Bresnan (Eds.), *Linguistic theory and psychological reality* (pp. 264–293). Cambridge, MA: MIT Press.

Carey, S., & Gelman, R. (Eds.). (1991). *The epigenesis of mind: Essays on biology and cognition.* Hillsdale, NJ: Erlbaum.

Carlson, B. E. (1984). The father's contribution to child care: Effects on children's perceptions of parental roles. *American Journal of Orthopsychiatry, 54*, 123–136.

Carlson, C. L., Lahey, B. B., & Neeper, R. (1984). Peer assessment of the social behavior of accepted, rejected, and neglected children. *Journal of Abnormal Child Psychology, 12*, 189–198.

Carlson, V., Cicchietti, D., Barnett, D., & Braunwald, K. (1989). Disorganized/disoriented attachment relationship in maltreated infants. *Child Development, 25*, 525–531.

Caron, A. J., Caron, R. F., & MacLean, D. J. (1988). Infant discrimination of naturalistic emotional expressions: The role of face and voice. *Child Development, 59*, 603–616.

Carpenter, C. J. (1983). Activity structure and play: Implications for socialization. In M. Liss (Ed.), *Social and cognitive skills: Sex roles and children's play* (pp. 117–145). New York: Academic Press.

Carpenter, C. J., Huston, A. C., & Holt, W. (1986). Modification of preschool sex-typed behaviors by participation in adult-structured activities. *Sex Roles, 14*, 603–615.

Carr, M., Borkowski, J. G., & Maxwell, S. E. (1991). Motivational components of underachievement. *Developmental Psychology, 27*, 108–118.

Carr, M., & Schneider, W. (1991). Long-term maintenance of organizational strategies in kindergarten children. *Contemporary Educational Psychology, 16*, 61–75.

Carr, S., Dabbs, J., & Carr, T. (1975). Mother-infant attachment: The importance of the mother's visual field. *Child Development, 46*, 331–338.

Carraher, T., Schliemann, A. D., & Carraher, D. W. (1988). Mathematical concepts in everyday life. In G. B. Saxe & M. Gearhart (Eds.), *New directions for child development* (Vol. 41, pp. 71–87). San Francisco: Jossey-Bass.

Carruth, B. R., Goldberg, D. L., & Skinner, J. D. (1991). Do parents and peers mediate the influence of television advertising on food-related purchases? *Journal of Adolescent Research, 6*, 253–271.

Carter, D. B., & Levy, G. D. (1988). Cognitive aspects of early sex-role development: The influence of gender schemas on preschoolers' memories and preferences for sex-typed toys and activities. *Child Development, 59*, 782–792.

Carter, D. B., & Levy, G. D. (1991). Gender schemas and the salience of gender: Individual differences in nonreversal discrimination learning. *Sex Roles, 25*, 555–567.

Carter, D. B., & Patterson, C. J. (1982). Sex roles as social conventions: The development of children's conceptions of sex-role stereotypes. *Developmental Psychology, 18*, 812–824.

Carter, K., Sabers, D., Cushing, K., Pinnegar, S., & Berliner, D. C. (1987). Processing and using information about students: A study of expert, novice, and postulant teachers. *Teaching & Teacher Education, 3*, 147–157.

Case, R. (1977). Responsiveness to conservation training as a function of induced subjective uncertainty, M-space, and cognitive style. *Canadian Journal of Behavioral Sciences, 9,* 12–25.

Case, R. (1978). Intellectual development from birth to adulthood: A neo-Piagetian approach. In R. S. Siegler (Ed.), *Children's thinking: What develops?* (pp. 37–71). Hillsdale, NJ: Erlbaum.

Case, R. (1985). *Intellectual development: A systematic reinterpretation.* New York: Academic Press.

Case, R. (1991). Stages in the development of the young child's first sense of self. *Developmental Review, 11,* 210–230.

Case, R. (1992). *The mind's staircase.* Hillsdale, NJ: Erlbaum.

Case, R., & Griffin, S. (1990). Child cognitive development: The role of central conceptual structures in the development of scientific and social thought. In C. A. Hauert (Ed.), *Developmental psychology: Cognitive, perceptuo-motor and neuropsychological perspectives* (pp. 193–230). Amsterdam: North Holland.

Case, R., Griffin, S., McKeough, A., & Okamoto, Y. (1992). Parallels in the development of children's social, numerical, and spatial thought. In R. Case (Ed.), *The mind's staircase* (pp. 269–284). Hillsdale, NJ: Erlbaum.

Casey, M. B. (1986). Individual differences in selective attention among prereaders: A key to mirror-image confusions. *Developmental Psychology, 22,* 58–66.

Casey, M. B., Tivnan, T., Riley, E., & Spenciner, L. (1991). Differentiating preschoolers' sequential planning ability from their general intelligence: A study of organization, systematic responding, and efficiency in young children. *Journal of Applied Developmental Psychology, 12,* 19–32.

Caspi, A., Elder, G. H., Jr., & Bem, D. J. (1987). Moving against the world: Life-course patterns of explosive children. *Developmental Psychology, 23,* 308–313.

Caspi, A., Elder, G. H., Jr., & Bem, D. J. (1988). Moving away from the world: Life-course patterns of shy children. *Developmental Psychology, 24,* 824–831.

Caspi, A., Lynam, D., Moffitt, T. E., & Silva, P. A. (1993). Unraveling girls' delinquency: Biological, dispositional, and contextual contributions to adolescent misbehavior. *Developmental Psychology, 29,* 19–30.

Cassidy, J., Parke, R. D., Butkovsky, L., & Braungart, J. M. (1992). Family-peer connections: The roles of emotional expressiveness within the family and children's understanding of emotions. *Child Development, 63,* 603–618.

Catherwood, D., Crassini, B., & Freiberg, K. (1989). Infant response to stimuli of similar hue and dissimilar shape: Tracing the origins of the categorization of objects by hue. *Child Development, 60,* 752–762.

Cattell, J. M. (1890). Mental tests and measurements. *Mind, 15,* 373–381.

Cattell, R. B. (1971). *Abilities: Their structure, growth and action.* Boston: Houghton Mifflin.

Cattell, R. B. (1987). *Intelligence: Its structure, growth and action.* Amsterdam: North-Holland.

Cauce, A. M. (1987). School and peer competence in early adolescence: A test of domain-specific self-perceived competence. *Developmental Psychology, 23,* 287–291.

Caudill, W. (1973). Psychiatry and anthropology: The individual and his nexus. In L. Nader & T. W. Maretzki (Eds.), *Cultural illness and health: Essays in human adaptation* (Anthropological Studies 9, pp. 67–77). Washington, DC: American Anthropological Association.

Caudill, W., & Frost, L. (1975). A comparison of maternal care and infant behavior in Japanese-American, American, and Japanese families. In U. Bronfenbrenner & M. A. Mahoney (Eds.), *Influences on human development* (2nd ed., pp. 329–342). Hinsdale, IL: Dryden.

Cazden, C. (1984). *Effective instructional practices in bilingual education.* Washington, DC: National Institute of Education.

Ceci, S. J. (1989). On domain specificity . . . more of less general and specific constraints on cognitive development. *Merrill-Palmer Quarterly, 35,* 131–142.

Ceci, S. J. (1990). *On intelligence . . . More or less.* Englewood Cliffs, NJ: Prentice-Hall.

Ceci, S. J. (1991). How much does schooling influence general intelligence and its cognitive components? A reassessment of the evidence. *Developmental Psychology, 27,* 703–722.

Cernoch, J. M., & Porter, R. H. (1985). Recognition of maternal axillary odors by infants. *Child Development, 56,* 1593–1598.

Chalmers, J. B., & Townsend, M. A. R. (1990). The effects of training in social perspective taking on socially maladjusted girls. *Child Development, 61,* 178–190.

Chamberlain, M. C., Nichols, S. L., & Chase, C. H. (1991). Pediatric AIDS: Comparative cranial MRI and CT scans. *Pediatric Neurology, 7,* 357–362.

Chandler, M. J. (1973). Egocentrism and antisocial behavior: The assessment and training of social perspective-taking skills. *Developmental Psychology, 9,* 326–332.

Chandler, M. J. (1988). Doubt and developing theories of mind. In J. W. Astington, P. L. Harris, & D. R. Olson (Eds.), *Developing theories of mind* (pp. 387–413). New York: Cambridge University Press.

Chandra, R. K. (1991). Interactions between early nutrition and the immune system. In *Ciba Foundation Symposium No. 156* (pp. 77–92). Chichester, England: Wiley.

Chang, H. (1992). *Adolescent life and ethos: An ethnography of a U.S. high school.* Washington, DC: Falmer.

Chao, P. (1982). *Chinese kinship.* London: Kegan Paul International.

Chapman, K. L., Leonard, L. B., & Mervis, C. B. (1986). The effect of feedback on young children's inappropriate word usage. *Journal of Child Language, 13,* 101–117.

Chapman, M., & Lindenberger, U. (1988). Functions, operations, and décalage in the development of transitivity. *Developmental Psychology, 24,* 542–551.

Chapman, M., & Skinner, E. A. (1989). Children's agency beliefs, cognitive performance, and conceptions of effort and ability: Individual and developmental differences. *Child Development, 60,* 1229–1238.

Chapman, M., Zahn-Waxler, C., Iannotti, R., & Cooperman, G. (1987). Empathy and responsibility in the motivation of children's helping. *Developmental Psychology, 23,* 140–145.

Charlesworth, R., & Hartup, W. W. (1967). Positive social reinforcement in the nursery school peer group. *Child Development, 38,* 993–1002.

Charlesworth, W. R., & Dzur, C. (1987). Gender comparisons of preschoolers' behavior and resource utilization in group problem-solving. *Child Development, 58,* 191–200.

Chasnoff, I. J., Griffith, D. R., MacGregor, S., Dirkes, K., & Burns, K. A. (1989). Temporal patterns of cocaine use in pregnancy: Perinatal outcome. *Journal of the American Medical Association, 261,* 1741–1744.

Chassin, L., Presson, C. C., Montello, D., Sherman, S. J., & McGrew, J. (1986). Changes in peer and parent influence during adolescence: Longitudinal versus cross-sectional perspectives on smoking initiation. *Developmental Psychology, 22,* 327–334.

Chatkupt, S., Mintz, M., Epstein, L. G., Bhansali, D., & Koenigsberger, M. R. (1989). Neuroimaging studies in children with human immunodeficiency virus type 1 infection. *Annals of Neurology, 26,* 453.

Cherlin, A. J., & Furstenberg, F. F., Jr. (1986). *The new American grandparent.* New York: Basic Books.

Cherlin, A. J., Furstenberg, F. F., Jr., Chase-Lansdale, P. L., Kiernan, K. E., Robins, P. K., Morrison, D. R., & Teitler, J. O. (1991). Longitudinal studies of effects of divorce on children in Great Britain and the United States. *Science, 252,* 1386–1389.

Chess, S., & Thomas, A. (1984). *Origins and evolution of behavior disorders.* New York: Brunner/Mazel.

Chi, M. T. H. (1978). Knowledge structures and memory development. In R. S. Siegler (Ed.), *Children's thinking: What develops?* (pp. 73–96). Hillsdale, NJ: Erlbaum.

Chi, M. T. H. (1982). Knowledge development and memory performance. In M. Friedman, J. P. Das, & N. O'Connor (Eds.), *Intelligence and learning* (pp. 221–229). New York: Plenum.

Chi, M. T. H., & Ceci, S. J. (1987). Content knowledge: Its role, representation, and restructuring in memory development. In H. W. Reese (Ed.), *Advances in child development and behavior* (Vol. 20, pp. 91–142). Orlando, FL: Academic Press.

Chi, M. T. H., & Koeske, R. D. (1983). Network representation of a child's dinosaur knowledge. *Developmental Psychology, 19,* 29–39.

Children's Defense Fund. (1990a, April). Improving the health of Medicaid-eligible children. *CDF Reports, 11(8),* 1–2.

Children's Defense Fund. (1990b, April). *S.O.S. America! A children's defense budget.* Washington, DC: Author.

Children's Defense Fund. (1991a). *The adolescent and young adult fact book.* Washington, DC: Author.

Children's Defense Fund. (1991b). *The state of America's children 1991.* Washington, DC: Author.

Children's Defense Fund. (1992a, March). Bush budget neglects children. *CDF Reports, 13(5),* pp. 1–3, 10.

Children's Defense Fund. (1992b). *The state of America's children 1992.* Washington, DC: Author.

Children's Defense Fund. (1993, March). Head Start at a glance. *CDF Reports, 14(4),* 3.

Childs, C. P., & Greenfield, P. M. (1982). Informal modes of learning and teaching: The case of Zinacanteco weaving. In N. Warren (Ed.), *Advances in cross cultural psychology* (Vol. 2, pp. 269–316). London: Academic Press.

Chin, S., Rona, R. J., & Price, C. E. (1989). The secular trend in height of primary school children in England and Scotland: 1972–79 and 1979–86. *Annals of Human Biology, 16,* 387–395.

Chisholm, J. S. (1989). Biology, culture, and the development of temperament: A Navajo example. In J. K. Nugent, B. M. Lester, & T. B. Brazelton (Eds.), *Biology, culture, and development* (Vol. 1, pp. 341–364). Norwood, NJ: Ablex.

Chiu, L-H. (1992-1993). Self-esteem in American and Chinese (Taiwanese) children. *Current Psychology: Research and Reviews, 11,* 309–313.

Choi, S. (1991). Early acquisition of epistemic meaning in Korean: A study of sentence-ending suffixes in the spontaneous speech of three children. *First Language, 11,* 93–120.

Chomsky, N. (1969). *The acquisition of syntax in children from five to ten.* Cambridge, MA: MIT Press.

Chomsky, N. (1957). *Syntactic structures.* The Hague: Mouton.

Chomsky, N. (1959). Review of B. F. Skinner's *Verbal Behavior. Language, 35,* 26–129.

Chomsky, N. (1981). *Lectures on government and binding.* Dordrecht, Holland: Foris.

Chomsky, N. A. (1976). *Reflections on language.* London: Temple Smith.

Christianson, S. (1992). Emotional stress and eyewitness memory: A critical review. *Psychological Bulletin, 112,* 284–309.

Christie, D. J., & Schumacher, G. M. (1975). Developmental trends in the abstraction and recall of relevant versus irrelevant thematic information from connected verbal materials. *Child Development, 46,* 598–602.

Cicchetti, D., & Aber, J. L. (1986). Early precursors of later depression: An organizational perspective. In L. P. Lipsitt & C. Rovee-Collier (Eds.), *Advances in infancy research* (Vol. 4, pp. 87–137). Norwood, NJ: Ablex.

Cicerelli, V. G., Evans, J. W., & Schiller, J. S. (1969). *The impact of Head Start: An evaluation of the effects of Head Start on children's cognitive and affective development* (Vols. 1–2). Athens, OH: Westinghouse Learning Corporation and Ohio University.

Clancy, P. (1985). Acquisition of Japanese. In D. I. Slobin (Ed.), *The crosslinguistic study of language acquisition: Vol. 1. The data* (pp. 323–524). Hillsdale, NJ: Erlbaum.

Clancy, P. (1989). Form and function in the acquisition of Korean wh- questions. *Journal of Child Language, 16,* 323–347.

Clark, E. V. (1973). Nonlinguistic strategies and the acquisition of word meanings. *Cognition, 2,* 161–182.

Clark, E. V. (1978). Strategies for communicating. *Child Development, 49,* 977–987.

Clark, E. V. (1983). Meanings and concepts. In P. H. Mussen (Ed.), *Handbook of child psychology: Vol. 3. Cognitive development* (pp. 787–840). New York: Wiley.

Clark, E. V. (1988). On the logic of contrast. *Journal of Child Language, 15,* 317–335.

Clark, E. V. (1990). On the pragmatics of contrast. *Journal of Child Language, 17,* 417–431.

Clark, E. V., & Hecht, B. F. (1982). Learning to coin agent and instrument nouns. *Cognition, 12,* 1–24.

Clark, M. L. (1991). Social identity, peer relations, and academic competence of African-American adolescents. *Education and Urban Society, 24,* 41–52.

Clarke-Stewart, K. A. (1973). Interactions between mothers and their young children: Characteristics and consequences. *Monographs of the Society for Research in Child Development, 38* (6–7, Serial No. 153).

Clarke-Stewart, K. A. (1978). Recasting the Lone Stranger. In J. Glick & K. A. Clarke-Stewart (Eds.), *The development of social understanding* (pp. 109–176). New York: Gardner Press.

Clarke-Stewart, K. A. (1989). Infant day care: Maligned or malignant? *American Psychologist, 44,* 266–273.

Claudy, J. G. (1984). The only child as a young adult: Results from Project Talent. In T. Falbo (Ed.), *The single-child family* (pp. 211–252). New York: Guilford.

Clausen, J. A. (1975). The social meaning of differential physical and sexual maturation. In S. E. Dragastin & G. H. Elder (Eds.), *Adolescence in the life cycle: Psychological change and the social context* (pp. 25–47). New York: Halsted.

Clavadetscher, J. E., Brown, A. M., Ankrum, C., & Teller, D. Y. (1988). Spectral sensitivity and chromatic discriminations in 3- and 7-week-old human infants. *Journal of the Optical Society of America, 5,* 2093–2105.

Clements, D. H. (1986). Effects of Logo and CAI environments on cognition and creativity. *Journal of Educational Psychology, 78,* 309–318.

Clements, D. H. (1990). Metacomponential development in a Logo programming environment. *Journal of Educational Psychology, 82,* 141–149.

Clements, D. H. (1991). Enhancement of creativity in computer environments. *American Educational Research Journal, 28,* 173–187.

Clements, D. H., & Nastasi, B. K. (1992). Computers and early childhood education. In M. Gettinger, S. N. Elliott, & T. R. Kratochwill (Eds.), *Advances in school psychology: Preschool and early childhood treatment directions* (pp. 187–246). Hillsdale, NJ: Erlbaum.

Clements, D. H., Nastasi, B. K., & Swaminathan, S. (1993, January). Young children and computers: Crossroads and directions from research. *Young Children, 48*(2), 56–64.

Clopton, N. A., & Sorell, G. T. (1993). Gender differences in moral reasoning: Stable or situational? *Psychology of Women Quarterly, 17,* 85–101.

Coakley, J. (1990). *Sport and society: Issues and controversies* (4th ed.). St. Louis: Mosby.

Cochi, S. L., Edmonds, L. E., Dyer, K., Greaves, W. L., Marks, J. S., Rovira, E. Z., Preblud, S. R., & Orenstein, W. A. (1989). Congenital rubella syndrome in the United States, 1970–1985: On the verge of elimination. *American Journal of Epidemiology, 129,* 349–361.

Cochran, M. M., & Brassard, J. A. (1979). Child development and personal social networks. *Child Development, 50,* 601–616.

Coe, C. L., Lubach, G. R., & Ershler, W. B. (1989). Immunological consequences of maternal separation in infant primates. In M. Lewis & J. Worobey (Eds.), *Infant stress and coping* (pp. 65–92). San Francisco: Jossey-Bass.

Coe, C. L., Lubach, G. R., Schneider, M. L., Dierschke, D. J., & Ershler, W. B. (1992). Early rearing conditions alter immune responses in the developing infant primate. *Pediatrics, 90,* 505–509.

Cohen, F. L. (1984). *Clinical genetics in nursing practice.* Philadelphia: Lippincott.

Cohen, S. E., & Parmelee, A. H. (1983). Prediction of five-year Stanford-Binet scores in preterm infants. *Child Development, 54,* 1242–1253.

Cohn, J. F., Campbell, S. B., Matias, R., & Hopkins, J. (1990). Face-to-face interactions of postpartum depressed and nondepressed mother–infant pairs at 2 months. *Developmental Psychology, 26,* 15–23.

Cohn, J. F., & Tronick, E. Z. (1988). Mother–infant face-to-face interaction: Influence is bidirectional and unrelated to periodic cycles in either partner's behavior. *Developmental Psychology, 24,* 386–392.

Coie, J. D., Dodge, K. A., & Coppotelli, H. (1982). Dimensions and types of social status: A cross-age perspective. *Developmental Psychology, 18,* 557–570.

Coie, J. D., & Krehbiel, G. (1984). Effects of academic tutoring on the social status of low-achieving, socially rejected children. *Child Development, 55,* 1465–1478.

Coie, J. D., & Kupersmidt, J. B. (1983). A behavioral analysis of emerging social status in boys' groups. *Child Development, 54,* 1400–1416.

Coker, D. R. (1984). The relationship among gender concepts and cognitive maturity in preschool children. *Sex Roles, 10,* 19–31.

Colby, A., & Kohlberg, L. (1987). *The measurement of moral judgment: Theoretical foundations and research validation* (Vol. 1). Cambridge: Cambridge University Press.

Colby, A., Kohlberg, L., Gibbs, J., & Lieberman, M. (1983). A longitudinal study of moral judgment. *Monographs of the Society for Research in Child Development, 48* (1-2, Serial No. 200).

Cole, C. B., & Loftus, E. F. (1987). The memory of children. In S. J. Ceci, M. P. Toglia, & D. F. Ross (Eds.), *Children's eyewitness memory* (pp. 178–208). New York: Springer-Verlag.

Cole, D. A. (1991). Change in self-perceived competence as a function of peer and teacher evaluation. *Developmental Psychology, 27,* 682–688.

Cole, J. R., & Zuckerman, H. (1987, February). Marriage, motherhood, and research performance in science. *Scientific American, 256*(2), 119–125.

Cole, M., & Scribner, S. (1977). Cross-cultural studies of memory and cognition. In R. V. Kail & J. W. Hagen (Eds.), *Perspectives on the development of memory and cognition* (pp. 239–271). Hillsdale, NJ: Erlbaum.

Coles, C. D., Platzman, K. A., Smith, I., James, M. E., & Falek, A. (1992). Effects of cocaine and alcohol use in pregnancy on neonatal growth and neurobehavioral status. *Neurotoxicology and Teratology, 14,* 23–33.

Collard, R. (1971). Exploratory and play behaviors of infants reared in an institution and in lower and middle class homes. *Child Development, 42,* 1003–1015.

Collins, R. (1993, January). Head Start: Steps toward a two-generation program strategy. *Young Children, 48*(2), 25–33.

Collins, W. A. (1983). Children's processing of television content: Implications for prevention of negative effects. *Prevention in Human Services, 2,* 53–66.

Collins, W. A., Berndt, T. V., & Hess, V. L. (1974). Observational learning of motives and consequences for television aggression: A developmental study. *Child Development, 45,* 799–802.

Collins, W. A., Wellman, H., Keniston, A. H., & Westby, S. D. (1978). Age-related aspects of comprehension and inference from a televised dramatic narrative. *Child Development, 49,* 389–399.

Colón, P. A., & Colón, A. R. (1989). The health of America's children. In F. J. Macchiarola & A. Gartner (Eds.), *Caring for America's children* (pp. 45–57). New York: Academy of Political Science.

Compas, B. E., Howell, D. C., Phares, V., Williams, R. A., & Ledoux, N. (1989). Parent and child stress symptoms: An integrative analysis. *Developmental Psychology, 25,* 550–559.

Condry, J. C., & Ross, D. F. (1985). Sex and aggression: The influence of gender label on the perception of aggression in children. *Child Development, 56,* 225–233.

Conger, R. D., Conger, K. J., Elder, G. H., Jr., Lorenz, F. O., Simons, R. L., & Whitbeck, L. B. (1992). A family process model of economic hardship and adjustment of early adolescent boys. *Child Development, 63,* 527–541.

Connolly, J. A., & Doyle, A. B. (1984). Relations of social fantasy play to social competence in preschoolers. *Developmental Psychology, 20,* 797–806.

Connolly, J. A., Doyle, A. B., & Reznick, E. (1988). Social pretend play and social interaction in preschoolers. *Journal of Applied Developmental Psychology, 9,* 301–313.

Connolly, K., & Dagleish, M. (1989). The emergence of a tool-using skill in infancy. *Developmental Psychology, 25,* 894–912.

Conoley, J. C. (1990). Review of the K-ABC: Reflecting the unobservable. *Journal of Psychoeducational Assessment, 8,* 369–375.

Constanzo, P. R., & Woody, E. Z. (1979). Externality as a function of obesity in children: Pervasive style or eating-specific attribute? *Journal of Personality and Social Psychology, 37,* 2286–2296.

Cooke, R. A. (1982). The ethics and regulation of research involving children. In B. B. Wolman (Ed.), *Handbook of developmental psychology* (pp. 149–172). Englewood Cliffs, NJ: Prentice-Hall.

Cooley, C. H. (1902). *Human nature and the social order.* New York: Scribner.

Coon, H., Fulker, D. W., DeFries, J. C., & Plomin, R. (1990). Home environment and cognitive ability of 7-year-old children in the Colorado Adoption Project: Genetic and environmental etiologies. *Developmental Psychology, 26,* 459–468.

Cooper, H. M. (1979). Pygmalion grows up: A model for teacher expectation communication and performance. *Review of Educational Research, 49,* 389–410.

Cooper, H. M. (1989). Does reducing student-to-instructor ratios affect achievement? *Educational Psychologist, 24,* 79–98.

Cooper, R. P., & Aslin, R. N. (1990). Preference for infant-directed speech in the first month after birth. *Child Development, 61,* 1584–1595.

Coopersmith, S. (1967). *The antecedents of self-esteem.* San Francisco: Freeman.

Corah, N. L., Anthony, E. J., Painter, P., Stern, J. A., & Thurston, D. L. (1965). Effects of perinatal anoxia after seven years. *Psychological Monographs, 79* (3, No. 596).

Coren, S., & Halpern, D. F. (1991). Left-handedness: A marker for decreased survival fitness. *Psychological Bulletin, 109,* 90–106.

Corman, H. H., & Escalona, S. K. (1969). Stages of sensorimotor development: A replication study. *Merrill-Palmer Quarterly, 15,* 351–360.

Cornell, E. H., & Bergstrom, L. I. (1983). Serial-position effects in infants' recognition memory. *Memory and Cognition, 11,* 494–499.

Cornell, E. H., & Gottfried, A. W. (1976). Intervention with premature human infants. *Child Development, 47,* 32–39.

Corrigan, R. (1987). A developmental sequence of actor-object pretend play in young children. *Merrill-Palmer Quarterly, 33,* 87–106.

Costabile, A., Smith, P. K., Matheson, L., Aston, J., Hunter, T., & Boulton, M. (1991). Cross-national comparison of how children distinguish serious and playful fighting. *Developmental Psychology, 27,* 881–887.

Cotton, P. (1990). Sudden infant death syndrome: Another hypothesis offered but doubts remain. *Journal of the American Medical Association, 263,* 2865, 2869.

Courage, M. L., & Adams, R. J. (1990). Visual acuity assessment from birth to three years using the acuity card procedures: Cross-sectional and longitudinal samples. *Optometry and Vision Science, 67,* 713–718.

Cox, M. J., Owen, M. T., Henderson, V. K., & Lewis, J. M. (1989). Marriage, adult adjustment, and early parenting. *Child Development, 60,* 1015–1024.

Cox, M. J., Owen, M. T., Henderson, V. K., & Margand, N. A. (1992). Prediction of infant–father and infant–mother attachment. *Developmental Psychology, 28,* 474–483.

Cox, M. J., Owen, M., Lewis, J. M., & Henderson, V. K. (1989). Marriage, adult adjustment, and early parenting. *Child Development, 60,* 1015–1024.

Craik, F. I. M., & Lockhart, R. S. (1972). Levels of processing: A framework for memory research. *Journal of Verbal Learning and Verbal Behavior, 11,* 671–684.

Craik, F. I. M., & Tulving, E. (1975). Depth of processing and the retention of words in episodic memory. *Journal of Experimental Psychology: General, 104,* 268–294.

Crain-Thoreson, C., & Dale, P. S. (1992). Do early talkers become early readers? Linguistic precocity, preschool language, and emergent literacy. *Developmental Psychology, 28,* 421–429.

Cratty, B. J. (1986). *Perceptual and motor development in infants and children* (3rd ed.). Englewood Cliffs, NJ: Prentice-Hall.

Crawley, S. B., & Spiker, D. (1983). Mother-child interactions involving two-year-olds with Down syndrome: A look at individual differences. *Child Development, 54,* 1312–1323.

Crick, N. R., & Ladd, G. W. (1993). Children's perceptions of their peer experiences: Attributions, loneliness, social anxiety, and social avoidance. *Developmental Psychology, 29,* 244–254.

Crockenberg, S. B. (1981). Infant irritability, mother responsiveness, and social support influences on the security of mother-infant attachment. *Child Development, 52,* 857–865.

Crockenberg, S. B. (1986). Are temperamental differences in babies associated with predictable differences in care-giving? In J. V. Lerner & R. M. Lerner (Eds.), *Temperament and social interaction in infants and children (New Dimensions in Child Development, No. 30* , pp. 75–88). San Francisco: Jossey-Bass.

Crockenberg, S., & Litman, C. (1990). Autonomy as competence in 2-year-olds: Maternal correlates of child defiance, compliance, and self-assertion. *Developmental Psychology, 26,* 961–971.

Crockett, L. J. (1990). Sex role and sex-typing in adolescence. In R. M. Lerner, A. C. Petersen, & J. Brooks-Gunn (Eds.), *The encyclopedia of adolescence* (Vol. 2, pp. 1007–1017). New York: Garland.

Crook, C. K., & Lipsitt, L. P. (1976). Neonatal nutritive sucking: Effects of taste stimulation upon sucking rhythm and heart rate. *Child Development, 47,* 518–522.

Cross, T. G. (1978). Mothers' speech and its association with rate of linguistic development in young children. In N. Waterson & C. E. Snow (Eds.), *The development of communication* (pp. 199–216). New York: Wiley.

Crowe, H. P., & Zeskind, P. S. (1992). Psychophysiological and perceptual responses to infant cries varying in pitch: Comparison of adults with low and high scores on the child abuse potential inventory. *Child Abuse & Neglect, 16,* 19–29.

Crowell, J. A., & Feldman, S. S. (1988). Mothers' internal models of relationships and children's behavioral and developmental status: A study of mother–child interaction. *Child Development, 59,* 1273–1283.

Crowell, J. A., & Feldman, S. S. (1991). Mothers' working models of attachment relationships and mother and child behavior during separation and reunion. *Developmental Psychology, 27,* 597–605.

Csikszentmihalyi, M., & Larson, R. (1984). *Being adolescent: Conflict and growth in the teenage years.* New York: Basic Books.

Cummings, E. M., Iannotti, R. J., & Zahn-Waxler, C. (1985). Influence of conflict between adults on the emotions and aggression of young children. *Developmental Psychology, 21,* 495–507.

Cummings, J. S., Pellegrini, D. S., Notarius, C. I., & Cummings, E. M. (1989). Children's responses to angry adult behavior as a function of marital distress and history of interparent hostility. *Child Development, 60,* 1035–1043.

Cummings, S., & Taebel, D. (1980). Sexual inequality and the reproduction of consciousness: An analysis of sex-role stereotyping among children. *Sex Roles, 6,* 631–644.

Cunningham, A. E., & Stanovich, K. E. (1990). Early spelling acquisition: Writing beats the computer. *Journal of Educational Psychology, 82,* 159–162.

Cunningham, F. G., MacDonald, P. C., & Gant, N. F. (1989). *Williams obstetrics* (18th ed.). Norwalk, CT: Appleton & Lange.

Cunningham, M. R. (1986). Measuring the physical in physical attractiveness: Quasi-experiments on the sociobiology of female facial beauty. *Journal of Personality and Social Psychology, 50,* 925–935.

Curran, D. K. (1987). *Adolescent suicidal behavior.* Washington, DC: Hemisphere.

Curtiss, S. (1977). *Genie: A psycholinguisitc study of a modern-day "wild child."* New York: Academic Press.

Curtiss, S. (1989). The independence and task-specificity of language. In M. H. Bornstein & J. S. Bruner (Eds.), *Interaction in human development* (pp. 105–137). Hillsdale, NJ: Erlbaum.

Cutts, F. T., Zell, E. R., Mason, D., Bernier, R. H., Dini, E. F., & Orenstein, W. A. (1992). Monitoring progress toward U.S. preschool immunization goals. *Journal of the American Medical Association, 267,* 1952–1955.

D

Damon, W. (1977). *The social world of the child.* San Francisco: Jossey-Bass.

Damon, W. (1988). *The moral child.* New York: Free Press.

Damon, W., & Hart, D. (1988). *Self-understanding in childhood and adolescence.* New York: Cambridge University Press.

Dannemiller, J. L. (1989). A test of color constancy in 9- and 20-week-old human infants following simulated illuminant changes. *Developmental Psychology, 25,* 171–184.

Dannemiller, J. L., & Stephens, B. R. (1988). A critical test of infant pattern preference models. *Child Development, 59,* 210–216.

Dansky, J. L. (1980). Make-believe: A mediator of the relationship between play and associative fluency. *Child Development, 51,* 576–579.

Darvill, D., & Cheyne, J. A. (1981, March). *Sequential analysis of responses to aggression: Age and sex effects.* Paper presented at the biennial meeting of the Society for Research in Child Development, Boston.

Darwin, C. (1877). Biographical sketch of an infant. *Mind, 2,* 285–294.

Darwin, C. (1936). *On the origin of species by means of natural selection.* New York: Modern Library. (Original work published 1859)

Das Gupta, P., & Bryant, P. E. (1989). Young children's causal inferences. *Child Development, 60,* 1138–1146.

Davidson, P., & Youniss, J. (1991). Which comes first, morality or identity? In W. M. Kurtines & J. L. Gewirtz (Eds.), *Handbook of moral behavior and development* (Vol. 1, pp. 105–121). Hillsdale, NJ: Erlbaum.

Davidson, R. J., & Fox, N. A. (1989). Frontal brain asymmetry predicts infants' response to maternal separation. *Journal of Abnormal Psychology, 98,* 127–131.

Day, R. H., & McKenzie, B. E. (1981). Infant perception of the invariant size of approaching and receding objects. *Developmental Psychology, 17,* 670–677.

De Lisi, R., & Gallagher, A. M. (1991). Understanding gender stability and constancy in Argentinean children. *Merrill-Palmer Quarterly, 37,* 483–502.

de Villiers, J. G. (1984, October). *Learning the passive from models: Some contradictory data.* Paper presented at the annual Boston University Conference on Language Development, Boston, MA.

de Villiers, J. G., & de Villiers, P. A. (1973). A cross-sectional study of the acquisition of grammatical morphemes in child speech. *Journal of Psycholinguistic Research, 2,* 267–278.

de Villiers, P. A., & de Villiers, J. G. (1992). Language develop-

ment. In M. H. Bornstein & M. E. Lamb (Eds.), *Developmental psychology: An advanced textbook* (3rd ed., pp. 337–418). Hillsdale, NJ: Erlbaum.

Deaux, K. (1985). Sex and gender. In M. R. Rosenzweig & L. W. Porter (Eds.) *Annual review of psychology* (Vol. 36, pp. 49–81). Palo Alto, CA: Annual Reviews.

Deaux, K. (1993). Commentary: Sorry, wrong number—A reply to Gentile's call. *Psychological Science, 4,* 125–126.

Deaux, K., & Lewis, L. L. (1984). Structure of gender stereotypes: Interrelationships among components and gender label. *Journal of Personality and Social Psychology, 46,* 991–1004.

DeCasper, A. J., & Spence, M. J. (1986). Prenatal maternal speech influences newborns' perception of speech sounds. *Infant Behavior and Development, 9,* 133–150.

Declercq, E. R. (1992). The transformation of American midwifery: 1975 to 1988. *American Journal of Public Health, 82,* 680–684.

DeFries, J. C., Plomin, R., & LaBuda, M. C. (1987). Genetic stability of cognitive development from childhood to adulthood. *Developmental Psychology, 23,* 4–12.

Degelman, D., Free, J. U., Scarlato, M., Blackburn, J. M., & Golden, T. (1986). Concept learning in preschool children: Effects of a short-term Logo experience. *Journal of Educational Computing Research, 2,* 199–205.

DeGroot, A. D. (1951). War and the intelligence of youth. *Journal of Abnormal and Social Psychology, 46,* 596–597.

Dekovic, M., & Janssens, J. M. A. M. (1992). Parents' child-rearing style and child's sociometric status. *Developmental Psychology, 28,* 925–932.

Delecki, J. (1985). Principles of growth and development. In P. M. Hill (Ed.), *Human growth and development throughout life* (pp. 33–48). New York: Wiley.

Delgado-Gaitan, C. (1992). School matters in the Mexican-American home: Socializing children to education. *American Educational Research Journal, 29,* 495–515.

Dellas, M., & Jernigan, L. P. (1990). Affective personality characteristics associated with undergraduate ego identity formation. *Journal of Adolescent Research, 5,* 306–324.

DeLoache, J. S., & Todd, C. M. (1988). Young children's use of spatial categorization as a mnemonic strategy. *Journal of Experimental Child Psychology, 46,* 1–20.

Delphi Communication Sciences. (1990). *Video game use symposium.* Los Angeles: Author.

DeMarie-Dreblow, D. (1991). Relation between knowledge and memory: A reminder that correlation does not imply causality. *Child Development, 62,* 484–498.

Denham, S. A. (1986). Social cognition, prosocial behavior, and emotion in preschoolers: Contextual validation. *Child Development, 57,* 194–201.

Denham, S. A., Renwick, S. M., & Holt, R. W. (1991). Working and playing together: Prediction of preschool social-emotional competence from mother-child interaction. *Child Development, 62,* 242–249.

Dennis, W. (1960). Causes of retardation among institutionalized children: Iran. *Journal of Genetic Psychology, 96,* 47–59.

Dennis, W. (1973). *Children of the Creche.* New York: Appleton-Century-Crofts.

Dennis, W., & Dennis, M. G. (1940). The effect of cradling practices upon the onset of walking in Hopi children. *Journal of Genetic Psychology, 56,* 77–86.

Dennis, W., & Najarian, P. (1957). Infant development under environmental handicap. *Psychological Monographs, 71,* 1–13.

Derdeyn, A. P. (1985). Grandparent visitation rights: Rendering family dissension more pronounced? *American Journal of Orthopsychiatry, 55,* 277–287.

Deutsch, W., & Pechmann, T. (1982). Social interaction and the development of definite descriptions. *Cognition, 11,* 159–184.

deVries, M. W. (1984). Temperament and infant mortality among the Masai of East Africa. *American Journal of Psychiatry, 141,* 1189–1194.

Dewsbury, D. A. (1992). Comparative psychology and ethology: A reassessment. *American Psychologist, 47,* 208–215.

Diamond, A., & Goldman-Rakic, P. S. (1989). Comparison of human infants and rhesus monkeys on Piaget's AB search task: Evidence for dependence on dorsolateral prefrontal cortex. *Experimental Brain Research, 74,* 24–40.

Diamond, M., Johnson, R., Young, D., & Singh, S. (1983). Age-related morphologic differences in the rat cerebral cortex and hippocampus: Male–female; right–left. *Experimental Neurology, 81,* 1–13.

Diaz, R. M. (1983). Thought and two languages: The impact of bilingualism on cognitive development. *Review of Research in Education, 10,* 23–54.

Diaz, R. M., & Berk, L. E. (Eds.). (1992). *Private speech: From social interaction to self-regulation.* Hillsdale, NJ: Erlbaum.

Dick-Read, G. (1959). *Childbirth without fear.* New York: Harper & Brothers.

Dickinson, D. K. (1984). First impressions: Children's knowledge of words gained from a single exposure. *Applied Psycholinguistics, 5,* 359–373.

Dietz, W. H., Jr., Bandini, L. G., & Gortmaker, S. (1990). Epidemiologic and metabolic risk factors for childhood obesity. *Klinische Pädiatrie, 202,* 69–72.

Dietz, W. H., Jr., & Gortmaker, S. L. (1985). Do we fatten our children at the television set? Obesity and television viewing in children and adolescents. *Pediatrics, 75,* 807–812.

DiLalla, L. F., & Watson, M. W. (1988). Differentiation of fantasy and reality: Preschoolers' reactions to interruptions in their play. *Developmental Psychology, 24,* 286–291.

Dirks, J. (1982). The effect of a commercial game on children's Block Design scores on the WISC-R test. *Intelligence, 6,* 109–123.

Dirks, J., & Gibson, E. (1977). Infants' perception of similarity between live people and their photographs. *Child Development, 48,* 124–130.

Dishion, T. J. (1990). The family ecology of boys' peer relations in middle childhood. *Child Development, 61,* 874–892.

Dishion, T. J., Patterson, G. R., Stoolmiller, M., & Skinner, M. L. (1991). Family, school, and behavioral antecedents to early adolescent involvement with antisocial peers. *Developmental Psychology, 27,* 172–180.

Dittrichova, J., Brichacek, V., Paul, K., & Tautermannova, M. (1982). The structure of infant behavior: An analysis of sleep and waking in the first months of life. In W. W. Hartup (Ed.), *Review of child development research* (Vol. 6, pp. 73–100). Chicago: University of Chicago Press.

Divine-Hawkins, P. (1981). *Family day care in the United States: National day care home study final report, executive summary.* Washington, DC: U.S. Government Printing Office.

Dixon, R. A., & Lerner, R. M. (1992). A history of systems in developmental psychology. In M. H. Bornstein & M. E. Lamb (Eds.), *Developmental psychology: An advanced textbook* (3rd ed., pp. 3–58). Hillsdale, NJ: Erlbaum.

Dodd, B. J. (1972). Effects of social and vocal stimulation on infant babbling. *Developmental Psychology, 7,* 80–83.

Dodge, K. A. (1980). Social cognition and children's aggressive behavior. *Child Development, 51,* 162–170.

Dodge, K. A. (1983). Behavioral antecedents of peer social status. *Child Development, 54,* 1386–1399.

Dodge, K. A. (1985). A social information processing model of social competence in children. In M. Perlmutter (Ed.), *Minnesota Symposia on Child Psychology* (Vol. 18, pp. 77–125). Hillsdale, NJ: Erlbaum.

Dodge, K. A. (1989). Coordinating responses to aversive stimuli: Introduction to a special section on the development of emotional regulation. *Developmental Psychology, 25,* 339–342.

Dodge, K. A., Bates, J. E., & Pettit, G. S. (1990). Mechanisms in the cycle of violence. *Science, 250,* 1678–1683.

Dodge, K. A., & Frame, C. L. (1983). Social cognitive biases and deficits in aggressive boys. *Child Development, 53,* 620–635.

Dodge, K. A., & Somberg, D. R. (1987). Hostile attributional biases among aggressive boys are exacerbated under conditions of threats to the self. *Child Development, 58,* 213–224.

Dodge, K. A., & Tomlin, A. M. (1987). Utilization of self-schemas as a mechanism of interpretational bias in aggressive children. *Social Cognition, 5,* 280–300.

Dodge, K. A., Pettit, G. S., McClaskey, C. L., & Brown, M. M. (1986). Social competence in children. *Monographs of the Society for Research in Child Development, 51* (2, Serial No. 213).

Dodwell, P. C., Humphrey, G. K., & Muir, D. W. (1987). Shape and pattern perception. In P. Salapatek & L. Cohen (Eds.), *Handbook of infant perception* (Vol. 2, pp. 1–77). Orlando, FL: Academic Press.

Doherty, W. J., & Needle, R. H. (1991). Psychological adjustment and substance use among adolescents before and after a parental divorce. *Child Development, 62,* 328–337.

Doi, L. T. (1973). *The anatomy of dependence* (J. Bester, Trans.). Tokyo: Kadansha International.

Dolgin, K. G., & Behrend, D. A. (1984). Children's knowledge about animates and inanimates. *Child Development, 55,* 1646–1650.

Dollaghan, C. (1985). Child meets word: "Fast mapping" in preschool children. *Journal of Speech and Hearing Research, 28,* 449–454.

Dornbusch, S. M., Carlsmith, J. M., Bushwall, S. J., Ritter, P. L., Leiderman, H., Hastorf, A. H., & Gross, R. T. (1985). Single parents, extended households, and the control of adolescence. *Child Development, 56,* 326–341.

Dornbusch, S. M., Ritter, P. L., Leiderman, P. H., Roberts, D. F., & Fraleigh, M. J. (1987). The relation of parenting style to adolescent school performance. *Child Development, 58,* 1244–1257.

Dorr, A., & Kovaric, P. (1980). Some of the people some of the time—But which people? Televised violence and its effects. In E. L. Palmer & A. Dorr (Eds.), *Children and the faces of television: Teaching, violence, selling* (pp. 183–199). New York: Academic Press.

Dorr, A., Kovaric, P., & Doubleday, C. (1989). Parent–child coviewing of television. *Journal of Broadcasting and Electronic Media, 33,* 35–51.

Dossey, J. A., Mullis, I. V. S., Lindquist, M. M., & Chambers, D. L. (1988). *The Mathematics Report Card: Are we measuring up?* Princeton, NJ: Educational Testing Service.

Douglas, V. I. (1983). Attentional and cognitive problems. In M. Rutter (Ed.), *Developmental neuropsychiatry* (pp. 280–329). New York: Guilford.

Downey, G., & Walker, E. (1989). Social cognition and adjustment in children at risk for psychopathology. *Developmental Psychology, 25,* 835–845.

Downs, A. C., & Fuller, M. J. (1991). Recollections of spermarche: An exploratory investigation. *Current Psychology: Research and Reviews, 10,* 93–102.

Downs, A. C., & Langlois, J. H. (1988). Sex typing: Construct and measurement issues. *Sex Roles, 18,* 87–100.

Drabman, R. S., Cordua, G. D., Hammer, D., Jarvie, G. J., & Horton, W. (1979). Developmental trends in eating rates of normal and overweight preschool children. *Child Development, 50,* 211–216.

Drabman, R. S., & Thomas, M. H. (1976). Does watching violence on television cause apathy? *Pediatrics, 57,* 329–331.

Draper, P., & Cashdan, E. (1988). Technological change and child behavior among the !Kung. *Ethnology, 27,* 339–365.

Drotar, D., Eckerle, D., Satola, J., Pallotta, J., & Wyatt, B. (1990). Maternal interactional behavior with nonorganic failure-to-thrive infants: A case comparison study. *Child Abuse and Neglect, 14,* 41–51.

Drotar, D., & Sturm, L. (1988). Prediction of intellectual development in young children with early histories of nonorganic failure-to-thrive. *Journal of Pediatric Psychology, 13,* 281–296.

DuBois, D. L., & Hirsch, B. J. (1990). School and neighborhood friendship patterns of black and whites in early adolescence. *Child Development, 61,* 524–536.

Dubow, E. F., & Tisak, J. (1989). The relation between stressful life events and adjustment in elementary school children: The role of social support and social problem-solving skills. *Child Development, 60,* 1412–1423.

Dubow, E. F., Tisak, J., Causey, D., Hryshko, A., & Reid, G. (1991). A two-year longitudinal study of stressful life events, social support, and social problem-solving skills: Contributions to children's behavioral and academic adjustment. *Child Development, 62,* 583–599.

Duncan, P., Ritter, P., Dornbusch, S., Gross, R., & Carlsmith, J. (1985). The effects of pubertal timing on body image, school behavior, and deviance. *Journal of Youth and Adolescence, 14,* 227–236.

Dunford, F. W., & Elliott, D. S. (1984). Identifying career offenders using self-reported data. *Journal of Research in Crime and Delinquency, 21,* 57–86.

Dunham, P., & Dunham, R. (1992). Lexical development during middle infancy: A mutually driven infant–caregiver process. *Developmental Psychology, 28,* 414–420.

Dunn, J. (1987). The beginnings of moral understanding: Development in the second year. In J. Kagan & S. Lamb (Eds.), *The emergence of morality in young children* (pp. 91–111). Chicago: University of Chicago Press.

Dunn, J. (1989). Siblings and the development of social understanding in early childhood. In P. G. Zukow (Ed.), *Sibling interaction across cultures* (pp. 106–116). New York: Springer-Verlag.

Dunn, J. (1992). Sisters and brothers: Current issues in developmental research. In F. Boer & J. Dunn (Eds.), *Children's sibling relationships* (pp. 1–17). Hillsdale, NJ: Erlbaum.

Dunn, J., Bretherton, I., & Munn, P. (1987). Conversations about feeling states between mothers and their young children. *Developmental Psychology, 23,* 132–139.

Dunn, J., Brown, J. H., & Beardsall, L. (1991). Family talk about feeling states and children's later understanding of others' emotions. *Developmental Psychology, 27,* 448–455.

Dunn, J., Brown, J., Slomkowski, C. T., & Youngblade, L. (1991). Young children's understanding of other people's feelings and beliefs: Individual differences and their antecedents. *Child Development, 62,* 1352–1366.

Dunn, J., & Kendrick, C. (1982). *Siblings: Love, envy and understanding.* Cambridge, MA: Harvard University Press.

Dunn, J., & Plomin, R. (1990). *Separate lives: Why siblings are so different.* New York: Basic Books.

Dunphy, D. C. (1963). The social structure of urban adolescent peer groups. *Sociometry, 26,* 230–246.

Dunst, C. J., & Linderfelt, B. (1985). Maternal ratings of temperament and operant learning in two- to three-month-old infants. *Child Development, 56,* 555–563.

Dweck, C. S. (1975). The role of expectations and attributions in the alleviation of learned helplessness. *Journal of Personality and Social Psychology, 31,* 674–685.

Dweck, C. S. (1991). Self-theories and goals: Their role in motivation, personality and development. In R. Dienstbier (Ed.), *Nebraska Symposia on Motivation* (Vol. 36, pp. 199–235). Lincoln: University of Nebraska Press.

Dweck, C. S., & Elliott, E. S. (1983). Achievement motivation. In E. M. Hetherington (Ed.), *Handbook of child psychology: Vol. 4. Socialization, personality, and social development* (4th ed., pp. 643–691). New York: Wiley.

Dweck, C. S., & Leggett, E. L. (1988). A social-cognitive approach to motivation and personality. *Psychological Review, 95,* 256–273.

Dye-White, E. (1986). Environmental hazards in the work setting: Their effect on women of child-bearing age. *American Association of Occupational Health and Nursing Journal, 34,* 76–78.

E

East, P. L., & Rook, K. S. (1992). Compensatory patterns of support among children's peer relationships: A test using school friends, nonschool friends, and siblings. *Developmental Psychology, 28,* 168–172.

Easterbrooks, M. A. (1989). Quality of attachment to mother and to father: Effects of perinatal risk status. *Child Development, 60,* 831–837.

Eaton, W. O., Von Bargen, D., & Keats, J. G. (1981). Gender understanding and dimensions of preschooler toy choice: Sex stereotype versus the activity level. *Canadian Journal of Behavioral Science, 13,* 203–209.

Eccles, J. S. (1990). Academic achievement. In R. M. Lerner, A. C. Petersen, & J. Brooks-Gunn (Eds.), *The encyclopedia of adolescence* (pp. 1–5). New York: Garland.

Eccles, J. S., & Harold, R. D. (1991). Gender differences in sport involvement: Applying the Eccles' expectancy-value model. *Journal of Applied Sport Psychology, 3,* 7–35.

Eccles, J. S., Jacobs, J. E., & Harold, R. D. (1990). Gender-role stereotypes, expectancy effects, and parents' role in the socialization of gender differences in self-perceptions and skill acquisition. *Journal of Social Issues, 46,* 183–201.

Eccles, J. S., & Midgley, C. (1989). Stage environment fit: Developmentally appropriate classrooms for young adolescents. In R. E. Ames & C. Ames (Eds.), *Research in motivation in education* (Vol. 3, pp. 139–186). New York: Academic Press.

Eccles, J. S., Wigfield, A., Flanagan, C., Miller, C., Reuman, D., & Yee, D. (1989). Self-concepts, domain values, and self-esteem: Relations and changes at early adolescence. *Journal of Personality and Social Psychology, 57,* 283–310.

Eckerman, C. O., Davis, C. C., & Didow, S. M. (1989). Toddlers' emerging ways of achieving social coordination with a peer. *Child Development, 60,* 440–453.

Eckerman, C. O., & Whatley, J. L. (1977). Toys and social interaction between infant peers. *Child Development, 48,* 1645–1656.

Eckerman, C. O., Whatley, J. L., & Kutz, S. L. (1975). Growth of social play with peers during the second year of life. *Developmental Psychology, 11*, 42–49.

Edelbrock, C., & Sugawara, A. I. (1978). Acquisition of sex-typed preferences in preschool-aged children. *Developmental Psychology, 14*, 614–623.

Edelman, M. W. (1989). Children at risk. In F. J. Macchiarola & A. Gartner (Eds.), Caring for America's children. *Proceedings of the Academy of Political Science, 37* (No. 32), 20–30.

Eder, D., & Parker, S. (1987). The cultural production and reproduction of gender: The effect of extracurricular activities on peer-group culture. *Sociology of Education, 60*, 200–213.

Eder, R. A. (1989). The emergent personologist: The structure and content of $3\frac{1}{2}$-, $5\frac{1}{2}$-, and $7\frac{1}{2}$-year-olds' concepts of themselves and other persons. *Child Development, 60*, 1218–1228.

Eder, R. A. (1990). Uncovering young children's psychological selves: Individual and developmental differences. *Child Development, 61*, 849–863.

Edwards, C. P. (1978). Social experiences and moral judgment in Kenyan young adults. *Journal of Genetic Psychology, 133*, 19–30.

Edwards, C. P. (1981). The comparative study of the development of moral judgment and reasoning. In R. L. Munroe, R. Munroe, & B. B. Whiting (Eds.), *Handbook of cross-cultural human development* (pp. 501–528). New York: Garland.

Edwards, J. N. (1991). New conceptions: Biosocial innovations and the family. *Journal of Marriage and the Family, 53*, 349–360.

Egeland, B., Jacobvitz, D., & Sroufe, L. A. (1988). Breaking the cycle of abuse. *Child Development, 59*, 1080–1088.

Egeland, B., & Sroufe, L. A. (1981). Developmental sequelae of maltreatment in infancy. In R. Rizley & D. Cicchetti (Ed.) *New directions for child development* (No. 11, pp. 77–92). San Francisco: Jossey-Bass.

Ehrhardt, A. A. (1975). Prenatal hormone exposure and psychosexual differentiation. In E. J. Sachar (Ed.), *Topics in psychoendocrinology* (pp. 67–82). New York: Grune & Stratton.

Ehrhardt, A. A., & Baker, S. W. (1974). Fetal androgens, human central nervous system differentiation, and behavior sex differences. In R. C. Friedman, R. M. Richart, & R. L. VandeWiele (Eds.), *Sex differences in behavior* (pp. 33–51). New York: Wiley.

Ehrhardt, A. A., Epstein, R., & Money, J. (1968). Fetal androgens and female gender identity in the early treated adrenogenital syndrome. *Johns Hopkins Medical Journal, 122*, 160–167.

Ehri, L. C. (1979). Linguistic insight: Threshold of reading acquisition. In T. G. Waller & G. E. MacKinnon (Eds.), *Reading research: Advances in theory and practice* (Vol. 1, pp. 63–114). New York: Harcourt Brace Jovanovich.

Eisenberg, L. (1984). The epidemiology of suicide in adolescents. *Pediatric Annals, 13*, 47–54.

Eisenberg, N. (1982). The development of reasoning regarding prosocial behavior. In N. Eisenberg (Ed.), *The development of prosocial behavior* (pp. 219–249). New York: Academic Press.

Eisenberg, N., Fabes, R. A., Schaller, M., Carlo, G., & Miller, P. A. (1991). The relations of parental characteristics and practices to children's vicarious emotional responding. *Child Development, 62*, 1393–1408.

Eisenberg, N., & Lennon, R. (1983). Sex differences in empathy and related capacities. *Psychological Bulletin, 94*, 100–131.

Eisenberg, N., Lennon, R., & Roth, K. (1983). Prosocial development: A longitudinal study. *Developmental Psychology, 19*, 846–855.

Eisenberg, N., & Miller, P. A. (1987). The relation of empathy to prosocial and related behaviors. *Psychological Bulletin, 101*, 91–119.

Eisenberg, N., Miller, P. A., Shell, R., McNalley, & Shea, C. (1991). Prosocial development in adolescence: A longitudinal study. *Developmental Psychology, 27*, 849–857.

Eisenberg, N., Shell, R., Pasternack, J., Lennon, R., Beller, R., & Mathy, R. M. (1987). Prosocial development in middle childhood: A longitudinal study. *Developmental Psychology, 23*, 712–718.

Eisenberg-Berg, N. (1979). Development of children's prosocial moral judgment. *Developmental Psychology, 15*, 128–137.

Eisenberg-Berg, N., & Hand, M. (1979). The relationship of preschoolers' reasoning about prosocial moral conflicts to prosocial behavior. *Child Development, 50*, 356–363.

Eisenberg-Berg, N., & Roth, K. (1980). The development of children's prosocial moral judgment: A longitudinal follow-up. *Developmental Psychology, 16*, 375–376.

Ekman, P., & Friesen, W. (1972). Constants across culture in the face of emotion. *Journal of Personality and Social Psychology, 17*, 124–129.

Elardo, R., Bradley, R. H., & Caldwell, B. M. (1975). The relation of infants' home environments to mental test performance from six to thirty-six months: A longitudinal analysis. *Child Development, 46*, 71–76.

Elardo, R., Bradley, R. H., & Caldwell, B. M. (1977). A longitudinal study of the relation of infants' home environments to language development at age 3. *Child Development, 48*, 595–603.

Elder, G. H., Jr. (1974). *Children of the Great Depression.* Chicago: University of Chicago Press.

Elder, G. H., Jr., & Caspi, A. (1988). Human development and social change: An emerging perspective on the life course. In N. Bolger, A. Caspi, G. Downey, & M. Moorehouse (Eds.), *Persons in context: Developmental processes* (pp. 77–113). Cambridge: Cambridge University Press.

Elder, G. H., Jr., Caspi, A., & Van Nguyen, T. (1986). Resourceful and vulnerable children: Family influences in hard times. In R. K. Silbereisen, K. Eysferth, & G. Rodinger (Eds.), *Development as action in context: Problem behavior and normal youth development* (pp. 167–186). New York: Springer-Verlag.

Elder, G. H., Jr., Liker, J. K., & Cross, C. E. (1984). Parent-child behavior in the Great Depression: Life course and intergenerational influences. In P. B. Baltes & O. G. Brim (Eds.), *Life-span development and behavior* (Vol. 6, pp. 109–158). New York: Academic Press.

Elder, G. H., Jr., Van Nguyen, T., & Caspi, A. (1985). Linking family hardship to children's lives. *Child Development, 56*, 361–375.

Elias, M. J., Gara, M., Ubriaco, M., Rothman, P. A., Clabby, J. F., & Schuyler, T. (1986). Impact of preventive social problem solving intervention on children's coping with middle-school stressors. *American Journal of Community Psychology, 14*, 259–276.

Elicker, J., Englund, M., & Sroufe, L. A. (1992). Predicting peer competence and peer relationships in childhood from early parent–child relationships. In R. D. Parke & G. W. Ladd (Eds.), *Family–peer relationships: Modes of linkage* (pp. 77–106). Hillsdale, NJ: Erlbaum.

Elkind, D. (1991, August). Attitudes toward homosexuality (14-through 18-year-olds). *Parents, 66*(8), p. 140.

Elkind, D., & Bowen, R. (1979). Imaginary audience behavior in children and adolescence. *Developmental Psychology, 15*, 33–44.

Elliott, E. S., & Dweck, C. S. (1988). Goals: An approach to motivation and achievement. *Journal of Personality and Social Psychology, 54,* 5–12.

Ellis, S., Rogoff, B., & Cromer, C. (1981). Age segregation in children's social interactions. *Developmental Psychology, 17,* 399–407.

Ellsworth, C. P., Muir, D. W., & Hains, S. M. J. (1993). Social competence and person-object differentiation: An analysis of the still-face effect. *Developmental Psychology, 29,* 63–73.

Emde, R. N. (1992). Individual meaning and increasing complexity: Contributions of Sigmund Freud and René Spitz to developmental psychology. *Developmental Psychology, 28,* 347–359.

Emde, R. N., Bioringen, Z., Clyman, R. B., & Oppenheim, D. (1991). The moral self of infancy: Affective core and procedural knowledge. *Developmental Review, 11,* 251–270.

Emde, R. N., & Buchsbaum, H. K. (1990). "Didn't you hear my mommy?" Autonomy with connectedness in moral self-emergence. In D. Cicchetti & M. Beeghly (Eds.), *Development of the self through transition* (pp. 35–60). Chicago: University of Chicago Press.

Emde, R. N., Johnson, W. F., & Easterbrooks, A. (1987). The do's and don'ts of early moral development: Psychoanalytic tradition and current research. In J. Kagan & S. Lamb (Eds.), *The emergence of morality in young children* (pp. 245–276). Chicago: University of Chicago Press.

Emde, R. N., Plomin, R., Robinson, J., Corley, R., DeFries, J., Fulker, D. W., Reznick, J. S., Campos, J., Kagan, J., & Zahn-Waxler, C. (1992). Temperament, emotion, and cognition at fourteen months: The MacArthur Longitudinal Twin Study. *Child Development, 63,* 1437–1455.

Emery, R. E. (1988). *Marriage, divorce, and children's adjustment.* Newbury Park, CA: Sage.

Emery, R. E. (1989). Family violence. *American Psychologist, 44,* 321–328.

Emery, R. E., & Wyer, M. M. (1987). Divorce mediation. *American Psychologist, 42,* 472–480.

Emmerich, W. (1981). Non-monotonic developmental trends in social cognition: The case of gender constancy. In S. Strauss (Ed.), *U-shaped behavioral growth* (pp. 249–269). New York: Academic Press.

Emory, E. K., & Toomey, K. A. (1988). Environmental stimulation and human fetal responsibility in late pregnancy. In W. P. Smotherman & S. R. Robinson (Eds.), *Behavior of the fetus* (pp. 141–161). Caldwell, NJ: Telford.

Engliert, C. S., & Palincsar, A. S. (1991). Reconsidering instructional research in literacy from a sociocultural perspective. *Learning Disabilities Research and Practice, 6,* 225–229.

Enright, R. D., Bjerstedt, A., Enright, W. F., Levy, W. M., Jr., Lapsley, D. K., Buss, R. R., Harwell, M., & Zindler, M. (1984). Distributive justice development: Cross-cultural, contextual, and longitudinal evaluations. *Child Development, 55,* 1737–1751.

Enright, R. D., Franklin, C. C., & Manheim, L. A. (1980). Children's distributive justice reasoning: A standardized and objective scale. *Developmental Psychology, 16,* 193–202.

Enright, R. D., Lapsley, D. K., & Shukla, D. (1979). Adolescent egocentrism in early and late adolescence. *Adolescence, 14,* 687–695.

Enright, R. D., & Sutterfield, S. J. (1980). An ecological validation of social cognitive development. *Child Development, 51,* 156–161.

Epstein, H. T. (1974a). Phrenoblysis: Special brain and mind growth periods. I. Human brain and skull development. *Developmental Psychobiology, 7,* 207–216.

Epstein, H. T. (1974b). Phrenoblysis: Special brain and mind growth periods. II. Human mental development. *Developmental Psychobiology, 7,* 217–224.

Epstein, H. T. (1980). EEG developmental stages. *Developmental Psychobiology, 13,* 629–631.

Epstein, J. L. (1983a). Selection of friends in differently organized schools and classrooms. In J. L. Epstein & N. Karweit (Eds.), *Friends in school* (pp. 73–92). New York: Academic Press.

Epstein, J. L. (1983b). The influence of friends on achievement and affective outcomes. In J. L. Epstein & N. L. Karweit (Eds.), *Friends in school* (pp. 177–200). New York: Academic Press.

Epstein, L. H., McCurley, J., Wing, R. R., & Valoski, A. (1990). Five-year follow-up of family-based treatments for childhood obesity. *Journal of Consulting and Clinical Psychology, 58,* 661–664.

Epstein, L. H., Wing, R. R., Koeske, R., & Valoski, A. (1987). Long-term effects of family-based treatment of childhood obesity. *Journal of Consulting and Clinical Psychology, 55,* 91–95.

Erickson, M. F., Sroufe, L. A., & Egeland, B. (1985). The relationship between quality of attachment and behavior problems in preschool in a high-risk sample. In I. Bretherton & E. Waters (Eds.), Growing points of attachment theory and research. *Monographs for the Society for Research in Child Development, 50* (1–2, Serial No. 209).

Erikson, E. H. (1950). *Childhood and society.* New York: Norton.

Erikson, E. H. (1968). *Identity, youth, and crisis.* New York: Norton.

Eron, L. D., Walder, L. O., Huesmann, L. R., & Lefkowitz, N. M. (1974). The convergence of laboratory and field studies of the development of aggression. In J. deWit & W. W. Hartup (Eds.), *Determinants and origins of aggressive behavior* (pp. 347–380). The Hague: Mouton.

Espenschade, A., & Eckert, H. (1974). Motor development. In W. R. Warren & E. R. Buskirk (Eds.), *Science and medicine of exercise and sport* (pp. 329–330). New York: Harper & Row.

Etaugh, C., Collins, G., & Gerson, A. (1975). Reinforcement of sex-typed behaviors of two-year-old children in a nursery school setting. *Developmental Psychology, 11,* 255.

Etaugh, C., & Harlow, H. (1975). Behaviors of male and female teachers as related to behaviors and attitudes of elementary school children. *Journal of Genetic Psychology, 127,* 163–170.

Etaugh, C., & Liss, M. B. (1992). Home, school, and playroom: Training grounds for adult gender roles. *Sex Roles, 26,* 129–147.

Etaugh, C., & Rose, S. (1975). Adolescents' sex bias in the evaluation of performance. *Developmental Psychology, 11,* 663–664.

Etzel, B., & Gewirtz, J. (1967). Experimental modification of caretaker-maintained high rate operant crying in a 6- and a 20-week-old infant (Infans tyrannotearus): Extinction of crying with reinforcement of eye contact and smiling. *Journal of Experimental Child Psychology, 5,* 303–317.

Eveleth, P. B., & Tanner, J. M. (1990). *Worldwide variation in human growth* (2nd ed.). Cambridge: Cambridge University Press.

F

Fabes, R. A., Eisenberg, N., McCormick, S. E., & Wilson, M. S. (1988). Preschoolers' attributions of the situational determinants of others' naturally occurring emotions. *Developmental Psychology, 24,* 376–385.

Fabes, R. A., Eisenberg, N., Nyman, M., & Michealieu, Q. (1991). Young children's appraisals of others' spontaneous emotional reactions. *Developmental Psychology, 27*, 858–866.

Fabricius, W. V., & Cavalier, L. (1989). The role of causal theories about memory in young children's memory strategy choice. *Child Development, 60*, 298–308.

Fabricius, W. V., & Wellman, H. M. (1993). Two roads diverged: Young children's ability to judge distance. *Child Development, 64*, 399–414.

Fackelmann, K. A. (1992, November 28). Finding Marfan syndrome in the womb. *Science News, 142(22)*, 382.

Fagan, J. F., III. (1973). Infant's delayed recognition memory and forgetting. *Journal of Experimental Child Psychology, 16*, 424–450.

Fagan, J. F., III. (1976). Infants' recognition of invariant features of faces. *Child Development, 47*, 627–638.

Fagan, J. F., III, & Montie, J. E. (1988). The behavioral assessment of cognitive well-being in the infant. In J. Kavanagh (Ed.), *Understanding mental retardation* (pp. 207–221). Baltimore: Paul H. Brookes.

Fagan, J. F., III, Shepherd, P. A., & Knevel, C. R. (1991). *Predictive validity of the Fagan Test of Infant Intelligence.* Paper presented at the biennial meeting of the Society for Research in Child Development, Seattle, WA.

Fagan, J. F., III, & Singer, L. T. (1979). The role of simple feature differences in infants' recognition of faces. *Infant Behavior and Development, 2*, 39–45.

Fagan, J. F., III, & Singer, L. T. (1983). Infant recognition memory as a measure of intelligence. In L. P. Lipsitt (Ed.), *Advances in infancy research* (Vol. 2, pp. 31–78). Norwood, NJ: Ablex.

Fagot, B. I. (1974). Sex differences in toddlers' behavior and parental reaction. *Developmental Psychology, 10*, 554–558.

Fagot, B. I. (1977). Consequences of moderate cross-gender behavior in preschool children. *Child Development, 48*, 902–907.

Fagot, B. I. (1978). The influence of sex of child on parental reactions to toddler children. *Child Development, 49*, 459–465.

Fagot, B. I. (1985a). Beyond the reinforcement principle: Another step toward understanding sex role development. *Developmental Psychology, 21*, 1097–1104.

Fagot, B. I. (1985b). Changes in thinking about early sex role development. *Developmental Review, 5*, 83–98.

Fagot, B. I., & Hagan, R. I. (1991). Observations of parent reactions to sex-stereotyped behaviors: Age and sex effects. *Child Development, 62*, 617–628.

Fagot, B. I., Hagan, R. I., Leinbach, M. D., & Kronsberg, S. (1985). Differential reactions to assertive and communicative acts of toddler boys and girls. *Child Development, 56*, 1499–1505.

Fagot, B. I., & Kavanaugh, K. (1990). The prediction of antisocial behavior from avoidant attachment classifications. *Child Development, 61*, 864–873.

Fagot, B. I., & Leinbach, M. D. (1989). The young child's gender schema: Environmental input, internal organization. *Child Development, 60*, 663–672.

Fagot, B. I., Leinbach, M. D., & Hagan, R. I. (1986). Gender labeling and the adoption of sex-typed behaviors. *Developmental Psychology, 22*, 440–443.

Fagot, B. I., Leinbach, M. D., & O'Boyle, C. (1992). Gender labeling, gender stereotyping, and parenting behaviors. *Developmental Psychology, 28*, 225–230.

Fagot, B. I., & Littman, I. (1976). Relation of pre-school sex-typing to intellectual performance in elementary school. *Psychological Reports, 39*, 699–704.

Fagot, B. I., & Patterson, G. R. (1969). An in vivo analysis of reinforcing contingencies for sex-role behaviors in the preschool child. *Developmental Psychology, 1*, 563–568.

Fahrmeier, E. D. (1978). The development of concrete operations among the Hausa. *Journal of Cross-Cultural Psychology, 9*, 23–44.

Falbo, T. (1992). Social norms and the one-child family: Clinical and policy implications. In F. Boer & J. Dunn (Eds.), *Children's sibling relationships* (pp. 71–82). Hillsdale, NJ: Erlbaum.

Falbo, T., & Polit, D. (1986). A quantitative review of the only-child literature: Research evidence and theory development. *Psychological Bulletin, 100*, 176–189.

Falbo, T., & Poston, D. L., Jr. (1993). The academic, personality, and physical outcomes of only children in China. *Child Development, 64*, 18–35.

Faller, K. C. (1990). *Understanding child sexual maltreatment.* Newbury Park, CA: Sage.

Fantz, R. L. (1961). The origin of form perception. *Scientific American, 204*, 66–72.

Fantz, R. L. (1963). Pattern vision in newborn infants. *Science, 140*, 296–297.

Farrar, M. J. (1990). Discourse and the acquisition of grammatical morphemes. *Journal of Child Language, 17*, 607–624.

Farrar, M. J., & Goodman, G. S. (1992). Developmental changes in event memory. *Child Development, 63*, 173–187.

Farrington, D. P. (1987). Epidemiology. In H. C. Quay (Ed.), *Handbook of juvenile delinquency* (pp. 33–61). New York: Wiley.

Faust, M. S. (1977). Somatic development of adolescent girls. *Monographs of the Society for Research in Child Development, 42*, (1, Serial No. 169).

Featherman, D. (1980). Schooling and occupational careers: Constancy and change in worldly success. In O. Brim, Jr., & J. Kagan (Eds.), *Constancy and change in human development* (pp. 675–738). Cambridge, MA: Harvard University Press.

Fee, E. (1990). Public health in practice: An early confrontation with the "silent epidemic" of childhood lead paint poisoning. *Journal of the History of Medicine and Allied Sciences, 45*, 570–606.

Feingold, A. (1988). Cognitive gender differences are disappearing. *American Psychologist, 43*, 95–103.

Feinman, S. (1982). Social referencing in infancy. *Merrill-Palmer Quarterly, 28*, 445–470.

Feis, C. L., & Simons, C. (1985). Training preschool children in interpersonal cognitive problem-solving skills: A replication. *Prevention in Human Services, 3*, 59–70.

Feldlaufer, H., Midgley, C., & Eccles, J. S. (1988). Student, teacher, and observer perceptions of the classroom environment before and after the transition to junior high school. *Journal of Early Adolescence, 8*, 133–156.

Feldman, D. H., & Goldsmith, L. T. (1991). *Nature's gambit.* New York: Teachers College Press.

Felner, R. D., & Adan, A. M. (1988). The School Transitional Environment Project: An ecological intervention and evaluation. In R. H. Price, E. L. Cowan, R. P. Lorion, & J. Ramos-McKay (Eds.), *14 ounces of prevention: A casebook for practitioners* (pp. 111–122). Washington, DC: American Psychological Association.

Fenema, E., & Sherman, J. (1977). Sex-related differences in mathematics achievement, spatial visualization, and affective factors. *American Educational Research Journal, 14*, 51–71.

Fenster, L., Eskenazi, B., Windham, G. C., & Swan, S. H. (1991). Caffeine consumption during pregnancy and spontaneous abortion. *Epidemiology, 2*, 168–174.

Fenton, N. (1928). The only child. *Journal of Genetic Psychology, 35,* 546–556.

Ferguson, L. R. (1978). The competence and freedom of children to make choices regarding participation in research: A statement. *Journal of Social Issues, 34,* 114–121.

Fergusson, D. M., Horwood, L. J., & Shannon, F. T. (1987). Breast-feeding and subsequent social adjustment in six- to eight-year-old children. *Journal of Child Psychology and Psychiatry, 28,* 378–386.

Fernald, A., Taeschner, T., Dunn, J., Papousek, M., Boysson-Bardies, B., & Fukui, I. (1989). A cross-language study of prosodic modifications in mothers' and fathers' speech to preverbal infants. *Journal of Child Language, 16,* 477–502.

Feshbach, N. D. (1987). Parental empathy and child adjustment/maladjustment. In N. Eisenberg & J. Strayer (Eds.), *Empathy and its development* (pp. 271–291). New York: Cambridge University Press.

Feshbach, N. D., & Feshbach, S. (1982). Empathy training and the regulation of aggression: Potentialities and limitation. *Academic Psychology Bulletin, 4,* 399–413.

Field, D. (1981). Can preschool children really learn to conserve? *Child Development, 52,* 326–334.

Field, T. M., Schanberg, S. M., Scafidi, F., Bauer, C. R., Vega-Lahr, N., Garcia, R., Nystrom, J., & Kuhn, C. M. (1986). Effects of tactile/kinesthetic stimulation on preterm neonates. *Pediatrics, 77,* 654–658.

Field, T. M., Woodson, R., Greenberg, R., & Cohen, D. (1982). Discrimination and imitation of facial expressions by neonates. *Science, 218,* 179–181.

Fiese, B. (1990). Playful relationships: A contextual analysis of mother-toddler interaction and symbolic play. *Child Development, 61,* 1648–1656.

Fine, B. A. (1990). *Strategies in genetic counseling: Reproductive genetics and new technologies.* White Plains, NY: March of Dimes Birth Defects Foundation.

Fine, G. A. (1980). The natural history of preadolescent male friendship groups. In H. C. Foot, A. J. Chapman, & J. R. Smith (Eds.), *Friendship and social relations in children* (pp. 293–320). Chichester, England: Wiley.

Finegan, J. K., Niccols, G. A., & Sitarenios, G. (1992). Relations between prenatal testosterone levels and cognitive abilities at 4 years. *Developmental Psychology, 28,* 1075–1089.

Finkelhor, D. (1984). *Child sexual abuse: New theory and research.* New York: Free Press.

Finman, R., Davidson, R. J., Colton, M. B., Straus, A. M., & Kagan, J. (1989). Psychophysiological correlates of inhibition to the unfamiliar in children. *Psychophysiology, 26,* S24.

Finn, J. D., & Achilles, C. M. (1990). Answers and questions about class size: A statewide experiment. *American Educational Research Journal, 27,* 557–577.

Fischer, K. W. (1987). Commentary—Relations between brain and cognitive development. *Child Development, 58,* 623–632.

Fischer, K. W., & Bidell, T. (1991). Constraining nativist inferences about cognitive capacities. In S. Carey & R. Gelman (Eds.), *The epigenesis of mind: Essays on biology and cognition* (pp. 199–235). Hillsdale, NJ: Erlbaum.

Fischer, K. W., & Farrar, M. J. (1987). Generalizations about generalizations: How a theory of skill development explains both generality and specificity. *International Journal of Psychology, 22,* 643–677.

Fischer, K. W., & Pipp, S. L. (1984). Processes of cognitive development: Optimal level and skill acquisition. In R. J. Sternberg (Ed.), *Mechanisms of cognitive development* (pp. 45–80). New York: Freeman.

Fisher, C. B., Bornstein, M. H., & Gross, G. G. (1985). Left-right coding skills related to beginning reading. *Journal of Developmental and Behavioral Pediatrics, 6,* 279–283.

Fitzgerald, J. (1987). Research on revision in writing. *Review of Educational Research, 57,* 481–506.

Fivush, R. (1984). Learning about school: The development of kindergartners' school scripts. *Child Development, 55,* 1697–1709.

Fivush, R. (1991). Gender and emotion in mother-child conversations about the past. *Journal of Narrative and Life History, 1,* 325–341.

Fivush, R., Gray, J. T., & Fromhoff, F. A. (1987). Two year olds talk about the past. *Cognitive Development, 2,* 393–409.

Fivush, R., Kuebli, J., & Clubb, P. A. (1992). The structure of events and event representations: A developmental analysis. *Child Development, 63,* 188–201.

Flanagan, C. A., & Eccles, J. S. (1993). Changes in parents' work status and adolescents' adjustment at school. *Child Development, 64,* 246–257.

Flavell, J. H. (1963). *The developmental psychology of Jean Piaget.* New York: Van Nostrand.

Flavell, J. H. (1976). Metacognitive aspects of problem solving. In L. B. Resnick (Ed.), *The nature of intelligence* (pp. 231–235). Hillsdale, NJ: Erlbaum.

Flavell, J. H. (1982). On cognitive development. *Child Development, 53,* 1–10.

Flavell, J. H. (1985). *Cognitive development* (2nd ed.). Englewood Cliffs, NJ: Prentice-Hall.

Flavell, J. H. (1992). Cognitive development: Past, present, and future. *Developmental Psychology, 28,* 998–1005.

Flavell, J. H., Botkin, P. T., Fry, C. L., Jr., Wright, J. W., & Jarvis, P. E. (1968). *The development of role-taking and communication skills in children.* New York: Wiley.

Flavell, J. H., Green, F. L., & Flavell, E. R. (1987). Development of knowledge about the appearance–reality distinction. *Monographs of the Society for Research in Child Development, 51* (1, Serial No. 212).

Flavell, J. H., Green, F. L., & Flavell, E. R. (1989). Young children's ability to differentiate appearance–reality and level 2 perspectives in the tactile modality. *Child Development, 60,* 201–213.

Fleming, P. J., Gilbert, R., Azaz, Y., Berry, P. J., Rudd, P. T., Stewart, A., & Hall, E. (1990). Interaction between bedding and sleep position in sudden infant death syndrome: A population-based control study. *British Medical Journal, 301,* 85–89.

Fodor, J. A. (1983). *Modularity of mind.* Cambridge, MA: MIT Press.

Fogel, A., Melson, G. F., Toda, S., & Mistry, T. (1987). Young children's responses to unfamiliar infants. *International Journal of Behavioral Development, 10,* 1071–1077.

Fogel, A., Toda, S., & Kawai, M. (1988). Mother–infant face-to-face interaction in Japan and the United States: A laboratory comparison using 3-month-old infants. *Developmental Psychology, 24,* 398–406.

Fonagy, P., Steele, H., & Steele, M. (1991). Maternal representations of attachment during pregnancy predict the organization of infant–mother attachment at one year of age. *Child Development, 62,* 891–905.

Food Research and Action Center. (1991). *Community Childhood Hunger Identification Project.* Washington, DC: Author.

Ford, C., & Beach, F. (1951). *Patterns of sexual behavior.* New York: Harper & Row.

Ford, D. Y., & Harris, J. J., III. (1990). On discovering the hidden treasure of gifted and talented black children. *Roeper Review, 13,* 27–32.

Forehand, R., Wierson, M., Thomas, A. M., Fauber, R., Armistead, L., Kempton, T., & Long, N. (1991). A short-term longitudinal examination of young adolescent functioning following divorce: The role of family factors. *Journal of Abnormal Child Psychology, 19,* 97–111.

Forman, E. A. (1987). Learning through peer interaction: A Vygotskian perspective. *Genetic Epistemologist, 15,* 6–15.

Forrest, J. D., & Singh, S. (1990). The sexual and reproductive behavior of American women, 1982–1988. *Family Planning Perspectives, 22,* 206–214.

Forrester, M. A. (1988). Young children's polyadic conversation monitoring skills. *First Language, 7,* 145–158.

Fox, N. A. (1989). Psychophysiological correlates of emotional reactivity during the first year of life. *Developmental Psychology, 25,* 364–372.

Fox, N. A. (1991). If it's not left, it's right: Electroencephalograph asymmetry and the development of emotion. *American Psychologist, 46,* 863–872.

Fox, N. A., Bell, M. A., & Jones, N. A. (1992). Individual differences in response to stress and cerebral asymmetry. *Developmental Neuropsychology, 8,* 161–184.

Fox, N. A., & Davidson, R. J. (1986). Taste-elicited changes in facial signs of emotion and the asymmetry of brain electrical activity in newborn infants. *Neuropsychologia, 24,* 417–422.

Fox, N. A., & Field, T. M. (1989). Individual differences in young children's adjustment to preschool. *Journal of Applied Developmental Psychology, 10,* 527–540.

Fox, N. A., & Fitzgerald, H. E. (1990). Autonomic function in infancy. *Merrill-Palmer Quarterly, 36,* 27–52.

Fox, N. A., Kimmerly, N. L., & Schafer, W. D. (1991). Attachment to mother/attachment to father: A meta-analysis. *Child Development, 62,* 210–225.

Francis, P. L., & McCroy, G. (1983). *Bimodal recognition of human stimulus configurations.* Paper presented at the biennial meeting of the Society for Research in Child Development, Detroit.

Frank, S. J., Pirsch, L. A., & Wright, V. C. (1990). Late adolescents' perceptions of their relationships with their parents: Relationships among deidealization, autonomy, relatedness, and insecurity and implications for adolescent adjustment and ego identity status. *Journal of Youth and Adolescence, 19,* 571–588.

Frankel, K. A., & Bates, J. E. (1990). Mother-toddler problem solving: Antecedents in attachment, home behavior, and temperament. *Child Development, 61,* 810–819.

Frankel, M. T., & Rollins, H. A. (1985). Associative and categorical hypotheses of organization in the free recall of adults and children. *Journal of Experimental Child Psychology, 40,* 304–318.

Frauenglass, M. II., & Diaz, R. M. (1985). Self-regulatory functions of children's private speech: A critical analysis of recent challenges to Vygotsky's theory. *Developmental Psychology, 21,* 357–364.

Frederiksen, J. R., & Warren, B. M. (1987). A cognitive framework for developing expertise in reading. In R. Glaser (Ed.), *Advances in instructional psychology* (Vol. 3, pp. 1–39). Hillsdale, NJ: Erlbaum.

Freedman, D. G. (1976). *Developmental psychobiology: The significance of infancy.* Hillsdale, NJ: Erlbaum.

Freedman, D. G., & Freedman, N. (1969). Behavioral differences between Chinese-American and European-American newborns. *Nature, 224,* 1227.

Freeman, D. (1983). *Margaret Mead and Samoa: The making and unmaking of an anthropological myth.* Cambridge, MA: Harvard University Press.

French, D. C. (1984). Children's knowledge of the social functions of younger, older, and same-age peers. *Child Development, 55,* 1429–1433.

French, D. C., & Waas, G. A. (1985). Behavior problems of peer-neglected and peer-rejected elementary age children: Parent and teacher perspectives. *Child Development, 56,* 246–252.

Freud, A. (1958). Adolescence. *Psychoanalytic Study of the Child, 13,* 255–278.

Freud, A., & Dann, S. (1951). An experiment in group upbringing. *Psychoanalytic Study of the Child, 6,* 127–168.

Freud, S. (1933). *New introductory lectures on psychoanalysis.* New York: Norton.

Freud, S. (1953). Three essays on the theory of sexuality. In J. Strachey (Ed.), *The standard edition of the complete psychological works of Sigmund Freud* (Vol. 7, pp. 125–248). London: Hogarth Press. (Original work published 1905)

Freud, S. (1961). Some psychological consequences of the anatomical distinction between the sexes. In J. Strachey (Ed.), *Standard edition of the complete psychological works of Sigmund Freud* (Vol. 19, pp. 248–258). London: Hogarth Press. (Original work published 1925)

Freud, S. (1973). *An outline of psychoanalysis.* London: Hogarth. (Original work published 1938)

Freud, S. (1974). *The ego and the id.* London: Hogarth. (Original work published 1923)

Frey, K. S., & Ruble, D. N. (1992). Gender constancy and the "cost" of sex-typed behavior: A test of the conflict hypothesis. *Developmental Psychology, 28,* 714–721.

Fried, P. A., & Makin, J. E. (1987). Neonatal behavioral correlates of prenatal exposure to marijuana, cigarettes, and alcohol in a low risk population. *Neurobehavioral Toxicology and Teratology, 9,* 1–7.

Fried, P. A., & O'Connell, C. M. (1987). A comparison of the effects of prenatal exposure to tobacco, alcohol, cannabis, and caffeine on birth size and subsequent growth. *Neurobehavioral Toxicology and Teratology, 9,* 79–85.

Fried, P. A., & Watkinson, B. (1990). 36- and 48-month neurobehavioral follow-up of children prenatally exposed to marijuana, cigarettes, and alcohol. *Journal of Developmental and Behavioral Pediatrics, 11,* 49–58.

Fried, P. A., Watkinson, B., & Dillon, R. F. (1987). Neonatal neurological status in a low-risk population after prenatal exposure to cigarettes, marijuana, and alcohol. *Journal of Developmental and Behavioral Pediatrics, 8,* 318–326.

Friedman, J. A., & Weinberger, H. L. (1990). Six children with lead poisoning. *American Journal of Diseases of Children, 144,* 1039–1044.

Friedman, L. (1989). Mathematics and the gender gap: A meta-analysis of recent studies on sex differences in mathematical tasks. *Review of Educational Research, 59,* 185–214.

Friedman, M., & Rosenman, R. H. (1959). Association of specific overt behavior patterns with blood and cardiovascular findings. *Journal of the American Medical Association, 169,* 1286–1296.

Friedrich-Cofer, L., & Huston, A. C. (1986). Television violence and aggression: The debate continues. *Psychological Bulletin, 100,* 364–371.

Friedrich-Cofer, L. K., Tucker, C. J., Norris-Baker, C., Farnsworth, J. B., Fisher, D. P., Hannington, C. M., & Hoxie, K. (1978). *Perceptions by adolescents of television heroines.* Paper presented at the annual meeting of the Southwestern Psychological Association, New Orleans.

Frisch, R. E., Gotz-Welbergen, A., McArthur, J. W., Albright, T., Witschi, J., Bullen, B., Birnholz, J., Reed, R. B., & Hermann, H. (1981). Delayed menarche and amenorrhea of college athletes in relation to age of onset of training. *Journal of the American Medical Association, 246,* 1559–1563.

Frodi, A. (1985). When empathy fails: Aversive infant crying and child abuse. In B. M. Lester & C. F. Z. Boukydis (Eds.), *Infant crying: Theoretical and research perspectives* (pp. 263–277). New York: Plenum.

Froggatt, P., Beckwith, J. B., Schwartz, P. J., Valdes-Dapena, M., & Southall, D. P. (1988). Cardiac and respiratory mechanisms that might be responsible for sudden infant death syndrome. In P. J. Schwartz, D. P. Southall, & M. Valdes-Dapena (Eds.), *The sudden infant death syndrome* (Annals of the New York Academy of Sciences, Vol. 533, pp. 421–426). New York: The New York Academy of Sciences.

Fuchs, I., Eisenberg, N., Hertz-Lazarowitz, R., & Sharabany, R. (1986). Kibbutz, Israeli city, and American children's moral reasoning about prosocial moral conflicts. *Merrill-Palmer Quarterly, 32,* 37–50.

Funder, D. C., Block, J. H., & Block, J. (1983). Delay of gratification: Some longitudinal personality correlates. *Journal of Personality and Social Psychology, 44,* 1198–1213.

Furman, W., & Buhrmester, D. (1992). Age and sex differences in perceptions of networks of personal relationships. *Child Development, 63,* 103–115.

Furrow, D., & Nelson, K. (1984). Environmental correlates of individual differences in language acquisition. *Journal of Child Language, 11,* 523–534.

Furstenberg, F. F., Jr., Brooks-Gunn, J., & Chase-Landsdale, L. (1989). Teenaged pregnancy and childbearing. *American Psychologist, 44,* 313–320.

Furstenberg, F. F., Jr., Brooks-Gunn, J., & Morgan, S. P. (1987). *Adolescent mothers and their children in later life.* Cambridge: Cambridge University Press.

Furstenberg, F. F., Jr., & Cherlin, A. J. (1991). *Divided families.* Cambridge, MA: Harvard University Press.

Furstenberg, F. F., Jr., & Crawford, D. B. (1978). Family support: Helping teenagers to cope. *Family Planning Perspectives, 10,* 322–333.

Furstenberg, F. F., Jr., Levine, J. A., & Brooks-Gunn, J. (1990). The children of teenage mothers: Patterns of early childbearing in two generations. *Family Planning Perspectives, 22,* 54–61.

Furstenberg, F. F., Jr., & Nord, C. W. (1985). Parenting apart: Patterns of childrearing after marital disruption. *Journal of Marriage and the Family, 47,* 893–904.

Fuson, K. C. (1988). *Children's counting and concepts of number.* New York: Springer-Verlag.

Fuson, K. C. (1992). Research on learning and teaching addition and subtraction of whole numbers. In G. Leinhardt, R. T. Putnam, & R. A. Hattrup (Eds.), *The analysis of arithmetic for mathematics teaching* (pp. 53–187). Hillsdale, NJ: Erlbaum.

Fuson, K. C., & Kwon, Y. (1992). Korean children's understanding of multidigit addition and subtraction. *Child Development, 63,* 491–506.

Fyans, L. J., Jr., Salili, F., Maehr, M. L., & Desai, K. A. (1983). A cross-cultural exploration into the meaning of achievement. *Journal of Personality and Social Psychology, 44,* 1000–1013.

G

Gaddis, A., & Brooks-Gunn, J. (1985). The male experience of pubertal change. *Journal of Youth and Adolescence, 14,* 61–69.

Gaensbauer, T. J. (1980). Anaclitic depression in a three-and-one-half month-old child. *American Journal of Psychiatry, 137,* 841–842.

Gagan, R. J. (1984). The families of children who fail to thrive: Preliminary investigations of parental deprivation among organic and non-organic cases. *Child Abuse and Neglect, 8,* 93–103.

Gage, N. (1978). The yield of research on teaching. *Phi Delta Kappan, 59,* 229–235.

Galambos, N. L., & Maggs, J. L. (1991). Children in self-care: Figures, facts, and fiction. In J. V. Lerner & N. L. Galambos (Eds.), *Employed mothers and their children* (pp. 131–157). New York: Garland.

Galambos, S. J., & Goldin-Meadow, S. (1990). The effects of learning two languages on levels of metalinguistic awareness. *Cognition, 34,* 1–56.

Galin, D., Johnstone, J., Nakell, L., & Herron, J. (1979). Development of the capacity for tactile information transfer between hemispheres in normal children. *Science, 204,* 1330–1332.

Galler, J. R., Ramsey, F., & Solimano, G. (1985a). A follow-up study of the effects of early malnutrition on subsequent development: I. Physical growth and sexual maturation during adolescence. *Pediatric Research, 19,* 518–523.

Galler, J. R., Ramsey, F., & Solimano, G. (1985b). A follow-up study of the effects of early malnutrition on subsequent development: II. Fine motor skills in adolescence. *Pediatric Research, 19,* 524–527.

Galler, J. R., Ramsey, F., Solimano, G., Kucharski, L. T., & Harrison, R. (1984). The influence of early malnutrition on subsequent behavioral development: IV. Soft neurological signs. *Pediatric Research, 18,* 826–832.

Gallimore, R., & Tharp, R. (1990). Teaching mind in society: Teaching, schooling, and literate discourse. In L. C. Moll (Ed.), *Vygotsky and education* (pp. 175–205). New York: Cambridge University Press.

Gallup, G. (1987). More today than in 1985 say premarital sex is wrong. *The Gallup Report, 263,* 20.

Galotti, K. M., Kozberg, S. F., & Farmer, M. C. (1991). Gender and developmental differences in adolescents' conceptions of moral reasoning. *Journal of Youth and Adolescence, 20,* 13–30.

Galton, F. (1883). *Inquiries into human faculty and its development.* London: Macmillan.

Gandour, M. J. (1989). Activity level as a dimension of temperament in toddlers: Its relevance for the organismic specificity hypothesis. *Child Development, 60,* 1092–1098.

Gannon, S., & Korn, S. J. (1983). Temperament, cultural variation, and behavior disorder in preschool children. *Child Psychiatry and Human Development, 13,* 203–212.

Garbarino, J., & Sherman, D. (1980). High risk neighborhoods and high-risk families: The human ecology of child maltreatment. *Child Development, 51,* 188–198.

Gardner, H. (1980). *Artful scribbles: The significance of children's drawings.* New York: Basic Books.

Gardner, H. (1983). *Frames of mind.* New York: Basic Books.

Gardner, H., & Hatch, T. (1989, November). Multiple intelligences go to school. *Educational Researcher, 18*(8), 4–10.

Gardner, M. J., Snee, M. P., Hall, A. J., Powell, C. A., Downes, S., & Terrell, J. D. (1990). Leukemia cases linked to fathers' radiation dose. *Nature, 343,* 423–429.

Gardner, R. A., &, Gardner, B. T. (1969). Teaching sign language to a chimpanzee. *Science, 165,* 664–672.

Garland, A. F., & Zigler, E. (1993). Adolescent suicide prevention: Current research and social policy implications. *American Psychologist, 48,* 169–182.

Garmezy, N. (1983). Stressors of childhood. In N. Garmezy & M. Rutter (Eds.), *Stress, coping, and development in children* (pp. 43–84). New York: McGraw-Hill.

Garn, S. M., & Clark, D. C. (1976). Trends in fatness and the origins of obesity. *Pediatrics, 57,* 443–456.

Garvey, C. (1974). Requests and responses in children's speech. *Journal of Child Language, 2,* 41–60.

Garvey, C. (1990). *Play.* Cambridge, MA: Harvard University Press.

Garwood, S. G., Phillips, D., Hartman, A., & Zigler, E. F. (1989). As the pendulum swings: Federal agency programs for children. *American Psychologist, 44,* 434–440.

Gathercole, S. E., Willis, C. S., Emslie, H., & Baddeley, A. D. (1992). Phonological memory and vocabulary development during the early school years: A longitudinal study. *Developmental Psychology, 28,* 887–898.

Gathercole, V. C. (1987). The contrastive hypothesis for the acquisition of word meaning: A reconsideration of the theory. *Journal of Child Language, 14,* 493–531.

Gauvain, M., & Rogoff, B. (1989). Collaborative problem solving and children's planning skills. *Developmental Psychology, 25,* 139–151.

Geary, D. C., & Burlingham-Dubree, M. (1989). External validation of the strategy choice model for addition. *Journal of Experimental Child Psychology, 47,* 175–192.

Gekoski, M. J., Rovee-Collier, C. K., & Carulli-Rabinowitz, V. (1983). A longitudinal analysis of inhibition of infant distress: The origins of social expectations? *Infant Behavior and Development, 6,* 339–351.

Gellatly, A. R. H. (1987). Acquisition of a concept of logical necessity. *Human Development, 30,* 32–47.

Gelles, R. J., & Cornell, C. P. (1983). International perspectives on child abuse. *Child Abuse & Neglect, 7,* 375–386.

Gelman, R. (1972). Logical capacity of very young children: Number invariance rules. *Child Development, 43,* 75–90.

Gelman, R., & Baillargeon, R. (1983). A review of some Piagetian concepts. In P. H. Mussen (Ed.), *Handbook of child psychology: Vol. 3. Cognitive development* (4th ed., pp. 167–230). New York: Wiley.

Gelman, R., & Gallistel, C. R. (1986). *The child's understanding of number.* Cambridge, MA: Harvard University Press.

Gelman, R., & Shatz, M. (1978). Appropriate speech adjustments: The operation of conversational constraints on talk to two-year-olds. In M. Lewis & L. A. Rosenblum (Eds.), *Interaction, conversation, and the development of language* (pp. 27–61). New York: Wiley.

Gelman, S. A., & Ebeling, K. S. (1989). Children's use of nonegocentric standards in judgments of functional size. *Child Development, 60,* 920–932.

Gentner, D. (1982). Why nouns are learned before verbs: Linguistic relativity versus natural partitioning. In S. A. Kuczaj II (Ed.), *Language development: Vol. 2. Language, thought, and culture* (pp. 301–332). Hillsdale, NJ: Erlbaum.

George, C., Kaplan, N., & Main, M. (1985). *The Adult Attachment Interview.* Unpublished manuscript, University of California at Berkeley.

Gerbner, G., Gross, L., Signorielli, N., & Morgan, M. (1986). *Television's mean world: Violence Profile No. 14–15.* Philadelphia: Annenberg School of Communications, University of Pennsylvania.

Gerbner, G., Gross, L., Signorielli, N., Morgan, M., & Jackson-Beeck, M. (1979). The demonstration of power: Violence Profile No. 10. *Journal of Communication, 29* (3), 177–195.

Gerken, L. A., Landau, B., & Remez, R. (1990). Function morphemes in young children's speech perception and production. *Developmental Psychology, 26,* 204–216.

Gershman, E. S., & Hayes, D. S. (1983). Differential stability of reciprocal friendships and unilateral relationships among preschool children. *Merrill-Palmer Quarterly, 29,* 169–177.

Gershon, E. S., Targum, S. D., Kessler, L. R., Mazure, C. M., & Bunney, W. E., Jr. (1977). Genetics studies and biologic strategies in affective disorders. *Progress in Medical Genetics, 2,* 103–164.

Gesell, A. (1933). Maturation and patterning of behavior. In C. Murchison (Ed.), *A handbook of child psychology.* Worcester, MA: Clark University Press.

Gesell, A., & Ilg, F. L. (1949). The child from five to ten. In A. Gesell & F. Ilg (Eds.), *Child development* (pp. 394–454). New York: Harper & Row.

Gewirtz, J. (1969). Mechanisms of social learning: some roles of stimulation and behavior in early human development. In D. A. Goslin (Eds.), *Handbook of socialization theory and research* (pp. 57–212). Skokie, IL: Rand McNally.

Gewirtz, J. L., & Boyd, E. F. (1977a). Does maternal responding imply reduced infant crying? A critique of the 1972 Bell and Ainsworth report. *Child Development, 48,* 1200–1207.

Gewirtz, J. L., & Boyd, E. F. (1977b). In reply to the rejoinder to our critique of the 1972 Bell and Ainsworth report. *Child Development, 48,* 1217–1218.

Ghiglieri, M. P. (1988). *East of the mountains of the moon: Chimpanzee society in the African rain forest.* New York: Free Press.

Giaconia, R. M., & Hedges, L. V. (1982). *Identifying features of open education.* Stanford, CA: Stanford University Press.

Gibbs, J. C. (1991). Toward an integration of Kohlberg's and Hoffman's theories of morality. In W. M. Kurtines & J. L. Gewirtz (Eds.), *Handbook of moral behavior and development* (Vol. 1, pp. 183–222). Hillsdale, NJ: Erlbaum.

Gibbs, J. C. (1993). Moral-cognitive interventions. In A. P. Goldstein & C. R. Huff (Eds.), *The gang intervention handbook* (pp. 159–185). Champaign, IL: Research Press.

Gibbs, J. C., Arnold, K. D., & Burkhart, J. E. (1984). Sex differences in the expression of moral judgment. *Child Development, 53,* 1040–1043.

Gibbs, J. C., Basinger, K. S., & Fuller, D. (1992). *Moral maturity: Measuring the development of sociomoral reflection.* Hillsdale, NJ: Erlbaum.

Gibbs, J. C., Clark, P. M., Joseph, J. A., Green, J. L., Goodrick, T. S., & Makowski, D. G. (1986). Relations between moral judgment, moral courage, and field independence. *Child Development, 57,* 185–193.

Gibbs, J. C., Potter, G., & Goldstein, A. P. (in press). *EQUIP: Motivating and equipping youth to help one another.* Champaign, IL: Research Press.

Gibbs, J. C., & Schnell, S. V. (1985). Moral development "versus" socialization. *American Psychologist, 40,* 1071–1080.

Gibbs, J. C., & Widaman, K. F. (1982). *Social intelligence: Measuring the development of sociomoral reflection.* Englewood Cliffs, NJ: Prentice-Hall.

Gibson, D., & Harris, A. (1988). Aggregated early intervention effects for Down's syndrome persons: Patterning and longevity of benefits. *Journal of Mental Deficiency Research, 32,* 1–7.

Gibson, E. J. (1970). The development of perception as an adaptive process. *American Scientist, 58,* 98–107.

Gibson, E. J., Schapiro, F., & Yonas, A. (1968). *Confusion matrices for graphic patterns obtained with a latency measure.* Final report, Cornell University and U.S. Office of Education Project No. 5-1213, Contract No. OE6–10–156.

Gibson, E. J., & Spelke, E. S. (1983). The development of perception. In P. H. Mussen (Ed.), *Handbook of child psychology: Vol. 3. Cognitive development* (pp. 1–76). New York: Wiley.

Gibson, E. J., & Walk, R. D. (1960). The "visual cliff." *Scientific American, 202,* 64–71.

Gibson, J. J. (1979). *The ecological approach to visual perception.* Boston: Houghton Mifflin.

Gil, D. G. (1987). Maltreatment as a function of the structure of social systems. In M. R. Brassard, R. Germain, & S. N. Hart (Eds.), *Psychological maltreatment of children and youth* (pp. 159–170). New York: Pergamon Press.

Gilbert, E. H., & DeBlassie, R. R. (1984). Anorexia nervosa: Adolescent starvation by choice. *Adolescence, 76,* 839–846.

Gilfillan, M. C., Curtis, L., Liston, W. A., Pullen, I., Whyte, D. A., & Brock, D. J. H. (1992). Prenatal screening for cystic fibrosis. *Lancet, 340,* 214–216.

Gilger, J. W., & Ho, H-Z. (1989). Gender differences in adult spatial information processing: Their relationship to pubertal timing, adolescent activities, and sex-typing of personality. *Cognitive Development, 4,* 197–214.

Gilligan, C. F. (1982). *In a different voice.* Cambridge, MA: Harvard University Press.

Gilligan, C. F., & Attanucci, J. (1989). Two moral orientations: Gender differences and similarities. *Merrill-Palmer Quarterly, 34,* 223–237.

Ginsburg, H. P., & Opper, S. (1988). *Piaget's theory of intellectual development* (3rd ed.). Englewood Cliffs, NJ: Prentice-Hall.

Glass, D. C., Krakoff, L. R., Contrada, R., Hilton, W. F., Kehoe, K., Mannucci, E. G., Collins, C., Snow, B., & Elting, E. (1980). Effect of harassment and competition upon cardiovascular and plasma catecholamine responses in Type A and Type B individuals. *Psychophysiology, 17,* 453–463.

Glass, G. V., Cahen, L. S., Smith, M. L., & Filby, N. N. (1982). *School class size.* Beverly Hills, CA: Sage.

Glick, J. (1975). Cognitive development in cross-cultural perspective. In F. Horowitz (Ed.), *Review of child development research* (Vol. 4, pp. 595–654). Chicago: University of Chicago Press.

Glick, P. C. (1990). American families: As they are and were. *Sociology and Social Research, 74,* 139–145.

Gnepp, J. (1983). Children's social sensitivity: Inferring emotions from conflicting cues. *Developmental Psychology, 19,* 805–814.

Gnepp, J., McKee, E., & Domanic, J. A. (1987). Children's use of situational information to infer emotion: Understanding emotionally equivocal situations. *Developmental Psychology, 23,* 114–123.

Goduka, I. N., Poole, D. A., & Aotaki-Phenice, L. (1992). A comparative study of black South African children from three different contexts. *Child Development, 63,* 509–525.

Goelman, H. (1986). The language environments of family day care. In S. Kilmer (Ed.), *Advances in early education and day care* (Vol. 4, pp. 153–179). Greenwich, CT: JAI Press.

Goffin, S. G. (1988, March). Putting our advocacy efforts into a new context. *Young Children, 43(3),* 52–56.

Goldberg, W. A., & Easterbrooks, M. A. (1988). Maternal employment when children are toddlers and kindergartners. In A. E. Gottfried & A. W. Gottfried (Eds.), *Maternal employment and children's development: Longitudinal research.* New York: Plenum.

Goldfield, B. A. (1987). The contributions of child and caregiver to referential and expressive language. *Applied Psycholinguistics, 8,* 267–280.

Goldfield, B. A., & Reznick, J. S. (1990). Early lexical acquisition: Rate, content, and the vocabulary spurt. *Journal of Child Language, 17,* 171–183.

Goldin-Meadow, S., & Morford, M. (1985). Gesture in early language: Studies of deaf and hearing children. *Merrill-Palmer Quarterly, 31,* 145–176.

Goldin-Meadow, S., & Mylander, C. (1983). Gestural communication in deaf children: Noneffect of parental input on language development. *Science, 221,* 372–374.

Goldman-Rakic, P. S. (1987). Development of cortical circuitry and cognitive function. *Child Development, 58,* 601–622.

Goldschmid, M. L., & Bentler, P. M. (1968). *Manual: Concept Assessment Kit—Conservation.* San Diego: Educational and Industrial Testing Service.

Goldsmith, H. H. (1987). Roundtable: What is temperament? Four approaches. *Child Development, 58,* 505–529.

Goldsmith, H. H., & Gottesman, I. I. (1981). Origins of variation in behavioral style: A longitudinal study of temperament in young twins. *Child Development, 52,* 91–103.

Goldstein, A. P. (1990). *Delinquents on delinquency.* Champaign, IL: Research Press.

Goleman, D. (1980, February). 1,528 little geniuses and how they grew. *Psychology Today, 13(9),* 28–53.

Golinkoff, R. M. (1983). The preverbal negotiation of failed messages: Insights into the transition period. In R. M. Golinkoff (Ed.), *The transition of prelinguistic to linguistic communication* (pp. 57–78). Hillsdale, NJ: Erlbaum.

Golinkoff, R. M., Hirsh-Pasek, K., Bailey, L. M., & Wenger, N. R. (1992). Young children and adults use lexical principles to learn new nouns. *Developmental Psychology, 28,* 99–108.

Gomez-Schwartz, B., Horowitz, J. M., & Cardarelli, A. P. (1990). *Child sexual abuse: Initial effects.* Newbury Park, CA: Sage.

Göncü, A. (1993). Development of intersubjectivity in the dyadic play of preschoolers. *Early Childhood Research Quarterly, 8,* 99–116.

Good, T. L., & Power, C. (1976). Designing successful classroom environments for different types of students. *Journal of Curriculum Studies, 8,* 45–69.

Goodall, J. (1990). *Through a window: My thirty years with the chimpanzees of Gombe.* Boston: Houghton Mifflin.

Goodenough, F. L. (1931). *Anger in young children.* Minneapolis: University of Minnesota Press.

Goodlad, J. I. (1984). *A place called school.* New York: McGraw-Hill.

Goodman, G. S., Hirschman, J. E., Hepps, D., & Rudy, L. (1991). Children's memory for stressful events. *Merrill-Palmer Quarterly, 37,* 109–158.

Goodman, G. S., Taub, E. P., Jones, D. P. H., England, P., Port, L. K., Rudy, L., & Prado, L. (1992). Testifying in criminal court: Emotional effects on child sexual assault victims. *Monographs of the Society for Research in Child Development, 57* (5, Serial No. 229).

Goodman, K. S. (1986). *What's whole in whole language?* Portsmouth, NH: Heinemann.

Goodman, R. A., & Whitaker, H. A. (1985). Hemispherectomy: A review (1928–1981) with special reference to the linguistic abilities and disabilities of the residual right hemisphere. In R. A. Goodman & H. A. Whitaker (Eds.), *Hemispheric function and collaboration in the child* (pp. 121–155). New York: Academic Press.

Goodz, N. S. (1989). Parental language mixing in bilingual families. *Infant Mental Health Journal, 10,* 25–44.

Goossens, F. A., & van IJzendoorn, M. H. (1990). Quality of infants' attachments to professional caregivers: Relation to infant–parent attachment and day-care characteristics. *Child Development, 61,* 832–837.

Gopnik, A., & Choi, S. (1990). Do linguistic differences lead to cognitive differences? A cross-linguistic study of semantic and cognitive development. *First Language, 11,* 199–215.

Gopnik, A., & Meltzoff, A. N. (1986). Relations between semantic and cognitive development in the one-word stage: The specificity hypothesis. *Child Development, 57,* 1040–1053.

Gopnik, A., & Meltzoff, A. N. (1987a). The development of categorization in the second year and its relation to other cognitive and linguistic developments. *Child Development, 58,* 1523–1531.

Gopnik, A., & Meltzoff, A. N. (1987b). Language and thought in the young child: Early semantic developments and their relationships to object permanence, means–ends understanding, and categorization. In K. Nelson & A. Van Kleeck (Eds.), *Children's language* (Vol. 6, pp. 191–212). Hillsdale, NJ: Erlbaum.

Gopnik, A., & Meltzoff, A. N. (1992). Categorization and naming: Basic-level sorting in eighteen-month-olds and its relation to language. *Child Development, 63,* 1091–1103.

Gordon, P., & Chafetz, J. (1990). Verb-based versus class-based accounts of actionality effects in children's comprehension of passives. *Cognition, 36,* 227–254.

Gordon, S., & Gilgun, J. F. (1987). Adolescent sexuality. In V. B. Van Hasselt & M. Hersen (Eds.), *Handbook of adolescent psychology* (pp. 147–167). New York: Pergamon Press.

Gorn, G. J., & Goldberg, M. E. (1982). Behavioral evidence of the effects of televised food messages on children. *Journal of Consumer Research, 9,* 200–205.

Gortmaker, S. L., Dietz, W. H., & Cheung, L. W. Y. (1990). Inactivity, diet, and the fattening of America. *Journal of the American Dietetic Association, 90,* 1247–1252.

Gortmaker, S. L., Dietz, W. H., Sobol, A. M., & Wehler, C. A. (1987). Increasing pediatric obesity in the United States. *American Journal of Diseases of Children, 141,* 535–540.

Gottesman, I. I. (1963). Genetic aspects of intelligent behavior. In N. R. Ellis (Ed.), *Handbook of mental deficiency* (pp. 253–296). New York: McGraw-Hill.

Gottesman, I. I., Carey, G., & Hanson, D. R. (1983). Pearls and perils in epigenetic psychopathology. In S. B. Guze, E. J. Earls, & J. E. Barrett (Eds.), *Childhood psychopathology and development* (pp. 287–300). New York: Raven Press.

Gottfried, A. E. (1991). Maternal employment in the family setting: Developmental and environmental issues. In J. V. Lerner & N. L. Galambos (Eds.), *Employed mothers and their children* (pp. 63–84). New York: Garland.

Gottfried, A. E., Gottfried, A. W., & Bathurst, K. (1988). Maternal employment, family environment, and children's development: Infancy through the school years. In A. E. Gottfried & A. W. Gottfried (Eds.), *Maternal employment and children's development: Longitudinal research* (pp. 11–58). New York: Plenum.

Gottlieb, G. (1991). Experiential canalization of behavioral development: Theory. *Developmental Psychology, 27,* 4–13.

Gottman, J. M., Gonso, J., & Rasmussen, B. (1975). Social interaction, social competence, and friendship in children. *Child Development, 46,* 709–718.

Gould, M. S. (1990). Cluster suicides. In R. M. Lerner, A. C. Petersen, & J. Brooks-Gunn (Eds.), *The encyclopedia of adolescence* (Vol. 2, pp. 1117–1122). New York: Garland.

Gove, W. R., & Zeiss, C. (1987). Multiple roles and happiness. In F. Crosby (Ed.), *Spouse, parent, worker* (pp. 125–137). New Haven: Yale University Press.

Goy, R. W., & Goldfoot, D. A. (1974). Experiential and hormonal factors influencing development of sexual behavior in the male rhesus monkey. In R. O. Schmitt & F. G. Worden (Eds.), *The neurosciences* (pp. 571–581). Cambridge, MA: MIT Press.

Graham, F. K., Ernhart, C. B., Thurston, D. L., & Craft, M. (1962). Development three years after perinatal anoxia and other potentially damaging newborn experiences. *Psychological Monographs, 76*(3, No. 522).

Graham, P. (1979). Epidemiological studies. In H. C. Quay & J. S. Werry (Eds.), *Psychopathological disorders of childhood* (pp. 185–246). New York: Wiley.

Graham, S., Doubleday, C., & Guarino, P. A. (1984). The development of relations between perceived controllability and the emotions of pity, anger, and guilt. *Child Development, 55,* 561–565.

Gralinski, J. H., & Kopp, C. B. (1993). Everyday rules for behavior: Mothers' requests to young children. *Developmental Psychology, 29,* 573–584.

Grant, J. P. (1992). *The state of the world's children.* New York: Oxford University Press (in cooperation with UNICEF).

Grantham-McGregor, S., Schofield, W., & Powell, C. (1987). Development of severely malnourished children who received psychosocial stimulation: Six-year follow-up. *Pediatrics, 79,* 247–254.

Grattan, M. P., De Vos, E., Levy, J., & McClintock, M. K. (1992). Asymmetric action in the human newborn: Sex differences in patterns of organization. *Child Development, 63,* 273–289.

Grau, P. N. (1985). Counseling the gifted girl. *Gifted Child Today, 38,* 8–11.

Graves, S. N. (1975). *How to encourage positive racial attitudes.* Paper presented at the biennial meeting of the Society for Research in Child Development, Denver.

Gray, W. M. (1978). A comparison of Piagetian theory and criterion-referenced measurement. *Review of Educational Research, 48,* 223–250.

Graziano, W. G., French, D., Brownell, C. A., & Hartup, W. W. (1976). Peer interaction in same- and mixed-age triads in relation to chronological age and incentive condition. *Child Development, 47,* 707–714.

Green, J. A., Jones, L. E., & Gustafson, G. E. (1987). Perception of cries by parents and nonparents: Relation to cry acoustics. *Developmental Psychology, 23,* 370–382.

Green, R. (1987). *The "sissy boy" syndrome and the development of homosexuality*. New Haven: Yale University Press.

Greenberg, M., & Morris, N. (1974). Engrossment: The newborn's impact upon the father. *American Journal of Orthopsychiatry, 44,* 520–531.

Greenberger, E., & Goldberg, W. A. (1989). Work, parenting, and the socialization of children. *Developmental Psychology, 25,* 22–35.

Greenberger, E., & Steinberg, L. (1986). *When teenagers work*. New York: Basic Books.

Greenbowe, T., Herron, J. D., Lucas, C., Nurrenbern, S., Staver, J. R., & Ward, C. R. (1981). Teaching preadolescents to act as scientists: Replication and extension of an earlier study. *Journal of Educational Psychology, 73,* 705–711.

Greenfield, P. (1992, June). *Notes and references for developmental psychology*. Conference on Making Basic Texts in Psychology More Culture-Inclusive and Culture-Sensitive, Western Washington University, Bellingham, WA.

Greenfield, P. M. (1984). *Mind and media: The effects of television, video games, and computers*. Cambridge, MA: Harvard University Press.

Greeno, J. G. (1989). A perspective on thinking. *American Psychologist, 44,* 134–141.

Greenough, W. T., Black, J. E., & Wallace, C. S. (1987). Experience and brain development. *Child Development, 58,* 539–559.

Greif, E. B. (1979). *Sex differences in parent–child conversations: Who interrupts who?* Paper presented at the annual meeting of the Society for Research in Child Development, Boston.

Greif, E. B., & Berko Gleason, J. (1980). Hi, thanks, and good-bye: More routine information. *Language in Society, 9,* 159–166.

Greif, E. B., & Ulman, K. (1982). The psychological impact of menarche on early adolescent females: A review. *Child Development, 53,* 1413–1430.

Grimes, D. A., & Mishell, D. R., Jr. (1988). Congenital limb reduction deformities and oral contraceptives [letter]. *American Journal of Obstetrics and Gynecology, 158,* 439–440.

Grossman, H. J. (Ed.). (1983). *Classification in mental retardation*. Washington, DC: American Association on Mental Deficiency.

Grossmann, K., Fremmer-Bombik, E., Rudolph, J., & Grossmann, K. E. (1988). Maternal attachment representations as related to patterns of infant-mother attachment and maternal care during the first year. In R. A. Hinde & J. Stevenson-Hinde (Eds.), *Relationships within families: Mutual influences* (pp. 241–260). Oxford: Clarendon.

Grossmann, K., Grossmann, K. E., Spangler, G., Suess, G., & Unzner, L. (1985). Maternal sensitivity and newborns' orientation responses as related to quality of attachment in Northern Germany. In I. Bretherton & E. Waters (Eds.), Growing points of attachment theory and research. *Monographs of the Society for Research in Child Development, 50* (1–2, Serial No. 209).

Grotevant, H. D. (1978). Sibling constellations and sex-typing of interests in adolescence. *Child Development, 49,* 540–542.

Grotevant, H. D., & Cooper, C. (1988). The role of family experience in career exploration during adolescence. In P. Baltes, D. Featherman, & R. Lerner (Eds.), *Life-span development and behavior* (Vol. 8, pp. 231–258). Hillsdale, NJ: Erlbaum.

Grotevant, H. D., & Cooper, C. R. (1981). *Assessing adolescent identity in the areas of occupation, religion, politics, friendships, dating, and sex roles: Manual for administration and coding of the interview*. Austin: University of Texas.

Grotevant, H. D., & Cooper, C. R. (1985). Patterns of interaction in family relationships and the development of identity exploration in adolescence. *Child Development, 56,* 415–428.

Grusec, J. E. (1988). *Social development: History, theory, and research*. New York: Springer-Verlag.

Grusec, J. E. (1992). Social learning theory and developmental psychology: The legacies of Robert Sears and Albert Bandura. *Developmental Psychology, 28,* 776–786.

Grusec, J. E., & Abramovitch, R. (1982). Imitation of peers and adults in a natural setting: A functional analysis. *Child Development, 53,* 636–642.

Grusec, J. E., Kuczynski, L., Rushton, J., & Simutis, Z. (1979). Learning resistance to temptation through observation. *Developmental Psychology, 15,* 233–240.

Grusec, J. E., & Redler, E. (1980). Attribution, reinforcement, and altruism: A developmental analysis. *Developmental Psychology, 16,* 525–534.

Grusec, J. E., & Walters, G. C. (1991). Psychological abuse and childrearing belief systems. In R. H. Starr, Jr., & D. A. Wolfe (Eds.), *The effects of child abuse and neglect* (pp. 186–202). New York: Guilford.

Gu, B., Poston, D. L., & Shu, J. (1987). *The People's Republic of China population data sheet*. Austin: University of Texas.

Guerra, N. G., & Slaby, R. G. (1990). Cognitive mediators of aggression in adolescent offenders: 2. Intervention. *Developmental Psychology, 26,* 269–277.

Guidubaldi, J., & Cleminshaw, H. K. (1985). Divorce, family health and child adjustment. *Family Relations, 34,* 35–41.

Guilford, J. P. (1967). *The nature of human intelligence*. New York: McGraw-Hill.

Guilford, J. P. (1985). The structure-of-intellect model. In B. B. Wolman (Ed.), *Handbook of intelligence* (pp. 225–266). New York: Wiley.

Guilford, J. P. (1988). Some changes in the structure-of-intellect model. *Educational and Psychological Measurement, 48,* 1–4.

Gurucharri, C., & Selman, F. L. (1982). The development of interpersonal understanding during childhood, preadolescence, and adolescence: A longitudinal follow-up study. *Child Development, 53,* 924–927.

Gusella, J. L., Muir, D. W., & Tronick, E. Z. (1988). The effect of manipulating maternal behavior during an interaction on 3- and 6-month-olds' affect and attention. *Child Development, 59,* 1111–1124.

Gustafson, G. E., & Harris, K. L. (1990). Women's responses to young infant's cries. *Developmental Psychology, 26,* 144–152.

Gutiérrez, R., & Slavin, R. E. (1992). Achievement effects of the nongraded elementary school: A best evidence synthesis. *Review of Educational Research, 62,* 333–376.

H

Haan, N., Aerts, E., & Cooper, B. (1985). *On moral grounds: The search for practical morality*. New York: New York University Press.

Hadwin, J., & Perner, J. (1991) Pleased and surprised. Children's cognitive theory of emotion. *British Journal of Developmental Psychology, 9,* 215–234.

Haft, W. L., & Slade, A. (1989). Affect attunement and maternal attachment: A pilot study. *Infant Mental Health Journal, 10,* 157–172.

Hagen, J. W., Hargrove, S., & Ross, W. (1973). Prompting and rehearsal in short-term memory. *Child Development, 44,* 201–204.

Hahn, W. K. (1987). Cerebral lateralization of function: From infancy through childhood. *Psychological Bulletin, 101,* 376–392.

Hainline, L. (1985). Oculomotor control in human infants. In R. Groner, G. W. McConkie, & C. Menz (Eds.), *Eye movements and human information processing* (pp. 71–84). Amsterdam: Elsevier.

Hakuta, K. (1986). *Mirror of language.* New York: Basic Books.

Hakuta, K., Ferdman, B. M., & Diaz, R. M. (1987). Bilingualism and cognitive development: Three perspectives. In S. Rosenberg (Ed.), *Advances in applied psycholinguistics: Vol. 2. Reading, writing, and language learning* (pp. 284–319). New York: Cambridge University Press.

Hakuta, K., & Garcia, E. E. (1989). Bilingualism and education. *American Psychologist, 44,* 374–379.

Halford, G. S. (1990). *Children's understanding: The development of mental models.* Hillsdale, NJ: Erlbaum.

Hall, D. G. (1991). Acquiring proper nouns for familiar and unfamiliar animate objects: Two-year-olds' word-learning biases. *Child Development, 62,* 1142–1154.

Hall, G. S. (1904). *Adolescence* (Vols. 1–2). New York: Appleton-Century-Crofts.

Hall, J. A. (1978). Gender effects in decoding nonverbal cues. *Psychological Bulletin, 85,* 845–857.

Hall, J. A., & Halberstadt, A. G. (1980). Masculinity and femininity in children: Development of the Children's Attributes Questionnaire. *Developmental Psychology, 16,* 270–280.

Hall, J. A., & Halberstadt, A. G. (1981). Sex roles and nonverbal communication skills. *Sex Roles, 7,* 273–287.

Hall, J. G., Sybert, V. P., Williamson, R. A., Fisher, N. L., & Reed, S. D. (1982). Turner's syndrome. *West Journal of Medicine, 137,* 32–44.

Hall, W. S. (1989). Reading comprehension. *American Psychologist, 44,* 157–161.

Halmi, K. A. (1987). Anorexia nervosa and bulimia. In V. B. Van Hasselt & M. Hersen (Eds.), *Handbook of adolescent psychology* (pp. 265–287). New York: Pergamon Press.

Halpern, D. F. (1986). *Sex differences in cognitive abilities.* Hillsdale, NJ: Erlbaum.

Halverson, H. M. (1931). An experimental study of prehension in infants by means of systematic cinema records. *Genetic Psychology Monographs, 10,* 107–286.

Hamer, D. H., Hu, S., Magnuson, V. L., Hu, N., & Pattatucci, A. M. L. (1993). A linkage between DNA markers on the X chromosome and male sexual orientation. *Science, 261,* 321–327.

Hamilton, S. F. (1990). *Apprenticeship for adulthood: preparing youth for the future.* New York: Free Press.

Hamilton, S. F. (1993). Prospects for an American-style youth apprenticeship system. *Educational Researcher, 22*(3), 11–16.

Hammersley, M. (1992). *What's wrong with ethnography?* New York: Routledge.

Hammill, D. D. (1990). On defining learning disabilities: An emerging consensus. *Journal of Learning Disabilities, 23,* 74–84.

Hanigan, W. C., Morgan, A. M., Stahlberg, L. K., & Hiller, J. L. (1990). Tentorial hemorrhage associated with vacuum extraction. *Pediatrics, 85,* 534–539.

Hareven, T. K. (1982). American families in transition: Historical perspectives on change. In F. Walsh (Ed.), *Normal family processes* (pp. 446–466). New York: Guilford.

Harlow, H. F. (1969). Age-mate or peer affectional system. In D. S. Lehrman, R. A. Hinde, & E. Shaw (Eds.), *Advances in the study of behavior* (Vol. 2, pp. 333–383). New York: Academic Press.

Harlow, H. F., & Zimmerman, R. (1959). Affectional responses in the infant monkey. *Science, 130,* 421–432.

Härnqvist, K. (1968). Changes in intelligence from 13 to 18. *Scandinavian Journal of Psychology, 9,* 50–82.

Harper, L. V., & Huie, K. S. (1985). The effects of prior group experience, age, and familiarity on the quality and organization of preschoolers' social relationships. *Child Development, 56,* 704–717.

Harris, J. F., Durso, F. T., Mergler, N. L., & Jones, S. K. (1990). Knowledge base influences on judgments of frequency of occurrence. *Cognitive Development, 5,* 223–233.

Harris, P. L. (1983). Infant cognition. In M. M. Haith & J. J. Campos (Eds.), *Handbook of child psychology: Vol. 2. Infancy and developmental psychobiology* (4th ed., pp. 689–782). New York: Wiley.

Harris, P. L. (1991). The work of the imagination. In A. Whiten (Ed.), *Natural theories of mind* (pp. 283–304). Oxford: Blackwell.

Harris, R. T. (1991, March/April). Anorexia nervosa and bulimia nervosa in female adolescents. *Nutrition Today, 26*(2), 30–34.

Harris, S., Mussen, P. H., & Rutherford, E. (1976). Some cognitive, behavioral, and personality correlates of maturity of moral judgment. *Journal of Genetic Psychology, 128,* 123–135.

Harrison, A. O., Wilson, M. N., Pine, C. J., Chan, S. Q., & Buriel, R. (1990). Family ecologies of ethnic minority children. *Child Development, 61,* 347–362.

Hart, B. (1991). Input frequency and children's first words. *First Language, 11,* 289–300.

Hart, C. H., Ladd, G. W., & Burleson, B. R. (1990). Children's expectations of the outcomes of social strategies: Relations with sociometric status and maternal disciplinary styles. *Child Development, 61,* 127–137.

Hart, S. N., & Brassard, M. R. (1987). A major threat to children's mental health. *American Psychologist, 42,* 160–165.

Harter, S. (1982). The perceived competence scale for children. *Child Development, 53,* 87–97.

Harter, S. (1983). Developmental perspectives on the self-system. In E. M. Hetherington (Ed.), *Handbook of child psychology: Vol. 4. Socialization, personality, and social development* (4th ed., pp. 275–385). New York: Wiley.

Harter, S. (1986). Processes underlying the construction, maintenance, and enhancement of self-concept in children. In S. Suhls & A. Greenwald (Eds.), *Psychological perspectives of the self* (Vol. 3, pp. 136–182). Hillsdale, NJ: Erlbaum.

Harter, S. (1990). Issues in the assessment of the self-concept of children and adolescents. In A. LaGreca (Ed.), *Through the eyes of a child* (pp. 292–325). Boston: Allyn and Bacon.

Harter, S., & Buddin, B. J. (1987). Children's understanding of the simultaneity of two emotions: A five-stage developmental acquisition sequence. *Developmental Psychology, 23,* 388–399.

Harter, S., Wright, K., & Bresnick, S. (1987, April). *A developmental sequence of the emergence of self affects: The understanding of pride and shame.* Paper presented at the biennial meeting of the Society for Research in Child Development, Baltimore.

Hartman, C. R., & Burgess, A. W. (1989). Sexual abuse of children: Causes and consequences. In D. Cicchetti & V. Carlson (Eds.), *Child maltreatment* (pp. 95–128). New York: Cambridge University Press.

Hartup, W. W. (1974). Aggression in childhood: Developmental perspectives. *American Psychologist, 29,* 336–341.

Hartup, W. W. (1983). Peer relations. In E. M. Hetherington (Ed.), *Handbook of child psychology: Vol. 4. Socialization, personality, and social development* (4th ed., pp. 103–196). New York: Wiley.

Hartup, W. W., & Moore, S. G. (1990). Early peer relations: Developmental significance and prognostic implications. *Early Childhood Research Quarterly, 5,* 1–17.

Haugaard, J. J., & Reppucci, N. D. (1988). *The sexual abuse of children.* San Francisco: Jossey-Bass.

Haviland, J., & Lelwica, M. (1987). The induced affect response: 10-week-old infants' responses to three emotion expressions. *Developmental Psychology, 23,* 97–104.

Hawke, S., & Knox, D. (1978). The one-child family: A new lifestyle. *The Family Coordinator, 27,* 215–219.

Hawkins, D. J., & Lam, T. (1987). Teacher practices, social development, and delinquency. In J. D. Burchard & S. N. Burchard (Eds.), *Prevention of delinquent behavior* (pp. 241–274). Newbury Park, CA: Sage.

Hawkins, J., & Sheingold, K. (1986). The beginnings of a story: Computers and the organization of learning in classrooms. In J. A. Culbertson & L. L. Cunningham (Eds.), *Microcomputers and education* (85th yearbook of the National Society for the Study of Education, pp. 40–58). Chicago: University of Chicago Press.

Hawkins, R. P., & Pingree, S. (1978). A developmental exploration of the fear of success phenomenon as cultural stereotype. *Sex Roles, 4,* 539–547.

Hay, D. F. (1984). Social conflict in early childhood. In G. Whitehurst (Ed.), *Annals of child development* (Vol. 1, pp. 1–44). Greenwich, CT: JAI Press.

Hay, D. F., Caplan, M., Castle, J., & Stimson, C. A. (1991). Does sharing become increasingly "rational" in the second year of life? *Developmental Psychology, 27,* 987–993.

Hayden-Thomson, L., Rubin, K. H., & Hymel, S. (1987). Sex preferences in sociometric choices. *Developmental Psychology, 23,* 558–562.

Hayes, C. D. (1982). *Making policies for children: A study of the federal process.* Washington, DC: National Academy Press.

Hayes, C. D. (Ed.). (1987). *Risking the future: Adolescent sexuality, pregnancy, and childbearing* (Vol. 1). Washington, DC: National Academy Press.

Hayes, R. M. (1989). Homeless children. In F. J. Macchiarola & A. Gartner (Eds.), Caring for America's children. *Proceedings of the Academy of Political Science, 37* (No. 32), 58–69.

Hayne, H., Rovee-Collier, C. K., & Perris, E. E. (1987). Categorization and memory retrieval by three-month-olds. *Child Development, 58,* 750–767.

Haynes, C. F., Cutler, C., Gray, J., O'Keefe, K., & Kempe, R. S. (1983). Nonorganic failure to thrive: Implications of placement through analysis of videotaped interactions. *Child Abuse and Neglect, 7,* 321–328.

Hearold, S. (1986). A synthesis of 1,043 effects of television on social behavior. In G. Comstock (Ed.), *Public communications and behavior* (Vol. 1, pp. 65–133). New York: Academic Press.

Heath, S. B. (1982). Questioning at home and at school: A comparative study. In G. Spindler (Ed.), *Doing the ethnography of schooling: Educational anthropology in action* (pp. 102–127). New York: Holt.

Heath, S. B. (1989). Oral and literate traditions among black Americans living in poverty. *American Psychologist, 44,* 367–373.

Heath, S. B. (1990). The children of Trackton's children: Spoken and written language and social change. In J. Stigler, G. Herdt, & R. A. Shweder (Eds.), *Cultural psychology: Essays on comparative human development* (pp. 496–519). New York: Cambridge University Press.

Hebb, D. O. (1946). On the nature of fear. *Psychological Review, 53,* 259–276.

Hebb, D. O. (1949). *The organization of behavior.* New York: Wiley.

Heckhausen, H. (1988). Becoming aware of one's competence in the second year: Developmental progression within the mother–child dyad. *International Journal of Behavioral Development, 11,* 305–326.

Hedges, L. V., Giaconia, R. M., & Gage, N. L. (1981). *Meta-analysis of the effects of open and traditional instruction.* Stanford, CA: Stanford University, Program on Teaching Effectiveness.

Heinl, T. (1983). *The baby massage book.* London: Coventure.

Heinonen, O. P., Slone, D., & Shapiro, S. (1977). *Birth defects and drugs in pregnancy.* Littleton, MA: PSG Publishing.

Hendrick, J., & Stange, T. (1991). Do actions speak louder than words? An effect of the functional use of language on dominant sex role behavior in boys and girls. *Early Childhood Research Quarterly, 6,* 565–576.

Hendrix, L., & Johnson, G. D. (1985). Instrumental and expressive socialization: A false dichotomy. *Sex Roles, 13,* 581–595.

Henggeler, S. W. (1989). *Delinquency in adolescence.* Newbury Park, CA: Sage.

Henker, B., & Whalen, C. K. (1989). Hyperactivity and attention deficits. *American Psychologist, 44,* 216–223.

Herdt, G. H., & Davidson, J. (1988). The Sambia "Turnim-Man": Sociocultural and clinical aspects of gender formation in male pseudohermaphrodites with 5-alpha-reductase deficiency in Papua New Guinea. *Archives of Sexual Behavior, 17,* 33–56.

Hess, R., & McGarvey, L. (1987). School-relevant effects of educational uses of microcomputers in kindergarten classrooms and homes. *Journal of Educational Computer Research, 3,* 269–287.

Hetherington, E. M. (1988). Parents, children and siblings: Six years after divorce. In R. A. Hinde & J. Stevenson-Hinde (Eds.), *Relationships within families* (pp. 311–331). Oxford: Oxford University Press.

Hetherington, E. M. (1989). Coping with family transitions: Winners, losers, and survivors. *Child Development, 60,* 1–14.

Hetherington, E. M. (1991). The role of individual differences and family relationships in children's coping with divorce and remarriage. In P. A. Cowan & M. Hetherington (Eds.), *Family transitions* (pp. 165–194). Hillsdale, NJ: Erlbaum.

Hetherington, E. M., & Clingempeel, W. G. (1992). Coping with marital transitions: A family systems perspective. *Monographs of the Society for Research in Child Development, 57* (2–3, Serial No. 227).

Hetherington, E. M., Cox, M., & Cox, R. (1982). Effects of divorce on parents and children. In M. E. Lamb (Ed.), *Nontraditional families: Parenting and child development* (pp. 233–288). Hillsdale, NJ: Erlbaum.

Hetherington, E. M., Cox, M., & Cox, R. (1985). Long-term effects of divorce and remarriage on the adjustment of children. *Journal of the American Academy of Child and Adolescent Psychiatry, 24,* 518–530.

Hetherington, E. M., Stanley-Hagan, M., & Anderson, E. R. (1989). Marital transitions: A child's perspective. *American Psychologist, 44,* 303–312.

Hetherington, S. E. (1990). A controlled study of the effect of prepared childbirth classes on obstetric outcomes. *Birth, 17,* 86–90.

Hewlett, B. S. (Ed.). (1992a). *Father-child relations.* New York: Aldine De Gruyter.

Hewlett, B. S. (1992b). Husband–wife reciprocity and the father–infant relationship among Aka pygmies. In B. S. Hewlett (Ed.), *Father–child relations: Cultural and biosocial contexts* (pp. 153–176). New York: Aldine de Gruyter.

Heyman, G. D., & Dweck, C. S. (1992). Achievement goals and intrinsic motivation: Their relation and their role in adaptive motivation. *Motivation and Emotion, 16,* 231–247.

Heyman, G. D., Dweck, C. S., & Cain, K. M. (1992). Young children's vulnerability to self-blame and helplessness: Relationship to beliefs about goodness. *Child Development, 63,* 401–415.

Heyns, B. (1978). *Summer learning and the effects of schooling.* San Diego: Academic Press.

Hickey, T. L., & Peduzzi, J. D. (1987). Structure and development of the visual system. In P. Salapatek & L. Cohen (Eds.), *Handbook of infant perception: Vol. 1. From sensation to perception* (pp. 1–42). New York: Academic Press.

Hier, D. B., & Crowley, W. F. (1982). Spatial ability in adrogen-deficient men. *New England Journal of Medicine, 302,* 1202–1205.

Higgins, A. (1991). The just community approach to moral education: Evolution of the idea and recent findings. In W. M. Kurtines & J. L. Gewirtz (Eds.), *Handbook of moral behavior and development* (Vol. 3, pp. 111–141). Hillsdale, NJ: Erlbaum.

Higley, J. D., Hopkins, W. D., Thompson, W. W., Byrne, E. A., Hirsch, R. M., & Suomi, S. J. (1992). Peers as primary attachment sources in yearling rhesus monkeys (Macaca mulatta). *Developmental Psychology, 28,* 1163–1171.

Hill, C. R., & Stafford, F. P. (1980). Parental care of children: Time diary estimate of quantity, predictability, and variety. *Journal of Human Resources, 15,* 219–239.

Hill, J., & Holmbeck, G. (1986). Attachment and autonomy during adolescence. In G. Whitehurst (Ed.), *Annals of child development* (Vol. 3, pp. 145–189). Greenwich, CT: JAI Press.

Hill, P. M., & Humphrey, P. (1982). *Human growth and development throughout life: A nursing perspective.* New York: Delmar.

Hillier, L., Hewitt, K. L., & Morrongiello, B. A. (1992). Infants' perception of illusions in sound localization: Reaching to sounds in the dark. *Journal of Experimental Child Psychology, 53,* 159–179.

Hillman, S. B., & Davenport, G. G. (1978). Teacher-student interactions in desegregated schools. *Journal of Educational Psychology, 70,* 545–553.

Hinde, R. A. (1989). Ethological and relationships approaches. In R. Vasta (Ed.), *Annals of child development* (Vol. 6, pp. 251–285). Greenwich, CT: JAI Press.

Hinde, R. A., Stevenson-Hinde, J., & Tamplin, A. (1985). Characteristics of 3- to 4-year-olds assessed at home and their interactions in preschool. *Developmental Psychology, 21,* 130–140.

Hines, M. (1982). Prenatal gonadal hormones and sex differences in human behavior. *Psychological Bulletin, 92,* 56–80.

Hines, M., & Green, R. (1991). Human hormonal and neural correlates of sex-typed behaviors. *Review of Psychiatry, 10,* 536–555.

Hirschi, T., & Hindelang, M. J. (1977). Intelligence and delinquency: A revisionist view. *American Sociological Review, 42,* 571–587.

Hirsh-Pasek, K., Kemler Nelson, D. G., Jusczyk, P. W., Cassidy, K. W., Druss, B., & Kennedy, L. (1987). Clauses are perceptual units for young infants. *Cognition, 26,* 269–286.

Hirshberg, L. M., & Svejda, M. (1990). When infants look to their parents: I. Infants' social referencing of mothers compared to fathers. *Child Development, 61,* 1175–1186.

Hiscock, M., & Kinsbourne, M. (1987). Specialization of the cerebral hemispheres: Implications for learning. *Journal of Learning Disabilities, 20,* 130–143.

Ho, H., Glahn, T. J., & Ho, J. (1988). The fragile-X syndrome. *Developmental Medicine and Child Neurology, 30,* 257–261.

Hobart, C. (1987). Parent-child relations in remarried families. *Journal of Family Issues, 8,* 259–277.

Hobart, C., & Brown, D. (1988). Effects of prior marriage children on adjustment in remarriages: A Canadian study. *Journal of Comparative Family Studies, 19,* 381–396.

Hock, E., & DeMeis, D. (1987). *Depression in mothers of infants: The role of maternal employment.* Paper presented at the biennial meeting of the Society for Research in Child Development, Baltimore.

Hodges, J., & Tizard, B. (1989). Social and family relationships of ex-institutional adolescents. *Journal of Child Psychology and Psychiatry, 30,* 77–97.

Hodges, R. M., & French, L. A. (1988). The effect of class and collection labels on cardinality, class-inclusion, and number conservation tasks. *Child Development, 59,* 1387–1396.

Hofferth, S. L. (1984). Long-term economic consequences for women of delayed childbearing and reduced family size. *Demography, 21,* 141–155.

Hoffman, L. W. (1974). Effects of maternal employment on the child—A review of the research. *Developmental Psychology, 10,* 204–228.

Hoffman, L. W. (1984). Work, family, and the socialization of the child. In R. E. Parke (Ed.), *Review of child development research* (Vol. 7, pp. 223–282). Chicago: University of Chicago Press.

Hoffman, L. W. (1985). The changing genetics/socialization balance. *Journal of Social Issues, 41,* 127–148.

Hoffman, L. W. (1989). Effects of maternal employment in the two-parent family. *American Psychologist, 44,* 283–292.

Hoffman, M. L. (1980). Moral development in adolescence. In J. Adelson (Ed.), *Handbook of adolescent psychology* (pp. 295–343). New York: Wiley.

Hoffman, M. L. (1983). Affective and cognitive processes in moral internalization. In E. T. Higgins, D. N. Ruble, & W. W. Hartup (Eds.), *Social cognition and social development: A sociocultural perspective* (pp. 236–274). Cambridge: Cambridge University Press.

Hoffman, M. L. (1984). Interaction of affect and cognition in empathy. In C. E. Izard, J. Kagan, & R. B. Zajonc (Eds.), *Emotions, cognition, and behavior* (pp. 103–131). Cambridge: Cambridge University Press.

Hoffman, M. L. (1988). Moral development. In M. H. Bornstein & M. E. Lamb (Eds.), *Developmental psychology: An advanced textbook* (2nd ed., pp. 497–548). Hillsdale, NJ: Erlbaum.

Hoffman, M. L. (1991). Empathy, cognition, and social action. In W. M. Kurtines & J. L. Gewirtz (Eds.), *Handbook of moral behavior and development* (Vol. 1, pp. 275–303). Hillsdale, NJ: Erlbaum.

Hoffner, C., & Badzinski, D. M. (1989). Children's integration of facial and situational cues to emotion. *Child Development, 60,* 411–422.

Hofstede, G. (1980). *Culture's consequences: International differences in work-related values.* London: Sage.

Hofsten, C. von. (1984). Developmental changes in the organization of prereaching movements. *Developmental Psychology, 20,* 378–388.

Hofsten, C. von. (1989). Motor development as the development of systems: Comments on the special section. *Developmental Psychology, 25,* 950–953.

Hofsten, C. von, & Spelke, E. S. (1985). Object perception and object-directed reaching in infancy. *Journal of Experimental Psychology: General, 114,* 198–212.

Holden, G. W. (1983). Avoiding conflict: Mothers as tacticians in the supermarket. *Child Development, 54,* 233–240.

Holden, G. W., & Ritchie, K. L. (1991). Linking extreme marital discord, child rearing, and child behavior problems: Evidence from battered women. *Child Development, 62,* 311–327.

Holden, G. W., & West, M. J. (1989). Proximate regulation by mothers: A demonstration of how differing styles affect young children's behavior. *Child Development, 60,* 64–69.

Hollenbeck, A. R. (1978). Television viewing patterns of families with young infants. *Journal of Social Psychology, 105,* 259–264.

Holmbeck, G. N., & Hill, J. P. (1991). Conflictive engagement, positive affect, and menarche in families with seventh-grade girls. *Child Development, 62,* 1030–1048.

Honzik, M. P. (1983). Measuring mental abilities in infancy: The value and limitations. In M. Lewis (Ed.), *Origins of intelligence* (2nd ed., pp. 67–105). New York: Plenum.

Honzik, M. P., Macfarlane, J. W., & Allen, L. (1948). The stability of mental test performance between two and eighteen years. *Journal of Experimental Education, 17,* 309–329.

Hook, E. B. (1980). Genetic counseling dilemmas: Down syndrome, paternal age, and recurrence risk after remarriage. *American Journal of Medical Genetics, 5,* 145.

Hook, E. B. (1982). Epidemiology of Down syndrome. In S. M. Pueschel & J. E. Rynders (Eds.), *Down syndrome: Advances in biomedicine and the behavioral sciences* (pp. 21–43). Cambridge, MA: Ware Press.

Hook, E. B. (1988). Evaluation and projection of rates of chromosome abnormalities in chorionic villus studies (c.v.s.). *American Journal of Human Genetics Supplement, 43,* A108.

Hooper, F. H., & DeFrain, J. D. (1980). On delineating distinctly Piagetian contributions to education. *Genetic Psychology Monographs, 191,* 151–181.

Hopkins, B., & Westra, T. (1988). Maternal handling and motor development: An intracultural study. *Genetic, Social and General Psychology Monographs, 14,* 377–420.

Horan, J. J., & Straus, L. K. (1987). Substance abuse in adolescence. In V. B. Ban Hasselt & M. Hersen (Eds.), *Handbook of adolescent psychology* (pp. 313–331). New York: Pergamon Press.

Horgan, D. (1978). The development of the full passive. *Journal of Child Language, 5,* 65–80.

Horn, J. M. (1983). The Texas Adoption Project: Adopted children and their intellectual resemblance to biological and adoptive parents. *Child Development, 54,* 268–275.

Horner, T. M. (1980). Two methods of studying stranger reactivity in infants: A review. *Journal of Child Psychology and Psychiatry, 21,* 203–219.

Horowitz, F. D. (1987). *Expooring developmental theories: Toward a structural/behavioral model of development.* Hillsdale, NJ: Erlbaum.

Horowitz, F. D. (1992). John B. Watson's legacy: Learning and environment. *Developmental Psychology, 28,* 360–367.

Horowitz, F. D., & O'Brien, M. (1986). Gifted and talented children: State of knowledge and directions for research. *American Psychologist, 41,* 1147–1152.

Hort, B. E., Leinbach, M. D., & Fagot, B. I. (1991). Is there coherence among the cognitive components of gender acquisition? *Sex Roles, 24,* 195–207.

Horwitz, R. A. (1979). Psychological effects of the open classroom. *Review of Educational Research, 49,* 71–86.

Hotaling, G. T., Finkelhor, D., Kirkpatrick, J. T., & Strauss, M. A. (Eds.). (1988). *Family abuse and its consequences: New directions in research.* Newbury Park, CA: Sage.

Howe, N. (1991). Sibling-directed internal state language, perspective taking, and affective behavior. *Child Development, 62,* 1503–1512.

Howe, N., & Ross, H. S. (1990). Socialization, perspective-taking, and the sibling relationship. *Developmental Psychology, 26,* 160–165.

Howes, C. (1988a). Peer interaction of young children. *Monographs of the Society for Research in Child Development, 53* (1, Serial No. 217).

Howes, C. (1988b). Relations between early child care and schooling. *Developmental Psychology, 24,* 53–57.

Howes, C. (1990). Can the age of entry into child care and the quality of child care predict adjustment in kindergarten? *Developmental Psychology, 26,* 292–303.

Howes, C., & Farver, J. (1987). Social pretend play in 2-year-olds: Effects of age of partner. *Early Childhood Research Quarterly, 2,* 305–314.

Howes, C., & Matheson, C. C. (1992). Sequences in the development of competent play with peers: Social and social pretend play. *Developmental Psychology, 28,* 961–974.

Howes, C., Phillips, D. A., & Whitebook, M. (1992). Thresholds of quality: Implications for the social development of children in center-based child care. *Child Development, 63,* 449–460.

Howes, C., Rodning, C., Galluzzo, D. C., & Myers, L. (1988). Attachment and child care: Relationships with mother and caregiver. *Early Childhood Research Quarterly, 3,* 403–416.

Howes, C., & Stewart, P. (1987). Child's play with adults, toys, and peers: An examination of family and child-care influences. *Developmental Psychology, 23,* 423–430.

Howes, P., & Markman, H. J. (1989). Marital quality and child functioning: A longitudinal investigation. *Child Development, 60,* 1044–1051.

Hoyseth, K. S., & Jones, P. J. H. (1989). Ethanol induced teratogenesis: Characterization, mechanisms, and diagnostic approaches. *Life Sciences, 44,* 643–649.

Hubel, D. H., & Wiesel, T. N. (1970). The period of susceptibility to the physiological effects of unilateral eye closure in kittens. *Journal of Physiology, 206,* 419–436.

Hubert, N., Wachs, T. D., Peters-Martin, P., & Gandour, M. (1982). The study of early temperament: Measurement and conceptual issues. *Child Development, 53,* 571–600.

Hudson, J. A. (1988). Children's memory for atypical actions in script-based stories: Evidence for a disruption effect. *Journal of Experimental Child Psychology, 46,* 159–173.

Hudson, J. A., & Fivush, R. (1991). As time goes by: Sixth graders remember a kindergarten experience. *Applied Cognitive Psychology, 5,* 347–360.

Hudson, J., & Nelson, K. (1983). Effects of script structure on children's story recall. *Developmental Psychology, 19,* 625–635.

Huesmann, L. R. (1986). Psychological processes promoting the relation between exposure to media violence and aggressive behavior by the viewer. *Journal of Social Issues, 12,* 125–139.

Huesmann, L. R., Eron, L. D., Lefkowitz, M. M., & Walder, L. O. (1984). Stability of aggression over time and generations. *Developmental Psychology, 20,* 1120–1134.

Hughes, M., & Macleod, H. (1986). Part II: Using LOGO with very young children. In R. Lawler, B. D. Boulay, M. Hughes, & H. Macleod (Eds.), *Cognition and computers: Studies in learning* (pp. 179–219). Chichester, England: Ellis Horwood Limited.

Humphrey, T. (1978). Function of the nervous system during prenatal life. In U. Stave (Ed.), *Perinatal physiology* (pp. 651–683). New York: Plenum.

Humphreys, A. P., & Smith, P. K. (1987). Rough and tumble, friendship, and dominance in schoolchildren: Evidence for continuity and change with age. *Child Development, 58,* 201–212.

Humphreys, L. G. (1989). Intelligence: Three kinds of instability and their consequences for policy. In R. L. Linn (Ed.), *Intelligence* (pp. 193–216). Urbana: University of Illinois Press.

Humphreys, L. G., Rich, S. A., & Davey, T. C. (1985). A Piagetian test of general intelligence. *Developmental Psychology, 21,* 871–877.

Hunt, J. McV. (1961). *Intelligence and experience.* New York: Ronald Press.

Hunt, J. McV., Mohandessi, K., Ghodessi, M., & Akeyama, M. (1976). The psychological development of orphanage-reared infants: Interventions with outcomes (Tehran). *Genetic Psychology Monographs, 94,* 177–226.

Hunter, J. E., & Hunter, R. F. (1984). Validity and utility of alternative predictors of job performance. *Psychological Bulletin, 96,* 72–98.

Hunter, R. S., & Kilstrom, N. (1979). Breaking the cycle in abusive families. *American Journal of Psychiatry, 136,* 1320–1322.

Huntington, L., Hans, S. L., & Zeskind, P. S. (1990). The relations among cry characteristics, demographic variables, and developmental test scores in infants prenatally exposed to methadone. *Infant Behavior and Development, 13,* 533–538.

Husén, T. (1967). *International study of achievement in mathematics: A comparison of twelve countries.* New York: Wiley.

Huston, A. C. (1983). Sex-typing. In E. M. Hetherington (Ed.), *Handbook of child psychology: Vol. 4. Socialization, personality, and social development* (4th ed., pp. 387–467). New York: Wiley.

Huston, A. C., & Alvarez, M. M. (1990). The socialization context of gender role development in early adolescence. In R. Montemayor, G. R. Adams, & T. P. Gullotta (Eds.), *From childhood to adolescence: A transitional period?* (pp. 156–179). Newbury Park, CA: Sage.

Huston, A. C., Greer, D., Wright, J. C., Welch, R., & Ross, R. (1984). Children's comprehension of televised formal features with masculine and feminine connotations. *Developmental Psychology, 20,* 707–716.

Huston, A. C., Watkins, B. A., & Kunkel, D. (1989). Public policy and children's television. *American Psychologist, 44,* 424–433.

Huston, A. C., Wright, J. C., Rice, M. L., Kerkman, D., & St. Peters, M. (1990). Development of television viewing patterns in early childhood: A longitudinal investigation. *Developmental Psychology, 26,* 409–420.

Huston-Stein, A., Fox, S., Greer, D., Watkins, B. A., & Whitaker, J. (1981). The effects of TV action and violence on children's social behavior. *Journal of Genetic Psychology, 138,* 183–191.

Huston-Stein, A., & Higgins-Trenk, A. (1978). Development of females from childhood through adulthood: Career and feminine role orientations. In P. B. Baltes (Ed.), *Life-span development and behavior* (Vol. 1, pp. 257–296). New York: Academic Press.

Huttenlocher, J., & Burke, D. (1976). Why does memory span increase with age? *Cognitive Psychology, 8,* 1–31.

Huttenlocher, J., Haight, W., Bryk, A., Seltzer, M., & Lyons, T. (1991). Early vocabulary growth: Relation to language input and gender. *Developmental Psychology, 27,* 236–248.

Huttunen, M. O., & Niskanen, P. (1978). Prenatal loss of father and psychiatric disorders. *Archives of General Psychiatry, 35,* 429–431.

Hyde, J. S. (1984). How large are gender differences in aggression? A developmental meta-analysis. *Developmental Psychology, 20,* 722–736.

Hyde, J. S., Fenema, E., & Lamon, S. J. (1990). Gender differences in mathematics performance: A meta-analysis. *Psychological Bulletin, 107,* 139–155.

Hyde, J. S., & Linn, M. C. (1988). Gender differences in verbal ability: A meta-analysis. *Psychological Bulletin, 104,* 53–69.

Hymel, S. (1983). Preschool children's peer relations: Issues in sociometric assessment. *Merrill-Palmer Quarterly, 19,* 237–260.

Hynd, G. W., Horn, K. L., Voeller, K. K., & Marshall, R. M. (1991). Neurobiological basis of attention-deficit hyperactivity disorder (ADHD). *School Psychology Review, 20,* 174–186.

I

Iannotti, R. J. (1985). Naturalistic assessment of prosocial behavior in preschool children: The influence of empathy and perspective taking. *Developmental Psychology, 21,* 46–55.

Imperato-McGinley, J., Peterson, R. E., Gautier, T., & Sturla, E. (1979). Steroid 5 alpha-reductase deficiency in man: An inherited form of male pseudohermaphroditism. *Science, 186,* 1213–1243.

Ingram, D. (1986). Phonological development: Production. In P. Fletcher & M. Garman (Eds.), *Language acquisition* (2nd ed., pp. 223–239). Cambridge: Cambridge University Press.

Inhelder, B., & Piaget, J. (1958). *The growth of logical thinking from childhood to adolescence: An essay on the construction of formal operational structures.* New York: Basic Books. (Original work published 1955)

Inoff-Germain, G., Arnold, G. S., Nottelman, E. D., Susman, E. J., Cutler, G. B., Jr., & Crousos, G. P. (1988). Relations between hormone levels and observational measures of aggressive behavior of young adolescents in family interactions. *Developmental Psychology, 24,* 129–139.

International Education Association. (1988). *Science achievement in seventeen countries: A preliminary report.* Oxford: Pergamon Press.

Intons-Peterson, M. J. (1988). *Gender concepts of Swedish and American youth.* Hillsdale, NJ: Erlbaum.

Irvine, J. J. (1986). Teacher–student interactions: Effects of student race, sex, and grade level. *Journal of Educational Psychology, 78,* 14–21.

Isaacs, S. (1933). *Social development in young children: A study of beginnings.* London: Routledge.

Isabella, R. A. (1993). Origins of attachment: Maternal interactive behavior across the first year. *Child Development, 64,* 605–621.

Isabella, R., & Belsky, J. (1991). Interactional synchrony and the origins of infant–mother attachment: A replication study. *Child Development, 62,* 373–384.

Istvan, J. (1986). Stress, anxiety, and birth outcomes: A critical review of the evidence. *Psychological Bulletin, 100,* 331–348.

Izard, C. E. (1979). *The maximally discriminative facial movement scoring system.* Unpublished manuscript, University of Delaware.

Izard, C. E. (1991). *The psychology of emotions.* New York: Plenum.

Izard, C. E., Haynes, O. M., Chisholm, G., & Baak, K. (1991). Emotional determinants of infant-mother attachment. *Child Development, 62,* 906–917.

Izard, C. E., Hembree, E. A., & Huebner, R. R. (1987). Infants' emotion expressions to acute pain. *Developmental Psychology, 23,* 105–113.

Izard, C. E., & Malatesta, C. Z. (1987). Perspectives on emotional development I: Differential emotions theory of early emotional development. In J. D. Osofsky (Ed.), *Handbook of infant development* (2nd ed., pp. 494–554). New York: Wiley.

J

Jacklin, C. N., & Maccoby, E. E. (1978). Social behavior at thirty-three months in same-sex and mixed-sex dyads. *Child Development, 49,* 557–569.

Jacklin, C. N., & Maccoby, E. E. (1983). Issues of gender differentiation in normal development. In M. D. Levine, W. B. Carey, A. C. Crocker, & R. T. Gross (Eds.), *Developmental-behavioral pediatrics* (pp. 175–184). Philadelphia: Saunders.

Jackson, P. W. (1968). *Life in classrooms.* New York: Holt, Rinehart and Winston.

Jacobs, F. H., & Davies, M. W. (1991). Rhetoric or reality? Child and family policy in the United States. *Social Policy Report of the Society for Research in Child Development, 5* (No. 4).

Jacobs, J. E. (1991). Influence of gender stereotypes on parent and child mathematics attitudes. *Journal of Educational Psychology, 83,* 518–527.

Jacobson, J. L., Jacobson, S. W., Fein, G., Schwartz, P. M., & Dowler, J. (1984). Prenatal exposure to an environmental toxin: A test of the multiple effects model. *Developmental Psychology, 20,* 523–532.

Jacobson, J. L., Jacobson, S. W., & Humphrey, H. E. B. (1990). Effects of in utero exposure to polychlorinated biphenyls on cognitive functioning in young children. *Journal of Pediatrics, 116,* 38–45.

Jacobson, J. L., Jacobson, S. W., Padgett, R. J., Brumitt, G. A., & Billings, R. L. (1992). Effects of prenatal PCB exposure on cognitive processing efficiency and sustained attention. *Developmental Psychology, 28,* 297–306.

Jacobson, J. L., Tianen, R. L., Wille, D. E., & Aytch, D. M. (1986). Infant-mother attachment and early peer relations: The assessment of behavior in an interactive context. In E. Mueller & C. Cooper (Eds.), *Process and outcome in peer relations* (pp. 57–78). New York: Academic Press.

Jacobson, S. W., Fein, G. G., Jacobson, J. L., Schwartz, P. M., & Dowler, J. (1985). The effect of intrauterine PCB exposure on visual recognition memory. *Child Development, 56,* 853–860.

James, W. (1963). *Psychology.* New York: Fawcett. (Original work published 1890)

Jencks, C. (1972). *Inequality: A reassessment of the effect of family and schooling in America.* New York: Basic Books.

Jensen, A. R. (1969). How much can we boost IQ and scholastic achievement? *Harvard Educational Review, 39,* 1–123.

Jensen, A. R. (1973). *Educability and group differences.* New York: Harper & Row.

Jensen, A. R. (1974). Cumulative deficit: A testable hypothesis. *Developmental Psychology, 10,* 996–1019.

Jensen, A. R. (1980). *Bias in mental testing.* New York: Free Press.

Jensen, A. R. (1985). The nature of the black-white difference on various psychometric tests: Spearman's hypothesis. *Behavioral and Brain Sciences, 8,* 193–219.

Jensen, A. R. (1987). Individual differences in the Hick paradigm. In P. A. Vernon (Ed.), *Speed of information processing and intelligence* (pp. 101–176). Norwood, NJ: Ablex.

Jensen, A. R. (1988). Speed of information processing and population differences. In S. H. Irvine & J. W. Berry (Eds.), *Human abilities in cultural context* (pp. 105–145). New York: Cambridge University Press.

Jensen, A. R., & Figueroa, R. A. (1975). Forward and backward digit-span interaction with race and IQ: Predictions from Jensen's theory. *Journal of Educational Psychology, 67,* 882–893.

Johnson, C. L., Stuckey, M. K., Lewis, L. D., & Schwartz, D. M. (1983). A survey of 509 cases of self-reported bulimia. In P. L. Darby (Ed.), *Anorexia nervosa: Recent developments in research* (pp. 159–171). New York: Alan R. Liss.

Johnson, E. S., & Meade, A. C. (1987). Developmental patterns of spatial ability: An early sex difference. *Child Development, 58,* 725–740.

Johnson, J. E., & Hooper, F. H. (1982). Piagetian structuralism and learning: Two decades of educational application. *Contemporary Educational Psychology, 7,* 217–237.

Johnson, J. S., & Newport, E. L. (1989). Critical period effects in second language learning: The influence of maturational state on the acquisition of English as a second language. *Cognitive Psychology, 21,* 60–99.

Johnston, F. E. (1980). The causes of malnutrition. In L. S. Greene & F. E. Johnston (Eds.), *Social and biological predictors of nutritional status, physical growth, and neurological development* (pp. 1–6). New York: Academic Press.

Johnston, J. R., Kline, M., & Tschann, J. M. (1989). Ongoing post-divorce conflict: Effects on children of joint custody and frequent access. *American Journal of Orthopsychiatry, 59,* 576–592.

Johnston, J. R., & Slobin, D. I. (1979). The development of locative expressions in English, Italian, Serbo-Croatian, and Turkish. *Journal of Child Language, 16,* 531–547.

Jones, C. P., & Adamson, L. B. (1987). Language use in mother–child–sibling interactions. *Child Development, 58,* 356–366.

Jones, E. F., Forrest, J. D., Goldman, N., Henshaw, S. K., Lincoln, R., Rosoff, J. I., Westoff, C. F., & Wulf, D. (1985). Teenage pregnancy in developed countries: Determinants and policy implications. *Family Planning Perspectives, 17,* 53–63.

Jones, G. P., & Dembo, M. H. (1989). Age and sex role differences in intimate friendships during childhood and adolescence. *Merrill-Palmer Quarterly, 35,* 445–462.

Jones, M. C. (1965). Psychological correlates of somatic development. *Child Development, 36,* 899–911.

Jones, M. C., & Bayley, N. (1950). Physical maturing among boys as related to behavior. *Journal of Educational Psychology, 41,* 129–148.

Jones, M. C., & Mussen, P. H. (1958). Self-conceptions, motivations, and interpersonal attitudes of early- and late-maturing girls. *Child Development, 29,* 491–501.

Jones, S. S., & Raag, T. (1989). Smile production in older infants: The importance of a social recipient for the facial signal. *Child Development, 60,* 811–818.

Jordan, B. (1980). *Birth in four cultures.* Montreal: Eden.

Jorgensen, M., & Keiding, N. (1991). Estimation of spermarche from longitudinal spermaturia data. *Biometrics, 47,* 177–193.

Jouriles, E. N., Murphy, C. M., Farris, A. M., Smith, D. A., Richters, J. E., & Waters, E. (1991). Marital adjustment, parental disagreements about child rearing, and behavior problems in boys: Increasing the specificity of the marital assessment. *Child Development, 62,* 1424–1433.

K

Kagan, J. (1980). Four questions in psychological development. *International Journal of Behavioral Development, 3,* 231–241.

Kagan, J. (1987). Introduction. In J. Kagan & S. Lamb (Eds.), *The emergence of morality in young children* (pp. ix–xx). Chicago: University of Chicago Press.

Kagan, J. (1989). *Unstable ideas: Temperament, cognition, and self.* Cambridge, MA: Cambridge University Press.

Kagan, J. (1992). Behavior, biology, and the meanings of temperamental constructs. *Pediatrics, 90,* 510–513.

Kagan, J., Kearsley, R. B., & Zelazo, P. R. (1978). *Infancy: Its place in human development.* Cambridge, MA: Harvard University Press.

Kagan, J., Klein, R. E., Finley, G. E., Rogoff, B., & Nolan, E. (1979). A cross-cultural study of cognitive development. *Monographs of the Society for Research in Child Development, 44* (5, Serial No. 180).

Kagan, J., Reznick, J. S., & Gibbons, J. (1989). Inhibited and uninhibited types of children. *Child Development, 60,* 838–845.

Kagan, J., & Snidman, N. (1991). Temperamental factors in human development. *American Psychologist, 46,* 856–862.

Kahn, P. H., Jr. (1992). Children's obligatory and discretionary moral judgments. *Child Development, 63,* 416–430.

Kail, R. (1988). Developmental functions for speeds of cognitive processes. *Journal of Experimental Child Psychology, 45,* 339–364.

Kail, R. (1990). *The development of memory in children* (3rd ed.). New York: Freeman.

Kail, R. (1991). Processing time declines exponentially during childhood and adolescence. *Developmental Psychology, 27,* 259–266.

Kain, E. L. (1990). *The myth of family decline.* Lexington, MA: Lexington Books.

Kaitz, M., Meschulach-Sarfaty, O., Auerbach, J., & Eidelman, A. (1988). A reexamination of newborns' ability to imitate facial expressions. *Developmental Psychology, 24,* 3–7.

Kaler, S. R., & Kopp, C. B. (1990). Compliance and comprehension in very young toddlers. *Child Development, 61,* 1997–2003.

Kalter, N., Riemer, B., Brickman, A., & Chen, J. W. (1985). Implications of parental divorce for female development. *Journal of the American Academy of Child Psychiatry, 24,* 538–544.

Kamerman, S. B. (1993). International perspectives on child care policies and programs. *Pediatrics, 91,* 248–252.

Kandall, S. R., & Gaines, J. (1991). Maternal substance use and subsequent sudden infant death syndrome (SIDS) in offspring. *Neurotoxicology and Teratology, 13,* 235–240.

Kandel, D. B. (1978a). Similarity in real-life adolescent friendship pairs. *Journal of Personality and Social Psychology, 36,* 306–312.

Kandel, D. B. (1978b). Homophily, selection, and socialization in adolescent friendships. *American Journal of Sociology, 84,* 427–436.

Kandel, D. B., & Lesser, G. S. (1972). *Youth in two worlds.* San Francisco: Jossey-Bass.

Kandel, D. B., Raveis, V. H., & Davies, M. (1991). Suicidal ideation in adolescence: Depression, substance use, and other risk factors. *Journal of Youth and Adolescence, 20,* 289–309.

Kanner, A. D., Feldman, S. S., Weinberger, D. A., & Ford, M. E. (1987). Uplifts, hassles, and adaptational outcomes in early adolescents. *Journal of Early Adolescence, 7,* 371–394.

Kantor, D., & Lehr, W. (1975). *Inside the family.* San Francisco: Jossey-Bass.

Kaplan, R. M. (1985). The controversy related to the use of psychological tests. In B. B. Wolman (Ed.), *Handbook of intelligence* (pp. 465–504). New York: Wiley.

Karadsheh, R. (1991, March). *This room is a junkyard! Children's comprehension of metaphorical language.* Paper presented at the biennial meeting of the Society for Research in Child Development, Seattle, WA.

Karmiloff-Smith, A. (1979). Language development after five. In P. Fletcher & M. Garman (Ed.), *Language acquisition* (pp. 307–323). New York: Cambridge University Press.

Katchadourian, H. (1977). *The biology of adolescence.* San Francisco: Freeman.

Katchadourian, H. (1990). Sexuality. In S. S. Feldman & G. R. Elliott (Eds.), *At the threshold: The developing adolescent* (pp. 330–351). Cambridge, MA: Harvard University Press.

Kaufman, A. S., Kamphaus, R. W., & Kaufman, N. L. (1985). New directions in intelligence testing: The Kaufman Assessment Battery for Children (K-ABC). In B. B. Wolman (Ed.), *Handbook of intelligence* (pp. 663–698). New York: Wiley.

Kaufman, A. S., & Kaufman, N. L. (1983). *Kaufman Assessment Battery for Children: Administration and scoring manual.* Circle Pines, MN: American Guidance Service.

Kavale, K. (1982). Meta-analysis of the relationship between visual perceptual skills and reading achievement. *Journal of Learning Disabilities, 15,* 42–51.

Kaye, K., Elkind, L., Goldberg, D., & Tytun, A. (1989). Birth outcomes for infants of drug abusing mothers. *New York State Journal of Medicine, 89,* 256–261.

Kaye, K., & Marcus, J. (1981). Infant imitation: The sensory-motor agenda. *Developmental Psychology, 17,* 258–265.

Kazdin, A. E. (1987). Treatment of antisocial behavior in children: Current status and future directions. *Psychological Bulletin, 102,* 187–203.

Kearins, J. M. (1981). Visual spatial memory in Australian aboriginal children of desert regions. *Cognitive Psychology, 13,* 434–460.

Keating, D. (1979). Adolescent thinking. In J. Adelson (Ed.), *Handbook of adolescent psychology* (pp. 211–246). New York: Wiley.

Keating, D., & Clark, L. V. (1980). Development of physical and social reasoning in adolescence. *Developmental Psychology, 16,* 23–30.

Keeney, T. J., Canizzo, S. R., & Flavell, J. H. (1967). Spontaneous and induced verbal rehearsal in a recall task. *Child Development, 38,* 953–966.

Keil, F. (1986). Conceptual domains and the acquisition of metaphor. *Cognitive Development, 1,* 72–96.

Keil, F. C. (1989). *Concepts, kinds, and cognitive development.* Cambridge, MA: MIT Press.

Keller, A., Ford, L. H., & Meacham, J. A. (1978). Dimensions of self-concept in preschool children. *Developmental Psychology, 14,* 483–489.

Keller, M., & Wood, P. (1989). Development of friendship reasoning: A study of interindividual differences and intraindividual change. *Developmental Psychology, 25,* 820–826.

Kelley, M. L., Power, T. G., & Wimbush, D. D. (1992). Determinants of disciplinary practices in low-income black mothers. *Child Development, 63,* 573–582.

Kempe, C. H., Silverman, B. F., Steele, P. W., Droegemueller, P. W., & Silver, H. K. (1962). The battered-child syndrome. *Journal of the American Medical Association, 181,* 17–24.

Kempe, R. S., & Kempe, C. H. (1984). *The common secret: Sexual abuse of children and adolescents.* New York: Freeman.

Kendler, K. S., & Robinette, C. D. (1983). Schizophrenia in the National Academy of Science—National Research Council twin registry: A 16-year update. *American Journal of Psychiatry, 140,* 1551–1563.

Kennell, J., Klaus, M., McGrath, S., Robertson, S., & Hinkley, C. (1991). Continuous emotional support during labor in a U.S. hospital. *Journal of the American Medical Association, 265,* 2197–2201.

Keogh, B. (1985). Temperament and schooling: Meaning of "Goodness of fit"? In J. V. Lerner & R. M. Lerner (Eds.), *Temperament and social interaction in infants and children (New Directions for Child Development, No. 31)* (pp. 89–108). San Francisco: Jossey-Bass.

Keogh, B. K. (1988). Improving services for problem learners. *Journal of Learning Disabilities, 21,* 6–11.

Kermoian, R., & Campos, J. J. (1988). Locomotor experience: A facilitator of spatial cognitive development. *Child Development, 59,* 908–917.

Kerns, K. A., & Berenbaum, S. A. (1991). Sex differences in spatial ability in children. *Behavior Genetics, 21,* 383–396.

Kerr, B. A. (1983). Raising the career aspirations of gifted girls. *Vocational Guidance Quarterly, 32,* 37–43.

Kessen, W. (1967). Sucking and looking: Two organized congenital patterns of behavior in the human newborn. In H. W. Stevenson, E. H. Hess, & H. L. Rheingold (Eds.), *Early behavior: Comparative and developmental approaches* (pp. 147–179). New York: Wiley.

Ketterlinus, R. D., Henderson, S. H., & Lamb, M. E. (1990). Maternal age, sociodemographics, prenatal health and behavior: Influences on neonatal risk status. *Journal of Adolescent Health Care, 11,* 423–431.

Kilbride, J. E., & Kilbride, P. L. (1975). Sitting and smiling behavior of Baganda infants. *Journal of Cross-Cultural Psychology, 6,* 88–107.

Kimball, M. M. (1986). Television and sex-role attitudes. In T. M. Williams (Ed.), *The impact of television* (pp. 265–301). New York: Academic Press.

Kinney, H. C., Brody, B. A., Finkelstein, D. M., Vawter, G. F., Mandell, F., & Gilles, F. H. (1991). Delayed central nervous system myelination in the sudden infant death syndrome. *Journal of Neuropathology and Experimental Neurology, 50,* 29–48.

Kinsey, A. C., Pomeroy, W. B., Martin, C. E., & Gebhard, P. H. (1953). *Sexual behavior in the human female..* Philadelphia: Saunders.

Kinsman, C. A., & Berk, L. E. (1979). Joining the block and housekeeping areas: Changes in play and social behavior. *Young Children, 35,* 66–75.

Kirby, D. (1992). School-based programs to reduce sexual risk-taking. *Journal of School Health, 62,* 280–287.

Kiser, L. J., Bates, J. E., Maslin, C. A., & Bayles, K. (1986). Mother–infant play at six months as a predictor of attachment security at thirteen months. *Journal of the American Academy of Child Psychiatry, 25,* 68–75.

Kisker, E. E. (1985). Teenagers talk about sex, pregnancy, and contraception. *Family Planning Perspectives, 17,* 83–90.

Klahr, D. (1992). Information-processing approaches to cognitive development. In M. H. Bornstein & M. E. Lamb (Eds.), *Developmental psychology: An advanced textbook* (3rd ed., pp. 273–335). Hillsdale, NJ: Erlbaum.

Klahr, D., Langley, P., & Neches, R. (1987). *Production system models of learning and development.* Cambridge, MA: MIT Press.

Klatzky, R. L. (1984). *Memory and awareness: An information processing perspective.* New York: Freeman.

Kleinke, C. L., & Nicholson, T. A. (1979). Black and white children's awareness of de facto race and sex differences. *Developmental Psychology, 15,* 84–86.

Klimes-Dougan, B., & Kistner, J. (1990). Physically abused preschoolers' responses to peers' distress. *Developmental Psychology, 26,* 599–602.

Klineberg, O. (1963). Negro-white differences in intelligence test performance: A new look at an old problem. *American Psychologist, 18,* 198–203.

Knittle, J. L., & Hirsch, J. (1968). Effect of early nutrition on the development of rat epididymal fat pads: Cellularity and metabolism. *Journal of Clinical Investigation, 47,* 2091–2098.

Knobloch, H., & Pasamanick, B. (Eds.). (1974). *Gesell and Amatruda's Developmental Diagnosis.* Hagerstown, MD: Harper & Row.

Knobloch, H., Stevens, F., & Malone, A. (1980). *A manual for developmental diagnosis.* New York: Harper & Row.

Kochanska, G. (1991). Socialization and temperament in the development of guilt and conscience. *Child Development, 62,* 1379–1392.

Kochanska, G. (1992). Children's interpersonal influence with mothers and peers. *Developmental Psychology, 28,* 491–499.

Kochanska, G. (1993). Toward a synthesis of parental socialization and child temperament in early development of conscience. *Child Development, 64,* 325–347.

Kochanska, G., Kuczynski, L., & Radke-Yarrow, M. (1989). Correspondence between mothers' self-reported and observed child-rearing practices. *Child Development, 60,* 56–63.

Kochanska, G., & Radke-Yarrow, M. (1992). Inhibition in toddlerhood and the dynamics of the child's interaction with an unfamiliar peer at age five. *Child Development, 63,* 325–335.

Kodroff, J. K., & Roberge, J. J. (1975). Developmental analysis of the conditional reasoning abilities of primary-grade children. *Developmental Psychology, 11,* 21–28.

Kogan, N. (1983). Stylistic variation in childhood and adolescence: Creativity, metaphor, and cognitive style. In J. H. Flavell & E. M. Markman (Ed.), *Handbook of child psychology: Vol. 3. Cognitive development* (pp. 630–708). New York: Wiley.

Kohlberg, L. (1966). A cognitive-developmental analysis of children's sex-role concepts and attitudes. In E. E. Maccoby (Ed.), *The development of sex differences* (pp. 82–173). Stanford, CA: Stanford University Press.

Kohlberg, L. (1969). Stage and sequence: The cognitive-developmental approach to socialization. In D. A. Goslin (Ed.), *Handbook of socialization theory and research* (pp. 347–480). Chicago: Rand McNally.

Kohlberg, L. (1976). Moral stages and moralization: The cognitive-developmental approach. In T. Lickona (Ed.), *Moral development and behavior: Theory, research, and social issues* (pp. 31–53). New York: Holt.

Kohlberg, L. (1984). *Essays on moral development. Vol. 2: The psychology of moral development.* San Francisco: Harper & Row.

Kohlberg, L., Levine, C., & Hewer, A. (1983). *Moral stages: A current formulation and a response to critics.* Basel: Karger.

Kohn, M. L. (1979). The effects of social class on parental values and practices. In D. Reiss & H. A. Hoffman (Eds.), *The American family: Dying or developing* (pp. 45–68). New York: Plenum.

Kojima, H. (1986). Childrearing concepts as a belief-value system of the society and the individual. In H. Stevenson, H. Azuma, & K. Hakuta (Eds.), *Child development and education in Japan* (pp. 39–54). New York: Freeman.

Kolata, G. B. (1989, May 14). Operating on the unborn. *The New York Times Magazine,* pp. 34–35, 46–48.

Koneya, M. (1976). Location and interaction in row-and-column seating arrangements. *Environment and Behavior, 8,* 265–282.

Kopp, C. (1983). Risk factors in development. In P. H. Mussen (Ed.), *Handbook of child psychology: Vol. 2. Infancy and developmental psychobiology* (pp. 1081–1188). New York: Wiley.

Kopp, C., & Kaler, S. R. (1989). Risk in infancy. *American Psychologist, 44,* 224–230.

Kopp, C. B. (1987). The growth of self-regulation: Caregivers and children. In N. Eisenberg (Ed.), *Contemporary topics in developmental psychology* (pp. 34–55). New York: Wiley.

Kopp, C. B. (1989). Regulation of distress and negative emotions: A developmental view. *Developmental Psychology, 25,* 343–354.

Kopp, C. B., & Krakow, J. B. (Eds.). (1982). *The child: Development in context.* Reading, MA: Addison-Wesley.

Korner, A. F., Constantinou, J., Dimiceli, S., Brown, B. W., Jr., & Thom, V. A. (1991). Establishing the reliability and developmental validity of a neurobehavioral assessment for preterm infants: A methodological process. *Child Development, 62,* 1200–1208.

Korner, A. F., Hutchinson, C. A., Koperski, J. A., Kraemer, H. C., & Schneider, P. A. (1981). Stability of individual differences of neonatal motor and crying pattern. *Child Development, 52,* 83–90.

Kornhaber, M., Krechevsky, M., & Gardner, H. (1991). Engaging intelligence. *Educational Psychologist, 25,* 177–199.

Kouba, V. L., Brown, C. A., Carpenter, T. P., Lindquist, M. M., Silver, E. A., & Swafford, J. O. (1988). Results of the fourth NAEP assessment of mathematics: Number, operations, and word problems. *Arithmetic Teacher, 35*(8), 14–19.

Kozol, J. (1991). *Savage inequalities.* New York: Crown.

Kozulin, A. (1990). *Vygotsky's psychology: A biography of ideas.* Cambridge, MA: Harvard University Press.

Kramer, M. D., Taylor, V., Hickok, D. E., Daling, J. R., Vaughan, T. L., & Hollenbach, K. A. (1991). Maternal smoking and placenta previa. *Epidemiology, 2,* 221–223.

Kranzler, J. H., & Jensen, A. R. (1989). Inspection time and intelligence: A meta-analysis. *Intelligence, 13,* 329–347.

Krebs, D., & Gillmore, J. (1982). The relationship among the first stages of cognitive development, role-taking abilities, and moral development. *Child Development, 53,* 877–886.

Kreitler, S., & Kreitler, H. (1987). Conceptions and processes of planning: The development of perspective. In S. L. Friedman, E. K. Scholnick, & R. R. Cocking (Eds.), *Blueprints for thinking: The role of planning in cognitive development* (pp. 205–272). Cambridge: Cambridge University Press.

Kremenitzer, J. P., Vaughan, H. G., Kurtzberg, D., & Dowling, K. (1979). Smooth-pursuit eye movements in the newborn infant. *Child Development, 50,* 441–448.

Kreutzer, M. A., Leonard, C., & Flavell, J. H. (1975). An interview study of children's knowledge about memory. *Monographs of the Society for Research in Child Development, 40* (1, Serial No. 159).

Kricker, A., Elliott, J. W., Forrest, J. M., & McCredie, J. (1986). Congenital limb reduction deformities and use of oral contraceptives. *American Journal of Obstetrics and Gynecology, 155,* 1072–1078.

Kristjansson, B., & Fried, P. A. (1989). Maternal smoking during pregnancy affects children's vigilance performance. *Drug and Alcohol Dependency, 24,* 11–19.

Kruger, A. C. (1992). The effect of peer and adult-child transactive discussions on moral reasoning. *Merrill-Palmer Quarterly, 38,* 191–211.

Kuczaj, S. A., II. (1977). The acquisition of regular and irregular past tense forms. *Journal of Verbal Learning and Verbal Behavior, 16,* 589–600.

Kuczaj, S. A., II. (1986). Thoughts on the intentional basis of early object word extension: Evidence from comprehension and production. In S. A. Kuczaj, II, & M. D. Barrett (Eds.), *The development of word meaning* (pp. 99–120). New York: Springer-Verlag.

Kuczynski, L. (1984). Socialization goals and mother-child interaction: Strategies for long-term and short-term compliance. *Developmental Psychology, 20,* 1061–1073.

Kuczynski, L., & Kochanska, G. (1990). Development of children's noncompliance strategies from toddlerhood to age 5. *Developmental Psychology, 26,* 398–408.

Kuczynski, L., Kochanska, G., Radke-Yarrow, M., & Girnius-Brown, O. (1987). A developmental interpretation of young children's noncompliance. *Developmental Psychology, 23,* 799–806.

Kuebli, J., & Fivush, R. (1992). Gender differences in parent-child conversations about past emotions. *Sex Roles, 27,* 683–698.

Kuhl, P. K., & Meltzoff, A. N. (1984). The intermodal representation of speech in infants. *Infant Behavior and Development, 7,* 361–381.

Kuhl, P. K., Williams, K. A., Lacerda, F., Stevens, K. N., & Lindblom, B. (1992). Linguistic experience alters phonetic perception in infants by 6 months of age. *Science, 255,* 606–608.

Kuhn, D. (1989). Children and adults as intuitive scientists. *Psychological Review, 96,* 674–689.

Kuhn, D. (1992). Cognitive development. In M. H. Bornstein & M. E. Lamb (Eds.), *Developmental psychology: An advanced textbook* (3rd ed., pp. 211–272). Hillsdale, NJ: Erlbaum.

Kuhn, D., Amsel, E., & O'Loughlin, M. (1988). *The development of scientific thinking skills.* Orlando, FL: Academic Press.

Kuhn, D., Ho, V., & Adams, C. (1979). Formal reasoning among pre- and late adolescents. *Child Development, 50,* 1128–1135.

Kuhn, D., Nash, S. C., & Brucken, L. (1978). Sex role concepts of two- and three-year-olds. *Child Development, 49,* 445–451.

Kull, J. A. (1986). Learning and Logo. In P. F. Campbell & G. G. Fein (Eds.), *Young children and microcomputers* (pp. 103–128). Englewood Cliffs, NJ: Prentice-Hall.

Kun, A. (1977). Development of the magnitude-covariation and compensation schemata in ability and effort attributions of performance. *Child Development, 48,* 862–872.

Kunzinger, E. L., III. (1985). A short-term longitudinal study of memorial development during early grade school. *Developmental Psychology, 21,* 642–646.

Kurdek, L. A. (1978). Relationship between cognitive perspective-taking and teachers' ratings of children's classroom behavior in grades one through four. *Journal of Genetic Psychology, 132,* 21–27.

Kurdek, L. A. (1980). Developmental relations among children's perspective-taking, moral judgment, and parent-rated behavior. *Merrill-Palmer Quarterly, 26,* 103–121.

L

LaBarre, W. (1954). *The human animal.* Chicago: University of Chicago Press.

Laboratory of Comparative Human Cognition. (1989). Kids and computers: A positive vision of the future. *Harvard Educational Review, 59,* 73–86.

Lackey, P. N. (1989). Adults' attitudes about assignments of household chores to male and female children. *Sex Roles, 20,* 271–281.

Ladd, G. W. (1981). Effectiveness of a social learning method for enhancing children's social interaction and peer acceptance. *Child Development, 52,* 171–178.

Ladd, G. W. (1990). Having friends, keeping friends, making friends, and being liked by peers in the classroom: Predictors of children's early school adjustment? *Child Development, 61,* 1081–1100.

Ladd, G. W., & Hart, C. H. (1992). Creating informal play opportunities: Are parents' and preschoolers' initiations related to children's competence with peers? *Developmental Psychology, 28,* 1179–1187.

Ladd, G. W., & Price, J. M. (1987). Predicting children's social and school adjustment following the transition from preschool to kindergarten. *Child Development, 58,* 1168–1189.

Lagercrantz, H., & Slotkin, T. A. (1986). The "stress" of being born. *Scientific American, 254,* 100–107.

Lamaze, F. (1958). *Painless childbirth.* London: Burke.

Lamb, M. E. (1976). Interaction between eight-month-old children and their fathers and mothers. In M. E. Lamb (Ed.), *The role of the father in child development* (pp. 307–327). New York: Wiley.

Lamb, M. E. (1987). *The father's role: Cross-cultural perspectives.* Hillsdale, NJ: Erlbaum.

Lamb, M. E., & Oppenheim, D. (1989). Fatherhood and father–child relationships: Five years of research. In S. H. Cath, A. Gurwitt, & L. Gunsberg (Eds.), *Fathers and their families* (pp. 11–26). Hillsdale, NJ: Erlbaum.

Lamb, M. E., Sternberg, K. J., & Prodromidis, M. (1992). Nonmaternal care and the security of infant–mother attachment: A reanalysis of the data. *Infant Behavior and Development, 15,* 71–83.

Lamb, M. E., Thompson, R. A., Gardner, W., Charnov, E. L., & Connell, J. P. (1985). *Infant–mother attachment: The origins and developmental significance of individual differences in Strange Situation behavior.* Hillsdale, NJ: Erlbaum.

Lamb, S. (1991). First moral sense: Aspects of and contributors to a beginning morality in the second year of life. In W. M. Kurtines & J. L. Gewirtz (Eds.), *Handbook of moral behavior and development:* (Vol. 2, pp. 171–189). Hillsdale, NJ: Erlbaum.

Lamborn, S. D., Mounts, N. S., Steinberg, L., & Dornbusch, S. M. (1991). Patterns of competence and adjustment among adolescents from authoritative, authoritarian, indulgent, and neglectful families. *Child Development, 62,* 1049–1065.

Lamborn, S. D., & Steinberg, L. (1993). Emotional autonomy redux: Revisiting Ryan and Lynch. *Child Development, 64,* 483–499.

Lampl, M., Veldhuis, J. D., & Johnson, M. L. (1992). Saltation and stasis: A model of human growth. *Science, 258,* 801–803.

Lancaster, J. B., & Whitten, P. (1980). Family matters. *The Sciences, 20,* 10–15.

Landau, R. (1982). Infant crying and fussing. *Journal of Cross-Cultural Psychology, 13,* 427–443.

Landau, S., Lorch, E. P., & Milich, R. (1992). Visual attention to and comprehension of television in attention-deficit hyperactivity disordered and normal boys. *Child Development, 63,* 928–937.

Landau, S., & McAninch, C. (1993, May). Young children with attention deficits. *Young Children, 48* (4), 49–58.

Landesman, S., & Ramey, C. (1989). Developmental psychology and mental retardation: Integrating scientific principles with treatment practices. *American Psychologist, 44,* 409–415.

Lane, D. M., & Pearson, D. A. (1982). The development of selective attention. *Merrill-Palmer Quarterly, 28,* 317–337.

Lange, G., & Pierce, S. H. (1992). Memory-strategy learning and maintenance in preschool children. *Developmental Psychology, 28,* 453–462.

Langlois, J. H., & Downs, A. C. (1979). Peer relations as a function of physical attractiveness: The eye of the beholder or behavioral reality? *Child Development, 50,* 409–418.

Langlois, J. H., & Downs, A. C. (1980). Mothers, fathers, and peers as socialization agents of sex-typed play behaviors in young children. *Child Development, 51,* 1237–1247.

Langlois, J. H., Ritter, J. M., Roggman, L. A., & Vaughn, L. S. (1991). Facial diversity and infant preferences for attractive faces. *Developmental Psychology, 27,* 79–84.

Langlois, J. H., & Roggman, L. A. (1990). Attractive faces are only average. *Psychological Science, 1,* 115–121.

Langlois, J. H., Roggman, L. A., & Rieser-Danner, L. A. (1990). Infants' differential social responses to attractive and unattractive faces. *Developmental Psychology, 26,* 153–159.

Langlois, J. H., & Stephan, C. (1977). The effects of physical attractiveness and ethnicity on children's behavioral attributions and peer preferences. *Child Development, 48,* 1694–1698.

Langlois, J. H., & Stephan, C. W. (1981). Beauty and the beast: The role of physical attractiveness in peer relationships and social behavior. In S. S. Brehm, S. M. Kassin, & S. X. Gibbons (Eds.), *Developmental social psychology: Theory and research* (pp. 152–168). New York: Oxford University Press.

Langlois, J. H., & Styczynski, L. E. (1979). The effects of physical attractiveness on the behavioral attributions and peer preferences of acquainted children. *International Journal of Behavioral Development, 2,* 325–342.

Laosa, L. M. (1981). Maternal behavior: Sociocultural diversity in modes of family interaction. In R. W. Henderson (Ed.), *Parent-child interaction: Theory, research, and prospects* (pp. 125–167). New York: Academic Press.

Lapsley, D. K. (1990). Egocentrism theory and the "new look" at the imaginary audience and personal fable in adolescence. In R. M. Lerner, A. C. Petersen, & J. Brooks-Gunn (Eds.), *The encyclopedia of adolescence* (pp. 281–286). New York: Garland.

Lapsley, D. K., Enright, R. D., & Serlin, R. C. (1989). Moral and social education. In J. Worell & F. Danner (Eds.), *The adolescent as decision-maker: Applications to development and education* (pp. 111–141). New York: Academic Press.

Lapsley, D. K., Jackson, S., Rice, K., & Shadid, G. (1988). Self-monitoring and the "new look" at the imaginary audience and personal fable: An ego-developmental analysis. *Journal of Adolescent Research, 3,* 17–31.

Lapsley, D. K., Milstead, M., Quintana, S., Flannery, D., & Buss, R. (1986). Adolescent egocentrism and formal operations: Tests of a theoretical assumption. *Developmental Psychology, 22,* 800–807.

Lapsley, D. K., Rice, K. G., & FitzGerald, D. P. (1990). Adolescent attachment, identity, and adjustment to college: Implications for the continuity of adaptation hypothesis. *Journal of Counseling and Development, 68,* 561–565.

Larson, R., & Ham, M. (1993). Stress and "storm and stress" in early adolescence: The relationship of negative events with dysphoric affect. *Developmental Psychology, 29,* 130–140.

Larson, R., & Lampman-Petraitis, C. (1989). Daily emotional states as reported by children and adolescents. *Child Development, 60,* 1250–1260.

Laudenslager, M. L., & Reite, M. R. (1984). Loss and separations: Immunological consequences and health implications. In P. Shaver (Ed.), *Review of personality and social psychology* (Vol. 5, pp. 285–311). Beverly Hills, CA: Sage.

Laupa, M. (1991). Children's reasoning about three authority attributes: Adult status, knowledge, and social position. *Developmental Psychology, 27,* 321–329.

Laupa, M., & Turiel, E. (1986). Children's concepts of adult and peer authority. *Child Development, 57,* 405–412.

Laupa, M., & Turiel, E. (1993). Children's concepts of authority and social contexts. *Journal of Educational Psychology, 85,* 191–197.

Lawler, K. A., Allen, M. T., Critcher, E. C., & Standard, B. A. (1981). The relationship of physiological responses to the coronary-prone behavior pattern in children. *Journal of Behavioral Medicine, 4,* 203–216.

Lazar, I., & Darlington, R. (1982). Lasting effects of early education: A report from the Consortium for Longitudinal Studies. *Monographs of the Society for Research in Child Development, 47* (2–3, Serial No. 195).

Leahy, R. L., & Eiter, M. (1980). Moral judgment and the development of real and ideal androgynous self-image during adolescence and young adulthood. *Developmental Psychology, 16,* 362–370.

Leaper, C. (1991). Influence and involvement in children's discourse. *Child Development, 62,* 797–811.

Lee, C. L., & Bates, J. E. (1985). Mother–child interaction at age two years and perceived difficult temperament. *Child Development, 56,* 1314–1325.

Lee, M., & Prentice, N. M. (1988). Interrelations of empathy, cognition, and moral reasoning with dimensions of juvenile delinquency. *Journal of Abnormal Child Psychology, 16,* 127–139.

Lee, V. E., Brooks-Gunn, J., & Schnur, E. (1988). Does Head Start work: A 1-year follow-up comparison of disadvantaged children attending Head Start, no preschool, and other preschool programs. *Developmental Psychology, 24,* 210–222.

Lee, V. E., Brooks-Gunn, J., Schnur, E., & Liaw, F. (1990). Are Head Start effects sustained? A longitudinal follow-up comparison of disadvantaged children attending Head Start, no preschool, and other preschool programs. *Child Development, 61,* 495–507.

Leeman, L. W., Gibbs, J. C., & Fuller, D. (1993). Evaluation of a multi-component group treatment program for juvenile delinquents. *Aggressive Behavior, 19,* 281–292.

Lefkowitz, M. M., Eron, L. D., Walder, L. O., & Huesmann, L. R. (1972). Television violence and child aggression: A follow-up study. In G. A. Comstock & E. A. Rubinstein (Eds.), *Television and social behavior* (Vol. 3, pp. 35–135). Washington, DC: U.S. Government Printing Office.

Lehman, D. R., & Nisbett, R. E. (1990). A longitudinal study of the effects of undergraduate training on reasoning. *Developmental Psychology, 26,* 952–960.

Leiter, M. P. (1977). A study of reciprocity in preschool play groups. *Child Development, 48,* 1288–1295.

LeMare, L. J., & Rubin, K. H. (1987). Perspective taking and peer interaction: Structural and developmental analyses. *Child Development, 58,* 306–315.

Lemire, R. J., Loeser, J. D., Leech, R. W., & Alvord, E. C. (1975). *Normal and abnormal development of the human nervous system.* New York: Harper & Row.

Lempert, H. (1989). Animacy constraints on preschoolers' acquisition of syntax. *Child Development, 60,* 237–245.

Lenneberg, E. H. (1967). *Biological foundations of language.* New York: Wiley.

Leonard, M. F., Rhymes, J. P., & Solnit, A. J. (1986). Failure to thrive in infants: A family problem. *American Journal of Diseases of Children, 111,* 600–612.

Lepper, M. R. (1985). Microcomputers in education: Motivational and social issues. *American Psychologist, 40,* 1–18.

Lepper, M. R., & Gurtner, J. (1989). Children and computers: Approaching the twenty-first century. *American Psychologist, 44,* 170–178.

Lerner, J. W. (1989). Educational interventions in learning disabilities. *Journal of the American Academy of Child and Adolescent Psychiatry, 28,* 326–331.

Lerner, R. M., & Brackney, B. (1978). The importance of inner and outer body parts attitudes in the self-concept of late adolescents. *Sex Roles, 4,* 225–238.

Lerner, R. M., Palermo, M., Spiro, A., & Nesselroade, J. (1982). Assessing the dimensions of temperamental individuality across the life-span: The Dimensions of Temperament Survey (DOTS). *Child Development, 53,* 149–160.

Lerner, R. M., & Schroeder, C. (1971). Physique identification, preference, and aversion in kindergarten children. *Developmental Psychology, 5,* 538.

Lerner, R. M., Spanier, G. B., & Belsky, J. (1982). The child in the family. In C. B. Kopp & J. B. Krakow (Eds.), *The child: Development in a social context* (pp. 393–455). Reading, MA: Addison-Wesley.

Leslie, A. M. (1988). Some implications of pretense for mechanisms underlying the child's theory of mind. In J. W. Astington, P. L. Harris, & D. R. Olson (Eds.), *Developing theories of mind* (pp. 19–46). New York: Cambridge University Press.

Lester, B. M. (1985). Introduction: There's more to crying than meets the ear. In B. M. Lester & C. F. Z. Boukydis (Eds.), *Infant crying* (pp. 1–27). New York: Plenum.

Lester, B. M. (1987). Developmental outcome prediction from acoustic cry analysis in term and preterm infants. *Pediatrics, 80,* 529–534.

Lester, B. M., & Dreher, M. (1989). Effects of marijuana use during pregnancy on newborn cry. *Child Development, 60,* 765–771.

Lester, B. M., Kotelchuck, M., Spelke, E., Sellers, M. J., & Klein, R. E. (1974). Separation protest in Guatemalan infants: Cross-cultural and cognitive findings. *Developmental Psychology, 10,* 79–85.

Leventhal, G. S. (1970). Influence of brothers and sisters on sex role behavior. *Journal of Personality and Social Psychology, 16,* 452–465.

Levin, J. A., Boruta, M. J., & Vasconellos, M. T. (1983). Microcomputer-based environments for writing: A writer's assistant. In A. C. Wilkinson (Ed.), *Classroom computers and cognitive science* (pp. 219–232). New York: Academic Press.

Levin, S. R., Petros, T. V., & Petrella, F. W. (1982). Preschoolers' awareness of television advertising. *Child Development, 53,* 933–937.

Levine, L. E. (1983). Mine: Self-definition in 2-year-old boys. *Developmental Psychology, 19,* 544–549.

LeVine, R. A., & LeVine, S. E. (1988). Parental strategies among the Gusii of Kenya. In R. A. LeVine, P. M. Miller, & M. M. West (Eds.), *Parental behavior in diverse societies* (pp. 27–35). San Francisco: Jossey-Bass.

Levitt, A. G., & Utmann, J. G. A. (1992). From babbling towards the sound systems of English and French: A longitudinal two-case study. *Journal of Child Language, 19,* 19–49.

Levitt, A. G., & Wang, Q. (1991). Evidence for language-specific rhythmic influences in the reduplicative babbling of French- and English-learning infants. *Language and Speech, 34,* 235–249.

Levy, G. D. (1989). Relations among aspects of children's social environments, gender schematization, gender role knowledge, and flexibility. *Sex Roles, 21,* 803–823.

Levy, G. D., & Carter, D. B. (1989). Gender schema, gender constancy, and gender-role knowledge: The roles of cognitive factors in preschoolers' gender-role stereotype attributions. *Developmental Psychology, 25,* 444–449.

Levy-Shiff, R., & Israelashvili, R. (1988). Antecedents of fathering: Some further exploration. *Developmental Psychology, 24,* 434–440.

Lewis, C. C. (1981). The effects of parental firm control: A reinterpretation of findings. *Psychological Bulletin, 90,* 547–563.

Lewis, C., & Osborne, A. (1990). Three-year-olds' problems with false belief: Conceptual deficit or linguistic artifact? *Child Development, 61,* 1514–1519.

Lewis, M. (1991). Ways of knowing: Objective self-awareness or consciousness. *Developmental Review, 11,* 231–243.

Lewis, M. (1992). The self in self-conscious emotions (commentary on Self-evaluation in young children). *Monographs of the Society for Research in Child Development, 57* (1, Serial No. 226).

Lewis, M., Alessandri, S. M., & Sullivan, M. W. (1992). Differences in shame and pride as a function of children's gender and task difficulty. *Child Development, 63,* 630–638.

Lewis, M., & Brooks, J. (1978). Self-knowledge and emotional development. In M. Lewis & L. A. Rosenblum (Ed.), *The development of affect* (pp. 205–226). New York: Plenum.

Lewis, M., & Brooks-Gunn, J. (1979). *Social cognition and the acquisition of self.* New York: Plenum.

Lewis, M., & Sullivan, M. W. (1985). Infant intelligence and its assessment. In B. B. Wolman (Ed.), *Handbook of infant intelligence* (pp. 505–599). New York: Wiley.

Lewis, M., Sullivan, M. W., & Ramsay, D. S. (1992). Individual differences in anger and sad expressions during extinction: Antecedents and consequences. *Infant Behavior and Development, 15,* 443–452.

Lewis, M., Sullivan, M. W., Stanger, C., & Weiss, M. (1989). Self development and self-conscious emotions. *Child Development, 60,* 146–156.

Lewis, M., Sullivan, M. W., & Vasen, A. (1987). Making faces: Age and emotion differences in the posing of emotional expressions. *Developmental Psychology, 23,* 690–697.

Lewontin, R. C. (1976). Race and intelligence. In N. J. Block & G. Dworkin (Eds.), *The IQ controversy* (pp. 78–92). New York: Pantheon Books.

Liben, L. S., & Downs, R. M. (1986). *Children's production and comprehension of maps: Increasing graphic literacy.* Washington, DC: National Institute of Education.

Liben, L. S., & Golbeck, S. L. (1984). Performance on Piagetian horizontality and verticality tasks: Sex-related differences in knowledge of relevant physical phenomena. *Developmental Psychology, 20,* 595–606.

Lickona, T. (1976). Research on Piaget's theory of moral development. In T. Lickona (Ed.), *Moral development and behavior* (pp. 219–240). New York: Holt, Rinehart and Winston.

Liebert, R. M. (1986). Effects of television on children and adolescents. *Developmental and Behavioral Pediatrics, 7,* 43–48.

Liebert, R. M., & Sprafkin, J. (1988). *The early window: Effects of television on children and youth* (3rd ed.). New York: Pergamon Press.

Light, P., & Perrett-Clermont, A. (1989). Social context effects in learning and testing. In A. R. H. Gellatly, D. Rogers, & J. Sloboda (Eds.), *Cognition and social worlds* (pp. 99–112). Oxford: Clarendon Press.

Lillard, A. S. (1993). Pretend play skills and the child's theory of mind. *Child Development, 64,* 348–371.

Lin, C. C., & Fu, V. R. (1990). A comparison of child-rearing practices among Chinese, immigrant Chinese, and Caucasian-American parents. *Child Development, 61,* 429–433.

Linde, E. V., Morrongiello, B. A., & Rovee-Collier, C. (1985).

Determinants of retention in 8-week-old infants. *Developmental Psychology, 21,* 601–613.

Lindell, S. G. (1988). Education for childbirth: A time for change. *Journal of Obstetrics, Gynecology, and Neonatal Nursing, 17,* 108–112.

Lindsay, P. (1984). High school size, participation in activities, and young adult social participation: Some enduring effects of schooling. *Educational Evaluation and Policy Analysis, 6,* 73–83.

Linn, M. C. (1985). Fostering equitable consequences from computer learning environments. *Sex Roles, 13,* 229–240.

Linn, M. C., & Hyde, J. S. (1989). Gender, mathematics, and science. *Educational Researcher, 18,* 17–27.

Linn, M. C., & Petersen, A. C. (1985). Emergence and characterization of sex differences in spatial ability: A meta-analysis. *Child Development, 56,* 1479–1498.

Linn, S., Lieberman, E., Schoenbaum, S. C., Monson, R. R., Stubblefield, P. G., & Ryan, K. J. (1988). Adverse outcomes of pregnancy in women exposed to diethylstilbestrol in utero. *Journal of Reproductive Medicine, 33,* 3–7.

Lipsitt, L. P. (1990). Learning and memory in infants. *Merrill-Palmer Quarterly, 36,* 53–66.

Lipsitt, L. P., Sturner, W. Q., & Burke, P. (1979). Perinatal indicators and subsequent crib death. *Infant Behavior and Development, 2,* 325–328.

Lipsitt, L. P., & Werner, J. S. (1981). The infancy of human learning processes. In E. S. Gollin (Ed.), *Developmental plasticity* (pp. 101–133). New York: Academic Press.

Liss, M. B., Reinhardt, L. C., & Fredriksen, S. (1983). TV heroes: The impact of rhetoric and deeds. *Journal of Applied Developmental Psychology, 4,* 175–187.

Litowitz, B. (1977). Learning to make definitions. *Journal of Child Language, 8,* 165–175.

Little, B. B., Snell, L. M., Klein, V. R., & Gilstrap, L. C., III. (1989). Cocaine abuse during pregnancy: Maternal and fetal implications. *Obstetrics and Gynecology, 73,* 157–160.

Livesley, W. J., & Bromley, D. B. (1973). *Person perception in childhood and adolescence.* London: Wiley.

Livson, N., & Peskin, H. (1980). Perspectives on adolescence from longitudinal research. In J. Adelson (Ed.), *Handbook of adolescent psychology* (pp. 47–98). New York: Wiley.

Lloyd, B., & Smith, C. (1985). The social representation of gender and young children's play. *British Journal of Developmental Psychology, 3,* 65–73.

Lloyd, P., Boada, H., & Forns, H. (1992). New directions in referential communication research. *British Journal of Developmental Psychology, 10,* 385–403.

Locke, J. (1892). Some thoughts concerning education. In R. H. Quick (Ed.), *Locke on education* (pp. 1–236). Cambridge: Cambridge University Press. (Original work published 1690)

Locke, J. L. (1989). Babbling and early speech: Continuity and individual differences. *First Language, 9,* 191–206.

Lockheed, M. E. (1986). Reshaping the social order: The case of gender segregation. *Sex Roles, 14,* 617–628.

Lockheed, M. E., & Harris, A. M. (1984). Cross-sex collaborative learning in elementary classrooms. *American Educational Research Journal, 21,* 275–294.

Loehlin, J. C. (1989). Partitioning environmental and genetic contributions to behavioral development. *American Psychologist, 44,* 1285–1292.

Loehlin, J. C., Horn, J. M., & Willerman, L. (1989). Modeling IQ change: Evidence from the Texas Adoption Project. *Child Development, 60,* 993–1004.

Loehlin, J. C., Willerman, L., & Horn, J. M. (1988). Human behavior genetics. *Annual Review of Psychology, 38,* 101–133.

Lohman, D. F. (1988). Spatial abilities as traits, processes, and knowledge. In R. J. Sternberg (Ed.), *Advances in the psychology of human intelligence* (Vol. 4, pp. 181–248). Hillsdale, NJ: Erlbaum.

Lombardi, J. (1993). Looking at the child care landscape. *Pediatrics, 91,* 179–188.

Long, N., & Forehand, R. (1987). The effects of parental divorce and marital conflict on children: An overview. *Journal of Developmental and Behavioral Pediatrics, 8,* 292–296.

Lorenz, K. Z. (1943). Die angeborenen Formen möglicher Erfahnrung. *Zeitschrift für Tierpsychologie, 5,* 235–409.

Lorenz, K. Z. (1952). *King Solomon's ring.* New York: Thomas Y. Crowell.

Lovejoy, C. O. (1981). The origin of man. *Science, 211,* 341–350.

Loveland, K. A. (1987). Behavior of young children with Down syndrome before the mirror: Exploration. *Child Development, 58,* 768–778.

Lozoff, B. (1989). Nutrition and behavior. *American Psychologist, 44,* 231–236.

Lozoff, B., Wolf, A., & Davis, N. (1984). Cosleeping in urban families with young children in the United States. *Pediatrics, 74,* 171–182.

Lucariello, J., & Nelson, K. (1985). Slot-filler categories as memory organizers for young children. *Developmental Psychology, 21,* 272–282.

Ludemann, P. M. (1991). Generalized discrimination of positive facial expressions by seven- and ten-month-old infants. *Child Development, 62,* 55–67.

Lummis, M., & Stevenson, H. W. (1990). Gender differences in beliefs about achievement: A cross-cultural study. *Developmental Psychology, 26,* 254–263.

Lundberg, U. (1983). Note on Type A behavior and cardiovascular responses to challenge in 3- 6-year old children. *Journal of Psychosomatic Research, 27,* 39–42.

Luria, A. R. (1961). *The role of speech in the regulation of normal and abnormal behavior.* New York: Pergamon Press.

Luster, T., & Dubow, E. (1992). Home environment and maternal intelligence as predictors of verbal intelligence: A comparison of preschool and school-age children. *Merrill-Palmer Quarterly, 38,* 151–175.

Luster, T., Rhoades, K., & Haas, B. (1989). The relation between parental values and parenting behavior. *Journal of Marriage and the Family, 51,* 139–147.

Lutz, P. (1983). The stepfamily: An adolescent perspective. *Family Relations, 32,* 367–375.

Lyons-Ruth, K., Alpern, L., & Repacholi, B. (1993). Disorganized infant attachment classification and maternal psychosocial problems as predictors of hostile–aggressive behavior in the preschool classroom. *Child Development, 64,* 572–585.

Lyons-Ruth, K., Connell, D. B., Grunebaum, H. U., & Botein, S. (1990). Infants at social risk: Maternal depression and family support services as mediators of infant development and security of attachment. *Child Development, 61,* 85–98.

Lysynchuk, L. M., Pressley, M., & Vye, N. J. (1990). Reciprocal teaching improves standardized reading-comprehension performance in poor comprehenders. *Elementary School Journal, 90,* 469–484.

Lytton, H., & Romney, D. M. (1991). Parents' sex-related differential socialization of boys and girls: A meta-analysis. *Psychological Bulletin, 109,* 267–296.

M

Maccoby, E. E. (1984a). Middle childhood in the context of the family. In W. A. Collins (Ed.), *Development during middle childhood* (pp. 184–239). Washington, DC: National Academy Press.

Maccoby, E. E. (1984b). Socialization and developmental change. *Child Development, 55,* 317–328.

Maccoby, E. E. (1988). Gender as a social category. *Developmental Psychology, 24,* 755–765.

Maccoby, E. E. (1990a). Gender and relationships. *American Psychologist, 45,* 513–520.

Maccoby, E. E. (1990b). The role of gender identity and gender constancy in sex-differentiated development. In D. Schrader (Ed.), *New directions for child development* (No. 47, pp. 5–20). San Francisco: Jossey-Bass.

Maccoby, E. E., & Jacklin, C. N. (1974). *The psychology of sex differences.* Stanford, CA: Stanford University Press.

Maccoby, E. E., & Jacklin, C. N. (1980). Sex differences in aggression: A rejoinder and reprise. *Child Development, 51,* 964–980.

Maccoby, E. E., & Jacklin, C. N. (1987). Gender segregation in childhood. In E. H. Reese (Ed.), *Advances in child development and behavior* (Vol. 20, pp. 239–287). New York: Academic Press.

Maccoby, E. E., & Martin, J. A. (1983). Socialization in the context of the family. In E. M. Hetherington (Ed.), *Handbook of Child Psychology: Vol. 4. Socialization, personality, and social development* (pp. 1–101). New York: Wiley.

MacDonald, K. (1992). Warmth as a developmental construct: An evolutionary analysis. *Child Development, 63,* 753–773.

MacFarlane, A. (1975). Olfaction in the development of social preferences in the human neonate. In *Parent-infant interaction: Ciba Foundation Symposium 33* (pp. 103–117). Amsterdam: Elsevier.

Macfarlane, J. (1971). From infancy to adulthood. In M. C. Jones, N. Bayley, J. W. Macfarlane, & M. P. Honzik (Eds.), *The course of human development* (pp. 406–410). Waltham, MA: Xerox College Publishing.

MacKinnon, C. E. (1989). An observational investigation of sibling interactions in married and divorced families. *Developmental Psychology, 25,* 36–44.

Macklin, M. C., & Kolbe, R. H. (1984). Sex role stereotyping in children's advertising: Current and past trends. *Journal of Advertising, 13,* 34–42.

MacMillan, D. L., Keogh, B. K., & Jones, R. L. (1986). Special educational research on mildly handicapped learners. In M. C. Wittrock (Ed.), *Handbook of research on teaching* (3rd ed., pp. 686–724). New York: Macmillan.

MacQuiddy, S. L., Maise, S. J., & Hamilton, S. B. (1987). Empathy and affective perspective taking skills in parent identified conduct disordered boys. *Journal of Clinical Child Psychology, 16,* 260–268.

Macrides, R., Bartke, A., & Dalterio, S. (1975). Strange females increase plasma testosterone levels in male mice. *Science, 189,* 1104–1105.

MacTurk, R., Vietze, P., McCarthy, M., McQuiston, S., & Yarrow, L. (1985). The organization of exploratory behavior in Down syndrome and nondelayed infants. *Child Development, 56,* 573–581.

Madden, N., & Slavin, R. (1983). Mainstreaming students with mild handicaps: Academic and social outcomes. *Review of Educational Research, 53,* 519–569.

Main, M., & Cassidy, J. (1988). Categories of response to reunion with the parent at age 6: Predictable from infant attachment classifications and stable over a 1-month period. *Developmental Psychology, 24,* 415–426.

Main, M., & Goldwyn, R. (in press). Interview-based adult attachment classifications: Related to infant–mother and infant–father attachment. *Developmental Psychology.*

Main, M., & Solomon, J. (1990). Procedures for identifying infants as disorganized/disoriented during the Ainsworth Strange Situation. In M. Greenberg, D. Cicchetti, & M. Cummings (Eds.), *Attachment in the preschool years: Theory, research, and intervention* (pp. 121–160). Chicago: University of Chicago Press.

Makin, J. W., & Porter, R. H. (1989). Attractiveness of lactating females' breast odors to neonates. *Child Development, 60,* 803–810.

Makin, J. W., Fried, P. A., & Watkinson, B. (1991). A comparison of active and passive smoking during pregnancy: Long-term effects. *Neurotoxicology and Teratology, 13,* 5–12.

Makinson, C. (1985). The health consequences of teenage fertility. *Family Planning Perspectives, 17,* 132–139.

Malatesta, C. Z., Culver, C., Tesman, J. R., & Shepard, B. (1989). The development of emotion expression during the first two years of life. *Monographs of the Society for Research in Child Development, 54* (1–2, Serial No. 219).

Malatesta, C. Z., Grigoryev, P., Lamb, C., Albin, M., & Culver, C. (1986). Emotion socialization and expressive development in preterm and full-term infants. *Child Development, 57,* 316–330.

Malatesta, C. Z., & Haviland, J. M. (1982). Learning display rules: The socialization of emotion expression in infancy. *Child Development, 53,* 991–1003.

Malina, R. M. (1975). *Growth and development: The first twenty years in man.* Minneapolis: Burgess Publishing.

Malina, R. M. (1990). Physical growth and performance during the transitional years (9–16). In R. Montemayor, G. R. Adams, & T. P. Gullotta (Eds.), *From childhood to adolescence: A transitional period?* (pp. 41–62). Newbury Park, CA: Sage.

Mallick, S. K., & McCandless, B. R. (1966). A study of catharsis of aggression. *Journal of Personality and Social Psychology, 4,* 591–596.

Malloy, M. H., Kao, T., & Lee, Y. J. (1992). Analyzing the effect of prenatal care on pregnancy outcome: A conditional approach. *American Journal of Public Health, 82,* 448–453.

Maloney, M., & Kranz, R. (1991). *Straight talk about eating disorders.* New York: Facts on File.

Manchester, D. (1988). Prehensile development: A contrast of mature and immature patterns. In J. E. Clark & J. H. Humphrey (Eds.), *Advances in motor development research* (pp. 165–199). New York: AMS Press.

Mandler, J. M. (1983). Representation. In P. H. Mussen (Ed.), *Handbook of child psychology: Vol. 3. Cognitive development* (pp. 420–494). New York: Wiley.

Mandler, J. M. (1984). *Stories, scripts, and scenes: Aspects of schema theory.* Hillsdale, NJ: Erlbaum.

Mandler, J. M. (1992a). The foundations of conceptual thought in infancy. *Cognitive Development, 7,* 273–285.

Mandler, J. M. (1992b). How to build a baby: II. Conceptual primitives. *Psychological Review, 99,* 587–604.

Mandler, J. M., & Bauer, P. J. (1988). The cradle of categorization: Is the basic level basic? *Cognitive Development, 2,* 339–354.

Mandler, J. M., Bauer, P. J., & McDonough, L. (1991). Separating the sheep from the goats: Differentiating global categories. *Cognitive Psychology, 23,* 263–298.

Mandler, J. M., & Robinson, C. A. (1978). Developmental changes in picture recognition. *Journal of Experimental Child Psychology, 26,* 122–136.

Mangelsdorf, S., Gunnar, M., Kestenbaum, R., Lang, S., & Andreas, D. (1990). Infant proneness-to-distress temperament, maternal pesonality, and mother–infant attachment: Associations and goodness of fit. *Child Development, 61,* 830–831.

Mant, C. M., & Perner, J. (1988). The child's understanding of commitment. *Developmental Psychology, 24,* 343–351.

Maqsud, M. (1977). The influence of social heterogeneity and sentimental credibility on moral judgments of Nigerian Muslim adolescents. *Journal of Cross-Cultural Psychology, 8,* 113–122.

Maratsos, M. P. (1983). Some current issues in the study of the acquisition of grammar. In P. H. Mussen (Ed.), *Handbook of child psychology* (Vol. 3, pp. 707–786). New York: Wiley.

Maratsos, M. P. (1989). Innateness and plasticity in language acquisition. In M. L. Rice & R. L. Schiefelbusch (Eds.), *The teachability of language* (pp. 105–125). Baltimore: Paul H. Brookes.

Maratsos, M. P., & Chalkley, M. A. (1980). The internal language of children's syntax: The ontogenesis and representation of syntactic categories. In K. Nelson (Ed.), *Children's language* (Vol. 2, pp. 127–214). New York: Gardner Press.

Marcella, S., & McDonald, B. (1990). The infant walker: An unappreciated household hazard. *Connecticut Medicine, 54,* 127–129.

Marcia, J. E. (1980). Identity in adolescence. In J. Adelson (Ed.), *Handbook of adolescent psychology* (pp. 159–187). New York: Wiley.

Marcia, J. E. (1988). Identity and intervention. *Journal of Adolescence, 12,* 401–410.

Marcus, D. E., & Overton, W. F. (1978). The development of cognitive gender constancy and sex role preferences. *Child Development, 49,* 434–444.

Marcus, G. F. (1993). Negative evidence in language acquistion. *Cognition, 46,* 53–85.

Marcus, G. F., Pinker, S., Ullman, M., Hollander, M., Rosen, T. J., & Xu, F. (1992). Overregularization in language acquisition. *Monographs for the Society for Research in Child Development, 57* (4, Serial No. 228).

Marcus, J., Maccoby, E. E., Jacklin, C. N., & Doering, C. H. (1985). Individual differences in mood in early childhood: Their relation to gender and neonatal sex steroids. *Developmental Psychobiology, 18,* 327–340.

Marcus, L. C. (1983). Preventing and treating toxoplasmosis. *Drug Therapy, 13,* 129–144.

Marcus, R. F., Telleen, S., & Roke, E. J. (1979). Relation between cooperation and empathy in young children. *Developmental Psychology, 15,* 346–347.

Marini, Z., & Case, R. (1989). Parallels in the development of preschoolers' knowledge about their physical and social worlds. *Merrill-Palmer Quarterly, 35,* 63–87.

Markman, E. M. (1989). *Categorization and naming in children.* Cambridge, MA: MIT Press

Markman, E. M. (1992). Constraints on word learning: Speculations about their nature, origins, and domain specificity. In M. R. Gunnar & M. P. Maratsos (Eds.), *Minnesota Symposia on Child Psychology* (Vol. 25, pp. 59–101). Hillsdale, NJ: Erlbaum.

Markovits, H., Schleifer, M., & Fortier, L. (1989). Development of elementary deductive reasoning in young children. *Developmental Psychology, 25,* 787–793.

Markovits, H., & Vachon, R. (1989). Reasoning with contrary-to-fact propositions. *Journal of Experimental Child Psychology, 47,* 398–412.

Markovits, H., & Vachon, R. (1990). Conditional reasoning, representation, and level of abstraction. *Developmental Psychology, 26*, 942–951.

Marsh, D. T., Serafica, F. C., & Barenboim, C. (1981). Interrelationships among perspective taking, interpersonal problem solving, and interpersonal functioning. *Journal of Genetic Psychology, 138*, 37–48.

Marsh, H. W. (1989a). Age and sex effects in multiple dimensions of self-concept: Preadolescence to early adulthood. *Journal of Educational Psychology, 81*, 417–430.

Marsh, H. W. (1989b). Sex differences in the development of verbal and mathematics constructs: The High School and Beyond study. *American Educational Research Journal, 26*, 191–225.

Marsh, H. W. (1990). The structure of academic self-concept: The Marsh/Shavelson model. *Journal of Educational Psychology, 82*, 623–636.

Marsh, H. W., Barnes, J., Cairns, L., & Tidman, M. (1984). Self-description questionnaire: Age and sex effects in the structure and level of self-concept for preadolescent children. *Journal of Educational Psychology, 76*, 940–956.

Marsh, H. W., Craven, R. G., & Debus, R. (1991). Self-concepts of young children 5 to 8 years of age: Measurement and multidimensional structure. *Journal of Educational Psychology, 83*, 377–392.

Marsh, H. W., & Gouvernet, P. J. (1989). Multidimensional self-concepts and perceptions of control: Construct validation of responses by children. *Journal of Educational Psychology, 81*, 57–69.

Marsh, H. W., Smith, I. D., & Barnes, J. (1985). Multidimensional self-concepts: Relations with sex and academic achievement. *Journal of Educational Psychology, 77*, 581–596.

Marshall, W. A., & Tanner, J. M. (1969). Variations in the pattern of pubertal changes in girls. *Archives of Disease in Childhood, 44*, 291–303.

Martin, C. L. (1989). Children's use of gender-related information in making social judgments. *Developmental Psychology, 25*, 80–88.

Martin, C. L., & Halverson, C. F., Jr. (1981). A schematic processing model of sex typing and stereotyping in children. *Child Development, 52*, 1119–1134.

Martin, C. L., & Halverson, C. F., Jr. (1983). The effects of sex-typing schemas on young children's memory. *Child Development, 54*, 563–574.

Martin, C. L., & Halverson, C. F., Jr. (1987). The role of cognition in sex role acquisition. In D. B. Carter (Ed.), *Current conceptions of sex roles and sex typing: Theory and research* (pp. 123–137). New York: Praeger.

Martin, C. L., & Little, J. K. (1990). The relation of gender understanding to children's sex-typed preferences and gender stereotypes. *Child Development, 61*, 1427–1439.

Martin, G. B., & Clark, R. D., III. (1982). Distress crying in neonates: Species and peer specificity. *Developmental Psychology, 18*, 3–9.

Martin, J. A. (1981). A longitudinal study of the consequences of early mother-infant interaction: A microanalytic approach. *Monographs of the Society for Research in Child Development, 46* (3, Serial No. 190).

Martin, J. B. (1987). Molecular genetics: Applications to the clinical neurosciences. *Science, 298*, 765–772.

Martin, R. M. (1975). Effects of familiar and complex stimuli on infant attention. *Developmental Psychology, 11*, 178–185.

Martin, S. L., Ramey, C. T., & Ramey, S. (1990). The prevention of a randomized trial of educational day care. *American Journal of Public Health, 80*, 844–847.

Masataka, N. (1992). Early ontogeny of vocal behavior of Japanese infants in response to maternal speech. *Child Development, 63*, 1177–1185.

Mason, M. G., & Gibbs, J. C. (1993). Social perspective taking and moral judgment among college students. *Journal of Adolescent Research, 8*, 109–123.

Massey, C. M., & Gelman, R. (1988). Preschoolers' ability to decide whether a photographed unfamiliar object can move itself. *Developmental Psychology, 24*, 307–317.

Mastroiacovo, P., & Cavalcanti, D. P. (1991). Limb reduction defects and chorion villus sampling. *Lancet, 337*, 1091.

Masur, E. F., McIntyre, C. W., & Flavell, J. H. (1973). Developmental changes in apportionment of study time among items in a multi-trial free recall task. *Journal of Experimental Child Psychology, 15*, 237–246.

Matas, L., Arend, R., & Sroufe, L. A. (1978). Continuity of adaptation in the second year: The relationship between quality of attachment and later competence. *Child Development, 49*, 547–556.

Matheny, A. P., Jr. (1989). Temperament and cognition: Relations between temperament and mental test scores. In G. A. Kohnstamm, J. E. Bates, & M. K. Rothbart (Eds.), *Temperament in childhood* (pp. 263–282). New York: Wiley.

Matthei, E. (1987). Subject and agent in emerging grammars: Evidence for a change in children's biases. *Journal of Child Language, 14*, 295–308.

Matthews, K. A., & Angulo, J. (1980). Measurement of the Type A behavior pattern in children: Assessment of children's competitiveness, impatience-anger, and aggression. *Child Development, 51*, 466–475.

Matute-Bianchi, M. E. (1986). Ethnic identities and patterns of school success and failure among Mexican-descent and Japanese-American students in a California high school: An ethnographic analysis. *American Journal of Education, 95*, 233–255.

Maurer, D. (1985). Infants' perception of facedness. In T. Fields & N. Fox (Eds.), *Social perception in infants* (pp. 73–100). Norwood, NJ: Ablex.

Mayers, M. M., Davenny, K., Schoenbaum, E. E., Feingold, A. R., Selwyn, P. A., Robertson, V., Ou, C. Y., Rogers, M. F., & Naccarato, M. (1991). A prospective study of infants of human immunodeficiency virus seropositive and seronegative women with a history of intravenous drug use or of intravenous drug-using sex partners, in the Bronx, New York City. *Pediatrics, 88*, 1248–1256.

Mayes, L. C., & Carter, A. S. (1990). Emerging social regulatory capacities as seen in the still-face situation. *Child Development, 61*, 754–763.

Mayes, L. C., & Zigler, E. (1992). An observational study of the affective concomitants of mastery in infants. *Journal of Child Psychology and Psychiatry, 33*, 659–667.

Maynard, R., & McGinnis, E. (1993). Policies to meet the need for high quality child care. In A. Booth (Ed.), *Child care for the '90s* (pp. 189–208). Hillsdale, NJ: Erlbaum.

McCabe, A. E., & Peterson, C. (1988). A comparison of adults' versus children's spontaneous use of *because* and *so*. *Journal of Genetic Psychology, 149*, 257–268.

McCabe, A. E., & Siegel, L. S. (1987). The stability of training effects in young children's class inclusion reasoning. *Merrill-Palmer Quarterly, 33*, 187–194.

McCall, R. B. (1977). Childhood IQs as predictors of adult educational and occupational status. *Science, 197*, 482–483.

McCall, R. B. (1983). Environmental effects on intelligence: The forgotten realm of discontinuous nonshared within-family factors. *Child Development, 54,* 408–415.

McCall, R. B. (1987). The media, society, and child development research. In J. D. Osofsky (Ed.), *Handbook of infant development* (pp. 1199–1255). New York: Wiley.

McCall, R. B., Appelbaum, M. I., & Hogarty, P. S. (1973). Developmental changes in mental performance. *Monographs for the Society for Research in Child Development, 38* (3, Serial No. 150).

McCall, R. B., Kennedy, C. B., & Appelbaum, M. I. (1977). Magnitude of discrepancy and the distribution of attention in infants. *Child Development, 48,* 772–785.

McCall, R., & McGhee, P. (1977). The discrepancy hypothesis of attention and affect. In F. Weizmann & I. Uzgiris (Eds.), *The structuring of experience* (pp. 179–210). New York: Plenum.

McCartney, K. (1984). The effect of quality of day care environment upon children's language development. *Developmental Psychology, 20,* 244–260.

McConaghy, M. J. (1979). Gender permanence and the genital basis of gender: Stages in the development of constancy of gender identity. *Child Development, 50,* 1223–1226.

McCormick, C. M., & Maurer, D. M. (1988). Unimanual hand preferences in 6-month-olds: Consistency and relation to familial-handedness. *Infant Behavior and Development, 11,* 21–29.

McCormick, M. C., Gortmaker, S. L., & Sobol, A. M. (1990). Very low birth weight children: Behavior problems and school difficulty in a national sample. *Journal of Pediatrics, 117,* 687–693.

McDonald, K. B. (Ed.). (1988). *Sociobiological perspectives on human development.* New York: Springer-Verlag.

McGee, L. M., & Richgels, D. J. (1990). *Literacy's beginnings: Supporting young readers and writers.* Boston: Allyn and Bacon.

McGhee, P. E. (1979). *Humor: Its origin and development.* San Francisco: Freeman.

McGhee-Bidlack, B. (1991). The development of noun definitions: A metalinguistic analysis. *Journal of Child Language, 18,* 417–434.

McGilly, K., & Siegler, R. S. (1990). The influence of encoding and strategic knowledge on children's choices among serial recall strategies. *Developmental Psychology, 26,* 931–941.

McGinty, M. J., & Zafran, E. I. (1988). *Surrogacy: Constitutional and legal issues.* Cleveland: Ohio Academy of Trial Lawyers.

McGroarty, M. (1992, March). The societal context of bilingual education. *Educational Researcher, 21*(2), 7–9.

McGue, M., & Bouchard, T. J., Jr. (1989). Genetic and environmental determinants of information processing and special mental abilities: A twin analysis. In R. J. Sternberg (Ed.), *Advances in the psychology of human intelligence* (Vol. 5, pp. 7–46). Hillsdale, NJ: Erlbaum.

McGuinness, D., & Pribram, K. H. (1980). The neuropsychology of attention: Emotional and motivational controls. In M. C. Wittcock (Ed.), *The brain and psychology* (pp. 95–139). New York: Academic Press.

McGuire, J. (1988). Gender stereotypes of parents with two-year-olds and beliefs about gender differences in behavior. *Sex Roles, 19,* 233–240.

McGuire, K. D., & Weisz, J. R. (1982). Social cognition and behavior correlates of preadolescent chumship. *Child Development, 53,* 1483–1484.

McHale, S. M., Bartko, W. T., Crouter, A. C., & Perry-Jenkins, M. (1990). Children's housework and psychosocial functioning: The mediating effects of parents' sex-role behaviors and attitudes. *Child Development, 61,* 68–81.

McKenna, M. C., Robinson, R. D., & Miller, J. W. (1990, November). Whole language: A research agenda for the nineties. *Educational Researcher, 19*(8), 3–6.

McKenzie, B. E., Tootell, H. E., & Day, R. H. (1980). Development of visual size constancy during the 1st year of human infancy. *Developmental Psychology, 16,* 163–174.

McKey, R. H., Condelli, L., Ganson, H., Barrett, B. J., McConkey, C., & Plantz, M. C. (1985). *The impact of Head Start on children, families, and communities.* Washington, DC: U.S. Government Printing Office.

McKnight, C. C., Crosswhite, F. J., Dossey, J. A., Kifer, E., Swafford, J. O., Travers, K. J., & Cooney, T. J. (1987). *The underachieving curriculum: Assessing U.S. school mathematics from an international perspective.* Champaign, IL: Stipes.

McKusick, V. A. (1990). *Mendelian inheritance in man: Catalogs of autosomal dominant, autosomal recessive, and X-linked phenotypes* (9th ed.). Baltimore: Johns Hopkins University Press.

McLean, J., & Snyder-McLean, L. (1978). *A transactional approach to early language training.* Columbus, OH: Merrill.

McLoyd, V. C. (1989). Socialization and development in a changing economy: The effects of paternal job and income loss on children. *American Psychologist, 44,* 293–302.

McLoyd, V. C. (1990). The impact of economic hardship on black families and children: Psychological distress, parenting, and socioemotional development. *Child Development, 61,* 311–346.

McLoyd, V. C., Warren, D., & Thomas, E. A. C. (1984). Anticipatory and fantastic role enactment in preschool triads. *Developmental Psychology, 20,* 807–814.

McManus, I. C., Sik, G., Cole, D. R., Mellon, A. F., Wong, J., & Kloss, J. (1988). The development of handedness in children. *British Journal of Developmental Psychology, 6,* 257–273.

McNamee, S., & Peterson, J. (1986). Young children's distributive justice reasoning, behavior, and role taking: Their consistency and relationship. *Journal of Genetic Psychology, 146,* 399–404.

Mead, G. H. (1934). *Mind, self, and society.* Chicago: University of Chicago Press.

Mead, M. (1928). *Coming of age in Samoa.* Ann Arbor, MI: Morrow.

Mead, M. (1963). *Sex and temperament in three primitive societies.* New York: Morrow. (Original work published 1935)

Mead, M., & Newton, N. (1967). Cultural patterning of perinatal behavior. In S. Richardson & A. Guttmacher (Eds.), *Childbearing: Its social and psychological aspects* (pp. 142–244). Baltimore: Williams & Wilkins.

Meany, M. J., Stewart, J., & Beatty, W. W. (1985). Sex differences in social play: The socialization of sex roles. In J. S. Rosenblatt, C. Bear, C. M. Busnell, & P. Slater (Eds.), *Advances in the study of behavior* (Vol. 15, pp. 1–58). New York: Academic Press.

Mebert, C. J. (1991). Dimensions of subjectivity in parents' ratings of infant temperament. *Child Development, 62,* 352–361.

Mehler, J., Jusczyk, P. W., Lambertz, G., Halsted, N., Bertoncini, J., & Amiel-Tison, C. (1988). A precursor of language acquisition in young infants. *Cognition, 29,* 143–178.

Meilman, P. W. (1979). Cross-sectional age changes in ego identity status during adolescence. *Developmental Psychology, 15,* 230–231.

Melson, G. F., & Fogel, A. (1988, January). Learning to care. *Psychology Today, 22*(1), 39–45.

Melton, G. B., & Thompson, R. A. (1987). Legislative approaches to psychological maltreatment: A social policy analysis. In M. R. Brassard, R. Germain, & S. N. Hart (Eds.), *Psychological maltreatment of children and youth* (pp. 203–216). New York: Pergamon Press.

Meltzoff, A., & Gopnik, A. (1993). The role of imitation in understanding persons and developing a theory of mind. In S. Baron-Cohen & H. Tager-Flusberg (Eds.), *Understanding other minds* (pp. 335–366). Oxford: Oxford University Press.

Meltzoff, A. N. (1988a). Imitation of televised models by infants. *Child Development, 59,* 1221–1229.

Meltzoff, A. N. (1988b). Infant imitation after a 1-week delay: Long-term memory for novel acts and multiple stimuli. *Developmental Psychology, 24,* 470–476.

Meltzoff, A. N. (1988c). Infant imitation and memory: Nine-month-olds in immediate and deferred tests. *Child Development, 59,* 217–255.

Meltzoff, A. N. (1990). Towards a developmental cognitive science. *Annals of the New York Academy of Sciences, 608,* 1–37.

Meltzoff, A. N., & Borton, R. W. (1979). Intermodal matching by human neonates. *Nature, 282,* 403–404.

Meltzoff, A. N., & Moore, M. K. (1977). Imitation of facial and manual gestures by human neonates. *Science, 198,* 75–78.

Meltzoff, A. N., & Moore, M. K. (1989). Imitation in newborn infants: Exploring the range of gestures imitated and the underlying mechanisms. *Developmental Psychology, 25,* 954–962.

Meltzoff, A. N., & Moore, M. K. (1992). Early imitation within a functional framework: The importance of person identity, movement, and development. *Infant Behavior and Development, 15,* 479–505.

Menn, L. (1989). Phonological development: Learning sounds and sound patterns. In J. Berko Gleason (Ed.), *The development of language* (2nd ed., pp. 59–100). Columbus, OH: Merrill.

Menyuk, P. (1977). *Language and maturation.* Cambridge, MA: MIT Press.

Meredith, N. V. (1978). *Human body growth in the first ten years of life.* Columbia, SC: State Printing.

Mervis, C. B. (1987). Child-basic object categories and early lexical development. In U. Neisser (Ed.), *Concepts and conceptual development: Ecological and intellectual factors in categorization* (pp. 201–233). Cambridge: Cambridge University Press.

Mervis, C. B., & Crisafi, M. A. (1982). Order of acquisition of subordinate-, basic-, and superordinate categories. *Child Development, 53,* 258–266.

Meyer, D. R., & Garasky, S. (1993). Custodial fathers: Myths, realities, and child support policy. *Journal of Marriage and the Family, 55,* 73–79.

Michaels, G. Y. (1988). Motivational factors in the decision and timing of pregnancy. In G. Y. Michaels & W. A. Goldberg (Eds.), *The transition to parenthood: Current theory and research* (pp. 23–61). New York: Cambridge University Press.

Michel, C. (1989). Radiation embryology. *Experientia, 45,* 69–77.

Micheli, R. (1985, June). Water babies. *Parents, 60*(6), 8–13.

Midgley, C., Feldlaufer, H., & Eccles, J. S. (1989). Student/teacher relations and attitudes toward mathematics before and after the transition to junior high school. *Child Development, 60,* 981–992.

Midlarsky, E., & Bryan, J. H. (1972). Affect expressions and children's imitative altruism. *Journal of Experimental Research in Personality, 6,* 195–203.

Milburn, N., & D'Ercole, A. (1991). Homeless women, children, and families. *American Psychologist, 46,* 1159–1160.

Miles, C. (1935). Sex in social psychology. In C. Murchison (Ed.), *Handbook of social psychology* (pp. 699–704). Worcester, MA: Clark University Press.

Miller, G. E., & Emihovich, C. (1986). The effects of mediated programming instruction on preschool children's self-monitoring. *Journal of Educational Computing Research, 2,* 283–297.

Miller, G. E., & Pressley, M. (1987). Partial picture effects on children's memory for sentences containing implicit information. *Journal of Experimental Child Psychology, 43,* 300–310.

Miller, K. F., & Baillargeon, R. (1990). Length and distance: Do preschoolers think that occlusion brings things together? *Developmental Psychology, 26,* 103–114.

Miller, N. B., Cowan, P. A., Cowan, C. P., Hetherington, E. M., & Clingempeel, W. G. (1993). Externalizing in preschoolers and early adolescents: A cross-study replication of a family model. *Developmental Psychology, 29,* 3–18.

Miller, P., & Sperry, L. L. (1987). The socialization of anger and aggression. *Merrill-Palmer Quarterly, 33,* 1–31.

Miller, P. H. (1989). *Theories of developmental psychology* (2nd ed.). New York: Freeman.

Miller, P. H., & Bigi, L. (1979). The development of children's understanding of attention. *Merrill-Palmer Quarterly, 25,* 235–250.

Miller, P. H., Kessel, F. S., & Flavell, J. H. (1970). Thinking about people thinking about people thinking about . . . : A study of social cognitive development. *Child Development, 41,* 613–623.

Miller, P. H., & Zalenski, R. (1982). Preschoolers' knowledge about attention. *Developmental Psychology, 18,* 871–875.

Miller, S. A. (1987). *Developmental research methods.* Englewood Cliffs, NJ: Prentice-Hall.

Miller, S. A., & Davis, T. L. (1992). Beliefs about children: A comparative study of mothers, teachers, peers, and self. *Child Development, 63,* 1251–1265.

Miller-Jones, D. (1989). Culture and testing. *American Psychologist, 44,* 360–366.

Mills, R., & Grusec, J. (1989). Cognitive, affective, and behavioral consequences of praising altruism. *Merrill-Palmer Quarterly, 35,* 299–326.

Minuchin, P. P. (1988). Relationships within the family: A systems perspective on development. In R. A. Hinde & J. Stevenson-Hinde (Eds.), *Relationships within families: Mutual influences* (pp. 7–26). New York: Oxford University Press.

Minuchin, P., Biber, B., Shapiro, E., & Zimiles, H. (1969). *The psychological impact of school experience.* New York: Basic Books.

Minuchin, P. P., & Shapiro, E. K. (1983). The school as a context for social development. In E. M. Hetherington (Ed.), *Handbook of child psychology: Vol. 4. Socialization, personality, and social development* (4th ed., pp. 197–274). New York: Wiley.

Mischel, H. N., & Liebert, R. M. (1966). Effects of discrepancies between observed and imposed reward criteria on their acquisition and transmission. *Journal of Personality and Social Psychology, 3,* 45–53.

Mischel, H. N., & Mischel, W. (1983). The development of children's knowledge of self-control strategies. *Child Development, 54,* 603–619.

Mischel, W. (1974). Processes in delay of gratification. In L. Berkowitz (Ed.), *Advances in experimental social psychology* (Vol. 7, pp. 249–292). New York: Academic Press.

Mischel, W., & Baker, N. (1975). Cognitive appraisals and transformations in delay behavior. *Journal of Personality and Social Psychology, 31,* 254–261.

Mischel, W., Shoda, Y., & Peake, P. K. (1988). The nature of adolescent competencies predicted by preschool delay of gratification. *Journal of Personality and Social Psychology, 54,* 687–696.

Mischel, W., Shoda, Y., & Rodriguez, M. L. (1989). Delay of gratification in children. *Science, 244,* 933–938.

Miscione, J. L., Marvin, R. S., O'Brien, R. G., & Greenburg, M. T. (1978). A developmental study of preschool children's understanding of the words "know" and "guess." *Child Development, 48,* 1107–1113.

Mitchell, G., & Shively, C. (1984). Natural and experimental studies of nonhuman primate and other animal families. In R. D. Parke (Ed.), *Review of child development research* (Vol. 7, pp. 20–41). Chicago: University of Chicago Press.

Mitchell, R. E., & Trickett, E. J. (1980). An analysis of the effects and determinants of social networks. *Community Mental Health Journal, 16,* 27–44.

Miyake, K., Chen, S., & Campos, J. J. (1985). Infant temperament, mother's mode of interaction, and attachment in Japan: An interim report. In I. Bretherton & E. Waters (Eds.), Growing points of attachment theory and research. *Monographs of the Society for Research in Child Development, 50* (1–2, Serial No. 209).

Mize, J., & Ladd, G. W. (1988). Predicting preschoolers' peer behavior and status from their interpersonal strategies: A comparison of verbal and enactive responses to hypothetical social dilemmas. *Developmental Psychology, 24,* 782–788.

Mize, J., & Ladd, G. W. (1990). A cognitive-social learning approach to social skill training with low-status preschool children. *Developmental Psychology, 26,* 388–397.

Moely, B. E. (1977). Organizational factors in the development of memory. In R. V. Kail & J. W. Hagen (Eds.), *Perspectives on the development of memory and cognition* (pp. 203–236). Hillsdale, NJ: Erlbaum.

Moely, B. E., Hart, S. S., Leal, L., Johnson, T., Rao, N., & Burney, L. (1986). How do teachers teach memory skills? *Educational Psychologist, 21,* 55–71.

Moerk, E. L. (1992). *A first language taught and learned.* Baltimore: Paul H. Brookes.

Moffitt, T. E., Caspi, A., Belsky, J., & Silva, P. A. (1992). Childhood experience and the onset of menarche: A test of a sociobiological model. *Child Development, 63,* 47–58.

Money, J. (1985). Pediatric sexology and hermaphroditism. *Journal of Sex and Marital Therapy, 11,* 139–156.

Money, J., & Ehrhardt, A. A. (1972). *Man and woman, boy and girl.* Baltimore: Johns Hopkins University Press.

Monroe, S., Goldman, P., & Smith, V. E. (1988). *Brothers: Black and poor—A true story of courage and survival.* New York: Morrow.

Montemayor, R., & Eisen, M. (1977). The development of self-conceptions from childhood to adolescence. *Developmental Psychology, 13,* 314–319.

Moore, C., Bryant, D., & Furrow, D. (1989). Mental terms and the development of certainty. *Child Development, 60,* 167–171.

Moore, E. G. J. (1986). Family socialization and the IQ test performance of traditionally and transracially adopted black children. *Developmental Psychology, 22,* 317–326.

Moore, K., Peterson, J., & Furstenberg, F. F., Jr. (1986). Parental attitudes and the occurrence of early sexual activity. *Journal of Marriage and the Family, 48,* 777–782.

Moore, K. L. (1993). *Before we are born* (4th ed.). Philadelphia: Saunders.

Moorehouse, M. J. (1991). Linking maternal employment patterns to mother-child activities and children's school competence. *Developmental Psychology, 27,* 295–303.

Moran, G. F., & Vinovskis, M. A. (1986). The great care of godly parents: Early childhood in Puritan New England. In A. B. Smuts & J. W. Hagen (Eds.), History and research in child development. *Monographs of the Society for Research in Child Development, 50* (4–5, Serial No. 211, pp. 24–37).

Moran, J. D., Milgram, R. M., Sawyers, J. K., & Fu, V. R. (1983). Original thinking in preschool children. *Child Development, 54,* 921–926.

Morelli, G., Rogoff, B., Oppenheim, D., & Goldsmith, D. (1992). Cultural variation in infants' sleeping arrangements: Questions of independence. *Developmental Psychology, 28,* 604–613.

Morgan, M. (1982). Television and adolescents' sex stereotypes: A longitudinal study. *Journal of Personality and Social Psychology, 43,* 947–955.

Morison, R., & Masten, A. S. (1991). Peer reputation in middle childhood as a predictor of adaptation in adolescence: A seven-year follow-up. *Child Development, 62,* 991–1007.

Morrongiello, B. A. (1986). Infants' perception of multiple-group auditory patterns. *Infant Behavior and Development, 9,* 307–319.

Moshman, D., & Franks, B. A. (1986). Development of the concept of inferential validity. *Child Development, 57,* 153–165.

Moss, M., Colombo, J., Mitchell, D. W., & Horowitz, F. D. (1988). Neonatal behavioral organization and visual processing at three months. *Child Development, 59,* 1211–1220.

Mott, F. L., & Marsiglio, W. (1985). Early childbearing and completion of high school. *Family Planning Perspectives, 17,* 234–237.

Mott, S. R., James, S. R., & Sperhac, A. M. (1990). *Nursing care of children and families.* Redwood City, CA: Addison-Wesley.

Mowrer, O. H. (1960). *Learning theory and behavior.* New York: Wiley.

Moynahan, E. D. (1973). The development of knowledge concerning the effect of categorization upon free recall. *Child Development, 44,* 238–246.

Muecke, L., Simons-Morton, B., Huang, I. W., & Parcel, G. (1992). Is childhood obesity associated with high-fat foods and low physical activity? *Journal of School Health, 62,* 19–23.

Mullis, I. V. S., Dossey, J. A., Foertsch, M. A., Jones, L. R., & Gentile, C. A. (1991). *Trends in academic progress.* Washington, DC: U.S. Government Printing Office.

Mullis, I. V. S., Dossey, J. A., Owen, E. H., & Phillips, G. W. (1991). *The state of mathematics achievement: Executive summary* (NAEP's 1990 assessment of the nation and the trial assessment of the states). Princeton, NJ: Educational Testing Service.

Munro, G., & Adams, G. R. (1977). Ego identity formation in college students and working youth. *Developmental Psychology, 13,* 523–524.

Murett-Wagstaff, S., & Moore, S. G. (1989). The Hmong in America: Infant behavior and rearing practices. In J. K. Nugent, B. M. Lester, & T. B. Brazelton (Eds.), *Biology, culture, and development* (Vol. 1, pp. 319–339). Norwood, NJ: Ablex.

Murray, A. D. (1985). Aversiveness is in the mind of the beholder. In B. M. Lester & C. F. Z. Boukydis (Eds.), *Infant crying* (pp. 217–239). New York: Plenum.

Murray, A. D., Dolby, R. M., Nation, R. L., & Thomas, D. B. (1981). Effects of epidural anesthesia on newborns and their mothers. *Child Development, 52,* 71–82.

Murray, A. D., Johnson, J., & Peters, J. (1990). Fine-tuning of utterance length to preverbal infants: Effects on later language development. *Journal of Child Language, 17,* 511–525.

Murry, V. M. (1992). Incidence of first pregnancy among black adolescent females over three decades. *Youth & Society, 23,* 478–506.

Mussen, P., & Eisenberg-Berg, N. (1977). *Roots of caring, sharing, and helping.* San Francisco: Freeman.

Myers, N. A., Clifton, R. K., & Clarkson, M. G. (1987). When they were very young: Almost-threes remember two years ago. *Infant Behavior and Development, 10,* 123–132.

N

Nadel, L., & Zola-Morgan, S. (1984). Infantile amnesia: A neurobiological perspective. In M. Moscovitch (Ed.), *Infant memory* (pp. 145–172). New York: Plenum.

Naeye, R. L., Blanc, W., & Paul, C. (1973). Effects of maternal nutrition on the human fetus. *Pediatrics, 52,* 494–503.

Naglieri, J. A., & Jensen, A. R. (1987). Comparison of black-white differences on the WISC-R and K-ABC: Spearman's hypothesis. *Intelligence, 11,* 21-43.

Nanez, J. (1987). Perception of impending collision in 3- to 6-week-old infants. *Infant Behavior and Development, 11,* 447–463.

Nash, J. E., & Persaud, T. V. N. (1988). Embryopathic risks of cigarette smoking. *Experimental Pathology, 33,* 65–73.

Nastasi, B. K., & Clements, D. H. (1991). Research on cooperative learning: Implications for practice. *School Psychology Review, 20,* 110–131.

Nastasi, B. K., Clements, D. H., & Battista, M. T. (1990). Social–cognitive interactions, motivation, and cognitive growth in logo programming and CAI problem-solving environments. *Journal of Educational Psychology, 82,* 1–9.

National Association for the Education of Young Children. (1984). *Accreditation criteria and procedures of the National Academy of Early Childhood Programs.* Washington, DC: Author.

National Center for Health Statistics. (1991). *Advance Report of Final Natality Statistics* (Vol. 42). Washington, DC: U.S. Government Printing Office.

National Commission for the Protection of Human Subjects. (1977). *Report and recommendations: Research involving children.* Washington, DC: U.S. Government Printing Office.

Neal, J. H. (1983). Children's understanding of their parents' divorce. In L. A. Kurdek (Ed.), *New directions for child development* (No. 19, pp. 3–14). San Francisco: Jossey-Bass.

Needleman, H. L., Gunnoe, C., Leviton, A., Reed, R., Peresie, H., Maher, C., & Barrett, B. S. (1979). Deficits in psychologic and classroom performance of children with elevated dentine lead levels. *New England Journal of Medicine, 300,* 689–695.

Needleman, H. L., Schell, A., Bellinger, D., Leviton, A., & Allred, E. N. (1990). The long-term effects of exposure to low doses of lead in childhood. *New England Journal of Medicine, 322,* 83–88.

Neisser, U. (1967). *Cognitive psychology.* Englewood Cliffs, NJ: Prentice-Hall.

Nelson, C. A. (1987). The recognition of facial expressions in the first year of life: Mechanisms of development. *Child Development, 58,* 889–909.

Nelson, G. (1993). Risk, resistance, and self-esteem: A longitudinal study of elementary school-aged children from mother custody and two-parent families. *Journal of Divorce and Remarriage, 19,* 99–119.

Nelson, J., & Aboud, F. E. (1985). The resolution of social conflict between friends. *Child Development, 56,* 1009–1017.

Nelson, J. R., Smith, D. J., & Dodd, J. (1990). The moral reasoning of juvenile delinquents: A meta-analysis. *Journal of Abnormal Child Psychology, 18,* 231–239.

Nelson, K. (1973). Structure and strategy in learning to talk. *Monographs for the Society for Research in Child Development, 38,* (1–2, Serial No. 149).

Nelson, K. (1976). Some attributes of adjectives used by young children. *Cognition, 4,* 13–30.

Nelson, K. (1981). Individual differences in language development: Implications for development and language. *Developmental Psychology, 17,* 170–187.

Nelson, K. E. (1989). Strategies for first language teaching. In M. L. Rice & R. L. Schiefelbusch (Eds.), *The teachability of language* (pp. 263–310). Baltimore: Paul H. Brookes.

Nelson, K. E., & Brown, A. L. (1978). The semantic-episodic distinction in memory development. In P. A. Ornstein (Ed.), *Memory development in children* (pp. 233–241). Hillsdale, NJ: Erlbaum.

Nelson, K. E., Denninger, M., Bonvillian, J., Kaplan, B., & Baker, N. (1984). Maternal adjustments and non-adjustments as related to children's linguistic advances and language acquisition theories. In A. Pelligrini & T. Yawkey (Eds.), *The development of oral and written languages: Readings in developmental and applied linguistics* (pp. 31–56). Norwood, NJ: Ablex.

Nelson, K. E., & Gruendel, J. (1981). Generalized event representations: Basic building blocks of cognitive development. In M. Lamb & A. Brown (Eds.), *Advances in developmental psychology* (Vol. 1, pp. 131–158). Hillsdale, NJ: Erlbaum.

Nelson, K. E., & Kosslyn, S. M. (1976). Recognition of previously labeled or unlabeled pictures by 5-year-olds and adults. *Journal of Experimental Child Psychology, 21,* 40–45.

Nelson-Le Gall, S. A. (1985). Motive-outcome matching and outcome foreseeability: Effects on attribution of intentionality and moral judgments. *Developmental Psychology, 21,* 332–337.

Nemerowicz, G. M. (1979). *Children's perceptions of gender and work roles.* New York: Praeger.

Nesher, P. (1988). Multiplicative school word problems: Theoretical approaches and empirical findings. In M. J. Behr & J. Hiebert (Eds.), *Research agenda in mathematical education: Number concepts and operations in the middle grades* (pp. 19–40). Reston, VA: National Council of Teachers of Mathematics.

Netley, C. T. (1986). Summary overview of behavioural development in individuals with neonatally identified X and Y aneuploidy. *Birth Defects, 22,* 293–306.

Newcomb, A. F., Bukowski, W. M., & Pattee, L. (1993). Children's peer relations: A meta-analytic review of popular, rejected, neglected, controversial, and average sociometric status. *Psychological Bulletin, 113,* 99–128.

Newcomb, M. D., & Bentler, P. M. (1989). Substance use and abuse among children and teenagers. *American Psychologist, 44,* 242–248.

Newcomb, M. D., Maddahian, E., & Bentler, P. M. (1986). Risk factors for drug use among adolescents: Concurrent and longitudinal analyses. *American Journal of Public Health, 76,* 525–531.

Newcombe, N. (1982). Development of spatial cognition and cognitive development. In R. Cohen (Ed.), *Children's conceptions of spatial relationships* (pp. 65–81). San Francisco: Jossey-Bass.

Newcombe, N., & Dubas, J. S. (1987). Individual differences in cognitive ability: Are they related to timing of puberty? In R. M. Lerner & T. T. Foch (Eds.), *Biological-psychosocial interactions in early adolescence: A life-span perspective* (pp. 249–302). Hillsdale, NJ: Erlbaum.

Newcombe, N., & Dubas, J. S. (1992). A longitudinal study of predictors of spatial ability in adolescent females. *Child Development, 63,* 37–46.

Newcombe, N., Dubas, J. S., & Baenninger, M. A. (1989). Associations of timing of puberty, spatial ability, and lateralization in adult women. *Child Development, 60,* 246–254.

Newcombe, N., Fox, N. A., & Prime, A. G. (1989). *Preschool memories: Through a glass darkly*. Paper presented at the annual meeting of the American Psychological Society, Alexandria, VA.

Newcombe, N., & Huttenlocher, J. (1992). Children's early ability to solve perspective-taking problems. *Developmental Psychology, 28*, 635–643.

Newman, L. S. (1990). Intentional and unintentional memory in young children: Remembering vs. playing. *Journal of Experimental Child Psychology, 50*, 243–258.

Newport, E. L. (1991). Contrasting conceptions of the critical period for language. In S. Carey & R. Gelman (Eds.), *The epigenesis of mind: Essays on biology and cognition* (pp. 111–130). Hillsdale, NJ: Erlbaum.

Newport, E. L., Gleitman, H., & Gleitman, L. R. (1977). Mother, I'd rather do it myself: Some effects and non-effects of maternal speech style. In C. A. Ferguson & C. E. Snow (Eds.), *Talking to children* (pp. 109–149). New York: Cambridge University Press.

Newson, J., & Newson, E. (1975). Intersubjectivity and the transmission of culture: On the social origins of symbolic functioning. *Bulletin of the British Psychological Society, 28*, 437–446.

Newson, J., & Newson, E. (1976). *Seven years old in the home environment*. London: Allen & Unwin.

Nicholls, A. L., & Kennedy, J. M. (1992). Drawing development: From similarity of features to direction. *Child Development, 63*, 227–241.

Nicholls, J. G. (1978). The development of concepts of effort and ability, perception of academic attainment, and the understanding that difficult tasks require more ability. *Child Development, 49*, 800–814.

Nichols, R. C. (1978). Heredity and environment: Major findings from twin studies of ability, personality, and interests. *Home, 29*, 158–173.

Nidorf, J. F. (1985). Mental health and refugee youths: A model for diagnostic training. In T. C. Owen (Ed.), *Southeast Asian mental health: Treatment, prevention, services, training, and research* (pp. 391–427). Washington, DC: National Institute of Mental Health.

Nielsen, A. C. (1990). *Annual Nielsen report on television: 1990*. New York: Nielsen Media Research.

Niemiec, R., & Walberg, H. J. (1987). Comparative effects of computer-assisted instruction: A synthesis of reviews. *Journal of Educational Computing Research, 3*, 19–37.

NIH/CEPH Collaborative Mapping Group. (1992). A comprehensive genetic linkage map of the human genome. *Science, 258*, 67–86.

Nilsson, L., & Hamberger, L. (1990). *A child is born*. New York: Delacorte.

Noddings, N. (1992). Gender and the curriculum. In P. W. Jackson (Ed.), *Handbook of research on curriculum* (pp. 659–684). New York: Macmillan.

Norbeck, J. S., & Tilden, V. P. (1983). Life stress, social support, and emotional disequilibrium in complications of pregnancy: A prospective, multivariate study. *Journal of Health and Social Behavior, 24*, 30–46.

Nottelmann, E. D. (1987). Competence and self-esteem during transition from childhood to adolescence. *Developmental Psychology, 23*, 441–450.

Nottelmann, E. D., Inoff-Germain, G., Susman, E. J., & Chrousos, G. P. (1990). Hormones and behavior at puberty. In J. Bancroft & J. M. Reinisch (Eds.), *Adolescence and puberty* (pp. 88–123). New York: Oxford University Press.

Nottelmann, E. D., Susman, E. J., Blue, J. H., Inoff-Germain, G., Dorn, L. D., Loriaux, D. L., Cutler, G. B., Jr., & Chrousos, G. P. (1987). Gonadal and adrenal hormone correlates of adjustment in early adolescence. In R. M. Lerner & T. T. Foch (Eds.), *Biological-psychosocial interactions in early adolescence: A life-span perspective* (pp. 303–323). Hillsdale, NJ: Erlbaum.

Nowakowski, R. S. (1987). Basic concepts of CNS development. *Child Development, 58*, 568–595.

Nucci, L. (1981). Conceptions of personal issues: A domain distinct from moral or societal concepts. *Child Development, 52*, 114–121.

Nucci, L., & Turiel, E. (1978). Social interactions and the development of social concepts in preschool children. *Child Development, 49*, 400–407.

Nuckolls, K. B., Cassel, J., & Kaplan, B. H. (1972). Psychosocial assets, life crisis, and the prognosis of pregnancy. *American Journal of Epidemiology, 95*, 431–441.

Nunnally, J. C. (1982). The study of human change: Measurement, research strategies, and methods of analysis. In B. B. Wolman (Ed.), *Handbook of developmental psychology* (pp. 133–148). Englewood Cliffs, NJ: Prentice-Hall.

O

O'Brien, M., & Huston, A. C. (1985). Development of sex-typed play behavior in toddlers. *Developmental Psychology, 21*, 866–871.

O'Connor, M., Foch, T., Sherry, T., & Plomin, R. (1980). A twin study of specific behavioral problems of socialization as viewed by parents. *Journal of Abnormal Child Psychology, 8*, 189–199.

O'Keefe, B. J., & Benoit, P. J. (1982). Children's arguments. In J. R. Cox & C. A. Willard (Eds.), *Advances in argumentation theory and research* (pp. 154–183). Carbondale, IL: Southern Illinois University Press.

O'Mahoney, J. F. (1989). Development of thinking about things and people: Social and nonsocial cognition during adolescence. *Journal of Genetic Psychology, 150*, 217–224.

O'Neill, D. K., Astington, J. W., & Flavell, J. H. (1992). Young children's understanding of the role that sensory experiences play in knowledge acquisition. *Child Development, 63*, 474–490.

Oakes, J., Gamoran, A., & Page, R. N. (1992). Curriculum differentiation: Opportunities, outcomes, and meanings. In P. W. Jackson (Ed.), *Handbook of research on curriculum* (pp. 570–608). New York: Macmillan.

Oakes, L. M., Madole, K. L., & Cohen, L. B. (1991). Infants' object examining: Habituation and categorization. *Cognitive Development, 6*, 377–392.

Oakland, T., & Parmelee, R. (1985). Mental measurement of minority-group children. In B. B. Wolman (Ed.), *Handbook of intelligence* (pp. 699–736). New York: Wiley.

Oates, R. K. (1984). Similarities and differences between nonorganic failure to thrive and deprivation dwarfism. *Child Abuse and Neglect, 8*, 438–445.

Oates, R. K., Peacock, A., & Forrest, D. (1985). Long-term effects of nonorganic failure to thrive. *Pediatrics, 75*, 36–40.

Oberg, C. N. (1988, Spring). Children and the uninsured. *Social Policy Report (Society for Research in Child Development), 3* (No. 1).

Ochs, E. (1988). *Culture and language development: Language acquisition and language socialization in a Samoan village*. Cambridge: Cambridge University Press.

Oettingen, G. (1985). The influence of kindergarten teachers on sex differences in behavior. *International Journal of Behavioral Development, 8,* 3–13.

Offer, D. (1988). *The teenage world: Adolescents' self-image in ten countries.* New York: Plenum.

Ogbu, J. (1988). Black education: A cultural-ecological perspective. In H. P. McAdoo (Ed.), *Black families* (pp. 169–186). Beverly Hills, CA: Sage.

Ogbu, J. U. (1985). A cultural ecology of competence among inner-city blacks. In M. B. Spencer, G. K. Brookins, & W. R. Allen (Eds.), *Beginnings: The social and affective development of black children* (pp. 45–66). Hillsdale, NJ: Erlbaum.

Okagaki, L., & Sternberg, R. J. (1993). Parental beliefs and children's school performance. *Child Development, 64,* 36–56.

Ollendick, T. H., Weist, M. D., Borden, M. C., & Greene, R. W. (1992). Sociometric status and academic, behavioral, and psychological adjustment: A five-year longitudinal study. *Journal of Consulting and Clinical Psychology, 60,* 80–87.

Oller, D. K., & Eilers, R. E. (1988). The role of audition in infant babbling. *Child Development, 59,* 441–449.

Olweus, D. (1978). *Aggression in the schools: Bullies and whipping boys.* Washington, DC: Hemisphere.

Olweus, D. (1980). Familial and temperamental determinants of aggressive behavior in adolescent boys: A causal analysis. *Developmental Psychology, 16,* 644–666.

Olweus, D. (1984). Aggressors and their victims: Bullying at school. In N. Frude & H. Gault (Eds.), *Disruptive behaviors in schools* (pp. 57–76). New York: Wiley.

Omer, H., & Everly, G. S. (1988). Psychological factors in preterm labor: Critical review and theoretical synthesis. *American Journal of Psychiatry, 145,* 1507–1513.

Oppenheim, D., Sagi, A., & Lamb, M. E. (1988). Infant-adult attachments on the kibbutz and their relation to socioemotional development 4 years later. *Developmental Psychology, 24,* 427–433.

Ornstein, P. A., Naus, M. J., & Liberty, C. (1975). Rehearsal and organizational processes in children's memory. *Child Development, 46,* 818–830.

Osherson, D. N., & Markman, E. M. (1975). Language and the ability to evaluate contradictions and tautologies. *Cognition, 2,* 213–226.

Oshima-Takane, Y. (1988). Children learn from speech not addressed to them: The case of personal pronouns. *Journal of Child Language, 15,* 95–108.

Oster, H., Hegley, D., & Nagel, L. (1992). Adult judgments and fine-grained analysis of infant facial expressions: Testing the validity of a priori coding formulas. *Developmental Psychology, 28,* 1115–1131.

Otaki, M., Durrett, M., Richards, P., Nyquist, L., & Pennebaker, J. (1986). Maternal and infant behavior in Japan and America: A partial replication. *Journal of Cross-Cultural Psychology, 17,* 251–268.

Owen, M. T., & Cox, M. (1988). Maternal employment and the transition to parenthood. In A. E. Gottfried & A. W. Gottfried (Eds.), *Maternal employment and children's development: Longitudinal research* (pp. 85–119). New York: Plenum.

Owen, M. T., Easterbrooks, M. A., Chase-Lansdale, L., & Goldberg, W. A. (1984). The relation between maternal employment status and the stability of attachments to mother and father. *Child Development, 55,* 1894–1901.

Owens, R. (1992). *Language development: An introduction* (3rd ed.). New York: Merrill.

Owens, T. (1982). Experience-based career education: Summary and implications of research and evaluation findings. *Child and Youth Services Journal, 4,* 77–91.

P

Padgham, J. J., & Blyth, D. A. (1990). Dating during adolescence. In R. M. Lerner, A. C. Peterson, & J. Brooks-Gunn (Eds.), *The encyclopedia of adolescence* (Vol. 1, pp. 196–198). New York: Garland.

Padilla, M. L., & Landreth, G. L. (1989). Latchkey children: A review of the literature. *Child Welfare, 68,* 445–454.

Page, D. C., Mosher, R., Simpson, E. M., Fisher, E. M. C., Mardon, G., Pollack, J., McGillivray, B., de la Chapelle, A., & Brown, L. G. (1987). The sex-determining region of the human Y chromosome encodes a finger protein. *Cell, 51,* 1091–1104.

Page, E. B., & Grandon, G. M. (1979). Family configuration and mental ability: Two theories contrasted with U.S. data. *American Educational Research Journal, 16,* 257–272.

Paget, K. F., & Kritt, D. (1986). The development of the conceptual organization of self. *Journal of Genetic Psychology, 146,* 333–341.

Paikoff, R. L., & Brooks-Gunn, J. (1991). Do parent–child relationships change during puberty? *Psychological Bulletin, 110,* 47–66.

Palincsar, A. S. (1992, April). *Beyond reciprocal teaching: A retrospective and prospective view.* Raymond B. Cattell Early Career Award Address at the annual meeting of the American Educational Research Association, San Francisco.

Palincsar, A. S., & Brown, A. L. (1984). Reciprocal teaching of comprehension-fostering and monitoring activities. *Cognition and Instruction, 1,* 117–175.

Palincsar, A. S., & Klenk, L. (1992). Fostering literacy learning in supportive contexts. *Journal of Learning Disabilities, 25,* 211–225.

Papini, D. R., Micka, J. C., & Barnett, J. K. (1989). Perceptions of intrapsychic and extrapsychic functioning as bases of adolescent ego identity statuses. *Journal of Adolescent Research, 4,* 462–482.

Parekh, U. C., Pherwani, A., Udani, P. M., & Mukherjee, S. (1970). Brain weight and head circumference in fetus, infant and children of different nutritional and socio-economic groups. *Indian Pediatrics, 7,* 347–358.

Parikh, B. (1980). Development of moral judgment and its relation to family environmental factors in Indian and American families. *Child Development, 51,* 1030–1039.

Paris, S. G., Lawton, T. A., Turner, J. C., & Roth, J. L. (1991). A developmental perspective on standardized achievement testing. *Educational Researcher, 20*(5), 12–20.

Paris, S. G., & Lindauer, B. K. (1977). Constructive processes in children's comprehension and memory. In R. V. Kail & J. W. Hagen (Eds.), *Perspectives on the development of memory and cognition* (pp. 35–60). Hillsdale, NJ: Erlbaum.

Parke, R. D. (1977). Punishment in children: Effects, side effects, and alternative strategies. In H. L. Hom, Jr., & A. Robinson (Eds.), *Psychological processes in early education* (pp. 71–97). New York: Academic Press.

Parke, R. D., & Collmer, C. W. (1975). Child abuse: An interdisciplinary analysis. In E. M. Hetherington (Ed.), *Review of child development research* (Vol. 5, pp. 509–590). Chicago: Chicago University Press.

Parke, R. D., MacDonald, K. B., Beitel, A., & Bhavnagri, N. (1988). The role of the family in the development of peer relations. In R. DeV. Peters & R. J. McMahan (Eds.), *Marriages and families: Behavioral treatment and processes* (pp. 17–44). New York: Brunner/Mazel.

Parke, R. D., & Slaby, R. G. (1983). The development of aggression. In E. M. Hetherington (Ed.), *Handbook of child psychology: Vol. 4. Socialization, personality, and social development* (4th ed., pp. 547–641). New York: Wiley.

Parke, R. D., & Tinsley, B. R. (1981). The father's role in infancy: Determinants of involvement in caregiving and play. In M. E. Lamb (Ed.), *The role of the father in child development* (pp. 429–458). New York: Wiley.

Parke, R. D., & Walters, R. H. (1967). Some factors determining the efficacy of punishment for inducing response inhibition. *Monographs of the Society for Research in Child Development, 32* (1, Serial No. 109).

Parker, J. G., & Asher, S. R. (1987). Peer relations and later personal adjustment: Are low-accepted children at risk? *Psychological Bulletin, 102,* 357–389.

Parkhurst, J. T., & Asher, S. R. (1992). Peer rejection in middle school: Subgroup differences in behavior, loneliness, and interpersonal concerns. *Developmental Psychology, 28,* 231–241.

Parmelee, A., Wenner, W., Akiyama, Y., Stern, E., & Flescher, J. (1967). Electroencephalography and brain maturation. In A. Minkowski (Ed.), *Symposium on regional development of the brain in early life* (pp. 459–476). Philadelphia: Davis.

Parrish, L. H. (1991). Community resources and dropout prevention. In L. L. West (Ed.), *Effective strategies for dropout prevention of at-risk youth* (pp. 217–232). Gaithersburg, MD: Aspen Publishers.

Parsons, J. E. (1982). Biology, experience, and sex-dimorphic behaviors. In W. R. Gove & G. R. Carpenter (Eds.), *The fundamental connection between nature and nurture* (pp. 137–170). Lexington, MA: Lexington Books.

Parsons, J. E., Adler, T. F., & Kaczala, C. M. (1982). Socialization of achievement attitudes and beliefs: Parental influences. *Child Development, 53,* 310–321.

Parten, M. (1932). Social participation among preschool children. *Journal of Abnormal and Social Psychology, 27,* 243–269.

Passman, R. H. (1987). Attachments to inanimate objects: Are children who have security blankets insecure? *Journal of Consulting and Clinical Psychology, 55,* 825–830.

Patterson, G. R. (1982). *Coercive family processes.* Eugene, OR: Castilia Press.

Patterson, G. (1988). Stress: A change agent for family process. In N. Garmezy & M. Rutter (Eds.), *Stress, coping, and development in children* (pp. 235–264). Baltimore: Johns Hopkins University Press.

Patterson, G. R. (1991, April). *Interaction of stress and family structure, and their relation to child adjustment: An example of across-site collaboration.* Paper presented at the biennial meeting of the Society for Research in Child Development, Seattle.

Patterson, G. R., DeBaryshe, B. D., & Ramsey, E. (1989). A developmental perspective on antisocial behavior. *American Psychologist, 44,* 329–335.

Patterson, G. R., & Fleishman, M. J. (1979). Maintenance of treatment effects: Some considerations concerning family systems and follow-up data. *Behavior Therapy, 10,* 168–185.

Patterson, G. R., Littman, R. A., & Bricker, W. (1967). Assertive behavior in children: A step toward a theory of aggression. *Monographs of the Society for Research in Child Development, 35* (5, Serial No. 113).

Patterson, G. R., Reid, J. B., Jones, R. R., & Conger, R. E. (1975). *A social learning approach: Vol. 1. Families with aggressive children.* Eugene, OR: Castilia Press.

Patteson, D. M., & Barnard, K. E. (1990). Parenting of low birth weight infants: A review of issues and interventions. *Infant Mental Health Journal, 11,* 37–56.

Pea, R. D., & Kurland, D. M. (1984). On the cognitive effects of learning computer programming. *New Ideas in Psychology, 2,* 137–168.

Pearson, J. L., Hunter, A. G., Ensminger, M. E., & Kellam, S. G. (1990). Black grandmothers in multigenerational households: Diversity in family structure and parenting involvement in the Woodlawn community. *Child Development, 61,* 434–442.

Peevers, B. H., & Secord, P. F. (1973). Developmental changes in attribution of descriptive concepts to persons. *Journal of Personality and Social Psychology, 27,* 120–128.

Penner, S. G. (1987). Parental responses to grammatical and ungrammatical utterances. *Child Development, 58,* 376–384.

Pennington, B. F., Bender, B., Puck, M., Salbenblatt, J., & Robinson, A. (1982). Learning disabilities in children with sex chromosome anomalies. *Child Development, 53,* 1182–1192.

Pennington, B. F., & Smith, S. D. (1988). Genetic influences on learning disabilities: An update. *Journal of Consulting and Clinical Psychology, 56,* 817–823.

Pepler, D. J., & Ross, H. S. (1981). The effects of play on convergent and divergent problem solving. *Child Development, 52,* 1202–1210.

Peres, Y., & Pasternack, R. (1991). To what extent can the school reduce the gaps between children raised by divorced and intact families? *Journal of Divorce and Remarriage, 15,* 143–158.

Perfetti, C. A. (1988). Verbal efficiency in reading ability. In M. Daneman, G. E. MacKinnon, & T. G. Waller (Eds.), *Reading research: Advances in theory and practice* (Vol. 6, pp. 109–143). San Diego: Academic Press.

Perlmutter, M. (1984). Continuities and discontinuities in early human memory: Paradigms, processes, and performances. In R. V. Kail, Jr., & N. R. Spear (Eds.), *Comparative perspectives on the development of memory* (pp. 253–287). Hillsdale, NJ: Erlbaum.

Perlmutter, M., Behrend, S. D., Kuo, F., & Muller, A. (1989). Social influences on children's problem solving. *Developmental Psychology, 25,* 744–754.

Perner, J. (1988). Higher-order beliefs and intentions in children's understanding of social interaction. In J. W. Astington, P. L. Harris, & D. R. Olson (Eds.), *Developing theories of mind* (pp. 271–294). New York: Cambridge University Press.

Perner, J. (1991). *Understanding the representational mind.* Cambridge, MA: Bradford/MIT Press.

Perry, D. G., Kusel, S. J., & Perry, L. C. (1988). Victims of peer aggression. *Developmental Psychology, 24,* 807–814.

Perry, D. G., Perry, L. C., & Rasmussen, P. (1986). Cognitive social learning mediators of aggression. *Child Development, 57,* 700–711.

Perry, D. G., Perry, L. C., & Weiss, R. J. (1989). Sex differences in the consequences that children anticipate for aggression. *Developmental Psychology, 25,* 171–184.

Perry, D. G., White, A. J., & Perry, L. C. (1984). Does early sex typing result from children's attempts to match their behavior to sex role stereotypes? *Child Development, 55,* 2114–2121.

Perry, D. G., Williard, J. C., & Perry, L. C. (1990). Peers' perceptions of the consequences that victimized children provide aggressors. *Child Development, 61,* 1310–1325.

Peshkin, A. (1978). *Growing up American: Schooling and the survival of the community.* Chicago: University of Chicago Press.

Petersen, A. C. (1985). Pubertal development as a cause of disturbance: Myths, realities, and unanswered questions. *Genetic, Social, and General Psychology Monographs, 111,* 205–232.

Peterson, L. (1982). An alternative perspective to norm-based explanations of modeling and children's generosity: A reply to Lipscomb, Larrieu, McAllister, and Bregman. *Merrill-Palmer Quarterly, 28,* 283–290.

Peterson, L. (1989). Latchkey children's preparation for self-care: Overestimated, underrehearsed, and unsafe. *Journal of Clinical Child Psychology, 18,* 36–43.

Petitto, L. A., & Marentette, P. F. (1991). Babbling in the manual mode: Evidence for the ontogeny of language. *Science, 251,* 1493–1496.

Pettit, G. S., Bakshi, A., Dodge, K. A., & Coie, J. D. (1990). The emergence of social dominance in young boys' play groups: Developmental differences and behavioral correlates. *Developmental Psychology, 26,* 1017–1025.

Pettit, G. S., Dodge, K. A., & Brown, M. M. (1988). Early family experience, social problem solving patterns, and children's social competence. *Child Development, 59,* 107–120.

Pezzullo, T. R., Thorsen, E. E., & Madaus, G. F. (1972). The heritability of Jensen's Level I and II and divergent thinking. *American Educational Research Journal, 9,* 539–546.

Phillips, D. A. (1987). Socialization of perceived academic competence among highly competent children. *Child Development, 58,* 1308–1320.

Phillips, D. A., & McCartney, K., & Scarr, S. (1987). Child-care quality and children's social development. *Developmental Psychology, 23,* 537–543.

Phillips, D. A., & Zimmerman, M. (1990). The developmental course of perceived competence and incompetence among competent children. In R. Sternberg & J. Kolligian (Eds.), *Competence considered* (pp. 41–66). New Haven: Yale University Press.

Phillips, K., & Fulker, D. W. (1989). Quantitative genetic analysis of longitudinal trends in adoption designs with application to IQ in the Colorado Adoption Project. *Behavior Genetics, 19,* 621–658.

Phinney, J. S. (1989). Stages of ethnic identity development in minority group adolescents. *Journal of Early Adolescence, 9,* 34–49.

Phinney, J., & Alipuria, L. (1990). Ethnic identity in college students from four ethnic groups. *Journal of Adolescence, 13,* 171–183.

Piaget, J. (1926). *The language and thought of the child.* New York: Harcourt, Brace & World. (Original work published 1923)

Piaget, J. (1928). *Judgment and reasoning in the child.* New York: Harcourt, Brace & World. (Original work published 1926)

Piaget, J. (1929). *The child's conception of physical causality.* New York: Harcourt, Brace & World. (Original work published 1926)

Piaget, J. (1930). *The child's conception the world.* New York: Harcourt, Brace & World. (Original work published 1926)

Piaget, J. (1950). *The psychology of intelligence.* New York: International Universities Press.

Piaget, J. (1951). *Play, dreams, and imitation in childhood.* New York: Norton. (Original work published 1945)

Piaget, J. (1952a). Jean Piaget (autobiographical sketch). In E. G. Boring, H. S. Langfeld, H. Werner, & R. M. Yerkes (Eds.), *A history of psychology in autobiography* (pp. 237–256). Worcester, MA: Clark University Press.

Piaget, J. (1952b). *The origins of intelligence in children.* New York: International Universities Press. (Original work published 1936)

Piaget, J. (1954). *The construction of reality in the child.* New York: Free Press.

Piaget, J. (1965). *The moral judgment of the child.* New York: Free Press. (Original work published 1932)

Piaget, J. (1967). *Six psychological studies.* New York: Vintage.

Piaget, J. (1970). *The child's conception of movement and speed.* London: Routledge & Kegan Paul. (Original work published 1946)

Piaget, J. (1971). *Biology and knowledge.* Chicago: University of Chicago Press.

Piaget, J. (1985). *The equilibration of cognitive structures: The central problem of intellectual development.* Chicago: University of Chicago Press.

Piaget, J., & Inhelder, B. (1956). *The child's conception of space.* London: Routledge & Kegan Paul. (Original work published 1948)

Piaget, J., & Inhelder, B. (1969). *The psychology of the child.* London: Routledge & Kegan Paul. (Original work published 1967)

Piaget, J., Inhelder, B., & Szeminska, A. (1960). *The child's conception of geometry.* New York: Basic Books. (Original work published 1948)

Pianta, R. C., Egeland, B., & Erickson, M. F. (1989). The antecedents of maltreatment: Results of the Mother-Child Interaction Research Project. In D. Cicchetti & V. Carlson (Eds.), *Child maltreatment* (pp. 203–253). New York: Cambridge University Press.

Pianta, R. C., Sroufe, L. A., & Egeland, B. (1989). Continuity and discontinuity in maternal sensitivity at 6, 24, and 42 months in a high-risk sample. *Child Development, 60,* 481–487.

Picariello, M. L., Greenberg, D. N., & Pillemer, D. B. (1990). Children's sex-related stereotyping of colors. *Child Development, 61,* 1453–1460.

Pick, A. D., & Frankel, G. W. (1974). A developmental study of strategies of visual selectivity. *Child Development, 45,* 1162–1165.

Pick, H. L., Jr. (1989). Motor development: The control of action. *Developmental Psychology, 25,* 867–870.

Pierce, R., & Pierce, L. H. (1985). The sexually abused child: A comparison of male and female victims. *Child Abuse & Neglect, 9,* 191–199.

Pillow, B. H. (1988a). Early understanding of perception as a source of knowledge. *Journal of Experimental Child Psychology, 47,* 116–129.

Pillow, B. H. (1988b). The development of children's beliefs about the mental world. *Merrill-Palmer Quarterly, 34,* 1–32.

Pillow, B. H. (1991). Children's understanding of biased social cognition. *Developmental Psychology, 27,* 539–551.

Pinker, S. (1981). On the acquisition of grammatical morphemes. *Journal of Child Language, 8,* 477–484.

Pinker, S. (1984). *Language learnability and language development.* Cambridge, MA: Harvard University Press.

Pinker, S., Lebeaux, D. S., & Frost, L. A. (1987). Productivity and constraints in the acquisition of the passive. *Cognition, 26,* 195–267.

Pipes, P. L. (1989). *Nutrition in infancy and childhood* (4th ed.). St. Louis: Mosby.

Pipp, S., & Haith, M. M. (1984). Infant visual responses to pattern: Which metric predicts best? *Journal of Experimental Child Psychology, 38,* 373–379.

Plomin, R. (1989). Environment and genes: Determinants of behavior. *American Psychologist, 44,* 105–111.

Plomin, R. (1990). *Nature and nurture: An introduction to behavior genetics.* Pacific Grove, CA: Brooks/Cole.

Plomin, R., Chipuer, H. M., & Loehlin, J. C. (1990). Behavior genetics and personality. In L. A. Pervin (Ed.), *Handbook of personality theory and research* (pp. 225–243). New York: Guilford.

Plomin, R., & DeFries, J. C. (1983). The Colorado Adoption Project. *Child Development, 54,* 276–289.

Plomin, R., DeFries, J. C., & McClearn, G. E. (1990). *Behavioral genetics: A primer* (2nd ed.). New York: Freeman.

Plomin, R., Loehlin, J. C., & DeFries, J. C. (1985). Genetic and environmental components of "environmental" influences. *Developmental Psychology, 21,* 391–402.

Podrouzek, W., & Furrow, D. (1988). Preschoolers' use of eye contact while speaking: The influence of sex, age, and conversational partner. *Journal of Psycholinguistic Research, 17,* 89–93.

Polansky, N. A., Gaudin, J. M., Ammons, P. W., & Davis, K. B. (1985). The psychological ecology of the neglectful mother. *Child Abuse & Neglect, 9,* 265–275.

Polit, D. F., Quint, J. C., & Riccio, J. A. (1988). *The challenge of service teenage mothers: Lessons from Project Redirection.* New York: Manpower Demonstration Research Corporation.

Pollock, L. (1987). *A lasting relationship: Parents and children over three centuries.* Hanover, NH: University Press of New England.

Pomerleau, A., Bolduc, D., Malcuit, G., & Cossette, L. (1990). Pink or blue: Environmental gender stereotypes in the first two years of life. *Sex Roles, 22,* 359–367.

Porter, F. L., Porges, S. W., & Marshall, R. E. (1988). Newborn pain cries and vagal tone: Parallel changes in response to circumcision. *Child Development, 59,* 495–505.

Porter, R. H., Makin, J. W., Davis, L. B., & Christensen, K. M. (1992). An assessment of the salient olfactory environment of formula-fed infants. *Physiology & Behavior, 50,* 907–911.

Poulin-Dubois, D., & Shultz, T. R. (1988). The development of the understanding of human behavior: From agency to intentionality. In J. W. Astington, P. L. Harris, & D. R. Olson (Eds.), *Developing theories of mind* (pp. 109–125). New York: Cambridge University Press.

Power, F. C., Higgins, A., & Kohlberg, L. (1989). *Lawrence Kohlberg's approach to moral education.* New York: Columbia University Press.

Powers, S. I., Hauser, S. T., & Kilner, L. A. (1989). Adolescent mental health. *American Psychologist, 44,* 200–208.

Pratt, M. W., Kerig, P., Cowan, P. A., & Cowan, C. P. (1988). Mothers and fathers teaching 3-year-olds: Authoritative parenting and adult scaffolding of young children's learning. *Developmental Psychology, 24,* 832–839.

Prechtl, H. F. R. (1958). Problems of behavioral studies in the newborn infant. In D. S. Lehrmann, R. A. Hinde, & E. Shaw (Eds.), *Advances in the study of behavior* (Vol. 1, pp. 75–98). New York: Academic Press.

Prechtl, H. F. R., & Beintema, D. (1965). *The neurological examination of the full-term newborn infant.* London: William Heinemann Medical Books.

Preisser, D. A., Hodson, B. W., & Paden, E. P. (1988). Developmental phonology: 18–29 months. *Journal of Speech and Hearing Disorders, 53,* 125–130.

Premack, A. J. (1976). *Why chimps can read.* New York: Harper & Row.

Pressley, M. (1982). Elaboration and memory development. *Child Development, 53,* 296–309.

Pressley, M. (1992). How not to study strategy discovery. *American Psychologist, 47,* 1240–1241.

Pressley, M., Cariglia-Bull, T., Deane, S., & Schneider, W. (1987). Short-term memory, verbal competence, and age as predictors of imagery instructional effectiveness. *Journal of Experimental Child Psychology, 43,* 194–211.

Pressley, M., & Ghatala, E. S. (1990). Self-regulated learning: Monitoring learning from text. *Educational Psychologist, 25,* 19–34.

Preston, R. C. (1962). Reading achievement of German and American children. *School and Society, 90,* 350–354.

Previc, F. H. (1991). A general theory concerning the prenatal origins of cerebral lateralization. *Psychological Review, 98,* 299–334.

Preyer, W. (1888). *The mind of the child* (2 vols.). New York: Appleton. (Original work published 1882)

Prior, M., Smart, D., Sanson, A., & Oberklaid, F. (1993). Sex differences in psychological adjustment from infancy to 8 years. *Journal of the American Academy of Child and Adolescent Psychiatry, 32,* 291–304.

Proffitt, D. R., & Bertenthal, B. I. (1990). Converging operations revisited: Assessing what infants perceive using discrimination measures. *Perception & Psychophysics, 47,* 1–11.

Pulkkinen, L. (1982). Self-control and continuity from childhood to late adolescence. In P. B. Baltes & O. G. Brim, Jr. (Eds.), *Life-span development and behavior* (Vol. 4, pp. 63–105). New York: Academic Press.

Putallaz, M., & Heflin, A. H. (1990). Parent–child interaction. In S. R. Asher & J. D. Coie (Eds.), *Peer rejection in childhood* (pp. 189–216). Cambridge: Cambridge University Press.

Q

Qazi, Q. H., Sheikh, T. M., Fikrig, S., & Menikoff, H. (1988). Lack of evidence for craniofacial dysmorphism in perinatal human immunodeficiency virus infection. *Journal of Pediatrics, 112,* 7–11.

Quadagno, D. M., Briscoe, R., & Quadagno, J. S. (1977). Effect of perinatal gonadal hormones on selected nonsexual behavior patterns: A critical assessment of the nonhuman and human literature. *Psychological Bulletin, 84,* 62–80.

Quarfoth, J. M. (1979). Children's understanding of the nature of television characters. *Journal of Communication, 29* (2), 210–218.

Quay, H. C. (1987). Institutional treatment. In H. C. Quay (Ed.), *Handbook of juvenile delinquency* (pp. 244–265). New York: Wiley.

Quay, L. C., & Jarrett, O. S. (1986). Teachers' interactions with middle- and lower-SES preschool boys and girls. *Journal of Educational Psychology, 78,* 495–498.

Quiggle, N. L., Garber, J., Panak, W. F., & Dodge, K. A. (1992). Social information processing in aggressive and depressed children. *Child Development, 63,* 1305–1320.R

R

Rabiner, D. L., & Coie, J. (1989). Effect of expectancy inductions on rejected children's acceptance by unfamiliar peers. *Developmental Psychology, 25,* 450–457.

Rabiner, D. L., Keane, S. P., & MacKinnon-Lewis, C. (1993). Children's beliefs about familiar and unfamiliar peers in relation to their sociometric status. *Developmental Psychology, 29,* 236–243.

Radford, A. (1988). Small children's small clauses. *Transactions of the Philological Society, 86,* 1–46.

Radke-Yarrow, M., Cummings, E. M., Kuczinski, L., & Chapman, M. (1985). Patterns of attachment in two and three-year-olds in normal families with parental depression. *Child Development, 56,* 884–893.

Radke-Yarrow, M., & Zahn-Waxler, C. (1984). Roots, motives and patterns in children's prosocial behavior. In J. Reykowski, J. Karylowski, D. Bar-Tel, & E. Staub (Eds.), *The development and maintenance of prosocial behaviors: International perspectives on positive mortality* (pp. 81–99). New York: Plenum.

Radziszewska, B., & Rogoff, B. (1988). Influence of adult and peer collaboration on the development of children's planning skills. *Developmental Psychology, 24,* 840–848.

Rafferty, Y., & Shinn, M. (1991). The impact of homelessness on children. *American Psychologist, 11,* 1170–1179.

Räikkönen, K., Keltikangas-Järvinen, L., & Pietikäinen, M. (1991). Type A behavior and its determinants in children, adolescents, and young adults with and without parental coronary heart disease: A case-control study. *Journal of Psychosomatic Research, 35,* 273–280.

Ramey, C. T., & Campbell, F. A. (1984). Preventive education for high-risk children: Cognitive consequences of the Carolina Abecedarian Project. *American Journal of Mental Deficiency, 88,* 515–523.

Ramey, C. T., & Ramey, S. L. (1990). Intensive educational intervention for children of poverty. *Intelligence, 14,* 1–9.

Ramos-Ford, V., & Gardner, H. (1990). Giftedness from a multiple intelligences perspective. In N. Colangelo & G. Davis (Eds.), *Handbook of gifted education* (pp. 55–64). Boston: Allyn and Bacon.

Ramphal, C. (1962). *A study of three current problems in education.* Unpublished doctoral dissertation, University of Natal, India.

Ramsay, D. S. (1985). Fluctuations in unimanual hand preference in infants following the onset of duplicated babbling. *Developmental Psychology, 21,* 318–324.

Ramsay, D. S., & McCune, L. (1984). *Fluctuations in bimanual handedness in the second year of life.* Unpublished manuscript, Rutgers University.

Ratner, N., & Bruner, J. S. (1978). Social exchange and the acquisition of language. *Journal of Child Language, 5,* 391–402.

Raymond, C. L., & Benbow, C. P. (1986). Gender differences in mathematics: A function of parental support and student sex typing? *Developmental Psychology, 22,* 808–819.

Rayner, K., & Pollatsek, A. (1989). *The psychology of reading.* Englewood Cliffs, NJ: Prentice-Hall.

Read, C. R. (1991). Achievement and career choices: Comparisons of males and females. *Roeper Review, 13,* 188–193.

Redd, W. H., Morris, E. K., & Martin, J. A. (1975). Effects of positive and negative adult-child interaction on children's social preferences. *Journal of Experimental Child Psychology, 19,* 153–164.

Reed, E. (1975). Genetic anomalies in development. In F. D. Horowitz (Ed.), *Review of child development research* (Vol. 4, pp. 59–99). Chicago: University of Chicago Press.

Reese, H. W. (1977). Imagery and associative memory. In R. V. Kail & J. W. Hagen (Eds.), *Perspectives on the development of memory and cognition* (pp. 113–116). Hillsdale, NJ: Erlbaum.

Reich, P. A. (1986). *Language development.* Englewood Cliffs, NJ: Prentice-Hall.

Reich, T., Van Eerdewegh, P., Riche, J., Jullaney, J., Endicott, J., & Klerman, G. L. (1987). The familial transmission of primary major depressive disorder. *Archives of General Psychology, 41,* 441–447.

Reid, B. V. (1990). Weighing up the factors: Moral reasoning and culture change in a Samoan community. *Ethos, 18,* 48–70.

Reid, J. B., Taplin, P. S., & Lorber, R. (1981). A social interactional approach to the treatment of abusive families. In R. B. Stuart (Ed.), *Violent behavior: Social learning approaches to prediction, management, and treatment* (pp. 83–101). New York: Brunner/Mazel.

Reinisch, J. M. (1981). Prenatal exposure to synthetic progestins increases potential for aggression in humans. *Science, 211,* 1171–1173.

Reis, S. M. (1989). Reflections on policy affecting the education of gifted and talented students: Past and future perspectives. *American Psychologist, 44,* 399–408.

Reis, S. M. (1991). The need for clarification in research designed to examine gender differences in achievement and accomplishment. *Roeper Review, 13,* 193–198.

Reiser, J., Yonas, A., & Wikner, K. (1976). Radial localization of odors by human neonates. *Child Development, 47,* 856–859.

Reisman, J. E. (1987). Touch, motion, and proprioception. In P. Salapatek & L. Cohen (Eds.), *Handbook of infant perception: Vol. 1. From sensation to perception* (pp. 265–303). Orlando, FL: Academic Press.

Reissland, N. (1988). Neonatal imitation in the first hour of life: Observations in rural Nepal. *Developmental Psychology, 24,* 464–469.

Reschly, D. J. (1981). Psychological testing in educational classification and placement. *American Psychologist, 36,* 1094–1102.

Rescorla, L. A. (1980). Category development in early language. *Journal of Child Language, 8,* 225–238.

Resnick, L. B. (1989). Developing mathematical knowledge. *American Psychologist, 44,* 162–169.

Resnick, S. M., Berenbaum, S. A., Gottesman, I. I., & Bouchard, T. J., Jr. (1986). Early hormonal influences on cognitive functioning in congenital adrenal hyperplasia. *Developmental Psychology, 22,* 191–198.

Rest, J. R. (1979a). *Development in judging moral issues.* Minneapolis: University of Minnesota Press.

Rest, J. R. (1979b). *Revised manual for the Defining Issues Test.* Minneapolis: Moral Research Projects.

Rest, J. R. (1983). Morality. In J. H. Flavell & E. M. Markman (Ed.), *Handbook of child psychology: Vol. 3. Cognitive development* (4th ed., pp. 556–629). New York: Wiley.

Rest, J. R. (1986). *Moral development: Advances in research and theory.* New York: Praeger.

Rest, J. R., & Narvaez, D. (1991). The college experience and moral development. In W. M. Kurtines & J. L. Gewirtz (Eds.), *Handbook of moral behavior and development* (Vol. 2, pp. 229–245). Hillsdale, NJ: Erlbaum.

Rest, J. R., & Thoma, S. J. (1985). Relation of moral judgment to formal education. *Developmental Psychology, 21,* 709–714.

Revelle, G. L., Karabenick, J. D., & Wellman, H. M. (1981). *Comprehension monitoring in preschool children.* Paper presented at the biennial meeting of the Society for Research in Child Development, Boston.

Reznick, J. S., Gibbons, J. L., Johnson, M. O., & McDonough, P. M. (1989). Behavioral inhibition in a normative sample. In J. S. Reznick (Ed.), *Perspectives on behavioral inhibition* (pp. 25–49). Chicago: University of Chicago Press.

Reznick, J. S., & Goldfield, B. A. (1992). Rapid change in lexical development in comprehension and production. *Developmental Psychology, 28,* 406–413.

Reznick, J. S., Kagan, J., Snidman, N., Gersten, M., Baak, K., & Rosenberg, A. (1986). Inhibited and uninhibited children: A follow-up study. *Child Development, 57,* 660–680.

Rheingold, H., Gewirtz, J., & Ross, H. (1959). Social conditioning of vocalizations in the infant. *Journal of Comparative and Physiological Psychology, 52,* 68–72.

Rhoads, G. G., Jackson, L. G., Schlesselman, S. E., de la Cruz, F. F., Desnick, R. J., Golbus, M. S., Ledbetter, D. H., Lubs, H. A., Mahoney, M. J., & Pergament, E. (1989). The safety and efficacy of chorionic villus sampling for early prenatal diagnosis of cytogenetic abnormalities. *New England Journal of Medicine, 320,* 609–617.

Ricciardelli, L. A. (1992). Bilingualism and cognitive development: Relation to threshold theory. *Journal of Psycholinguistic Research, 21,* 301–316.

Ricco, R. B. (1989). Operational thought and the acquisition of taxonomic relations involving figurative dissimilarity. *Developmental Psychology, 25,* 996–1003.

Rice, M. L. (1989). Children's language acquisition. *American Psychologist, 44,* 149–156.

Rice, M. L., Huston, A. C., Truglio, R., & Wright, J. (1990). Words from "Sesame Street": Learning vocabulary while viewing. *Developmental Psychology, 26,* 421–428.

Rice, M. L., Huston, A. C., & Wright, J. C. (1982). The forms of television: Effects on children's attention, comprehension, and social behavior. In D. Pearl, L. Bouthilet, & J. Lazar (Eds.), *Television and behavior: Ten years of scientific progress and implications for the eighties* (Vol. 2, pp. 24–38). Washington, DC: U.S. Government Printing Office.

Rice, M. L., Huston, A. C., & Wright, J. C. (1986). Replays as repetitions: Young children's interpretation of television forms. *Journal of Applied Developmental Psychology, 7,* 61–76.

Rice, M. L., & Woodsmall, L. (1988). Lessons from television: Children's word learning when viewing. *Child Development, 59,* 420–429.

Richards, D. D., & Siegler, R. S. (1986). Children's understandings of the attributes of life. *Journal of Experimental Child Psychology, 42,* 1–22.

Richardson, J. L., Dwyer, K., McGuigan, K., Hansen, W. B., Dent, C., Johnson, C. A., Sussman, S. Y., Brannon, B., & Flay, B. (1989). Substance use among eighth-grade students who take care of themselves after school. *Pediatrics, 84,* 556–566.

Richardson, S. A., Koller, H., & Katz, M. (1986). Factors leading to differences in the school performance of boys and girls. *Developmental and Behavioral Pediatrics, 7,* 49–55.

Richman, A. L., Miller, P. M., & LeVine, R. A. (1992). Cultural and educational variations in maternal responsiveness. *Developmental Psychology, 28,* 614–621.

Ridley, C. A., & Vaughn, R. (1982). Interpersonal problem solving: An intervention program for preschool children. *Journal of Applied Developmental Psychology, 3,* 177–190.

Riese, M. L. (1987). Temperament stability between the neonatal period and 24 months. *Developmental Psychology, 23,* 216–222.

Ritts, V., Patterson, M. L., & Tubbs, M. E. (1992). Expectations, impressions, and judgments of physically attractive students: A review. *Review of Educational Research, 62,* 413–426.

Robbins, L. C. (1963). The accuracy of parental recall of aspects of child development and of child rearing practices. *Journal of Abnormal and Social Psychology, 66,* 261–270.

Robert, M. (1989). Reduction of demand characteristics in the measurement of certainty during modeled conservation. *Journal of Experimental Child Psychology, 47,* 451–466.

Roberton, M. A. (1984). Changing motor patterns during childhood. In J. R. Thomas (Ed.), *Motor development during childhood and adolescence* (pp. 48–90). Minneapolis: Burgess Publishing.

Roberts, K. (1988). Retrieval of a basic-level category in prelinguistic infants. *Developmental Psychology, 24,* 21–27.

Robinson, B. E. (1988). *Teenage fathers.* Lexington, MA: Lexington Books.

Robinson, B. E., & Canaday, H. (1978). Sex-role behaviors and personality traits of male day care teachers. *Sex Roles, 4,* 853–865.

Robinson, C. C., & Morris, J. T. (1986). The gender-stereotyped nature of Christmas toys received by 36-, 48-, and 60-month-old children: A comparison between nonrequested vs. requested toys. *Sex Roles, 15,* 21–32.

Robinson, J. L., Kagan, J., Reznick, J. S., & Corley, R. (1992). The heritability of inhibited and uninhibited behavior: A twin study. *Developmental Psychology, 28,* 1030–1037.

Robinson, J. P. (1988). Who's doing the housework? *American Demographics, 10,* 24–63.

Rochat, P. (1989). Object manipulation and exploration in 2- to 5-month-old infants. *Developmental Psychology, 25,* 871–884.

Roche, A. F. (1979). Secular trends in stature, weight, and maturation. In A. F. Roche (Ed.), *Secular trends in human growth, maturation, and development. Monographs of the Society for Research in Child Development, 44* (3–4, Serial No. 179).

Roche, A. F. (1981). The adipocyte-number hypothesis. *Child Development, 52,* 31–43.

Rodriguez, M. L., Mischel, W., & Shoda, Y. (1989). Cognitive and personality variables in the delay of gratification of older children at risk. *Journal of Personality and Social Psychology, 57,* 358–367.

Roffwarg, H. P., Muzio, J. N., & Dement, W. C. (1966). Ontogenetic development of the human sleep-dream cycle. *Science, 152,* 604–619.

Rogoff, B. (1990). *Apprenticeship in thinking.* New York: Oxford University Press.

Rogoff, B., & Mistry, J. (1985). Memory development in cultural context. In M. Pressley & C. Brainerd (Eds.), *Cognitive learning and memory in children* (pp. 117–142). New York: Springer-Verlag.

Rogoff, B., & Morelli, G. (1989). Culture and American children: Section introduction. *American Psychologist, 44,* 341–342.

Rogoff, B., & Waddell, K. J. (1982). Memory for information organized in a scene by children from two cultures. *Child Development, 53,* 1224–1228.

Rohlen, T. P. (1983). Japan's high schools. Berkeley, CA: University of California Press.

Rohner, R. P. & Rohner, E. C. (1981). Parental acceptance-rejection and parental control: Cross-cultural codes. *Ethnology, 20,* 245–260.

Roopnarine, J. L., Talukder, E., Jain, D., Joshi, P., & Srivastave, P. (1990). Characteristics of holding, patterns of play, and social behaviors between parents and infants in New Delhi, India. *Developmental Psychology, 26,* 667–673.

Roosa, M. W. (1984). Maternal age, social class, and the obstetric performance of teenagers. *Journal of Youth and Adolescence, 13,* 365–374.

Rose, R. M., Holaday, J. W., & Bernstein, I. S. (1976). Plasma testosterone, dominance rank and aggressive behavior in male rhesus monkeys. *Nature, 231,* 366–368.

Rose, S. A. (1988). Shape recognition in infancy: Visual integration of sequential information. *Child Development, 59,* 1161–1176.

Rose, S. A., Feldman, J. F., & Wallace, I. F. (1988). Individual differences in infant information processing: Reliability, stability, and prediction. *Child Development, 59,* 1177–1197.

Rose, S. A., Feldman, J. F., & Wallace, I. F. (1992). Infant information processing in relation to six-year cognitive outcome. *Child Development, 63,* 1126–1141.

Rosen, A. B., & Rozin, P. (1993). Now you see it, now you don't: The preschool child's conception of invisible particles in the context of dissolving. *Developmental Psychology, 29,* 300–311.

Rosen, A. C., & Rekers, G. A. (1980). Toward a taxonomic framework for variables of sex and gender. *Genetic Psychology Monographs, 102,* 191–218.

Rosen, K. S., & Rothbaum, F. (1993). Quality of parental caregiving and security of attachment. *Developmental Psychology, 29,* 358–367.

Rosen, W. D., Adamson, L. B., & Bakeman, R. (1992). An experimental investigation of infant social referencing: Mothers' messages and gender differences. *Developmental Psychology, 28,* 1172–1178.

Rosenberg, M. (1979). *Conceiving the self.* New York: Basic Books.

Rosenberg, M. S., & Reppucci, N. D. (1985). Primary prevention of child abuse. *Journal of Consulting and Clinical Psychology, 53,* 576–585.

Rosenberg, R. N., & Pettegrew, J. W. (1983). Genetic neurologic diseases. In R. N. Rosenberg (Ed.), *The clinical neurosciences* (pp. 33–165). New York: Churchill Livingstone.

Rosenfield, P., Lambert, N. M., & Black, A. (1985). Desk arrangement effects on pupil classroom behavior. *Journal of Educational Psychology, 77,* 101–108.

Rosenkrantz, P., Vogel, S., Bee, H., Broverman, I., & Broverman, D. (1968). Sex-role stereotypes and self-concepts in college students. *Journal of Consulting and Clinical Psychology, 32,* 287–295.

Rosenstein, D., & Oster, H. (1988). Differential facial responses to four basic tastes in newborns. *Child Development, 59,* 1555–1568.

Rosenthal, D. A. (1987). Ethnic identity development in adolescents. In J. S. Phinney & M. J. Rotheram (Eds.), *Children's ethnic socialization* (pp. 156–179). Newbury Park, CA: Sage.

Rosenthal, R., & Jacobson, L. (1968). *Pygmalion in the classroom: Teacher expectation and pupils' intellectual development.* New York: Holt, Rinehart and Winston.

Ross, G. S. (1980). Categorization in 1- to 2-year-olds. *Developmental Psychology, 16,* 391–396.

Ross, H. S., & Goldman, B. D. (1977). Infants' sociability toward strangers. *Child Development, 48,* 638–642.

Ross, R. P., Campbell, T., Huston-Stein, A., & Wright, J. C. (1984). Nutritional misinformation of children: A developmental and experimental analysis of the effects of televised food commercials. *Journal of Applied Developmental Psychology, 1,* 329–347.

Rotenberg, K. J., Simourd, L., & Moore, D. (1989). Children's use of a verbal-nonverbal consistency principle to infer truth and lying. *Child Development, 60,* 309–322.

Rothbart, M. K. (1981). Measurement of temperament in infancy. *Child Development, 52,* 569–578.

Rothbart, M. K., & Rothbart, M. (1976). Birth-order, sex of child and maternal help giving. *Sex Roles, 2,* 39–46.

Rotheram-Borus, M. J. (1989). Ethnic differences in adolescents' identity status and associated behavior problems. *Journal of Adolescence, 12,* 361–374.

Rotheram-Borus, M. J. (in press). Bicultural reference group orientation and adjustment. In M. Bernal & G. Knight (Eds.), *Ethnic identity.* Albany: State University of New York Press.

Rourke, B. P. (1988). Socioemotional disturbances of learning disabled children. *Journal of Consulting and Clinical Psychology, 56,* 801–810.

Rousseau, J. J. (1955). *Emile.* New York: Dutton. (Original work published 1762)

Rovee-Collier, C. K. (1987). Learning and memory. In J. D. Osofsky (Ed.), *Handbook of infant development* (2nd ed., pp. 98–148). New York: Wiley.

Rovee-Collier, C. K., & Hayne, H. (1987). Reactivation of infant memory: Implications for cognitive development. In H. W. Reese (Ed.), *Advances in child development and behavior* (Vol. 20, pp. 185–238). New York: Academic Press.

Rovee-Collier, C. K., Patterson, J., & Hayne, H. (1985). Specificity in the reactivation of infant memory. *Developmental Psychobiology, 18,* 559–574.

Rovee-Collier, C. K., & Shyi, G. (1992). A functional and cognitive analysis of infant long-term retention. In C. J. Brainerd, M. L. Howe, & V. Reyna (Eds.), *Development of long-term retention* (pp. 3–55). New York: Springer-Verlag.

Royce, J. M., Darlington, R. B., & Murray, H. W. (1983). Pooled analyses: Findings across studies. In Consortium for Longitudinal Studies (Ed.), *As the twig is bent: Lasting effects of preschool programs* (pp. 411–459). Hillsdale, NJ: Erlbaum.

Rozin, P. (1990). Development in the food domain. *Developmental Psychology, 26,* 555–562.

Rubin, J. Z., Provenzano, F. J., & Luria, Z. (1974). The eye of the beholder: Parents' views on sex of newborns. *American Journal of Orthopsychiatry, 44,* 512–519.

Rubin, K. H. (1972). Relationship between egocentric communication and popularity among peers. *Developmental Psychology, 7,* 364.

Rubin, K. H. (1982). Nonsocial play in preschoolers: Necessarily evil? *Child Development, 53,* 651–657.

Rubin, K. H., & Daniels-Bierness, T. (1983). Concurrent and predictive correlates of sociometric status in kindergarten and grade one children. *Merrill-Palmer Quarterly, 29,* 279–282.

Rubin, K. H., Fein, G. G., & Vandenberg, B. (1983). Play. In E. M. Hetherington (Ed.), *Handbook of child psychology: Vol. 4. Socialization, personality, and social development* (4th ed., pp. 693–744). New York: Wiley.

Rubin, K. H., & Krasnor, L. R. (1985). Social-cognitive and social behavioral perspectives on problem solving. In M. Perlmutter (Ed.), *Minnesota Symposia on Child Psychology* (Vol. 18, pp. 1–68). Hillsdale, NJ: Erlbaum.

Rubin, K. H., LeMare, L., & Lollis, S. (1990). Social withdrawal in childhood: Developmental pathways to peer rejection. In S. R. Asher & J. D. Coie (Eds.), *Peer rejection in childhood* (pp. 217–252). New York: Cambridge University Press.

Rubin, K. H., & Maioni, T. (1975). Play preference and its relationship to egocentrism, popularity, and classification skills in preschoolers. *Merrill-Palmer Quarterly, 21,* 171–180.

Rubin, K. H., Maioni, T. L., & Hornung, M. (1976). Free play behaviors in middle- and lower-class preschoolers: Parten and Piaget revisited. *Child Development, 47,* 414–419.

Rubin, K. H., Watson, K. S., & Jambor, T. W. (1978). Free-play behaviors in preschool and kindergarten children. *Child Development, 49,* 534–536.

Ruble, D. N. (1987). The acquisition of self-knowledge: A self-socialization perspective. In N. Eisenberg (Ed.), *Contemporary topics in developmental psychology* (pp. 243–270). New York: Wiley.

Ruble, D. N. (1988). Sex-role development. In M. H. Bornstein & M. E. Lamb (Eds.), *Developmental psychology: An advanced textbook* (2nd ed., pp. 411–460). Hillsdale, NJ: Erlbaum.

Ruble, D. N., Boggiano, A. K., Feldman, N. S., & Loebl, J. H. (1980). Developmental analysis of the role of social comparison in self-evaluation. *Developmental Psychology, 16,* 105–115.

Ruble, D. N., & Frey, K. S. (1991). Changing patterns of comparative behavior as skills are acquired: A functional model of self-evaluation. In J. Suls & T. Wills (Eds.), *Social comparison: Contemporary theory and research* (pp. 79–116). Hillsdale, NJ: Erlbaum.

Ruble, D. N., & Ruble, T. L. (1982). Sex stereotypes. In A. G. Miller (Ed.), *In the eye of the beholder* (pp. 188–252). New York: Praeger.

Ruble, T. L. (1983). Sex stereotypes: Issues of change in the 1970s. *Sex Roles, 9,* 397–402.

Rudel, R. G., & Teuber, H. L. (1963). Discrimination of direction of line in children. *Journal of Comparative and Physiological Psychology, 56,* 892–898.

Rudy, L., & Goodman, G. S. (1991). Effects of participation on children's reports: Implications for children's testimony. *Developmental Psychology, 27,* 527–538.

Ruff, H. A., Bijur, P. E., Markowitz, M., Ma, Y-C., & Rosen, J. F. (1993). Declining blood lead levels and cognitive changes in moderately lead-poisoned children. *Journal of the American Medical Association, 269,* 1641–1646.

Ruff, H. A., & Lawson, K. R. (1990). Development of sustained, focused attention in young children during free play. *Developmental Psychology, 26,* 85–93.

Ruff, H. A., Lawson, K. R., Parrinello, R., & Weissberg, R. (1990). Long-term stability of individual differences in sustained attention in the early years. *Child Development, 61,* 60–75.

Ruff, H. A., Saltarelli, L. M., Capozzoli, M., & Dubiner, K. (1992). The differentiation of activity in infants' exploration of objects. *Developmental Psychology, 28,* 851–861.

Rugh, R., & Shettles, L. B. (1971). *From conception to birth: The drama of life's beginnings.* New York: Harper & Row.

Ruiz, R. (1988). Bilingualism and bilingual education in the United States. In C. B. Paulston (Ed.), *International handbook of bilingualism and bilingual education* (pp. 539–560). New York: Greenwood Press.

Rumbaugh, D. M. (1977). *Language learning by a chimpanzee: The Lana project.* New York: Academic Press.

Runco, M. A. (1990). The divergent thinking of young children: Implications of the research. *Gifted Child Today, 13*(4), 37–39.

Ruopp, R., Travers, J., Glantz, F., & Coelen, C. (1979). *Children at the center: Final report of the national day care study.* Cambridge, MA: Abt Books.

Russell, A., & Finnie, V. (1990). Preschool children's social status and maternal instructions to assist group entry. *Developmental Psychology, 26,* 603–611.

Russell, J. A. (1990). The preschooler's understanding of the causes and consequences of emotion. *Child Development, 61,* 1872–1881.

Rutter, M. (1987). Psychosocial resilience and protective mechanisms. *American Journal of Orthopsychiatry, 57,* 316–331.

Rutter, M., Graham, P., Chadwick, O. F. D., & Yule, W. (1976). Adolescent turmoil: Fact or fiction. *Journal of Child Psychology and Psychiatry, 17,* 35–56.

Rutter, M., & Madge, N. (1976). *Cycles of disadvantage.* London: Heinemann.

Ryan, K. J. (1989). Ethical issues in reproductive endocrinology and infertility. *American Journal of Obstetrics and Gynecology, 160,* 1415–1417.

S

Saarni, C. (1979). Children's understanding of display rules for expressive behavior. *Developmental Psychology, 15,* 424–429.

Saarni, C. (1989). Children's understanding of strategic control of emotional expression in social transactions. In C. Saarni & P. L. Harris (Eds.), *Children's understanding of emotion* (pp. 181–208). New York: Cambridge University Press.

Sadler, T. W. (1990). *Langman's medical embryology* (6th ed.). Baltimore: Williams & Wilkins.

Saigal, S., Rosenbaum, P., Szatmari, P., & Campbell, D. (1991). General health, cognitive abilities, and school performance of extremely low birthweight children and matched term controls at 8 years: A regional study. *Journal of Pediatrics, 118,* 751–760.

Salapatek, P. (1975). Pattern perception in early infancy. In L. B. Cohen & P. Salapatek (Eds.), *Infant perception: From sensation to cognition* (pp. 133–248). New York: Academic Press.

Salapatek, P., & Cohen, L. (Eds.). (1987). *Handbook of infant perception: Vol 2. From perception to cognition.* Orlando, FL: Academic Press.

Salomon, G. (1979). *Interaction of media, cognition, and learning.* San Francisco: Jossey-Bass.

Salomon, J. B., Mata, L. J., & Gordon, J. E. (1968). Malnutrition and the common communicable diseases of childhood in rural Guatemala. *American Journal of Health, 58,* 505–516.

Saltzstein, H. D. (1976). Social influence and moral development: A perspective on the role of parents and peers. In T. Lickona (Ed.), *Moral development and behavior: Theory, research and social issues* (pp. 253–265). New York: Holt, Rinehart and Winston.

Salzinger, S., Feldman, R. S., Hammer, M., & Rosario, M. (1993). The effects of physical abuse on children's social relationships. *Child Development, 64,* 169–187.

Samenow, S. E. (1984). *Inside the criminal mind.* New York: Random House.

Sameroff, A. J. (1968). The components of sucking in the human newborn. *Journal of Experimental Child Psychology, 6,* 607–623.

Sameroff, A. J., Seifer, R., Baldwin, A., & Baldwin, C. (1993). Stability of intelligence from preschool to adolescence: The influence of social and family risk factors. *Child Development, 64,* 80–97.

Samson, L. F. (1988). Perinatal viral infections and neonates. *Journal of Perinatal Neonatal Nursing, 1,* 56–65.

Samuels, S. J. (1985). Toward a theory of automatic information processing in reading: Updated. In H. Singer & R. B. Ruddell (Eds.), *Theoretical models and processes of reading* (3rd ed., pp. 719–721). Newark, DE: International Reading Association.

Sandberg, D. E., Ehrhardt, A. A., Ince, S. E., & Meyer-Bahlberg, H. F. L. (1991). Gender differences in children's and adolescent's career aspirations. *Journal of Adolescent Research, 6,* 371–386.

Sandqvist, K. (1992). Sweden's sex-role scheme and commitment to gender equality. In S. Lewis, D. N. Izraeli, & H. Hottsmans (Eds.), *Dual-earner families: International perspectives.* London: Sage.

Santelli, J. S., & Beilenson, P. (1992). Risk factors for adolescent sexual behavior, fertility, and sexually transmitted diseases. *Journal of School Health, 62,* 271–279.

Santrock, J. W., & Warshak, R. A. (1979). Father custody and social development in boys and girls. *Journal of Social Issues, 35,* 112–125.

Santrock, J. W., & Warshak, R. A. (1986). Development of father custody relationships and legal/clinical considerations in father-custody families. In M. E. Lamb (Ed.), *The father's role: Applied perspectives* (pp. 135–166). New York: Wiley.

Sarason, I. G. (1980). *Test anxiety: Theory, research, and applications.* Hillsdale, NJ: Erlbaum.

Sattler, J. M. (1988). *Assessment of children's intelligence and special abilities* (3rd ed.). San Diego: Author.

Satz, P., & Bullard-Bates, C. (1981). Acquired aphasia in children. In M. T. Sarno (Ed.), *Acquired aphasia* (pp. 399–426). New York: Academic Press.

Saudino, K., & Eaton, W. O. (1991). Infant temperament and genetics: An objective twin study. *Child Development, 62,* 1167–1174.

Savage-Rumbaugh, E. S., Murphy, J., Sevcik, R. A., Brakke, K. E., Williams, S. L., & Rumbaugh, D. M. (1993). Language comprehension in ape and child. *Monographs of the Society for Research in Child Development, 58,* (3–4, Serial No. 233).

Savage-Rumbaugh, E. S., Sevcik, R. A., Brakke, K. E., Rumbaugh, D. M., & Greenfield, P. (1990). Symbols: Their communicative use, comprehension, and combination by bonobos *(Pan paniscus).* In C. Rovee-Collier & L. P. Lipsitt (Eds.), *Advances in infancy research* (Vol. 6, pp. 221–271). Norwood, NJ: Ablex.

Savin-Williams, R. C. (1979). Dominance hierarchies in groups of early adolescents. *Child Development, 50,* 923–935.

Savin-Williams, R. C. (1980). Dominance hierarchies in groups of middle to late adolescent males. *Journal of Youth and Adolescence, 9,* 75–85.

Savin-Williams, R. C. (1990). *Gay and lesbian youth: Expresssions of identity.* New York: Hemisphere.

Savin-Williams, R. C., & Berndt, T. J. (1990). Friendship and peer relations. In S. S. Feldman & G. R. Elliott (Eds.), *At the threshold: The developing adolescent* (pp. 277–307). Cambridge, MA: Harvard University Press.

Saxe, G. B. (1988, August–September). Candy selling and math learning. *Educational Researcher, 17*(6), 14–21.

Saxe, G. B., Guberman, S. R., & Gearhart, M. (1987). Social processes in early number development. *Monographs of the Society for Research in Child Development, 52* (2, Serial No. 216).

Saxe, L., Cross, T., & Silverman, N. (1988). Children's mental health: The gap between what we know and what we do. *American Psychologist, 43,* 800–807.

Saywitz, K. J. (1987). Children's testimony: Age-related patterns of memory errors. In S. J. Ceci, M. P. Toglia, & D. F. Ross (Eds.), *Children's eyewitness memory* (pp. 36–52). New York: Springer-Verlag.

Saywitz, K. J., Goodman, G. S., Nicholas, E., & Moan, S. F. (1991). Children's memories of a physical examination involving genital touch: Implications for reports of child sexual abuse. *Journal of Consulting and Clinical Psychology, 59,* 682–691.

Scarr, S. (1985). Constructing psychology: Making facts and fables for our times. *American Psychologist, 40,* 499–512.

Scarr, S. (1988). How genotypes and environments combine: Development and individual differences. In N. Bolger, A. Caspi, G. Downey, & M. Moorehouse (Eds.), *Persons in context: Developmental processes* (pp. 217–244). Cambridge: Cambridge University Press.

Scarr, S., & Kidd, K. K. (1983). Developmental behavior genetics. In M. M. Haith & J. J. Campos (Eds.), *Handbook of child psychology: Vol. 2. Infancy and developmental psychobiology* (pp. 345–433). New York: Wiley.

Scarr, S., & McCartney, K. (1983). How people make their own environments: A theory of genotype → environment effects. *Child Development, 54,* 424–435.

Scarr, S., Phillips, D. A., & McCartney, K. (1990). Facts, fantasies, and the future of child care in America. *Psychological Science, 1,* 26–35.

Scarr, S., Phillips, D., McCartney, K., & Abbott-Shim, M. (1993). Quality of child care as an aspect of family and child care policy in the United States. *Pediatrics, 91,* 182–188.

Scarr, S., & Weinberg, R. A. (1976). IQ test performance of black children adopted by white families. *American Psychologist, 31,* 726–739.

Scarr, S., & Weinberg, R. A. (1978). The influence of "family background" on intellectual attainment. *American Sociological Review, 43,* 674–692.

Scarr, S., & Weinberg, R. A. (1983). The Minnesota Adoption Studies: Genetic differences and malleability. *Child Development, 54,* 260–267.

Schachter, F. F., & Stone, R. K. (1985). Difficult sibling, easy sibling: Temperament and the within-family environment. *Child Development, 56,* 1335–1344.

Schaefer, M., Hatcher, R. P., & Bargelow, P. D. (1980). Prematurity and infant stimulation. *Child Psychiatry and Human Development, 10,* 199–212.

Schaffer, H. R. (1979). Acquiring the concept of the dialogue. In M. H. Bornstein & W. Kessen (Eds.), *Psychological development from infancy: Image to intention* (pp. 279–305). Hillsdale, NJ: Erlbaum.

Schaffer, H. R., & Emerson, P. E. (1964). The development of social attachments in infancy. *Monographs of the Society for Research in Child Development, 29* (3, Serial No. 94).

Schaie, K. W., & Hertzog, C. (1982). Longitudinal methods. In B. B. Wolman (Ed.), *Handbook of developmental psychology* (pp. 91–115). Englewood Cliffs, NJ: Prentice-Hall.

Schaivi, R. C., Theilgaard, A., Owen, D., & White, D. (1984). Sex chromosome anomalies, hormones, and aggressivity. *Archives of General Psychiatry, 41,* 93–99.

Schaivo, R. S., & Solomon, S. K. (1981). *The effect of summer contact on preschoolers' friendships with classmates.* Paper presented at the annual meeting of the Eastern Psychological Association, New York.

Schanberg, S., & Field, T. M. (1987). Sensory deprivation stress and supplemental stimulation in the rat pup and preterm human neonate. *Child Development, 58,* 1431–1447.

Schauble, L. (1990). Belief revision in children: The role of prior knowledge and strategies for generating evidence. *Journal of Experimental Child Psychology, 49,* 31–57.

Schieffelin, B. B., & Ochs, E. (1987). *Language socialization across cultures.* New York: Cambridge University Press.

Schlegel, A., & Barry, H., III. (1991). *Adolescence: An anthropological inquiry.* New York: Free Press.

Schneider, W., & Bjorklund, D. F. (1992). Expertise, aptitude, and strategic remembering. *Child Development, 63,* 461–473.

Schneider, W., & Pressley, M. (1989). *Memory development between 2 and 20.* New York: Springer-Verlag.

Schnur, E., Brooks-Gunn, J., & Shipman, V. C. (1992). Who attends programs serving poor children? The case of Head Start attendees and nonattendees. *Journal of Applied Developmental Psychology, 13,* 405–421.

Schrag, S. G., & Dixon, R. L. (1985). Occupational exposures associated with male reproductive dysfunction. *Annual Review of Pharmacology and Toxicology, 25,* 567–592.

Schramm, W., Barnes, D., & Bakewell, J. (1987). Neonatal mortality in Missouri home births. *American Journal of Public Health, 77,* 930–935.

Schunk, D. H. (1983). Ability versus effort attributional feedback: Differential effects on self-efficacy and achievement. *Journal of Educational Psychology, 75,* 848–856.

Schwartz-Bickenbach, D., Schulte-Hobein, B., Abt, S., Plum, C., & Nau, H. (1987). Smoking and passive smoking during pregnancy and early infancy: Effects on birth weight, lactation period, and cotinine concentrations in mother's milk and infant's urine. *Toxicology Letters, 35,* 73–81.

Schweinhart, L. J., & Weikart, D. P. (1986, January). What do we know so far? A review of the Head Start Synthesis Project. *Young Children, 41*(2), 49–55.

Scribner, S. (1977). Modes of thinking and ways of speaking: Culture and logic reconsidered. In P. N. Johnson-Laird & P. C.

Wason (Eds.), *Thinking: Readings in cognitive science* (pp. 483–500). London: Cambridge University Press.

Sears, R. R. (1975). *Your ancients revisited: A history of child development.* Chicago: University of Chicago Press.

Sears, R. R., Maccoby, E. E., & Levin, H. (1957). *Patterns of child rearing.* New York: Harper & Row.

Seay, B., Alexander, B. K., & Harlow, H. F. (1964). Maternal behavior of socially deprived rhesus monkeys. *Journal of Abnormal and Social Psychology, 69,* 345–354.

Sebald, H. (1986). Adolescents' shifting orientation toward parents and peers: A curvilinear trend over recent decades. *Journal of Marriage and the Family, 48,* 5–13.

Seligman, M. E. P. (1975). *Helplessness: On depression, development, and death.* San Francisco: Freeman.

Seligmann, J. (1991, December 9). Condoms in the classroom. *Newsweek,* p. 61.

Selkow, P. (1984). Effects of maternal employment on kindergarten and first-grade children's vocational aspirations. *Sex Roles, 11,* 677–690.

Selman, R. L. (1976). Social-cognitive understanding: A guide to educational and clinical practice. In T. Lickona (Ed.), *Moral development and behavior: Theory, research, and social issues* (pp. 299–316). New York: Holt, Rinehart and Winston.

Selman, R. L. (1980). *The growth of interpersonal understanding.* New York: Academic Press.

Selman, R. L. (1981). The child as a friendship philosopher. In S. R. Asher & J. M. Gottman (Eds.), *The development of friendships* (pp. 242–272). New York: Cambridge University Press.

Selman, R. L., & Byrne, D. F. (1974). A structural-developmental analysis of levels of role taking in middle childhood. *Child Development, 45,* 803–806.

Selman, R. L., & Demorest, A. P. (1984). Observing troubled children's interpersonal negotiation strategies: Implications of and for a developmental model. *Child Development, 55,* 288–304.

Seltzer, V., & Benjamin, F. (1990). Breast-feeding and the potential for human immunodeficiency virus transmission. *Obstetrics and Gynecology, 75,* 713–715.

Serbin, L. A., Connor, J. M., & Citron, C. C. (1978). Environmental control of independent and dependent behaviors in preschool girls and boys: A model for early independence training. *Sex Roles, 4,* 867–875.

Serbin, L. A., Connor, J. M., & Iler, I. (1979). Sex-stereotyped and nonstereotyped introductions of new toys in the preschool classroom: An observational study of teacher behavior and its effects. *Psychology of Women Quarterly, 4,* 261–265.

Serbin, L. A., O'Leary, K. D., Kent, R. N., & Tonick, I. J. (1973). A comparison of teacher response to the preacademic and problem behavior of boys and girls. *Child Development, 44,* 796–804.

Serbin, L. A., Powlishta, K. K., & Gulko, J. (1993). The development of sex typing in middle childhood. *Monographs of the Society for Research in Child Development, 58* (2, Serial No. 232).

Serbin, L. A., & Sprafkin, C. (1986). The salience of gender and the process of sex-typing in three- to seven-year-old children. *Child Development, 57,* 1188–1199.

Serbin, L. A., Tonick, I. J., & Sternglanz, S. H. (1977). Shaping cooperative cross-sex play. *Child Development, 48,* 924–929.

Sever, J. L. (1983). Maternal infections. In C. C. Brown (Ed.), *Childhood learning disabilities and prenatal risk* (pp. 31–38). New York: Johnson & Johnson.

Shaffer, D. (1985). Depression, mania, and suicidal acts. In M. Rutter & L. Hersov (Eds.), *Child and adolescent psychiatry: Modern approaches* (pp. 698–719). New York: Guilford.

Shaffer, D., Garland, A., Gould, M., Fisher, P., & Trautman, P. (1988). Preventing teenage suicide: A critical review. *Journal of the American Academy of Child and Adolescent Psychiatry, 27,* 675–687.

Shahar, S. (1990). *Childhood in the Middle Ages.* London: Routledge & Kegan Paul.

Shainess, N. (1961). A re-evaluation of some aspects of femininity through a study of menstruation: A preliminary report. *Comparative Psychiatry, 2,* 20–26.

Shannon, D. C., Kelly, D. H., Akselrod, S., & Kilborn, K. M. (1987). Increased respiratory frequency and variability in high risk babies who die of sudden infant death syndrome. *Pediatric Research, 22,* 158–162.

Shaughnessy, M. F. (1990). Cognitive structures of the gifted: Theoretical perspectives, factor analysis, triarchic theories of intelligence, and insight issues. *Gifted Education International, 6,* 149–151.

Shavelson, R., Hubner, J. J., & Stanton, J. C. (1976). Self-concept: Validation of construct interpretations. *Review of Educational Research, 46,* 407–441.

Shedler, J., & Block, J. (1990). Adolescent drug use and psychological health: A longitudinal inquiry. *American Psychologist, 45,* 612–630.

Sherif, M., Harvey, O. J., White, B. J., Hood, W. R., & Sherif, C. W. (1961). *The Robbers Cave experiment: Intergroup conflict and cooperation.* Norman, OK: University of Oklahoma Press.

Sherman, M., & Key, C. B. (1932). The intelligence of isolated mountain children. *Child Development, 3,* 279–290.

Sherman, T. (1985). Categorization skills in infants. *Child Development, 56,* 1561–1573.

Shettles, L. B., & Rorvik, D. M. (1984). *How to choose the sex of your baby.* New York: Doubleday.

Shields, J. W. (1972). The trophic function of lymphoid elements. Springfield, IL: Charles C. Thomas.

Shields, P. J., & Rovee-Collier, C. K. (1992). Long-term memory for context-specific category information at six months. *Child Development, 63,* 245–259.

Shiffrin, R. M., & Atkinson, R. C. (1969). Storage and retrieval processes in long-term memory. *Psychological Review, 76,* 179–193.

Shiller, V., Izard, C. E., & Hembree, E. A. (1986). Patterns of emotion expression during separation in the Strange Situation. *Developmental Psychology, 22,* 378–382.

Shinn, M. W. (1900). *The biography of a baby.* Boston: Houghton Mifflin.

Shipman, G. (1971). The psychodynamics of sex education. In R. Muuss (Ed.), *Adolescent behavior and society* (pp. 326–339). New York: Random House.

Shoda, Y., Mischel, W., & Peake, P. K. (1990). Predicting adolescent cognitive and self-regulatory competencies from preschool delay of gratification: Identifying diagnostic conditions. *Developmental Psychology, 26,* 978–986.

Shucard, J., Shucard, D., Cummins, K., & Campos, J. (1981). Auditory evoked potentials and sex-related differences in brain development. *Brain and Language, 13,* 91–102.

Shultz, T. R. (1980). Development of the concept of intention. In W. A. Collins (Ed.), *Minnesota Symposia on Child Psychology* (Vol. 13, pp. 131–164). Hillsdale, NJ: Erlbaum.

Shweder, R. A., Mahapatra, M., & Miller, J. G. (1990). Culture and moral development. In J. Stigler, R. A. Shweder, & G. Herdt (Eds.), *Cultural psychology: Essays on comparative human development* (pp. 130–204). New York: Cambridge University Press.

Siegal, M., & Beattie, K. (1992). Where to look first for children's knowledge of false beliefs. *Cognition, 38,* 1–12.

Siegal, M., & Robinson, J. (1987). Order effects in children's gender-constancy responses. *Developmental Psychology, 23,* 283–286.

Siegel, A. W. (1981). The externalization of cognitive maps by children and adults: In search of ways to ask better questions. In L. S. Liben, A. H. Patterson, & N. Newcombe (Eds.), *Spatial representation and behavior across the life span* (pp. 167–194). New York: Academic Press.

Siegel, I. E. (1987). Does hothousing rob children of their childhood? *Early Childhood Research Quarterly, 2,* 211–225.

Siegler, R. S. (1981). Developmental sequences within and between concepts. *Monographs for the Society for Research in Child Development, 46* (2, Serial No. 189).

Siegler, R. S. (1983). Information processing approaches to development. In W. Kessen (Ed.), *Handbook of child psychology: Vol. 1. History, theory, and methods* (pp. 129–212). New York: Wiley.

Siegler, R. S. (1986). Unities in strategy choices across domains. In M. Perlmutter (Ed.), *Minnesota Symposia on Child Psychology* (Vol. 19, pp. 1–48). Hillsdale, NJ: Erlbaum.

Siegler, R. S. (1988). Individual differences in strategy choices: Good students, not-so-good students, and perfectionists. *Child Development, 59,* 833–851.

Siegler, R. S. (1989). How domain-general and domain-specific knowledge interact to product strategy choices. *Merrill-Palmer Quarterly, 35,* 1–26.

Siegler, R. S. (1991). *Children's thinking* (2nd ed.). Englewood Cliffs, NJ: Prentice-Hall.

Siegler, R. S. (1992). The other Alfred Binet. *Developmental Psychology, 28,* 179–190.

Siegler, R. S., & Crowley, K. (1991). The microgenetic method: A direct means for studying cognitive development. *American Psychologist, 46,* 606–620.

Siegler, R. S., & Crowley, K. (1992). Microgenetic methods revisited. *American Psychologist, 47,* 1241–1243.

Siegler, R. S., & Jenkins, E. (1989). *How children discover new strategies.* Hillsdale, NJ: Erlbaum.

Siegler, R. S., & Richards, D. D. (1980). *College students' prototypes of children's intelligence.* Paper presented at the annual meeting of the American Psychological Association, New York.

Siegler, R. S., & Richards, D. D. (1982). The development of intelligence. In R. J. Sternberg (Ed.), *Handbook of human intelligence* (pp. 897–971). Cambridge: Cambridge University Press.

Siegler, R., & Shrager, J. (1984). Strategy choices in addition and subtraction: How do children know what to do? In C. Sophian (Ed.), *Origins of cognitive skills* (pp. 229–294). Hillsdale, NJ: Erlbaum.

Sigelman, C. K., & Waitzman, K. A. (1991). The development of distributive justice orientations: Contextual influences on children's resource allocations. *Child Development, 62,* 1367–1378.

Signorella, M. L. (1987). Gender schemata: Individual differences and context effects. In L. S. Liben & M. L. Signorella (Eds.), *Children's gender schemata* (pp. 23–37). San Francisco: Jossey-Bass.

Signorella, M. L., Bigler, R. S., & Liben, L. S. (1993). Developmental differences in children's gender schemata about others: A meta-analytic review. *Developmental Review, 13,* 147–183.

Signorella, M. L., & Jamison, W. (1986). Masculinity, femininity, androgyny, and cognitive performance: A meta-analysis. *Psychological Bulletin, 100,* 207–228.

Signorella, M. L., & Liben, L. S. (1984). Recall and reconstruction of gender-related pictures: Effects of attitude, task difficulty, and age. *Child Development, 55,* 393–405.

Signorielli, N. (1989). Television and conceptions about sex roles: Maintaining conventionality and the status quo. *Sex Roles, 21,* 341–360.

Simkin, P., Whalley, J., & Keppler, A. (1984). *Pregnancy, childbirth, and the newborn.* New York: Meadowbrook.

Simmons, R. G., & Blyth, D. A. (1987). *Moving into adolescence.* New York: Aldine De Gruyter.

Simons, R. L., Conger, R. D., & Whitbeck, L. B. (1988). A multistage social learning model of the influences of family and peers upon adolescent substance use. *Journal of Drug Issues, 18,* 293–316.

Simons, R. L., Lorenz, F. O., Wu, C-I., & Conger, R. D. (1993). Social network and marital support as mediators and moderators of the impact of stress and depression on parental behavior. *Developmental Psychology, 29,* 368–381.

Simons, R. L., Lorenz, R. O., Conger, R. D., & Wu, C–I. (1992). Support from spouse as a mediator and moderator of the disruptive influence of economic strain on parenting. *Child Development, 63,* 1282–1301.

Simons, R. L., Whitbeck, L. B., Conger, R. D., & Chyi-In, W. (1991). Intergenerational transmission of harsh parenting. *Developmental Psychology, 27,* 159–171.

Singer, D. G., & Singer, J. L. (1990). *The house of make-believe.* Cambridge, MA: Harvard University Press.

Singer, J. L., & Singer, D. G. (1981). *Television, imagination, and aggression: A study of preschoolers.* Hillsdale, NJ: Erlbaum.

Singer, J. L., & Singer, D. G. (1983). Psychologists look at television. *American Psychologist, 38,* 826–834.

Singer, J. L., Singer, D. G., & Rapaczynski, W. (1984). Family patterns and television viewing as predictors of children's beliefs and aggression. *Journal of Communication, 34,* 73–89.

Siqueland, E. R., & Lipsitt, L. P. (1966). Conditioned head-turning behavior in newborns. *Journal of Experimental Child Psychology, 3,* 356–376.

Skinner, B. F. (1957). *Verbal behavior.* New York: Appleton-Century-Crofts.

Skodak, M., & Skeels, H. M. (1949). A follow-up study of one hundred adopted children. *The Journal of Genetic Psychology, 75,* 85–125.

Skouteris, H., McKenzie, B. E., & Day, R. H. (1992). Integration of sequential information for shape perception by infants: A developmental study. *Child development, 63,* 1164–1176.

Slaby, R. G., & Frey, K. S. (1975). Development of gender constancy and selective attention to same-sex models. *Child Development, 46,* 849–856.

Slade, A. (1987). A longitudinal study of maternal involvement and symbolic play during the toddler period. *Child Development, 58,* 367–375.

Slater, A. M., Morison, V., Town, C., & Rose, D. (1985). Movement perception and identity constancy in the new-born baby. *British Journal of Developmental Psychology, 3,* 211–220.

Slater, A. M., & Morison, V. (1985). Shape constancy and slant perception at birth. *Perception, 14,* 337–344.

Slavin, R. E. (1987). Ability grouping and student achievement in elementary schools: A best evidence synthesis. *Review of Educational Research, 57,* 293–336.

Slobin, D. I. (1982). Universal and particular in the acquisition of language. In L. R. Gleitman & H. E. Wanner (Eds.), *Language acquisition: The state of the art* (pp. 128–170). Cambridge: Cambridge University Press.

Slobin, D. I. (1985). Crosslinguistic evidence for the language-making capacity. In D. I. Slobin (Ed.), *The crosslinguistic study of language acquisition: Vol. 2. Theoretical issues* (pp. 1157–1256). Hillsdale, NJ: Erlbaum.

Slomkowski, C. L., Nelson, K., Dunn, J., & Plomin, R. (1992). Temperament and language: Relations from toddlerhood to middle childhood. *Developmental Psychology, 28*, 1090–1095.

Smalley, S. L., Thompson , A. L., Spence, M. A., Judd, W. J., & Sparkes, R. S. (1989). Genetic influences on spatial ability: Transmission in an extended kindred. *Behavior Genetics, 19*, 229–240.

Smetana, J. G. (1981). Preschool children's conceptions of moral and social rules. *Child Development, 52*, 1333–1336.

Smetana, J. G. (1985). Preschool children's conceptions of transgressions: Effects of varying moral and conventional domain-related attributes. *Developmental Psychology, 21*, 18–29.

Smetana, J. G. (1989). Toddlers' social interactions in the context of moral and conventional transgressions in the home. *Developmental Psychology, 25*, 499–508.

Smetana, J. G., & Braeges, J. L. (1990). The development of toddlers' moral and conventional judgments. *Merrill-Palmer Quarterly, 36*, 329–346.

Smilansky, S. (1968). *The effects of sociodramatic play on disadvantaged children: Preschool children.* New York: Wiley.

Smith, C. L., & Tager-Flusberg, H. (1982). Metalinguistic awareness and language development. *Journal of Experimental Child Psychology, 34*, 449–468.

Smith, H. (1992). The detrimental health effects of ionizing radiation. *Nuclear Medicine Communications, 13*, 4–10.

Smith, H. W. (1973). Some developmental interpersonal dynamics through childhood. *American Sociological Review, 38*, 343–352.

Smith, J., & Russell, G. (1984). Why do males and females differ? Children's beliefs about sex differences. *Sex Roles, 11*, 1111–1119.

Smith, L. D. (1992). On prediction and control: B. F. Skinner and the technological ideal of science. *American Psychologist, 47*, 216–223.

Smith, M. C. (1978). Cognizing the behavior stream: The recognition of intentional action. *Child Development, 49*, 736–743.

Smith, M. L., & Glass, G. V. (1980). Meta-analysis of research on class size and its relationship to attitudes and instruction. *American Educational Research Journal, 17*, 419–433.

Smith, M. S., & Bissell, J. S. (1970). Report analysis: The impact of Head Start. *Harvard Educational Review, 40*, 51–104.

Smith, P. K. (1978). A longitudinal study of social participation in preschool children: Solitary and parallel play reexamined. *Developmental Psychology, 14*, 517–523.

Smith, P. K., & Boulton, M. (1990). Rough-and-tumble play, aggression and dominance: Perception and behavior in children's encounters. *Human Development, 33*, 271–282.

Smith, P. K., & Connolly, K. J. (1980) *The ecology of preschool behaviour.* Cambridge: Cambridge University Press.

Smith, S. (1991, Spring). Two-generation program models: A new intervention strategy. *Social Policy Report of the Society for Research in Child Development, 5,*(1).

Smolucha, F. (1992). Social origins of private speech in pretend play. In R. M. Diaz & L. E. Berk (Eds.), *Private speech: From social interaction to self-regulation* (pp. 123–141). Hillsdale, NJ: Erlbaum.

Smuts, B. B., & Gubernick, D. J. (1992). Male–infant relationships in nonhuman primates: Paternal investment or mating effort? In B. S. Hewlett (Ed.), *Father-child relations: Cultural and biosocial contexts* (pp. 1–30). New York: Aldine De Gruyter.

Snarey, J. R., & Keljo, K. (1991). In a gemeinschaft voice: The cross-cultural expansion of moral development theory. In W. M. Kurtines & J. L. Gewirtz (Eds.), *Handbook of moral behavior and development* (Vol. 1, pp. 395–424). Hillsdale, NJ: Erlbaum.

Snarey, J. R., Reimer, J., & Kohlberg, L. (1985). The development of social-moral reasoning among Kibbutz adolescents: A longitudinal cross-cultural study. *Developmental Psychology, 20*, 3–17.

Snow, C. E., & Hoefnagel-Höhle, M. (1978). The critical period for language acquisition: Evidence from second language learning. *Child Development, 49*, 1114–1128.

Snyder, J. J., Dishion, T. J., & Patterson, G. R. (1986). Determinants and consequences of associating with deviant peers during preadolescence and adolescence. *Journal of Early Adolescence, 6*, 20–43.

Sobesky, W. E. (1983). The effects of situational factors on moral judgments. *Child Development, 54*, 575–584.

Society for Research in Child Development, Committee for Ethical Conduct in Child Development Research. (1990, Winter). SRCD ethical standards for research with children. *SRCD Newsletter.* Chicago: Society for Research in Child Development.

Sockett, H. (1992). The moral aspects of the curriculum. In P. W. Jackson (Ed.), *Handbook of research on curriculum* (pp. 543–569). New York: Macmillan.

Sodian, B., Taylor, C., Harris, P. L., & Perner, J. (1991). Early deception and the child's theory of mind: False trails and genuine markers. *Child Development, 62*, 468–483.

Sodian, B., & Wimmer, H. (1987). Children's understanding of inference as a source of knowledge. *Child Development, 58*, 424–433.

Soken, H. H., & Pick, A. D. (1992). Intermodal perception of happy and angry expressive behaviors by seven-month-old infants. *Child Development, 63*, 787–795.

Sokoloff, B. Z. (1987). Alternative methods of reproduction: Effects on the child. *Clinical Pediatrics, 26*, 11–17.

Sommerville, J. (1982). *The rise and fall of childhood.* Beverly Hills, CA: Sage.

Sonenstein, F. L., Pleck, J. H., & Ku, L. C. (1991). Levels of sexual activity among adolescent males in the United States. *Family Planning Perspectives, 23*, 162–167.

Sonenschein, S. (1986a). Development of referential communication: Deciding that a message is uninformative. *Developmental Psychology, 22*, 164–168.

Sonenschein, S. (1986b). Development of referential communication skills: How familiarity with a listener affects a speaker's production of redundant messages. *Developmental Psychology, 22*, 549–552.

Sonenschein, S. (1988). The development of referential communication: Speaking to different listeners. *Child Development, 59*, 694–702.

Sontag, C. W., Baker, C. T., & Nelson, V. L. (1958). Mental growth and personality development: A longitudinal study. *Monographs for the Society for Research in Child Development, 23* (2, Serial No. 68).

Sophian, C. (1988). Early developments in children's understanding of number: Inferences about numerosity and one-to-one correspondence. *Child Development, 59*, 1397–1414.

Sorce, J., Emde, R., Campos, J., & Klinnert, M. (1985). Maternal emotional signaling: Its effect on the visual cliff behavior of 1-year-olds. *Developmental Psychology, 21,* 195–200.

Sosa, R., Kennell, J., Klaus, M., Robertson, S., & Urrutia, J. (1980). The effect of a supportive companion on perinatal problems, length of labor, and mother-infant interaction. *New England Journal of Medicine, 303,* 597–600.

Spearman, C. (1927). *The abilities of man: Their nature and measurement.* New York: Macmillan.

Speer, J. R., & Flavell, J. H. (1979). Young children's knowledge of the relative difficulty of recognition and recall memory tasks. *Developmental Psychology, 15,* 214–217.

Spelke, E. S. (1987). The development of intermodal perception. In P. Salapatek & L. Cohen (Eds.), *Handbook of infant perception: Vol 2. From perception to cognition* (pp. 233–273). Orlando, FL: Academic Press.

Spelke, E. S., Hofsten, C. von, & Kestenbaum, R. (1989). Object perception in infancy: Interaction of spatial and kinetic information for object boundaries. *Developmental Psychology, 25,* 185–196.

Spellacy, W. N., Miller, S. J., & Winegar, A. (1986). Pregnancy after 40 years of age. *Obstetrics and Gynecology, 68,* 452–454.

Spence, J. T., Helmreich, R., & Stapp, J. (1975). Ratings of self and peers on sex role attributes and their relation to self-esteem and conceptions of masculinity and femininity. *Journal of Personality and Social Psychology, 32,* 29–39.

Spence, M. J., & DeCasper, A. J. (1987). Prenatal experience with low-frequency maternal voice sounds influences neonatal perception of maternal voice samples. *Infant Behavior and Development, 10,* 133–142.

Spencer, C., Blades, M., & Morsley, K. (1989). *The child in the physical environment.* Chichester, England: Wiley.

Spencer, M. B., & Dornbusch, S. M. (1990). Challenges in studying minority youth. In S. S. Feldman & G. R. Elliott (Eds.), *At the threshold: The developing adolescent* (pp. 123–146). Cambridge, MA: Harvard University Press.

Spinetta, J., & Rigler, D. (1972). The child-abusing parent: A psychological review. *Psychological Bulletin, 77,* 296–304.

Spirito, A., Brown, L., Overholser, J., & Fritz, G. (1989). Attempted suicide in adolescence: A review and critique of the literature. *Child Psychology Review, 9,* 336–363.

Spitz, R. A. (1945). Hospitalism: An inquiry into the genesis of psychiatric conditions in early childhood. *Psychoanalytic Study of the Child, 1,* 113–117.

Spitz, R. A. (1946). Anaclitic depression. *Psychoanalytic Study of the Child, 2,* 313–342.

Spivack, G., & Shure, M. B. (1974). *Social adjustment of young children: A cognitive approach to solving real life problems.* San Francisco: Jossey-Bass.

Spivack, G., & Shure, M. B. (1985). ICPS and beyond: Centripetal and centrifugal forces. *American Journal of Community Psychology, 13,* 226–243.

Spock, B., & Rothenberg, M. B. (1985). *Dr. Spock's baby and child care.* New York: Pocket Books.

Spreen, O., Tupper, D., Risser, A., Tuokko, H., & Edgell, D. (1984). *Human developmental neuropsychology.* New York: Oxford University Press.

Sroufe, L. A. (1979). The ontogenesis of emotion. In J. D. Osofsky (Ed.), *Handbook of infant development* (pp. 462–516). New York: Wiley.

Sroufe, L. A. (1983). Infant–caregiver attachment and patterns of adaptation in preschool: The roots of maladaptation. In M.

Perlmutter (Ed.), *Minnesota Symposia on Child Psycholog, (Vol. 16,* pp. 41–83). Hillsdale, NJ: Erlbaum.

Sroufe, L. A. (1985). Attachment classification from the perspective of infant–caregiver relationships and infant temperament. *Child Development, 56,* 1–14.

Sroufe, L. A. (1988). A developmental perspective on day care. *Early Childhood Research Quarterly, 3,* 293–292.

Sroufe, L. A., Egeland, B., & Kreutzer, T. (1990). The fate of early experience following developmental change: Longitudinal approaches to individual adaptation. *Child Development, 61,* 1363–1373.

Sroufe, L. A., & Waters, E. (1976). The ontogenesis of smiling and laughter: A perspective on the organization of development in infancy. *Psychological Review, 83,* 173–189.

Sroufe, L. A., & Wunsch, J. P. (1972). The development of laughter in the first year of life. *Child Development, 43,* 1324–1344.

St James-Roberts, I. (1989). Persistent crying in infancy. *Journal of Child Psychology and Psychiatry, 30,* 189–195.

St James-Roberts, I., & Halil, T. (1991). Infant crying patterns in the first year: Normal community and clinical findings. *Journal of Child Psychology and Psychiatry, 32,* 951–968.

St. Peters, M., Fitch, M., Huston, A. C., Wright, J. C., & Eakins, D. J. (1991). Television and families: What do young children watch with their parents? *Child Development, 62,* 1409–1423.

Staats, A. (1971). Linguistic-mentalistic theory versus an explanatory S-R learning theory of language development. In D. Slobin (Ed.), *The ontogenesis of grammar* (pp. 103–152). New York: Academic Press.

Stack, D. M., & Muir, D. W. (1992). Adult tactile stimulation during face-to-face interactions modulates five-month-olds' affect and attention. *Child Development, 63,* 1509–1525.

Stanbury, J. B., Wyngaarden, J. B., & Frederickson, D. S. (1983). *The metabolic basis of inherited disease.* New York: McGraw-Hill.

Stangor, C., & Ruble, D. N. (1989). Differential influences of gender schemata and gender constancy on children's information processing and behavior. *Social Cognition, 7,* 353–372.

Stanhope, L., Bell, R. Q., & Parker-Cohen, N. Y. (1987). Temperament and helping behavior in preschool children. *Developmental Psychology, 23,* 347–353.

Stankov, L., Horn, J. L., Roy, T. (1980). On the relationship between Gf/Gc theory and Jensen's Level I/Level II theory. *Journal of Educational Psychology, 72,* 796–809.

Stark, L. J., Allen, K. D., Hurst, M., Nash, D. A., Rigney, B., & Stokes, T. F. (1989). Distraction: Its utilization and efficacy with children undergoing dental treatment. *Journal of Applied Behavior Analysis, 22,* 297–307.

Starkey, P., Spelke, E. S., & Gelman, R. (1983). Detection of intermodal numerical correspondences by human infants. *Science, 10,* 179–181.

Stattin, H., & Magnusson, D. (1990). *Pubertal maturation in female development.* Hillsdale, NJ: Erlbaum.

Stechler, G., & Halton, A. (1982). Prenatal influences on human development. In B. B. Wolman (Ed.), *Handbook of developmental psychology* (pp. 175–189). Englewood Cliffs, NJ: Prentice-Hall.

Stein, A. H. (1971). The effects of sex-role standards for achievement and sex-role preference on three determinants of achievement motivation. *Developmental Psychology, 4,* 219–231.

Stein, A. H., & Smithells, J. (1969). Age and sex differences in children's sex-role standards about achievement. *Developmental Psychology, 1,* 252–259.

Stein, Z., Susser, M., Saenger, G., & Marolla, F. (1975). *Famine and human development: The Dutch hunger winter of 1944–1945.* New York: Oxford University Press.

Steinberg, L. (1984). The varieties and effects of work during adolescence. In M. Lamb, A. Brown, & B. Rogoff (Eds.), *Advances in developmental psychology* (Vol. 3, pp. 1–37). Hillsdale, NJ: Erlbaum.

Steinberg, L. (1986). Latchkey children and susceptibility to peer pressure: An ecological analysis. *Developmental Psychology, 22,* 433–439.

Steinberg, L. (1988). Stability of Type A behavior from early childhood to young adulthood. In P. B. Baltes, D. L. Featherman, & R. M. Lerner (Eds.), *Life-span development and behavior* (Vol. 8, pp. 129–161). Hillsdale, NJ: Erlbaum.

Steinberg, L. D. (1987). The impact of puberty on family relations: Effects of pubertal status and pubertal timing. *Developmental Psychology, 23,* 451–460.

Steinberg, L. D. (1990). Interdependence in the family: Autonomy, conflict, and harmony in the parent–adolescent relationship. In S. S. Feldman & G. R. Elliott (Eds.), *At the threshold: The developing adolescent* (pp. 255–276). Cambridge, MA: Harvard University Press.

Steinberg, L. D. (1993). *Adolescence* (3rd ed.). New York: McGraw-Hill.

Steinberg, L., & Dornbusch, S. M. (1991). Negative correlates of part-time employment during adolescence: Replication and elaboration. *Developmental Psychology, 27,* 304–313.

Steinberg, L., Elman, J. D., & Mounts, N. S. (1989). Authoritative parenting, psychosocial maturity, and academic success among adolescents. *Child Development, 60,* 1424–1436.

Steinberg, L., Lamborn, S. D., Dornbusch, S. M., & Darling, N. (1992). Impact of parenting practices on adolescent achievement: Authoritative parenting, school involvement, and encouragement to succeed. *Child Development, 63,* 1266–1281.

Steinberg, L., Mounts, N. S., Lamborn, S. D., & Dornbusch, S. M. (1991). Authoritative parenting and adolescent adjustment across varied ecological niches. *Journal of Research on Adolescence, 1,* 19–36.

Steinberg, L., & Silverberg, S. (1986). The vicissitudes of autonomy in early adolescence. *Child Development, 57,* 841–851.

Steiner, J. E. (1979). Human facial expression in response to taste and smell stimulation. In H. W. Reese & L. P. Lipsitt (Eds.), *Advances in child development and behavior* (Vol. 13, pp. 257–295). New York: Academic Press.

Stenberg, C., & Campos, J. (1990). The development of anger expressions in infancy. In N. Stein, B. Leventhal, & T. Trabasso (Eds.), *Psychological and biological approaches to emotion* (pp. 247–282). Hillsdale, NJ: Erlbaum.

Stenberg, C., Campos, J., & Emde, R. (1983). The facial expression of anger in seven-month-old infants. *Child Development, 54,* 178–184.

Stene, J., Stene, E., & Stengel-Rutkowski, S. (1981). Paternal age and Down's syndrome. Data from prenatal diagnosis (DFG). *Human Genetics, 59,* 119–124.

Stern, D. N. (1985). *The interpersonal world of the infant: A view from psychoanalysis and developmental psychology.* New York: Basic Books.

Stern, M., & Karraker, K. H. (1989). Sex stereotyping of infants: A review of gender labeling studies. *Sex Roles, 20,* 501–522.

Sternberg, K. J., Lamb, M. E., Greenbaum, C., Cicchetti, D., Dawud, S., Cortes, R. M., Krispin, O., & Lorey, F. (1993). Effects of domestic violence on children's behavior problems and depression. *Developmental Psychology, 29,* 44–52.

Sternberg, R. J. (1982, April). Who's intelligent? *Psychology Today, 16*(4), 30–39.

Sternberg, R. J. (1984a). Evaluation of the Kaufman Assessment Battery for Children from an information processing perspective. *Journal of Special Education, 18,* 269–279.

Sternberg, R. J. (1984b). Mechanisms of cognitive development: A componential approach. In R. J. Sternberg (Ed.), *Mechanisms of cognitive development* (pp. 163–186). New York: Freeman.

Sternberg, R. J. (1985). *Beyond IQ: A triarchic theory of human intelligence.* New York: Cambridge University Press.

Sternberg, R. J. (1988). A triarchic view of intelligence in cross-cultural perspective. In S. H. Irvine & J. W. Berry (Eds.), *Human abilities in cultural context* (pp. 60–85). New York: Cambridge University Press.

Sternberg, R. J. (1989). Domain-generality and domain-specificity: The life and impending death of a false dichotomy. *Merrill-Palmer Quarterly, 35,* 115–130.

Sternberg, R. J., & Davidson, J. E. (Eds.). (1986). *Conceptions of giftedness.* New York: Cambridge University Press.

Stevens, J. H. (1984). Black grandmothers' and black adolescent mothers' knowledge about parenting. *Developmental Psychology, 20,* 1017–1025.

Stevenson, H. W. (1992, December). Learning from Asian schools. *Scientific American, 267,* 32–38.

Stevenson, H. W., & Baker, D. P. (1987). The family-school relation and the child's school performance. *Child Development, 58,* 1348–1357.

Stevenson, H. W., Chen, C., & Lee, S-Y. (1993). Mathematics achievement of Chinese, Japanese, and American children: Ten years later. *Science, 259,* 53–58.

Stevenson, H. W., & Lee, S-Y. (1990). Contexts of achievement: A study of American, Chinese, and Japanese children. *Monographs of the Society for Research in Child Development, 55* (1–2, Serial No. 221).

Stevenson, H. W., & Stigler, J. W. (1992). *The learning gap.* New York: Summit.

Stevenson, H. W., Stigler, J. W., Lee, S., Lucker, G. W., Litamura, S., & Hsu, C. (1985). Cognitive performance and academic achievement of Japanese, Chinese, and American children. *Child Development, 56,* 718–734.

Stevenson, R., & Pollitt, C. (1987). The acquisition of temporal terms. *Journal of Child Language, 14,* 533–545.

Stewart, A. J., & Healy, J. M., Jr. (1989). Linking individual development and social changes. *American Psychologist, 44,* 30–42.

Stewart, D. A. (1982). *Children with sex chromosome aneuploidy: Follow-up studies.* New York: Alan R. Liss.

Stiefvater, K., Kurdek, L. A., & Allik, J. (1986). Effectiveness of a short-term social problem-solving program for popular, rejected, neglected, and average fourth-grade children. *Journal of Applied Developmental Psychology, 7,* 33–43.

Stifter, C. A., & Fox, N. A. (1990). Infant reactivity: Physiological correlates of newborn and 5-month temperament. *Developmental Psychology, 26,* 582–588.

Stigler, J. W., Smith, S., & Mao, L. W. (1985). The self-perception of competence by Chinese children. *Child Development, 56,* 1259–1270.

Stillman, R. J. (1982). In utero exposure to diethylstilbestrol: Adverse effects on the reproductive tract and reproductive performance in male and female offspring. *American Journal of Obstetrics and Gynecology, 142,* 905–921.

Stipek, D. J. (1981). Children's perceptions of their own and their classmates' ability. *Journal of Educational Psychology, 73,* 404–410.

Stipek, D. J. (1984). Sex differences in children's attributions for success and failure on math and spelling tests. *Sex Roles, 11,* 969–981.

Stipek, D. J., Gralinski, J. H., & Kopp, C. B. (1990). Self-concept development in the toddler years. *Developmental Psychology, 26,* 972–977.

Stipek, D. J., & Kowalski, P. S. (1989). Learned helplessness in task-orienting versus performance-orienting testing conditions. *Journal of Educational Psychology, 81,* 384–391.

Stipek, D., & MacIver, D. (1989). Developmental change in children's assessment of intellectual competence. *Child Development, 60,* 531–538.

Stipek, D., Recchia, S., & McClintic, S. (1992). Self-evaluation in young children. *Monographs of the Society for Research in Child Development, 57* (1, Serial No. 226).

Stjernfeldt, M., Berglund, K., Lindsten, J., & Ludvigsson, J. (1992). Maternal smoking and irradiation during pregnancy as risk factors for child leukemia. *Cancer Detection and Prevention, 16,* 129–135.

Stoch, M. B., Smythe, P. M., Moodie, A. D., & Bradshaw, D. (1982). Psychosocial outcome and CT findings after growth undernourishment during infancy: A 20-year developmental study. *Developmental Medicine and Child Neurology, 24,* 419–436.

Stocker, C., Dunn, J., & Plomin, R. (1989). Sibling relationships: Links with child temperament, maternal behavior, and family structure. *Child Development, 60,* 715–727.

Stocker, C. M., & McHale, S. M. (1992). The nature and family correlates of preadolescents' perceptions of their sibling relationships. *Journal of Social and Personal Relationships, 9,* 179–195.

Stockman, I. J., & Vaughn-Cooke, F. (1992). Lexical elaboration in children's locative action expressions. *Child Development, 63,* 1104–1125.

Stoddart, T., & Turiel, E. (1985). Children's concepts of cross-gender activities. *Child Development, 56,* 1241–1252.

Stodolsky, S. S. (1974). How children find something to do in preschools. *Genetic Psychology Monographs, 90,* 245–303.

Stodolsky, S. S. (1988). *The subject matters.* Chicago: University of Chicago Press.

Stoel-Gammon, C., & Otomo, K. (1986). Babbling development of hearing-impaired and normally hearing subjects. *Journal of Speech and Hearing Disorders, 51,* 33–41.

Stone, L. (1977). *The family, sex, and marriage in England, 1500–1800.* New York: Harper & Row.

Stoneman, Z., Brody, G. H., & MacKinnon, C. E. (1986). Same-sex and cross-sex siblings: Activity choices, roles, behavior, and gender stereotypes. *Sex Roles, 15,* 495–511.

Strain, P. S. (1977). An experimental analysis of peer social initiation on the behavior of withdrawn preschool children: Some training and generalization effects. *Journal of Abnormal Child Psychology, 5,* 445–455.

Strasburger, V. C. (1989). Adolescent sexuality and the media. *Adolescent Gynecology, 36,* 747–773.

Strauss, M. S., & Curtis, L. E. (1984). Development of numerical concepts in infancy. In C. Sophian (Ed.), *The origins of cognitive skills* (pp. 131–155). Hillsdale, NJ: Erlbaum.

Streissguth, A. P., Barr, H. M., Sampson, P. D., Darby, B. L., & Martin, D. C. (1989). IQ at age 4 in relation to maternal alcohol use and smoking during pregnancy. *Developmental Psychology, 25,* 3–11.

Streissguth, A. P., Treder, R., Barr, H. M., Shepard, T., Bleyer, W. A., Sampson, P. D., & Martin, D. (1987). Aspirin and acetaminophen use by pregnant women and subsequent child IQ and attention decrements. *Teratology, 35,* 211–219.

Strickland, D. S., & Ascher, C. (1992). Low-income African-American children and public schooling. In P. W. Jackson (Ed.), *Handbook of research on curriculum* (pp. 609–625). New York: Macmillan.

Strober, M., McCracken, J., & Hanna, G. (1990). Affective disorders. In R. M. Lerner, A. C. Petersen, & J. Brooks-Gunn (Eds.), *The encyclopedia of adolescence* (Vol. 1, pp. 18–25). New York: Garland.

Strutt, G. F., Anderson, D. R., & Well, A. D. (1975). A developmental study of the effects of irrelevant information on speeded classification. *Journal of Experimental Child Psychology, 20,* 127–135.

Stunkard, A. J., Foch, T. T., & Hrubec, Z. (1986). A twin study of human obesity. *Journal of the American Medical Association, 314,* 193–198.

Suess, G. J., Grossmann, K. E., & Sroufe, L. A. (1992). Effects of infant attachment to mother and father on quality of adaptation in preschool: From dyadic to individual organisation of self. *International Journal of Behavioral Development, 15,* 43–65.

Sullivan, H. S. (1953). *The interpersonal theory of psychiatry.* New York: Norton.

Sullivan, J. W., & Horowitz, F. D. (1983). The effects of intonation on infant attention: The role of the rising intonation contour. *Journal of Child Language, 10,* 521–534.

Sullivan, L. W. (1987). The risks of the sickle-cell trait: Caution and common sense. *New England Journal of Medicine, 317,* 830–831.

Suomi, S. J. (1982). Biological foundations and developmental psychobiology. In C. B. Kopp & J. B. Krakow (Eds.), *The child: Development in a social context* (pp. 42–91). Reading, MA: Addison-Wesley.

Suomi, S. J., & Harlow, H. F. (1978). Early experience and social development in rhesus monkeys. In M. E. Lamb (Ed.) *Social and personality development* (pp. 252–271). New York: Holt, Rinehart, and Winston.

Super, C. M. (1981). Behavioral development in infancy. In R. H. Monroe, R. L. Monroe, & B. B. Whiting (Eds.), *Handbook of cross-cultural human development* (pp. 181–270). New York: Garland.

Super, C. M., & Harkness, S. (1982). The infant's niche in rural Kenya and metropolitan America. In L. L. Adler (Ed.), *Cross-cultural research at issue* (pp. 247–255). New York: Academic Press.

Susman, E. J., Inoff-Germain, G., Nottelmann, E. D., Loriaux, D. L., Cutler, G. B., Jr., & Chrousos, G. P. (1987). Hormones, emotional dispositions, and aggressive attributes in young adolescents. *Child Development, 58,* 1114–1134.

Swanson, H. L. (1990). Influence of metacognitive knowledge and aptitude on problem solving. *Journal of Educational Psychology, 82,* 306–314.

T

Tager-Flusberg, H. (1989). Putting words together: Morphology and syntax in the preschool years. In J. Berko Gleason (Ed.), *The development of language* (pp. 135–165). Columbus, OH: Merrill.

Tager-Flusberg, H. (1992). Autistic children's talk about psychological states: Deficits in the early acquisition of a theory of mind. *Child Development, 63,* 161–172.

Taitz, L. S. (1983). *The obese child.* Boston: Blackwell.

Takahashi, K. (1990). Are the key assumptions of the "Strange Situation" procedure universal? A view from Japanese research. *Human Development, 33,* 23–30.

Takanishi, R., DeLeon, P., & Pallak, M. S. (1983). Psychology and public policy affecting children, youth, and families. *American Psychologist, 38,* 67–69.

Tamis-LeMonda, C. S., & Bornstein, M. H. (1989). Habituation and maternal encouragement of attention in infancy as predictors of toddler language, play and representational competence. *Child Development, 60,* 738–751.

Tanner, J. M. (1990). *Foetus into man* (2nd ed.). Cambridge, MA: Harvard University Press.

Tanner, J. M., & Inhelder, B. (Eds.). (1956). *Discussions on child development* (Vol. 1). London: Tavistock.

Tanner, J. M., & Whitehouse, R. H. (1975). Revised standards for triceps and subscapular skinfolds in British children. *Archives of Disease in Childhood, 50,* 142–145.

Tanner, J. M., Whitehouse, R. H., Cameron, N., Marshall, W. A., Healey, M. J. R., & Goldstein, H. (1983). *Assessment of skeletal maturity and prediction of adult height [TW 2 Method]* (2nd ed.). London: Academic Press.

Task Force on Pediatric AIDS. (1989). Pediatric AIDS and human immunodeficiency virus infection. *American Psychologist, 44,* 258–264.

Tauber, M. A. (1979). Parental socialization techniques and sex differences in children's play. *Child Development, 50,* 225–234.

Taylor, A. R., Asher, S. R., & Williams, G. A. (1987). The social adaptation of mainstreamed mildly retarded children. *Child Development, 58,* 1321–1334.

Taylor, M., Cartwright, B. S., & Bowden, T. (1991). Perspective taking and theory of mind: Do children predict interpretive diversity as a function of differences in observers' knowledge? *Child Development, 62,* 1334–1351.

Taylor, M., & Gelman, S. A. (1988). Adjectives and nouns: Children's strategies for learning new words. *Child Development, 59,* 411–419.

Taylor, M., & Gelman, S. A. (1989). Incorporating new words into the lexicon: Preliminary evidence for language hierarchies. *Child Development, 60,* 625–636.

Taylor, M. C., & Hall, J. A. (1982). Psychological androgyny: Theories, methods, and conclusions. *Psychological Bulletin, 92,* 347–366.

Taylor, R. D., Casten, R., & Flickinger, S. M. (1993). Influence of kinship social support on the parenting experiences and psychosocial adjustment of African-American adolescents. *Developmental Psychology, 29,* 382–388.

Teberg, A. J., Walther, F. J., & Pena, I. C. (1988). Mortality, morbidity, and outcome of the small-for-gestational-age infant. *Seminar in Perinatology, 12,* 84–94.

Tedder, J. L. (1991). Using the Brazelton Neonatal Assessment Scale to facilitate the parent-infant relationship in a primary care setting. *Nurse Practitioner, 16,* 27–36.

Templin, M. C. (1957). Certain language skills in children: Their development and interrelationships. *University of Minnesota Institute of Child Welfare Monograph, 26.*

Tennes, K., Emde, R., Kisley, A., & Metcalf, D. (1972). The stimulus barrier in early infancy: An exploration of some formulations of John Benjamin. In R. Holt and E. Peterfreund (Eds.), *Psychoanalysis and contemporary science* (Vol. 1, pp. 206–234). New York: Macmillan.

Tenney, Y. J. (1975). The child's conception of organization and recall. *Journal of Experimental Child Psychology, 19,* 100–114.

Terman, L., & Oden, M. H. (1959). *Genetic studies of genius: Vol. 4. The gifted group at midlife.* Stanford, CA: Stanford University Press.

Terrace, H. S., Petitto, L. A., Sanders, R. J., & Bever, T. G. (1980). On the grammatical capacity of apes. In K. E. Nelson (Ed.), *Children's language* (Vol. 2, pp. 371–495). New York: Cambridge University Press.

Teti, D. M., & Ablard, K. E. (1989). Security of attachment and infant–sibling relationships: A laboratory study. *Child Development, 60,* 1519–1528.

Tharp, R. G., & Gallimore, R. (1988). *Rousing minds to life: Teaching, learning, and schooling in social context.* New York: Cambridge University Press.

Thatcher, R. W., Walker, R. A., & Giudice, S. (1987). Human cerebral hemispheres develop at different rates and ages. *Science, 236,* 1110–1113.

The Psychological Corporation. (1993). *Assessment focus.* San Antonio, TX: Author.

Thelen, E. (1983). Learning to walk is still an "old" problem: A reply to Zelazo. *Journal of Motor Behavior, 15,* 139–161.

Thelen, E. (1989). The (re)discovery of motor development: Learning new things from an old field. *Developmental Psychology, 25,* 946–949.

Thelen, E., & Adolph, K. E. (1992). Arnold Gesell: The paradox of nature and nurture. *Developmental Psychology, 28,* 368–380.

Thelen E., Fisher, D. M., & Ridley-Johnson, R. (1984). The relationship between physical growth and a newborn reflex. *Infant Behavior and Development, 7,* 479–493.

Theorell, K., Prechtl, H., & Vos, J. (1974). A polygraphic study of normal and abnormal newborn infants. *Neuropaediatrie, 5,* 279–317.

Thevenin, D. M., Eilers, R. E., Oller, D. K., & Lavoie, L. (1985). Where's the drift in babbling drift? A cross-linguistic study. *Applied Psycholinguistics, 6,* 3–15.

Thoma, S. J. (1986). Estimating gender differences in the comprehension and preference of moral issues. *Developmental Review, 6,* 165–180.

Thomas, A., & Chess, S. (1977). *Temperament and development.* New York: Brunner/Mazel.

Thomas, A., Chess, S., & Birch, H. G. (1968). *Temperament and behavior disorders in children.* New York: New York University Press.

Thomas, A., Chess, S., & Birch, H. G. (1970, August). The origins of personality. *Scientific American, 223* (2), 102–109.

Thomas, N. G., & Berk, L. E. (1981). Effects of school environments on the development of young children's creativity. *Child Development, 52,* 1152–1162.

Thomas, R. M. (1992). *Comparing theories of child development* (3rd ed.). Belmont, CA: Wadsworth.

Thompson, J. G., & Myers, N. A. (1985). Inferences and recall at ages four and seven. *Child Development, 56,* 1134–1144.

Thompson, L. A., Detterman, D. K., & Plomin, R. (1991). Associations between cognitive abilities and scholastic achievement: Genetic overlap but environmental differences. *Psychological Science, 2,* 158–165.

Thompson, R. A. (1990a). On emotion and self-regulation. In R. A. Thompson (Ed.), *Nebraska Symposium on Motivation* (Vol. 36, pp. 383–483). Lincoln: University of Nebraska Press.

Thompson, R. A. (1990b). Vulnerability in research: A developmental perspective on research risk. *Child Development, 61,* 1–16.

Thompson, R. A., Connell, J. P., & Bridges, L. (1988). Temperament, emotion, and social interactive behavior in the Strange Situation: A component process analysis of attachment system functioning. *Child Development, 59,* 1102–1110.

Thompson, R. A., Lamb, M., & Estes, D. (1982). Stability of infant–mother attachment and its relationship to changing life circumstances in an unselected middle-class sample. *Child Development, 53,* 144–148.

Thompson, R. A., & Limber, S. (1991). "Social anxiety" in infancy: Stranger wariness and separation distress. In H. Leitenberg (Ed.), *Handbook of social and evaluation anxiety* (pp. 85–137). New York: Plenum.

Thompson, R. A., Tinsley, B. R., Scalora, M. J., & Parke, R. D. (1989). Grandparents' visitation rights: Legalizing the ties that bind. *American Psychologist, 44,* 1217–1222.

Thorndike, R. L., Hagen, E. P., & Sattler, J. M. (1986). *The Stanford-Binet Intelligence Scale: Fourth edition. Guide for administering and scoring.* Chicago: Riverside Publishing.

Thornton, M., & Taylor, R. (1988). Black American perceptions of black Africans. *Ethnic and Racial Studies, 11,* 139–150.

Thurstone, L. L. (1938). *Primary mental abilities.* Chicago: University of Chicago Press.

Tietjen, A., & Walker, L. (1985). Moral reasoning and leadership among men in a Papua New Guinea village. *Developmental Psychology, 21,* 982–992.

Tizard, B., & Hodges, J. (1978). The effect of early institutional rearing on the behaviour problems and affectional relationships of four-year-old children. *Journal of Child Psychology and Psychiatry, 19,* 99–118.

Tizard, B., & Rees, J. (1975). The effect of early institutional rearing on the behaviour problems and affectional relationships of four-year-old children. *Journal of Child Psychology and Psychiatry, 16,* 61–73.

Tobias, P. V. (1975). Anthropometry among disadvantaged people: Studies in southern Africa. In E. S. Watts, F. E. Johnston, & G. W. Lasker (Eds.), *Biosocial interrelations in population adaptation: World anthropology series* (pp. 287–305). The Hague: Mouton.

Tolson, T. F. J., & Wilson, M. N. (1990). The impact of two- and three-generational black family structure on perceived family climate. *Child Development, 61,* 416–428.

Tomasello, M. (1990). The role of joint attentional processes in early language development. *Language Sciences, 10,* 68–88.

Tomasello, M., Mannle, S., & Kruger, A. C. (1986). Linguistic environment of 1- to 2-year-old twins. *Developmental Psychology, 22,* 169–176.

Toner, I. J., Parke, R. D., & Yussen, S. R. (1978). The effect of observation of model behavior on establishment and stability of resistance to deviation in children. *Journal of Genetic Psychology, 132,* 283–290.

Toner, I. J., & Smith, R. A. (1977). Age and overt verbalization in delay maintenance behavior in children. *Journal of Experimental Child Psychology, 24,* 123–128.

Torrance, E. P. (1980). *The Torrance Tests of Creative Thinking.* New York: Scholastic Testing Service.

Touwen, B. C. L. (1978). Variability and stereotype in normal and deviant development. In J. Apley (Ed.), *Care of the handicapped child* (pp. 99–110). Philadelphia: Lippincott.

Touwen, B. C. L. (1984). Primitive reflexes—conceptual or semantic problem? In H. F. R. Prechtl (Ed.), *Continuity of neural functions from prenatal to postnatal life* (Clinics in developmental medicine No. 94, pp. 115–125). Philadelphia: Lippincott.

Tower, R. B., Singer, D. G., Singer, J. L., & Biggs, A. (1979). Differential effects of television programming on preschoolers' cognition, imagination, and social play. *American Journal of Orthopsychiatry, 49,* 265–281.

Trause, M. A. (1977). Stranger responses: Effects of familiarity, stranger's approach, and sex of infant. *Child Development, 48,* 1657–1661.

Trautner, H. M., Helbing, N., Sahm, W. B., & Lohaus, A. (1989, April). *Beginning awareness-rigidity-flexibility: A longitudinal analysis of sex-role stereotyping in 4- to 10-year-old children.* Paper presented at the biennial meeting of the Society for Research in Child Development, Kansas City.

Trevethan, S. D., & Walker, L. J. (1989). Hypothetical versus real-life moral reasoning among psychopathic and delinquent youth. *Development and Psychopathology, 1,* 91–103.

Trickett, P. K., Aber, J. L., Carlson, V., & Cicchetti, D. (1991). Relationship of socioeconomic status to the etiology and developmental sequelae of physical child abuse. *Developmental Psychology, 27,* 148–158.

Trickett, P. K., & Kuczynski, L. (1986). Children's misbehaviors and parental discipline strategies in abusive and nonabusive families. *Developmental Psychology, 22,* 115–123.

Trieber, F. A., Mabe, P. A., Riley, W. T., McDuffie, M., Strong, W. B., & Levy, M. (1990). Children's Type A behavior: The role of parental hostility and family history of cardiovascular disease. *Journal of Social Behavior and Personality, 5,* 183–189.

Trivers, R. L. (1971). The evolution of reciprocal altruism. *Quarterly Review of Biology, 46,* 35–57.

Tronick, E. Z. (1989). Emotions and emotional communication in infants. *American Psychologist, 44,* 115–123.

Tronick, E. Z., & Cohn, J. F. (1989). Infant-mother face-to-face interaction: Age and gender differences in coordination and the occurrence of miscoordination. *Child Development, 60,* 85–92.

Tronick, E. Z., Cohn, J. F., & Shea, E. (1986). The transfer of affect between mothers and infants. In T. B. Brazelton & M. W. Yogman (Eds.), *Affect development in infancy* (pp. 11–25). New York: Cambridge University Press.

Troy, M., & Sroufe, L. A. (1987). Victimization among preschoolers: Role of attachment relationship history. *Journal of the American Academy of Child and Adolescent Psychiatry, 26,* 166–172.

Tudge, J. R. H. (1992). Processes and consequences of peer collaboration: A Vygotskian analysis. *Child Development, 63,* 1364–1379.

Tudge, J. R. H., & Rogoff, B. (1987). Peer influences on cognitive development: Piagetian and Vygotskian perspectives. In M. H. Bornstein & J. S. Bruner (Eds.), *Interaction in human development* (pp. 17–40). Hillsdale, NJ: Erlbaum.

Tulving, E. (1972). Episodic and semantic memory. In E. Tulving & W. Donaldson (Eds.), *Organization of memory* (pp. 382–403). New York: Academic Press.

Tulviste, P. (1991). *Cultural-historical development of verbal thinking: A psychological study.* Commack, NY: Nova Science Publishers.

Tunmer, W. E., & Nesdale, A. R. (1982). The effects of digraphs and pseudo-words on phonemic segmentation in young children. *Journal of Applied Psycholinguistics, 3,* 299–311.

Turiel, E. (1983). *The development of social knowledge: Morality and convention.* New York: Cambridge University Press.

Turiel, E., Smetana, J. G., & Killen, M. (1991). Social contexts in social cognitive development. In W. M. Kurtines & J. L. Gewirtz (Eds.), *Handbook of moral behavior and development* (Vol. 2, pp. 307–332). Hillsdale, NJ: Erlbaum.

Turkheimer, E., & Gottesman, I. I. (1991). Individual differences and the canalization of human behavior. *Developmental Psychology, 27,* 18–22.

U

U.S. Bureau of the Census. (1992). *Statistical abstract of the United States* (112th ed.). Washington, DC: U.S. Government Printing Office.

U.S. Centers for Disease Control. (1992). *HIV/AIDS surveillance.* Washington, DC: U.S. Government Printing Office.

U.S. Centers for Disease Control. (1992, January 3). Sexual behavior among high school students—United States, 1990. *Morbidity and Mortality Weekly Report, 40,* 885–888.

U.S. Centers for Disease Control. (1993, July). *HIV/AIDS surveillance.* Atlanta: Author.

U.S. Department of Health and Human Services. (1990). *Drug abuse among youth: Findings from the 1988 national household survey on drug abuse.* Washington, DC: U.S. Government Printing Office.

U.S. Department of Health and Human Services. (1991). *Drug use among American high school seniors, college students and young adults, 1975–1990* (Vol. 1). Washington, DC: U.S. Government Printing Office.

U.S. Department of Health and Human Services. (1992a). *Advance data from vital and health statistics of the National Center for Health Statistics.* Washington, DC: U.S. Government Printing Office.

U.S. Department of Health and Human Services. (1992b). *Vital Statistics of the United States, 1989.* Washington, DC: U.S. Government Printing Office.

U.S. Department of Justice. (1992). *Crime in the United States.* Washington, DC: U.S. Government Printing Office.

U.S. Department of Labor, Bureau of Labor Statistics. (1993, February). Consumer Price Index. *Monthly Labor Review, 116* (2), 105.

U.S. Office of Management and Budget. (1992). *Historical tables, budget of the United States.* Washington, DC: U.S. Government Printing Office.

Udry, J. R. (1990). Hormonal and social determinants of adolescent sexual initiation. In J. Bancroft & J. M. Reinisch (Eds.), *Adolescence and puberty* (pp. 70–87). New York: Oxford University Press.

Ullian, D. Z. (1976). The development of conceptions of masculinity and femininity. In B. Lloyd & J. Archer (Eds.), *Exploring sex differences* (pp. 25–47). London: Academic Press.

Underwood, M. K., Coie, J. D., & Herbsman, C. R. (1992). Display rules for anger and aggression in school-age children. *Child Development, 63,* 366–380.

Unger, R., Kreeger, L., & Christoffel, K. K. (1990). Childhood obesity: Medical and familial correlates and age of onset. *Clinical Pediatrics, 29,* 368–372.

Unger, R. K., & Crawford, M. (1993). Sex and gender—The troubled relationship between terms and concepts. *Psychological Science, 4,* 122–124.

Ungerer, J. A., Zelazo, P. R., Kearsley, R. B., & O'Leary, K. (1981). Developmental changes in the representation of objects in symbolic play from 19–34 months of age. *Child Development, 52,* 186–195.

Urberg, K. A. (1979, March). *The development of androgynous sex-role concepts in young children.* Paper presented at the biennial meeting of the Society for Research in Child Development, San Francisco.

Uttal, D. H., & Wellman, H. M. (1989). Young children's representation of spatial information acquired from maps. *Developmental Psychology, 25,* 128–138.

Uzgiris, I. C., & Hunt, J. McV. (1975). *Assessment in infancy: Ordinal scales of psychological development.* Urbana: University of Illinois Press.

V

Vaidyanathan, R. (1988). Development of forms and functions of interrogatives in children: A language study of Tamil. *Journal of Child Language, 15,* 533–549.

Valian, V. (1986). Syntactic categories in the speech of young children. *Developmental Psychology, 22,* 562–579.

Valian, V. V. (1993). *Parental replies: Linguistic status and didactic role.* Cambridge, MA: MIT Press.

Valleroy, L. A., Harris, J. R., & Way, P. O. (1990). The impact of HIV infection on child survival in the developing world. *AIDS, 4,* 667–672.

Van Dyke, D. C., Lang, D. J., Heide, F., van Duyne, S., & Soucek, M. J. (Eds.). (1990). *Clinical perspectives in the management of Down syndrome.* New York: Springer-Verlag.

van der Veer, R., & Valsiner, J. (1991). *Understanding Vygotsky: A quest for synthesis.* London: Routledge.

van IJzendoorn, M. H., Goldberg, S., Kroonenberg, P. M., & Frenkel, O. J. (1992). The relative effects of maternal and child problems on the quality of attachment: A meta-analysis of attachment in clinical samples. *Child Development, 63,* 840–858.

van IJzendoorn, M. H., Kranenburg, M. J., Zwart-Woudstra, A., van Busschbach, A. M., & Lambermon, M. W. E. (1991). Parental attachment and children's socio-emotional development: Some findings on the validity of the adult attachment interview in The Netherlands. *International Journal of Behavioral Development, 14,* 375–394.

van IJzendoorn, M. H., & Kroonenberg, P. M. (1988). Cross-cultural patterns of attachment: A meta-analysis of the Strange Situation. *Child Development, 59,* 147–156.

Vandell, D. L., & Corasaniti, M. A. (1988). The relation between third-graders' after school care and social, academic, and emotional functioning. *Child Development, 59,* 868–875.

Vandell, D. L., & Ramanan, J. (1991). Children of the National Longitudinal Survey of Youth: Choices in after-school care and child development. *Developmental Psychology, 27,* 637–643.

Vandell, D. L., & Wilson, K. S. (1987). Infants' interactions with mother, sibling, and peer: Contrasts and relations between interaction systems. *Child Development, 58,* 176–186.

Vandell, D. L., Wilson, K. S., & Buchanan, N. R. (1980). Peer interaction in the first year of life: An examination of its structure, content, and sensitivity to toys. *Child Development, 51,* 481–488.

Vanfossen, B., Jones, J., & Spade, J. (1987). Curriculum tracking and status maintenance. *Sociology of Education, 60,* 104–122.

Vasudev, J., & Hummel, R. C. (1987). Moral stage sequence and principled reasoning in an Indian sample. *Human Development, 30,* 105–118.

Vaughn, B. E., Bradley, C. F., Joffe, L. S., Seifer, R., & Barglow, P. (1987). Maternal characteristics measured prenatally are predictive of ratings of temperament "difficulty" on the Carey Infant Temperament Questionnaire. *Developmental Psychology, 23,* 152–161.

Vaughn, B. E., Kopp, C. B., & Krakow, J. B. (1984). The emergence and consolidation of self-control from eighteen to thirty months of age: Normative trends and individual differences. *Child Development, 55,* 990–1004.

Vaughn, B. E., Lefever, B. G., Seifer, R., & Barglow, P. (1989).

Attachment behavior, attachment security, and temperament during infancy. *Child Development, 60,* 728–737.

Vaughn, B. E., Stevenson-Hinde, J., Waters, E., Kotsaftis, A., Lefever, G. B., Shouldice, A., Trudel, M., & Belsky, J. (1992). Attachment security and temperament in infancy and early childhood: Some conceptual clarifications. *Developmental Psychology, 28,* 463–373.

Vaughn, B. E., & Waters, E. (1990). Attachment behavior at home and in the lab: Q-sort observations and Strange Situation classifications of one-year-olds. *Child Development, 61,* 1965–1973.

Veerula, G. R., & Noah, P. K. (1990). Clinical manifestations of childhood lead poisoning. *Journal of Tropical Medicine and Hygiene, 93,* 170–177.

Vega-Lahr, N., Field, T., Goldstein, S., & Carran, D. (1988). Type A behavior in preschool children. In T. M. Field, P. M. McCabe, & N. Schneiderman (Eds.), *Stress and coping across development* (pp. 89–107). Hillsdale, NJ: Erlbaum.

Ventura, S. J. (1989). Trends and variations in first births to older women in the United States, 1970–86. *Vital and Health Statistics* (Series 21). Hyattsville, MD: U.S. Department of Health and Human Services.

Verlinsky, Y., Rechitsky, S., Evsikov, S., White, M., Cieslak, J., Lifchez, A., Valle, J., Moise, J., & Strom, C. M. (1992). Preconception and preimplantation diagnosis for cystic fibrosis. *Prenatal Diagnosis, 12,* 103–110.

Vernon, P. A. (1981). Level I and Level II: A review. *Educational Psychologist, 16,* 45–64.

Vernon, P. A. (1987). Level I and Level II revisited. In S. Modgil & C. Modgil (Eds.), *Arthur Jensen: Consensus and controversy* (pp. 17–24). New York: Falmer Press.

Vietze, P., Falsey, S., O'Connor, S., Sandler, H., Sherrod, K., & Altemeier, W. (1980). Newborn behavioral and interactional characteristics of nonorganic failure-to-thrive infants. In T. Field, S. Goldberg, D. Stern, & A. Sostek (Eds.), *High-risk infants and children* (pp. 5–23). New York: Academic Press.

Vihman, M., (1993). Phonological development. In J. E. Bernthal & N. Bankson (Eds.), *Articulation disorders* (pp. 63–146). Englewood Cliffs, NJ: Prentice-Hall.

Vinovskis, M. A. (1988). *An "epidemic" of adolescent pregnancy?* New York: Oxford University Press.

Vitaro, F., & Pelletier, D. (1991). Assessment of children's social problem-solving skills in hypothetical and actual conflict situations. *Journal of Abnormal Child Psychology, 19,* 505–518.

Vogel, D. A., Lake, M. A., Evans, S., & Karraker, H. (1991). Children's and adults' sex-stereotyped perceptions of infants. *Sex Roles, 24,* 605–616.

Vohr, B. R., & Garcia-Coll, C. T. (1988). Follow-up studies of high-risk low-birth-weight infants: Changing trends. In H. E. Fitzgerald, B. M. Lester, & M. W. Yogman (Eds.), *Theory and research in behavioral pediatrics* (pp. 1–65). New York: Plenum.

Volling, B. L., & Belsky, J. (1992). Contribution of mother–child and father–child relationships to the quality of sibling interaction: A longitudinal study. *Child Development, 63,* 1209–1222.

Vorhees, C. V. (1986). Principles of behavioral teratology. In E. P. Riley & C. V. Vorhees (Eds.), *Handbook of behavioral teratology* (pp. 23–48). New York: Plenum.

Vorhees, C. V., & Mollnow, E. (1987). Behavioral teratogenesis: Long-term influences on behavior from early exposure to environmental agents. In J. D. Osofsky (Ed.), *Handbook of infant development* (2nd ed., pp. 913–971). New York: Wiley.

Voydanoff, P., & Donnelly, B. W. (1990). *Adolescent sexuality and pregnancy.* Newbury Park, CA: Sage.

Vuchinich, S., Hetherington, E. M., Vuchinich, R. A., & Clingempeel, W. G. (1991). Parent-child interaction and gender differences in early adolescents' adaptation to stepfamilies. *Developmental Psychology, 27,* 618–626.

Vurpillot, E. (1968). The development of scanning strategies and their relation to visual differentiation. *Journal of Experimental Child Psychology, 6,* 632–650.

Vurpillot, E., Ruel, J., & Castrec, A. (1977). L'organization perceptive chez le nourrisson: Réponse au tout au á ses éléments. *Bulletin de Psychologie, 327,* 396–405.

Vygotsky, L. S. (1978). *Mind in society: The development of higher mental processes.* Cambridge, MA: Harvard University Press. (Original works published 1930, 1933, and 1935)

Vygotsky, L. S. (1986). *Thought and language* (A. Kozulin, Trans.). Cambridge, MA: MIT Press. (Original work published 1934)

W

Waas, G. A. (1988). Social attributional biases of peer-rejected and aggressive children. *Child Development, 59,* 969–975.

Waber, D. P. (1976). Sex differences in cognition: A function of maturation rate? *Science, 192,* 572–574.

Wachs, T. D. (1975). Relation of infants' performance on Piaget scales between twelve and twenty-four months and their Stanford-Binet performance at thirty-one months. *Child Development, 46,* 929–935.

Waddington, C. H. (1957). *The strategy of the genes.* London: Allen and Unwin.

Waggoner, J. E., & Palermo, D. S. (1989). Betty is a bouncing bubble: Children's comprehension of emotion-descriptive metaphors. *Developmental Psychology, 25,* 152–163.

Wagner, B. M., & Phillips, D. A. (1992). Beyond beliefs: Parent and child behaviors and children's perceived academic competence. *Child Development, 63,* 1380–1391.

Wagner, M. E., Schubert, H. J. P., & Schubert, D. S. P. (1985). Family size effects: A review. *Journal of Genetic Psychology, 146,* 65–78.

Wagner, M. E., Schubert, H. J. P., & Schubert, D. S. P. (1993). Sex-of-sibling effects: Part 1. Gender role, intelligence, achievement, and creativity. In Hayne W. Reese (Ed.), *Advances in child development and behavior* (Vol. 24, pp. 181–214). San Diego: Academic Press.

Walberg, H. J. (1986). Synthesis of research on teaching. In M. C. Wittrock (Ed.), *Handbook of research on teaching* (3rd ed., pp. 214–229). New York: Macmillan.

Walden, T. A., & Ogan, T. A. (1988). The development of social referencing. *Child Development, 59,* 1230–1240.

Walk, R. D., & Gibson, E. J. (1961). A comparative and analytic study of visual depth perception. *Psychological Monographs, 75* (15, Serial No. 519).

Walker, L. J. (1980). Cognitive and perspective-taking prerequisites for moral development. *Child Development, 51,* 131–139.

Walker, L. J. (1988). The development of moral reasoning. In R. Vasta (Ed.), *Annals of child development* (Vol. 5, pp. 33–78). Greenwich, CT: JAI Press.

Walker, L. J. (1989). A longitudinal study of moral reasoning. *Child Development, 60,* 157–166.

Walker, L. J. (1991). Sex differences in moral reasoning. In W. M. Kurtines & J. L. Gewirtz (Eds.), *Handbook of moral behavior and development* (Vol. 2, pp. 333–364). Hillsdale, NJ: Erlbaum.

Walker, L. J., & Moran, T. J. (1991). Moral reasoning in a Communist Chinese society. *Journal of Moral Education, 20,* 139–155.

Walker, L. J., & Richards, B. S. (1979). Stimulating transitions in moral reasoning as a function of stage of cognitive development. *Developmental Psychology, 15,* 95–103.

Walker, L. J., & Taylor, J. H. (1991a). Family interactions and the development of moral reasoning. *Child Development, 62,* 264–283.

Walker, L. J., & Taylor, J. H. (1991b). Stage transitions in moral reasoning: A longitudinal study of developmental processes. *Developmental Psychology, 27,* 330–337.

Walker-Andrews, A. S. (1986). Intermodal perception of expressive behaviors: Relation of eye and voice? *Developmental Psychology, 22,* 373–377.

Walker-Andrews, A. S., & Grolnick, W. (1983). Discrimination of vocal expressions by young infants. *Infant Behavior and Development, 6,* 491–498.

Wallace, J. R., Cunningham, T. F., & Del Monte, V. (1984). Change and stability in self-esteem between late childhood and early adolescence. *Journal of Early Adolescence, 4,* 253–257.

Wallach, G. P. (1984). Later language learning: Syntactic structures and strategies. In G. P. Wallach & K. G. Butler (Eds.), *Language learning disabilities in school age children* (pp. 82-102). Baltimore: Williams and Wilkins.

Wallach, M. A. (1985). Creativity testing and giftedness. In F. D. Horowitz & M. O'Brien (Eds.), *The gifted and talented: Developmental perspectives* (pp. 99–123). Washington, DC: American Psychological Association.

Wallerstein, J. S. (1983). Children of divorce: The psychological tasks of the child. *American Journal of Orthopsychiatry, 53,* 230–243.

Wallerstein, J. S. (1991). The long-term effects of divorce on children: A review. *Journal of the American Academy of Child and Adolescent Psychiatry, 30,* 349–360.

Wallerstein, J. S., & Corbin, S. B. (1989). Daughters of divorce: Report from a ten-year follow-up. *American Journal of Orthopsychiatry, 59,* 593–604.

Wallerstein, J. S., Corbin, S. B., & Lewis, J. M. (1988). Children of divorce: A ten-year study. In E. M. Hetherington & J. Arasteh (Eds.), *Impact of divorce, single parenting, and stepparenting on children* (pp. 198–214). Hillsdale, NJ: Erlbaum.

Wallerstein, J. S., & Kelly, J. B. (1980). *Surviving the break-up: How children and parents cope with divorce.* New York: Basic Books.

Walters, R. H., & Andres, D. (1967). *Punishment procedures and self-control.* Paper presented at the annual meeting of the American Psychological Association, Washington, DC.

Wanska, S. K., & Bedrosian, J. L. (1985). Conversational structure and topic performance in mother-child interaction. *Journal of Speech and Hearing Research, 28,* 579–584.

Warburton, D. (1989). The effect of maternal age on the frequency of trisomy: Change in meiosis or in utero selection? In T. J. Hassold & C. J. Epstein (Eds.), *Molecular and cytogenetic studies of nondisjunction* (pp. 165–181). New York: Alan R. Liss.

Ward, S., Wackman, D., & Wartella, E. (1977). *How children learn to buy: The development of consumer information-processing skills.* Beverly Hills, CA: Sage.

Warren, A. R., & Tate, C. S. (1992). Egocentrism in children's telephone conversations. In R. M. Diaz & L. E. Berk (Eds.), *Private speech: From social interaction to self-regulation* (pp. 245–264). Hillsdale, NJ: Erlbaum.

Warren-Leubecker, A., & Bohannon, J. N., III. (1989). Pragmatics: Language in social contexts. In J. Berko Gleason (Ed.), *The development of language* (2nd ed., pp. 327–368). Columbus, OH: Merrill.

Washington, J., Minde, K., & Goldberg, S. (1986). Temperament in preterm infants: Style and stability. *Journal of the American Academy of Child and Adolescent Psychiatry, 25,* 493–502.

Waterman, A. S. (1985). Identity in context of adolescent psychology. In A. S. Waterman (Ed.), *New Directions for Child Development* (No. 30, pp. 5–24). San Francisco: Jossey-Bass.

Waterman, A. S. (1989). Curricula interventions for identity change: Substantive and ethical considerations. *Journal of Adolescence, 12,* 389–400.

Waters, E. (1978). The reliability and stability of individuals differences in infant-mother attachment. *Child Development, 49,* 483–494.

Waters, H. F. (1993, July 12). Networks under the gun. *Newsweek,* pp. 64–66.

Watkins, B., & Bentovim, A. (1992). The sexual abuse of male children and adolescents: A review of current research. *Journal of Child Psychology and Psychiatry, 33,* 197–248.

Watson, D. J. (1989). Defining and describing whole language. *Elementary School Journal, 90,* 129–141.

Watson, J. B., & Raynor, R. (1920). Conditioned emotional reactions. *Journal of Experimental Psychology, 3,* 1–14.

Watson, J. D., & Crick, F. H. C. (1953). Molecular structure of nucleic acids. *Nature, 171,* 737–738.

Waxman, S. R., & Hatch, T. (1992). Beyond the basics: Preschool children label objects flexibly at multiple hierarchical levels. *Journal of Child Language, 19,* 153–166.

Waxman, S. R., & Senghas, A. (1992). Relations among word meanings in early lexical development. *Developmental Psychology, 28,* 862–873.

Wechsler, D. (1989). *Manual for the Wechsler Preschool and Primary Scale of Intelligence–Revised.* New York: The Psychological Corporation.

Wechsler, D. (1991). *Manual for the Wechsler Intelligence Test for Children–III.* New York: The Psychological Corporation.

Wegman, M. E. (1992). Annual summary of vital statistics—1991. *Pediatrics, 90,* 835–845.

Wehren, A., De Lisi, R., & Arnold, M. (1981). The development of noun definition. *Journal of Child Language, 8,* 165–175.

Weideger, P. (1976). *Menstruation and menopause.* New York: Knopf.

Weil, W. B. (1975). Infantile obesity. In M. Winick (Ed.), *Childhood obesity* (pp. 61–72). New York: Wiley.

Weinraub, M., Clemens, L. P., Sockloff, A., Ethridge, T., Gracely, E., & Myers, B. (1984). The development of sex role stereotypes in the third year: Relationships to gender labeling, gender identity, sex-typed toy preference, and family characteristics. *Child Development, 55,* 1493–1503.

Weinraub, M., & Lewis, M. (1977). The determinants of children's responses to separation. *Monographs of the Society for Research in Child Development, 42* (4, Serial No. 172).

Weinstein, R. S., Marshall, H. H., Sharp, L., & Botkin, M. (1987). Pygmalion and the student: Age and classroom differences in children's awareness of teacher expectations. *Child Development, 58,* 1079–1093.

Weisner, T. S., & Gallimore, R. (1977). My brother's keeper: Child and sibling caretaking. *Current Anthropology, 18,* 169–190.

Weisner, T. S., & Wilson-Mitchell, J. E. (1990). Nonconventional family life-styles and sex typing in six-year-olds. *Child Development, 61,* 1915–1933.

Weiss, B., Dodge, K. A., Bates, J. E., & Pettit, G. S. (1992). Some consequences of early harsh discipline: Child aggression and a maladaptive social information processing style. *Child Development, 63,* 1321–1335.

Weissman, G. (1991). Working with pregnant women at high risk for HIV infections: Outreach and intervention. *Bulletin of the New York Academy of Medicine, 167,* 291–300.

Wellman, H. M. (1977). Preschoolers' understanding of memory relevant variables. *Child Development, 48,* 13–21.

Wellman, H. M. (1985). The child's theory of mind: The development of conceptions of cognition. In S. R. Yussen (Ed.), *The growth of reflection in children* (pp. 169–206). Orlando, FL: Academic Press.

Wellman, H. M. (1988a). First steps in the child's theorizing about mind. In J. W. Astington, P. L. Harris, & D. R. Olson (Eds.), *Developing theories of mind* (pp. 64–92). Cambridge: Cambridge University Press.

Wellman, H. M. (1988b). The early development of memory strategies. In F. E. Weinert & M. Perlmutter (Eds.), *Memory development: Universal changes and individual differences* (pp. 3–30). Hillsdale, NJ: Erlbaum.

Wellman, H. M. (1990). *Children's theories of mind.* Cambridge, MA: MIT Press.

Wellman, H. M., & Banerjee, M. (1991). Mind and emotion: Children's understanding of the emotional consequences of beliefs and desires. *British Journal of Developmental Psychology, 9,* 191–214.

Wellman, H. M., & Bartsch, K. (1988). Young children's reasoning about beliefs. *Cognition, 30,* 239–277.

Wellman, H. M., & Gelman, S. A. (1992). Cognitive development: Foundational theories of core domains. *Annual Review of Psychology, 43,* 337–375.

Wellman, H. M., Somerville, S. C., & Haake, R. J. (1979). Development of search procedures in real-life spatial environments. *Developmental Psychology, 15,* 530–542.

Wellman, H. M., & Woolley, J. (1990). From simple desires to ordinary beliefs: The early development of everyday psychology. *Cognition, 35,* 245–275.

Wells, G. (1985). Preschool literacy-related activities and success in school. In D. R. Olson, N. Torrance, & A. Hildyard (Eds.), *Literacy, language, and learning* (pp. 229–255). Cambridge: Cambridge University Press.

Welsh, M. C., Pennington, B. F., Ozonoff, S., Rouse, B., & McCabe, E. R. B. (1990). Neuropsychology of early-treated phenylketonuria: Specific executive function deficits. *Child Development, 61,* 1697–1713.

Werker, J. F. (1989). Becoming a native listener. *American Scientist, 77,* 54–59.

Werner, E. E. (1989). Children of the Garden Island. *Scientific American, 260*(4), 106–111.

Werner, E. E., & Smith, R. S. (1982). *Vulnerable but invincible.* New York: McGraw-Hill.

Werner, E. E., & Smith, R. S. (1992). *Overcoming the odds: High risk children from birth to adulthood.* Ithaca, NY: Cornell University Press.

Werner, J. S., & Siqueland, E. R. (1978). Visual recognition memory in the preterm infant. *Infant Behavior and Development, 1,* 79–94.

Wertsch, J. V., & Tulviste, P. (1992). L. S. Vygotsky and contemporary developmental psychology. *Developmental Psychology, 28,* 548–557.

Wetzel, J. R. (1987). *American youth: A statistical snapshot.* Washington, DC: William T. Grant Foundation.

Wexler, K., & Culicover, P. (1980). *Formal principles of language acquisition.* Cambridge, MA: MIT Press.

Whalen, C. K. (1983). Hyperactivity, learning problems, and the attention deficit disorders. In T. H. Ollendick & M. Hersen (Eds.), *Handbook of child psychopathology* (pp. 155–199). New York: Plenum.

Whalen, C. K., & Henker, B. (1991). Therapies for hyperactive children: Comparisons, combinations, and compromises. *Journal of Consulting and Clinical Psychology, 59,* 126–137.

Wheeler, M. D. (1991). Physical changes of puberty. *Endocrinology and Metabolism Clinics of North America, 20,* 1–14.

Whisnant, L., & Zegans, L. (1975). A study of attitudes toward menarche in white middle-class American adolescent girls. *American Journal of Psychiatry, 132,* 809–814.

White, B. (1990). *The first three years of life.* New York: Prentice-Hall.

White, B., & Held, R. (1966). Plasticity of sensorimotor development in the human infant. In J. F. Rosenblith & W. Allinsmith (Eds.), *The causes of behavior* (pp. 60–70). Boston: Allyn and Bacon.

White, K. R., Taylor, M. J., & Moss, V. D. (1992). Does research support claims about the benefits of involving parents in early intervention programs? *Review of Educational Research, 62,* 91–125.

White, R. W. (1959). Motivation reconsidered: The concept of competence. *Psychological Review, 66,* 297–333.

White, S. H. (1992). G. Stanley Hall: From philosophy to developmental psychology. *Developmental Psychology, 28,* 25–34.

White, S. H., & Pillemer, D. B. (1979). Childhood amnesia and the development of a socially accessible memory system. In J. F. Kihlstrom & F. J. Evans (Eds.), *Functional disorders of memory* (pp. 29–73). Hillsdale, NJ: Erlbaum.

Whitehurst, G. J. (1982). Language development. In B. B. Wolman (Ed.), *Handbook of developmental psychology* (pp. 367–386). New York: Wiley.

Whitehurst, G. J., Fischel, J. E., Caulfield, M. B., DeBaryshe, B. D., & Valdez-Menchaca, M. C. (1989). Assessment and treatment of early expressive language delay. In P. R. Zelazo & R. Barr (Eds.), *Challenges to developmental paradigms: Implications for assessment and treatment* (pp. 113–135). Hillsdale, NJ: Erlbaum.

Whitehurst, G. J., & Valdez-Menchaca, M. C. (1988). What is the role of reinforcement in early language acquisition? *Child Development, 59,* 430–440.

Whitehurst, G. J., & Vasta, R. (1975). Is language acquired through imitation? *Journal of Psycholinguistic Research, 4,* 37–59.

Whitelaw, A. (1990). Kangaroo baby care: Just a nice experience or an important advance for preterm infants? *Pediatrics, 85,* 604–605.

Whiting, B., & Edwards, C. P. (1988a). *Children of different worlds.* Cambridge, MA: Harvard University Press.

Whiting, B., & Edwards, C. P. (1988b). A cross-cultural analysis of sex differences in the behavior of children aged 3 through 11. In G. Handel (Ed.), *Childhood socialization* (pp. 281–297). New York: Aldine De Gruyter.

Whiting, J. W. M., Burbank, V. K., & Ratner, M. S. (1986). The duration of maidenhood across cultures. In J. B. Lancaster & B. Hamburg (Eds.), *School-age pregnancy and parenthood: Biosocial dimensions* (pp. 273–302). New York: Aldine De Gruyter.

Whitley, B. E. (1983). Sex role orientation and self-esteem: A critical meta-analytic review. *Journal of Personality and Social Psychology, 44,* 765–778.

Wilcox, A. J., & Skjoerven, R. (1992). Birth weight and perinatal mortality: The effect of gestational age. *American Journal of Public Health, 83,* 378–382.

Wilensky, H. L. (1983). Evaluating research and politics: Political legitimacy and consensus as missing variables in the assessment of social policy. In E. Spiro and E. Yuchtman-Yaar (Eds.), *Evaluating the welfare state: Social and political perspectives* (pp. 51–74). New York: Academic Press.

Wille, D. E. (1991). Relation of preterm birth with quality of infant–mother attachment at one year. *Infant Behavior and Development, 14,* 227–240.

Willems, E. P. (1967). Sense of obligation to high school activities as related to school size and marginality of student. *Child Development, 38,* 1247–1260.

Willer, B., Hofferth, S. L., Kisker, E. E., Divine-Hawkins, P., Farquhar, E., & Glantz, F. B. (1991). *The demand and supply of child care in 1990: Joint findings from the National Child Care Survey 1990 and A Profile of Child Care Settings.* Washington, DC: National Association for the Education of Young Children.

Willerman, L. (1979). Effects of families on intellectual development. *American Psychologist, 34,* 923–929.

Williams, B. C. (1990). Immunization coverage among preschool children: The United States and selected countries. *Pediatrics, 86* (6, Part 2), 1052–1055.

Williams, E., & Radin, N. (1993). Paternal involvement, maternal employment, and adolescents' academic achievement: An 11-year follow-up. *American Journal of Orthopsychiatry, 63,* 306–312.

Williams, E., Radin, N., & Allegro, T. (1992). Sex-role attitudes of adolescents reared primarily by their fathers: An 11-year follow-up. *Merrill-Palmer Quarterly, 38,* 457–476.

Williams, J. E., & Best, D. L. (1982). *Measuring sex stereotypes: A thirty-nation study.* Beverly Hills, CA: Sage.

Williams, T. M. (1986). *The impact of television: A natural experiment in three communities.* Orlando, FL: Academic Press.

Wilson, A. L., & Neidich, G. (1991). Infant mortality and public policy. *Social Policy Report of the Society for Research in Child Development, 5*(2).

Wilson, E. O. (1975). *Sociobiology: The new synthesis.* Cambridge, MA: Harvard University Press.

Wilson, M. N. (1986). The black extended family: An analytical consideration. *Developmental Psychology, 22,* 246–258.

Wilson, M. N. (1989). Child development in the context of the black extended family. *American Psychologist, 44,* 380–385.

Wilson, M. N., & Tolson, T. F. J. (1985). *An analysis of adult–child interaction patterns in three-generational black families.* Charlottesville, VA: University of Virginia, Department of Psychology.

Wilson, R. S. (1976). Concordance in physical growth for monozygotic and dizygotic twins. *Annals of Human Biology, 3,* 1–10.

Wilson, R. S. (1983). The Louisville Twin Study: Developmental synchronies in behavior. *Child Development, 54,* 298–316.

Wilson, W. J. (1987). *The truly disadvantaged: The inner city, the underclass, and public policy.* Chicago: University of Chicago Press.

Wimmer, H., & Hartl, M. (1991). Against the Cartesian view of mind: Young children's difficulty with own false beliefs. *British Journal of Developmental Psychology, 9,* 125–138.

Winch, R. F. (1971). *The modern family* (3rd ed.). New York: Holt, Rinehart and Winston.

Winer, G., Craig, R. K., & Weinbaum, E. (1992). Adults' failure on misleading weight-conservation tests: A developmental analysis. *Developmental Psychology, 28,* 109–120.

Winick, M., & Noble, A. (1966). Cellular response in rats during malnutrition at various ages. *Journal of Nutrition, 89,* 300–306.

Winick, M., Rosso, P., & Waterlow, J. (1970). Cellular growth of cerebrum, cerebellum, and brain stem in normal and marasmic children. *Experimental Neurology, 26,* 393–400.

Winner, E. (1986, August). Where pelicans kiss seals. *Psychology Today, 20*(8), 25–35.

Winner, E. (1988). *The point of words: Children's understanding of metaphor and irony.* Cambridge, MA: Harvard University Press.

Winthrop, R. H. (1991). *Dictionary of concepts in cultural anthropology.* New York: Greenwood Press.

Witelson, S. F., & Kigar, D. L. (1988). Anatomical development of the corpus callosum in humans: A review with reference to sex and cognition. In D. L. Molfese & S. J. Segalowitz (Eds.), *Brain lateralization in children* (pp. 35–57). New York: Guilford.

Witherell, C. S., & Edwards, C. P. (1991). Moral versus social-conventional reasoning: A narrative and culture critique. *Journal of Moral Education, 20,* 293–304.

Wohlwill, J. F. (1973). *The study of behavioral development.* New York: Academic Press.

Wolf, A., & Lozoff, B. (1989). Object attachment, thumbsucking, and the passage to sleep. *Journal of the American Academy of Child and Adolescent Psychiatry, 28,* 287–292.

Wolff, P. H. (1963). Observations on the early development of smiling. In B. M. Foss (Ed.), *Determinants of infant behavior* (Vol. 2, pp. 113–138). London: Methuen.

Wolff, P. H. (1966). The causes, controls and organization of behavior in the neonate. *Psychological Issues, 5* (1, Serial No. 17).

Wong-Fillmore, L., Ammon, P., McLaughlin, B., & Ammon, M. S. (1985). *Learning English through bilingual instruction.* Rosslyn, VA: National Clearinghouse for Bilingual Education.

Wood, D. J. (1989). Social interaction as tutoring. In M. H. Bornstein & J. S. Bruner (Eds.), *Interaction in human development.* Hillsdale, NJ: Erlbaum.

Woolley, J. D., & Wellman, H. M. (1990). Young children's understanding of realities, nonrealities, and appearances. *Child Development, 61,* 946–961.

Worobey, J., & Blajda, V. M. (1989). Temperament ratings at 2 weeks, 2 months, and 1 year: Differential stability of activity and emotionality. *Developmental Psychology, 25,* 257–263.

Wright, J. D., Huston, A. C., Ross, R. P., Clavert, S. L., Rolandelli, D., Weeks, L. A., Raeissi, P., & Potts, R. (1984). Pace and continuity of television programs: Effects on children's attention and comprehension. *Developmental Psychology, 20,* 653–666.

Y

Yarrow, M. R., Campbell, J. D., & Burton, R. V. (1970). Recollections of childhood: A study of the retrospective method. *Monographs of the Society for Research in Child Development, 35* (5, Serial No. 138).

Yarrow, M. R., Scott, P. M., & Waxler, C. Z. (1973). Learning concern for others. *Developmental Psychology, 8,* 240–260.

Yazigi, R. A., Odem, R. R., & Polakoski, K. L. (1991). Demonstration of specific binding of cocaine to human spermatozoa. *Journal of the American Medical Association, 266,* 1956–1959.

Yeates, K. O., MacPhee, D., Campbell, F. A., & Ramey, C. T. (1983). Maternal IQ and home environment as determinants of early childhood intellectual competence: A developmental analysis. *Developmental Psychology, 19,* 731–739.

Yeates, K. O., Schultz, L. H., & Selman, R. L. (1991). The development of interpersonal negotiation strategies in thought and action: A social-cognitive link to behavioral adjustment and social status. *Merrill-Palmer Quarterly, 37,* 369–405.

Yogman, M. W. (1981). Development of the father–infant relationship. In H. Fitzgerald, B. Lester, & M. W. Yogman (Eds.), *Theory and research in behavioral pediatrics* (Vol. 1, pp. 221–279). New York: Plenum.

Yonas, A., Arterberry, M. E., & Granrud, C. E. (1987). Four-month-old infants' sensitivity to binocular and kinetic information for three-dimensional-object shape. *Child Development, 58,* 910-917.

Yonas, A., Granrud, E. C., Arterberry, M. E., & Hanson, B. L. (1986). Infants' distance perception from linear perspective and texture gradients. *Infant Behavior and Development, 9,* 247–256.

Yonas, A., & Hartman, B. (1993). Perceiving the affordance of contact in four- and five-month-old infants. *Child Development, 64,* 298–308.

Young, K. T. (1990). American conceptions of infant development from 1955 to 1984: What the experts are telling parents. *Child Development, 61,* 17–28.

Youniss, J. (1980). *Parents and peers in social development: A Piagetian-Sullivan perspective.* Chicago: University of Chicago Press.

Youniss, J., & Smollar, J. (1986). *Adolescent relations with mothers, fathers, and friends.* Chicago: University of Chicago Press.

Yuill, N., & Perner, J. (1988). Intentionality and knowledge in children's judgments of actor's responsibility and recipient's emotional reaction. *Developmental Psychology, 24,* 358–365.

Z

Zahavi, S., & Asher, S. R. (1978). The effect of verbal instructions on preschool children's aggressive behavior. *Journal of School Psychology, 16,* 146–153.

Zahn-Waxler, C., Cole, P. M., & Barrett, K. C. (1991). Guilt and empathy: Sex differences and implications for the development of depression. In J. Garber & K. A. Dodge (Eds.), *The development of emotion regulation and dysregulation* (pp. 243–272). Cambridge: Cambridge University Press.

Zahn-Waxler, C., Kochanska, G., Krupnick, J., & McKnew, D. (1990). Patterns of guilt in children of depressed and well mothers. *Developmental Psychology, 26,* 51–59.

Zahn-Waxler, C., & Radke-Yarrow, M. (1990). The origins of empathic concern. *Motivation and Emotion, 14,* 107–130.

Zahn-Waxler, C., Radke-Yarrow, M., & King, R. M. (1979). Childrearing and children's prosocial initiations toward victims of distress. *Child Development, 50,* 319–330.

Zahn-Waxler, C., Radke-Yarrow, M., Wagner, E., & Chapman, M. (1992). Development of concern for others. *Developmental Psychology, 28,* 126–136.

Zahn-Waxler, C., Robinson, J. L., & Emde, R. N. (1992). The development of empathy in twins. *Developmental Psychology, 28,* 1038–1047.

Zajonc, R. B. (1976). Family configuration and intelligence. *Science, 192,* 227–236.

Zajonc, R. B., & Markus, G. B. (1975). Birth order and intellectual development. *Psychological Review, 82,* 74–88.

Zajonc, R. B., Markus, H., & Markus, G. B. (1979). The birth order puzzle. *Journal of Personality and Social Psychology, 37,* 1325–1341.

Zarbatany, L., Hartmann, D., & Gelfand, D. (1985). Why does

children's generosity increase with age: Susceptibility to experimenter influence or altruism? *Child Development, 56,* 746–756.

Zaslow, M. J. (1989). Sex differences in children's response to parental divorce: 2. Samples, variables, ages, and sources. *American Journal of Orthopsychiatry, 59,* 118–141.

Zaslow, M. J., Rabinovich, B. A., & Suwalsky, J. T. (1991). From maternal employment to child outcomes: Preexisting group differences and moderating variables. In J. V. Lerner & N. L. Galambos (Eds.), *Employed mothers and their children* (pp. 237–282). New York: Garland.

Zelazo, P. R. (1983). The development of walking: New findings on old assumptions. *Journal of Motor Behavior, 2,* 99–137.

Zelazo, P. R., Zelazo, N. A., & Kolb, S. (1972). "Walking" in the newborn. *Science, 176,* 314–315.

Zeskind, P. S., & Ramey, C. T. (1978). Fetal malnutrition: An experimental study of its consequences on infant development in two caregiving environments. *Child Development, 49,* 1155–1162.

Zeskind, P. S., & Ramey, C. T. (1981). Preventing intellectual and interactional sequelae of fetal malnutrition: A longitudinal, transactional, and synergistic approach to development. *Child Development, 52,* 213–218.

Zhang, J., Cai, W., & Lee, D. J. (1992). Occupational hazards and pregnancy outcomes. *American Journal of Industrial Medicine, 21,* 397–408.

Zigler, E. F., Abelson, W. D., & Seitz, V. (1973). Motivational factors in the performance of economically disadvantaged children on the Peabody Picture Vocabulary Test. *Child Development, 44,* 294–303.

Zigler, E. F., & Finn-Stevenson, M. (1992). Applied developmental psychology. In M. H. Bornstein & M. E. Lamb (Eds.), *Developmental psychology: An advanced textbook* (3rd ed., pp. 677–729). Hillsdale, NJ: Erlbaum.

Zigler, E. F., & Gilman, E. (1993). Day care in America: What is needed? *Pediatrics, 91,* 175–178.

Zigler, E. F., & Hall, N. W. (1989). Physical child abuse in America: Past, present, and future. In D. Cicchetti & V. Carlson (Eds.), *Child maltreatment* (pp. 203–253). New York: Cambridge University Press.

Zigler, E.F., & Seitz, V. (1982). Social policy and intelligence. In R. J. Sternberg (Ed.), *Handbook of human intelligence* (pp. 586–641). Cambridge: Cambridge University Press.

Zimmerman, B. J. (1990). Self-regulation learning and academic achievement: An overview. *Educational Psychologist, 25,* 3–18.

Zuckerman, B., Frank, D. A., & Hingson, R. (1989). Effects of maternal marijuana and cocaine use on fetal growth. *New England Journal of Medicine, 320,* 762–768.

Zukow, P. G. (1986). The relationship between interaction with the caregiver and the emergence of play activities during the one-word period. *British Journal of Developmental Psychology, 4,* 223–234.

Zukow, P. G. (1989). Siblings as effective socializing agents: Evidence from central Mexico. In P. G. Zukow (Ed.), *Sibling interaction across cultures* (pp. 79–105). New York: Springer-Verlag.

Zuraivin, S. J. (1991). Research definitions of child physical abuse and neglect: Current problems. In R. H. Starr, Jr., & D. A. Wolfe (Eds.), *The effects of child abuse and neglect* (pp. 100–128). New York: Guilford.

Name Index

Hudson, J. A., 285, 289
Huebner, R. R., 397
Huesmann, L. R., 508n, 509, 624, 625n
Hughes, M., 600
Huie, K. S., 607
Hummel, R. C., 496
Humphrey, G. K., 163
Humphrey, H. E. B., 103
Humphrey, P., 183n
Humphrey, T., 154
Humphreys, A. P., 605
Humphreys, L. G., 318, 322
Hunt, J. McV., 36, 171, 231, 319
Hunter, J. E., 325
Hunter, R. F., 325
Hunter, R. S., 592
Huntington, L., 139
Husén, T., 643
Huston, A. C., 411, 518, 519, 520, 521, 522, 523, 524, 528, 532, 533, 539, 540, 549, 621, 623, 624, 625, 626, 627
Huston-Stein, A., 540, 627
Huttenlocher, J., 240, 287, 365
Huttunen, M. O., 105
Hwang, P., 412
Hyde, J. S., 544n, 545, 548, 549
Hymel, S., 527, 608
Hynd, G. W., 279

I

Iannotti, R. J., 56n, 57, 460, 551
Iler, I., 532, 533
Ilg, F. L., 11
Imperato-McGinley, J., 528
Ingersoll, G. M., 443
Ingram, D., 361, 362n
Inhelder, B., 222, 235, 243, 245, 248, 250
Inoff-Germain, G., 550
International Education Association, 643
Intons-Peterson, M. J., 526
Irvine, J. J., 447
Isaacs, S., 613
Isabella, R. A., 413, 421
Israelashvili, R., 425
Istvan, J., 105
Izard, C. E., 392, 395, 396n, 397, 398, 422

J

Jacklin, C. N., 365, 527, 532, 543, 549
Jackson, P. W., 638
Jackson-Cook, C., 85, 86
Jacobs, F. H., 428
Jacobs, J. E., 180, 522, 530
Jacobs, J. W., 281
Jacobson, J. L., 102, 103, 602

Jacobson, L., 640
Jacobson, S. W., 103
Jacobvitz, D., 594
Jambor, T. W., 603, 603n
James, S. R., 181, 210
James, W., 434
Jamison, W., 540
Janssens, J. M. A. M., 609
Jarrett, O. S., 640
Jencks, C., 327
Jenkins, E., 297
Jensen, A. R., 122, 310n, 313, 323, 326, 327, 330, 331, 332, 338
Jensen, M. D., 104
Jernigan, L. P., 450
Johnson, C. L., 201
Johnson, E. S., 546
Johnson, G. D., 525
Johnson, Jacqueline S., 356, 356n
Johnson, James E., 253
Johnson, Jeanne, 359
Johnson, M. L., 178
Johnson, W. F., 477
Johnston, F. E., 209n
Johnston, J. R., 372, 581
Jones, C. P., 379
Jones, E. F., 34n, 195
Jones, G. P., 465
Jones, J., 641
Jones, L. E., 137
Jones, M. C., 193
Jones, N. A., 409
Jones, P. J. H., 100
Jones, R. L., 642
Jones, S. S., 396
Jordan, B., 109
Jorgensen, M., 189
Jouriles, E. N., 561
Jusczyk, P. W., 156, 358

K

Kaczala, C. M., 446
Kagan, J., 170, 283, 283n, 391, 409, 410, 417n, 422, 473
Kahn, P. H., Jr., 496
Kail, R., 270, 271n, 280
Kain, E. L., 573
Kaitz, M., 146
Kaler, S. R., 98, 114, 502
Kalter, N., 580
Kamerman, S. B., 27, 117, 588
Kamphaus, R. W., 323, 334
Kandall, S. R., 144
Kandel, D. B., 451, 465, 465n, 568, 618
Kanner, A. D., 465
Kantor, D., 560, 561
Kao, T., 117
Kaplan, B. H., 105
Kaplan, N., 424

Kaplan, R. M., 332
Karabenick, J. D., 380
Karadsheh, R., 368
Karmiloff-Smith, A., 376
Karraker, K. H., 529
Katchadourian, H., 180, 189, 199
Katz, M., 81
Katz, V. L., 112
Kaufman, A. S., 318, 323, 334
Kaufman, N. L., 318, 323, 334
Kavale, K., 275
Kavanaugh, K., 427
Kawai, M., 412
Kaye, K., 99, 226
Kazdin, A. E., 512
Keane, S. P., 610
Kearins, J. M., 260
Kearsley, R. B., 391, 417n
Keating, D., 251, 458
Keats, J. G., 539
Keeney, T. J., 280
Keiding, N., 189
Keil, F. C., 274, 368
Keljo, K., 494
Keller, A., 438
Keller, M., 463
Kelley, M. L., 571
Kelly, J. B., 579
Keltikangas-Järvinen, L., 394
Kempe, C. H., 591, 595
Kempe, R. S., 595
Kendrick, C., 574, 575
Kennedy, C. B., 391
Kennedy, J. M., 234
Kennell, J., 111
Keogh, B. K., 412, 642
Keppler, A., 113
Kermoian, R., 161
Kerns, K. A., 546
Kerr, B. A., 531
Kessel, F. S., 459, 459n, 460
Kessen, W., 132, 158
Kestenbaum, R., 167
Ketterlinus, R. D., 106
Key, C. B., 324
Kidd, K. K., 121, 330
Kigar, D. L., 206
Kilbride, J. E., 152
Kilbride, P. L., 152
Killen, M., 499
Kilner, L. A., 189, 443
Kilstrom, N., 592
Kimball, M. M., 625
Kimmerly, N. L., 422
King, R. M., 476
Kinney, H. C., 144
Kinsbourne, M., 205
Kinsey, A. C., 197
Kinsman, C. A., 45
Kirby, D., 200
Kiser, L. J., 421
Kisker, E. E., 196, 197, 586n

Kistner, J., 405
Klahr, D., 22, 23, 266, 276
Klatzky, R. L., 269
Kleinke, C. L., 524
Klenk, L., 258
Klimes-Dougan, B., 405
Kline, M., 581
Klineberg, O., 322
Knevel, C. R., 319
Knittle, J. L., 212
Knobloch, H., 11n, 131n, 132
Knox, D., 577n
Kochanska, G., 51, 410, 476, 503, 507, 606
Kodroff, J. K., 251
Koeske, R. D., 21
Kogan, N., 343, 344
Kohlberg, L., 485, 487, 488, 489, 489n, 490, 492, 493, 494, 495, 496, 538
Kohn, M. L., 569
Kojima, H., 411
Kolata, G. B., 88n
Kolb, S., 132
Kolbe, R. H., 625
Koller, H., 81
Koneya, M., 632
Kopp, C. B., 26n, 83, 98, 114, 400, 436, 502, 503, 503n, 504n, 505
Korn, S. J., 413
Korner, A. F., 139, 410
Kornhaber, M., 345
Koslowski, B., 140
Kosslyn, S. M., 284
Kouba, V. L., 299
Kovaric, P., 624, 628n
Kowalski, P. S., 447
Kozberg, S. F., 496
Kozol, J., 340
Kozulin, A., 254
Krakow, J. B., 26n, 503, 503n
Kramer, M. D., 113
Kramer, R., 404
Kramer, T. L., 465
Kranz, R., 201
Kranzler, J. H., 313
Krasnor, L. R., 467
Krebs, D., 458, 490
Krechevsky, M., 345
Kreeger, L., 212
Krehbiel, G., 612
Kreitler, H., 313
Kreitler, S., 313
Kremenitzer, J. P., 157
Kreutzer, M. A., 292
Kreutzer, T., 171, 171n
Kricker, A., 101
Kristjansson, B., 100
Kritt, D., 439
Kroonenberg, P. M., 420
Kruger, A. C., 379, 500

Schubert, H. J. P., 535, 573
Schul, Y., 617
Schultz, L. H., 467
Schumacher, G. M., 286
Schunk, D. H., 447
Schwartz, S. S., 629
Schwartz-Bickenbach, D., 100
Schweinhart, L. J., 340
Scott, P. M., 57, 478
Scribner, S., 252, 282
Sears, R. R., 16, 18, 50, 415
Seay, B., 415
Sebald, H., 618
Secord, P. F., 454
Segal, N. L., 331
Seitz, V., 323, 324, 331, 334
Seligman, M. E. P., 144
Seligmann, J., 200
Selkow, P., 534
Sellers, C., 195
Selman, R. L., 457, 455, 457,
    457n, 458, 458n, 461, 462,
    463, 467, 490
Seltzer, V., 210
Senghas, A., 369
Serafica, F. C., 460
Serbin, L. A., 522, 523, 523n,
    524, 527, 532, 533, 534, 539
Serlin, R. C., 497
Sever, J. L., 102n
Shaffer, D., 451
Shahar, S., 8
Shainess, N., 190
Shannon, D. C., 144
Shannon, F. T., 210
Shapiro, E. K., 634, 638
Shapiro, S., 106
Shatz, M., 240
Shaughnessy, M. F., 344
Shavelson, R., 442n
Shea, E., 421
Shedler, J., 619
Sheingold, K., 631
Shepherd, P. A., 319
Sherif, M., 613
Sherman, D., 561, 593
Sherman, J., 524
Sherman, M., 324
Sherman, T., 230
Shettles, L. B., 81, 93
Shields, J. W., 183
Shields, P. J., 143
Shiffrin, R. M., 22, 266, 267n, 268
Shiffrin, V., 397
Shinn, Marybeth, 570
Shinn, Millicent W., 10
Shipman, G., 190
Shipman, V. C., 339
Shively, C., 559
Shoda, Y., 504, 505, 507
Shrager, J., 297
Shu, J., 576

Shucard, J., 545
Shukla, D., 251
Shultz, T. R., 437, 454
Shure, M. B., 467, 469
Shweder, R. A., 499
Shyi, G., 146
Sidle, A. L., 240
Siegal, M., 437, 538
Siegel, A. W., 245
Siegel, I. E., 171
Siegel, L. S., 242
Siegler, R. S., 12, 24, 63, 64, 240,
    242, 253, 266, 268, 270,
    273, 280, 285, 287, 295,
    297, 298, 308, 309n, 322
Sigafoos, A. D., 146
Sigelman, C. K., 500
Sigman, M. D., 146
Signorella, M. L., 523, 524, 540,
    542
Signorielli, N., 534
Sikora, D. M., 66
Silverberg, S., 567
Silverman, N., 33
Simkin, P., 113
Simmons, R. G., 193, 194, 443,
    637, 637n, 638
Simons, C., 469
Simons, R. L., 27, 561, 570n,
    592, 593
Simourd, L., 455
Simpson, J. A., 451
Singer, D. G., 234, 604, 622,
    624, 627
Singer, J. L., 234, 604, 622, 624,
    627
Singer, L. T., 145, 145n, 327
Singh, S., 195
Siqueland, E. R., 143, 145
Sitarenios, G., 547
Skeels, H. M., 330
Skinner, B. F., 18, 351
Skinner, E. A., 445
Skinner, J. D., 213
Skinner, M. L., 580
Skjoerven, R., 114
Skodak, M., 330
Skouteris, H., 164
Slaby, R. G., 508, 509, 513, 538,
    624
Slade, A., 257, 424
Slater, A., 166, 167
Slavin, R. E., 635, 641, 642
Slobin, D. I., 357, 370, 372, 373,
    376
Slomkowski, C. L., 412
Slone, D., 106
Slotkin, T. A., 108
Smetana, J. G., 484, 498, 499
Smilansky, S., 604n
Smiley, S. S., 277
Smith, Carole L., 381

Smith, Caroline, 535
Smith, D. J., 510
Smith, H. W., 605
Smith, I. D., 443
Smith, J., 523, 524
Smith, L. D., 4, 101
Smith, M. C., 455, 603n
Smith, M. L., 633
Smith, M. S., 338
Smith, P. K., 605, 606
Smith, Robin, 623
Smith, Romanyne A., 505
Smith, Ruth S., 118, 561
Smith, Shelley D., 642
Smith, Shiela, 342, 443
Smith, V. E., 453
Smithells, J., 522
Smollar, J., 465
Smolucha, F., 257
Smoot, D. L., 610
Smuts, B. B., 558
Snarey, J. R., 489, 494, 496
Snidman, N., 409
Snow, C. E., 353, 355
Snyder, J. J., 510
Snyder, L., 365, 412
Snyder-McLean, L., 356
Sobesky, W. E., 490
Sobol, A. M., 114
Society for Research in Child
    Development, 65, 66n
Sockett, H., 495
Sodian, B., 291, 437
Soken, H. H., 168
Sokoloff, B. Z., 87
Solimano, G., 211
Solnit, A. J., 214
Solomon, J., 418
Solomon, S. K., 464
Somberg, D. R., 456
Somerville, S. C., 277n, 278
Sommerville, J., 7
Sonenstein, F. L., 195
Sonnenschein, S., 380
Sontag, C. W., 322
Sophian, C., 297
Sorce, J., 402
Sorell, G. T., 496
Sosa, R., 111
Spade, J., 641
Spanier, G. B., 559
Spearman, C., 311
Speer, J. R., 292
Spelke, E. S., 167, 168, 274, 297
Spellacy, W. N., 106
Spence, J. T., 536, 537
Spence, M. J., 96, 156
Spencer, C., 245
Spencer, M. B., 453
Sperhac, A. M., 181, 210
Sperry, L. L., 53, 401
Spiker, D., 84

Spinetta, J., 591
Spirito, A., 451
Spitz, R. A., 398, 420
Spivack, G., 467, 469
Spock, B., 135
Sprafkin, C., 522
Sprafkin, J., 512, 621n, 624,
    626, 628
Spreen, O., 202, 203, 206
Spuhl, S., 257
Sroufe, L. A., 171, 171n, 395,
    396, 399, 423, 424, 426,
    427, 428, 565, 594, 611
St James-Roberts, I., 138, 139n
St. Peters, M., 49, 628n
Staats, A., 352
Stabb, S. D., 612
Stack, D. M., 155
Stafford, F. P., 566
Stanbury, J. B., 78n
Stange, T., 533, 53n
Stangor, C., 539
Stanhope, L., 47
Stankov, L., 328
Stanley, J. C., 544n, 547
Stanley-Hagan, M., 578, 579, 580
Stanovich, K. E., 630
Stanowicz, L., 377
Stanton, J. C., 442n
Stapp, J., 536, 537
Stark, L. J., 19
Starkey, P., 297
Stattin, H., 193, 194
Stechler, G., 113
Steele, H., 424
Steele, M., 424
Stein, A. H., 522
Stein, Z., 104
Steinberg, L. D., 192, 193, 394,
    564, 567, 568, 586, 589, 647
Steiner, J. E., 142, 155
Stenberg, C., 397
Stene, E., 84
Stene, J., 84
Stengel-Rutkowski, S., 84
Stephan, C. W., 193, 609
Stephens, B. R., 165
Sterling, C. W., 631n
Stern, D. N., 421
Stern, M., 529
Sternberg, K. J., 428, 593
Sternberg, R. J., 274, 308, 314,
    315, 318, 331, 332, 342, 344
Sternglanz, S. H., 534
Stevens, F., 11n
Stevens, J. H., 572
Stevenson, H. W., 27, 447, 522,
    545, 643, 644, 645n, 646
Stevenson, R., 367
Stevenson-Hinde, J., 412
Stewart, A. J., 61
Stewart, D. A., 84

Wallace, J. R., 442
Wallach, G. P., 376
Wallach, M. A., 342, 343, 344
Wallerstein, J. S., 578, 579, 580
Walters, G. C., 590
Walters, R. H., 480
Walther, F. J., 114
Wang, Q., 359
Wanska, S. K., 378
Warburton, D., 84
Ward, S., 626
Warren, A. R., 380
Warren, B. M., 295, 295n
Warren, D., 606
Warren, M. P., 192
Warren-Leubecker, A., 353, 357, 380
Warshak, R. A., 534, 580
Wartella, E., 626
Washington, J., 413
Waterlow, J., 104
Waterman, A. S., 451, 452
Waters, E., 396, 419
Waters, H. F., 624
Watkins, Bill, 591
Watkins, Bruce A., 621, 626, 627
Watkinson, B., 99, 100
Watson, D. J., 296
Watson, J. B., 18, 390
Watson, J. D., 72
Watson, K. S., 603, 603n
Watson, M. W., 242
Waxler, C. Z., 57, 478
Waxman, S. R., 369, 370
Way, P. O., 103
Wechsler, D., 317
Wegman, M. E., 33, 34n, 117n
Wehren, A., 368
Weideger, P., 190
Weikart, D. P., 340
Weil, W. B., 212
Weinbaum, E., 247, 247n
Weinberg, M., 197
Weinberg, R. A., 120, 122, 124, 329n, 331, 332
Weinberger, H. L., 208

Weinraub, M., 417, 520, 524, 534
Weinstein, R. S., 640
Weiskopf, S., 158
Weisner, T. S., 532, 601
Weiss, B., 456
Weiss, R. J., 551
Weissman, G., 103
Weisz, J. R., 244, 401, 464
Well, A. D., 277, 277n
Wellman, H. M., 242, 245, 274, 277n, 278, 280, 291, 292, 380, 436, 437
Wells, G., 297
Welsh, M. C., 77
Werker, J. F., 358
Werner, E. E., 118, 561
Werner, J. S., 143, 145
Wertsch, J. V., 29, 254, 260, 261
West, M. J., 480
Westra, T., 152, 152n
Wetzel, J. R., 37
Wexler, K., 357
Whalen, C. K., 26, 279
Whalley, J., 113
Whatley, J. L., 602
Wheeler, M. D., 179, 188
Whisnant, L., 191
Whitaker, H. A., 205
Whitbeck, L. B., 570n, 593
White, A. J., 524
White, B., 153, 171, 391
White, K. R., 341
White, R. W., 444
White, S. H., 11, 285
Whitebook, M., 587
Whitehouse, R. H., 180, 182n
Whitehurst, G. J., 19, 352, 363
Whitelaw, A., 115
Whiting, B., 508, 525, 527, 531, 601, 607
Whiting, J. W. M., 189
Whitley, B. E., 537
Whitten, P., 558, 559
Wiesel, T. N., 207
Wikner, K., 155
Wilcox, A. J., 114

Wilensky, H. L., 35
Wille, D. E., 422
Willems, E. P., 634
Willer, B., 585, 586n, 587
Willerman, L., 121, 329, 331, 331n
Williams, B. C., 213, 214n
Williams, E., 584, 585
Williams, G. A., 642
Williams, J. E., 519
Williams, T. M., 621
Williard, J. C., 611
Wilson, A. L., 144
Wilson, E. O., 474
Wilson, K. S., 602
Wilson, M. N., 571, 572
Wilson, R. S., 124, 208, 328, 329n
Wilson, W. J., 340
Wilson-Mitchell, J. E., 532
Wimbush, D. D., 571
Wimmer, H., 291, 437
Winch, R. F., 559
Winegar, A., 106
Winer, G., 247, 247n
Winick, M., 104, 212
Winner, E., 234, 235n, 368, 369, 381
Winthrop, R. H., 52
Witelson, S. F., 206
Witherell, C. S., 499
Wohlwill, J. F., 59
Wolf, A., 135
Wolff, P. H., 134n, 396
Wong Fillmore, L., 384
Wood, D. J., 256
Wood, P., 463
Woodsmall, L., 365
Woodward, L., 112
Woody, E. Z., 212
Woolley, J. D., 242, 436
Worobey, J., 409
Wright, H. F., 601
Wright, J. C., 623
Wright, J. D., 623
Wright, K., 399

Wright, V. C., 450, 567
Wunsch, J. P., 396
Wyer, M. M., 581
Wyngaarden, J. B., 78n

Y

Yarrow, M. R., 46, 50, 57, 478
Yazigi, R. A., 99
Yeates, K. O., 336, 467
Yogman, M. W., 425
Yonas, A., 151, 155, 159, 160, 160n, 275
Young, K. T., 12n
Youniss, J., 461, 465, 486
Yuill, N., 483
Yussen, S. R., 616

Z

Zafran, E. I., 87
Zahavi, S., 512
Zahn-Waxler, C., 56n, 57, 404, 405, 476, 544n, 548, 549, 551
Zajonc, R. B., 337
Zakin, D. F., 194
Zalar, M. K., 104
Zalenski, R., 292
Zarbatany, L., 478, 534
Zaslow, M. J., 580, 584
Zegans, L., 191
Zeiss, C., 584
Zelazo, N. A., 132
Zelazo, P. R., 132, 391, 417n
Zeskind, P. S., 105, 137, 139
Zhang, J., 81
Zigler, E. F., 36, 37, 148, 323, 324, 331, 334, 428, 451, 587, 593, 594
Zimmerman, B. J., 293
Zimmerman, M., 447
Zimmerman, R., 415
Zola-Morgan, S., 285
Zuckerman, B., 99
Zuckerman, H., 531
Zukow, P. G., 257
Zuraivin, S. J., 590

Subject Index

Child care. *See* Day care
Child Development (journal of the Society for Research in Child Development), 13
Child development
  basic themes and issues, 3–6
  field of, 2–3, 13, 22, 254
  historical foundations, 6–13
Childhood, historical views of, 7–10
Child maltreatment, 590–595
  and attachment, 415, 421–422
  causes of, 27, 590–593
  and community characteristics, 593
  crisis intervention for, 594
  forms of
    emotional neglect, 565, 590
    physical abuse, 405, 590, 592
    physical neglect, 590
    psychological abuse, 590
    sexual abuse, 590, 591
  incidence, 590, 591
  infants at risk for, 114
  intergenerational continuity of, 591, 594
  of preterm infants, 114
  preventing, 593–595
  proving in court, 594
  public policy and, 33
  victims of, 355, 415, 421–422, 593
  see also Neglected children
Child neglect. *See* Child maltreatment; Neglected children
Child rearing
  adapting to children's development, 566–568
  advice of experts on, 11–12
  consistency in, 413, 561, 566
  costs of, 559
  historical views of, 8
  inconsistency in, 413
  peer-only rearing, 600–601
  styles of (*see* Parenting styles)
  see also Child-rearing practices
Child-rearing practices
  in African-American families, 571, 572
  and behaviorism, 18
  in Chinese families, 570–571
  culture and, 413, 570–571
  dimensions of, 563
  and empathy, 405
  ethnic differences in, 570–571
  gender stereotyping in, 529–532
  among the !Kung, 30

and moral reasoning, 493
and parents' social networks, 561
research methods, 50
and self-esteem, 443–444
temperament and, 413
see also Child rearing; Parent–child relationship
Children's Defense Fund, 37–38
Child support payments, 37
Chimpanzees. *See* Apes and monkeys
China
  education in, 641
  only children in, 576, 577
  population growth in, 576, 577
Chinese infants
  language acquisition in, 356
  temperament in, 411
Chorion, 92
Chorionic villus sampling, 86, 88, 89, 92n
Chromosomal abnormalities, 81–86, 87
Chromosomes, 72
  mapping, 88
  mosaic pattern, in Down syndrome, 83
  pairs of, 72–73
  sex, 76, 84–86
Chronological age (CA), 320
Circular reaction
  primary, 224, 225
  secondary, 224, 226, 228
  tertiary, 224, 227
Circumcision, 155
Classical conditioning, 18, 141
  in emotional development, 390
  extinction in, 142
  of infants, 18, 141–143
  in language development, 352
  states of arousal and, 143
Classification, 21, 239, 241
  hierarchical, 243, 244
Classrooms
  ability grouping in, 641
  computers in, 628–631
  KEEP, 259, 635
  Piagetian, 21, 253, 258
  seating arrangements in, 632
  traditional versus open, 634–635
  Vygotskian, 258
  see also Schooling; Teachers
Cleft palate, 105
Clinical interview
  Kohlberg's use of, 482, 485–486, 490

limitations of, 46, 50–51
Piaget's use of, 46, 49–51, 481–482
Clinical method, 16, 51–52
Cliques, 614
Cocaine
  and prenatal development, 99
Codominance, 80
Cognition, 18–19, 219
  emotion and, 392–393
  see also Social cognition
Cognitive abilities. *See* Intelligence
Cognitive development
  bilingualism and, 385
  emotional development and, 391–392, 404
  empathy and, 404
  and gender constancy, 538
  and gender stereotypes, 521–523
  gender-role identity and, 538–540
  and identity formation, 452
  language development and, 219–220, 231–232, 254–257
  peer interaction and, 255, 603
  perception and, 169, 275–276
  and perspective taking, 458
  play and, 232–234, 257
  self-control and, 503–505
  and social cognition, 433–434
  social origins of, 26, 256–257
  and temperament, 412
  see also Information-processing approach; Intellectual development; Piaget's theory of cognitive development; Sociocultural theory (Vygotsky's)
Cognitive-developmental discrepancy theory, 391–392
Cognitive maps, 245
Cohort effects, 60–61, 62
Color blindness, 81
Color perception, 157–158
Compliance, 502
  self-control and, 502–503
  sex-related differences in, 544, 549
  see also Conformity
Componential analyses, of IQ scores, 313
Comprehension, language, 363, 367, 370
Comprehension monitoring, 293, 380
Computer-assisted instruction (CAI), 629–630

Computer programming, 630
Computers, 628–632
  advantages of, 629–630
  concerns about, 631
  video games, 631
Concordance rate, 120–122
Concrete operational stage (Piaget's), 20
  conservation in, 243, 244, 246
  decentration in, 243, 244
  hierarchical classification in, 243, 244
  horizontal décalage in, 243, 246
  limitations of, 245–246
  recent research on, 246–247
  reversibility in, 243, 244
  seriation in, 243, 244
  spatial operations in, 243, 244, 246
  transitive inference in, 243, 244, 246
Conditioned response (CR), 142–143
Conditioned stimulus (CS), 142–143
Confluence model, 337–338, 379
Conformity
  in adolescence, 617–618
  to peer group norms, 613, 614–615
  to social norms, and moral development, 480–481
Conscience
  development of, 476, 477n
  Erikson's concept of, 477n
  ethical principles of, 489
  Freud's concept of, 14, 475–476
  recent psychoanalytic ideas, 477
Conservation, 236, 238
  concrete operational stage and, 243, 244
  cultural differences in, 246
  gender constancy and, 538
  of liquid, 236–237, 244, 272–273
  of mass, 273
  of number, 297n
  order of tasks, 246
  preoperational stage and, 236–238
  of weight, 247, 273
Consortium for Longitudinal Studies, 339
Construction, and moral development, 481
Constructivist approach, to memory, 286
Contexts for development, 24, 26–27, 557–648

Contingency cues, and infant self-recognition, 435
Continuous development, 5, 6, 8, 22
  and stance of major developmental theories, 31
Contraception
  access to, adolescents', 200
  sex education and, 199
  use of, adolescents', 196
Contrast sensitivity, 161–163
Control deficiency, in memory strategies, 280
Control processes, or mental strategies, 267
Conventional level, in Kohlberg's theory, 488, 496, 497–498
Convergent thinking, 312, 342–343
Conversation
  and language development, 378, 379
  prelinguistic, 360–361
  strategies for engaging in, 378
Cooing, 359
Cooley's anemia, 78
Cooperative learning, 258–260, 642
Cooperative play, 602, 604
Coregulation, 566–567
Corpus callosum, 185, 206
Corpus luteum, 90
Correlation, genetic–environmental, 123–124
  active, 124
  evocative, 123–124
  passive, 123–124
Correlation coefficient, 55
Correlational design, 54–56
Cosleeping, parent–infant, 135
Counting skills, 297
Court proceedings
  on child maltreatment, 594
  children's eyewitness memory in, 290
  and grandparent visitation rights, 581
Cradle-board infants, 150
Crawling, 150, 158
  and depth perception, 160–161
Creativity
  assessing, 311–312
  effect of television viewing on, 626–627
  and giftedness, 342–344
  intelligence and, 343
  make-believe play and, 344
  traditional versus open classrooms and, 635

Creoles, 353
Crisis intervention, for child maltreatment, 594
Critical period, 24. *See also* Sensitive period
Cross-fostering studies. *See* Adoption studies
Crossing over, in meiosis, 74
Cross-sectional design, 61–62
  combining with longitudinal approach, 62–63
  strengths and limitations of, 62, 65
Crowd, 614–615
Crying, infant, 134, 136–139, 404
  abnormal patterns of, 139
  adult responsiveness to, 137–138, 143
  causes of, 136–137, 155
  soothing and, 137
Crystallized intelligence, 312–313, 315, 317
Cultural bias, in intelligence testing, 308, 313, 315, 331–335
Cultural differences
  in adolescence, 189–190, 191
  in approaches to childbirth, 109–110
  in attachment, 420
  in child development, 28
  in child rearing, 30, 570–571
  in conservation, 246
  in early and late maturation, 194
  in health care, 213
  in identity development, 453
  in language development, 361, 365, 373, 380
  in learned helplessness, 447
  in maternal responsiveness, 137–138
  in memory, 282–283
  in moral development, 494–495
  in motor development, 152
  in newborn behavior, 139–140
  in physical growth, 183–184
  in sanctioning violence, 593
  in school achievement, 643–644, 645, 646
  in self-concept, 440
  in sex education, 195, 198
  in sexual practices, 195
  in temperament, 413–414
  see also Cultural influences
Cultural influences
  on child development, 28
  on child maltreatment, 593, 594
  on child rearing, 413
  on mathematical abilities, 298–299

on nutrition in pregnancy, 105
on self-esteem, 443
see also Cultural differences
Culturally specific practices, and child development, 29
Culture, 29
  political, and public policy, 35
Cumulative deficit hypothesis, 322–323
Cystic fibrosis, 78, 88
Cytomegalovirus, and prenatal development, 102, 103
Cytoplasm, 74

D
Darwin's theory. *See* Evolution, theory of
Day care, 585–588
  and attachment, 427–428
  and child development, 586–587
  European standards of, 27, 429, 587–588
  family day-care homes, 585–586, 587
  high-quality, 429, 586–588
  inadequate, 428
  infant, 428
  public policy and, 33, 37, 585, 587–588
Deaf children, language development of, 353, 359
Deaf parents, and language development, 365
Debriefing, in research, 67
Decentration, 243, 244
Deception, in research, 67
Decoding, 266
Delay of gratification, 503, 505, 507
Delinquency, 120, 194, 325, 510
Dental development, and physical maturity, 181
Deoxyribonucleic acid (DNA), 72–74
Dependent variable, 56
Depression
  in adolescence, 450
  concordance for severe, 120
  in infancy, 421
  maternal, 422
Deprivation. *See* Emotional deprivation; Maternal deprivation; Socioeconomic factors
Deprivation dwarfism, 214
Depth, in drawings, 234
Depth cues, 159

Depth perception, 158–161, 166
  binocular depth cues, 159
  independent movement and, 159–161
  kinetic depth cues, 159
  pictorial depth cues, 159, 160
  visual cliff and, 158, 231
DES (Diethylstilbestrol), 101
Developing countries, 34
  breast-feeding in, 210, 416
  infectious diseases in, 213
  malnutrition in, 211–212
  physical growth in, 184, 185
Developmental psychology, 2
Developmental research designs, 58–64
Deviation IQ, 320
Diabetes, forms of, 79, 88
Diet
  in infancy, 210–211
  phenylketonuria (PKU), 77
  pregnancy and, 104
  see also Nutrition
Diethylstilbestrol (DES), 101
Difficult child, 407
Digit span, 272
Dilation and effacement of the cervix, 107
Disadvantaged children. *See* Deprivation; Minority children; Socioeconomic factors
Discipline
  coercive, 476
  of divorced parents, 579, 580
  family size and, 573
  induction, 476
  love withdrawal, 476
  power assertion, 476
  punishment, 8, 479–480 (*see also* Punishment)
  Puritans and, 8
Discontinuous development, 5, 6, 9
  and stance of major developmental theories, 31
Discovery learning, 253
Disease(s)
  dominant and recessive, 77–80
  immunization against, 33
  infectious, 102, 104, 213
  malnutrition and, 211–212
  maternal, and prenatal development, 102, 103–106
  and physical growth, 211–212
  sexually transmitted, 103
Disequilibrium, and Piaget's theory, 222, 487, 491–492
Dishabituation, 319. *See also* Habituation–dishabituation studies

Gays, 197. *See also* Homosexuality

Gender
labeling, 521, 538, 539, 541
versus sex, 518–519
"Gender-appropriate" behavior, 529, 532–533, 534, 535, 538–539
modeling of, 539

Gender consistency, 538

Gender constancy
development of, 538
as predictor of gender-role adoption, 538–539

Gender differences. *See* Sex-related differences

Gender identity. *See* Gender-role identity

Gender labeling, 538, 539, 541

Gender-role adoption
biological influences on, 525–528
effect of gender stereotypes on, 524–525
environmental influences on, 529–536
gender constancy as predictor of, 538–539
reducing, 551
sex hormones and, 526–529
see also Gender roles

Gender-role identity, 519, 536
in adolescence, 540–541
androgyny and, 536, 539–540
cognitive-developmental theory of, 538
emergence of, 537–539
gender schema theory and, 541–543
gender typing and, 536
individual differences in, 536, 540–541
and psychological adjustment, 536–537
see also Gender roles

Gender roles, 519
cultural differences in, 525–526
evolutionary origins of, 558–559
and gender stereotypes, 519–525
see also Gender-role adoption; Gender-role identity

Gender schema theory, 518, 541–543

Gender stability, 538

Gender stereotypes, 519
in academic achievement, 522
in adolescence, 521–523
biological influences on, 525–528

cognitive intervention to reduce, 551–553, 542
in early childhood, 519–521
environmental influences on, 529–536
flexibility in, 522–523, 542
and gender-role adoption, 524–525
and gender roles, 519–525
gender schema theory and, 542
group differences in, 523–524
individual differences in, 523–524
masculine and feminine personality characteristics, 520, 521
in the media, 534
in middle childhood, 521–523
in occupations, 531
parental influences on, 529–532
racial differences in, 524
sex-related differences in, 523–524, 543–551
on television, 625
see also Gender typing

Gender typing, 518
cross-cultural research on, 525–526
cultural reversals of, 526
environmental influences on, 542
experience and, 526
gender constancy and, 539
gender-role identity and, 536
models, 533–534
by parents, 529–532
siblings and, 535–536
theories of, 518
see also Gender stereotypes

Gene mapping, 197

General factor, "g," 311, 312, 316, 323, 328

General growth curve, 182–183

Generalized other, 439–440

Generativity versus stagnation, 17

Genes, 72–74
dominant–recessive, 77–80
modifier, 81–82
mutations, 80–81, 208
see also Genetic influences; Genetics

Gene splicing, 88

Genetic code, 72–74, 81

Genetic counseling, 86

Genetic disorders, 77–80, 528
sex-related differences in, 81

Genetic engineering, 88

Genetic–environmental correlation, 123–124

Genetic influences
on attention-deficit hyperactivity disorder (ADHD), 279
on brain lateralization, 205
concordance and, 120–122
heritability estimates and, 120, 121–122
on homosexuality, 197
on intelligence, 59, 83, 122, 323, 326, 328–330
on obesity, 212
on personality, 120
on physical growth, 208–209
on temperament, 410–412

Genetics
and adaptation, 74
behavior, 119–122
codominance, 80
dominant–recessive relationships, 77–80
genetic code, 72–74
genotype, 72
Mendel's work in, 72
modifier genes, 82
mutations, 80–81
patterns of inheritance, 77–82
phenotypes, 72
pleiotropism, 81–82
polygenic inheritance, 82
sex cells, 74–75
sex determination, 76–77
X-linked inheritance, 81

Genital abnormalities, 101, 528

Genital stage, 14, 15

Genitals, growth of, 183

German measles, and prenatal development, 102, 103

Gestural communication, 360–361, 380

Gifted children, 316
assessment of, 342–345
creativity of, 342–344
educating, 344–345
special programs for, 345, 531
talent of, 344

Glial cells, 95, 202–203

Goal-directed (intentional) behavior, in Piaget's sensorimotor stage, 226

Goodness-of-fit model, 413, 423

Government programs. *See* Social policy

Grammar
creole, 353
universal, 352–353, 356

Grammatical development, 351, 370–377, 382–383
complex grammatical forms, 374–375
environmental influences on, 376, 377

expansions, 377
first word combinations, 370–371
infinitive phrases, 376
language acquisition device (LAD), 352–353
language-making capacity (LMC), 376
morphemes, 372, 372n, 373, 374
negation, 374
overregularization, 372–373
passive voice, 375–376
question forms, 374–375
recasts and, 377
semantic bootstrapping hypothesis, 376
telegraphic speech, 370–371
two-word utterances, 371–372

Grammatical morphemes, 372, 373, 374

Grammatical rules, 352

Grandparents
and child rearing, 561, 572
visitation rights of, 581

Grasping
and cognitive development, 152
development of, 151–152
reflex, 132
visual stimulation and, 155

Great Depression, children of, 61

Gross motor development, 148
sex-related differences in, 180

Gross national product, 34, 34n

Groups. *See* Peer groups

Growth. *See* Physical growth

Growth curves
distance, 177–178
general, 182–183
velocity, 178

Growth hormone (GH), 185–186, 208, 214

Growth norms, 177–178

Growth spurt, 188–189
in brain development, 206–207

Guatemala, childbirth in, 111

Guidance Study, 58–59

Guilt, 399, 476
in Freud's theory, 475, 476–477

H

Habituation, 144–146

Habituation–dishabituation studies
on color perception, 157–158
on combining pattern elements, 163
on early categorization, 230
on face perception, 165

Marital conflict, 27
  and child rearing, 561
Masai, infant survival among, 414
Masculinity
  cultural differences in, 526
  effect of sex hormones on, 528
  and gender-role identity, 536–537
  personality characteristics of, 520, 521, 537
Mastery-oriented attributions, 445–446
Matching, in experimental designs, 57
Maternal age
  and Down syndrome, 84
  and trends in childbirth, 105–106
Maternal blood analysis, 87, 88
Maternal deprivation
  attachment and, 214, 420–421, 427
  and growth disorders, 214–215
  infant response to, 397–398
Maternal disease, and prenatal development, 102, 103–106
Maternal employment
  effect on child development, 584–585
  and day care, 427–428, 584
  divorce and, 583
  effect on mother–infant attachment, 584
  public policy on, 585
  and self-care children, 588–589
  sex-related differences in response to, 584–585
  social-class differences in response to, 585
  social support for, 585
  in Sweden, 526
  in two-parent families, 583–584
Maternal leave, 117
Maternal responsiveness, 137–138, 141
Maternal separation, 409, 417, 418, 422
Mathematical abilities
  cultural influences on, 29, 298–299
  environmental influences on, 548
  handedness and, 206
  sex-related differences in, 547–548
Mathematics achievement
  cross-national research on, 298–299, 643–644, 645

information processing and, 23, 297–299
  in Korea, 299
  in the United States, 643–644, 646
Maturation, 9
  brain lateralization and, 546–547
  in cognitive-developmental theory, 222
  early versus late pubertal, 193–194, 638n
  genetic influences on physical, 209
  language development and, 359
  long-term studies of, 194
  of motor skills, 150, 152–153
  and pattern perception, 222
  secular trends in physical, 184–185
  sexual, 186–187
  and visual perception, 164
Maturational timing and puberty, 193–194
Mayans
  childbirth practices of, 109
  memory skills of, 282–283
Mean, or average, 320
Mechanistic theories, 4, 6, 8
  and stance of major developmental theories, 31
Media. See Computers; Television
Medications
  during childbirth, 109–110, 112, 146
  and prenatal development, 98–100
Medieval times, view of childhood, 6–8
Meiosis, 74, 75
Memory, 23
  conscious and unconscious, 285
  constructivist approach to, 286
  context-dependent, in infancy, 146
  emotion and, 392–393
  episodic, 289
  eyewitness, 290
  in infancy, 143, 144–146, 268, 285
  involuntary associations in, 281
  knowledge base and, 287–289
  long-term, 283–290
  phonological, 369
  recall, 146, 280, 284–285, 363
  recognition, 146, 284–285, 363
  reconstruction, 285–287, 289
  rehearsal, 280

retrieval, 268
  scripts and, 289–290
  semantic, 289
  short-term, 267, 268, 280–283
  strategies (see Memory strategies)
  stress and, 290
  of traumatic events, 290
  working, 268, 269, 273, 280–283, 369
Memory strategies, 280–282
  elaboration, 281–282
  environmental contexts and, 282–283
  knowledge of, 292
  organization, 281
  rehearsal, 280
Menarche, 106, 188
  age of, 188
  reactions to, 190
  secular trends in, 184
  in twins, 209
Menstrual cycle, 90, 187, 188
  malnutrition and, 200
Menstruation, 187, 188
Mental abilities
  hierarchical model of, 311
  racial and social-class differences in, 327–328
  see also Intelligence
Mental age (MA), 319–320
Mental inferences, children's awareness of, 291
Mental representation, 224, 227–228, 229–230, 254
Mental retardation
  causes of, 83–85, 102, 113, 186
  genetic transmission of, 77–79
  mainstreaming and, 642
Mental space, or M-space, 272
Mental strategies, 267
Mental testing movement. See Intelligence tests
Mercury, and prenatal development, 101–102
Mesoderm, 93
Mesosystem, 27
Metacognition, 291–295, 300, 434
  comprehension monitoring and, 293
  and intelligence, 313
  knowledge of cognitive capacities, 291–292
  knowledge of strategies and task variables, 292, 505
  self-regulation and, 292–294
Metacognitive training, 293
Metalinguistic awareness, 381, 382–383

Metaphors, use of, 367–368
Methadone and prenatal development, 99
Microcomputers. See Computers
Microgenetic design, 63–64
  strengths and weaknesses of, 65
Microsystem, 26
Minority children
  adolescent sexual activity, 195, 196
  bilingual education for, 384
  educational programs for, 259
  ethnic identity, 453, 572
  intelligence testing of, 317, 318, 333–334
  IQ scores, 322, 332
  low-birth-weight, 114
  and poverty, 32, 569–570, 572
  public policy and, 33
  teacher reactions to, 640–641
  teenage pregnancy and, 199
Miscarriage, 84, 87, 99, 101
  infectious disease and, 102
  See also Abortion
Mitosis, 74
Mobiles, 143, 145, 230, 436
Modeling
  and aggression, 479
  and emotional development, 390
  of gender-role behavior, 533–534
  and moral development, 478
  peer, 616–617
  in social skills training, 612
  and substance abuse, 618–619
  see also Imitation; Observational learning
Model of strategy choice, Siegler's, 295–296, 297–298
Models, effectiveness of, 18, 478
Modifier genes, 82
Monkeys. See Apes and monkeys
Moodiness, adolescent, 192
Moral development
  assessing, 485–487
  behaviorist view of, 478
  biological perspective on, 474
  cognitive-developmental perspective on, 481–498
  construction and, 481
  cultural differences in, 473–474, 494–495
  effects of punishment on, 479–480
  Freud's theory of, 476–477
  induction and, 476

Obesity (continued)
  treating, 213
Object-hiding tasks, and
    Piaget's sensorimotor
    stage, 152, 153
Object perception, 165–167
  objects as distinct, bounded
    wholes, 166–167
Object permanence, 224, 226,
    227, 228–229
Object words, in early vocabu-
    lary, 366
Observation
  naturalistic, 46–47, 49, 58
  participant, 52
  structured, 46, 47
  systematic, 46–49
Observational learning, 18
  and gender typing, 533–534
  See also Imitation; Modeling
Observer bias, 49, 51
Observer influence, in system-
    atic observation, 49
Occupational attainment, IQ
    and, 324–325
Occupations, sex-related differ-
    ences in, 531
Odors. See Smell
Oedipal conflict, 17, 475, 476
Only children, 576–577
Open classroom, 634–635
Operant conditioning, 18, 143
  and attachment, 415
  and emotional development,
    390
  in infancy, 143–144, 226, 390
  and language development,
    351–352
  and moral development, 478
  and punishment, 143
Operant-conditioning model
    of attachment, 415
Operations, in Piaget's theory,
    234, 244
Optic nerve, 157
Oral contraceptives, and pre-
    natal development, 101
Oral stage, 14, 15, 416
Organismic theories, 4, 6
  and stance of major develop-
    mental theories, 31
Organization
  memory strategy of, 281, 286
  in Piaget's theory, 222
  semantic, 281
  spatial, 281
Overextension, in language
    development, 367
Overregularization, in lan-
    guage development,
    372–373

Overstimulation, in infancy,
    153, 171
Overweight, at risk for, 212.
    See also Obesity
Ovum, 74, 90
Oxygen deprivation, 80
  during childbirth, 108,
    112–113

P
Pacifiers, 132, 137, 167
Pain, newborn sensitivity to,
    155
Palmar grasp reflex, 130, 131,
    132
Parallel play, 602, 603
Parasitic infections, 102, 104
Parental consent, for research
    participation, 67
Parent–child relationship
  and education, 646
  effect of third parties on, 27
  family size and, 573–574
  and identity, 452
  and intellectual develop-
    ment, 335–336
  and language development,
    378, 379
  and moral development, 477
  and obesity, 212
  and peer relations, 606
  puberty and, 192–193
  see also Attachment;
    Parenting; Parents
Parenting
  in adolescence, 192–193,
    567–568, 618
  advice on, 12
  discipline and, 560
  divorce and, 578–579
  and gender typing, 532
  in middle childhood, 566–567
  punishment and, 479–480,
    560
  regulating television view-
    ing, 628
  responsiveness and, 563, 564
  social support for, 561–562
  social class and, 569–570
  styles of (see Parenting
    styles)
  see also Child rearing; Child-
    rearing practices;
    Parent–child relation-
    ship; Parents
Parenting styles, 558, 563–565
  authoritarian, 564
  authoritative, 563–564, 568,
    572, 618, 626
  permissive, 565
  uninvolved, 565

see also Child-rearing prac-
    tices
Parents
  abusive, 592, 593
  of anorexics, 201
  deaf, 365
  gender stereotyping by,
    529–532
  low-income, 37, 568–569
  of maltreated children,
    590–593
  of preterm infants, 114–115
  as social planners, 606
  socialization by, 562–566
  systematic observation by, 49
  teenage, 33, 198–200, 572
Parents Anonymous, 594
Parents Without Partners,
    580–581
Parents magazine, 12
Participant observation, 52
Passive genetic–environmen-
    tal correlation, 123–124
Passive voice, use of, 375–376
Paternal age, and Down syn-
    drome, 84
Pattern perception, 161–164,
    169
  combining pattern elements,
    163–164
  contrast sensitivity, 161–163
Pavlov's research. See
    Classical conditioning
PCBs (Polychlorinated-
    biphenyls), 102
Pedigree, in genetic counsel-
    ing, 86
Peer acceptance, 608–612
  aggression and, 611
  assessing, sociometric tech-
    niques in, 608, 609–612
  controversial children, 608,
    610
  interventions for, 612
  mainstreamed children, 642
  neglected children, 608,
    610–611, 611, 612
  physical appearance and,
    609–610
  popular children, 608, 610
  and psychological adjust-
    ment, 608–609
  rejected children, 608–609,
    610, 611, 612, 642
  and school adjustment, 636
  social behavior and, 610–612
Peer collaboration, 258–260
Peer groups, 613–616
  cliques, 614
  conformity in, 617–618
  crowds, 614–615

dominance hierarchies in,
    615–616
  formation of, 613–614
  intergroup rivalry, 613
  leaders in, 613, 616
  norms in, 613, 614–615
  Robbers Cave experiment,
    613–614, 616
  social structures in, 615–616
  superordinate goals of,
    613–614
Peer interaction
  development of, 620
  familiarity of associates and,
    607–608
  friendship (see Friendship)
  and gender typing, 534–535
  in groups (see Peer groups)
  importance of, 600–601
  in Kohlberg's theory, 492
  mixed-age, 601, 606–607
  parental influences on, 606
  and peer acceptance (see Peer
    acceptance)
  in Piaget's theory, 607
  play materials and, 606
  same-sex, 465n, 534–535
  situational influences on,
    606–608
  sociability and (see Peer
    sociability)
  socialization and (see Peer
    socialization)
  social norms and, 604
  in Vygotsky's theory, 607
Peer-only rearing, 600–601
Peer pressure
  in adolescence, 617–618
  on self-care children 589
Peer(s)
  as authority figures, 484
  defined, 601
Peer sociability, 600, 601–605
  in adolescence, 604–606
  age mix of children, 606–607
  associative play, 602
  cooperative play, 602, 604
  development of, 602–606
  familiarity of peers and,
    607–608
  in infancy and toddlerhood,
    602
  in middle childhood, 604–606
  nonsocial activity, 602, 603
  parallel play, 602, 603
  parental influences on, 606
  play materials, 606
  in preschool years, 602–604
  rough-and-tumble play, 605
Peer socialization, 600, 601,
    616–620

conformity and, 617–618, 619
  modeling and, 616–617
  reinforcement and, 616–617
Pendulum problem, and
    Piaget's formal opera-
    tional stage, 248–249
Penis, pubertal growth of, 188,
    189
Perception
  categorical speech, 358
  depth, 158–161, 166
  face, 161, 163, 164–165, 169
  intermodal, 167–168
  of moving objects, 167
  object, 165–167
  of objects as distinct, bounded
      wholes, 166–167
  person, 454
  see also Perceptual develop-
      ment
Perception-bound thought,
    and Piaget's preopera-
    tional stage, 236, 237
Perceptual constancies, 166–167
Perceptual development
  differentiation theory of,
      168–169
  experience and, 160, 164
  of hearing, 156
  in infancy, 20, 145, 154–169,
      396
  intermodal, 167–168
  invariant features and, 168–169
  maturation and, 164
  nature–nurture debate on, 154
  and reading, 274–275
  research methods, 154
  of taste and smell, 155–156
  of touch, 154–155
  of vision, 156–167, 168
  see also Perception
Permissive child rearing, 565
  and Gesell's theory, 11
  and Rousseau's philosophy,
      9
Personal fable, 250
Personality traits, 59, 519,
    521–522
  environmental influences on,
      411
  gender stereotyping of, 537,
      539–540
  genetic influences on, 120,
      410, 411–412
  sex-related differences in,
      548–551
  stability over time, 59
Personality development
  Erikson's theory of, 15–16, 17
  Freud's theory of, 14–16
  see also Temperament

Person perception, 454
Perspective taking, 196, 434
  cognitive development and,
      458
  development of, 440,
      455–461
  and empathy, 404, 460
  games, 458–460
  in Kohlberg's theory, 487,
      490–491
  in middle childhood, 604
  and recursive thought,
      459–460
  Selman's stages of, 455–460,
      491
  and social behavior, 460
  training in, 460–461
Phallic stage, 475, 477n
Phenotypes, 72
Phenylalanine, 77, 81
Phenylketonuria (PKU)
  dietary treatment for, 77
  inheritance of, 77–80, 81
Phonemes, 358, 372n, 381
Phonological development,
    350, 361–363, 382–383
Phonological store, in work-
    ing memory, 369
Phonology, 350
Physical appearance, and peer
    acceptance, 609–610
Physical attractiveness. See
    Attractiveness
Physical growth
  in adolescence, 177, 187–202
  in animals, 176
  asynchronies in, 182–183
  brain development, 202–207
  changes in body composi-
      tion, 179–180
  changes in body propor-
      tions, 178–179
  changes in body size,
      176–178
  in childhood, 180, 183
  course of, 176–187
  cultural differences in, 183–184
  in developing countries, 184,
      185
  disease and, 213
  disorders of, 214–215, 393
  emotional well-being and,
      214–215
  hormonal influences on,
      185–187
  individual differences in,
      180–181, 183–184
  in infancy, 176, 178–179,
      182–183
  malnutrition and, 211–212,
      214

norms, 177–178, 184
  nutrition and, 209–213
  prenatal, 94–97, 178
  secular trends in, 184–185
  sex-related differences in,
      178, 179–181
  skeletal development,
      180–182
  see also Growth curves;
      Maturation; Puberty
Physical neglect, 590. See also
    Child maltreatment;
    Neglected children
Piaget's theory of cognitive
    development, 219–254,
    243–247
  background, 9, 19, 219–220
  compared to information
      processing, 266, 301–303
  educational implications of,
      253–254
  evaluation of, 21–22, 30, 31,
      252–253
  formal operational stage,
      248–252
  key concepts in, 220–222, 255
  methods of study and, 20–21
  notion of stages in, 20–21, 221,
      222–223, 252–253, 490
  preoperational stage, 231–242
  sensorimotor stage, 223–231
  Vygotsky's challenges to,
      223, 252, 254–261
  see also Cognitive develop-
      ment; Information pro-
      cessing; Sociocultural
      theory; names of stages
Piaget's theory of moral
    development, 481–485
  evaluation of, 483–485
  immanent justice in, 482
  intentions and moral judg-
      ments in, 483
  Kohlberg's extension of,
      485–489
  peer interaction in, 492
  realism in, 482
  reciprocity in, 483
  stages of moral understand-
      ing, 484–485
    autonomous morality,
        482–483
    heteronomous morality,
        482
Pictorial depth cues, 159
Pictorial representation, 234,
    235
Pidgins, 353
Pincer grasp, 152, 153
Pituitary gland, 185
PKU. See Phenylketonuria

Placenta, 92
  delivery of, 107, 108
  previa, 113
Plasticity, of the brain, 204–205
Play
  associative, 602
  cognitive maturity of,
      603–604
  cooperative, 602, 604
  creativity and, 344
  cultural differences in, 30
  environments, 45
  "gender-appropriate," 529,
      532–533, 534, 535, 539
  gender-typed (same-sex), 45,
      518
  in infancy, 223, 225, 227, 228
  make-believe, 228, 232–234,
      242, 257, 437–438, 604
  parallel, 602, 603
  and recall, 282
  rough-and-tumble, 605
  sociodramatic, 233, 234, 604
  solitary, 257, 603
Play materials, and peer socia-
    bility, 606
Pleiotropism, 80, 81
Political culture, and public
    policy, 35
Pollution, and prenatal devel-
    opment, 101–103
Polychlorinated-biphenyls
    (PCBs), and prenatal
    development, 102
Polygenic inheritance, 82, 119
Popular children, 608, 610
Postconventional level, in
    Kohlberg's theory,
    488–489, 497
Poverty
  and child-rearing practices,
      569
  and development, 170
  and IQ scores, 322
  and social policy, 32
Poverty line, 32
Practice effects, 60
Pragmatic development, 351,
    377–381, 382–383
  conversation abilities, 378
  referential communication
      skills, 378, 380
  sociolinguistic understand-
      ing, 380–381
Pragmatics, 351
Preconventional level, in
    Kohlberg's theory,
    487–488
Preformationism, 7
Pregnancy
  age trends in, 105–106

inductive, 476
logical, 242
mathematical, 297
moral, 484, 495–497, 495–502
preoperational, 236, 237–239, 240–241, 241, 242
prosocial, 501–502
scientific, 299–300
transductive, 236, 237–239, 241
see also Piaget's theory of cognitive development
Recall memory, 280, 284–285
in infancy, 146
Recasts, of children's utterances, 377
Reciprocal teaching, 258
Reciprocity, moral, 483
Recoding, 266
Recognition memory, 283–284
in infancy, 146
Reconstruction, memory, 285–287, 289
Recursive thought, 459–460
Red-green color blindness, 81
Referential communication skills, 378
Referential style, of language development, 365–366
Reflexes
adaptive value of, 132
assessment of, 133
and motor development, 132–133, 151
newborn, 130–133, 140, 154, 223–225
Reflexive schemes, 223–225
Reformation, and philosophy of child rearing, 7–8
Rehearsal, 280
Reinforcement
aggression and, 509
of gender-role behavior, 529, 532, 534, 535–536
in moral development, 478
in peer socialization, 616–617
Reinforcers, 18, 143
Rejected children, 608–609, 610, 611, 612, 642
interventions with, 612
Rejected-aggressive children, 610
Rejected-withdrawn children, 610
Relaxation techniques, for childbirth, 110
Reliability, 53–54
Religion
functions of, 559
Protestantism, and philosophy of child rearing, 8
Remarriage, 578

factors related to adjustment in, 582
stepparents and, 582–583
REM sleep. See Rapid-eye-movement sleep
Repression, 15
Reproductive technologies, 86, 87
pros and cons of, 87
Research
bias in, 10, 51, 52
in child development, 36
collaboration with practitioners, 45
cross-cultural, 28–30
early, 3, 9–10
equipment and recording devices, 48–49
planning, 44
and public policy, 36–37
reliability in, 53–54
rights, 65–67
theory and hypothesis in, 44–46
validity in, 54
see also Research designs; Research methods
Research designs, 44, 54–58
combining, 62–63, 64
correlational, 54–56
cross-sectional, 61–62
developmental, 58–64
experimental, 56–58
improving, 62–64
longitudinal, 58–61
longitudinal-sequential, 62
microgenetic, 63–64
strengths and limitations of, 65
see also Research; Research methods
Research methods, 44, 45–53
of behavior geneticists, 120–121
clinical, 46, 51–52
ethnography, 46, 52–53
self-reports, 46, 49–51
strengths and limitations of, 46
systematic observation, 46–49
Research questions, 44
Resistant attachment, 419, 424
Resource room, and mainstreaming, 642
Respiratory distress syndrome, 113
Respiratory infections, 144
Respiratory system
prenatal development of, 96
sex-related differences in capacity of, 180
and sudden infant death syndrome (SIDS), 144

Reticular formation, 185, 206
Retina, 157
Retrieval, 268, 283
recall and, 284–285
recognition and, 283–284
reconstruction and, 285–286
Reversibility, 237, 243, 244
Rh factor, 113
RhoGam, 113
Rite of passage, adolescent, 191
Robbers Cave experiment, 613–614, 616
Rooting reflex, 131, 132
Rough-and-tumble play, 605
Rubella (German measles), and prenatal development, 102, 103

S

Sadness, in infancy, 396–398
Samoa
adolescence in, 189
language development in, 361
Sampling
biased, 60
event, 48
time, 48
Sarcasm, 368–369
Scaffolding, 256, 257, 260
Scandinavia, childbirth leave in, 117
Scanning, visual, 157, 163
Schemes
developmental changes in, 221–222
in information processing, 272, 275
organization in, 222
preoperational, 233–234
reflexive, 223–225
sensorimotor, 221–226, 231
symbolic, 233–234
Schizophrenia, 120n
twin studies of, 120
Scholastic achievement. See Academic achievement
Scholastic Aptitude Test (SAT), 507, 547, 634
School achievement. See Academic achievement
School attendance, 324
School dropouts, 34, 324, 634
Schooling, 632–643
ability grouping, 641
classroom seating arrangements, 632–633
class size, 633–634
feminine bias in, 532
level of
and child-rearing practices, 569

and moral development, 493–494
and peer sociability, 604
social class and, 640–641
student body size, 633–634
teacher expectations, 639–640
teacher–pupil interaction, 638–641
textbooks in, 534
traditional versus open philosophies, 634–635
transitions
in adolescence, 636–638
early adjustment to school, 636–637
peer relations and, 636
school change, 636–637
school to work, 647–648, 648
and self-esteem, 637
timing of, 637
see also Academic achievement; Teacher–pupil interaction; Education; Teachers; Teaching
Scientific reasoning, 299–300
Scientific verification, 3
Screening, for developmental problems, 319
Scripts, 289–290
Scrotum, pubertal growth of, 188
Secondary, or learned, drives, 18
Secondary sexual characteristics, 187–188
Secular trends in physical growth, 184–185
Secure attachment, 418–419, 424, 425–427
factors affecting, 420–425
interactional synchrony and, 421
Secure base, 398
Self
categorical, 436
existential, 434
inner, 436
and other, distinguishing between, 436
psychological, 436
social, 439
thinking about the, 434–453
Self-awareness, 434
emergence of, 394
see also Self-recognition
Self-care children, 588–589
Self-concept, 438
development of, 438–440
influences on, 439–440
and self-esteem, 440–444

SI–17

IQs of
    biological and adopted, 120
    birth order and, 337
    nonshared environmental influences on, 336–338
    and language development, 379
    temperament and personality, 410–411
    and socialization, 574
    see also Sibling relationships
Sickle cell anemia, 79, 80, 81
Sickle cell trait, 80
Simultaneous processing, 318
Single mothers, adolescent, 198–199
Single-parent households, 577–578, 582
Size constancy, 165–166
Skeletal age, 181–182
Skeletal growth, 180–182
    sex hormones and, 179
    skull, 182, 202, 207
Skill theory, 272–273
Skin, of newborns, 109, 130, 140
Skull, 202, 207
    in infancy, 182
Sleep
    autostimulation theory of, 135–136
    in infancy, 133–136
    non-rapid-eye movement (NREM), 134–136
    parent–infant cosleeping, 133–134, 135
    rapid-eye movement (REM), 134–136
Slow-to-warm-up child, 407
Small-for-date infants, 114
Smell, 155–156
    animals' sense of, 155–156
    recognizing the mother's, 155–156
Smiles
    in infancy, 395–396
    social, 396
Smoking
    passive, 100
    and prenatal development, 100
Social acceptance. See Peer acceptance
Social behavior
    distributive justice and, 500
    emotions and, 393, 394
    peer acceptance and, 610–612
    perspective taking and, 460
    temperament and, 412

Social class
    and child rearing, 568–569
    and gender stereotyping, 524
    and IQ, 326–328, 330
    teacher's reaction to, 640–641
    see also Socioeconomic factors
Social cognition, 433–434
    information processing approach to, 466
Social-cognitive deficits, and aggression, 510–511, 512–513
Social-cognitive development, 19
    attributions, 444–447
    friendship, 461–466
    identity, in adolescence, 447–453
    intentions, understanding, 454–455
    person perception, 454
    perspective taking, 434, 455–461
    self-concept, 438–440
    self-esteem, 440–444
    self-recognition, 435–436
    social problem solving, 466–469
    theory of mind and, 436–438
    thinking about other people, 454–461, 468
    thinking about relations between people, 461–469, 468
    thinking about the self, 434–453, 468
Social-cognitive interventions, for aggression, 512–513
Social comparisons, 442, 443
Social conflict. See Social problem solving
Social conformity. See Conformity; Social conventions; Social norms
Social contract orientation, in Kohlberg's theory, 488–489
Social conventions, 498–499
Social development. See Peer sociability; Peer socialization
Social dilemmas, 455–457
Social interaction, in Vygotsky's theory, 29
Socialization
    development of, 563
    of emotional expression, 401–402
    of gender typing, 529–536
    within the family, 559, 562–572

of moral behavior, peer (see Peer socialization)
    and self-control, 503–504, 507
    siblings and, 574
Social learning theory, 18–19, 30, 31, 220
    contributions and limitations of, 19
    and emotional development, 390–391
    and gender constancy, 539
    and gender-role identity, 537–538
    and gender typing, 518
    and moral development, 474, 478–480
    and social skills training, 512, 612
    and treating aggression, 512
Social policy, 32–38
    policy-making process, 34–37
    see also Public policy
Social problem solving, 466–469
    development of, 467–469
    information-processing approach to, 466
    strategies, 407
    training in, 467–469
Social referencing, 402–403
Social skills training, 512, 612
Social smile, 396
Social support
    for divorced parents, 578, 580–581
    effect on pregnancy, 105
    for employed mothers, 585
    for natural childbirth, 111
    for parents, 561–562, 593–594
Social systems perspective
    on child abuse and neglect, 592
    on the family, 560, 561
Societal norms, morality as the adoption of, 475–481
Societal values, and public policy, 35
Society for Research in Child Development, 13
    ethical guidelines, 65
Sociobiology, 474
    and moral development, 474–475
Sociocultural theory (Vygotsky's), 29, 219, 252, 254–257
    background, 254
    cross-cultural research and, 28–30
    evaluation of, 31, 260–261

impact on education, 258–260, 635
    private speech in, 254–255, 293
    scaffolding in, 256, 257, 260
    and social origins of cognitive development, 256
    and zone of proximal development, 256, 257, 258, 259
Sociodramatic play, 233, 234, 604
Socioeconomic factors
    in ability grouping, 641
    in computer use, 631
    economic hardship, 61
    in family size, 573–574
    in intelligence, 326–328, 330, 331
    in lead poisoning, 208
    in malnutrition, 211
    in obesity, 212
    in parenting, 569–570
    in sexual activity, 196, 199
    in television viewing, 621–622
    see also Deprivation; Social class
Sociolinguistic understanding, 351, 380–381
Sociometric techniques, 608, 609–612
Sociomoral Reflection Measure–Short Form (SRM–SF), 485, 486–487
Solitary play, 257, 603
Somatomedin, 185
Spatial abilities, 260
    assessment of, 546
    biological influences on, 546
    brain lateralization and, 204, 546–547
    environmental influences on, 547
    sex-related differences in, 544, 545–547
    Turner Syndrome and, 84
Spatial operations, and Piaget's concrete operational stage, 243, 244
Spatial organization, 281
Spatial tasks, 546
Special-interest groups, and public policy, 35–38
Special needs children, 641–642
Special Supplemental Food Program for Women, Infants, and Children, 36, 37, 105
Specific factor, "s," in intelligence testing, 311